NAVIGATOR Britain

www.philips-maps.co.uk

First published in 1994 by Philip's
a division of Octopus Publishing Group Ltd
www.octopusbooks.co.uk
2–4 Heron Quays London E14 4JP
An Hachette Livre UK Company
www.hachettelivre.co.uk

Eighth edition 2009
First impression 2009

ISBN 978-1-84907-037-9

Cartography by Philip's
Copyright © 2009 Philip's

Ordnance Survey®

This product includes mapping data licensed from Ordnance
Survey®, with the permission of the Controller of Her
Majesty's Stationery Office. © Crown copyright 2009.
All rights reserved. Licence number 100011710

Data for the speed cameras provided by
PocketGPSWorld.com Ltd.

Information for National Parks, Areas of Outstanding Natural
Beauty, National Trails and Country Parks in Wales supplied
by the Countryside Council for Wales.

Information for National Parks, Areas of Outstanding Natural
Beauty, National Trails and Country Parks in England
supplied by Natural England. Data for Regional Parks, Long
Distance Footpaths and Country Parks in Scotland provided
by Scottish Natural Heritage.

Information for Forest Parks supplied by the
Forestry Commission

Information for the RSPB reserves provided by the RSPB

Gaelic name forms used in the Western Isles provided by
Comhairle nan Eilean.

Data for the National Nature Reserves in England provided
by Natural England. Data for the National Nature Reserves in
Wales provided by Countryside Council for Wales. Darparwyd
data'n ymwneud â Gwarchodfeydd Natur Cenedlaethol
Cymru gan Gyngor Cefn Gwlad Cymru.

Information on the location of National Nature Reserves in
Scotland was provided by Scottish Natural Heritage.

Data for National Scenic Areas in Scotland provided by
the Scottish Executive Office. Crown copyright material is
reproduced with the permission of the Controller of HMSO
and the Queen's Printer for Scotland. Licence number
C02W0003960.

Printed in China

*Navigator was the best-selling UK Road Atlas title by value in
2007/08 based on Nielsen BookScan Total Consumer Market.

Contents

Road map symbols

M25	Motorway
16 17	Motorway junctions – full access, restricted access
	Toll motorway
Pease Pottage Services	Motorway service area
	Motorway under construction
S	Primary route – dual, single carriageway, services – under construction, narrow
Cardiff	Primary destination
25 26	Numbered junctions – full, restricted access
	A road – dual, single carriageway – under construction, narrow
	B road – dual, single carriageway – under construction, narrow
	Minor road – dual, single carriageway
	Drive or track
	Roundabout, multi-level junction
2	Distance in miles
	Tunnel
Toll	Toll, steep gradient – points downhill
40 40	Speed camera – single, multiple
CLEVELAND WAY	National trail – England and Wales
GREAT GLEN WAY	Long distance footpath – Scotland
YATTON ROPLEY	Railway with station, level crossing, tunnel / Preserved railway with level crossing, station, tunnel / Tramway
	National boundary
	County or unitary authority boundary
	Car ferry, catamaran
	Passenger ferry, catamaran
CALAIS 1:30	Ferry destination, journey time – hours: minutes
	Hovercraft
(V) (P)	Internal ferry – car, passenger
✈ ✈	Principal airport, other airport or airfield
MENDIP HILLS	Area of outstanding natural beauty, National Forest – England and Wales, Forest park, National park, National scenic area – Scotland, Regional park
	Woodland
	Beach – sand, shingle
KENNET AND AVON CANAL	Navigable river or canal
6 6	Lock, flight of locks, canal bridge number
☼ ▲965	Viewpoint, spot height – in metres
	Linear antiquity
P&R	Park and ride
29	Adjoining page number
SY 80 70	Ordnance Survey National Grid reference – see page 402

Tourist information

BYLAND ABBEY	✠ Abbey or priory	HOLTON HEATH	National nature reserve
WOODHENGE	Ancient monument		⚓ Marina
SEALIFE CENTRE	Aquarium or dolphinarium	NAT MARITIME MUSEUM	Maritime or military museum
CITY MUSEUM AND ART GALLERY	Art collection or museum	SILVERSTONE	Motor racing circuit
TATE ST IVES	Art gallery	CUMBERLAND PENCIL MUSEUM	Museum
1644	Battle site and date		Picnic area
ABBOTSBURY SWANNERY	Bird sanctuary or aviary	WEST SOMERSET RAILWAY	Preserved railway
	Å Camping site	THIRSK	Racecourse
	Caravan site	LEAHILL TURRET	Roman antiquity
BAMBURGH CASTLE	Castle	BOYTON MARSHES	RSPB reserve
YORK MINSTER	✝ Cathedral	THRIGBY HALL	Safari park
SANDHAM MEMORIAL CHAPEL	Church of interest	FREEPORT BRAINTREE	Shopping village
SEVEN SISTERS / LOCHORE MEADOWS	Country park – England and Wales – Scotland	MILLENNIUM STADIUM	Sports venue
ROYAL BATH & WEST SHOWGROUND	County show ground	ALTON TOWERS	Theme park
MONK PARK FARM	Farm park		Tourist information centre i – open all year i – open seasonally
HILLIER GARDENS AND ARBORETUM	❀ Garden, arboretum	NATIONAL RAILWAY MUSEUM	Transport collection
ST ANDREWS	Golf course – 18-hole	LEVANT MINE	World heritage site
TYNTESFIELD	Historic house	HELMSLEY	△ Youth hostel
SS GREAT BRITAIN	Historic ship	MARWELL	Zoo
HATFIELD HOUSE	House and garden	SUTTON BANK VISITOR CENTRE	⋰ Other place of interest
MUSEUM OF DARTMOOR LIFE	Local museum	GLENFIDDICH DISTILLERY	

Approach map symbols

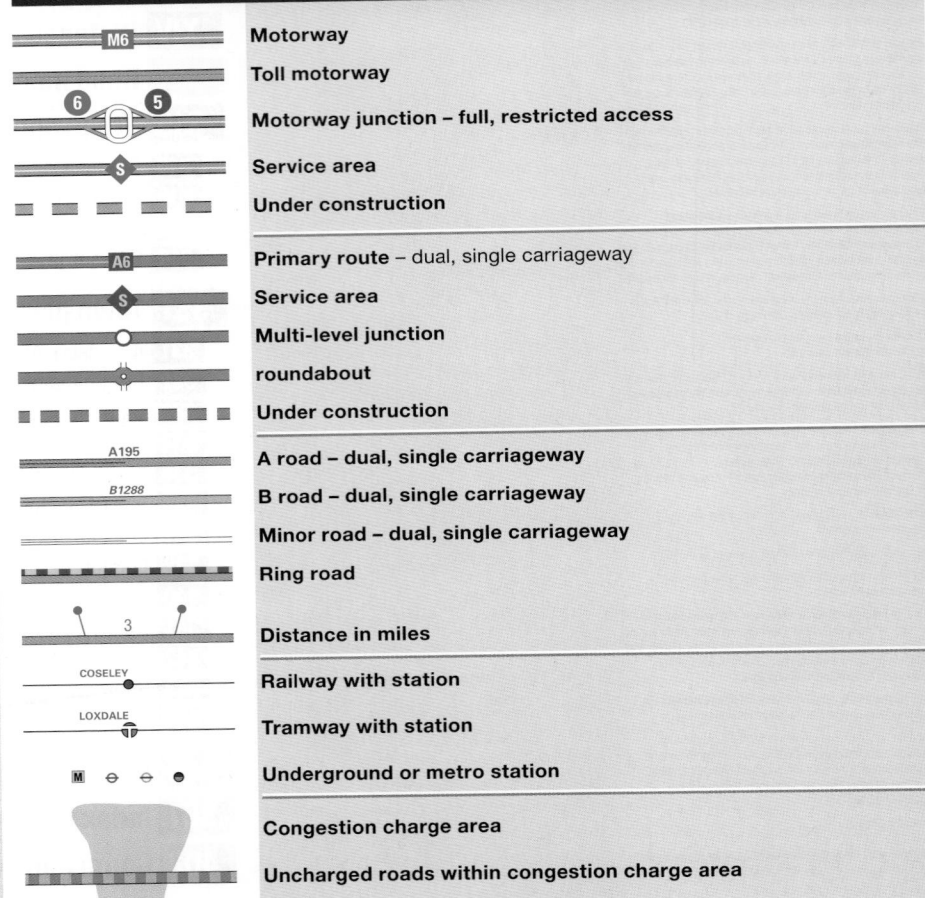

M6	Motorway
	Toll motorway
6 5	Motorway junction – full, restricted access
S	Service area
	Under construction
A6	Primary route – dual, single carriageway
S	Service area
	Multi-level junction
	roundabout
	Under construction
A195	A road – dual, single carriageway
B1288	B road – dual, single carriageway
	Minor road – dual, single carriageway
	Ring road
3	Distance in miles
COSELEY	Railway with station
LOXDALE	Tramway with station
M ⊖ ⊕ ⦿	Underground or metro station
	Congestion charge area
	Uncharged roads within congestion charge area

Road map scale 1 : 100 000 or 1.58 miles to 1 inch

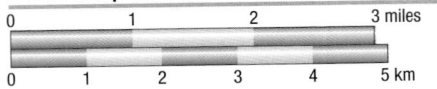

0   1   2   3 miles
0   1   2   3   4   5 km

Road map scale (Isle of Man and parts of Scotland)
1 : 200 000 or 3.15 miles to 1 inch

0   1   2   3   4   5   6 miles
0   1   2   3   4   5   6   7   8   9   10 km

Speed Cameras

Fixed camera locations are shown using the 40 symbol. In congested areas the 40 symbol is used to show that there are two or more cameras on the road indicated.

Due to the restrictions of scale the camera locations are only approximate and cannot indicate the operating direction of the camera. Mobile camera sites, and cameras located on roads not included on the mapping are not shown. Where two or more cameras are shown on the same road, drivers are warned that this may indicate that a SPEC system is in operation. These cameras use the time taken to drive between the two camera positions to calculate the speed of the vehicle.

Save £1000 off your annual motoring costs

Seven Top Tips from motoring journalist Andrew Charman

In today's cost-conscious motoring environment, is it possible to slice serious money from the cost of running a car? With the right preparation, it could well be.

Jonathan Maddock / iStockphoto.com

Ask any motorist whether they get good value from their driving and most will likely say no – many argue that motoring has never been more expensive. Drivers fight a constant battle against many enemies including fluctuating fuel prices, aggressive tax rates and an ever-expanding epidemic of safety cameras that many believe are present to generate revenue from fines first, and slow speeds second.

Some 60% of the drivers questioned for the 2008 Annual Report on Motoring compiled by the RAC believed that rising costs were the biggest minus of running a car in Britain today. Those drivers will be surprised to hear that, in fact, motoring is getting cheaper – the report concluded that even rocketing fuel prices have not stopped the overall cost of motoring falling in the past two decades.

The RAC research concluded that such factors as cheaper purchase and maintainance prices for cars have resulted in motoring costs decreasing in real terms by 18% since 1988, despite fuel costs rising 210%. Take those fuel price rises out of the equation and motoring today is 28% cheaper than 20 years ago.

This little bit of good news, however, does not mean that you can't save money on your motoring – and I intend to show you how some simple moves could put significant cash back into your pocket each year – possibly more than £1000.

Different cars, different homes

Saving big money on your motoring costs starts even before you buy the car. The vehicle you choose and how you buy it can make a difference of thousands of pounds, as shown in the panel on page V. But have no fear, because whether you've just bought a brand-new car or have used the same vehicle for many years, you can still save a packet on your motoring costs.

Of course, I can't say exactly what you will save by following the advice in these pages – so many varying factors affect one's motoring expenses. For example, I used to live in commuter-belt Surrey. Every morning I drove my children 8 miles to school, a journey of around half an hour on congested roads. Now I live in Mid-Wales and drive my wife to work, coincidentally also around 8 miles; it takes less than 15 minutes and I use 10–15% less fuel.

Similarly, potential savings in such areas as tyre life will be affected by your car, the way you drive and the roads you drive on. What I can confidently predict, however, is that by following even some of the advice on these pages, you will leave a noticeable amount of cash in your pocket.

In order to calculate these savings, we've devised 'Mr Average Motorist'. He drives a petrol-powered car – because, despite diesel soaring in popularity in recent times, the majority of cars on today's roads still run on petrol. Our man owns a Ford Mondeo family car, which is regularly one of the UK's top ten most popular

buys and averages 35mpg in fuel consumption. So, if he clocks up the national average of around 12,000 miles a year, he will use 1558 litres of fuel costing, at current prices, around £1402.

Preparation is everything

Fuel prices are the most visible and most obvious indicator of the cost of motoring today. As I write, the price of a litre of unleaded has plummeted to around 90p, having spent months steadily rising to over £1.20. But by the time you read this, prices could be soaring again and generally they are on the rise – remember that 210% figure within 20 years? We can't change fuel prices – but we can make the best use of every litre we buy.

You might think, then, that the first obvious move is to buy fuel from the cheapest source – but it's not. Before you put any fuel in your tank, you need to check that your car is in the best condition, both mechanically and otherwise, to stretch those litres. Skimping on servicing is NOT a way to save money on motoring. If your engine is not correctly tuned, it uses more fuel. In particular, clean fresh oil not only helps reduce fuel consumption but also wear caused by the friction of moving engine parts. Allow such parts to keep wearing and you could end up with a failure – and all your savings will be wiped out by an expensive repair bill. Ideally, on a petrol car you should change the oil at least once a year, and a diesel engine benefits from a change every six months.

But by far the biggest mechanical influence on fuel economy comes courtesy of what the car stands on – its tyres. Incorrectly inflated tyres, particularly containing too little pressure, leads to less mpg – and, incredibly, research by the tyre industry suggests that half of all tyres running on today's roads are under-inflated. Tyre manufacturers have calculated that for every 6psi a tyre is under-inflated, an extra 1% is added to consumption, and in roadside checks many cars have been found to have tyres under-inflated by as much as 20%.

◄ **Checking your tyre pressures is simple, and could greatly improve fuel economy.**

▼ **Under-inflated or damaged tyres could end up costing you more than a bigger fuel bill.**
Photographs courtesy of TyreSafe

Seven Top Tips to save money

1 SLOWING DOWN
average annual saving: up to £532

The first, most obvious area to watch is speed. We are always being told to slow down, but apart from the risk of paying out big money in fines having been caught by a safety camera, there's a far more obvious reason to ease back on that right-hand pedal – it saves money!

The effect is most noticeable on motorways. The national speed limit in Britain is 70mph, but on many a motorway that seems to be treated as a minimum, with traffic charging along at 80mph-plus. However, above 70mph aerodynamic drag becomes a serious issue, really eating into your fuel. If you adopt a more radical attitude, though, cruising along at 50mph instead of 70mph, your fuel costs will plummet, by an astonishing 38% in the average car.

Of course, many drivers will consider slowing down that much, particularly on a clear motorway, as a step too far, but even keeping firmly within speed limits will greatly influence your fuel costs. And there is much more you can do.

Smooth is good – don't, for example, floor the throttle the moment you see a clear stretch of road open up ahead of you. Harsh acceleration, and the resultant equally harsh braking, burns up those litres. Keep a good distance back from the car in front, so you can slow down gently when they do.

Powering around to the red line on your rev counter is another no-no – today's engines work most efficiently at speeds between 1500–2000rpm, and on modern petrol cars changing up a gear at around 2500rpm (2000rpm on a diesel) is both safe, smooth and fuel-friendly.

2 FUEL'S GOLD
average annual saving: up to £420

Find a bargain. Fuel prices charged by garages vary enormously – within a 20-mile radius of my home the differences add up to 5p per litre. And at the time of writing prices are changing almost daily. Clearly the trick is to buy from the cheapest source, but don't drive around looking for cheap prices – you could use as much as you save. Online resources, such as www.petrolprices.com, are a good way of finding out where fuel costs the least in your area, and while prices change constantly, the cheapest garages tend to remain cheapest.

When you've found your cheap supplier, try not to make a special trip to fill up – it's an unnecessary journey that uses fuel. Plan your motoring, factoring in a visit to the garage on the way to or from

Myth buster

A few motoring savings that are not always true....

? Buy your fuel from a busy garage because the fuel is used quicker, so has no time to age and lose quality

Not necessarily so – The big issue affecting fuel quality is water getting into the tanks through, for example, condensation. Garages periodically remove this water and busier garages may have less chance to do so compared to quieter rural outlets. Fuel quality depends on an individual garage's 'housekeeping' standards and there is no general standard. Also, by going to a busy garage you may lose any potential tiny saving from better-quality fuel while sitting in the queue with your engine running.

? When buying fuel in the early morning or evening, you get more for your money because in cooler conditions each litre of liquid becomes denser

False – Most garages keep their fuel in underground tanks, where temperature changes throughout the day are miniscule.

? Coasting down hills with the car in neutral saves fuel

False – At least with modern cars. Modern fuel systems cut off the supply to the engine the moment you come off the accelerator, but whether you are in gear or not a tiny amount is still used to ensure the engine does not stall. And without a gear, you have no engine braking, and less control.

? It's cheaper to get your car serviced at an independent

Not necessarily so – While independents might appear cheaper than a franchised dealer, because they don't specialize in a particular brand they don't know that brand so well, and crucially often don't possess the same level of diagnostic equipment as a franchised dealer. Therefore, tracing any faults can take significantly longer, which will be charged in service hours.

? A fast-fit supplier is the cheapest place to buy new tyres

Not necessarily so – Many franchised dealers are actively price-matching tyres to fast-fit opposition, and if you are told new tyres are needed during a service at the dealer, driving to a fast-fit supplier to find what you expect to be cheaper tyres can be an unnecessary, fuel-using journey.

▲ Recent on the scene are low-rolling-resistance tyres that extend fuel economy by causing less drag on the road surface. Photo courtesy Mercedes-Benz

▼ Neglecting servicing is not a way to save money – in fact it will end up exactly the opposite. Photo courtesy ATA

◀ Nice luggage, but leave the bags in the boot when you don't need them and you are simply adding fuel-using weight. Photo courtesy Volkswagen UK

▶ Roof racks are useful, but left atop the car when not in use, they simply ruin the aerodynamics, and the fuel economy. Photo courtesy GM UK

somewhere else. It's also prudent to visit the garage more often and only run on half a tank instead of a full one, if doing so suits your schedule, because all that extra liquid in a full tank is extra weight.

3 CUTTING DRAG
average annual saving: up to £140

Surely we can't change a car's aerodynamics? Oh yes, we can. Did you fit a roof rack to take all the extras for the family holiday last summer? Is it still bolted to the roof? The extra drag from such a large, anything-but-aerodynamic item could be costing you as much as 30% in fuel consumption.

The same goes for bike racks hung on the back of a car – they don't have the same dramatic effect as a roof rack, but they will unsettle the air ahead of them, thus affecting the aerodynamics of the rear end. Even running with your windows open harms the aerodynamics, interrupting the flow along the sides of the car. Do you tow a caravan and use those wing-mirror extensions to see around it? Well, if you haven't got the van hitched behind, take them off – they act like a couple of airbrakes.

4 AVOID THE CON
average annual saving: up to £140

Remember how it was advised to keep your windows closed for the best aerodynamics? Well, this next tip will go against the grain. Most modern cars have air-conditioning and many drivers leave it permanently switched on. But in doing so they can use up to 10% more fuel. Use the fans on cool without the system switched on, or have the window open just a little. If it's really hot, use the air-con for short periods instead of leaving it switched on and forgetting about it.

5 CLEVER FUELLING
average annual saving: up to £78

Planning ahead saves fuel and first you need to ask, 'Do I really need to make this trip?' Cars take a while to warm up during which they use the most fuel, which is why you should drive gently, avoiding stressing the engine, for the first few miles of any journey. But if said trip is merely nipping down to the shops for, say, a pint of milk, the car never has a chance to warm up, and your fuel economy suffers greatly. So for such short journeys consider walking, or perhaps cycling – it will benefit your health, as well as your car and your wallet. Alternatively, why not combine a number of short journeys in the week – visiting the family one night and doing the shopping on another – into one longer trip, perhaps popping into the garage for fuel at the same time.

Planning ahead comes into its own on longer journeys, especially if travelling to somewhere unfamiliar – you need to know exactly

where you are going, to avoid driving around trying to find a destination and eating up extra miles in the process.

Try to avoid congestion hotspots, because sitting in traffic queues not only wastes fuel but also tries one's patience, and when the jam clears we then drive more aggressively, and less fuel-efficiently, to try and make up time. Check where the problems are likely to be – Traffic England, the Highways Agency's website (www.trafficengland.com), carries constantly updated information on traffic issues and even has a facility where one can look at the view from the roadside CCTV cameras to see how heavy the traffic is. Once in the car, listen out for traffic reports on the radio so you can plan ahead and avoid the hot spots. Don't forget to take this road atlas with you so you can use it to detour around problems.

6 PRESSURE POINTS
average annual saving: up to £42

Under-inflated tyres cause increased wear, which as well as becoming dangerous (a bald tyre will harm grip in anything but totally dry conditions, as well as further increasing fuel consumption) reduces the life of the tyre by as much as 30%. You should also check the alignment of your wheels – simply hitting a pothole or a kerb can knock the alignment out, which again will increase tyre wear.

A recent advance in tyre technology, used extensively on the new breed of 'eco' cars, is to cut the tyre's rolling resistance, which is basically the force required to move the rubber over the road. Lower-rolling-resistance tyres require less force and so aid fuel economy, by around 2.5%. Now, less rolling resistance would suggest less grip, which is not very desirable, but these tyres use silica in their construction which effectively puts the grip back. And, surprisingly, such tyres do not generally carry a big price premium over traditional counterparts.

7 CAR WEIGHTWATCHERS
average annual saving: up to £35

Of all the battles fought by motorsport car designers, two areas stand out – reducing the weight of their cars by as much as possible, and making them as smooth as possible, so they slice more efficiently through the air. Exactly the same principles apply to road cars, not for speed, but for economy, and while we would not advocate slicing bits from your car, or trying to add wings and things to a body shape honed over many hours in a wind tunnel by professionals, there are distinct steps one can take that will have major effects on efficiency.

Have you looked in the back of your car recently? Do you know what is in there? Carrying around a lot of unnecessary weight greatly affects fuel economy, and thus your motoring costs – in some cases by as much as 10%. So if you play golf and your clubs and bag live in the boot, or you've been for a day out and left the deckchairs in the car, along with the picnic basket, that weight is squeezing your wallet. Go through the car looking for those pounds that can be shed. You might not think, for example, that a glovebox full of CDs weighs very much, but it all adds up.

Out on the road

There are still big savings to be made, but the onus is now firmly on you and the way you drive the car. So, if you are a bit of a speed merchant, like to use your throttle and brakes, can't remember the last time you checked your tyre pressures, and throw your cases on the roof rack because there's no room left in the boot, following the economy regime above could save you at least £1000 in a year! But even if you are a conscientious motorist who only needs to follow a couple of these Top Tips, you could still save significant money.

◀ Whether filling up with petrol, diesel or the latest biofuels, a little preparation will make the most of your visit to the garage. Photo courtesy GM UK

Road warrior approximately 40,000 miles per year

Supermini	Family hatch	Company car	Sports car	4x4 SUV	MPV
Up to £3500	Up to £4100	Up to £3650	Up to £5100	Up to £5200	Up to £4200

Professional driver approximately 22,000 miles per year

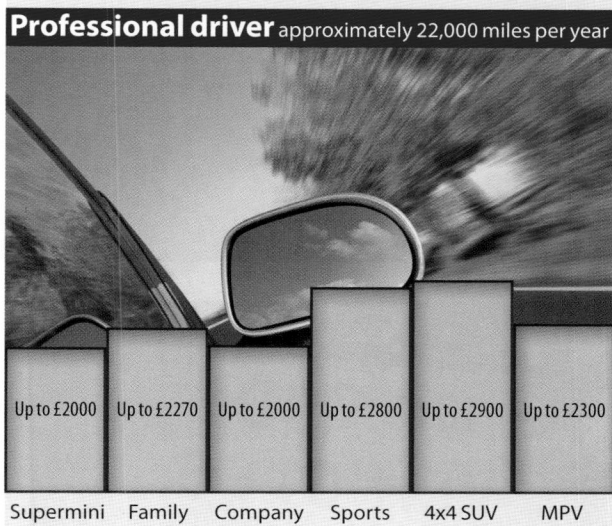

Supermini	Family hatch	Company car	Sports car	4x4 SUV	MPV
Up to £2000	Up to £2270	Up to £2000	Up to £2800	Up to £2900	Up to £2300

Family runabout approximately 12,000 miles per year

Supermini	Family hatch	Company car	Sports car	4x4 SUV	MPV
Up to £1150	Up to £1200	Up to £1100	Up to £1500	Up to £1500	Up to £1300

Just for shopping approximately 6000 miles per year

Supermini	Family hatch	Company car	Sports car	4x4 SUV	MPV
Up to £560	Up to £620	Up to £540	Up to £750	Up to £780	Up to £630

Buying a car

Most of us don't buy a new car every year, but when we do, there are thousands of pounds we can potentially save, as long as we do our homework first. Recent research by the AA found that a person spending up to £10,000 on a car could end up with a vehicle returning anything from 33 to almost 70mpg. Over a year, the difference in fuel costs for our average driver would add up to more than £700. When the AA compared the mpg figures for cars costing between £20,000 and £30000, the potential fuel savings came close to £2000! In addition, smaller, greener cars attract lower insurance premiums, and cheaper annual road tax – depending on your model, the cost of a tax disc can vary from £0 to £400 a year.

- **Think carefully before making your choice**. Do you really need a seven-seat people carrier? It might be useful on the few occasions your children bring friends home from school, but most of the time you will be carrying around extra, fuel-burning weight. Do you really want that sporty convertible? Folding roof mechanisms add weight, and as well as being less mpg-friendly to start with, performance engines encourage 'performance' driving, which gobble up those litres.

- **Many manufacturers are now producing new 'eco' versions** of their most popular models, with such refinements as low-rolling-resistance tyres, remapped engine electronics and reshaped aerodynamics to further stretch that fuel economy, and slash CO_2 emissions to levels that qualify for free road tax. But they can sometimes cost significantly more to buy than traditional counterparts.

- **The most economical cars will generally be diesel-powered**. Diesel engines travel a lot further on each litre of fuel and they produce less CO_2. But diesel fuel costs on average around 12p per litre more than the equivalent unleaded petrol – and the majority of diesel-powered cars come with a price premium over their petrol counterparts.

- **Spend time working out your annual mileage** and how far you will need to drive a diesel before you start saving money. Used-car specialist Parkers Guide recently launched a very useful fuel-cost calculator on its website (www.parkers.co.uk), which enables an instant check on how much individual car models will cost you in a year, and it can throw up surprises – for example, at current fuel prices and car list prices, a BMW 318d diesel would take close to 300,000 miles to recoup the £2790 more that it costs over the 318i petrol version.

- **Consider depreciation** when buying. Be sure to check the 'residual value' – which is an industry-quoted figure, easily found on internet sites such as Parkers, predicting how much the car will be worth after three years' use. Many factors influence such values – the make of car, its reliability, additional equipment installed, even in some cases the colour – so it's worth checking carefully to save money down the line.

Wasted fuel...

You could be using more than double the amount of fuel you need to! This chart shows how much cash you could be wasting by not attending to basic economy measures. Excess speed, for example, can increase fuel use by more than a third.

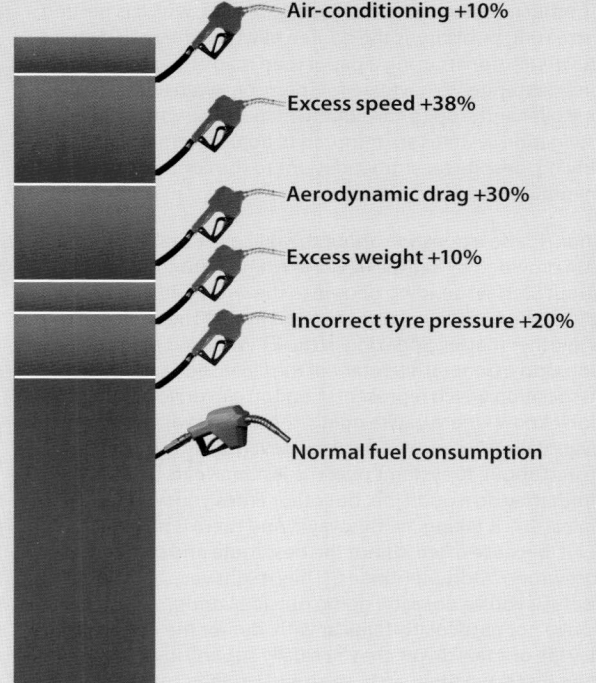

Air-conditioning +10%

Excess speed +38%

Aerodynamic drag +30%

Excess weight +10%

Incorrect tyre pressure +20%

Normal fuel consumption

- **Do you need to buy new?** New cars lose a significant amount of their value – sometimes 20-25% – the moment they are driven off the showroom forecourt. Yet there are many buyers who change their car every year, which adds excellent vehicles to a dealer's nearly-new selection. Many have at least a year of the manufacturer's warranty remaining – some substantially more with several makers moving to five-year and, in the case of Hyundai, seven-year warranties.

- **If you do buy used**, it's crucial to spend a little money, usually no more than £30–£40, on a vehicle data check, which will show up any irregularities in the car's history – whether it has outstanding finance owing on it, for example. This could avoid costing you a big bill, or even your car, later on.

- **Whether you buy new or used**, never accept the price stated at face value. With car sales having plummeted in the second half of 2008, dealers are desperate to sell – which puts the buyer in a very strong position to haggle over the price. Even persuading the dealer to fill the car with a tank of fuel is a significant saving at today's prices. And if you have hard cash available, this can encourage the dealer to offer you savings.

- **Shopping around for car insurance is essential**, and made easier these days thanks to a number of well-advertised internet price-comparison sites, but don't take these at face value – do your own research too. The choice of car is crucial to how much it will cost you in premiums, but insurers also like cars that are kept off the road, even better if you have a garage available. So if you have a garage full of junk with the car parked outside, why not have a clear out?

- **Also, think beyond the obvious**. If your eldest offspring has reached 17, passed their test and bought themselves an old banger to run around in, do they really need to be on the family car insurance too? If they are, it will send the premium rocketing. You might also consider taking an advanced driving course. While this will cost you money in the first place, insurers tend to give discounts to drivers with advanced qualifications, and along the way you learn driving techniques that will also help your overall economy.

- **Keeping your licence clean** can make a big difference to your insurance costs. You don't want penalty points, so don't use a handheld mobile phone at the wheel, and keep within speed limits – doing so offers a potential double saving, in fuel and insurance costs.

▲ All new cars on display in showrooms now include this chart giving the potential buyer a guide to their annual motoring cost.

▼ Careful driving really does save fuel. In the annual MPG challenge 400-mile endurance marathon, this Toyota Yaris diesel recorded 84.66mpg, almost 35% higher than its official combined fuel consumption figure. Photo courtesy Toyota GB

Why you can't rely on your SatNav alone

Satellite navigation aids utilizing the Global Positioning System (GPS) have become an essential accessory for many drivers in the last few years, and British motorists have readily embraced in-car satellite navigation systems despite their widely reported shortcomings.

When SatNavs first appeared in the mid 1990s, they were considered a luxury gadget and the ultimate 'boy's toy', reserved for top-of-the-range cars only. However, the situation started to change in the mid 2000s when TomTom, a software company based in Amsterdam, launched a pocket-sized, portable device aimed squarely at the mass market. Initially, the devices were relatively expensive – at around £400 – but as prices fell with improved technology and greater competition, sales started to soar and today portable SatNav units are widely available for less than £100.

In 2008, satellite navigation aids were more popular in the UK than in any other nation, with 35% of cars on UK roads carrying the technology compared with 24% for Western Europe and 16% for the United States – even Japan, where almost all new cars coming on to the market are now fitted with a SatNav, lagged behind the UK on 33%.

300,000 motorists using a SatNav said that it had caused them to have a crash or a near miss

So why is the SatNav so popular with motorists? There are several reasons: here is a device that promises to take the pressure out of driving, making getting from A to B a more relaxing experience, and saving motorists both the time and fuel costs that they would otherwise have wasted searching for their destination. The many proponents of the SatNav say that it gives them added confidence to drive into unfamiliar territory without getting lost, and that the technology's use of post codes and street names means that they can be directed to a precise location.

But is it really that simple?

The answer to that question is becoming clearer. In July 2008, the Daily Mirror reported on findings made by the insurance company Direct Line. Their research reported that a staggering 300,000 motorists using a SatNav said that it had caused

them to have a crash or a near miss; 1.5 million car drivers had veered dangerously or illegally while following its directions; and 5 million drivers had been sent the wrong way down a one-way street. A spokesperson for Brake, the road safety charity, said that the organization had 'very serious concerns' about SatNavs and the effects that they had on motorists. There were fears that users were putting lives in peril by slavishly following their instructions and neglecting road safety. Barely a week goes by without a story in the national press about accidents and near misses where the blame can be attributed to drivers suspending reasonable judgement by following the directions of their satellite navigation aid.

'Some of the guys just leave them on to see how bad they are'

Another negative aspect of SatNav devices, which is getting increasing publicity, is the degree to which they can distract drivers. Motorists using a paper road map either tend to rely on a passenger to navigate for them, or, when necessary, will pull over and stop to consult the map. Those with satellite navigation systems are tempted to adjust them while they are driving, despite recommendations to the contrary made by the manufacturers themselves.

There is also a question about the reliability of the information provided by SatNav devices. What of the complaints about SatNavs sending people to the wrong destination or giving them incorrect directions en route? The choice of route is another matter. Speaking in the FT Weekend Magazine, Bob Oddy, General Secretary of the Licensed Taxi Drivers Association which represents London cab drivers, said, 'If you don't know where you're going, the SatNav will get you there eventually. My caveat is the word "eventually". I must have tested about 30 systems over the last ten years or so and sometimes they do a good job, but other times you wonder: "Why on earth is it taking me this way?" And there is no explanation for it, because often it's not the best route and sometimes it's just wrong.' Oddy continues, 'They might very occasionally be useful if you've got a job going outside London or to a suburb you're not particularly familiar with, but for the normal, everyday life of a taxi driver, they're totally superfluous. Some of the guys just leave them on to see how bad they are.'

NO WIDE VEHICLES Do Not Follow SAT NAV

SINGLE TRACK ROAD No Passing Places

Our 10 of the best – or worst – SatNav stories, as reported in the national press:

1 Paula Ceely, 20, a student from Redditch, swore never to listen to her SatNav again after she was directed into the path of a speeding train at the Ffynnongain level crossing on the South Wales main line. Fortunately for Ceely, she had got out to close the gate behind her by the time a train smashed into her car. Miraculously, the driver and all the train passengers escaped injury too.

2 Police and rescue teams spent nine hours recovering the car of Robert Jones from Doncaster, which was left teetering on the edge of a 100 ft cliff in Todmorden, West Yorkshire, after he followed instructions from his SatNav that told him the steep, narrow footpath he was travelling down was a road.

3 A cabbie taking a fare – a daughter of Earl Spencer – from Althorp in Northamptonshire to watch Chelsea play at Stamford Bridge, in West London, ended up in Yorkshire. Rather than making the 85-mile trip to London, the driver went 146 miles in the wrong direction, ending up in the village of Stamford Bridge, in the East Riding of Yorkshire.

4 Another taxi driver, another near miss – this time with the driver stranded after following the device's instructions to drive up the River Nar near Swaffham, Norfolk. The cabbie persevered on his ill-fated journey for 200 yards before his minibus got stuck in the muddy riverbed and had to be rescued by a tractor. Keith Jarvis, owner of the Streamline taxi firm, said of the driver, 'He was in the car with his trousers rolled up. Fish were swimming around the headlights.'

5 Syrian truck driver Needet Bakimci was left red-faced after ending up 1600 miles adrift of his intended destination when driving from Turkey to Gibraltar. The driver had failed to appreciate that his SatNav had directed him to Gibraltar Point Nature Reserve near Skegness, Lincolnshire.

6 In January 2009, a 60 ft articulated lorry crashed into the country cottage of Carol and Tom Krosnar in Litton Cheney, Dorset, after the Hungarian driver was directed off a dual carriageway by his satellite navigation device. The lorry was wedged fast against the building, causing both external and internal damage to the house.

7 A Belgian truck driver blamed his electronic wayfinder after leaving a £20,000 trail of destruction in his wake in Wadebridge, Cornwall. Directed by his SatNav into an unsuitable cul-de-sac, the hapless trucker put his foot down in a panic, ending his turning manoeuvre by ploughing over a mini roundabout, getting a car trapped under his lorry, and destroying five more vehicles.

8 Lorries are becoming increasingly responsible for wreaking havoc on the roads in cases where their SatNavs have directed them in tall vehicles under low bridges, with catastrophic results. In 2007, three railway bridges within a 1-mile radius in the town of Grantham, Lincolnshire, were hit by lorries a total of 62 times.

9 From bridges getting in the way, to a bridge that was never even there – hundreds of drivers a year followed their SatNavs' instructions towards a bridge across the River Severn at Hampton Loade, Shropshire, that has never even existed. Drivers are having to make U-turns after driving miles out of their way to find that the 'bridge' is actually a ferry for foot passengers only.

10 Although some SatNav stories may make us laugh as we read of the scrapes that drivers get themselves into by blindly following the instructions from their devices, sadly every so often we come across a genuine SatNav horror story. In July 2008, a motorist confused by his satellite navigation system killed a woman after driving the wrong way along a dual carriageway and smashing into her car on the A413 in Buckinghamshire. The driver who caused the crash had misunderstood his SatNav's instructions and ignored road signs that should have made him realize his error. Sergeant Dominic Mahon of Thames Valley Police said, 'This is a tragic case that highlights the dangers of over-reliance on SatNavs.'

While SatNavs can make driving easier, safer and less stressful, serious driver errors may occur when obedience to the instructions of a digital device prevails over common sense. This may result in inconvenience to drivers and rescue workers, pollution for those who live in villages whose local roads become a rat-run for drivers on a shortcut, as well as damage to homes, railway lines and bridges – and sometimes tragic loss of life.

SatNav users beware!

Driven to distraction As SatNav technology has advanced, the temptation for manufacturers has been to cram more and more information on to the screen. As well as the mapping, most systems now show a dizzying array of extra information, such as speed limits, driving speed, locations of speed cameras, points of interest, estimated time of arrival, and traffic updates. These features are designed to help the driver, but they are all flashing up on screen while you should be concentrating on the road ahead. Other extra features, such as alternative routes, looking for local petrol stations or even simply resetting the device, can be a temptation for drivers to adjust their devices while on the move, which is potentially just as distracting and dangerous as using a mobile phone.

Out-of-date data Road networks change all the time – new roads are built, the layout of junctions are altered and side streets are made 'one-way only'. A SatNav, though, can only ever be as reliable as the mapping data it is based on. In North London, some devices will still offer to send you down Ashburton Grove, a road that was demolished several years ago to make way for Arsenal's new football stadium. 'Live' features that are now included on many devices, such as traffic information, may also be of limited reliability – quite often you will be in a queue of traffic before the device has had time to receive the latest information and warn you of a hold-up ahead. Alternatively, you may be sent on a diversion while your original route will have already cleared.

Stuck in the mud It's quite unlikely that your SatNav will be able to tell you the difference between a good-quality unclassified road and a poor one, so when you're driving through the countryside you run the risk of being directed down tracks or lanes that are really only suitable for tractors or other off-road vehicles.

An irritating bug An assumption sometimes made by SatNav systems is that the through-road is the one that goes straight ahead, when in fact you need to turn in order to follow the road.

More haste, less speed SatNavs may tell you the shortest or the fastest route to your destination, but often vehicles are sent along routes that are entirely inappropriate for them, resulting in lorries becoming stuck in small villages and providing unnecessary hazards to those towing caravans, horse boxes and trailers, for example.

Why you should always use and carry a map in your car

There are many benefits from using SatNav technology. The use of post codes can direct you door-to-door whereas a printed map can only get you as far the road you need, not the exact location, and when a SatNav is used with discretion, it can help you save time and money. But, a SatNav isn't infallible and it doesn't make you a better driver. Like all developing technologies, it has its flaws and sometimes things can go wrong.

These flaws can be compounded by the driver's over-reliance on the technology at the expense of common sense.

As a result, you should not rely on your SatNav alone and should always use it alongside a good, up-to-date road atlas.

- **By planning your route on a road atlas** before you leave, you can visualize your whole journey ahead and be confident that you are heading in the right direction.

- **When you read a paper map, you don't give up your common sense.** It's usually SatNav drivers, not map readers, who drive into rivers or get stuck in farm tracks. Road atlas users travelling alone are also far more like to pull over at the side of the road to consult their map to confirm where they are going.

- **With an atlas you can easily plan a journey** with several stops and check if there are places near to your route that you would like to visit. A SatNav is designed to get you from A to B in the quickest time possible and doesn't work as well as an atlas for leisure driving.

- **Road atlas users don't have to follow the herd.** When a SatNav gives prior warning of a traffic hold-up, hundreds of vehicles can be redirected on to the same route. A road atlas will allow the driver to choose alternatives.

- **Atlases don't lose signal, 'hang' or need recharging.** If a system crashes, it can leave hapless SatNav users high and dry – carrying an atlas means that you have a more reliable source of information to turn to in times of need.

- **It's quicker and easier to use a map when two people are travelling together.** According to Which?Computing maga-

◀ It is unlikely anyone will break into your car to steal your road atlas Monteverde / Alamy

zine, a driver and navigator covering a set route using an atlas went a distance of 67 miles in 1 hour and 35 minutes. Using SatNav, a different car took 8 minutes longer and covered more than 70 miles to complete the same journey.

- **Road atlases are inexpensive,** and Philip's road atlases are updated on a regular basis using the most up-to-date data available from the Ordnance Survey. Even the most rudimentary SatNav device will cost five times as much as a good road atlas – and that's before SatNav users have to think about paying annual subscription charges to update their mapping data and other information. Making sure you have an up-to-date road atlas is much cheaper. What's more, it is unlikely anyone will break into your car to steal your road atlas!

- **Good news for truckers!** By using the new Philip's Trucker's Navigator Britain atlas, there should be no reason to get stuck under a low bridge or drive along a road that is simply unsuitable for the size of your vehicle. As well as containing the unrivalled level of detail of the highly regarded Philip's Navigator Britain atlas, this new atlas includes additional bridge-height information and indicates bridges with width and weight restrictions to help plan your journey.

So our advice to all careful drivers is this: use and enjoy your SatNav to get you from A to B, but always carry an up-to-date road atlas in your car, make a conscious effort to check every journey with your atlas before you set out to make sure you are going the best way, and don't be afraid to question your route if you're in any doubt.

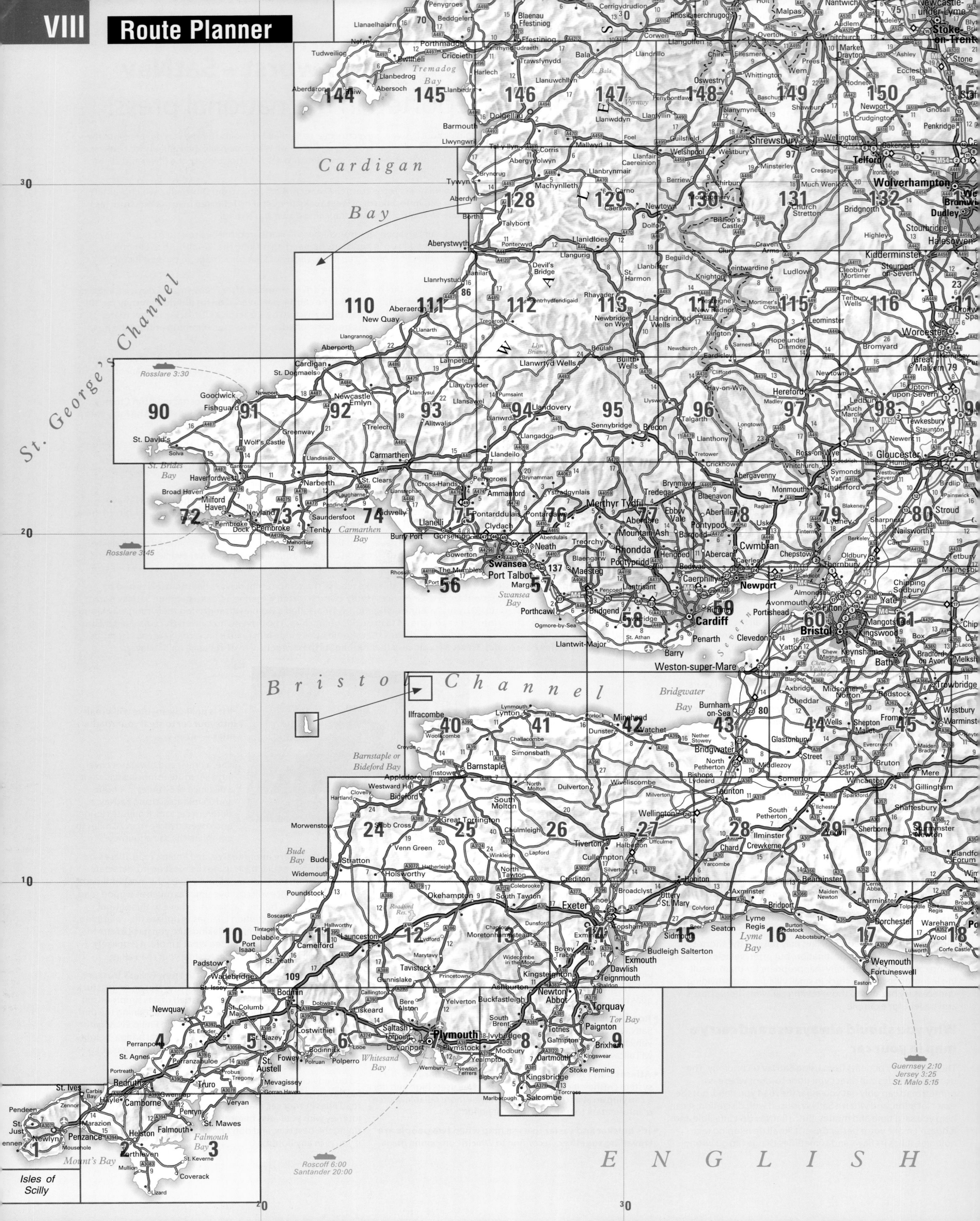

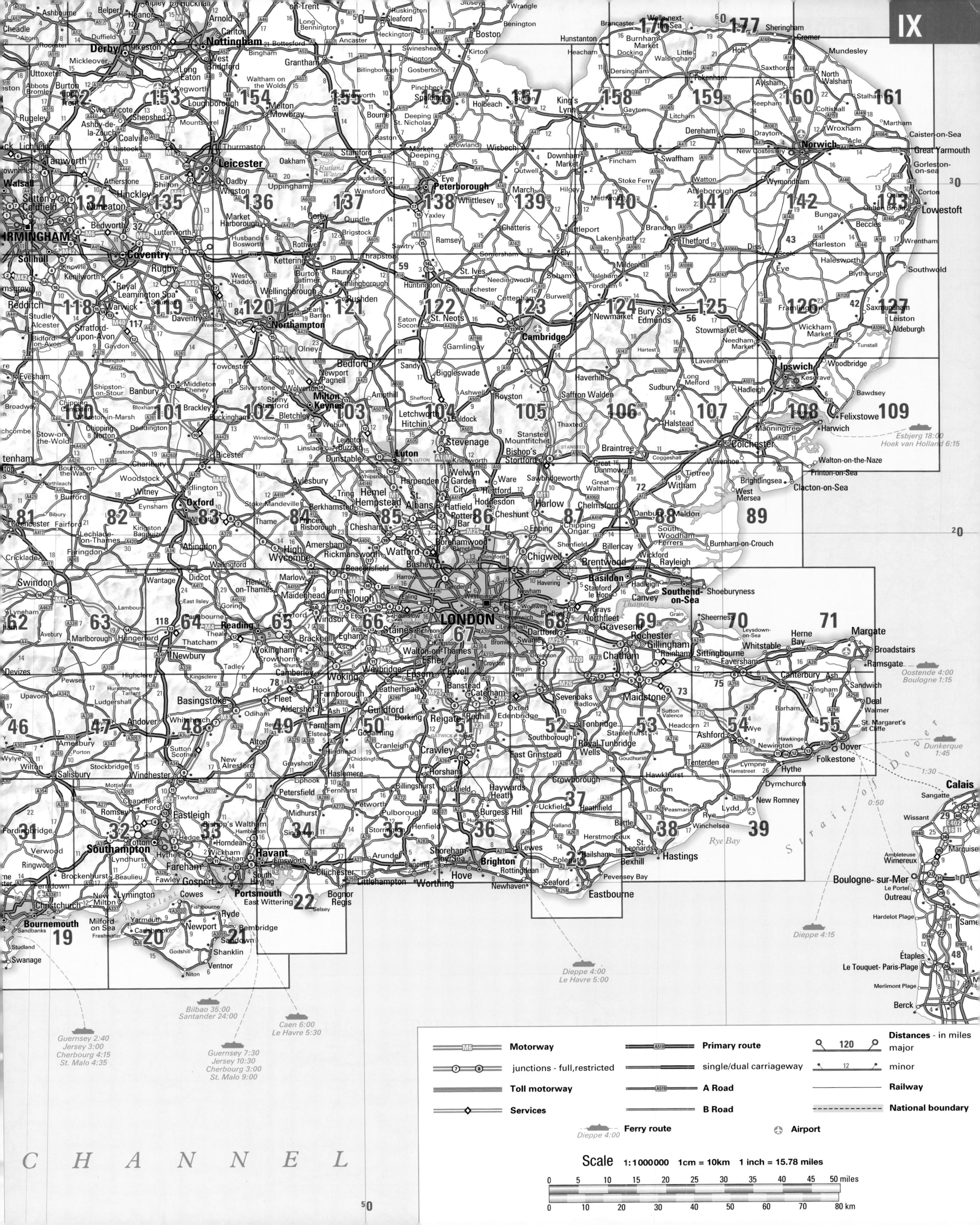

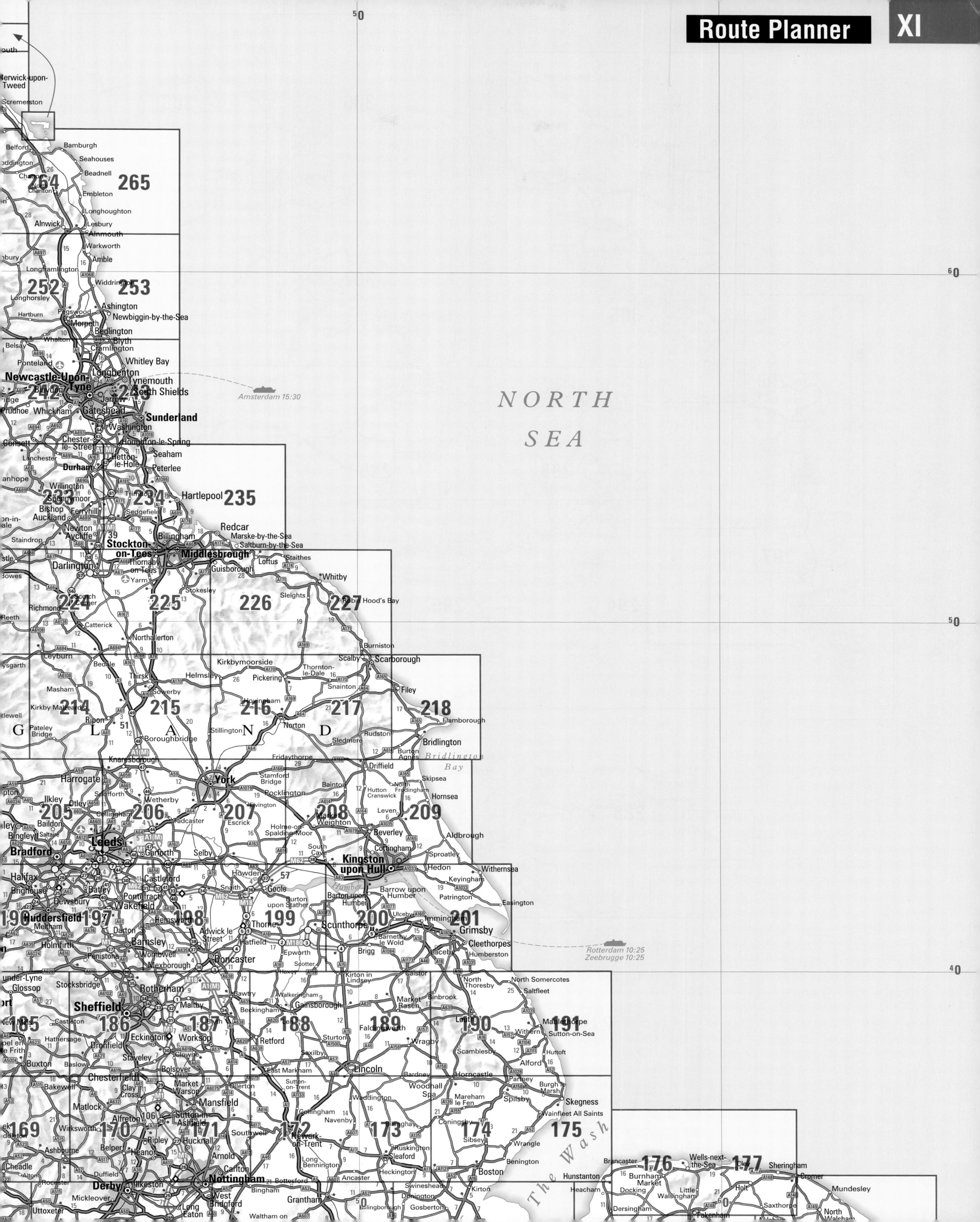

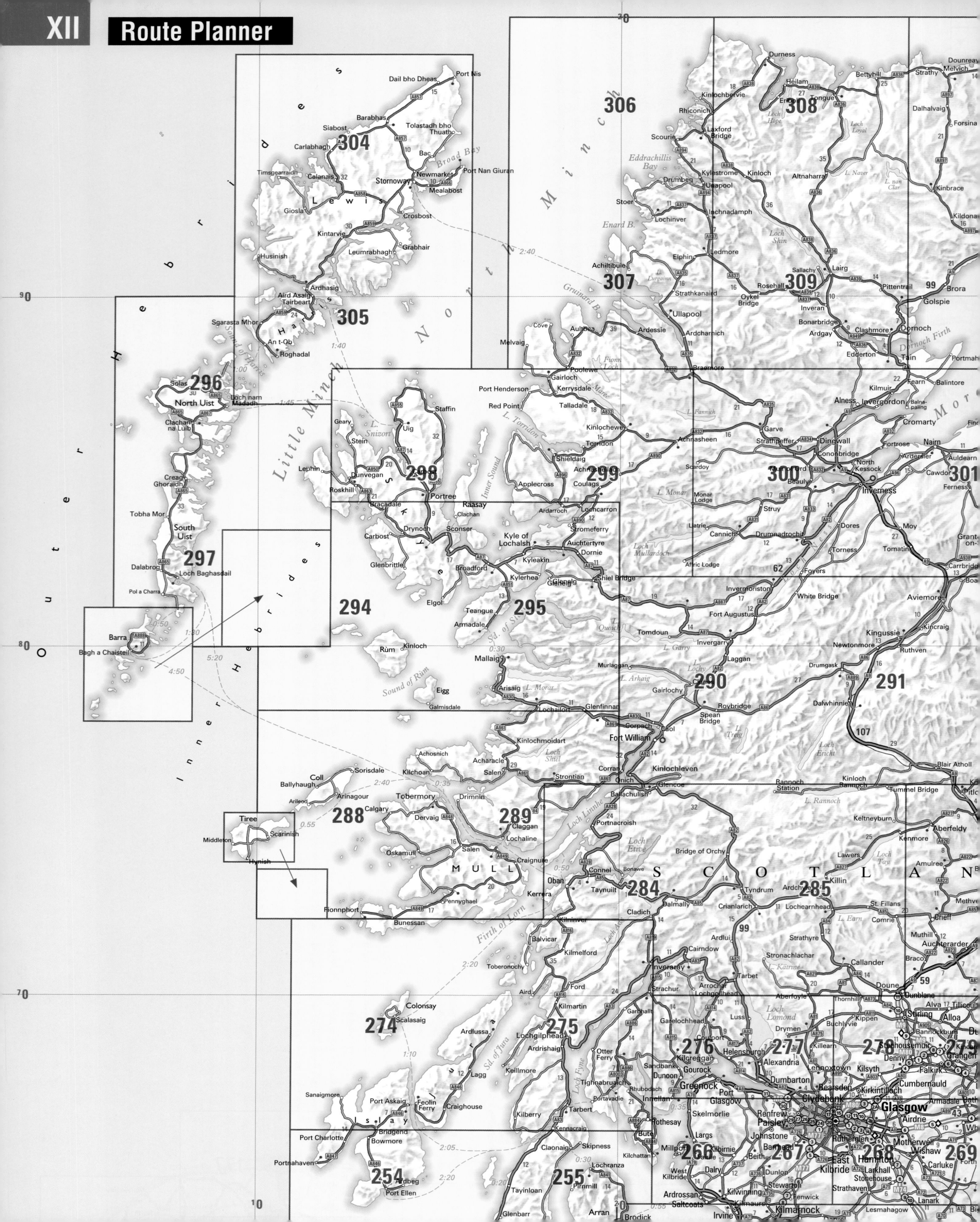

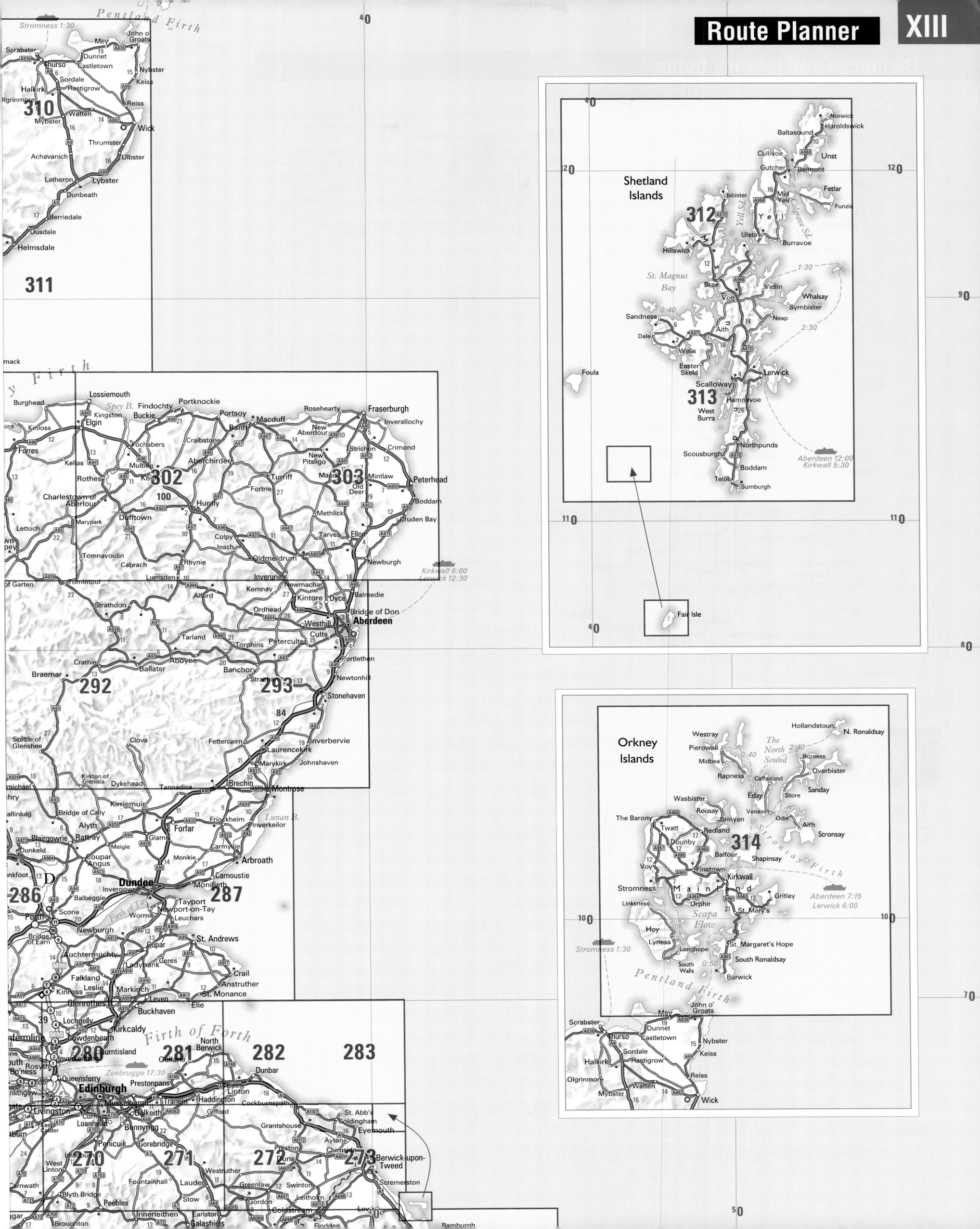

Distances and journey times

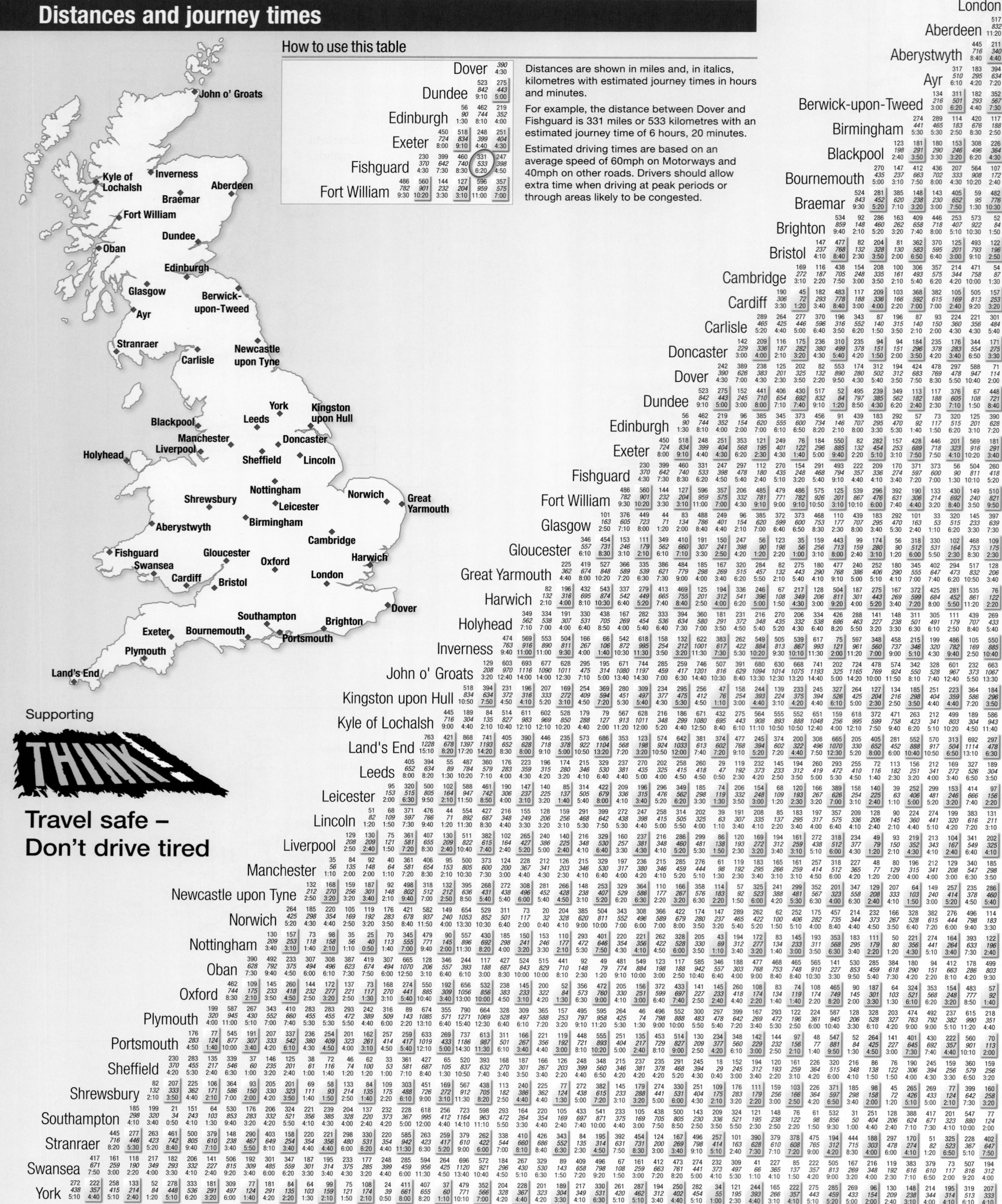

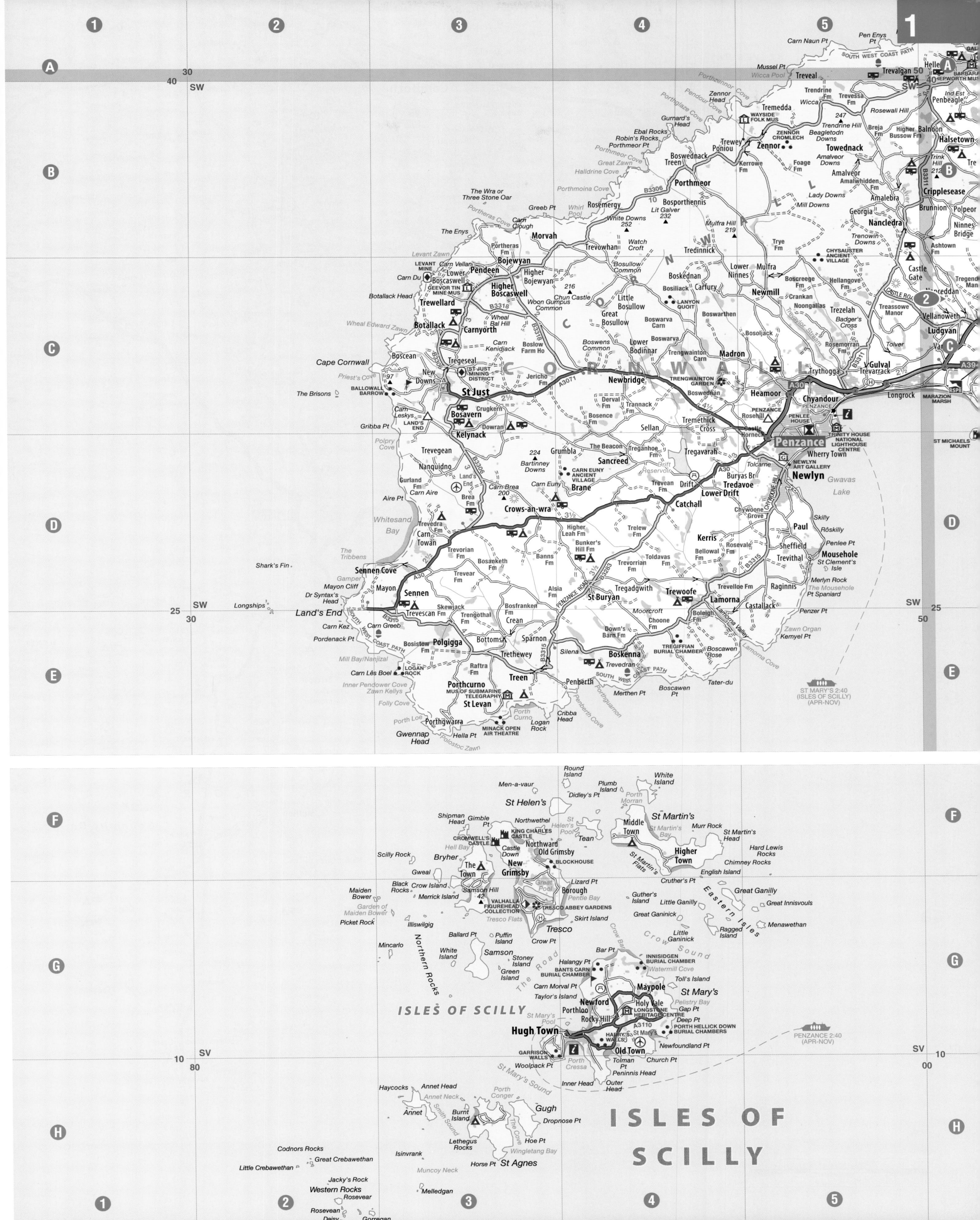

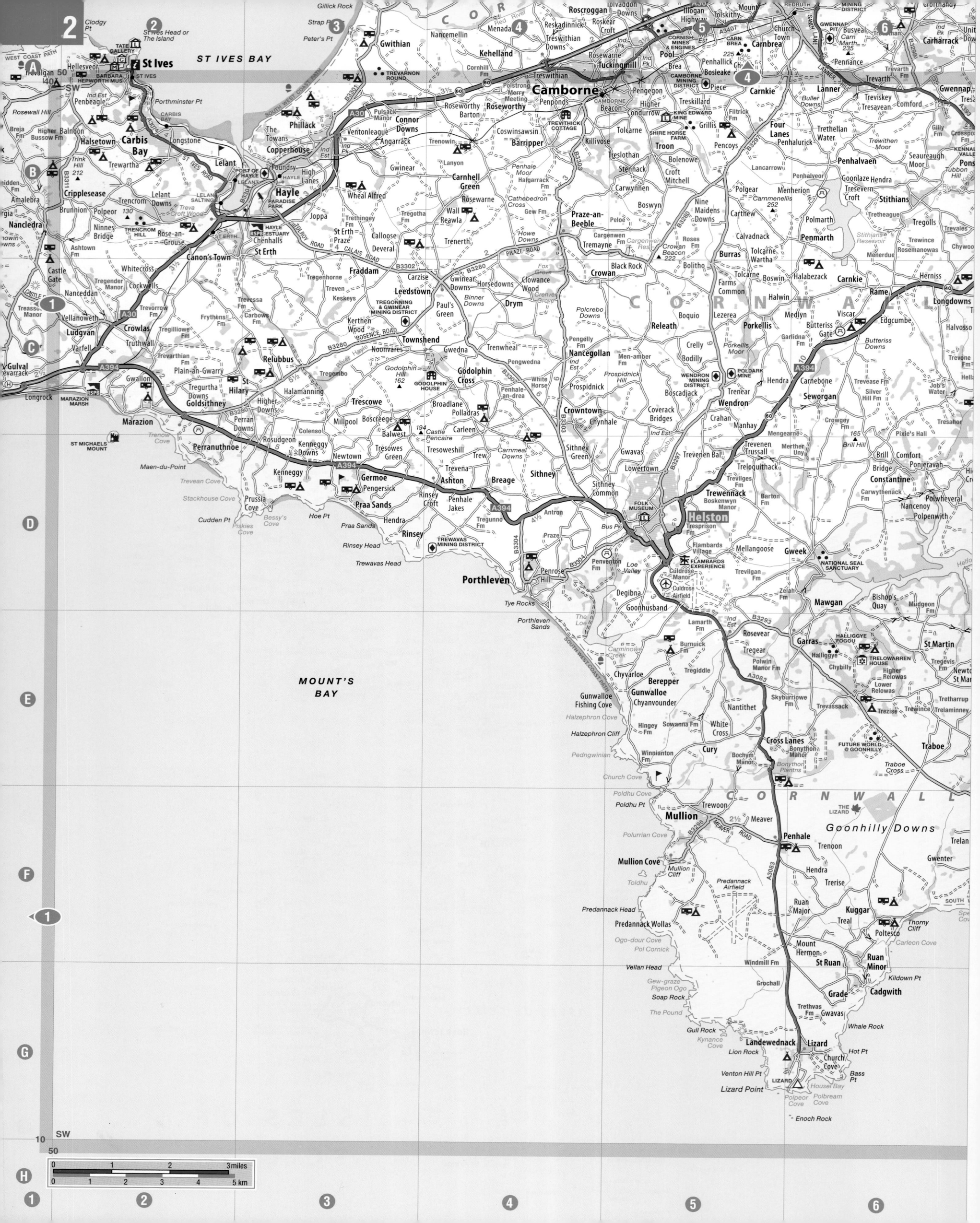

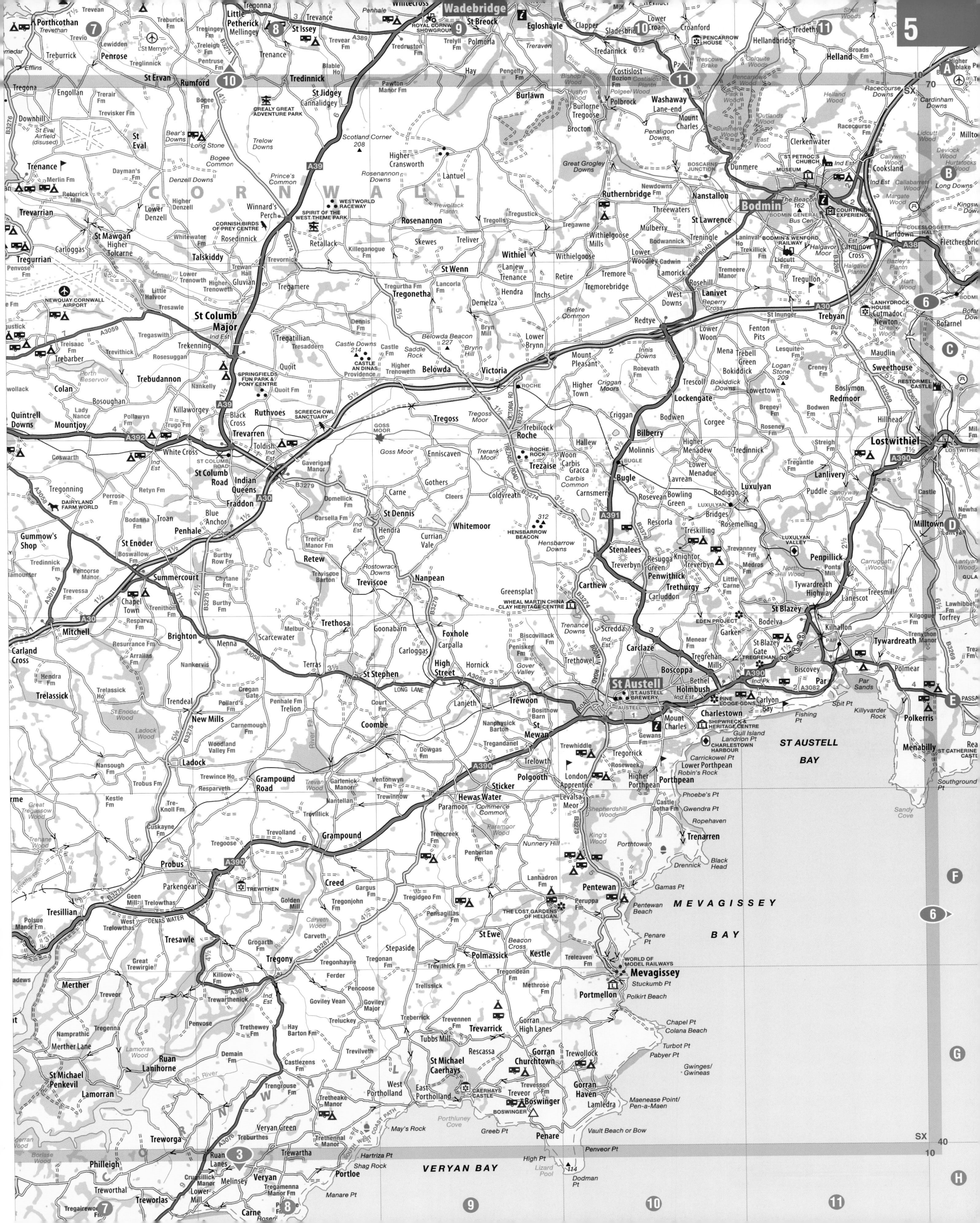

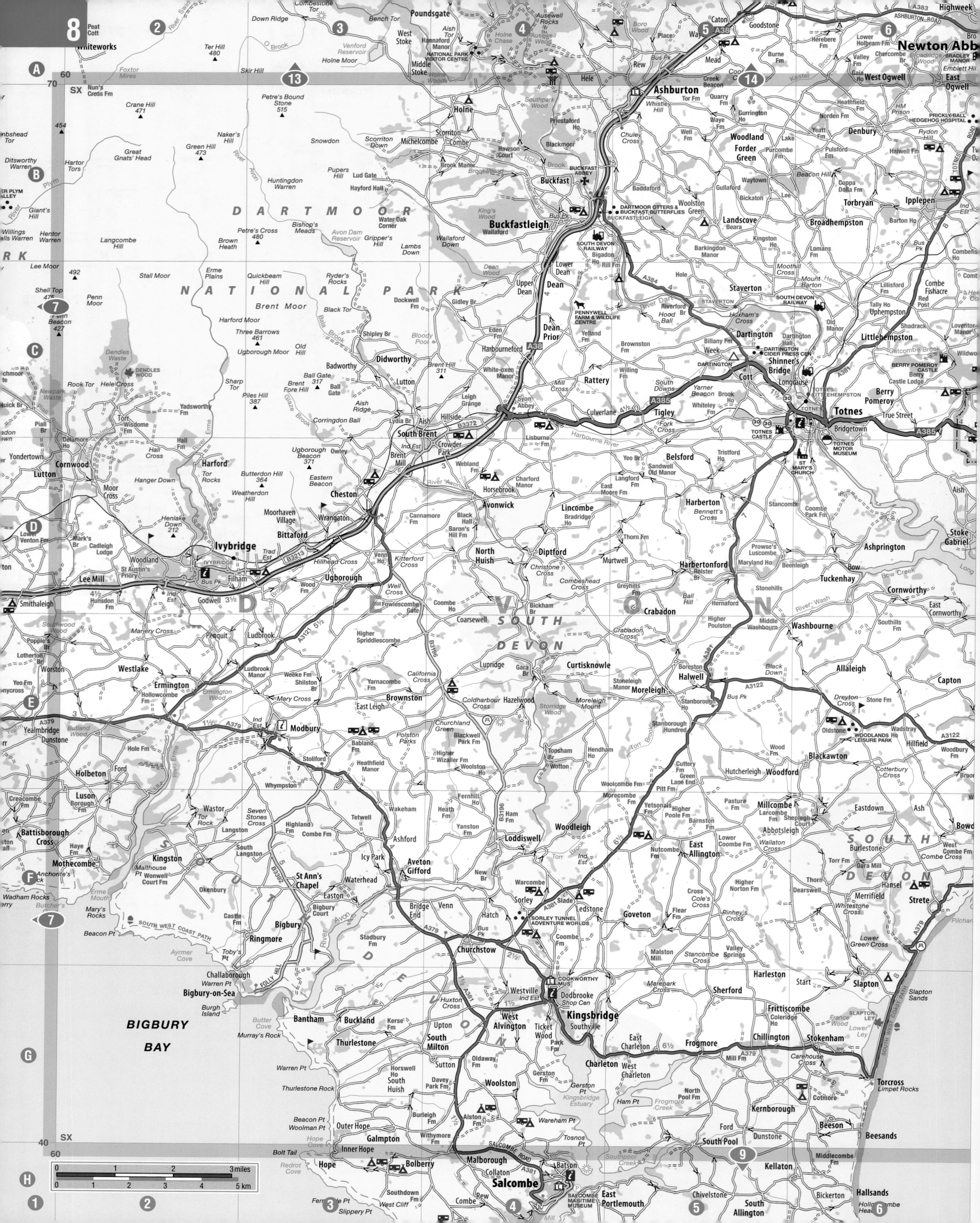

The Island
Tintagel Head
Glebe
Dunderhole Pt   Ti
                    TINTAGEL
Penhallic Pt

Tre
Trebarwi
Stra
Gull Rock   Port
            William
Dennis Pt
Backways Cove

Start Pt   Tr

Trerubies
Cove
Jacket's Pt   Tregardock
            Cliff
Crookmoyle Rock
Delabole Pt   West
Port   Dannonchapel
Isaac Bay   Barrett's Zawn

Rumps   The Mouls
Pt
Newland   Kellan   Varley
        Com   Head   Head
        Head   Scarnor   Lobber
    Pentire Pt   Port Quin Bay   Pt   Ranie Pt   Tresungers
        83   Pentire   Doyden   Pt
            Fm   Carnweather   Pt   Reedy
                Pt   Trevan   Pt   Port
Pentireglaze   Pt   Port Isaac   Port Gaverne
Haven   Port Quin   Trewetha
Padstow Bay   New Polzeath   Pendoggett
Gulland Rock   Hayle Bay   Trenant   Porteath   Scarrabine
                        Fm   LONG CROSS
            Polzeath   Carruan   VICTORIAN GDNS   Trelights
        Shilla   Plain   St
        Mill   Street   Endellion   Poltreworgey
    Pepper   Stepper Pt   Trebetherick   Pennytinney   Trelill
    Hole   The   St Minver   Gunvenna   Gunvenna   Lanow
    Narrows   Treglyn Down   Fm
Butter Hole   Tregellist   Trewethern
    Gunver   Trewiston   Trevanger   Tredrizzick   Trevine
    Head   Harbour   Fm   Pityme   St Minver   Trequite
Trevose Head   Cove   Daymer   Splatt   Treglyn   Rooke Fm   Trewethern   St Kew
Merope Rocks   Trebetherick   Bay   Penmayne   Chapel   Carclaze   Greater
Round Hole   Porthmissen   Gun Pt   Rock   Tresfra   Amble   Brighter Fm
Stinking Cove   Bridge   Round   Blakes   Penpont Fm   Hendra
Dinas Head   Tregirls Fm   Hole   Stoptide   Keiro   St Kew
Quies   PRIDEAUX   Crugmeer   Porthilly   Lower   Highway
        PLACE   Trethillick   Porthilly Cove   Gutt Bridge   Amble   Trevisquite
    Toll   Harlyn   Treator   PADSTOW   Trevelver   Trewornan   Fm
Booby's Bay   Harlyn   Trevone   MUSEUM   Town Bar   Tregorden   Kelly
Constantine   Treyarnon   Windmill   Padstow   NATIONAL   Rocksea   Dinham's
Bay   Constantine   Bay   B3276   Ind Est   LOBSTER HATCHERY   Fm   Br
    Treyarnon Pt   Bay   Dinas   River Camel   Tregunna   Burniere   Tregad
Trethias Island   TREYARNON   St Merryn   Dennis   Cant Cove   Perlees Fm   Bodieve   Three
Warren Cove   BAY   Treraval   Hill   Oldtown   Oldtown   Trevanson   Ball   Holes
Pepper Cove   Treyarnon   Towan   Fm   Sea   Cove   Tregunna   Edmonton   Dunveth   Cross   St Mabyn
Fox Cove   Trehemborne   Carnevas   Mills   Trevorrick   Bodellick   Ind Est   Hingham   Trevilder   Trethick
Minnows Islands   Shop   Burgois   CORNWALL   Penhale   Whitecross   Wadebridge   Mill   Cross
Will's Rock   Trevorrick   Highlanes   Tregonna   ROYAL CORNWALL   St Breock   Egloshayle   Clapper   Lower
Porthcothan   Trevean   Tregona   Little   Trevance   SHOWGROUND   Sladesbridge   Croan   Cranford
Bay   Treburrick   Tregingey   Petherick   Pengelly   Tredannick   PENCARROW
Trescore Islands   Porthcothan   Fm   Mellingey   St Issey   Trevear   A389   Tredruston   Hay   Fm   Teraven   Park   HOUSE
        Trevethan   Lewidden   Fm   Pawton   Trelyll   Polmorla   Trescowe
Porth Mear   Trevio   Treleigh   Trenance   Manor Fm   Polbrock   Brake
High Cove   Trevemedar   Penrose   St Merryn   Pentruse   Blable   Costislost
Park Head   Treglinnick   Fm   Trenance   Fm   Hay   Bozion   Penaligon
Diggory's Island   Tregona   Rumford   St Jidgey   Pengelly   Wood   Washaway   Downs
Queen Bess Rock   ollan   Trerair   Bogee   CREALY GREAT   Scotland Corner   Burlorne   Polbrock
REDRUTHAN STEPS   Fm   Fm   ADVENTURE PARK   208   Tregoose   Lane-end
    wnhill   Trevisker Fm   Higher   Brocton   Mount
High Cove   St Eval   Penaligon   Charles
Trenance Pt   Airfield   Bear's   Trelow   Downs
        (disused)   St Eval   Downs   Long Stone   Downs   Bogee
                            Common

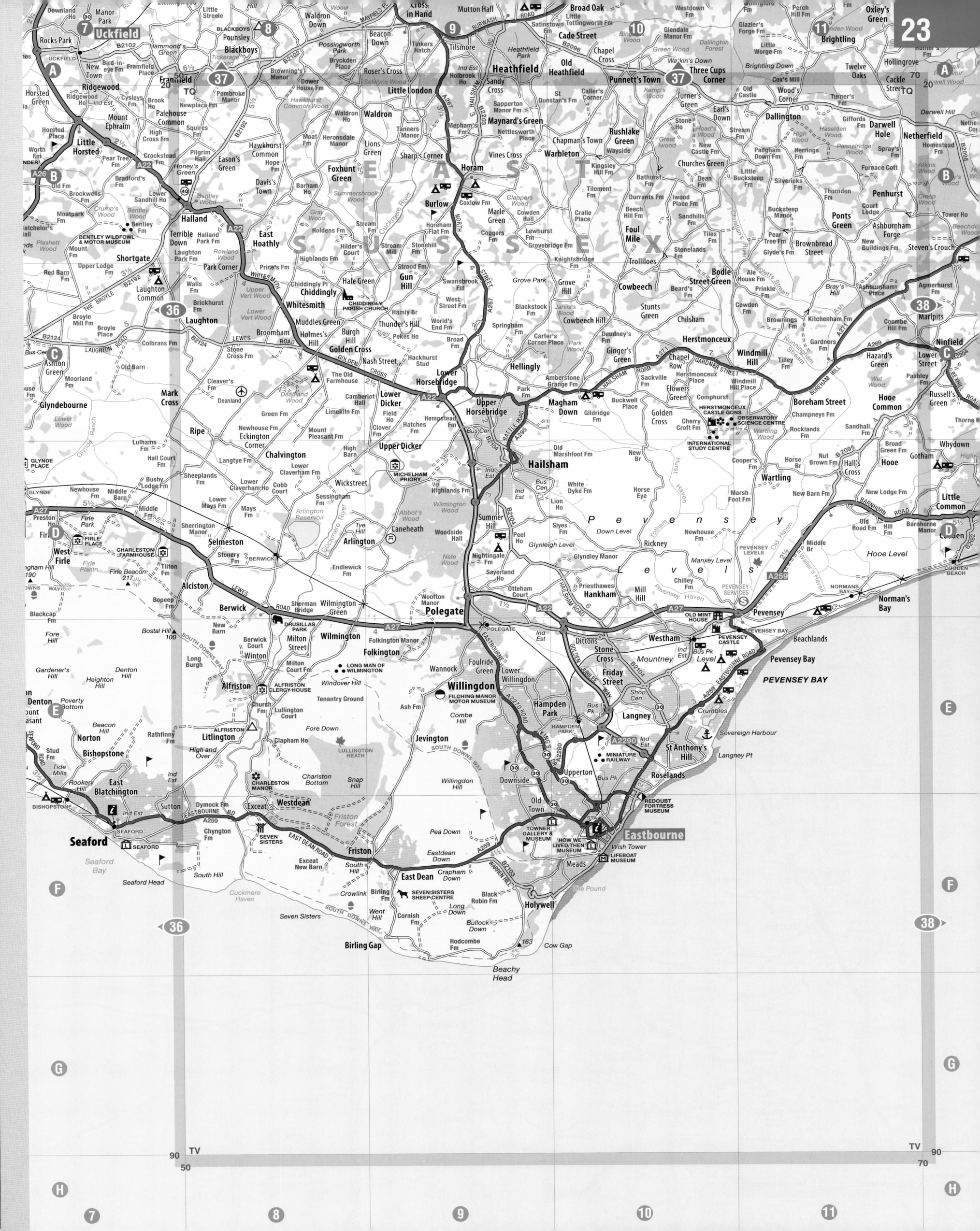

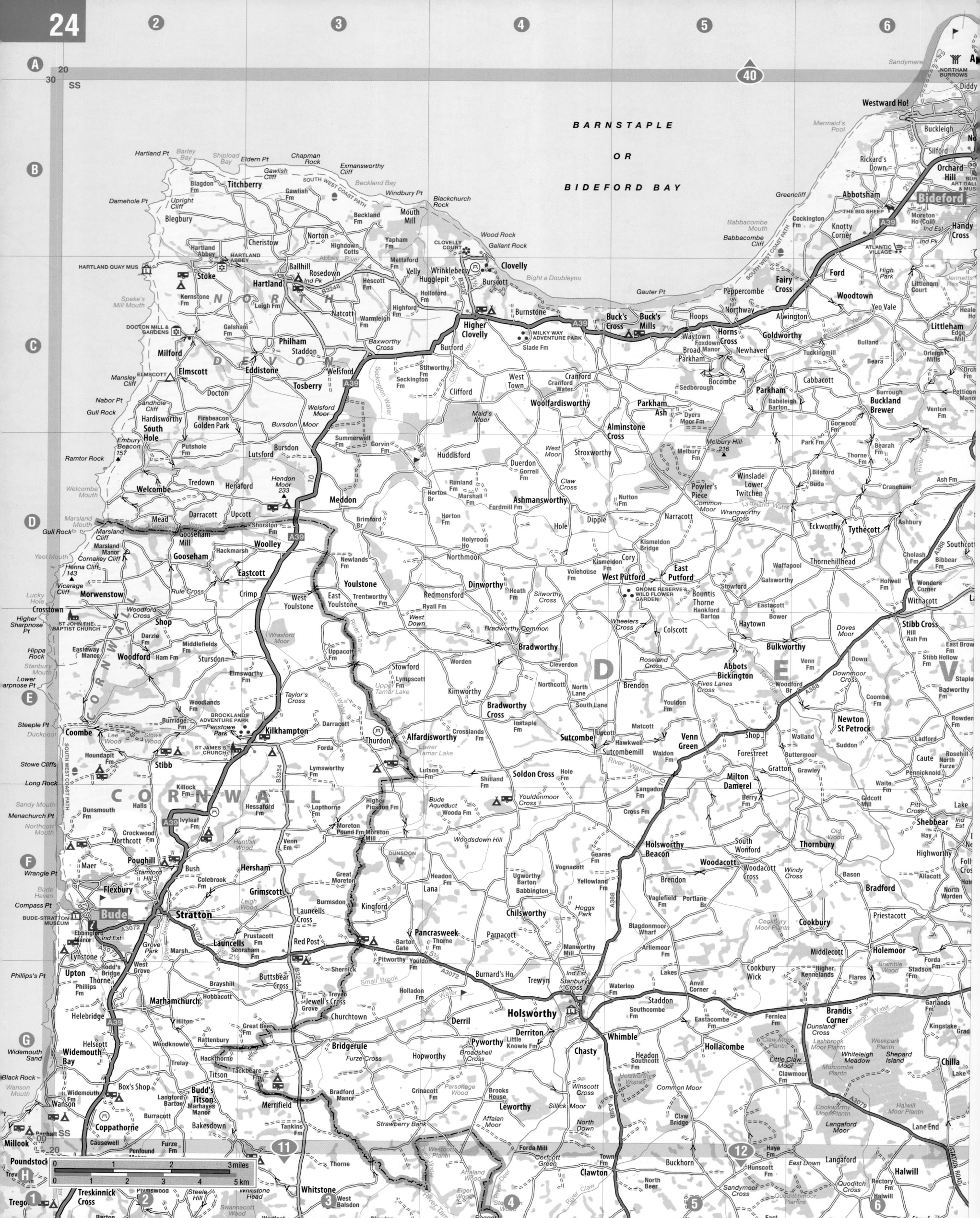

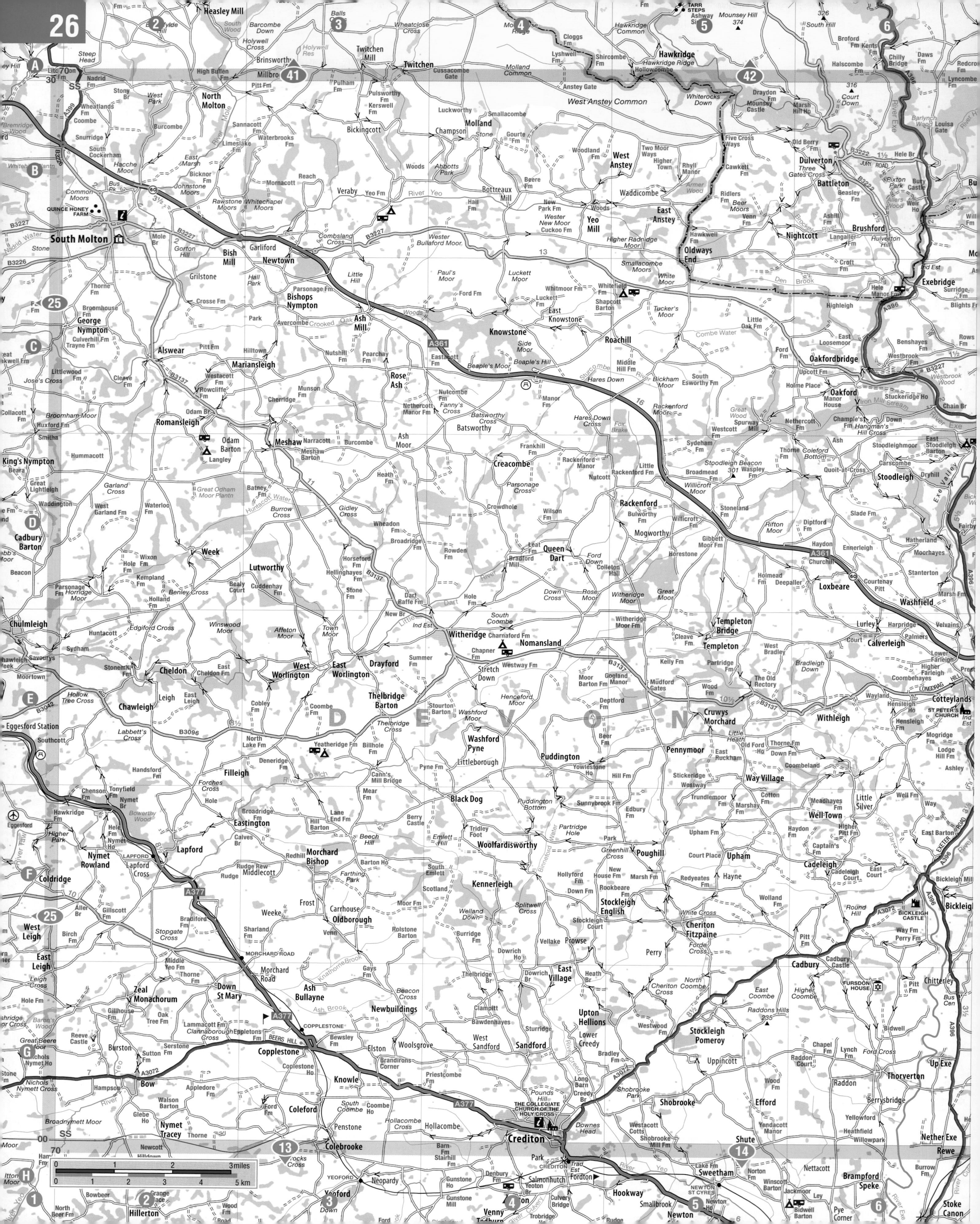

41   42

A

Steep Head
Little 70 Fm
30
SS
Heasley Mill
Fylde
Balls
Wheatclose Cross
Twitchen Mill
Twitchen
Moorhouse Ridge
Cloggs
Lyshwell
Shircombe
Hawkridge Common
Hawkridge
Hawkridge Ridge
Hollowcombe
TARR STEPS
Ashway Side
Mounsey Hill 374
South Hill
Broford Fm
Kents
Chilly Bridge
Daws Fm
Redcro
Lyncom
6

B
Bremridge Wood
Whiteh Plantn
B3226
Nadrid Fm
Wheatlands Coombe
Stony Br
West Park
High Bullen
Brinsworthy
Millbro
Pulham
Pulsworthy
Kerswell
Cussacombe Gate
Molland Common
West Anstey Common
Whiterocks Down
Draydon
Mounsey Castle
316
Court Down
River Exe
Barlynch Wood
Louisa Gate
North Molton
Pitt Fm
Luckworthy
Smallacombe
Molland
Champson
Stone
Gourte Fm
Anstey Gate
Two Moor Ways
Higher Town
Rhyll Manor
Old Berry
Five Cross Ways
Cawkett
Hawkwell
Dulverton
Three Gates Cross
Battleton
JURY ROAD
Pixton Park
Bury Castle
B
Snurridge
South Cockerham
Hacche Moor
East Marsh
Bicknor Moors
Reach
Mornacott
Veraby
Yeo Fm
River Yeo
Hall Mill
Bottreaux Mill
Beere Fm
New Park Fm
Wester New Moor
Cuckoo Fm
West Anstey
Woods
Waddicombe
East Anstey
Beer Moors
Venn
Ashill Fm
Nightcott
Langaller
Hulverton Hill
Brushford
Beasley Fm
Aller Cross
Weir Fm

Common Moors
QUINCE HONEY FARM
South Molton
B3227
Bish Mill
Garliford
Newtown
Grilstone
Hall Park
Little Hill
Bishops Nympton
Parsonage Fm
Combslang Cross
Ash Mill
B3227
Paul's Moor
Ford Fm
Knowstone
Side Moor
Luckett Moor
Whitmoor Fm
Shapcott Barton
East Knowstone
Tucker's Moor
Whitefield
Roachill
Oldways End
Hawkwell Moor
Higher Radnidge Moor
Smallacombe Moors
White Moor
Exebridge
Surridge
Highleigh
Oakfordbridge
Oakford
25
George Nympton
Broomhouse Fm
Culverhill Fm Trayne Fm
Alswear
Pitt Fm
Hilltown
Nutshill
Pearchay
Eastacott
Beaple's Moor
Beaple's Hill
Middle Hill Fm
Hares Down
South Esworthy Fm
Bickham Moor
Rackenford Moor
Great Wood
Spurway Fm
Westcott Fm
Nethercott
Chample's Fm
Down
Hangman's Hill Cross
Stuckeridge Ho
Chain Br
C
Littlewood
Jose's Cross
Cleave Fm
Cherridge
Romansleigh
Odam Br
Munson
Rose Ash
Nutcombe
Nethercott Manor Fm
Fanny's Cross
Batsworthy Cross
Batsworthy
Manor Fm
Hares Down Cross
Fox Brake
Rackenford Manor
Little Rackenford Fm
Willicroft Moor
Stoodleigh Beacon 301
Wasply
Quoit-at-Cross
Oakford Manor House
Holme Place
Thorne Coleford Bottom
Ash
Stoodleighmoor
East Stoodleigh Barton
Dryhill
Rows Fm

D
Cadbury Barton
Beara
King's Nympton
Great Lightleigh
Hummacott
Huxford Fm
Broomham Moor
Smitha
Meshaw
Narracott
Burcombe
Ash Moor
Heath Fm
Frankhill Fm
Creacombe
Parsonage Fm
Nutcott
Crowdhole
Wilson Fm
Rackenford
Bulworthy Fm
Willicroft
Mogworthy
Stoneland
Gibbett Moor Fm
Horestone
Rifton Moor
Diptford
Slade Fm
Stoodleigh
Churchill
Loxbeare
A361
Haydon Fm
Hatherland
Moorhayes
Stanterton
Courtenay Pitt
Washfield
Fairby
Waddington
West Garland Fm
Garland Cross
Waterloo Fm
Week
Lutworthy
Kempland
Benley Cross
Cuddenhay Fm
Stone
Dart Raffe Fm
Hole Fm
South Coombe
Down Cross
Rose Moor
Witheridge Moor
Great Moor
Holmead
Deepaller
Ennerleigh
Chawleigh
E
Hollow Tree Cross
Leigh
East Leigh
Cheldon
East Cheldon Fm
Cobley Fm
Coombe
Winswood Moor
Affeton Moor
Town Moor
Horseford Fm
Hellinghayes
Broadridge
Rowden Fm
Bradford Mill
Queen Dart
Colleton Hall
Witheridge
Nomansland
Chapner Fm
Charnaford Fm
Witheridge Moor Fm
Cleave Fm
Templeton Bridge
Lurley
Harpridge
Palmers
Calverleigh
West Bradley
Bradleigh Down
Higher Farleigh
Lower Farleigh
Coombehayes
Cotteylands
Henslea Ho
ST PETER'S CHURCH
Eggesford Station
Southcott
B3096
B3137
Labbett's Cross
North Lake Fm
Stonemill Fm
West Worlington
East Worlington
Drayford
Thelbridge Barton
Thelbridge Cross
Summer Moor
Stretch Down
Henceford Moor
Westway Fm
Moor Barton Fm
Gogland Manor
Kelly Fm
Partridge Fm
The Old Rectory
Templeton
Wood Fm
Mudford Gates
D E V O N
Cruwys Morchard
Withleigh
Wayland
Henslea Ho

F
Eggesford
Hawkridge
Higher Park
Chenson Fm
Tonyfield
Nymet Br
Nymet Ho
Filleigh
Deneridge Fm
Yeatheridge Fm
Billhole Fm
Cann's Mill Bridge
Mear Fm
Pyne Fm
Littleborough
Puddington
Yowlestone Ho
Hill Fm
Pennymoor
East Ruckham
Down Fm
Coombeland
Stickeridge Fm
Way Village
Westway
Trundlemoor Fm
Cotton Fm
Marshay Fm
Meadhayes Fm
Little Silver
Well Town
Way
Haydon
Higher Pitt Fm
Ashley
East Barton
Bickleigh
Coldridge
Nymet Rowland
Lapford
Lapford Cross
Bowerthy Wood
Hole
Broadridge
Eastington
Hill Barton
Lane End Fm
Beech Hill
Berry Castle
Emlett Hill
Black Dog
Tridley Foot
Partridge Hole
Park
Greenhill Cross
Upham Fm
New House Fm
Marsh Fm
Hollyford Fm
Poughill
Woolfardisworthy
Sunnybrook Fm
Edbury Fm
Redyeates Fm
Rookbeare Fm
Upham
Cadeleigh
East Court
Captain's Fm
Wolland Fm
Cadeleigh Court
EXETER RD
Bickleigh
G
West Leigh
East Leigh
Coldridge
25
A377
Aller Br
Gillscott Fm
Birch Fm
Bradiford
Stopgate Cross
Frost
Weeke
Carrhouse
Oldborough
Morchard Bishop
Rudge Rew
Middlecott
Rudge
Farthing Park
South Emlett
Scotland
Barton Ho
Kennerleigh
Welland Down
Splitwell Cross
Stockleigh English
Stockleigh Court
Vellake
Prowse
Hayne
White Cross
Cheriton Fitzpaine
Forde Cross
Pitt Fm
Cadbury
Cadbury Castle
East Coombe
Higher Coombe
FURSDON HOUSE
Round Hill
BICKLEIGH CASTLE
Way Fm
Perry Fm
Bickle
Chitterley
Bus Cen
West Leigh
East Leigh
Hole Fm
Middle Yeo Fm
Thorne Fm
Leigh Cross
Down St Mary
Morchard Road
Zeal Monachorum
MORCHARD ROAD
Ash Bullayne
Venn
Sharland
Rolstone Barton
Burridge
Dowrich Br
East Village
Cheriton Cross
North Coombe
East Coombe
Higher Coombe
Upton Hellions
Westwood
Stockleigh Pomeroy
Uppincott
Raddons Hills 235
Chapel Fm
Lynch Cross
Ford Cross
Bidwell
H
Nichols Nymett Cross
Hampson
Bow
Appledore
Walson Barton
Oak Tree Fm
Gillhouse
Lammacott Fm
Clannaborough Cross
Eppletons Cross
BEERS HILL
A377
Copplestone
Bewsley Fm
Elston
Woolsgrove
Brandirons Corner
West Sandford
Sandford
Long Barn
Creedy
Bradley Fm
Shobrooke Park
Shobrooke
Westcott Cotts
Shobrooke Mill Fm
Efford
Yeoford
Yellowford
Winscott Barton
Heathfield
Willowpark
Nether Exe
Rewe
Thorverton
Raddon
Berrysbridge
Up Exe
Great Beere Moor
Reeve Castle
Burston
Sutton Fm
Nichols Nymet Ho
Coldridge
A3072
Coleford
Penstone
Hollacombe Cross
Hollacombe
Knowle
South Coombe
Coombe Fm
A377
Colebrooke
Newbuildings
Clampitt
Bawdenhayes
Sturridge
Lower Creedy
THE COLLEGIATE CHURCH OF THE HOLY CROSS
Crediton
Downes Head
13   14

miles 0 1 2 3
km 0 1 2 3 4 5
00
70
SS

1
North Beer Fm
Bowbeer
2
Hillerton
Grange Place
Yeoford
Neopardy
3
Yenford
Wood Fm
Denbury
Yeoton
Salmonhutch
Fordton
Hookway
Smallbrook
CREDITON
4
Venny Tedburn
Gunstone Mill
Culvery Bridge
Trobridge Ho
Lake Fm
River Yeo
Trad Est
5
NEWTON ST CYRES
Newton
Sweetham
Norton
Winscott Barton
Jackmoor
Ley
6
Brampford Speke
Burrow Fm
Stoke Canon
Pye Corner
Bidwell Barton

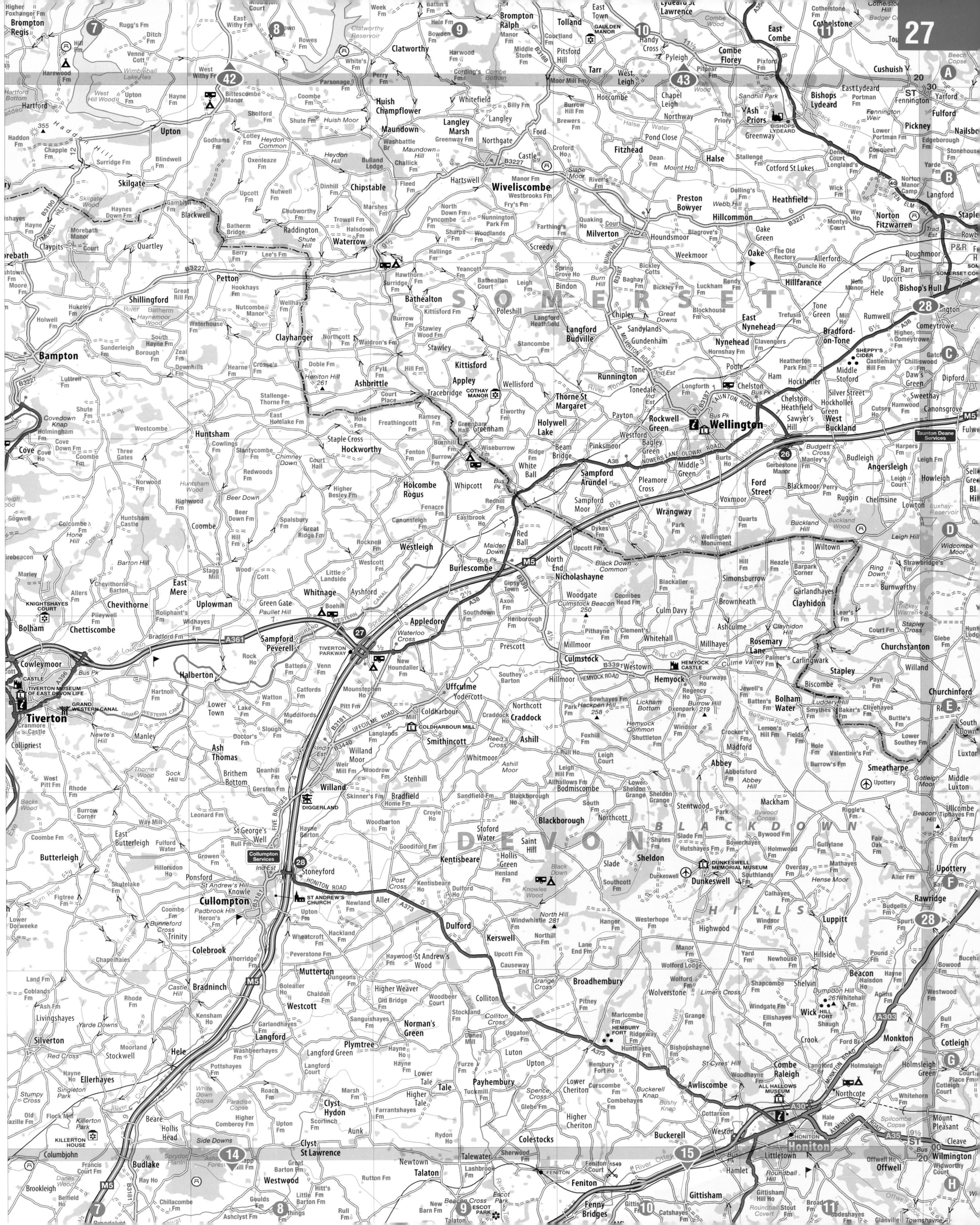

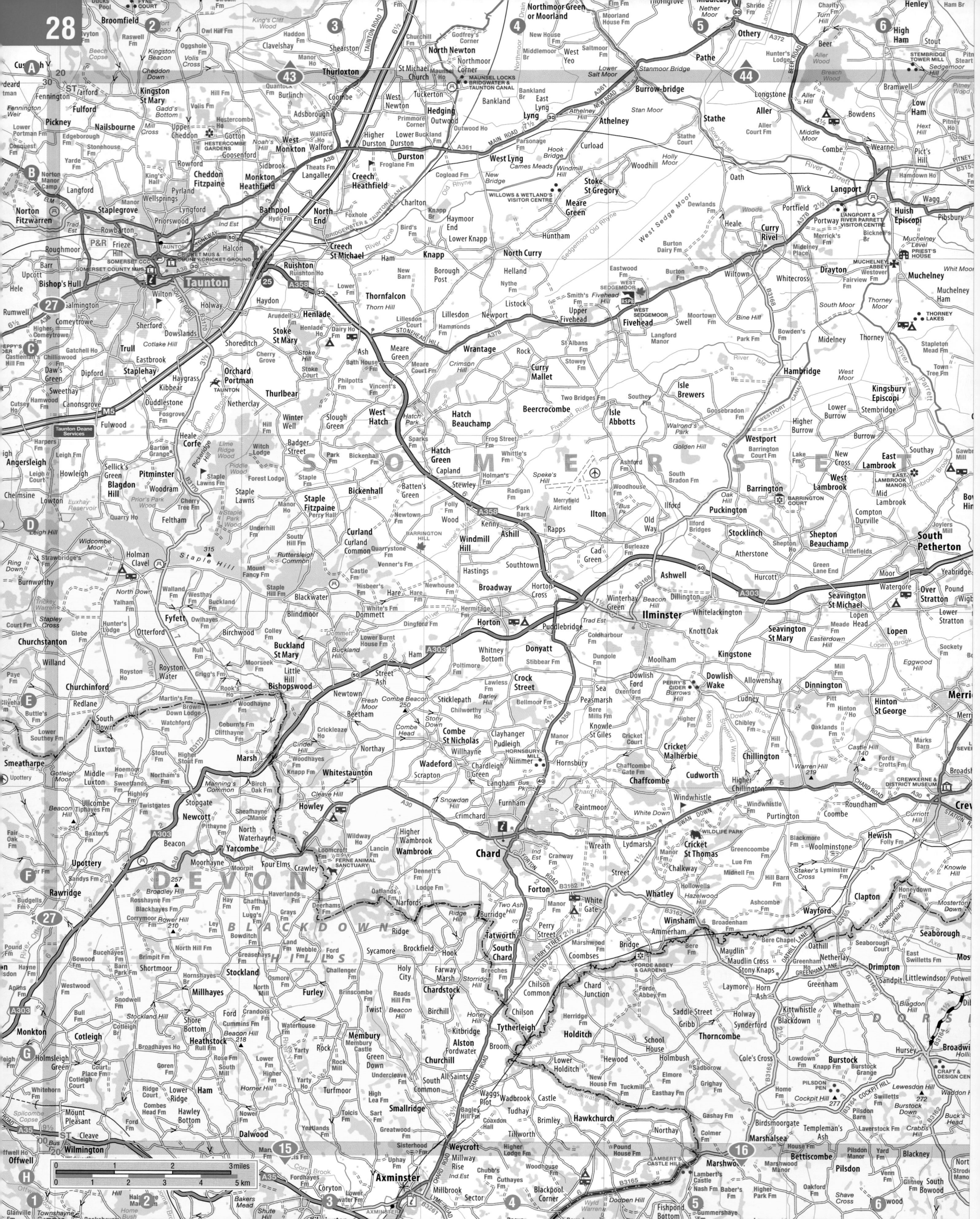

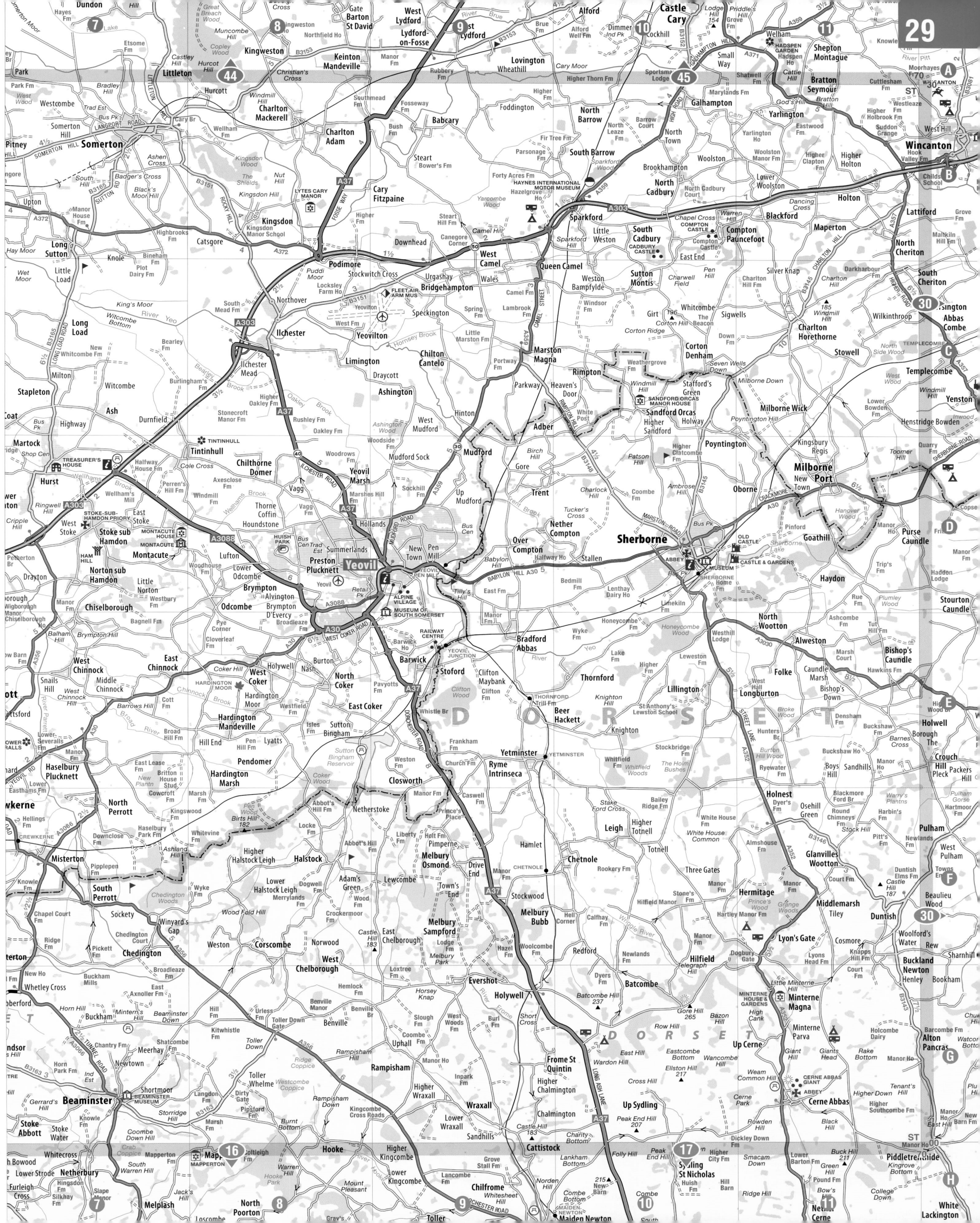

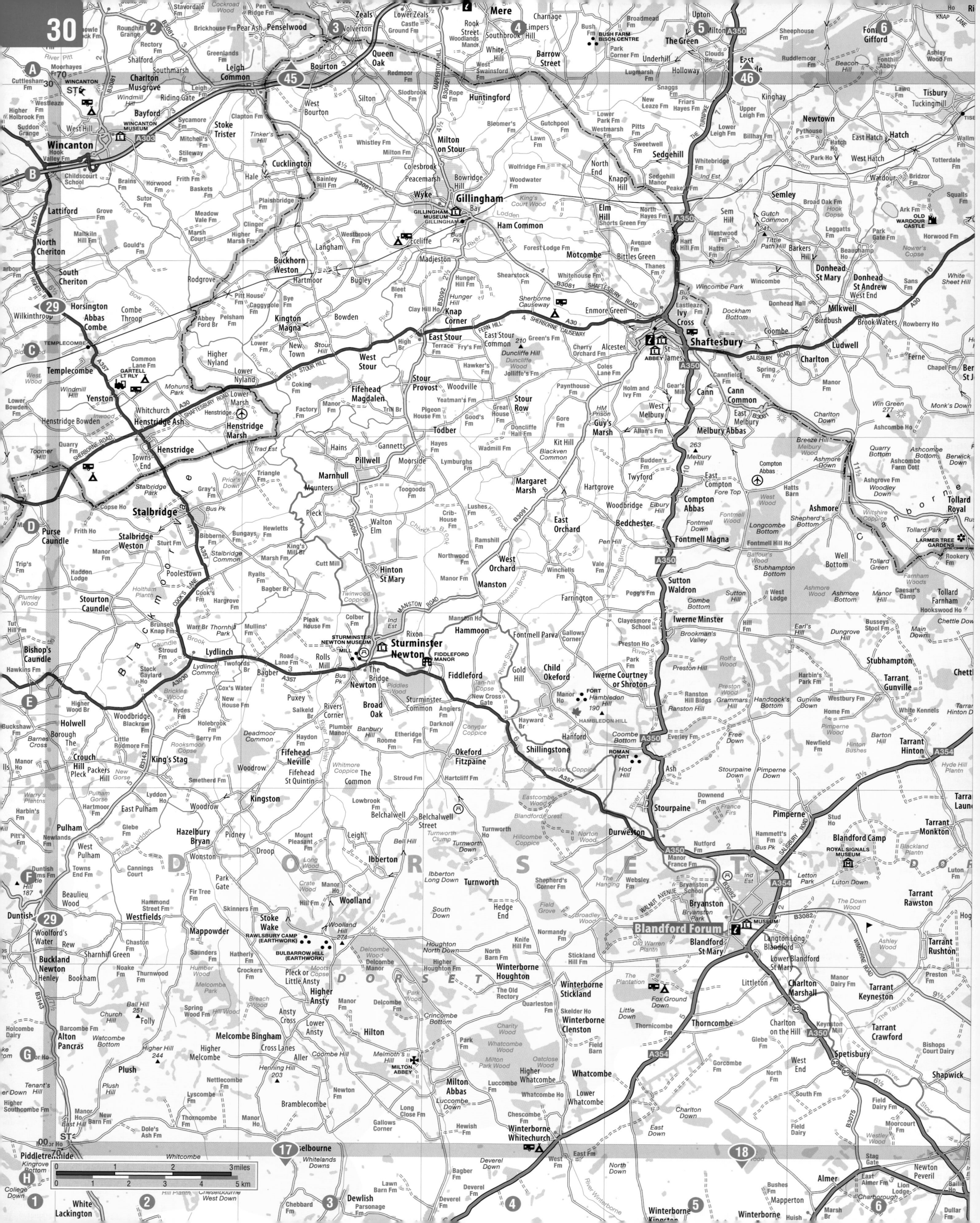

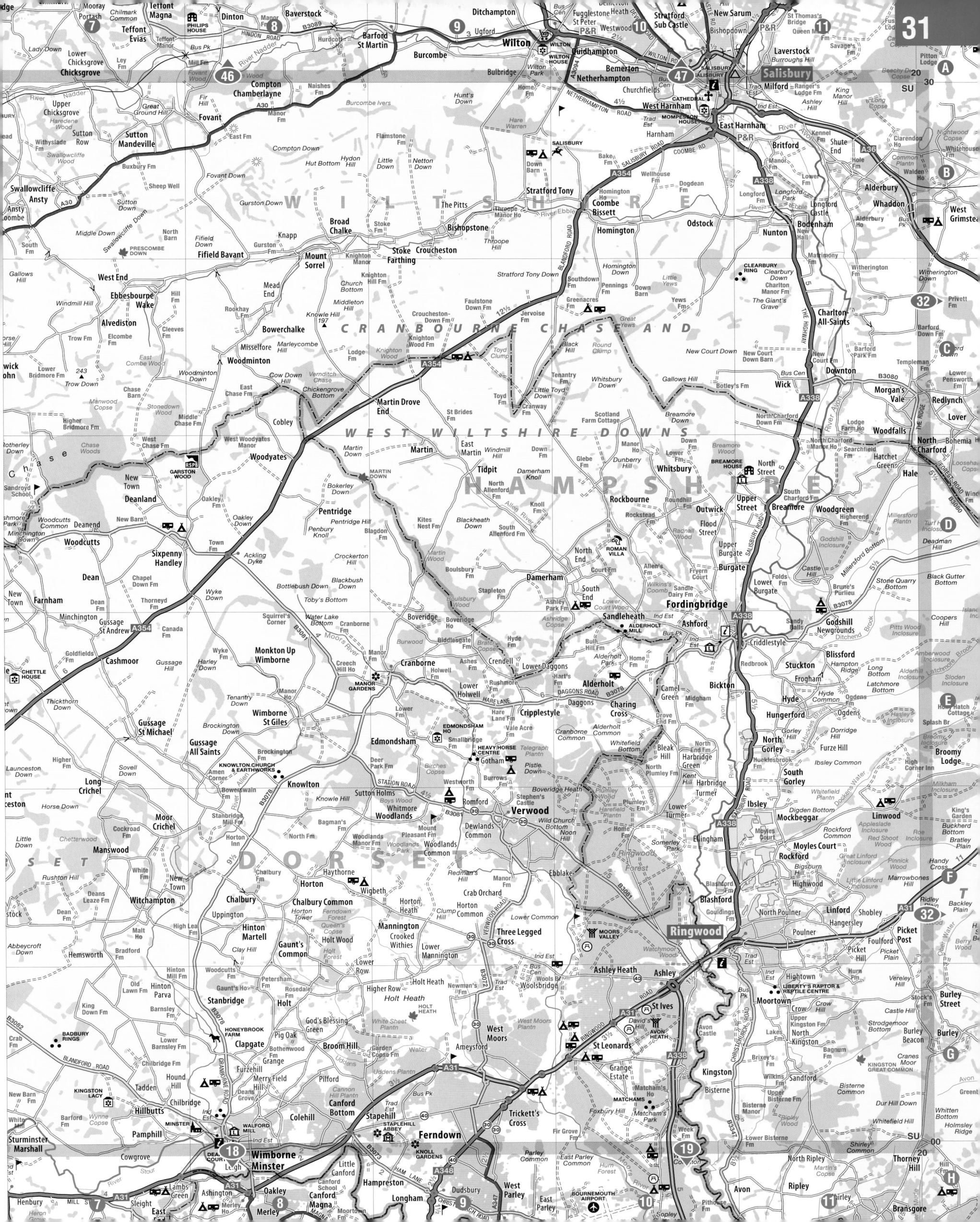

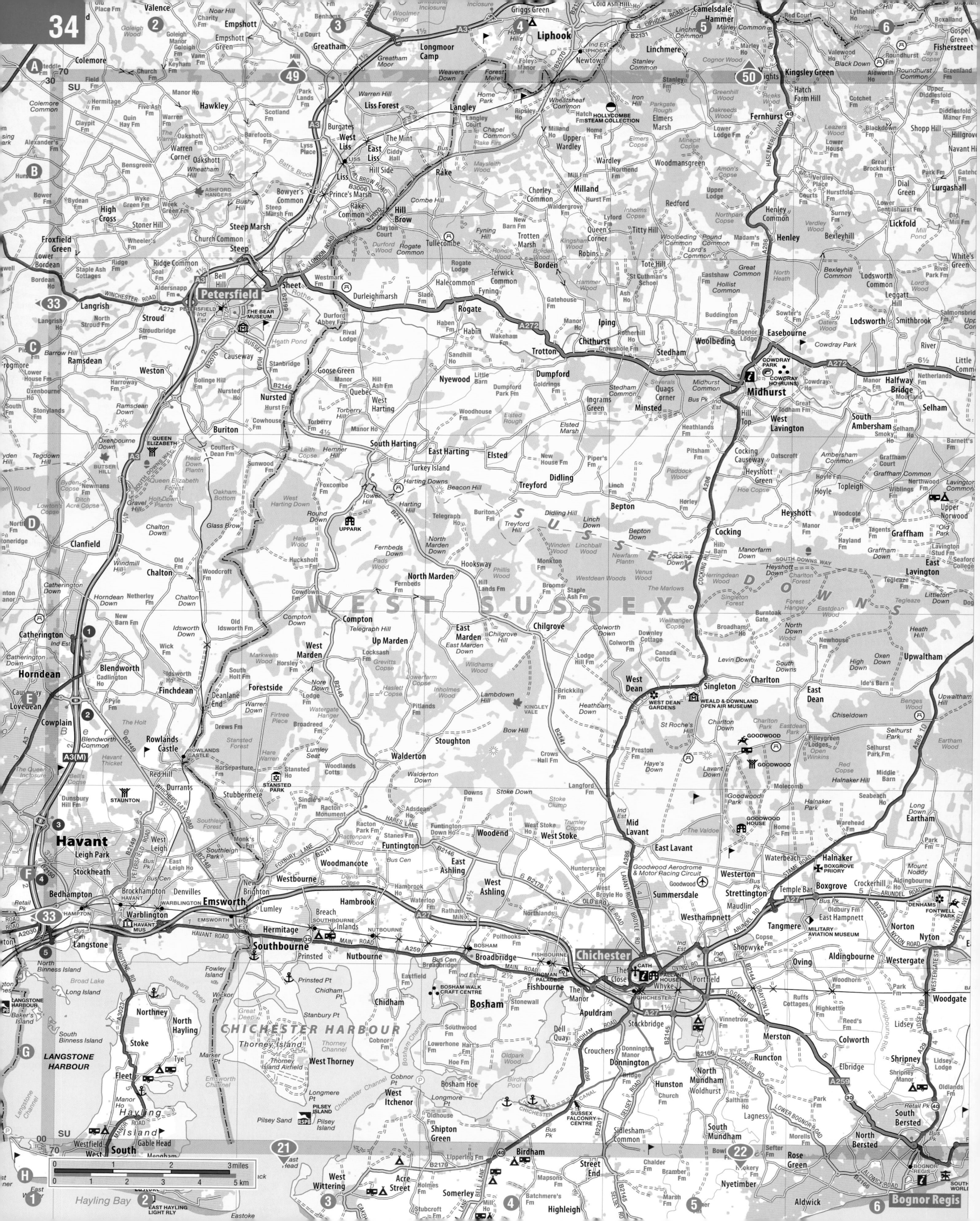

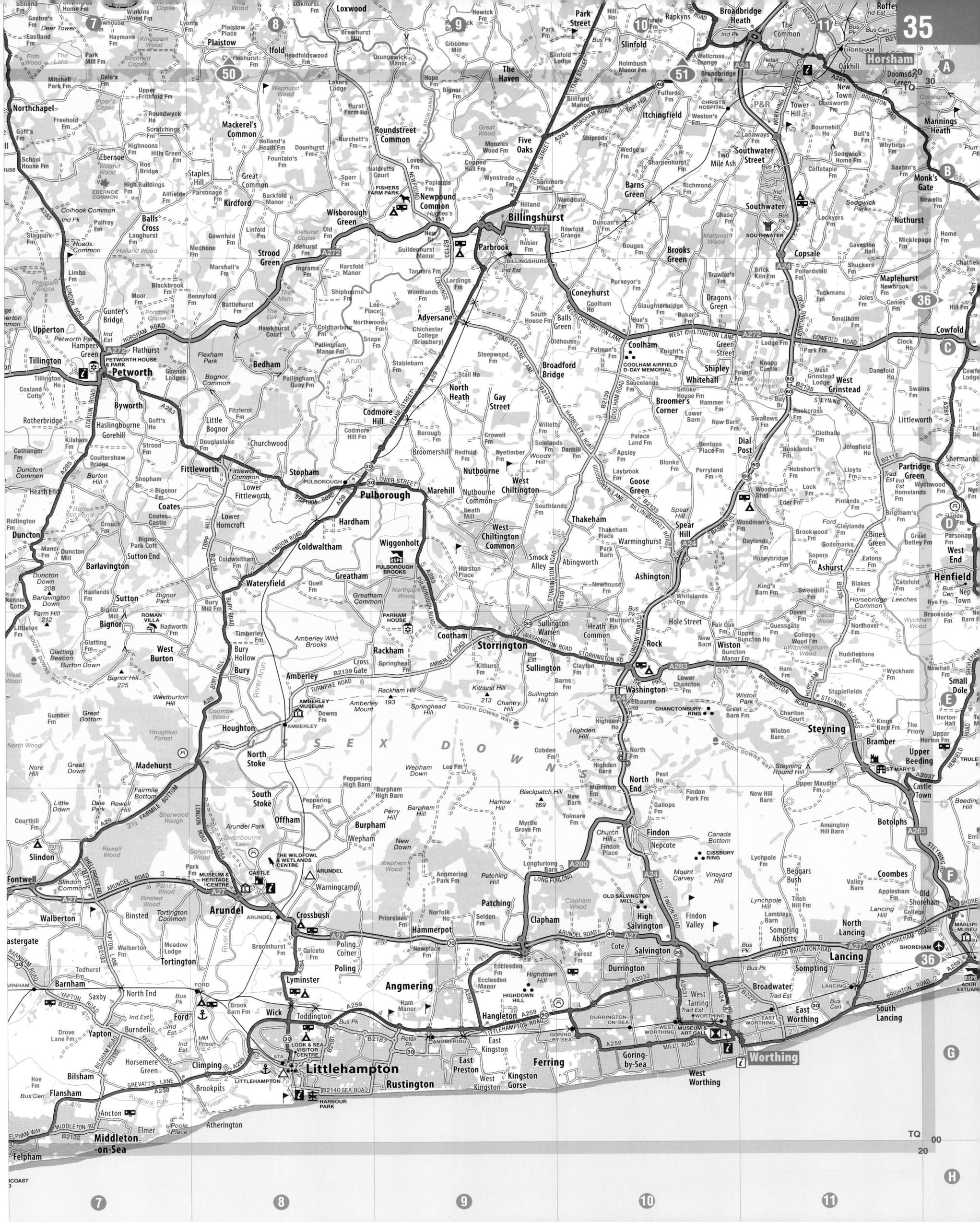

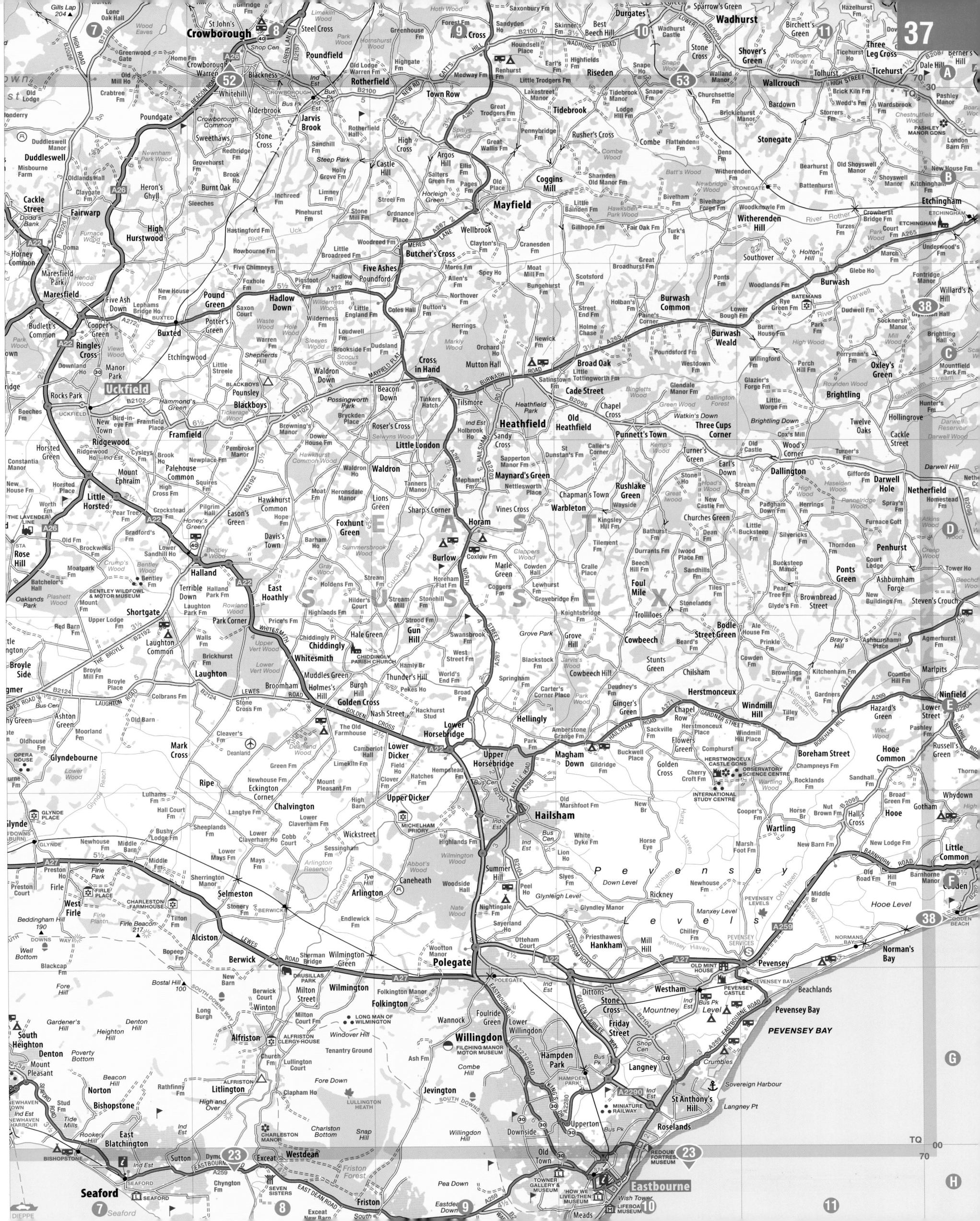

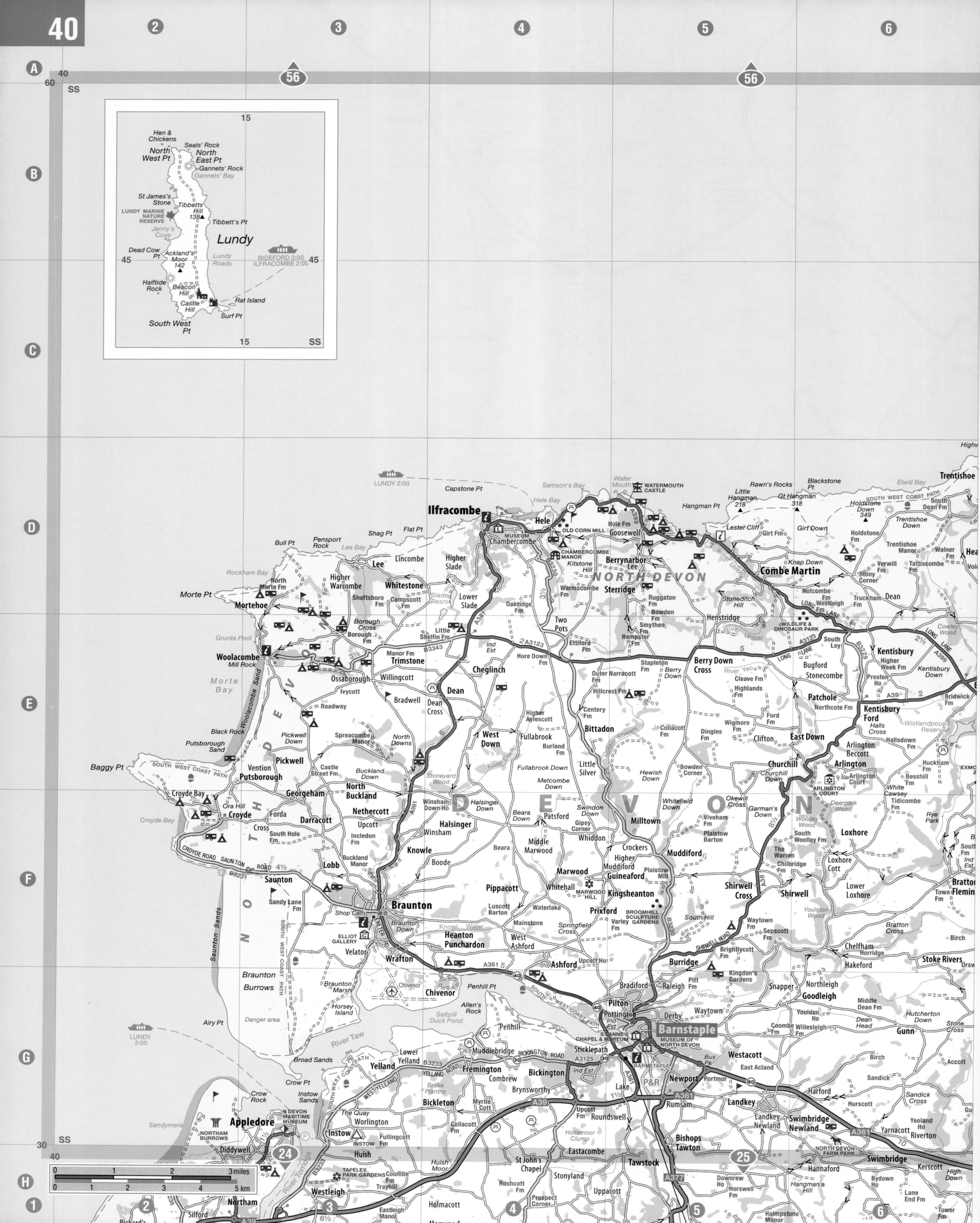

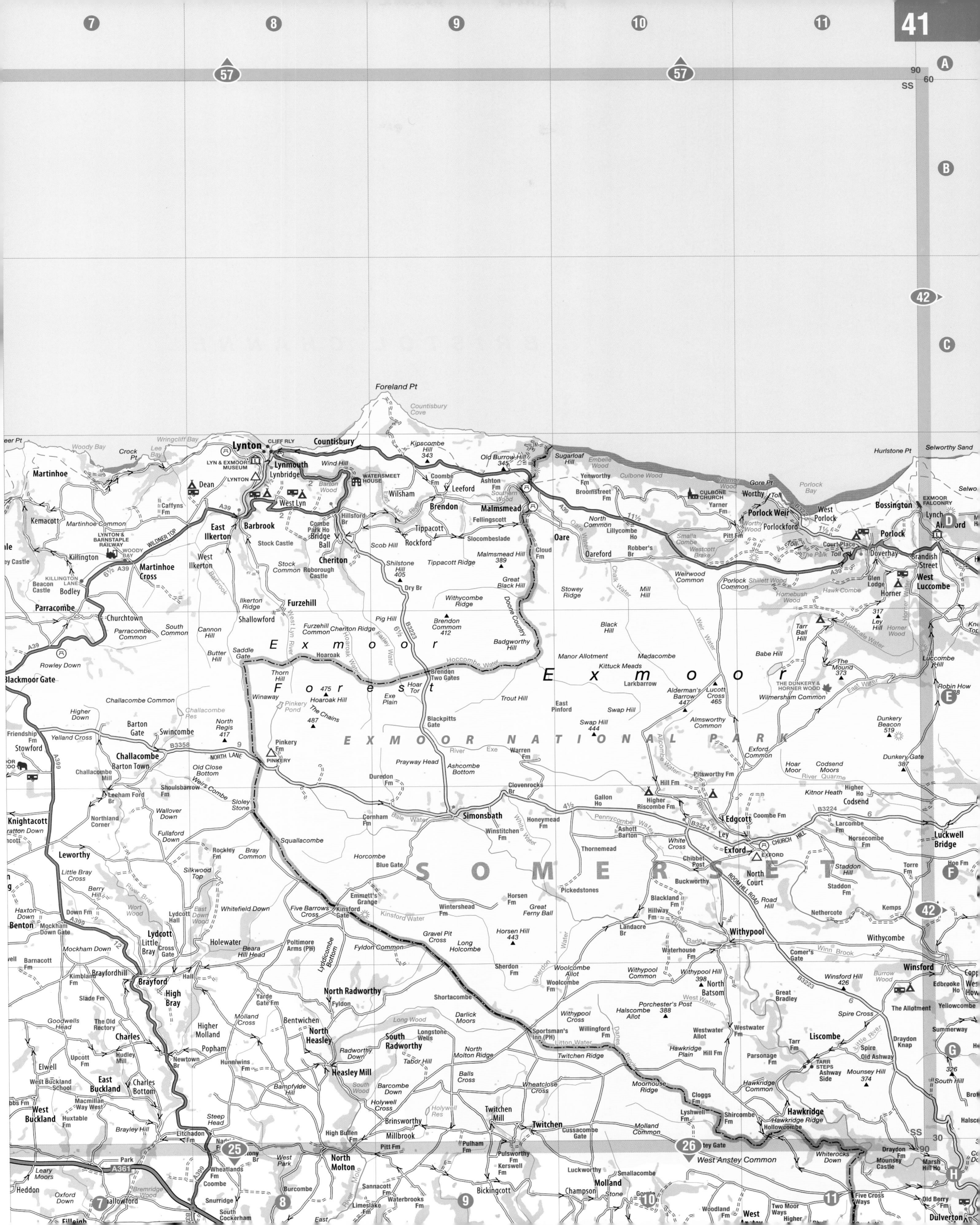

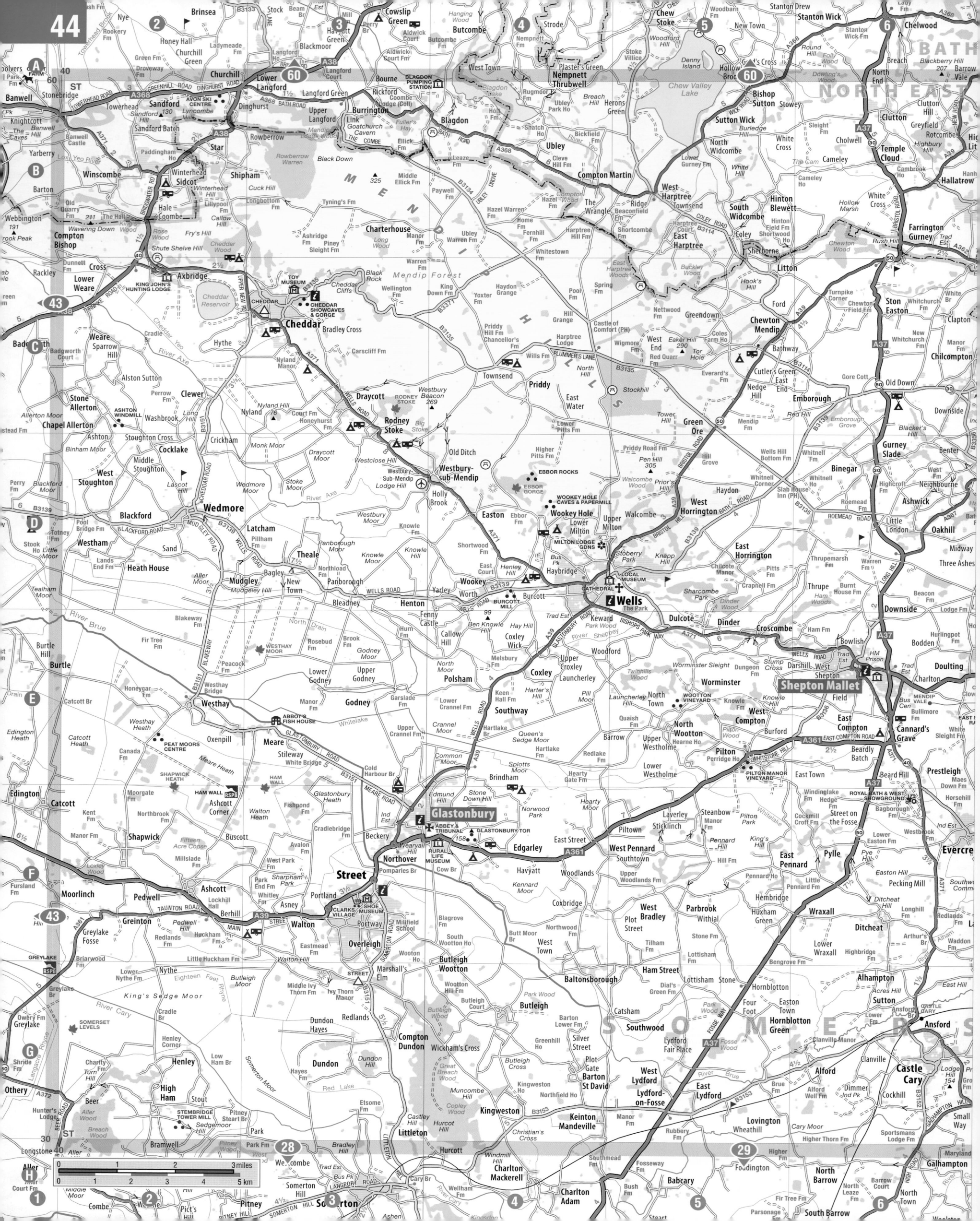

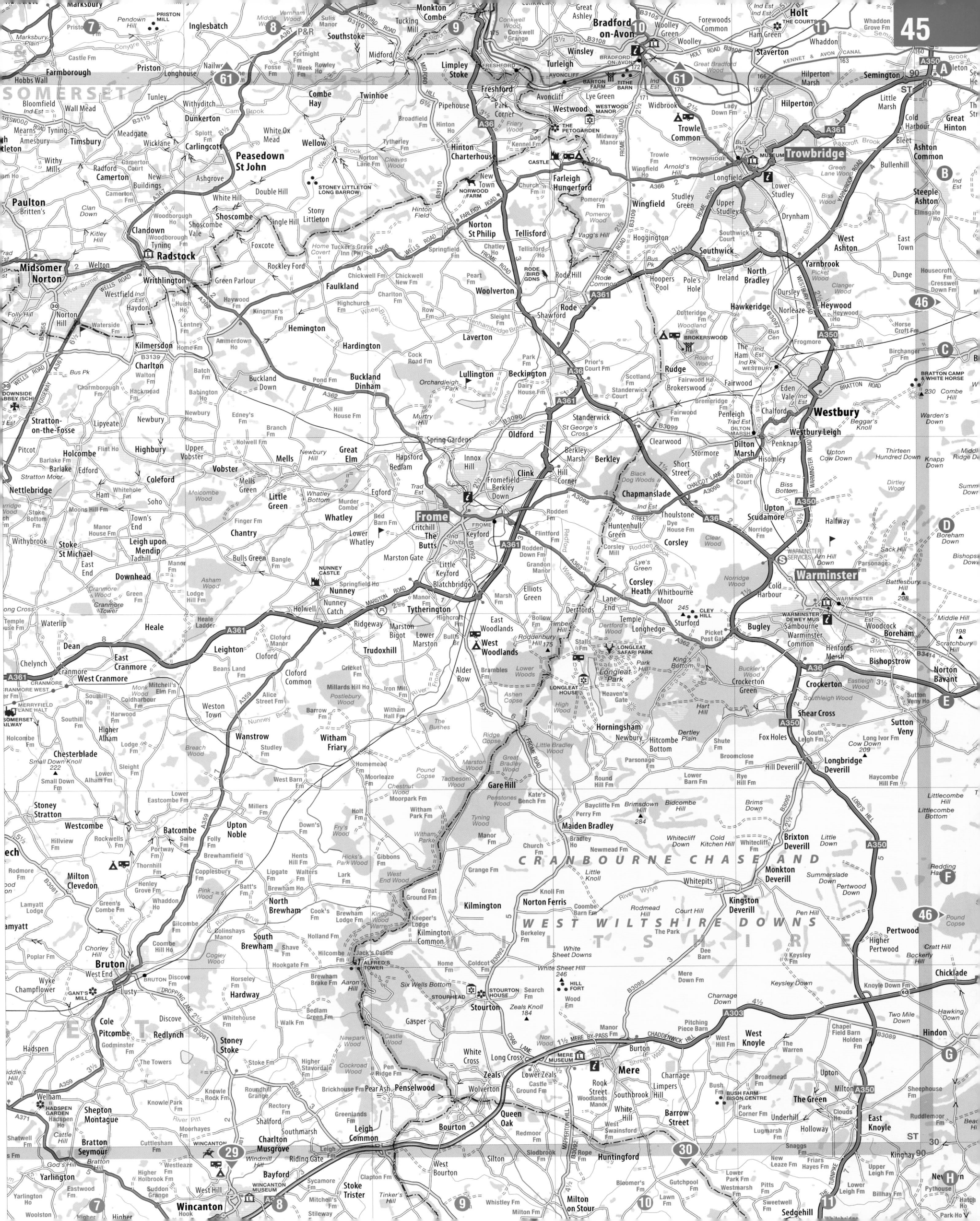

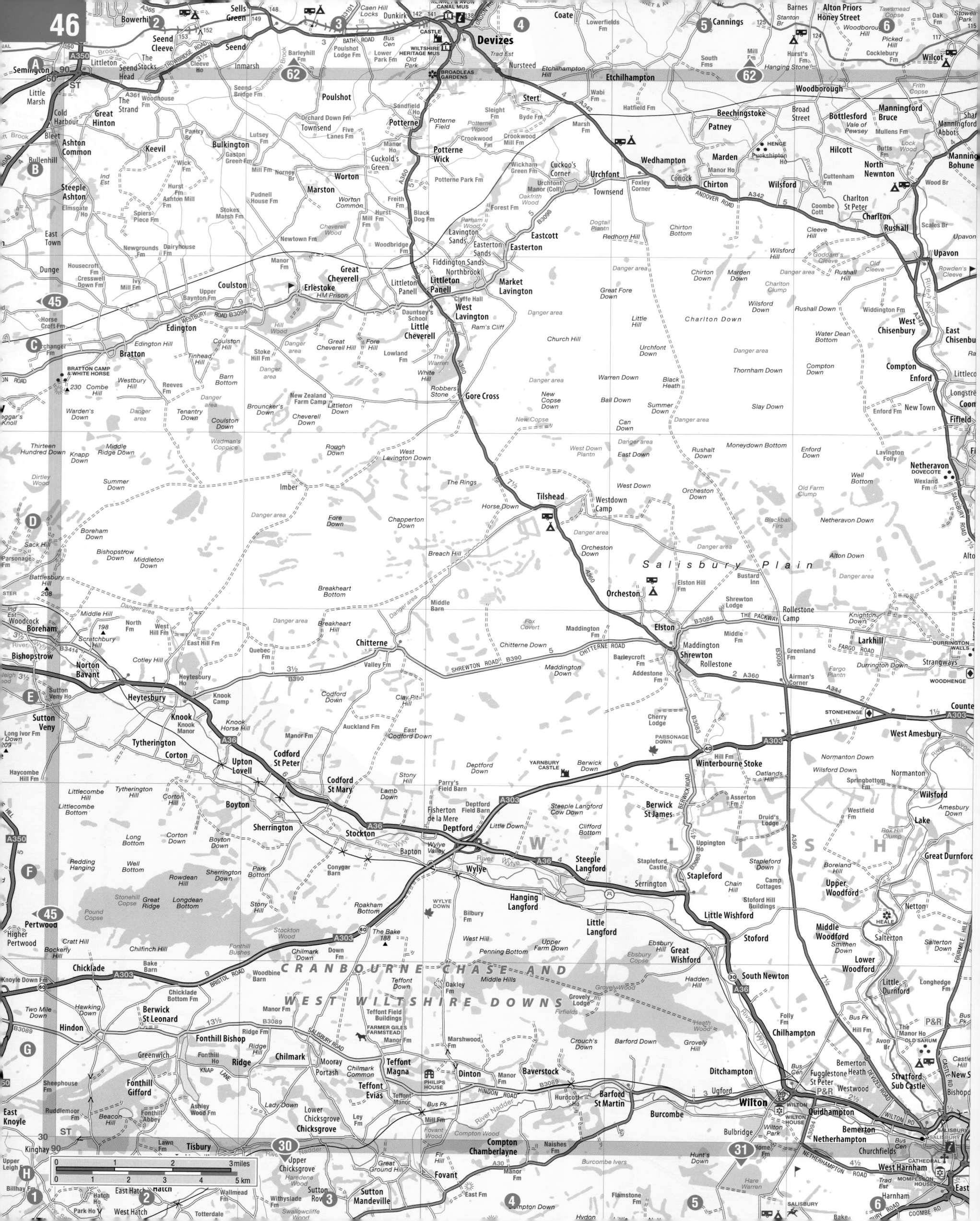

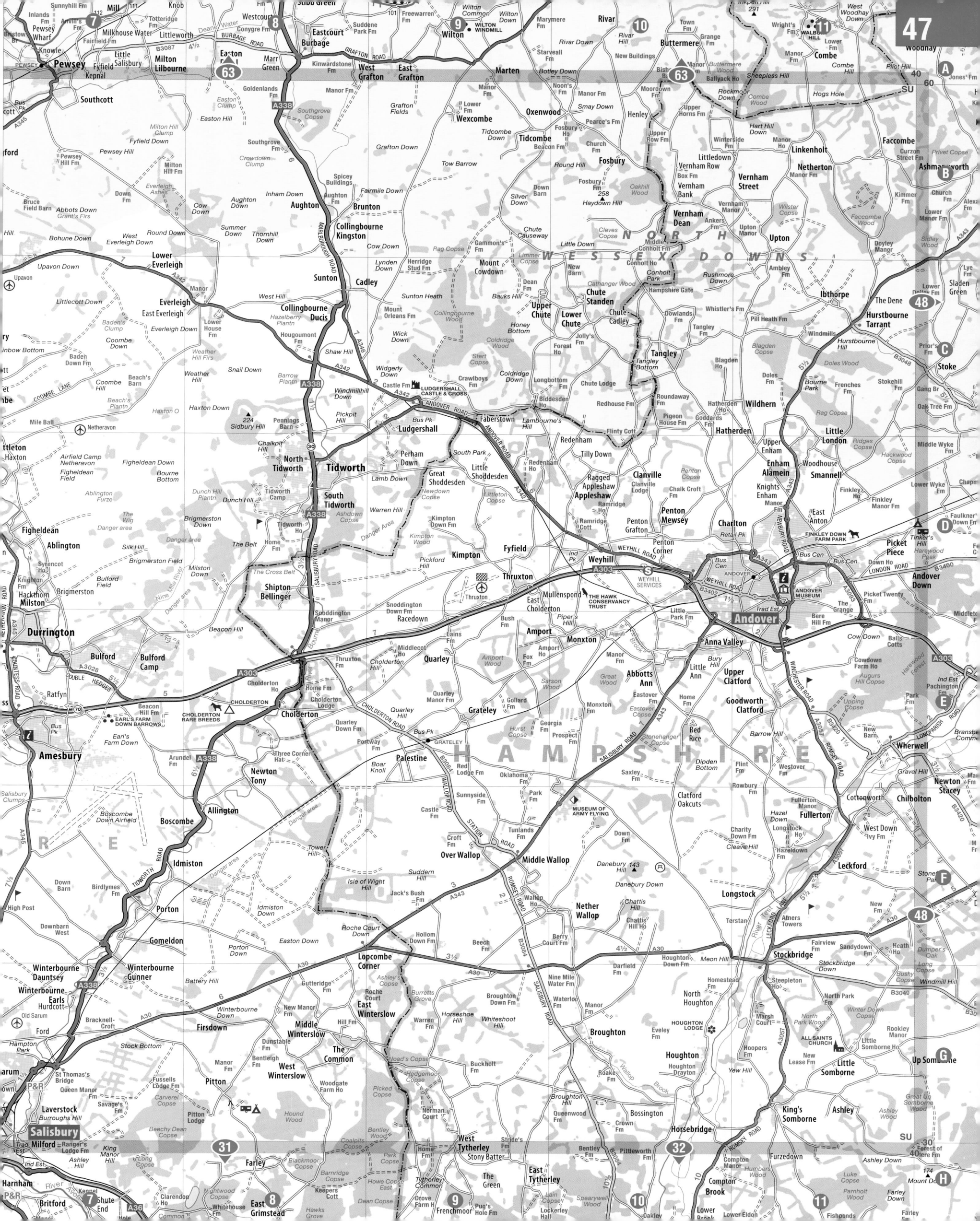

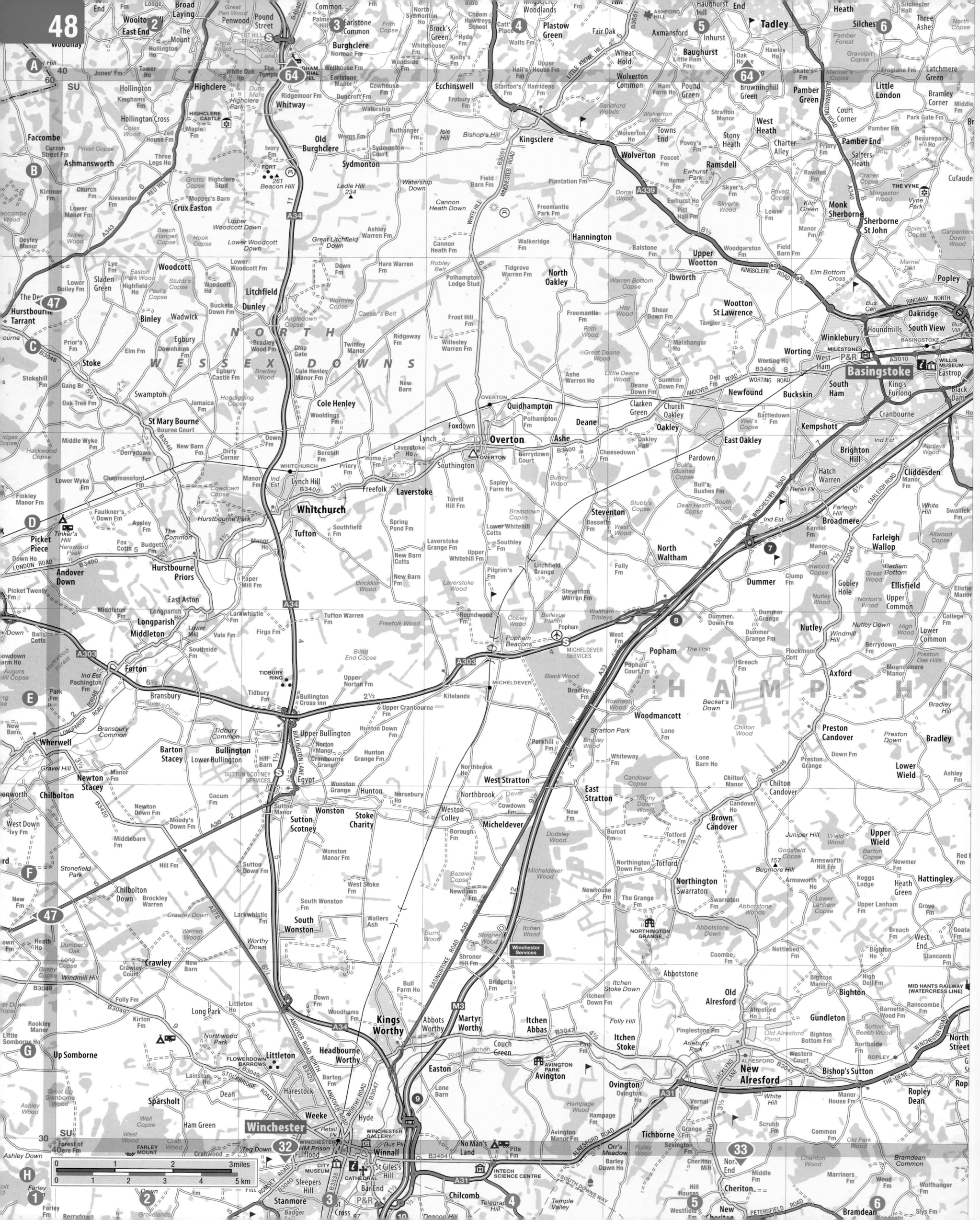

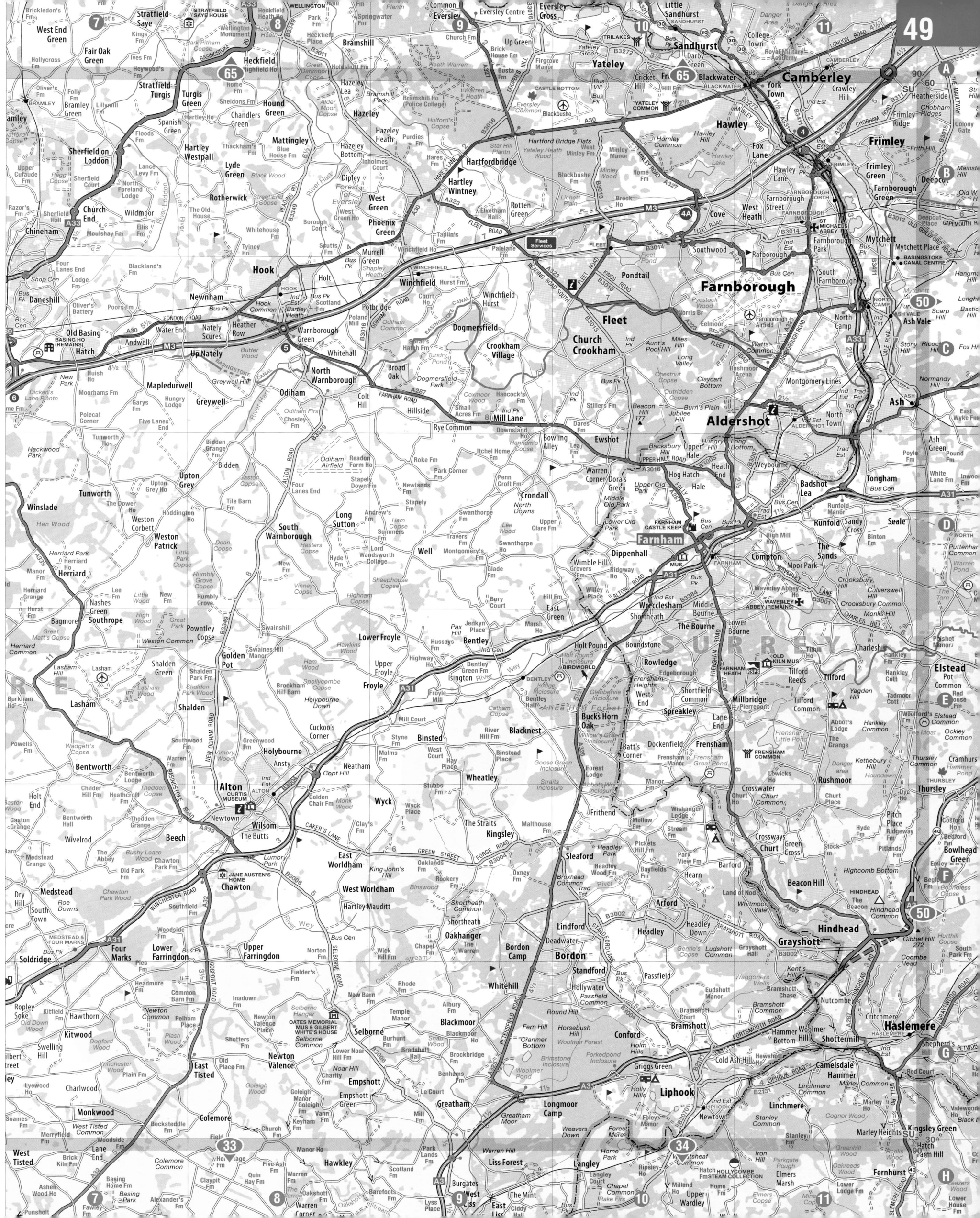

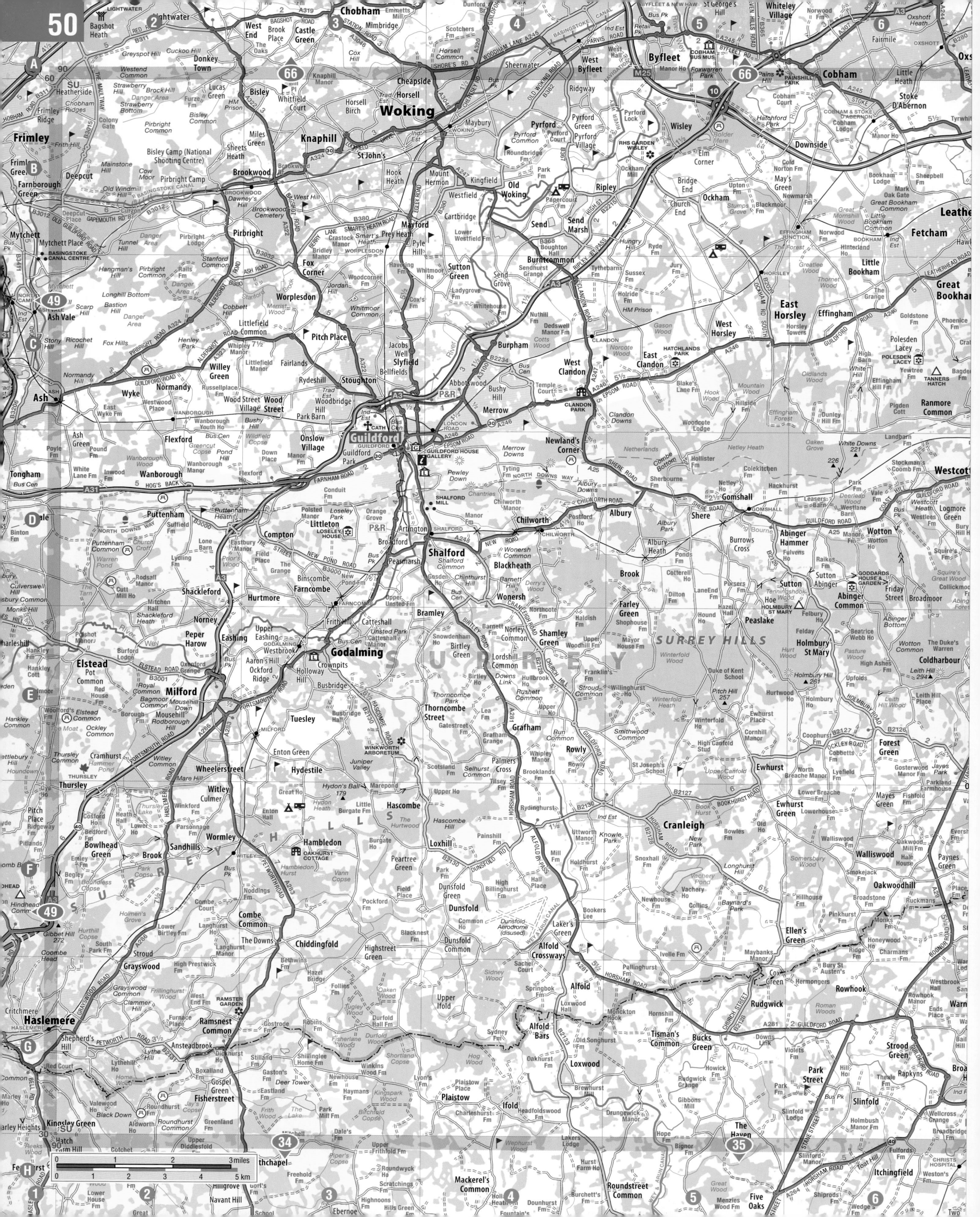

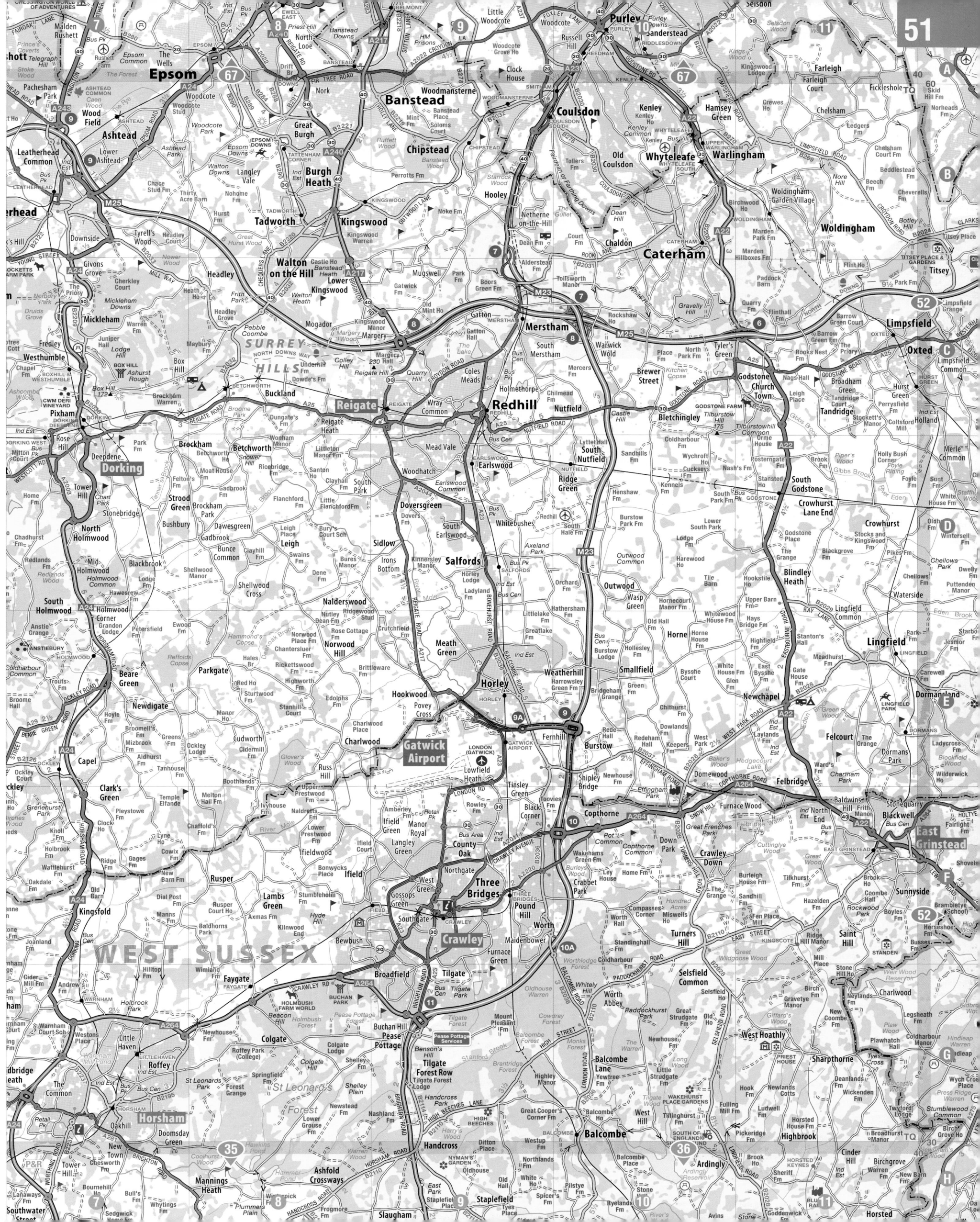

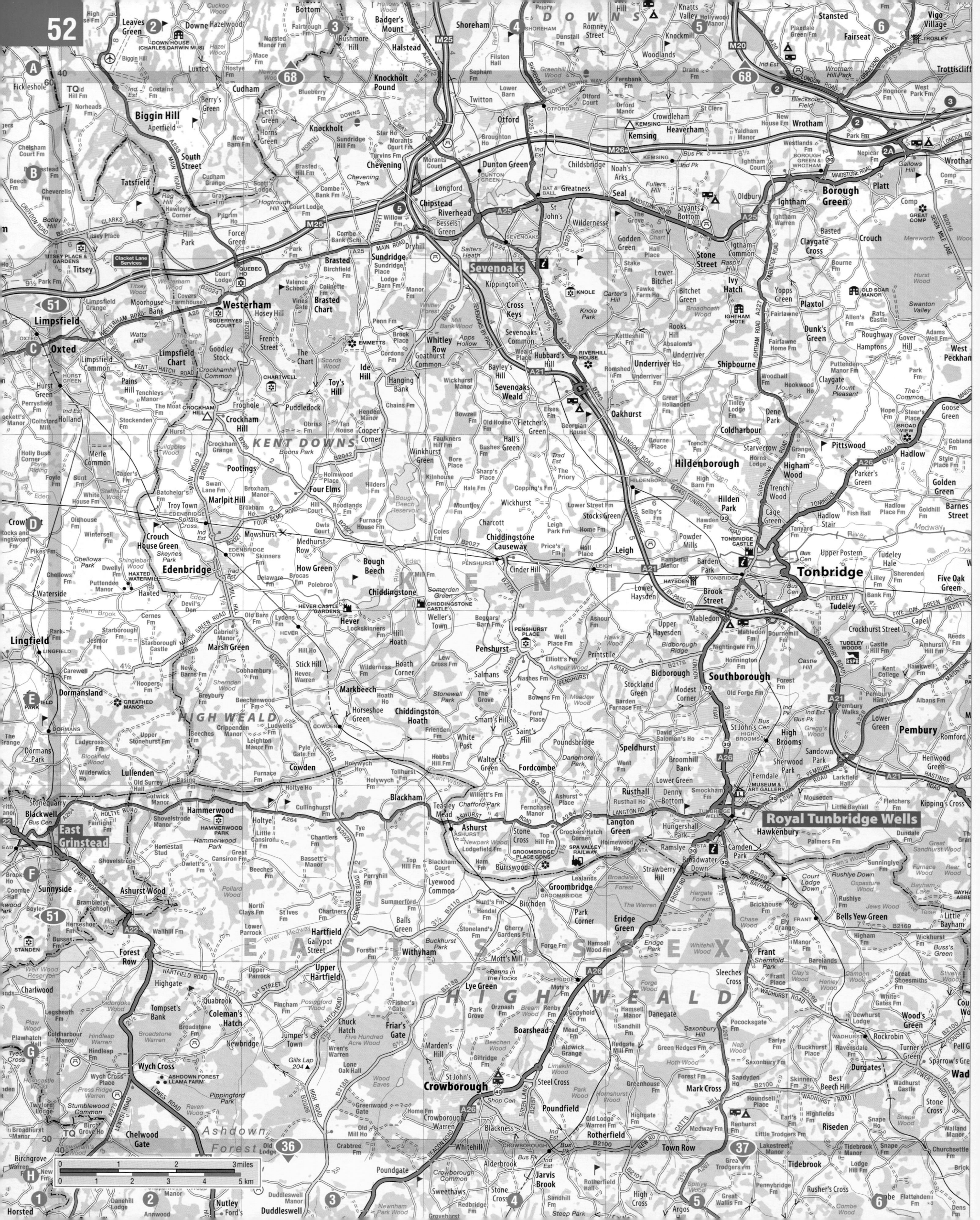

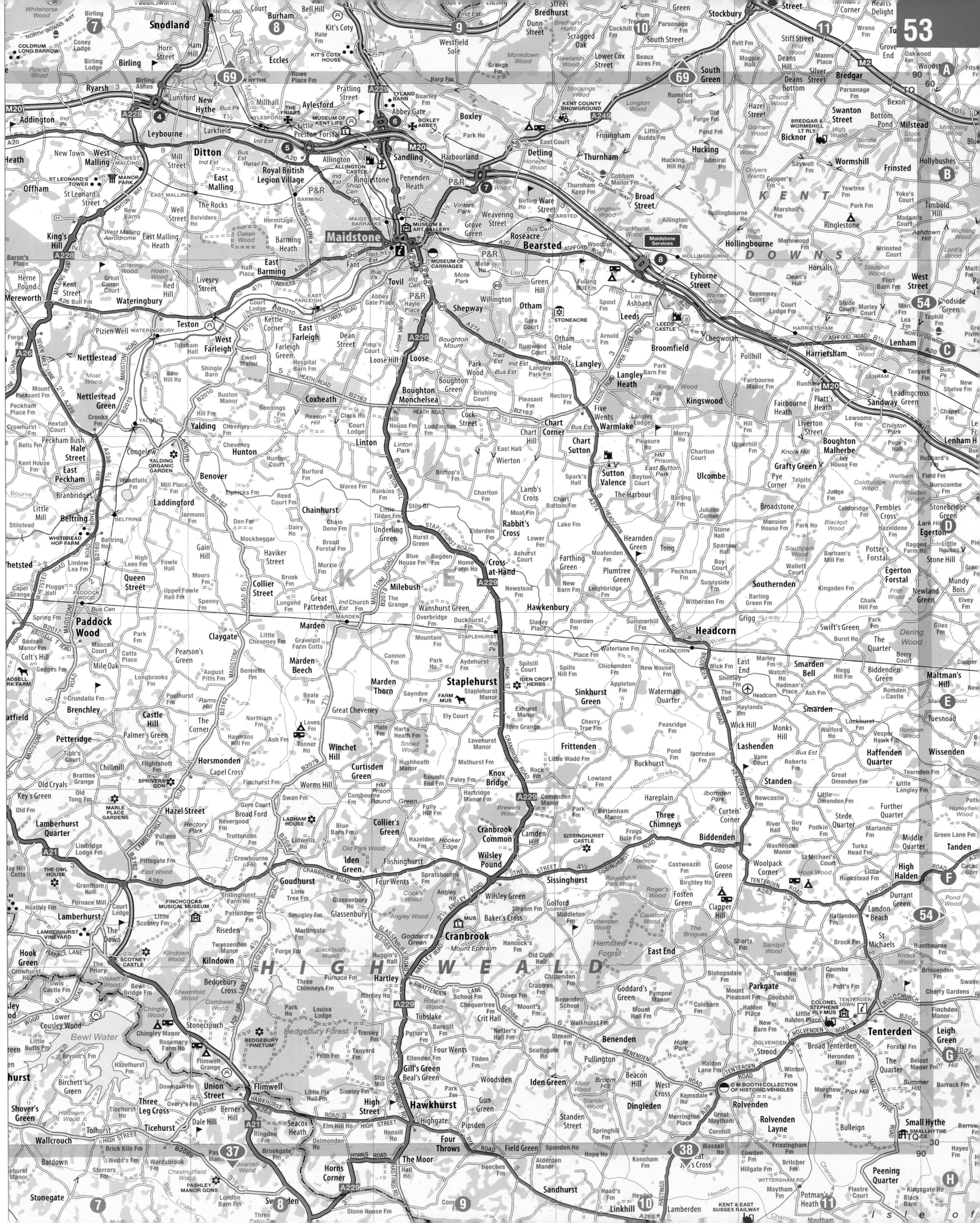

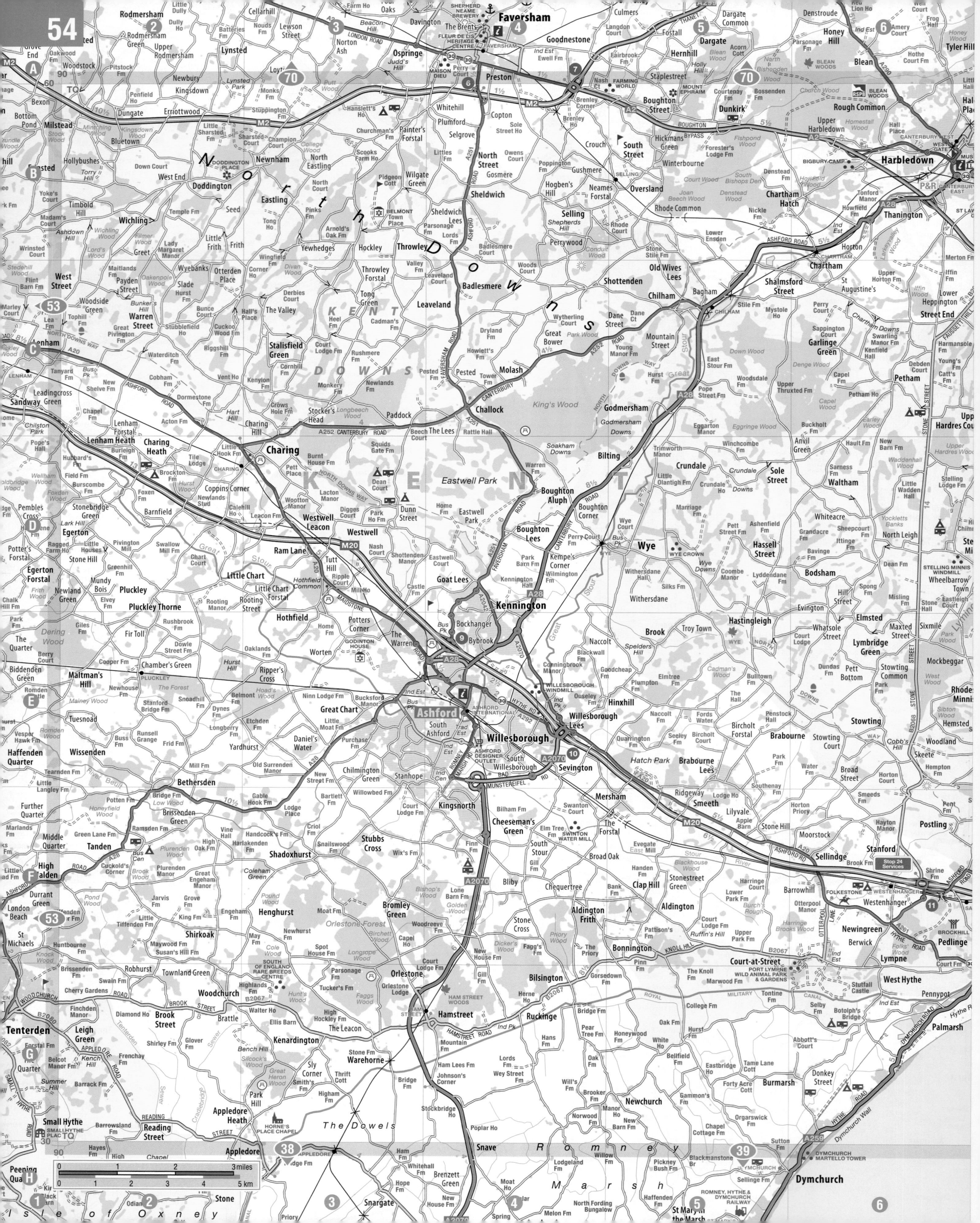

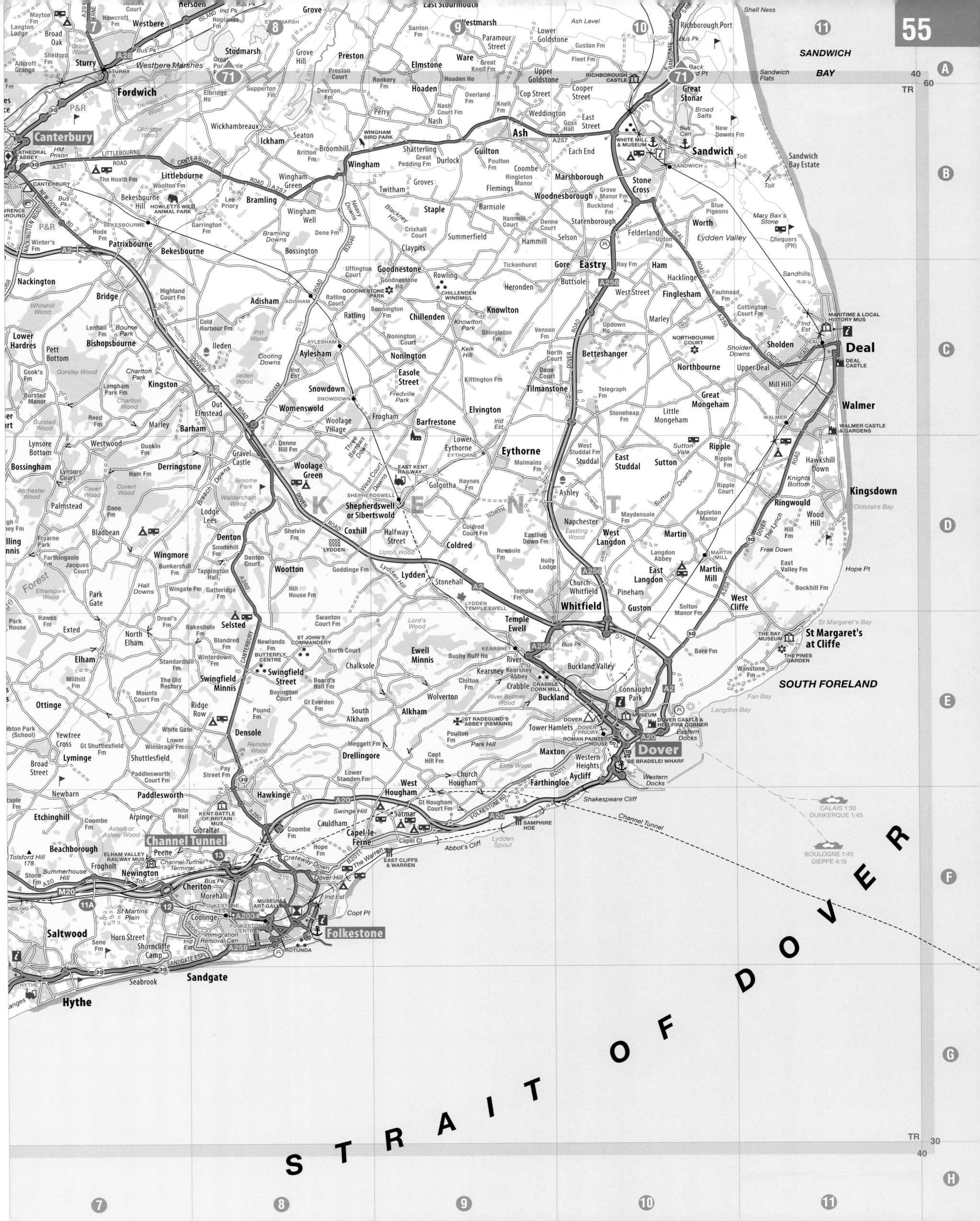

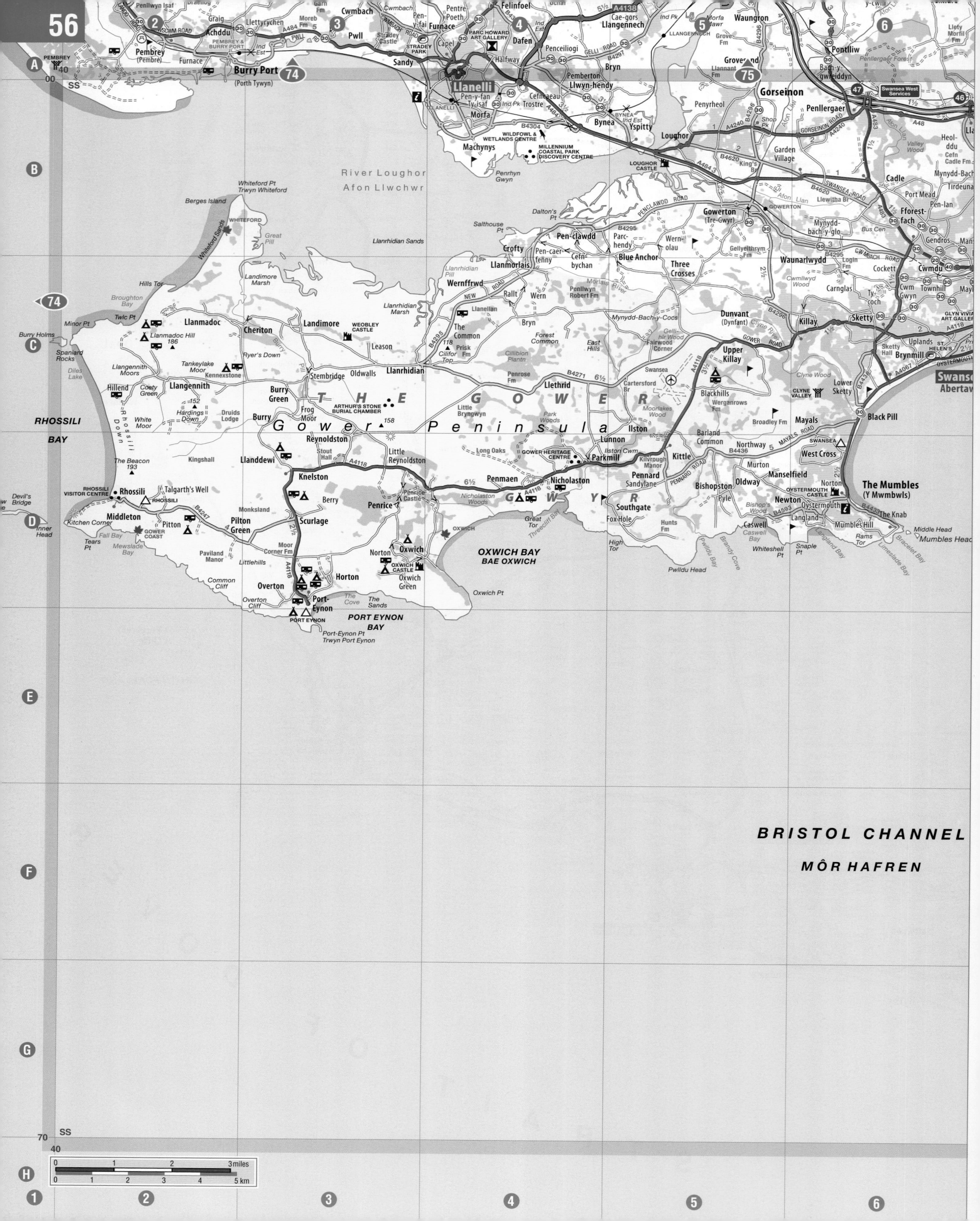

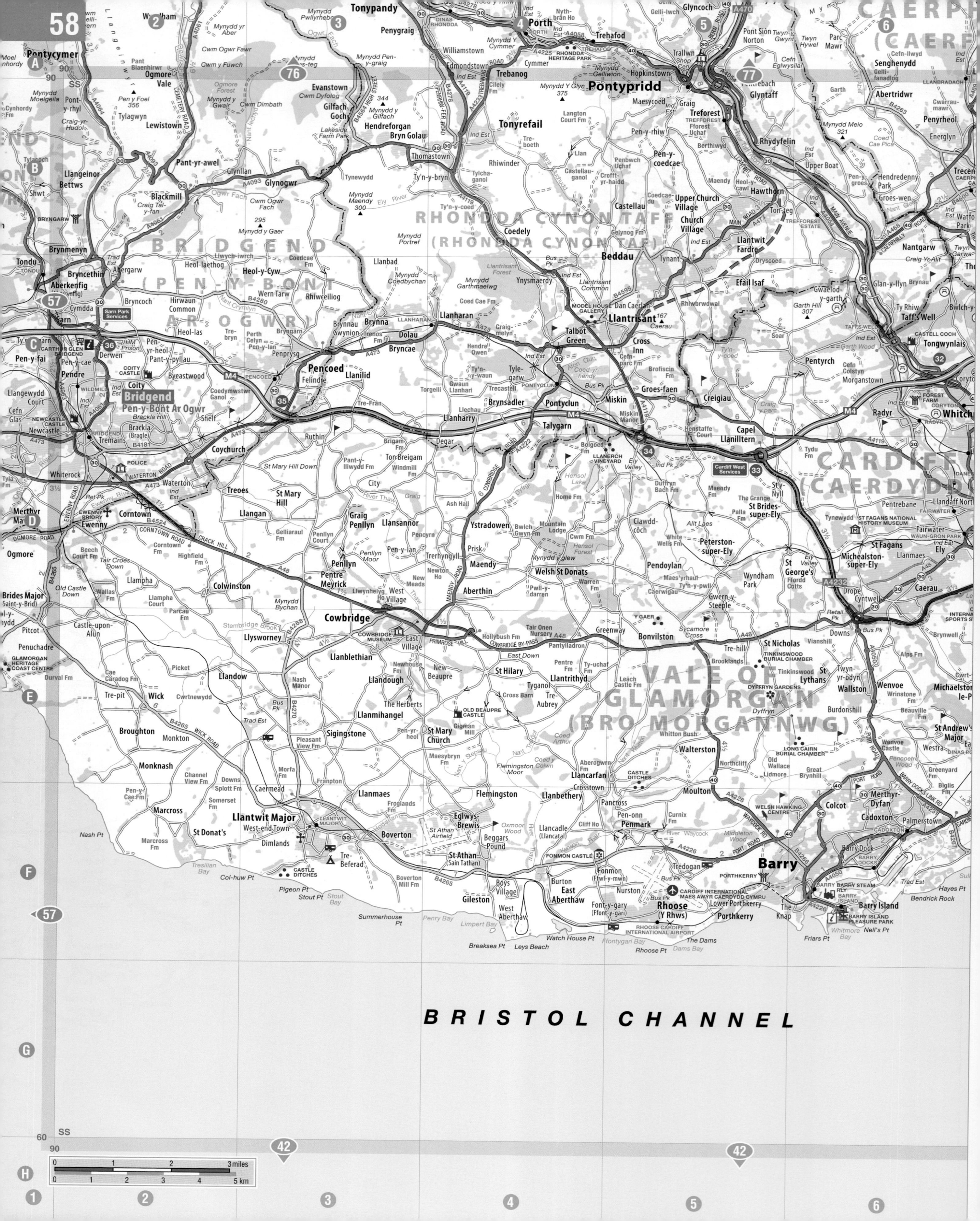

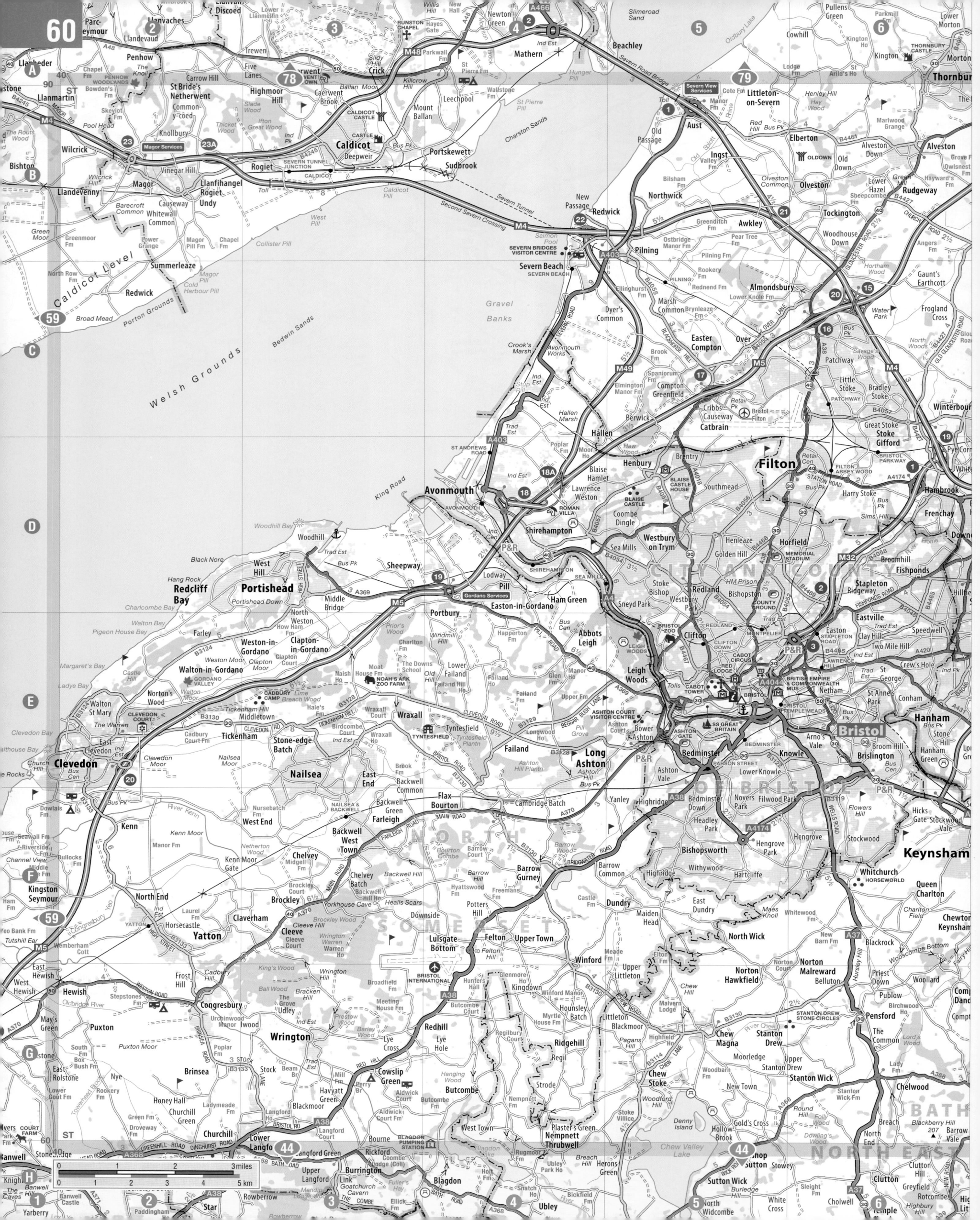

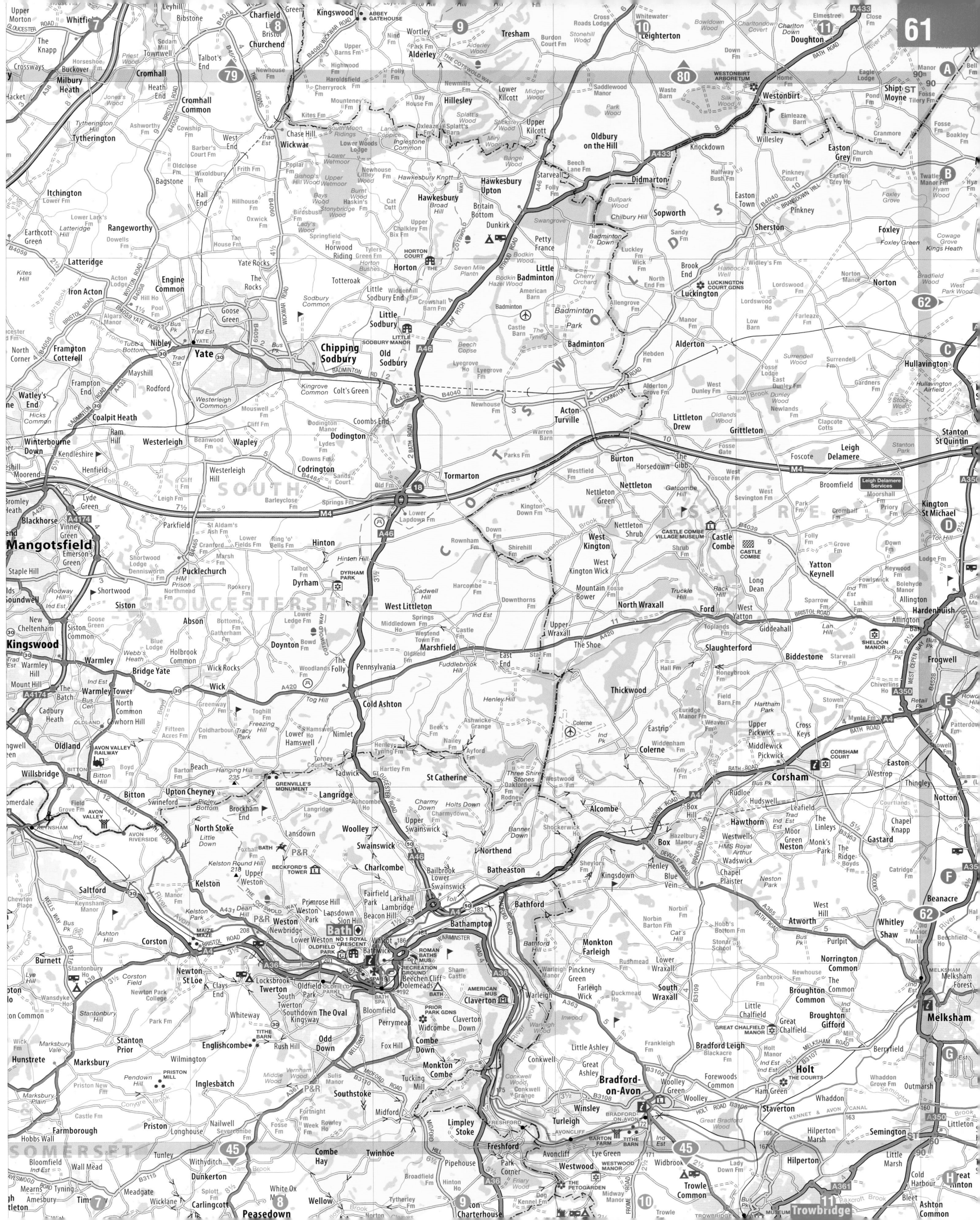

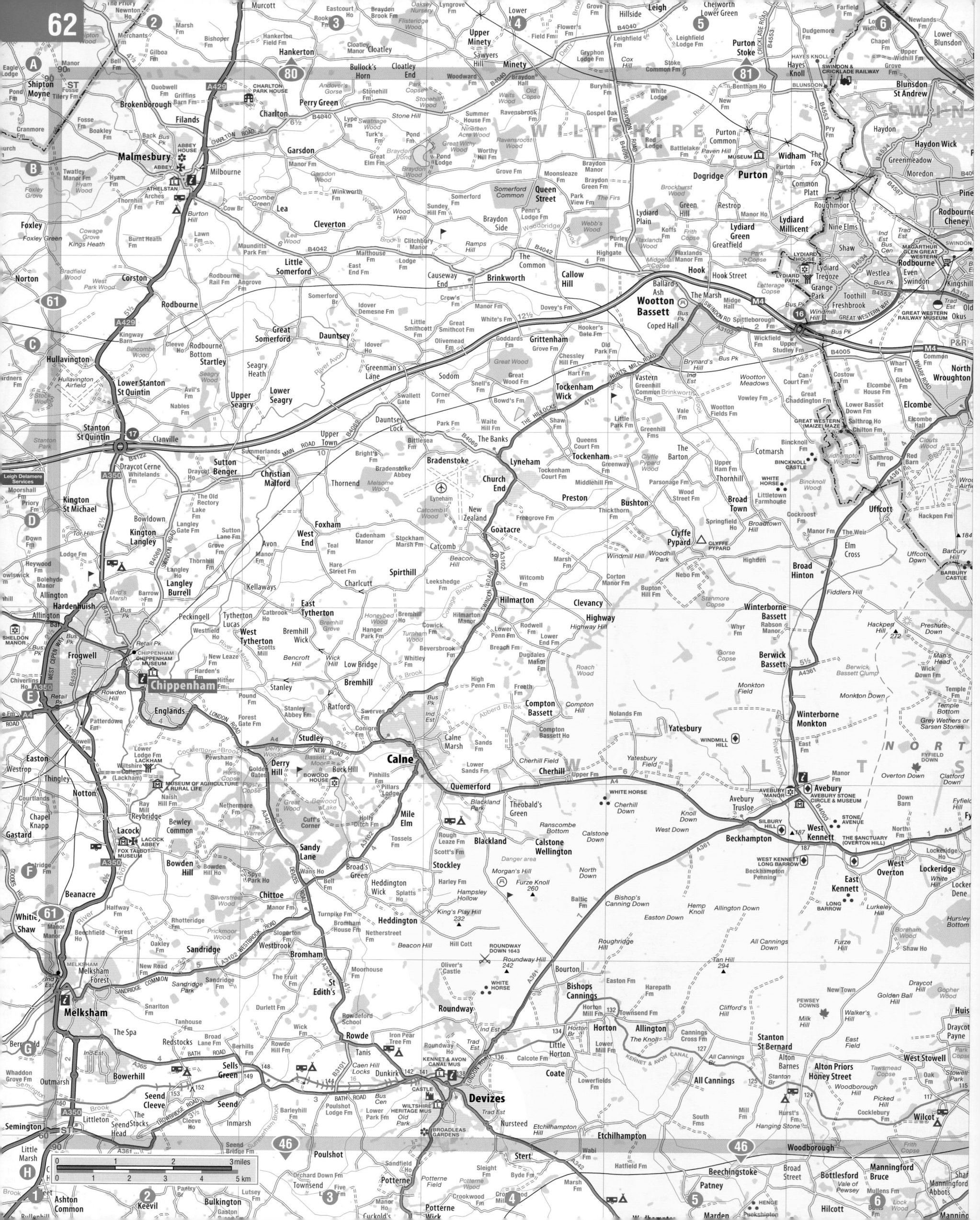

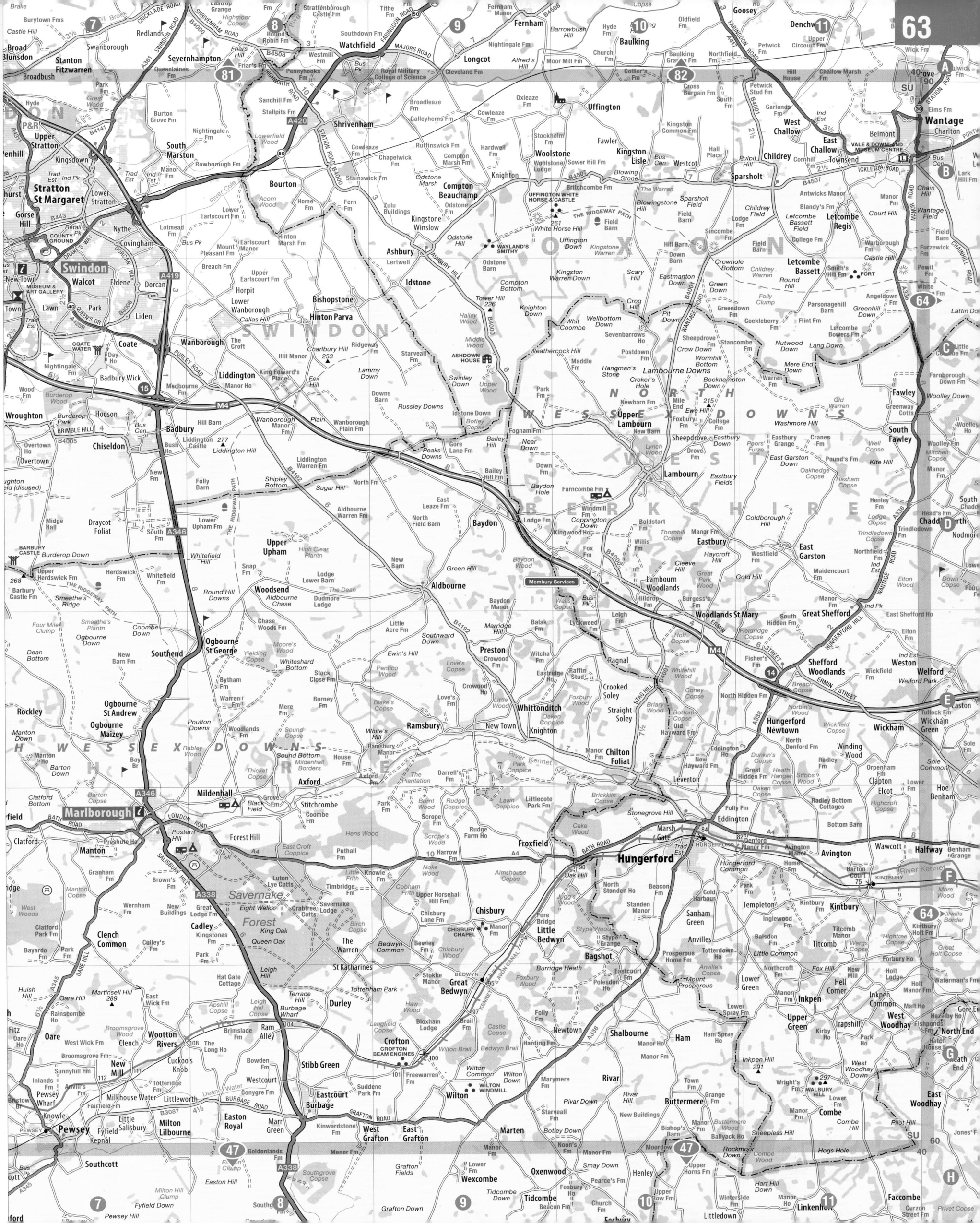

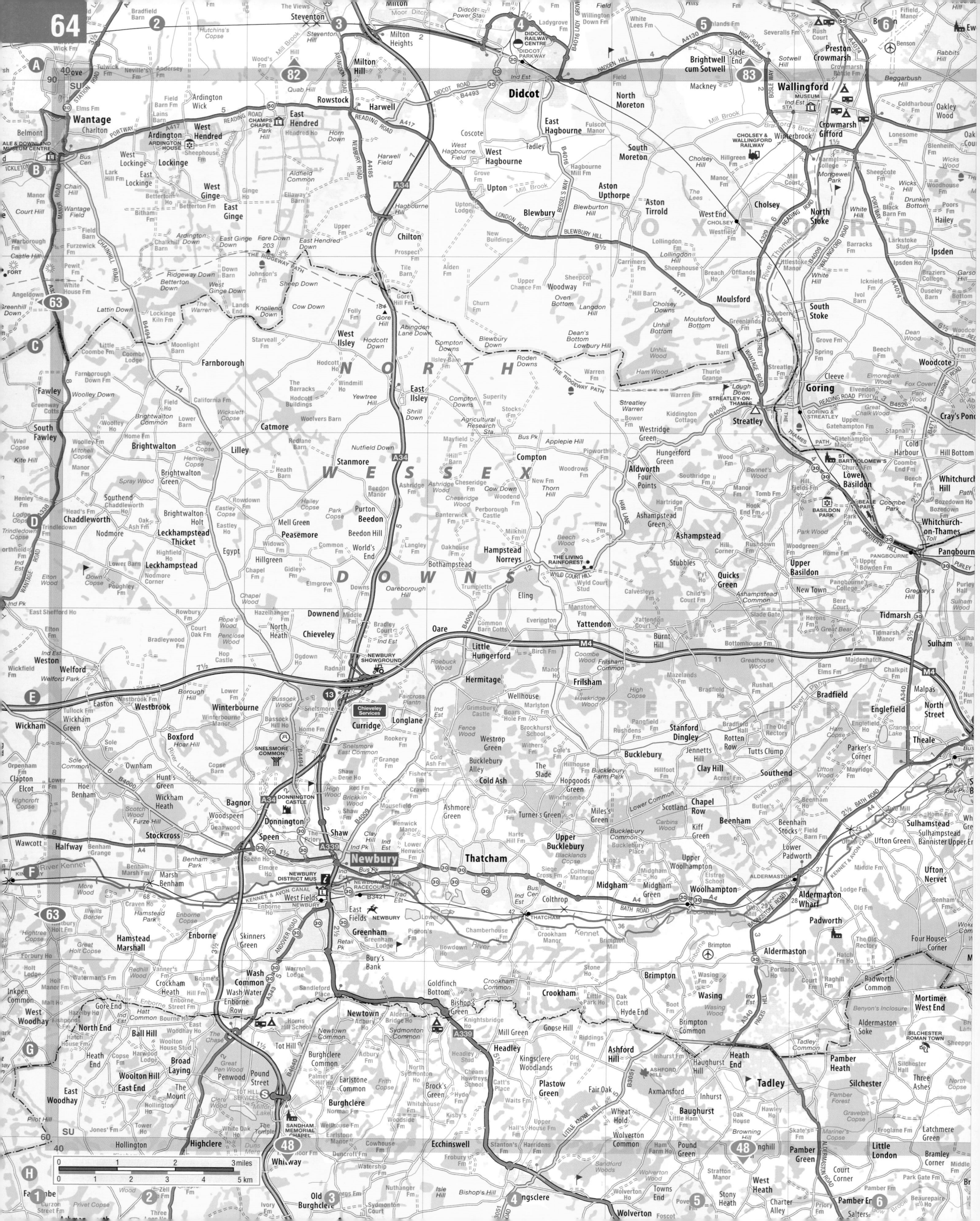

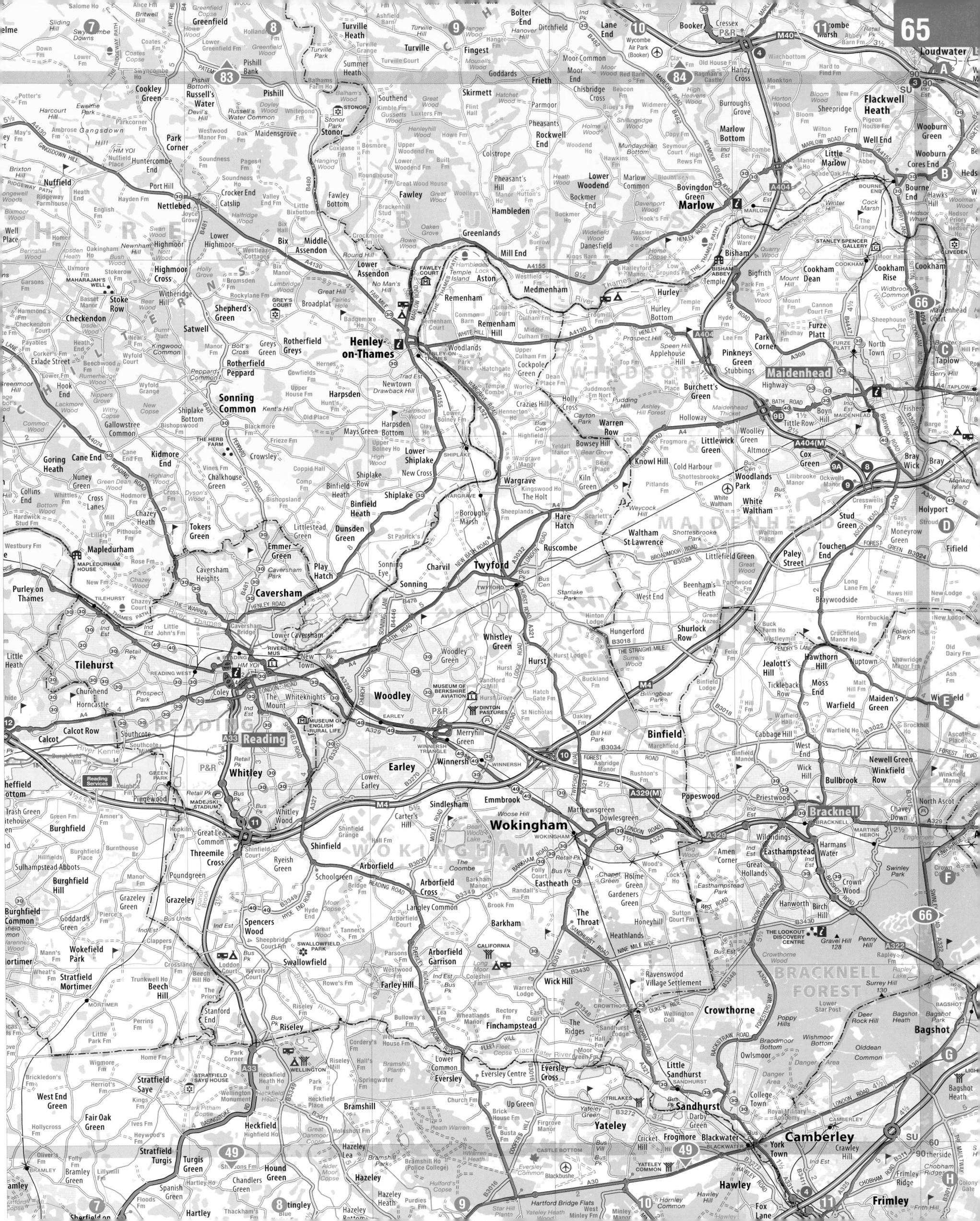

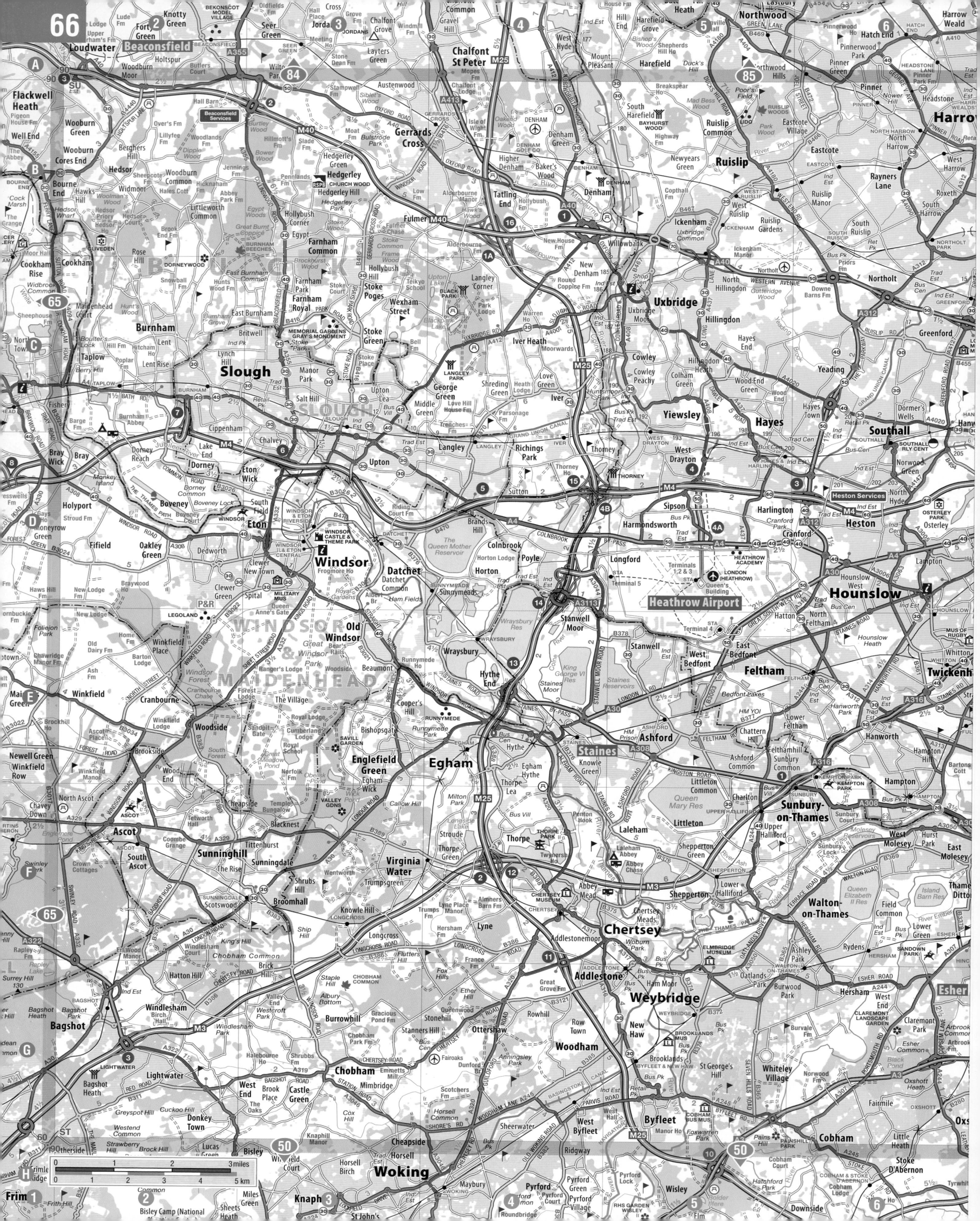

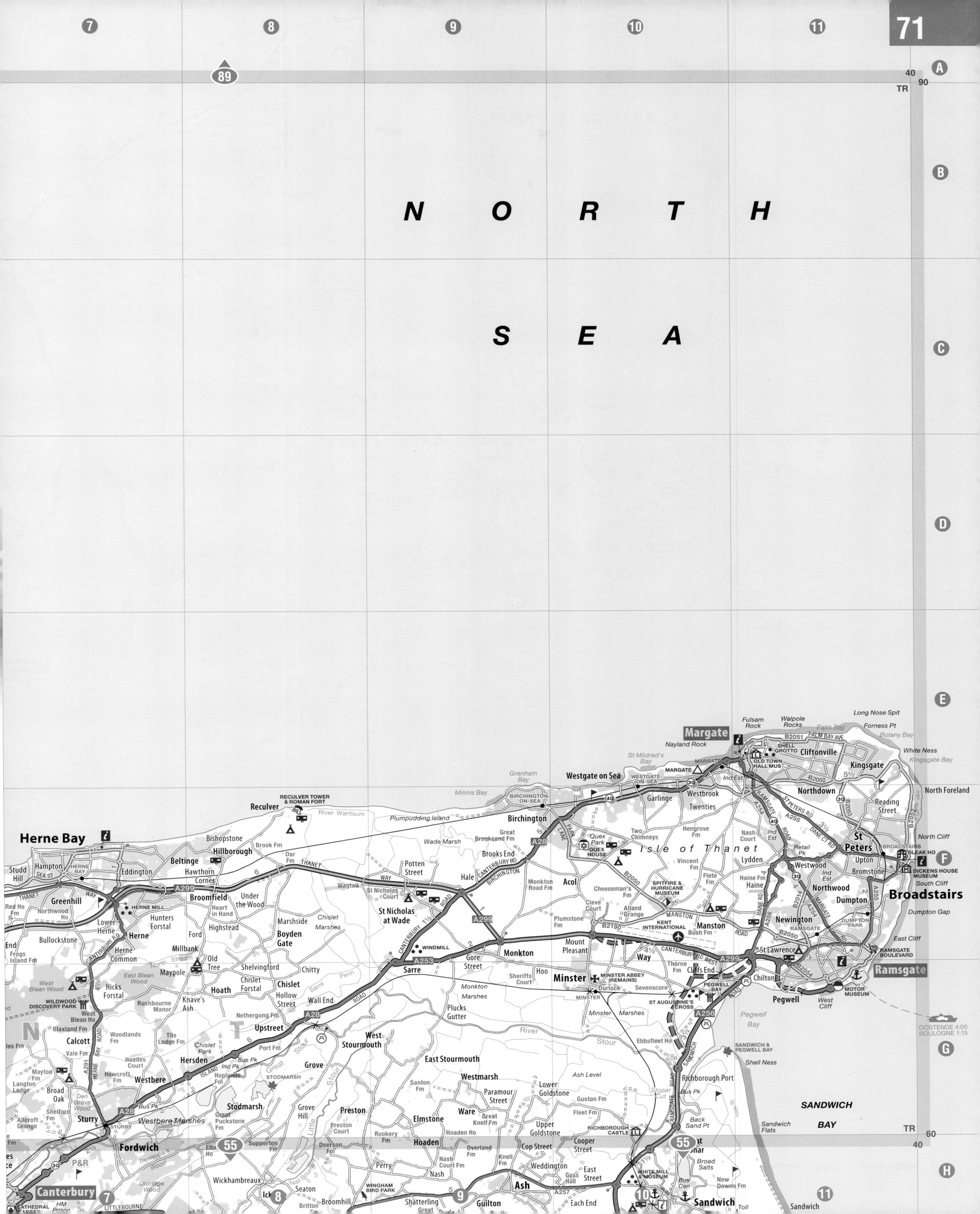

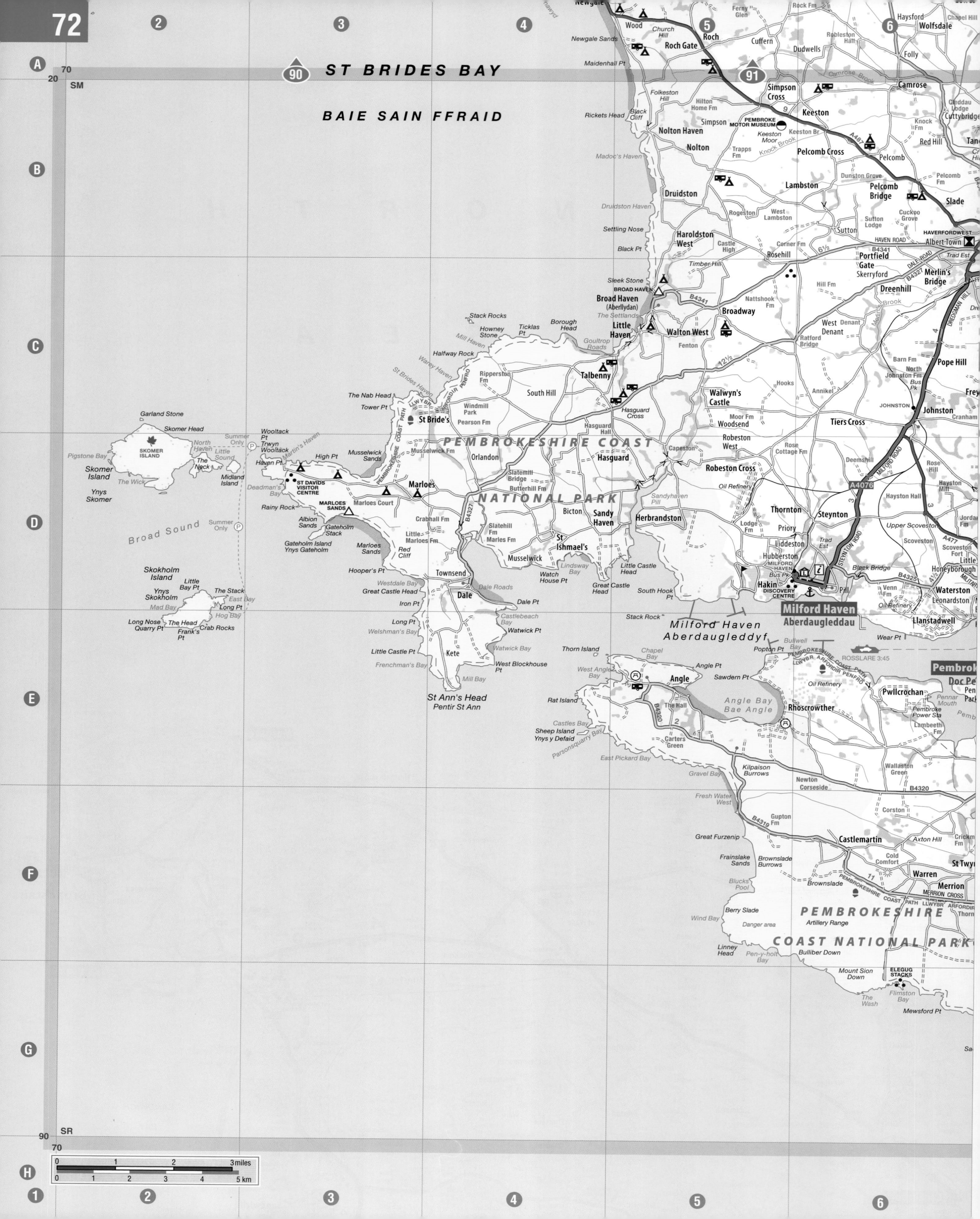

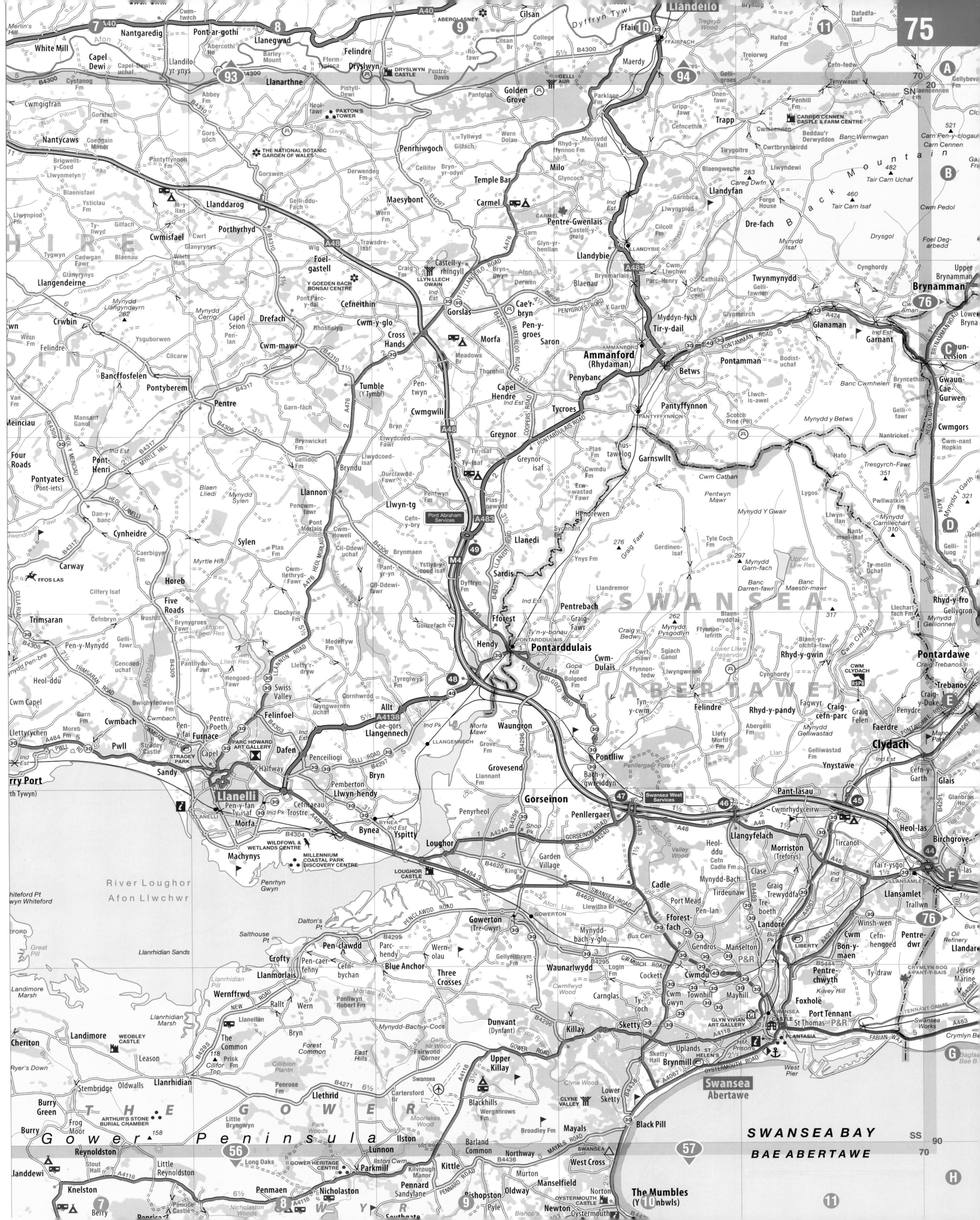

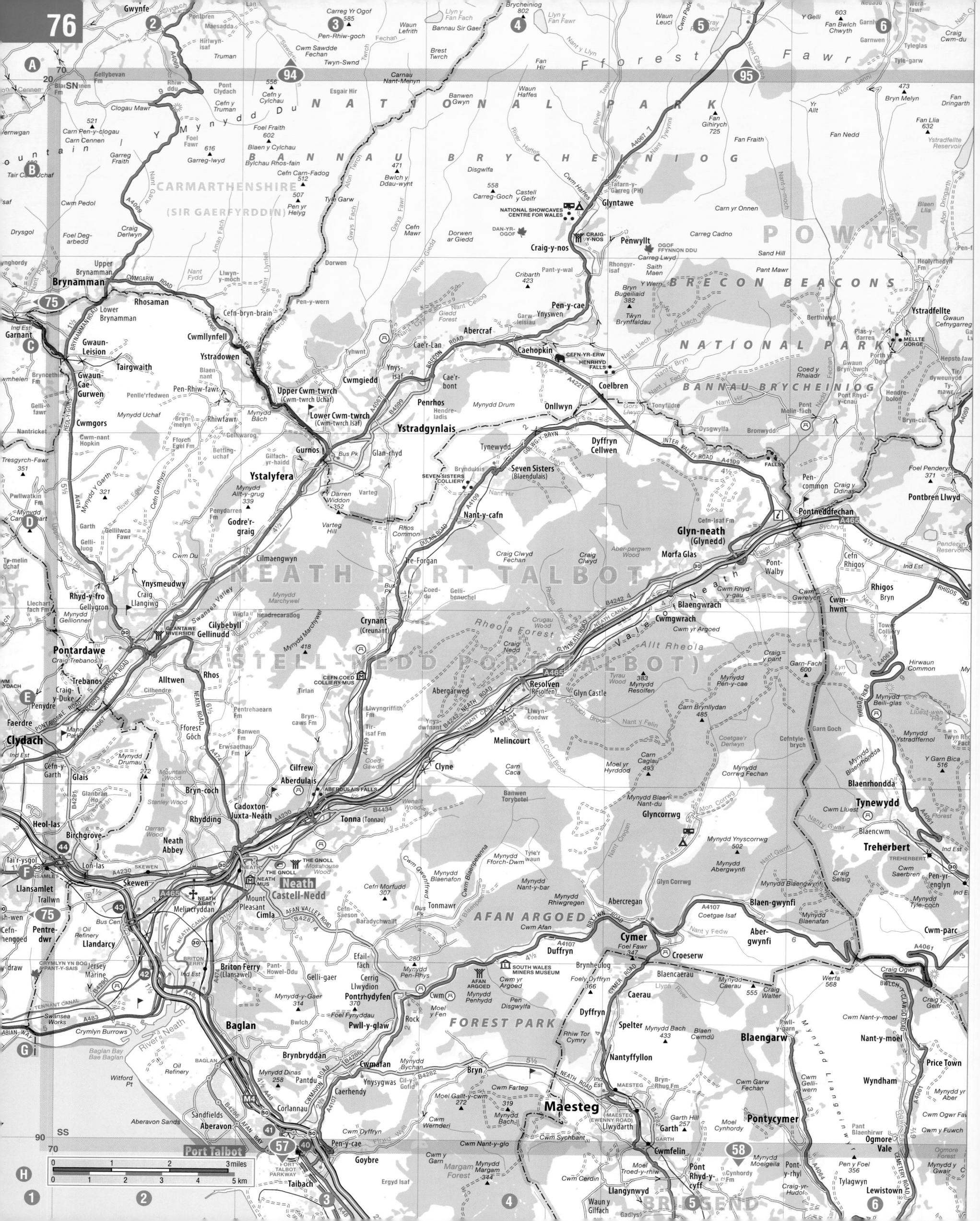

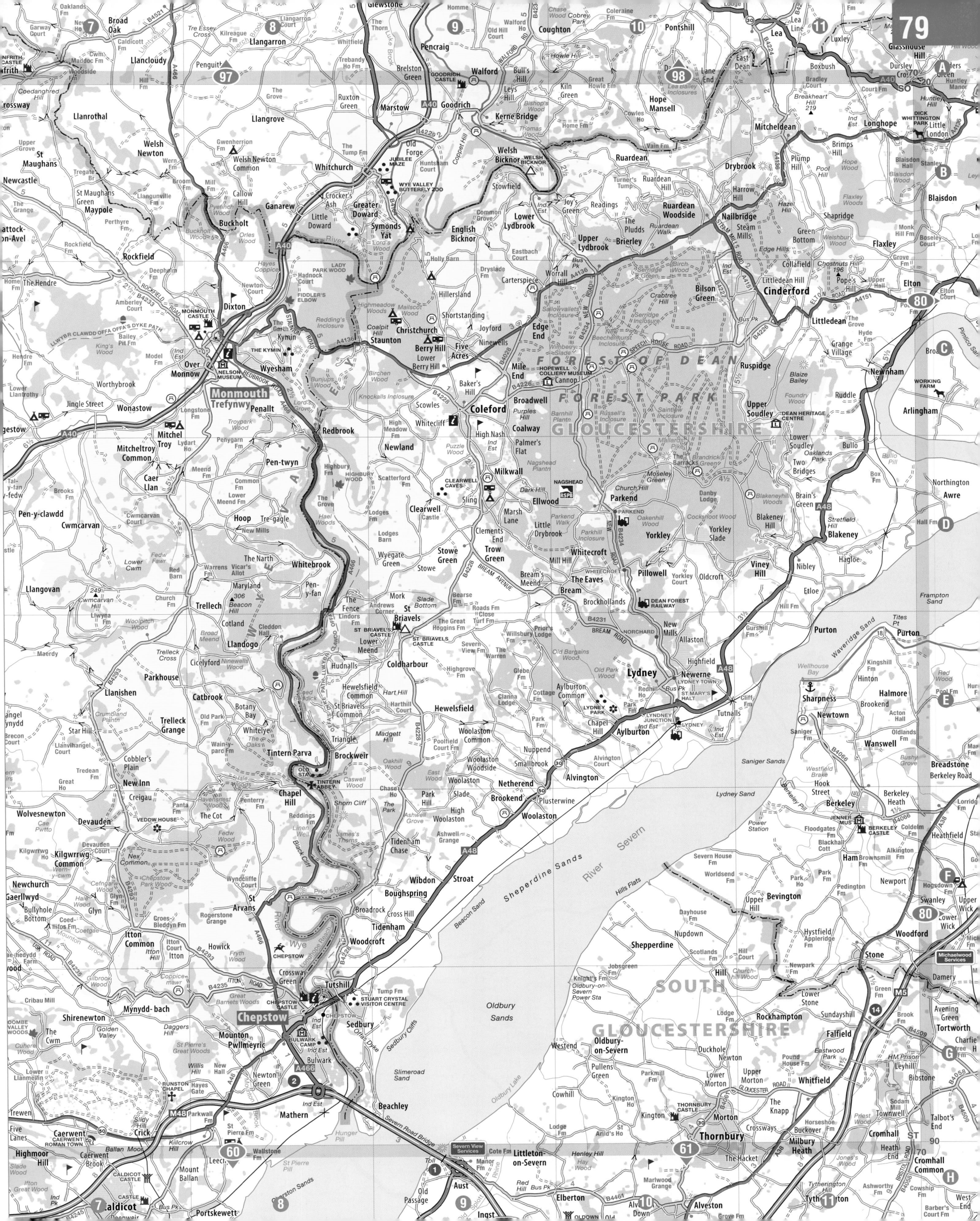

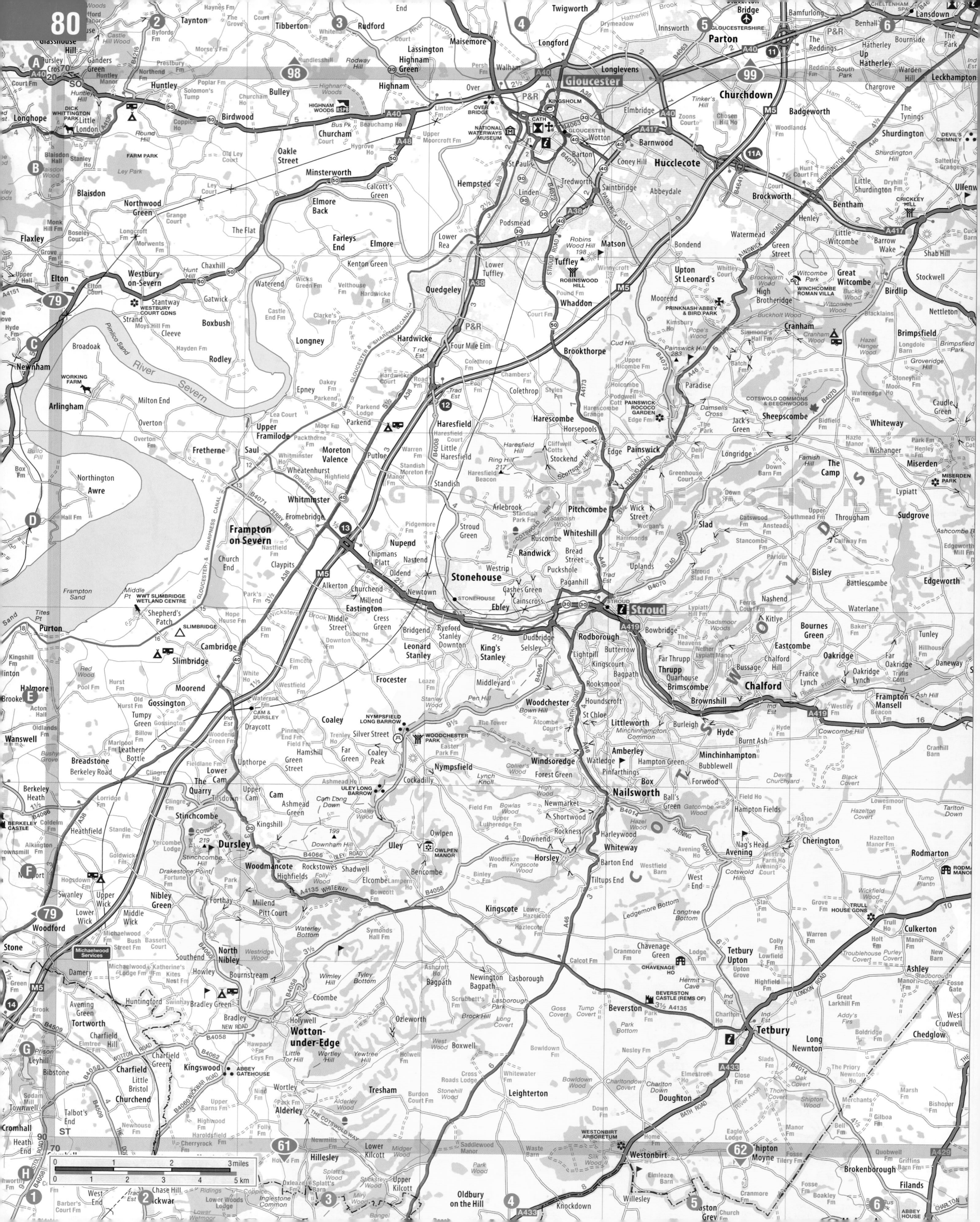

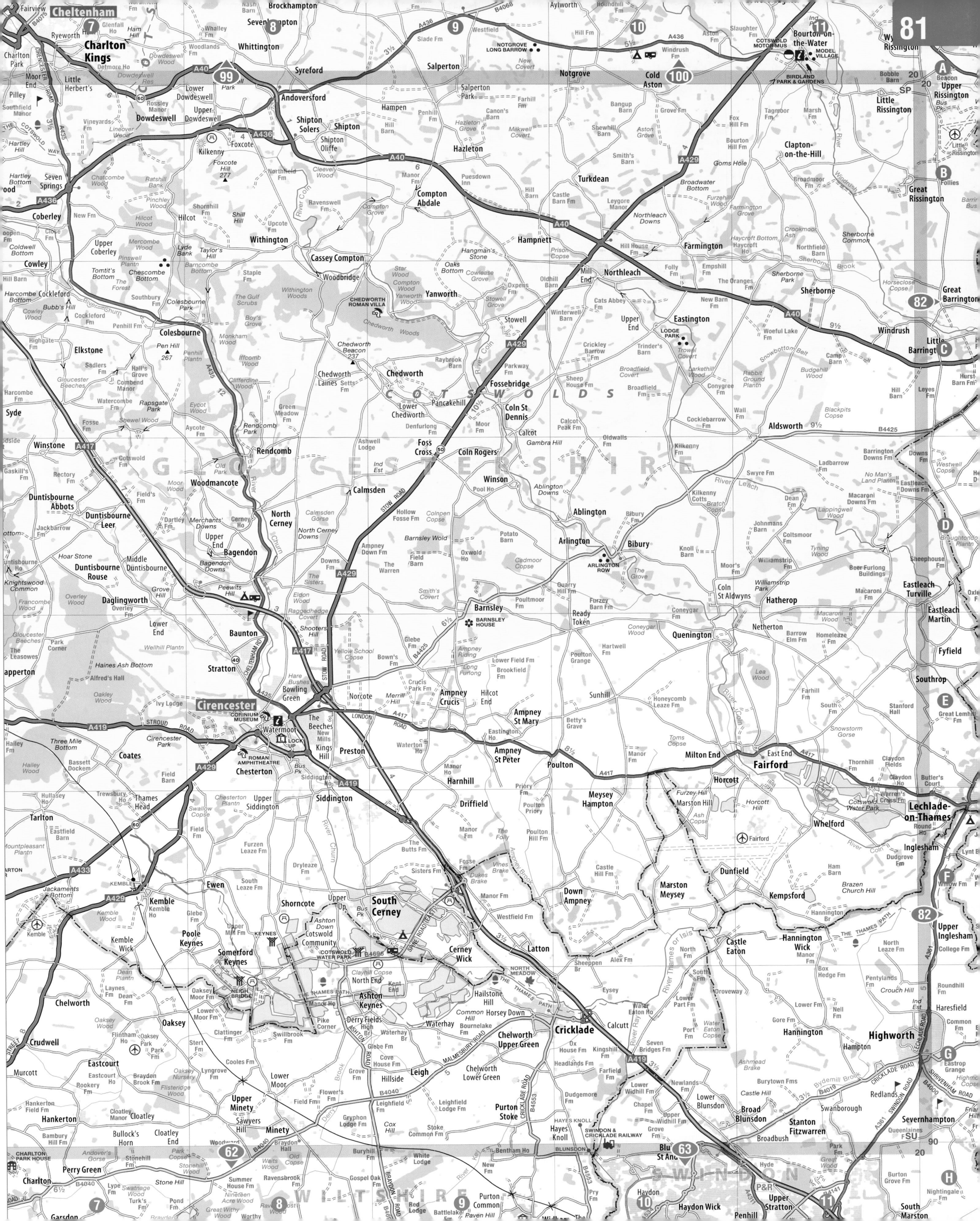

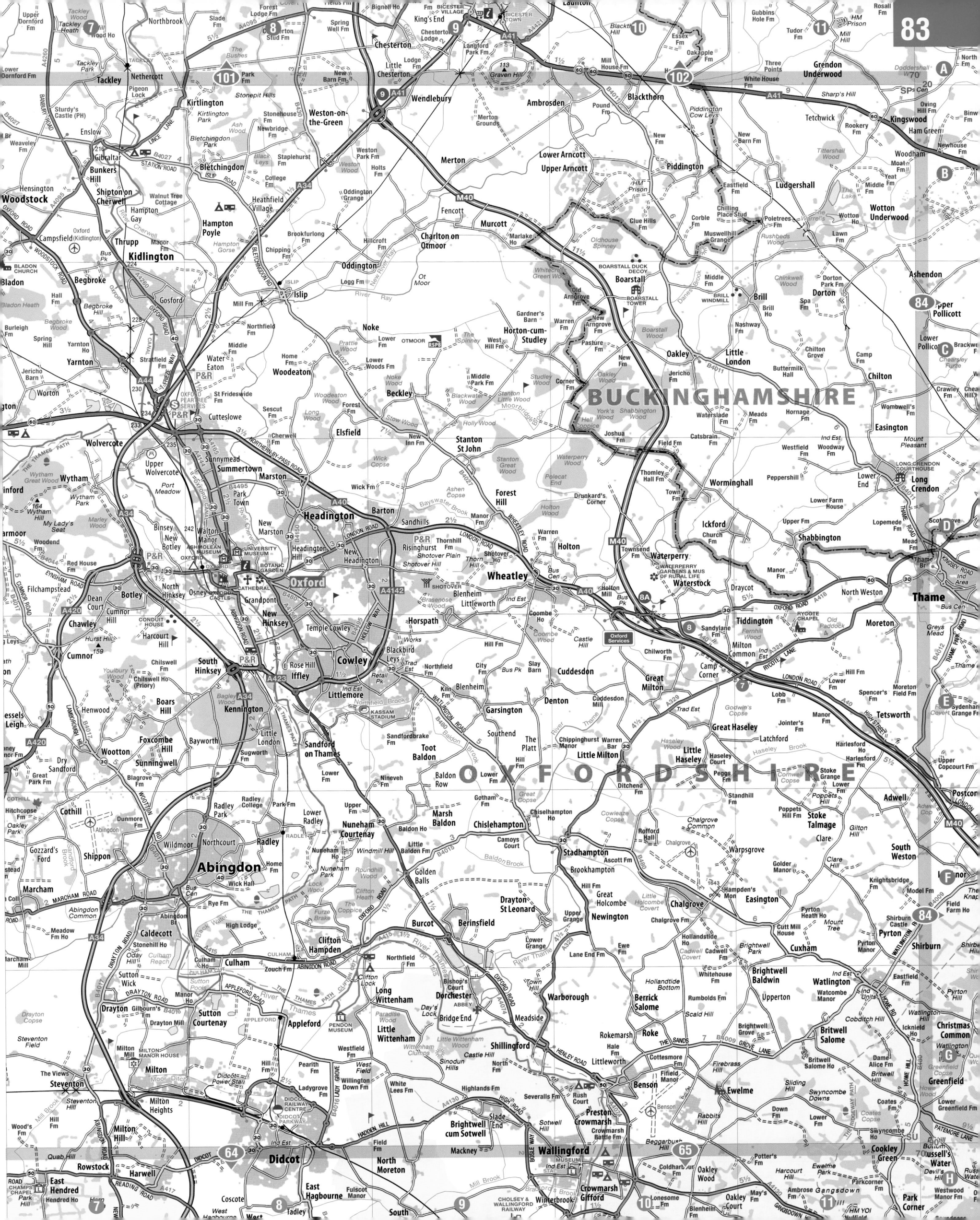

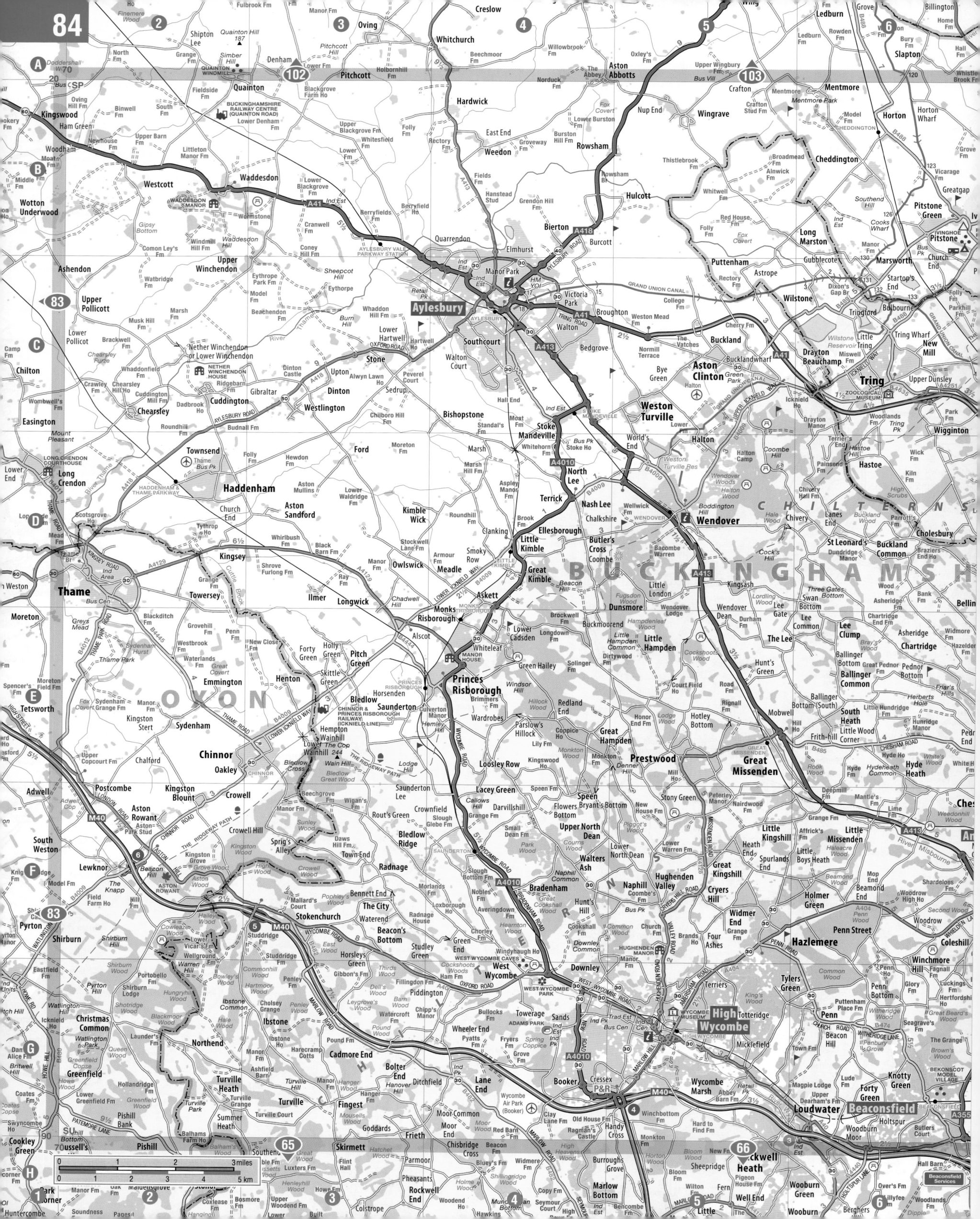

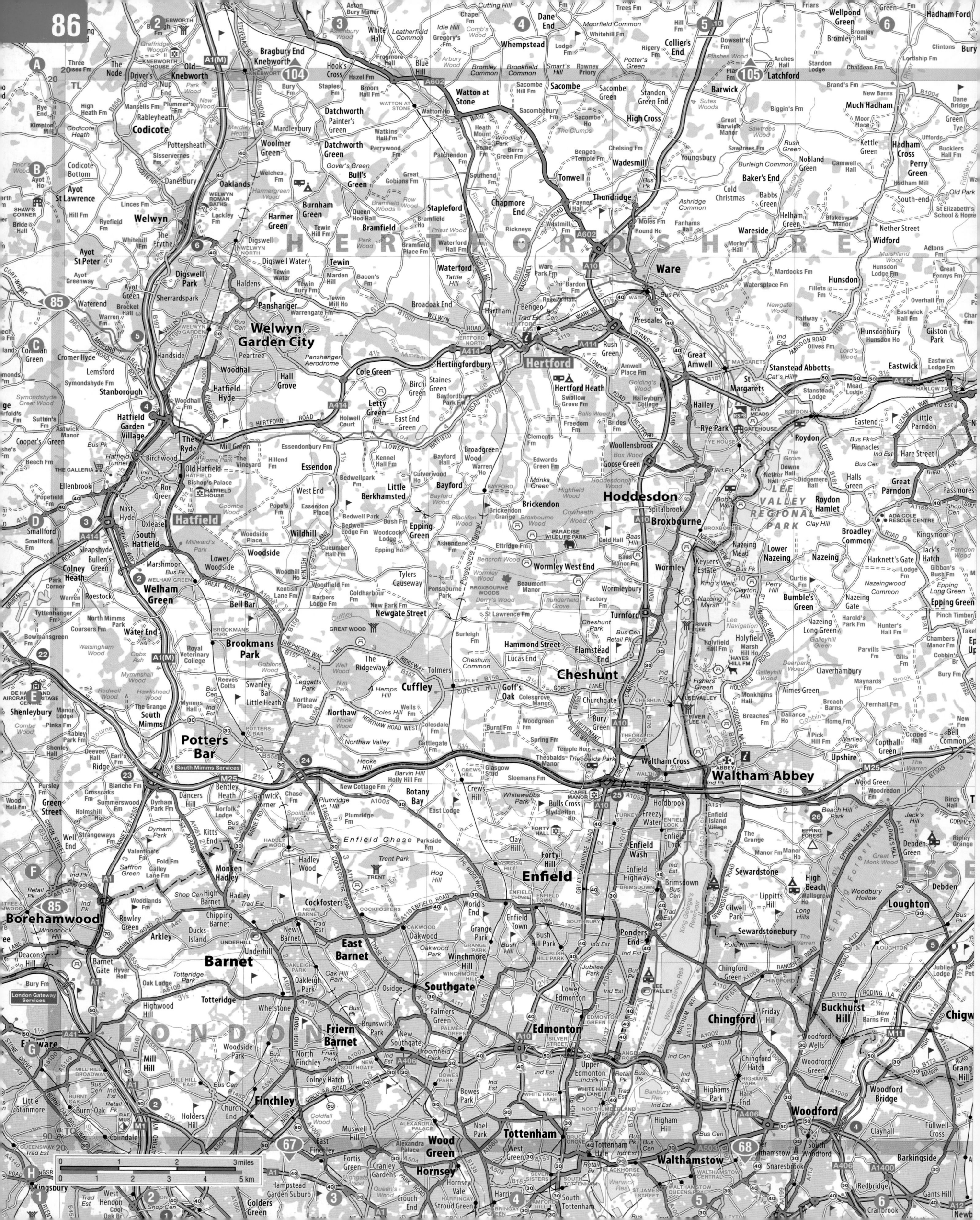

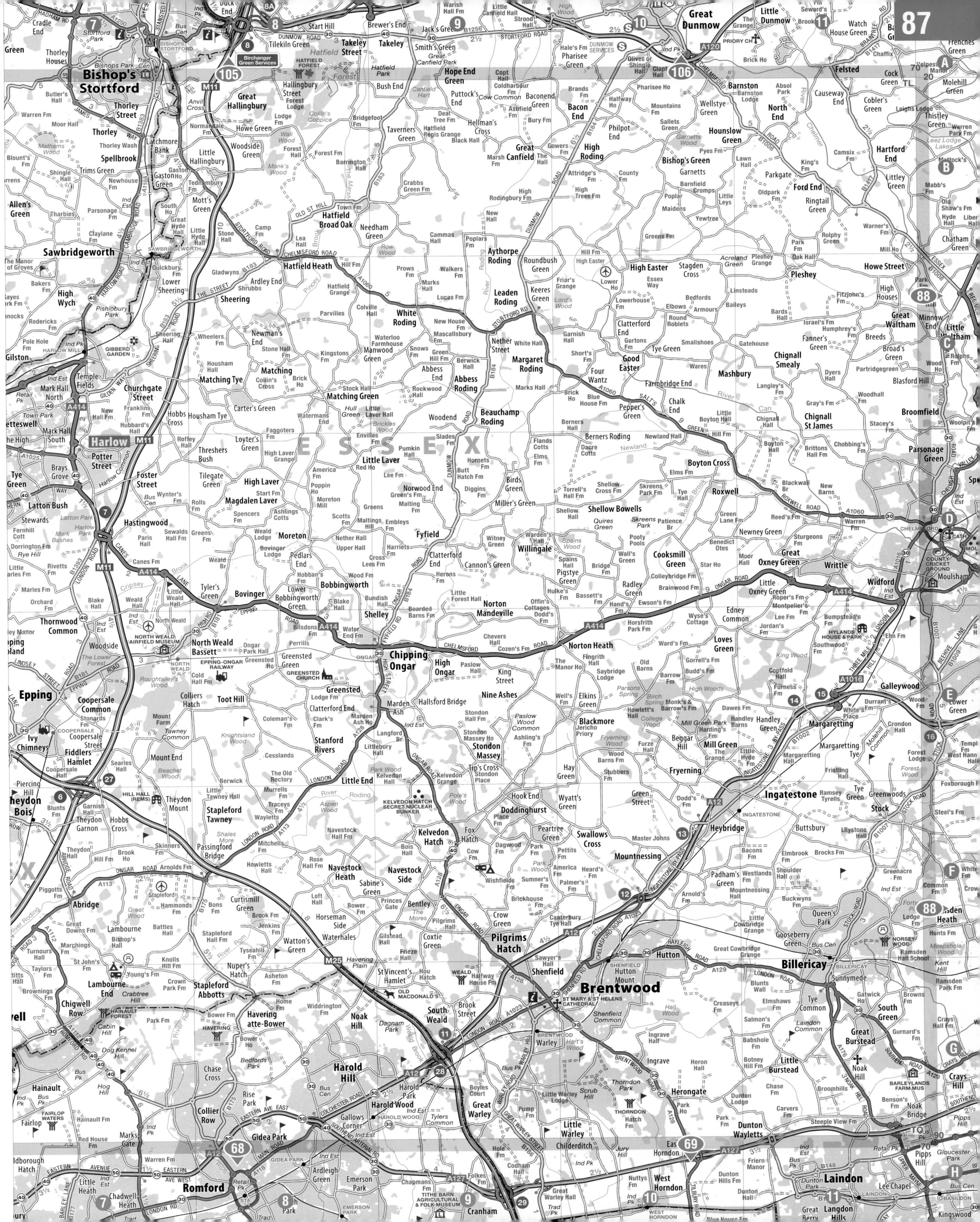

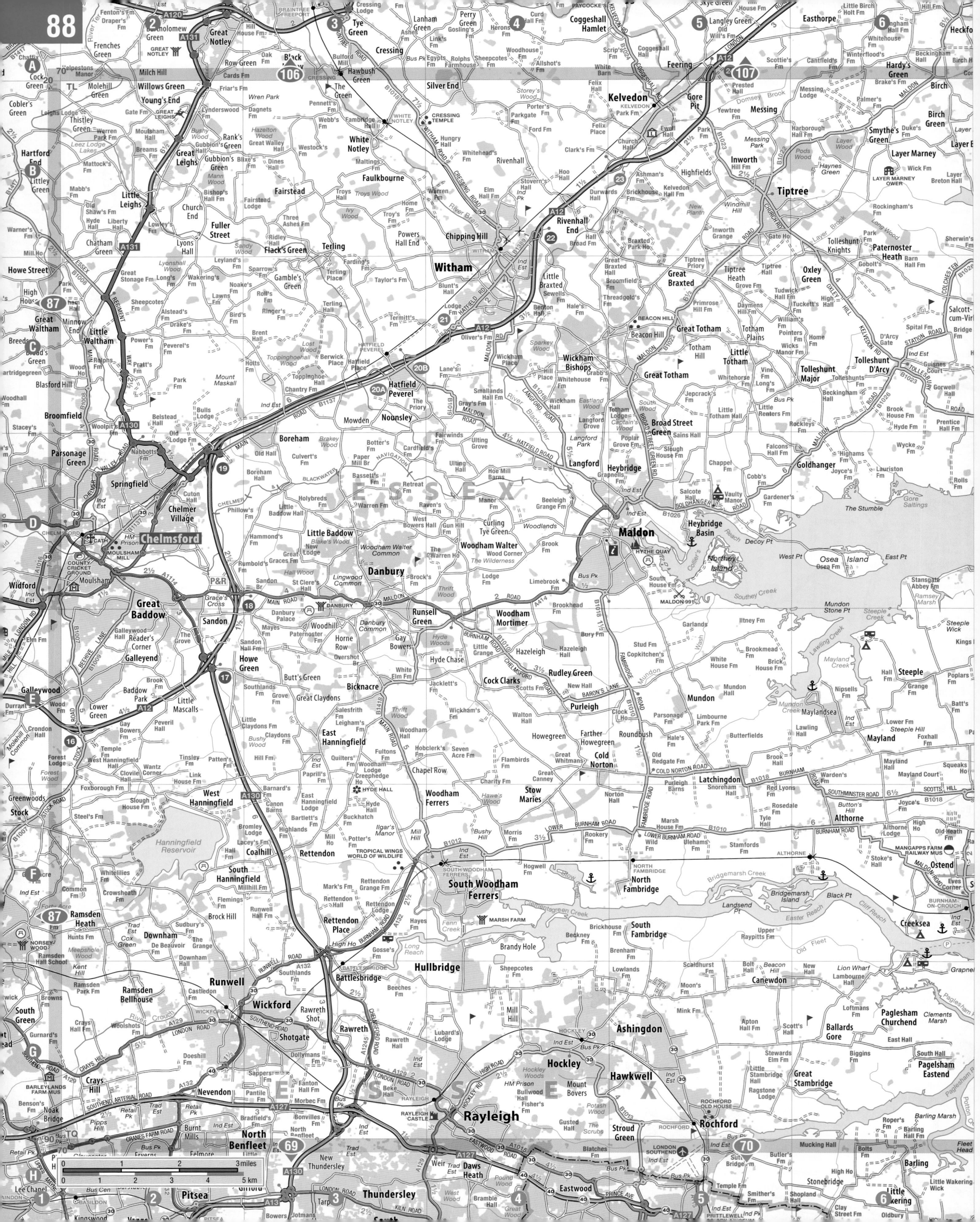

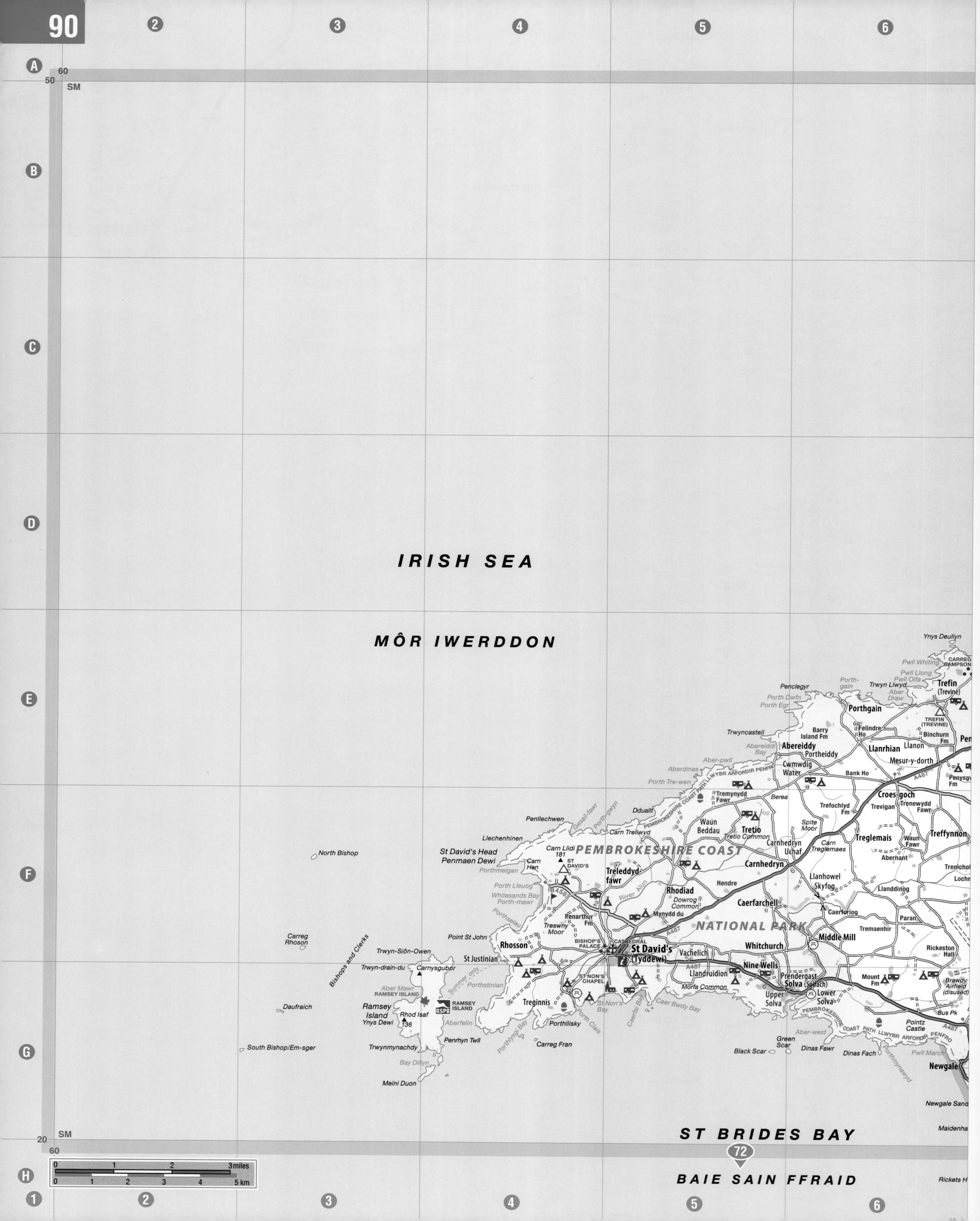

IRISH SEA

MÔR IWERDDON

Ynys Deullyn

Pwll Whiting
CARREG
SAMPSON
Pwll Llong
Pwll Olfa
Porth-
gain
Trwyn Llwyd
Trefin
(Trevine)
Penclegyr
Porth Dwfn
Porth Egr
Aber
Draw
TREFIN
(TREVINE)

Porthgain

Trwyncastell
Abereiddi
Bay
Barry
Island Fm
Felindre
Ho
Binchurn
Fm
Pen

Aber-pwll
Abereiddi
Bay
Abereiddy
Portheiddy
Llanrhian
Llanon
Mesur-y-dorth
Penysgw

Aberdinas
Cwmwdig
Water
Bank Ho
A487

Porth Tre-wen
PEMBROKESHIRE COAST PATH LLWYBR ARFORDIR PENFR
Berea
Croes-goch
Trevigan
Trenewydd
Fawr

North Bishop
Penllechwen
Gesail-fawr
Porth-gwyn
Ddualit
Tremynydd
Fawr
**Waun
Beddau**
Tretio
Tretio Common
Carnhedryn
Uchaf
Carn
Treglemaes
Trefochlyd
Fm
Treglemais
Waun
Fawr
Treffynnon

Llechenhinen
Carn Treliwyd
Spite
Moor
Abernant

St David's Head
Penmaen Dewi
Carn
Hen
Carn Llidi
181
ST
DAVID'S
PEMBROKESHIRE COAST
Carnhedryn
Carnhedryn
Tremichol
Lochn

Porthmelgan
**Treleddyd
fawr**
Llanhowel
Skyfog
Llanddinog
Paran

Porth Lleuog
Whitesands Bay
Porth-mawr
River Alun
Rhodiad
Dowrog
Common
Hendre
Caerfarchell
NATIONAL PARK
Tremaenhir

Porthsely
Renarthur
Fm
Mynydd du
Caerforiog
Rickeston
Hall

Carreg
Rhoson
Point St John
Treswny
Moor
A487
Whitchurch
Middle Mill

Bishops and Clerks
Trwyn-Siôn-Owen
Rhosson
BISHOP'S
PALACE
CATHEDRAL
St David's
(Tyddewi)
Vachelch

Trwyn-drain-du
Carnysgubor
Summer only
Porthstinian
St Non's
Bay
Morfa Common
Nine Wells
Caer Bwdy Bay
Prendergast
Fm
Mount
Brawdy
Airfield
(disused)

Daufraich
Aber Mawr
RAMSEY ISLAND
St Non's
Chapel
Llandruidion
Upper
Solva
Solva (Solfach)
Lower
Solva
Bus Pk

**Ramsey
Island**
Ynys Dewi
Rhod Isaf
136
RSPB
RAMSEY
ISLAND
Treginnis
Porthlisky
Caerfai Bay
PEMBROKESHIRE
COAST
LLWYBR ARFORDIR
PENFRO
Pointz
Castle
A487

South Bishop/Em-sger
Aberfelin
Porthysgol Bay
Caerfai
Porth Clais
Aber-west
Pwll March

Trwynmynachdy
Penrhyn Twll
Carreg Fran
Green
Scar
Black Scar
Dinas Fawr
Dinas Fach
Porthmynaewyd
Newgale

Bay Dillyn
Meini Duon
Newgale Sand

0   1   2   3miles
0   1   2   3   4   5 km

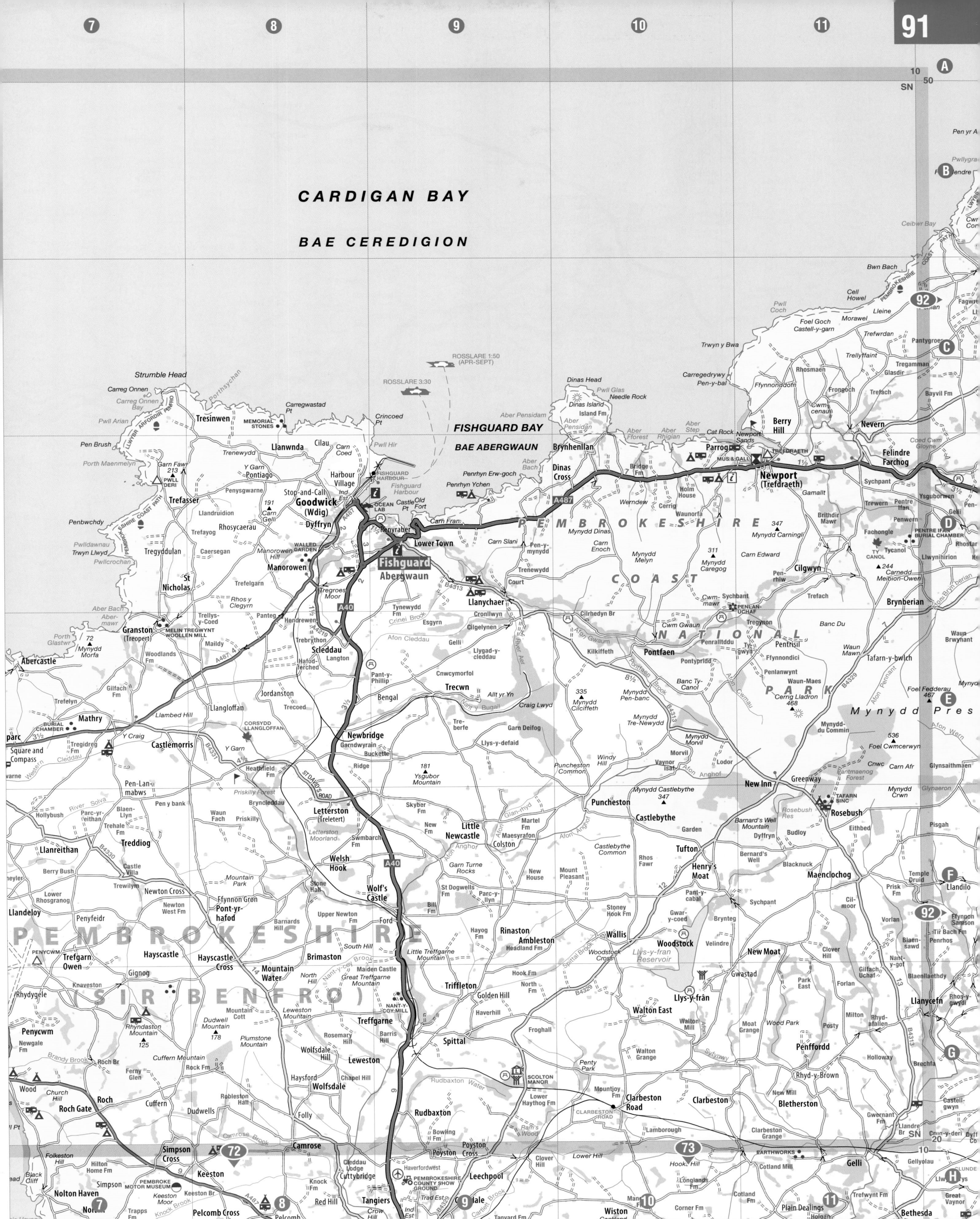

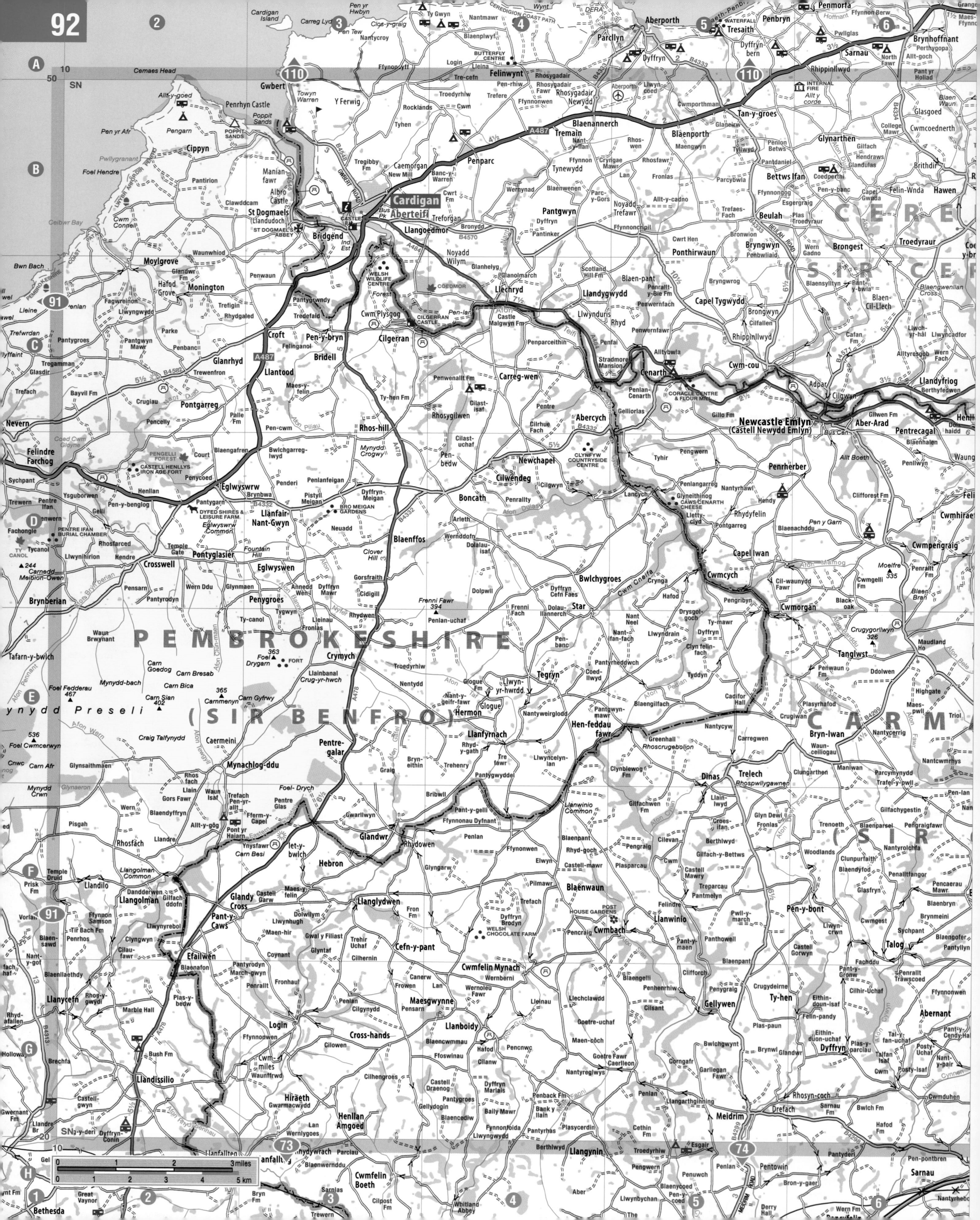

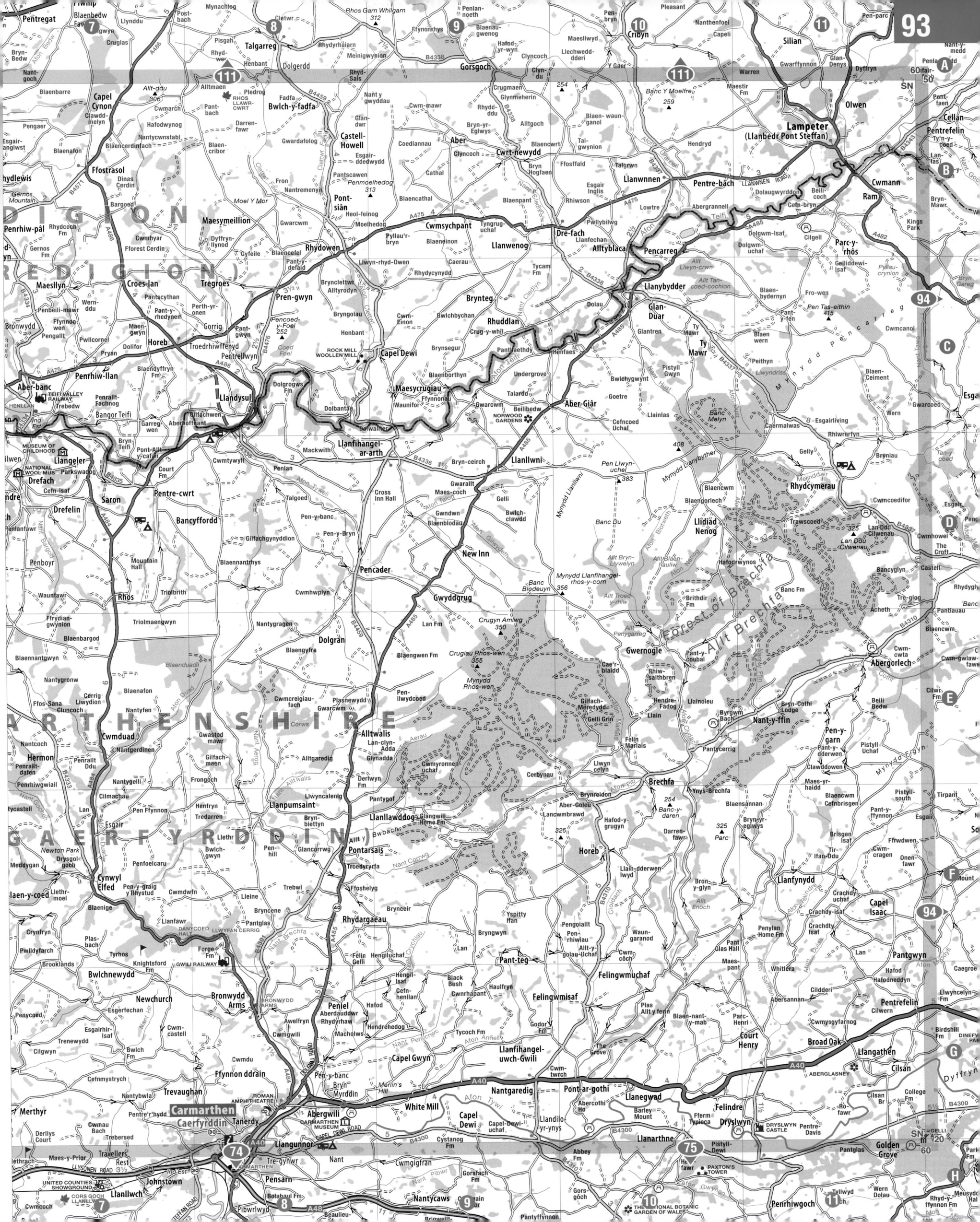

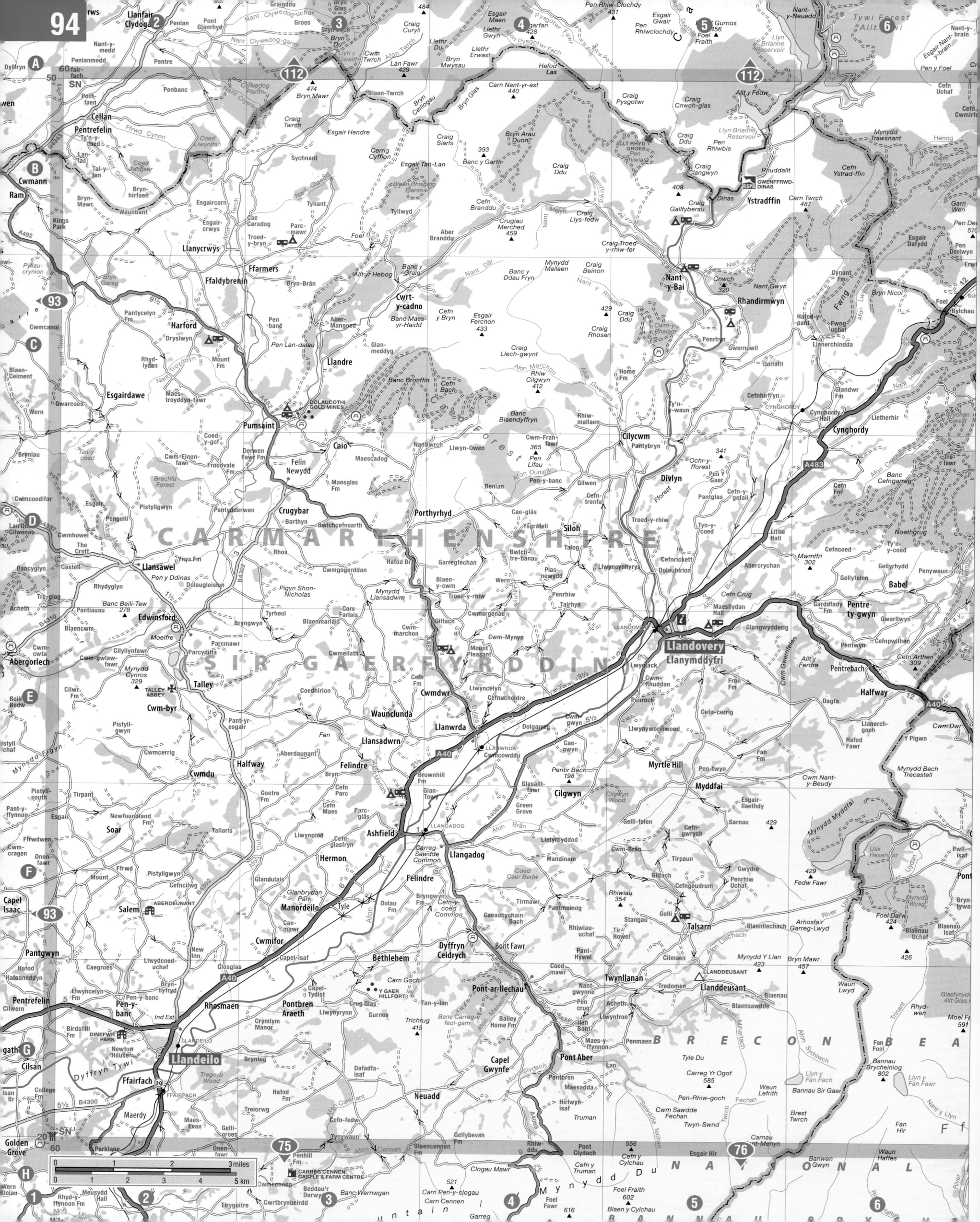

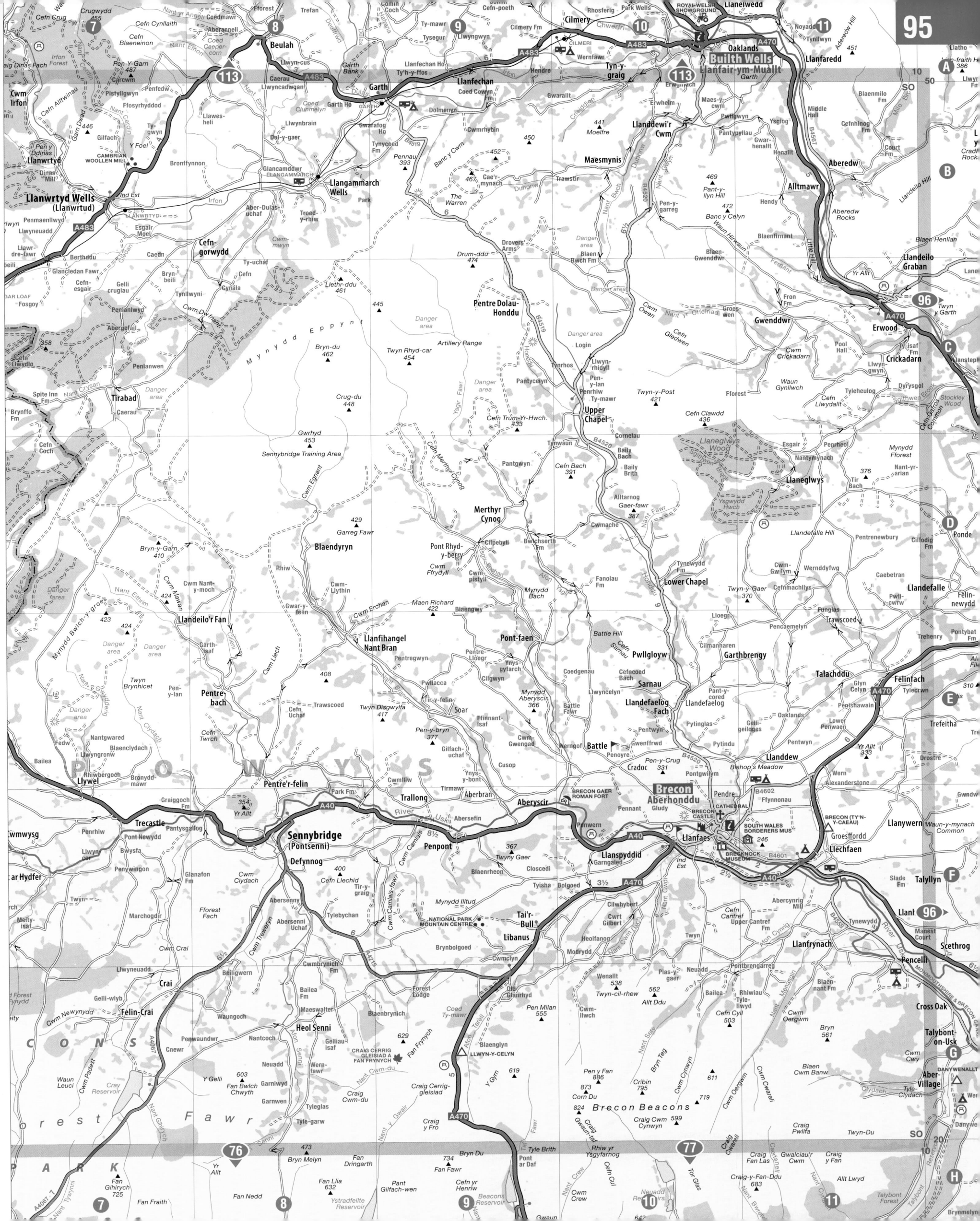

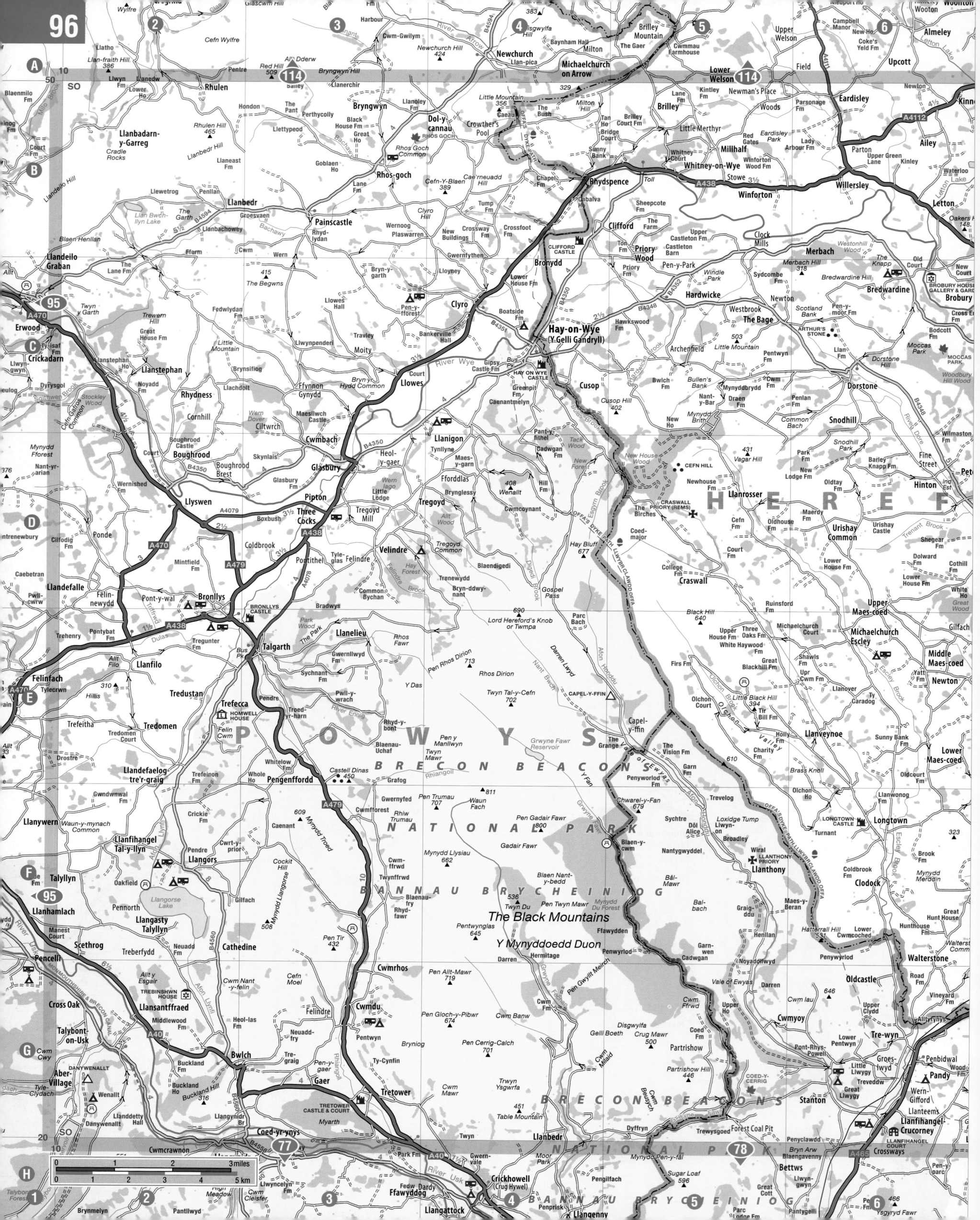

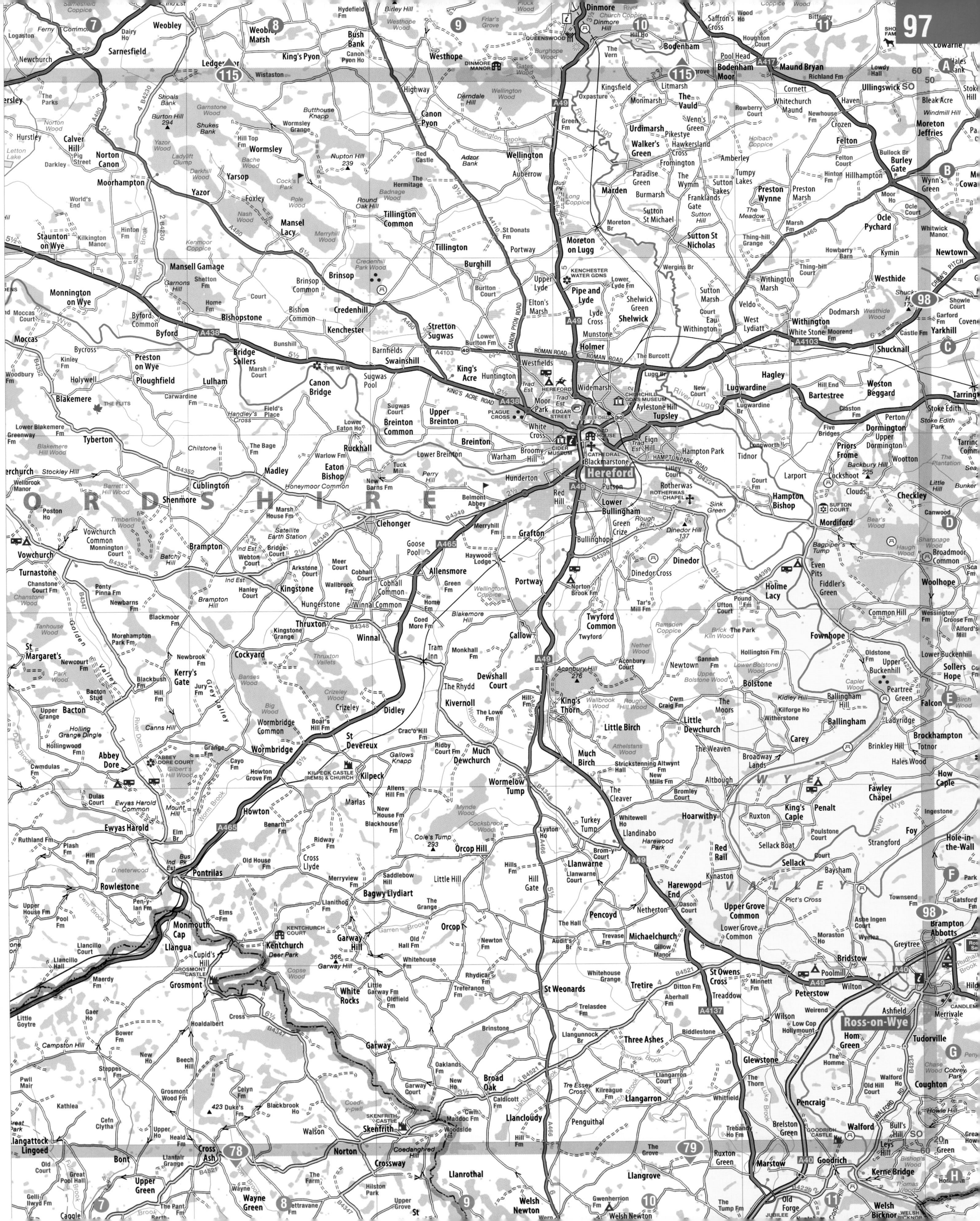

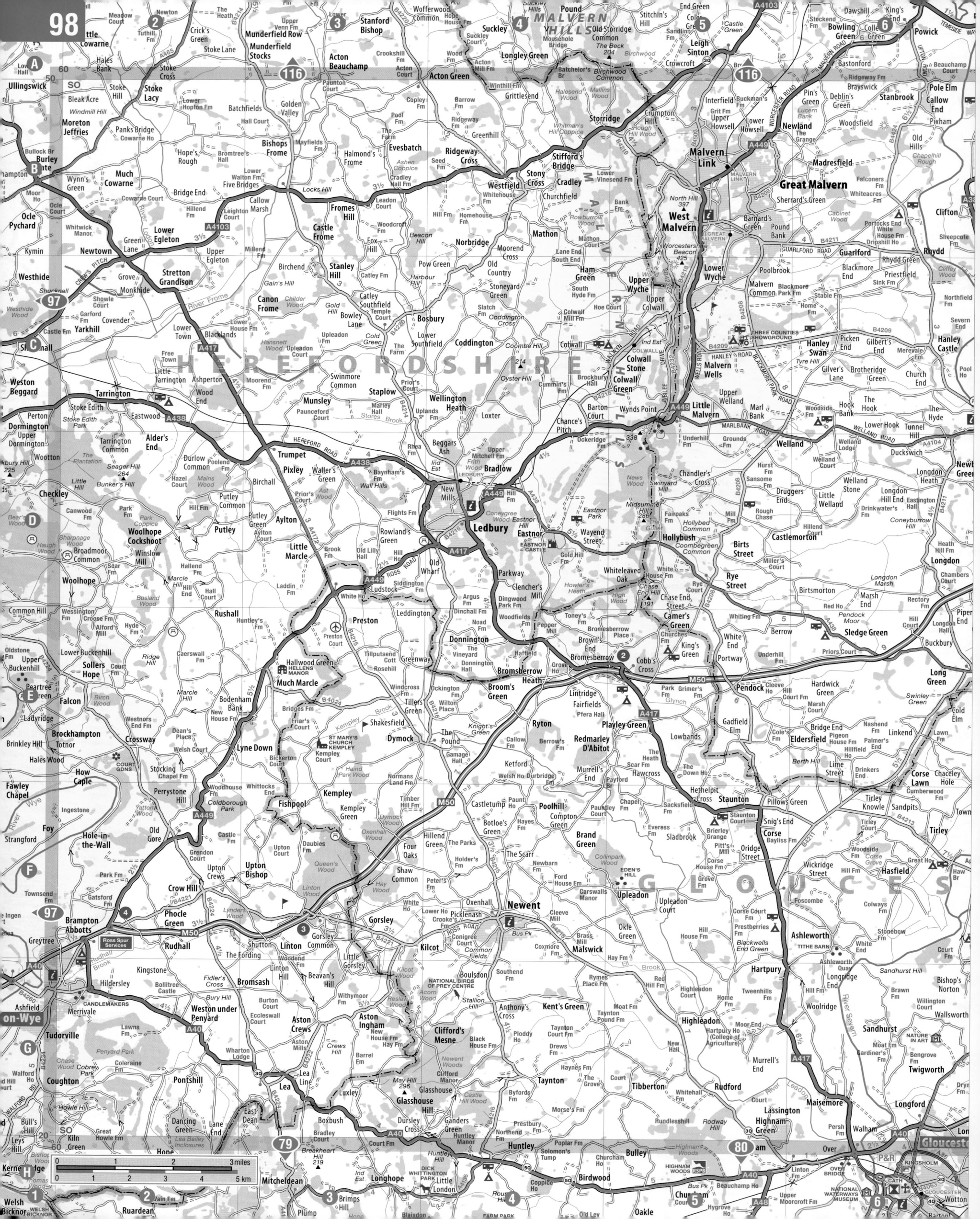

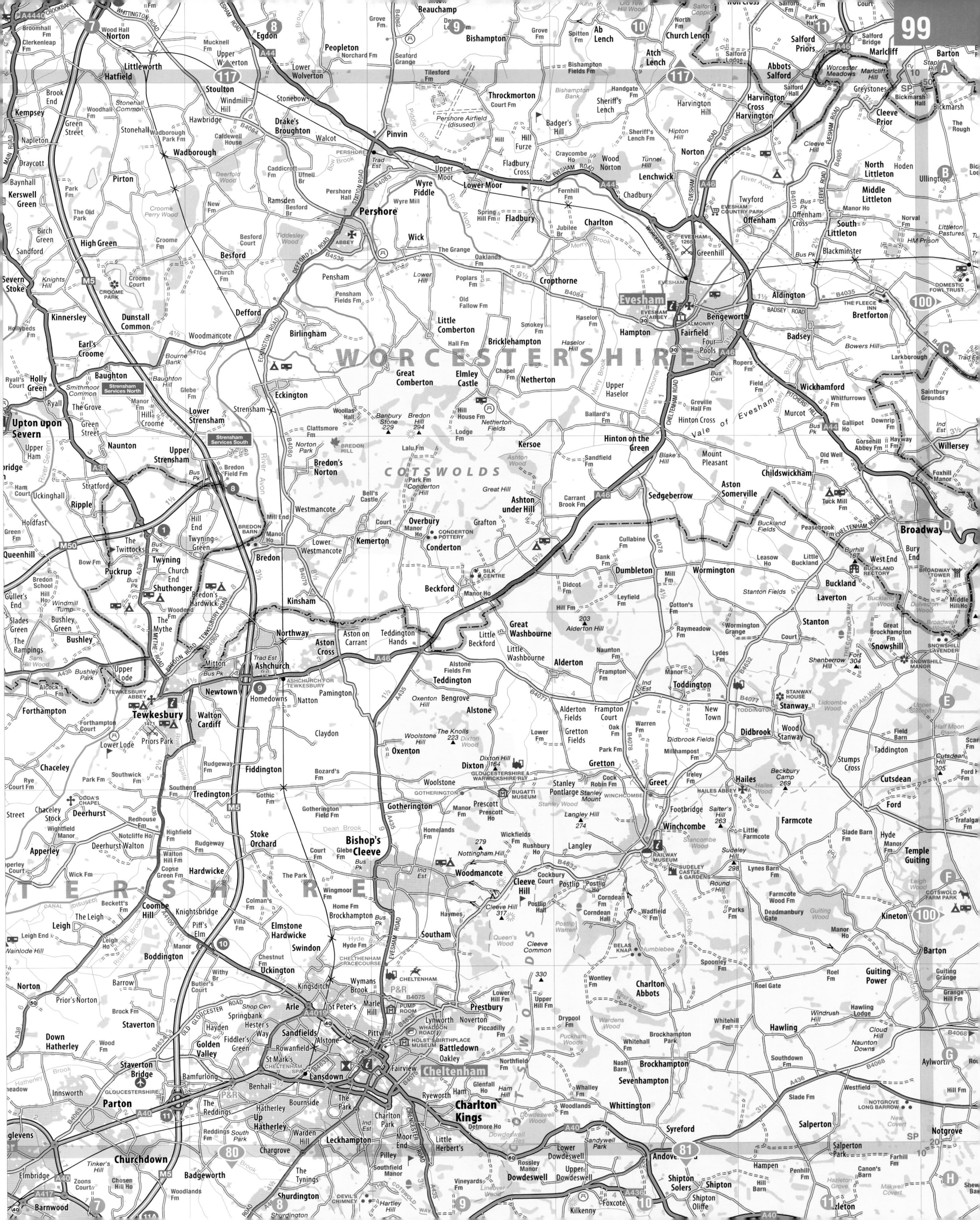

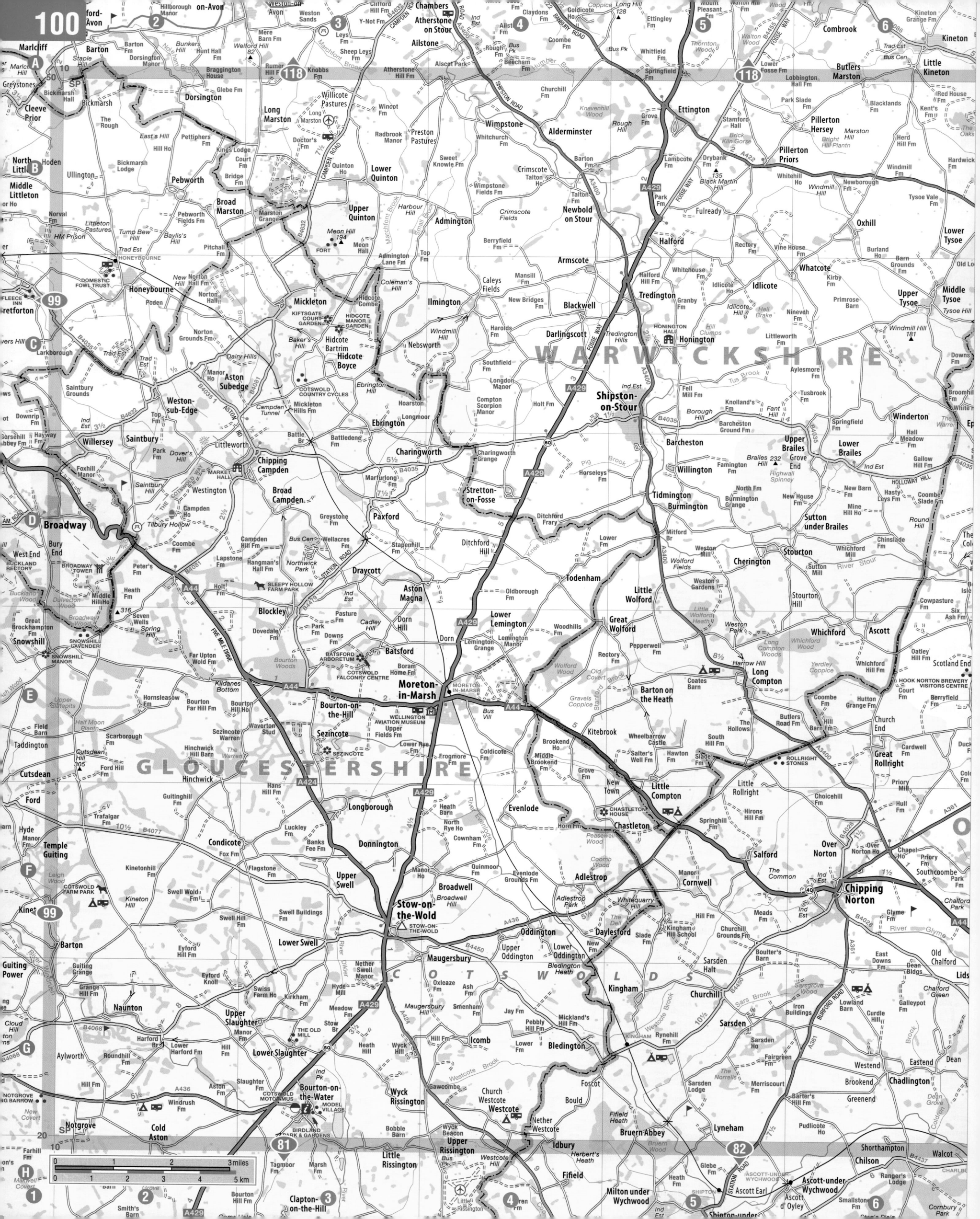

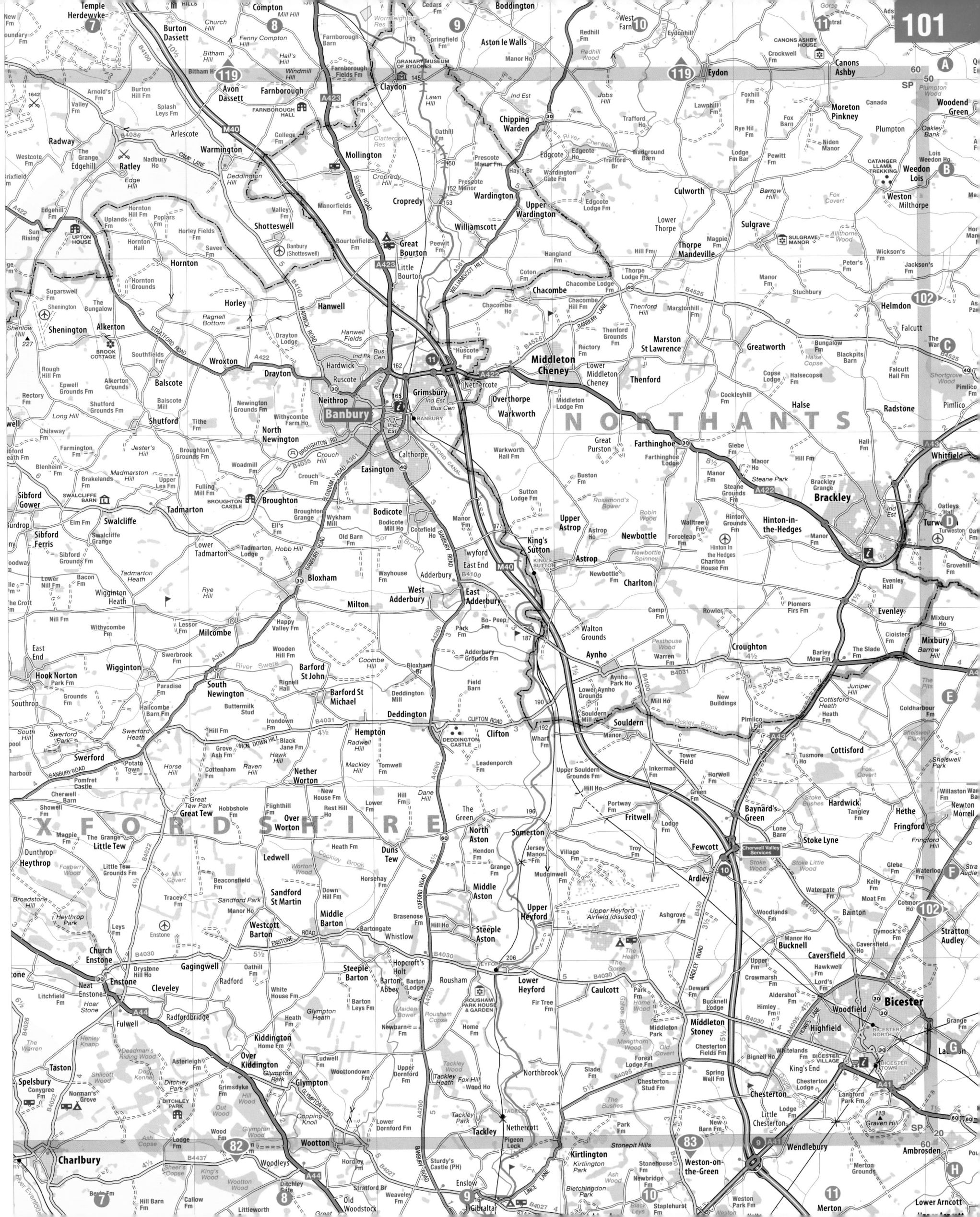

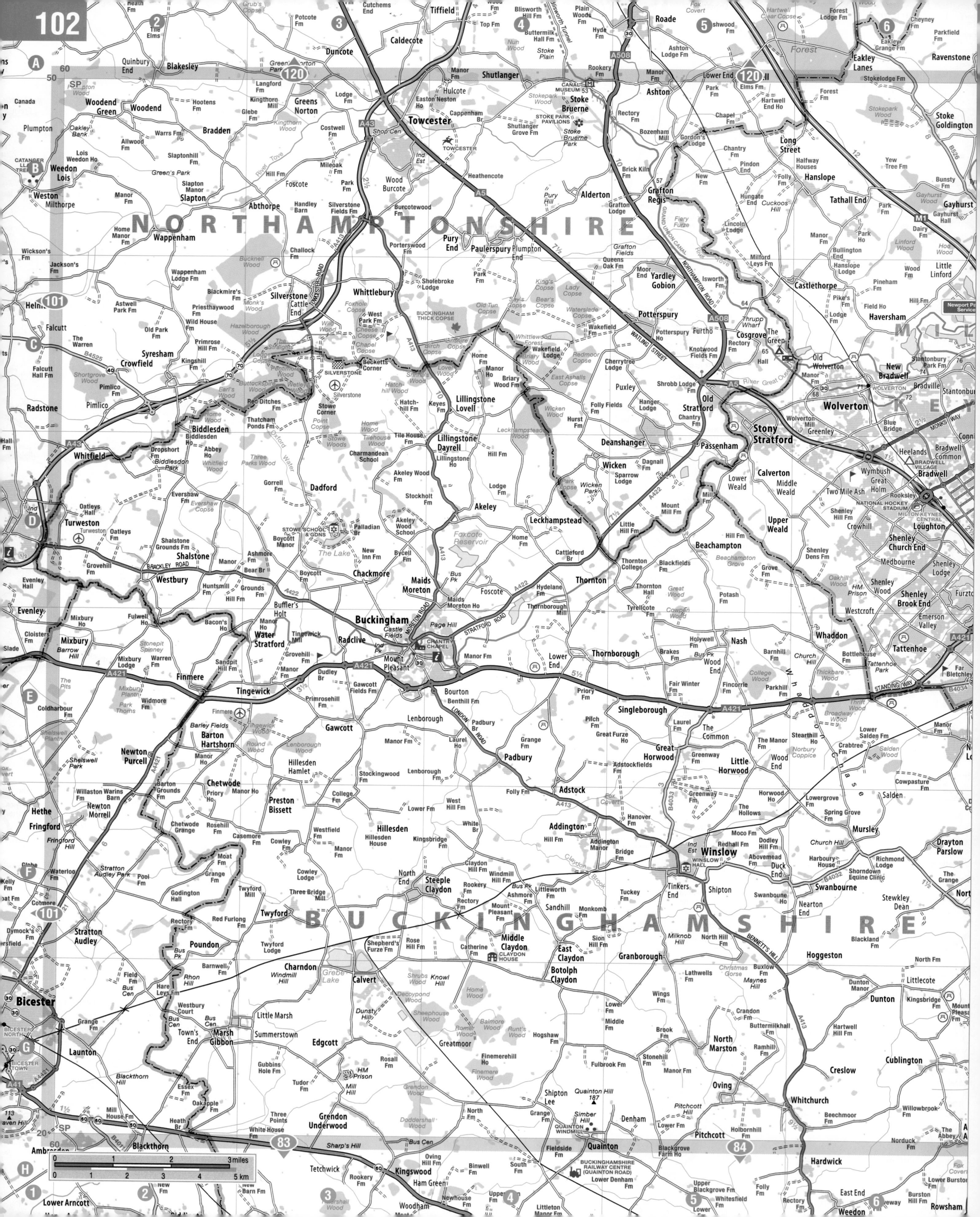

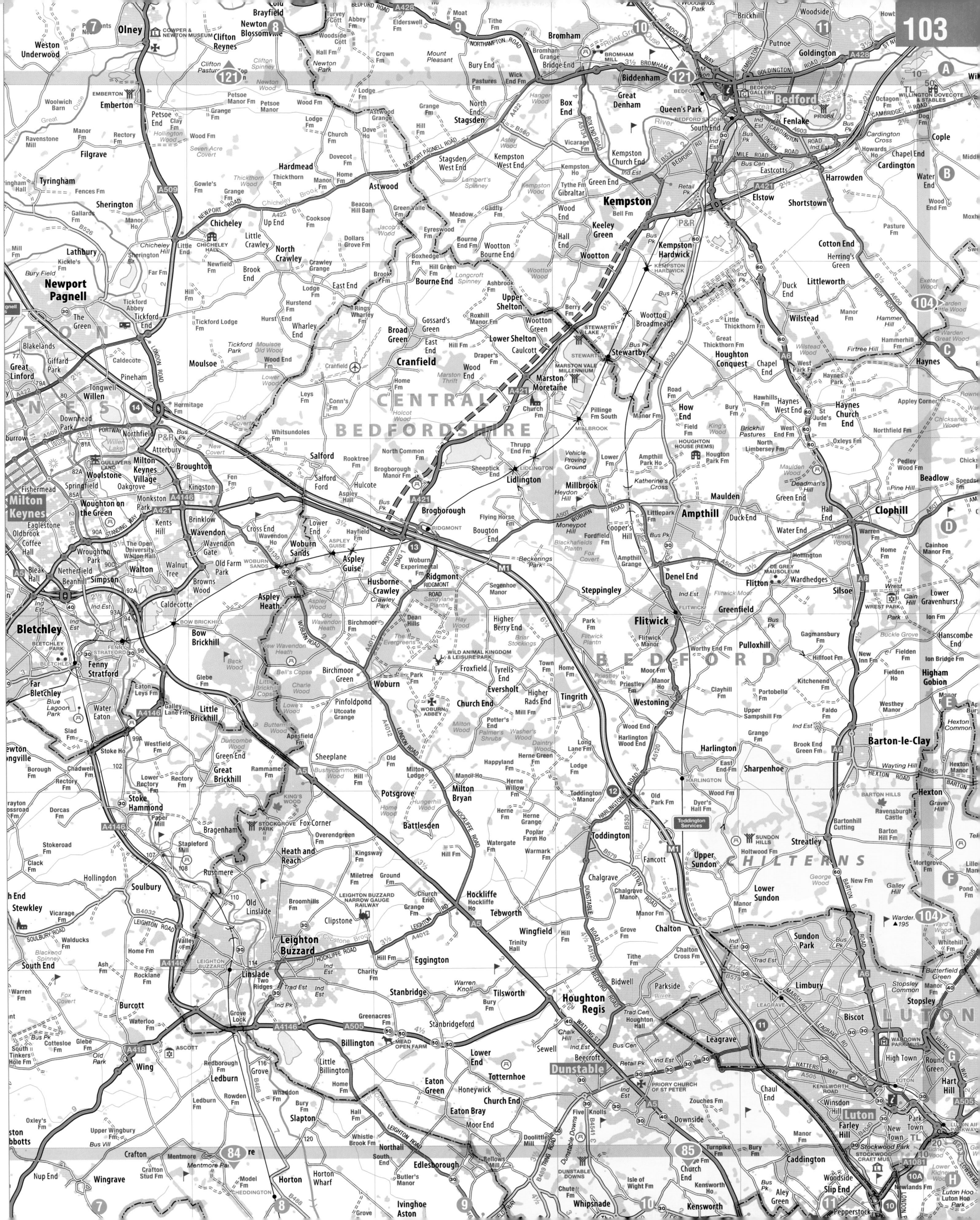

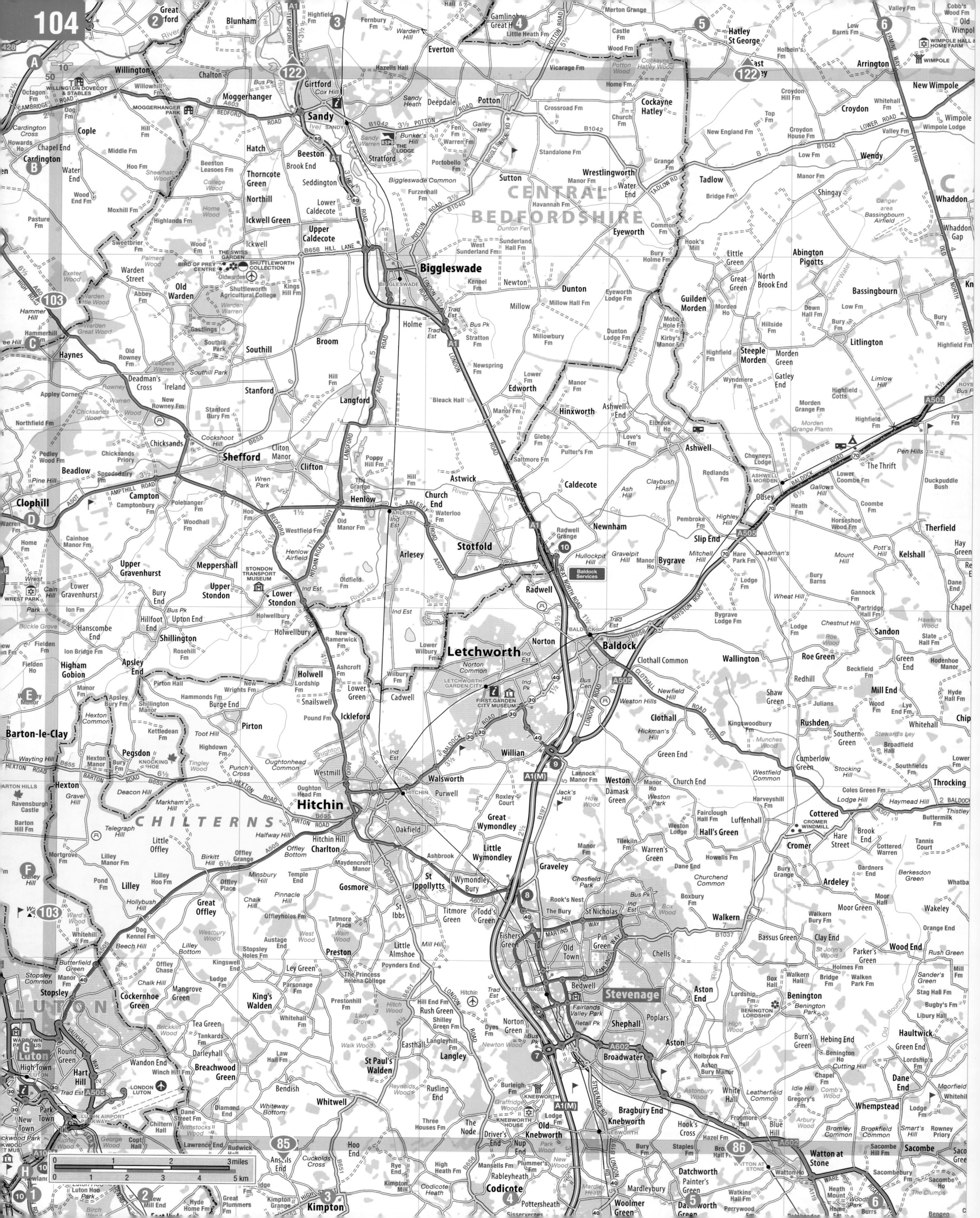

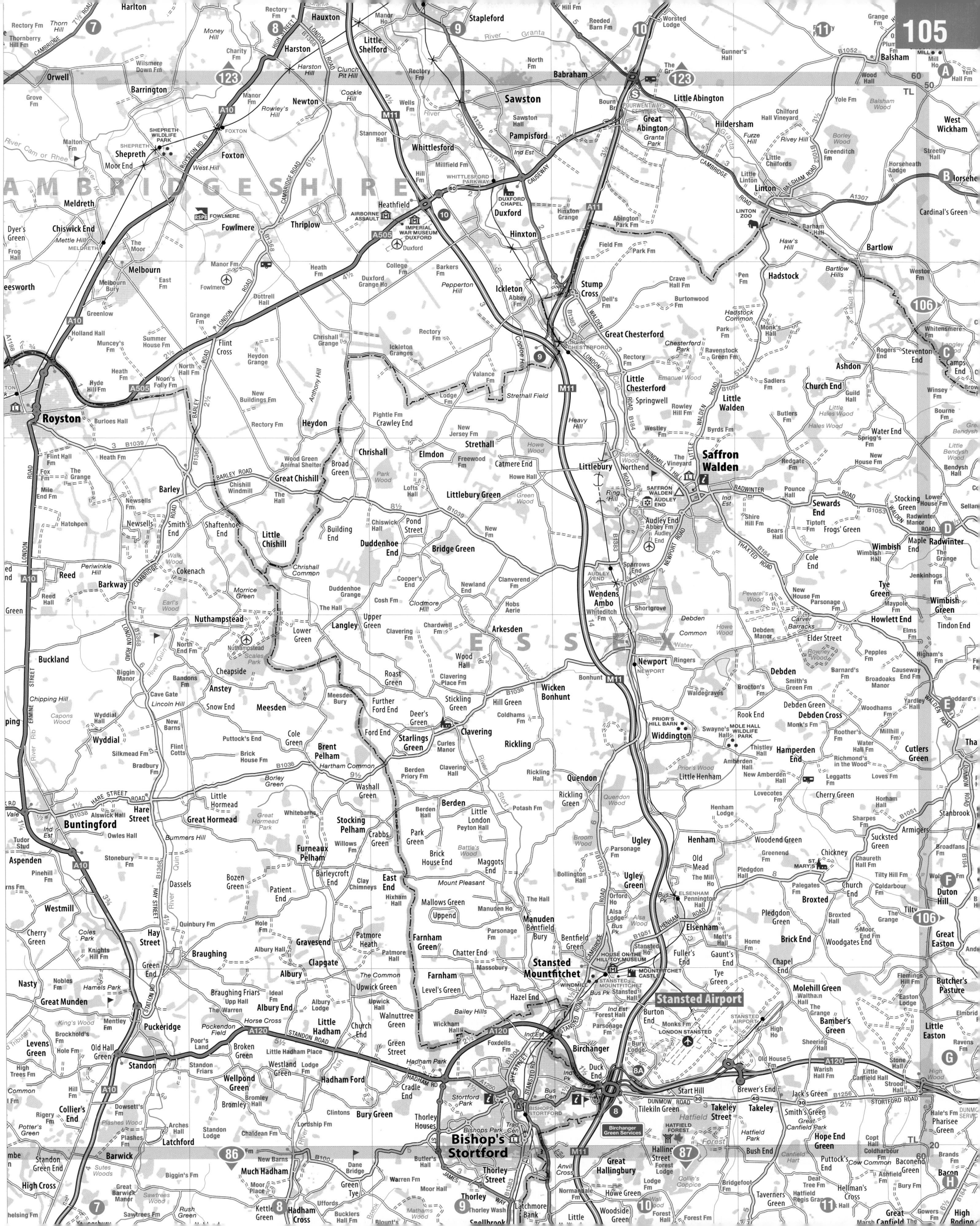

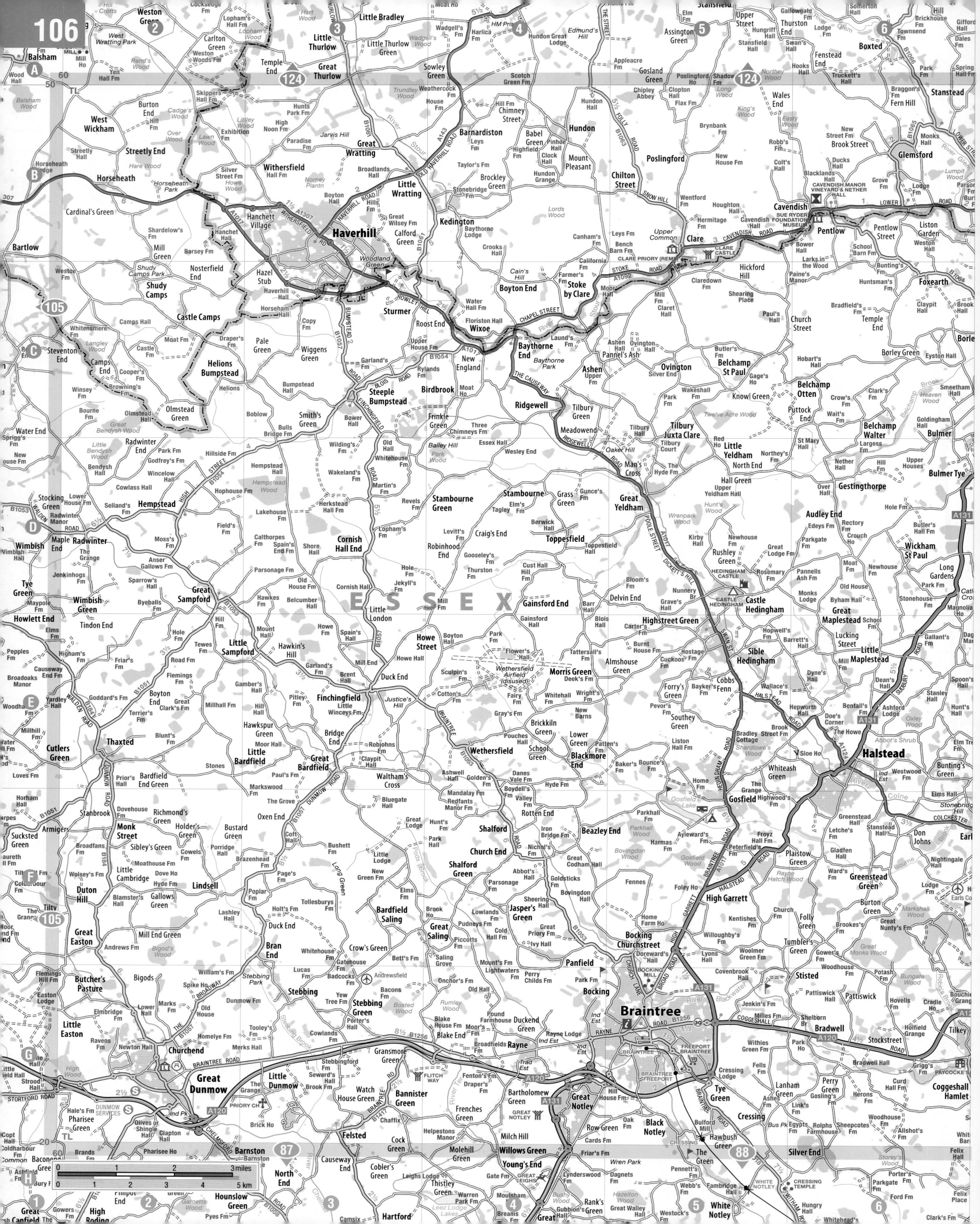

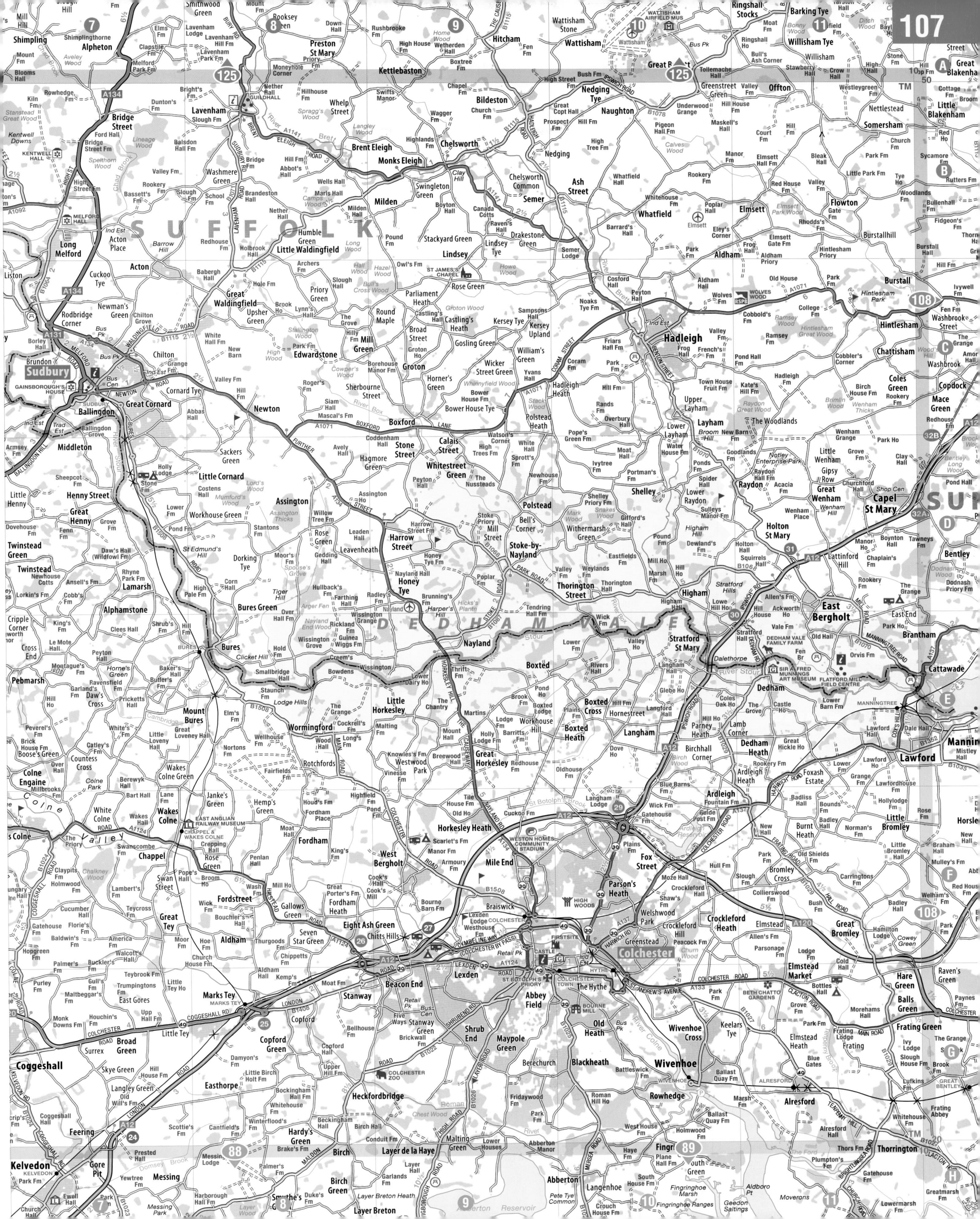

NORTH

SEA

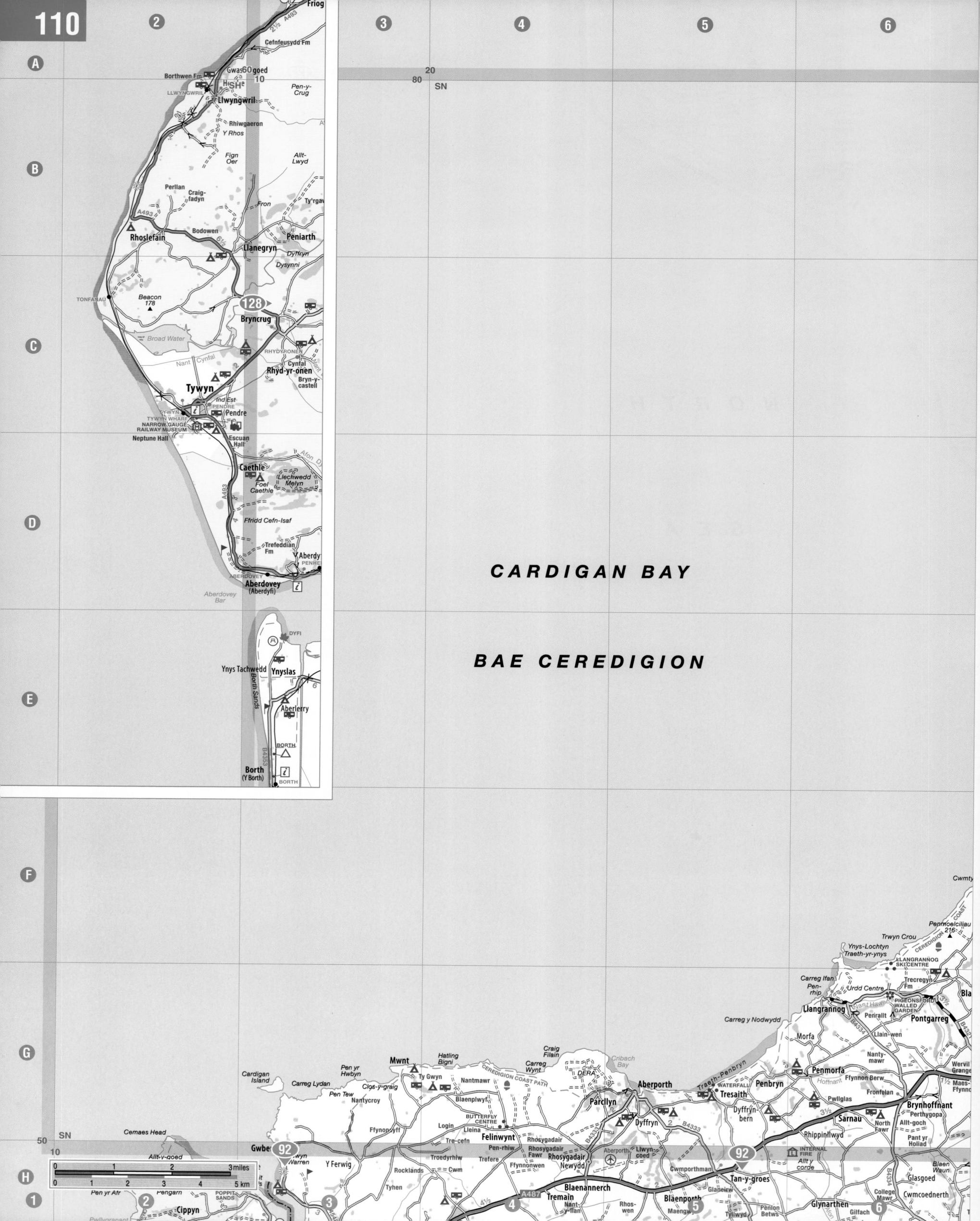

CARDIGAN BAY

BAE CEREDIGION

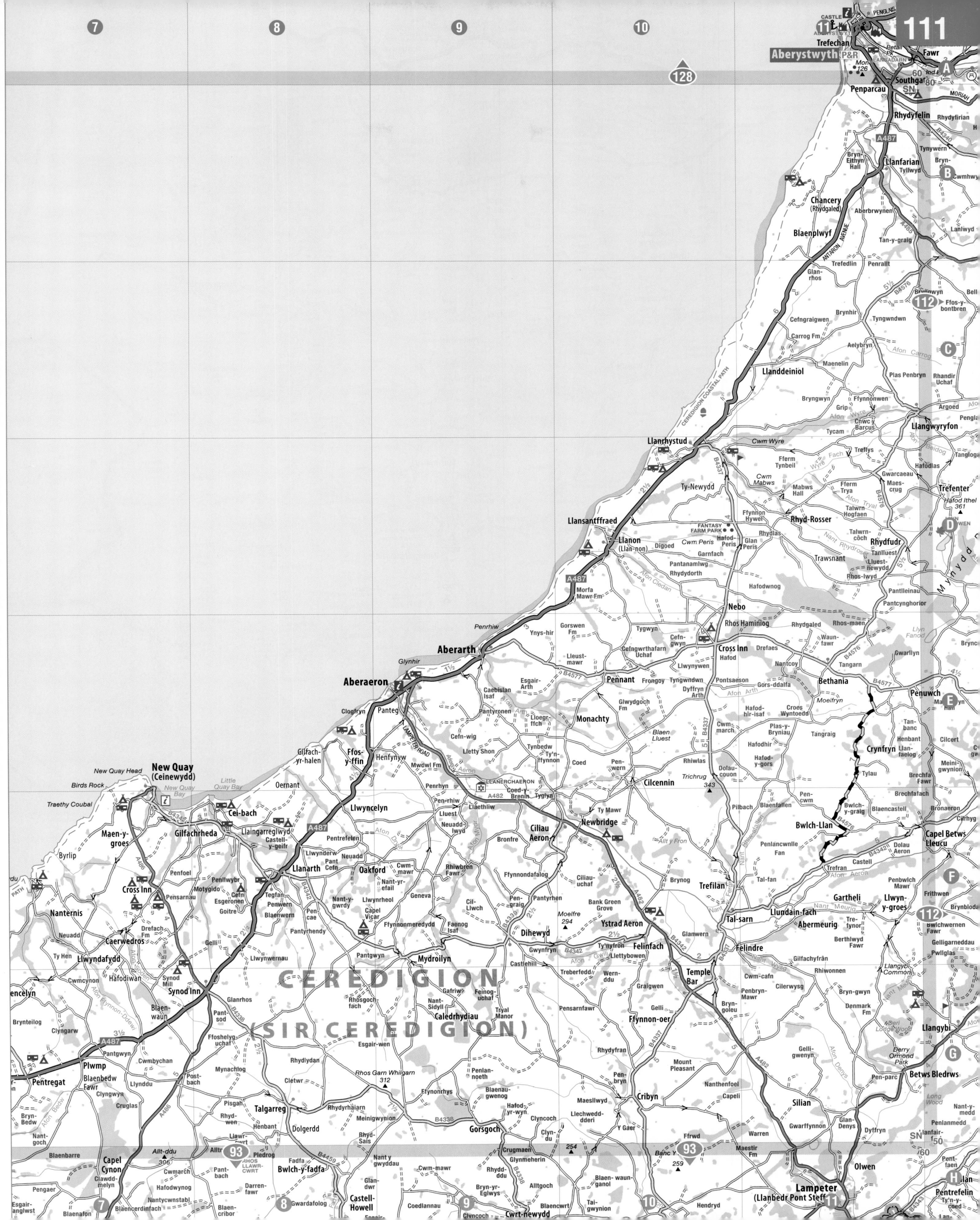

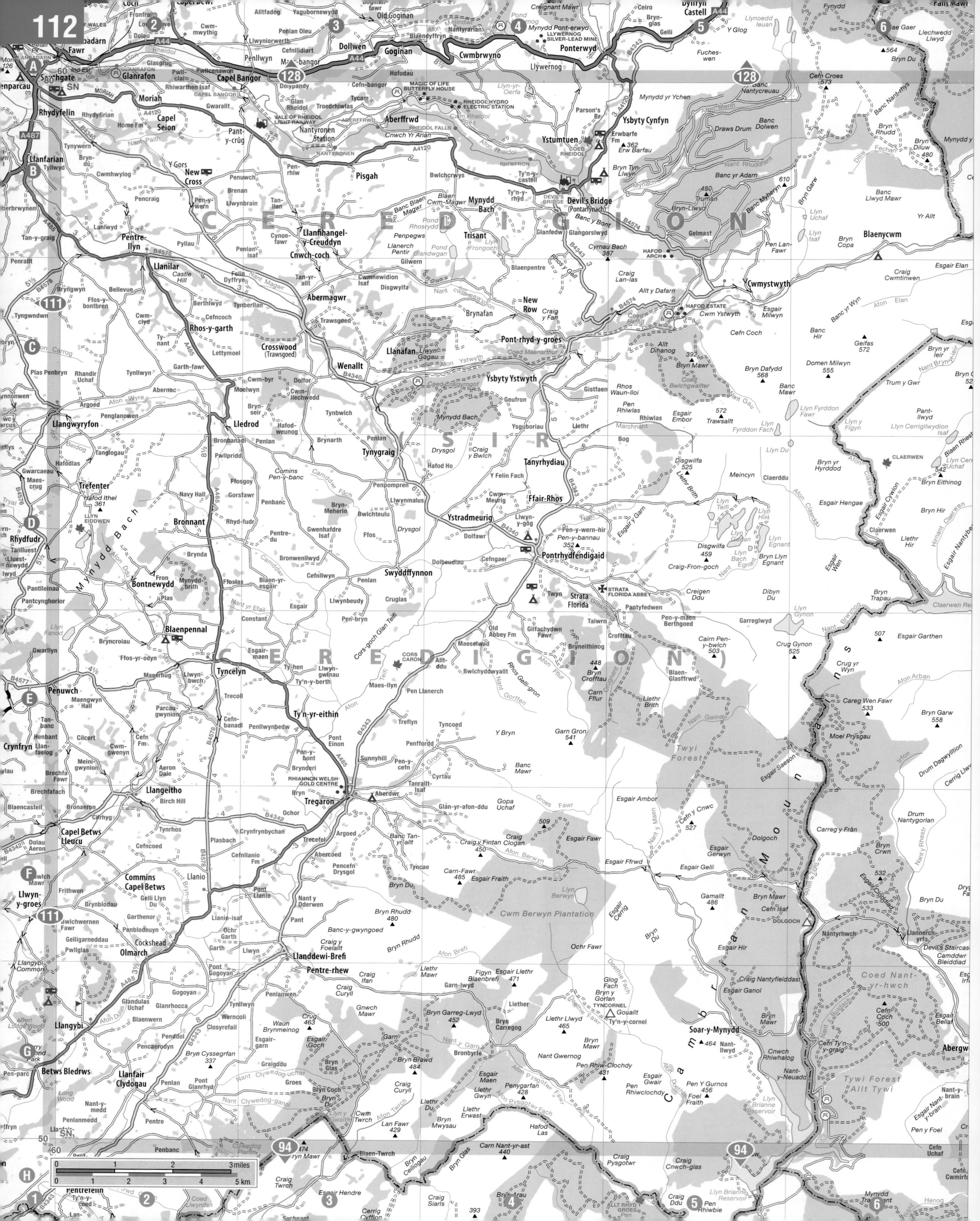

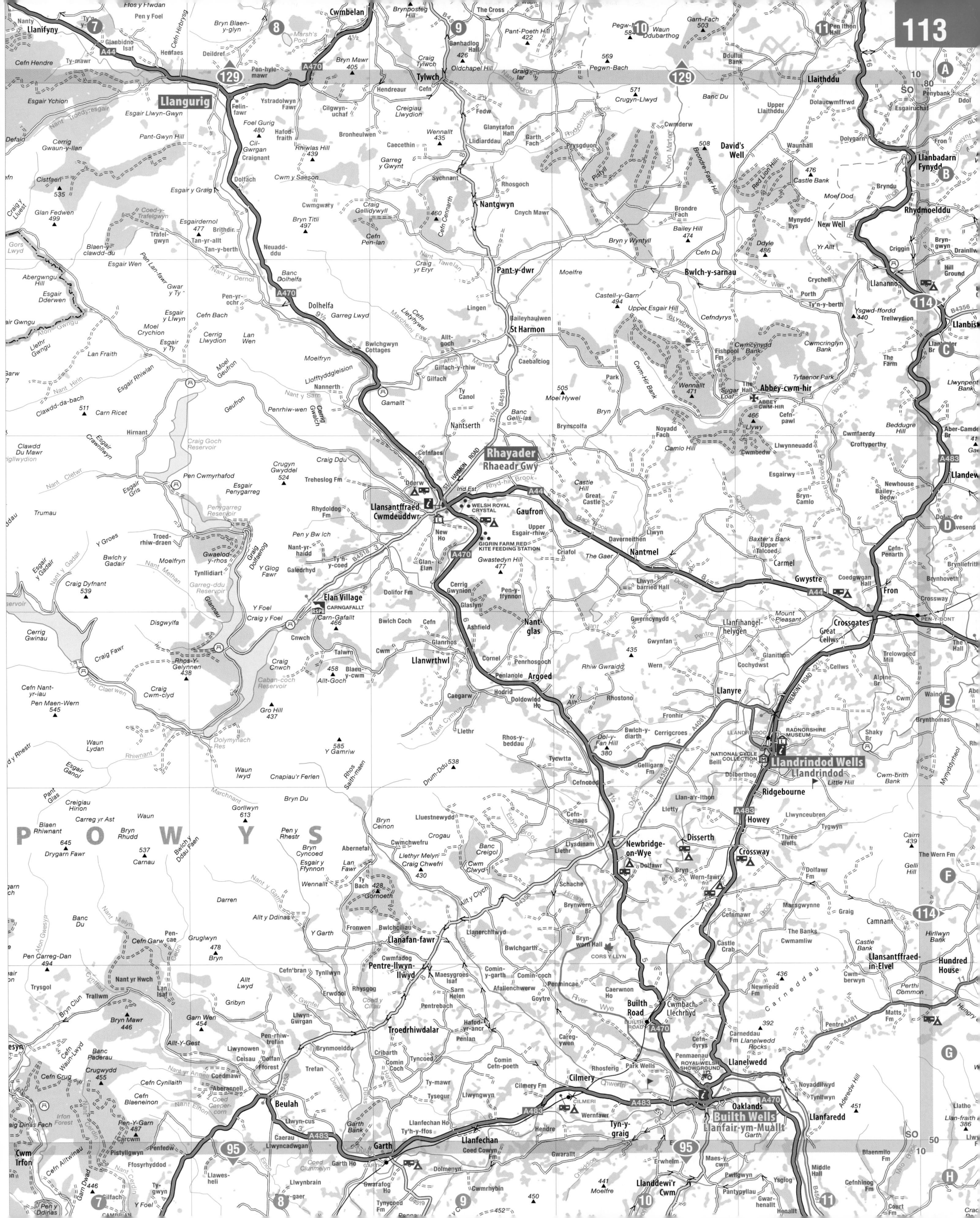

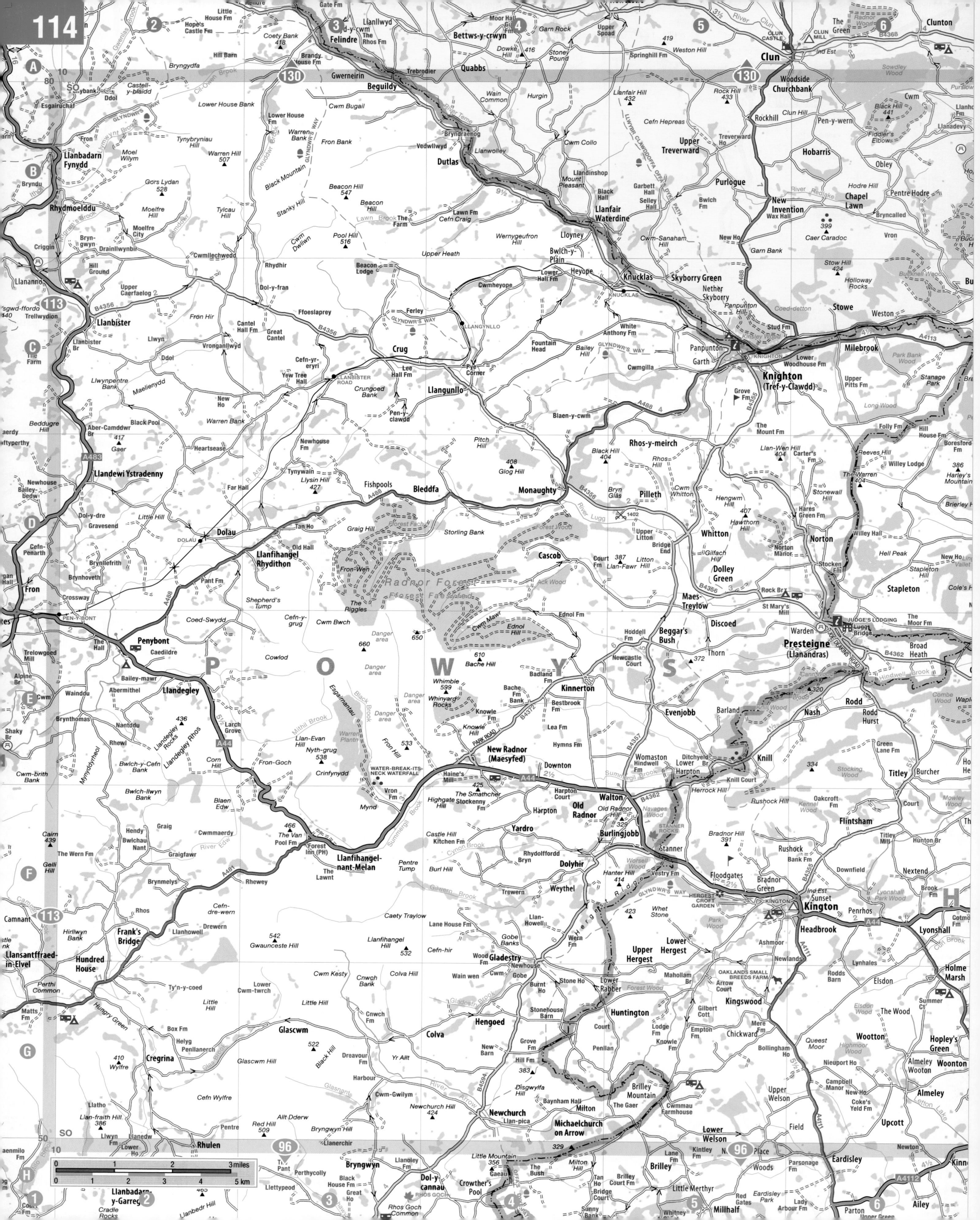

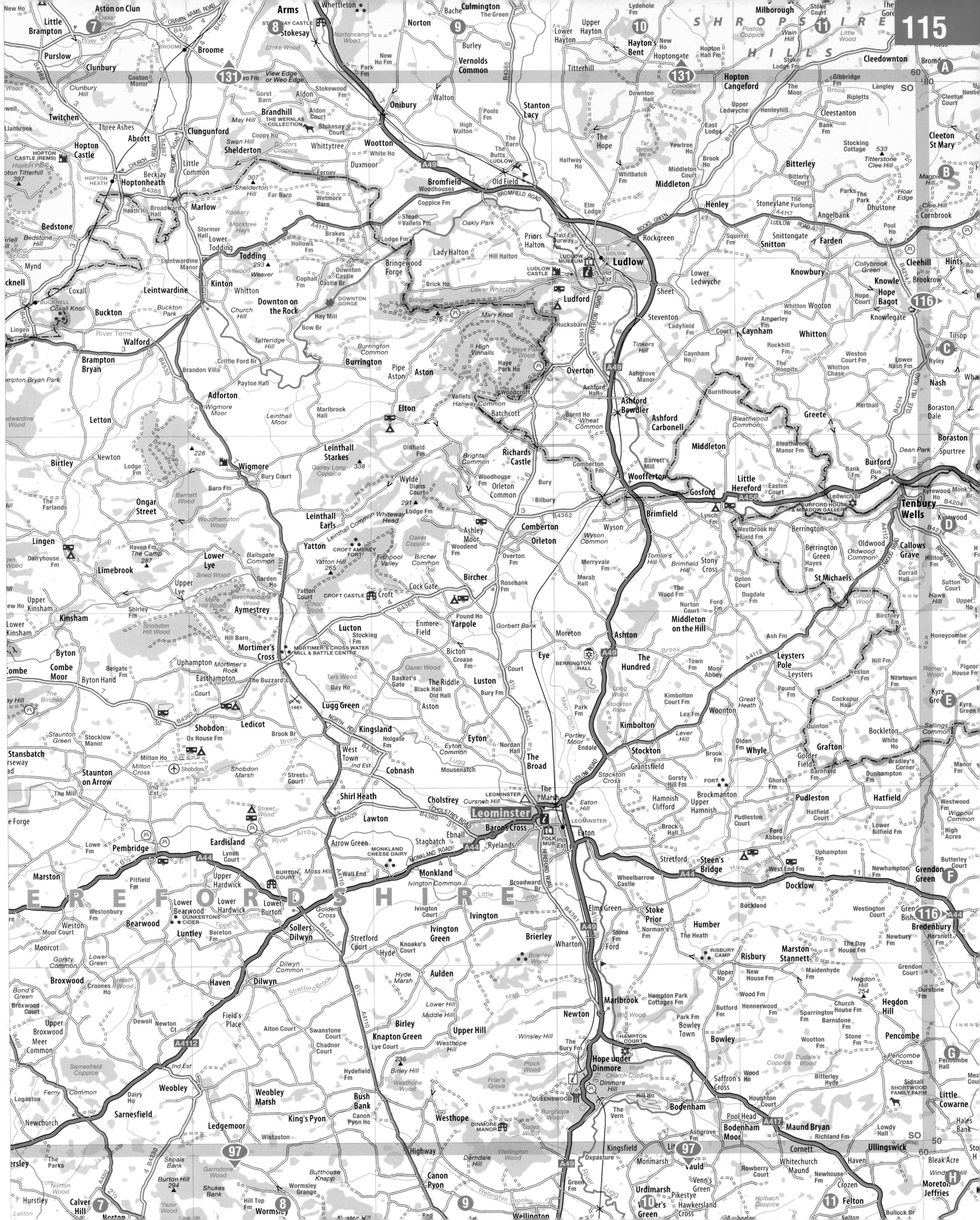

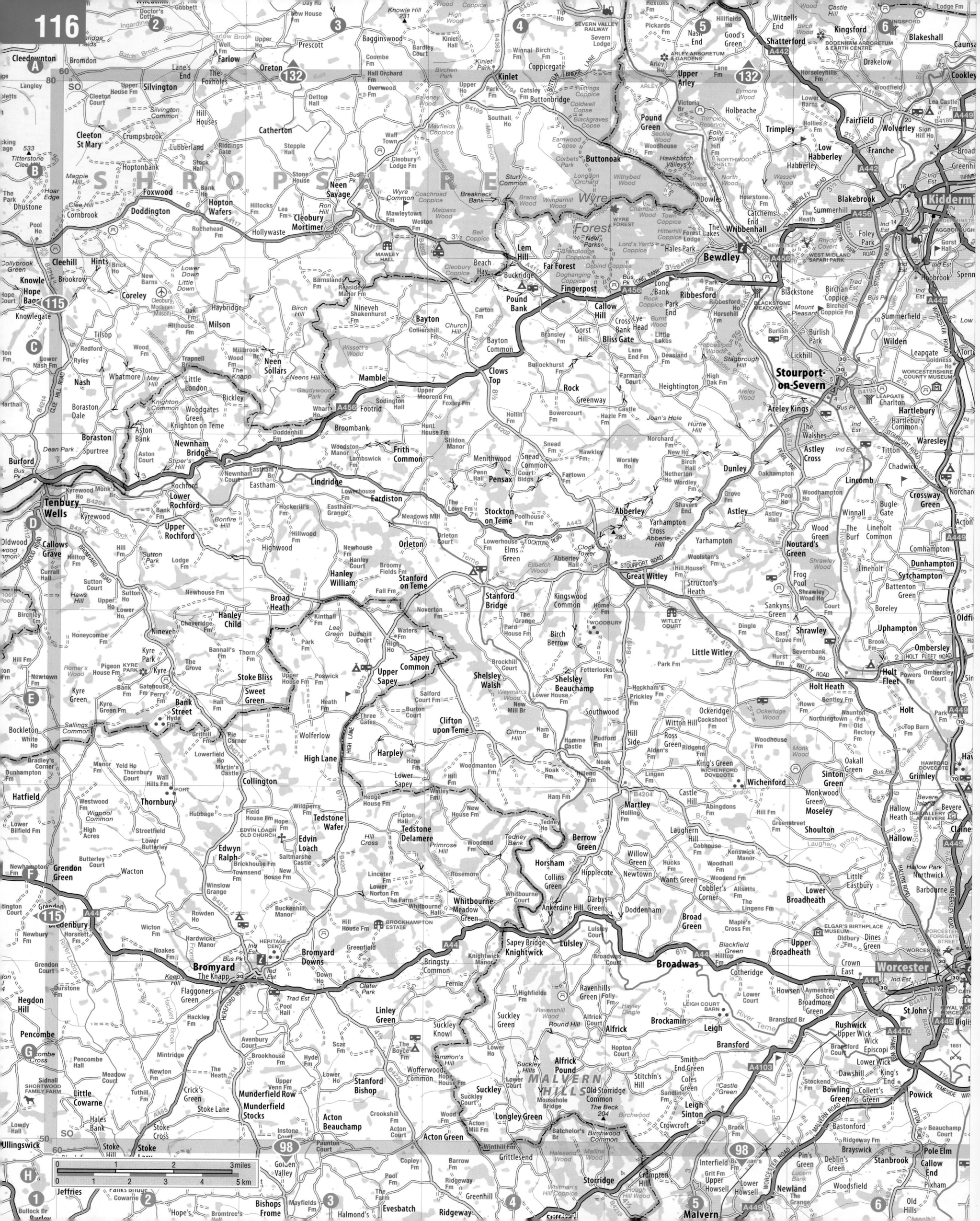

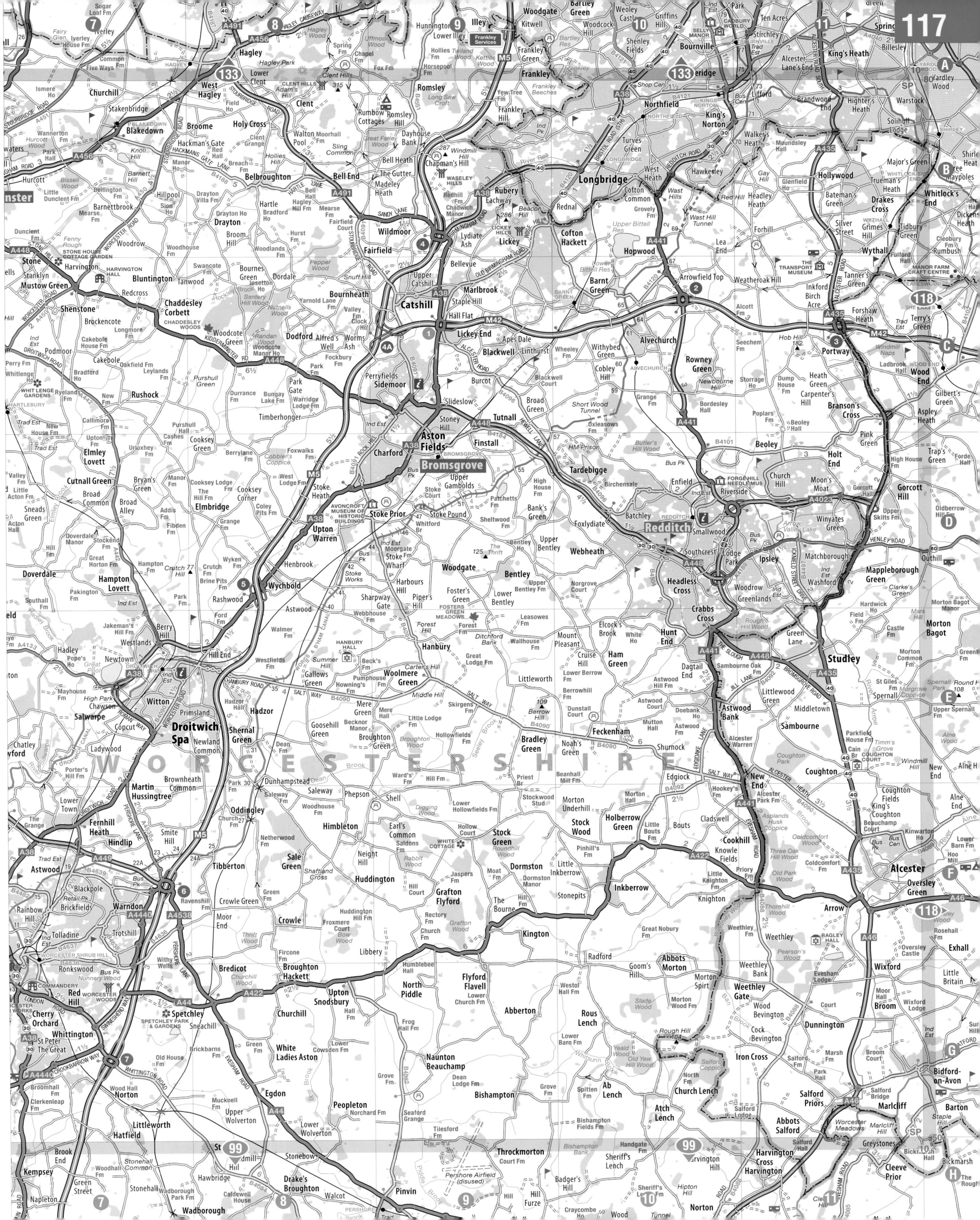

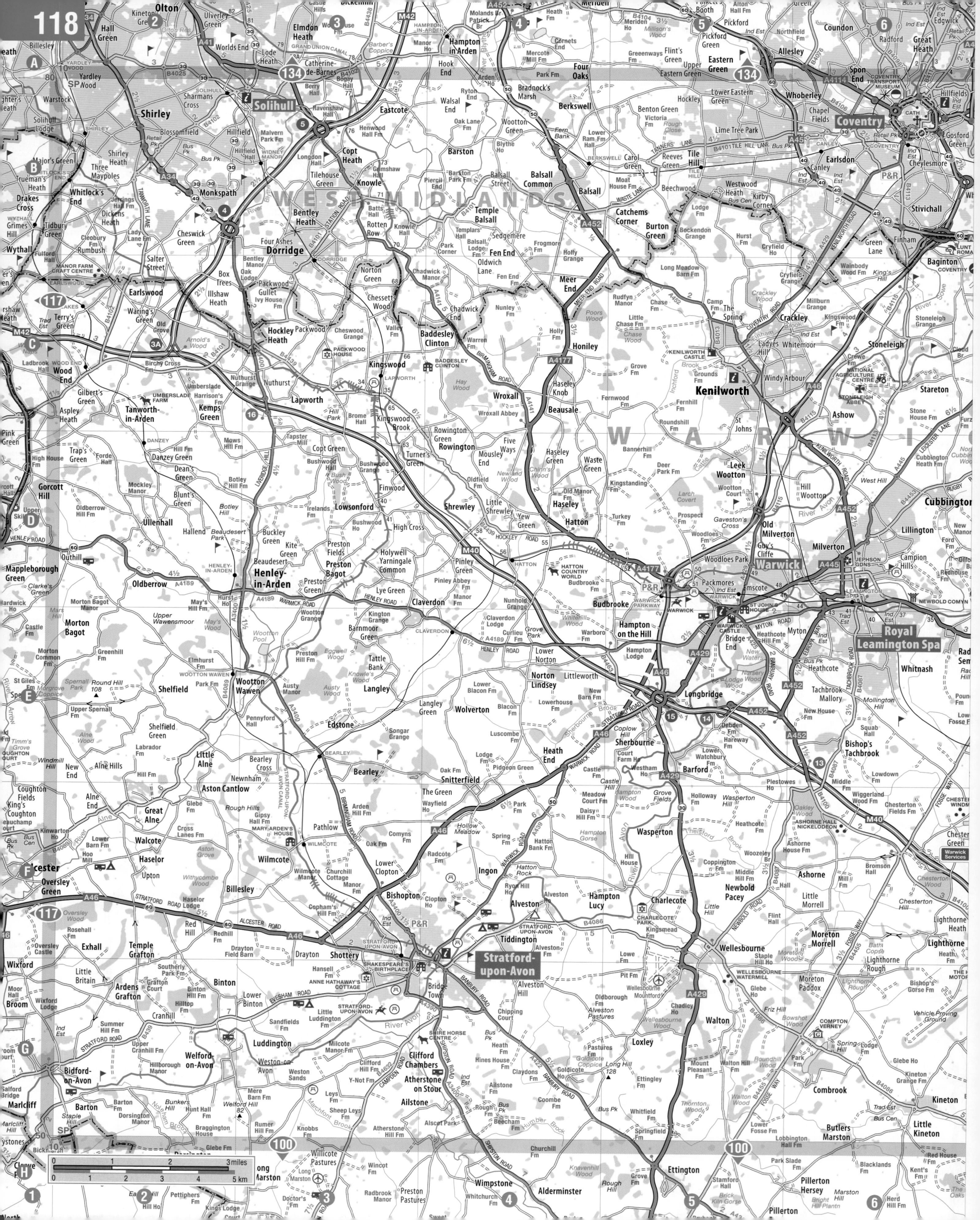

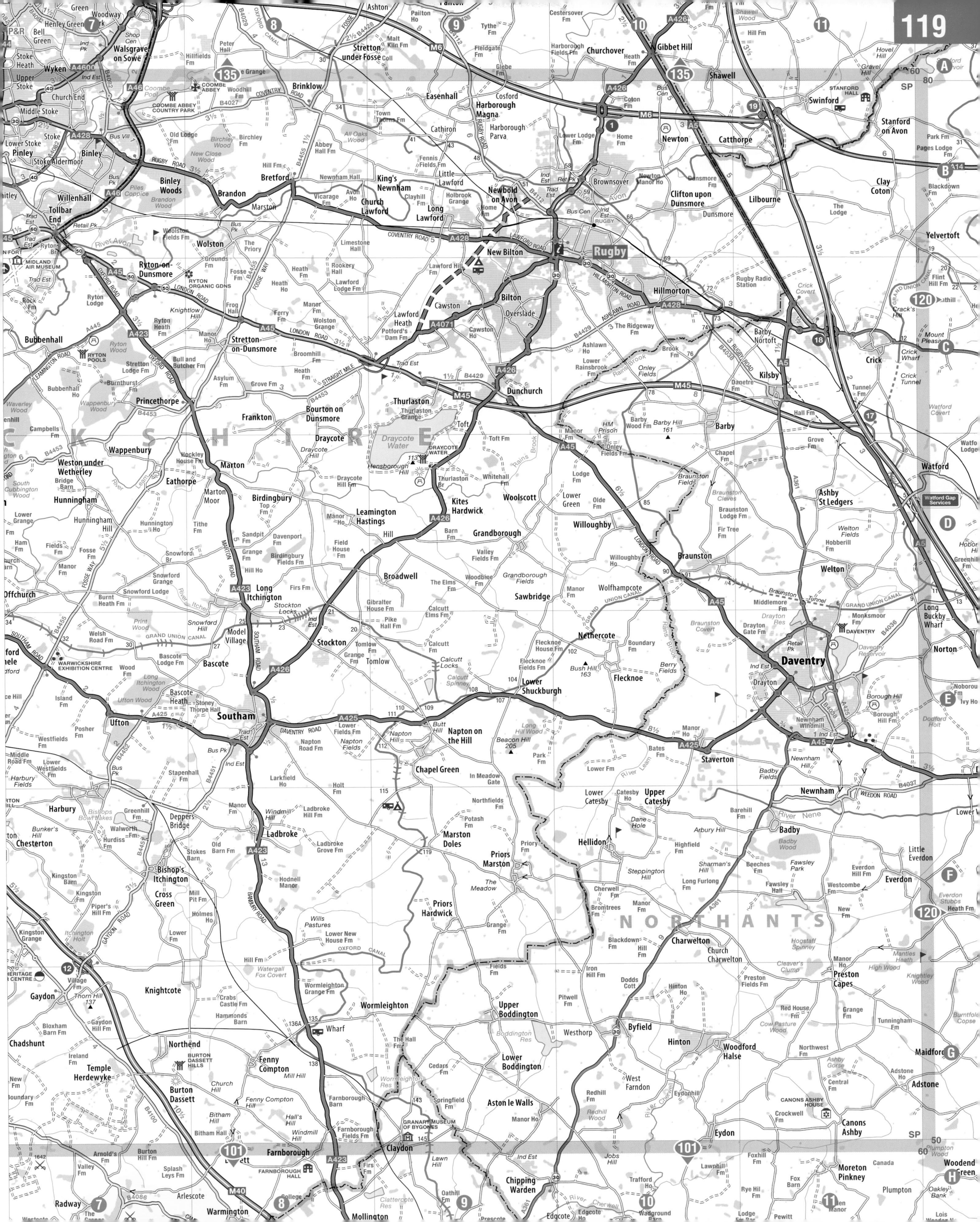

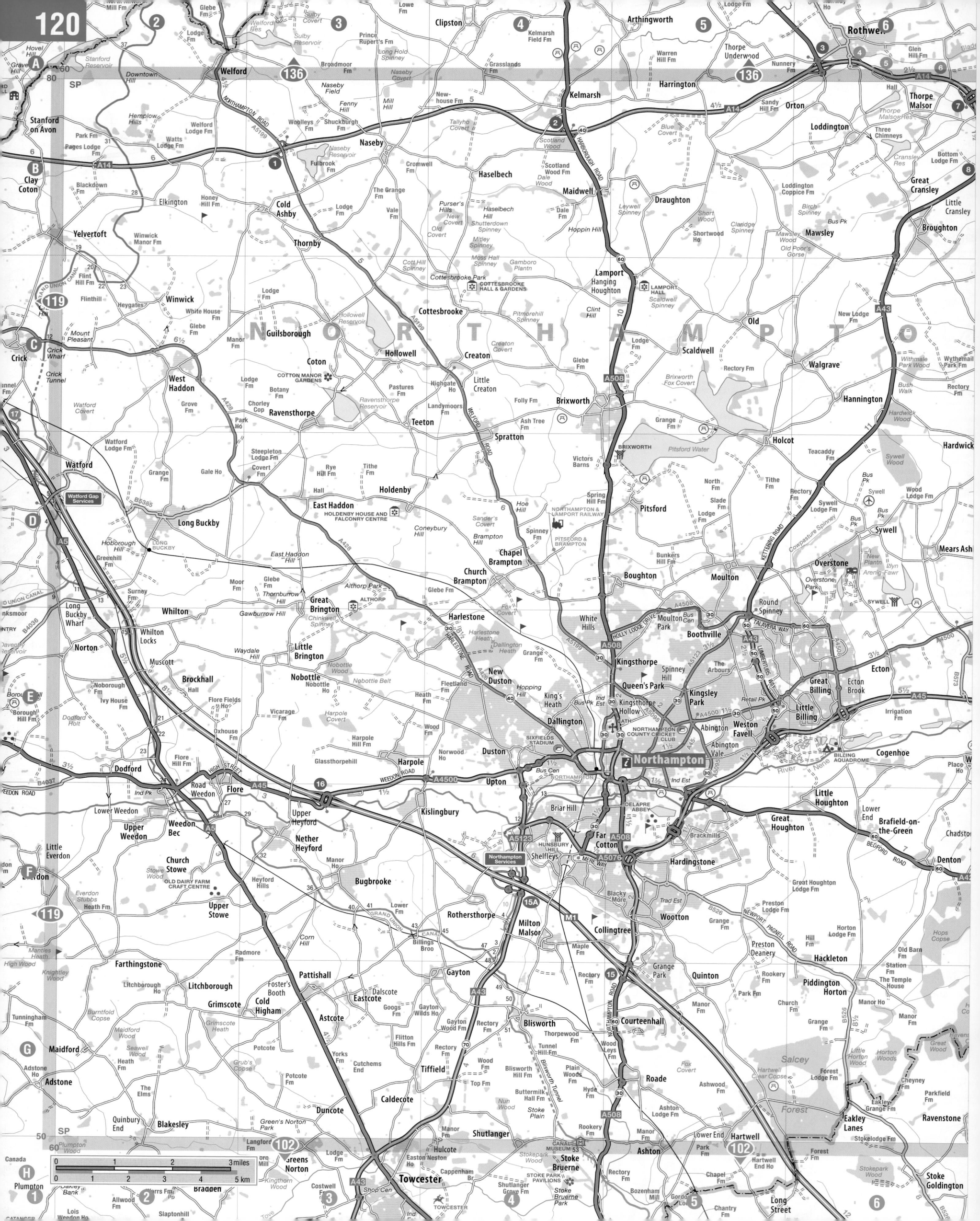

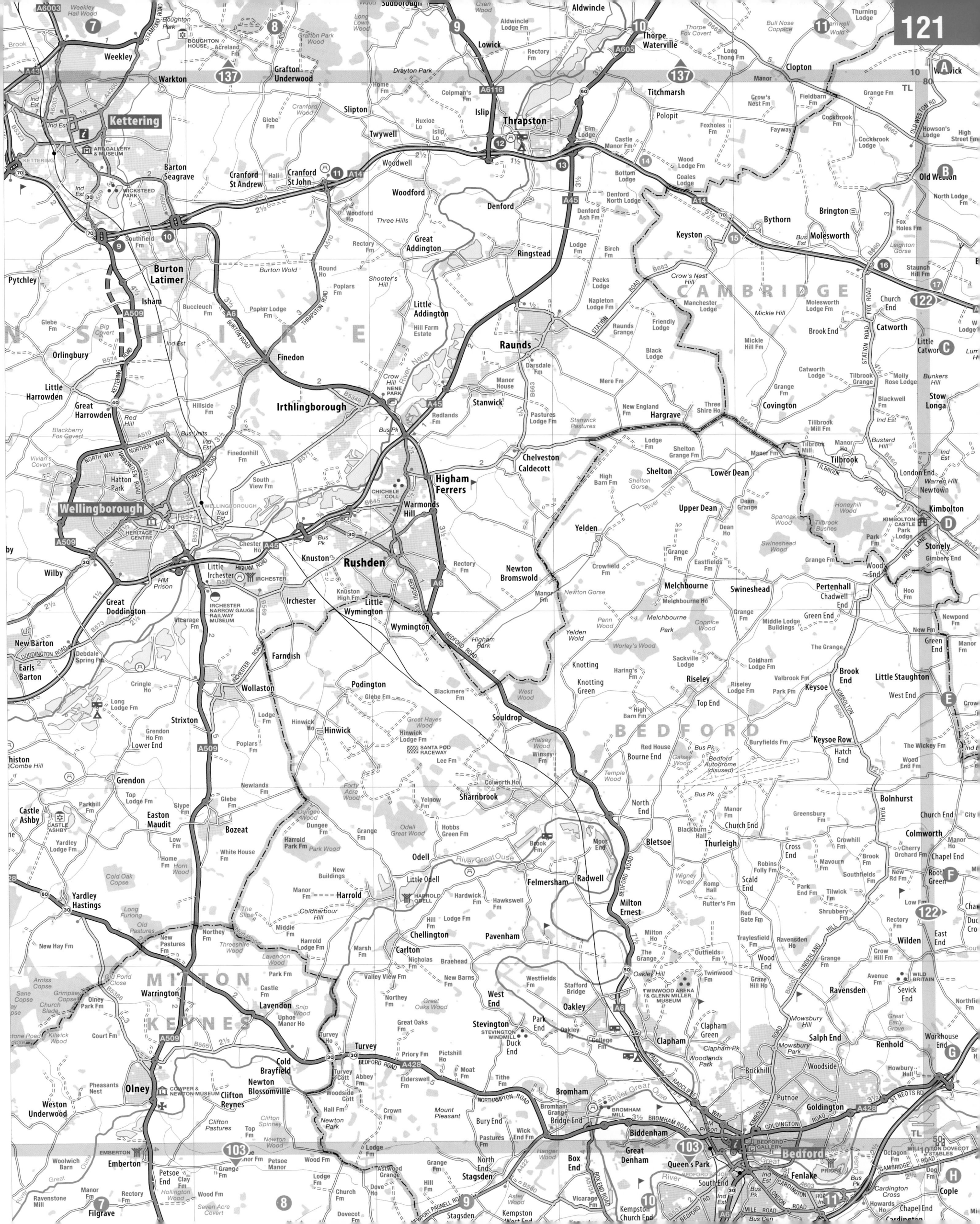

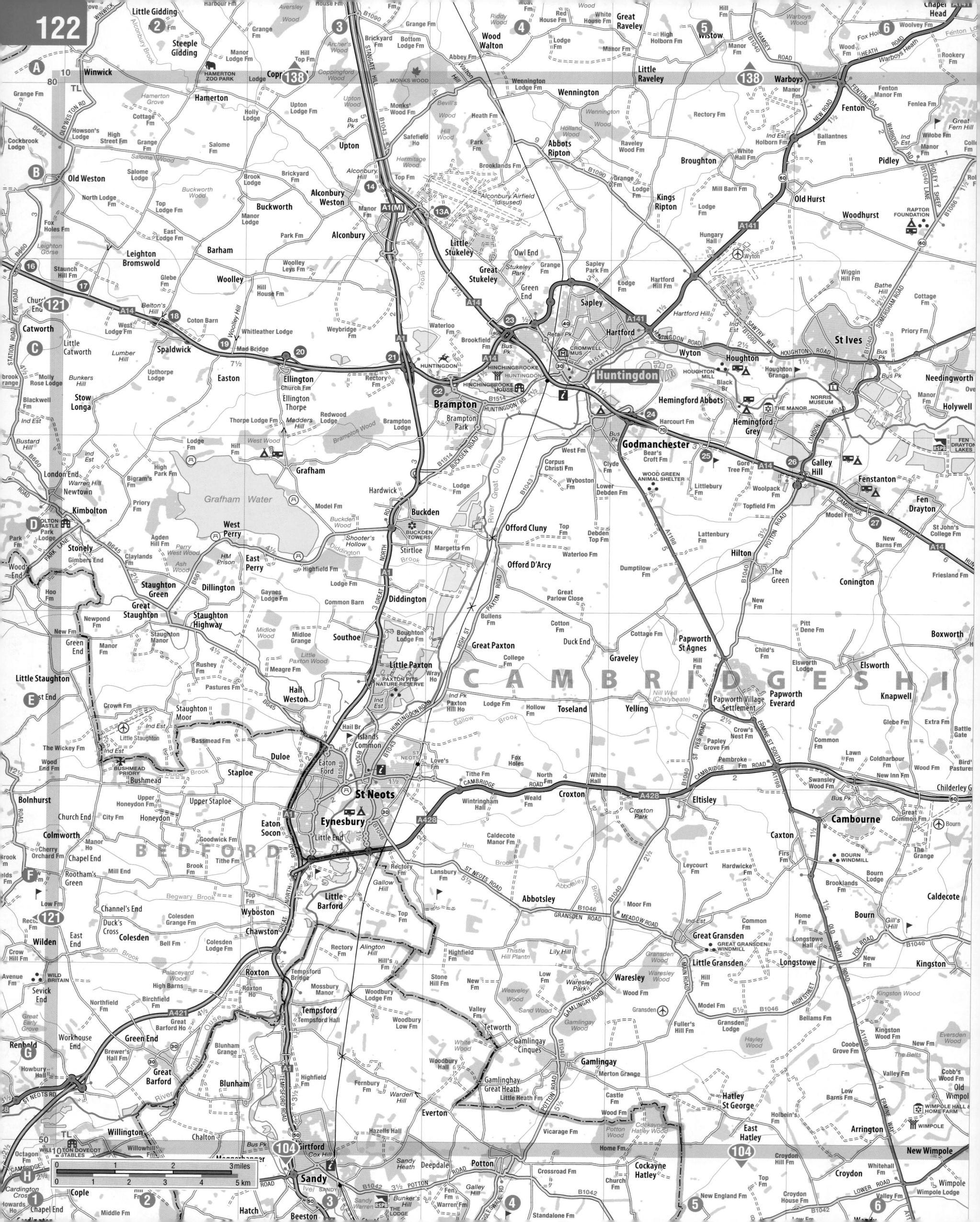

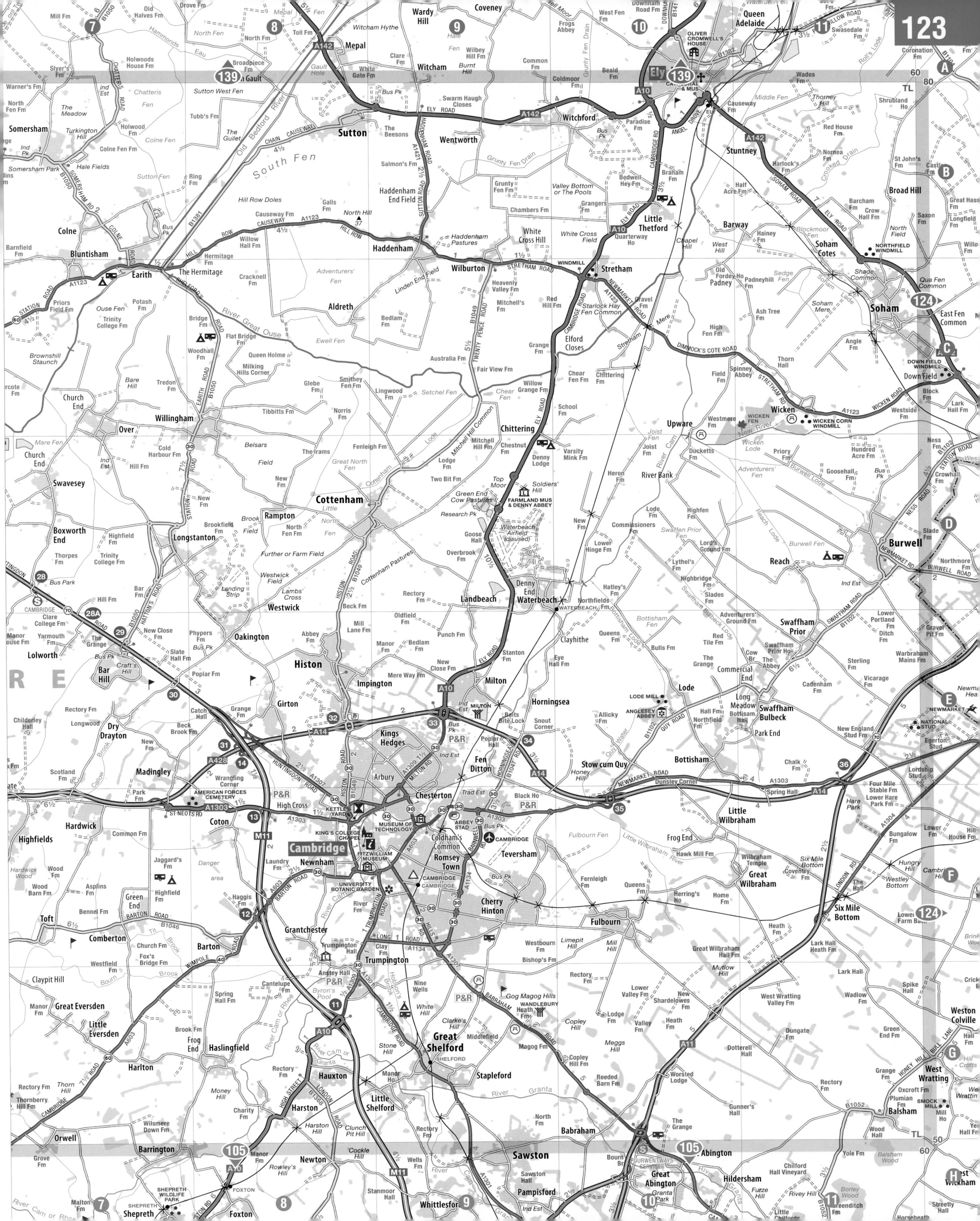

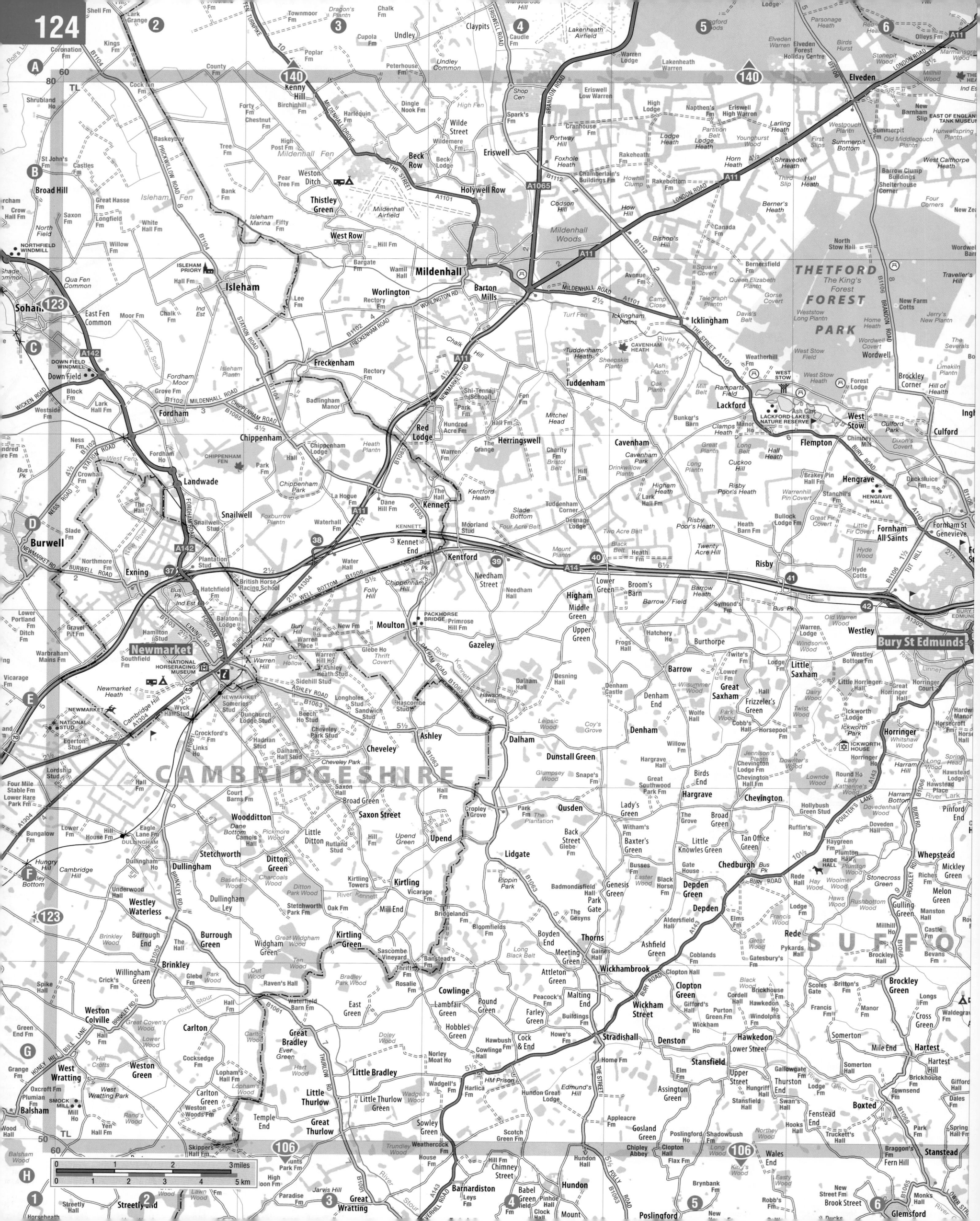

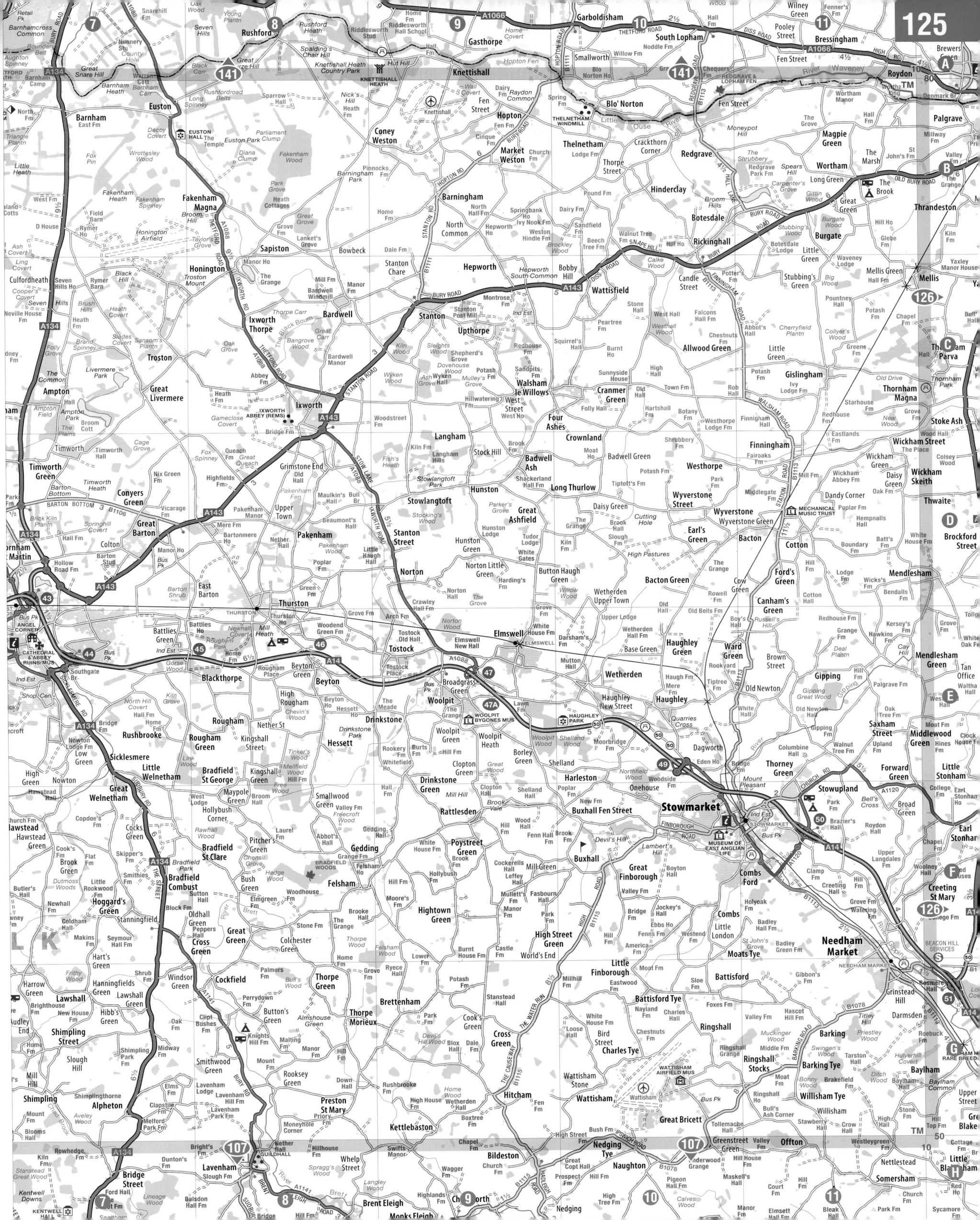

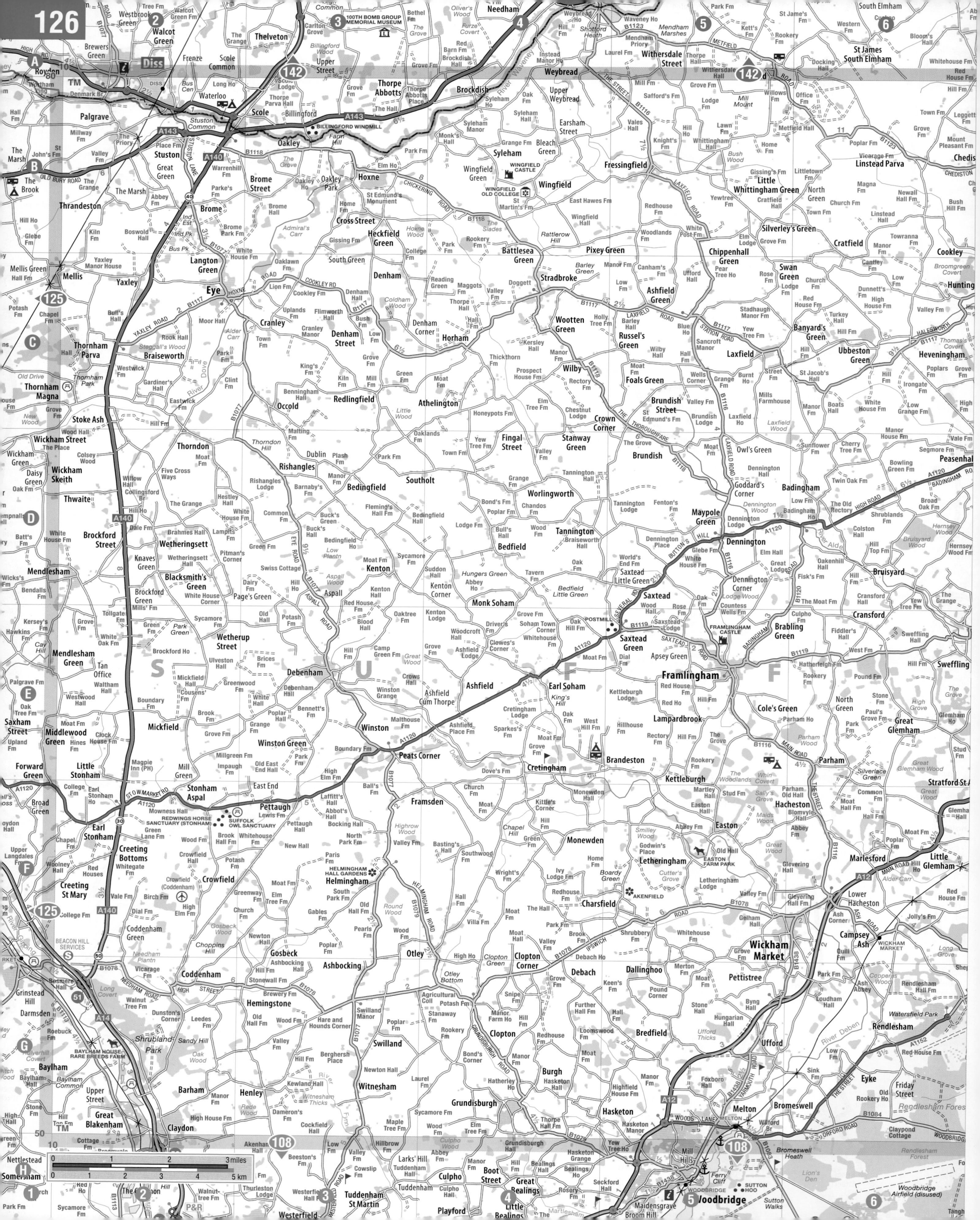

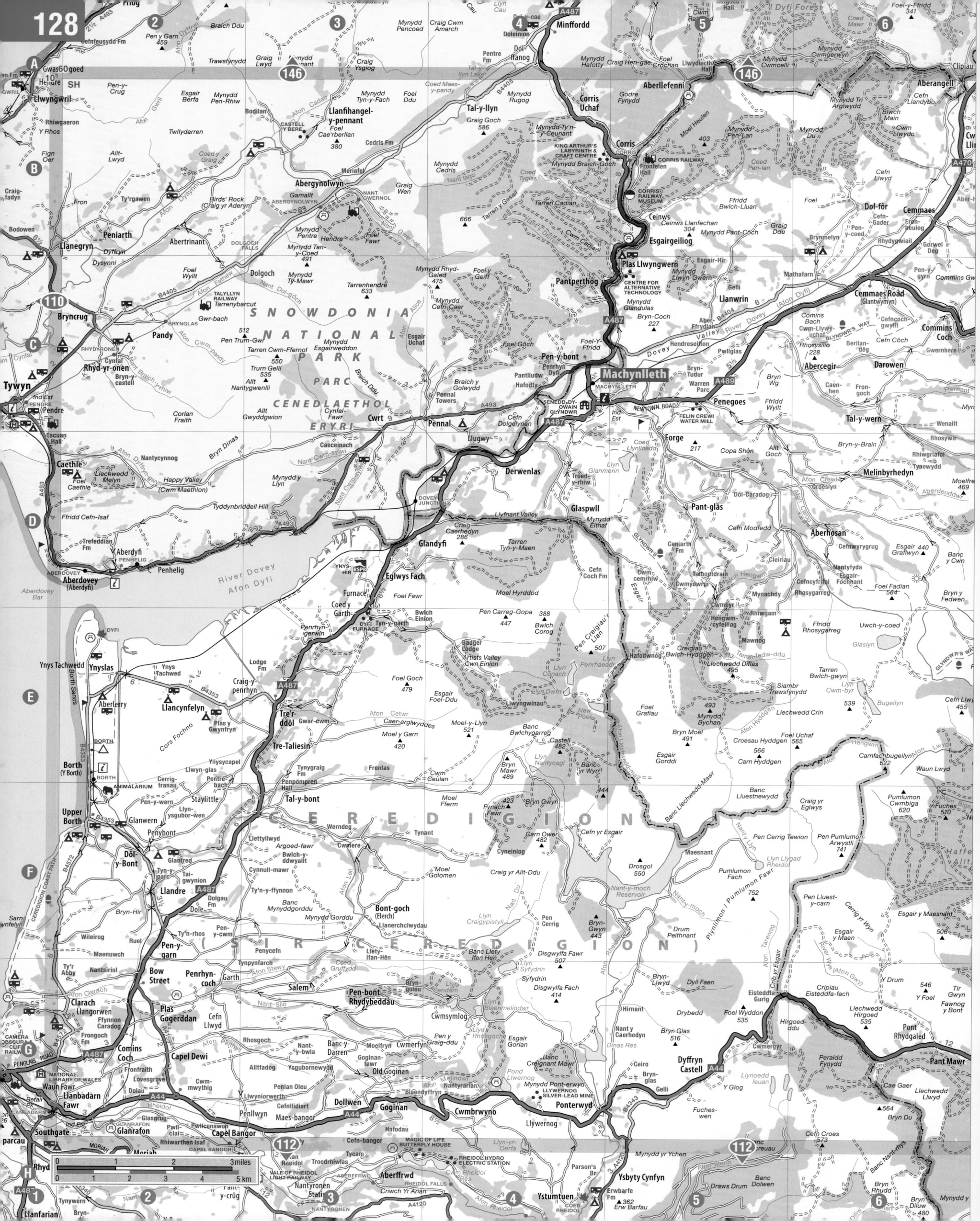

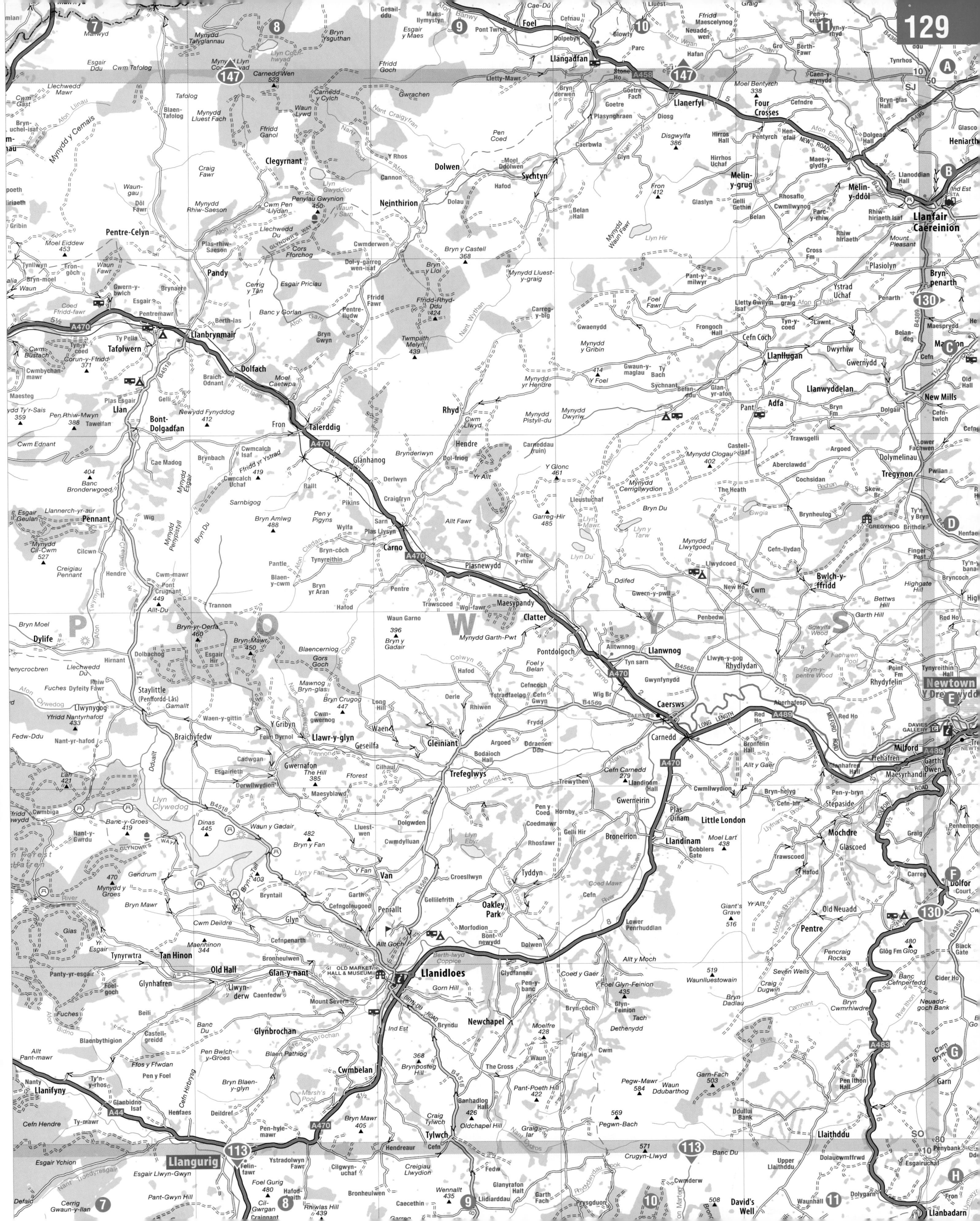

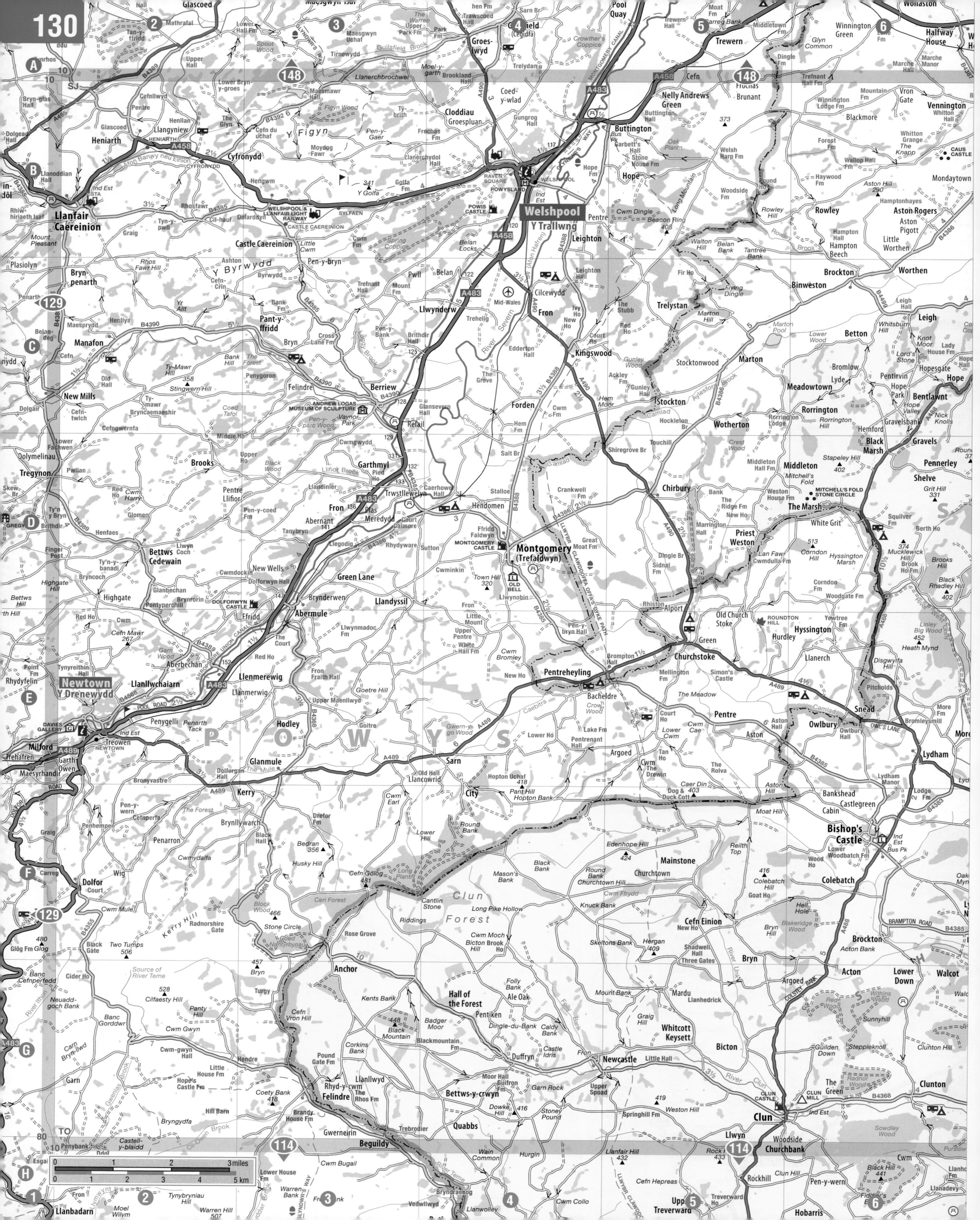

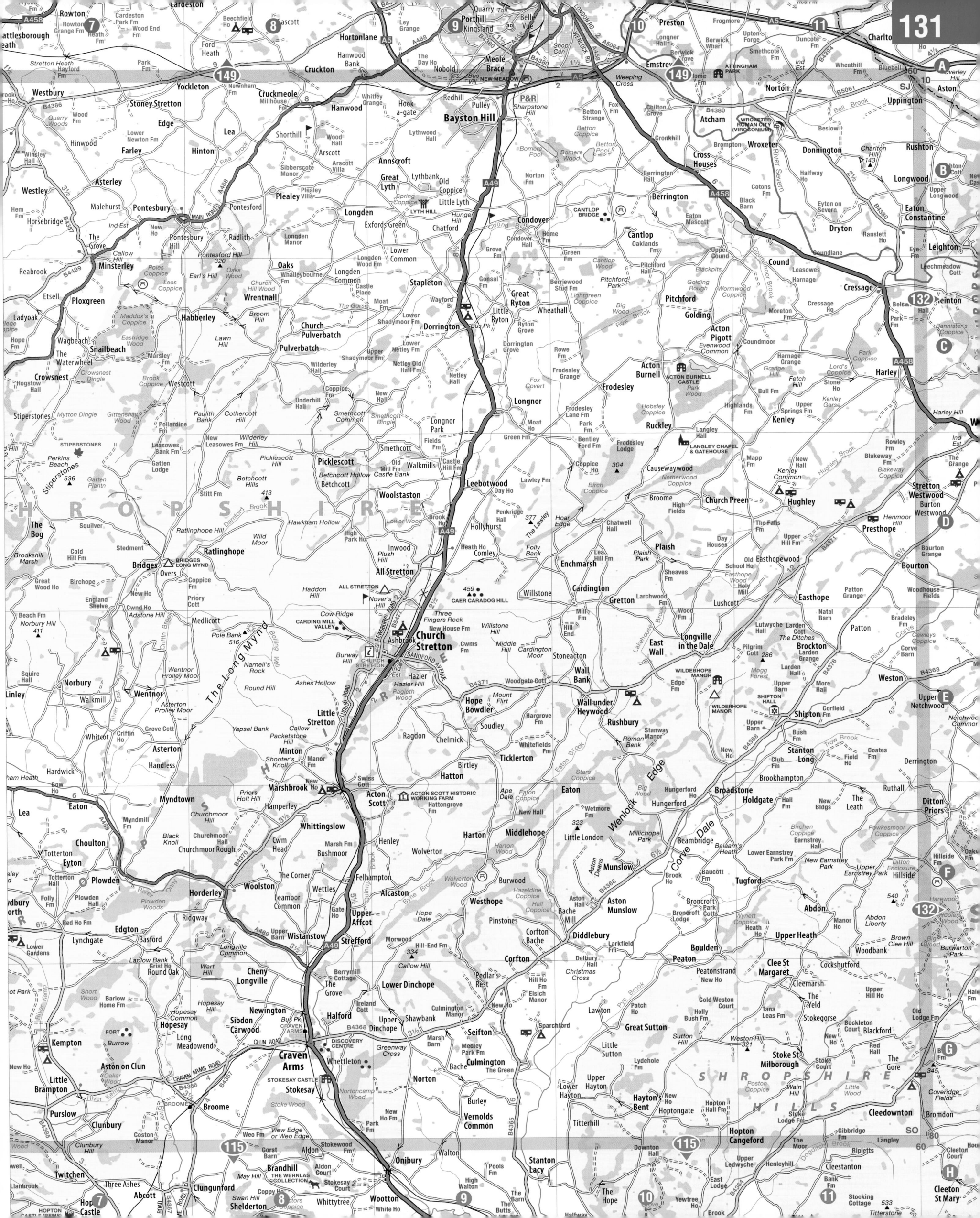

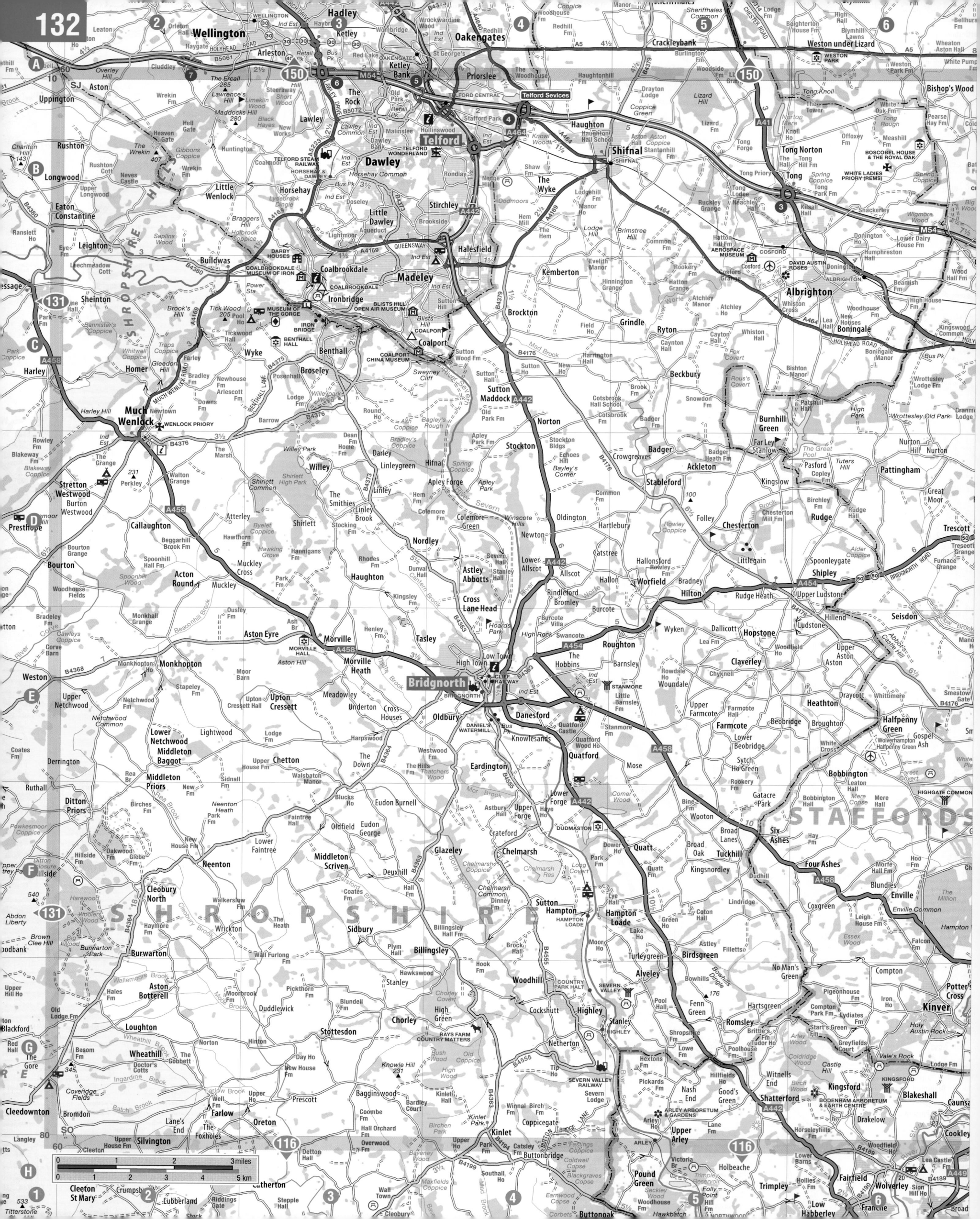

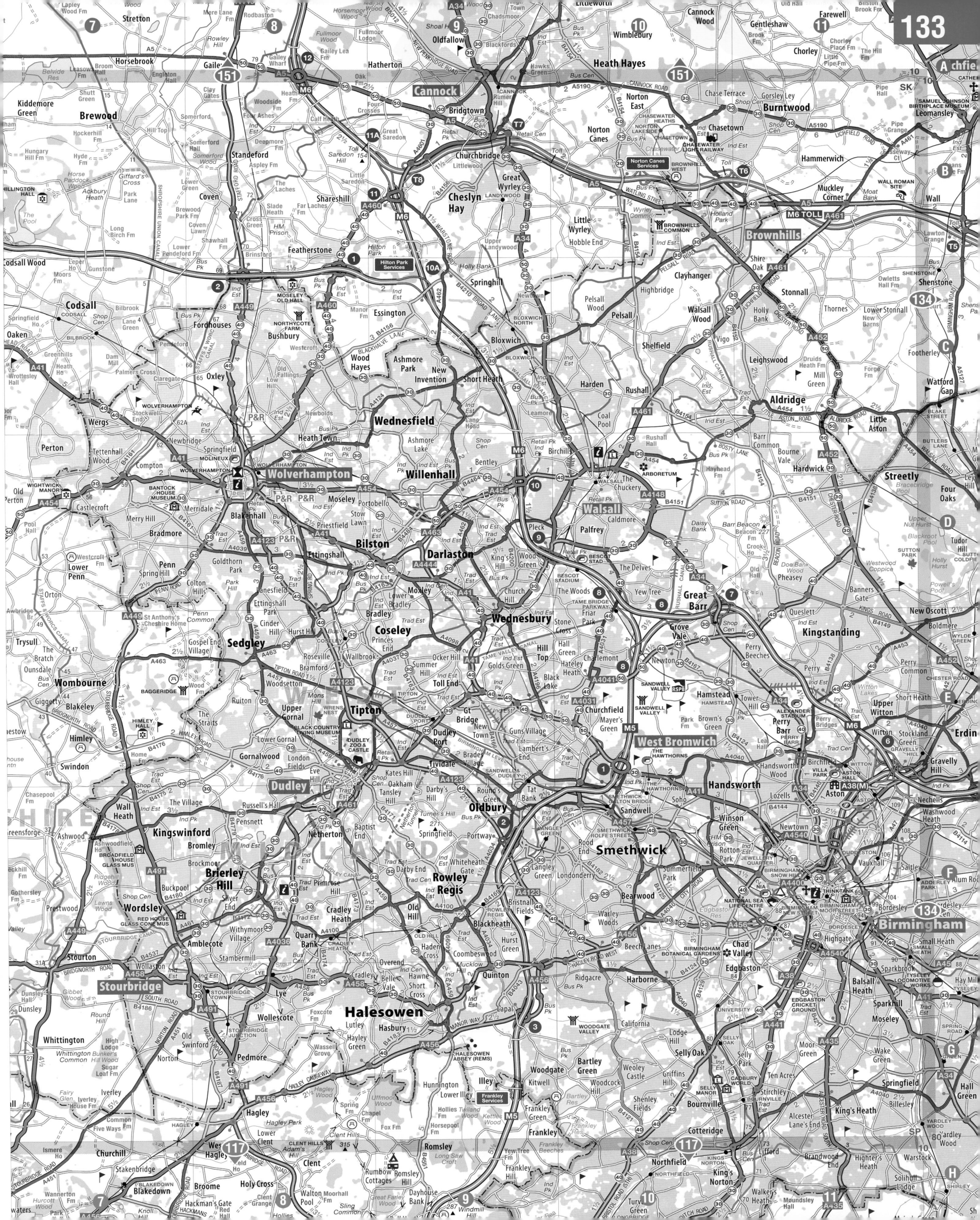

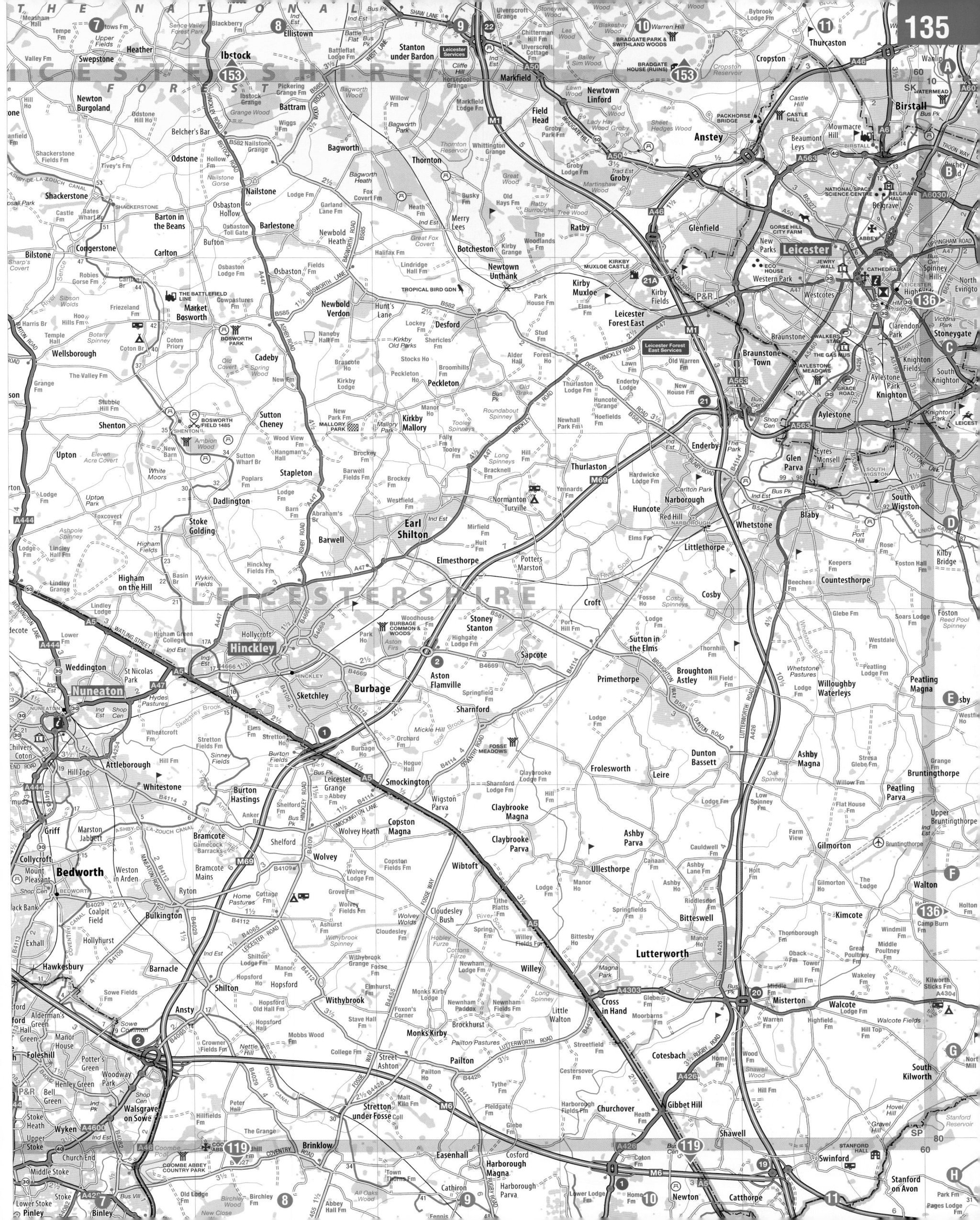

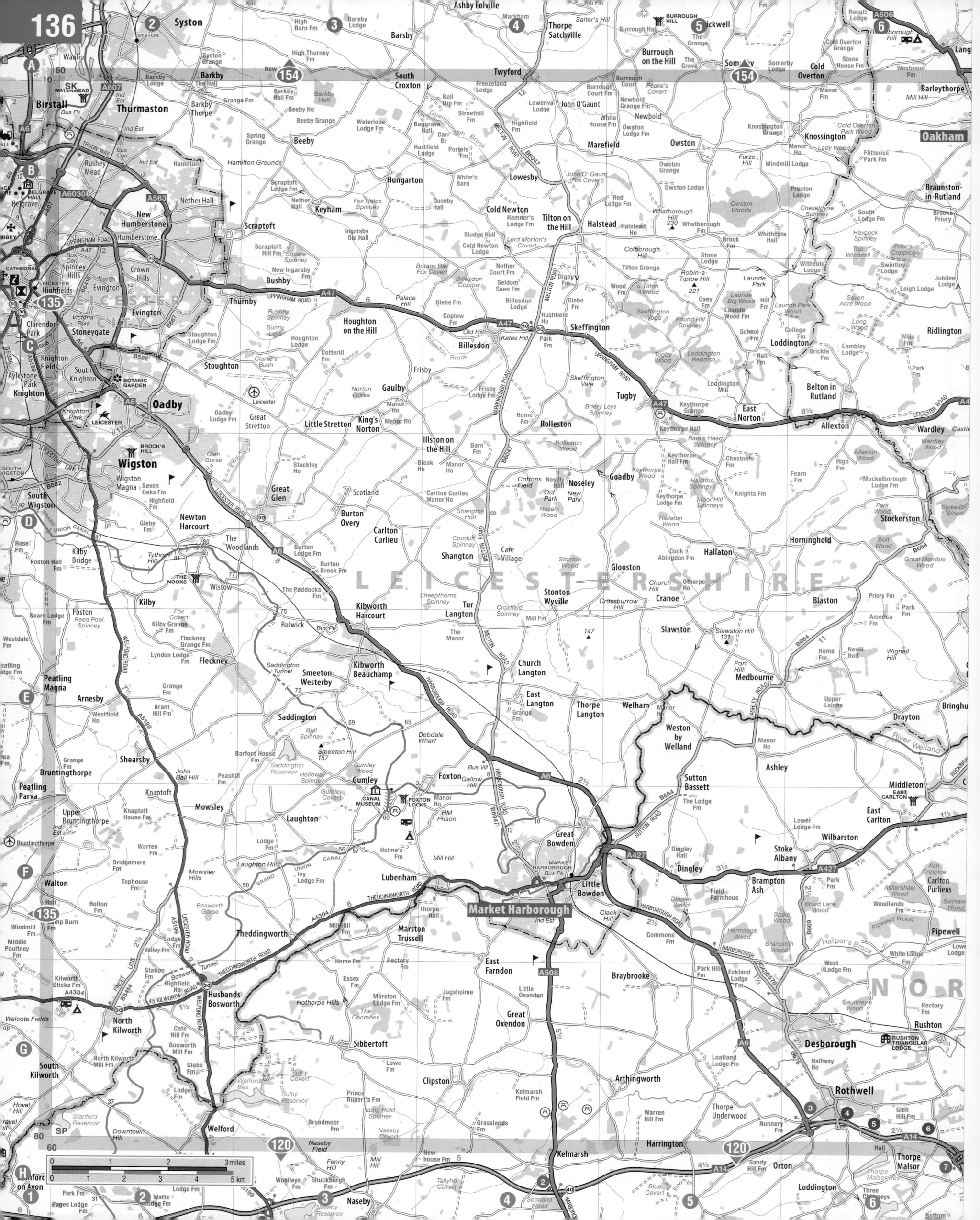

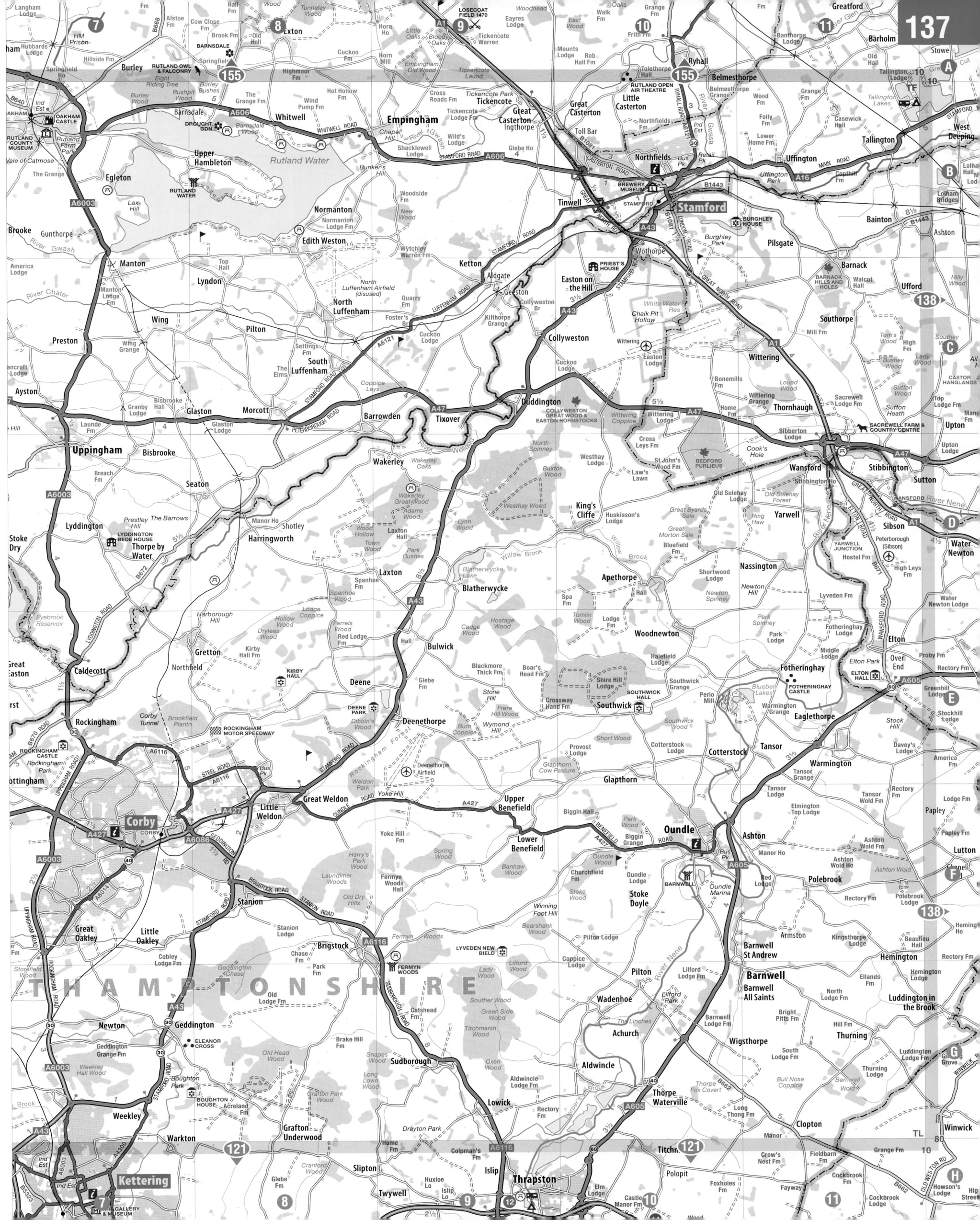

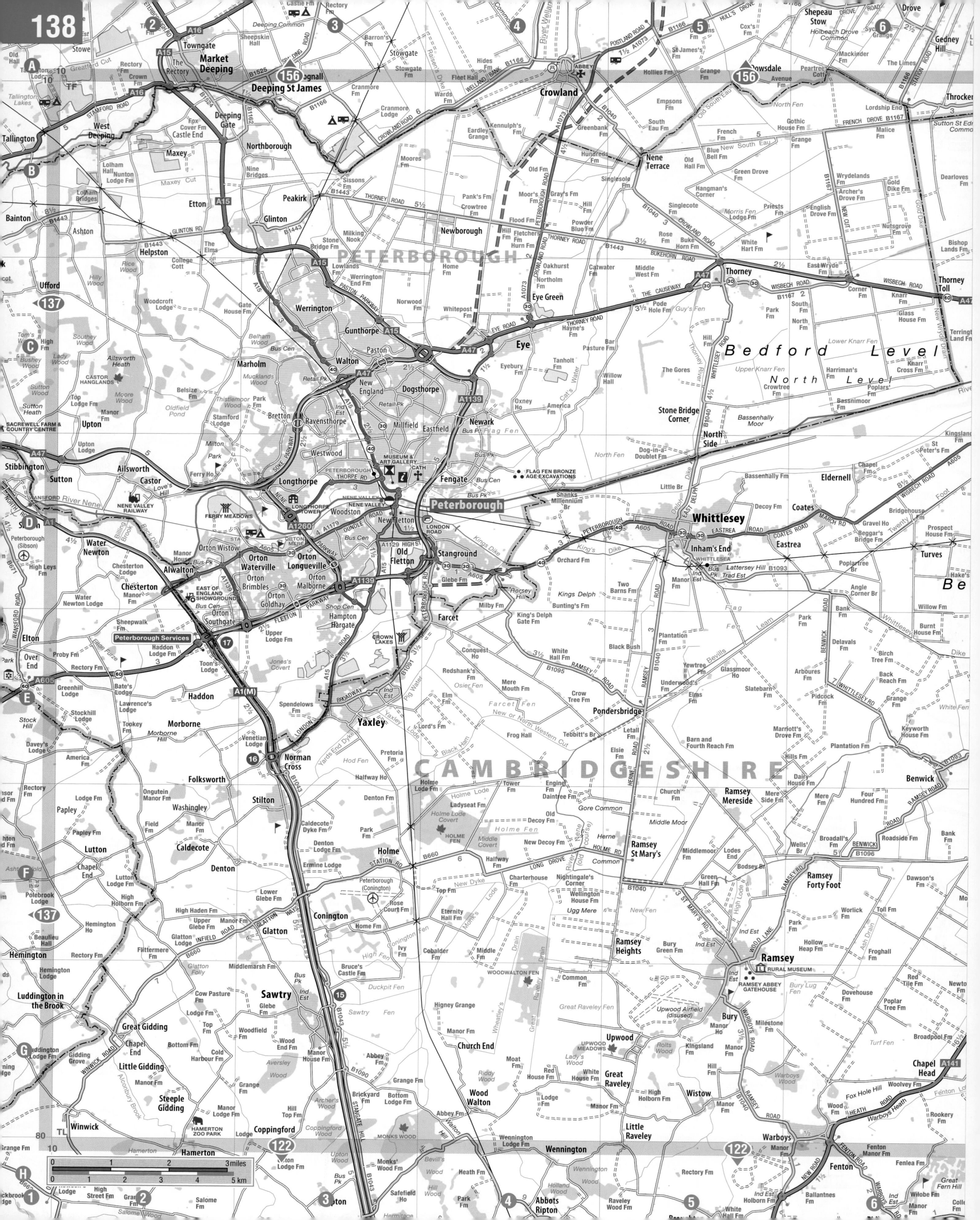

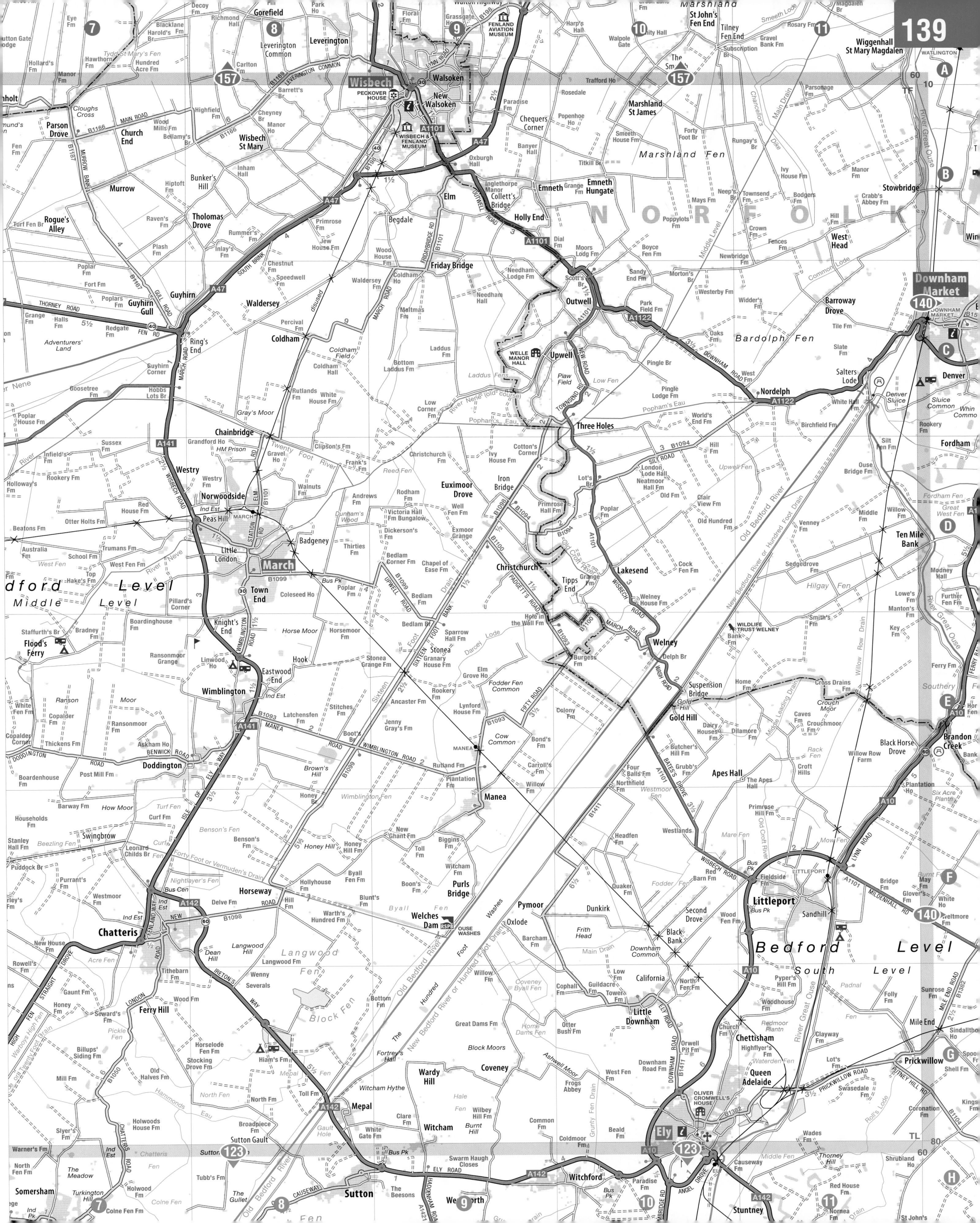

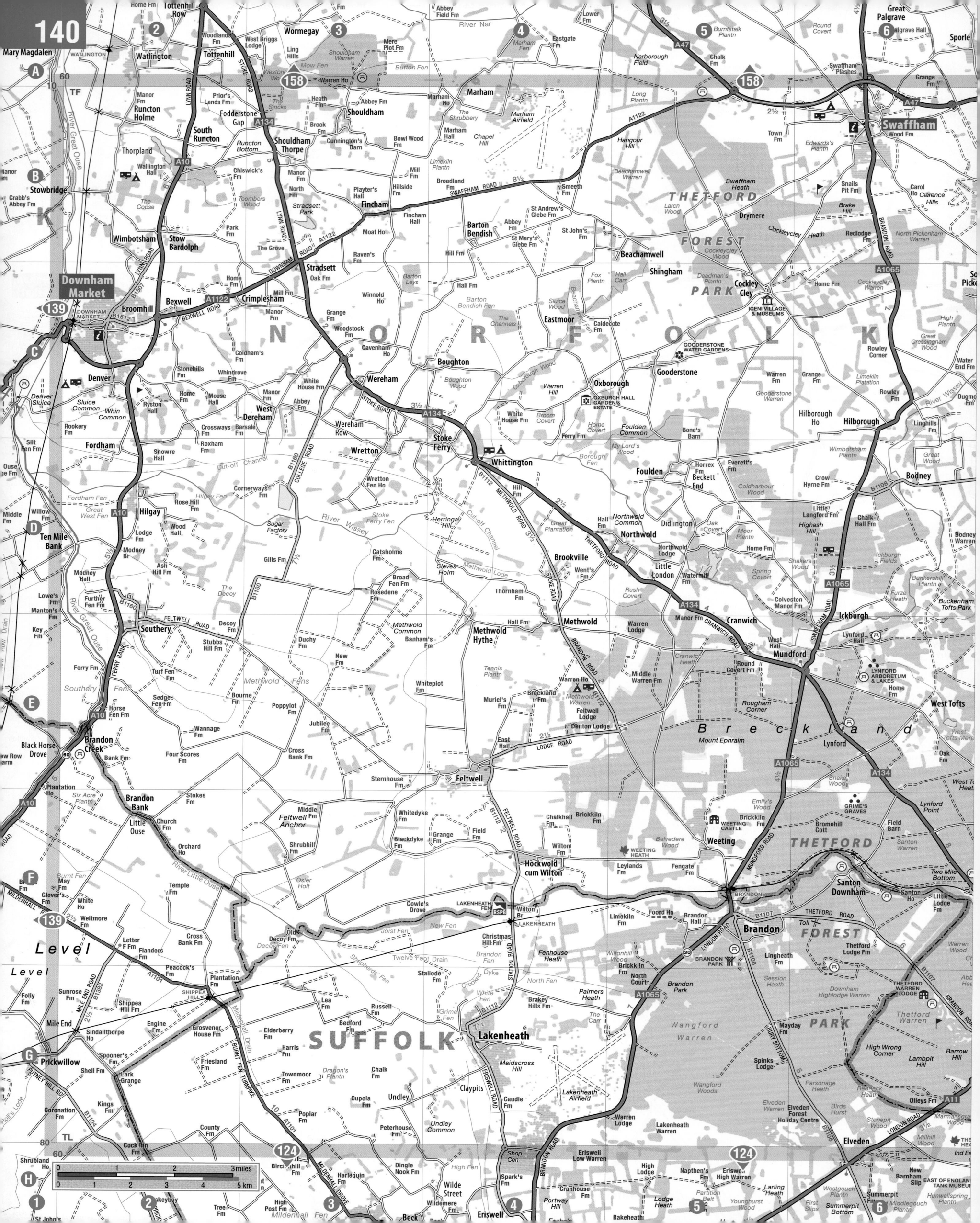

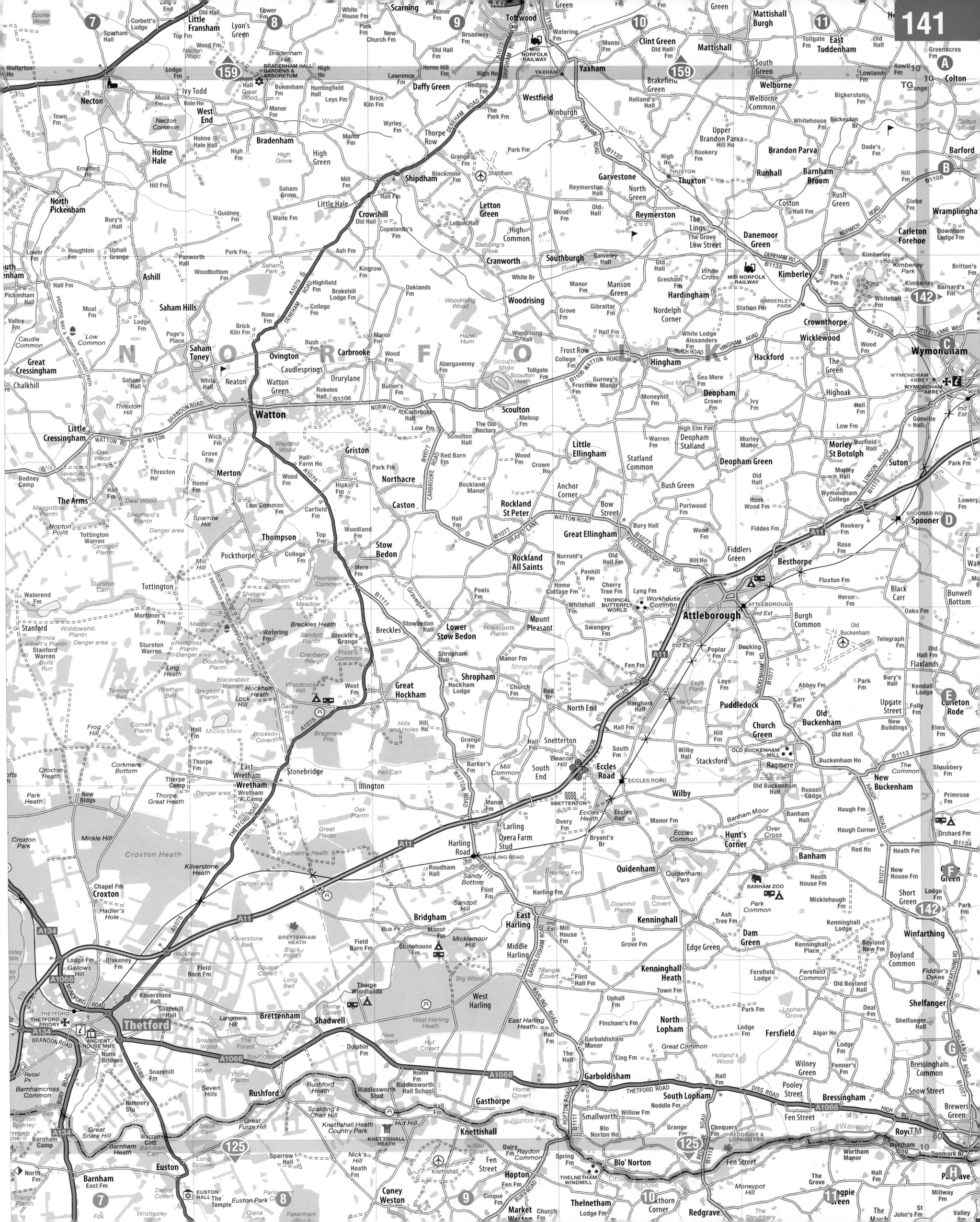

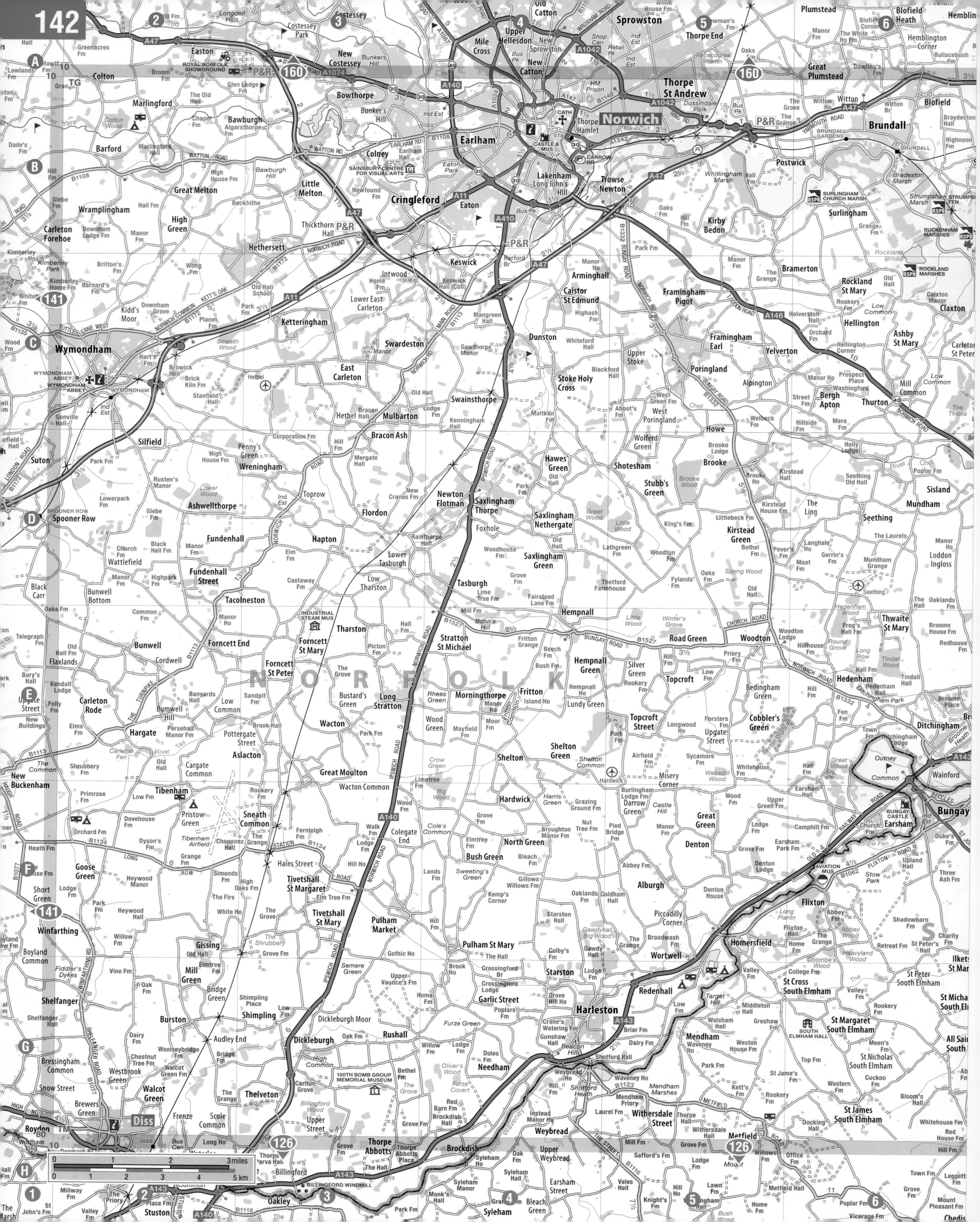

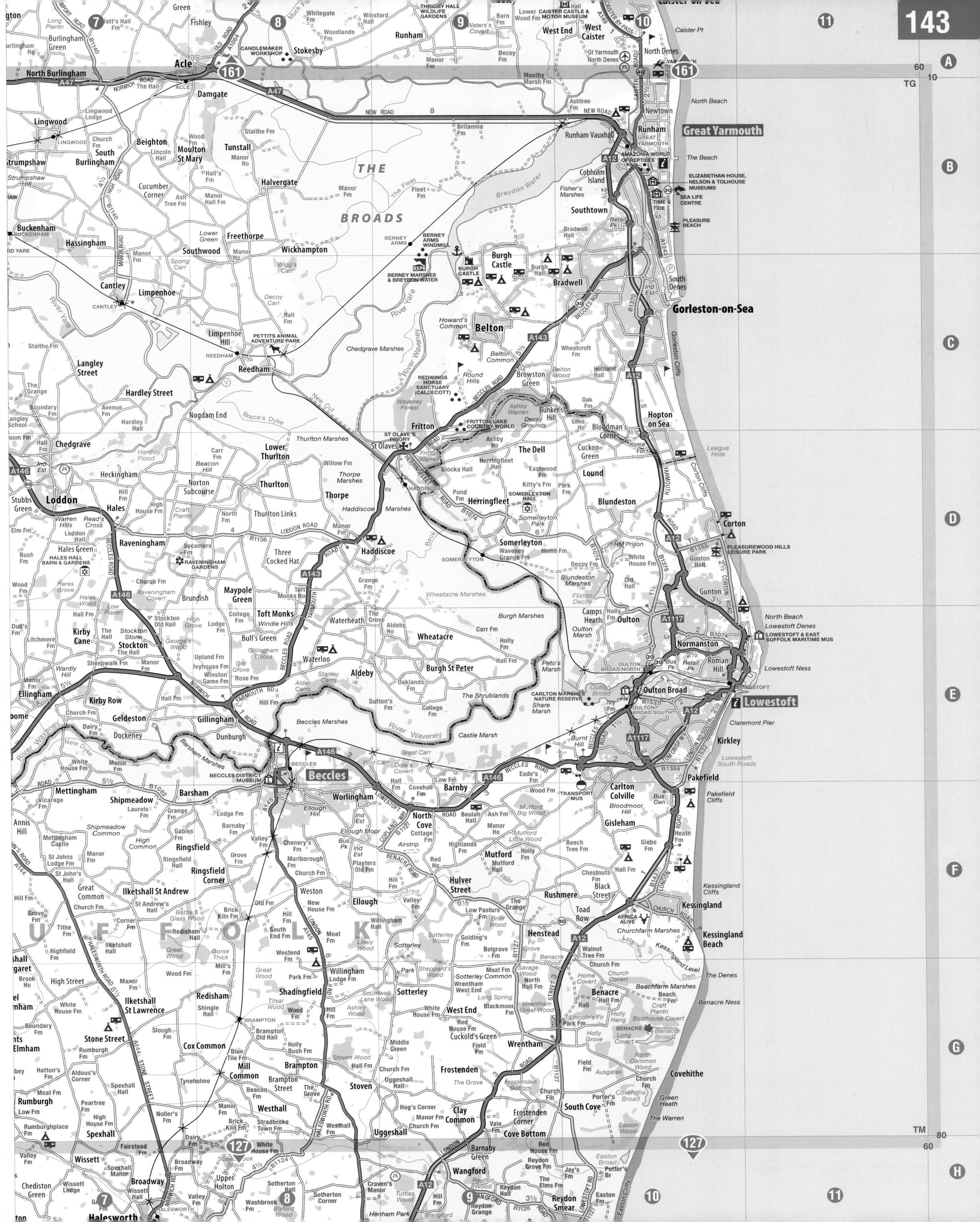

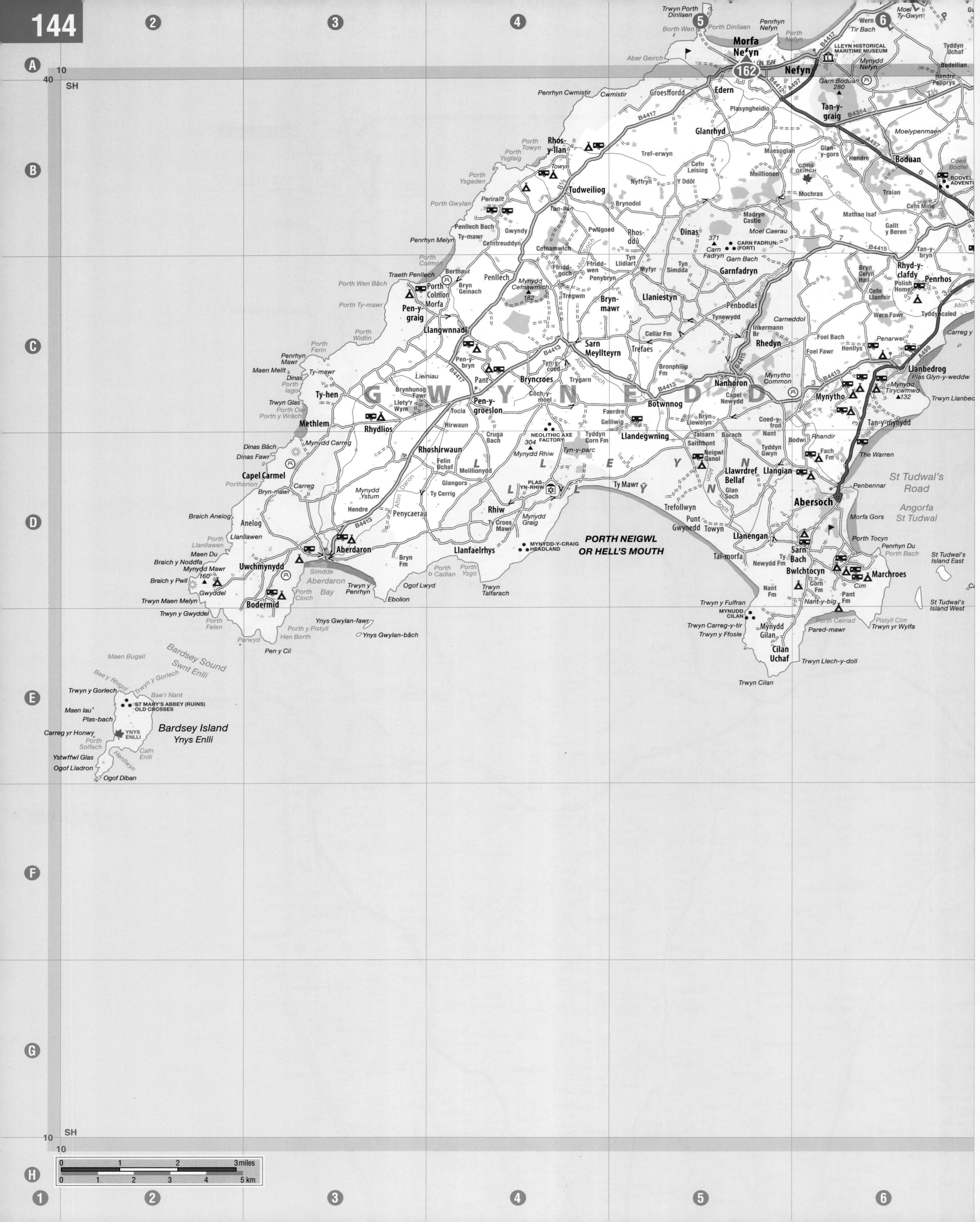

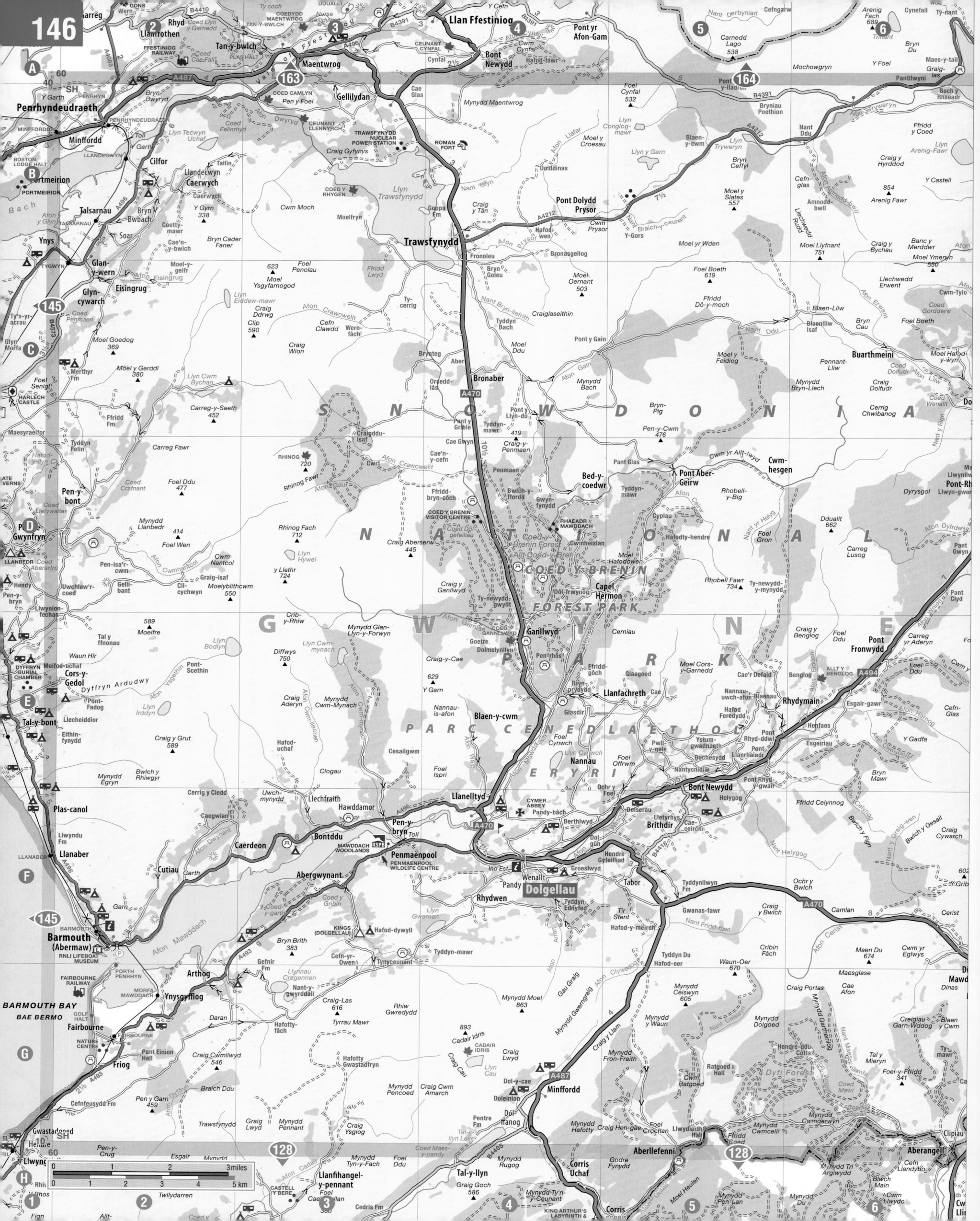

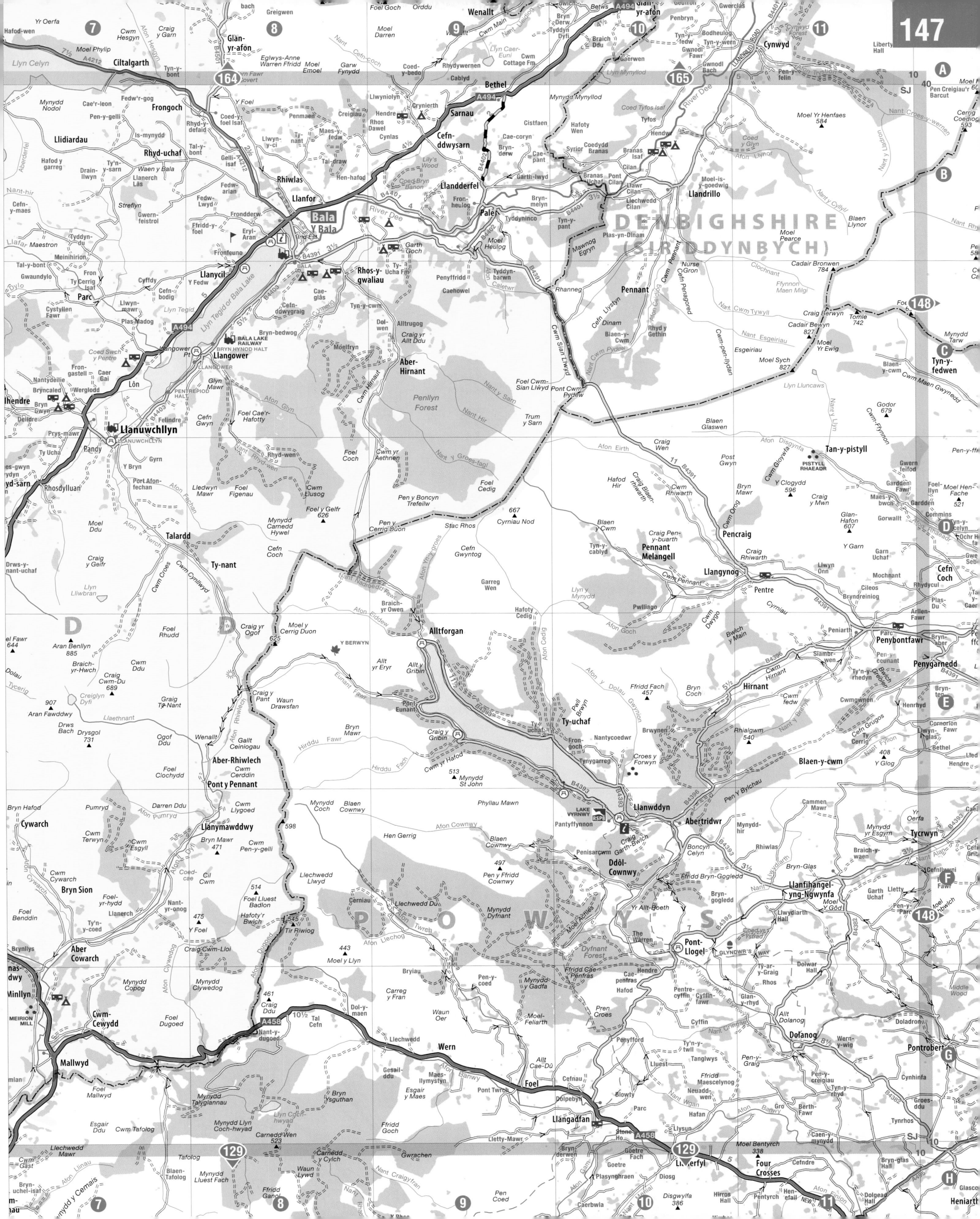

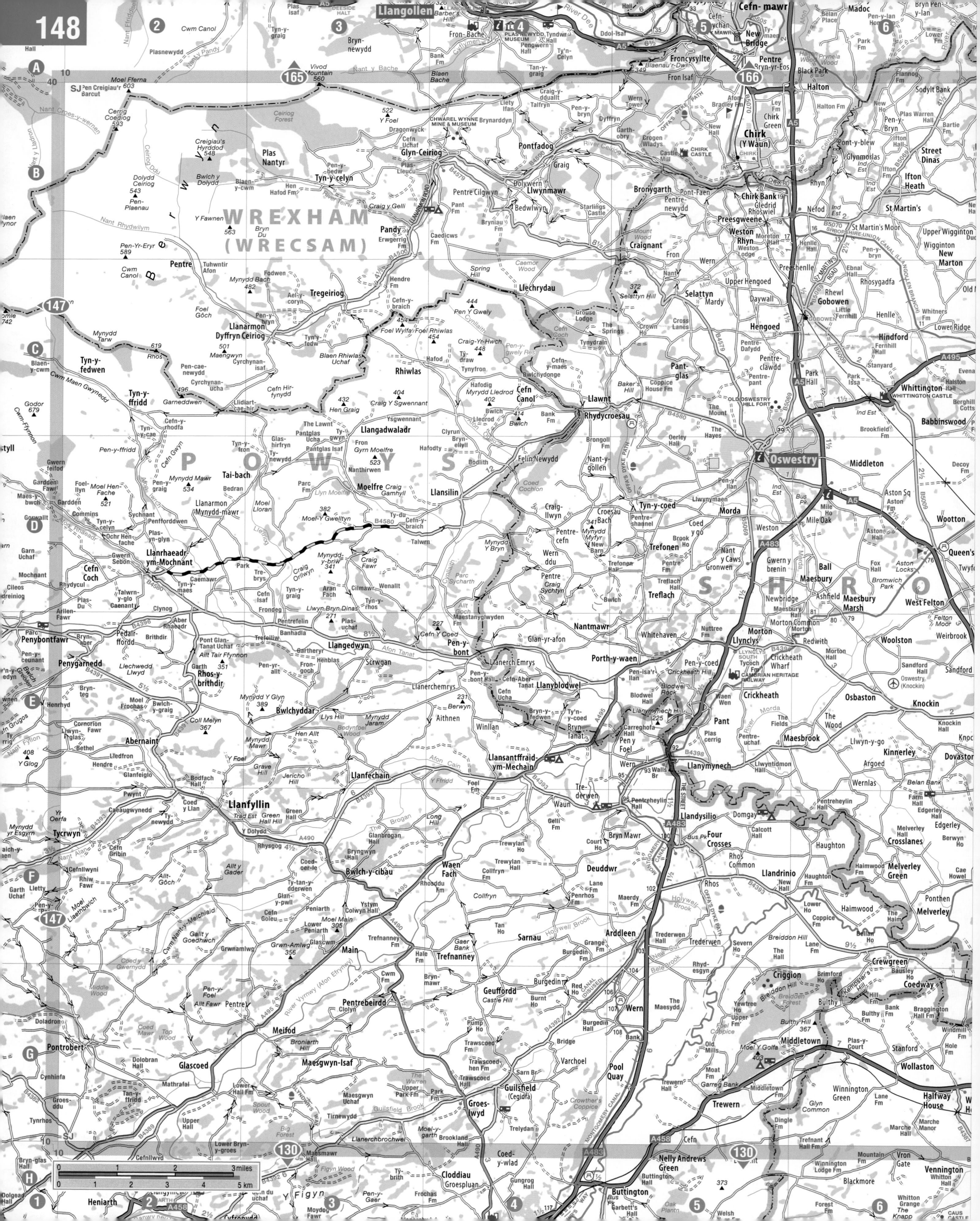

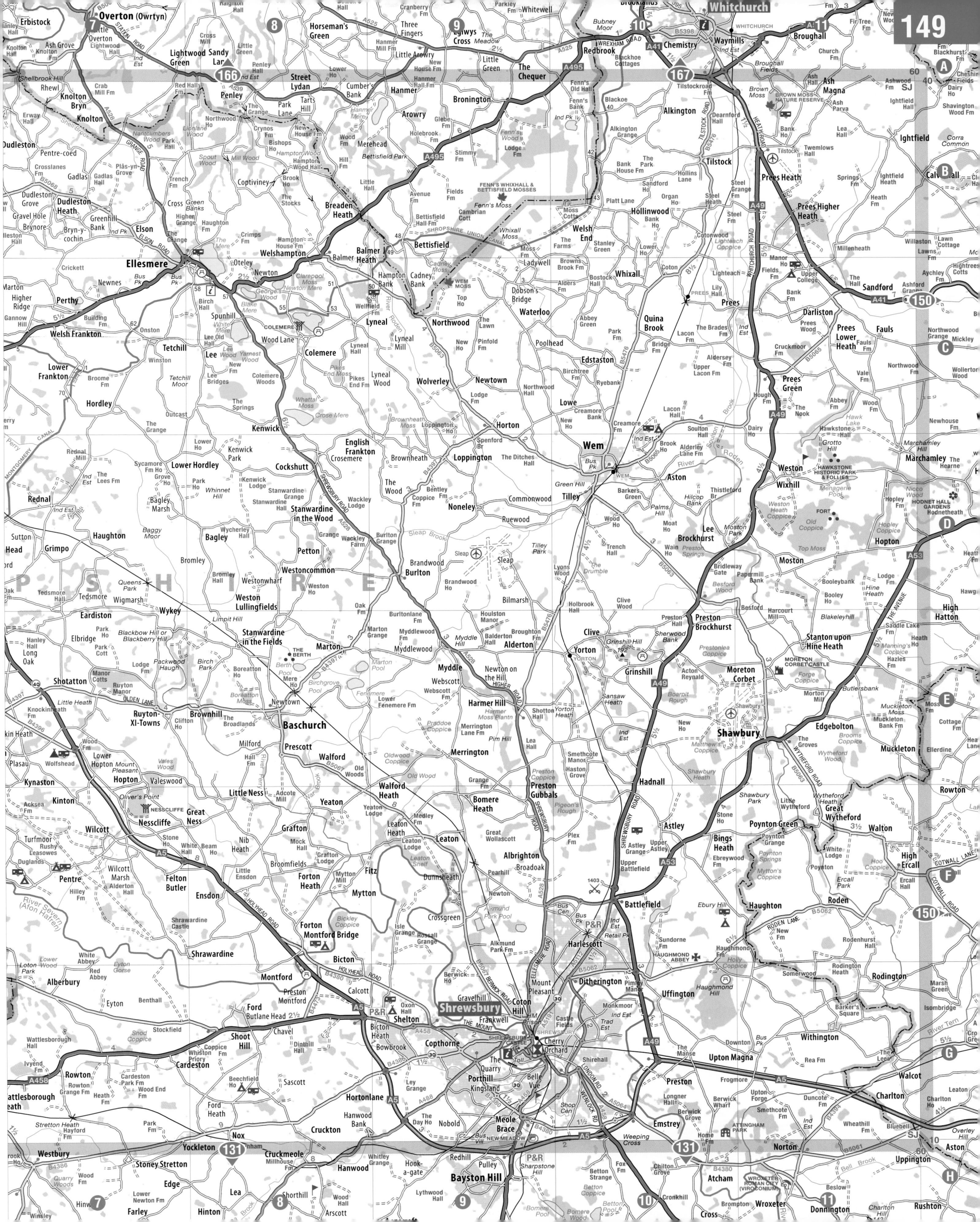

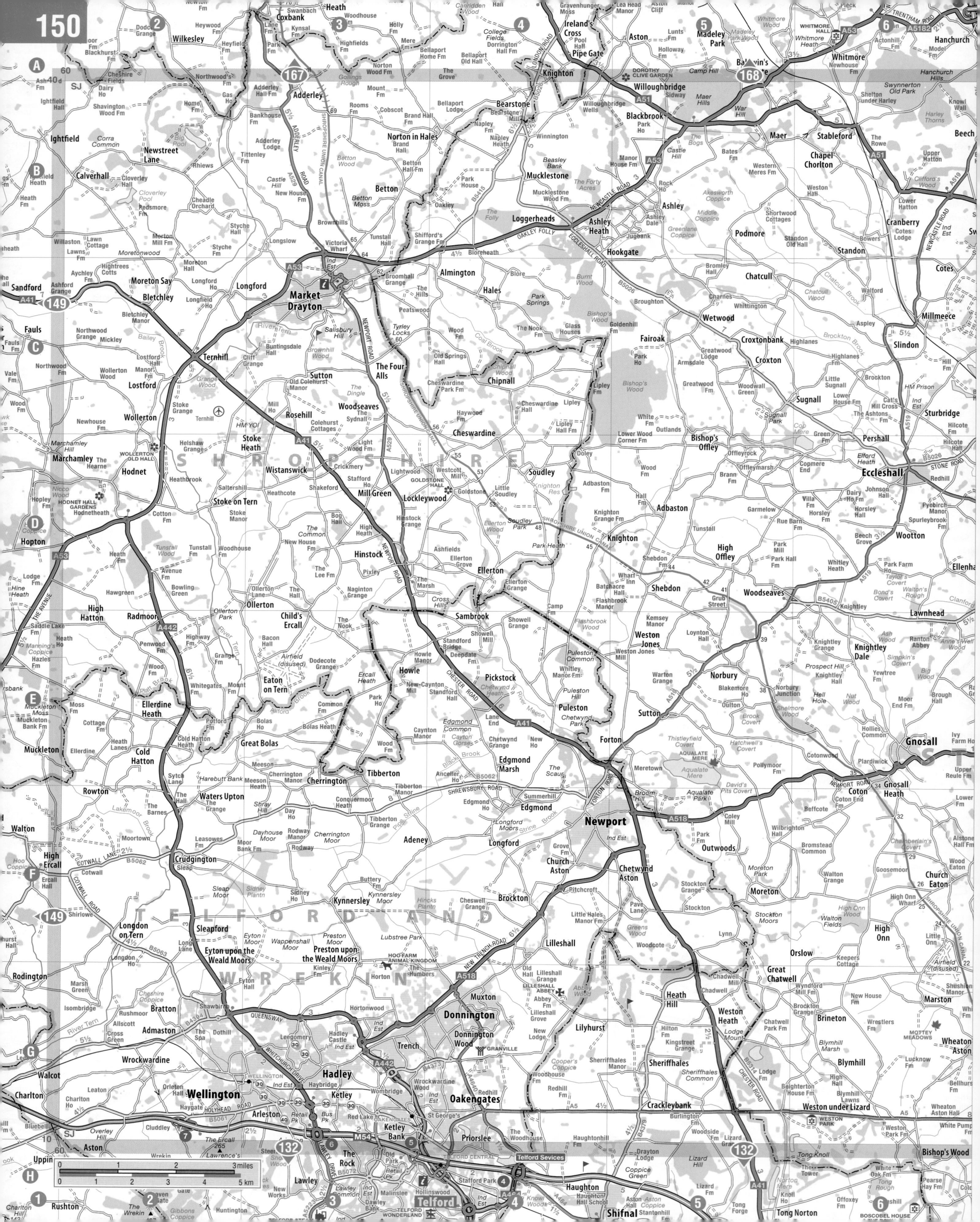

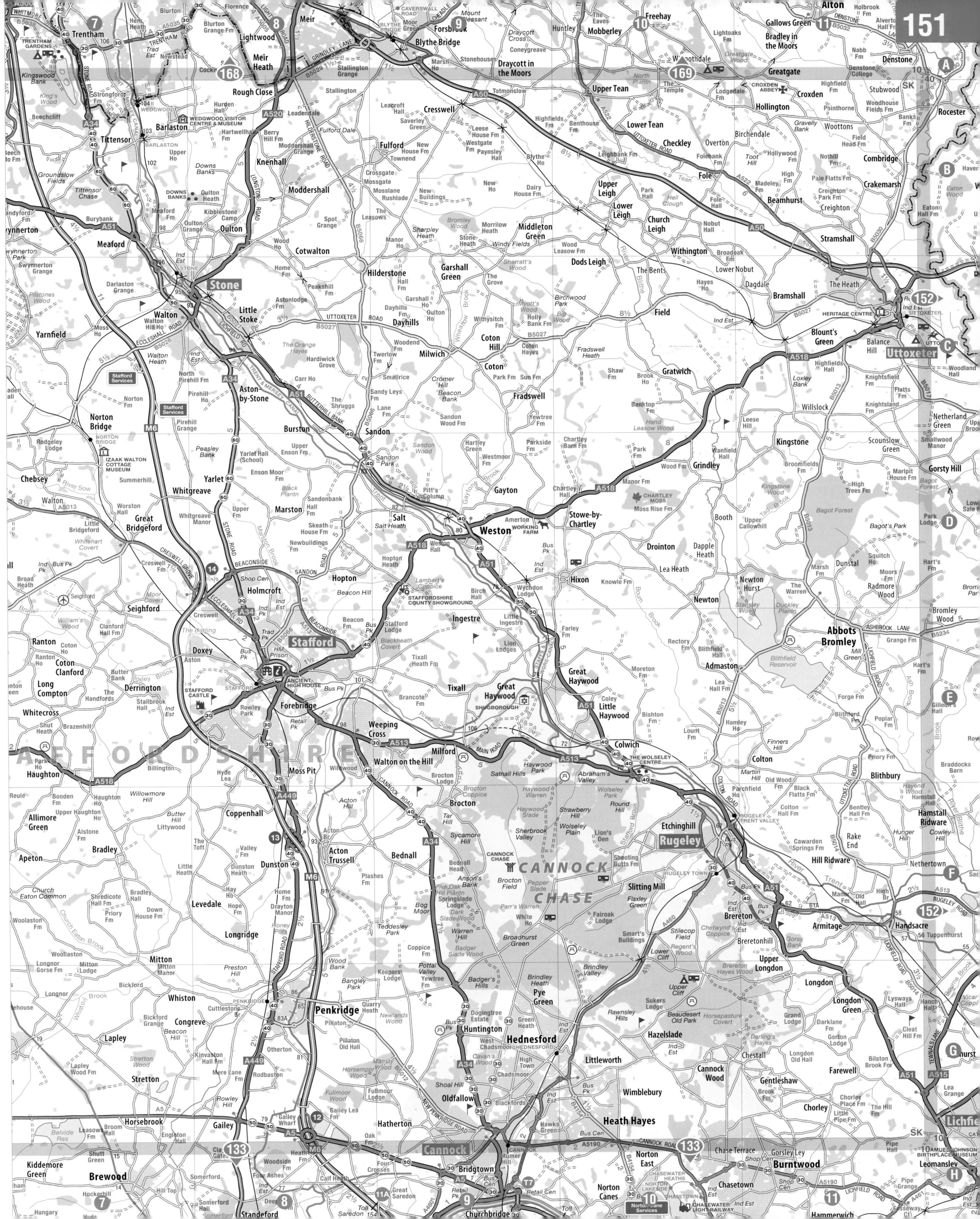

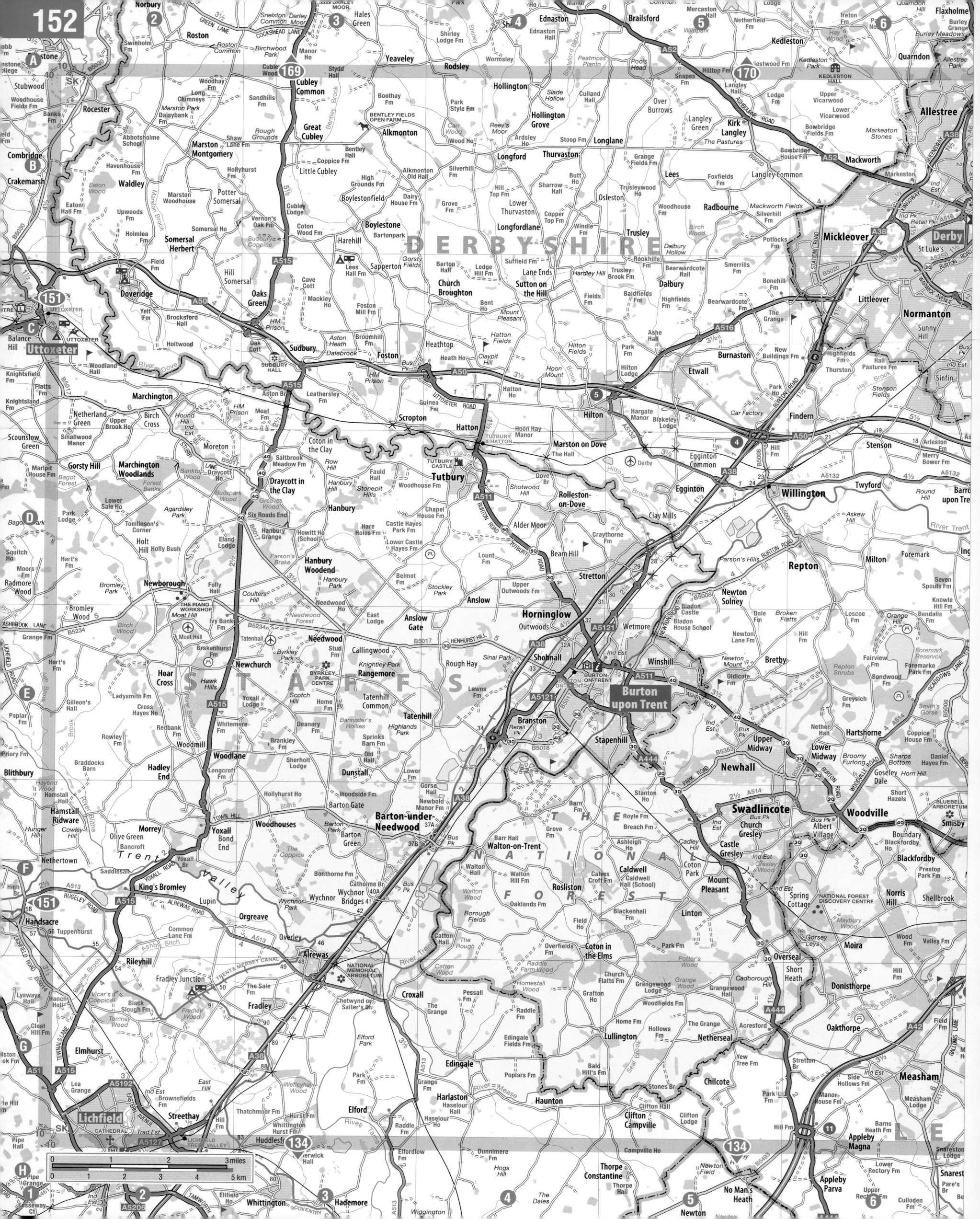

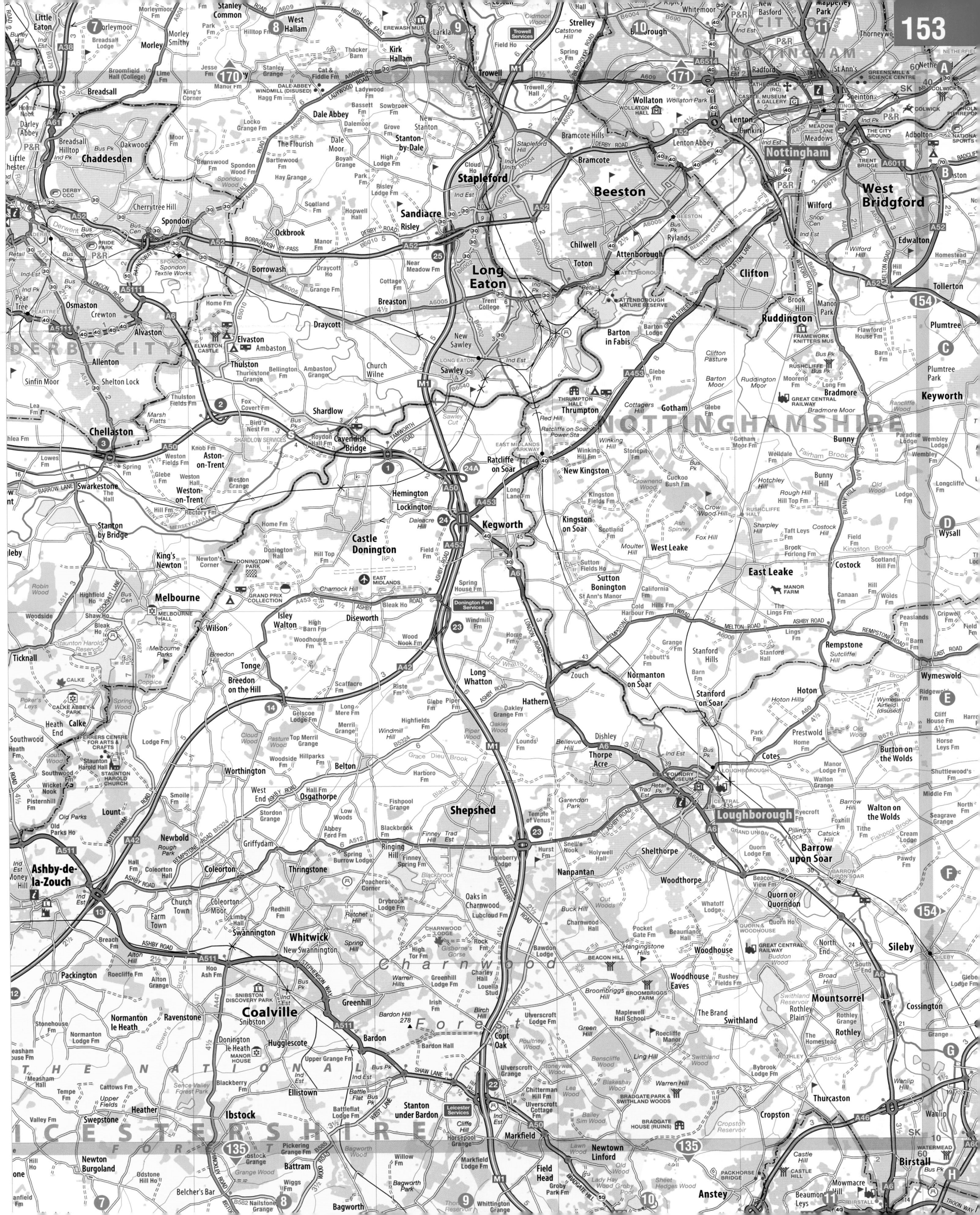

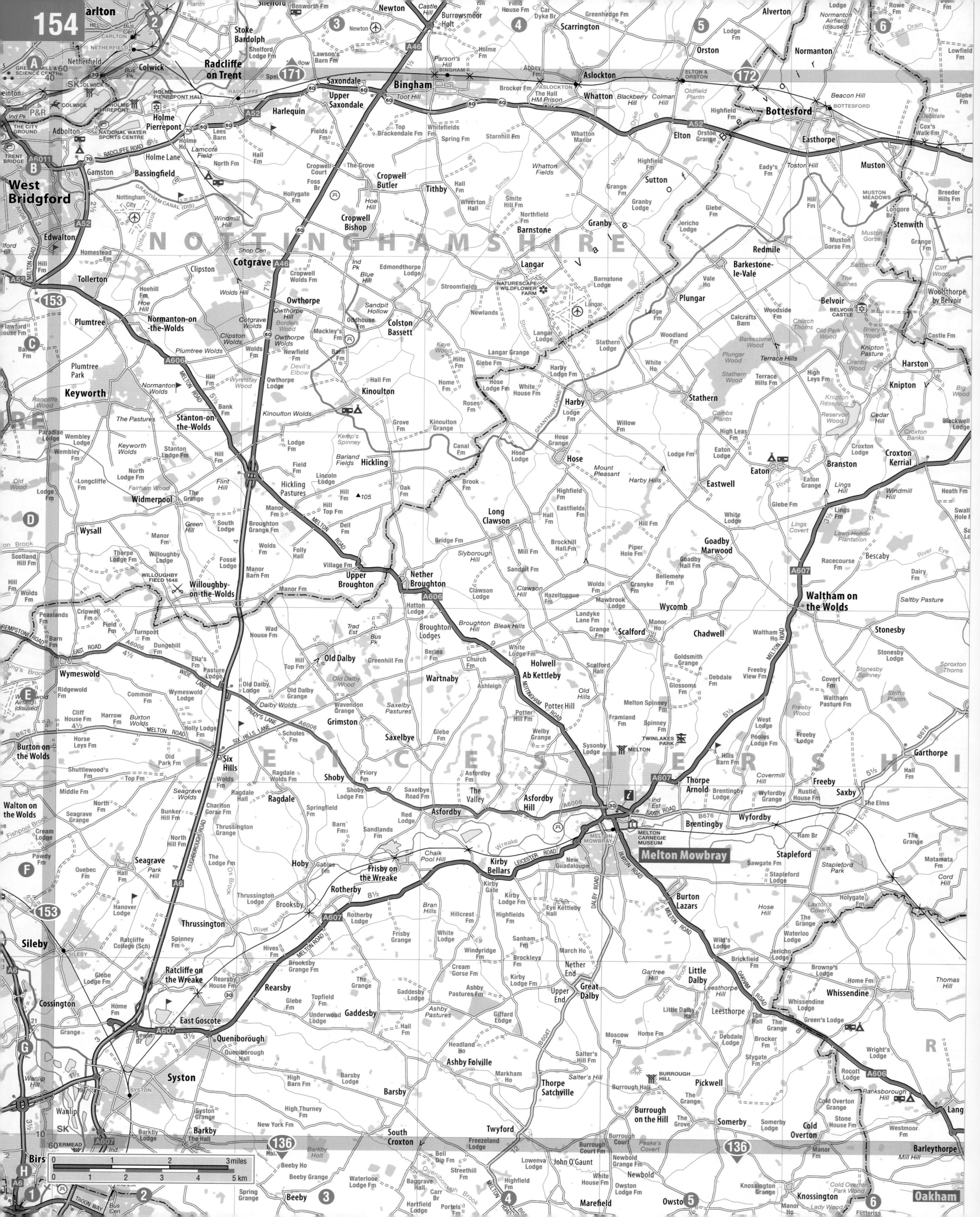

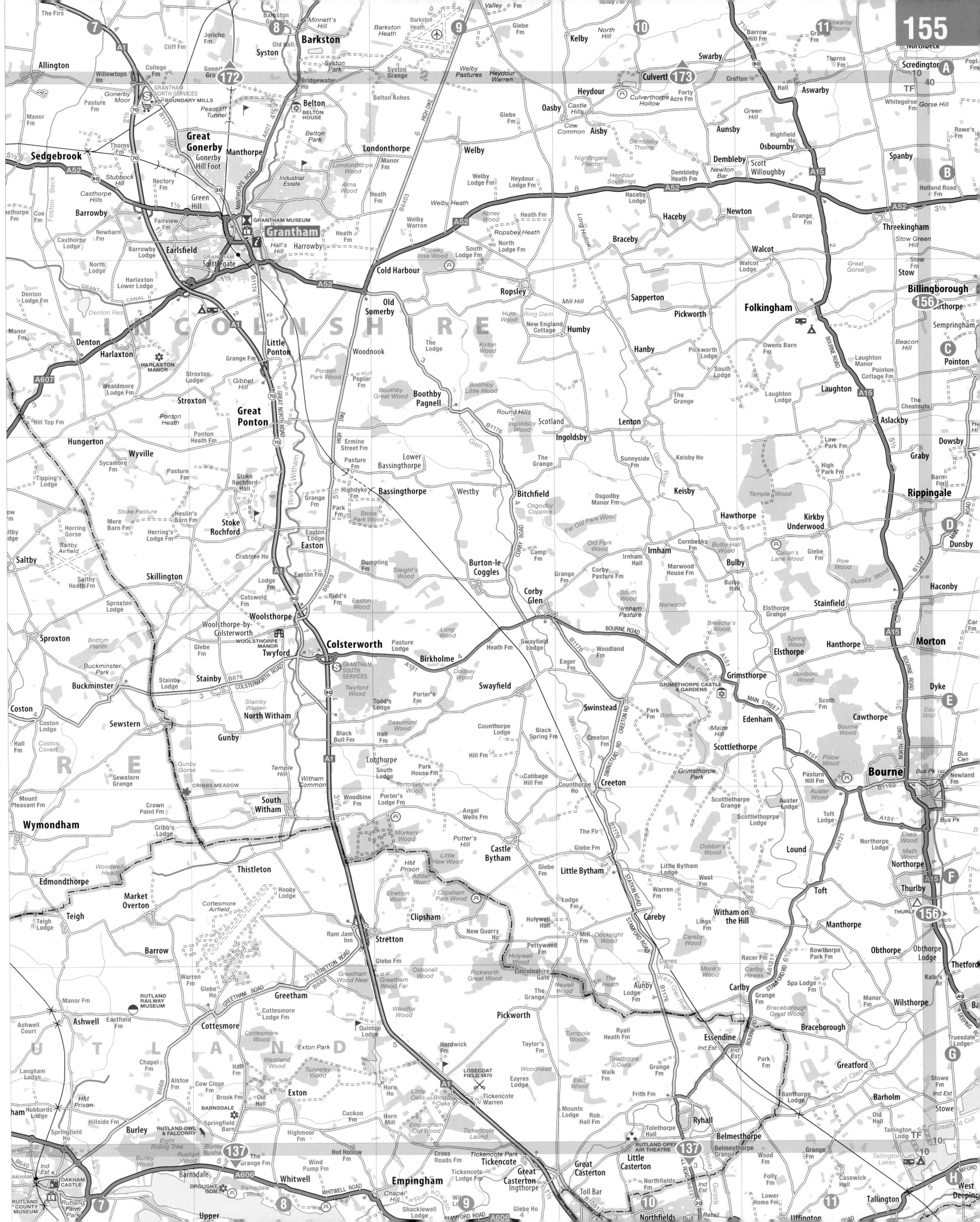

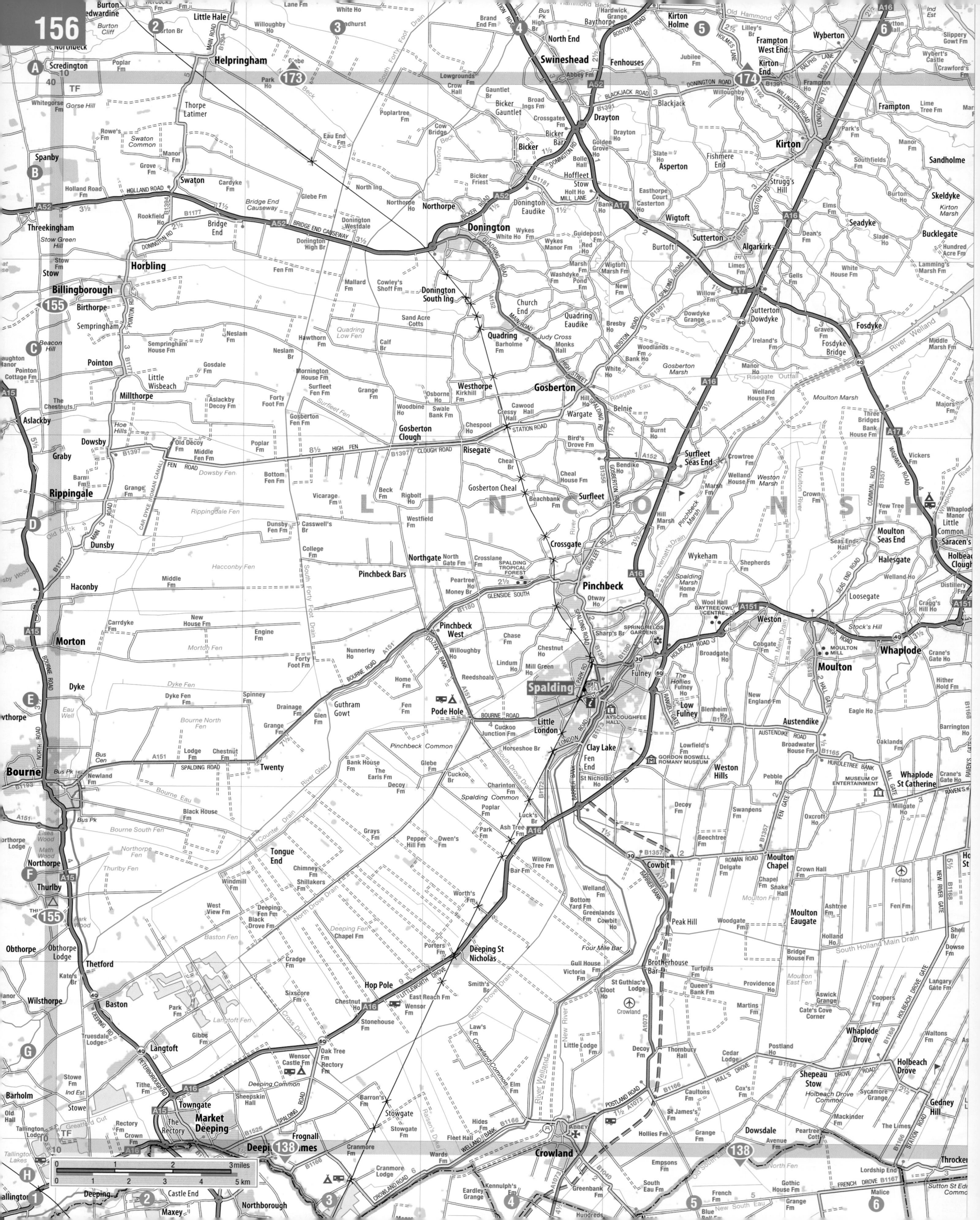

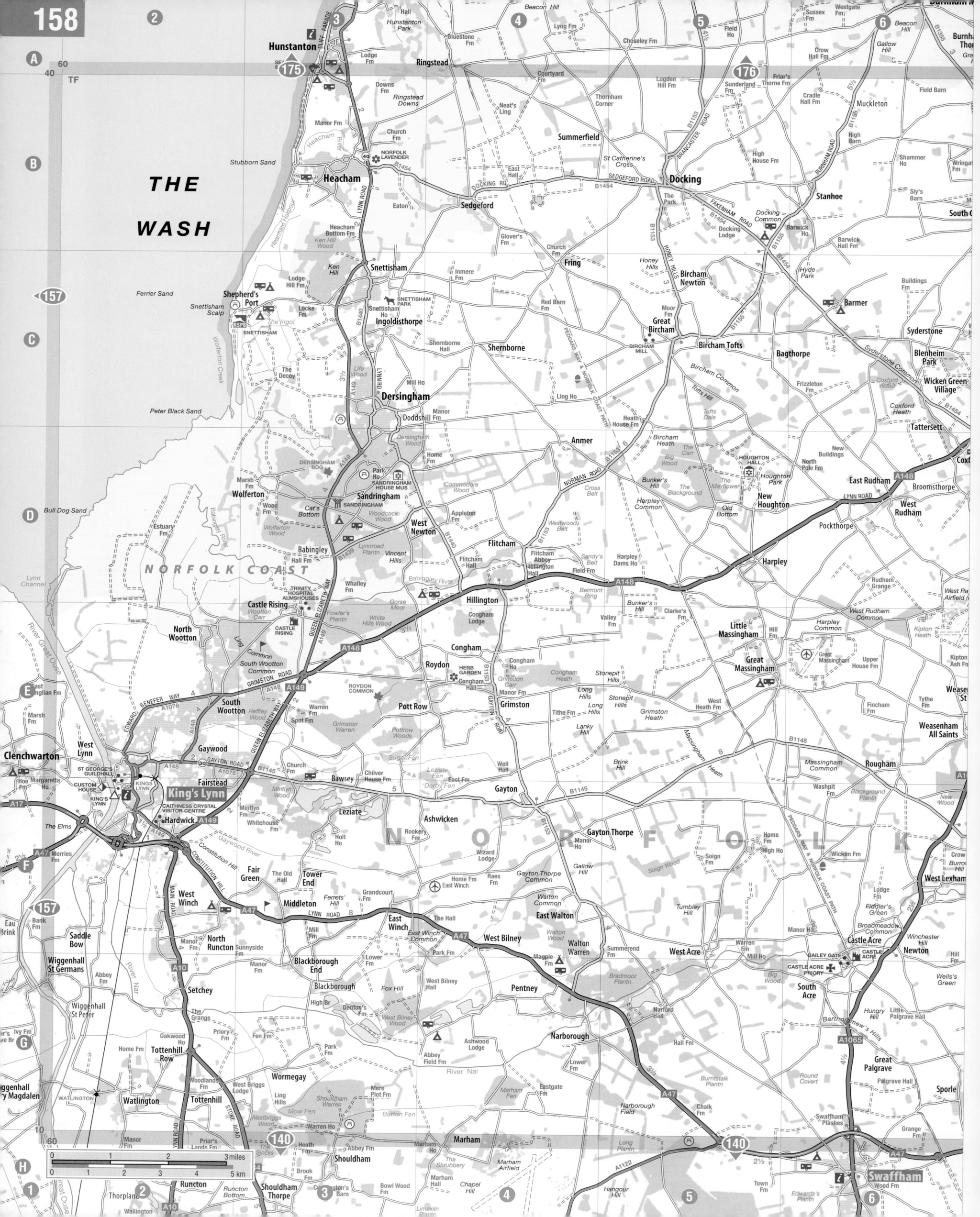

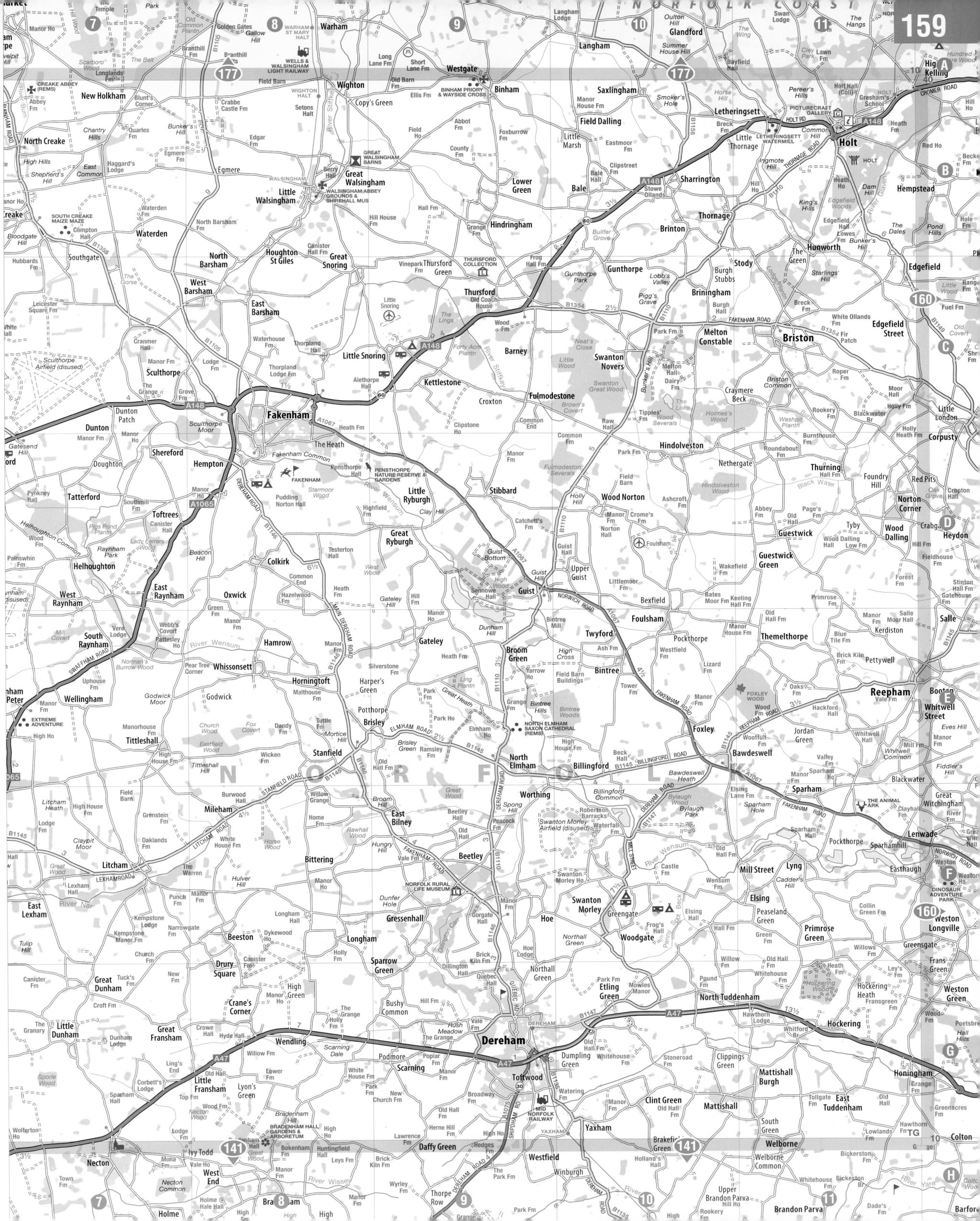

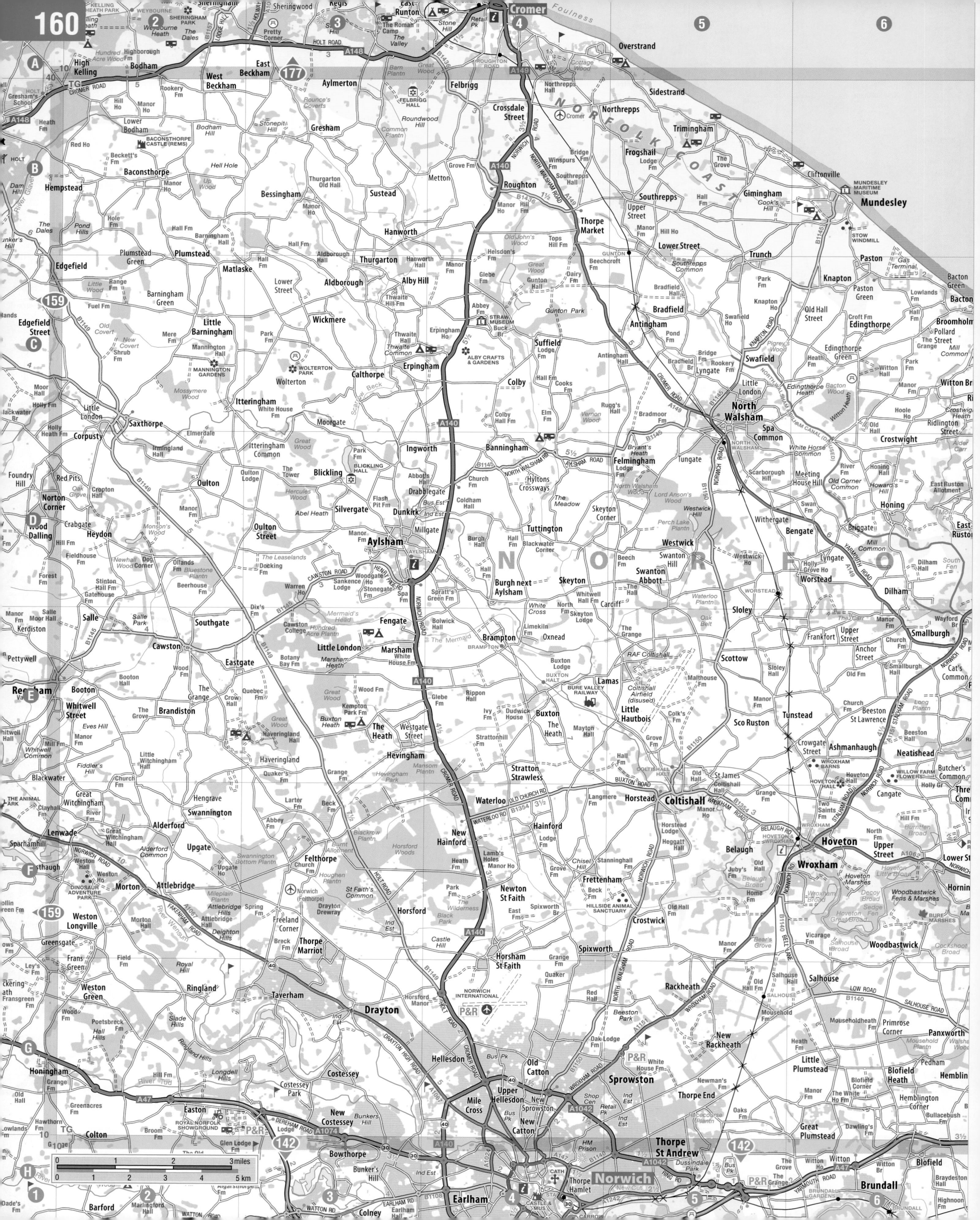

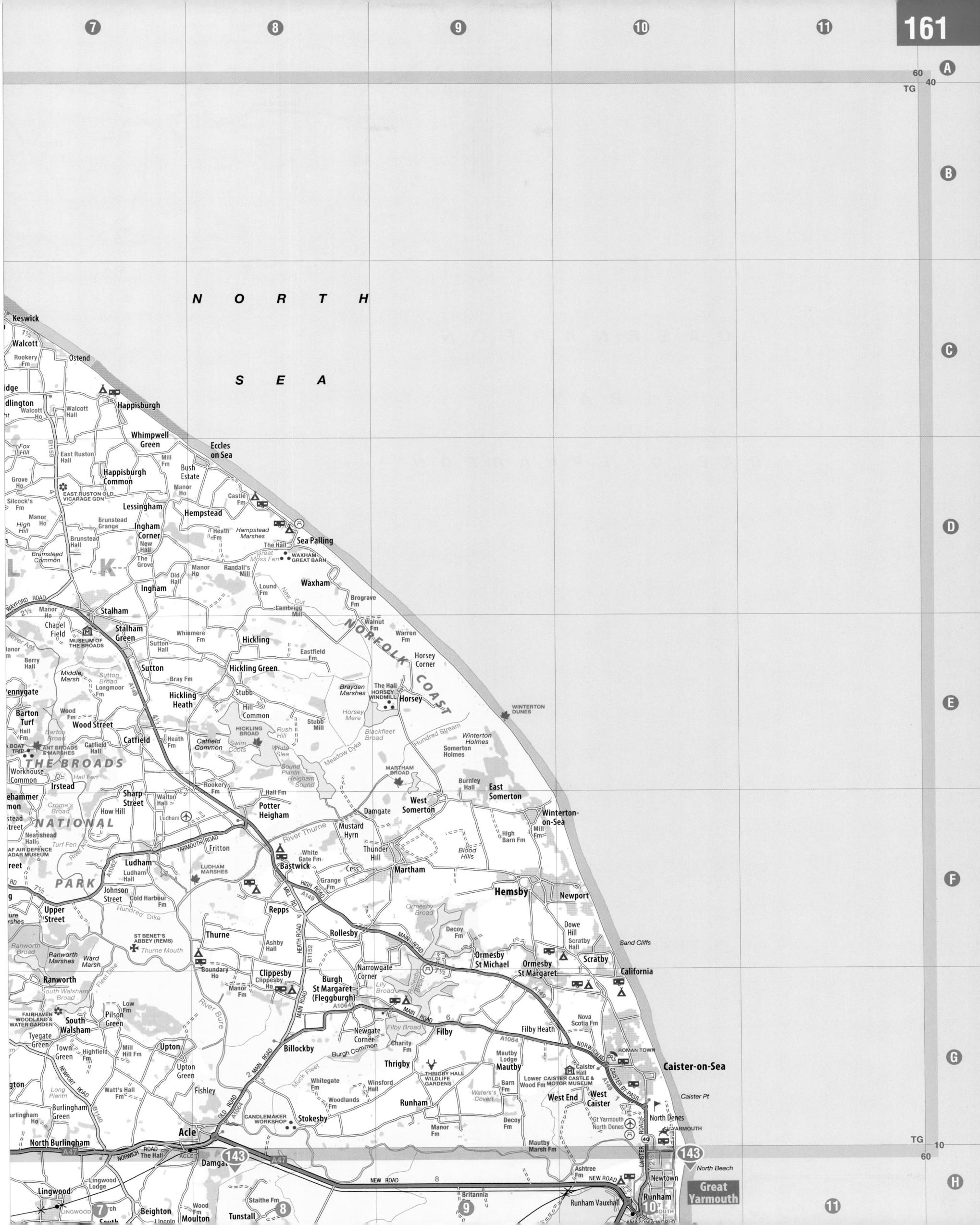

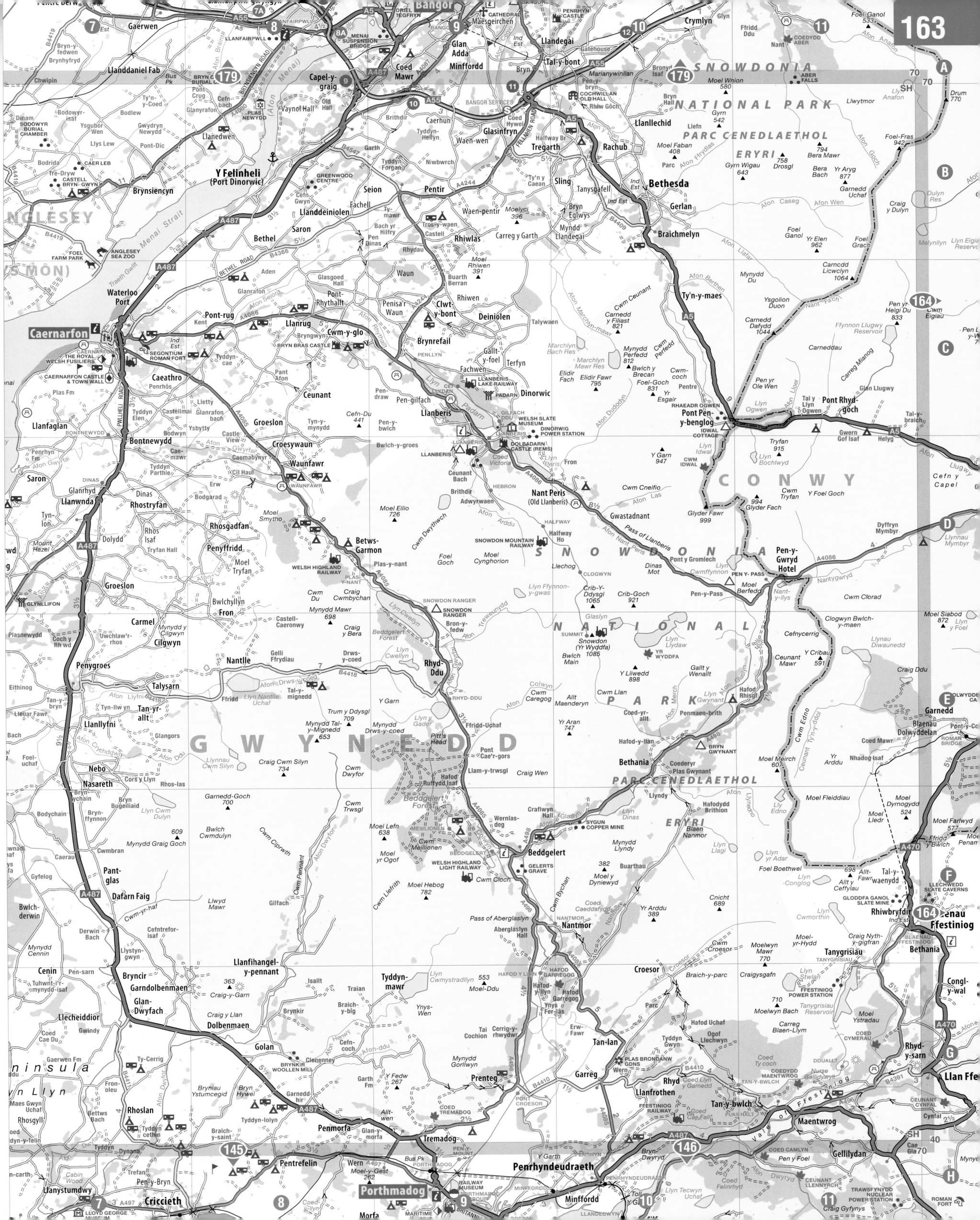

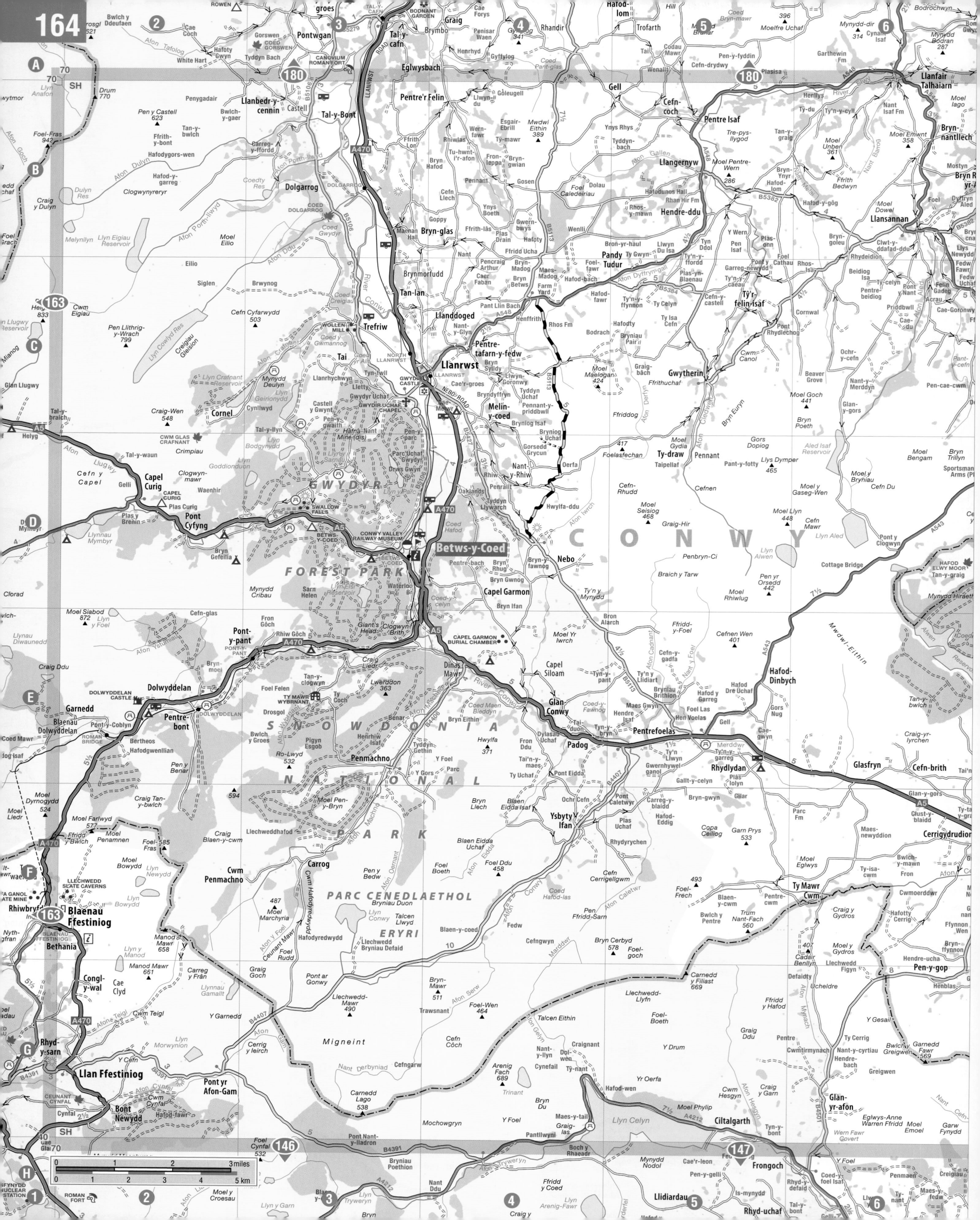

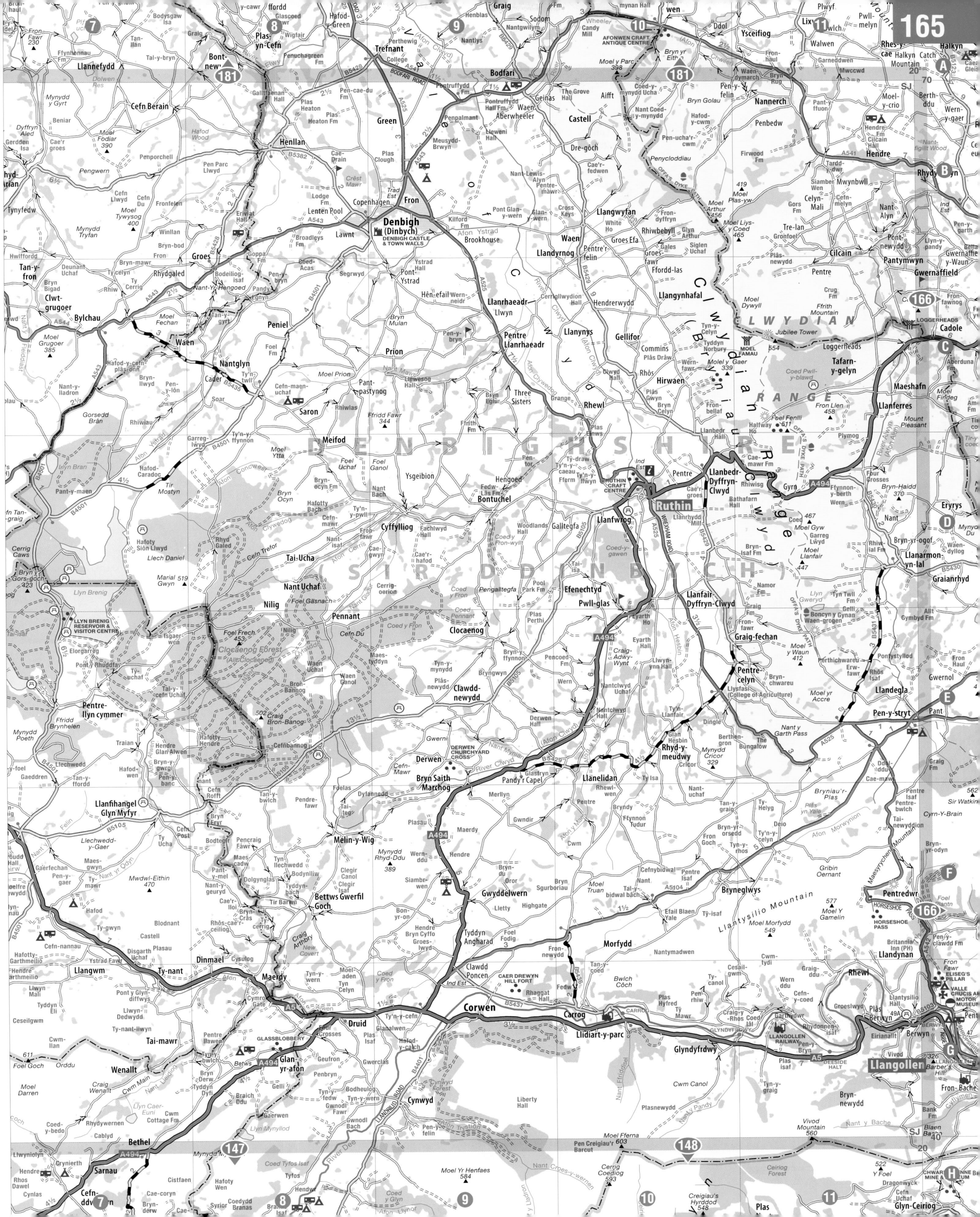

A55 A5117 A5104 A494 A483 A5156 A534 A483 A5 A539 A541 A494 A525 A542

SJ

FLINTSHIRE (SIR Y FFLINT)

WREXHAM (WRECSAM)

Chester
Chester Cathedral
Chester Castle & Walls
Deva Roman Experience
Chester Zoo
Handbridge
Hoole
Newton
Upton Heath
Upton
Mickle Trafford
Littleton

Mold (Yr-Wyddgrug)
Buckley (Bwcle)
Connah's Quay
Shotton
Queensferry
Hawarden (Penarlâg)
Ewloe
Ewloe Green
Flint Mountain (Mynydd Fflint)
Halkyn
Oakenholt
Northop (Llan-eurgain)
Northop Hall
Rhosesmor
Rhydymwyn
Soughton (Sychdyn)
New Brighton
Alltami
Mynydd-isa
Prenbrigog
Drury
Burntwood Pentre
Garden City
Sealand
Saughall
Mollington
Blacon
Saltney
Broughton
Bretton
Balderton
Eccleston
Belgrave
Dodleston
Kinnerton
Higher Kinnerton
Lower Kinnerton
Gorstella
Pulford
Poulton
Lavister
Rossett
Marford
Gresford
Trevalyn
Burton Green
Aldford
Churton
Farndon
Holt
Crewe-by-Farndon

Wrexham / Wrecsam
Rhosddu
Rhosnesni
The Dunks
Acton
Garden Village
Llay
Gwersyllt
Rhosrobin
Summerhill
Moss
Bradley
New Broughton
Coedpoeth
Minera
Bwlchgwyn
Brymbo
Bersham
Rhostyllen
Talwrn
Johnstown
Rhosllanerchrugog
Rhosymedre
Cefn-mawr
Ruabon (Rhiwabon)
Penycae
Acrefair
Trevor
Garth
Froncysyllte
Pontcysyllte
New Bridge
Chirk (Y Waun)
King's Mills
Marchwiel
Sontley
Cross Lanes
Pickhill
Bangor-is-y-coed
Overton (Owrtyn)
Overton Bridge
Eyton
Cock Bank
Worthenbury
Threapwood
Tallarn Green
Shocklach
Bowling Bank

Llangollen
Valle Crucis Abbey
Eliseg's Pillar
Castell Dinas Bran
Plas Newydd Museum
Berwyn
Llantysilio
Trevor Rocks
Pentredwr
Horseshoe Pass
World's End
Llandegla
Pen-y-stryt
Gwynfryn
Coedpoeth
Ffrith
Cymau
Cefn-y-bedd
Caergwrle
Hope (Yr Hôb)
Llanfynydd
Treuddyn
Coed-Talon
Leeswood (Coed-Llai)
Pontblyddyn
Nercwys
Gwernymynydd
Cadole
Loggerheads
Llanferres
Maeshafn
Eryrys
Graianrhyd
Llanarmon-yn-Ial
Rhydtalog
Bwlchgwyn
Four Crosses
Penyffordd
Penymynydd
Hendre
Rhydymwyn
Glyn-Ceiriog

River Dee
River Alyn / Afon Alyn
River Clywedog
River Ceiriog
River Dee (Afon Dyfrdwy)

Scale:
0 1 2 3 miles
0 1 2 3 4 5 km

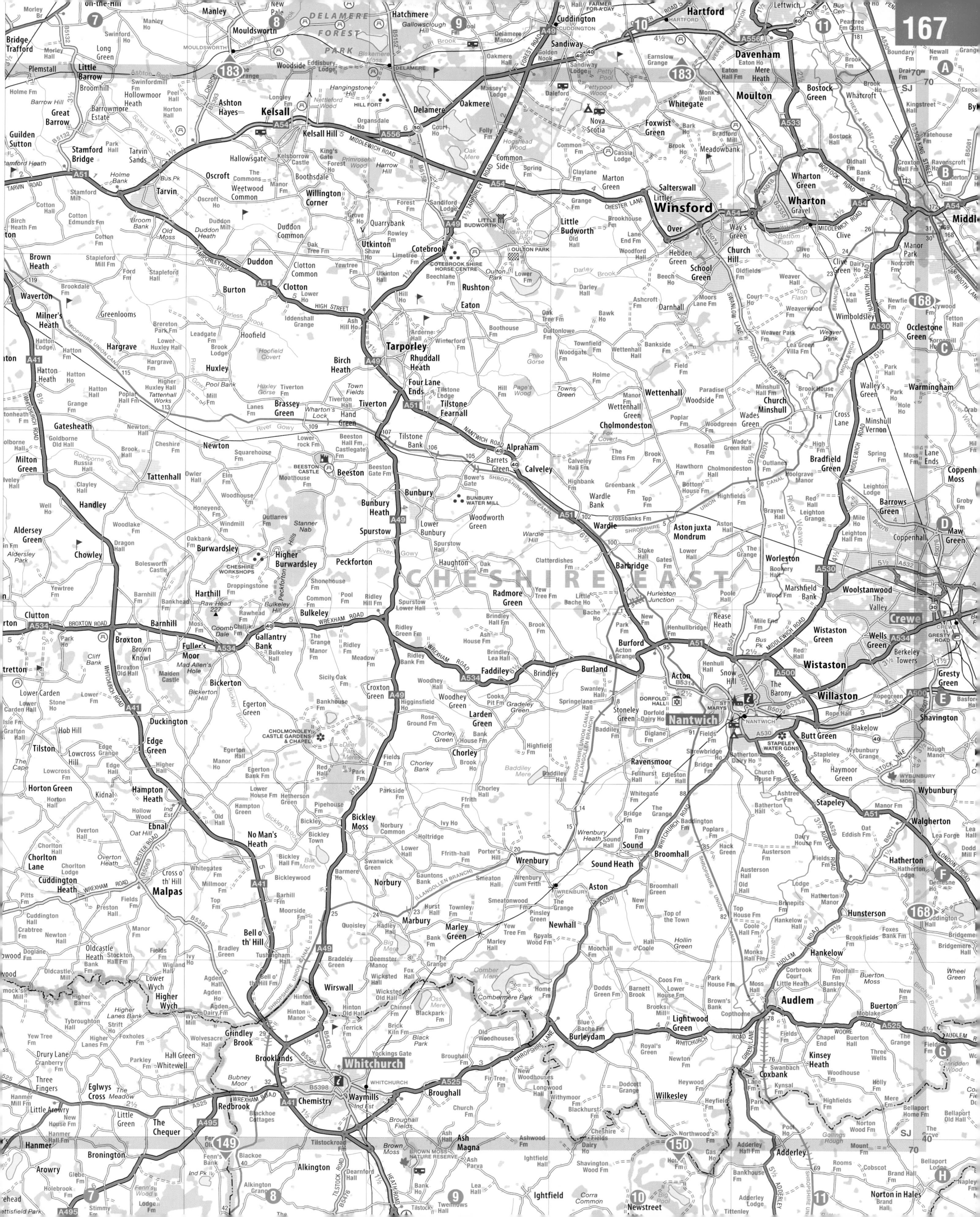

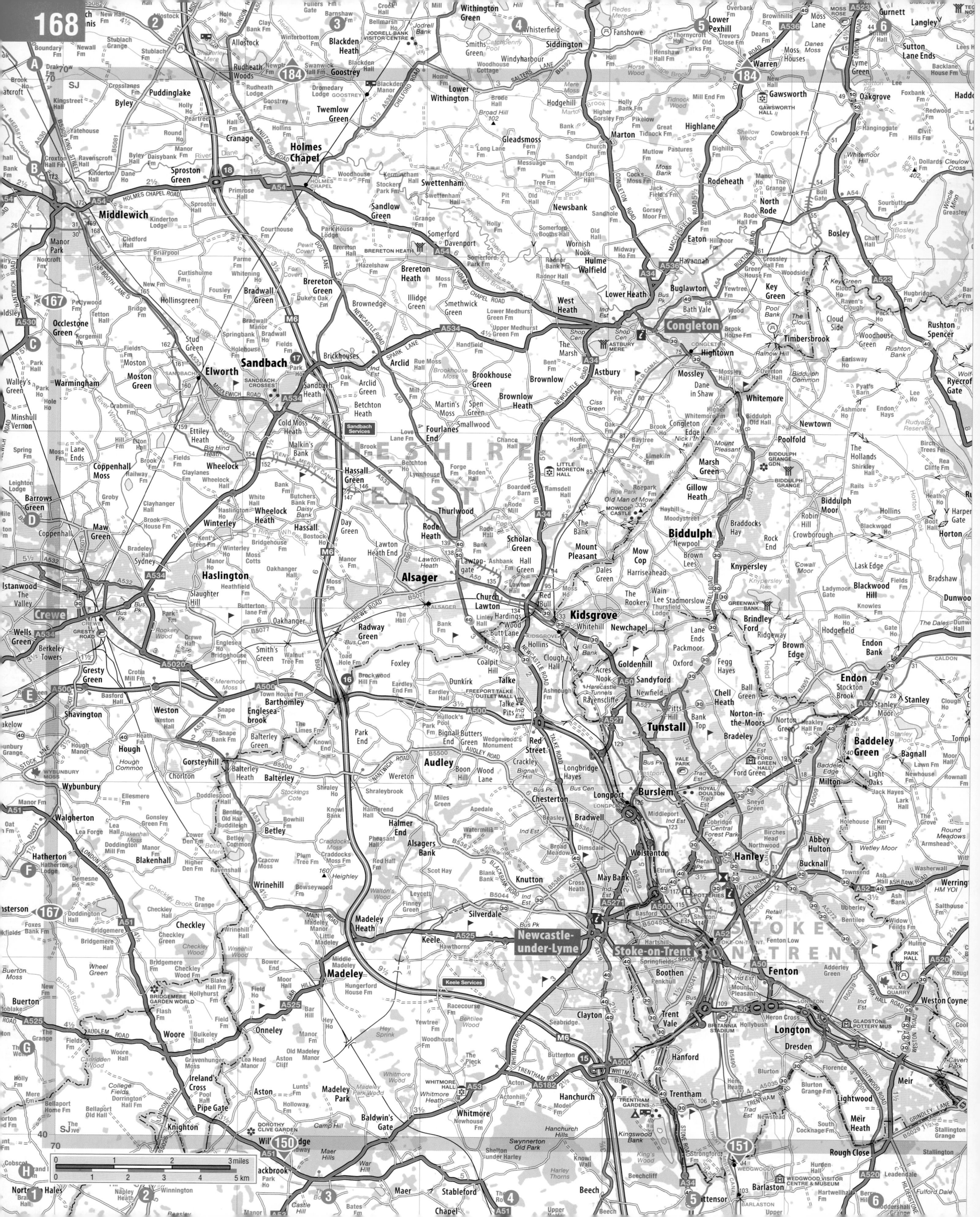

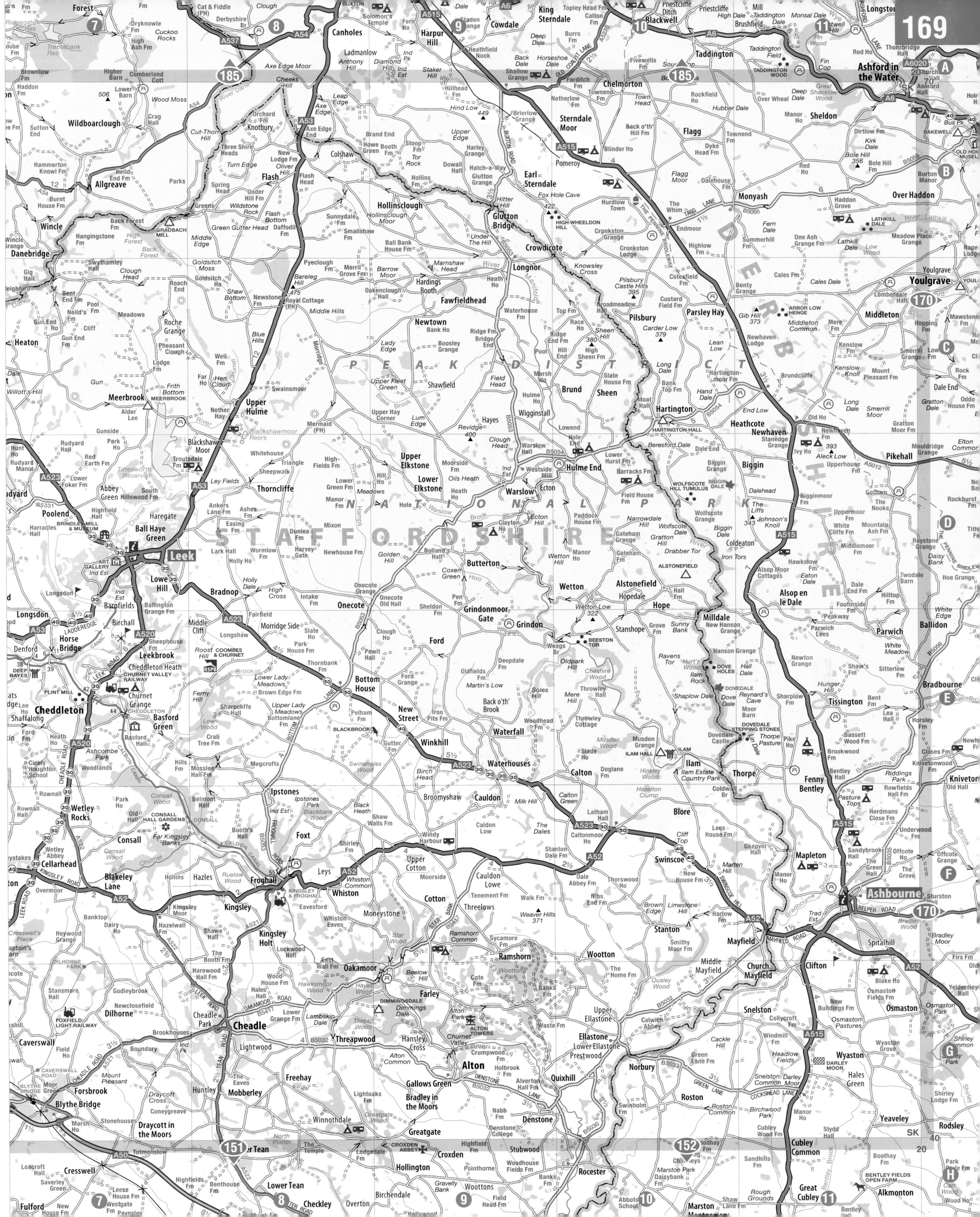

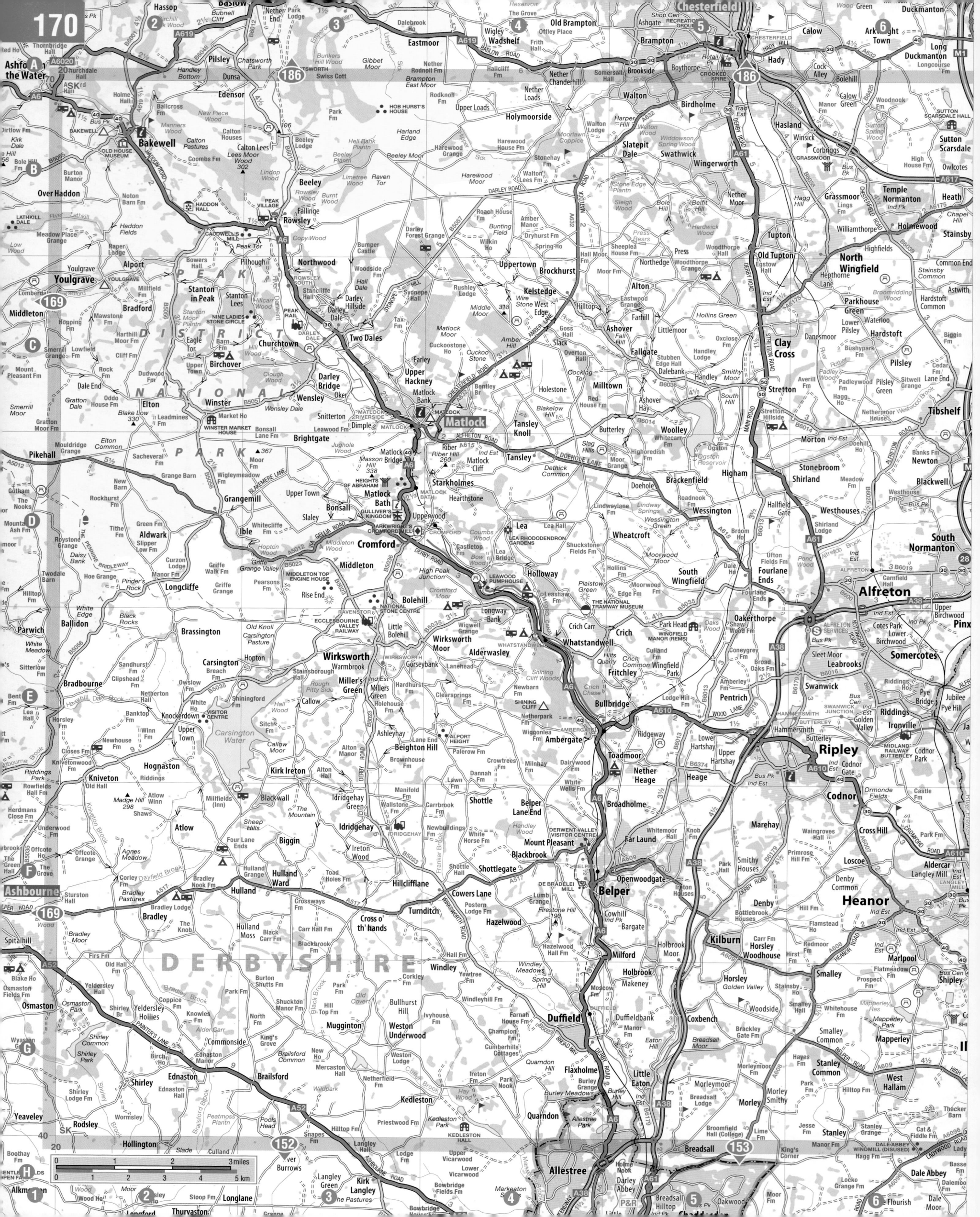

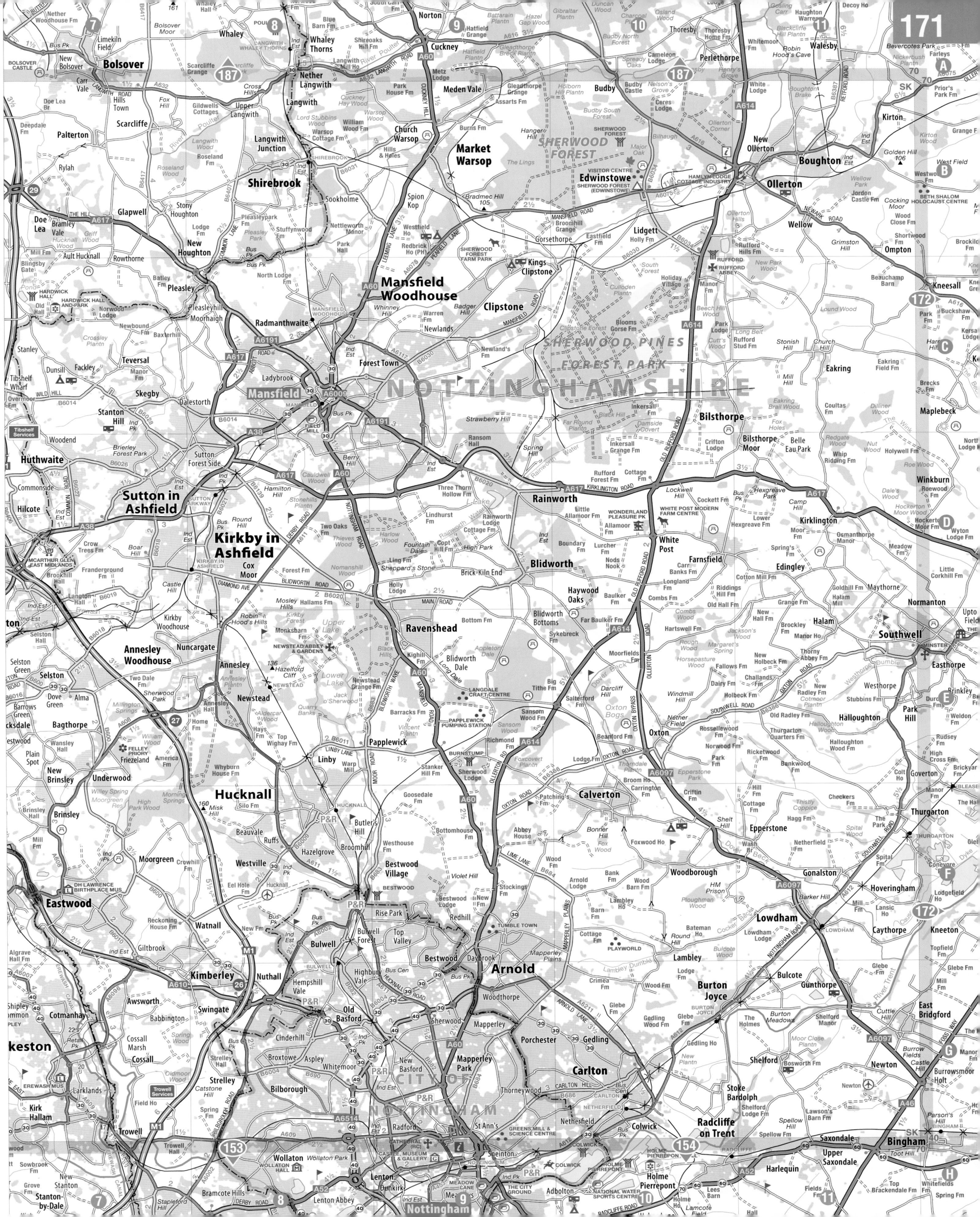

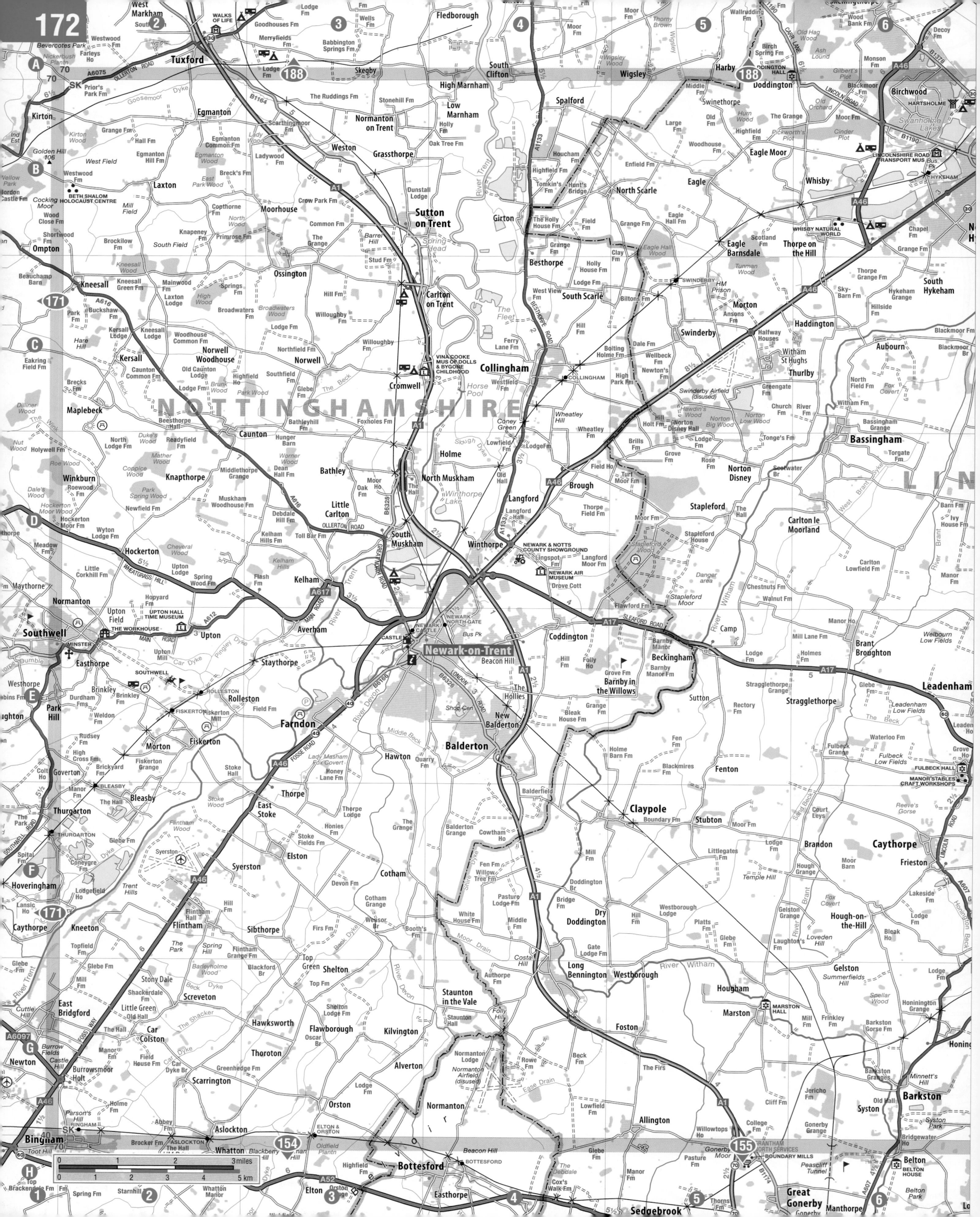

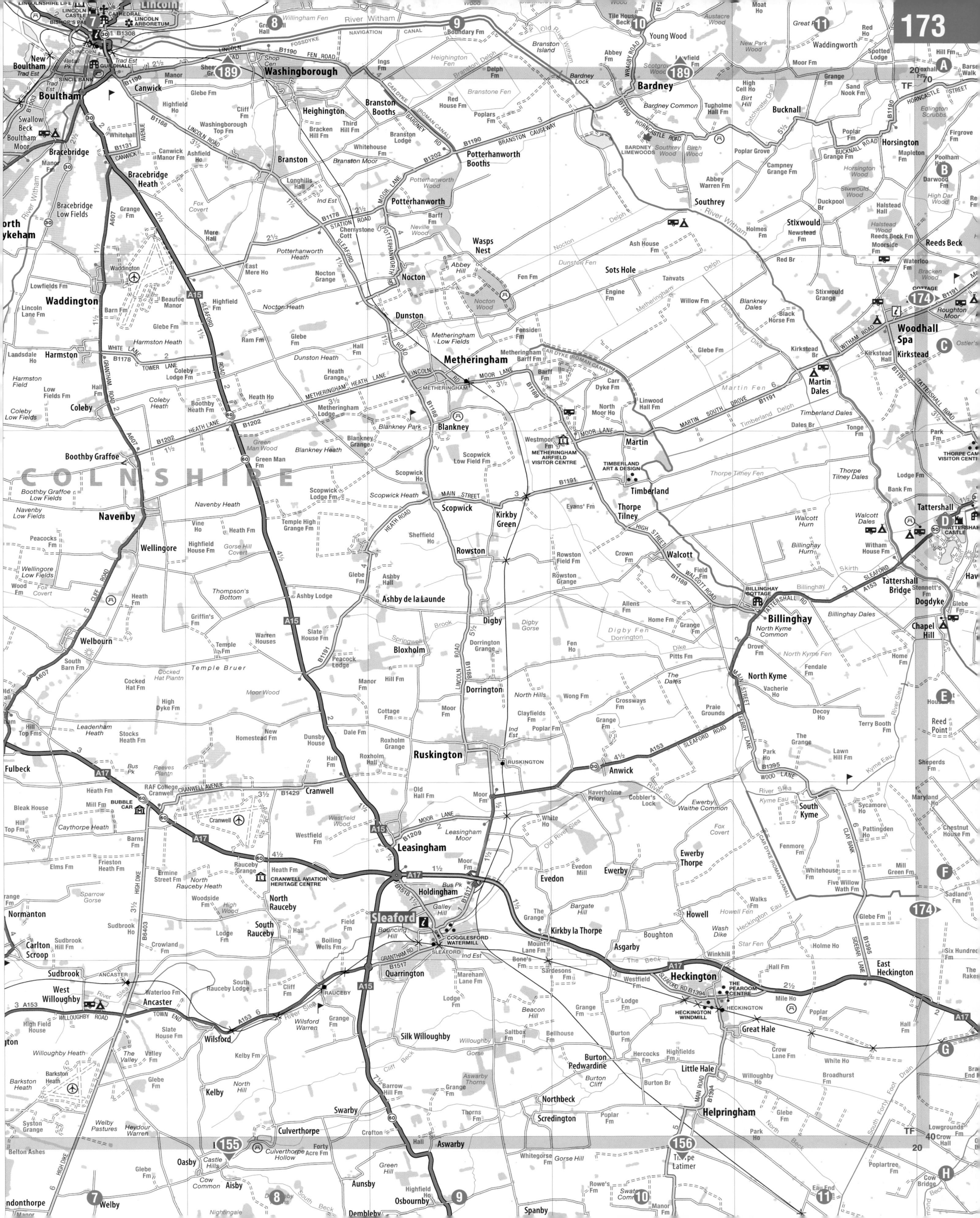

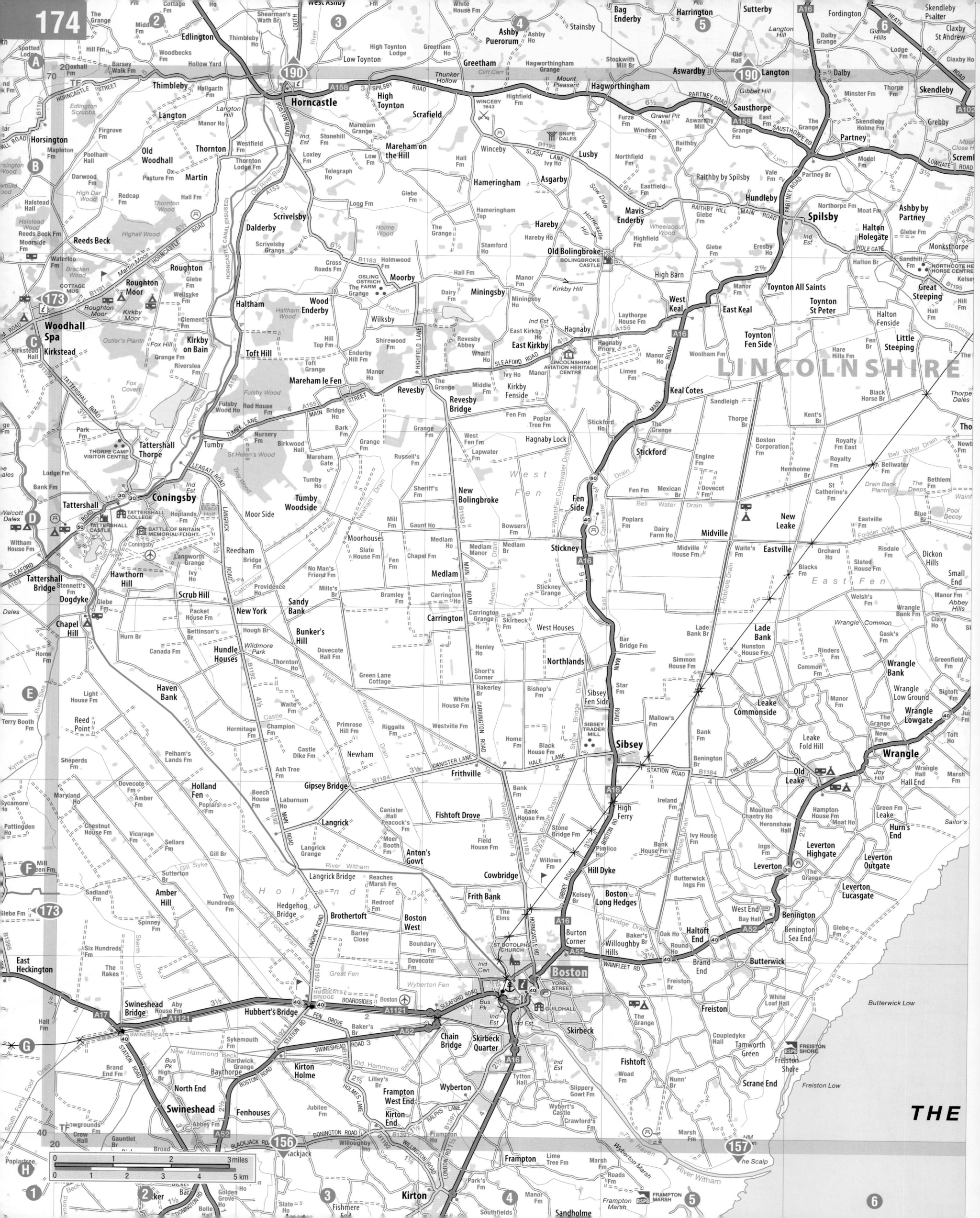

7 8 9 10 11

A
20
60
TG

B

C

D

Blakeney Pit

Warham Hole

West Sand Cabbage Creek
South Side Pits Pt The Marrams
Stiffkey Freshes BLAKENEY

Stiffkey Salt Marshes
Morston Salt Marshes
Great Barnett
Agar Creek New Cut
Stiffkey Salt Marshes BLAKENEY Cley Mill COAST PEDDARS WAY AND NORFOLK COAST PATH
NORFOLK COAST PATH GUILDHALL Cley next ROAD Salthouse
Warborough Stiffkey Greens 7½ BLAKENEY the Sea A149 Sheringham NORFOLK SHIRE
Hill RD Morston Blakeney MUCKLEBURGH Weybourne HORSE CENTRE
A149 Cockthorpe Joe's Wiveton Newgate COLLECTION Sheringham
Battledore Common Hill Gravelpit Gallow 1½ Weybourne Sheringham West
Hill Stiffkey Wiveton Hill Hill A149 Oak Park Runton
Cockthorpe Downs Kelling Wood Upper Sheringham WEST
NORFOLK COAST Sheringham Sheringham Beeston RUNTON East
Langham Oulton Swan Lowes The NORTH NORFOLK Hall Weybourne Regis WEST Runton CROMER
Long Lodge Hill Lodge Fm Hangs RAILWAY KELLING Weybourne The Dales RUNTON The Roman The
Lane Fm Short Glandford The HEATH PARK Kelling Heath Sheringwood Stone Camp Valley
Lane Fm Langham Summer Wing Kelling Hundred Highborough Hill Pretty Hill Stone Pela
Old Barn House Hill Cley Lawn Heath Acre Wood Fm Corner HOLT ROAD Hill Felbrigg
Westgate BINHAM PRIORY Park Fm High Bodham West East 3 A148
Ellis Fm & WAYSIDE CROSS Bayfield Kelling Beckham Beckham Barn Great Felbrigg
Binham Saxlingham Hall Pereer's Holt Hall Bodham Plantn Wood Aylmerton FELBRIGG
Field Manor Smoker's Hills (Coll) HOLT Rookery Hill Bodham Roundwood HALL
Field Ho House Fm Hole Horse Gresham's Fm Hill Ho Manor Stonepit Gresham Hill
Abbot Letheringsett Hill School CROMER Hill Ho Ho Hill Common
Fm Little Breck LETHERINGSETT GALLERY Heath Lower Bounce's Plantn
Foxburrow Little Fm WATERMILL PICTURECRAFT A148 Fm Bodham BACONSTHORPE Coverts
Fm Marsh Thornage HOLT RD Common Red Ho Beckett's CASTLE (REMS)
County Eastmoor Ingmote Road HOLT Heath Baconsthorpe Bodham Metton
Fm Fm Clipstreet Hill HOLT Hill Manor Hell Hole Thurgarton Sustead
GREAT Bale Fm Sharrington B1110 THORNAGE ROAD Dam Fm Up Old Hall Bessingham 160
SNORING Hall Stowe Heath Hill Wood
BARNS Bale Ollands Ho River Glaven Hole Manor
Lower 3½ King's Edgefield Fm Ho Hanworth
Green Hindringham Bullfer Hills Edgefield The Pond Plumstead Hall Fm Aldborough Alby Hill
Hall Fm 60 Grove Thornage Woods Dales Hills Green Barningham Thwaite
Hill House Brinton Hempstead Edgefield Plumstead Hall Hanworth Hill Fm
Fm Grange Hunworth Hall Lowes Bunker's Matlaske Lower Thurgarton
Fm The Fm Hill Hole Street Wickmere Abbt
Vinepark THURSFORD Frog Gunthorpe Stody Green Starlings' Edgefield Fm Range Barningham Alby & Gal
Thursford COLLECTION Hall Fm Park Lobb's Burgh Hill Fm Little Green
Green Gunthorpe Valley Stubbs Briningham Breck Wood Barningham
Thursford Pigg's Briningham White Ollands Fuel Fm Park
Little Old Coach B1354 2½ Grave Burgh Fm Edgefield Shrub
Snoring House 2 Hall FAKENHAM ROAD Street New Fm Erpingham
The Wood Park Fm Melton Briston B1354 Covert Ho
Lings Fm Neat's Constable Briston Fir Mere Thwaite
A148 Close Little Patch Mannington Park Thwaite Hall Erpingham
Barney Swanton Wood Briston Fm Hall Fm Common
snoring Novers Melton Oak Calthorpe TG
Kettlestone Fulmodeston Swanton Hall Roper Moor Covert MANNINGTON WOLTERTON 30
Croxton Severals Great Wood Dairy Fm Hall Shrub GARDENS PARK Erpingham A140
thorpe Bunker's Craymere Briston Fm Fm Mossymere Wolterton
Clipstone Brown's Hill Beck Common Holly Wood Itteringham
Common Covert Tippies' River Rookery Blackwater Little White House Moorgate PENSTHORPE
End Raw Wood Fm Br London Fm Blickling NATURE RESERVE
Hall Holmes's Washpit Holly Saxthorpe Itteringham Ingworth & GARDENS
Little Fm Wood Plantn Heath 160 Common Great
Ryburgh Manor Severals Burnthouse Fm Corpusty Irmingland Wood Park BLICKLING
Common Fm 159 Fm Hall Itteringham Fm HALL
Wensu Fm Hindolveston Park Fm Roundabout B1149 Hale Common
Stibbard Field Fm Oulton The
Holly Barn Thurning Lodge Tower Abbots
Hill Wood Nort Ashcroft Hill Foundry Red Pits Cropton Norton Hercules Hall Drabblegate
Hindolveston Hall Fm Hill Oak Grove Hall Corner Wood Hall Coldham
Wood Black Water Page's Abbey Manor Silvergate Flash Bus Est
Pit Fm

E
TON RD
CROMER
Reta Pk

F
Metton

G

H

7 8 9 10 11

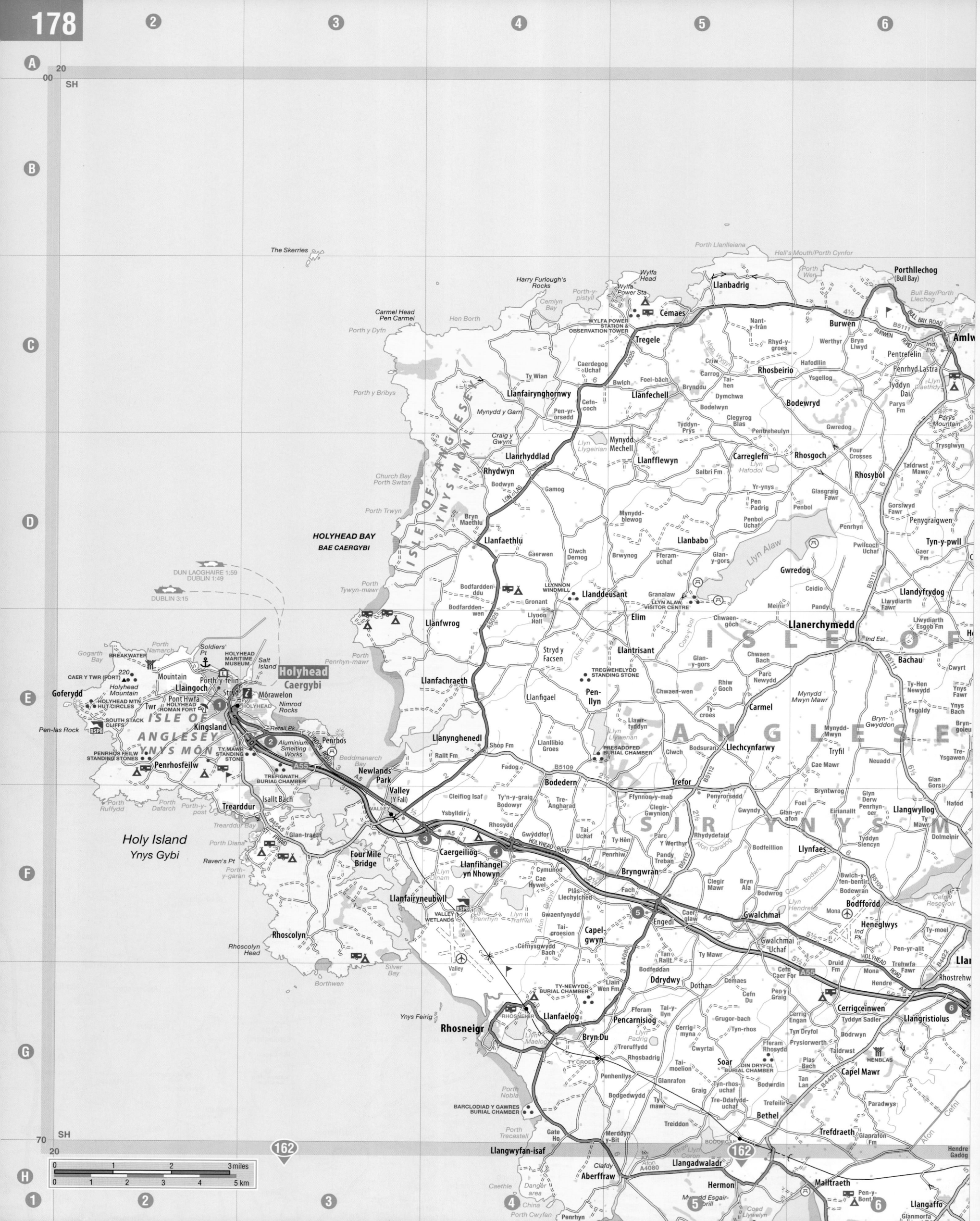

2   3   4   5   6

A

70
00
SH

B

◁ 179

C

IRISH SEA

MÔR IWERDDON

D

Hornby Cave   Great Ormes Head
Pen-y-Gogarth

GREAT ORME
Llandudno Bay
or Ormes Bay

Cregiau
Rhiwledyn   Little Ormes
Head

GREAT ORME
RAILWAY   CABIN LIFT

GREAT ORME
COPPER MINE   Toll   141

GREAT ORME

E   THE PARADE   COLWYN   ROAD   Penrhyn Bay
(Bae Penrhyn)

Llandudno   ALICE IN
WONDERLAND   Llandudno   Penrhynside   Penrhyn
4½   B5115   Rhôs Pt

ORIEL
MOSTYN   Craig-
y-don   Penrhyn-
side   Bus Pk   Rhôs-on-Sea

Conwy
Sands   Llanrhos   Bryn
Maelgwyn   Coed
Isaf   Dinarth
Hall   Bryn Euryn
131   Llandrillo-yn-Rhos

Deganwy   Bryn
Pydew   Glanwydden   20

Glan Conwy   Llangwstenin
Hall   Colwyn Bay
(Bae Colwyn)

DEGANWY   COLWYN BAY

16A   17   BUTTERFLY
JUNGLE   Tywyn   Llandudno
Junction
(Cyffordd
Llandudno)   WELSH
MOUNTAIN
ZOO   22   Penmaen
Rhôs

F   Allt-
Wen   Penmaen-
Bach   247   18   ABERGELE   7½   ROAD   ABERGELE
& PENSARN
Ind Esta

16   A55   255   245   ABERCONWY HOUSE /
PLAS MAWR   LLANDUDNO
JUNCTION   21   Old Colwyn   Mochdre   23   Llanddulas   23A

Dwygyfylchi   CONWY   CONWY
CASTLE   19   Dolwyd   Fron
Fm   Pentre-
uchaf   Bryn
Dulas   Cefn Yr
Ogof   Abergele

15A   Foel Lus   Pensychnant   Conwy   RSPB   Dolwyd   Mynydd   Llysfaen   Rhyd-
y-foel   Tyddyn
uchaf

179   Penmaenmawr   362   Gyffin   GLAN
CONWY   Bryn-rhys   B5381   Bryn-
y-maen   Llanelian-
yn-Rhos   Cefn
Castell   Nant Fawr

15   Garizim   Capelulo   Llechan
Ucha   Llechwedd   Bryn-y-maen
Fm   Llety'r   Twnan   Ffernant   Pant
Idda   Ffynhonnau

Llanfairfechan   Penmaenan   Craigyfedwen   Llansanffraid
Glan Conwy   Adar   Uchaf   Cefn Isaf

Nant-y-pandy   Craig Hafodwen   Hafodty   Henryd   Pentrefelin   C O N W Y   Dowlen

Moelfre
435   Cefn Côch   Bryn
Derwydd   Cymerau   Tynllwyn
Hir   Mynydd
Llanelian   Bryncar   Betws-yn-Rhos

Carreg Fawr
356   Cerrig
Gwynion   SNOWDONIA
NATIONAL PARK   Tanrallt Fm   Eirianws
Fm   Nant-y-cywarch   Dolgraian   Ffrith
Hen   Bethgeth   Ty Celyn

G   Cammarnaint   PARC CENEDLAETHOL
ERYRI   Cefn Du
347   Ddol
Bach   Coed
Bryndansi   B5381   Mynydd
Glyn-Lws   Ty-mawr

Foel Lwyd   Tal
y Fan   Coed Mawr Hall   Erw
Goch   Penoros   Hafod-
Iom   Baron
Hill   Mynydd
Bodrochwyn

Drosgl
621   Bwlch y
Ddeufaen   Rowen   Grugfryn   Dawn   Trofarth   396   Moelfre Uchaf   Mynydd-
dir   Cynant
Isaf   Mynydd
Bodran
287

Cae
Coch   ROWEN   TAL-Y-
CAFN   BODNANT
GARDEN   Chwefforddd   Gofer   Codau
Mawr   Bon
Gwyn

White Hart   Gorswen   Tyddyn Bach   Graig   Cae Forys   Moel
Gyffylog
341   Pen-y-fyddin   Cefn-drydwy   Garthewin
Fm

Afon Tafolog   COED
GORSWEN   Penisar
Waen   Tal   Coed
Pant-glas   Plasisa   Llanfair
Talhaiarn

Pontwgan   B5279   Tal-y-
cafn   Brymbo   Rhandir   Wenallt   Nant Isaf Fm   Mynydd
Iago

CANOVIUM
ROMAN FORT   Henrhyd   Gyffylog   Cefn-
coch   Ty-du   Bryn-
nantllech

H   0   1   2   3 miles   Eglwysbach   Llwyn-
du   Goleugell   Gell   Henllys   Moel Emwnt
361

0   1   2   3   4   5 km   164   Pentre'r Felin   Pentre Isaf   164

Drum
770   Tal-y-Bont   Esgair-
Ebrill   Mwdwl
Eithin
389   Ynys Rhys   Tan-y-
graig   Ty-pys-
llygod   Moel
358

1   Fôr
Fras   2   Hafodygors-wen   Carreg-
y-fford   3   A470   Wern-
fawr   Ty-ma   4   Tu-hwnt-
Fron-   5   6

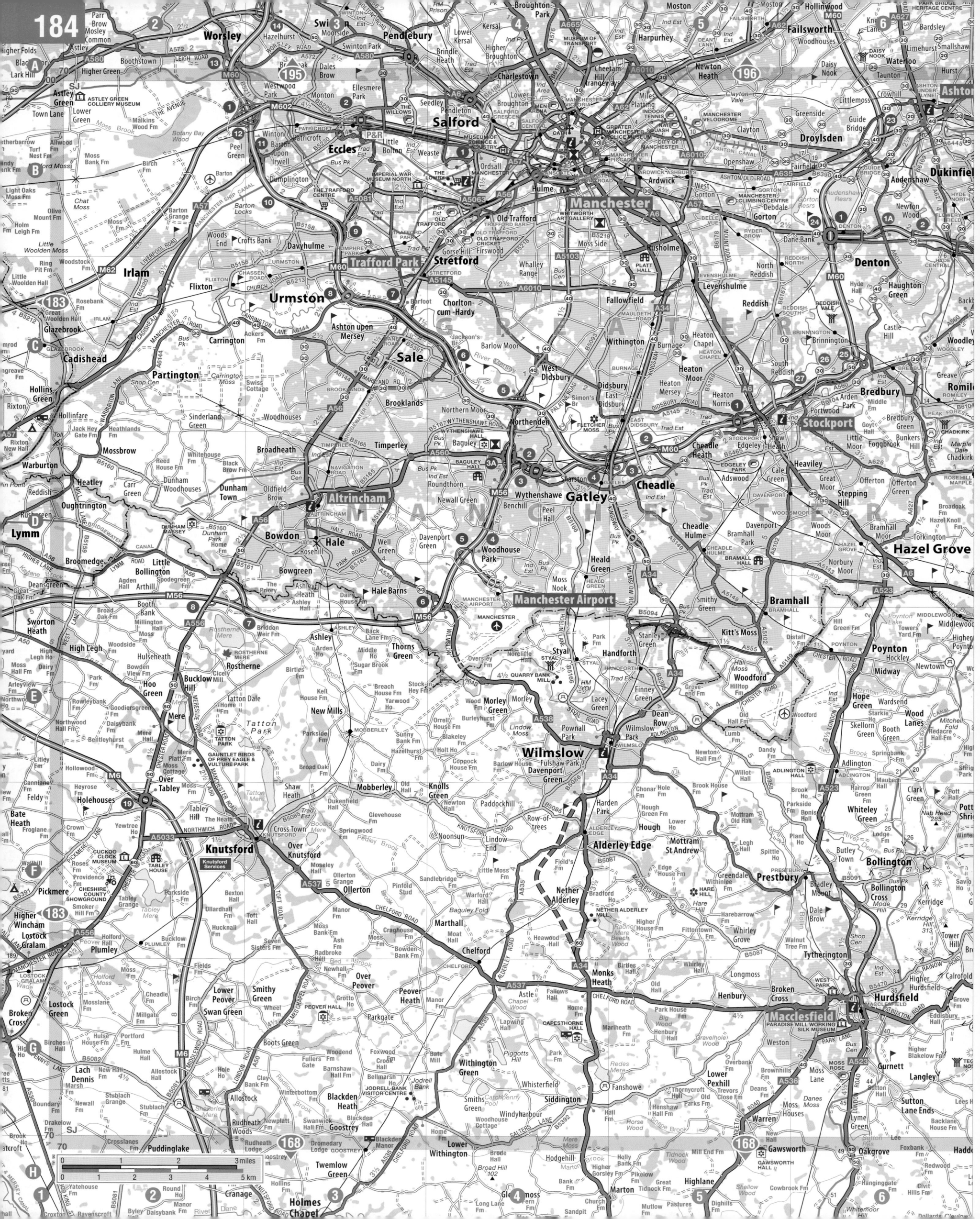

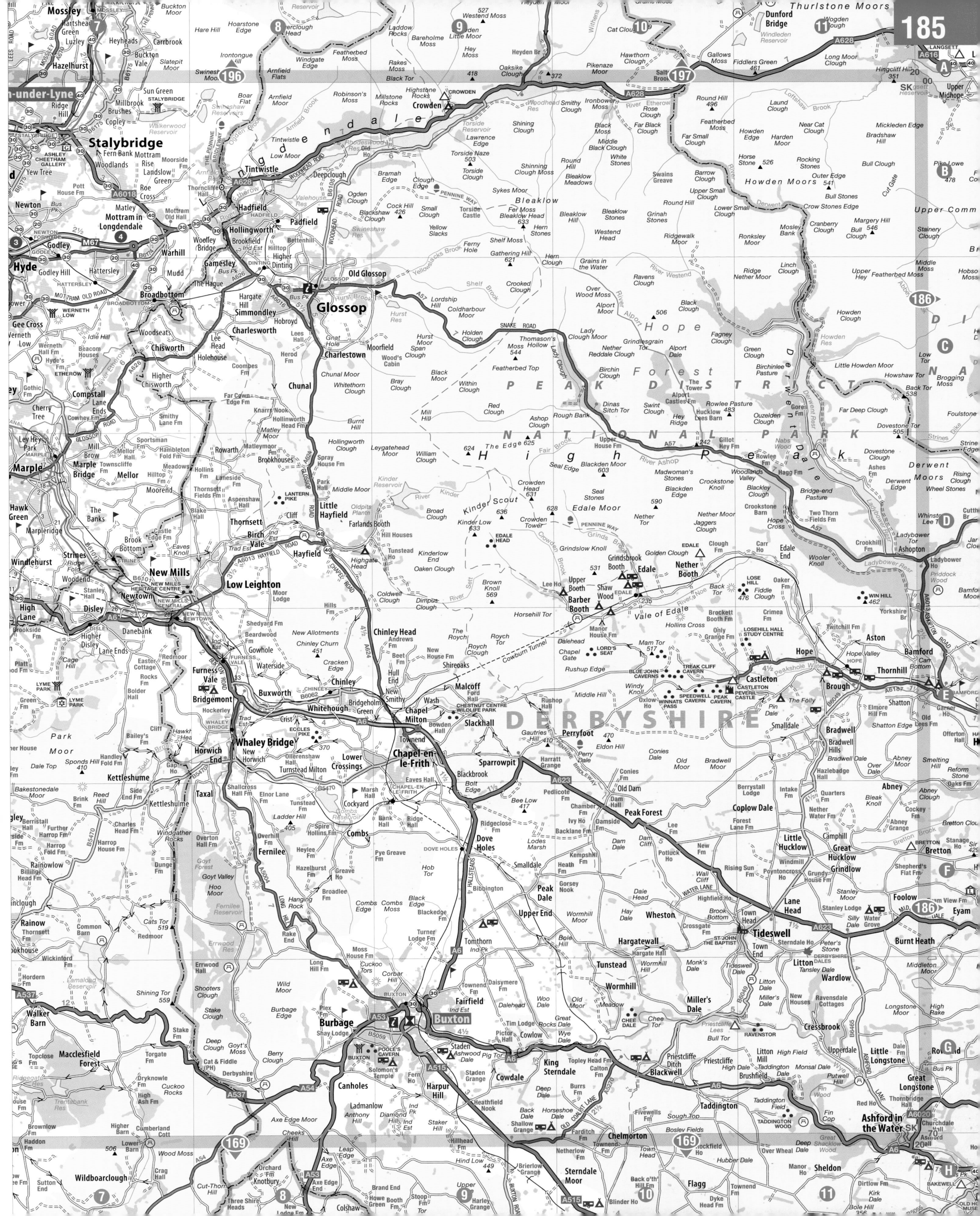

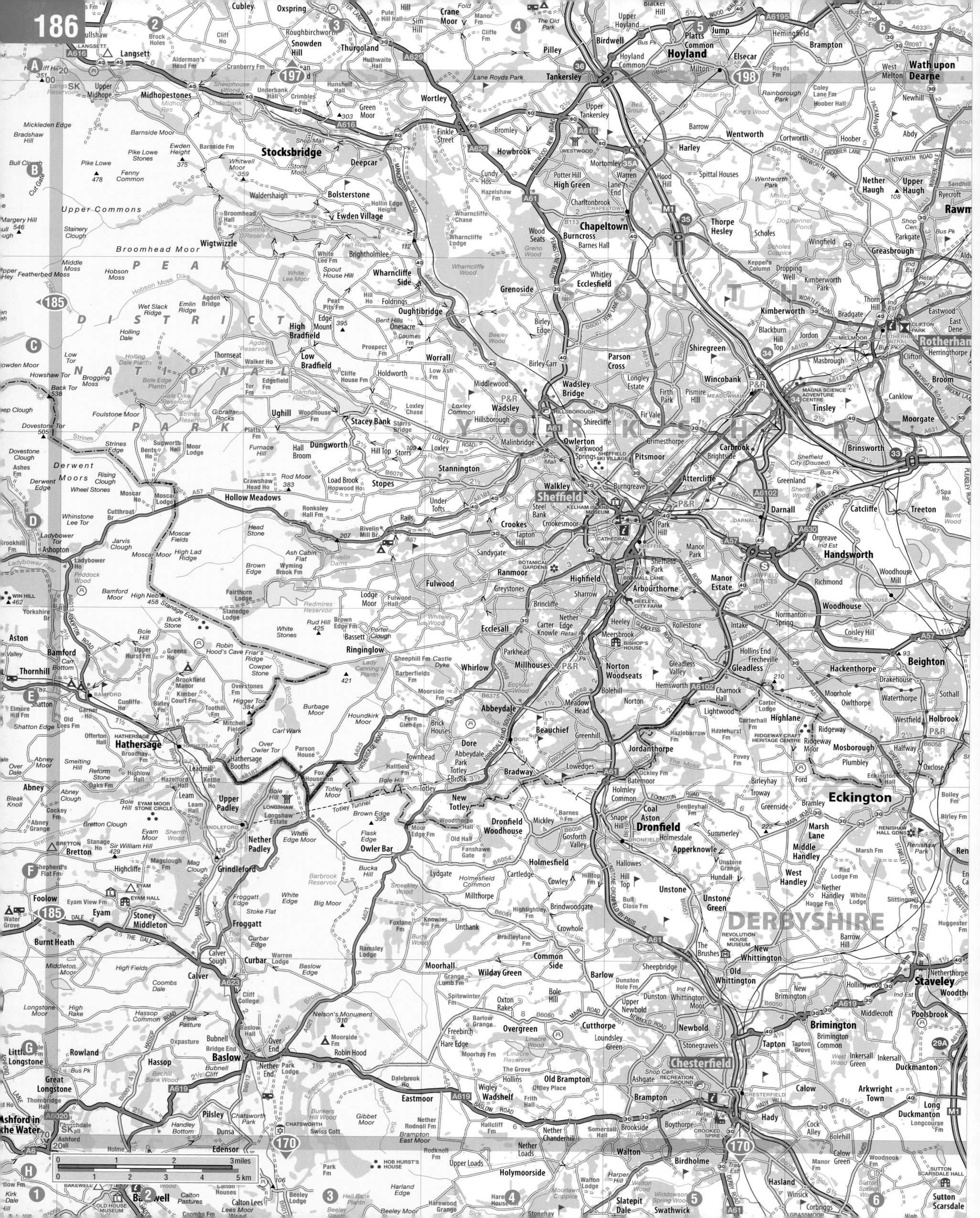

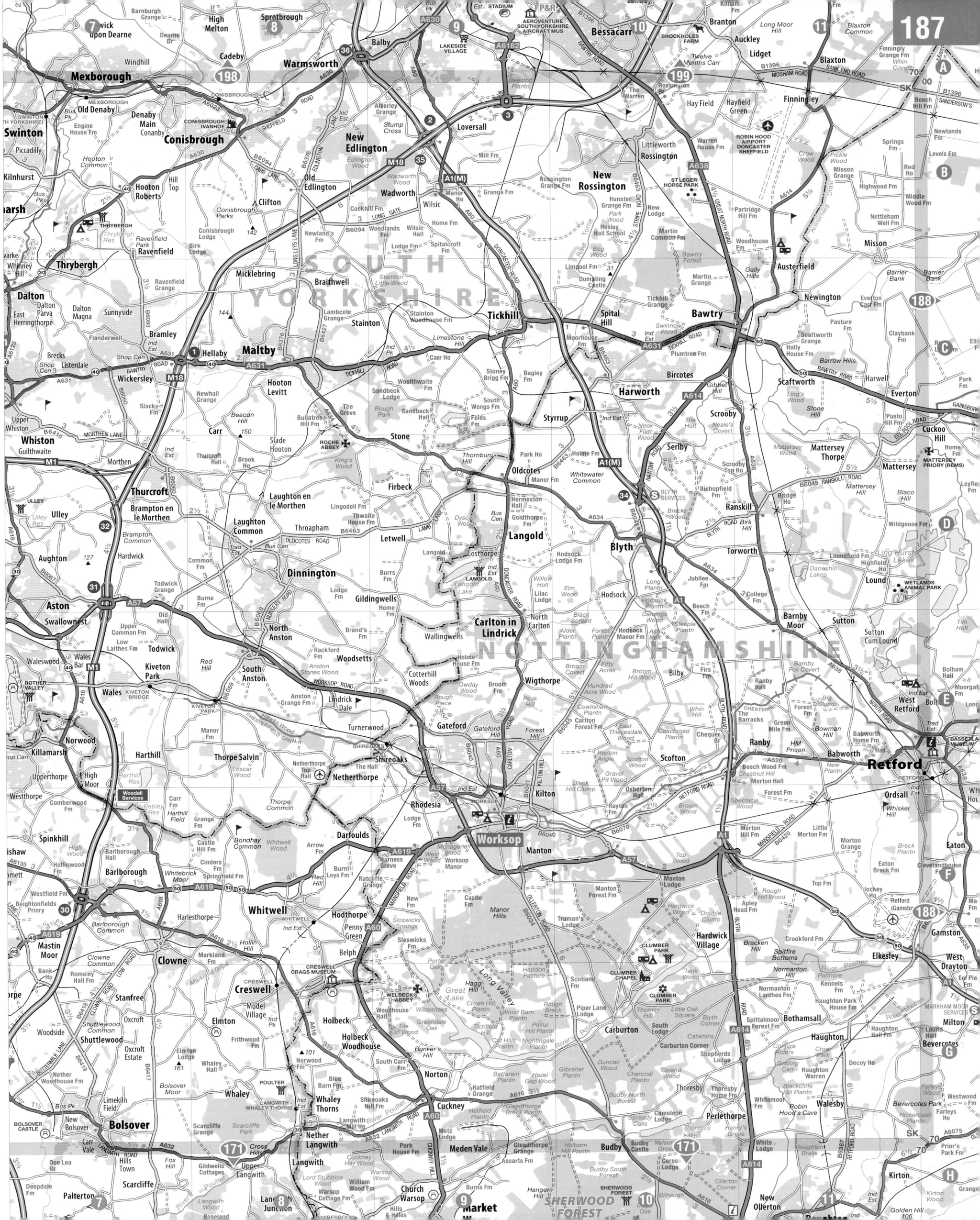

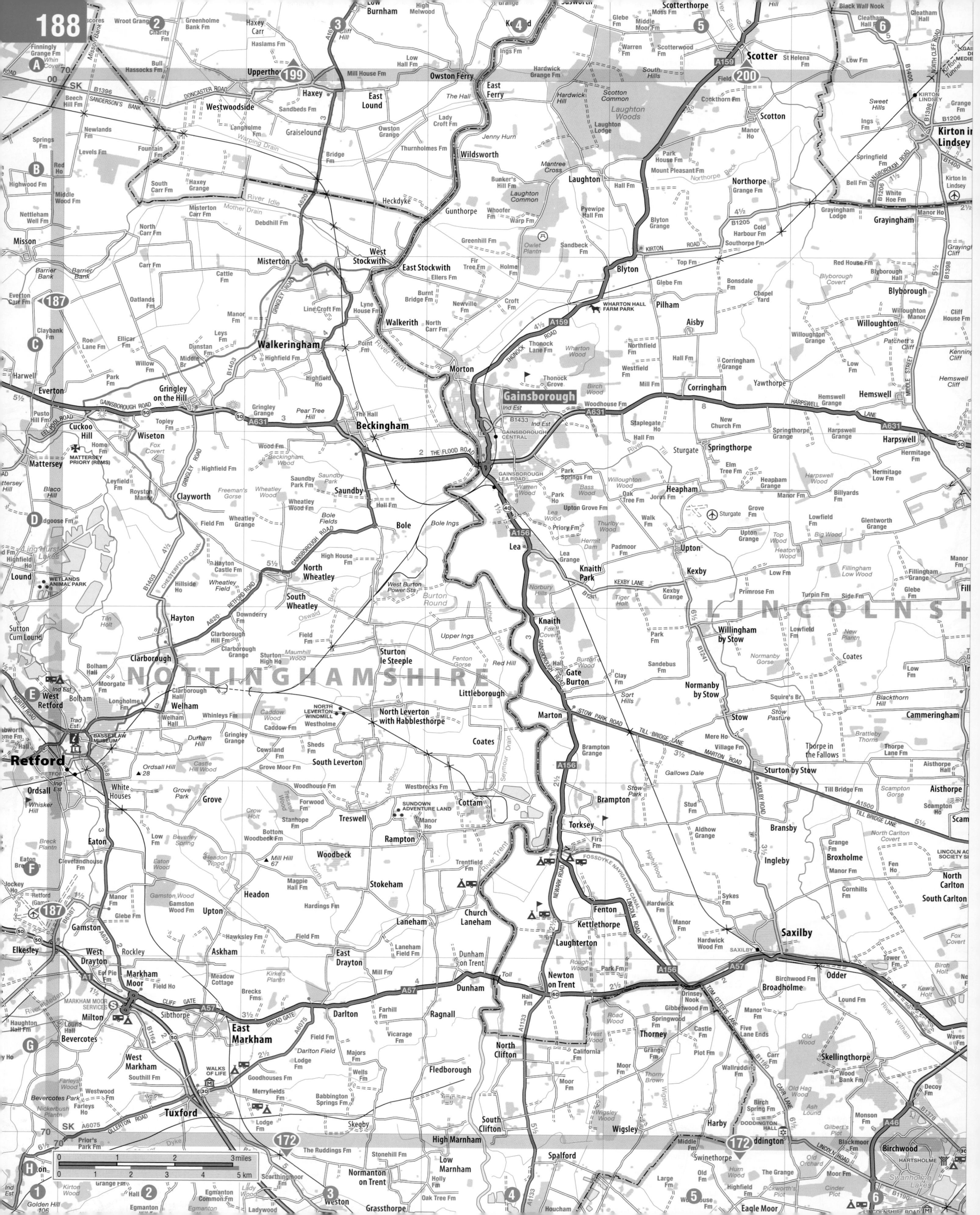

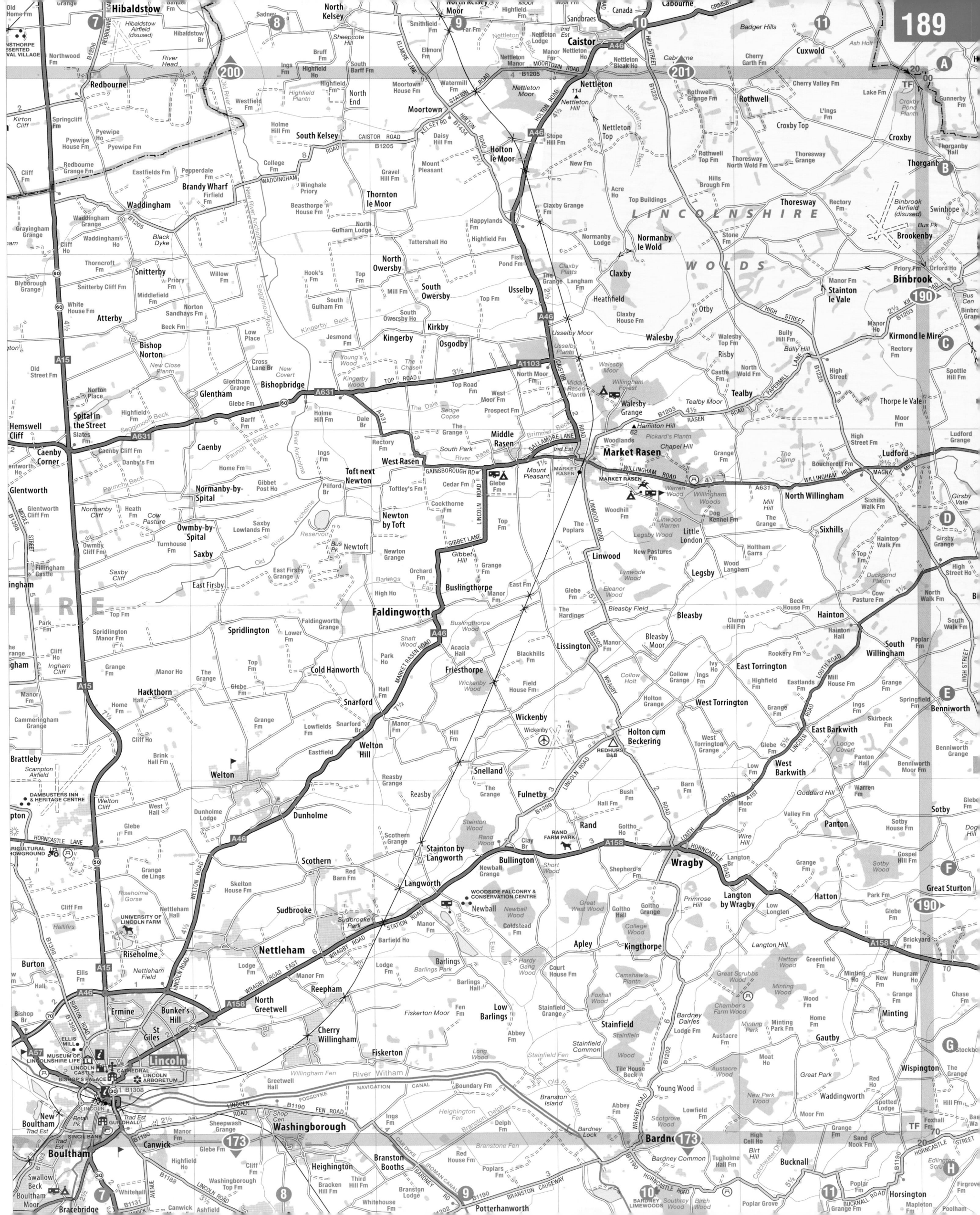

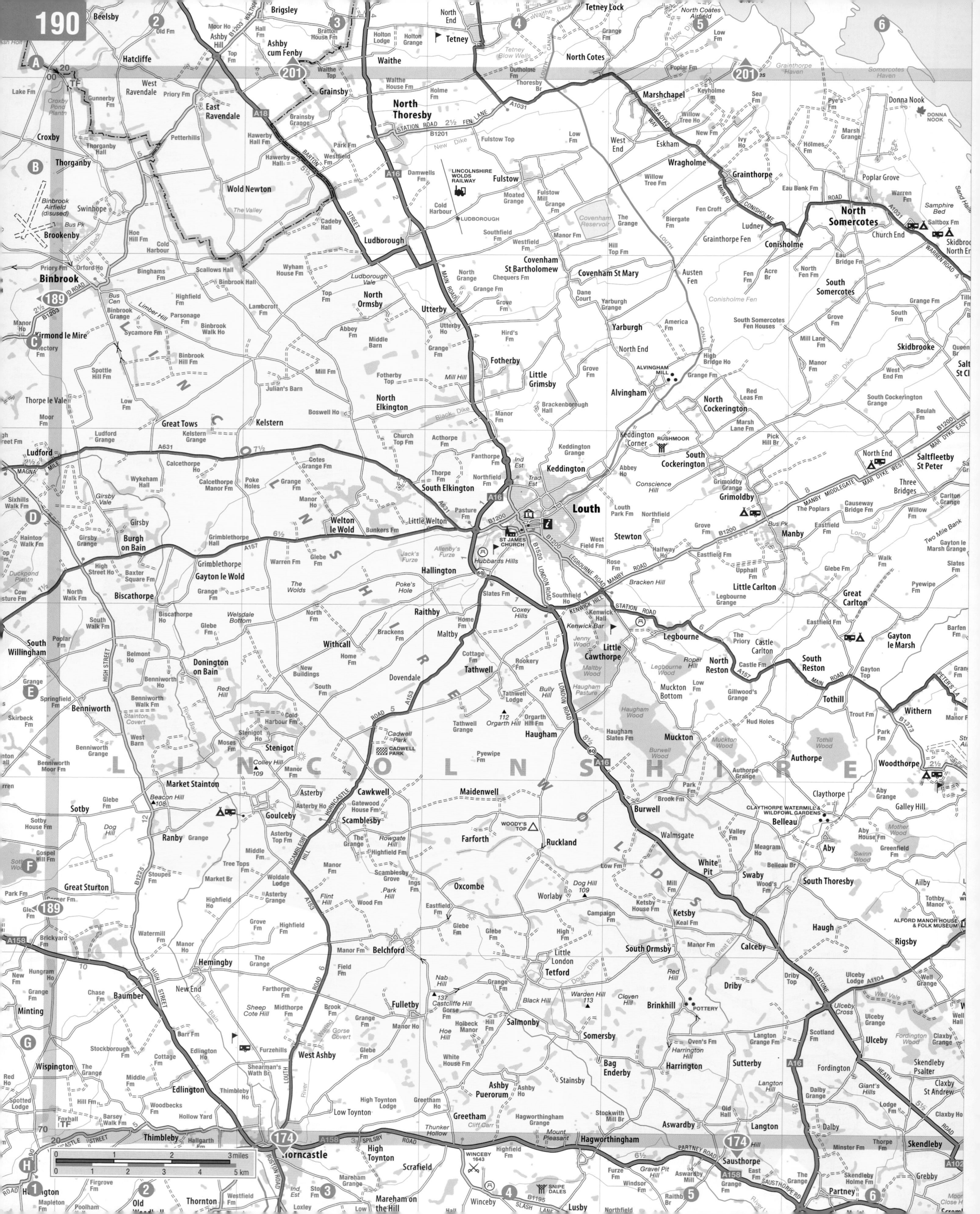

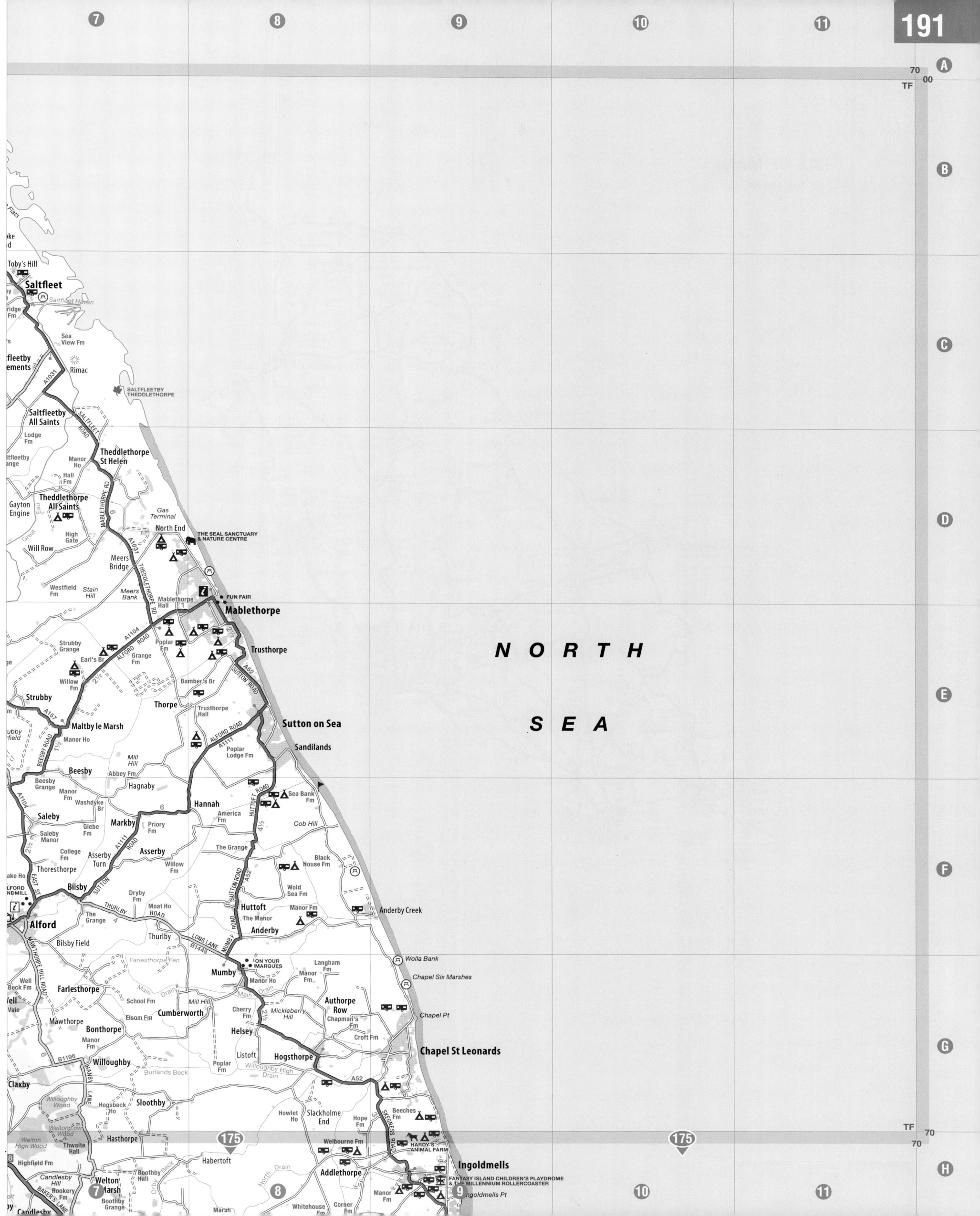

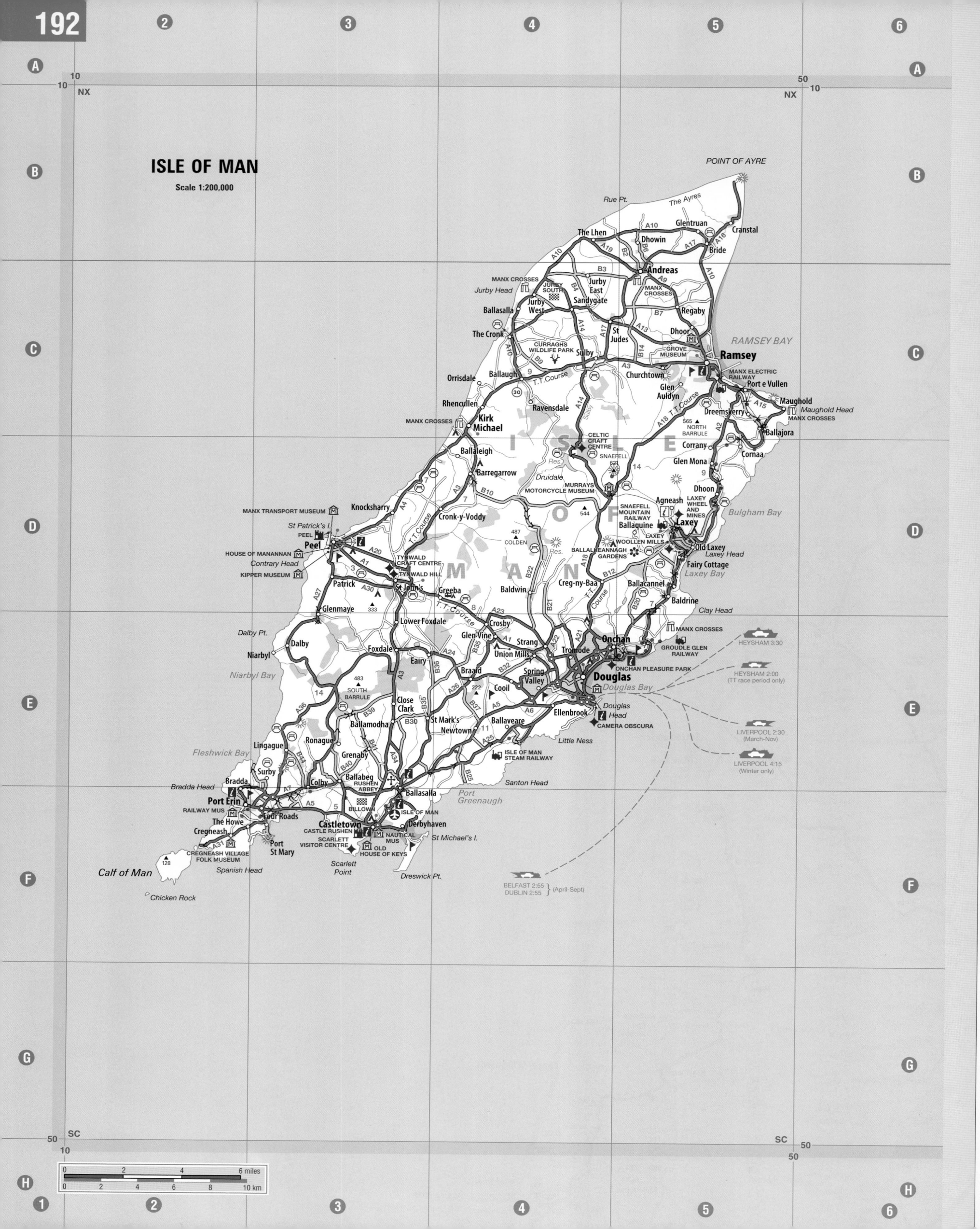

ISLE OF MAN

Scale 1:200,000

POINT OF AYRE

Rue Pt.
The Ayres

RAMSEY BAY

MANX CROSSES
Jurby Head

The Lhen
Dhowin
Glentruan
Cranstal
Bride

Andreas
Jurby
South
Jurby
East
Sandygate
Jurby
West
Ballasalla
Regaby
The Cronk
St Judes
Dhoor
CURRAGHS
WILDLIFE PARK
Sulby
GROVE
MUSEUM
Ramsey
MANX ELECTRIC
RAILWAY
Orrisdale
Ballaugh
Churchtown
Port e Vullen
Maughold
T.T. Course
Glen
Auldyn
Dreemskerry
Maughold Head
MANX CROSSES
Rhencullen
Ravensdale
NORTH
BARRULE
Ballajora
MANX CROSSES
Kirk
Michael
CELTIC
CRAFT
CENTRE
Corrany
Cornaa
Ballaleigh
SNAEFELL
Glen Mona
Barregarrow
Druidale
MURRAYS
MOTORCYCLE MUSEUM
Dhoon
SNAEFELL
MOUNTAIN
RAILWAY
Agneash
Knocksharry
Cronk-y-Voddy
BALLALHEANNAGH
GARDENS
Ballaquine
LAXEY
WHEEL
AND
MINES
MANX TRANSPORT MUSEUM
COLDEN
Laxey
St Patrick's I.
PEEL
LAXEY
WOOLLEN MILLS
Old Laxey
Laxey Head
Peel
HOUSE OF MANANNAN
Baldwin
Creg-ny-Baa
Ballacannel
Fairy Cottage
Laxey Bay
Contrary Head
TYNWALD
CRAFT CENTRE
KIPPER MUSEUM
Greeba
Baldrine
Clay Head
Patrick
TYNWALD HILL
St John's
Glenmaye
Lower Foxdale
Crosby
MANX CROSSES
Dalby Pt.
Glen Vine
Strang
Onchan
GROUDLE GLEN
RAILWAY
HEYSHAM 3:30
Niarbyl
Dalby
Foxdale
Union Mills
Tromode
HEYSHAM 2:00
(TT race period only)
Niarbyl Bay
Eairy
Braaid
Spring
Valley
Douglas
Douglas Bay
SOUTH
BARRULE
Close
Clark
Cooil
Douglas
Head
LIVERPOOL 2:30
(March-Nov)
Lingague
Ballamodha
St Mark's
Newtown
Ballaveare
Ellenbrook
CAMERA OBSCURA
LIVERPOOL 4:15
(Winter only)
Fleshwick Bay
Ronague
Grenaby
Little Ness
ISLE OF MAN
STEAM RAILWAY
Surby
Colby
Ballabeg
RUSHEN
ABBEY
Ballasalla
Port
Greenaugh
Santon Head
Bradda
Bradda Head
BILLOWN
ISLE OF MAN
Port Erin
RAILWAY MUS
Four Roads
Castletown
CASTLE RUSHEN
Derbyhaven
The Howe
Cregneash
SCARLETT
VISITOR CENTRE
NAUTICAL
MUS
St Michael's I.
CREGNEASH VILLAGE
FOLK MUSEUM
Port
St Mary
OLD
HOUSE OF KEYS
Calf of Man
Spanish Head
Scarlett
Point
Dreswick Pt.
BELFAST 2:55
DUBLIN 2:55
(April-Sept)
Chicken Rock

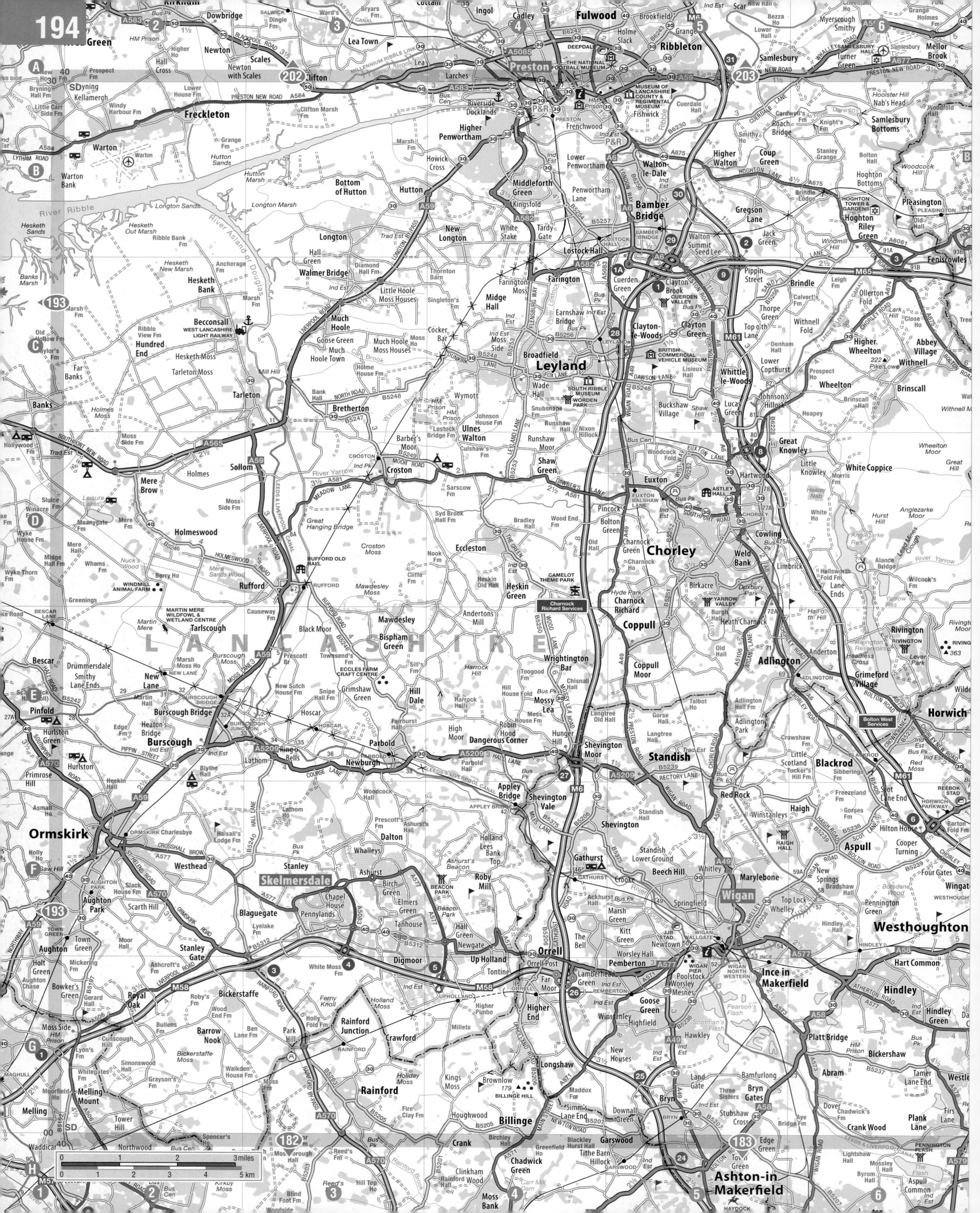

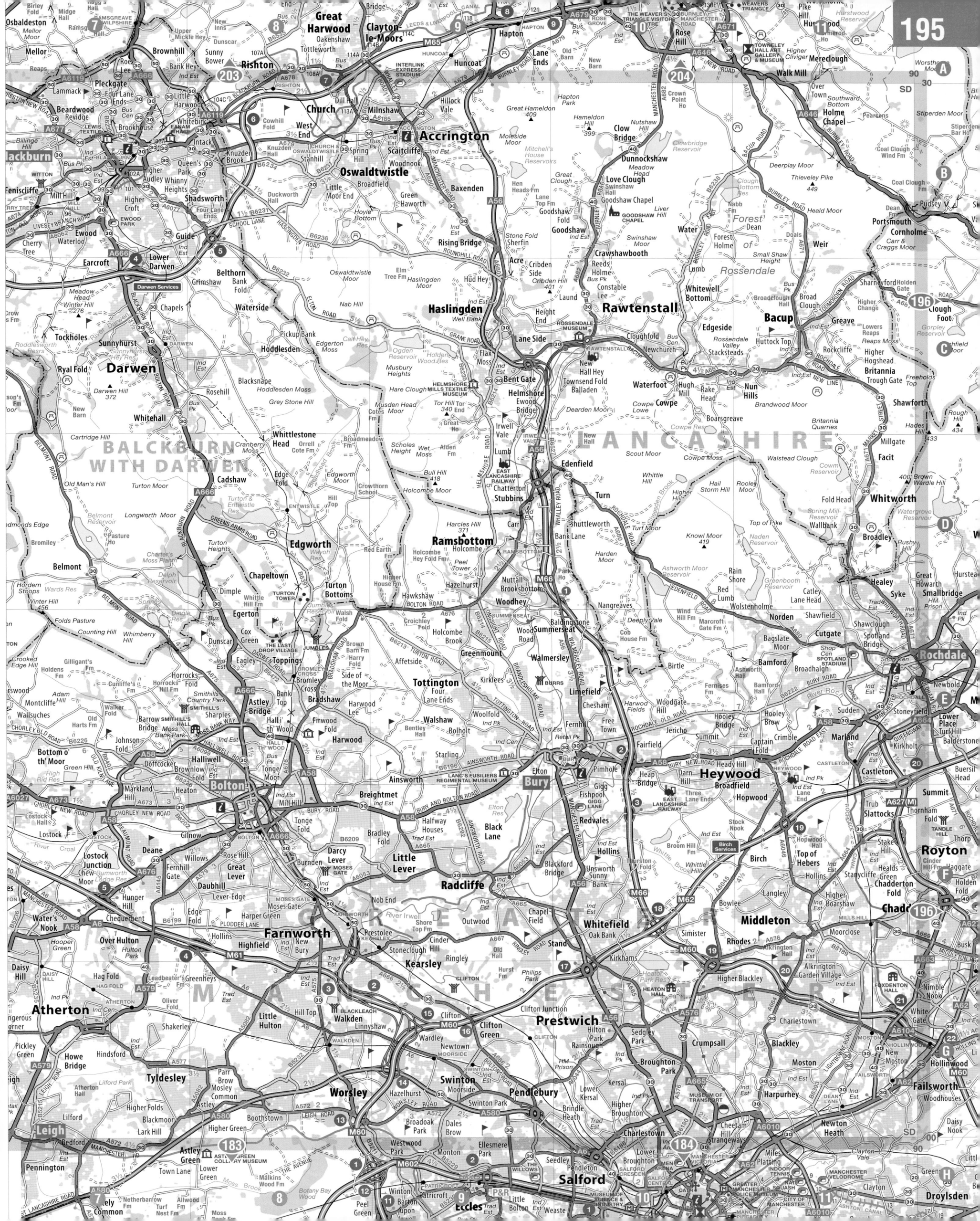

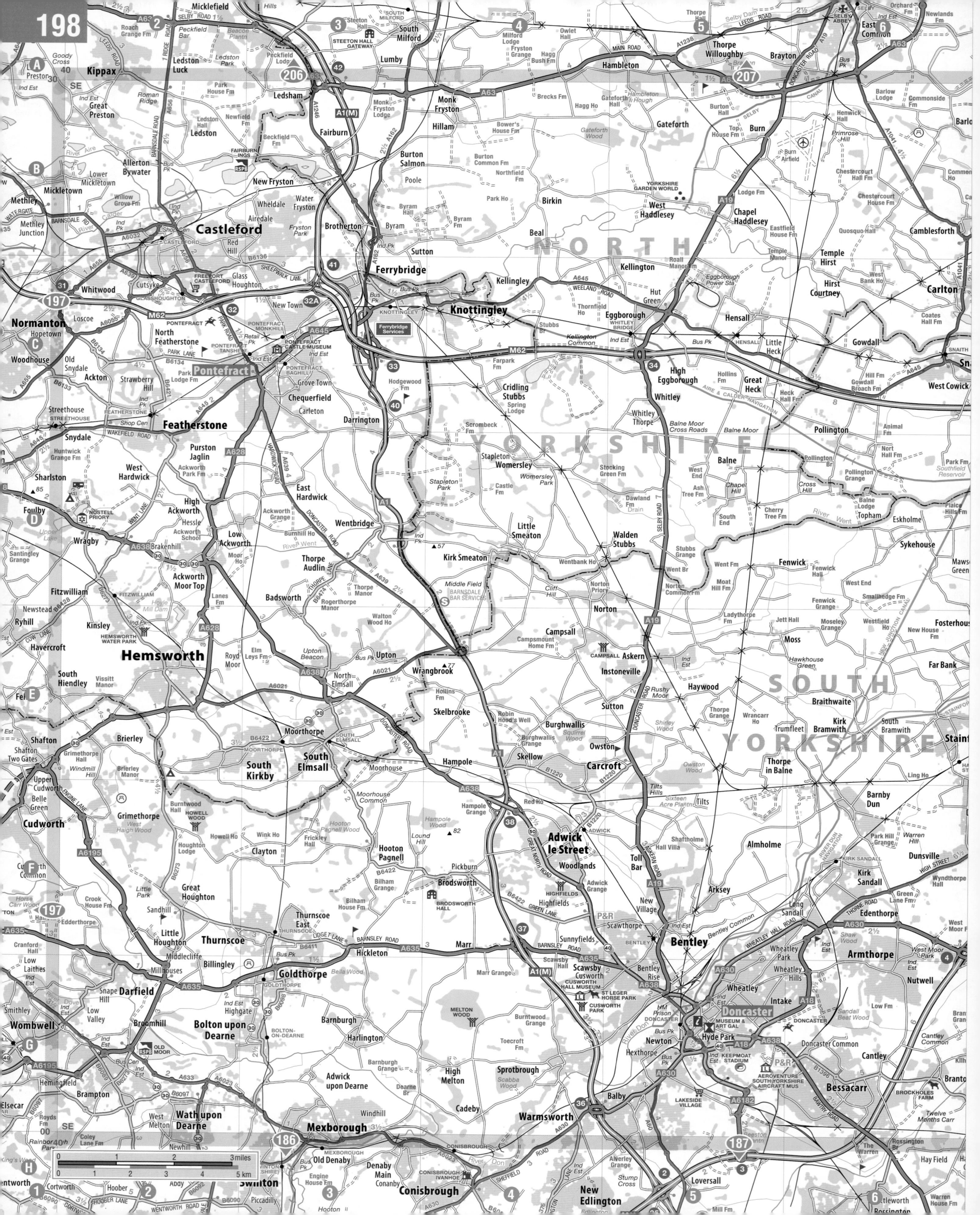

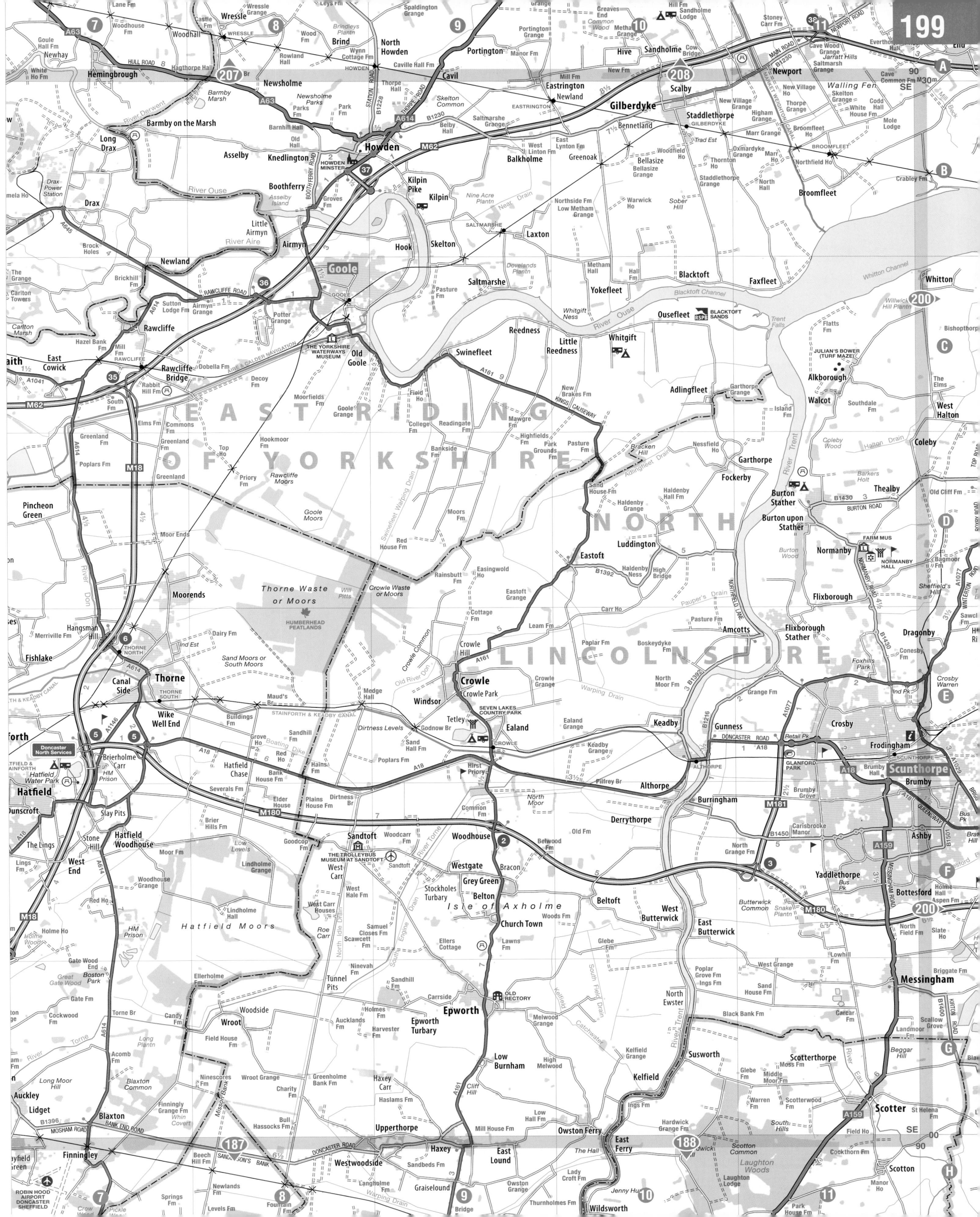

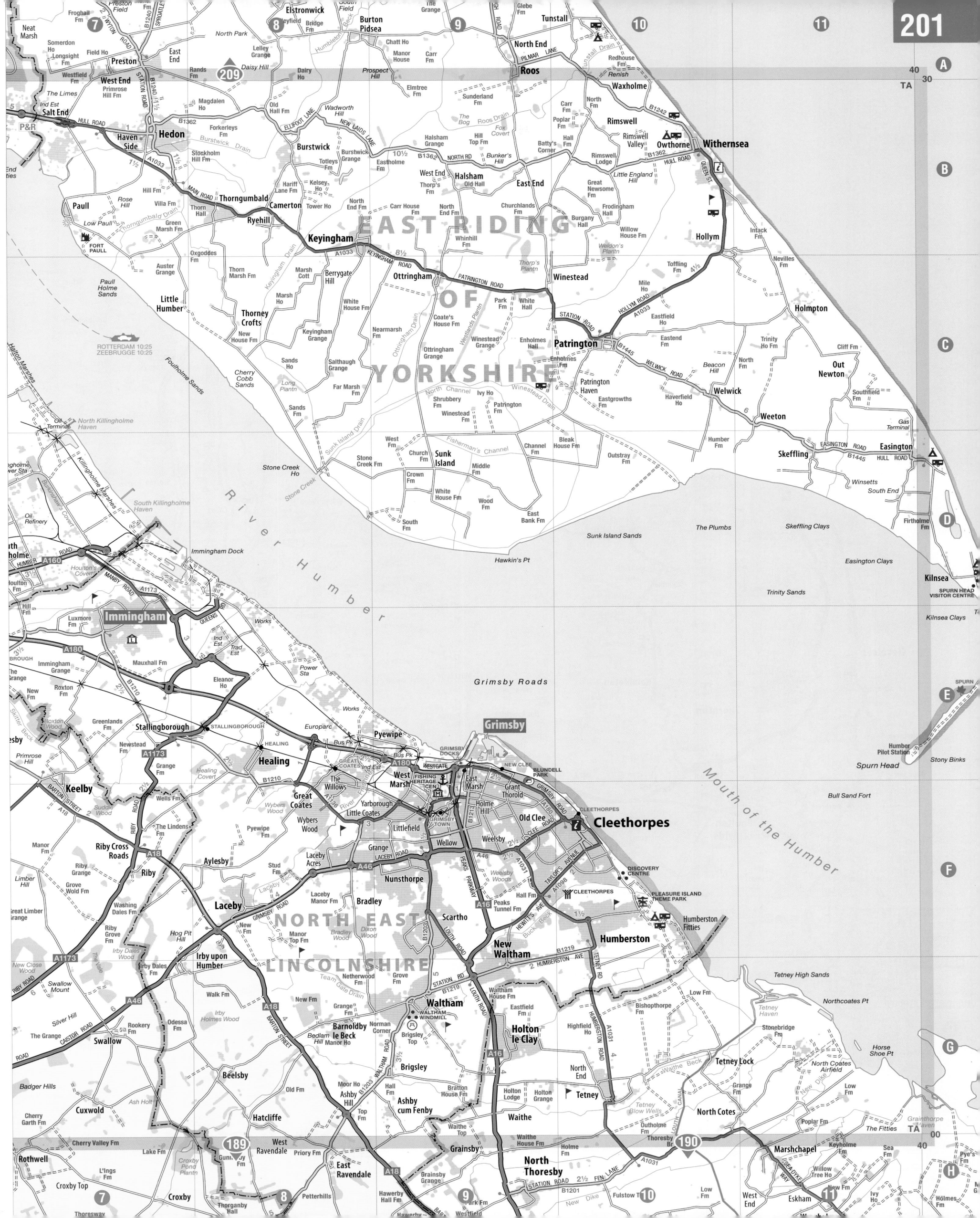

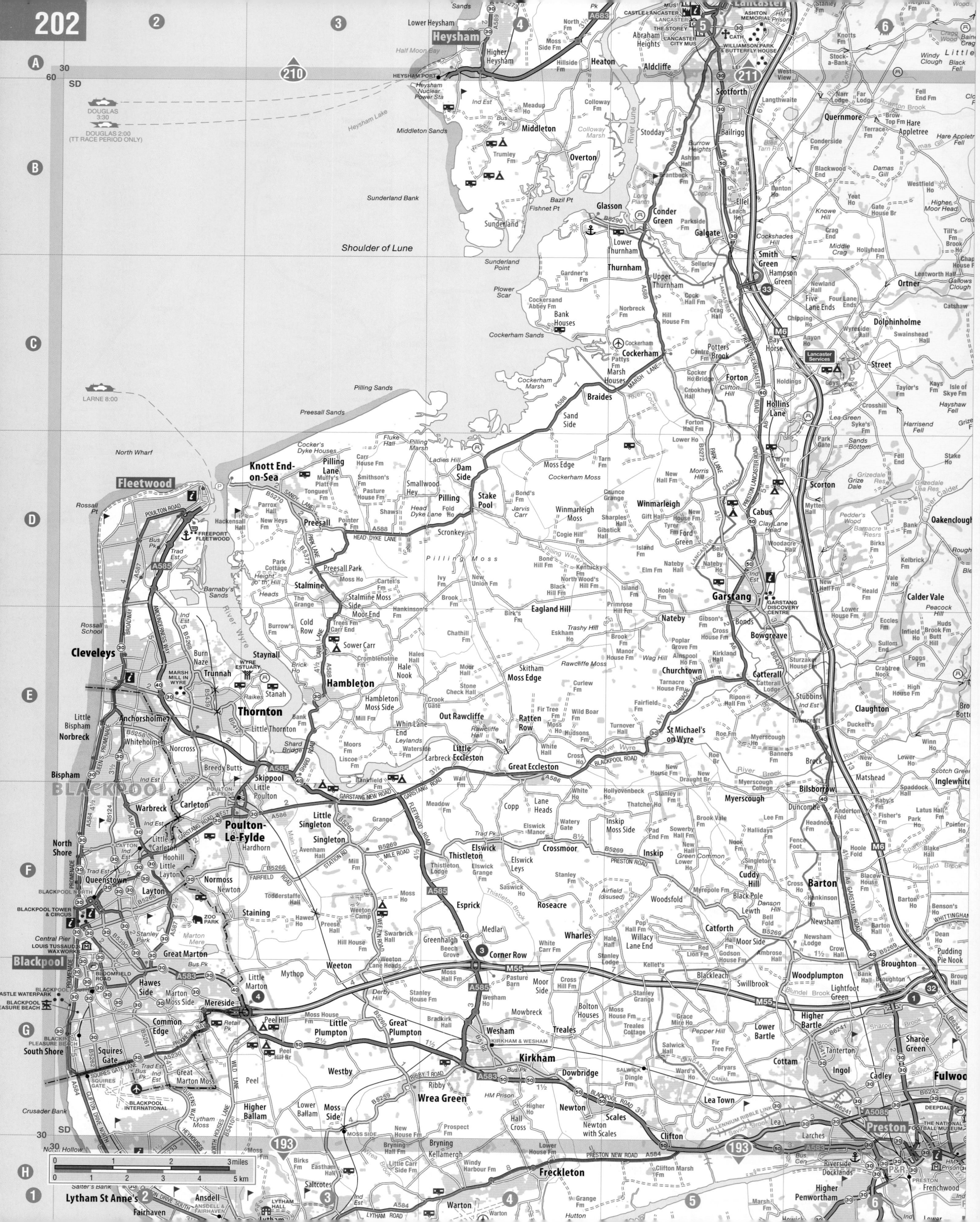

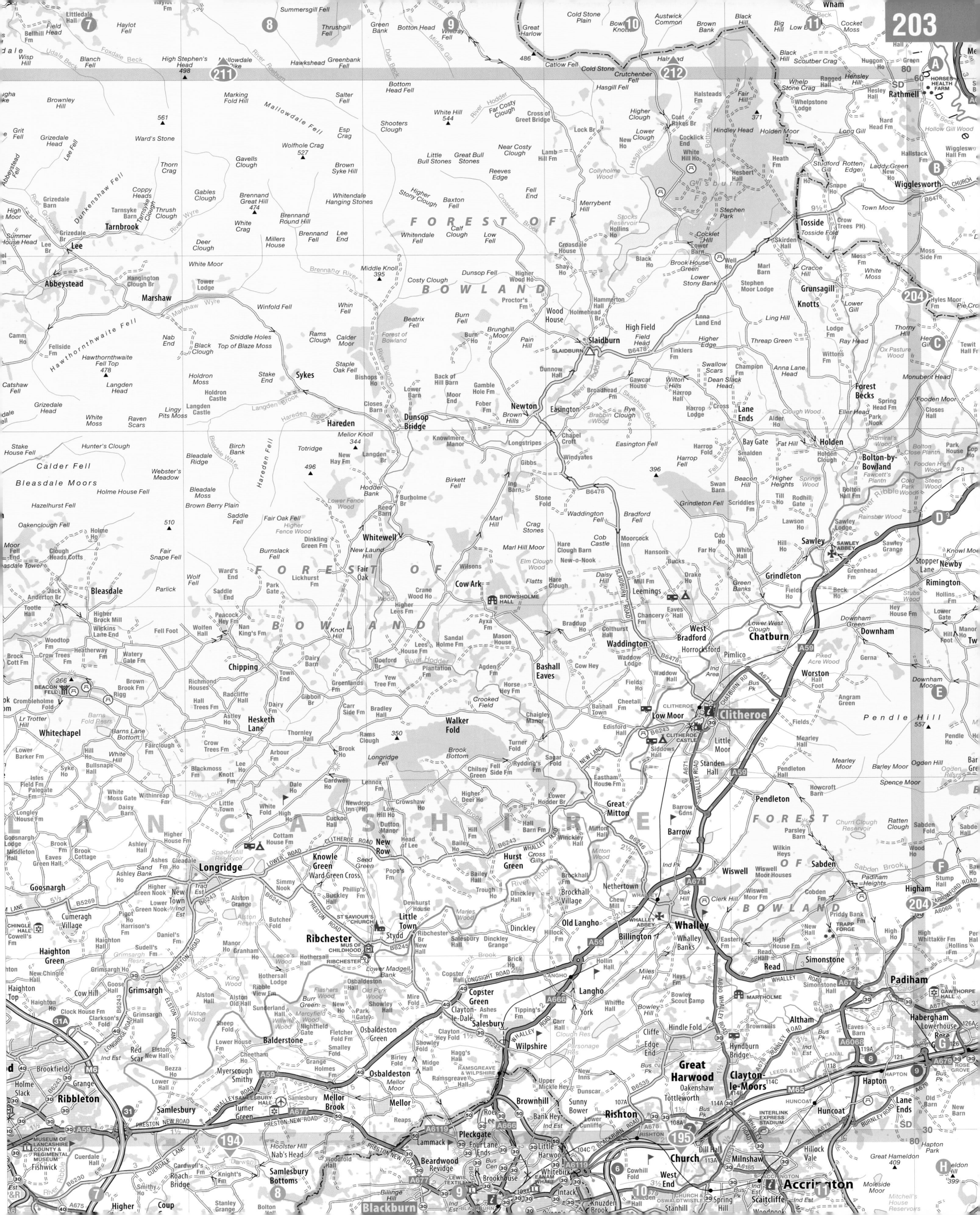

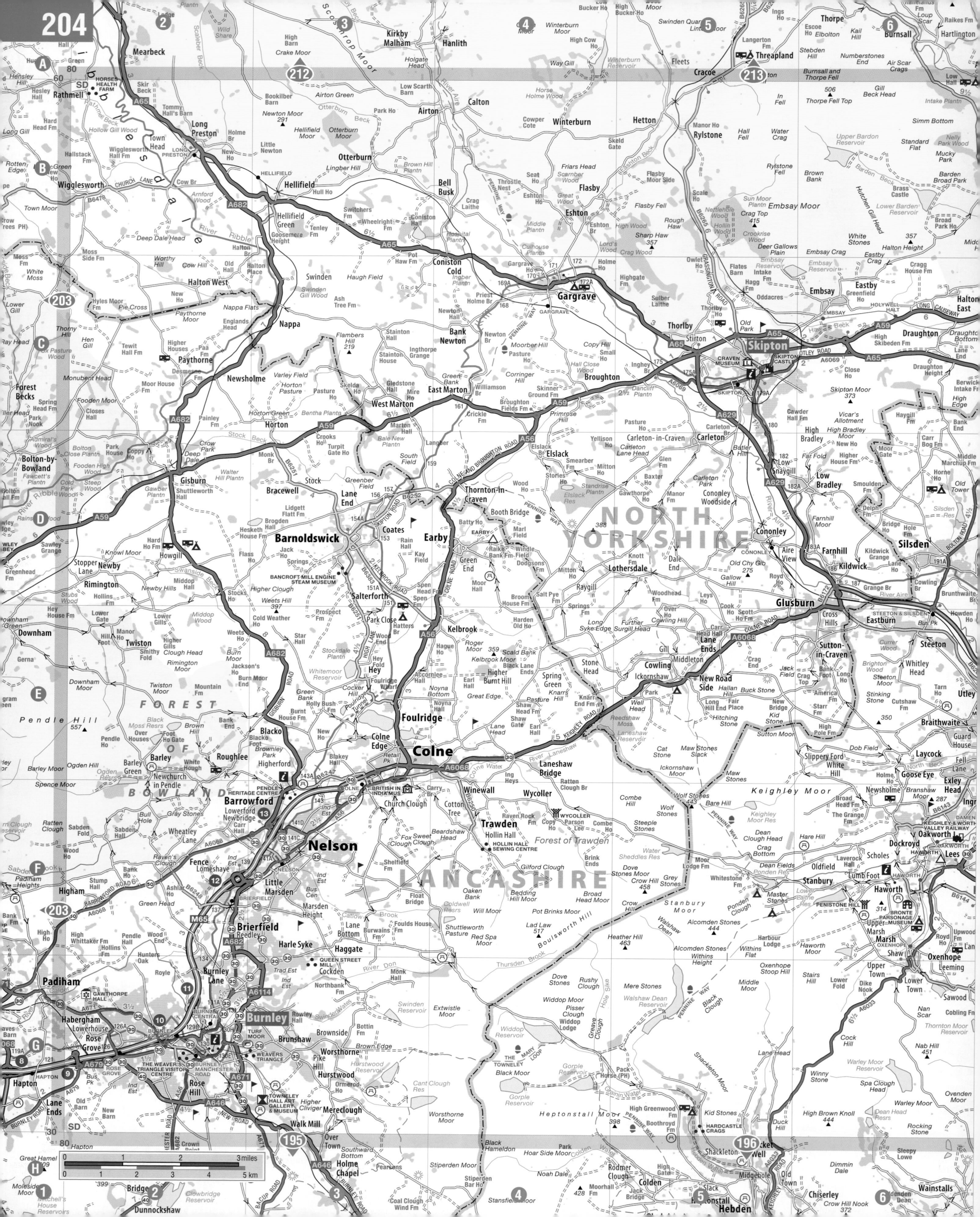

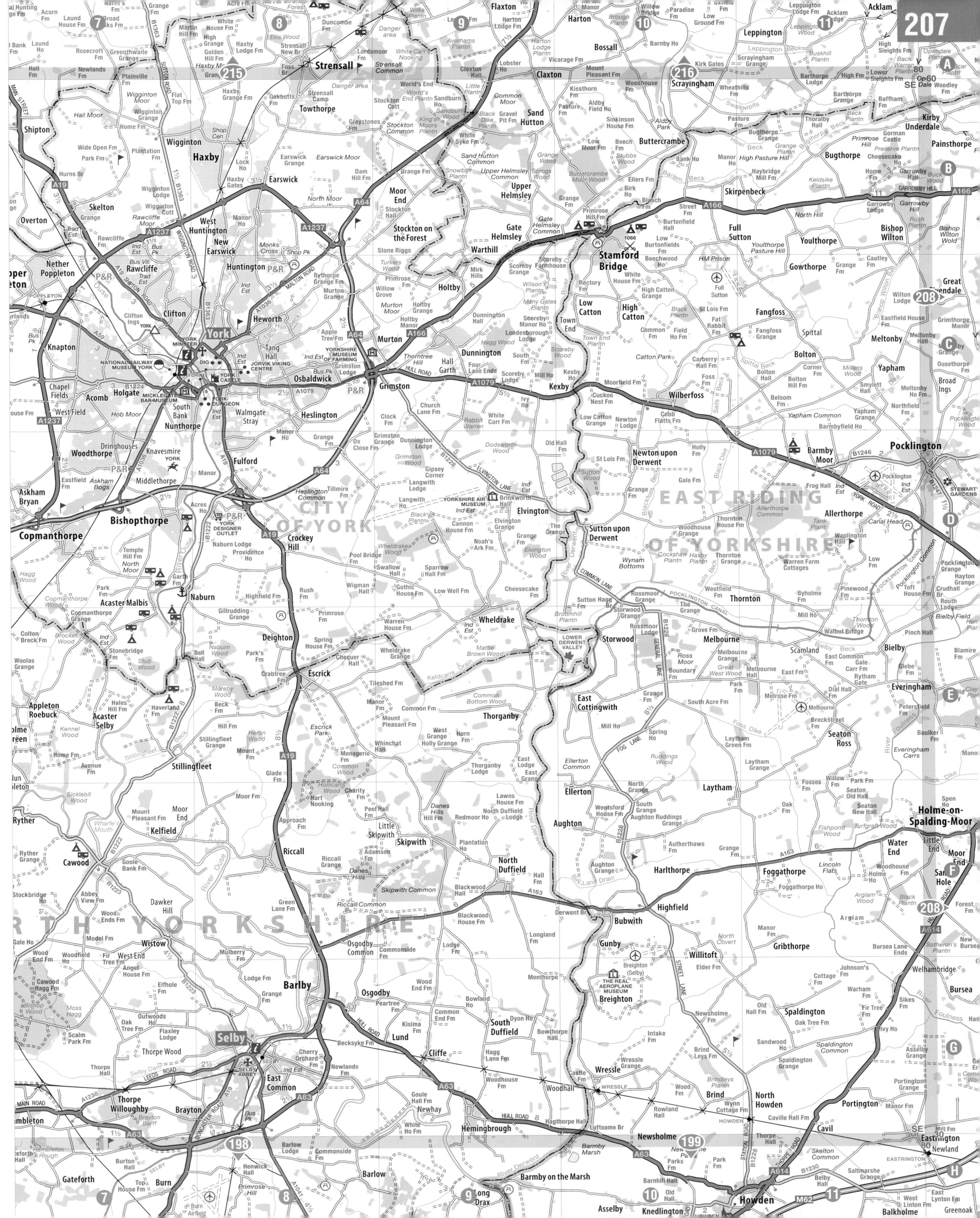

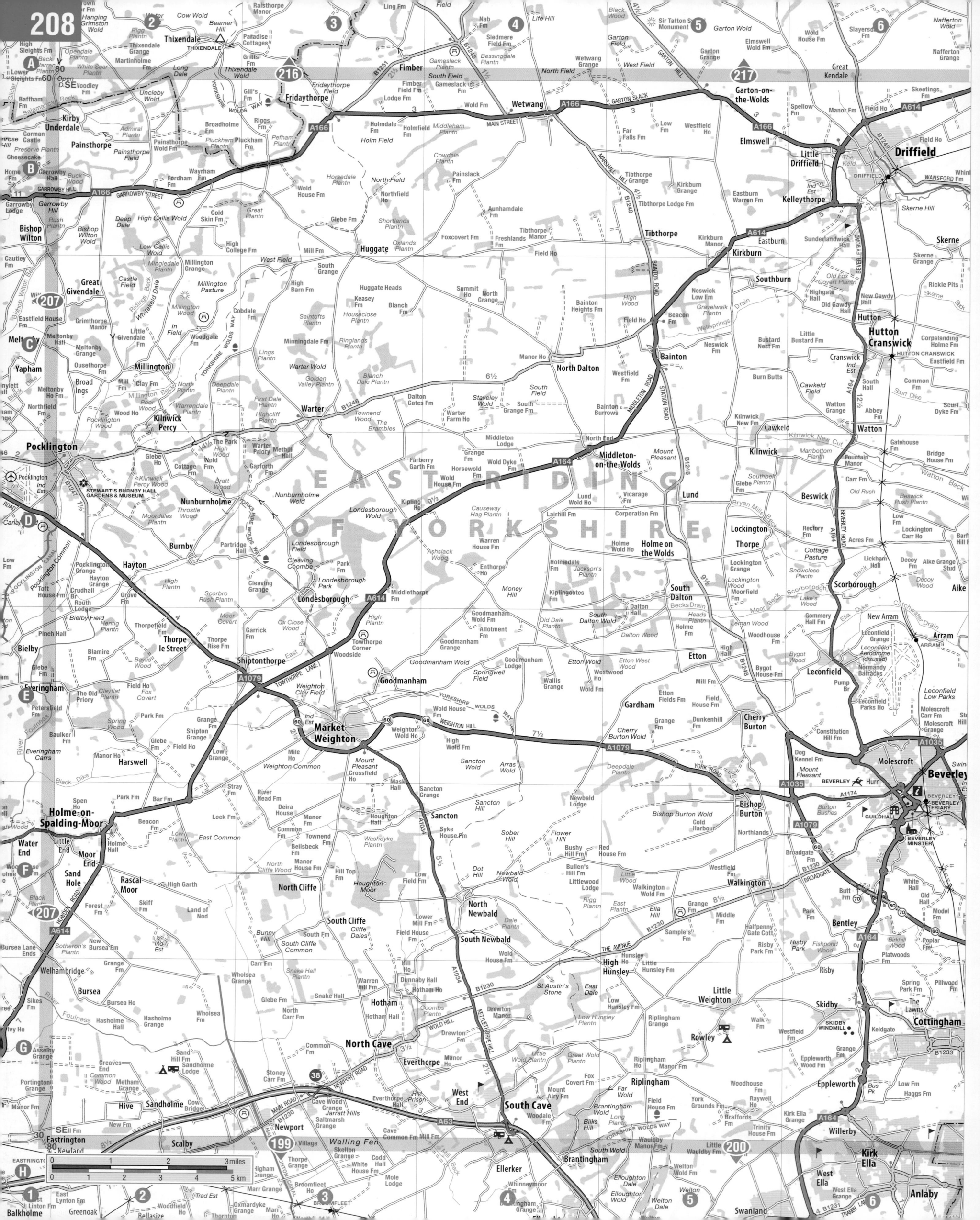

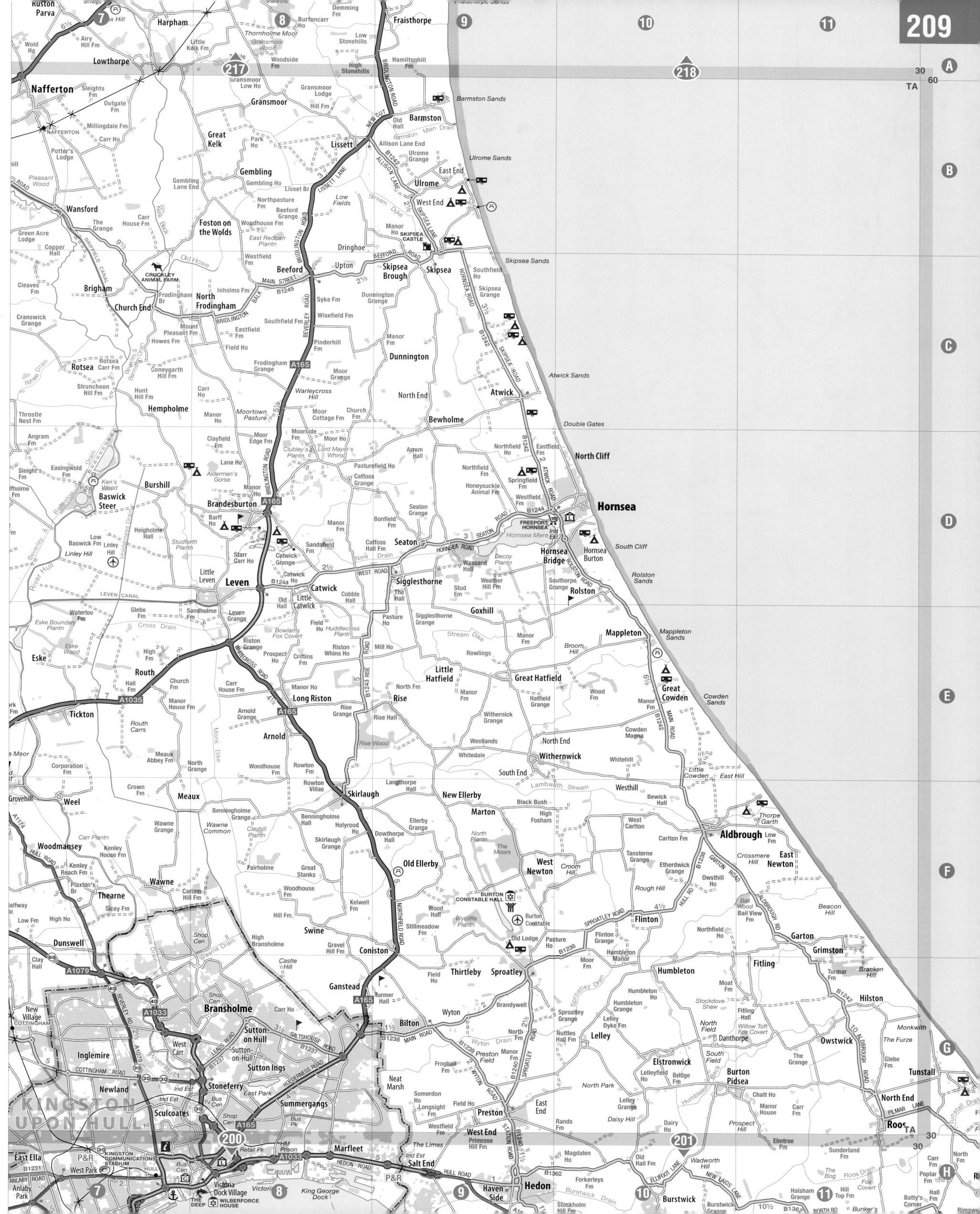

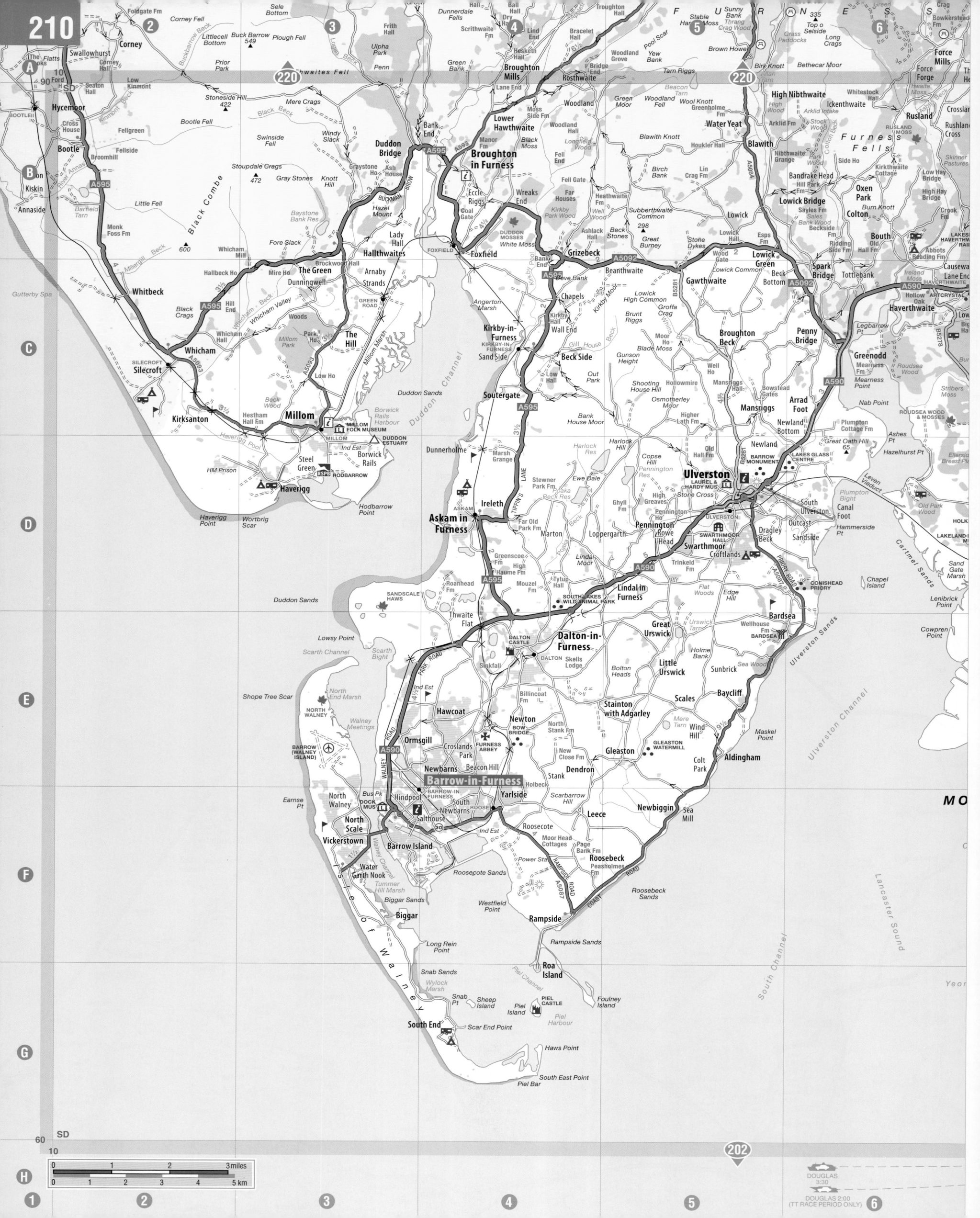

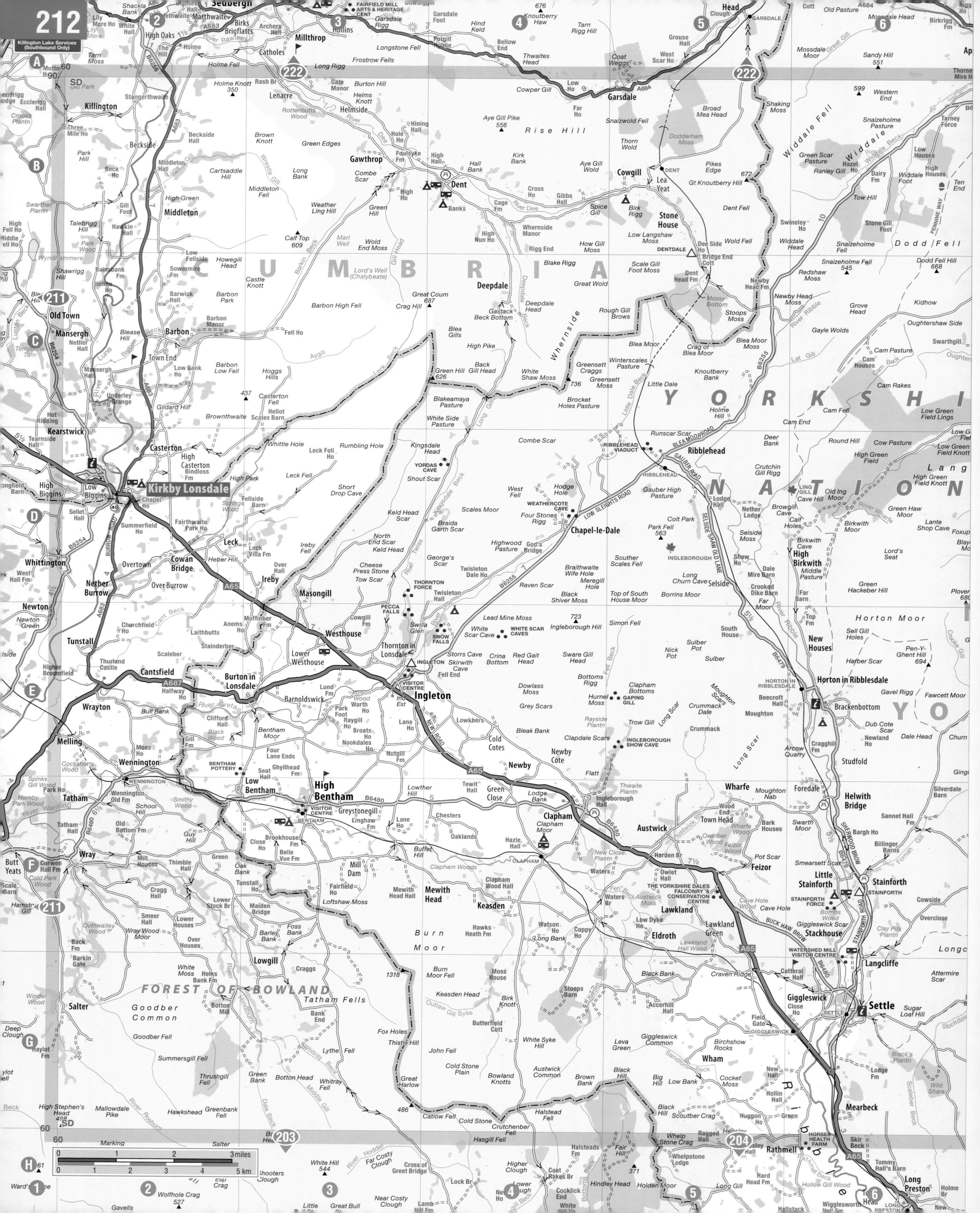

CUMBRIA

YORKSHIRE

NATIONAL

FOREST OF BOWLAND

Sedbergh · Millthrop · Catholes · Hollins · Lenacre · Helmside · Gawthrop · Dent · Cowgill · Stone House · Garsdale · Head · Garsdale

Killington · Middleton · Old Town · Mansergh · Barbon · Deepdale · Dentdale · Bridge End Cott · Widdale · Dodd Fell

Kearstwick · Casterton · Kirkby Lonsdale · Leck · Ireby · Masongill · Westhouse · Thornton in Lonsdale · Ingleton · Chapel-le-Dale · Ingleborough · Ribblehead · Ribblehead Viaduct · Selside

Whittington · Nether Burrow · Newton · Tunstall · Cantsfield · Burton in Lonsdale · Ingleborough Show Cave · Horton in Ribblesdale · New Houses · Brackenbottom

Melling · Wennington · Wrayton · Low Bentham · High Bentham · Newby · Clapham · Austwick · Wharfe · Helwith Bridge · Foredale

Tatham · Wray · Keasden · Lawkland · Eldroth · Feizor · Little Stainforth · Stainforth · Stackhouse

Butt Yeats · Salter · Lowgill · Wham · Giggleswick · Settle · Langcliffe · Mearbeck

Long Preston · Rathmell

Whernside · Rise Hill · Widdale Fell · Snaizeholme · Horton Moor · Pen-Y-Ghent Hill 694

Rise Hill · Great Coum 687 · Crag Hill · Green Hill 626 · Ingleborough Hill · Simon Fell

Scale 0 1 2 3 miles / 0 1 2 3 4 5 km

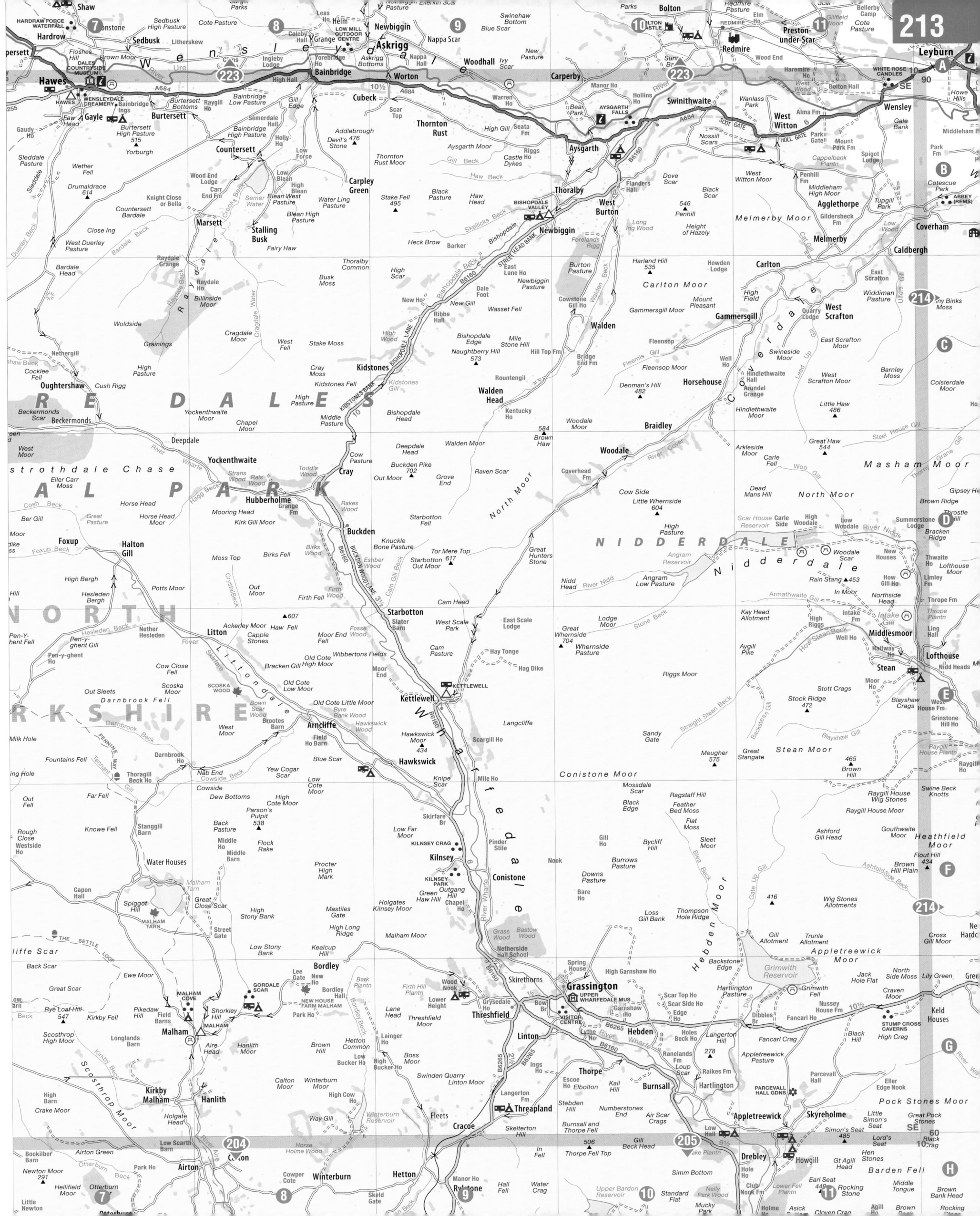

Leyburn · Wensley · Middleham · Spennithorne · Harmby · Constable Burton · Finghall · Patrick Brompton · Crakehall · Little Crakehall · Great Crakehall · Kirkbridge · Langthorne · Leeming Bar · Leeming · Aiskew · Bedale · Exelby · Firby · Burrill

Coverham · Caldbergh · East Witton · Jervaulx Abbey · Thornton Steward · Thornton Watlass · Thirn · Snape · Thornton Grange · Well · Theakston · Burneston · Carthorpe · Gatenby · Maunby

Colsterdale · Ellingstring · High Ellington · Low Ellington · Fearby · Healey · Masham · Low Burton · Theakston Brewery Visitor Centre · Uredale Glass · Swinton · Binsoe · West Tanfield · Nosterfield · Thornborough · Sutton Howgrave · Middleton Quernhow · Kirklington · Sinderby

Masham Moor · Leighton · Leighton Reservoir · Ilton · Warthermarske · Swinton Green · Marmion Tower · Sleningford Mill · North Stanley · Mickley · Wath · Melmerby

Middlesmoor · Lofthouse · Stean · Ramsgill · Gouthwaite Reservoir · Kirby Malzeard · Laverton · Galphay · Azerley · Winksley · Grewelthorpe · Dallow · Carlesmoor · Swetton · Greygarth · Lightwater Valley · North Lees · Sutton Grange · Nunwick · Hutton Conyers

Dallow Moor · Nidderdale · Heathfield Moor · Wath · Bouthwaite · Dacre · Fountains Abbey · Studley Royal · Grantley · Low Grantley · High Grantley · Aldfield · Risplith · Sawley · Eavestone · Galphay · Markenfield Hall · Bishopton · Ripon · Sharow · Copt Hewick · Bridge Hewick · Littlethorpe · Studley Roger

Ashfold Side · Pateley Bridge · Nidderdale Museum · Bewerley · Greenhow · Greenhow Hill · Wilsill · Glasshouses · Smelthouses · Low Laithe · Brimham Rocks · Summerbridge · Dacre Banks · New York · Bishop Thornton · Shaw Mills · Markington · Wormald Green · Burton Leonard · South Stainley · Copgrove · Bishop Monkton

Stump Cross Caverns · High Crag · Pock Stones Moor · Heyshaw Moor · Thornthwaite · Padside · Darley · Thruscross · Birstwith · Hampsthwaite · Clint · Burnt Yates · Bedlam · Bishop Thornton · Killinghall · Ripley · Ripley Castle · Scotton · Scriven · Brearton · Nidd

Wensleydale Railway · Wensley · River Ure · River Nidd · River Swale · River Skell · Fountains Earth Moor · Kirby Malzeard Moor · Pateley Moor

A684 · A6108 · A1 · A61 · A6055 · A6265 · A6108 · B6267 · B6268 · B6165 · B6451 · B6265

0 1 2 3 miles
0 1 2 3 4 5 km

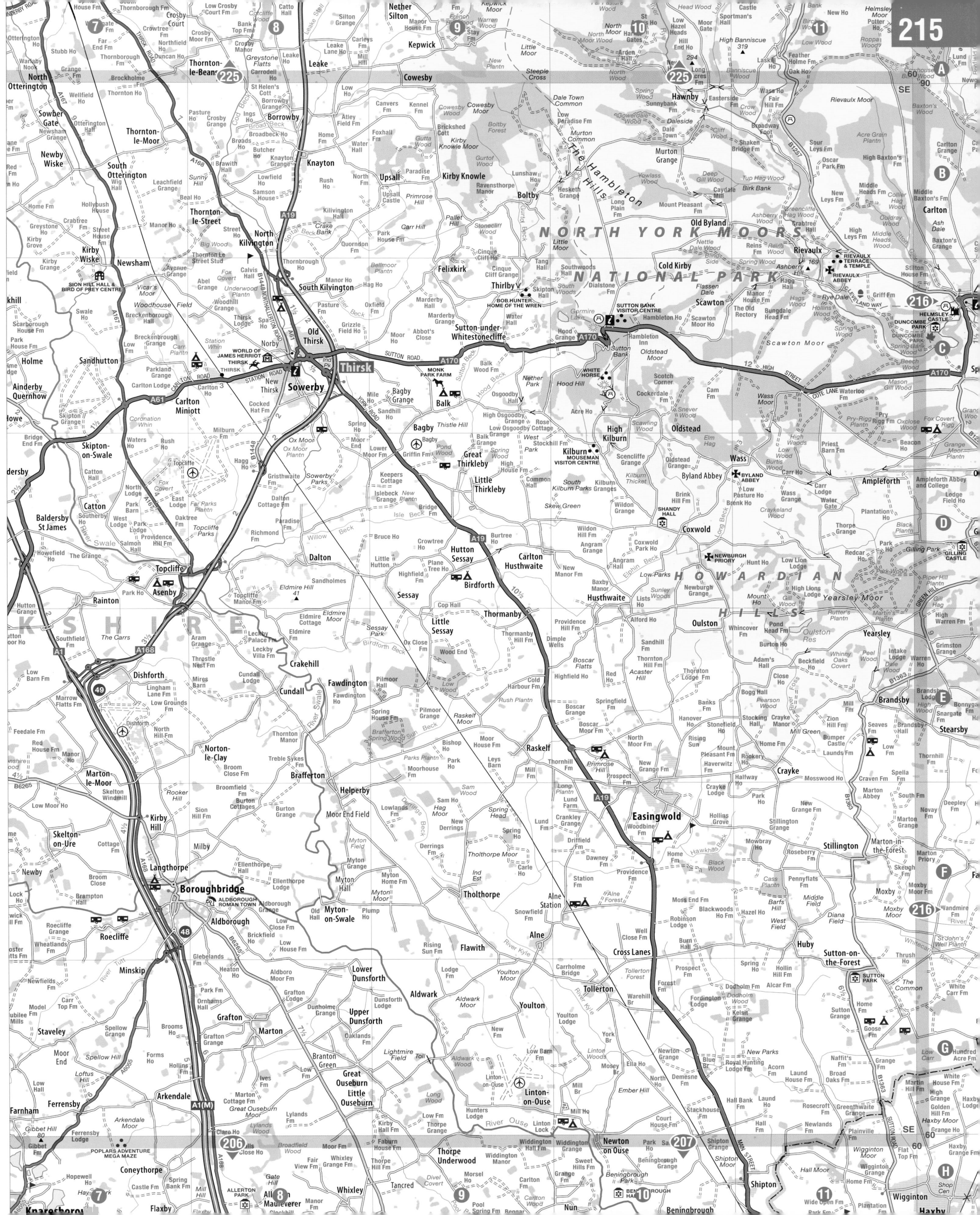

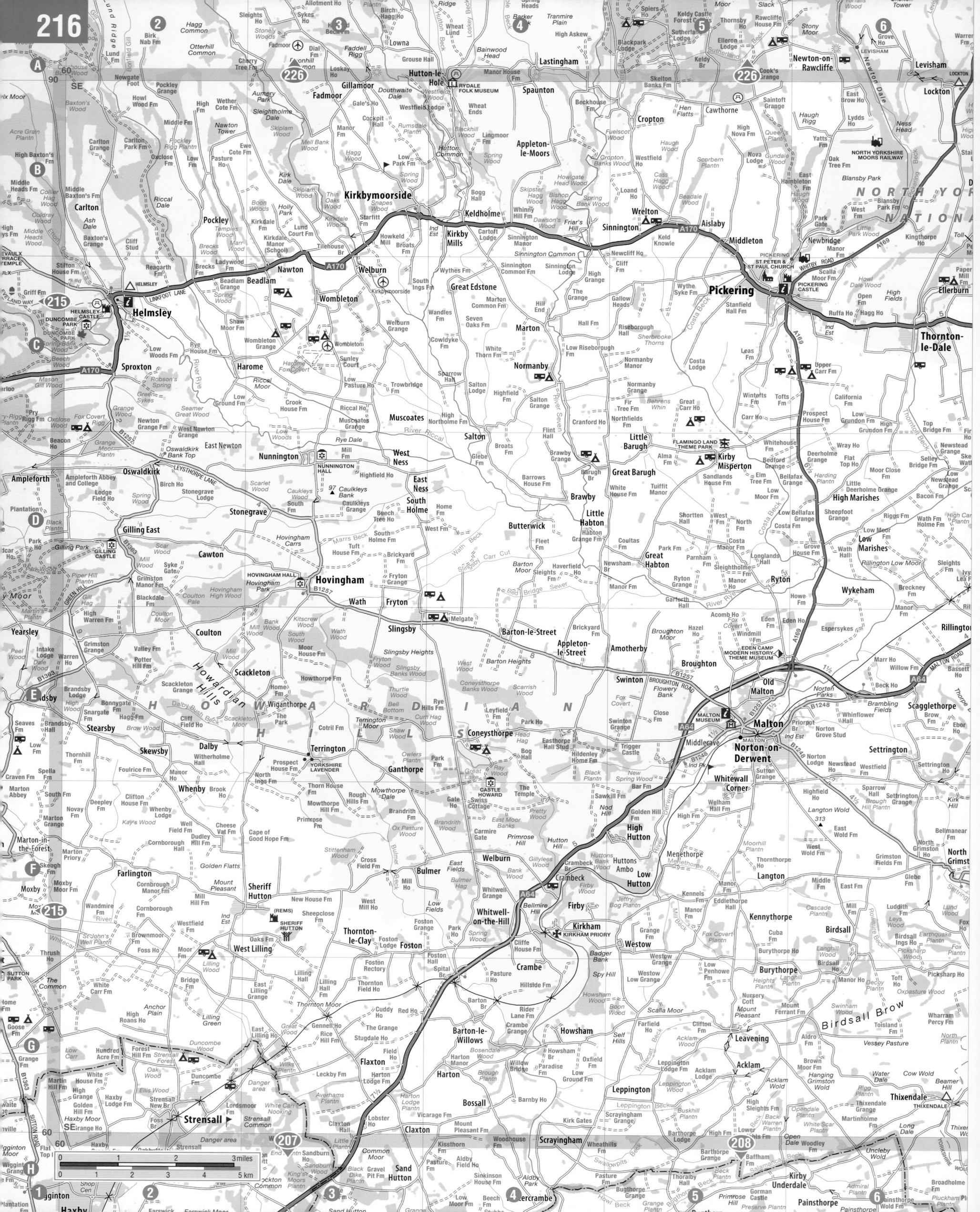

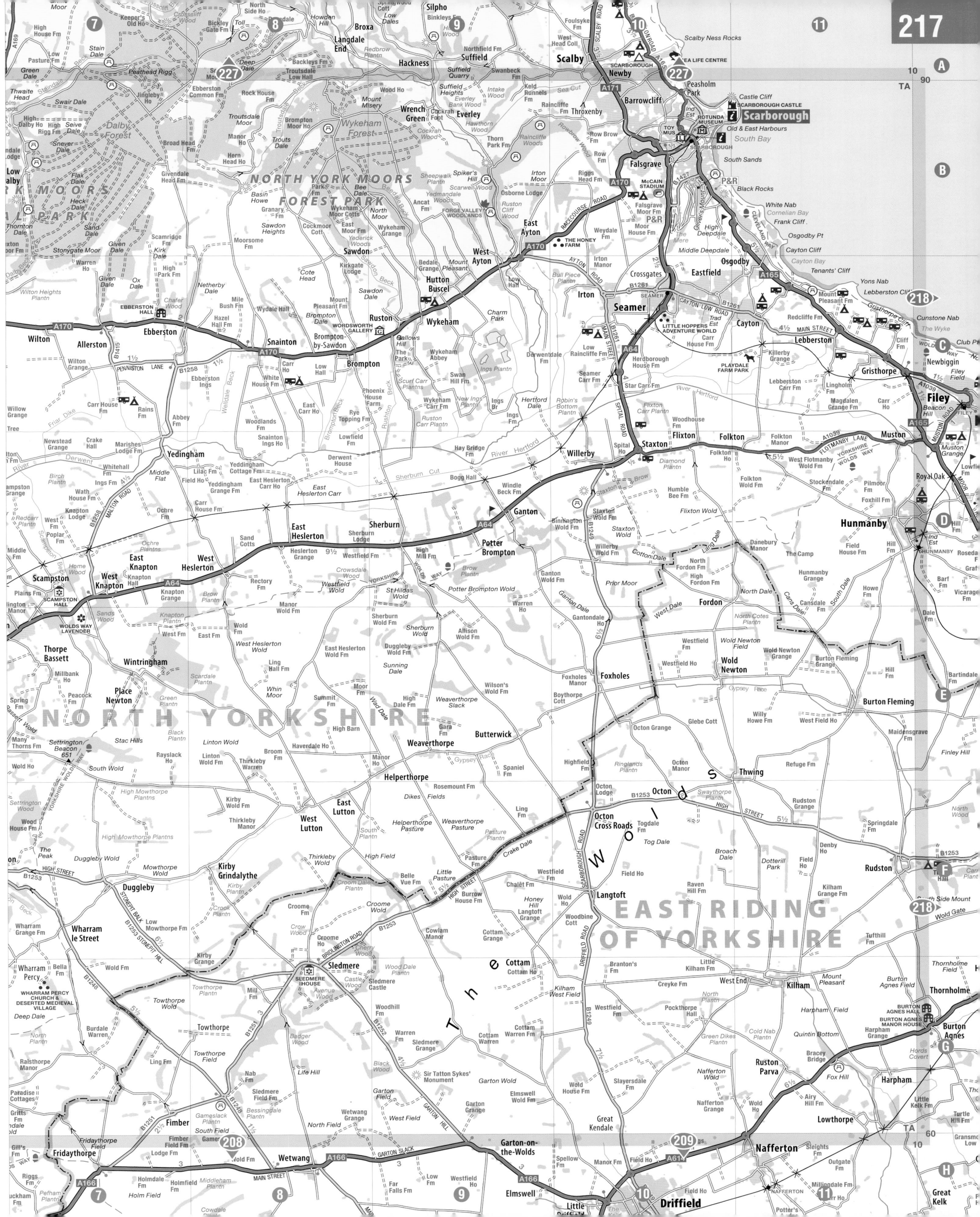

NORTH SEA

FILEY BAY

BRIDLINGTON BAY

EAST RIDING OF YORKSHIRE

Yons Nab
Lebberston Cliff
Cunstone Nab
The Wyke
217
Cliff Fm
WOLDS WAY
Club Pt
North Cliff
Newbiggin
Gristhorpe
Filey Field
Filey Brigg
Brigg End
1½
A1039
Filey
Filey Sands
Carr Ho
Beacon Hill
A165
Muston
Muston Grange
Muston Sands
LANE
Royal Oak
Lowfield Fm
Pilmoor Fm
Hunmanby Sands
Foxhill Fm
Primrose Valley
Hunmanby Gap
Airy Hill Fm
Hunmanby Moor
Hunmanby
HUNMANBY
Ind Est
Hill Fm
Rosedale Fm
Moor Fm
Reighton Sands
Howe Fm
Graffitoe Fm
Moor Ho
Reighton Gap
Dale Fm
Barf Fm
Moor Fm
Speeton Sands
Vicarage Fm
Reighton
Speeton Hills
Hill Fm
Reighton Field
Speeton
Speeton Cliffs
Buckton Cliffs
A165
Speeton Grange
Speeton Moor
Bartindale Fm
Speeton
Wasters Plantn
Field Greenlands
Buckton Hall
BEMPTON CLIFFS
Scale Nab
Cat Nab
Burton Fleming
Grindale Field
North Dale
High Huntow Fm
Standard Hill
RSPB
Gull Nook
Bempton Grange
Wandale Fm
Thornwick Bay
Maidensgrave Fm
Grindale
East Leys Fm
Buckton
North Cliff
Finley Hill
Newsham Field
Butterwicks
DANE'S DYKE
North Landing
Cradle Head
Fox Covert Plantn
North Mount
High Barn
BEMPTON
North Moor
Stottle Bank Nook
Springdale Fm
East Crags Wood
Charlestone Fm
Field Ho
Lynhams
Flatmere Plantn
Selwicks Bay
Boynton
Eastfield
High Easton Fm
The Crofts
FLAMBOROUGH ROAD
Flamborough Head
Binsdale Fm
Ind Est
FLAMBOROUGH
Old Fall Plantn
FLAMBOROUGH HEAD LIGHTHOUSE
B1253
Wandale Fm
Danes Dyke Fm
Flamborough
1½
High Stacks
Ruds
Thorpe Hall
Carr Plantn
West Lane Wood
Fish Ponds Wood
Sands Wood
Beacon Fm
Beacon Hill
Highcliffe Manor
PRIORY
BAYLE MUS
Old Town
Sewerby
SEWERBY HALL & GARDEN
Sewerby Rocks
South Landing
South Side Mount
Temple Fm
Carnaby Temple
High Wood
Hallowkiln Wood
BONDSVILLE MODEL VILLAGE
217
West Hill
Ind Est
The Spa
BRIDLINGTON
Bridlington
OLD PENNY MEMORIES
Tufthill Fm
Carnaby
Bessingby
Hilderthorpe
Haisthorpe Field
KINGSGATE
Thornholme Field
A614
Haisthorpe
Wilsthorpe
South Sands
Burton Agnes Field
Ind Est
PARK ROSE BIRD OF PREY CENTRE
Carnaby Moor
Auburn Fm
Thornholme
Oak Wood Fm
Brackendale Fm
BURTON AGNES HALL
BURTON AGNES MANOR HOUSE
Harpham Grange
Burton Agnes
Burton Agnes Stud Fm
6½
A165
Hords Covert
Demming
Fraisthorpe
Fraisthorpe Sands
Harpham
Little Kelk Fm
Thornholme Moor
Low Stonehills
Turtle Hill Fm
Gransmoor Wood
Woodside Fm
High Stonehills
Hamiltonhill Fm
Gransmoor Low Ho
209
Barmston Sands
Great Kelk
Park Fm
Barmston
Barmston Main Drain
Lissett
Allison Lane End
Ulrome
Ulrome Sands

0 1 2 3 miles
0 1 2 3 4 5 km

TA 90 · TA 90
TA 60 · TA 60
10 · 30

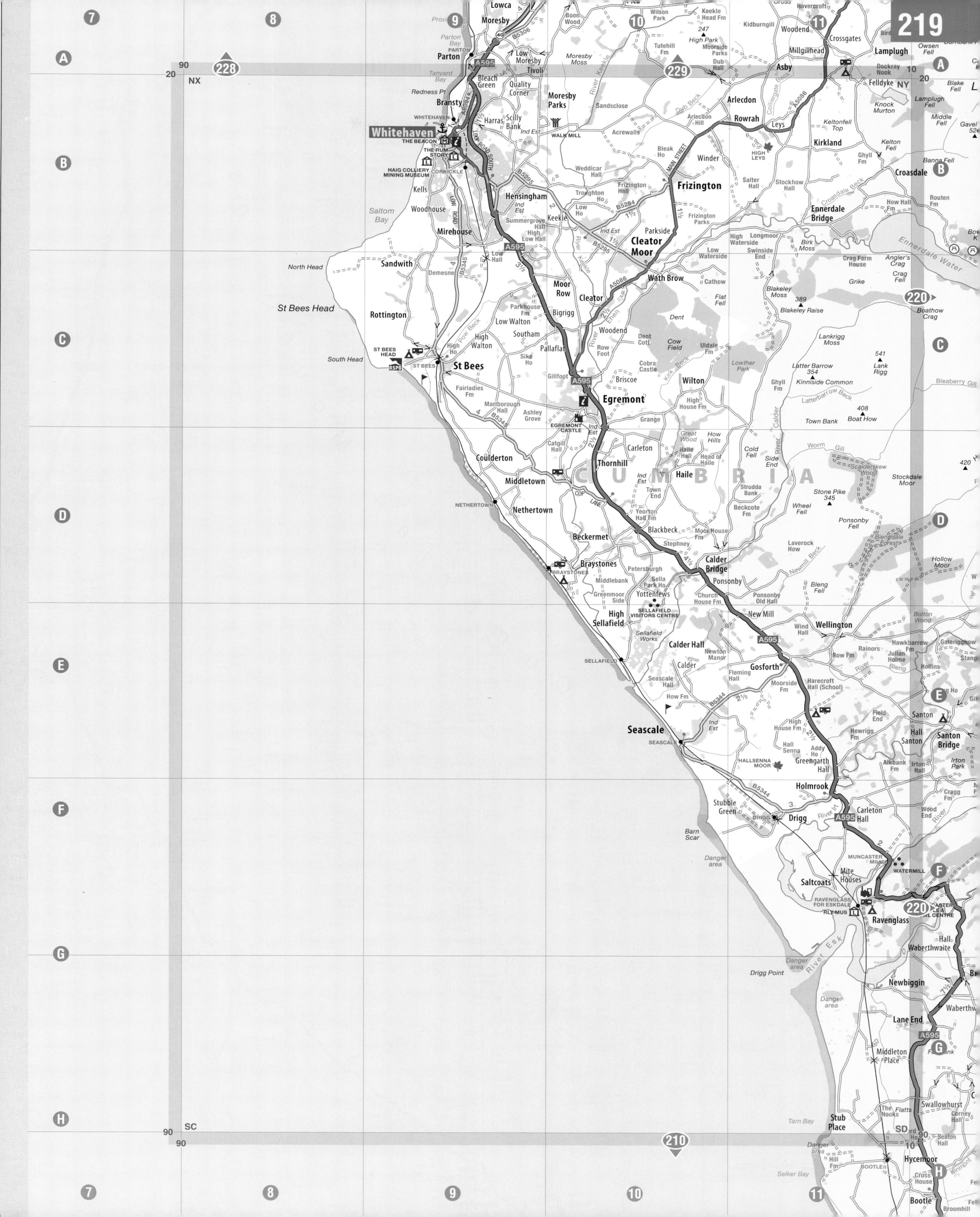

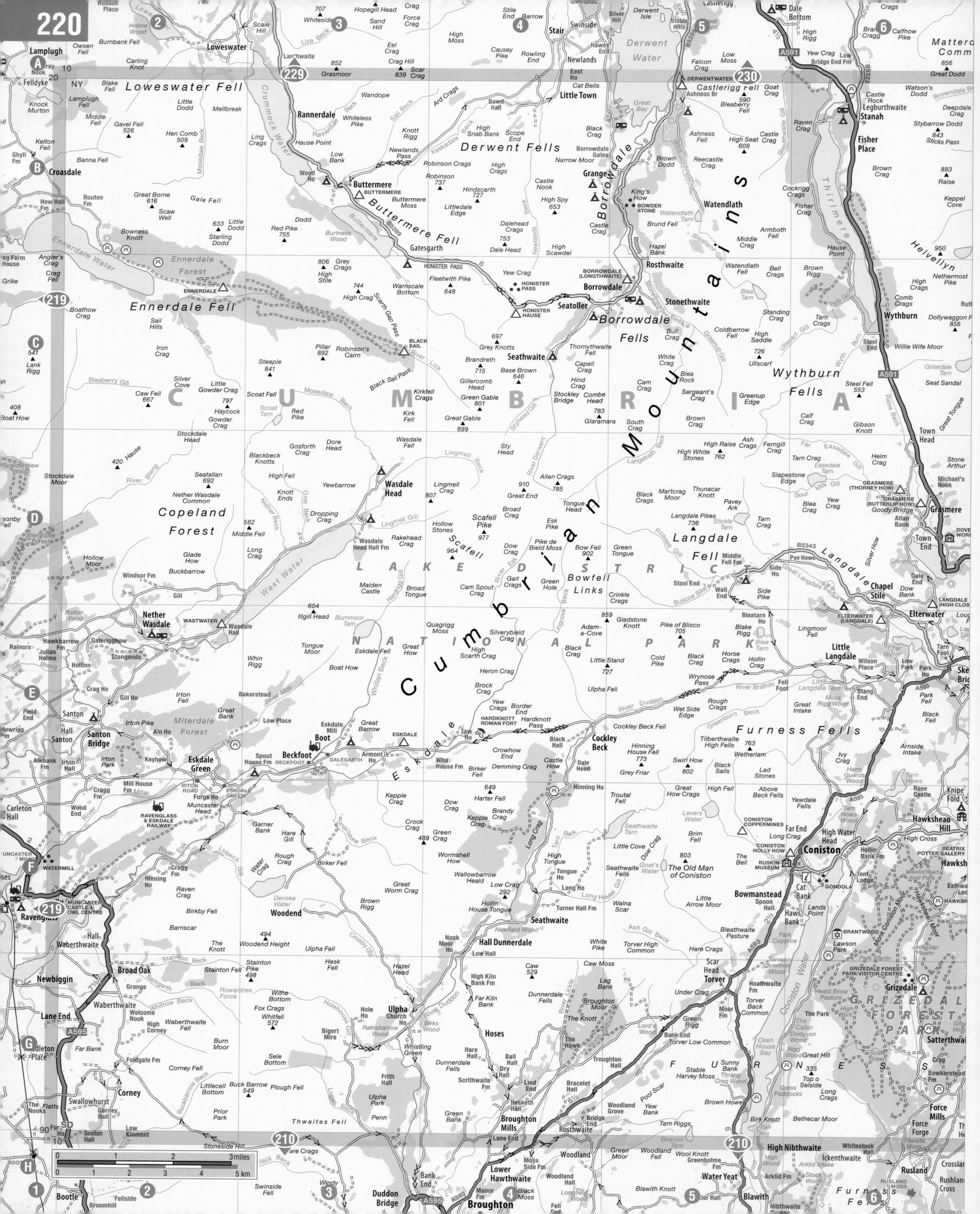

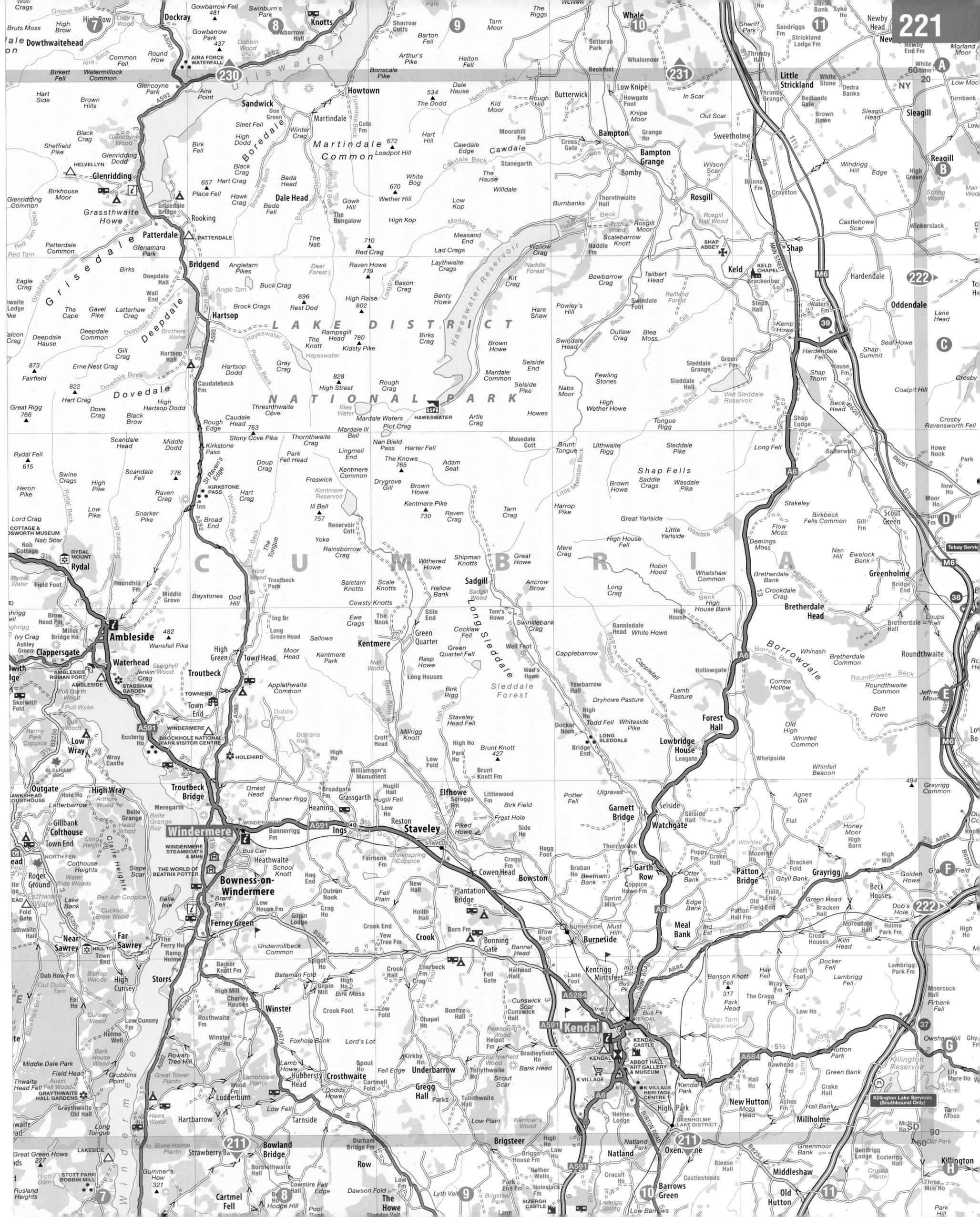

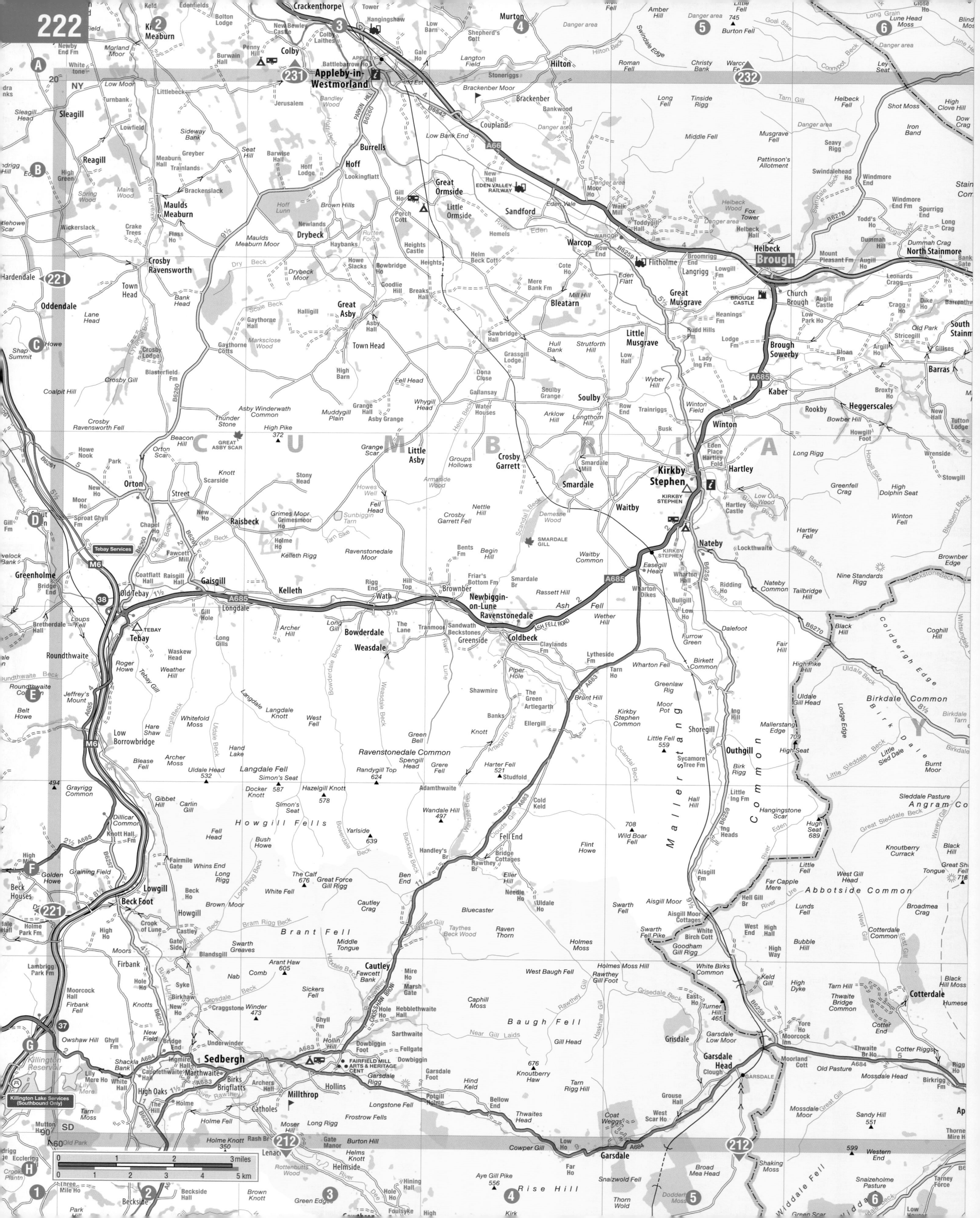

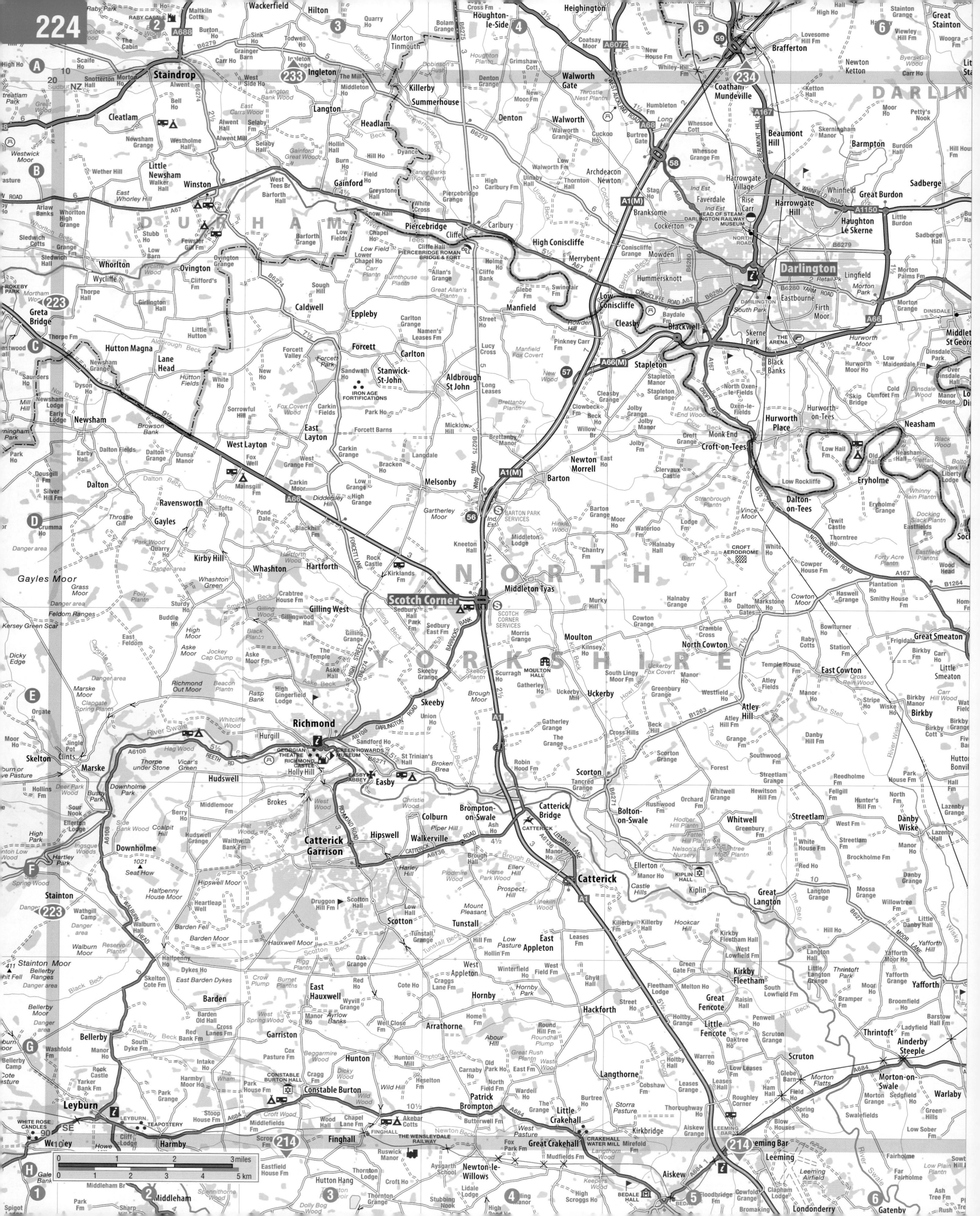

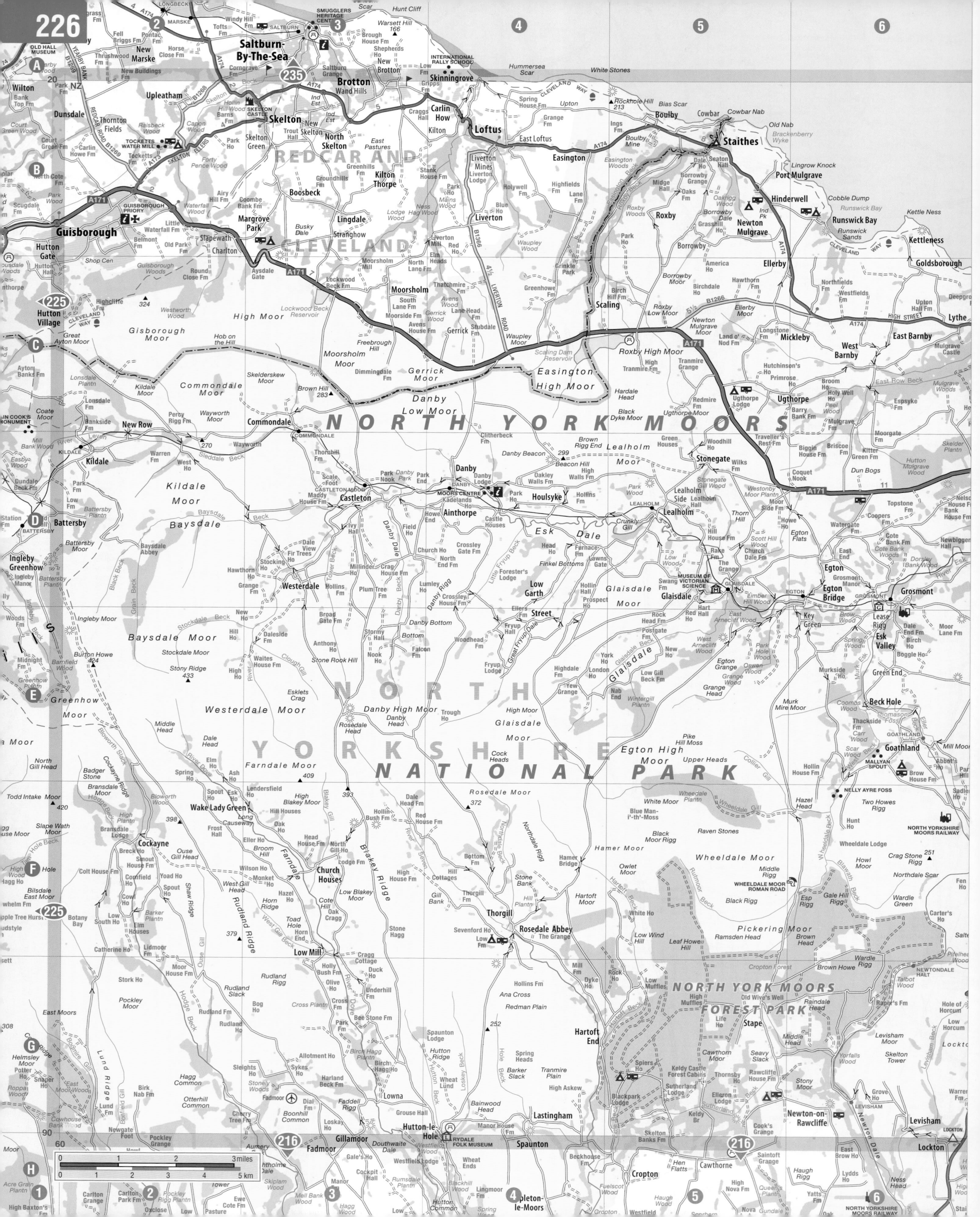

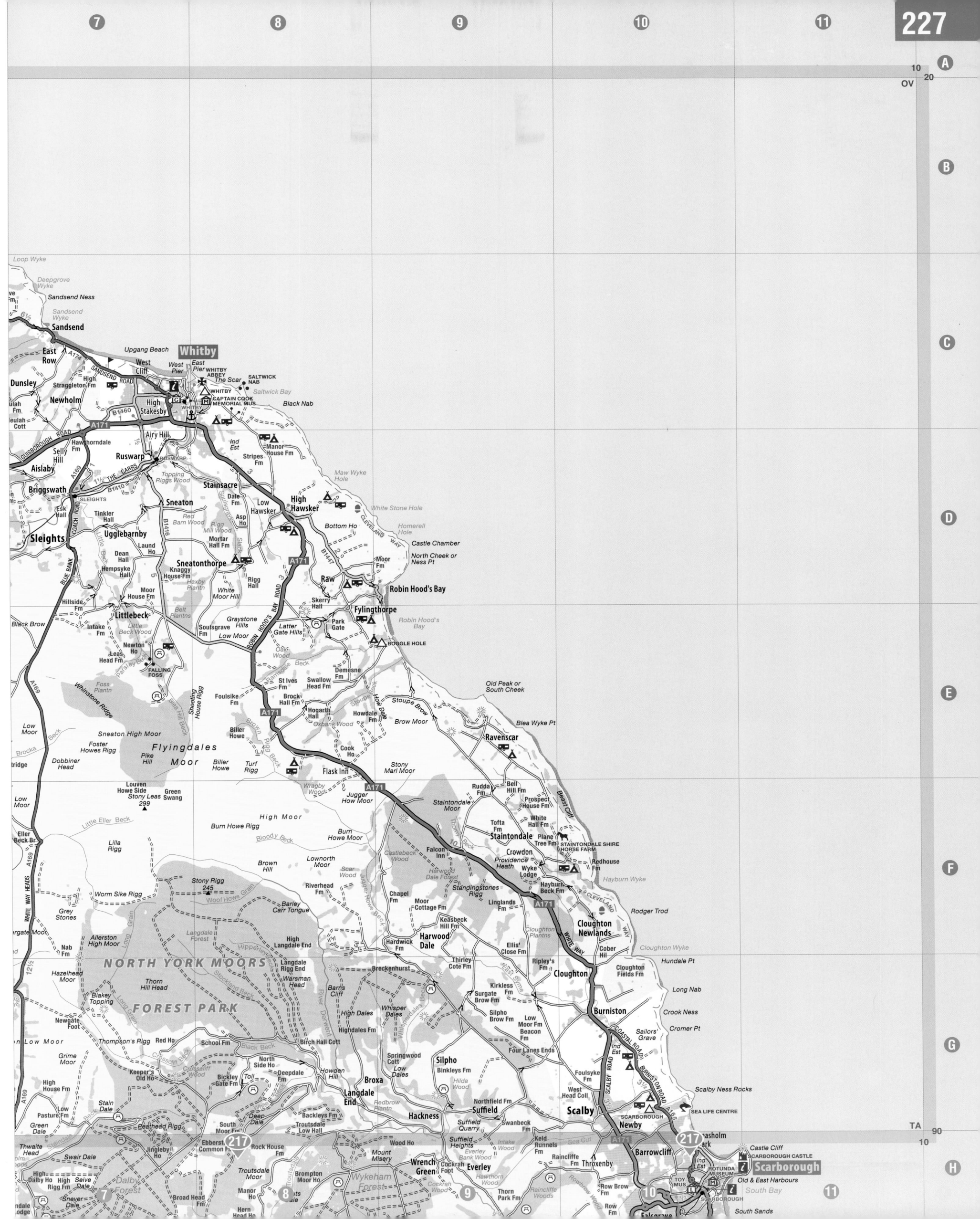

EAST STEWARTRY COAST

Auchencairn
Moyl
White Port
Almorness Pt
Hestan Island
Drungans
Auchencairn
50
80 Auchencairn Ho
NX
Cairn Hill
Balcary Bay
Nether Hazelfield
Airds Cott
Airds
Balcary Pt
Rascarrel
Airds Pt
Rascarrel Bay
Castle Muir Pt
Barlocco Bay

237
238

237

237

Bank End

SENHOUSE ROMAN MUSEUM
LAKE DISTRICT COAST AQUARIUM
MARITIME MUS
Maryport
THE WAVE CENTRE
MARYPORT
Ind Est
Netherton
Ewanrigg
Ellenb
Risehow Fm
Risehow
Woodside
Fothergill
Risehow
FLIMBY
Ind Est
Flimby
Standingsti

St Helens
MAIN ROAD
Camerton Grange
A596
Stud Fm
Siddick
Seaton
Camerton
Camerton Hall
Ribton Hall
Bus Pk
North Side
Hawk Hill
Salmon Hall
Stainburn Hall Fm
Great Clifton
Barepot
Clifton Hall
WORKINGTON HALL
Stainburn
Workington
A66
Close End
2½
HELENA THOMPSON MILL MUSEUM
Moorclose
Schoose
Quarry Hill
Mossbay
A596
Westfield
East Town End Fm
3½
Lostrigg Beck
Moss Bay
A592
2½
Salterbeck
Winscales
A595
Harrington
HARRINGTON
High Harrington
Gale Ho
Lucy Close Fm
Wythemoor Ho
Grayson Green
West Ghyll End Fm
Lillyhall Industrial Estate
Distington Works
Wythemoor Head
Branthwaite Row Fm
Harrington Parks
Kelmore Head
Park Ho
Hill Fm
Distington
Gilgarran
Cunning Pt
Barngill Ho
Common End
High House Fm
Pica
Lowca
Moresby
Boon Wood
Wilson Park
Keekle Head Fm
Providence Bay
40
B5306
247
High Park
Moorside Parks
Parton Bay
Moresby Moss
Tutehill Fm
Dub Hall
PARTON
A595
Low Moresby
Tivoli
Parton
Moresby Moss
Tanyard Bay
Blea Grea
219
Quality Corner
Moresby Parks
Sandsclose
Redness Pt
Bransty
20
80
NX
River Keekle
Dub Beck
WHITEHAVEN
THE BEACON
Whitehaven
Harras Bank
Scilly Bank
Ind Est
WALK MILL
Acrewa
Arlecdon
Bleak
THE RUM

0   1   2   3 miles
0 1 2 3 4 5 km

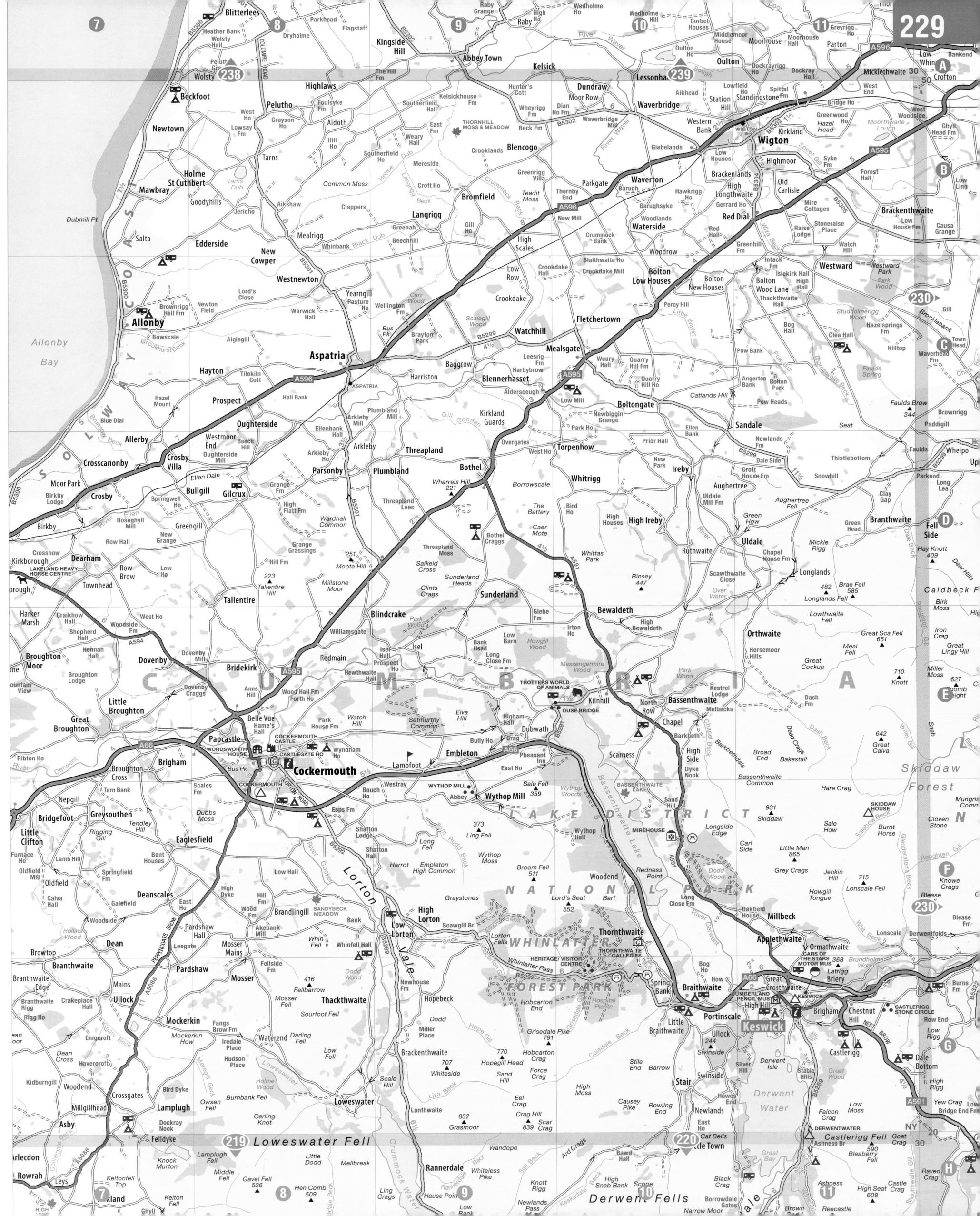

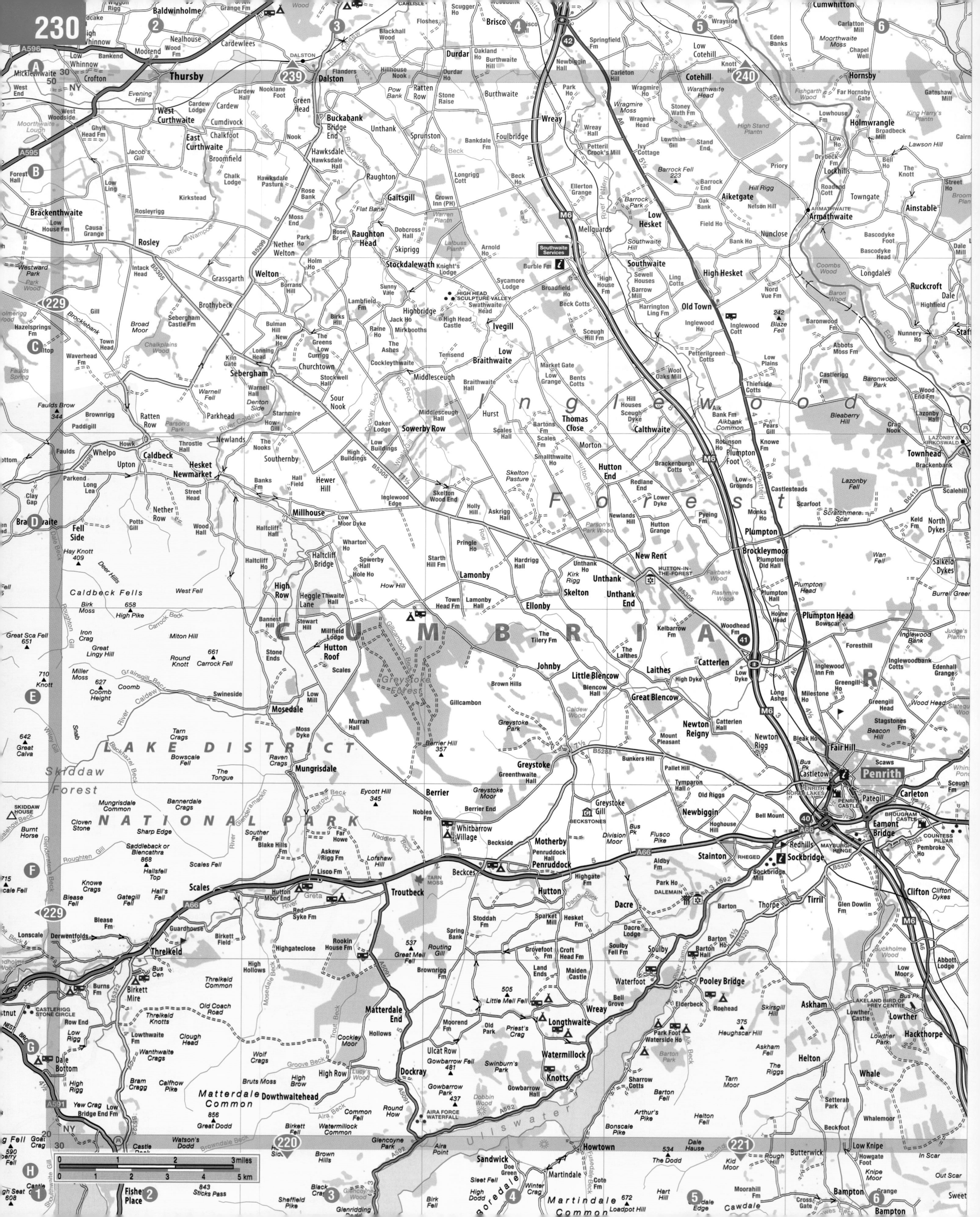

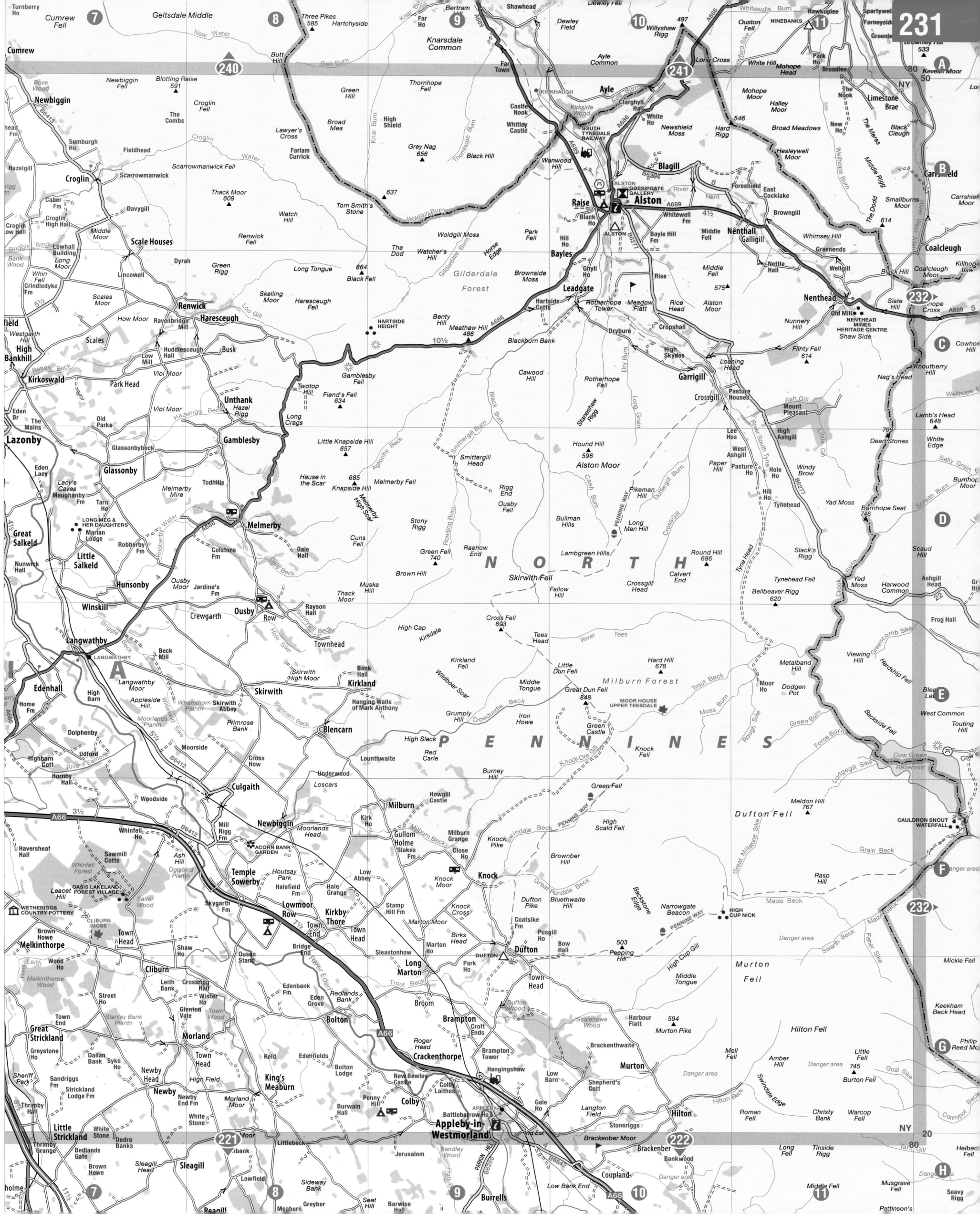

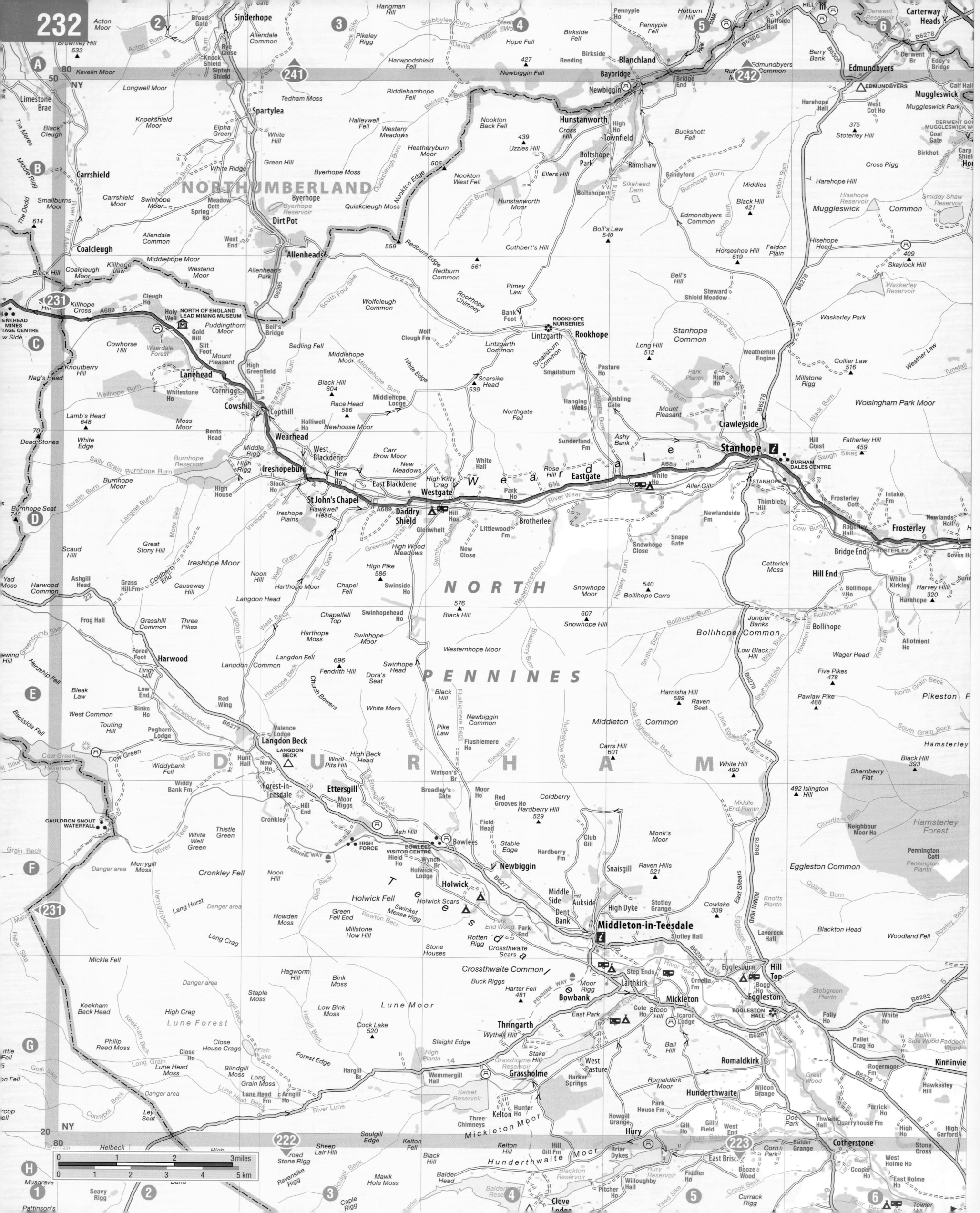

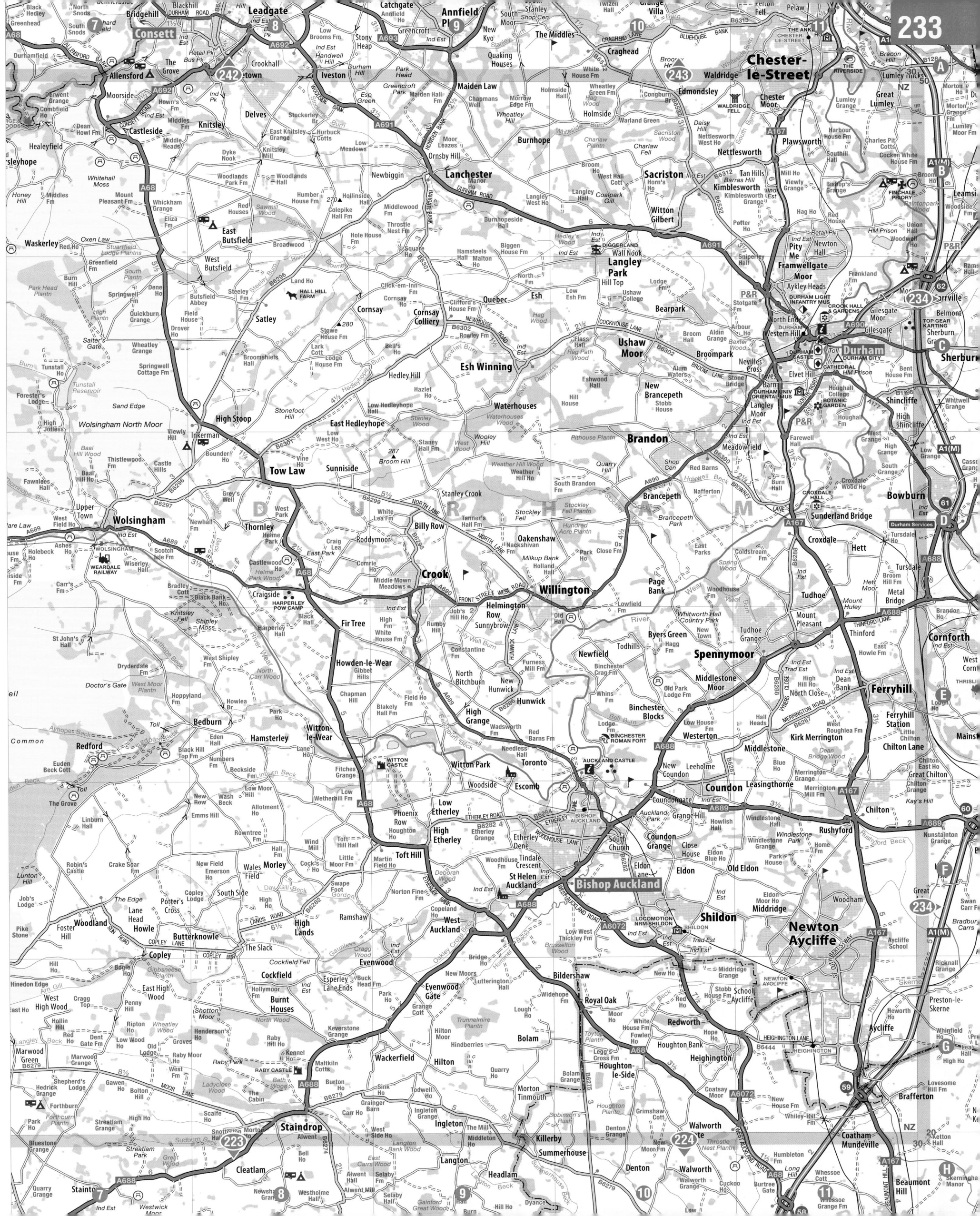

NORTH SEA

TEES BAY

Bran
Sands

Coatham Sands

Grangetown
Works

West Scar   Salt Scar
Warrenby   Redcar
Coatham   Rocks   The Flashes
REDCAR-CENTRAL
BRITISH STEEL
REDCAR
Westfield   Redcar
TRUNK ROAD   Redcar   **Redcar**   Mill Howle
Racecourse

Dormanstown   REDCAR LANE   EAST COAST ROAD   Scanbeck Howle

**Marske-by-
the-Sea**

Kirkleatham   Greygrass Fm   Stone Gap
LONGBECK
MARSKE   Windy Hill   Saltburn   Hunt Cliff
Fm   Scar
Fell   Pontac   Tofts   SMUGGLERS   Warsett Hill
Yearby   Briggs Fm   Fm   Fm   SALTBURN   HERITAGE   166
New   Horse   **Saltburn-**   CENTRE   Brough
Marske   Thrushwood   Close Fm   **By-The-Sea**   House Fm   Shepherds
Fm   Corngrave   Saltburn   Ho   INTERNATIONAL
New Buildings   Grange   New   Low   RALLY SCHOOL
Lazenby   Yearby   Brotton   Fm
Bank   Gripps   Hummersea   White Stones
Wilton   Park   **Brotton**   Spring   Scar   Skinningrove
Old Hall   Fm   Wand Hills   House Fm
Grangetown   225   Upleatham   226   WAY
Lazenby   Wilton   Redcar Road   Carlin   Rockhole Hill
Bank   Thornton   SKELTON   How   213   Bias Scar   Boulby
Dunsdale   Fields   Capon   CASTLE   Ind   Kilton   Grange   Cowbar   Cowbar Nab
Wood   Holme   Est   Craggs   Fm
Court   **Skelton**   Hill Wood   Ind   Hall   Ings   Boulby   Old Nab
Green Wood   Barns   Skelton   Est   **Loftus**   Fm   Mine   Brackenberry
242   Skelton   New   East   East Loftus   Wyke
Court   Carlin   Green   Skelton   Pastures   A174   **Staithes**
Fm   Howe Fm   Tocketts   Liverton   Easington   Boulby
Park Ho   Easington
REDCAR AND

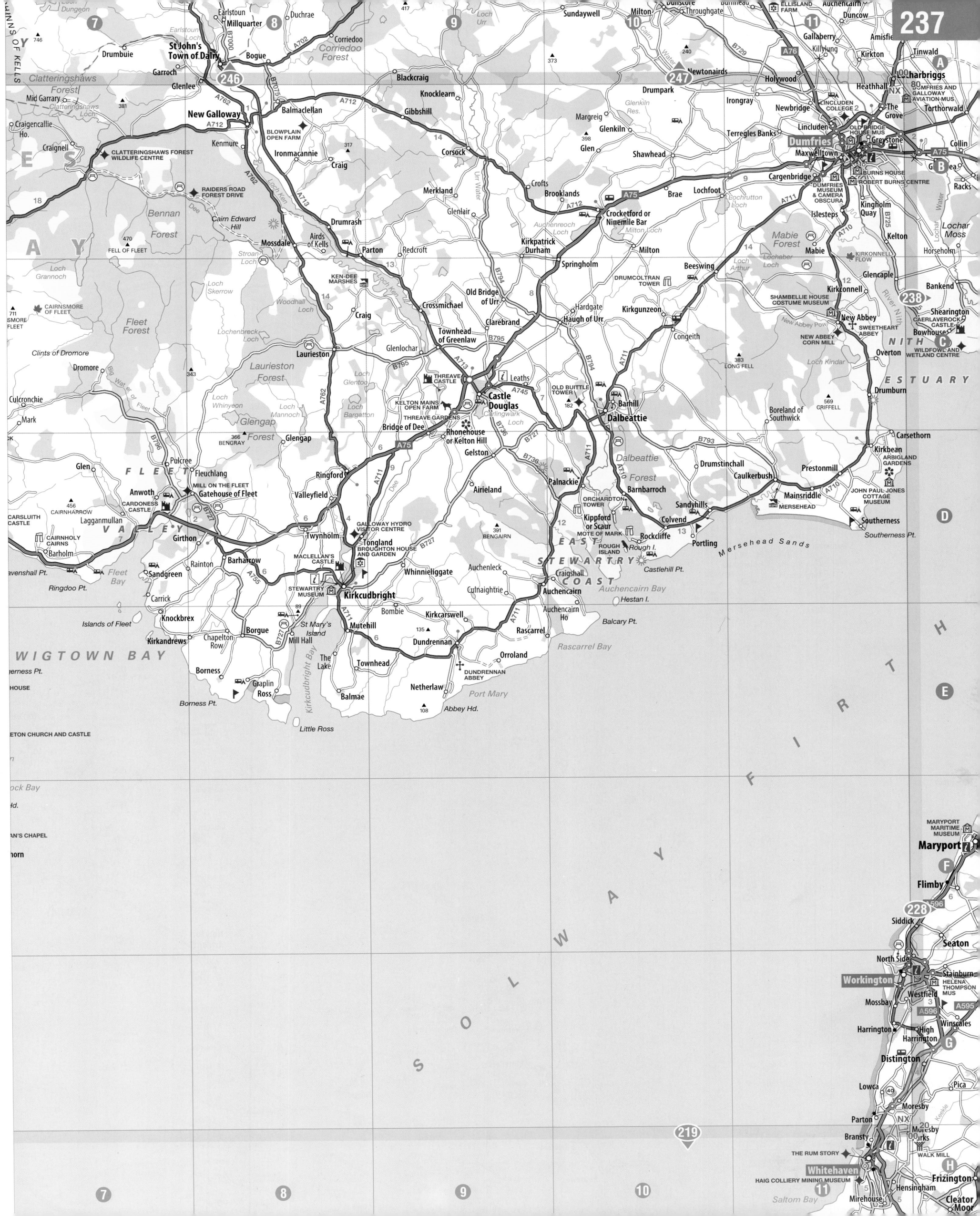

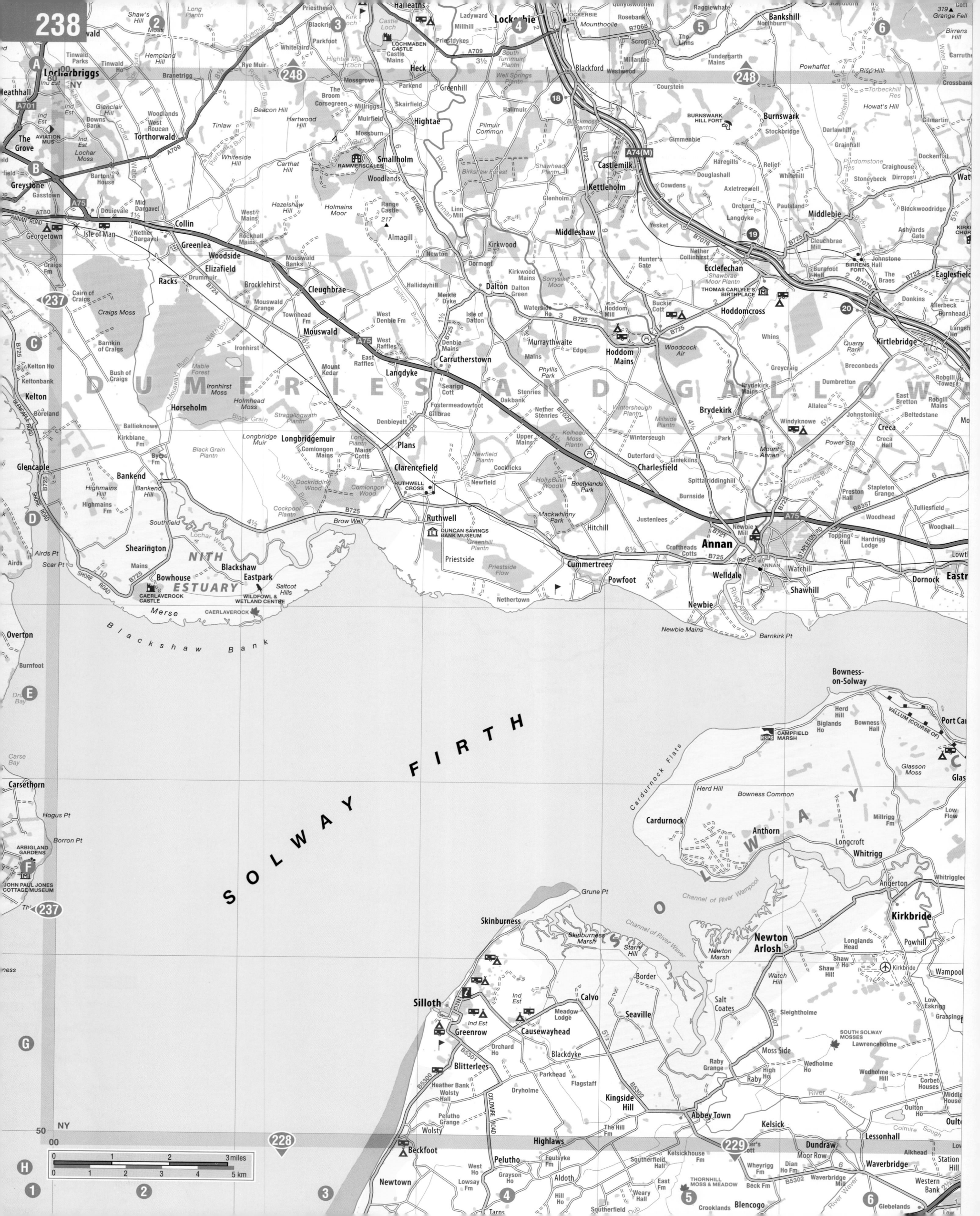

DUMFRIES AND GALLOWAY

SOLWAY FIRTH

Lockerbie

Annan

Silloth

Kirkbride

Newton Arlosh

Bowness-on-Solway

Lochmaben Castle

Caerlaverock Castle
Wildfowl & Wetland Centre

John Paul Jones Cottage Museum

Thomas Carlyle's Birthplace

Birrens Fort

Burnswark Hill Fort

Ecclefechan

Kirtlebridge

Middlebie

Eaglesfield

Cummertrees

Powfoot

Newbie

Ruthwell
Duncan Savings Bank Museum

Clarencefield

Bankend

Glencaple

Shearington

Blackshaw

Eastpark

Bowhouse

Carsethorn

Overton

Burnfoot

Carrutherstown

Dalton

Mouswald

Collin

Torthorwald

Lochfoot

Lochlarbriggs

Greystone

Georgetown

Carsegowan

Brydekirk

Hoddomcross

Hoddom Mains

Charlesfield

Beckfoot

Blitterlees

Greenrow

Causewayhead

Skinburness

Calvo

Seaville

Abbey Town

Kingside Hill

Waverbridge

Dundraw

Kelsick

Anthorn

Cardurnock

Whitrigg

Longcroft

Port Carlisle

Campfield Marsh

South Solway Mosses

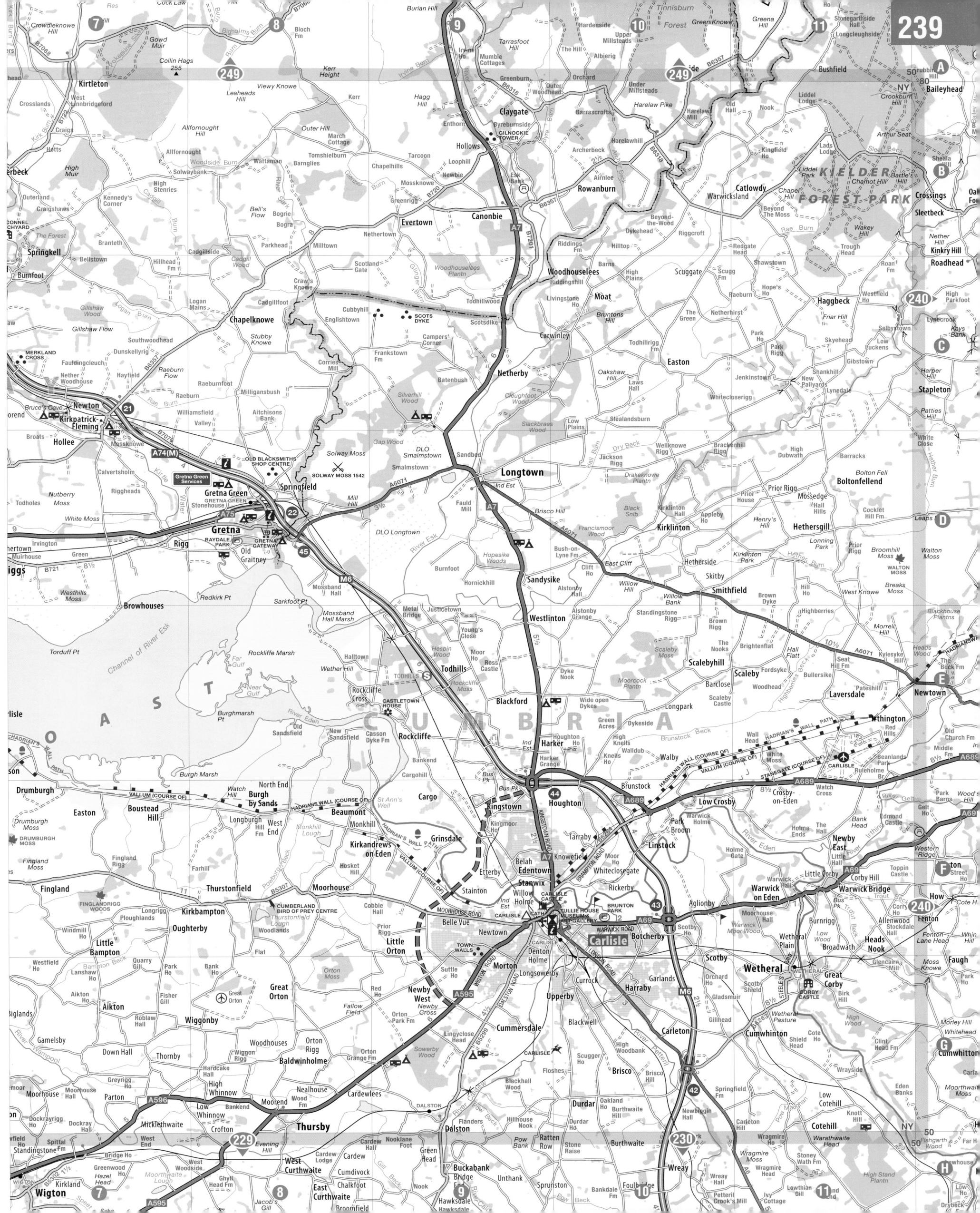

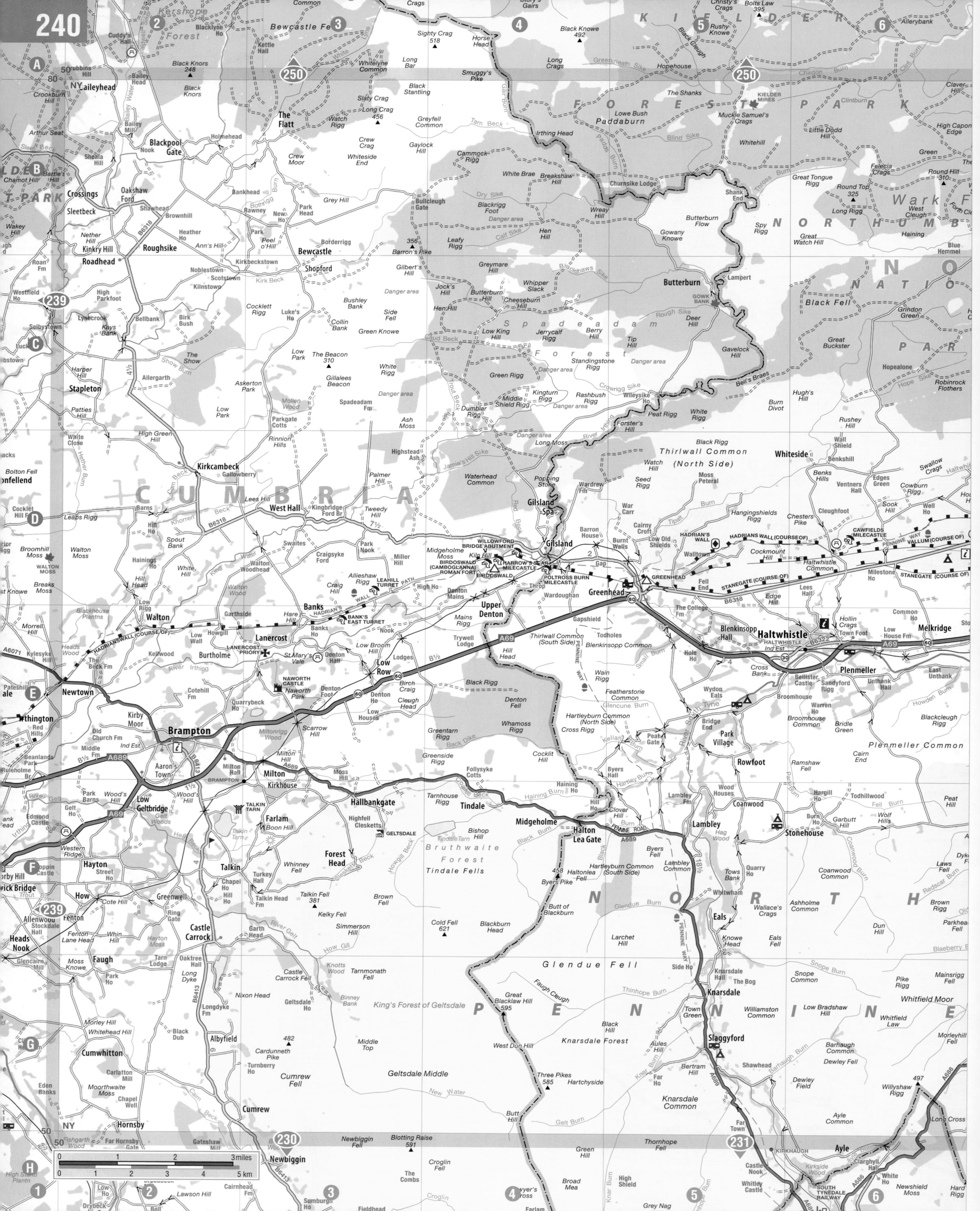

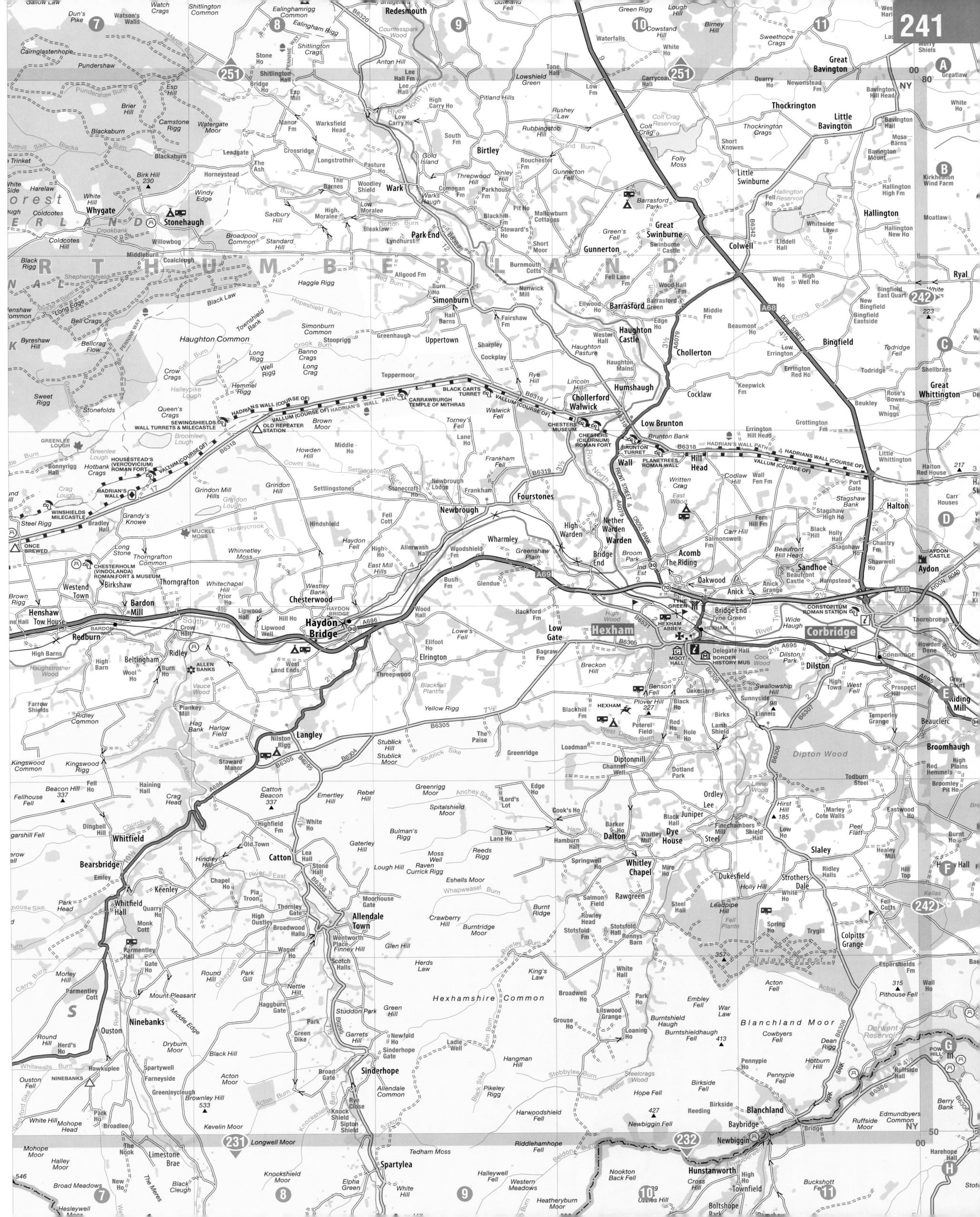

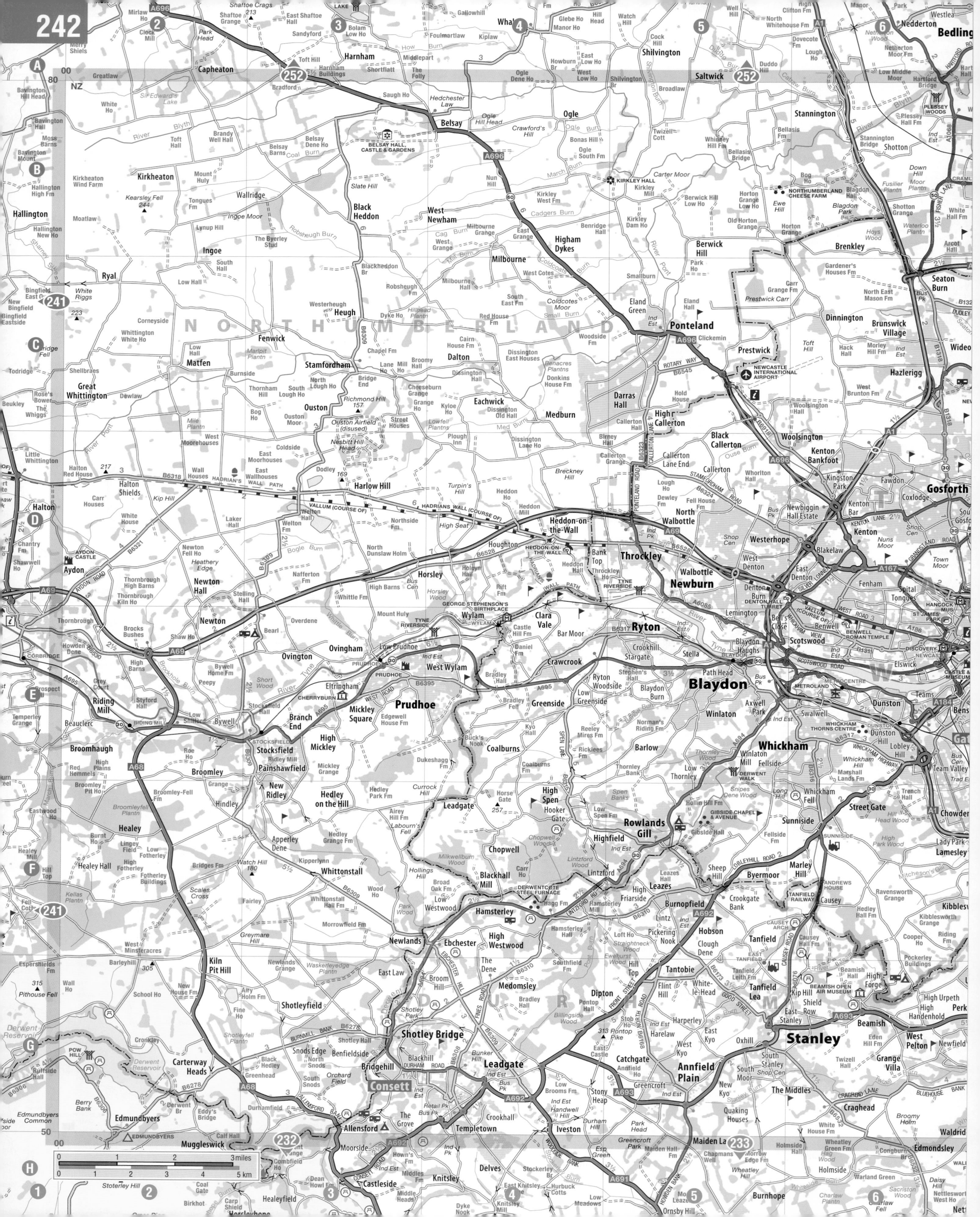

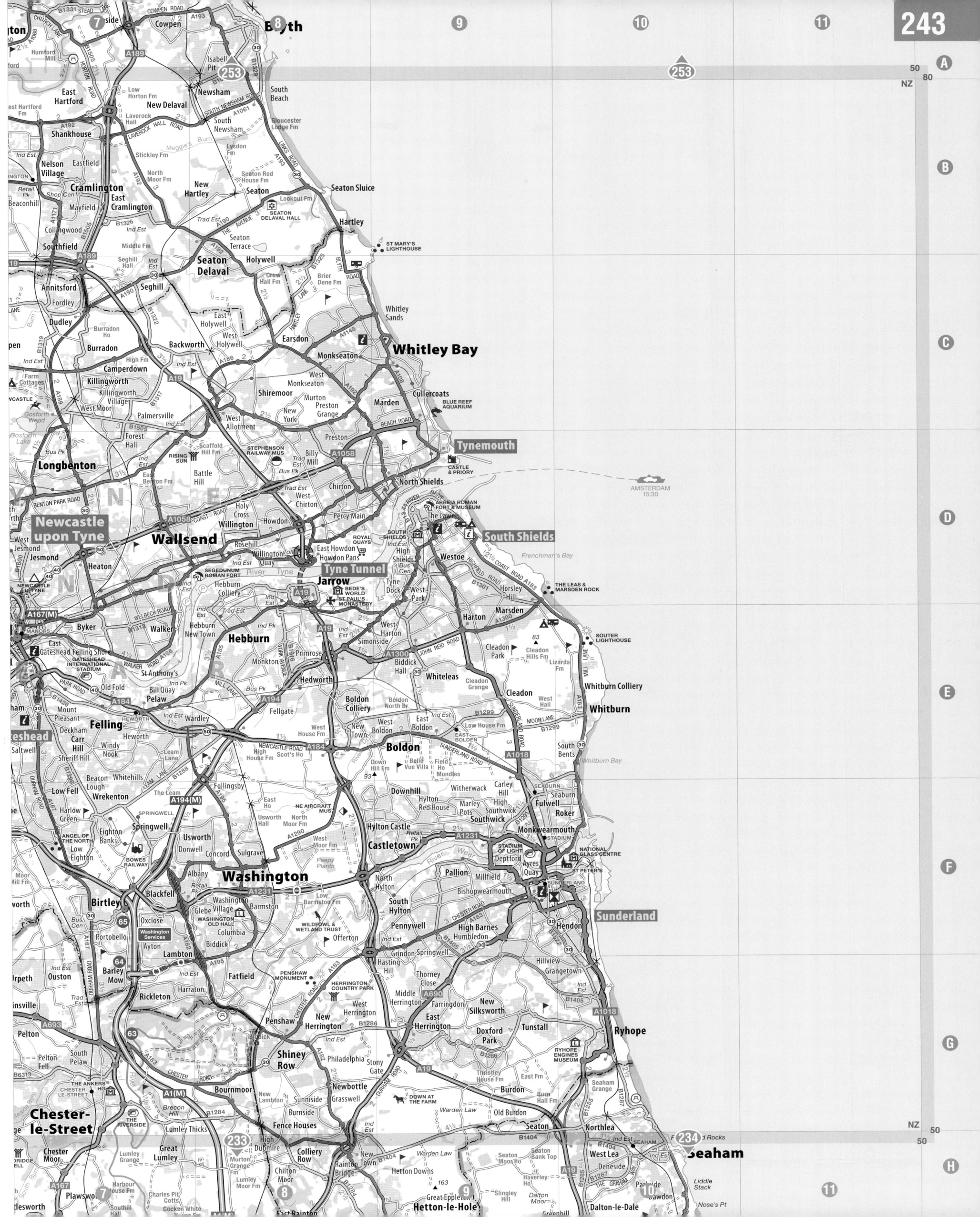

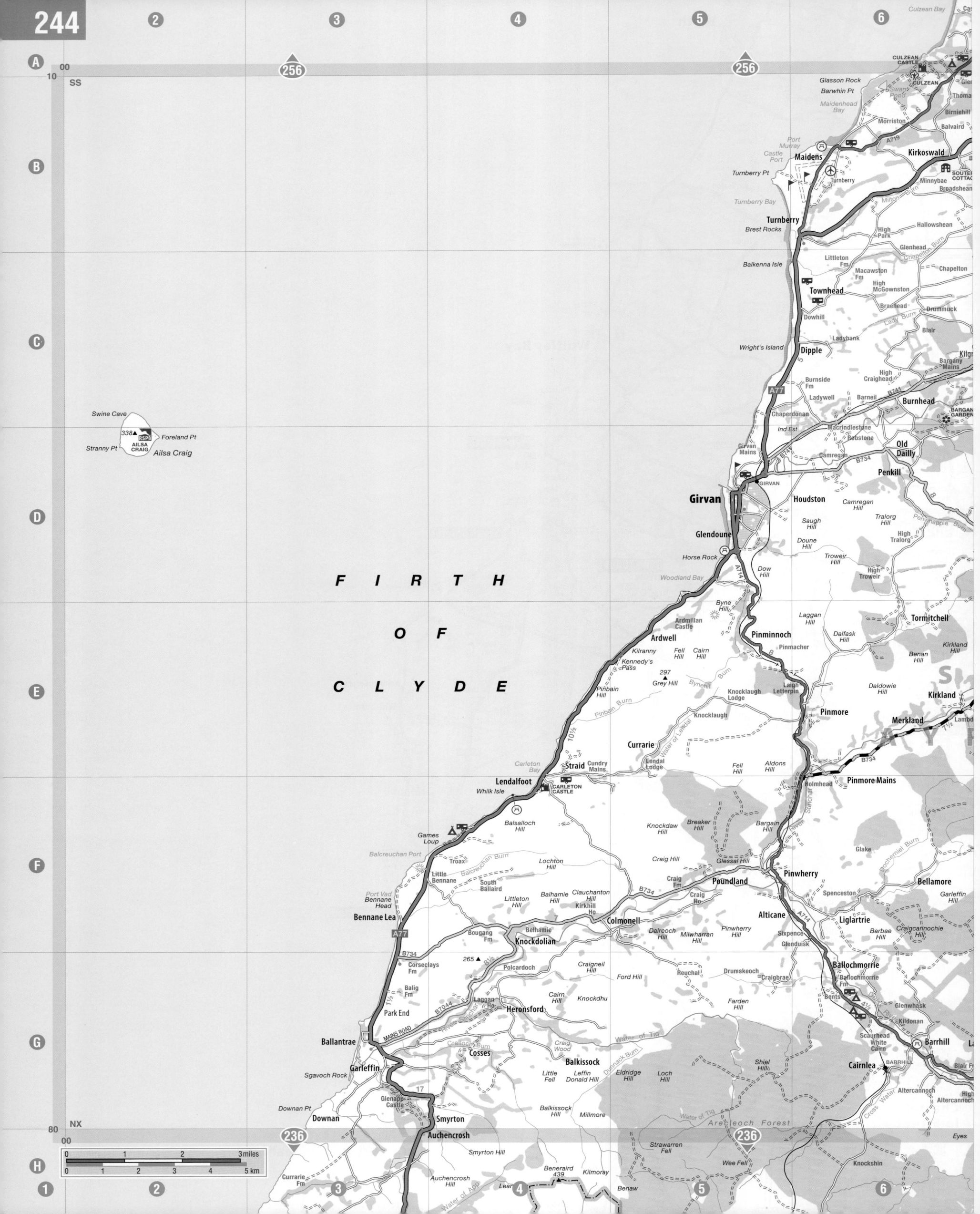

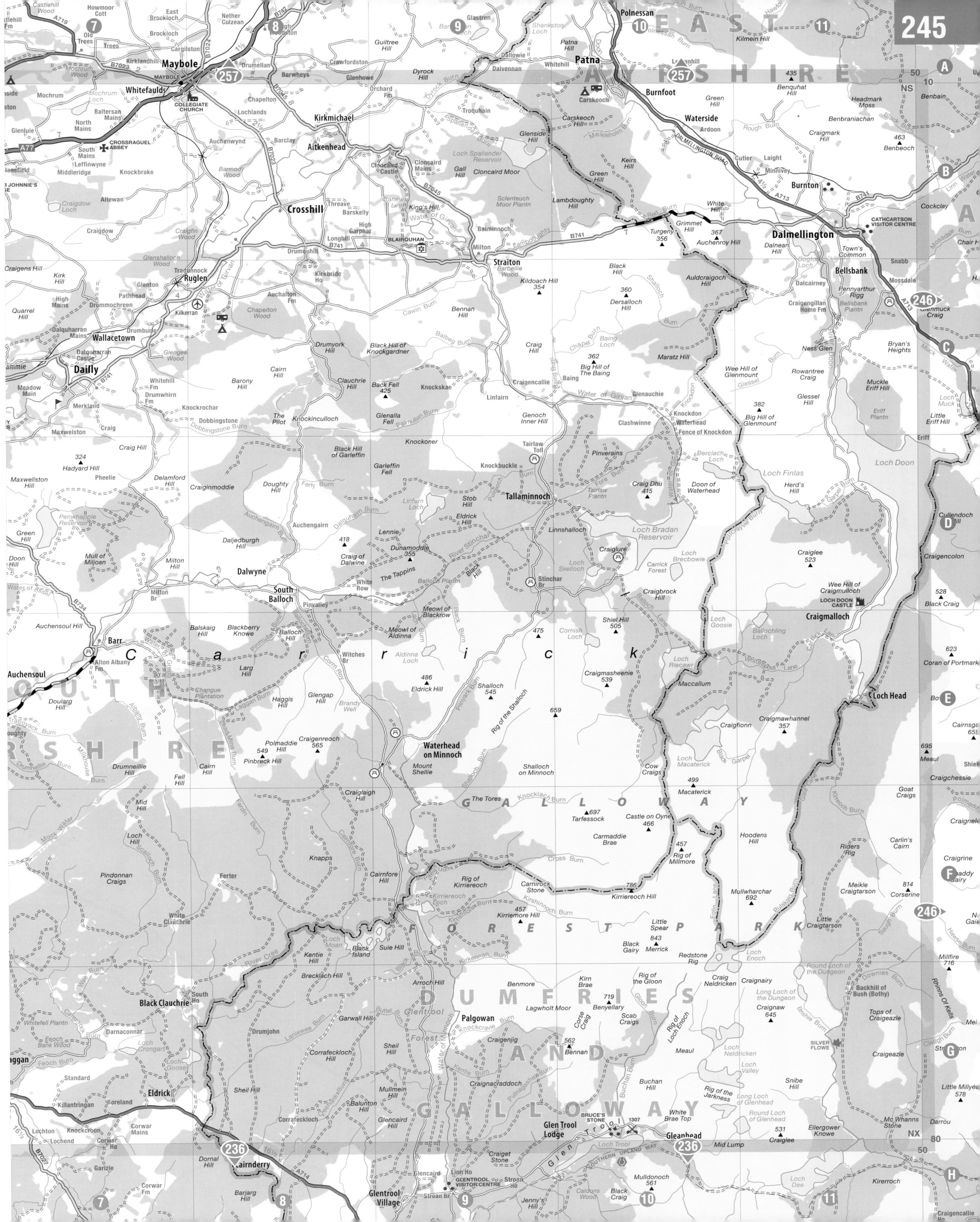

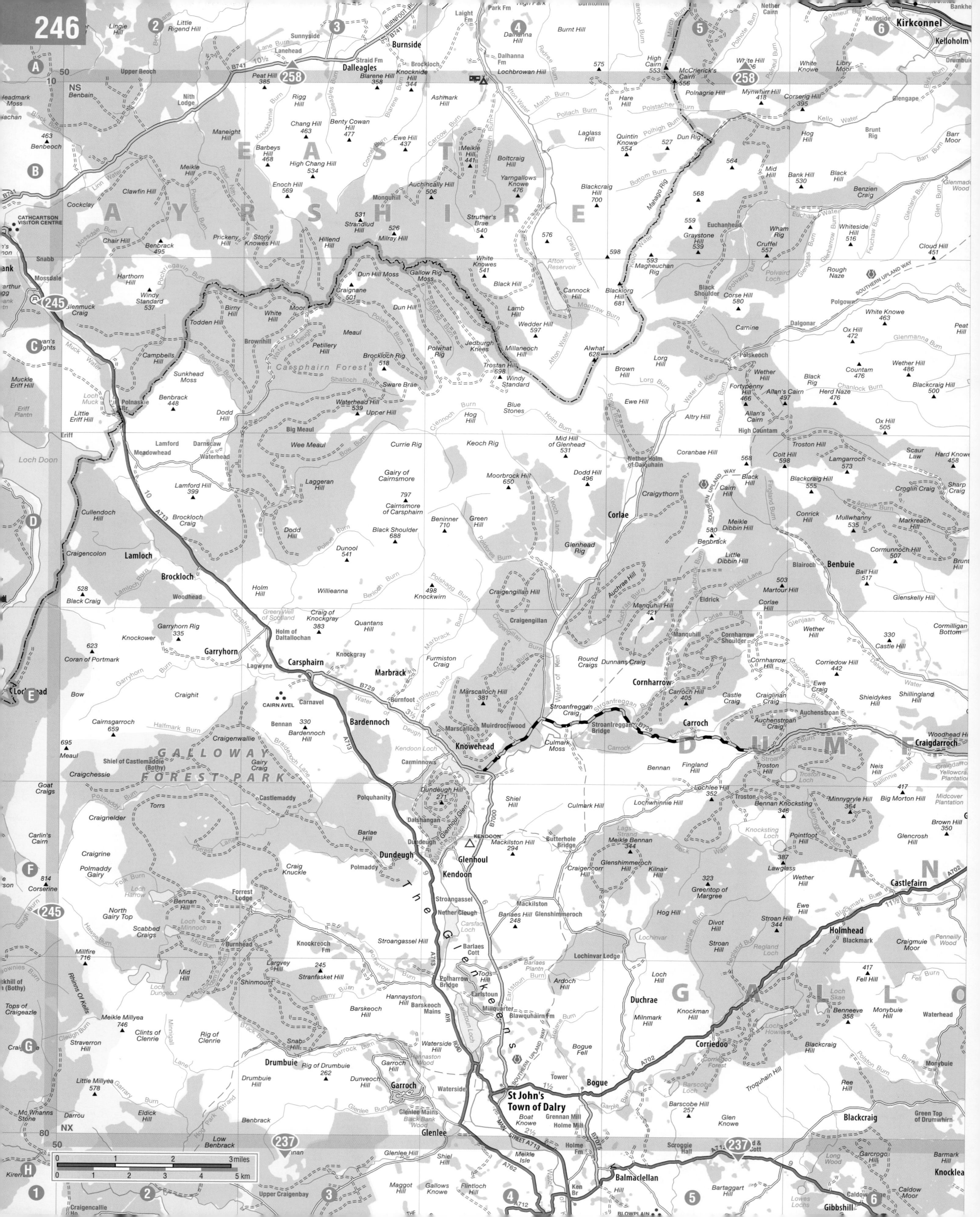

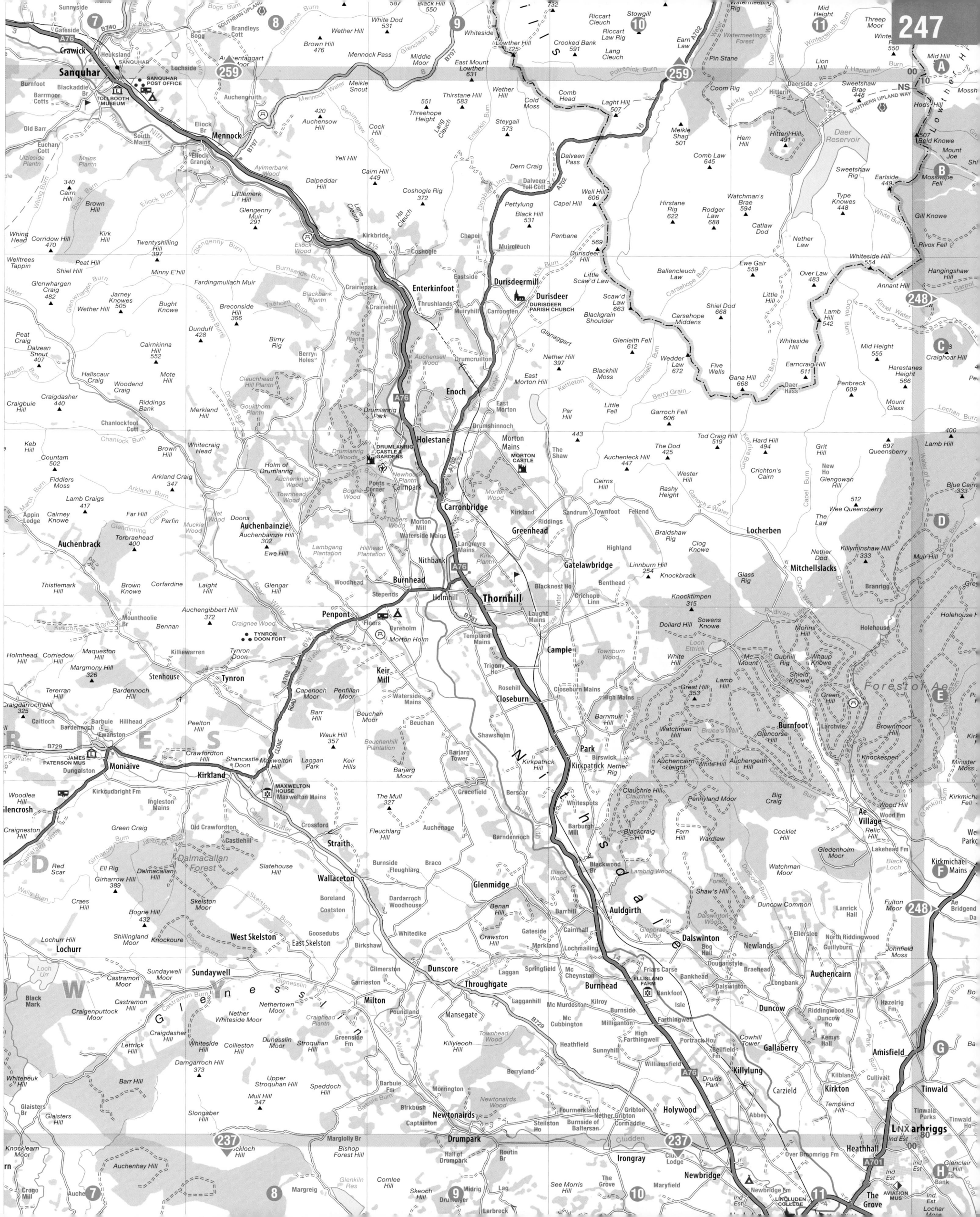

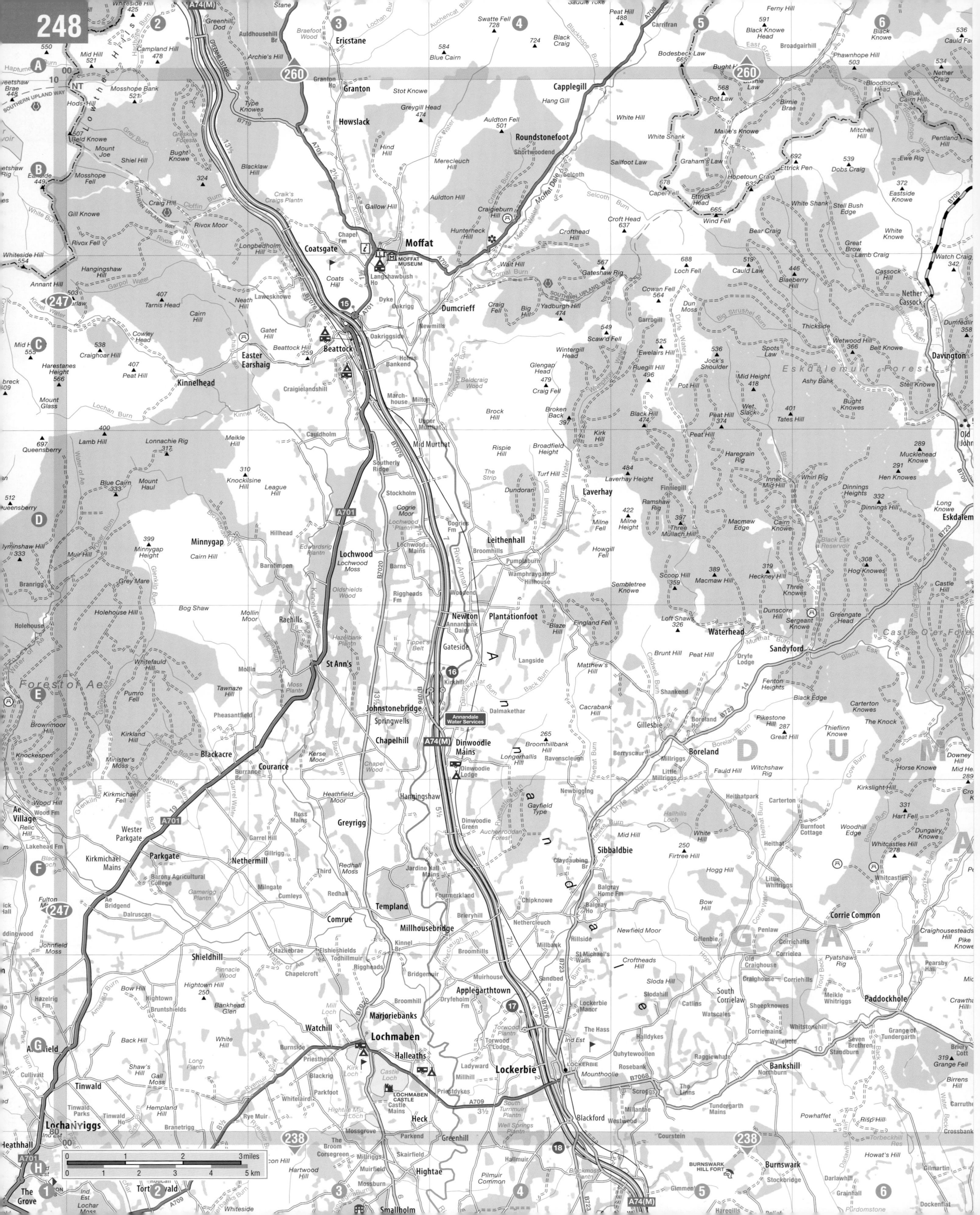

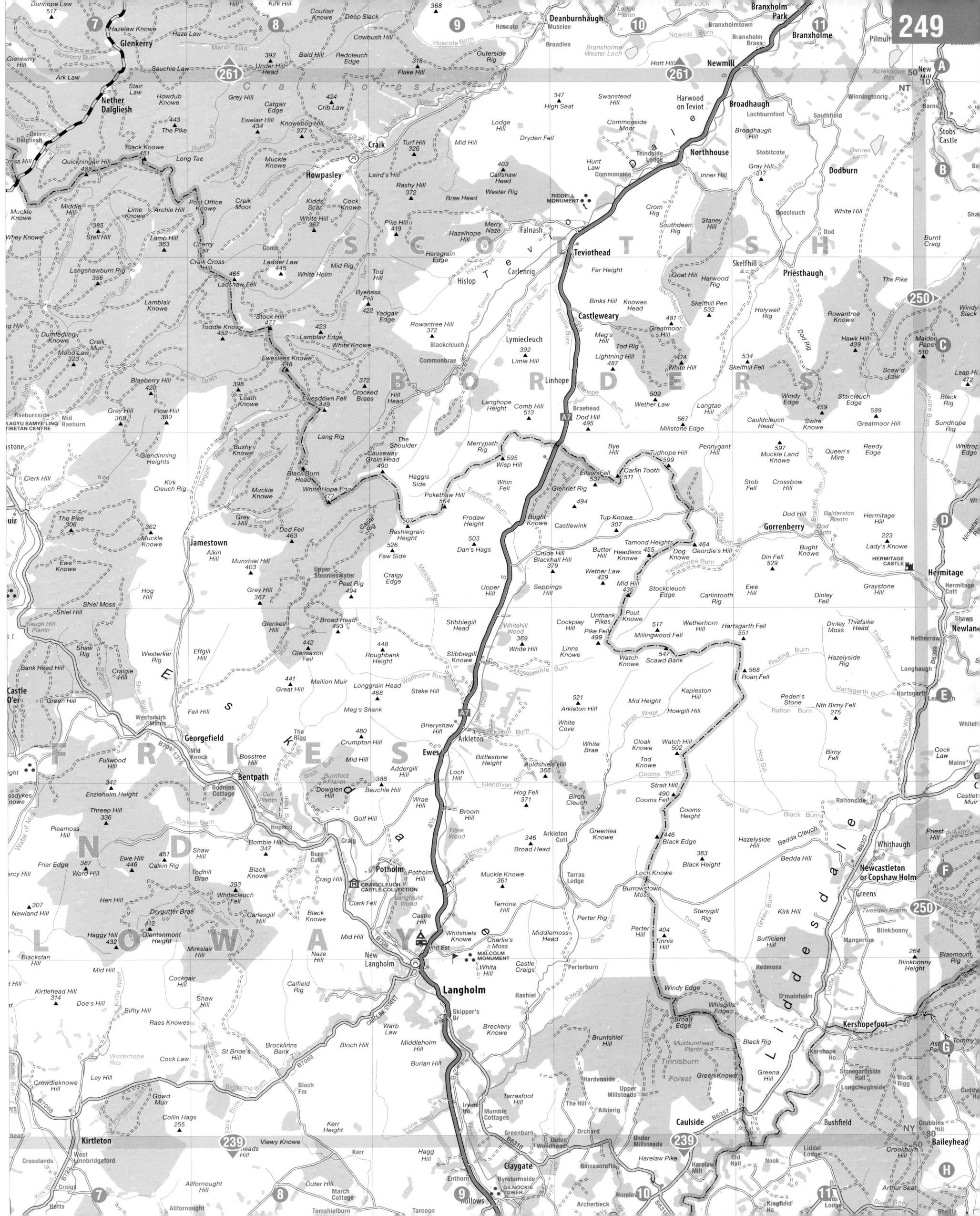

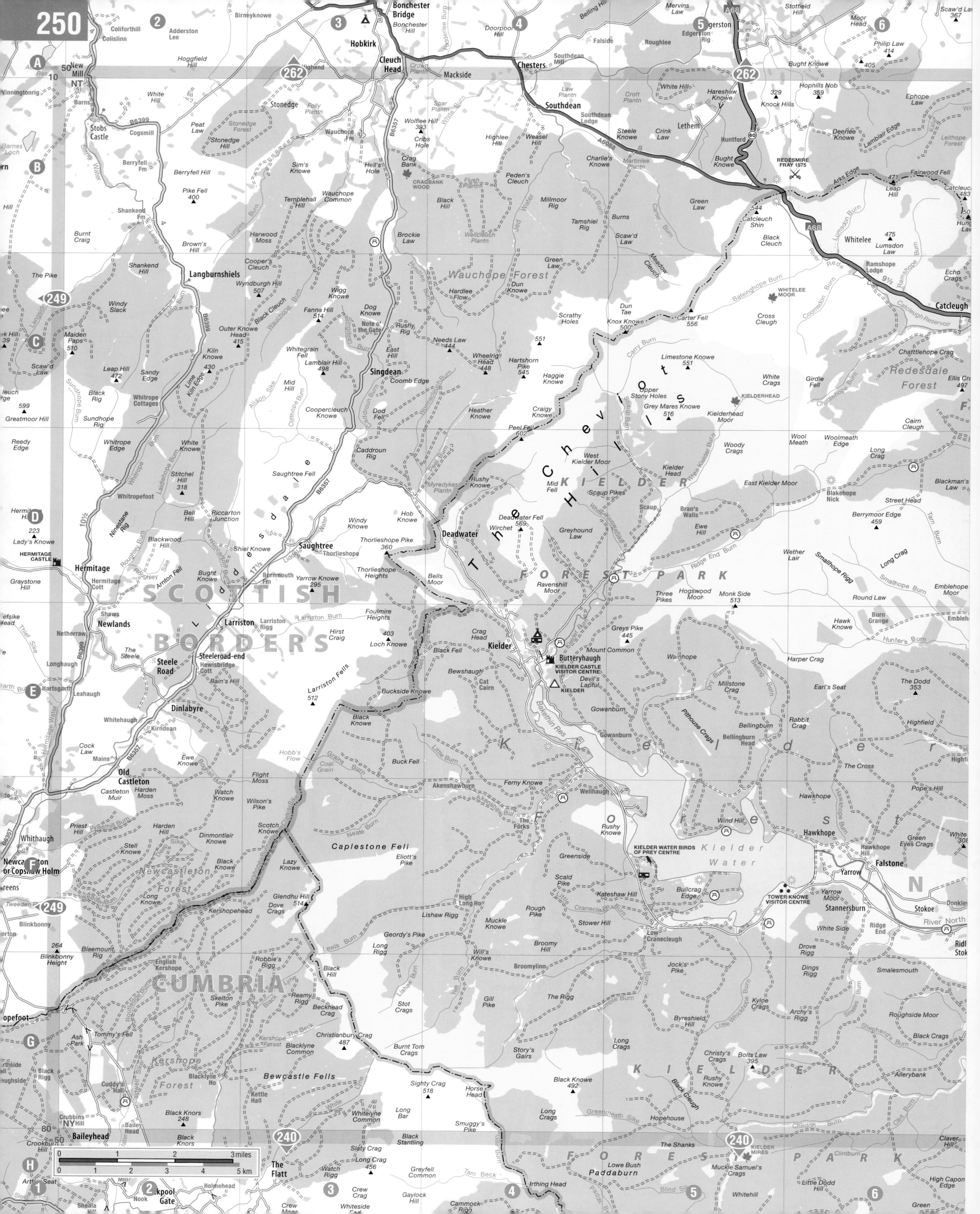

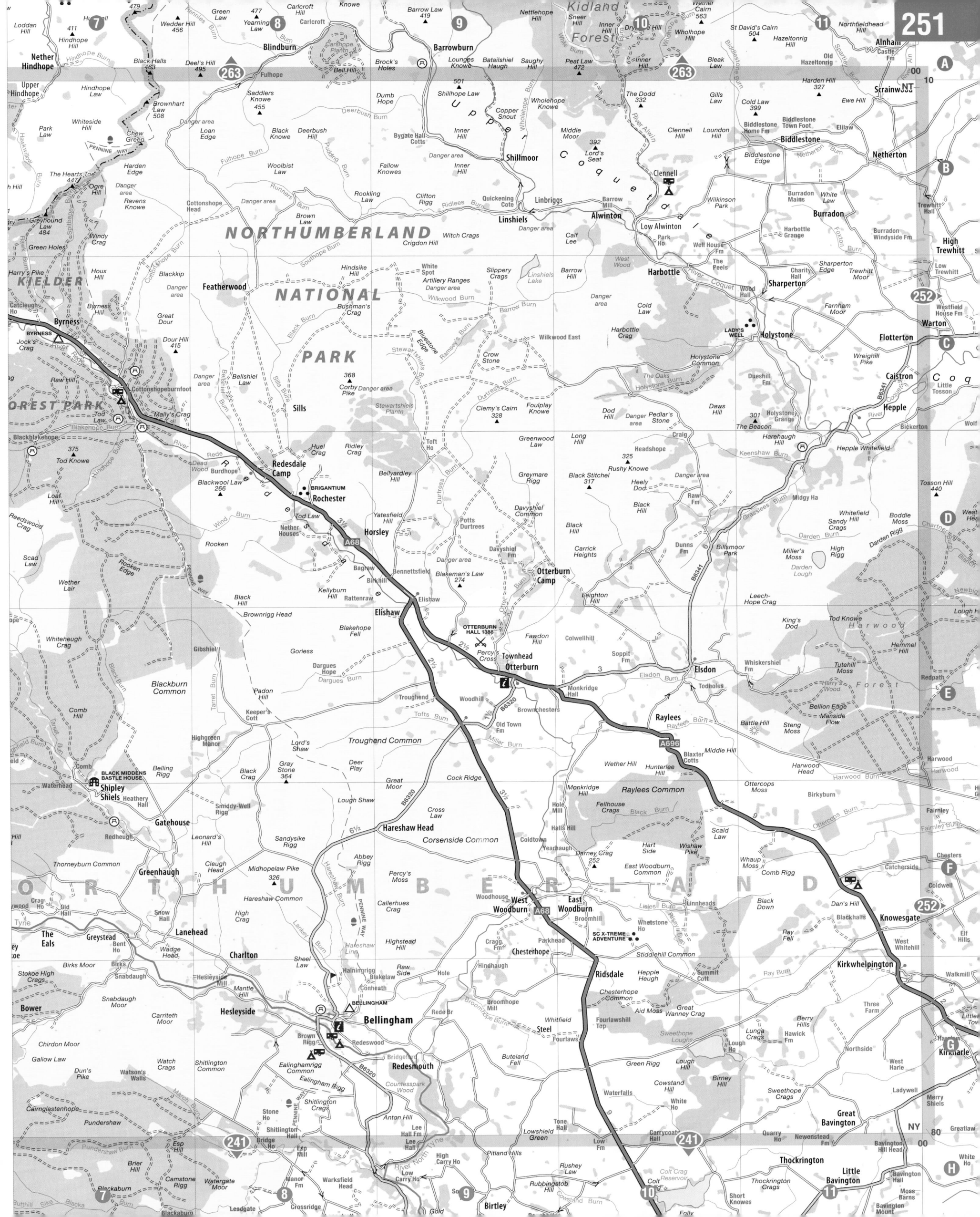

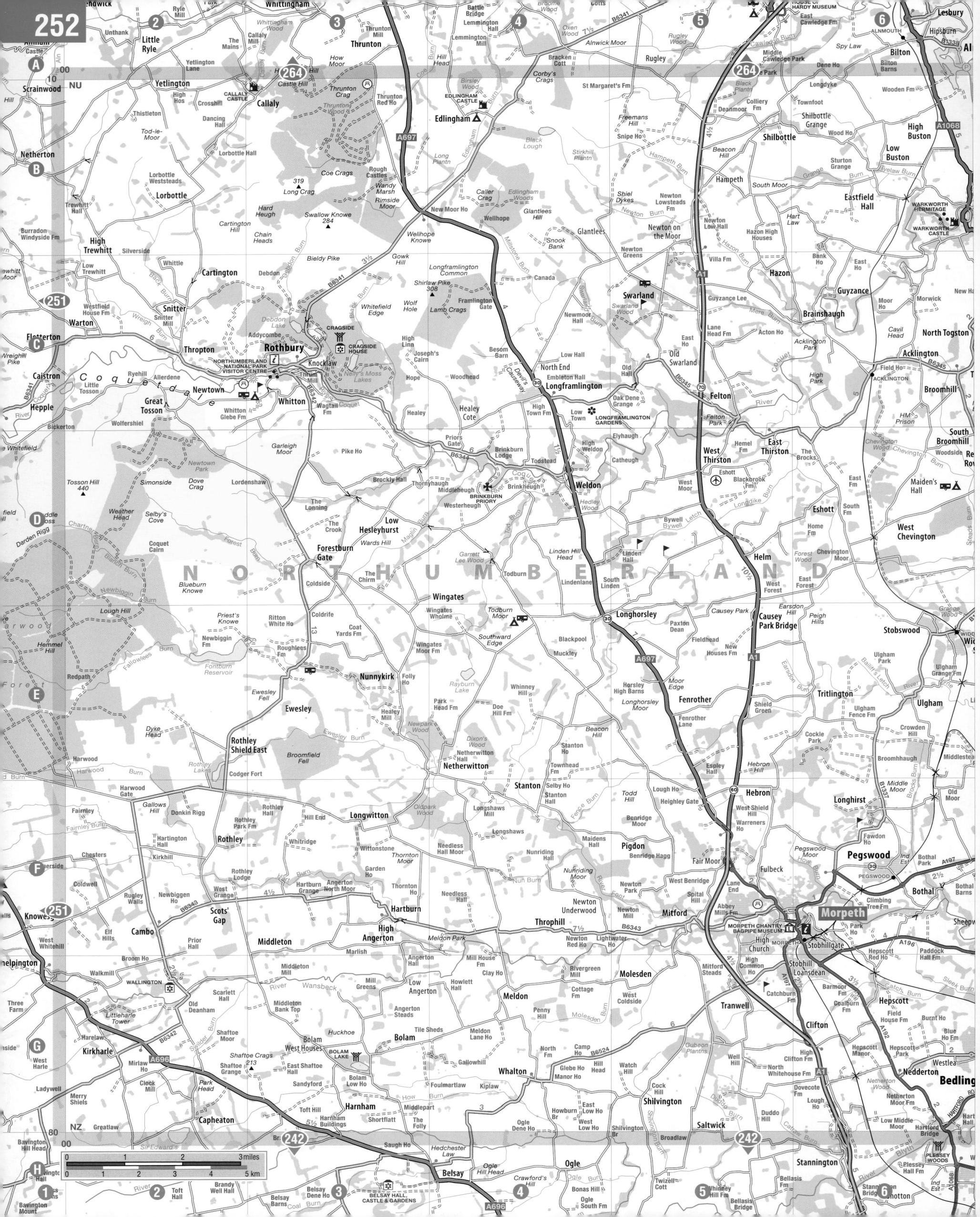

NORTH

SEA

North Blyth

Blyth

Amble

High Hauxley

Low Hauxley

Radcliffe

Togston
East Fm

Togston
Hall

Togston
Barns

ogston

Gloster
Hill

Moorhouse
Fm

Danger
area

Ladyburn
Lake

Hadston

DRURIDGE
BAY

Druridge
Bay

Whitefield
Ho

Chibburn
Fm

High Chibburn

Widdrington

Hemscott Hill

A1068

ddrington
Station

Highthorn

Cresswell

Warkworthlane
Cott

North
inton Fm

Hagg
House

Ellington

Cresswell
Home Fm

Linton

Lynemouth

East
Moor Fm

Potland
Fm

Works

QUEEN
ELIZABETH II

WOODHORN
COLLIERY MUS

A189

Woodhorn

WOODHORN
CHURCH MUS

Bus Cen

Woodbridge

Ashington

Newbiggin-by-the-Sea

Hirst

North
Seaton

Newbiggin Bay

WANSBECK

North Seaton
Colliery

Stakeford

STAKEFORD LANE

West
Sleekburn

Guide Post

Scotland
Gate

Bomarsund

Choppington

Cambois

East
Sleekburn

Bedlington
Station

Mount
Pleasant Fm

B1331 STEAD

Bebside

CHURCH LANE

COWPEN ROAD

Cowpen

A193

ton

A1068

Humford
Mill

A189

Isabella
Pit

243

243

East
Hartford

Low
Horton Fm

New Delaval

Newsh

South
Beach

est Hartford

Laverock
Hall

South
Newsham

A1061

Gloucester
Lodge Fm

A192

Shankhouse

Lysdon
Fm

Marden Rocks

Alnmouth
Bay

nmouth

265

265

50
10
NU

Birling

Warkworth

Warkworth
Harbour

Beal
Bank

Pan
Pt

Wellhaugh
Pt

Coquet
Island

A1068

NZ
80
50

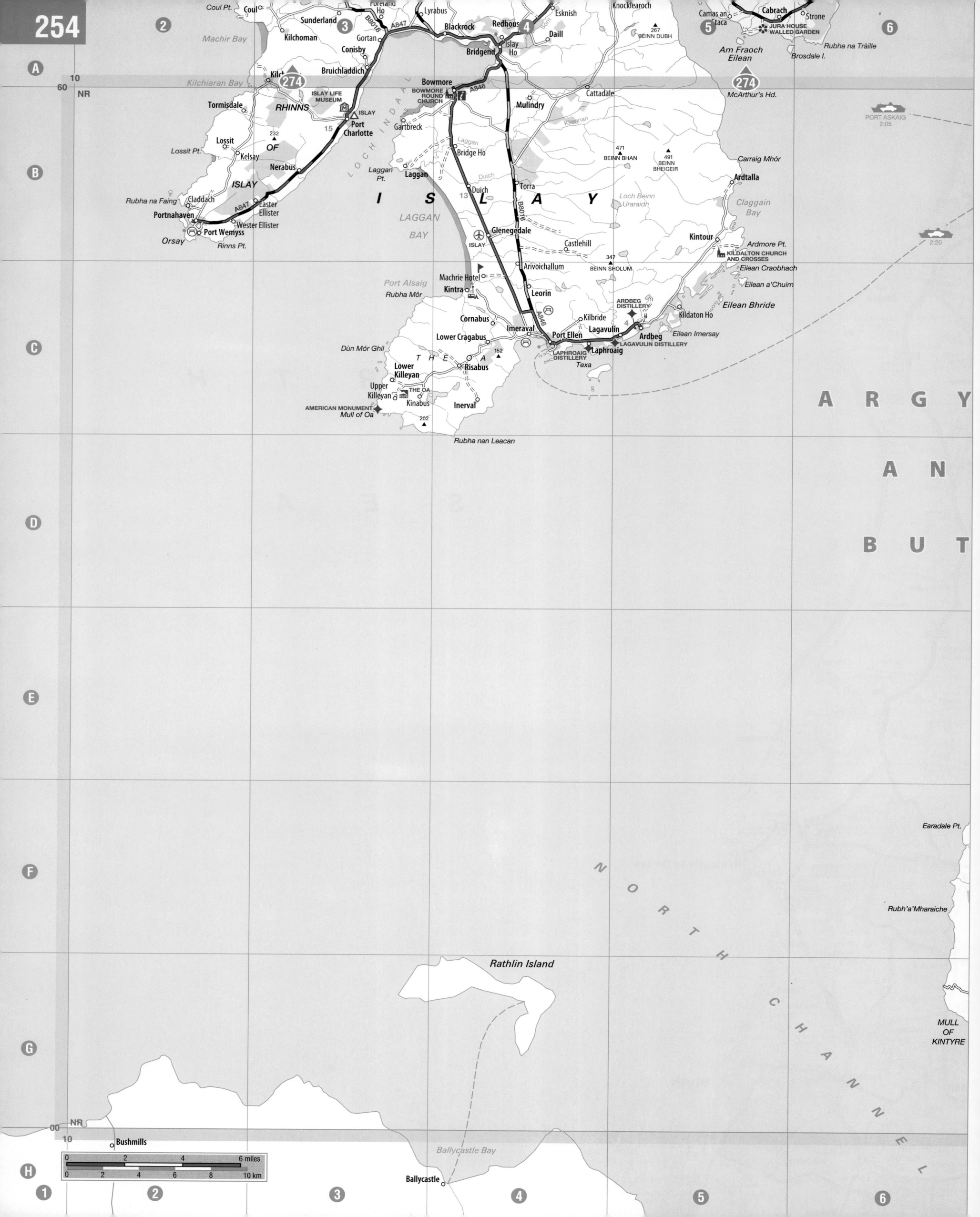

A 10
   60
   NR

B

C

D

E

F

G

   NR
   10

H

1   **2**   **3**   **4**   **5**   **6**

Coul Pt. Coul
Foreland Ho
Sunderland
Kilchoman
Conisby
Gortan
Lyrabus
Blackrock
Redhous
Esknish
Knocklearoch
Camas an
Staca
Cabrach
Strone
JURA HOUSE
WALLED GARDEN
Rubha na Tràille
Brosdale I.

Bridgend
Islay Ho
Daill
267
BEINN DUBH
Am Fraoch
Eilean

Bowmore
BOWMORE
ROUND CHURCH
A846
McArthur's Hd.
274
PORT ASKAIG
2:05

Kilchiaran Bay
Kilc
274
Bruichladdich
ISLAY LIFE
MUSEUM
ISLAY
Cattadale

Tormisdale
RHINNS
Mulindry
Kiennan
471
BEINN BHAN
491
BEINN
BHEIGEIR
Carraig Mhór

Lossit
OF
232
Port
Charlotte
15
Gartbreck
Loch
INDAAL
Laggan
Bridge Ho
Beinn
BEINN
BHEIGEIR
Ardtalla

Lossit Pt.
Kelsay
Laggan
Pt.
Laggan
Duich
13
Loch Beinn
Uraraidh
Claggain
Bay

Nerabus
ISLAY
Duich
Torra
Rubha na Faing
Claddach
Easter
Ellister
Portnahaven
Wester Ellister
Port Wemyss
A847
LAGGAN
BAY
ISLAY
Glenegedale
ISLAY
Kintour
Ardmore Pt.
KILDALTON CHURCH
AND CROSSES
Eilean Craobhach

Orsay
Rinns Pt.
Castlehill
347
BEINN SHOLUM
Eilean a'Chuirn
Eilean Bhride

Port Alsaig
Rubha Mór
Machrie Hotel
Kintra
Arivoichallum
Leorin
ARDBEG
DISTILLERY
4
Eilean Imersay
A

Dùn Mór Ghil
Cornabus
Lower Cragabus
Imeraval
Kilbride
Kildaton Ho
THE
O A
152
Risabus
Port Ellen
Lagavulin
Ardbeg
LAGAVULIN DISTILLERY
R G Y

Lower
Killeyan
Upper
Killeyan
THE OA
Kinabus
Inerval
LAPHROAIG
DISTILLERY
Laphroaig
Texa

AMERICAN MONUMENT
Mull of Oa
202
Rubha nan Leacan
A N

B U T

Earadale Pt.

N O R T H

Rubh'a'Mharaiche

Rathlin Island

C H A N N E L
MULL
OF
KINTYRE

Bushmills

Ballycastle Bay

0   2   4   6 miles
0   2 4 6 8 10 km

Ballycastle

A

B

C

D

E

F

G

H

1 2 3 4 5 6

Isle
of
Arran

NORTH

AYRSHIRE

F I R T H

O F

C L Y D E

40
NS
00

255 266

Port nam
Balach

BRODICK 0:55

Saltcoats

ARDROSSAN
HARBOUR

ARDROSSAN
SOUTH BEACH

ARDROSSAN
TOWN

NORTH AYRSHIRE MUSEUM

South Bay

Outer
Nebbock

Maol Donn
368

Merkland

Merkland
Wood

Merkland Pt
Wine Port

BRODICK
Cladach
Old Quay
ARRAN AROMATICS
VISITOR CENTRE

ISLE OF ARRAN
HERITAGE MUSEUM

Glenshant
Hill

Creag
Rosa

Torr
Breac

Glenrosa

Glen Shurig

THE STRING

B880

Glen Cloy

A841

BRODICK
CASTLE

Brodick

ARDROSSAN 0:55

Corriegills Pt

Strathwhillan

Fairy
Glen

North
Corriegills

Dun
Dubh

South
Corriegills

Clauchland
Hills

Clauchland
Fm

Clauchlands Pt

Clauchlands

Kerr's
Port

Hamilton Isle

255

Glen Ormidale

Sgiath
Bhan

Cnoc
Breac

Cnoc
Dubh

Meall
Buidhe

Margnaheglish

Clauchlands

Benlister Glen

Benlister Burn

Blairbeg

Lamlash

The Ross
311

Monamore
Br

Cordon

White Pt

Mullach
Beag

Holy Island

314
Mullach Mor

Pillar Rock Pt

Monamore Glen

A841

Gortonallister

Cnoc
Dubh

Invein

Urie
Loch

The Knowe
Fm

Auchencairn

Knockenkelly

Kingscross
Pt

Kingscross

Glas
Choirein

Allt Garbh

Borrach

North Kiscadale

Sandbraes

Cnoc
Donn

Cnoc an
Fheidh

Cnoc Mòr

South Kiscadale

Whiting Bay

Aucharoch

GLENASHDALE
FALLS

Glenashdale Burn

Largymore

Kilmory Water

Largymeanoch

Cnoc
Craobhach

Cnoc na
Garbad

Cnoc na
Comhairle

Largybeg

Largybeg Pt

Port na
Gaillin

Torr
bh Mòr

Torr a'
annain

Margenaish
Fm

Levencorroch
Hill

Dippin Head

Dippin

Southbank

East
Bennan

West
Bennan

Levencorroch

Auchenhew

Drumla

Porta
Leacach

STRUEY
ROCKS

Port a'Ghillie
Ghlais

Porta Buidhe

Port
Dearg

Kildonan

Bennan Head

Sound of Pladda

Pladda

255

10
NS
00

244 244

Dur

Broad Craig

Culzean Bay

CULZEAN
CASTLE

CULZEAN

Glasson Rock

Barwhin Pt

Maidenhead
Bay

Balvaird

Morriston

Birniehill

Port
Mutray

A719

0   1   2   3miles
0   1   2   3   4   5 km

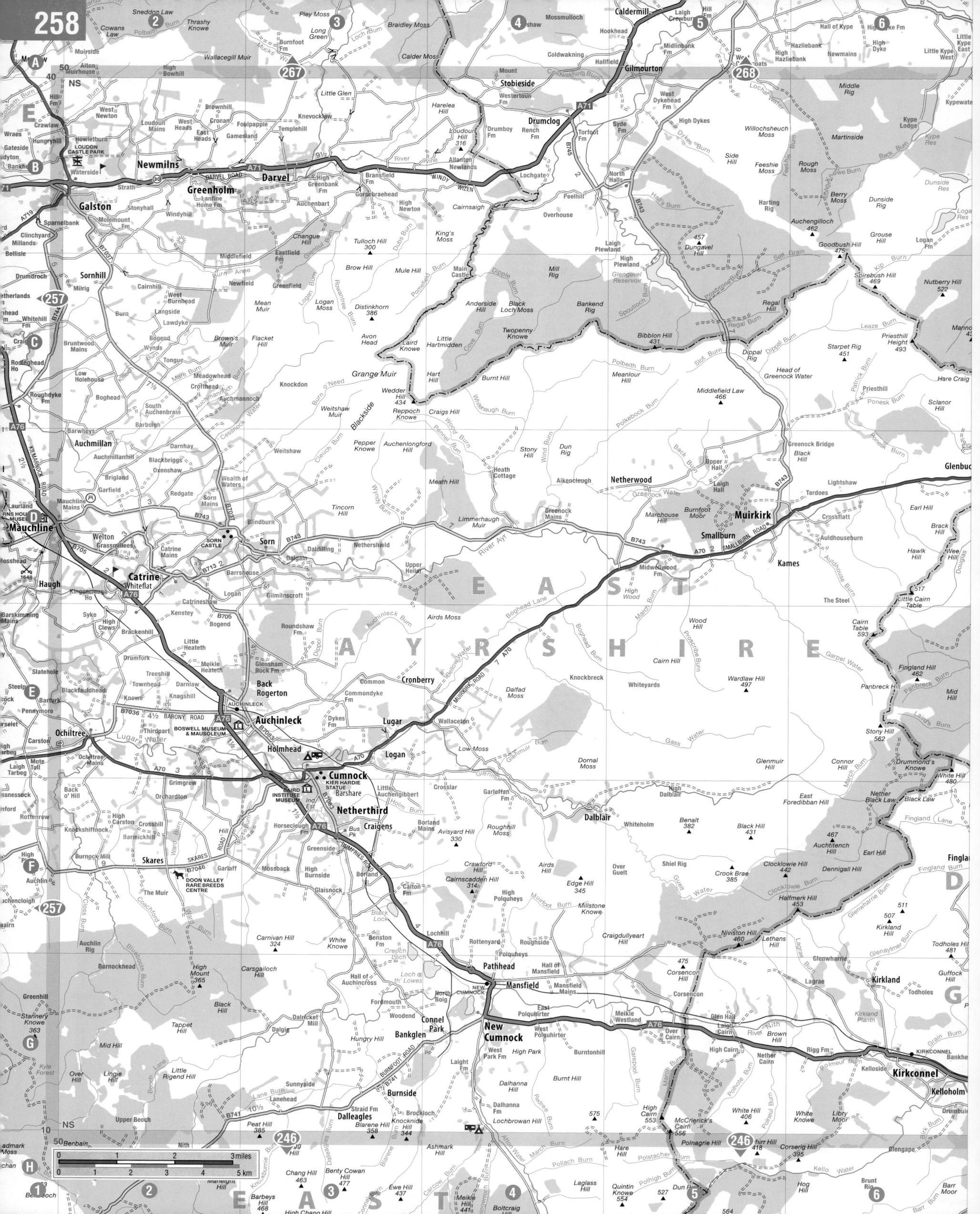

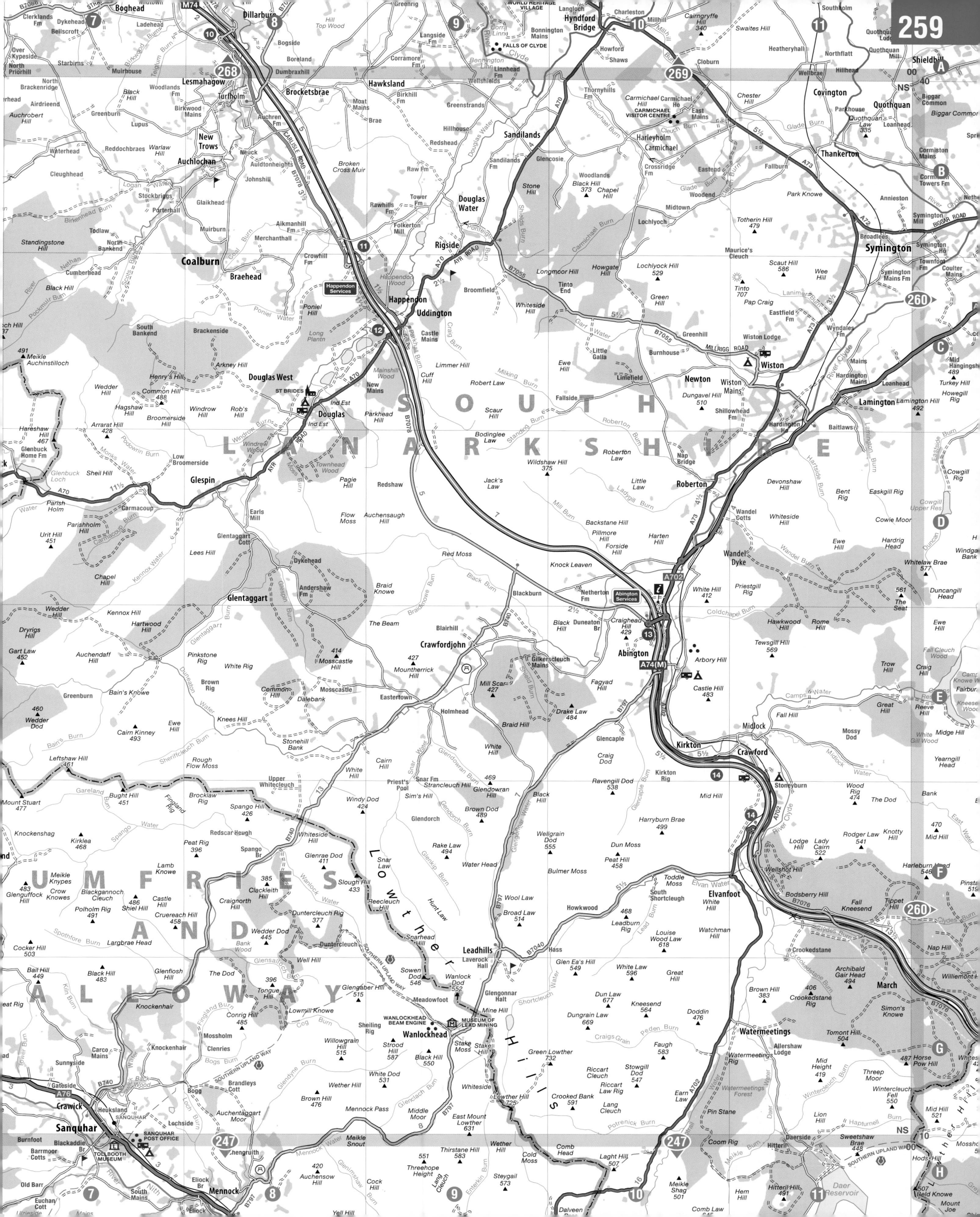

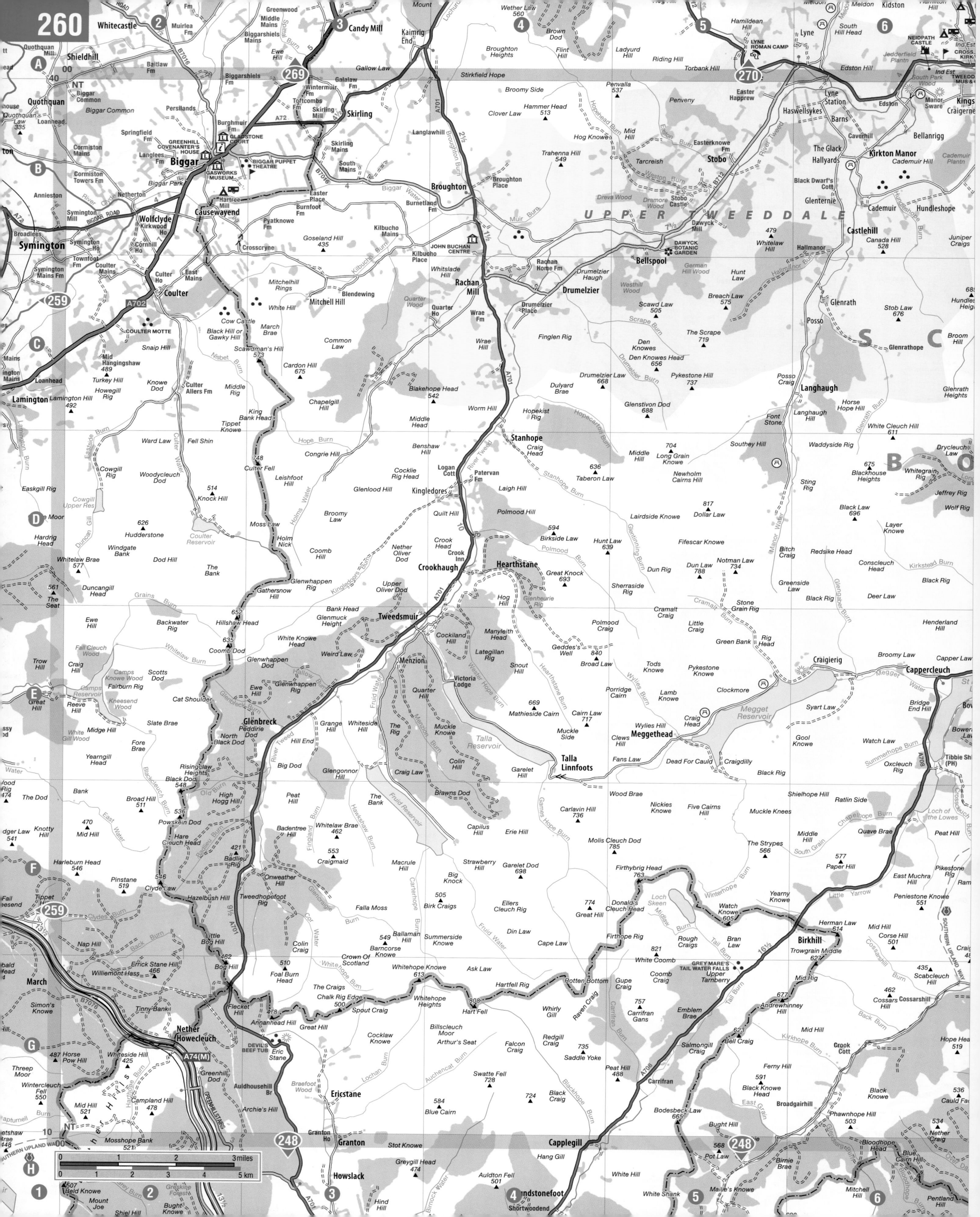

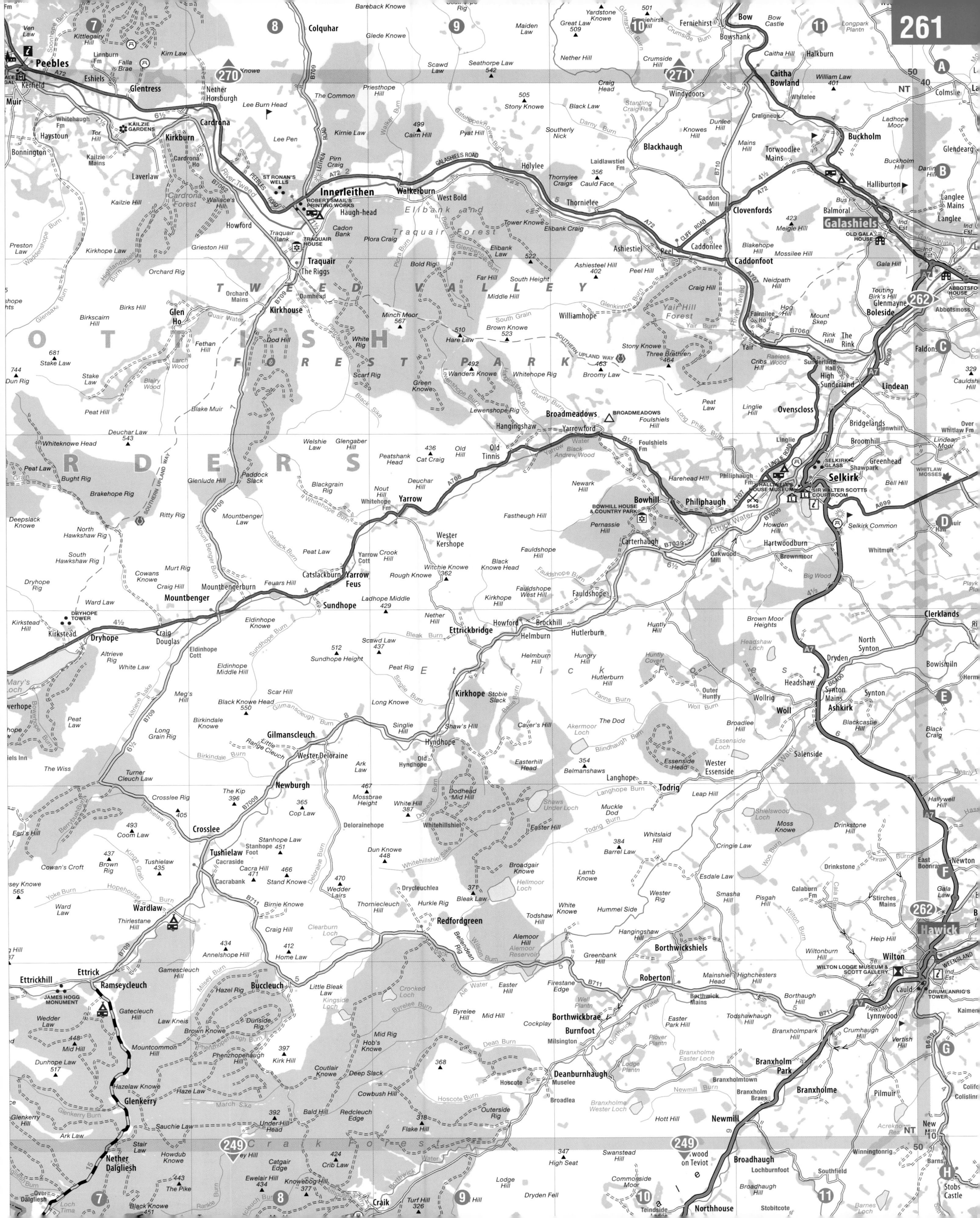

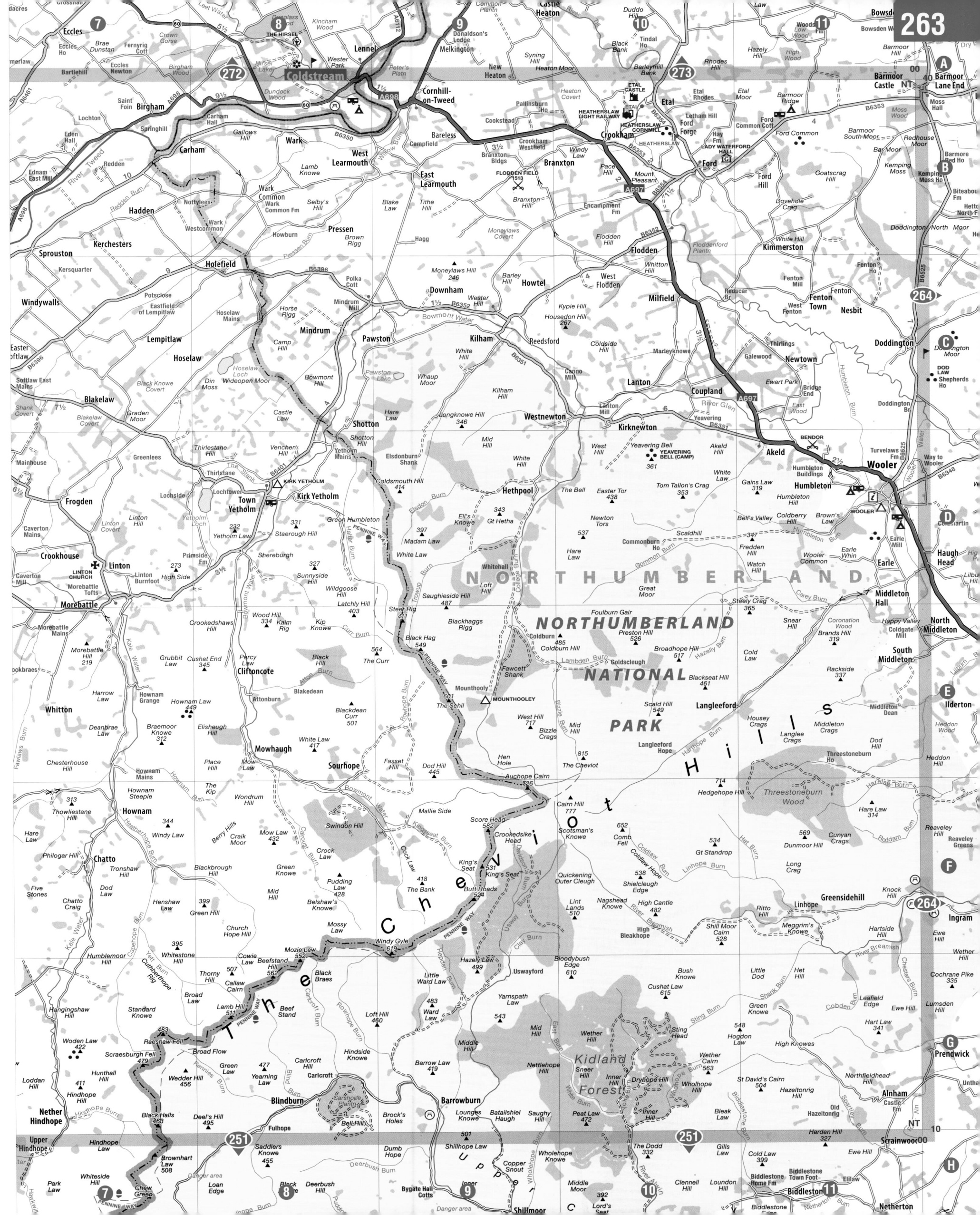

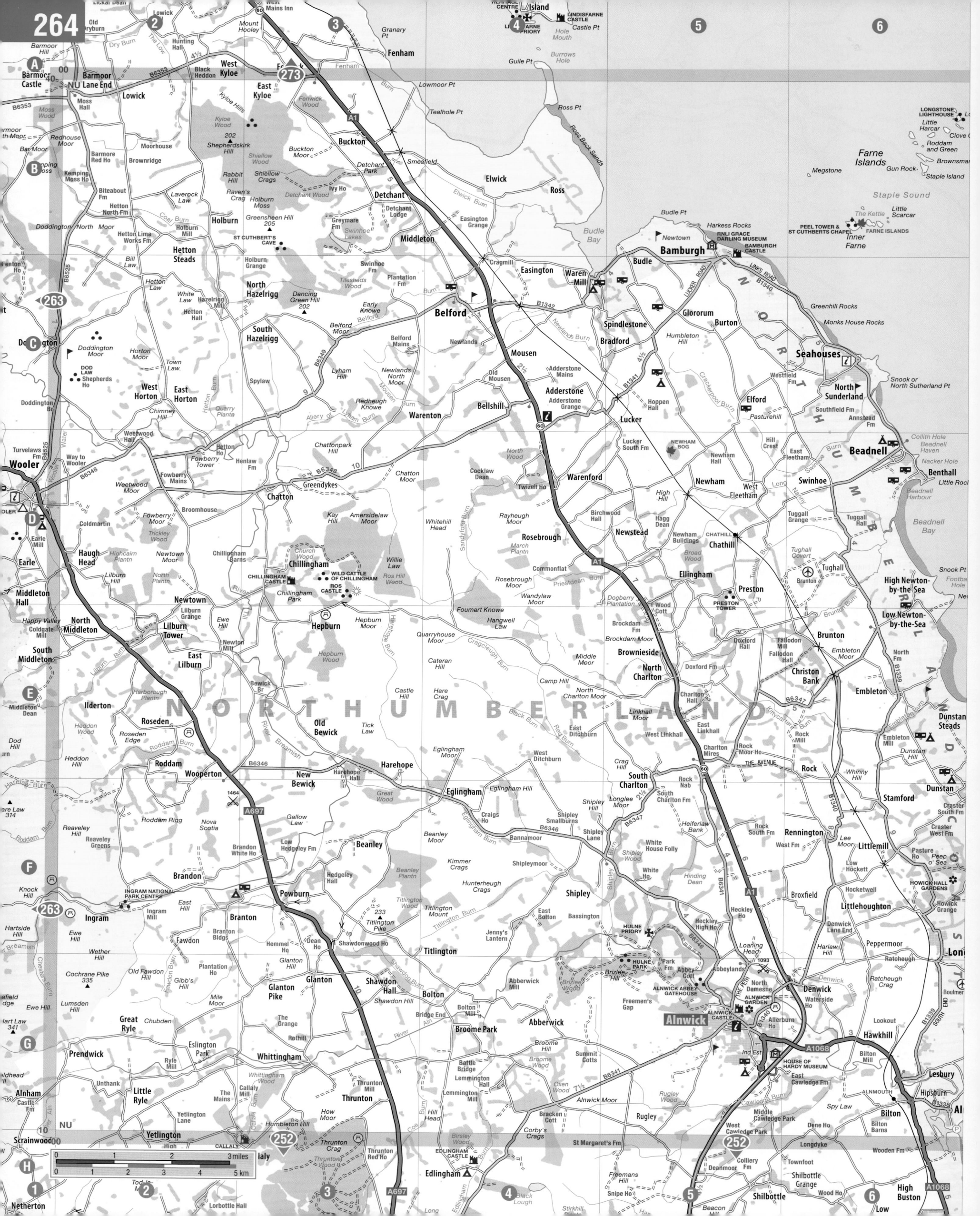

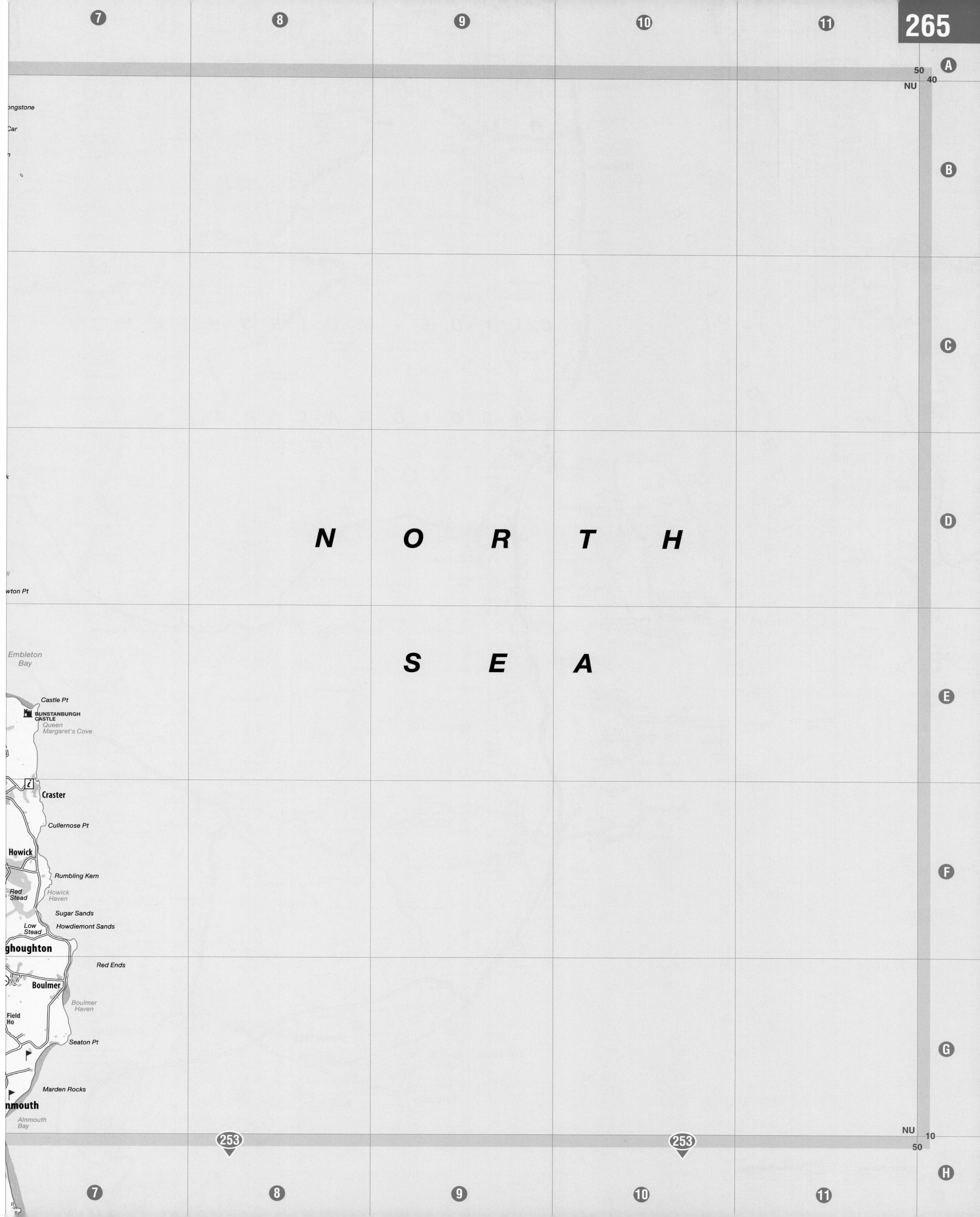

N O R T H

S E A

Embleton
Bay

Castle Pt
DUNSTANBURGH
CASTLE
Queen
Margaret's Cove

Craster

Cullernose Pt

Howick

Rumbling Kern

Red
Stead

Howick
Haven

Sugar Sands

Low
Stead

Howdiemont Sands

ghoughton

Red Ends

Boulmer

Boulmer
Haven

Field
Ho

Seaton Pt

Marden Rocks

nmouth

Alnmouth
Bay

ongstone

Car

wton Pt

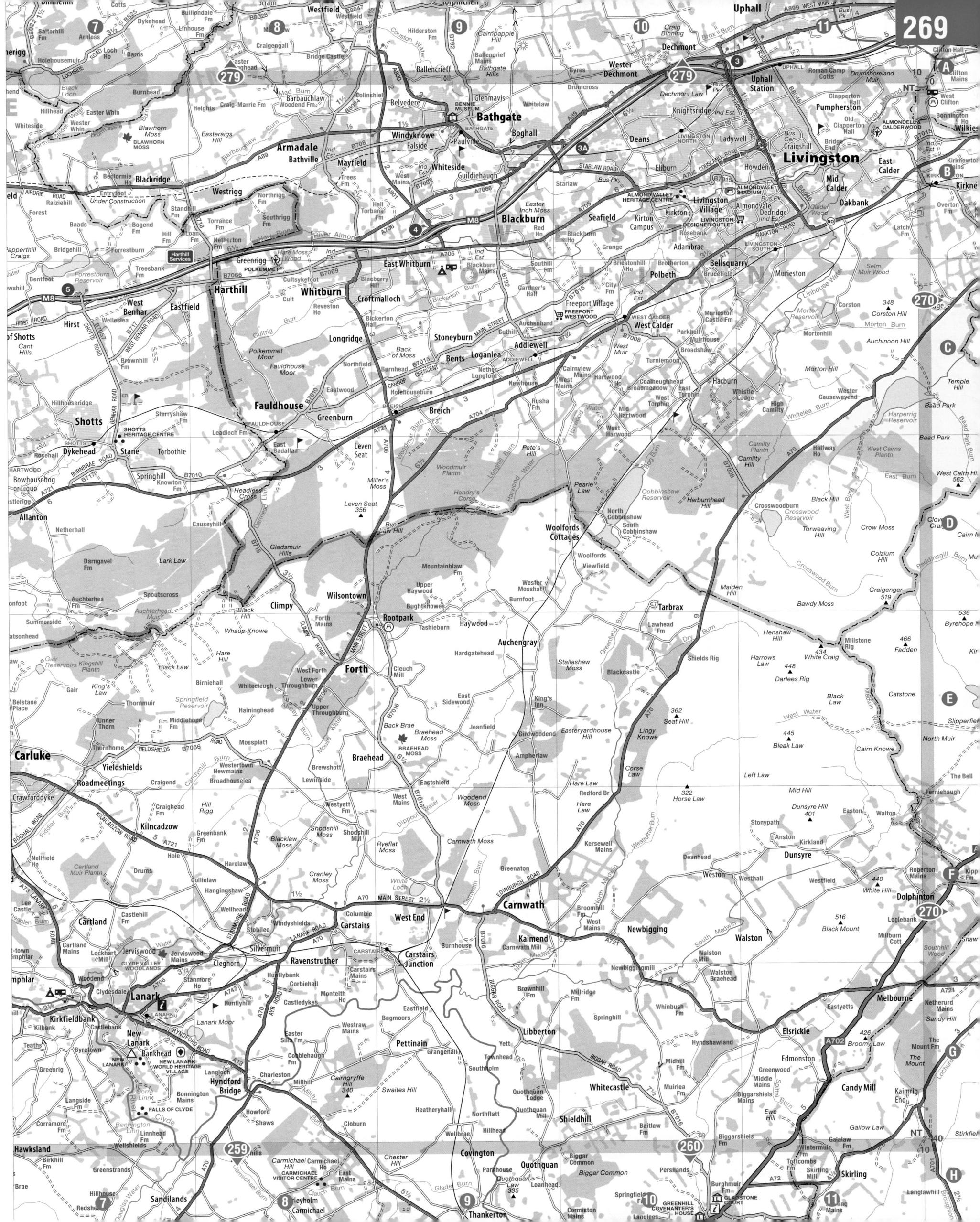

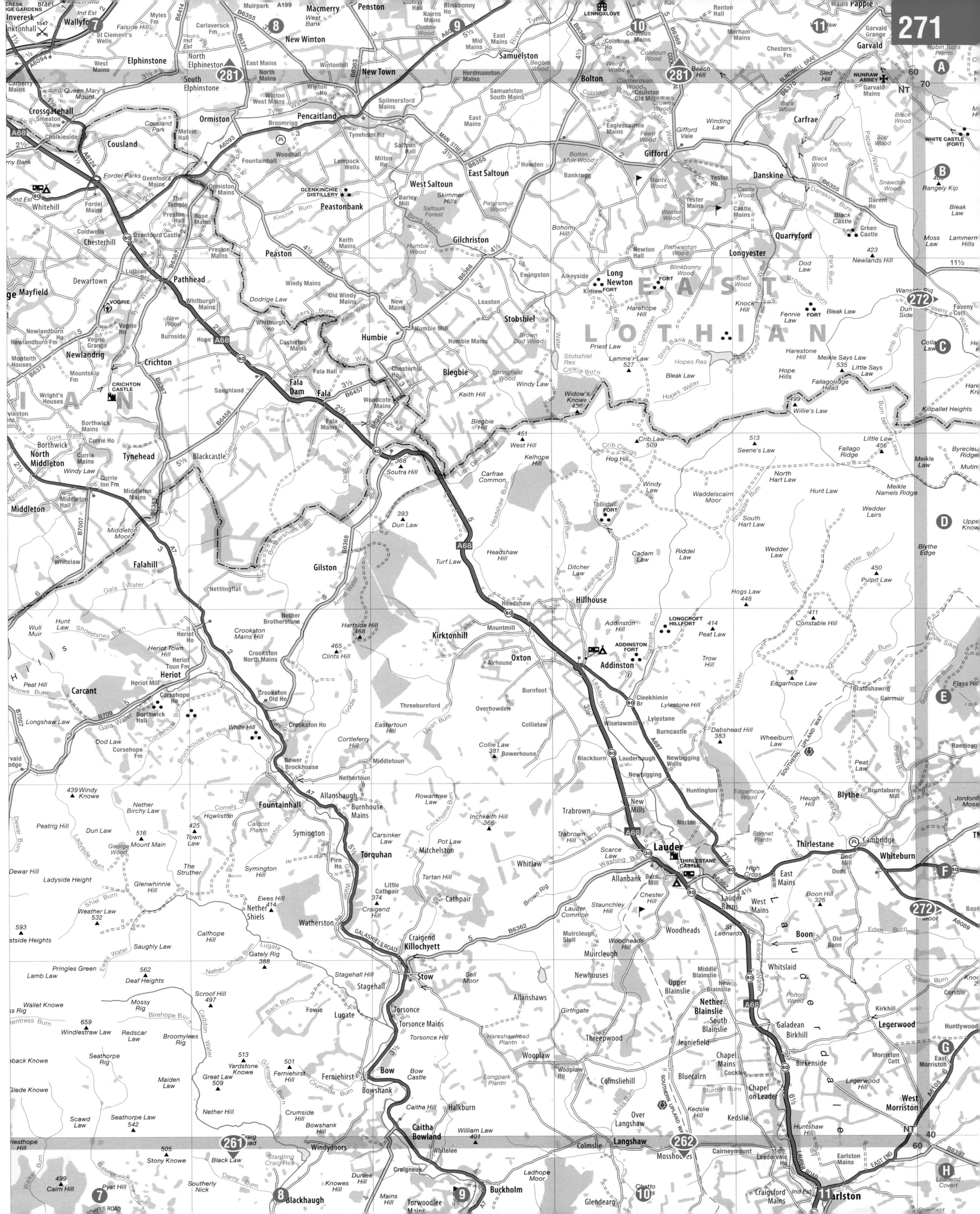

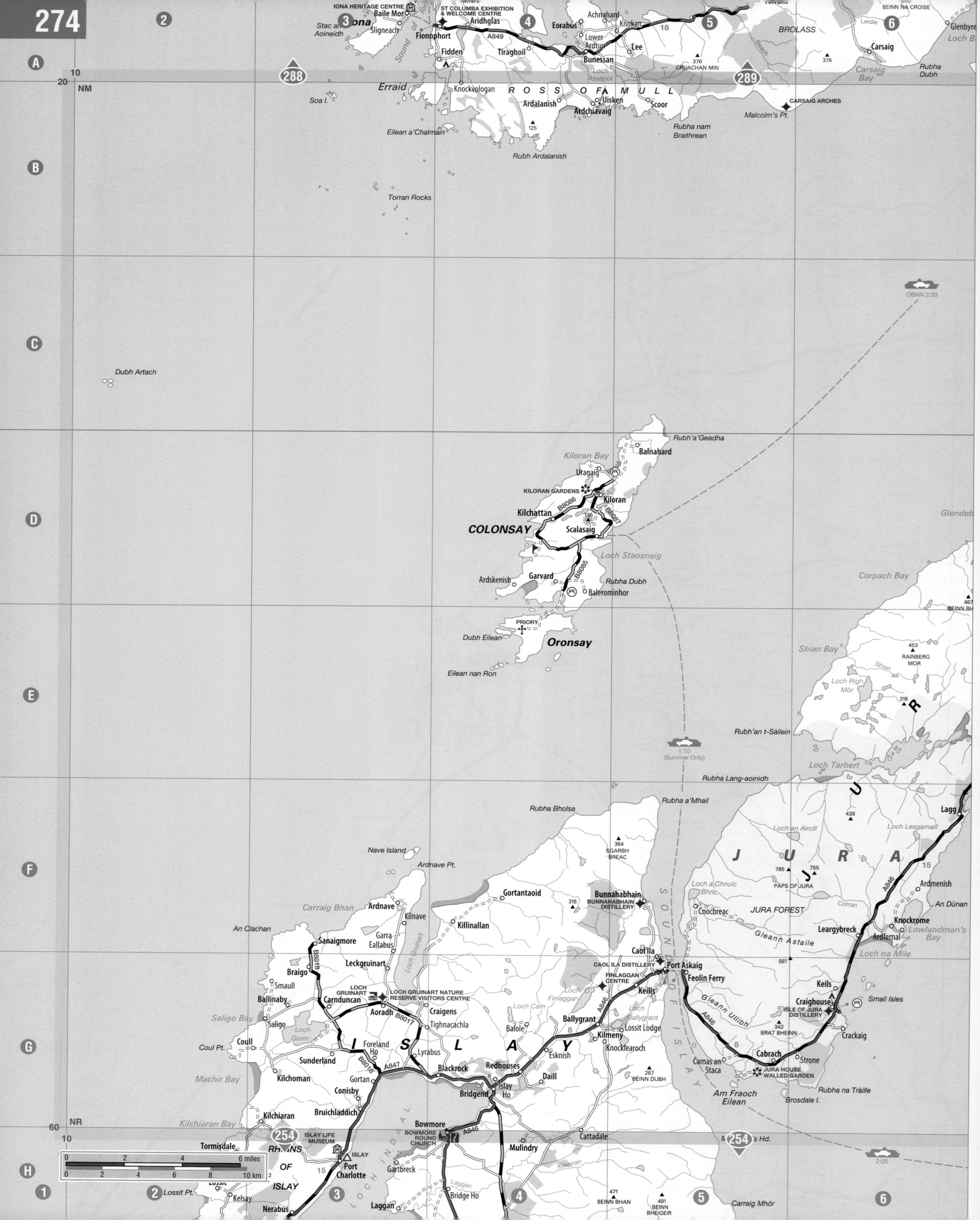

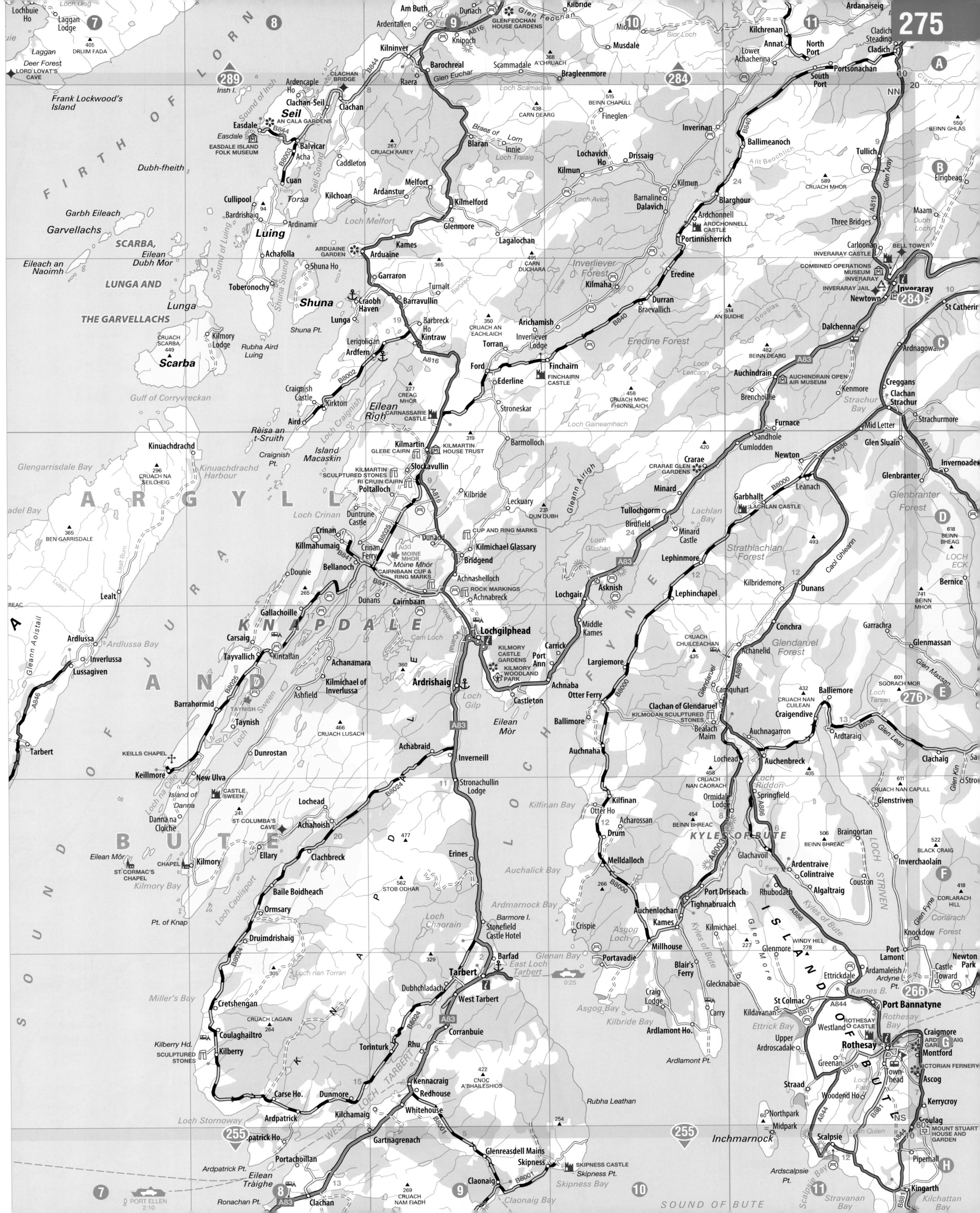

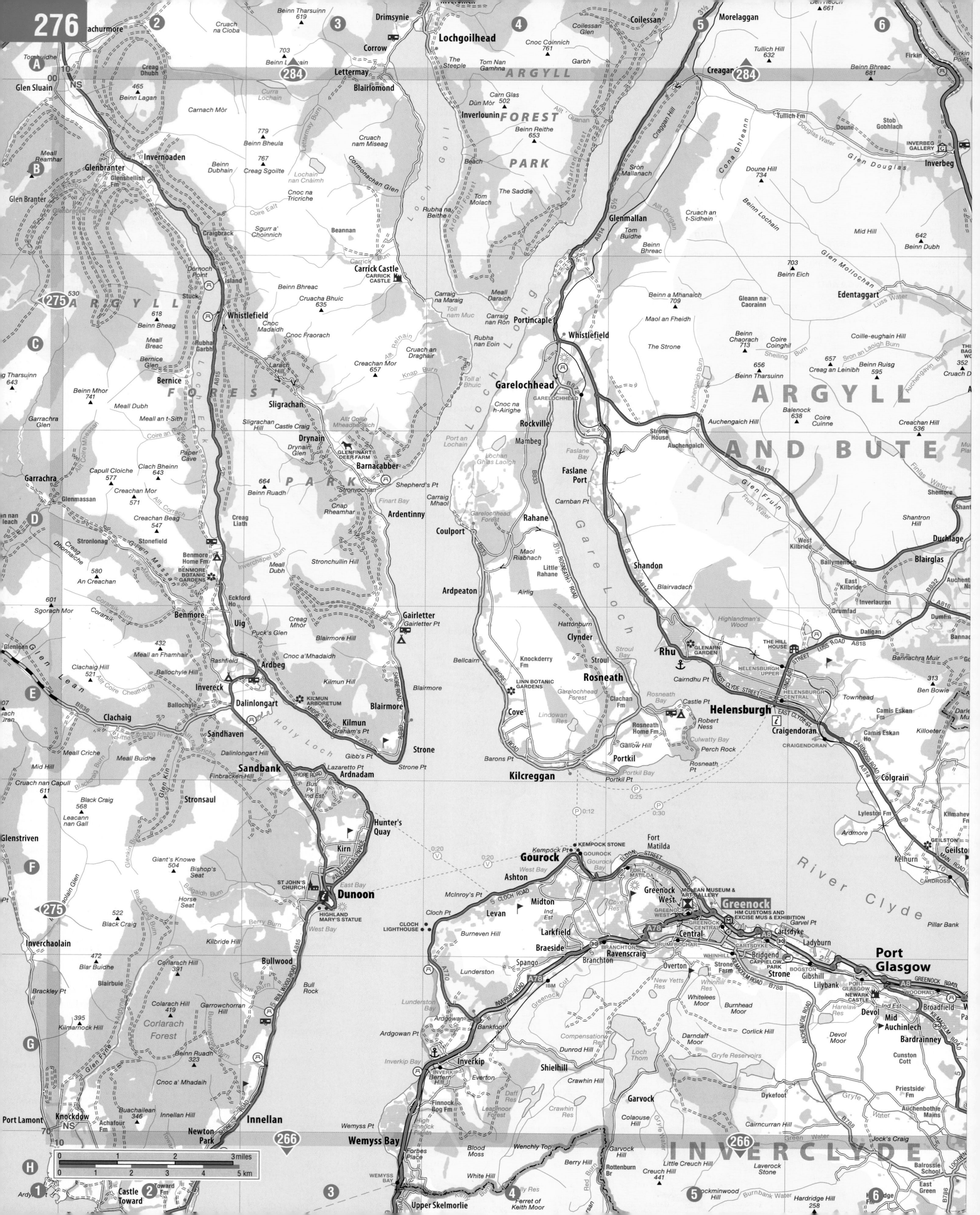

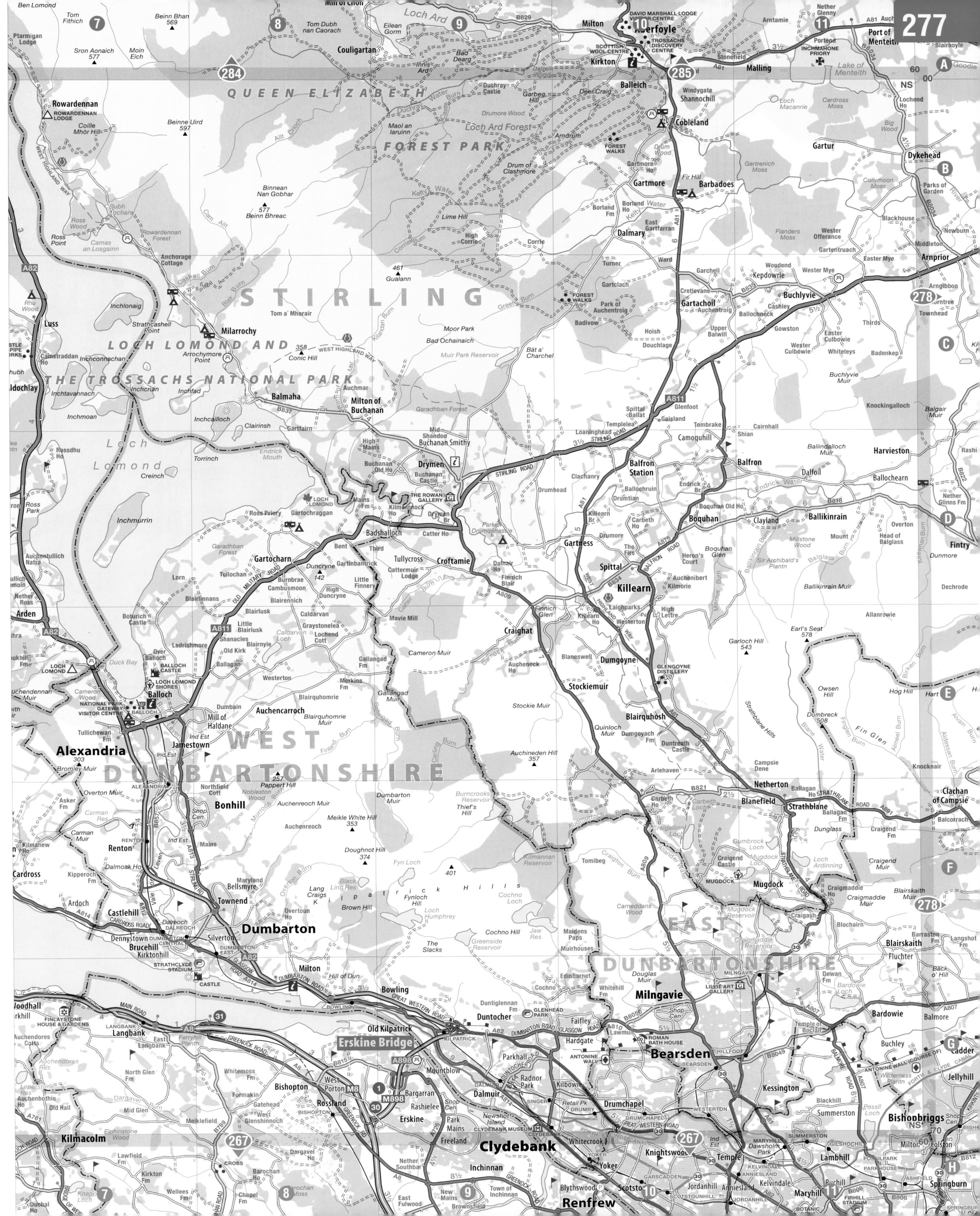

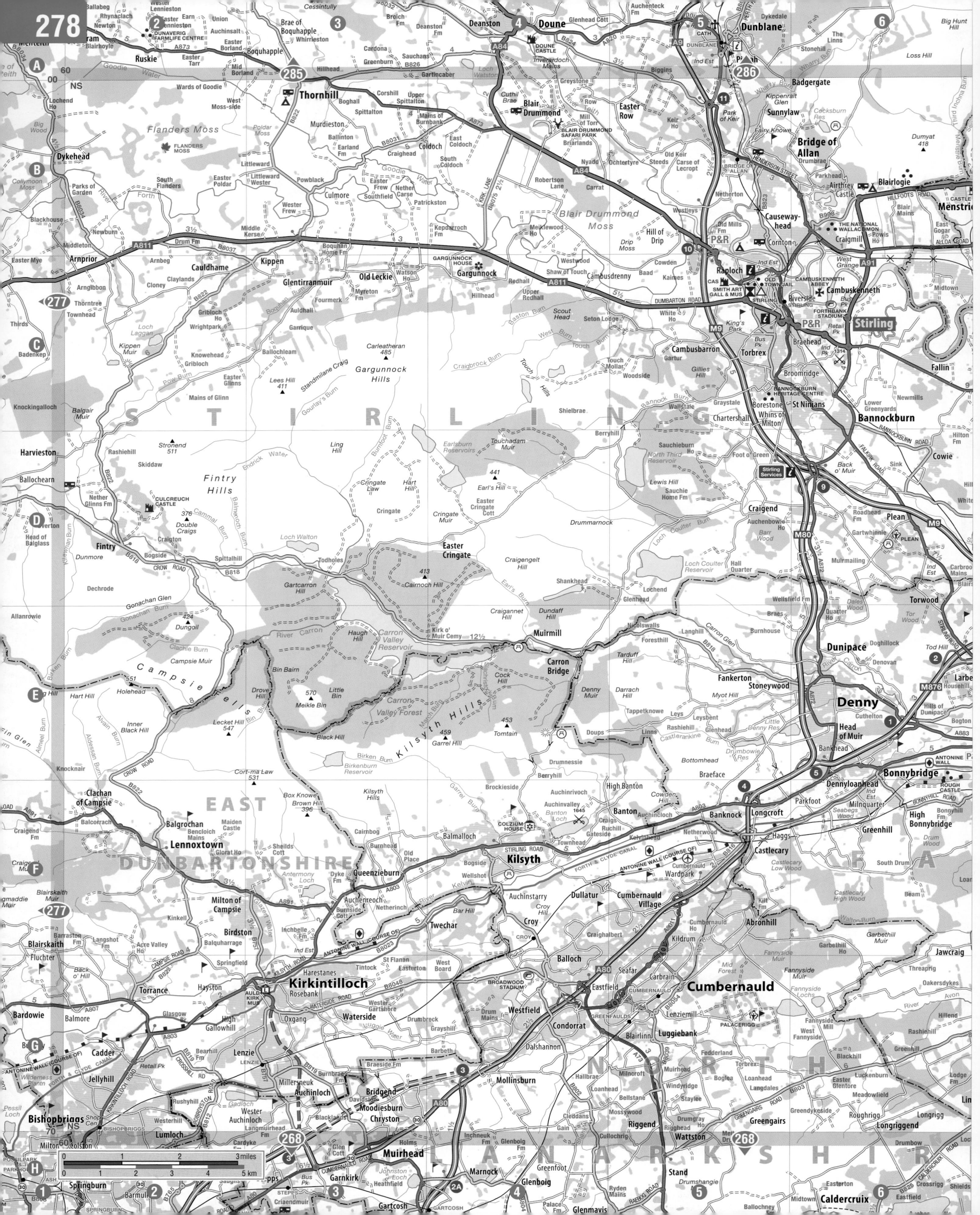

2   3   4   5   6

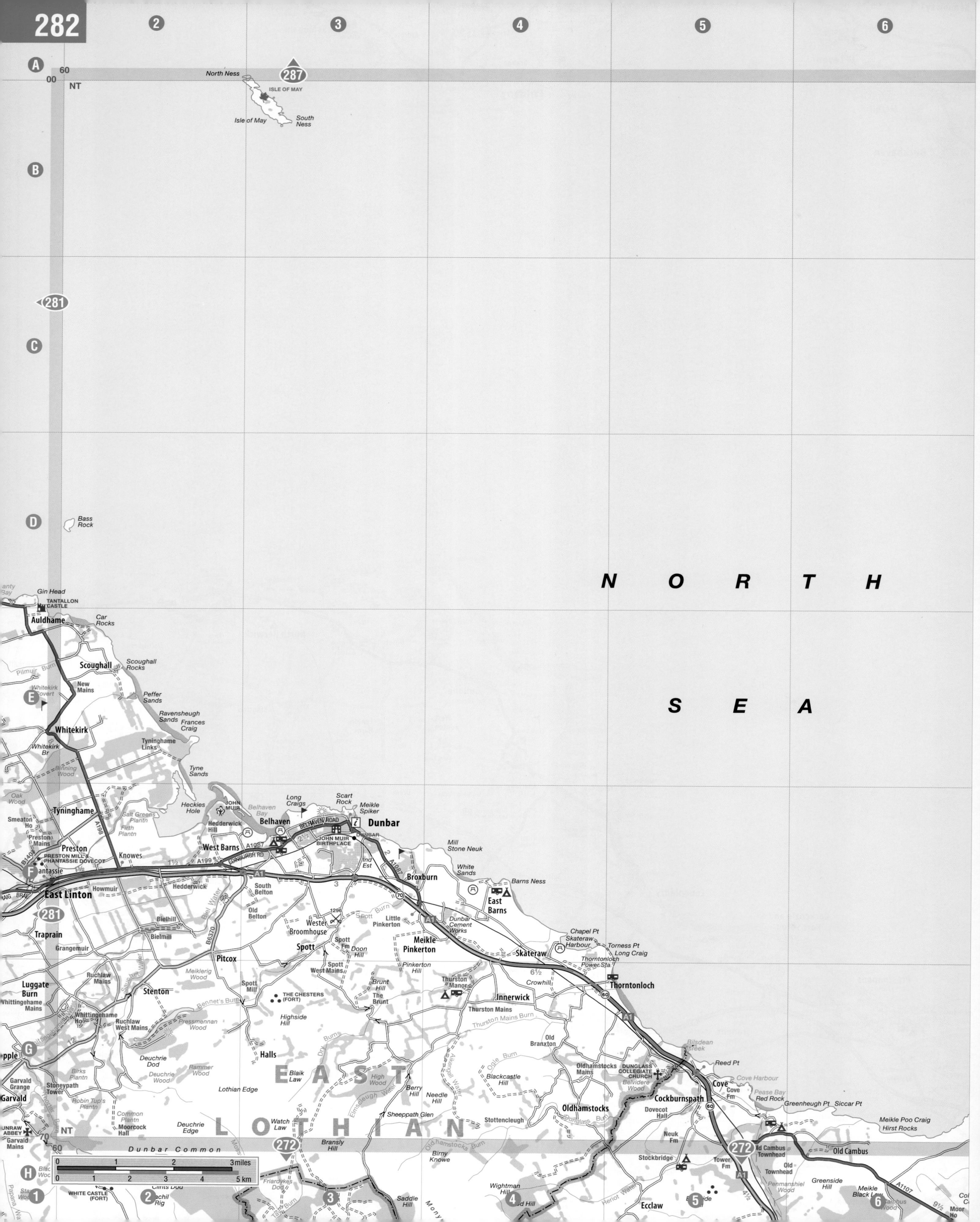

A

60
00
NT

North Ness
287
ISLE OF MAY
Isle of May
South Ness

B

281

C

D

Bass
Rock

N O R T H

anty Bay
Gin Head
TANTALLON CASTLE
Auldhame
Car Rocks

S E A

Scoughall Rocks
Scoughall
New Mains
Peffer Sands
Whitekirk Covert
Ravensheugh Sands
Frances Craig

E

Whitekirk
Whitekirk Br
Tyninghame Links
Tyne Sands

Oak Wood
Binning Wood

Heckies Hole
JOHN MUIR
Long Craigs
Scart Rock
Meikle Spiker

Smeaton Ho
Tyninghame
Salt Greens Plantn
Firth Plantn
Hedderwick Hill
Belhaven
BELHAVEN ROAD
Dunbar
DUNBAR
Mill Stone Neuk

Preston Mains
Preston
PRESTON MILL PHANTASSIE DOVECOT
Knowes
West Barns
A1087
JOHN MUIR BIRTHPLACE
2½
EDINBURGH RD
A199
Ind Est

F

antassie
East Linton
1½
A1
3
Broxburn
2
A1087
White Sands
Barns Ness

281
Howmuir
Hedderwick
South Belton
1296
Dunbar Cement Works
A1
70
Dunbar Burn
East Barns
Barns Ness

Traprain
Bielhill
Bielmill
Old Belton
Wester Broomhouse
Little Pinkerton
Meikle Pinkerton
Chapel Pt
Skateraw Harbour
Torness Pt
Long Craig

Grangemuir
Pitcox
Meiklerig Wood
Spott
Spott Fm
Doon Hill
Pinkerton Hill
Thurston Manor
Skateraw
Thorntonloch Power Sta.

Luggate Burn
Ruchlaw Mains
Stenton
Spott Mill
Spott West Mains
Brunt Hill
The Brunt
Thurston Mains
Innerwick
6½
Crowhill
Thorntonloch
60

Whittingehame Mains
Whittingehame Ho
Ruchlaw West Mains
THE CHESTERS (FORT)
Highside Hill
Thurston Mains Burn

G

apple
Birks Plantn
Pressmennan Wood
Rammer Wood
Halls
Blaik Law
Bell Water
High Wood
Berry Hill
Needle Hill
Old Branxton
Blackcastle Hill
Oldhamstocks Mains
DUNGLASS COLLEGIATE CHURCH
Belvidere Wood
Bilsdean Creek
Reed Pt
Cove
Cove Harbour
Pease Bay
Red Rock
Greenheugh Pt
Siccar Pt

Garvald Grange
Stoneypath Tower
Deuchrie Dod
Deuchrie Wood
Lothian Edge
E A S T
Watch Law
Sheeppath Glen
Oldhamstocks Burn
Oldhamstocks
Cockburnspath
Dovecot Fm
Meikle Poo Craig
Hirst Rocks

Garvald
UNRAW ABBEY
Garvald Mains
70
60
NT
Robin Tup's Plantn
Common Plantn
Moorcock Hall
Deuchrie Edge
L O T H I A N
Stottencleugh
Neuk Fm
60
272
d Cambus Townhead
Old Cambus

Blin Woo
Dunbar Common
Bransly Hill
Birny Knowe
Old amstocks Burn
Dunglass Burn
Stockbridge
Tower Fm
Old Townhead
A1
Penmanshiel Wood
Greenside Hill
A1107
Meikle Black Law
ol C

H

0 1 2 3 miles
0 1 2 3 4 5 km

Sta Woo
Papana Wa
WHITE CASTLE (FORT)
achil Rig
Clints Dod
272
Friardykes Dod
Saddle Hill
Mory
Wightman Hill
d Hill
Ecclaw
5side
Meikle mbus Wood
9½

1   2   3   4   5   6

7   8   9   10   11

A

NT

B

C

D

E

F

G

Fast Castle
Head   Wheat Stack

Telegraph
Hill   FAST
CASTLE

NT

10

Oatlee Hill

Dowlaw Burn

Lumsdaine

273   St Abb's Head

ST ABB'S HEAD

273

Horsecastle Bay

H

Lumsdaine
Moor   Coldingham Loch

Mire
Loch

dingham
ommon

Cross
Law

Bell
Hill   Starney Bay

Moorside
Plantn

7   8   9   10   11

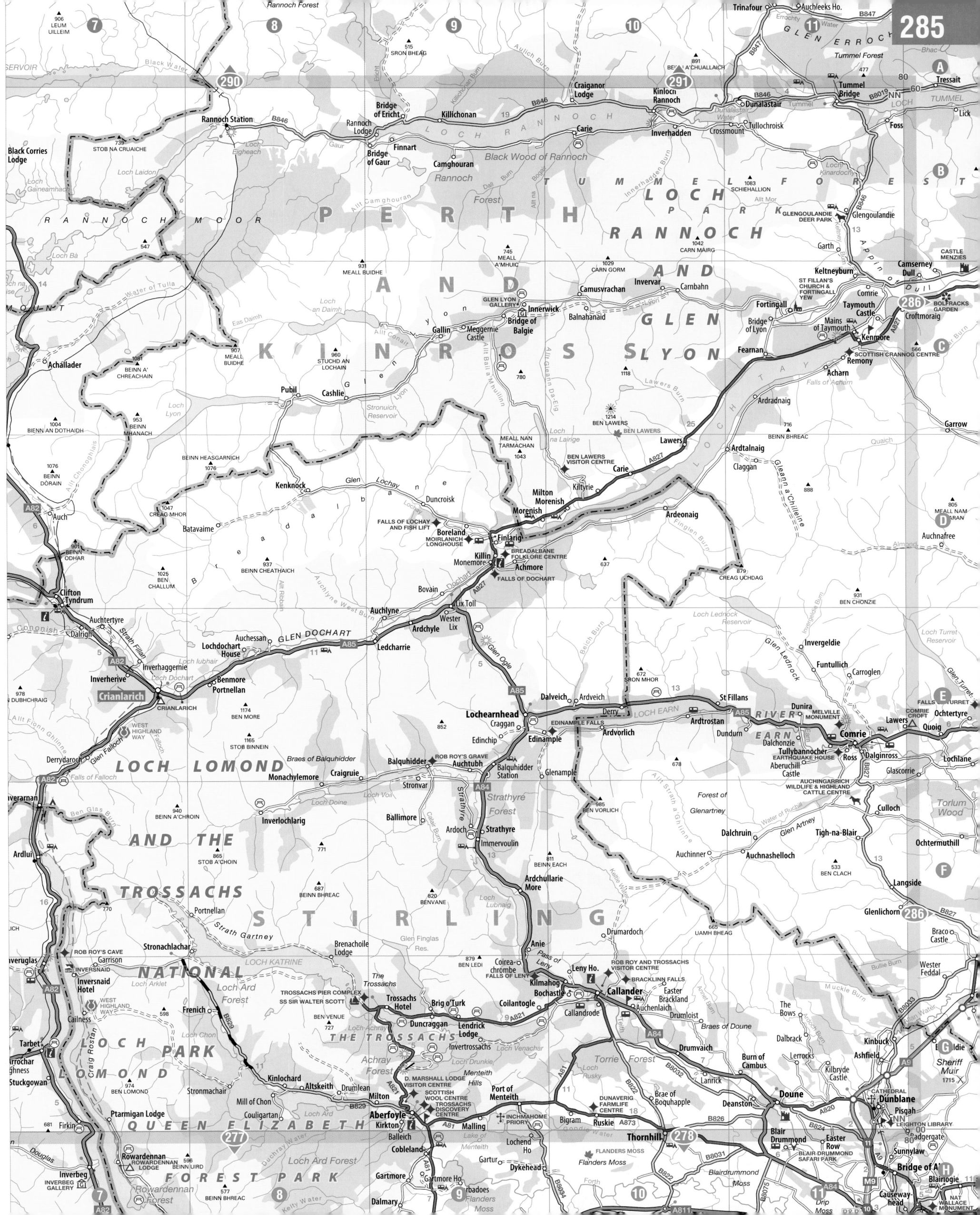

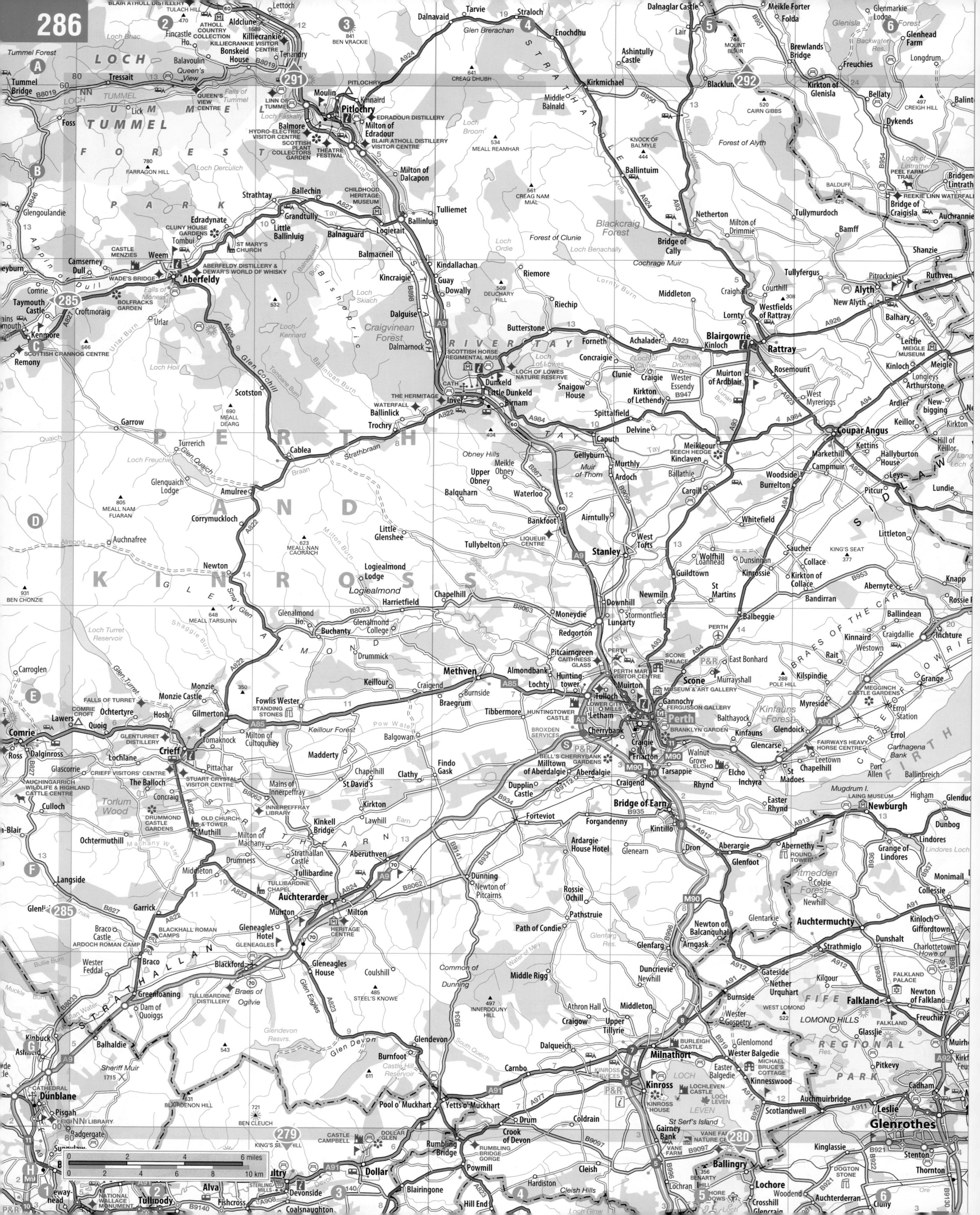

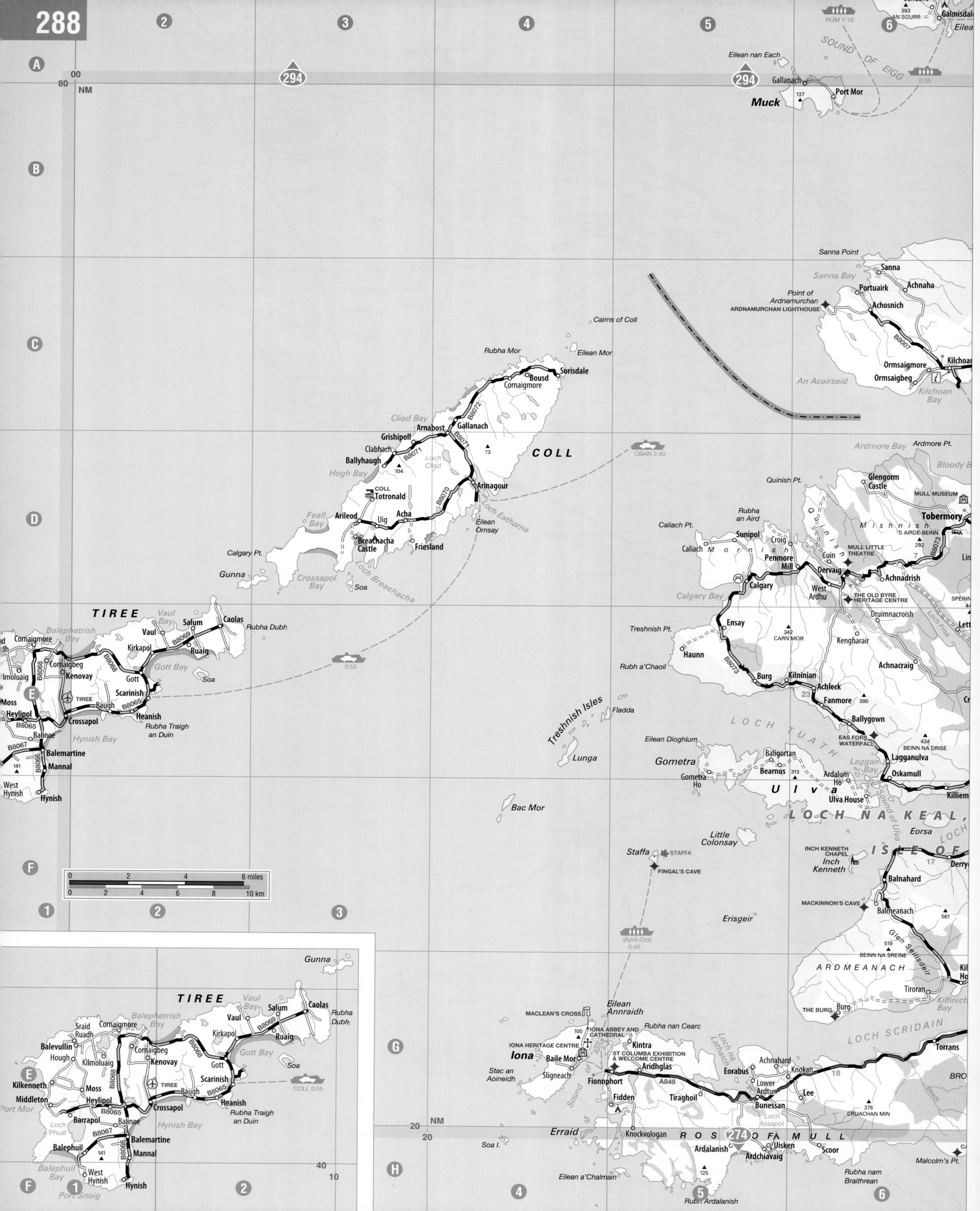

SOUND OF EIGG

RÚM 1:10

AN SGURR

Galmisdal

393

Eilea

Eilean nan Each

294

Gallanach

Port Mor

137

Muck

Sanna Point

Sanna Bay

Sanna

Achnaha

Portuairk

Achosnich

Point of
Ardnamurchan
ARDNAMURCHAN LIGHTHOUSE

B8007

Cairns of Coll

Rubha Mor

Eilean Mor

Bousd

Sorisdale

Cornaigmore

B8072

Arnabost

Gallanach

B8071

Grishipoll

Clabhach

B8071

Ballyhaugh

104

Loch
Clad

73

COLL

OBAN 2:40

Ormsaigmore

Ormsaigbeg

Kilchoar

Kilchoan
Bay

Ardmore Bay

Ardmore Pt.

Bloody B

Cliad Bay

Hogh Bay

COLL

Totronald

B8070

Loch Eatharna

Arinagour

Quinish Pt.

Glengorm
Castle

MULL MUSEUM

Arileod

Uig

Acha

Feall
Bay

Breachacha
Castle

Friesland

Eilean
Ornsay

Loch
Breachacha

Caliach Pt.

Rubha
an Aird

Sunipol

Croig

Penmore
Mill

Cuin

Dervaig

Mornish

Mishnish

'S AIRDE-BEINN

Tobermory

292

B8073

7

MULL LITTLE
THEATRE

Achnadrish

SPEINN

44

Calgary Pt.

TIREE

Gunna

Calgary
Bay

Soa

Crossapol
Bay

Calgary

West
Ardhu

THE OLD BYRE
HERITAGE CENTRE

Druimnacroish

Loch Frisa

Lett

Vaul
Bay

Salum

Caolas

Cornaigmore

Vaul

Kirkapol

B8069

Ruaig

Rubha Dubh

Treshnish Pt.

Ensay

342
CARN MOR

Kengharair

Achnacraig

Cr

Balephetrish
Bay

d

Cornaigbeg

Kenovay

B8068

Gott

Gott Bay

Soa

Rubh a'Chaoil

Haunn

B8073

Burg

Kilninian

Achleck

Fanmore

390

Imoluaig

dh

Moss

Scarinish

Heylipol

TIREE

Baugh

B8065

Heanish

Rubha Traigh
an Duin

Treshnish Isles

Fladda

Eilean Dioghlum

Ballygown

EAS FORS
WATERFALL

424
BEINN NA DRISE

Lagganulva

Balinoe

B8067

Balemartine

141

B8066

Mannal

Hynish Bay

Lunga

Baligortan

Bearnus

313

Gometra

Ardalum
Ho

Loch
Gometra
Ho

424

Laggan
Bay

Oskamull

LOCH TUATH

Ulva

West
Hynish

Hynish

Bac Mor

Ulva House

Killiem

LOCH NA KEAL,

Erraid

Staffa

STAFFA

STAFFA
CHAPEL

FINGAL'S CAVE

Little
Colonsay

INCH KENNETH
CHAPEL

Inch
Kenneth

ISLE OF

Derry

17

Eorsa

Loch

MACKINNON'S CAVE

Balnahard

Balmeanach

561

Erisgeir

(April-Oct)
0:45

Glen Sellisdeir

519

BEINN NA SREINE

ARDMEANACH

THE BURG

Burg

Kil
Ho

Tiroran

Kilfinich
Bay

MACLEAN'S CROSS

Eilean
Annraidh

Rubha nan Cearc

IONA ABBEY AND
CATHEDRAL

100

IONA HERITAGE CENTRE

Kintra

Achnahard

Knokan

376
CRUACHAN MIN

Iona

Baile Mor

ST COLUMBA EXHIBITION
& WELCOME CENTRE

Aridhglas

Eorabus

Lower
Ardtun

Lee

Torrans

BRO

Stac an
Aoineidh

Sligneach

Fionnphort

A849

Tiraghoil

Bunessan

18

Loch
na
Lathaich

Loch
Scridain

Fidden

NM

Knockvologan

ROSS OF MULL

274

Soa I.

Ardalanish

Uisken

Scoor

Eilean a'Chalmain

125

Ardchiavaig

Malcolm's Pt.

Rubha Ardalanish

Rubha nam
Braithrean

Inset map (bottom left): TIREE

Gunna

TIREE

Vaul
Bay

Salum

Caolas

Sraid
Ruadh

Cornaigmore

Vaul

Kirkapol

B8069

Ruaig

Rubha
Dubh

Balevullin

Hough

Kilmoluaig

Balephetrish
Bay

Cornaigbeg

Kenovay

B8068

Gott

Gott Bay

Soa

COLL 0:55

Kilkenneth

Middleton

Moss

Heylipol

TIREE

Scarinish

Port Mor

Loch
a'Phuill

Barrapol

B8065

Balinoe

Baugh

B8065

Heanish

Rubha Traigh
an Duin

Balephuil

B8067

Balemartine

141

B8066

Mannal

Hynish Bay

Balephuil
Bay

West
Hynish

Hynish

Port Snoig

NM

20

20

40

10

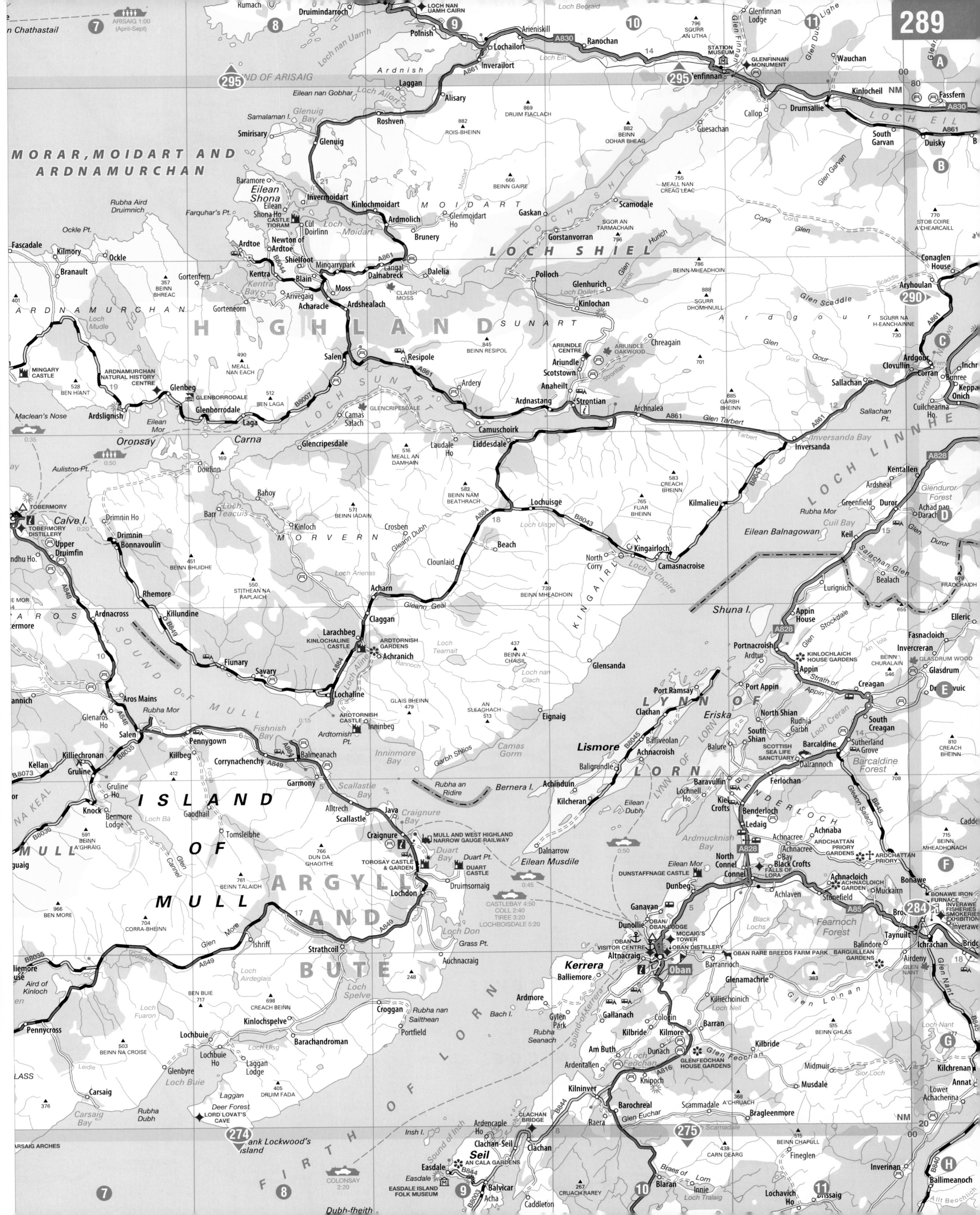

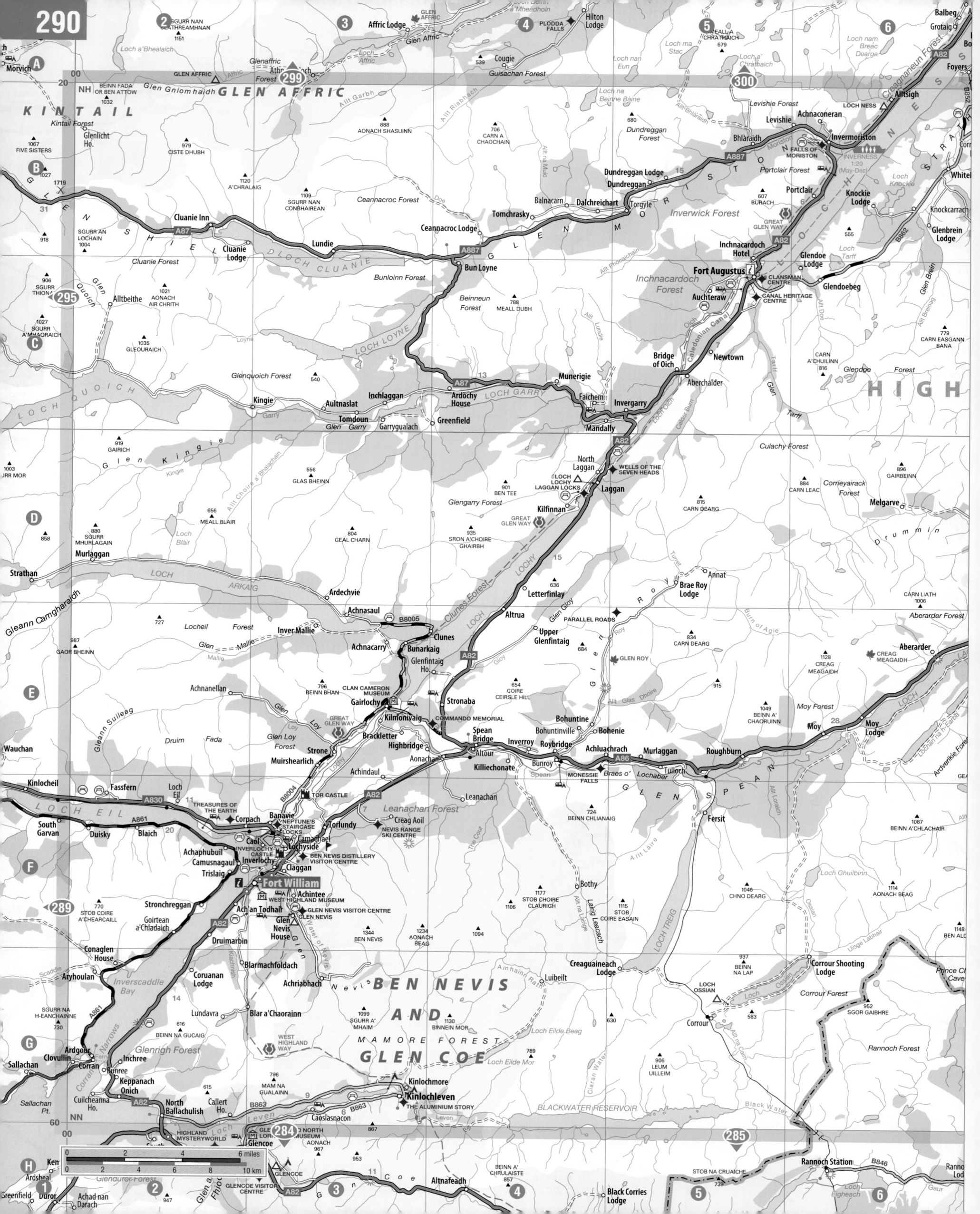

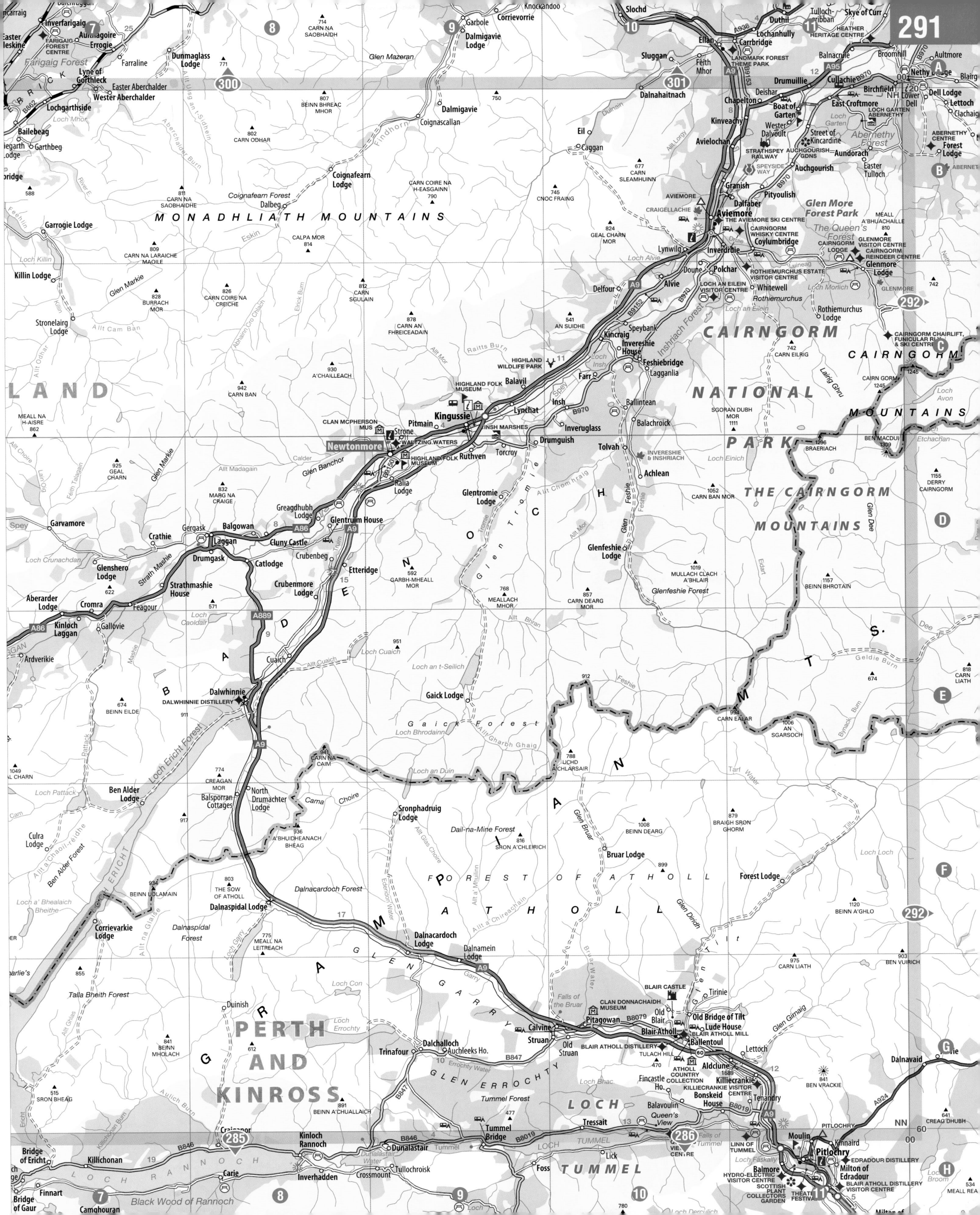

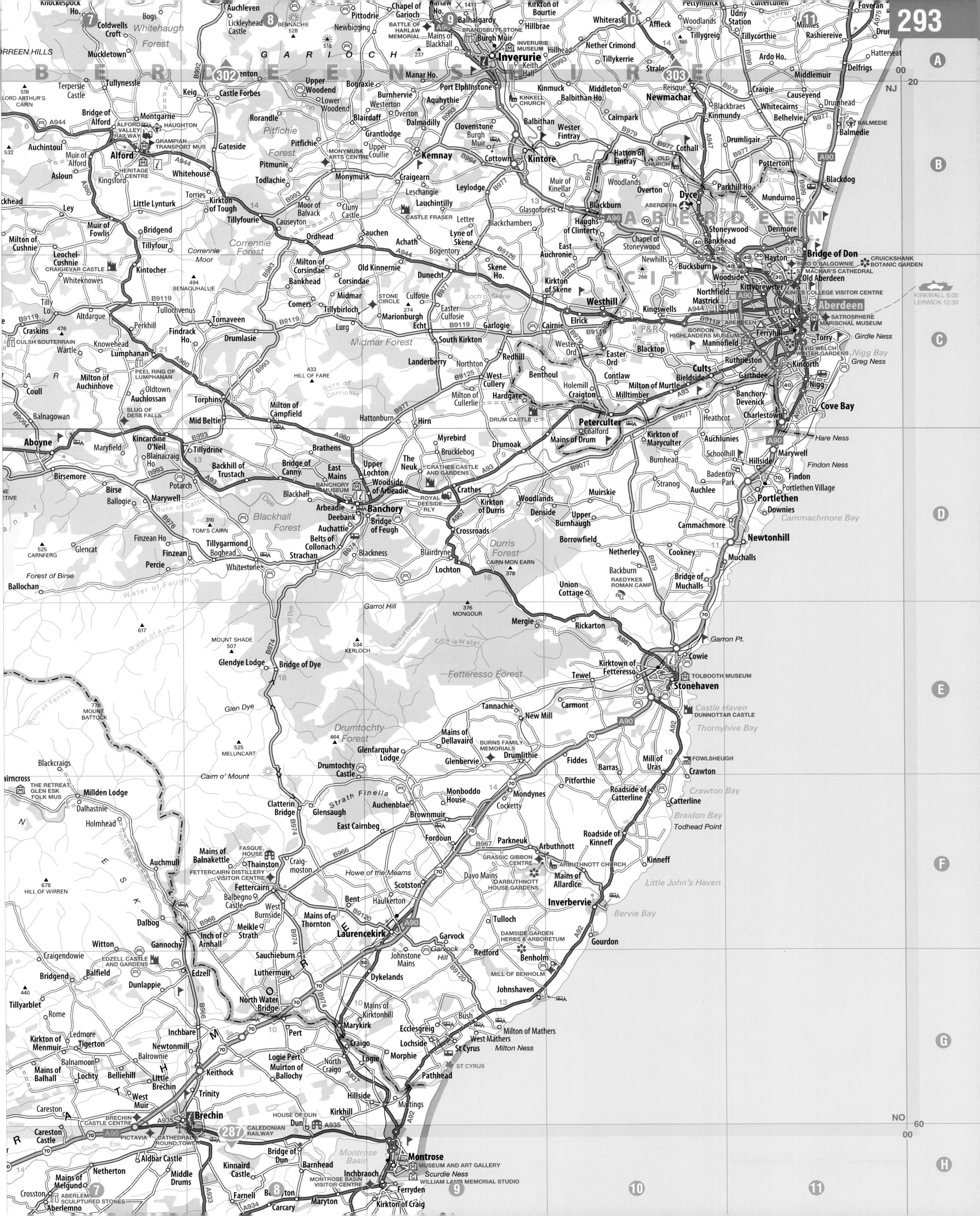

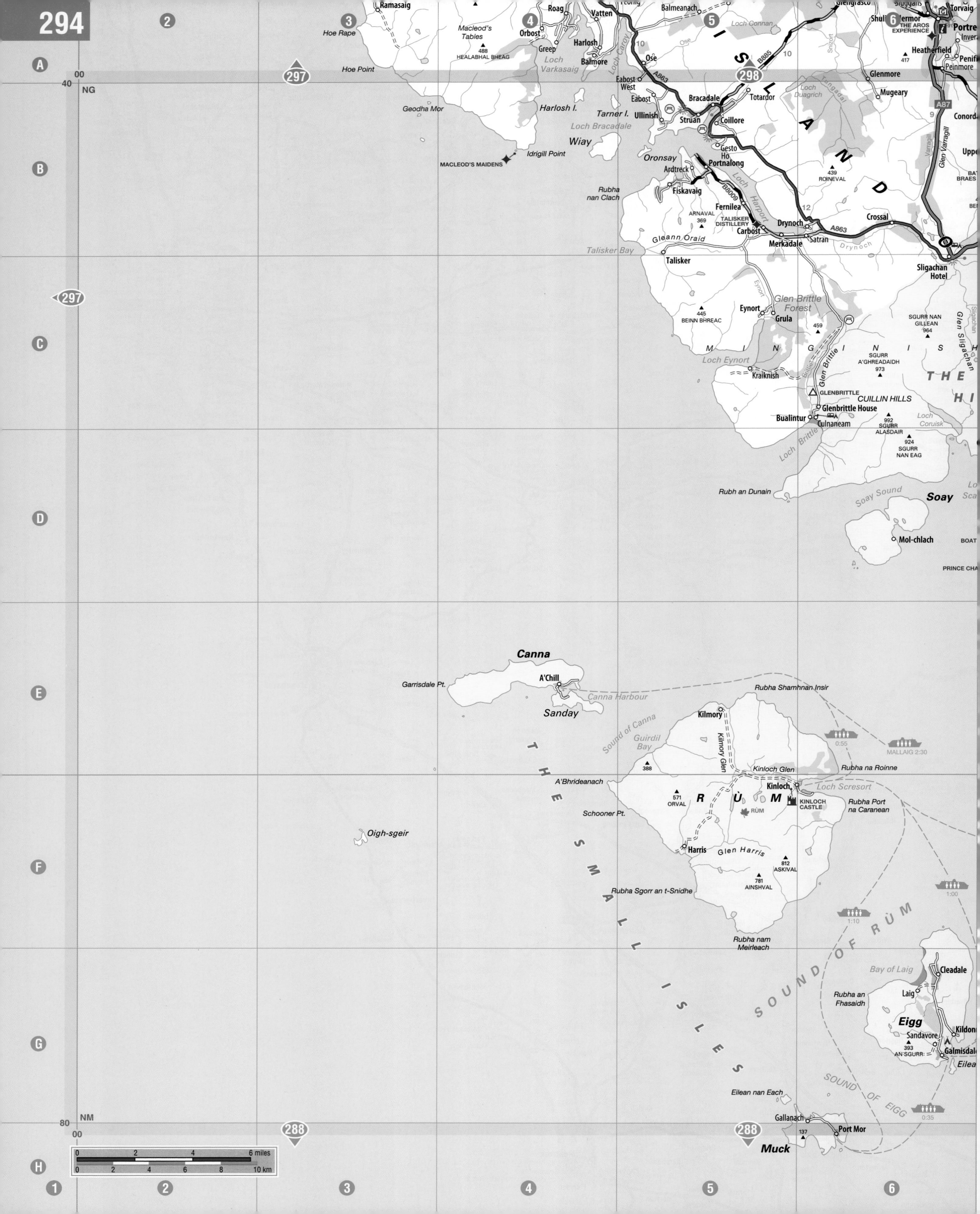

Ramasaig
Roag
Vatten
Balmeanach
Glengrasco
Sluggans
Torvaig
Portree
Macleod's Tables
Hoe Rape
Orbost
Greep
Harlosh
Ose
10
Loch Connan
Shul
THE AROS EXPERIENCE
Inver
Heatherfield
Penifi
488
HEALABHAL BHEAG
Loch Varkasaig
Balmore
Eabost West
A863
10
Glenmore
417
Peinmore

00
40
NG
Hoe Point
297
298
A87
Mugeary
9
Conord

Harlosh I.
Tarner I.
Eabost
Bracadale
Totardor
Loch Duagrich
Loch Tungadal

Ullinish
Struan
Coillore
Geodha Mor
Wiay
Loch Bracadale
439
ROINEVAL
Upp

MACLEOD'S MAIDENS
Idrigill Point
Oronsay
Gesto Ho
Portnalong
BAT
BRAES
BE

Ardtreck
Rubha nan Clach
Fiskavaig
Fernilea
ARNAVAL
369
TALISKER DISTILLERY
Carbost
Drynoch
Crossal
A863

Gleann Oraid
Merkadale
Satran
Drynoch

Talisker Bay
Talisker
Sligachan Hotel

445
BEINN BHREAC
Eynort
Glen-Brittle Forest
459
SGURR NAN GILLEAN
964
Glen Sligachan

Loch Eynort
Grula
SGURR A'GHREADAIDH
973
THE

Kraiknish
GLENBRITTLE
CUILLIN HILLS
MINGINISH
HI

Bualintur
Glenbrittle House
Culnaneam
992
SGURR ALASDAIR
924
SGURR NAN EAG
Loch Coruisk

Rubh an Dunain
Soay Sound
Soay
Lo
Sca

Mol-chlach
BOAT

PRINCE CHA

Canna
A'Chill
Rubha Shamhnan Insir

Garrisdale Pt.
Canna Harbour
Kilmory
0:55
MALLAIG 2:30

Sanday
Sound of Canna
Guirdil Bay
Kilmory Glen
Kinloch Glen
Rubha na Roinne

388
A'Bhrideanach
Kinloch
Loch Scresort

Oigh-sgeir
571
ORVAL
R Ù M
KINLOCH CASTLE
Rubha Port na Caranean

Schooner Pt.
RÙM

Harris
Glen Harris
812
ASKIVAL
1:00

781
AINSHVAL
1:10

Rubha Sgorr an t-Snidhe

Rubha nam Meirleach
SOUND OF RÙM

Bay of Laig
Cleadale

Rubha an Fhasaidh
Laig

Eigg
Kildon

Sandavore
393
AN SGURR
Galmisdale

Eilea

Eilean nan Each
SOUND OF EIGG

80
NM
00
288
288
Gallanach
0:35

Muck
137
Port Mor

0   2   4   6 miles
0 2 4 6 8 10 km

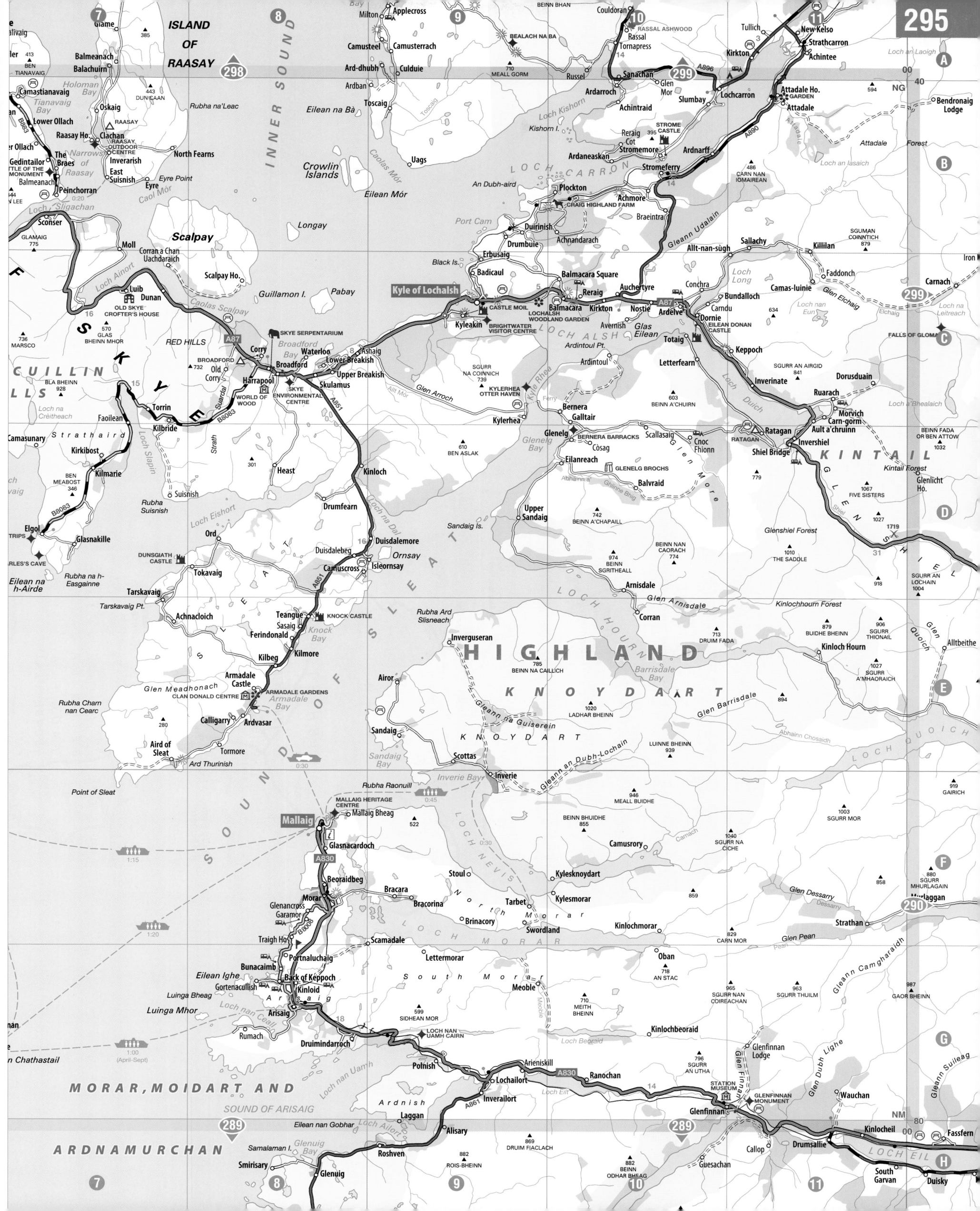

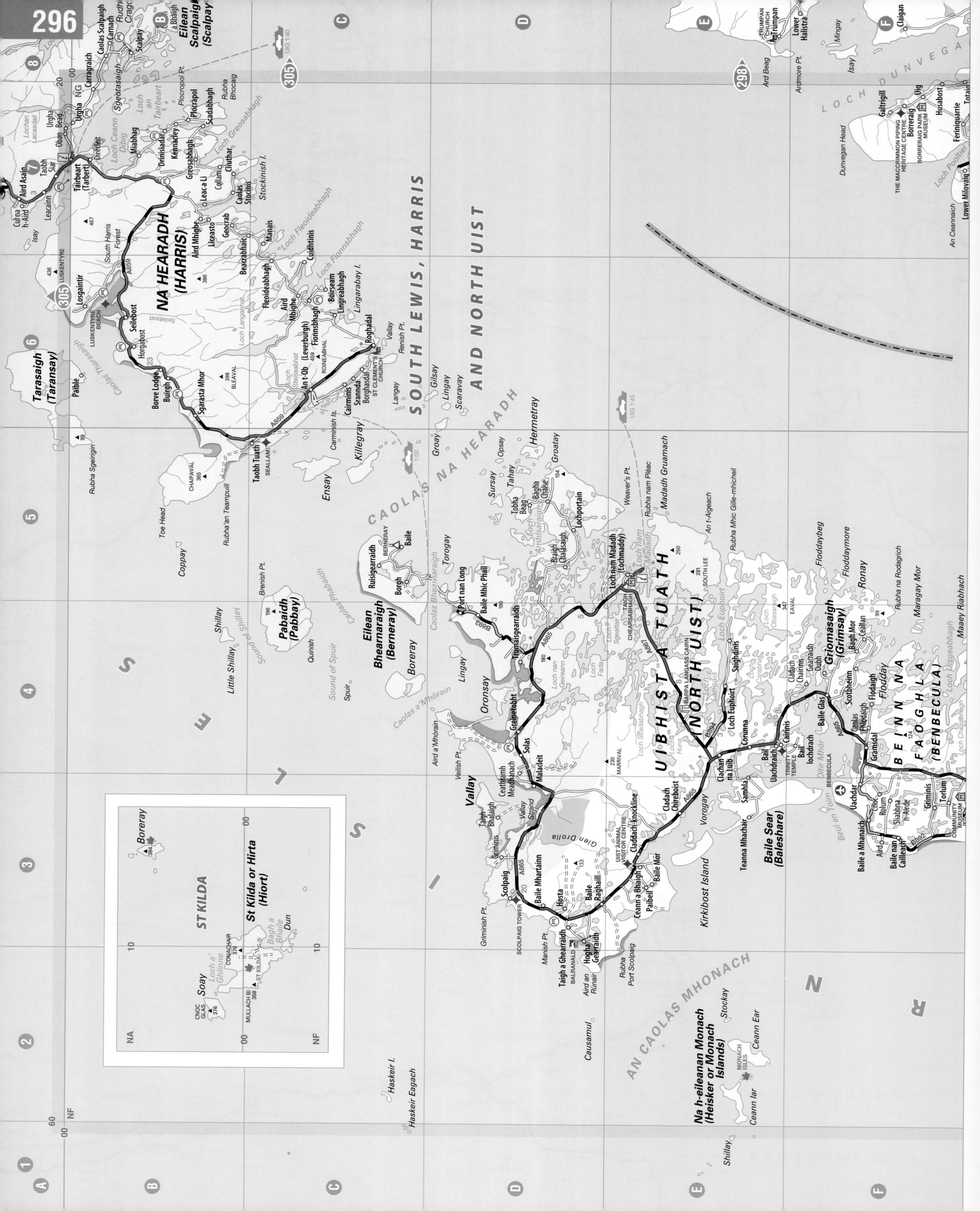

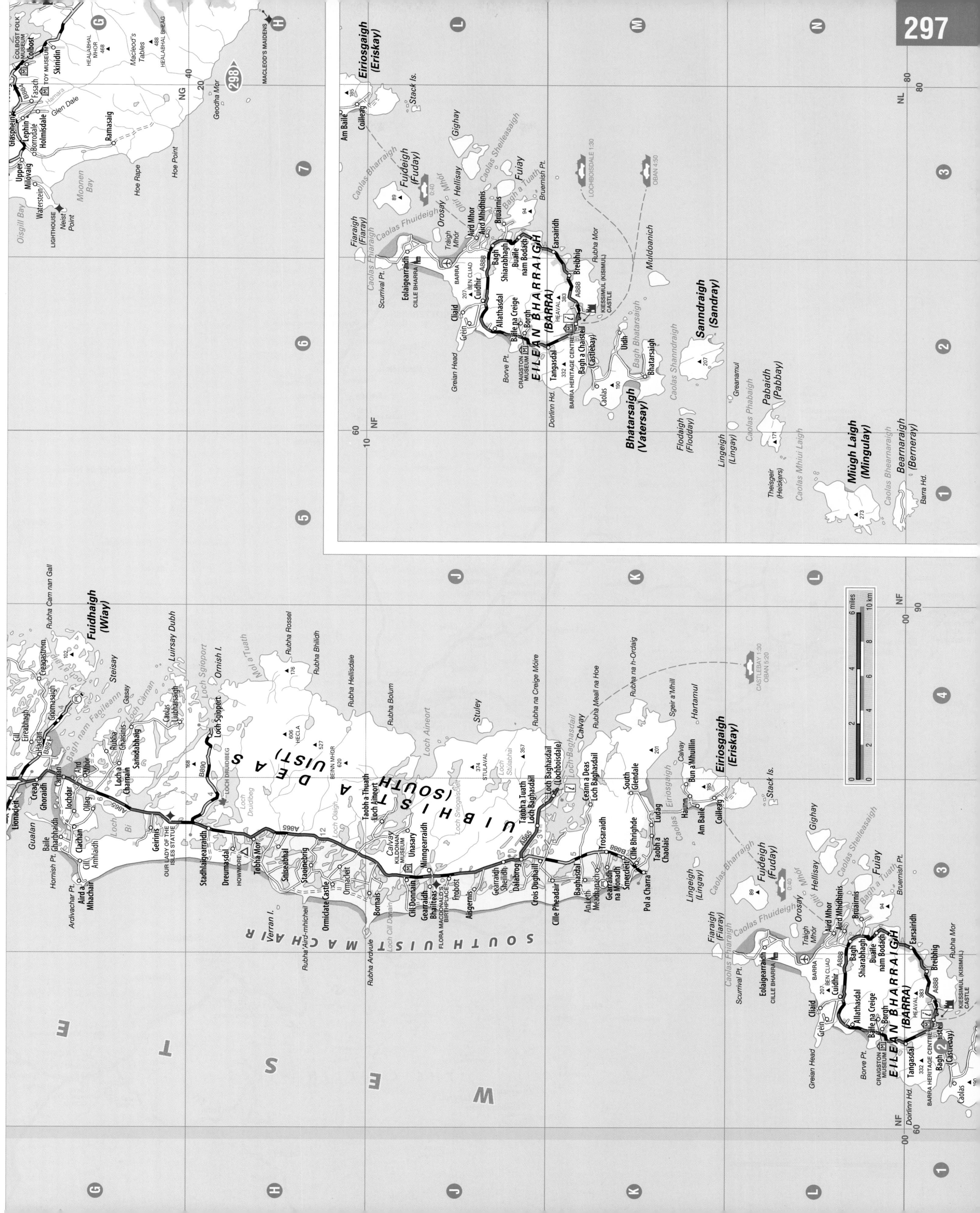

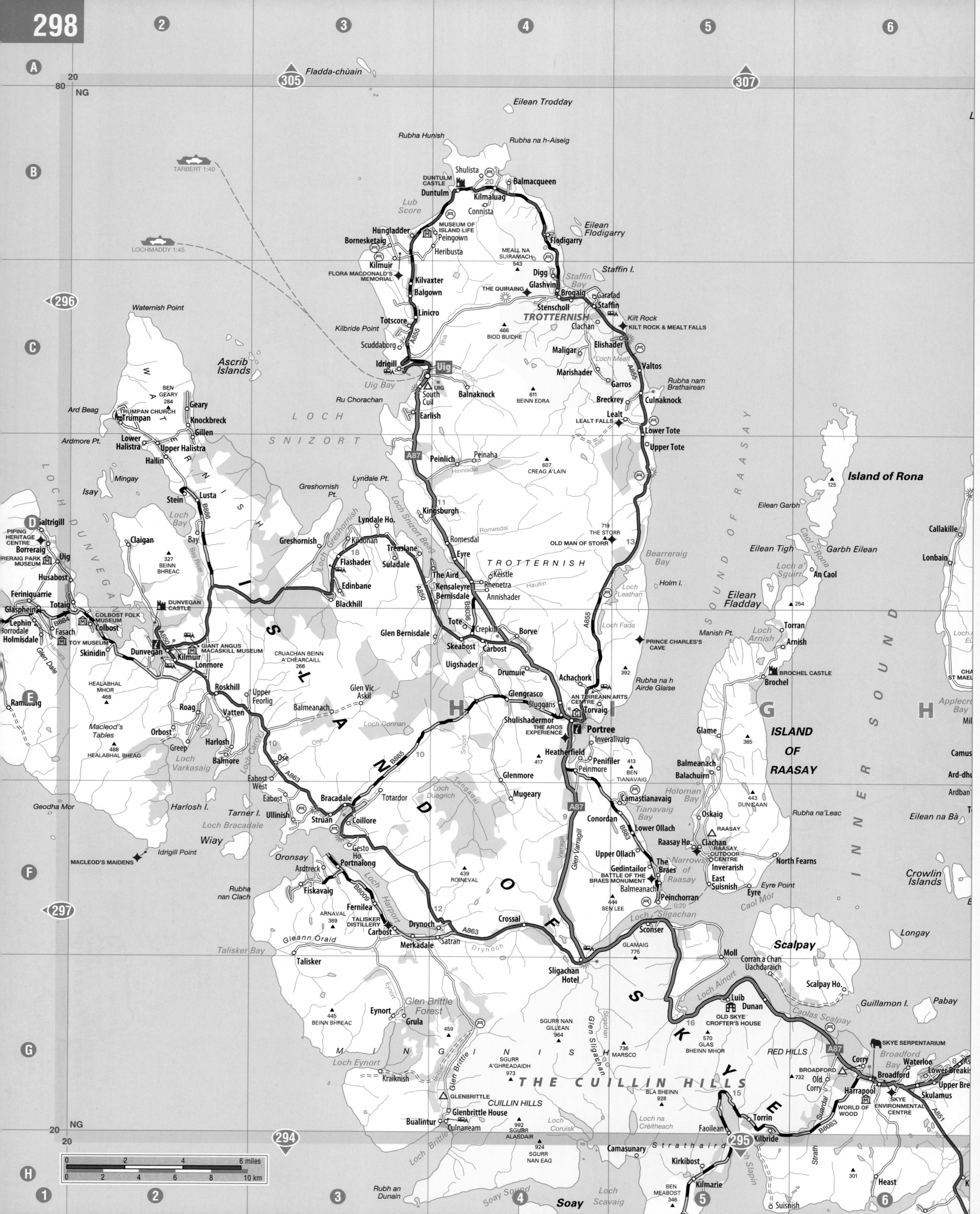

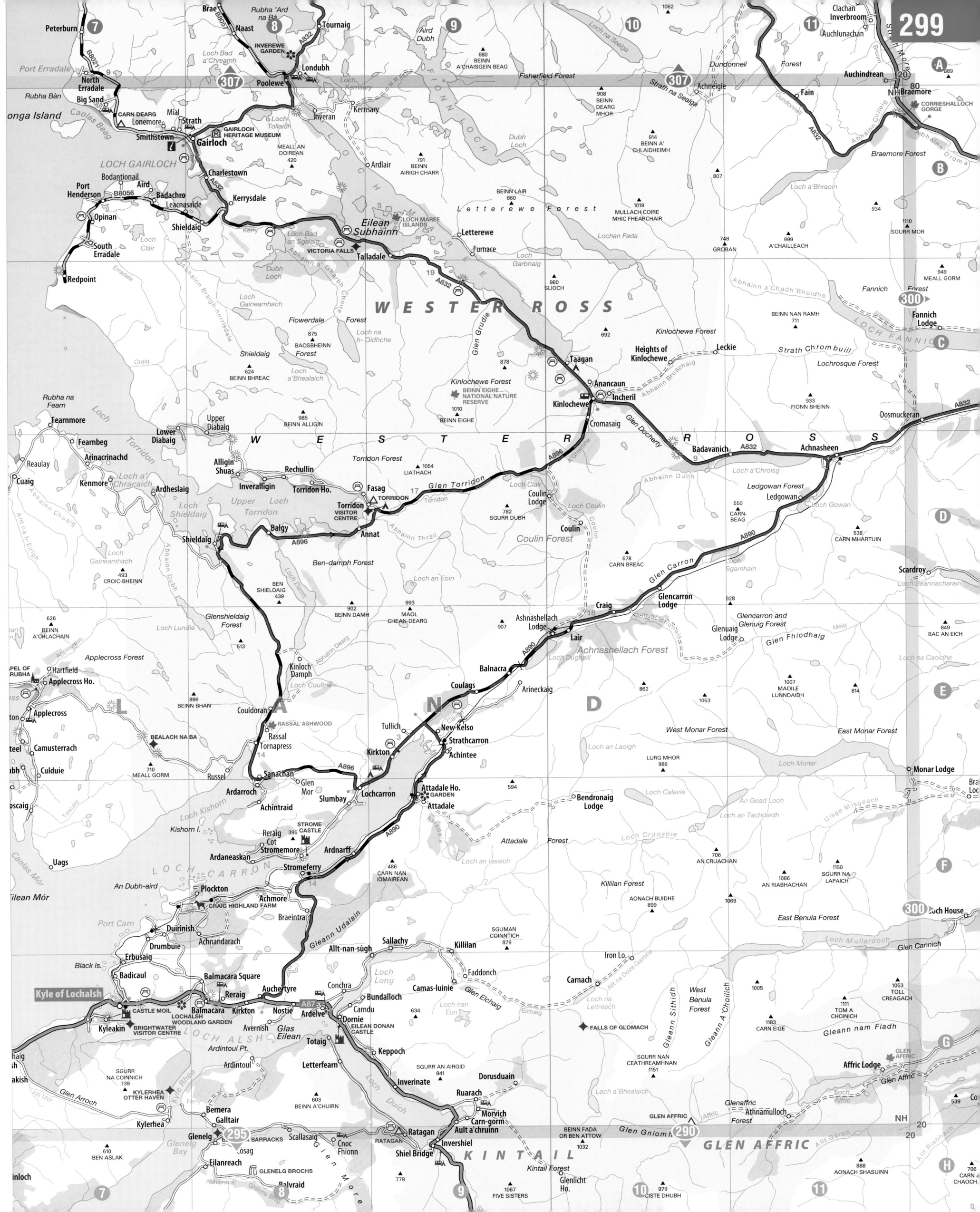

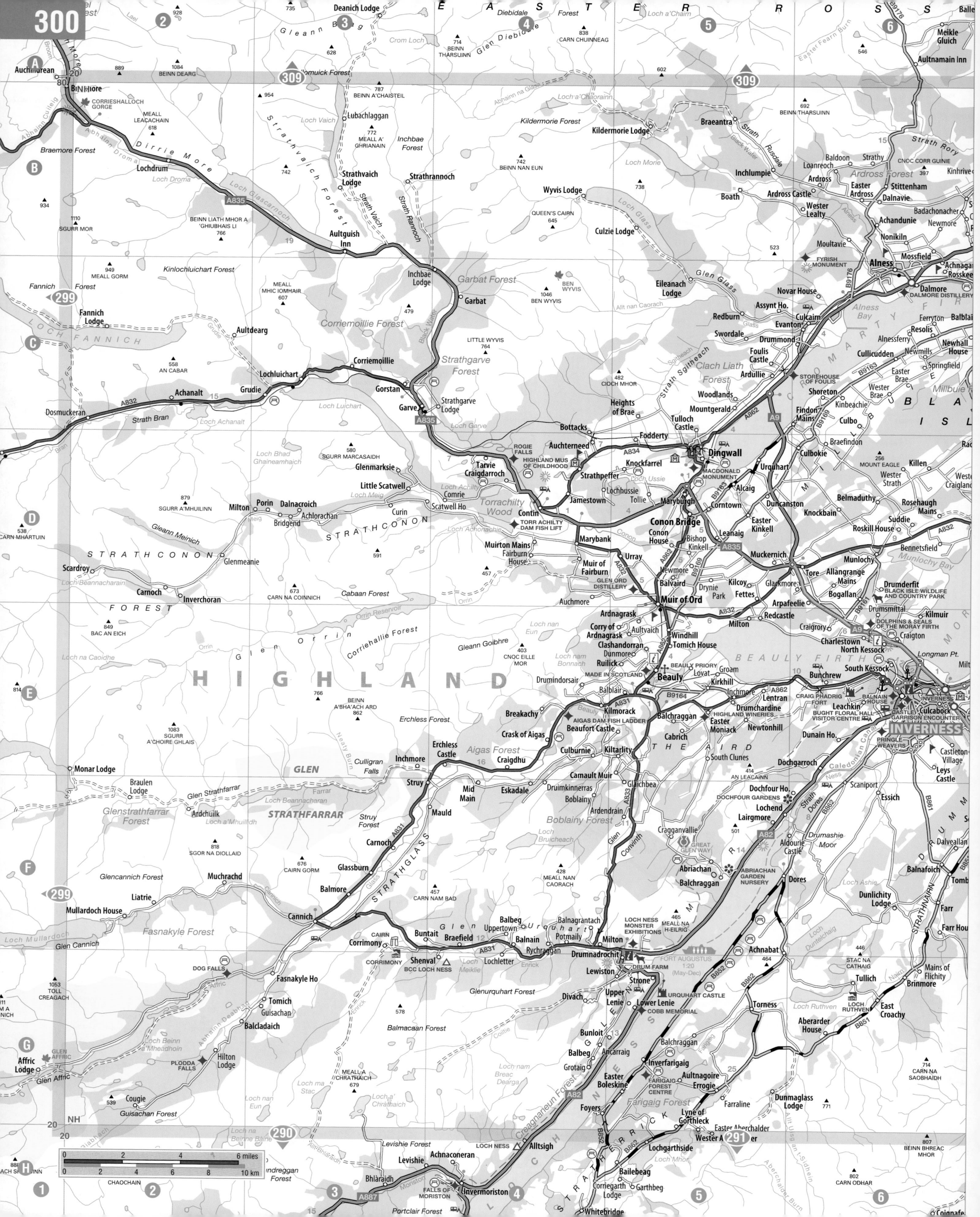

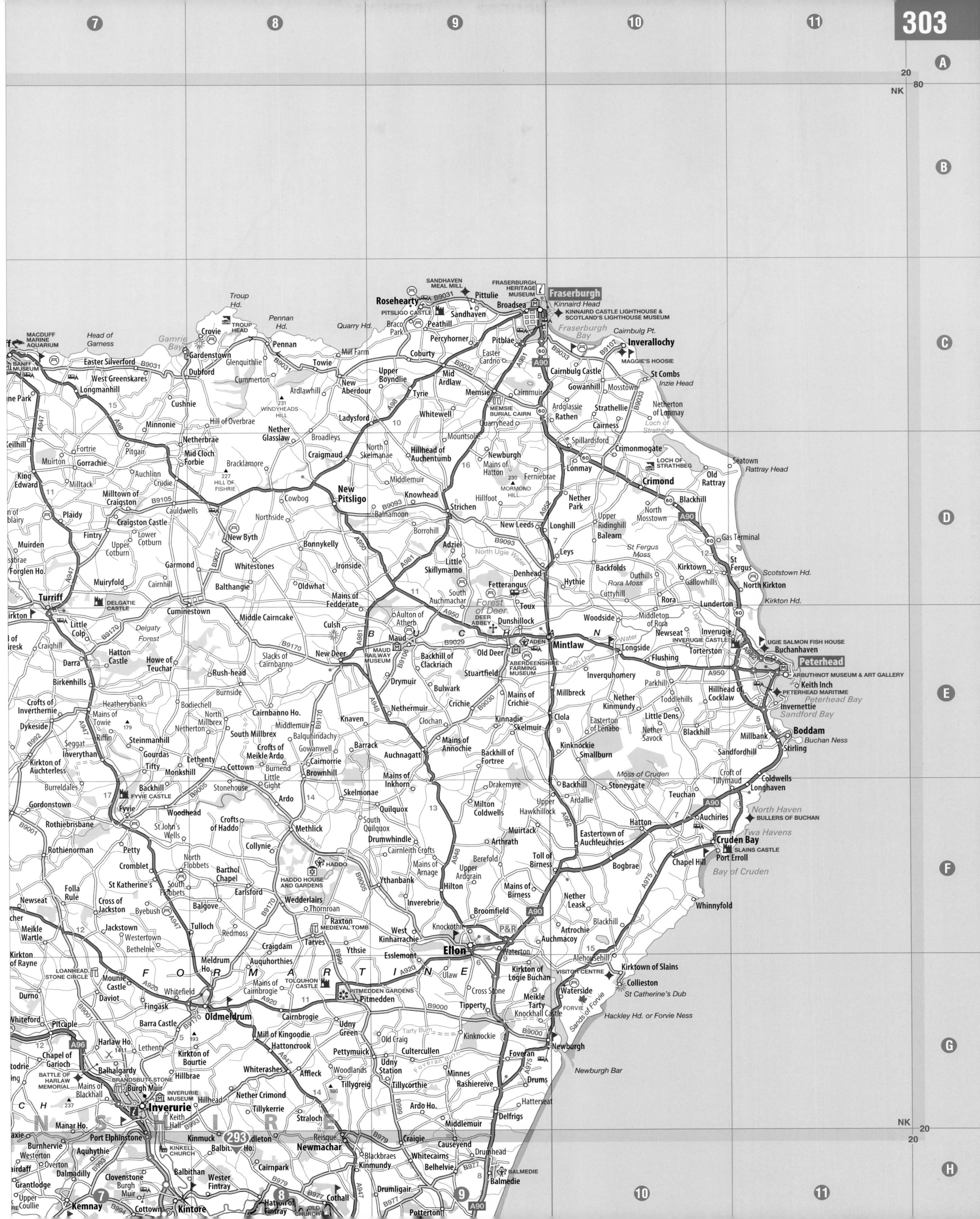

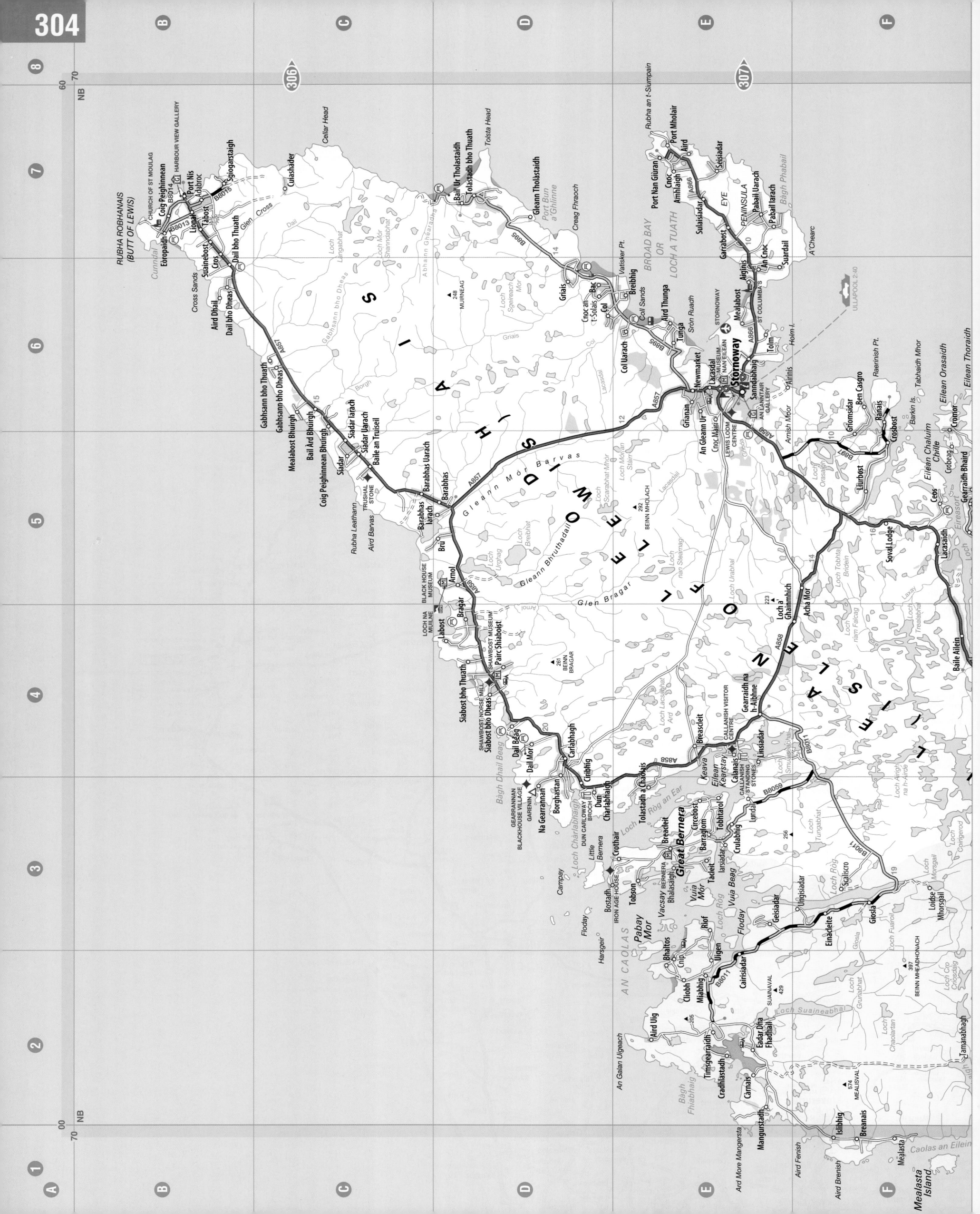

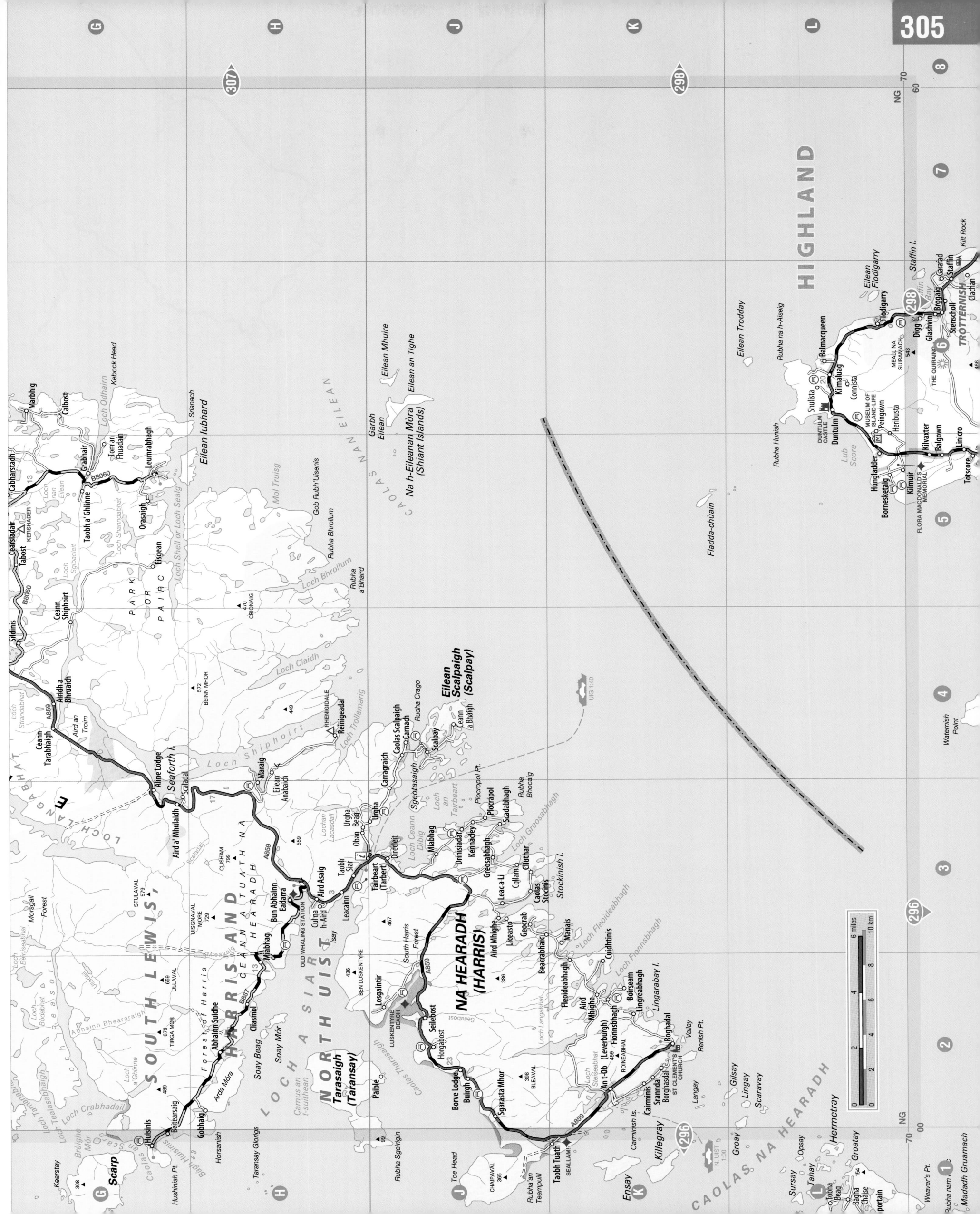

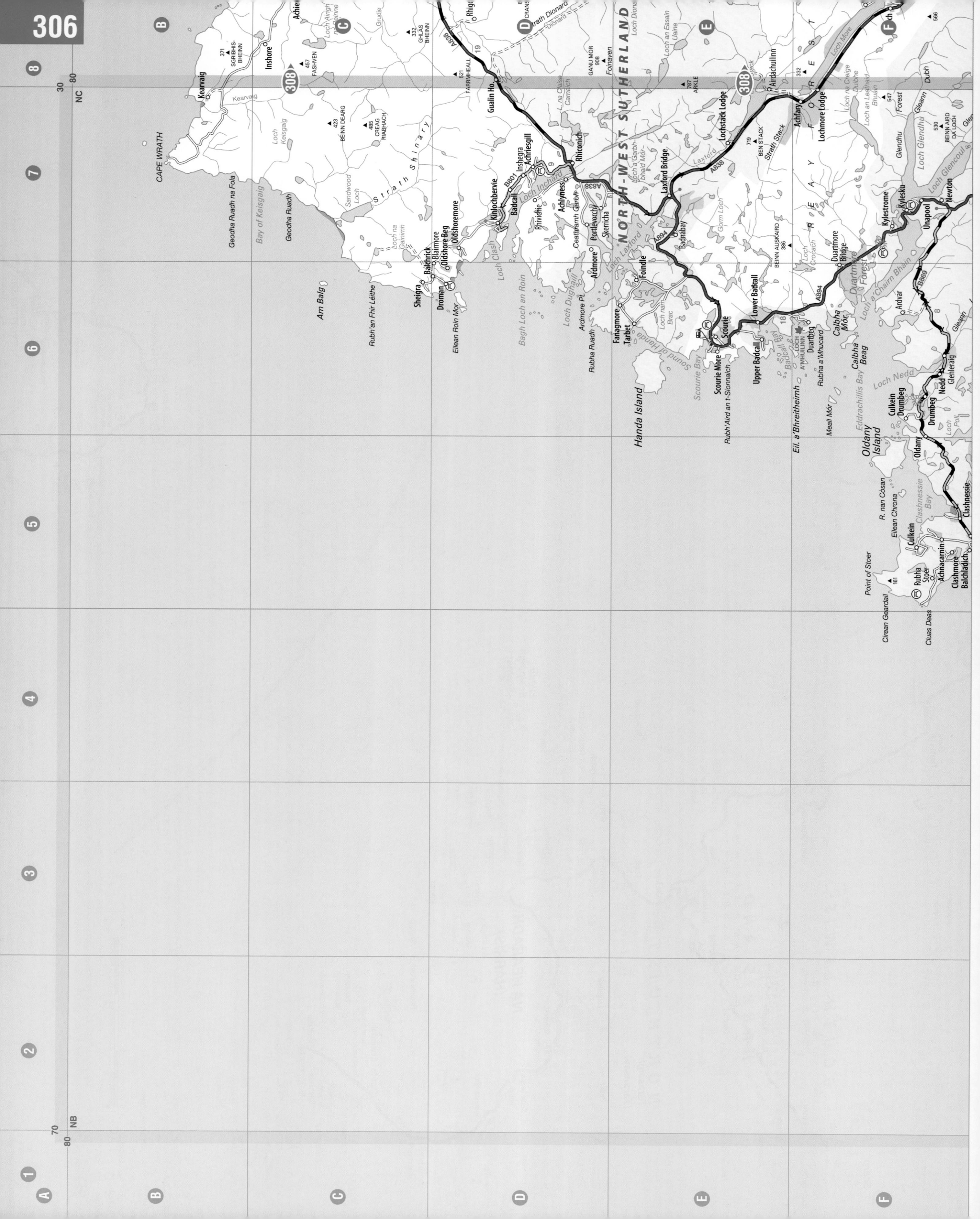

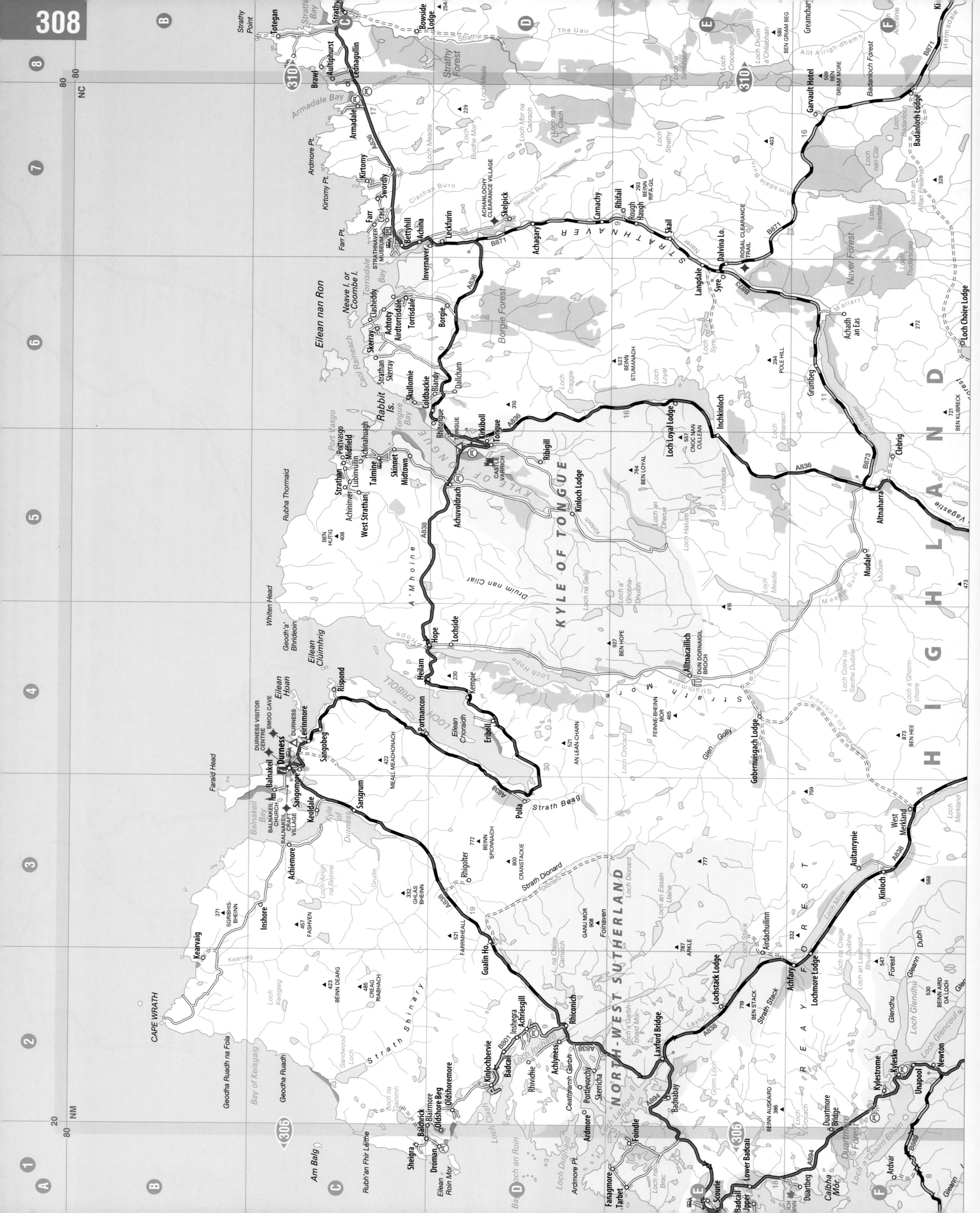

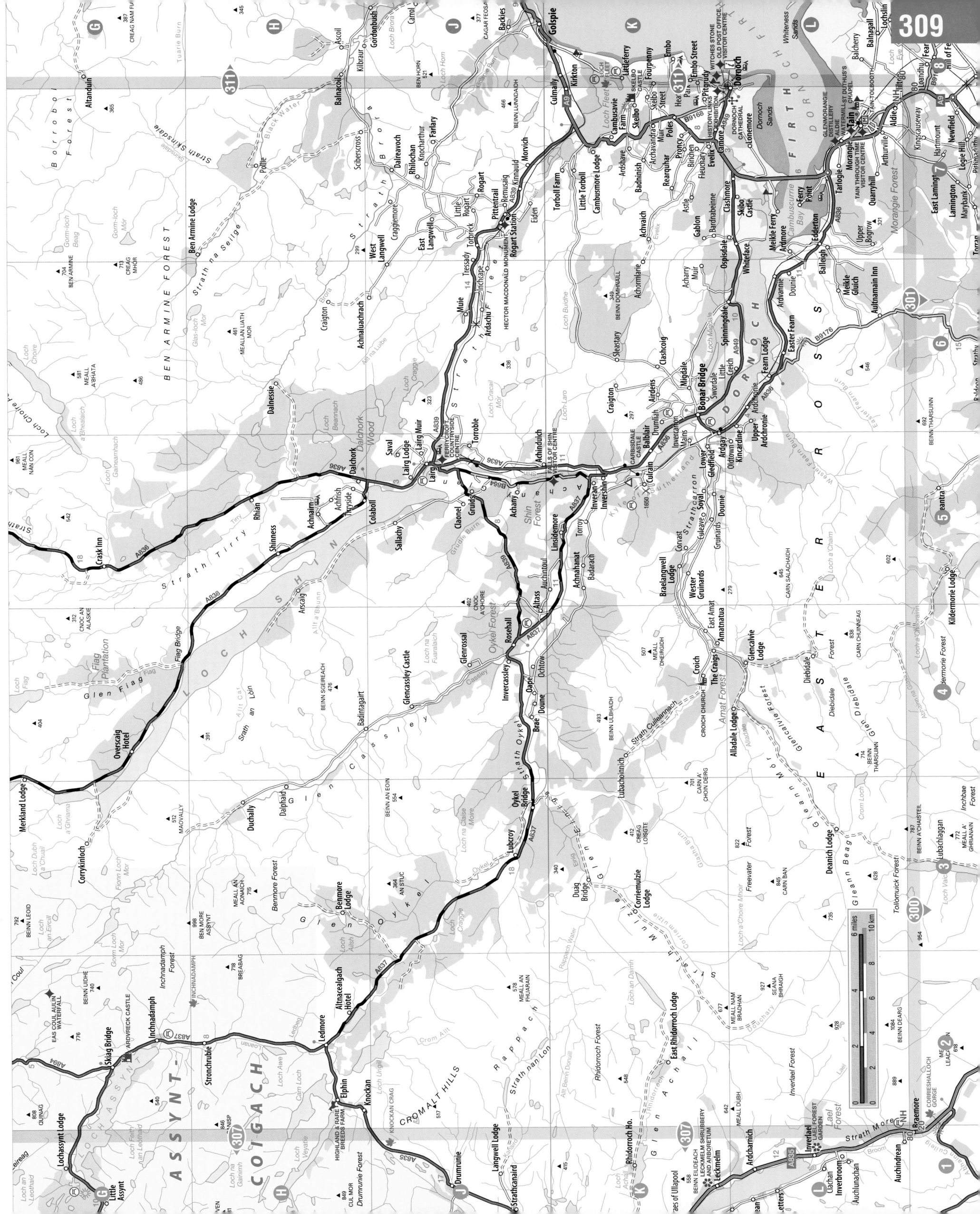

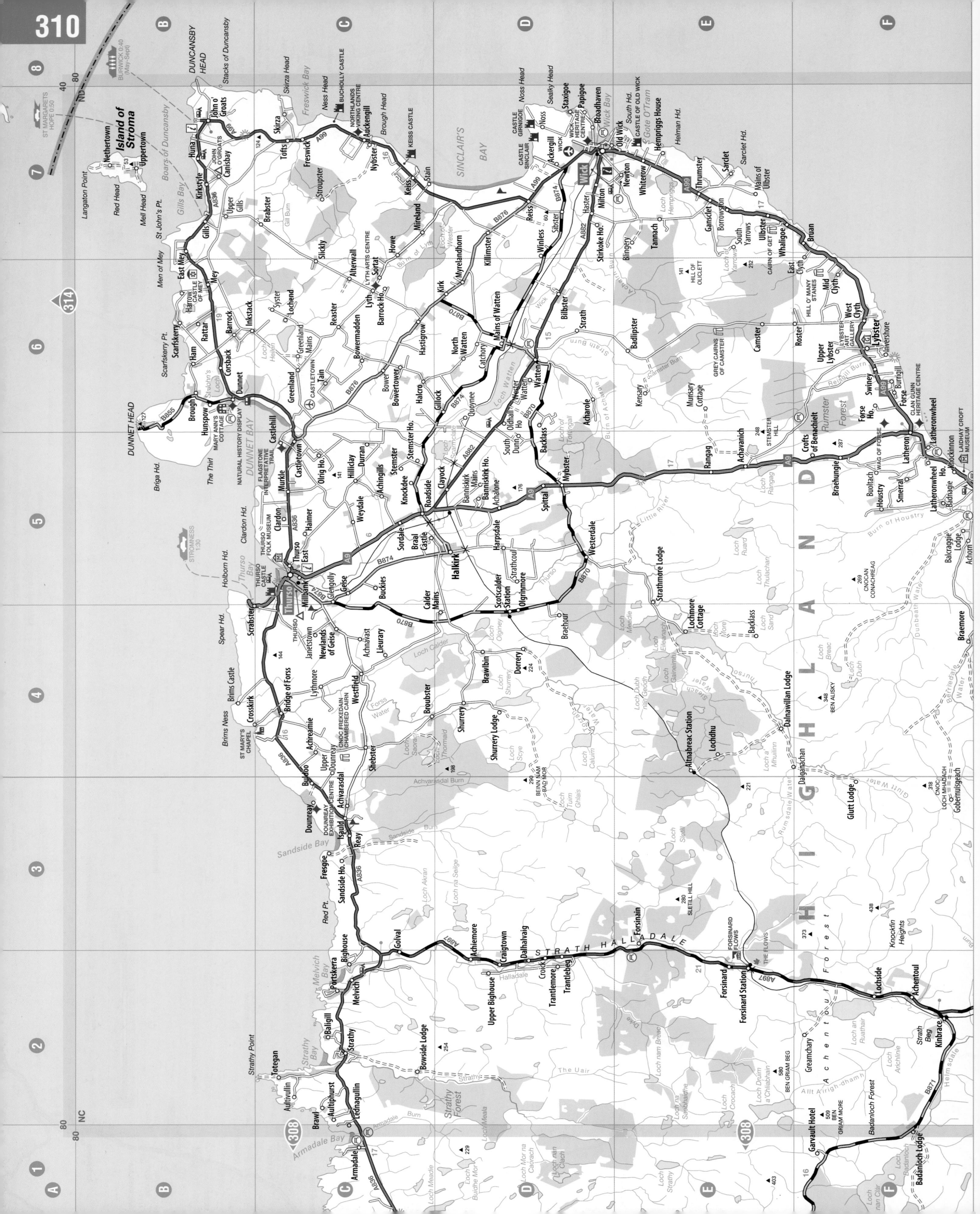

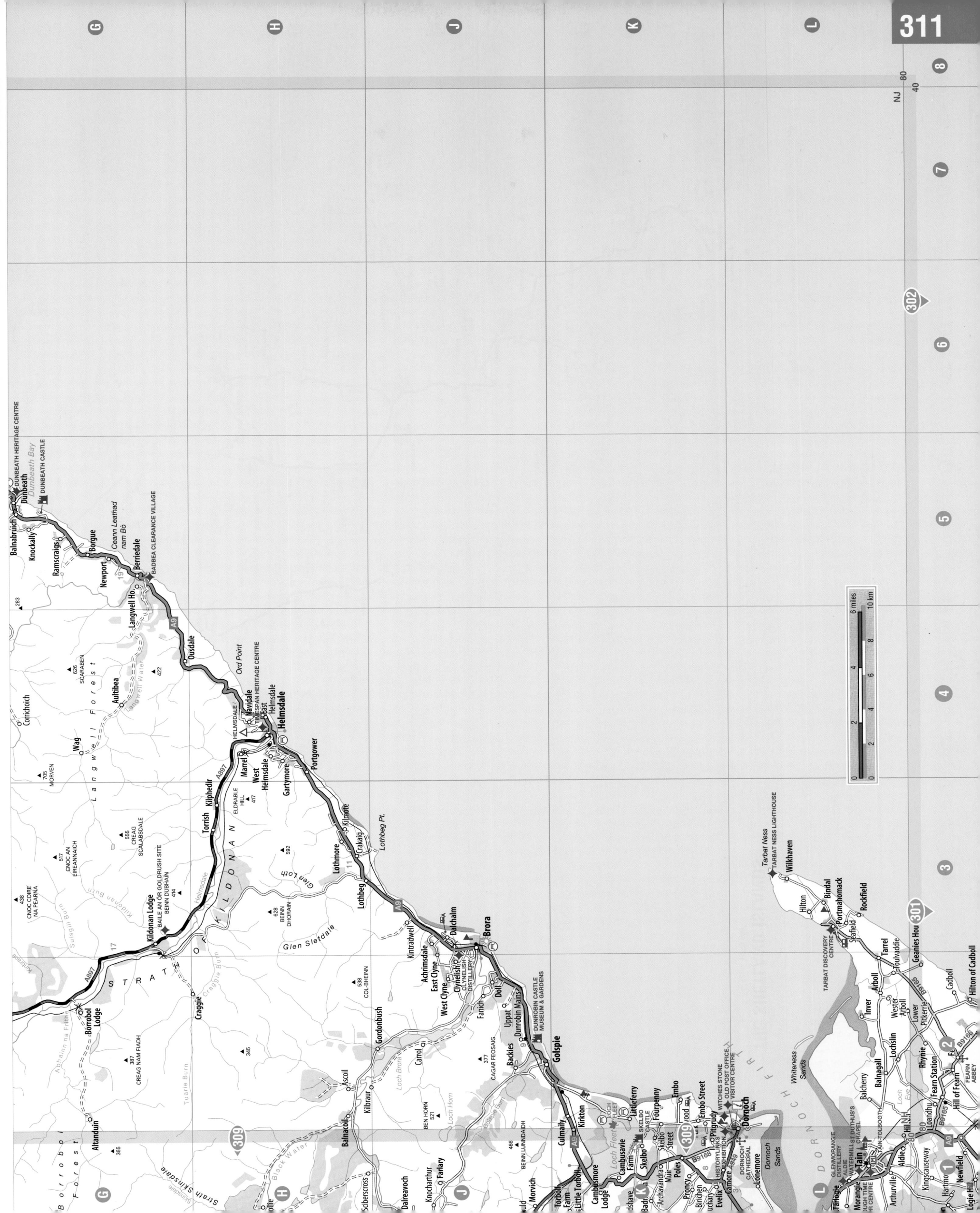

G H J K L

NJ 40 80

302

309

301

Map labels:

Dunbeath
DUNBEATH HERITAGE CENTRE
Dunbeath Bay
DUNBEATH CASTLE

Balnabruaich
Knockally
Ramscraigs
Borgue
Ceann Leathad nam Bò
Newport
Berriedale
BADBEA CLEARANCE VILLAGE
Langwell Ho.
283
Ousdale
A9
Corrichoich
Aultibea
626 SCARABEN
422
Wag
705 MORVEN
Kildonan Lodge
BAILE AN OR GOLDRUSH SITE
BEINN DUBHAIN 414
517 CNOC AN EIREANNAICH
CNOC COIRE NA PEARNA
438

Ord Point
HELMSDALE
Navidale
TIMESPAN HERITAGE CENTRE
Helmsdale East
Helmsdale
Marrel
West Helmsdale
ELDRABLE HILL 417
Gartymore
Portgower
Kilphedir
Torrish
A897
555 CREAG SCALABSDALE
592
Lothmore
Kilmote
Crakaig
Lothbeg Pt.
Lothbeg
628 BEINN DHORAIN
Glen Loth

STRATH OF KILDONAN

Borrobol Lodge
Altanduin 385
387
CREAG NAM FIADH
A897
Craggie
Craggie Burn
Gordonbush
Kintradwell
Achrimsdale
East Clyne
West Clyne
Clynelish
CLYNELISH DISTILLERY
Dalchalm
Brora
538 COL-BHEINN
Fanich
Doll
Uppat
DUNROBIN CASTLE MUSEUM & GARDENS

Tarbat Ness
TARBAT NESS LIGHTHOUSE
Wilkhaven
Hilton
Bindal
Portmahomack
Rockfield
TARBAT DISCOVERY CENTRE
Seafield
Geanies Hou
Inver
Wester Arboll
Arboll
Lower Pitkerrie
Tarrel
Loulvaddie
Cadboll
Hilton of Cadboll

Borrobol Forest
Abhainn na Frìth
Tuarie Burn
STRATH OF KILDONAN
Helmsdale
Kildonan Burn
Susgill Burn

Dalreavoch
Knocharthur
Ascoil
Kilbraur
Carrol
Loch Brora
BEN HORN 521
Loch Horn
345
377
CAGAR FEOSAIG
Backies
9
Golspie
WITCHES STONE

Borrobol
Balnacoil
BREACHD

STRATH SKINSDALE
Black Water
Strath Skinsdale

Balnazeich
466 BEINN LUNNDAIDH
Culmaily
Kirkton
LOCH FLEET
Littleferry
Foupenny
Embo
Embo Street
Pitgrudy
DORNOCH
Skelbo
Skelbo Street
Proncy
Cambusmore Lodge
Whiteness Sands

DORNOCH CASTLE
HISTORYLINKS
OLD POST OFFICE
VISITOR CENTRE
Dornoch Sands
DORNOCH CATHEDRAL

Morvich
Torboll
Little Torboll
Cambusavie
Morangie
Tain

GLENMORANGIE DISTILLERY
ALOE WATERMILL
ST DUTHUS'S CHAPEL
Tarlogie
Arthurville
Inver
Newfield
Logie Hill
Fearn
FEARN STATION
Loandhu
Hill of Fearn
Balchery
Balnagall
Rhynie
Lochslin

DORNOCH FIRTH
Kingscauseway

Scale bar:
6 miles
10 km
0 2 4 6 8
0 2 4 6 8

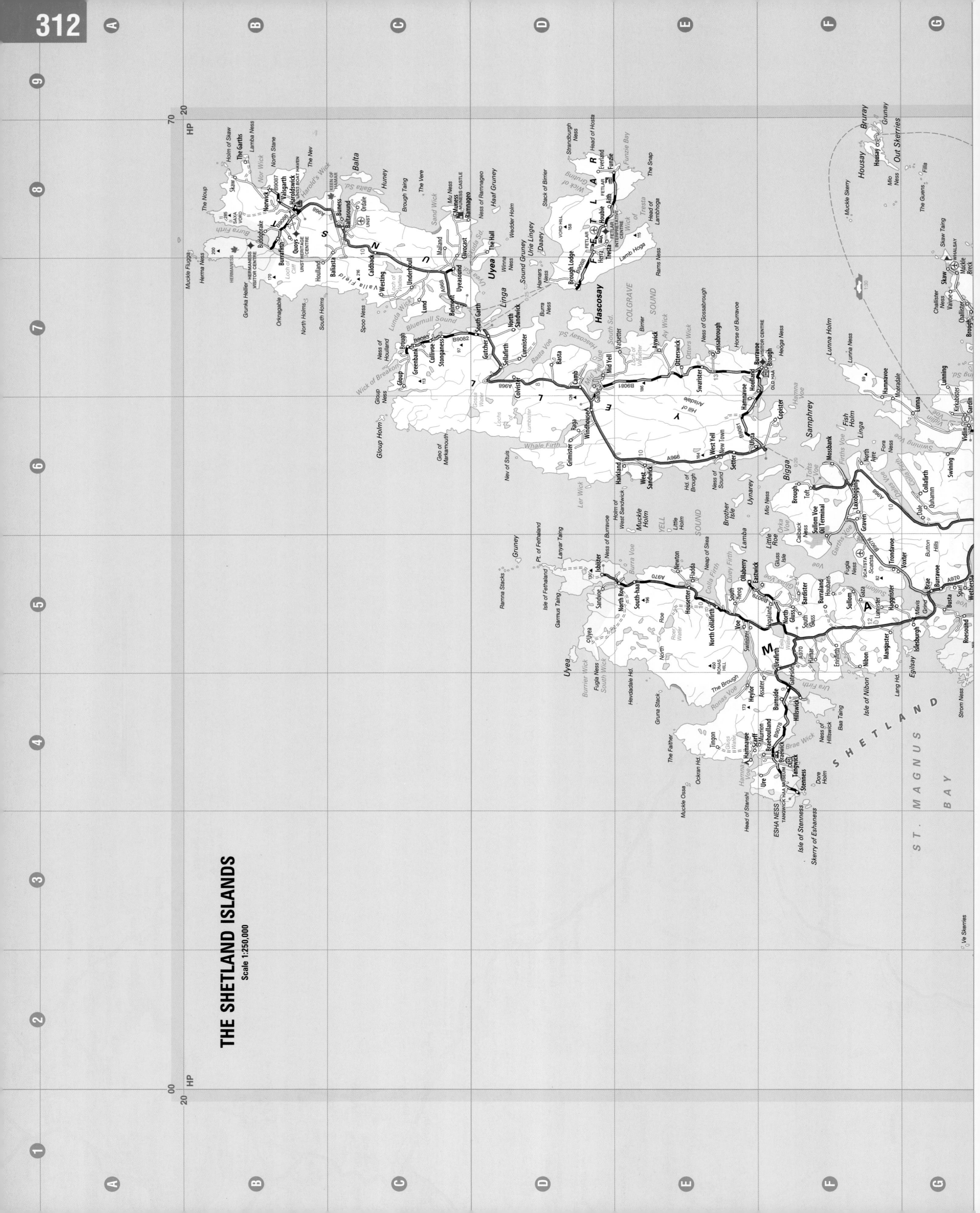

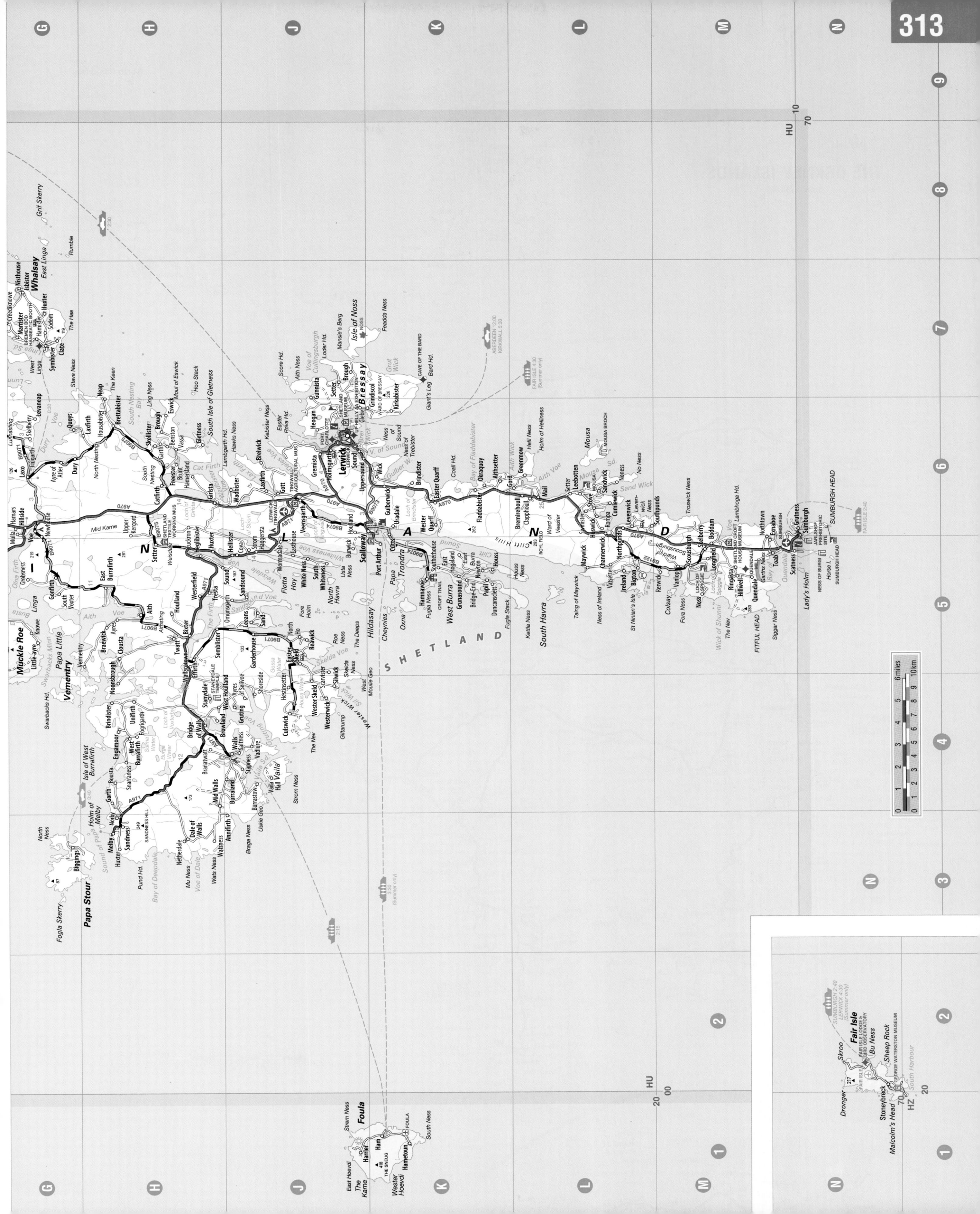

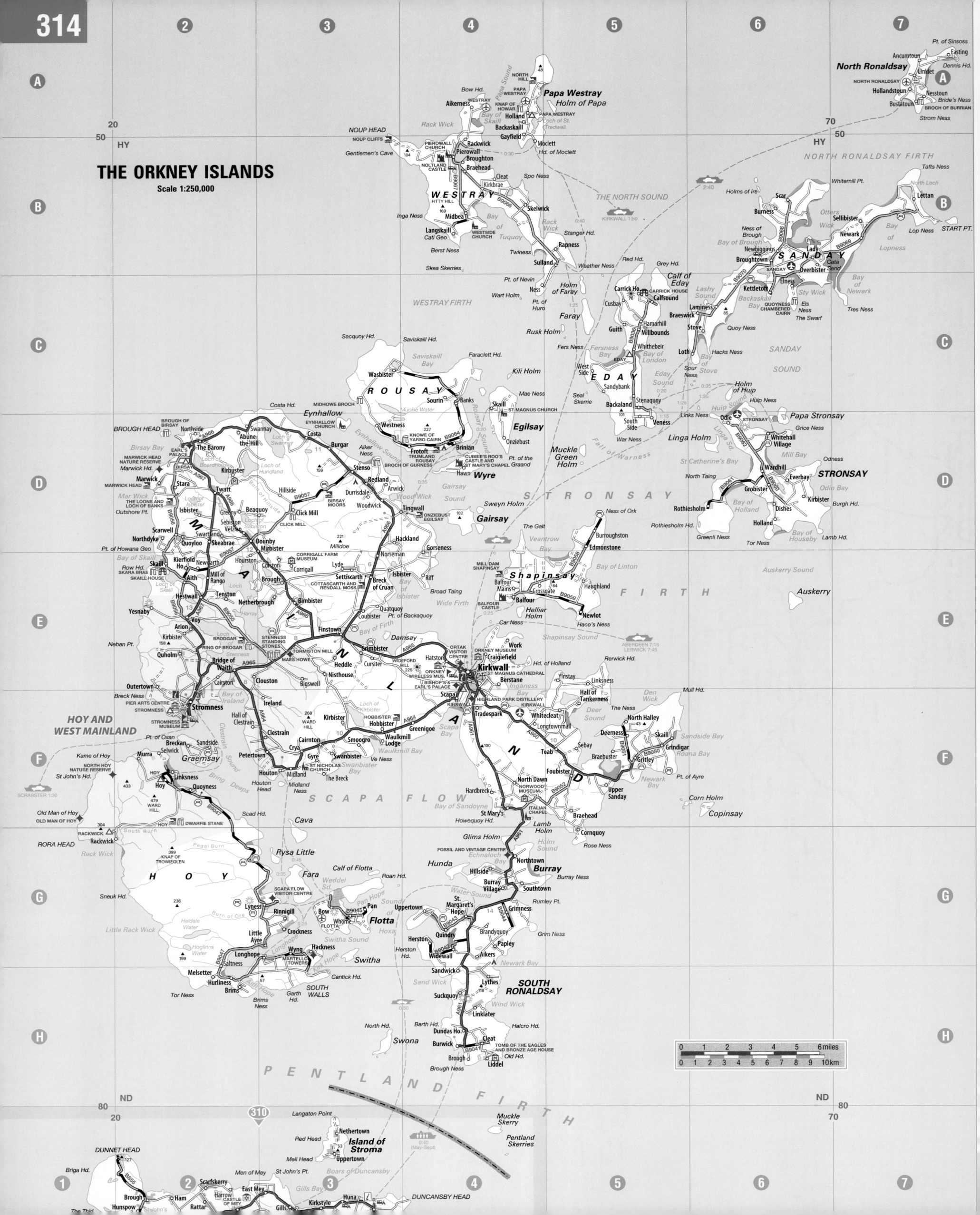

THE ORKNEY ISLANDS
Scale 1:250,000

HOY AND WEST MAINLAND

North Ronaldsay

Papa Westray
Holm of Papa

WESTRAY
FITTY HILL

SANDAY

EDAY
Calf of Eday

ROUSAY
Egilsay
Wyre
Gairsay

STRONSAY
Papa Stronsay
Linga Holm

Shapinsay

Kirkwall

M A I N L A N D

Stromness

SCAPA FLOW

HOY
Graemsay
Fara
Flotta

Burray

SOUTH RONALDSAY

PENTLAND FIRTH

Island of Stroma

DUNNET HEAD

DUNCANSBY HEAD

| 0 | 1 | 2 | 3 | 4 | 5 | 6 miles |
| 0 | 1 2 3 4 5 6 7 8 9 | | | | | 10km |

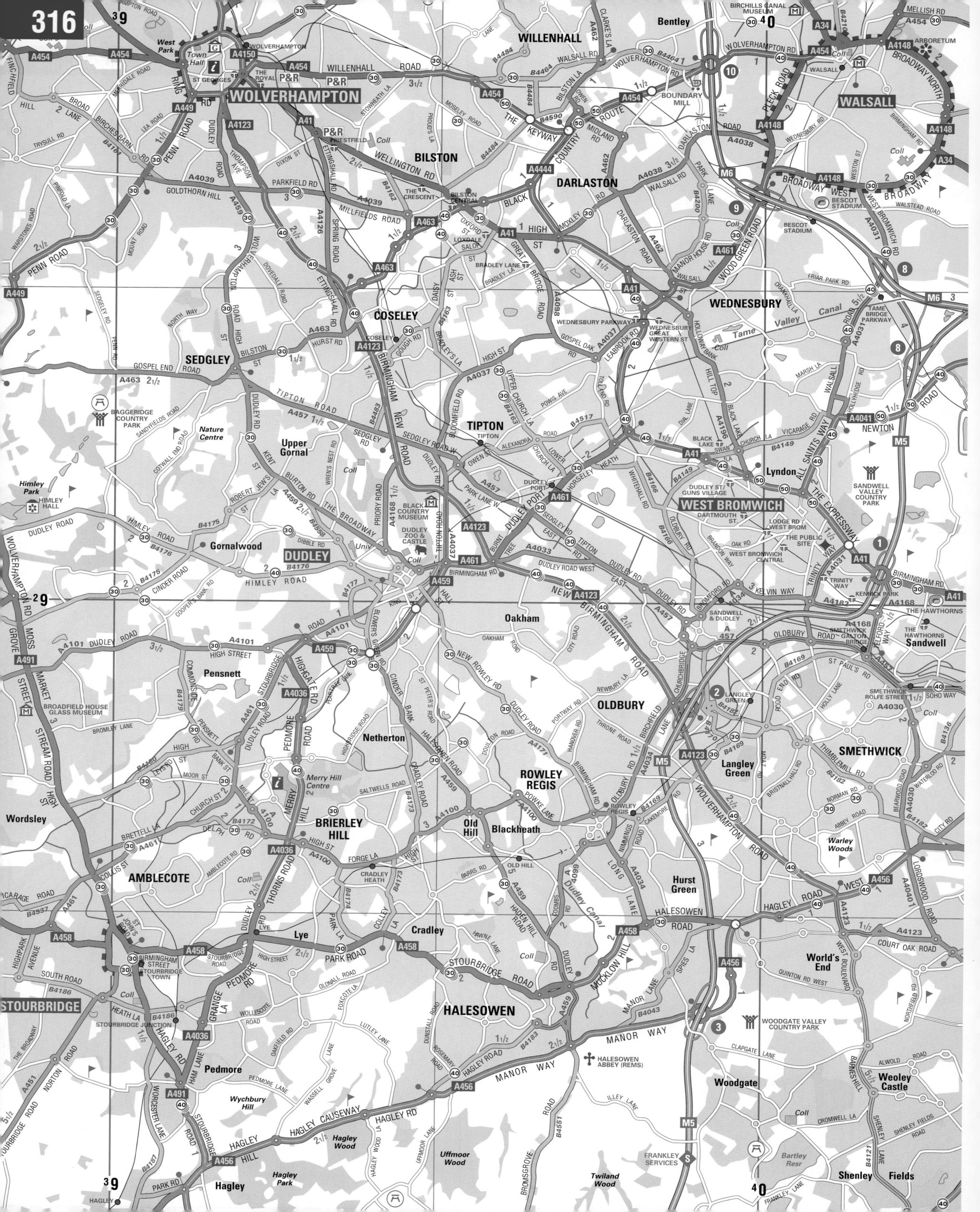

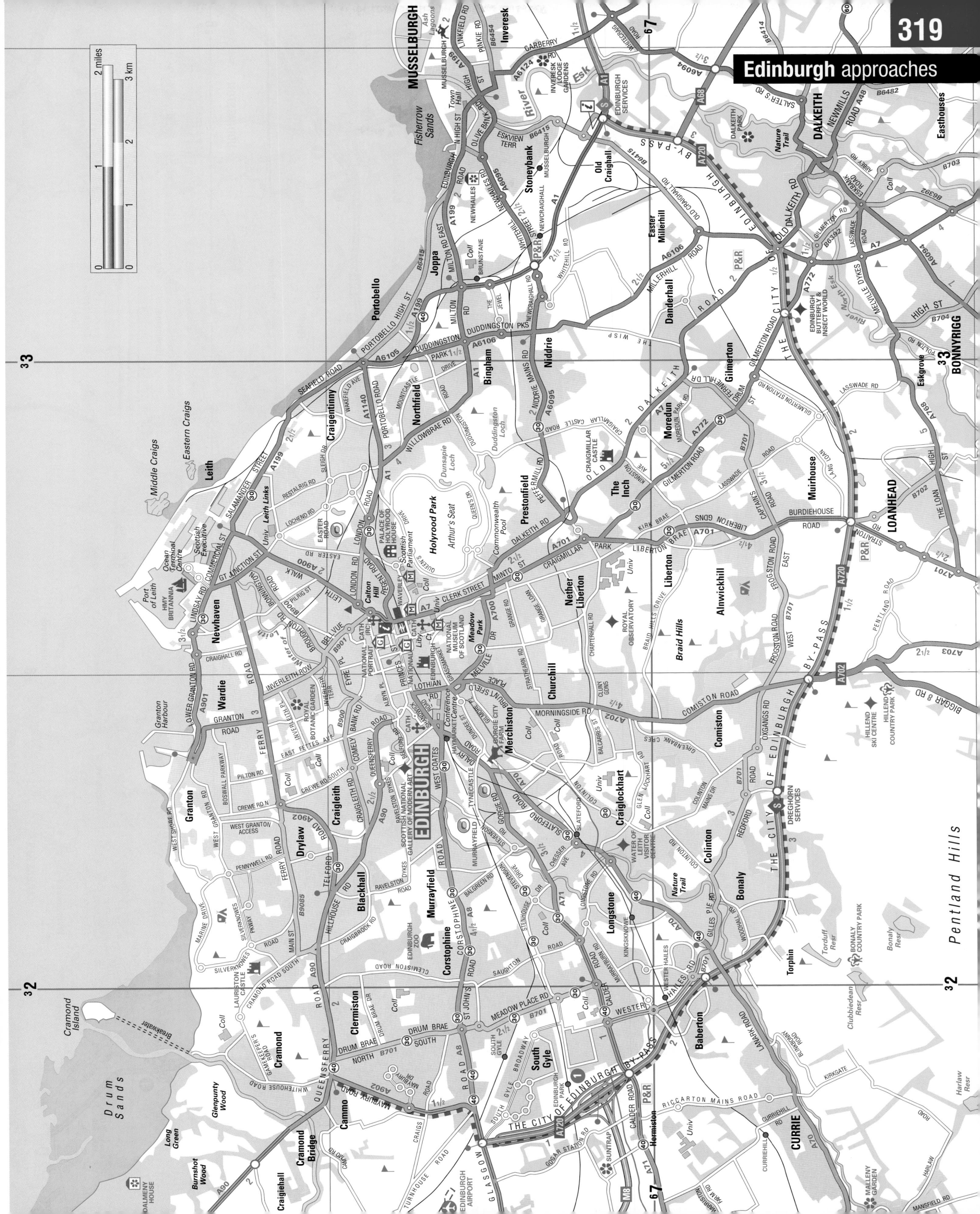

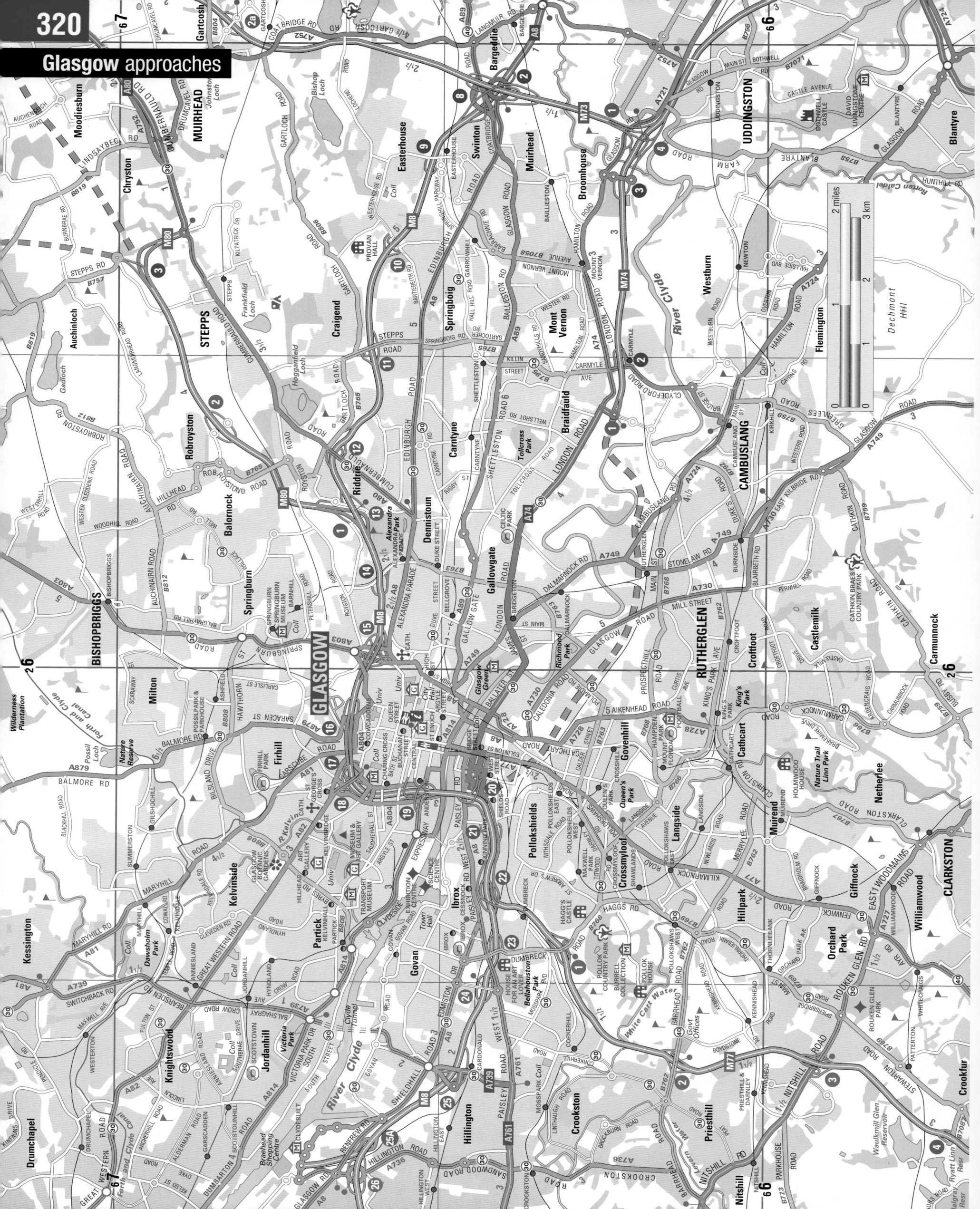

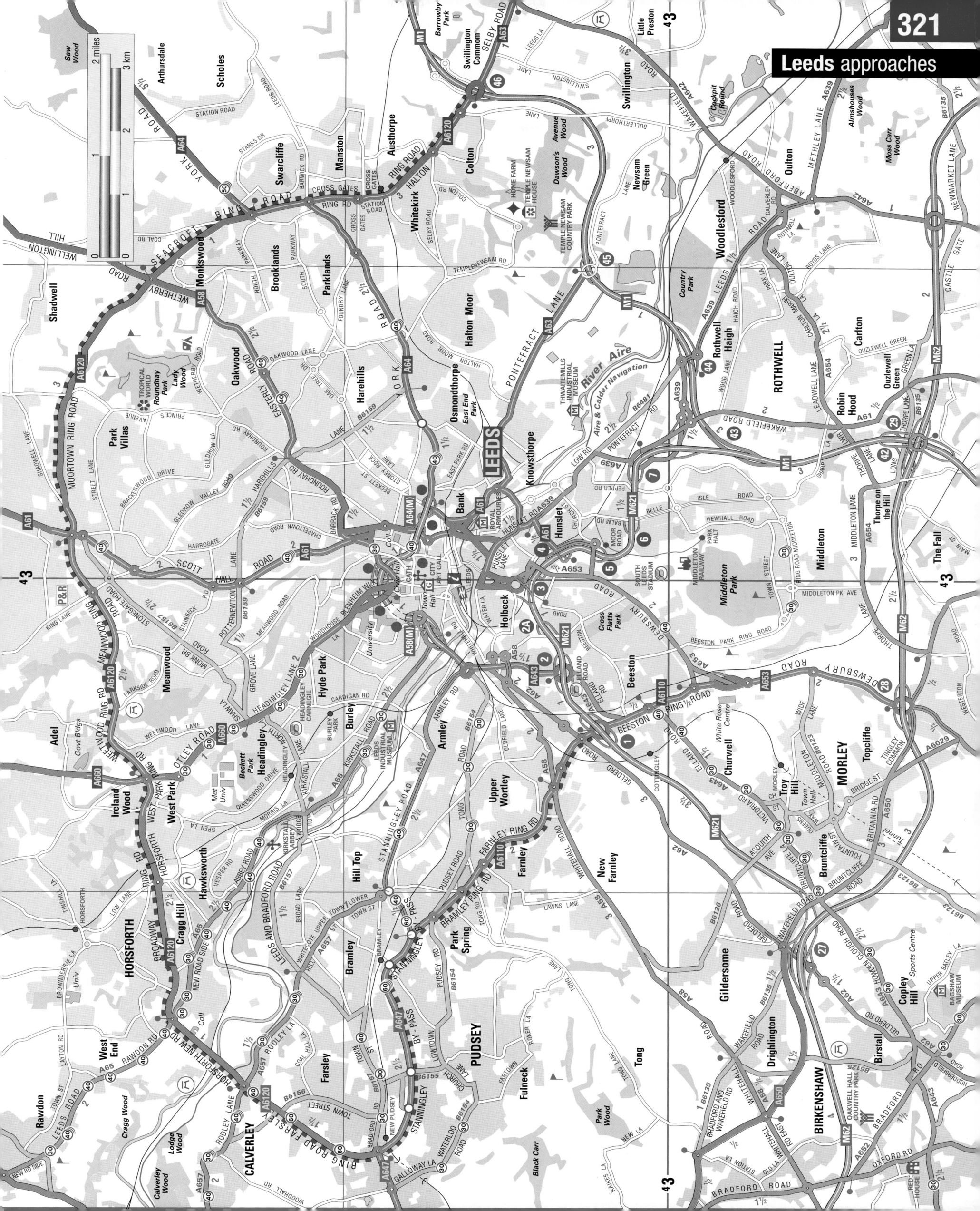

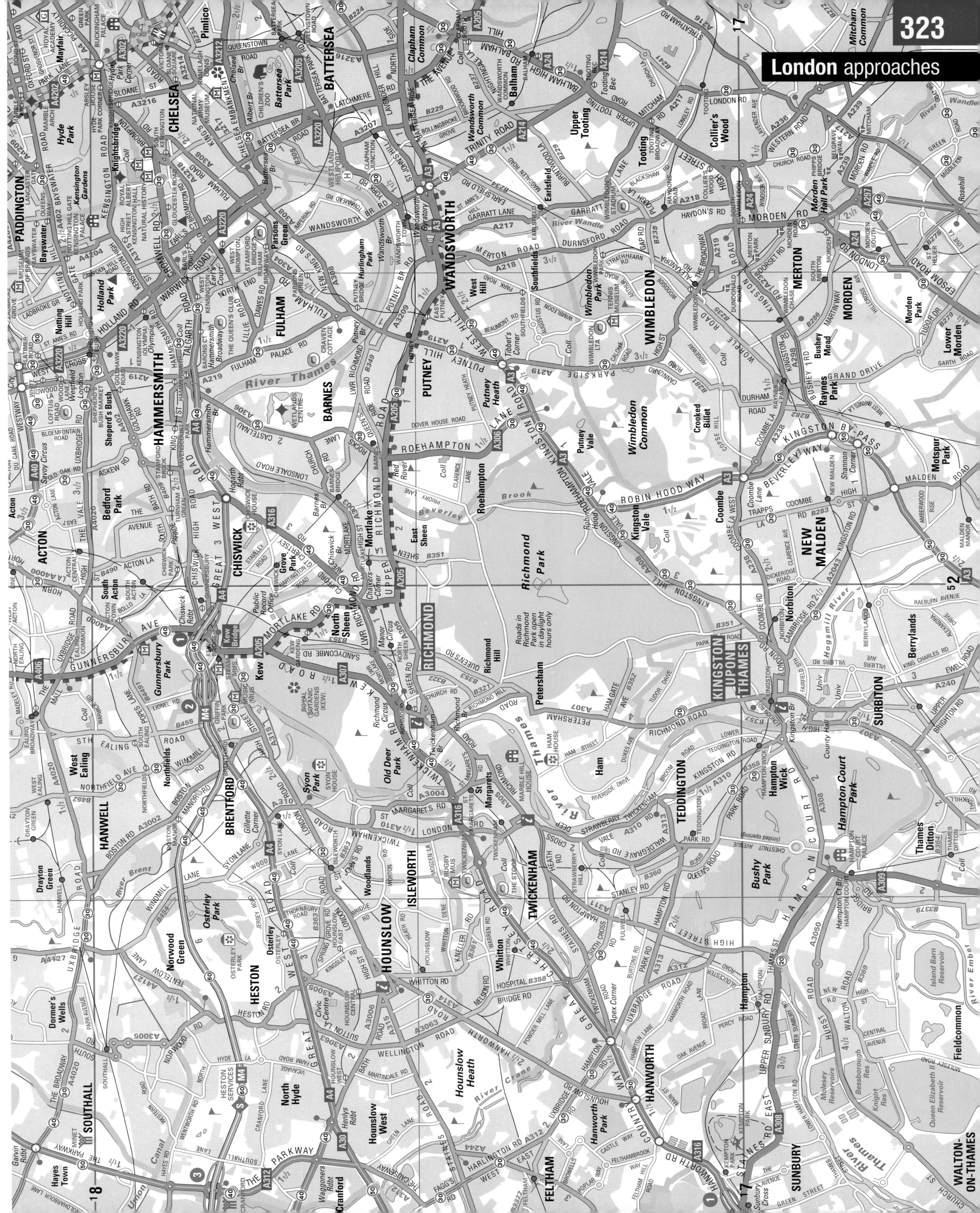

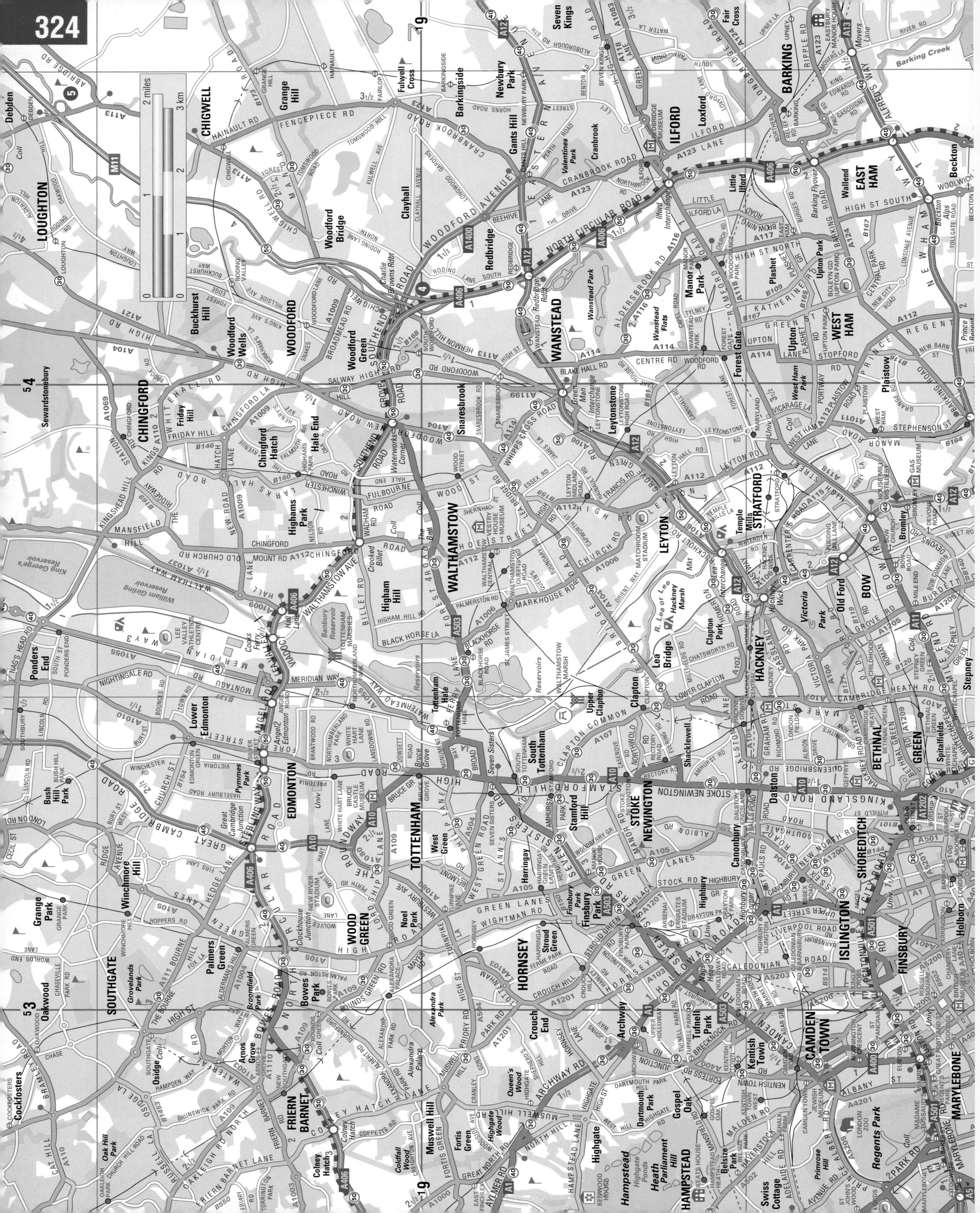

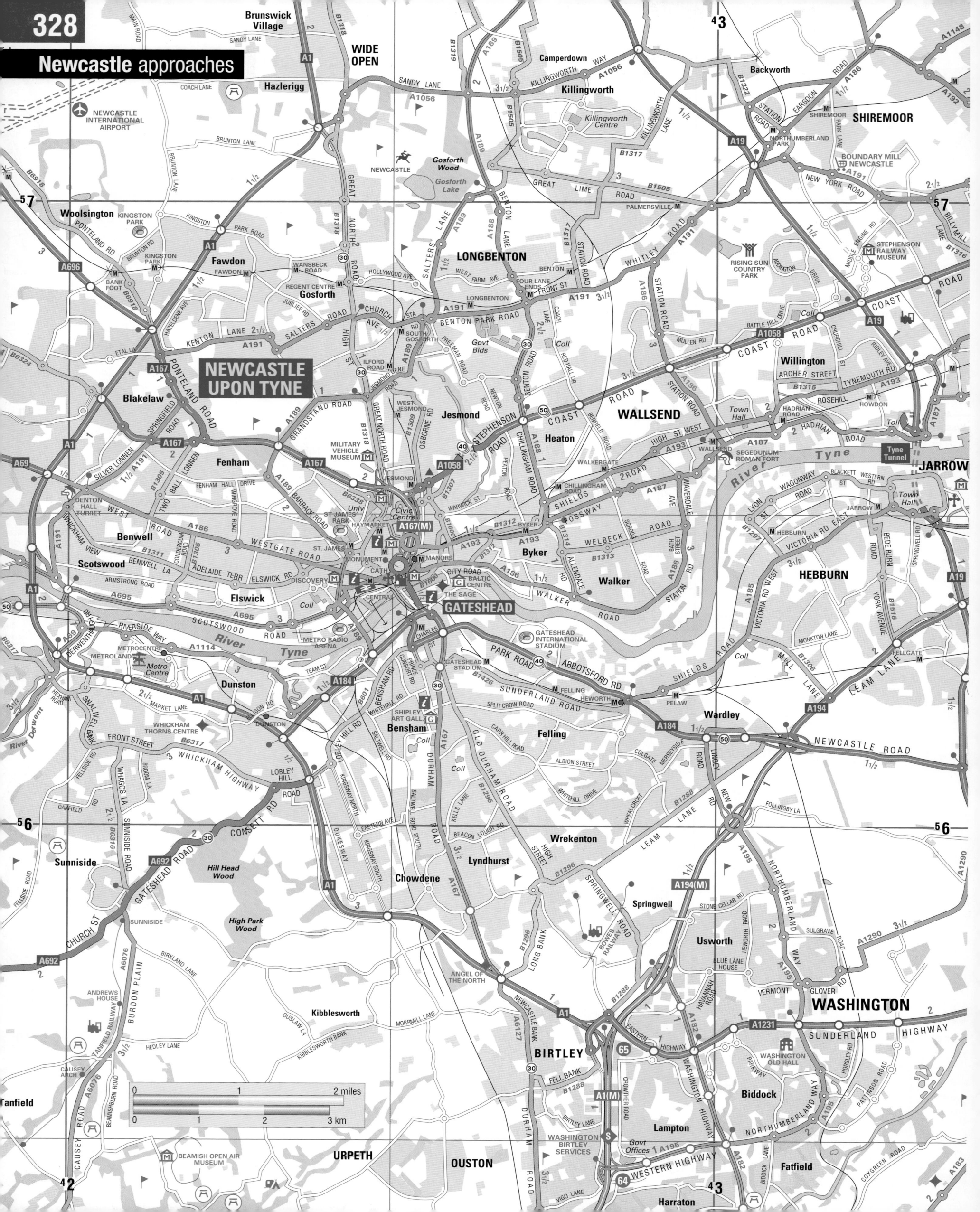

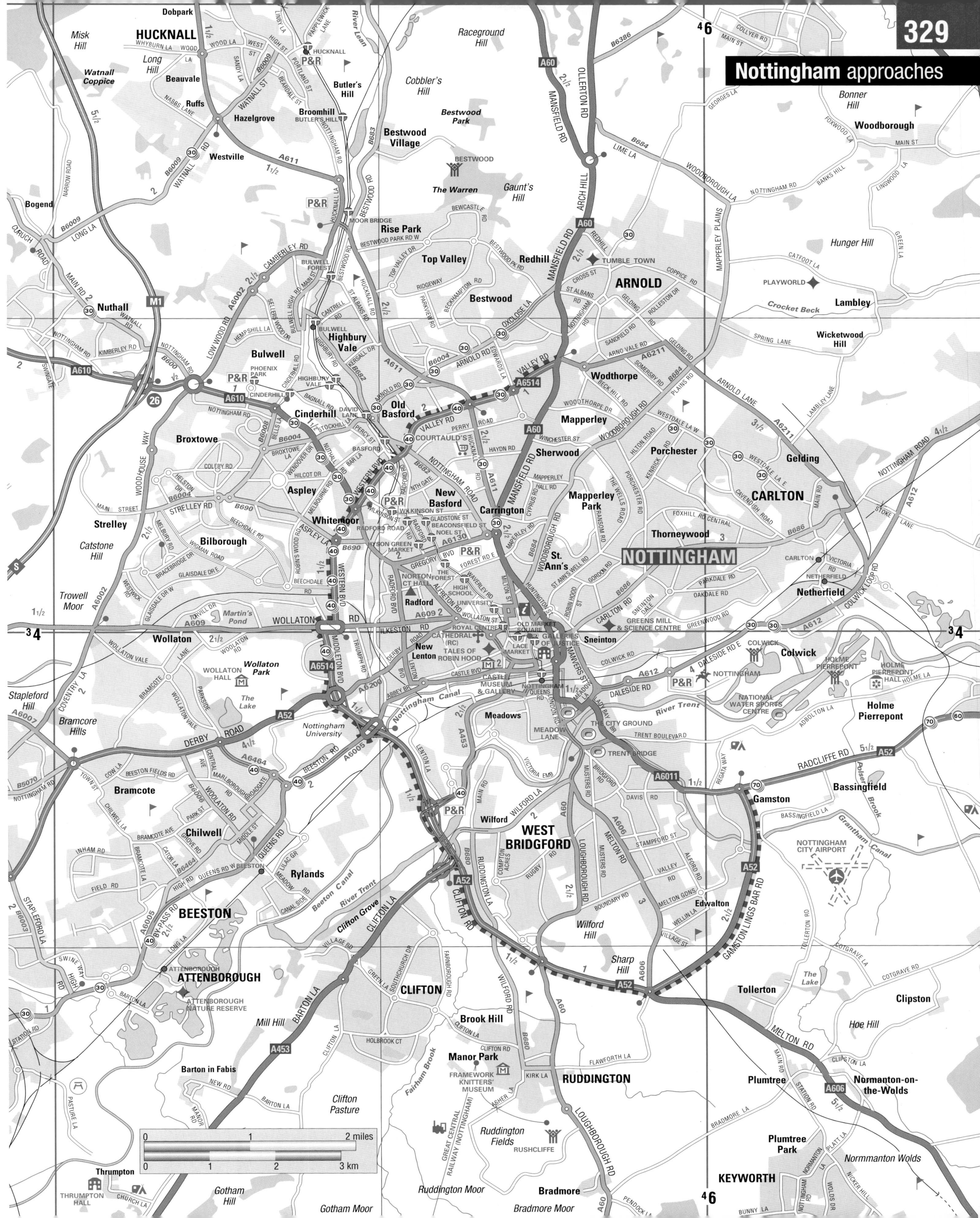

Aberdeen page 293 • Aberystwyth page 128 • Ashford page 54 • Ayr page 257 • Bangor page 179 • Barrow-in-Furness page 210 • Bath page 61 • Berwick-upon-Tweed page 273

331

Town plan symbols

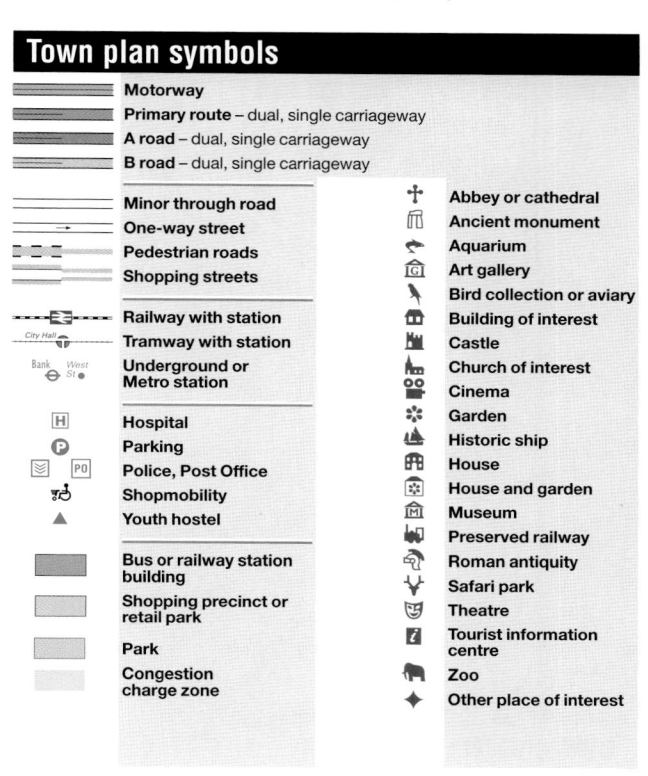

Aberdeen

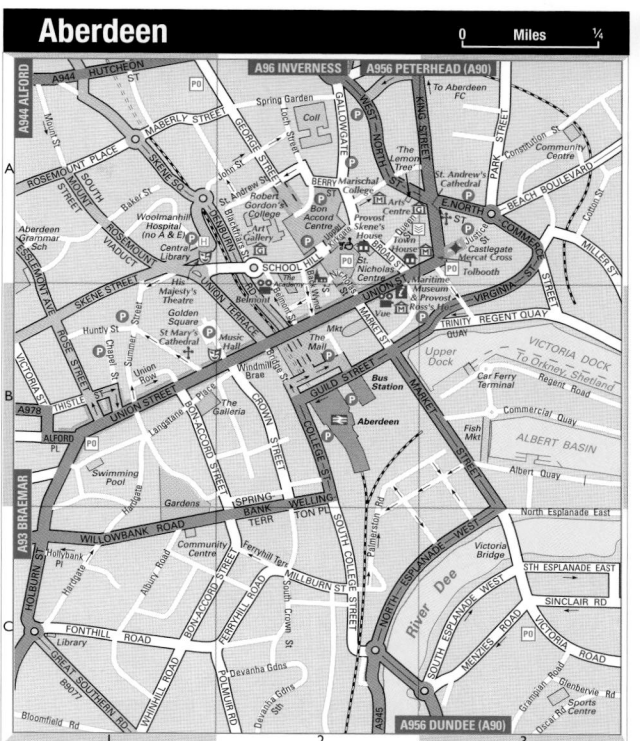

Aberystwyth

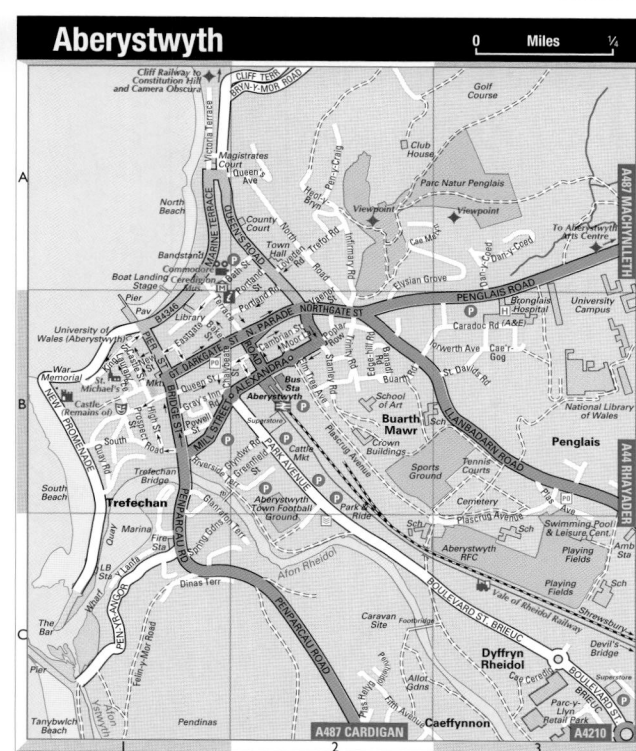

Ashford

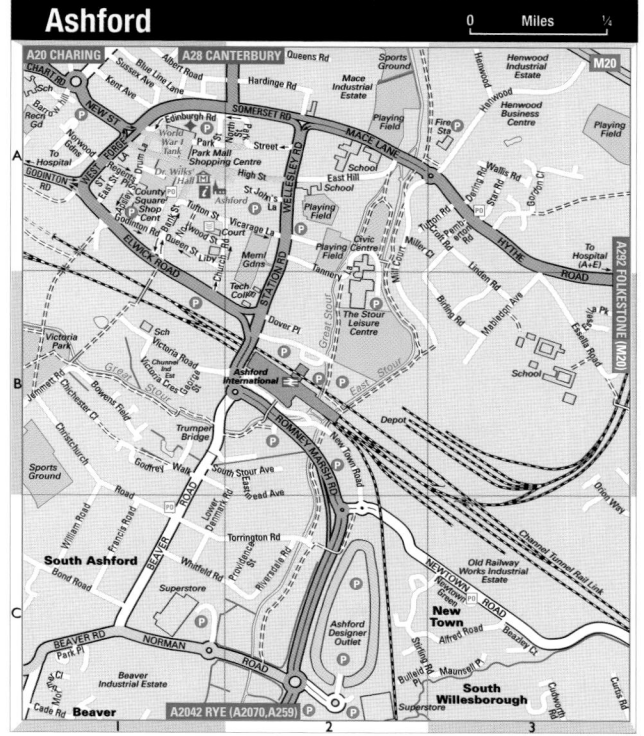

Ayr

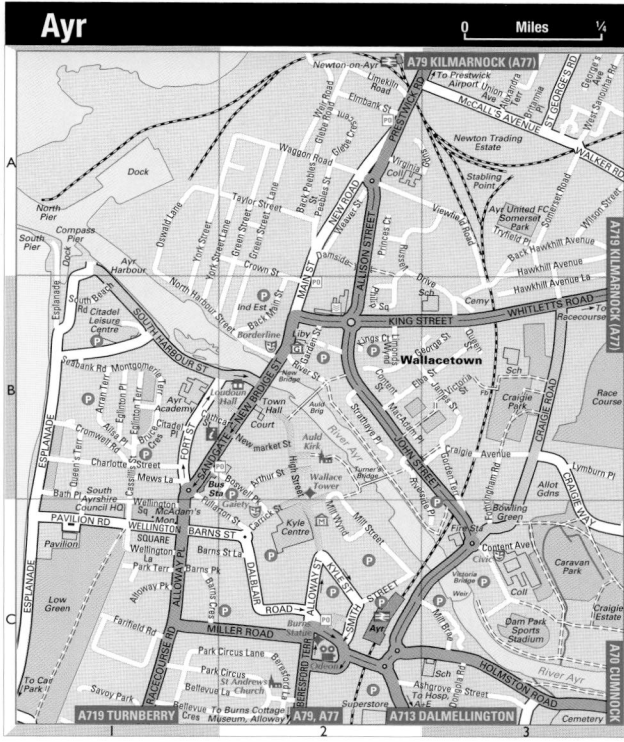

Bangor

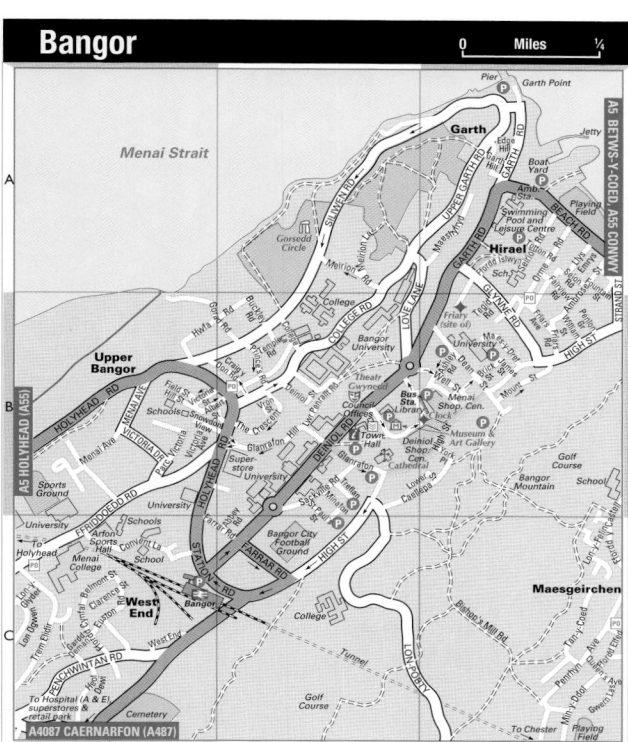

Barrow-in-Furness

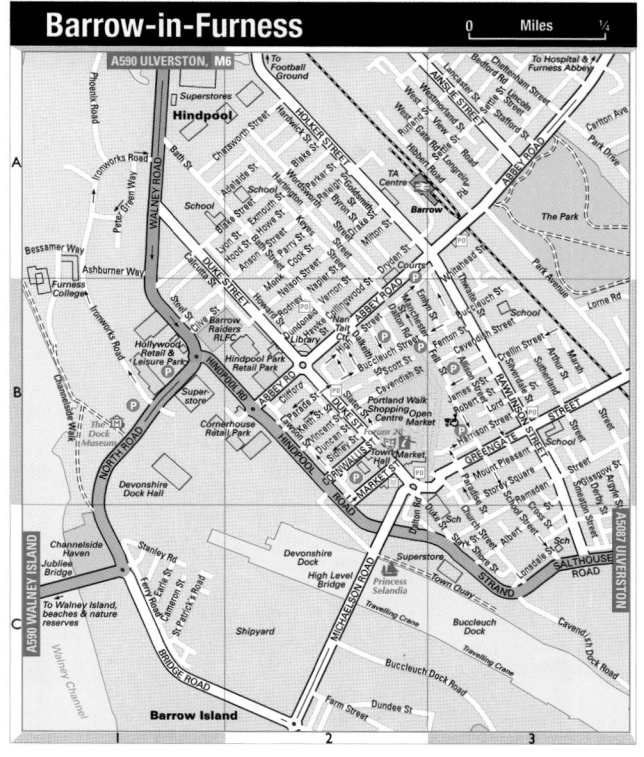

Bath

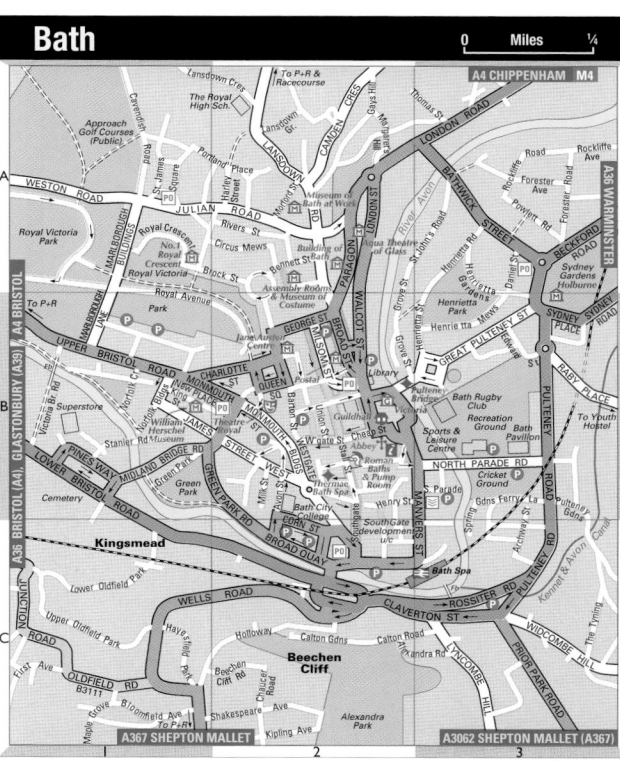

Berwick-upon-Tweed

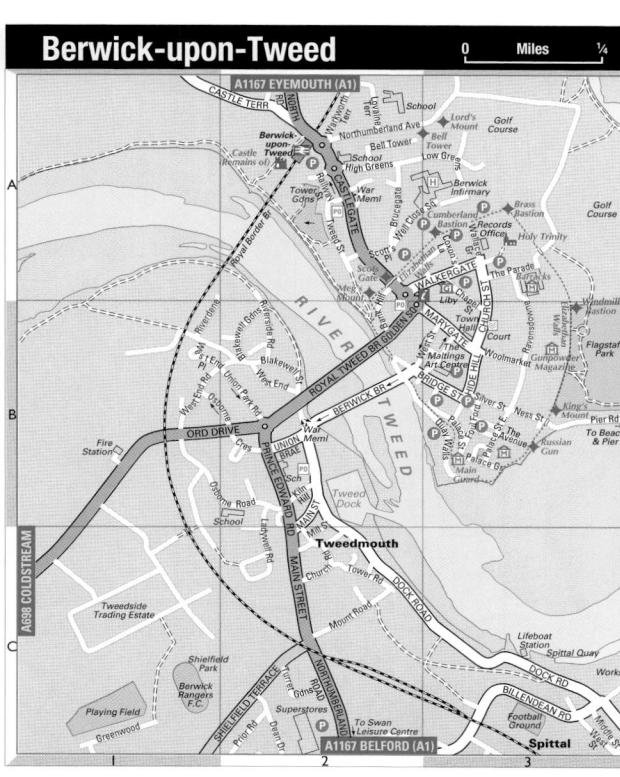

Birmingham

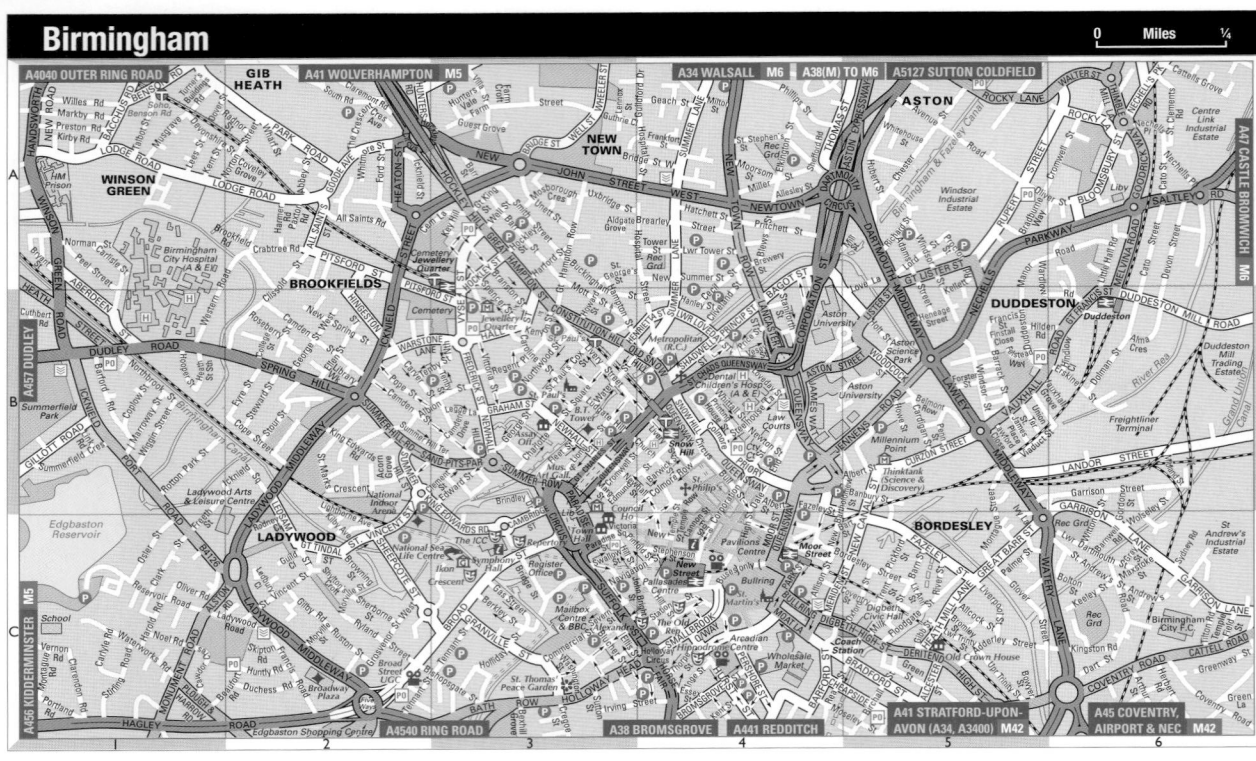

Blackpool

Bournemouth

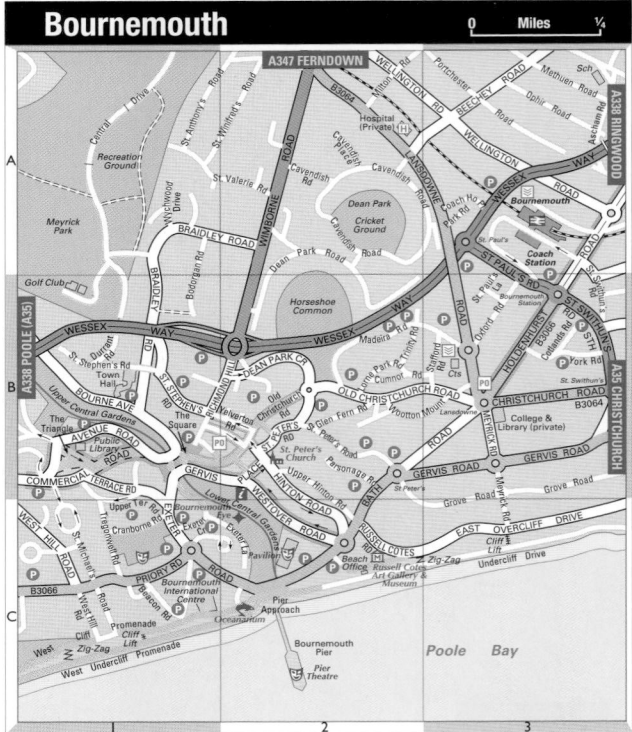

Bradford

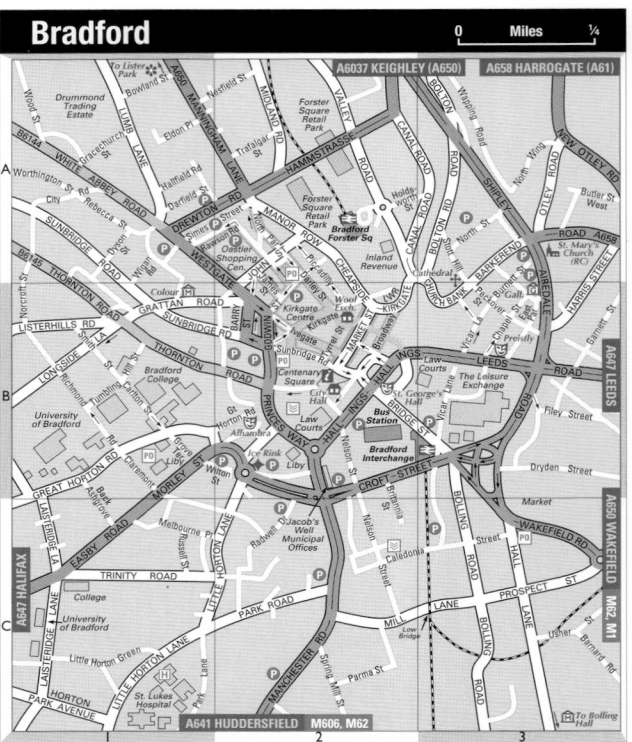

Brighton

Bristol

Bury St Edmunds

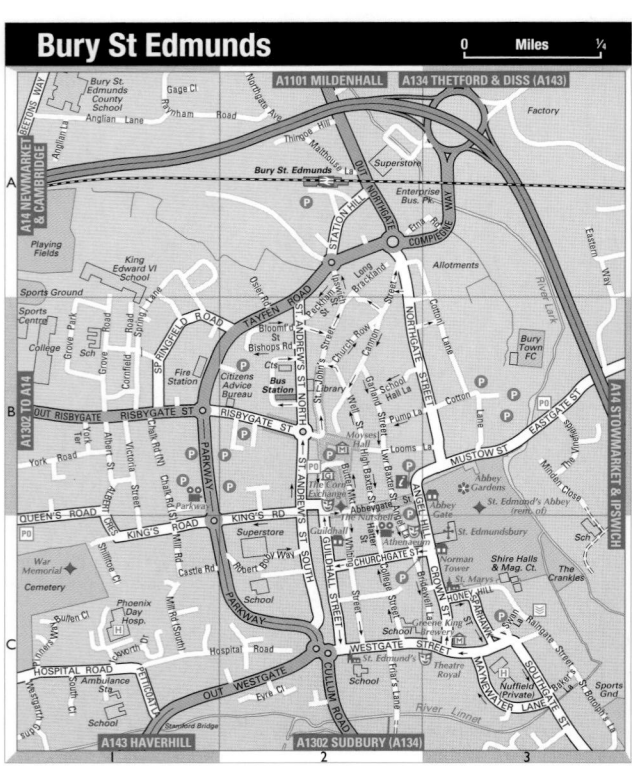

Cambridge page 123 ● **Canterbury** page 54 ● **Cardiff** page 59 ● **Carlisle** page 239 ● **Chelmsford** page 88 ● **Cheltenham** page 99 ● **Chester** page 166 ● **Chichester** page 22 ● **Colchester** page 107

333

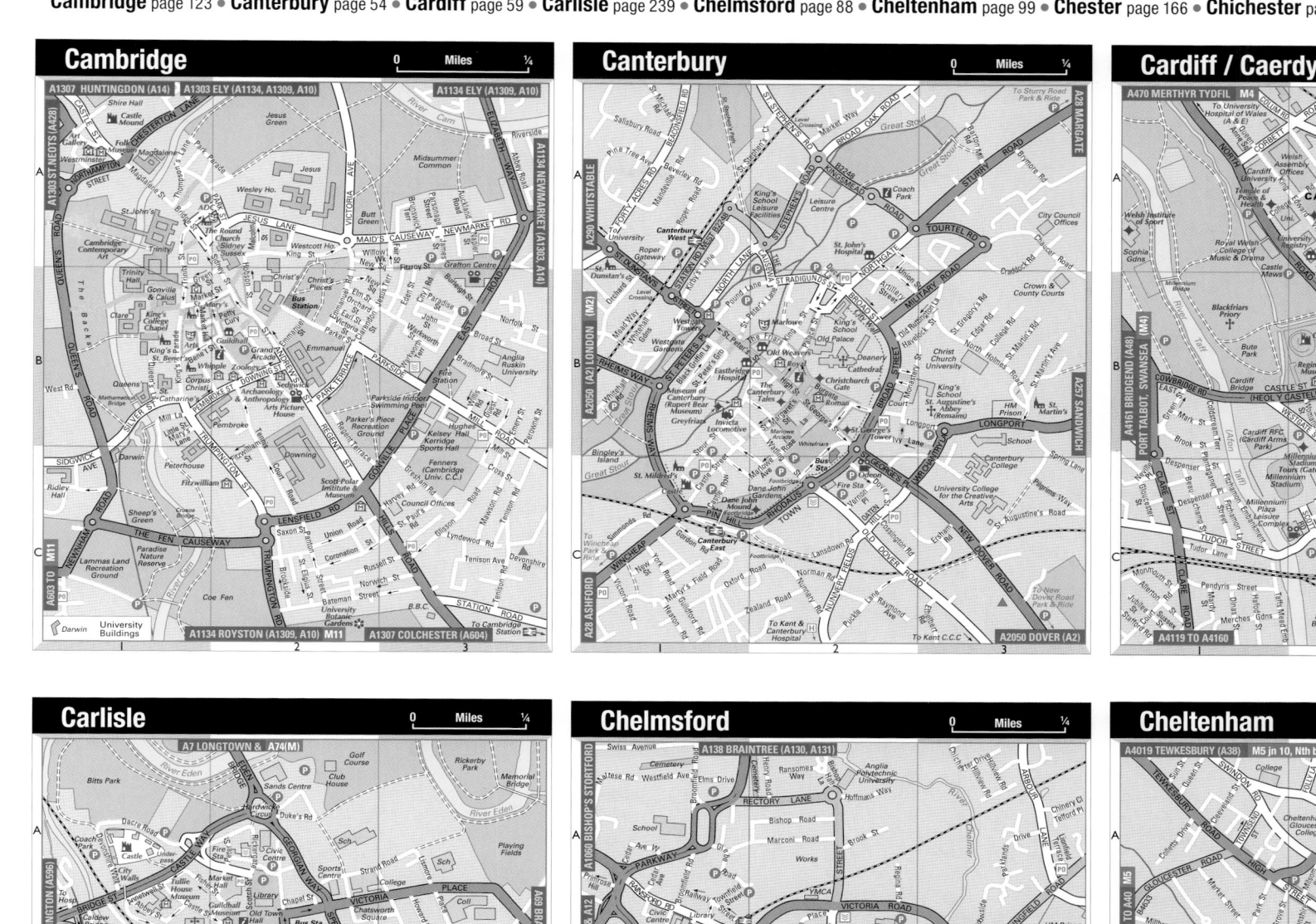

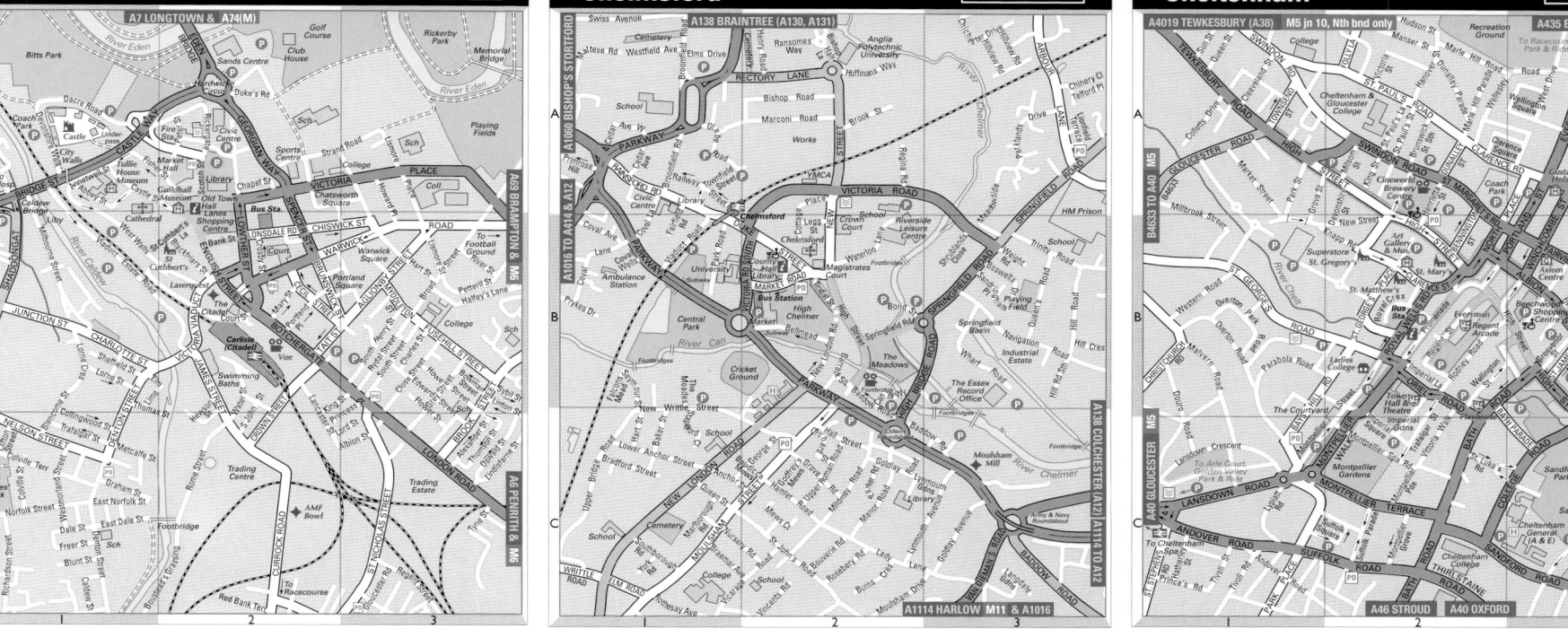

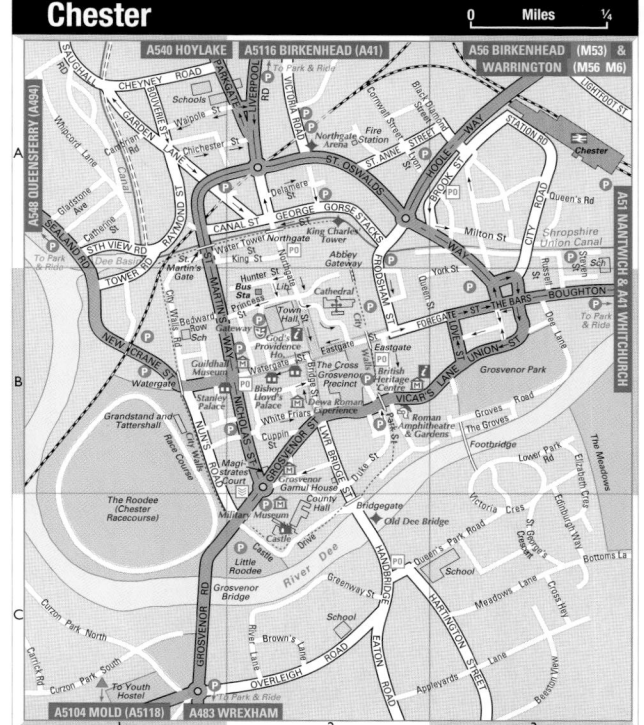

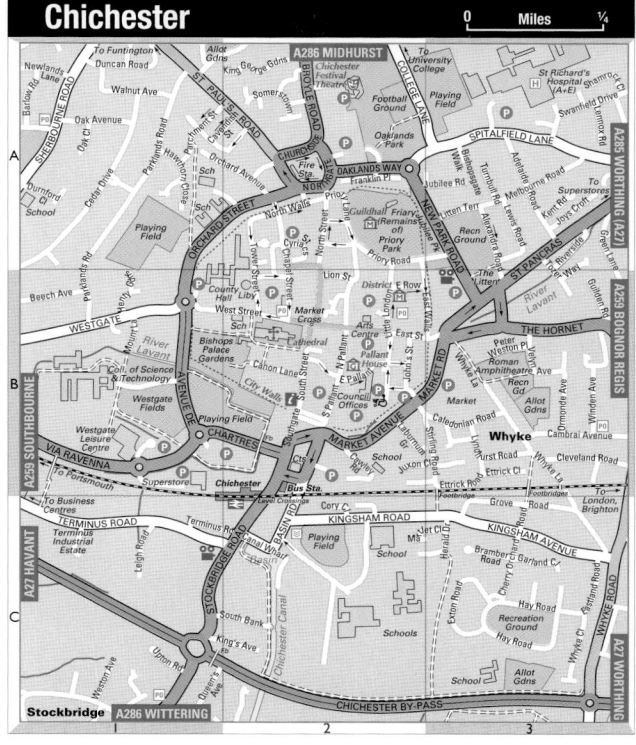

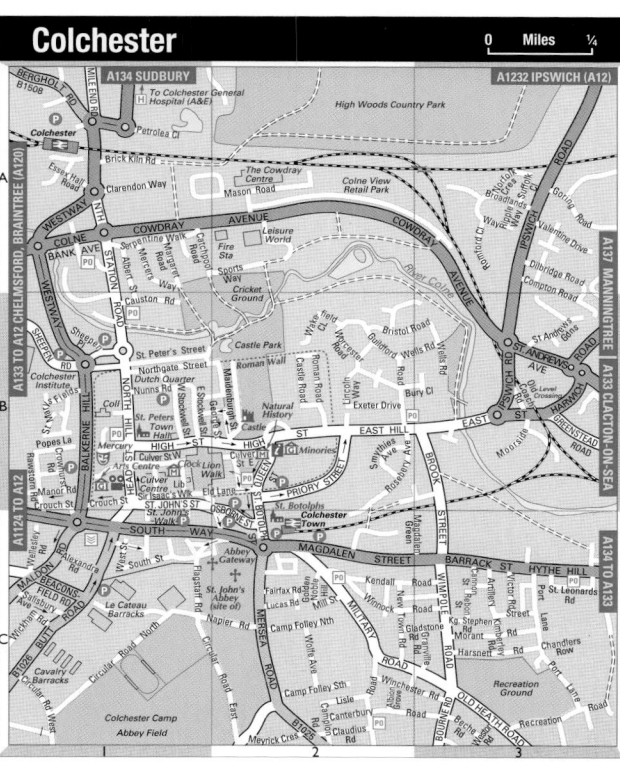

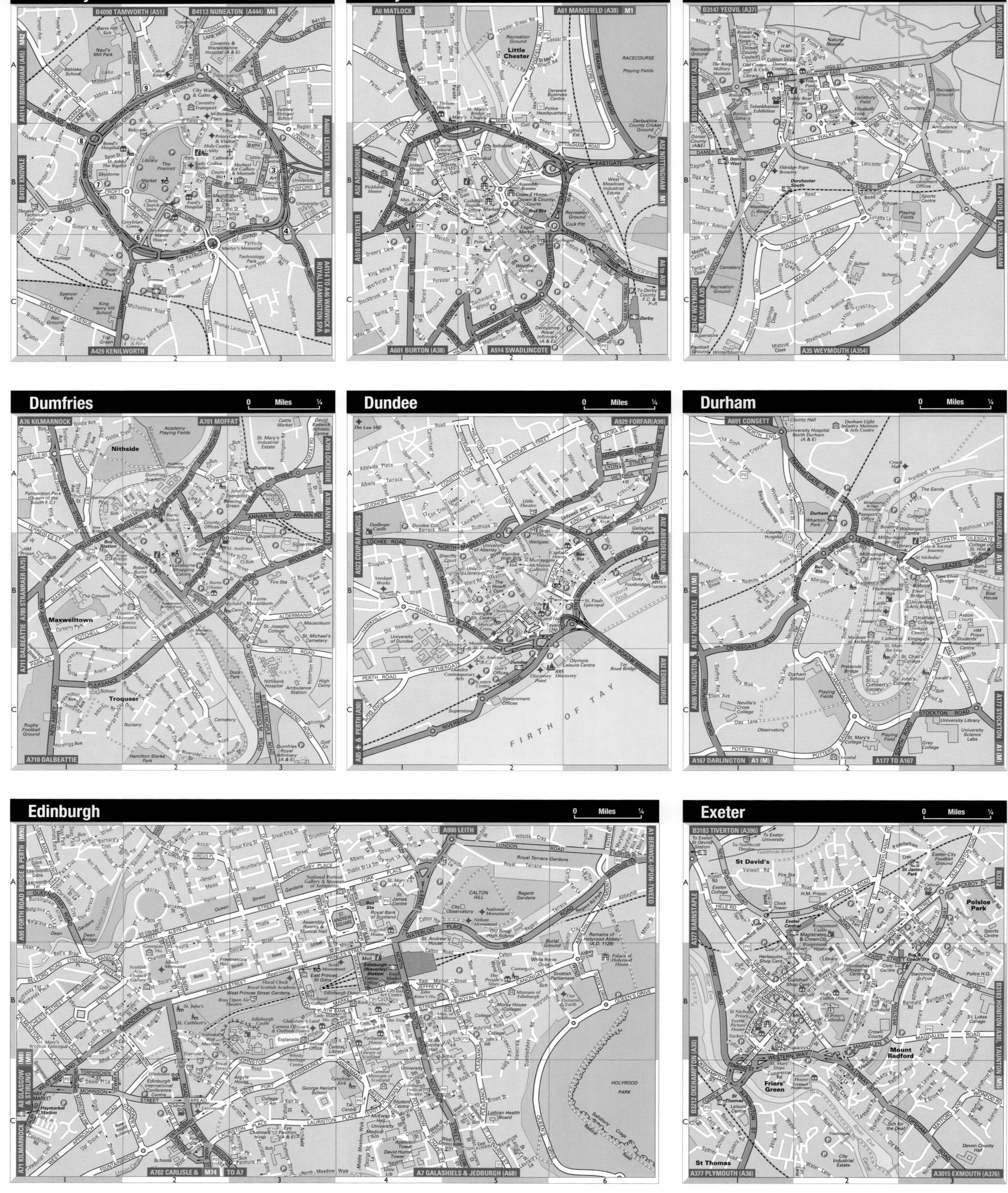

Fort William page 290 ● **Glasgow** page 267 ● **Gloucester** page 80 ● **Grimsby** page 201 ● **Hanley (Stoke-on-Tent)** page 168 ● **Harrogate** page 206 ● **Holyhead** page 178 ● **Hull** page 200

335

Fort William

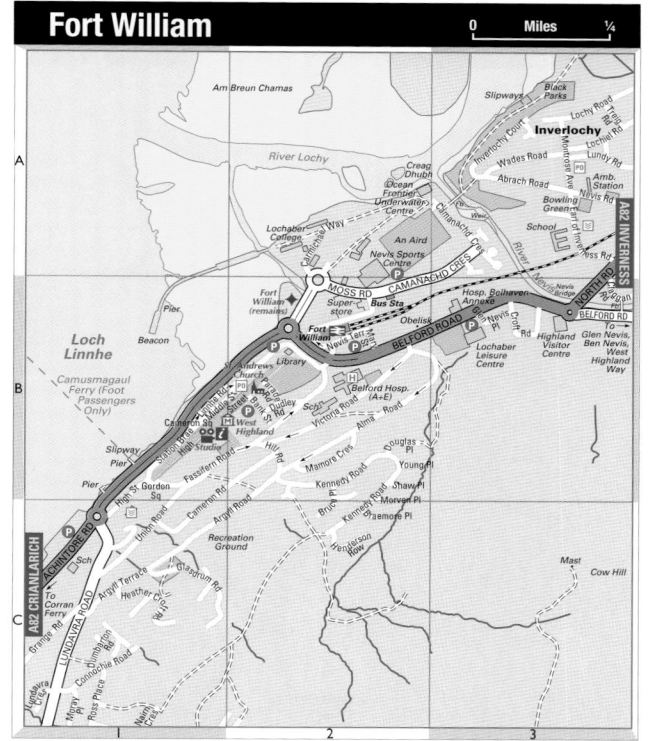

Glasgow

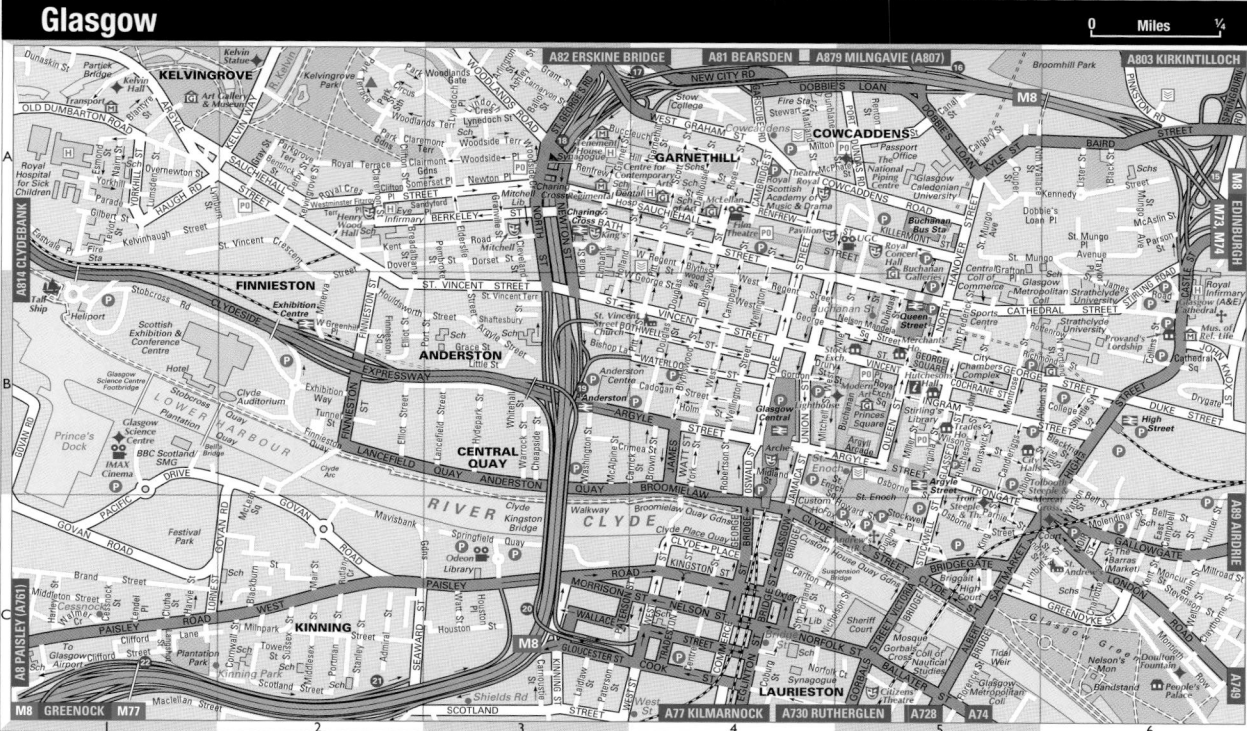

Gloucester

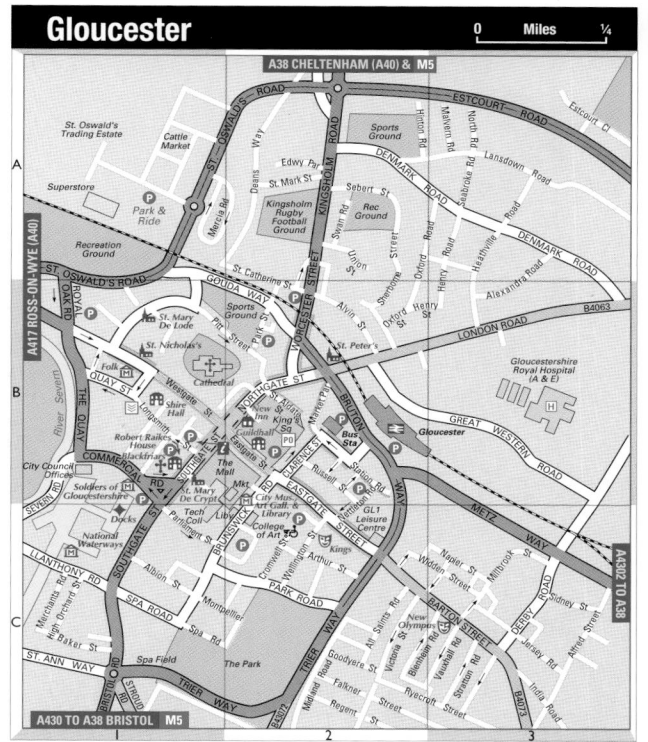

Grimsby

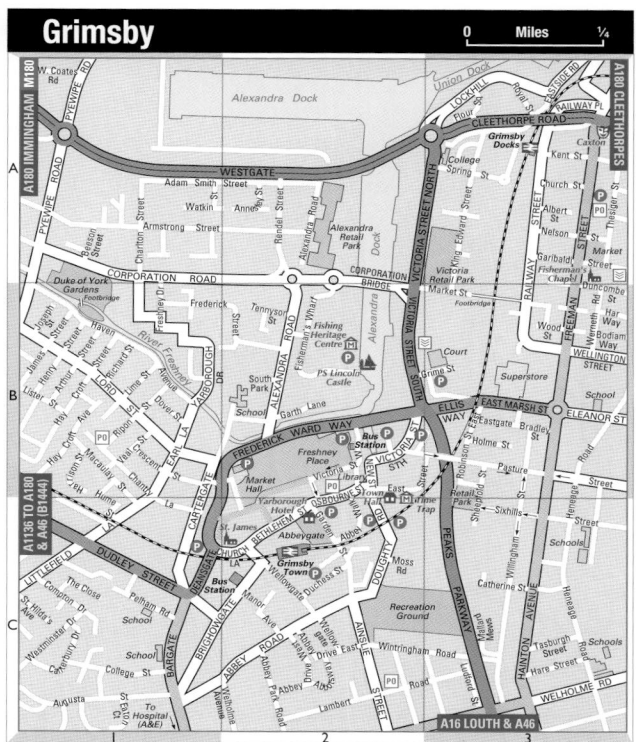

Hanley (Stoke-on-Trent)

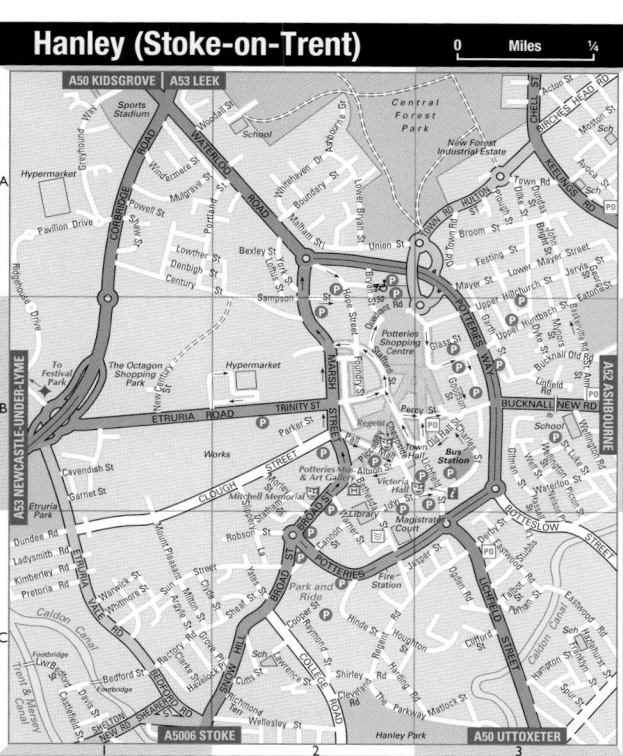

Harrogate

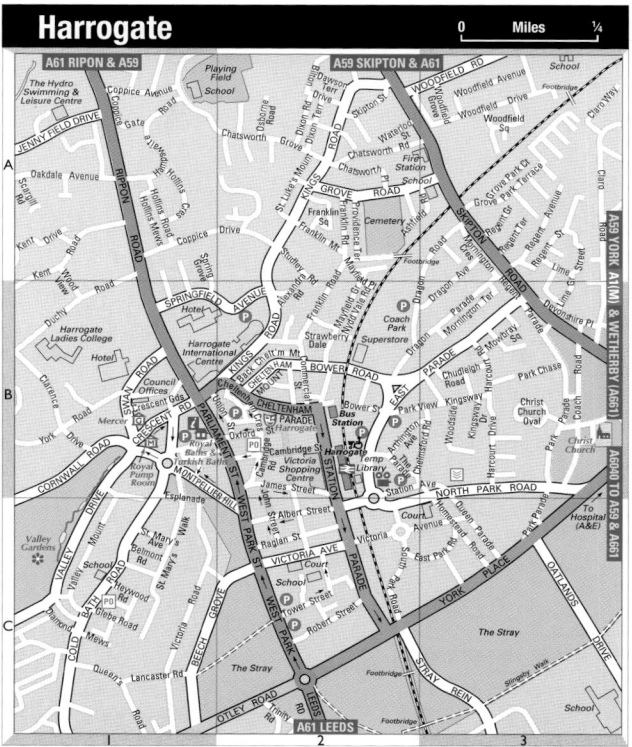

Holyhead / Caergybi

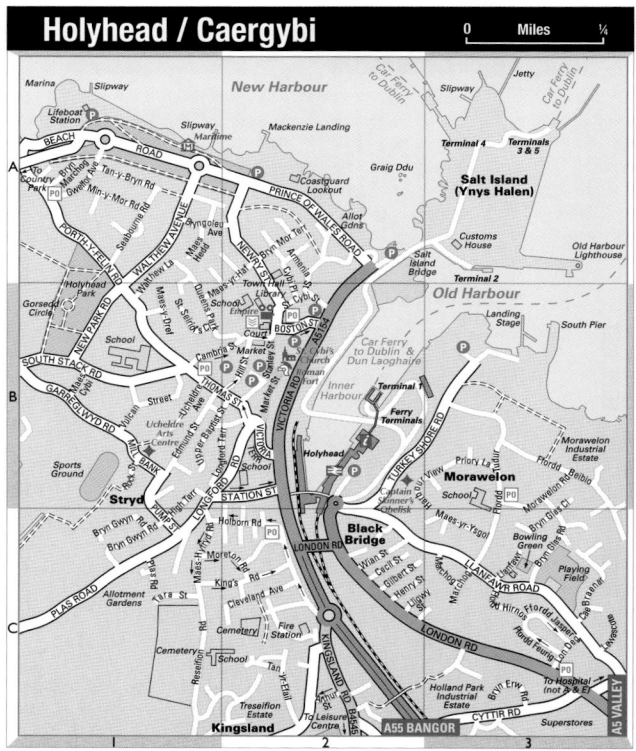

Hull

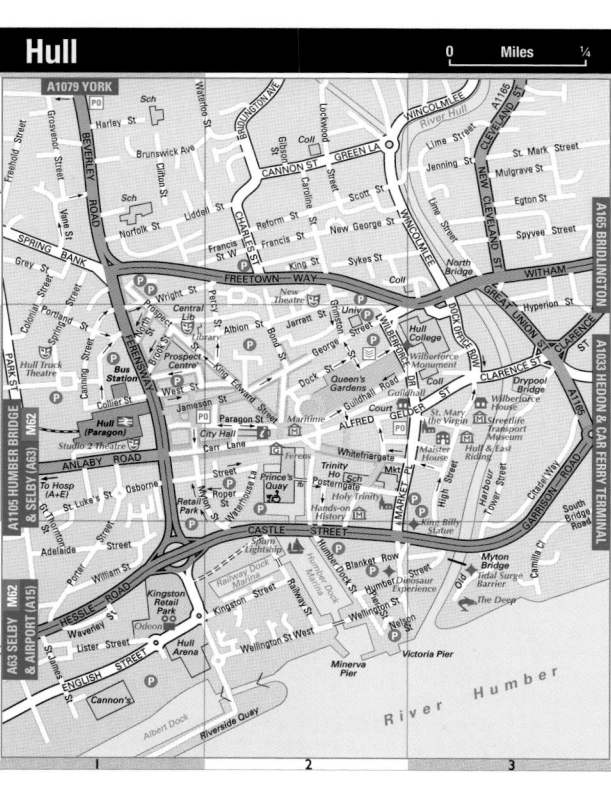

Inverness
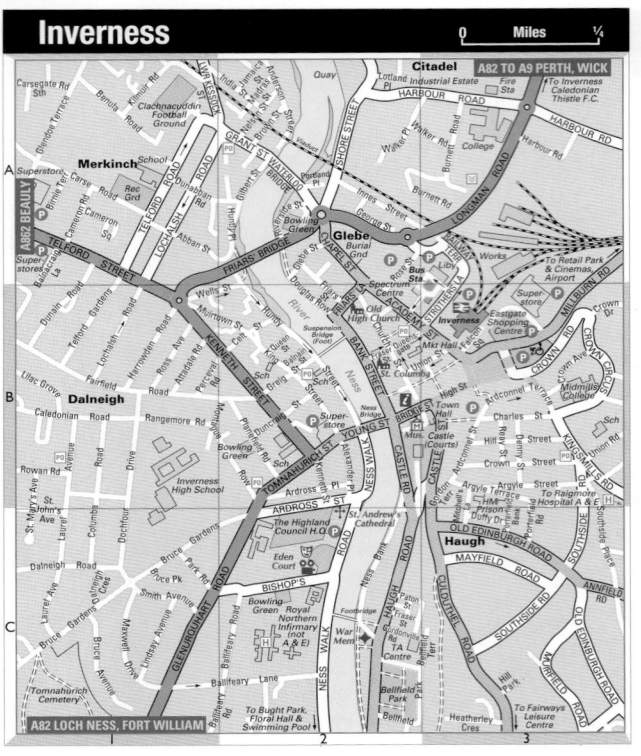

Ipswich
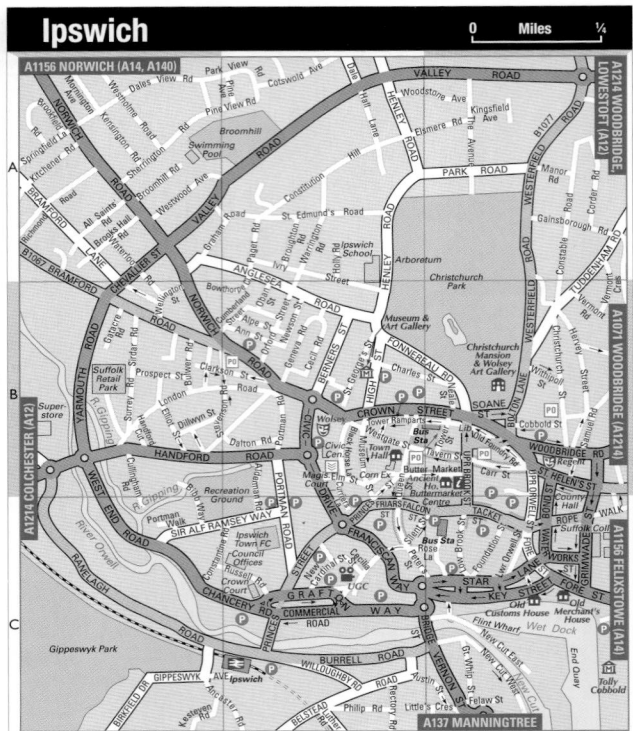

Kendal
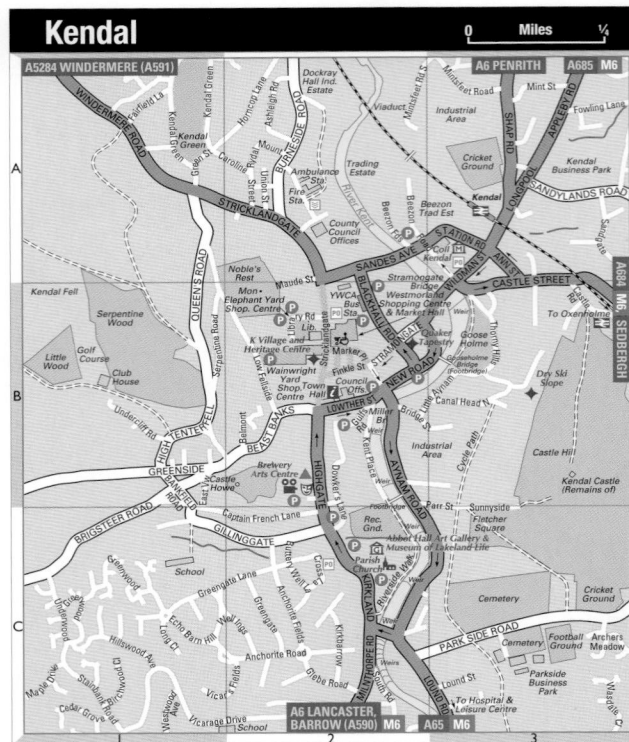

King's Lynn
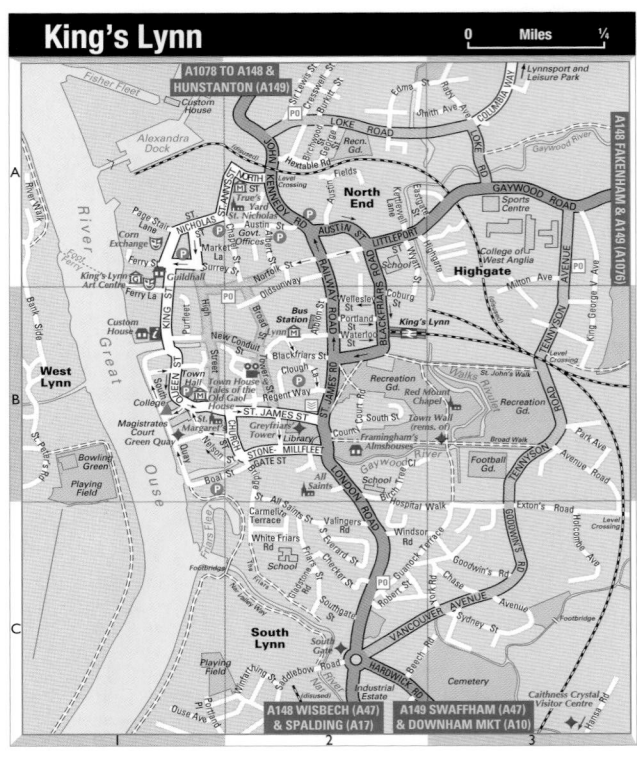

Leeds
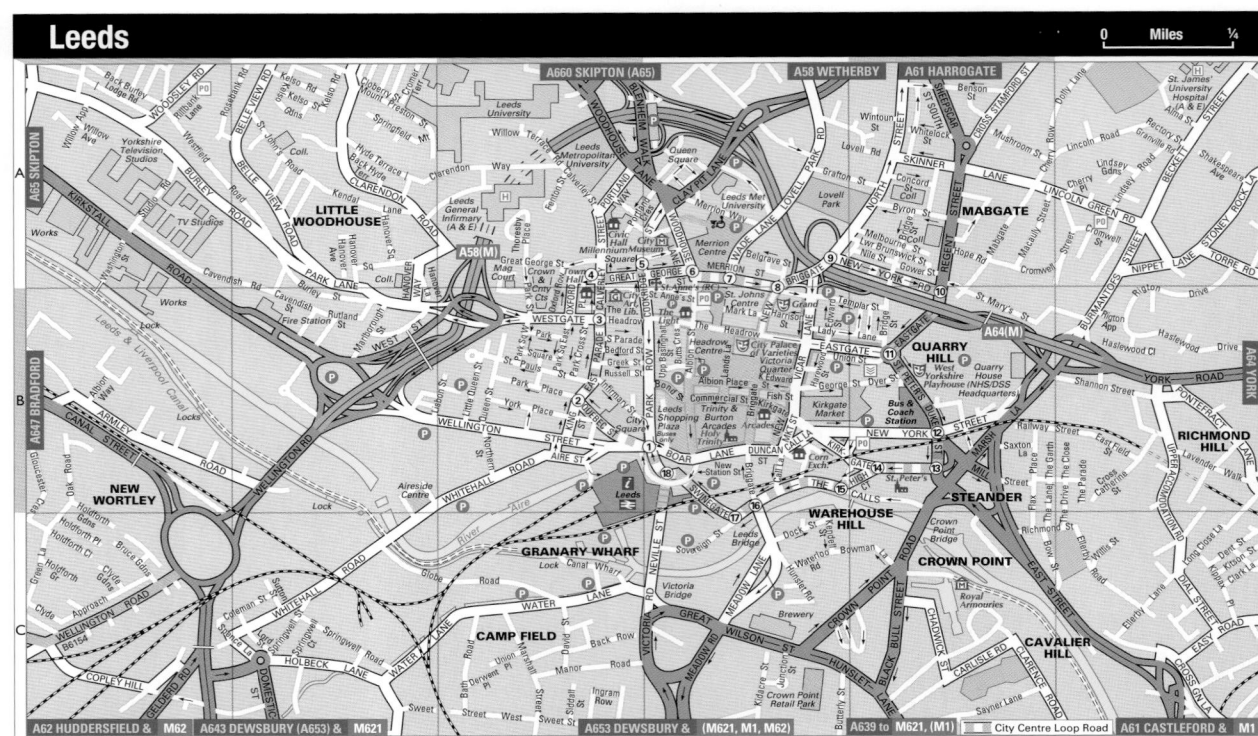

Lancaster
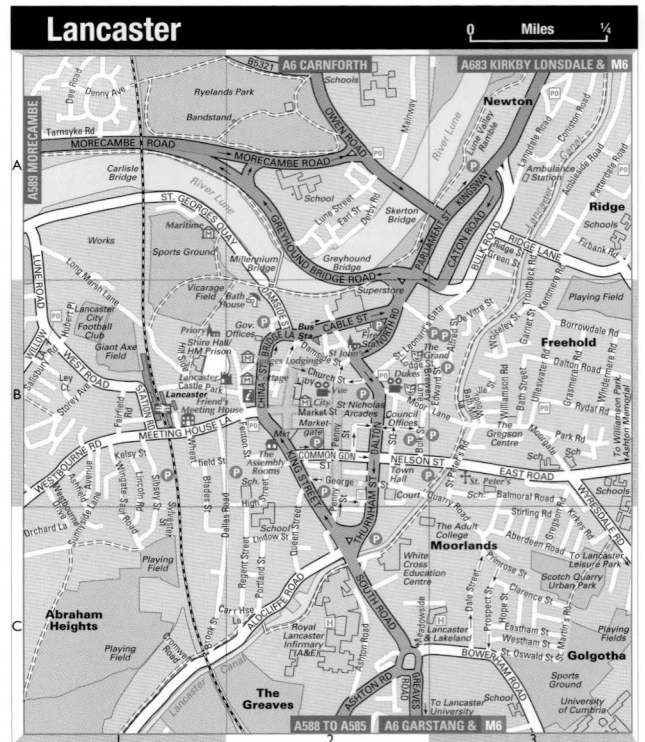

Leicester
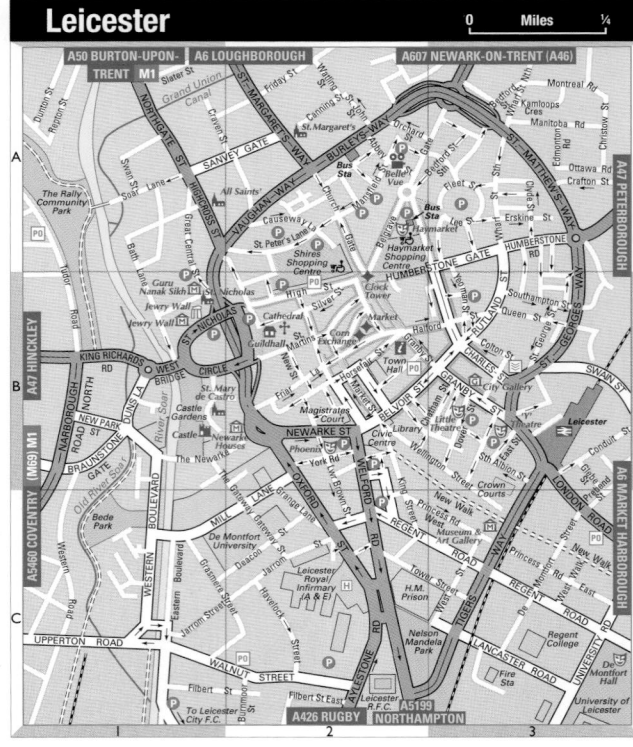

Lewes
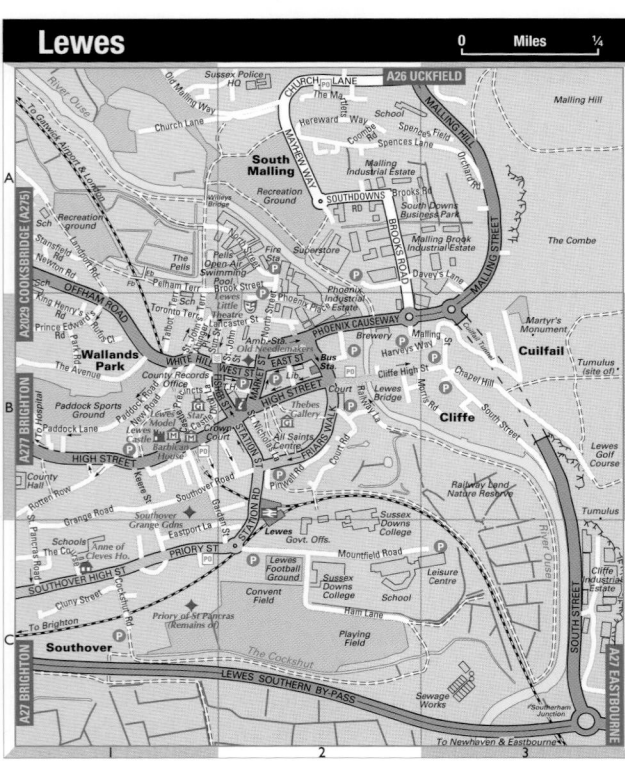

Lincoln page 189 • Liverpool page 182 • Llandudno page 180 • Llanelli page 56 • Luton page 103 • Macclesfield page 184 • Manchester page 184

337

Lincoln

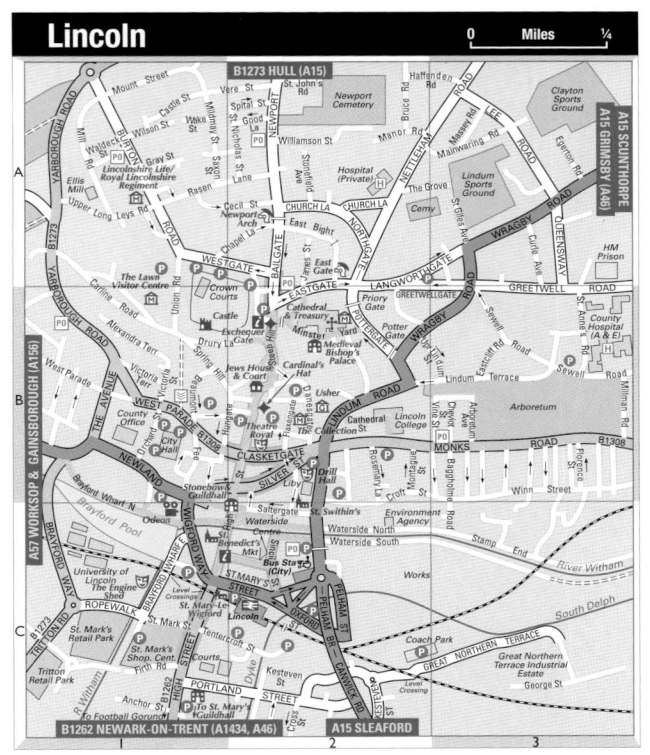

Liverpool

Llandudno

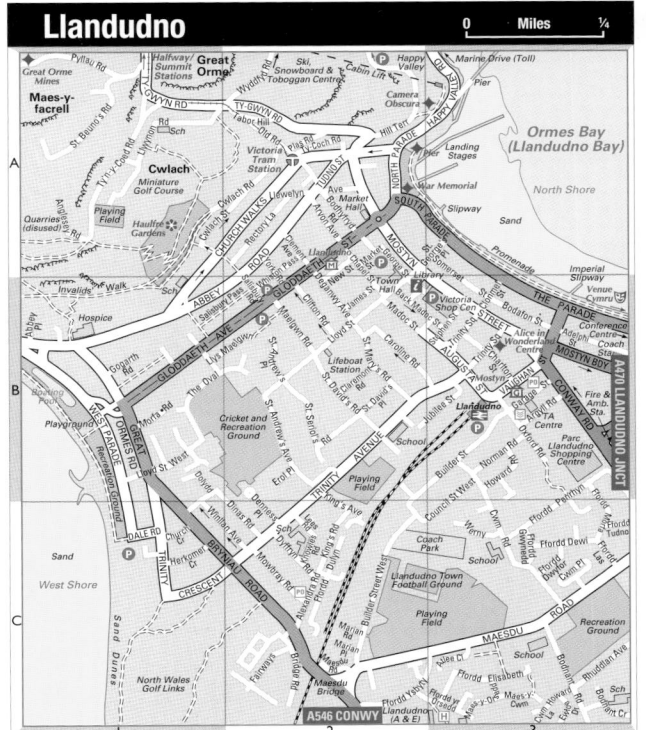

Llanelli

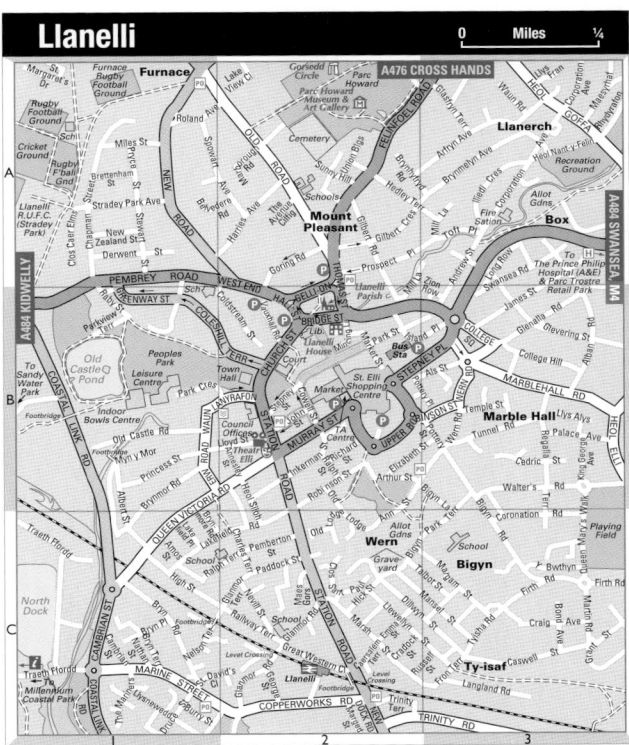

Luton

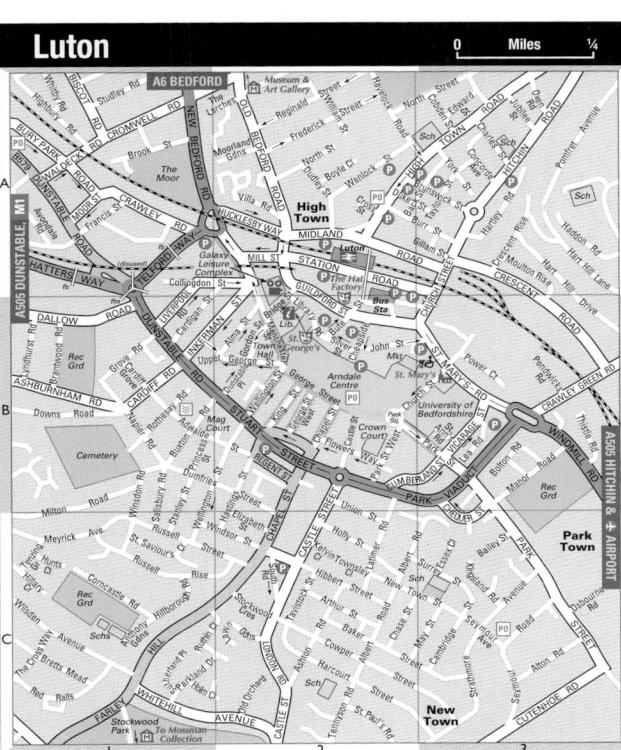

Macclesfield

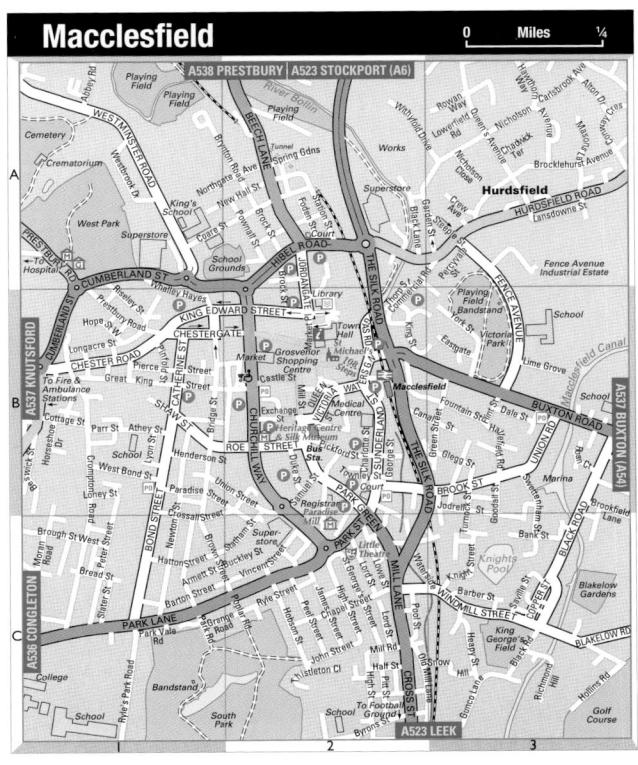

Manchester

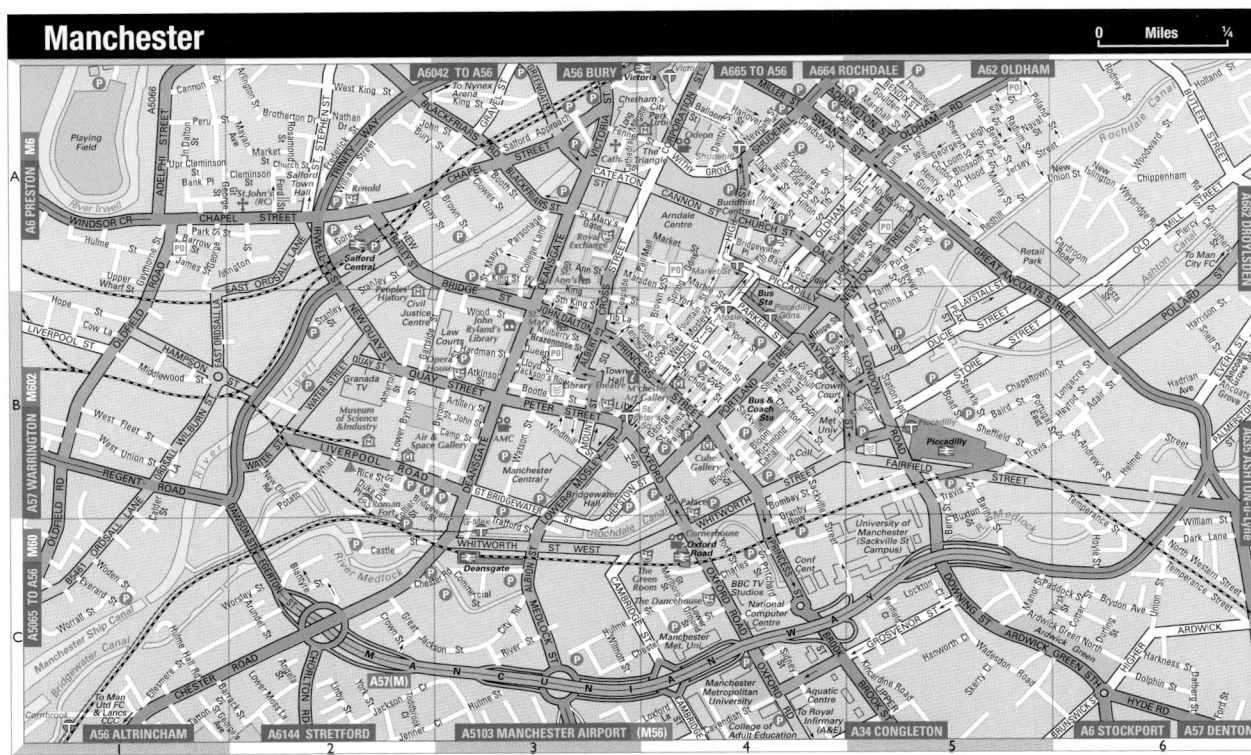

340

Maidstone p 53 • Merthyr Tydfil p 77 • Middlesbrough p 234 • Milton Keynes p 103 • Newcastle upon Tyne p 242 • Newport p 59 • Newquay p 4 • Newtown p 130 • Northampton p 120

Maidstone

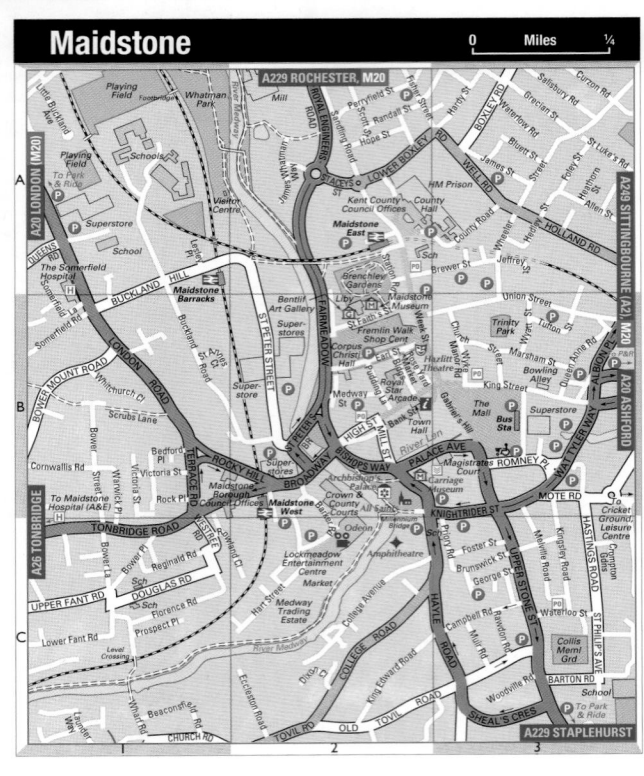

Merthyr Tydfil / Merthyr Tudful

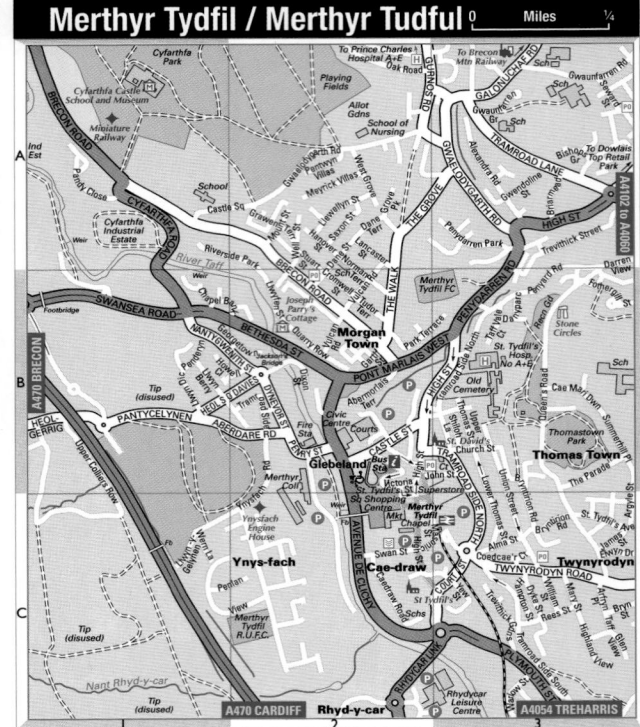

Middlesbrough

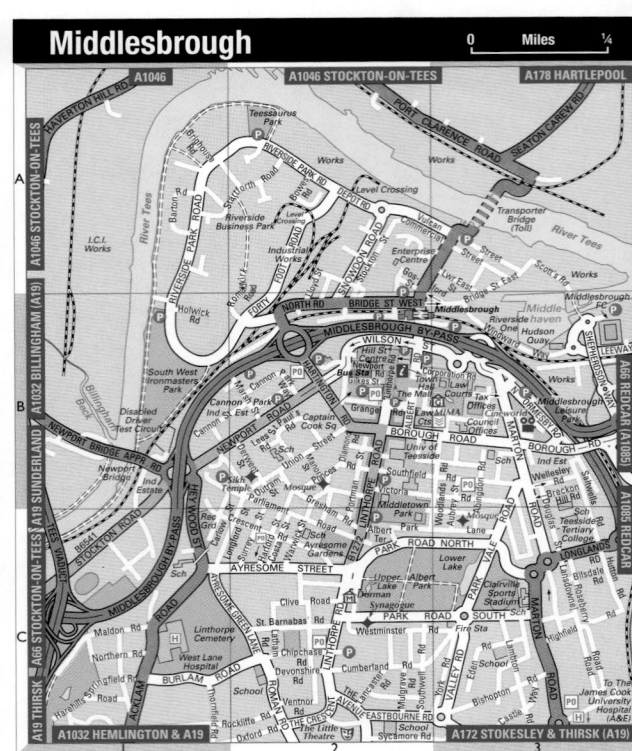

Milton Keynes

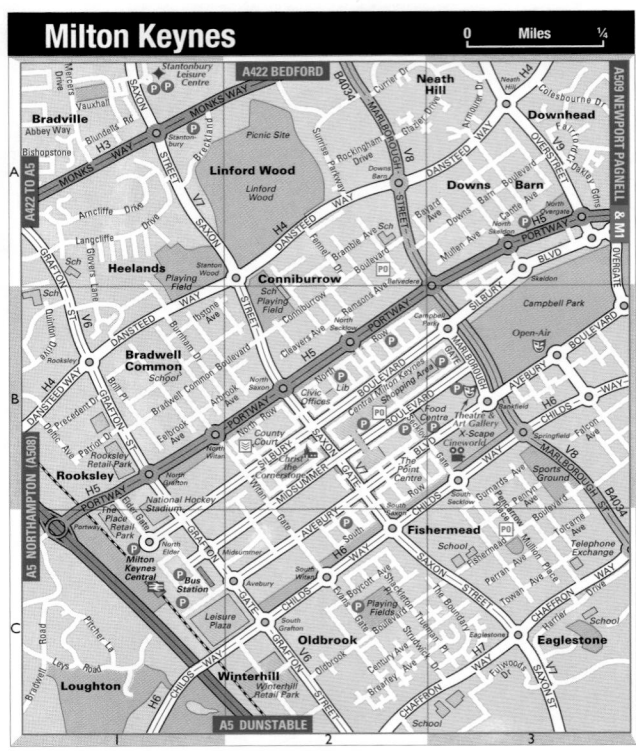

Newcastle upon Tyne

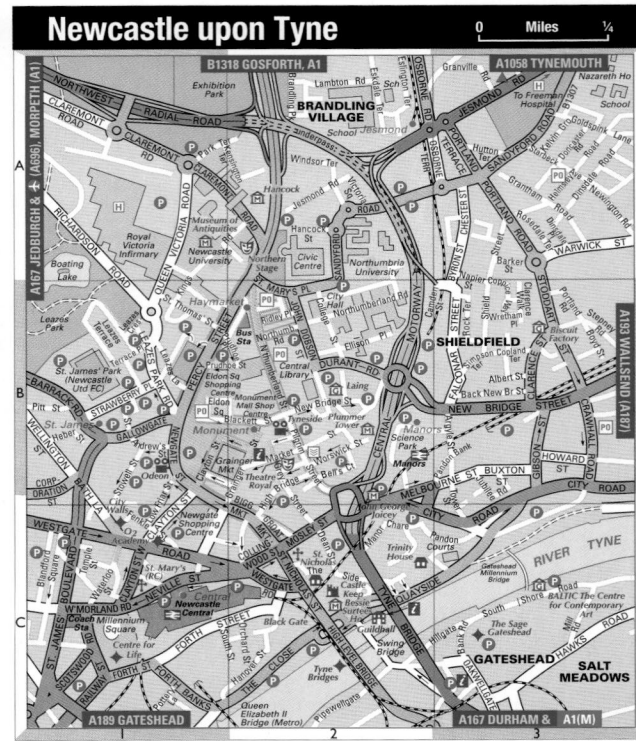

Newport / Casnewydd

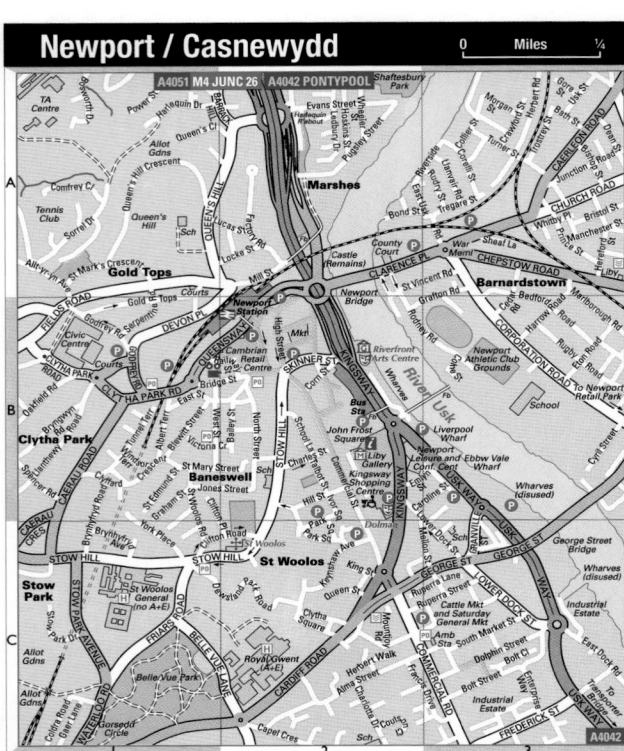

Newquay

Newtown / Y Drenewydd

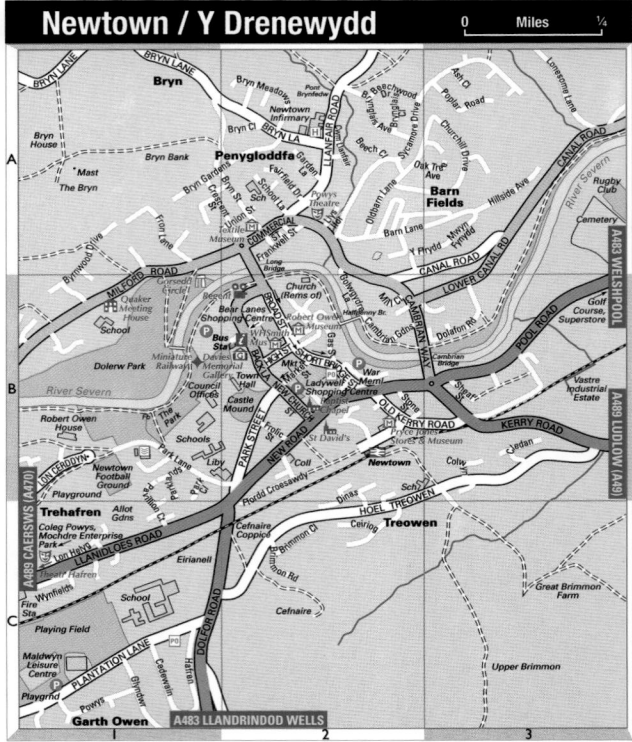

Northampton

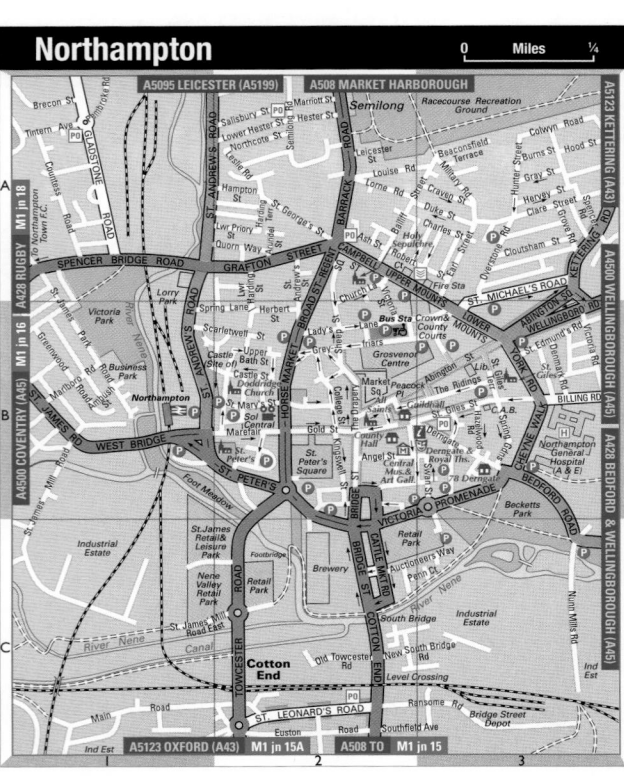

Norwich page 142 ● **Nottingham** page 153 ● **Oban** page 289 ● **Oxford** page 83 ● **Perth** page 286 ● **Peterborough** page 138 ● **Plymouth** page 7 ● **Poole** page 18 ● **Portsmouth** page 21

341

Norwich
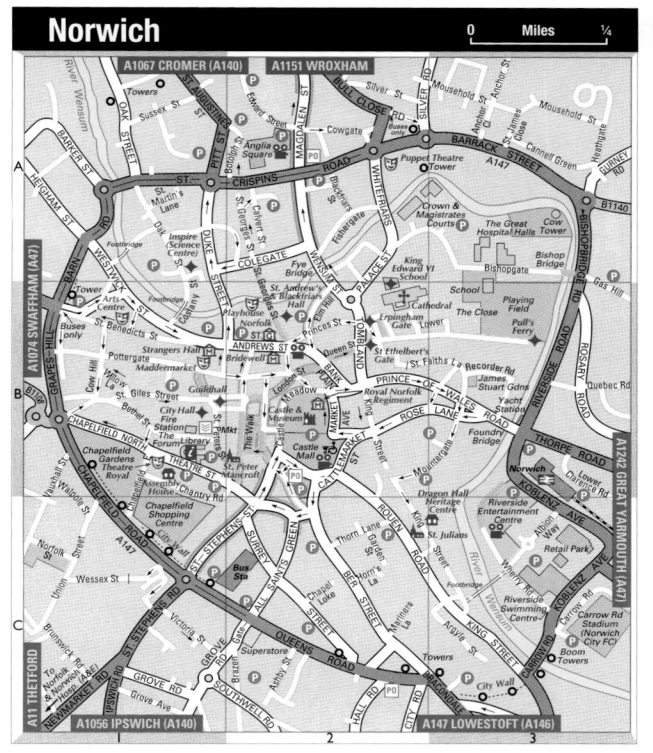

Nottingham
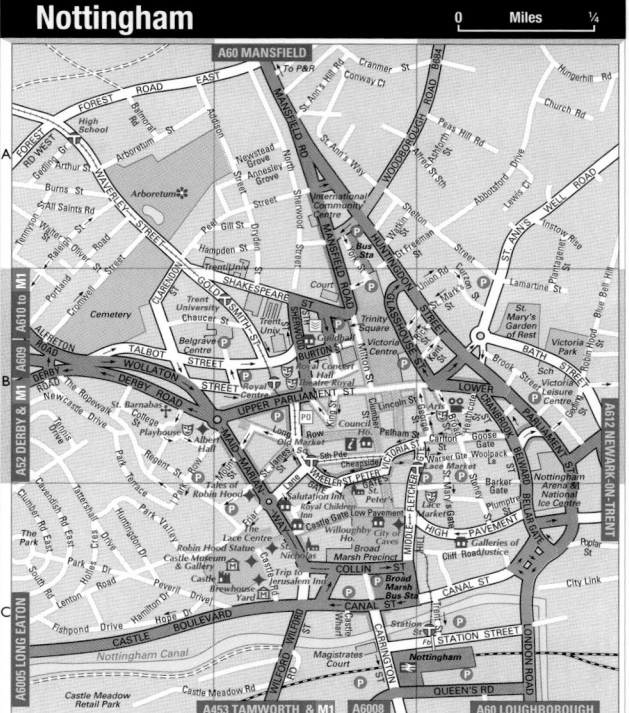

Oban
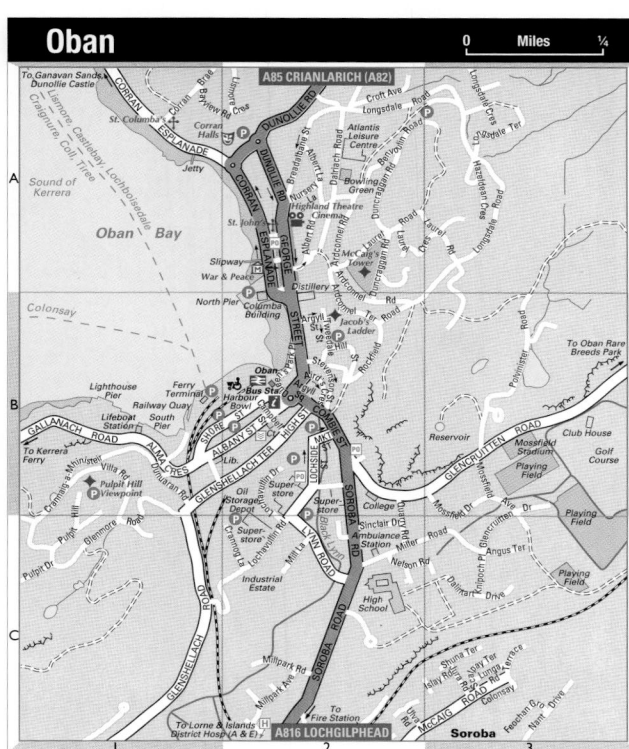

Oxford
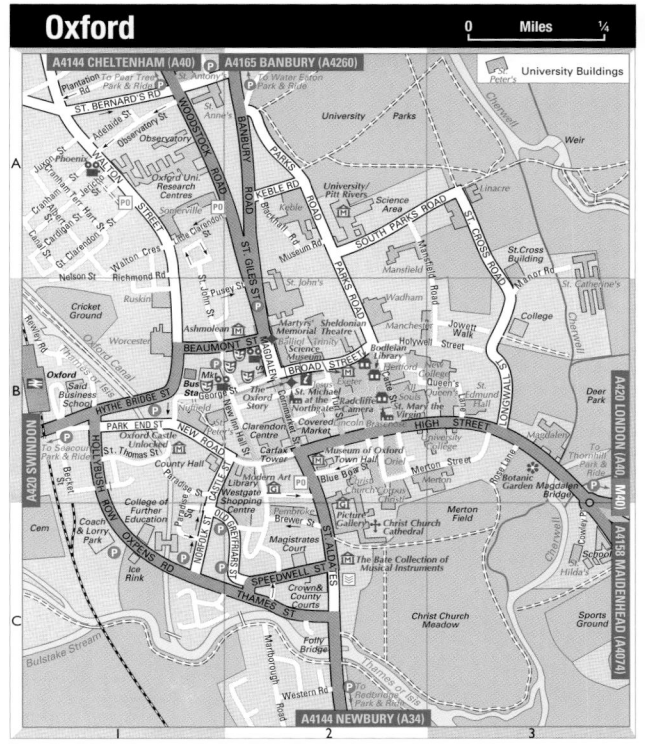

Perth
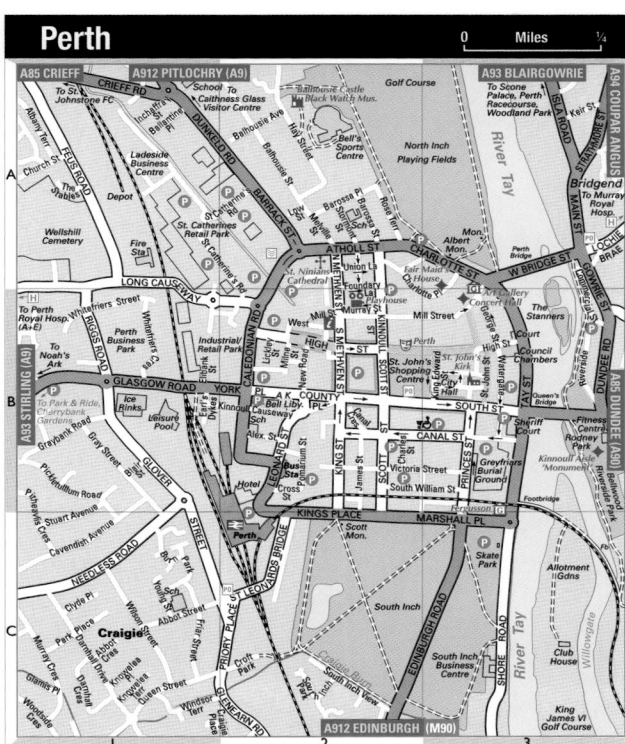

Peterborough
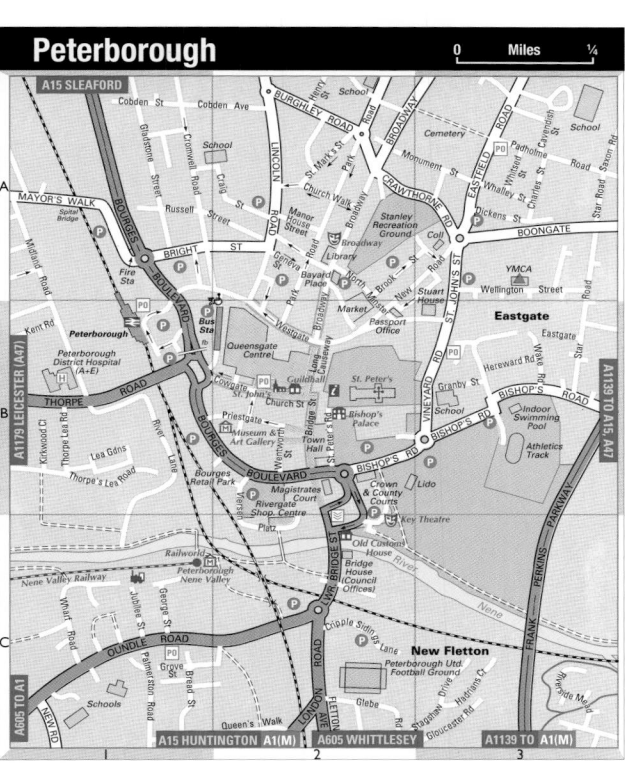

Plymouth
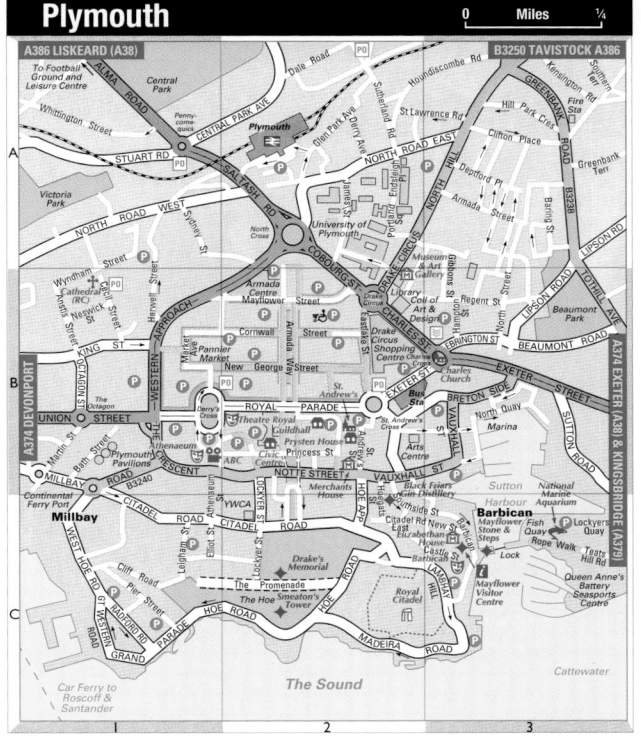

Poole
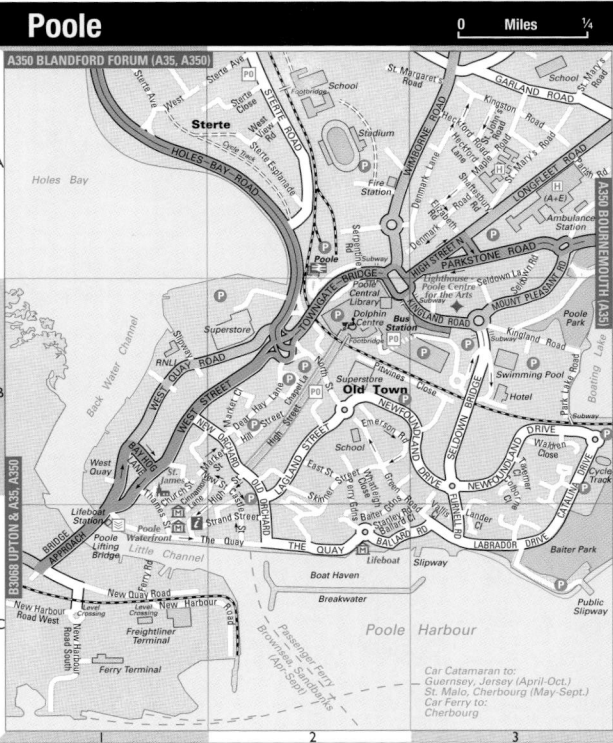

Portsmouth
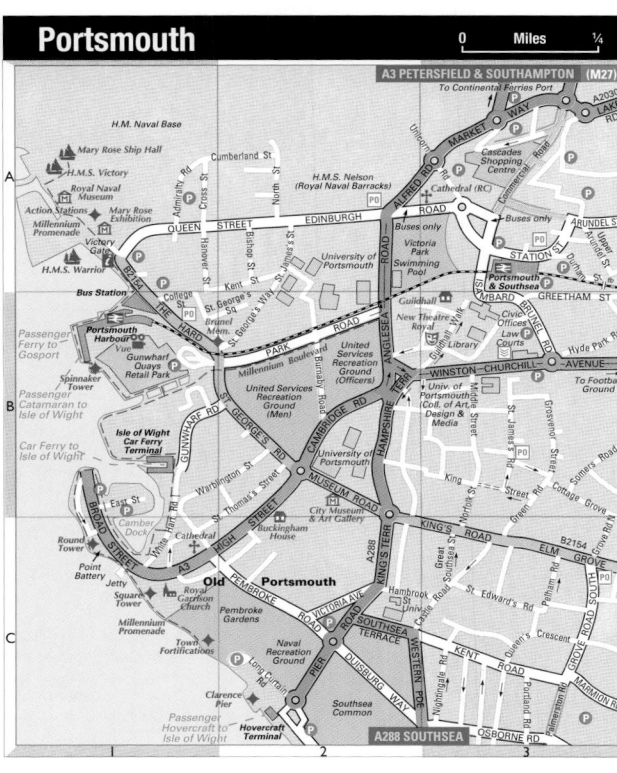

Preston

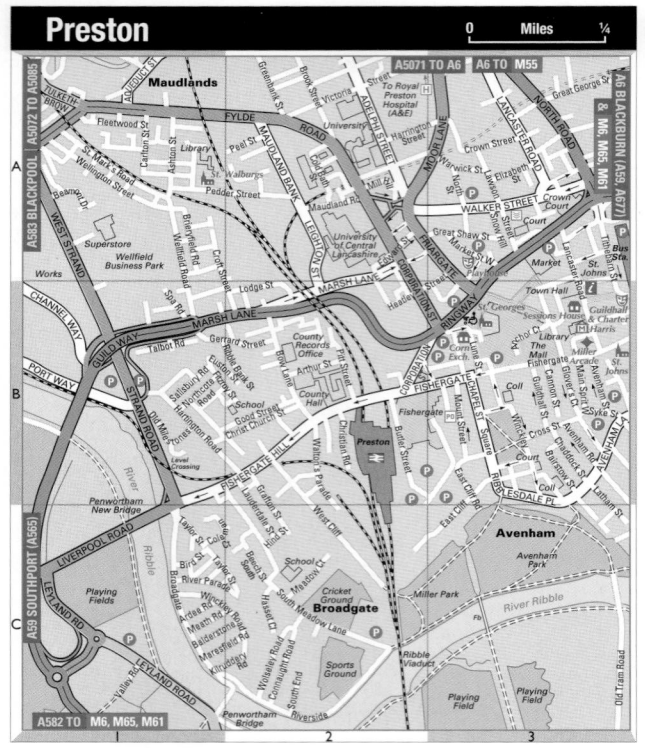

Reading

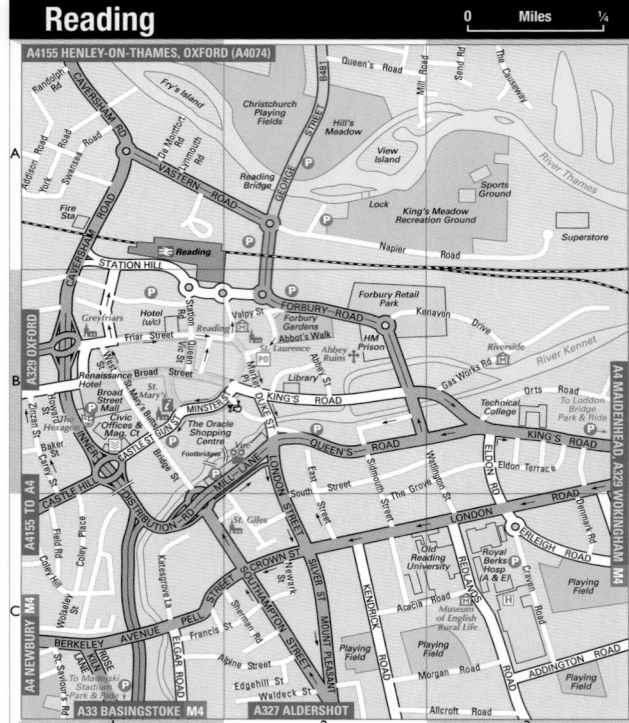

St Andrews

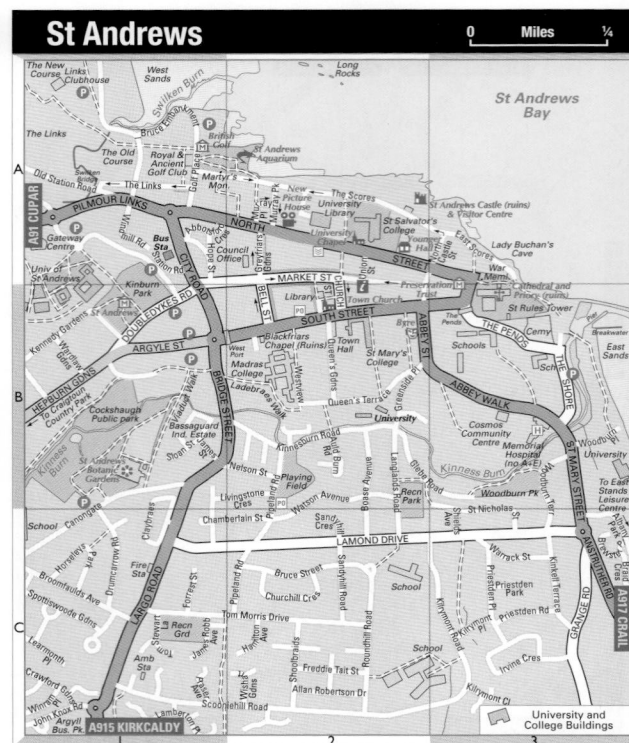

Salisbury

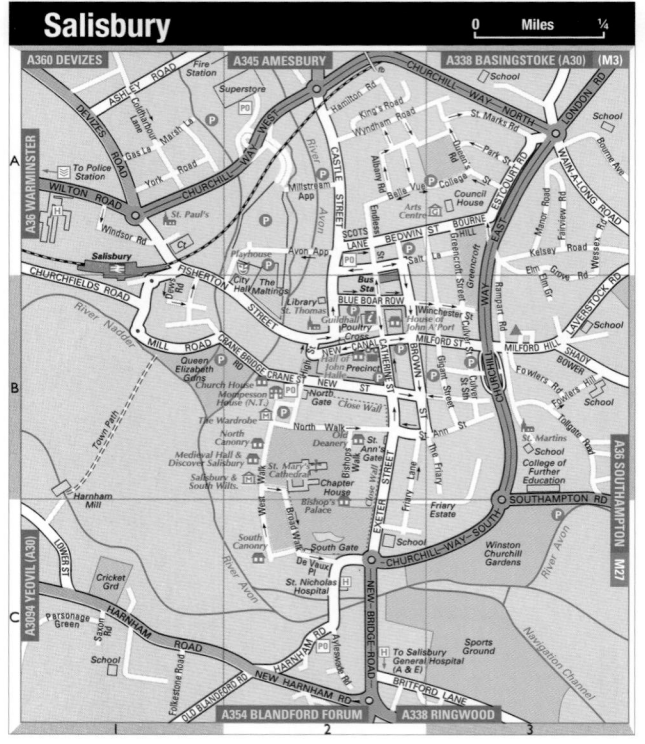

Scarborough

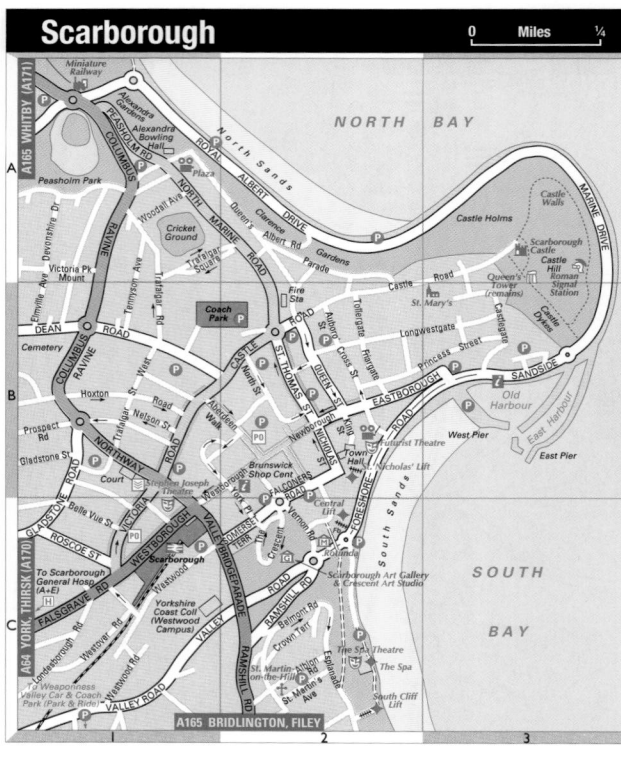

Shrewsbury

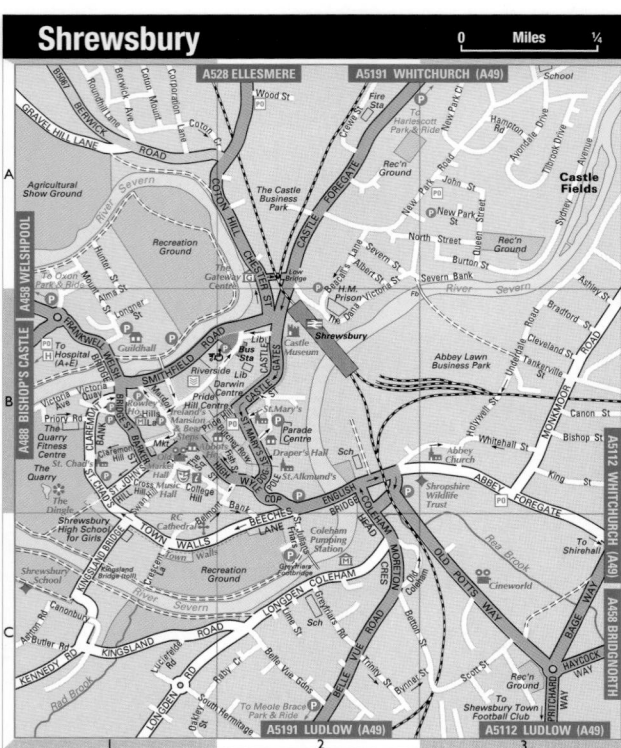

Sheffield

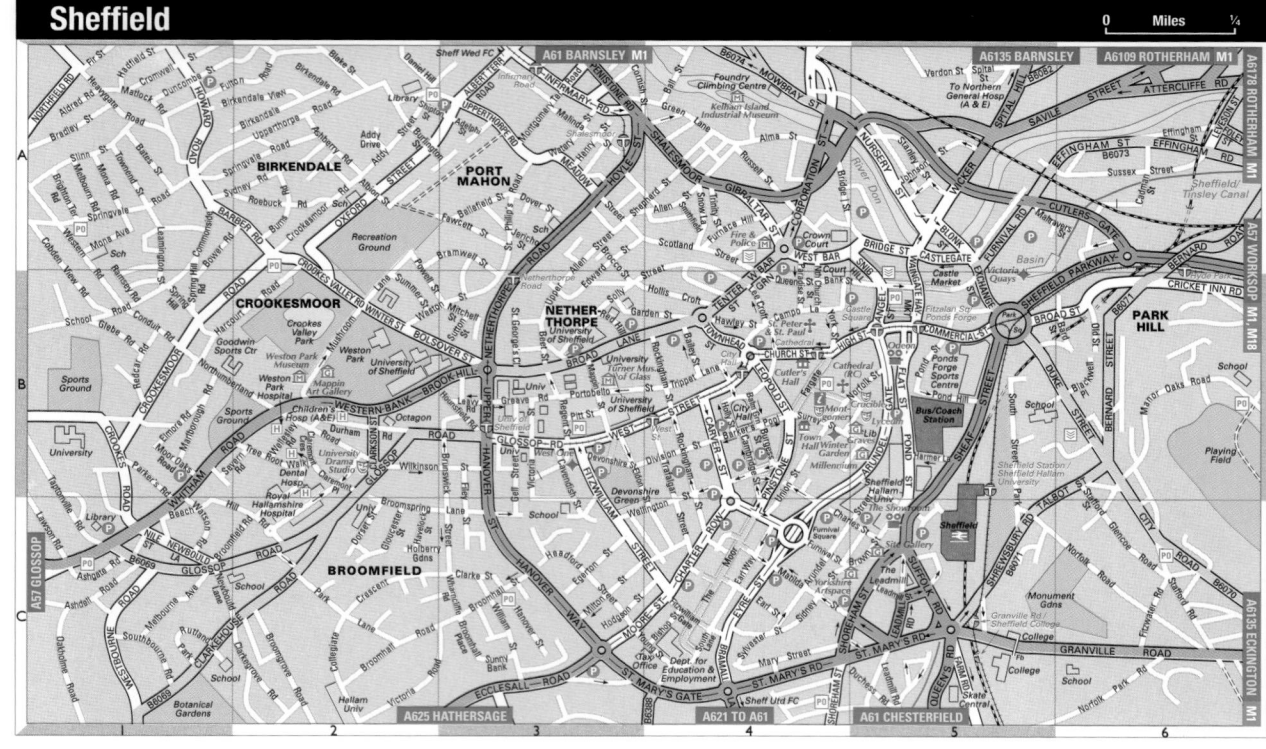

Southampton

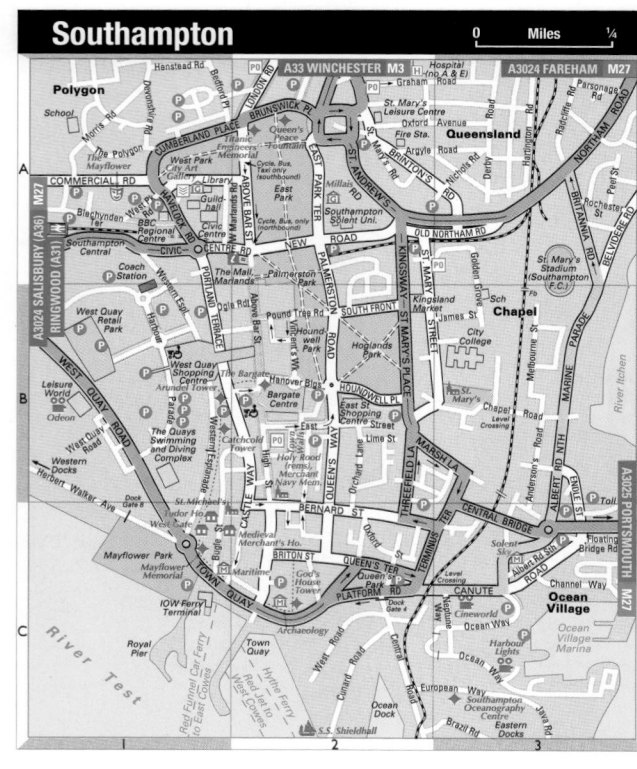

Southend page 69 ● Stirling page 278 ● Stoke page 168 ● Stratford-upon-Avon page 118 ● Sunderland page 243 ● Swansea page 56 ● Swindon page 63 ● Taunton page 28 ● Telford page 132

343

Southend-on-Sea

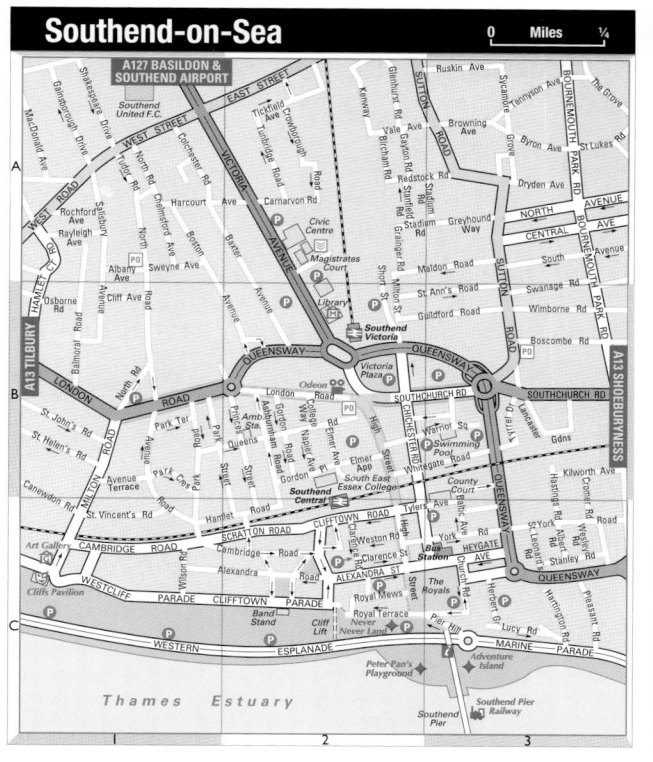

Stirling

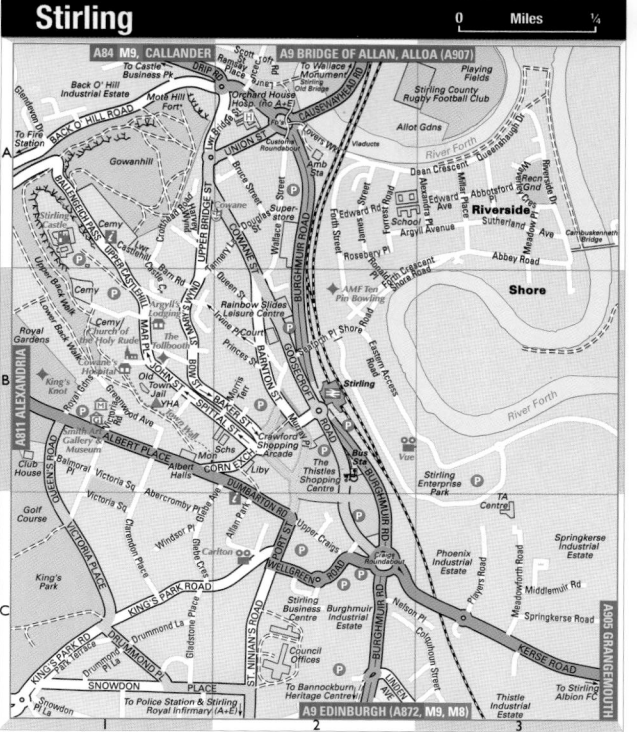

Stoke

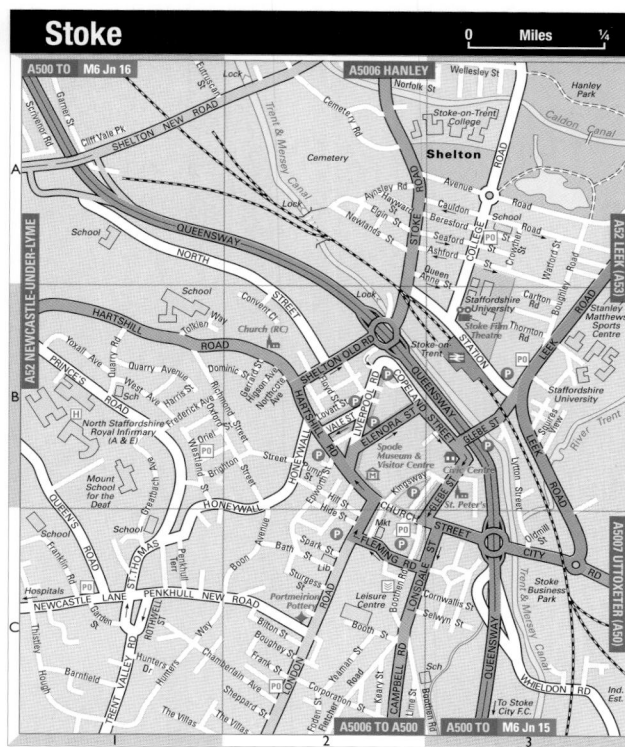

Stratford-upon-Avon

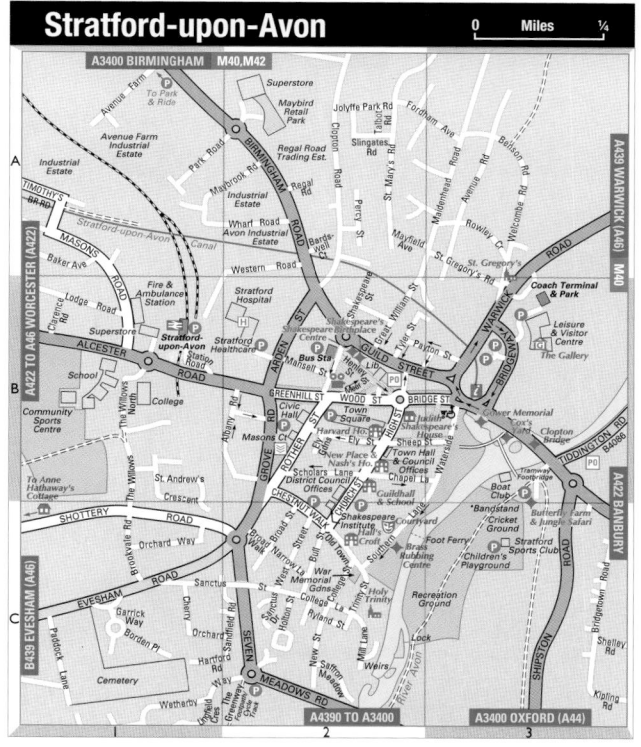

Sunderland

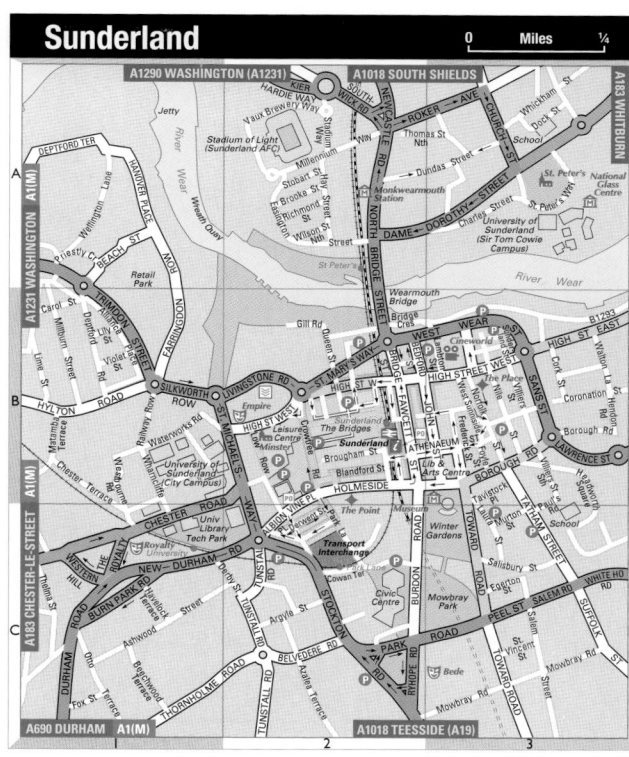

Swansea / Abertawe

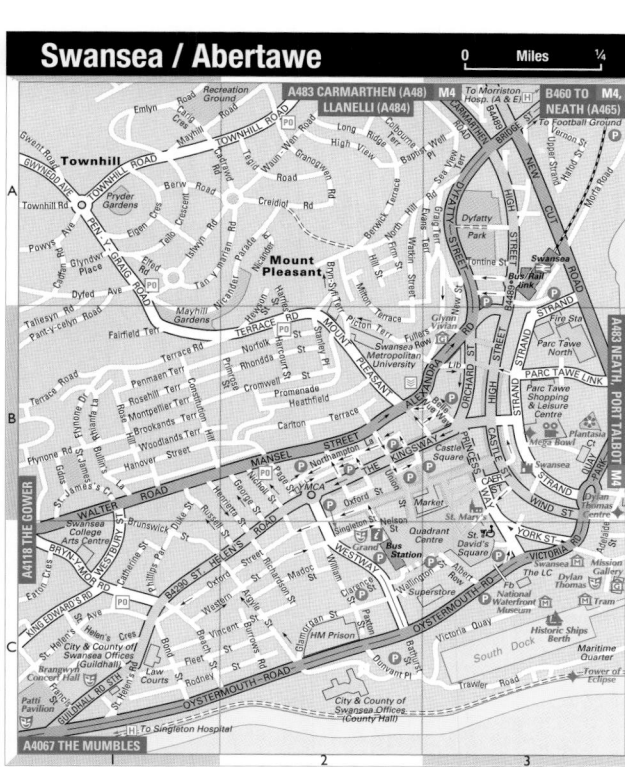

Swindon

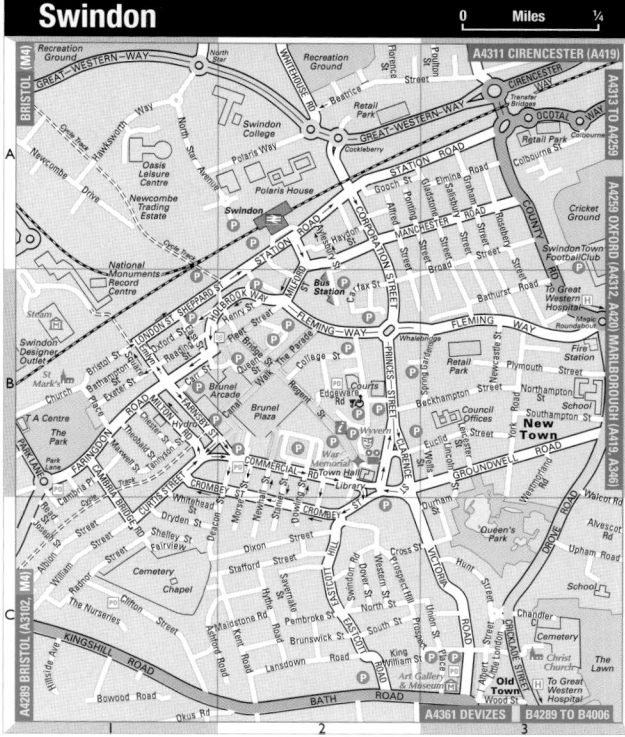

Taunton

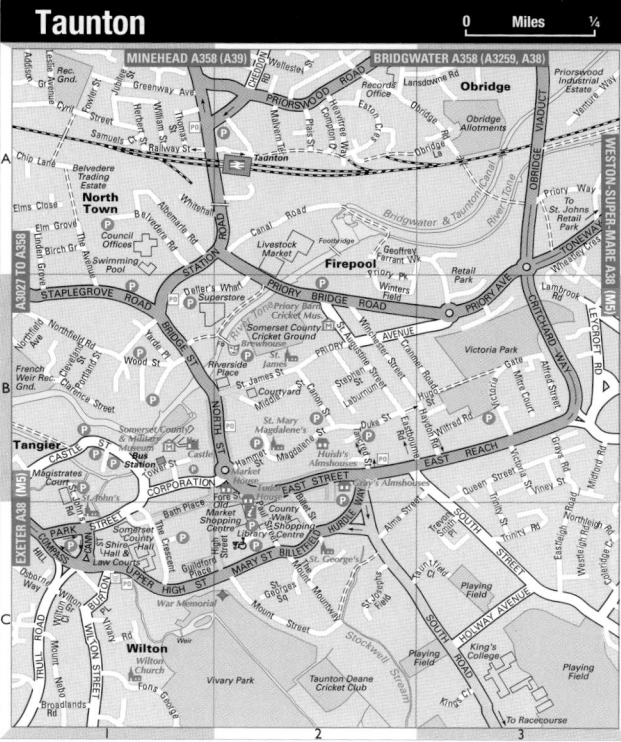

Telford

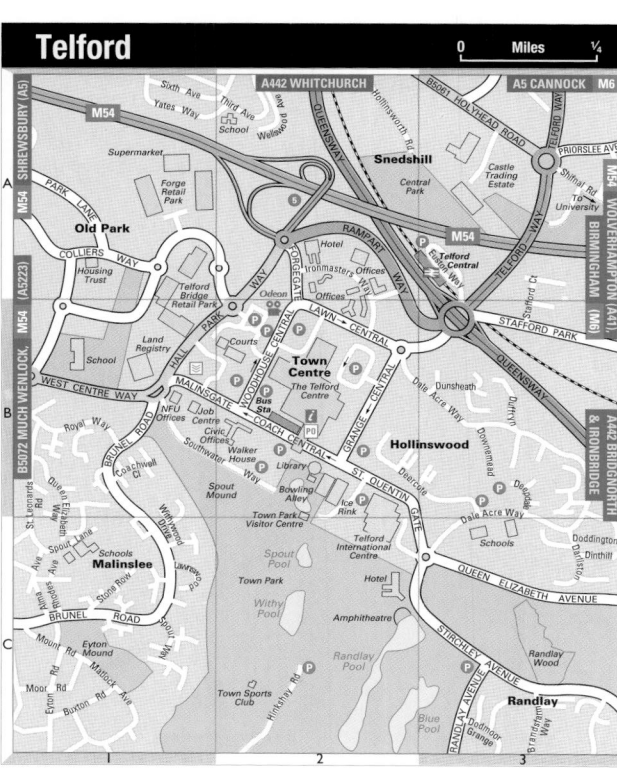

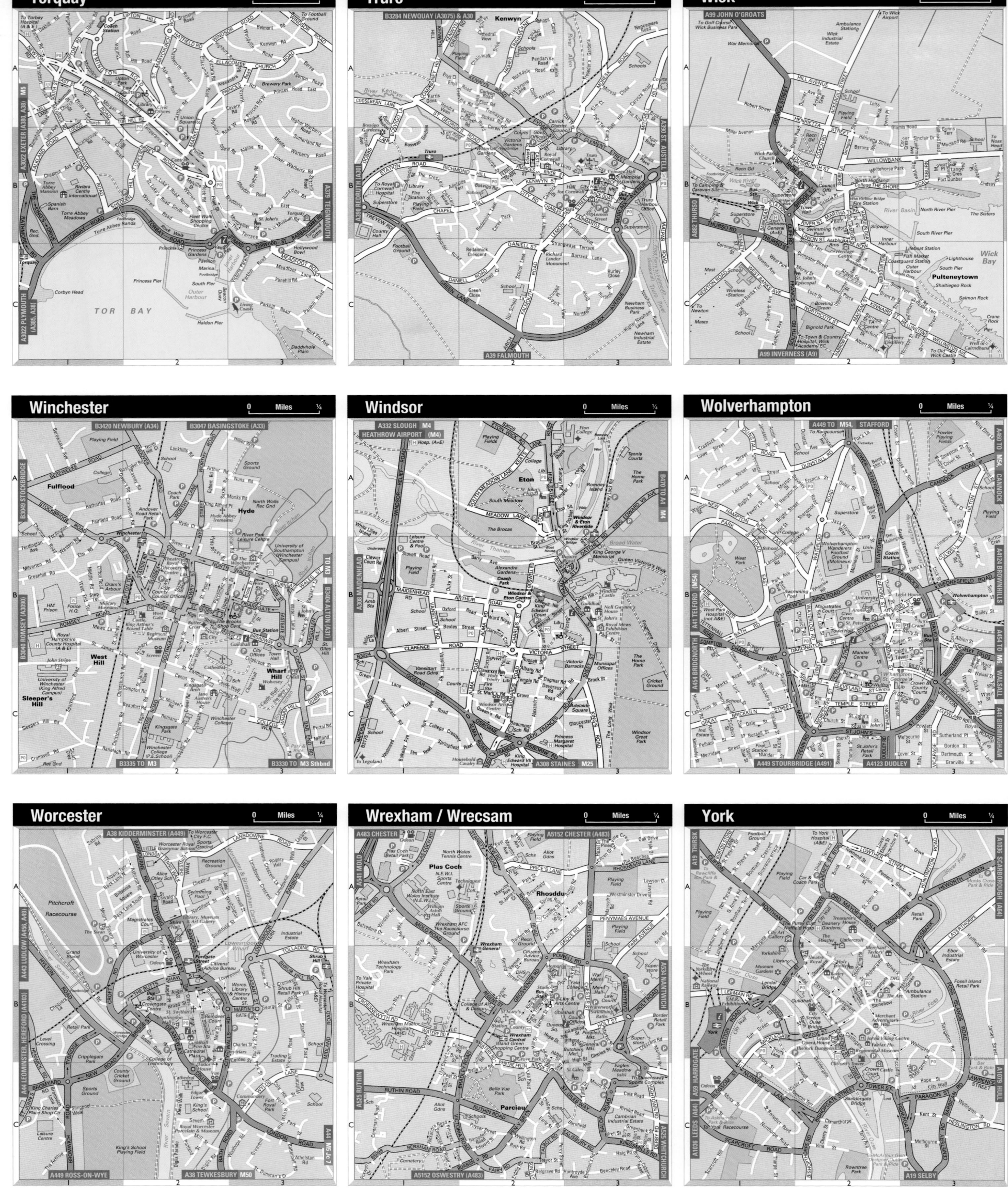

Town plan indexes

346 Blackpool • Bournemouth • Bradford • Brighton • Bristol

Alston Rd C1
Arcadian Centre C4
Arthur St C6
Assay Office B3
Aston Expressway A5
Aston Science Park B5
Aston St B4
Aston University B4/B5
Avenue Rd A5
BT Tower B3
Bacchus Rd A1
Bagot St B4
Banbury St B5
Barford Rd B1
Barford St C4
Barn St C5
Barnwell Rd C6
Barr St A3
Barrack St B5
Bartholomew St C4
Barwick St B4
Bath Row C3
Beaufort Rd C1
Belmont Row B5
Benson Rd A1
Berkley St C3
Bexhill Gr C3
Birchall St C5
Birmingham City FC C6
Birmingham City Hospital (A&E) A1
Bishopsgate St C3
Blews St A4
Bloomsbury St A6
Blucher St C3
Bordesley St C4
Bowyer St C5
Bradburne Way A5
Bradford St C5
Branston St A3
Brearley St A4
Brewery St A4
Bridge St A3
Bridge St C3
Bridge St West A4
Brindley Dr B3
Broad St C3
Broad St UGC C2
Broadway Plaza C2
Bromley St C5
Bromsgrove St C4
Brookfield Rd A2
Browning St C2
Bryant St A1
Buckingham St A3
Bullring C4
Bull St B4
Cambridge St C3
Camden Dr B3
Camden St B2
Cannon St C4
Cardigan St B5
Carlisle St A1
Carlyle Rd C1
Caroline St B3
Carver St B2
Cato St A6
Cattell Rd C6
Cattells Gr A6
Cawdor Cr C1
Cecil St B4
Cemetery A2/B2
Cemetery La A2
Centre Link Industrial Estate A6
Charlotte St B3
Cheapside C4
Chester St A5
Children's Hospital (A&E) B4
Church St B4
Claremont Rd A2
Clarendon Rd C1
Clark St C1
Clement St B3
Clissold St B2
Cliveland St B4
Coach Station C5
College St B2
Colmore Circus B4
Colmore Row B4
Commercial St C3
Constitution Hill B3
Convention Centre, The C3
Cope St B2
Coplow St B1
Corporation St B4
Council House B3
County Court B4
Coveley Gr A2
Coventry Rd C6
Coventry St C5
Cox St B3
Crabtree Rd A2
Cregoe St C3
Crescent Ave A2
Crescent Theatre C3
Cromwell St A6
Cromwell St B3
Curzon St B5
Cuthbert Rd B1
Dale End B4
Dart St C6
Dartmouth Circus A4
Dartmouth Middleway A5
Dental Hosp B4
Deritend C5
Devon St A6
Devonshire St A1
Digbeth Civic Hall C5
Digbeth High St C4
Dolman St B6
Dover St A1
Duchess Rd C2
Duddeston B6
Duddeston Manor Rd B5
Duddeston Mill Rd B6
Duddeston Mill Trading Estate B6
Dudley Rd B1
Edgbaston Shopping Centre C2
Edmund St B3
Edward St B3
Elkington St A4
Ellen St B2
Ellis St C3
Erskine St B6
Essex St C4
Eyre St B2
Farm Croft A3
Farm St A3
Fazeley St B4/C5
Felstead Way B5
Finstall Cl B5
Five Ways C2
Fleet St B3
Floodgate St C5
Ford St A2
Fore St C4
Forster St B5
Francis Rd C2
Francis St B5
Frankfort St A4
Frederick St B3
Freeth St C1
Freightliner Terminal B6
Garrison La C6
Garrison St B6
Gas St C3
Geach St A4
George St B3
George St West B2
Gibb St C5
Gillott Rd B1
Gilby Rd C2
Glover St C5
Goode Ave A2
Goodrick Way A6
Gordon St B6
Graham St B3
Granville St C3
Gray St C6
Great Barr St C5
Great Charles St B3
Great Francis St B6
Great Hampton Row A3
Great Hampton St A3
Great King St A3
Great Lister St A5
Great Tindal St C2
Green La C6
Green St C5
Greenway St C6
Grosvenor St West C2
Guest Gr A3
Guild Cl C2
Guildford Dr A4
Guthrie Cl A3
Hagley Rd C1
Hall St B3
Hampton St A3
Handsworth New Rd A1
Hanley St B4
Harford St A3
Harmer Rd A2
Harold Rd C1
Hatchett St A4
Heath Mill La C5
Heath St B1
Heath St South B1
Heaton St A2
Heneage St B5
Henrietta St B4
Herbert Rd C6
High St C4
High St C5
Hilden Rd B5
Hill St C3/C4
Hindlow Cl B6
Hingeston St B2
Hippodrome Theatre C4
HM Prison A1
Hockley Circus A2
Hockley Hill A3
Hockley St A3
Holliday St C3
Holloway Circus C4
Holloway Head C3
Holt St B5
Hooper St B1
Horse Fair C4
Hospital St A4
Howard St B3
Howe St B5
Hubert St A5
Hunters Rd A2
Hunters Vale A3
Huntly Rd C2
Hurst St C4
Icknield Port Rd B1
Icknield Sq B2
Icknield St A2/B2
Ikon Gallery C3
Information Ctr C4
Inge St C4
Irving St C3
Ivy La C5
James Watt Queensway B4
Jennens Rd B5
Jewellery Quarter A3
Jewellery Quarter Mus B3
John Bright St C4
Keeley St C6
Kellett Rd B5
Kent St C4
Kenyon St B3
Key Hill A3
Kilby Ave C2
King Edwards Rd B2
King Edwards Rd C3
Kingston Rd C6
Kirby Rd A1
Ladywood Arts & Leisure Centre B1
Ladywood Middleway C2/C3
Ladywood Rd C1
Lancaster St B4
Landor St B6
Law Courts B4
Lawford Cl B5
Lawley Middleway B5
Ledbury Cl C2
Ledsam St B2
Lees St A1
Legge La B3
Lennox St A3
Library A6/C3
Library Walk B2
Lighthorne Ave B2
Link Rd B1
Lionel St B3
Lister St B5
Little Ann St C5
Little Hall Rd A6
Liverpool St C5
Livery St B3/B4
Lodge Rd A1
Lord St A5
Love La A5
Loveday St B4
Lower Dartmouth St C6
Lower Loveday St B4
Lower Tower St A4
Lower Trinity St C5
Ludgate Hill B3
Mailbox Centre & BBC C3
Margaret St B3
Markby Rd A1
Marroway St B1
Maxstoke St C6
Melvina Rd A6
Meriden St C4
Metropolitan (RC) B5
Midland St B6
Milk St C5
Mill St A5
Millennium Point B5
Miller St A4
Milton St A4
Moat La C4
Montague Rd C1
Montague St C5
Monument Rd C1
Moor Street C4
Moor St Queensway C4
Moorsom St A4
Morville St C2
Mosborough Cr A3
Moseley St C4
Mott St B3
Mus & Art Gallery B3
Musgrave Rd A1
National Indoor Arena C2
National Sea Life Centre C3
Navigation St C3
Nechell's Park Rd A6
Nechells Parkway B5
Nechells Pl A6
New Bartholomew St C4
New Canal St C5
New John St West A3
New Spring St B2
New St C4
New Street C4
New Summer St A4
New Town Row A4
Newhall Hill B3
Newhall St B3
Newton St B4
Newtown A4
Noel Rd C1
Norman St A1
Northbrook St B1
Northwood St B3
Norton St A2
Old Crown House C5
Old Rep Theatre, The C4
Old Snow Hill B4
Oliver Rd C1
Oliver St A5
Osler St C1
Oxford St C5
Pallasades Centre C4
Palmer St C5
Paradise Circus C3
Paradise St C3
Park Rd A2
Park St C4
Pavilions Centre C4
Paxton Rd A2
Peel St A1
Penn St B5
Pershore St C4
Phillips St A4
Pickford St C5
Pinfold St C4
Pitsford St A2
Plough & Harrow Rd C1
Police Station A4/B1/B4/C2/C4
Pope St B2
Portland Rd C1
Post Office A3/A5/B1/B3/B4/B5/C2/C3/C5
Preston Rd A1
Price St B4
Princip St B4
Printing House St B4
Priory Queensway B4
Pritchett St A4
Proctor St A5
Queensway B3
Radnor St A2
Rea St C4
Regent Pl B3
Register Office C3
Repertory Theatre C3
Reservoir Rd C1
Richard St A5
River St C5
Rocky La A5/A6
Rodney Cl C2
Roseberry St B2
Rotton Park St B1
Rupert St A5
Ruston St C2
Ryland St C2
St Andrew's Industrial Estate C6
St Andrew's Rd C6
St Andrew's St C6
St Bolton St C6
St Chads Queensway B4
St Clements Rd A6
St George's St A3
St James Pl B5
St Marks Cr B2
St Martin's C4
St Paul's B3
St Paul's (Metro station) B3
St Paul's Sq B3
St Philip's B4
St Stephen's St A4
St Thomas' Peace Garden C3
St Vincent St C2
Saltley Rd A6
Sand Pits Pde B3
Severn St C3
Shadwell St B4
Sheepcote St C2
Shefford Rd A4
Sherborne St C2
Shylton's Croft C2
Skipton Rd C2
Smallbrook Queensway C4
Smith St A3
Snow Hill B4
Snow Hill Queensway B4
Soho, Benson Rd (Metro station) A1
South Rd A2
Spencer St B3
Spring Hill B2
Staniforth St B4
Station St C4
Steelhouse La B4
Stephenson St C4
Steward St B2
Stirling Rd C1
Stour St B2
Suffolk St C3
Summer Hill Rd B2
Summer Hill St B2
Summer Hill Terr B2
Summer La A4
Summer Row B3
Summerfield Cr B1
Summerfield Park B1
Sutton St C3
Swallow St C3
Sydney Rd C6
Symphony Hall C3
Talbot St A1
Temple Row C4
Temple St C4
Templefield St C6
Tenby St B3
Tenby St North B2
Tennant St C2/C3
The Crescent A2
Thimble Mill La A6
Thinktank (Science & Discovery) B5
Thomas St A4
Thorpe St C4
Tilton Rd C6
Tower St A4
Town Hall C3
Trent St C5
Turner's Buildings A1
Unett St A3
Union Terr B5
Upper Trinity St C5
Uxbridge St A3
Vauxhall Gr B5
Vauxhall Rd B5
Vernon Rd C1
Vesey St B4
Viaduct St B5
Victoria Sq C3
Villa St A3
Vittoria St B3
Vyse St B3
Walter St A6
Wardlow Rd A5
Warstone La B2
Washington St C3
Water St B3
Waterworks Rd C1
Watery La C5
Well St A3
Western Rd B1
Wharf St A2
Wheeler St A3
Whitehouse St A5
Whitmore St A2
Whittall St B4
Wholesale Market C4
Wiggin St B1
Willes Rd A1
Windsor Industrial Estate A5
Windsor St A5
Windsor St B5
Winson Green Rd A1
Witton St C6
Wolseley St C6
Woodcock St B5

Blackpool 332
Abingdon St A1
Addison Cr A3
Adelaide St B1
Albert Rd B2
Alfred St B2
Ascot Rd A3
Ashton Rd C2
Auburn Gr C3
Bank Hey St B1
Banks St A1
Beech Ave A3
Bela Gr C2
Belmont Ct B2
Birley St A1
Blackpool & Fleetwood Tram B1
Blackpool FC C2
Blackpool North A2
Blackpool Tower B1
Blundell St C1
Bonny St B1
Breck Rd B3
Bryan Rd A3
Buchanan St A2
Cambridge Rd A3
Caunce St A2/A3
Central Dr B1/C2
Central Pier C1
Central Pier (Tram stop) C1
Central Pier Theatre C1
Chapel St C1
Charles St A2
Charnley Rd B2
Church St A1/A2
Clinton Ave B2
Coach Station A2/C1
Cocker St A1
Cocker St (Tram stop) A1
Coleridge Rd A3
Collingwood Ave A3
Condor Gr C3
Cookson St A2
Coronation St B1
Corporation St A1
Courts B1
Cumberland Ave B3
Cunliffe Rd C3
Dale St C1
Devonshire Rd A3
Devonshire Sq A3
Dickson Rd A1
Elizabeth St A2
Ferguson Rd C3
Forest Gate B3
Foxhall Rd C1
Foxhall Sq (Tram stop) C1
Freckleton St C2
George St A2
Gloucester Ave B3
Golden Mile, The C1
Gorse Rd B3
Gorton St A2
Granville Rd A2
Grasmere Rd C2
Grosvenor St A2
Grundy Art Gallery A1
Harvey Rd B3
Hornby Rd B2
Hounds Hill Shopping Centre B1
Hull Rd B1
Ibbison Ct C2
Information Ctr A1
Kent Rd C2
Keswick Rd C2
King St A2
Knox Gr C3
Laycock Gate A3
Layton Rd A3
Leamington Rd B2
Leeds Rd B3
Leicester Rd B2
Levens Gr C2
Library A1
Lifeboat Station B1
Lincoln Rd B2
Liverpool Rd B3
Livingstone Rd B2
London Rd A3
Louis Tussaud's Waxworks B1
Lune Gr C2
Lytham Rd C1
Manchester Sq (Tram stop) C1
Manor Rd B3
Maple Ave B3
Market St A1
Marlboro Rd B3
Mere Rd B3
Milbourne St A2
Newcastle Ave B3
Newton Dr A3
North Pier A1
North Pier Theatre A1
Odeon C2
Olive Gr B3
Palatine Rd B2
Park Rd B2/C3
Peter St A2
Police Station B1
Post Office A1/A3B1/B2/B3
Princess Pde A1
Princess St C1/C2
Promenade A1/C1
Queen St A1
Queen Victoria Rd C2
Raikes Pde B2
Read's Ave B2
Regent Rd B2
Ribble Rd B2
Rigby Rd C1/C2
Ripon Rd B3
St Albans Rd B3
St Ives Ave C3
St Vincent Ave C3
Salisbury Rd B3
Salthouse Ave C2
Sands Way C2
Sealife Centre B1
Seaside Way C1
Selbourne Rd A2
Sharrow Gr C3
Somerset Ave C3
Springfield Rd A1
South King St B2
Sutton Pl B2
Talbot Rd A1/A2
Talbot Sq (Tram stop) A1
Thornber Gr C2
Topping St A1
Tower (Tram stop) B1
Town Hall A1
Tram Depot C1
Tyldesley Rd C1
Vance Rd B1
Victoria St B1
Victory Rd A2
Wayman Rd A3
Westmorland Ave C2/C3
Whitegate Dr B3
Winter Gardens Theatre & Opera House B1
Woodland Gr B3
Woolman Rd B2

Bournemouth 332
Ascham Rd A3
Avenue Rd B1
Bath Rd C2
Beacon Rd C1
Beach Office C2
Beechey Rd A3
Bodorgan Rd B1
Bourne Ave B1
Bournemouth A3
Bournemouth Eye C2
Bournemouth International Ctr C1
Bournemouth Pier C2
Bournemouth Station (r'about) B3
Braidley Rd A1
Cavendish Place A2
Cavendish Rd A2
Central Drive A1
Christchurch Rd B3
Cliff Lift C1/C3
Coach House Pl A3
Coach Station A3
College & Library (private) B3
Commercial Rd B1
Cotlands Rd B3
Courts B3
Cranborne Rd C1
Cricket Ground A2
Cumnor Rd B2
Dean Park A2
Dean Park Cr B2
Dean Park Rd A2
Durrant Rd B1
East Overcliff Dr C3
Exeter Cr C1
Exeter La C2
Exeter Rd C1
Gervis Place B1
Gervis Rd B3
Glen Fern Rd B2
Golf Club B2
Grove Rd B3
Hinton Rd C2
Holdenhurst Rd B3
Horseshoe Common B2
Hospital (Private) A2
Information Ctr B2
Lansdowne (r'about) B3
Lansdowne Rd A2
Lorne Park Rd B2
Lower Central Gdns B1/C2
Madeira Rd B2
Methuen Rd A3
Meyrick Park A1
Meyrick Rd B3
Milton Rd A2
Oceanarium C2
Old Christchurch Rd B2
Ophir Rd A3
Oxford Rd B3
Park Rd A3
Parsonage Rd B2
Pavilion C2
Pier Approach C2
Pier Theatre C2
Police Station A3/B3
Portchester Rd A3
Post Office B1/B3
Priory Rd C1
Recreation Ground A1
Richmond Hill Rd B1
Russell Cotes Art Gallery & Mus C2
Russell Cotes Rd C2
St Anthony's Rd A1
St Michael's Rd C1
St Paul's (r'about) A3
St Paul's La B3
St Paul's Rd A3
St Peter's B2
St Peter's (r'about) B2
St Peter's Rd B2
St Stephen's Rd B1/B2
St Swithun's (r'about) B3
St Swithun's Rd B3
St Swithun's Rd South B3
St Valerie Rd A2
St Winifred's Rd A2
Stafford Rd B3
Terrace Rd B1
The Square B1
The Triangle B1
Town Hall B1
Tregonwell Rd C1
Trinity Rd B2
Undercliff Drive C3
Upper Central Gdns B1
Upper Hinton Rd B2
Upper Terr Rd C1
Wellington Rd A2/A3
Wessex Way A3/B1/B2
West Cliff Promenade C1
West Hill Rd C1
West Undercliff Promenade C1
Westover Rd B2
Wimborne Rd A2
Wootton Mount B2
Wychwood Dr A1
Yelverton Rd B2
York Rd B3
Zig-Zag Walks C1/C3

Bradford 332
Alhambra B2
Back Ashgrove B1
Barkerend Rd A3
Barnard Rd C3
Barry St B2
Bolling Rd C3
Bolton Rd A3
Bowland St A1
Bradford College B1
Bradford Forster Sq A2
Bradford Interchange B3
Bridge St B2
Britannia St B2
Broadway B2
Burnett St B3
Bus Station B2
Butler St West A3
Caledonia St C2
Canal Rd A2
Carlton St B1
Cathedral A3
Centenary Sq B2
Chapel St B3
Cheapside A2
Church Bank B3
City Hall B2
City Rd A1
Claremont B1
Colour Mus B1
Croft St B2
Darfield St A1
Darley St A2
Drewton Rd A1
Drummond Trading Estate A1
Dryden St B3
Dyson St A1
Easby Rd C1
East Parade B3
Eldon Pl A1
Filey St B3
Forster Square Retail Park A2
Gallery B3
Garnett St B3
Godwin St B2
Gracechurch St A1
Grattan Rd B1
Great Horton Rd B1/B2
Grove Terr B1
Hall Ings B2
Hall La C3
Hallfield Rd A1
Hammstrasse A2
Harris St B3
Holdsworth St A2
Ice Rink B2
Information Ctr B2
Ivegate B2
Inland Revenue A2
Jacob's Well Municipal Offices B2
James St A2
John St A2
Kirkgate B2
Kirkgate Centre B2
Laisteridge La C1
Law Courts B2/B3
Leeds Rd B3
Library B1/B2
Listerhills Rd B1
Little Horton La C1
Little Horton Gn C1
Longside La B1
Lower Kirkgate B2
Lumb La A1
Manchester Rd C2
Manningham La A1
Manor Row A2
Market C3
Market St B2
Melbourne Place C1
Midland Rd A2
Mill La C2
Morley St B1
Nelson St B2/C2
Nesfield St A2
New Otley Rd A3
Norcroft St B1
North Parade A2
North St A3
North Wing A3
Oastler Shopping Centre A2
Otley Rd A3
Park Ave C1
Park La C1
Park Rd C2
Parma St C2
Peckover St B3
Piccadilly A2
Police Station B2/C2
Post Office A2/B1/B2/C3
Priestley B3
Princes Way B2
Prospect St C3
Radwell Drive C2
Rawson Rd A1
Rebecca St A1
Richmond Rd B1
Russell St C1
St George's Hall B2
St Lukes Hosp C1
St Mary's A3
Shipley Airedale Rd A3/B3
Simes St A1
Smith St B1
Spring Mill St C2
Stott Hill A3
Sunbridge Rd A1/B1/B2
The Leisure Exchange B3
Thornton Rd A1/B1
Trafalgar St A2
Trinity Rd C1
Tumbling Hill St B1
Tyrrel St B2
University of Bradford B1/C1
Usher St C3
Valley Rd A2
Vicar La B3
Wakefield Rd C3
Wapping Rd A3
Westgate A1
White Abbey Rd A1
Wigan Rd A1
Wilton St B1
Wood St A1
Wool Exchange B2
Worthington St A1

Brighton 332
Addison Rd A1
Albert Rd B2
Albion Hill B3
Albion St B3
Ann St A3
Art Gallery & Mus B3
Baker St A3
Brighton A2
Brighton Centre C2
Broad St C3
Buckingham Pl A2
Buckingham Rd B2
Cannon Pl C1
Carlton Hill B3
Chatham Pl A1
Cheapside A3
Church St B2
Churchill Square Shopping Centre B2
Clifton Hill B1
Clifton Pl B1
Clifton Rd B1
Clifton Terr B1
Clock Tower B2
Clyde Rd A3
Coach Park C3
Compton Ave A2
Davigdor Rd A1
Denmark Terr B1
Ditchling Rd A3
Dome, The B2
Duke St B2
Duke's La C2
Dyke Rd A1/B2
East St C2
Edward St B3
Elmore Rd B3
Frederick St B2
Fruit & Veg Market (wholesale) B3
Gardner St B2
Gloucester Pl B3
Gloucester Rd B2
Goldsmid Rd A1
Grand Junction Rd C2
Grand Pde B3
Hampton Pl B1
Hanover Terr A3
High St C3
Highdown Rd A1
Information Ctr C2
John St B3
Kemp St B2
Kensington Pl B2
Kings Rd C1
Law Courts B3
Lewes Rd A3
Library (temp) A2
London Rd A3
Madeira Dr C3
Marine Pde C3
Middle St C2
Montpelier Pl B1
Montpelier Rd B1
Montpelier St B1
New England Rd A2
New England St A2
New Rd B2
Newhaven St A3
Nizells Ave A1
Norfolk Rd B1
Norfolk Terr B1
North Rd B2
North St B2
Old Shoreham Rd A1
Old Steine C3
Osmond Rd A1
Over St B2
Oxford St A3
Paddling Pool C1
Palace Pier C3
Park Crescent Terr A3
Police Station B3
Post Office A1/A2/A3/B1/B2/B3/C3
Preston Rd A2
Preston St B1
Prestonville Rd A1
Queen's Rd B2
Regency Sq C1
Regent St B2
Richmond Pl B3
Richmond St B3
Richmond Terr A3
Rose Hill Terr A3
Royal Alexandra Hosp B1
Royal Pavilion B2
St Bartholomew's A3
St James' St C3
St Nicholas' B2
St Peter's A3
Sea Life Centre C3
Shaftesbury Rd A3
Sillwood Rd B1
Sillwood St B1
Southover St A3
Spring Gdns B2
Stanford Rd A1
Stanley Rd A3
Sussex St B3
Sussex Terr B3
Swimming Pool B3
Sydney St B3
Temple Gdns B1
Terminus Rd A2
The Lanes C2
Theatre Royal B2
Tidy St B2
Town Hall C2
Toy & Model Mus A2
Trafalgar St B2
Union Rd A3
University of Brighton B3
Upper Lewes Rd A3
Upper North St B1
Viaduct Rd A3
Victoria Gdns B3
Victoria Rd B1
Volk's Electric Railway C3
West Pier (Closed to the Public) C1
West St C2
Western Rd B1
Whitecross St B2
York Ave B1
York Pl B3

Bristol 332
Acramans Rd C4
Albert Rd C6
Alfred Hill A4
All Saint's St A4
All Saints' B4
Allington Rd C3
Alpha Rd C4
Ambra Vale B1
Ambra Vale East B2
Ambrose Rd B2
Amphitheatre C3
Anchor Rd B3
Anvil St B6
Architecture Centre B4
Argyle Pl B2
Arlington Villas A2
Arnolfini Arts Centre, The B4
Art Gallery A3
Ashton Gate Rd C2
Ashton Rd C1
at-Bristol B3
Avon Bridge C1
Avon Cr C1
Avon St B6
Baldwin St B4
Baltic Wharf C2
Baltic Wharf Leisure Centre & Caravan Park C2
Barossa Pl C4
Barton Manor B6
Barton Rd B6
Barton Vale B6
Bath Rd C6
Bathurst Basin C4
Bathurst Parade C4
Beauley Rd C3
Bedminster Bridge C5
Bedminster Parade C4
Bellevue B2
Bellevue Cr B2
Bellevue Rd C6
Berkeley Pl A2
Berkeley Sq A3
Birch Rd C2
Blackfriars A4
Bond St A5
Braggs La A6
Brandon Hill B3
Brandon Steep B3
Bristol Bridge B5
Bristol Cathedral (CE) B3
Bristol Central Library B3
Bristol Eye Hospital (A & E) A4
Bristol Grammar School A3
Bristol Harbour Railway C3
Bristol Marina C2
Bristol Royal Children's Hosp A4
Bristol Royal Infirmary (A & E) A4
Bristol Temple Meads Station B6
Broad Plain B6
Broad Quay B4
Broad St A4
Broad Weir A5
Broadcasting House A3
Broadmead A5
Brunel Way C1
Brunswick Sq A5
Burton Cl C5
Bus Station A4
Butts Rd B3
Cabot Tower B3

Bury St Edmunds • Cambridge • Canterbury • Cardiff • Carlisle 347

Caledonia Pl ... B1
Callowhill Ct ... A5
Cambridge St ... C6
Camden Rd ... C3
Camp Rd ... A1
Canada Way ... C2
Cannon St ... A4
Canon's Rd ... B3/B4
Canon's Way ... B3
Cantock's Cl ... A3
Canynge Rd ... A1
Canynge Sq ... A1
Castle Park ... A5
Castle St ... A5
Catherine Meade St ... C4
Cattle Market Rd ... C6
Charles Pl ... B1
Charlotte St ... B3
Charlotte St South ... B3
Chatterton House ... B5
Chatterton Sq ... C5
Chatterton St ... C5
Cheese La ... B5
Christchurch ... A4
Christchurch Rd ... A1
Christmas Steps ✦ ... A4
Church La ... B2/B5
Church St ... B5
City Museum ... A3
City of Bristol College ... B3
Clare St ... B4
Clarence Rd ... C5
Cliff Rd ... C1
Clift House Rd ... C1
Clifton Cathedral (RC) † ... A2
Clifton Down ... A1
Clifton Down Rd ... A1
Clifton Hill ... B2
Clifton Park ... A1/A2
Clifton Park Rd ... A1
Clifton Rd ... A2
Cliftonwood Cr ... B2
Cliftonwood Rd ... B2
Cliftonwood Terr ... B2
Clifton Vale ... B1
Cobblestone Mews ... A1
College Green ... B3
College Rd ... A1
College St ... B3
Colston Almshouses ... A4
Colston Ave ... B4
Colston Hall ... B4
Colston Parade ... C5
Colston St ... A4
Commercial Rd ... C4
Commonwealth Mus ... B5
Constitution Hill ... B2
Cooperage La ... C2
Corn St ... B4
Cornwallis Ave ... B1
Cornwallis Cr ... B1
Coronation Rd ... C2/C4
Council House ... B3
Counterslip ... B5
Courts ... A4
Create Centre, The ✦ ... C1
Crosby Row ... B2
Culver St ... B3
Cumberland Basin ... C1
Cumberland Cl ... C2
Cumberland Rd ... C2/C3
Dale St ... A6
David St ... A6
Dean La ... C4
Deanery Rd ... B3
Denmark St ... B4
Dowry Sq ... B1
East St ... A5
Eaton Cr ... A2
Elmdale Rd ... A3
Elton Rd ... A3
Eugene St ... A4/A6
Exchange, The and St Nicholas' Mkts ... B4
Fairfax St ... A4
Fire Station ... B5
Floating Harbour ... C3
Foster Almshouses ... A4
Frayne Rd ... C1
Frederick Pl ... A2
Freeland Pl ... B1
Frogmore St ... B3
Fry's Hill ... B2
Gas La ... B6
Gasferry Rd ... C3
General Hosp ... C4
Georgian House ... B3
Glendale ... B1
Glentworth Rd ... B2
Gloucester St ... A1
Goldney Hall ... B2
Goldney Rd ... B1
Gordon Rd ... A2
Granby Hill ... B1
Grange Rd ... A1
Great Ann St ... A6
Great George St ... A6/B3
Great George Rd ... B3
Great Western Way ... B6
Green St North ... B1
Green St South ... B1
Greenay Bush La ... C2
Greenbank Rd ... C2
Greville Smyth Park ... C1
Guildhall ... A4
Guinea St ... C4
Hamilton Rd ... C3
Hanbury Rd ... A2
Hanover Pl ... C2
Harbour Way ... B3
Harley Pl ... A1
Haymarket ... A5
Hensman's Hill ... B1
High St ... B4
Highbury Villas ... A3
Hill St ... B3
Hill St ... C6
Hippodrome ... B4
Hopechapel Hill ... B1
Horfield Rd ... A4
Horton St ... B6
Host St ... A4
Hotwell Rd ... B1/B2
Houlton St ... A6
Howard Rd ... C3
Ice Rink ... B3
IMAX Cinema ... B4
Information Ctr ... B4
Islington Rd ... C3
Jacob St ... A5/A6
Jacob's Wells Rd ... B2
John Carr's Terr ... B2
John Wesley's Chapel ... A5
Joy Hill ... B1
Jubilee St ... B6
Kensington Pl ... A2
Kilkenny St ... B6
King St ... B4
Kingsland Rd ... B6
Kingston Rd ... C3
Lamb St ... A6
Lansdown Rd ... A2
Lawford St ... A6
Lawfords Gate ... A6
Leighton Rd ... C3
Lewins Mead ... A4
Lime Rd ... C2
Little Ann St ... A6
Little Caroline Pl ... B1
Little George St ... A6
Little King St ... B4
Litfield Rd ... A1
Llandoger Trow ... B4
Lloyds' Building, The ... C3
Lodge St ... A4
Lord Mayor's Chapel, The ... B4
Lower Castle St ... A5
Lower Church La ... A4
Lower Clifton Hill ... B2
Lower Guinea St ... C4
Lower Lamb St ... B3
Lower Maudlin St ... A4
Lower Park Rd ... A4
Lower Sidney St ... C2
Lucky La ... C4
Lydstep Terr ... C3
Mall (Galleries Shopping Ctr), The ... A5
Manilla Rd ... A1
Mardyke Ferry Rd ... C2
Maritime Heritage Centre ... B3
Marlborough Hill ... A4
Marlborough St ... A4
Marsh St ... B4
Mead St ... C5
Meadow St ... A5
Merchant Dock ... B2
Merchant Seamen's Almshouses ... B4
Merchant St ... A5
Merchants Rd ... A1
Merchants Rd ... C1
Meridian Pl ... A2
Meridian Vale ... A2
Merrywood Rd ... C3
Midland Rd ... A6
Milford St ... C3
Millennium Sq ... B3
Mitchell La ... B5
Mortimer Rd ... A1
Murray Rd ... C4
Myrtle Rd ... A3
Narrow Plain ... B5
Narrow Quay ... B4
Nelson St ... A4
New Charlotte St ... C4
New Kingsley Rd ... B6
New Queen St ... C5
New St ... A6
Newfoundland St ... A5
Newgate ... A5
Newton St ... A6
Norland Rd ... A1
North St ... C2
Oakfield Gr ... A2
Oakfield Pl ... A2
Oakfield Rd ... A2
Old Bread St ... B6
Old Market St ... A6
Old Park Hill ... A4
Oldfield Rd ... B1
Orchard Ave ... B4
Orchard La ... B4
Orchard St ... B4
Osbourne Rd ... C3
Oxford St ... B6
Park Pl ... A2
Park Rd ... C3
Park Row ... A3
Park St ... A3
Passage St ... B5
Pembroke Gr ... A2
Pembroke Rd ... A2
Pembroke Rd ... C3
Pembroke St ... A5
Penn St ... A5
Pennywell Rd ... A6
Percival Rd ... A1
Pero's Bridge ... B4
Perry Rd ... A4
Pip & Jay ... A5
Plimsoll Bridge ... B1
Police Sta ... A4/A6
Polygon Rd ... B1
Portland St ... A1
Portwall La ... B5
Post Office ... A1/A3/A4/A5/A6/B1/B4/C4/C5
Prewett St ... C5
Prince St ... B4
Prince St Bridge ... C4
Princess St ... C5
Princess Victoria St ... B1
Priory Rd ... A3
Pump La ... C5
QEH Theatre ... A2
Queen Charlotte St ... B4
Quakers Friars ... A5
Quay St ... A4
Queen Elizabeth Hospital School ... B2
Queen Sq ... B4
Queen St ... A5
Queen's Ave ... A3
Queen's Parade ... B3
Queen's Rd ... A2/A3
Raleigh Rd ... C2
Randall Rd ... B2
Redcliffe Backs ... B5
Redcliffe Bridge ... B4
Redcliffe Hill ... C5
Redcliffe Parade ... C4
Redcliffe St ... B5
Redcliffe Way ... B5
Redcross La ... A6
Redcross St ... A6
Redgrave Theatre ... A1
Red Lodge ... A4
Regent St ... B1
Richmond Hill ... A2
Richmond Hill Ave ... A2
Richmond La ... A2
Richmond Park Rd ... A2
Richmond St ... C6
Richmond Terr ... A2
River St ... A6
Rownham Mead ... B2
Royal Fort Rd ... A3
Royal Park ... A2
Royal West of England Academy ... A3
Royal York Cr ... B1
Royal York Villas ... B1
Rupert St ... A4
Russ St ... B6
St Andrew's Walk ... B2
St George's ... B3
St George's Rd ... B3
St James ... A4
St John's ... A4
St John's Rd ... C4
St Luke's Rd ... C5
St Mary Redcliffe ... C5
St Mary's Hosp ... A3
St Matthias Park ... A6
St Michael's Hill ... A3
St Michael's Hosp ... A3
St Michael's Park ... A3
St Nicholas St ... B4
St Paul St ... A5
St Paul's Rd ... A2
St Peter's (ruin) ... A5
St Philip's Bridge ... B5
St Philips Rd ... A6
St Stephen's ... B4
St Stephen's St ... B4
St Thomas St ... B5
St Thomas the Martyr ... B5
Sandford Rd ... B1
Sargent St ... C5
Saville Pl ... B1
Ship La ... C5
Silver St ... A4
Sion Hill ... A1
Small St ... A4
Smeaton Rd ... C1
Somerset Sq ... C5
Somerset St ... C5
Southernhay Ave ... B2
Southville Rd ... C4
Spike Island Artspace ... C2
Spring St ... C5
SS Great Britain and The Matthew ... B2
Stackpool Rd ... C3
Staight St ... B6
Stillhouse La ... C4
Stracey Rd ... C2
Stratton St ... A5
Sydney Row ... C2
Tankard's Cl ... A3
Temple Back ... B5
Temple Boulevard ... B5
Temple Bridge ... B5
Temple Church ... B5
Temple Circus ... B5
Temple Gate ... C5
Temple St ... B5
Temple Way ... B5
Terrell St ... A4
The Arcade ... A5
The Fosseway ... A2
The Grove ... B4
The Horsefair ... A5
The Mall ... A1
Theatre Royal ... B4
Thomas La ... B5
Three Kings of Cologne ... A4
Three Queens La ... B5
Tobacco Factory, The ... C2
Tower Hill ... B5
Tower La ... A4
Trenchard St ... A4
Triangle South ... A3
Triangle West ... A3
Trinity Rd ... A6
Trinity St ... A6
Tucker St ... A5
Tyndall Ave ... A3
Union St ... A5
Union St ... B6
Unity St ... A6
Unity St ... B3
University of Bristol ... A3
University Rd ... A3
Upper Maudlin St ... A4
Upper Perry Hill ... C3
Upper Byron Pl ... A3
Upton Rd ... C2
Valentine Bridge ... B6
Victoria Gr ... C5
Victoria Rd ... C6
Victoria Rooms ... A2
Victoria Sq ... A2
Victoria St ... B5
Vyvyan Rd ... A1
Vyvyan Terr ... A1
Wade St ... A6
Walter St ... C2
Wapping Rd ... C4
Water La ... B5
Waterloo Rd ... A6
Waterloo St ... A1
Waterloo St ... A6
Watershed, The ✦ ... B4
Welling Terr ... B1
Wellington Rd ... A6
Welsh Back ... B4
West Mall ... A1
West St ... A6
Westfield Pl ... A1
Wetherell Pl ... A2
Whitehouse Pl ... C5
Whitehouse St ... C5
Whiteladies Rd ... A2
Whitson St ... A4
William St ... C5
Willway St ... C5
Windsor Pl ... B1
Windsor Terr ... B1
Wine St ... A4
Woodland Rise ... A3
Woodland Rd ... A3
Worcester Rd ... A1
Worcester Terr ... A1
YHA ▲ ... B4
York Gdns ... B1
York Pl ... A2
York Rd ... C5

Bury St Edmunds 332

Abbey Gardens ... B3
Abbey Gate ... B3
Abbeygate St ... B2
Albert Cr ... B1
Albert St ... B1
Ambulance Sta ... C1
Angel Hill ... B2
Angel La ... B2
Anglian Lane ... A1
Athenaeum ... C2
Baker's La ... C3
Beetons Way ... A1
Bishops Rd ... B2
Bloomfield St ... B2
Bridewell La ... C2
Bullen Cl ... C1
Bury St Edmunds County School ... A1
Bury St Edmunds ⇌ ... A2
Bury Town FC ... A3
Bus Station ... B2
Butter Mkt ... B2
Cannon St ... B2
Castle Rd ... C1
Cemetery ... C1
Chalk Rd (N) ... B1
Chalk Rd (S) ... B1
Church Row ... B2
Churchgate St ... C2
Citizens Advice Bureau ... B2
College St ... C2
Compiegne Way ... A3
Corn Exchange, The ... B2
Cornfield Rd ... B1
Cotton Lane ... B3
Courts ... B2
Crown St ... C3
Cullum Rd ... C2
Eastern Way ... A3
Eastgate St ... B3
Enterprise Business Park ... A2
Etna Rd ... A2
Eyre Cl ... C2
Fire Station ... B1
Friar's Lane ... C2
Gage Cl ... A1
Garland St ... B2
Greene King Brewery ... C3
Grove Park ... B1
Grove Rd ... B1
Guildhall ... C2
Guildhall St ... C2
Hatter St ... C2
High Baxter St ... B2
Honey Hill ... C3
Hospital Rd ... C1/C2
Ickworth Dr ... C1
Information Ctr ... B2
Ipswich St ... A2
King Edward VI Sch ... A1
King's Rd ... C1/B2
Library ... B2
Long Brackland ... A2
Looms La ... B2
Lwr Baxter St ... B2
Malthouse La ... A2
Manor House ... C3
Maynewater La ... C3
Mill Rd ... C1
Mill Rd (South) ... C1
Minden Close ... B3
Moyses Hall ... B2
Mustow St ... B3
Norman Tower ... C3
Northgate Ave ... A2
Northgate St ... B2
Nuffield (Private) ... B3
Nutshell, The ... B2
Osier Rd ... A2
Out Northgate ... A2
Out Risbygate ... B1
Out Westgate ... C2
Parkway ... B1/C2
Parkway ... B1
Peckham St ... B2
Petticoat La ... C1
Phoenix Day Hosp ... C1
Pinners Way ... C1
Police Station ... C3
Post Office ... B2/B3
Pump La ... B2
Queen's Rd ... B1
Raingate St ... C3
Raynham Rd ... A1
Risbygate St ... B1/B2
Robert Boby Way ... C2
St Andrew's St North ... B2
St Andrew's St South ... B2
St Botolph's La ... C3
St Edmund's ... C2
St Edmund's Abbey (Remains) ✦ ... B3
St Edmundsbury † ... C3
St John's St ... B2
St Marys ... C3
School Hall La ... B2
Shillitoe Cl ... C1
Shire Halls & Magistrates Ct ... C3
South Cl ... C1
Southgate St ... C3
Sparhawk St ... C3
Spring Lane ... B1
Springfield Rd ... B1
Station Hill ... A2
Swan La ... C3
Tayfen Rd ... B2
The Vinefields ... B3
Theatre Royal ... C3
Thingoe Hill ... A2
Victoria St ... B1
War Memorial ✦ ... C1
Well St ... B2
Westgarth Gdns ... C1
Westgate St ... C2
Whiting St ... C2
York Rd ... B1
York Terr ... B1

Cambridge 333

Abbey Rd ... A3
ADC ... A2
Anglia Ruskin University ... B3
Archaeology & Anthropology ... B2
Art Gallery ... A1
Arts Picture House ... B2
Arts Theatre ... B1
Auckland Rd ... A3
Bateman St ... C2
BBC ... C3
Bene't St ... B1
Bradmore St ... B3
Bridge St ... A1
Broad St ... B3
Brookside ... C2
Brunswick Terr ... A3
Burleigh St ... B3
Bus Station ... B2
Butt Green ... A2
Cambridge Contemporary Art Gallery ... B1
Castle Mound ... A1
Castle St ... A1
Chesterton La ... A1
Christ's (Coll) ... B2
Christ's Pieces ... B2
City Rd ... B3
Clare (Coll) ... B1
Clarendon St ... B2
Coe Fen ... C2
Coronation St ... C2
Corpus Christi (Coll) ... B1
Council Offices ... C3
Cross St ... C3
Crusoe Bridge ... C1
Darwin (Coll) ... C1
Devonshire Rd ... C3
Downing (Coll) ... C2
Downing St ... B2
Earl St ... B2
East Rd ... B3
Eden St ... B3
Elizabeth Way ... A3
Elm St ... B2
Emery St ... B3
Emmanuel (Coll) ... B2
Emmanuel Rd ... B2
Emmanuel St ... B2
Fair St ... A3
Fenners (Cambridge Univ C C) ... C3
Fire Station ... B3
Fitzroy St ... A3
Fitzwilliam Mus ... C2
Fitzwilliam St ... C2
Folk Mus ... A1
Glisson Rd ... C3
Gonville & Caius (Coll) ... B1
Gonville Place ... C2
Grafton Centre ... A3
Grand Arcade ... B2
Gresham Rd ... C3
Green St ... B1
Guest Rd ... B3
Guildhall ... B2
Harvey Rd ... C3
Hills Rd ... C3
Hobson St ... B2
Hughes Hall (Coll) ... B3
Information Ctr ... B2
James St ... A3
Jesus (Coll) ... A2
Jesus Green ... A2
Jesus La ... A2
Jesus Terr ... B3
John St ... B3
Kelsey Kerridge Sports Hall ... B3
King St ... A2
King's (Coll) ... B1
King's College Chapel ... B1
King's Parade ... B1
Lammas Land Recreation Ground ... C1
Lensfield Rd ... C2
Little St Mary's La ... B1
Lyndewod Rd ... C3
Magdalene (Coll) ... A1
Magdalene St ... A1
Maid's Causeway ... A3
Malcolm St ... A2
Market Hill ... B1
Market St ... B1
Mathematical Bridge ... B1
Mawson Rd ... C3
Midsummer Common ... A3
Mill La ... B1
Mill Rd ... B3
Mill St ... C3
Napier St ... A3
New Square ... A3
Newmarket Rd ... A3
Newnham Rd ... C1
Norfolk St ... B3
Northampton St ... A1
Norwich St ... C2
Orchard St ... B2
Panton St ... C2
Paradise Nature Reserve ... C1
Paradise St ... B3
Park Parade ... A1
Park St ... A2
Park Terr ... B2
Parker St ... B2
Parker's Piece ... B2
Parkside ... B3
Parkside Indoor Swimming Pool ... B3
Parsonage St ... A3
Pembroke (Coll) ... B2
Pembroke St ... B1
Perowne St ... B3
Peterhouse (Coll) ... C1
Petty Cury ... B2
Police Station ... B3
Post Office ... A1/A3/B2/B3/C1/C2/C3
Queens' (Coll) ... B1
Queen's La ... B1
Queen's Rd ... B1
Regent St ... B2
Regent Terr ... B2
Ridley Hall (Coll) ... C1
Riverside ... A3
Round Church, The ... A1
Russell St ... C2
St Andrew's St ... B2
St Benet's ... B1
St Catharine's (Coll) ... B1
St Eligius St ... C2
St John's (Coll) ... A1
St Mary's ... B1
St Paul's Rd ... C3
Saxon St ... C2
Scott Polar Institute & Mus ... C2
Sedgwick Mus ... B2
Sheep's Green ... C1
Shire Hall ... A1
Sidgwick Ave ... C1
Sidney St ... A2
Sidney Sussex (Coll) ... A2
Silver St ... B1
Station Rd ... C3
Tenison Ave ... C3
Tenison Rd ... C3
Tennis Court Rd ... B2
The Backs ... B1
The Fen Causeway ... C1
Thompson's La ... A1
Trinity (Coll) ... A1
Trinity Hall (Coll) ... B1
Trinity St ... B1
Trumpington Rd ... C2
Trumpington St ... B1
Union Rd ... C2
University Botanic Gardens ... C2
Victoria Ave ... A2
Victoria St ... B2
Warkworth St ... B3
Warkworth Terr ... B3
Wesley House (Coll) ... A2
West Rd ... B1
Westcott House (Coll) ... A2
Westminster (Coll) ... A1
Whipple ... B2
Willis Rd ... B3
Willow Walk ... A2
Zoology ... B2

Canterbury 333

Artillery St ... B2
Barton Mill Rd ... A3
Beaconsfield Rd ... A1
Beverley Rd ... A1
Bingley's Island ... B1
Black Griffin La ... B1
Broad Oak Rd ... A2
Broad St ... B2
Brymore Rd ... A3
Burgate ... B2
Bus Station ... C2
Canterbury College ... C3
Canterbury East ⇌ ... C1
Canterbury Tales, The ✦ ... B2
Canterbury West ⇌ ... A1
Castle ... C1
Castle Row ... C1
Castle St ... C1
Cathedral † ... B2
Chaucer Rd ... A3
Christ Church University ... B3
Christchurch Gate ✦ ... B2
City Council Offices ... A3
City Wall ... B2
Coach Park ... A2
College Rd ... B3
Cossington Rd ... C2
Court ... B2
Craddock Rd ... A3
Crown & County Courts ... B3
Dane John Gdns ... C2
Dane John Mound ✦ ... C1
Deanery ... B2
Dover St ... C2
Duck La ... B2
Eastbridge Hospital ... B1
Edgar Rd ... B3
Ersham Rd ... C3
Ethelbert Rd ... C3
Fire Station ... C2
Forty Acres Rd ... A1
Gordon Rd ... C1
Greyfriars ✦ ... B1
Guildford Rd ... C1
Havelock St ... B2
Heaton Rd ... C1
High St ... B2
HM Prison ... B3
Information Ctr ... A2/B2
Invicta Locomotive ... B1
Ivy La ... B2
King St ... B2
King's School ... B2/B3
King's School Leisure Facilities ... A2
Kingsmead Rd ... A2
Kirby's La ... B1
Lansdown Rd ... C2
Leisure Centre ... A2
Longport ... B3
Lower Chantry La ... C3
Mandeville Rd ... A1
Market Way ... A2
Marlowe Arcade ... B2
Marlowe Ave ... C2
Marlowe Theatre ... B2
Martyr's Field Rd ... C1
Mead Way ... B1
Military Rd ... B2
Monastery St ... B2
Mus of Canterbury (Rupert Bear Mus) ... B1
New Dover Rd ... C3
New St ... C1
Norman Rd ... C2
North Holmes Rd ... B3
North La ... B1
Northgate ... A2
Nunnery Fields ... C2
Nunnery Rd ... C2
Oaten Hill ... C2
Odeon Cinema ... C2
Old Dover Rd ... C2
Old Palace ... B2
Old Ruttington La ... B2
Old Weavers ... B2
Orchard St ... B1
Oxford Rd ... C1
Palace St ... B2
Pilgrims Way ... C3
Pin Hill ... C1
Pine Tree Ave ... A1
Police Station ... C2
Post Office ... B2/C1/C2
Pound La ... B1
Puckle La ... C2
Raymond Ave ... C2
Rheims Way ... B1
Rhodaus Town ... C2
Roman Mus ... B2
Roper Gateway ... A1
Roper Rd ... A1
Rose La ... B2
Royal Mus ... B2
St Augustine's Abbey (remains) † ... B3
St Augustine's Rd ... C3
St Dunstan's ... A1
St Dunstan's St ... A1
St George's Pl ... C2
St George's St ... B2
St George's Tower ✦ ... B2
St Gregory's Rd ... B3
St John's Hospital ... A2
St Margaret's St ... B2
St Martin's ... B3
St Martin's Ave ... B3
St Martin's Rd ... B3
St Michael's Rd ... A1
St Mildred's ... C1
St Peter's Gr ... B1
St Peter's La ... B2
St Peter's Pl ... B1
St Peter's St ... B1
St Radigunds St ... B2
St Stephen's Ct ... A1
St Stephen's Path ... A1
St Stephen's Rd ... A2
Salisbury Rd ... A1
Simmonds Rd ... C1
Spring La ... C3
Station Rd West ... B1
Stour St ... B1
Sturry Rd ... A3
The Causeway ... A2
The Friars ... B2
Tourtel Rd ... A3
Union St ... B2
University College for the Creative Arts ... C3
Vernon Pl ... C2
Victoria Rd ... C1
Watling St ... B2
Westgate Gdns ... B1
Westgate Towers ... B1
Whitefriars ... B2
Whitehall Gdns ... B1
Whitehall Rd ... B1
Wincheap ... C1
York Rd ... C1
Zealand Rd ... C2

Cardiff *Caerdydd* 333

Adam St ... B3
Alexandra Gdns ... A2
Allerton St ... C1
Arran St ... A3
ATRiuM (Univ of Glamorgan) ... C3
Beauchamp St ... C1
Bedford St ... A3
Blackfriars Priory † ... B1
Boulevard De Nantes ... B2
Brains Brewery ... C2
Brook St ... B1
Bus Station ... C2
Bute Park ... B1
Bute St ... C2
Bute Terr ... C3
Callaghan Sq ... C2/C3
Capitol Shopping Centre, The ... B3
Cardiff Bridge ... B1
Cardiff Castle ... B2
Cardiff Central Station ⇌ ... C2
Cardiff Centre Trading Estate ... C3
Cardiff International Arena ✦ ... C3
Cardiff Rugby Football Ground ... B1
Cardiff University ... A1/A2/B3
Cardiff University Student's Union ... A2
Caroline St ... C2
Castle Green ... B2
Castle Mews ... A1
Castle St (Heol y Castell) ... B1
Cathays Station ⇌ ... A2
Celerity Drive ... C3
Central Sq ... C2
Charles St (Heol Siarl) ... B3
Churchill Way ... B3
City Hall ... A2
City Rd ... A3
Clare Rd ... C1
Clare St ... C1
Coburn St ... A3
Coldstream Terr ... B1
College Rd ... A1
Colum Rd ... A1
Court ... C2
Court Rd ... C1
Craiglee Drive ... C3
Cranbrook St ... A3
Customhouse St ... C2
Cyfartha St ... A3
Despenser Place ... C1
Despenser St ... C1
Dinas St ... C1
Duke St (Heol y Dug) ... B2
Dumfries Place ... B3
East Grove ... A3
Ellen St ... C3
Fire Station ... B3
Fitzalan Place ... B3
Fitzhamon Embankment ... C1
Fitzhamon La ... C1
Gloucester St ... C1
Glynrhondda St ... A2
Gordon Rd ... A3
Gorsedd Gdns ... B2
Green St ... B1
Greyfriars Rd ... B2
HM Prison ... B3
Hafod St ... C1
Herbert St ... C3
High St ... B2
Industrial Estate ... C3
John St ... C3
Jubilee St ... C1
King Edward VII Ave ... A1
Kingsway (Ffordd y Brenin) ... B2
Knox Rd ... B3
Law Courts ... B2
Library ... B2
Llanbleddian Gdns ... A2
Llantwit St ... A2
Lloyd George Ave ... C3
Lower Cathedral Rd ... B1
Lowther Rd ... A3
Magistrates Court ... B3
Mansion House ... A3
Mardy St ... C1
Mark St ... B1
Market ... B2
Mary Ann St ... C3
Merches Gdns ... C1
Mill La ... C2
Millennium Bridge ... B1
Millennium Plaza Leisure Complex ... C1
Millennium Stadium ... C1
Millennium Stadium Tours (Gate 3) ✦ ... B2
Miskin St ... A2
Monmouth St ... C1
Museum Ave ... A2
Museum Place ... A2
National Mus of Wales ... A2
National War Memorial ✦ ... A2
Neville Place ... C1
New Theatre ... B2
Newport Rd ... B3
Northcote La ... A3
Northcote St ... A3
Park Grove ... A4
Park Place ... A2
Park St ... C2
Penarth Rd ... C2
Pendyris St ... C1
Plantaganet St ... C1
Quay St ... B2
Queen Anne Sq ... A1
Queen St (Heol y Frenhines) ... B2
Queen St Station ⇌ ... B3
Regimental Mus ... B2
Rhymney St ... A3
Richmond Rd ... A3
Royal Welsh College of Music and Drama ... A1
Russell St ... A3
Ruthin Gdns ... A2
St Andrews Place ... A2
St David's † ... B2
St David's 2 ... C2
St David's Centre ... B2
St David's Hall ✦ ... B2
St John The Baptist ... B2
St Mary St (Heol Eglwys Fair) ... B2
St Peter's St ... A3
Salisbury Rd ... A3
Sandon St ... B3
Schooner Way ... C3
Scott Rd ... C2
Scott St ... C2
Senghennydd Rd ... A2
Sherman Theatre ... A2
Sophia Gardens ... A1
South Wales Baptist College ... A3
Stafford Rd ... C1
Station Terr ... B3
Stuttgarter Strasse ... B2
Sussex St ... C1
Taffs Mead Embankment ... C1
Talworth St ... A3
Temple of Peace & Health ✦ ... A1
The Friary ... B2
The Hayes ... B2
The Parade ... A3
The Walk ... A3
Treharris St ... A3
Trinity St ... B2
Tudor La ... C1
Tudor St ... C1
Welsh Assembly Offices ... A1
Welsh Institute of Sport ✦ ... A1
West Grove ... A3
Westgate St (Heol y Porth) ... B2
Windsor Place ... B3
Womanby St ... B2
Wood St ... C2
Working St ... B2
Wyeverne Rd ... A2

Carlisle 333

Abbey St ... A1
Aglionby St ... B3
Albion St ... C3
Alexander St ... C3
AMF Bowl ✦ ... C2
Annetwell St ... A1
Bank St ... B2
Bitts Park ... A1
Blackfriars St ... B2
Blencome St ... C1
Blunt St ... C1
Botchergate ... B2
Boustead's Grassing ... C2
Bowman St ... B3
Broad St ... B3
Bridge St ... A1
Brook St ... C3
Brunswick St ... B2
Bus Station ... B2
Caldew Bridge ... A1
Caldew St ... C1
Carlisle (Citadel) Station ⇌ ... B2
Castle ... A1
Castle St ... A1
Castle Way ... A1
Cathedral † ... A1
Cecil St ... B2
Chapel St ... A2
Charles St ... B3
Charlotte St ... B1
Chatsworth Square ... A2
Chiswick St ... B2
Citadel, The ... B2
City Walls ... A1
Civic Centre ... A2
Clifton St ... C1
Close St ... B3
Collingwood St ... C1
Colville St ... C1
Colville Terr ... C1
Court ... B2
Court St ... B2
Crosby St ... B2
Crown St ... C2
Currock Rd ... C2
Dacre Rd ... A1
Dale St ... C1
Denton St ... C1
Devonshire Walk ... A1
Duke's Rd ... A2
East Dale St ... C1
East Norfolk St ... C1
Eden Bridge ... A2
Edward St ... B3
Elm St ... B1
English St ... B2
Fire Station ... A2
Fisher St ... A1
Flower St ... B3

Freer St C1
Fusehill St B3
Georgian Way A2
Gloucester Rd C3
Golf Course A2
Graham St C1
Grey St B3
Guildhall Mus A2
Halfey's La B3
Hardwicke Circus A2
Hart St B3
Hewson St C2
Howard Pl A3
Howe St B3
Information Ctr A2
James St B2
Junction St B1
King St B2
Lancaster St B2
Lanes Shopping Centre B2
Laserquest ✦ B2
Library A2/B1
Lime St B1
Lindisfarne St C3
Linton St B3
Lismore Pl A3
Lismore St B3
London Rd C3
Lonsdale Rd B2
Lord St C3
Lorne Cres B1
Lorne St B1
Lowther St B2
Market Hall A2
Mary St B2
Memorial Bridge A3
Metcalfe St C1
Milbourne St B1
Myddleton St B3
Nelson St C1
Norfolk St C1
Old Town Hall A2
Oswald St C3
Peter St A2
Petteril St B3
Police Station A2
Portland Pl B2
Portland Sq B2
Post Office A2/B2/B3/C1/C3
Princess St C2
Pugin St B1
Red Bank Terr C2
Regent St C3
Richardson St C1
Rickerby Park A3
Rickergate A2
River St B3
Rome St C2
Rydal St B3
St Cuthbert's B2
St Cuthbert's La B2
St James' Park C1
St James' Rd C1
St Nicholas St C3
Sands Centre A2
Scotch St A2
Shaddongate B1
Sheffield St B1
South Henry St B3
South John St C2
South St B3
Spencer St B2
Sports Centre A2
Strand Rd A2
Swimming Baths B2
Sybil St B3
Tait St B2
Thomas St B1
Thomson St C3
Trafalgar St C1
Tullie House Mus A1
Tyne St C3
Viaduct Estate Rd B1
Victoria Pl A2
Victoria Viaduct B2
Vue B2
Warwick Rd B2
Warwick Sq B3
Water St B2
West Walls B1
Westmorland St C1

Chelmsford 333

Ambulance Station B1
Anchor St C1
Anglia Polytechnic University A2
Arbour La A3
Baddow Rd B2/C3
Baker St C1
Barrack Sq B2
Bellmead B2
Bishop Hall La A2
Bishop Rd A2
Bond St B2
Boswells Dr B3
Boudicca Mews C2
Bouverie Rd C2
Bradford St C1
Braemar Ave C1
Brook St A2
Broomfield Rd A1
Burns Cres C2
Bus Station B1
Can Bridge Way B2
Cedar Ave A1
Cedar Ave West A1
Cemetery A1
Cemetery A2
Cemetery C1
Central Park B1
Chelmsford + B2
Chelmsford (rail) A1
Chichester Dr A3
Chinery Cl A3
Cinema B2
Civic Centre A1
College C1
Cottage Pl A2
County Hall B2
Coval Ave B1
Coval La B1
Coval Wells B1
Cricket Ground B2
Crown Court B2
Duke St B2
Elm Rd C1
Elms Dr A1
Essex Record Office, The B3
Fairfield Rd B1
Falcons Mead B1
George St C2
Glebe Rd A1
Godfrey's Mews C2
Goldlay Ave C3
Goldlay Rd C2
Grove Rd C2
HM Prison A3
Hall St C2
Hamlet Rd C2
Hart St C1
Henry Rd A2
High Bridge Rd B2
High Chelmer Shopping Centre B2
High St B2
Hill Cres B3
Hill Rd Sth B3
Hill Rd B3
Hillview Rd A3
Hoffmans Way A2
Hosp A2
Information Ctr B2
Lady La C2
Langdale Gdns C3
Legg St B2
Library A1
Library B2
Library C2
Lionfield Terr A3
Lower Anchor St C1
Lynmouth Ave C2
Lynmouth Gdns C3
Magistrates Court B2
Maltese Rd A1
Manor Rd C2
Marconi Rd A2
Market B2
Market Rd B2
Marlborough Rd C1
Meadows Shopping Centre, The B2
Meadowside A3
Mews Ct C2
Mildmay Rd C2
Moulsham Dr C2
Moulsham Mill ✦ C3
Moulsham St C1/C2
Navigation Rd B3
New London Rd B2/C1
New St A2/B2
New Writtle St C1
Nursery Rd C2
Orchard St C2
Park Rd B1
Parker Rd C2
Parklands Dr A3
Parkway A1/B1/B2
Police Station A2
Post Office A3/B2/C2
Primrose Hill A1
Prykes Dr B1
Queen St C1
Queen's Rd B3
Railway St A1
Rainsford Rd A1
Ransomes Way A2
Rectory La A2
Regina Rd A2
Riverside Leisure Centre B2
Rosebery Rd C2
Rothesay Ave C1
St John's Rd C2
Sandringham Pl B3
Seymour St B1
Shrublands Cl B3
Southborough Rd C1
Springfield Basin B3
Springfield Rd A3/B2/B3
Stapleford Cl C1
Swiss Ave A1
Telford Pl A3
The Meades B1
Tindal St B2
Townfield St A1
Trinity Rd B3
University B1
Upper Bridge Rd C1
Upper Roman Rd C2
Van Dieman's Rd C3
Viaduct Rd B1
Vicarage Rd C1
Victoria Rd A2
Victoria Rd South B2
Vincents Rd C2
Waterloo La B2
Weight Rd B3
Westfield Ave A1
Wharf Rd B3
Writtle Rd C1
YMCA A2
York Rd C1

Cheltenham 333

Albert Rd A3
Albion St B3
All Saints Rd B3
Andover Rd C1
Art Gallery & Mus B2
Axiom Centre B3
Bath Pde B2
Bath Rd C2
Bays Hill Rd C1
Beechwood Shopping Centre B3
Bennington St B2
Berkeley St B3
Brewery Centre A2
Brunswick St South A2
Bus Station B2
Carlton St B3
Central Cross Road A3
Cheltenham & Gloucester College A2
Cheltenham College C2
Cheltenham FC A3
Cheltenham General (A & E) C3
Christchurch Rd B1
Cineworld A2
Clarence Rd A2
Clarence Sq A2
Clarence St B2
Cleeveland St A1
Coach Park A2
College Rd C2
Colletts Dr A1
Corpus St C3
Devonshire St A2
Douro Rd B1
Duke St B3
Dunalley Pde A2
Dunalley St A2
Everyman B2
Evesham Rd A3
Fairview Rd B3
Fairview St B3
Folly La A2
Gloucester Rd A1
Grosvenor St B3
Grove St A1
Gustav Holst A3
Hanover St A2
Hatherley St C1
Henrietta St A2
Hewlett Rd B3
High St B2/B3
Hudson St A2
Imperial Gdns C2
Imperial La B2
Imperial Sq C2
Information Ctr B2
Keynsham Rd C3
King St A2
Knapp Rd B2
Ladies College B2
Lansdown Cr C1
Lansdown Rd C1
Leighton Rd B3
London Rd C3
Lypiatt Rd C1
Malvern Rd B1
Manser St A2
Market St A1
Marle Hill Pde A2
Marle Hill Rd A2
Millbrook St A1
Milsom St A2
Montpellier Gdns C2
Montpellier Gr C2
Montpellier Pde C2
Montpellier Spa Rd C2
Montpellier St C1
Montpellier Terr C2
Montpellier Walk C2
New St B2
North Pl B2
Old Bath Rd C3
Oriel Rd B2
Overton Park Rd B1
Overton Rd B1
Oxford St C3
Parabola Rd B1
Park Pl C1
Park St A1
Pittville Circus A3
Pittville Cr A3
Pittville Lawn A3
Playhouse B2
Police Station B1/C1
Portland St B3
Post Office B2/C1/C2
Prestbury Rd A3
Prince's Rd C1
Priory St B3
Promenade B2
Queen St A1
Recreation Ground A2
Regent Arcade B2
Regent St B2
Rodney Rd B2
Royal Cr B2
Royal Wells Rd B2
St George's Pl B2
St George's Rd B1
St Gregory's B2
St James St B3
St John's Ave B3
St Luke's Rd C2
St Margaret's Rd A2
St Mary's B2
St Matthew's B2
St Paul's La A2
St Paul's Rd A2
St Paul's St A2
St Stephen's Rd C1
Sandford Lido C3
Sandford Mill Road C3
Sandford Park C3
Sandford Rd C2
Selkirk St A3
Sherborne Pl B3
Sherborne St B3
Suffolk Pde C2
Suffolk Rd C1
Suffolk Sq C1
Sun St A1
Swindon Rd B2
Sydenham Villas Rd C3
Tewkesbury Rd A1
The Courtyard B1
Thirlstaine Rd C2
Tivoli Rd C1
Tivoli St C1
Town Hall & Theatre B2
Townsend St A1
Trafalgar St C2
Victoria Pl B3
Victoria St A2
Vittoria Walk C2
Wellesley Rd A2
Wellington Rd A3
Wellington Sq A3
Wellington St B2
West Drive A3
Western Rd B1
Winchcombe St B3

Chester 333

Abbey Gateway A2
Appleyards La C3
Bedward Row B1
Beeston View C3
Bishop Lloyd's Palace B2
Black Diamond St A2
Bottoms La C3
Boughton B3
Bouverie St A1
Bridge St B2
Bridgegate C2
British Heritage Centre B2
Brook St A3
Brown's La C2
Bus Station B2
Cambrian Rd A1
Canal St A2
Carrick Rd C1
Castle C2
Castle Dr C2
Cathedral + B2
Catherine St A1
Chester (rail) A3
Cheyney Rd A1
Chichester St A1
City Rd A3
City Walls B1/B2
City Walls Rd B1
Cornwall St A2
County Hall C2
Cross Hey C3
Cuppin St B2
Curzon Park North C1
Curzon Park South C1
Dee Basin A1
Dee La B3
Delamere St A2
Dewa Roman Experience B2
Duke St B2
Eastgate B2
Eastgate St B2
Eaton Rd C2
Edinburgh Way C3
Elizabeth Cr B3
Fire Station A2
Foregate St B2
Frodsham St B2
Gamul House B2
Garden La A1
Gateway Theatre B2
George St A2
Gladstone Ave A1
God's Providence House B2
Gorse Stacks A2
Greenway St C2
Grosvenor Bridge C1
Grosvenor Mus B2
Grosvenor Park B3
Grosvenor Precinct B2
Grosvenor Rd C1
Grosvenor St B2
Groves Rd B3
Guildhall Mus B1
Handbridge C2
Hartington St C3
Hoole Way A2
Hunter St B2
Information Ctr B2
King Charles' Tower ✦ A2
King St A2
Library B2
Lightfoot St A3
Little Roodee C2
Liverpool Rd A2
Love St B3
Lower Bridge St B2
Lower Park Rd B3
Lyon St A2
Magistrates Court B2
Meadows La C3
Military Mus C2
Milton St A3
New Crane St B1
Nicholas St B2
Northgate A2
Northgate Arena ✦ A2
Northgate St A2
Nun's Rd B1
Old Dee Bridge ✦ C2
Overleigh Rd C2
Park St B2
Police Station B2
Post Office A2/A3/B2/C2
Princess St B2
Queen St B2
Queen's Park Rd C3
Queen's Rd A3
Race Course B1
Raymond St A1
River La C2
Roman Amphitheatre & Gardens B2
Roodee, The (Chester Racecourse) B1
Russell St A3
St Anne St A2
St George's Cr C3
St Martin's Gate A1
St Martin's Way B1
St Oswalds Way A2
Saughall Rd A1
Sealand Rd A1
South View Rd A1
Stanley Palace B1
Station Rd A3
Steven St A3
The Bars B3
The Cross B2
The Groves B3
The Meadows B3
Tower Rd B1
Town Hall B2
Union St B3
Vicar's La B2
Victoria Cr C3
Victoria Rd A2
Walpole St A1
Water Tower St A1
Watergate B1
Watergate St B2
Whipcord La A1
White Friars B2
York St B3

Chichester 333

Adelaide Rd A3
Alexandra Rd A3
Arts Centre B2
Ave de Chartres B1/B2
Barlow Rd A1
Basin Rd C2
Beech Ave B1
Bishops Palace Gardens B2
Bishopsgate Walk A3
Bramber Rd C3
Broyle Rd A2
Bus Station B2
Caledonian Rd B3
Cambrai Ave B3
Canal Wharf C2
Canon La B2
Cathedral + B2
Cavendish St A1
Cawley Rd B2
Cedar Dr A1
Chapel St A2
Cherry Orchard Rd C3
Chichester By-Pass C2/C3
Chichester Festival A2
Chichester (rail) B2
Churchside A2
Cinema B3/C1
City Walls B2
Cleveland Rd B3
College La A2
Coll of Science & Technology B1
Cory Cl C2
Council Offices B2
County Hall B2
Courts B2
District B2
Duncan Rd A1
Durnford Cl A1
East Pallant B2
East Row B2
East St B2
East Walls B3
Eastland Rd C3
Ettrick Cl B3
Ettrick Rd B3
Exton Rd C3
Fire Station A2
Football Ground A2
Franklin Pl A2
Friary (Rems of) A2
Garland Cl C3
Green La A3
Grove Rd C3
Guilden Rd B3
Guildhall A2
Hawthorn Cl A1
Hay Rd C3
Henty Gdns B1
Herald Dr C3
Information Ctr B2
John's St B2
Joys Croft A3
Jubilee Pk A3
Jubilee Rd A3
Juxon Cl B1
Kent Rd A3
King George Gdns A2
King's Ave C2
Kingsham Ave C3
Kingsham Rd C2
Laburnum Gr B2
Leigh Rd C1
Lennox Rd A3
Lewis Rd A3
Library B2
Lion St B2
Litten Terr A3
Little London B2
Lyndhurst Rd B3
Market B3
Market Ave B2
Market Cross B2
Market Rd B3
Martlet Cl C2
Melbourne Rd A3
Mount La B1
New Park Rd A3
Newlands La A1
North Pallant B2
North St A2
North Walls A2
Northgate A2
Oak Ave A1
Oak Cl A1
Oaklands Park A2
Oaklands Way A2
Orchard Ave A1
Orchard St A1
Ormonde Ave B3
Pallant House B2
Parchment St A1
Parklands Rd A1/B1
Peter Weston Pl B3
Police Station C2
Post Office A1/B2/B3
Priory La A2
Priory Park A2
Priory Rd A2
Queen's Ave C1
Riverside A3
Roman Amphitheatre B3
St Cyriacs A2
St Pancras A3
St Paul's Rd A2
St Richard's Hospital (A+E) A3
Shamrock Cl A3
Sherbourne Rd A1
Somerstown A2
South Bank C2
South Pallant B2
South St B2
Southgate B2
Spitalfield La A3
Stirling Rd B3
Stockbridge Rd C1/C2
Swanfield Dr A3
Terminus Industrial Estate C1
Terminus Rd C1
The Hornet B3
The Litten A3
Tower St A2
Tozer Way A3
Turnbull Rd A3
Upton Rd C1
Velyn Ave B3
Via Ravenna B1
Walnut Ave A1
West St B2
Westgate B1
Westgate Fields B1
Westgate Leisure Centre B1
Weston Ave C1
Whyke Cl C3
Whyke La B3
Whyke Rd C3
Winden Ave B3

Colchester 333

Abbey Gateway + C2
Albert St A1
Albion Grove C2
Alexandra Rd C1
Artillery St C3
Arts Centre B1
Balkerne Hill B1
Barrack St C3
Beaconsfield Rd C1
Beche Rd C3
Bergholt Rd A1
Bourne Rd C3
Brick Kiln Rd A1
Bristol Rd B2
Broadlands Way A3
Brook St B3
Bury Cl B2
Butt Rd C1
Camp Folley North C2
Camp Folley South C2
Campion Rd C2
Cannon St C3
Canterbury Rd C2
Castle B2
Castle Park B2
Castle Rd B2
Catchpool Rd A1
Causton Rd B1
Cavalry Barracks C1
Chandlers Row C3
Circular Rd East C2
Circular Rd North C1
Circular Rd West C1
Clarendon Way A1
Claudius Rd C2
Clock B1
Colchester Camp Abbey Field C1
Colchester Institute B1
Colchester (rail) A1
Colchester Town (rail) C2
Colne Bank Ave A1
Colne View Retail Park A2
Compton Rd A3
Cowdray Ave A1/A2
Cowdray Centre, The A2
Crouch St B1
Crowhurst Rd B1
Culver Centre B1
Culver St East B2
Culver St West B1
Dilbridge Rd A3
East Hill B2
East St B3
East Stockwell St B1
Eld La B1
Essex Hall Rd A1
Exeter Dr B2
Fairfax Rd C2
Fire Station A2
Flagstaff Rd C1
George St B2
Gladstone Rd C2
Golden Noble Hill C2
Goring Rd A3
Granville Rd C3
Greenstead Rd B3
Guildford Rd B2
Harsnett Rd C3
Harwich Rd B3
Head St B1
High St B1/B2
High Woods Country Park A2
Hythe Hill C3
Information Ctr B2
Ipswich Rd A3
Kendall Rd C2
Kimberley Rd C3
King Stephen Rd C3
Le Cateau Barracks C1
Leisure World A2
Library B1
Lincoln Way B2
Lion Walk Shopping Centre B1
Lisle Rd C2
Lucas Rd C2
Magdalen Green C3
Magdalen St C2
Maidenburgh St B2
Maldon Rd C1
Manor Rd B1
Margaret Rd A1
Mason Rd A2
Mercers Way A1
Mercury B1
Mersea Rd C2
Meyrick Cr C2
Mile End Rd A1
Military Rd C2
Mill St C2
Minories B2
Moorside B3
Morant Rd C3
Napier Rd C2
Natural History B2
New Town Rd C2
Norfolk Cr A3
North Hill B1
North Station Rd A1
Northgate St B1
Nunns Rd B1
Odeon B1
Old Coach Rd B3
Old Heath Rd C3
Osborne St B2
Petrolea Cl A1
Police Station C1
Popes La B1
Port La C3
Post Office A1/B1/B2/C2/C3
Priory St B2
Queen St B2
Rawstorn Rd B1
Rebon St C3
Recreation Rd C3
Ripple Way A3
Roman Rd B2
Roman Wall B2
Romford Cl A3
Rosebery Ave B2
St Andrews Ave B3
St Andrews Gdns B3
St Botolph St B2
St Botolphs B2
St John's Abbey (site of) + C2
St John's St B1
St John's Walk Shopping Centre B1
St Leonards Rd C3
St Marys Fields B1
St Peters B1
St Peter's St B1
Salisbury Ave C1
Serpentine Walk A1
Sheepen Pl B1
Sheepen Rd B1
Sir Isaac's Walk B1
Smythies Ave B2
South St C1
South Way C1
Sports Way A2
Suffolk Cl A3
Town Hall B1
Valentine Dr A3
Victor Rd C3
Wakefield Cl B2
Wellesley Rd C1
Wells Rd B2/B3
West St C1
West Stockwell St B1
Weston Rd C3
Westway A1
Wickham Rd C1
Wimpole Rd C3
Winchester Rd C2
Winnock Rd C2
Wolfe Ave C2
Worcester Rd B2

Coventry 334

Abbots La A1
Albany Rd B1
Alma St B3
Art Faculty B3
Asthill Grove C2
Bablake School A1
Barras La A1/B1
Barrs Hill School A1
Belgrade B2
Bishop Burges St A2
Bond's Hospital B1
Broad Gate B2
Broadway C1
Bus Station A3
Butts Radial B1
Canal Basin ✦ A2
Canterbury St A3
Cathedral + B3
Chester St A1
Cheylesmore Manor House B2
Christ Church Spire ✦ B2
City Walls & Gates ✦ A2
Corporation St B2
Council House B2
Coundon Rd A1
Coventry & Warwickshire Hospital (A&E) A2
Coventry Station (rail) C2
Coventry Transport Mus A2
Cox St A3
Croft Rd B1
Dalton Rd C1
Deasy Rd C3
Earl St B2
Eaton Rd C2
Fairfax St B2
Foleshill Rd A2
Ford's Hospital B2
Fowler Rd A1
Friars Rd C2
Gordon St C1
Gosford St B3
Greyfriars Green ✦ B2
Greyfriars Rd B2
Gulson Rd B3
Hales St A2
Harnall Lane East A3
Harnall Lane West A2
Herbert Art Gallery & Mus B3
Hertford St B2
Hewitt Ave A1
High St B2
Hill St B1
Holy Trinity B2
Holyhead Rd A1
Howard St A3
Huntingdon Rd C1
Information Ctr B2
Jordan Well B3
King Henry VIII School C1
Lady Godiva Statue ✦ B2
Lamb St A2
Leicester Row A2
Library B2
Little Park St B2
London Rd C3
Lower Ford St B3
Magistrates & Crown Courts B2
Manor House Drive B2
Manor Rd C2
Market B2
Martyr's Memorial ✦ C2
Meadow St B1
Meriden St A1
Michaelmas Rd C2
Middleborough Rd A1
Mile La C3
Millennium Place ✦ A2
Much Park St B3
Naul's Mill Park A1
New Union B2
Park Rd C2
Parkside C3
Police HQ C3
Post Office B2
Primrose Hill St A3
Priory Gardens & Visitor Centre B2
Priory St B3
Puma Way C3
Quarryfield La C3
Queen's Rd B1
Quinton Rd C2
Radford Rd A2
Raglan St B3
Retail Park C1
Ringway (Hill Cross) A1
Ringway (Queens) B1
Ringway (Rudge) B1
Ringway (St Johns) B3
Ringway (St Nicholas) A2
Ringway (St Patricks) C2
Ringway (Swanswell) A2
Ringway (Whitefriars) B3
St John St B2
St John The Baptist B2
St Nicholas St A2
Skydome B1
Spencer Ave C1
Spencer Park C1
Spon St B1
Sports Centre B3
Stoney Rd C2
Stoney Stanton Rd A3
Swanswell Pool A3
Sydney Stringer School A3
Technical College B1
Technology Park C3
The Precinct B2
Theatre B1
Thomas Landsdail St C2
Tomson Ave A1
Top Green C1
Toy Mus B3
Trinity St B2
University B3
Upper Hill St A1
Upper Well St A2
Victoria St A3
Vine St A3
Warwick Rd C2
Waveley Rd B1
Westminster Rd C1
White St A3
Windsor St B1

Derby 334

Abbey St C1
Agard St B1
Albert St B2
Albion St B2
Ambulance Station B1
Arthur St A1
Ashlyn Rd B3
Assembly Rooms B2
Babington La C2
Becket St B1
Belper Rd A1
Bold La B1
Bradshaw Way C2
Bridge St B1
Brook St B1
Burrows Walk C2
Burton Rd C1
Bus Station B2
Caesar St A2
Canal St C3
Carrington St C3
Cathedral + B2
Cathedral Rd B1
Charnwood St C2
Chester Green Rd A2
City Rd A2
Clarke St A3
Cock Pitt B3
Council House B2
Courts B1
Cranmer Rd B3
Crompton St C1
Crown & County Courts B2
Crown Walk C2
Curzon St B1
Darley Grove A1
Derby (rail) C3
Derbyshire County Cricket Ground B3
Derbyshire Royal Infirmary (A&E) C2
Derwent Business Centre A2
Derwent St B2
Devonshire Walk C2
Drewry La C1
Duffield Rd A1
Duke St A2
Dunton Cl B3
Eagle Market C2
Eastgate B3
East St B2
Exeter St B2
Farm St C1
Ford St B1
Forester St C1
Fox St A2
Friar Gate B1
Friary St B1
Full St B2
Gerard St C1
Gower St C2
Green La C2
Grey St C1
Guildhall B2
Harcourt St C1
Highfield Rd A1
Hill La C2
Industrial B2
Information Ctr B2
Iron Gate B2
John St C3
Joseph Wright Centre B1
Kedleston Rd A1
Key St B2
King Alfred St C1
King St A1
Kingston St A1
Leopold St C2
Library B1
Liversage St C3
Lodge La B1
London Rd C2
Macklin St C1
Mansfield Rd A2
Market B2
Market Pl B2
May St C1
Meadow La B3
Melbourne St C2
Midland Rd C3
Monk St C1
Morledge B2
Mount St C1
Mus & Art Gallery B2
Noble St C3
North Parade A1
North St A1
Nottingham Rd A3
Osmaston Rd C2
Otter St A1
Park St C3
Parker St A1
Pickfords House B1
Playhouse C2
Police HQ A2
Police Station B2
Post Office A1/A2/B1/B2/C2/C3
Pride Parkway C3
Prime Parkway A2
Queens Leisure Centre B1
Racecourse A3
Railway Terr C3
Register Office B2
Sacheverel St C2
Sadler Gate B1
St Alkmund's Way B1/B2
St Helens House ✦ A1
St Mary's A1
St Mary's Bridge A2
St Mary's Bridge Chapel A2
St Mary's Gate B1
St Paul's Rd A2
St Peter's C2
St Peter's St C2
Siddals Rd C3
Sir Frank Whittle Rd A3
Spa La C1
Spring St C1
Stafford St B1
Station Approach C3
Stockbrook St C1
Stores Rd A3
Traffic St C2
Wardwick B1
Werburgh St C1

Dorchester • Dumfries • Dundee • Durham • Edinburgh • Exeter 349

West Ave A1
Westfield Centre C2
West Meadows Industrial Estate B3
Wharf Rd A2
Wilmot St C2
Wilson St C1
Wood's La C1

Dorchester 334

Ackerman Rd B3
Acland Rd A2
Albert Rd A1
Alexandra Rd B1
Alfred Place B3
Alfred Rd B2
Alington Ave B3
Alington Rd B3
Ambulance Station B3
Ashley Rd B1
Balmoral Cres C3
Barnes Way B2/C2
Borough Gdns A1
Bridport Rd A1
Buckingham Way C3
Caters Place A1
Cemetery A3/C1
Charles St A2
Coburg Rd B1
Colliton St A1
Cornwall Rd A1
Cromwell Rd B1
Culliford Rd B2
Culliford Rd North B2
Dagmar Rd B1
Damer's Rd B1
Diggory Cres C2
Dinosaur Mus A2
Dorchester Bypass C2
Dorchester South Station B1
Dorchester West Station B1
Dorset County Council Offices A1
Dorset County (A+E) A1
Dorset County Mus A1
Duchy Close C3
Duke's Ave B2
Durngate St A2
Durnover Court A3
Eddison Ave B3
Edward Rd B1
Egdon Rd C2
Eldridge Pope Brewery ✦ B1
Elizabeth Frink Statue ✦ B2
Farfrae Cres B2
Friary Hill A2
Friary Lane A2
Frome Terr A2
Garland Cres C3
Glyde Path Rd A1
Government Offices B3
Gt Western Rd B1
Grosvenor Cres C1
Grosvenor Rd C1
H M Prison A1
Herringston Rd C1
High St East A2
High Street Fordington A2
High Street West A1
Holloway Rd A2
Icen Way A2
Keep Military Mus, The A1
Kings Rd A3/B3
Kingsbere Cres C2
Lancaster Rd B2
Library A1
Lime Cl C1
Linden Ave B2
London Cl A3
London Rd A2/A3
Lubbecke Way A3
Lucetta La B2
Maiden Castle Rd C1
Manor Rd C2
Maumbury Rd B1
Maumbury Rings B1
Mellstock Ave C2
Mill St A3
Miller's Cl A1
Mistover Cl C1
Monmouth Rd B1/B2
Nature Reserve A2
North Sq A2
Northernhay A1
Old Crown Court & Cells A1
Olga Rd B1
Orchard St A2
Police Station A1
Post Office A1/B1/B2
Pound Lane A2
Poundbury Rd A1
Prince of Wales Rd B2
Prince's St A1
Queen's Ave B1
Roman Town House A1
Roman Wall A1
Rothesay Rd C2
St George's Rd B3
Salisbury Field A2
Shaston Cres C2
Smokey Hole La B3
South Court Ave C1
South St B1
South Walks Rd B2
Sports Centre B3
Superstore C3
Teddy Bear House A1
Temple Cl C1
The Grove A1
Town Hall A2
Town Pump ✦ A2
Trinity St A1
Tutankhamun Exhibition A1
Victoria Rd B1
Weatherbury Way C2
Wellbridge Cl C1
West Mills Rd A1
West Walks Rd A1
Weymouth Ave C1
Williams Ave B1
Winterbourne Hosp C1
Wollaston Rd A2
York Rd B2

Dumfries 334

Academy St A2
Aldermanhill Rd B3
Ambulance Station C3
Annan Rd A3
Ardwall Rd A3
Ashfield Dr A1
Atkinson Rd C1
Averill Cres C1
Balliol Ave C1
Bank St B2
Bankend Rd C3
Barn Slaps B3
Barrie Ave B3
Beech Ave A1
Bowling Green A3
Brewery St B2
Bridge House B1
Brodie Ave C2
Brooke St B2
Broomlands Dr C1
Brooms Rd B3
Buccleuch St A2
Burns House B2
Burns Mausoleum B3
Burns St B2
Burns Statue ✦ A2
Bus Station B1
Cardoness St A3
Castle St A2
Catherine St A2
Cattle Market A3
Cemetery B3
Cemetery C2
Church Cres A2
Church St B2
College Rd A1
College St A1
Corbelly Hill B1
Convent, The B1
Corberry Park B1
Cornwall Mt A3
County Offices A2
Court A2
Craigs Rd C3
Cresswell Ave B3
Cresswell Hill B3
Cumberland St B3
David Keswick Athletic Centre A3
David St B1
Dock Park C3
Dockhead B2
Dumfries Station A3
Dumfries Academy A2
Dumfries Mus & Camera Obscura B2
Dumfries Royal Infirmary (A & E) C3
East Riverside Dr C3
Edinburgh Rd A2
English St B2
Fire Station B3
Friar's Vennel A2
Galloway St B1
George Douglas Dr C1
George St A2
Gladstone Rd C2
Glasgow St A1
Glebe St B3
Glencaple Rd C3
Goldie Ave A1
Goldie Cres A1
Golf Course C3
Greyfriars A2
Grierson Ave B3
HM Prison B1
Hamilton Ave C1
Hamilton Starke Park C2
Hazelrigg Ave C1
Henry St B3
Hermitage Dr C1
High Cemetery C3
High St A2
Hill Ave C2
Hill St B1
Holm Ave C2
Hoods Loaning A3
Howgate St B1
Huntingdon Rd A3
Information Ctr B2
Irish St B2
Irving St A2
King St A1
Kingholm Rd C3
Kirkpatrick Ct C2
Laurieknowe B1
Leafield Rd B3
Library A2
Lochfield Rd A1
Loreburn Pk A3
Loreburn St A2
Loreburne Shopping Centre B2
Lover's Walk A2
Martin Ave B3
Maryholm Dr A1
Mausoleum B3
Maxwell St B1
McKie Ave B3
Mews La A2
Mill Green B2
Mill Rd B1
Moat Rd C2
Moffat Rd A3
Mountainhall Pk C3
Nelson St B1
New Abbey Rd B1/C1
New Bridge B1
Newall Terr A2
Nith Ave A2
Nith Bank C3
Nithbank Hosp C3
Nithside Ave A1
Odeon B2
Old Bridge B1
Palmerston Park (Queen of the South FC) A1
Park Rd C1
Pleasance Ave C1
Police HQ A3
Police Station A2
Portland Dr A1
Post Office A2/B1/B2/B3/B3
Priestlands Dr C1
Primrose St B1
Queen St B3
Queensberry St A2
Rae St A2
Richmond Ave C2
Robert Burns Centre B2
Roberts Cres C1
Robertson Ave C3
Robinson Dr C1
Rosefield Rd C2
Rosemount St B1
Rotchell Park C1
Rotchell Rd B1
Rugby Football Ground C1
Ryedale Rd C2
St Andrews B2
St John the Evangelist A2
St Josephs College B3
St Mary's Industrial Estate A3
St Mary's St A3
St Michael St B2
St Michael's B2
St Michael's Bridge B2
St Michael's Bridge Rd B2
St Michael's Cemetery B3
Shakespeare St B2
Solway Dr C2
Stakeford St A1
Stark Cres C2
Station Rd A3
Steel Ave A1
Sunderries Ave A1
Sunderries Rd A1
Suspension Brae B2
Swimming Pool A1
Terregles St B1
Theatre Royal B2
Troqueer Rd C2
Union St A1
Wallace St B3
Welldale B2
West Riverside Dr C2
White Sands B2

Dundee 334

Adelaide Pl A1
Airlie Pl C1
Albany Terr A1
Albert St A3
Alexander St A2
Ann St A2
Arthurstone Terr A3
Bank St B2
Barrack Rd A1
Barrack St B2
Bell St B2
Blackscroft A3
Blinshall St B1
Brown St B1
Bus Station B3
Caird Hall B2
Camperdown St B3
Candle La B3
Carmichael St A1
City Churches B2
City Quay B3
City Sq B2
Commercial St B2
Constable St A3
Constitution Ct A1
Constitution Cres A1
Constitution St A1/B2
Cotton Rd A3
Courthouse Sq B1
Cowgate A3
Crescent St A3
Crichton St B2
Dens Brae A3
Dens Rd A3
Discovery Point ✦ C2
Douglas St B1
Drummond St A1
Dudhope Castle A1
Dudhope St A2
Dudhope Terr A1
Dundee Station C2
Dundee College A1
Dundee Contemporary Arts ✦ C2
Dundee High School B2
Dura St A3
East Dock St B3
East Whale La B3
East Marketgait B3
Erskine St A3
Euclid Cr B2
Forebank Rd A2
Foundry La A3
Gallagher Retail Park B3
Gellatly St B3
Government Offices C2
Guthrie St B1
Hawkhill B1
Hilltown A2
HMS Unicorn ✦ B3
Howff Cemetery, The B2
Information Ctr B2
King St A3
Kinghorne Rd A1
Ladywell Ave A3
Laurel Bank A2
Law Hill, The ✦ A1
Law Rd A1
Law St A1
Library A2
Little Theatre A2
Lochee Rd B1
Lower Princes St A3
Lyon St A3
McManus Galleries B2
Meadow Side B2
Meadowside St Pauls B2
Mercat Cross ✦ B2
Murraygate B2
Nelson St A2
Nethergate B2/C1
North Marketgait B2
North Lindsay St B2
Old Hawkhill B1
Olympia Leisure Centre C3
Overgate Shopping Centre B2
Park Pl B1
Perth Rd C1
Police Station A2/B1
Post Office B2
Princes St A3
Prospect Pl A2
Reform St B2
Repertory C2
Riverside Dr C2
Roseangle C1
Rosebank St A2
RRS Discovery C2
St Andrew's † C2
St Pauls Episcopal † B3
Science Centre ✦ C2
Seagate B2
Sheriffs Court B1
South George St A2
South Marketgait B3
South Tay St B2
South Ward Rd B2
Steps A2
Tay Road Bridge ✦ C3
Tayside House B2
Trades La B3
Union St B2
Union Terr A1
University Library B2
University of Abertay B2
University of Dundee B1
Upper Constitution St A1
Verdant Works ✦ B1
Victoria Dock B3
Victoria Rd A2
Victoria St A3
West Marketgait B1/B2
Ward Rd B1
Wellgate B2
West Bell St B1
Westfield Pl C1
William St A3
Wishart Arch ✦ A3

Durham 334

Alexander Cr B2
Allergate B2
Archery Rise C1
Assize Courts B3
Back Western Hill A1
Bakehouse La A3
Baths B3
Baths Bridge B3
Boat House B3
Bowling A2
Boyd St C3
Bus Station B2
Castle B2
Castle Chare B2
Cathedral † B2
Church St C3
Clay La C1
Claypath B3
College of St Hild & St Bede B3
County Hall A1
County Hosp B1
Crook Hall ✦ A3
Crossgate B2
Crossgate Peth C1
Darlington Rd C1
Durham Station A2
Durham Light Infantry Mus & Arts Centre A2
Durham School C2
Ellam Ave C1
Elvet Bridge B3
Elvet Court B3
Farnley Hey B1
Ferens Cl A3
Fieldhouse La A1
Flass St B1
Framwelgate A2
Framwelgate Bridge B2
Framwelgate Peth A2
Framwelgate Waterside A2
Frankland La A3
Freeman's Pl A3
Gala & Sacred Journey B3
Geoffrey Ave C1
Gilesgate B3
Grey College C3
Grove St C2
Hallgarth St C3
Hatfield College B3
Hawthorn Terr B1
Heritage Centre B3
HM Prison B3
Information Ctr B3
John St B1
Kingsgate Bridge B3
Laburnum Terr B1
Lawson Terr B1
Leazes Rd B2/B3
Library B2
Margery La B2
Mavin St C3
Millburngate B2
Millburngate Bridge B2
Millburngate Centre B2
Millennium Bridge (foot/cycle) A2
Mus of Archaeology B2
Neville's Cross College C1
Nevilledale Terr B1
New Elvet B3
New Elvet Bridge B3
North Bailey B3
North End A1
North Rd A1/B2
Observatory C1
Old Elvet B3
Oriental Mus C2
Passport Office A2
Percy Terr B1
Pimlico C2
Police Station B3
Post Office A1/B2
Potters Bank C1/C2
Prebends Bridge C2
Prebends Walk C2
Prince Bishops Shopping Centre B3
Princes St A1
Providence Row A3
Quarryheads La C2
Redhills La B1
Redhills Terr B1
Saddler St B3
St Chad's College C3
St Cuthbert's Society C2
St John's College C2
St Margaret's B2
St Mary The Less C2
St Mary's College C2
St Monica Grove B1
St Nicholas' B3
St Oswald's C3
Sidegate A2
Silver St B2
South Bailey C2
South Rd C3
South St B2
Springwell Ave A1
Stockton Rd C3
Students' Rec Centre B3
Sutton St B2
The Avenue B1
The Crescent A1
The Grove A1
The Sands A3
Town Hall B2
Treasury Mus B2
University ✦ B2
University Arts Block B3
University Library C3
University Science Labs C3
Walkergate Centre A3
Wearside Dr A3
Western Hill A1
Wharton Park A2
Whinney Hill C3

Edinburgh 334

Abbey Strand B6
Abbeyhill A6
Abbeyhill Cr B6
Abbeymount A6
Abercromby Pl A3
Adam St C5
Albany La A4
Albany St A4
Albert Memorial ✦ B2
Albyn Pl A2
Alva Pl A6
Alva St B1
Ann St A1
Appleton Tower C4
Archibald Pl C3
Argyle House C3
Assembly Rooms & Musical Hall A3
Atholl Cr B1
Atholl Crescent La C1
Bank St B4
Barony St A4
Beaumont Pl C5
Belford Rd B1
Belgrave Cr A1
Belgrave Crescent La A1
Bell's Brae B1
Blackfriars St B4
Blair St B4
Bread St C2
Bristo Pl C4
Bristo St C4
Brougham St C2
Broughton St A4
Brown St C5
Brunton Terr A6
Buckingham Terr A1
Burial Ground A6
Bus Station A4
Caledonian Cr C1
Caledonian Rd C1
Calton Hill A4
Calton Hill A5
Calton Rd B4
Camera Obscura & Outlook Tower ✦ B3
Candlemaker Row C4
Canning St B2
Canongate B5
Canongate B5
Carlton St A1
Carlton Terr A6
Carlton Terrace La A6
Castle St B2
Castle Terr B2
Castlehill B3
Central Library B4
Chalmers Hosp C3
Chalmers St C3
Chambers St C4
Chapel St C4
Charles St C4
Charlotte Sq B2
Chester St B1
Circus La A2
Circus Pl A2
City Art Centre B4
City Chambers B4
City Observatory A5
Clarendon Cr A1
Clerk St C5
Coates Cr B1
Cockburn St B4
College of Art C3
Comely Bank Ave A1
Comely Bank Row A1
Cornwall St C2
Cowans Cl C5
Cowgate B4
Cranston St B5
Crichton St C4
Croft-An-Righ A6
Cumberland St A2
Dalry Pl C1
Dalry Rd C1
Danube St A1
Darnawy St A2
David Hume Tower C4
Davie St C5
Dean Bridge A1
Dean Gdns A1
Dean Park Cr A1
Dean Park Mews A1
Dean Park St A1
Dean Path B1
Dean St A1
Dean Terr A1
Dewar Pl C1
Dewar Place La C1
Doune Terr A2
Drummond Pl A3
Drummond St C5
Drumsheugh Gdns B1
Dublin Mews A3
Dublin St A4
Dublin Street Lane South A4
Dumbiedykes Rd B5
Dundas St A3
Earl Grey St C2
East Crosscauseway C5
East Market St B4
East Norton Pl A6
East Princes St Gdns B3
Easter Rd A6
Edinburgh (Waverley) Station B4
Edinburgh Castle B3
Edinburgh Dungeon ✦ B4
Edinburgh Festival Theatre C4
Edinburgh International Conference Ctr C2
Elder St A4
Esplanade B3
Eton Terr A1
Eye Pavilion C3
Festival Office B3
Filmhouse C2
Fire Station C2
Floral Clock ✦ B3
Forres St A2
Forth St A4
Fountainbridge C2
Frederick St A3
Freemasons' Hall B3
Fruit Market B4
Gardner's Cr C2
George Heriot's School C3
George IV Bridge B4
George Sq C4
George Sq La C4
George St B3
Georgian House B2
Gladstone's Land B3
Glen St C3
Gloucester La A2
Gloucester Pl A2
Gloucester St A2
Graham St C3
Grassmarket C3
Great King St A3
Great Stuart B1
Greenside La A5
Greenside Row A5
Greyfriars Kirk C4
Grindlay St C2
Grosvenor St C1
Grove St C1
Gullan's Cl B5
Guthrie St B4
Hanover St A3
Hart St A4
Haymarket C1
Haymarket Station C1
Heriot Pl C3
Heriot Row A2
High School Yard B5
High St B4
Hill Pl C5
Hill St A2
Hillside Cr A5
Holyrood Park C6
Holyrood Rd B5
Home St C2
Hope St B2
Horse Wynd B6
Howden St C5
Howe St A2
India Pl A2
India St A2
Infirmary St B4
Information Ctr B4
Jamaica Mews A2
Jeffrey St B4
John Knox's House B4
Johnston Terr C3
Keir St C3
Kerr St A2
King's Stables Rd B2
Lady Lawson St C3
Lady Stair's House B4
Laserquest ✦ C2
Lauriston Gdns C3
Lauriston Park C3
Lauriston Pl C3
Lauriston St C3
Lawnmarket B3
Learmonth Gdns A1
Learmonth Terr A1
Leith St A4
Lennox St A1
Lennox St La A1
Leslie Pl A2
London Rd A5
Lothian Health Board C5
Lothian Rd B2
Lothian St C4
Lower Menz Pl A6
Lynedoch Pl B1
Manor Pl B1
Market St B4
Marshall St C4
Maryfield A6
Maryfield Pl A6
McEwan Hall C4
Medical School C4
Melville St B1
Meuse La B4
Middle Meadow Walk C4
Milton St A6
Montrose Terr A6
Moray House (college) B5
Moray Place A2
Morrison Link C1
Morrison St C1
Mound Pl B3
Mus of Childhood B5
Mus of Edinburgh B5
National Gallery B3
National Library of Scotland B4
National Monument ✦ A5
National Mus of Scotland C4
National Portrait Gallery & Mus of Antiquities A3
Nelson Monument ✦ A5
Nelson St A3
New St B5
Nicolson Sq C4
Nicolson St C4
Niddry St B4
North Bridge B4
North Meadow Walk C3
North Bank St B3
North Castle St A2
North Charlotte St A2
North St Andrew St A4
North St David St A3
North West Circus Pl A2
Northumberland St A3
Odeon C2
Old Royal High School A5
Old Tolbooth Wynd B5
Our Dynamic Earth ✦ B6
Oxford Terr A1
Palace of Holyrood House B6
Palmerston Pl B1
Panmure Pl C3
Parliament House B4
Parliament Sq B4
People's Story, The B5
Playhouse Theatre A4
Pleasance C5
Police Station A4
Ponton St C2
Post Office A3/A4/B5/C1/C2/C4/C5
Potterrow C4
Princes Mall B4
Princes St B3
Queen St A2
Queen Street Gdns A3
Queen's Dr B6/C6
Queensferry Rd A1
Queensferry St B1
Queensferry Street La B2
Radical Rd C6
Randolph Cr B1
Regent Gdns A5
Regent Rd B5
Regent Rd Park A6
Regent Terr A5
Register House A4
Remains of Holyrood Abbey (AD 1128) A6
Richmond La C5
Richmond Pl C5
Rose St B2
Rosemount Bldgs C1
Ross Open Air Theatre B3
Rothesay Pl B1
Rothesay Terr B1
Roxburgh Pl C5
Roxburgh St C5
Royal Bank of Scotland A4
Royal Circus A2
Royal Lyceum C2
Royal Scottish Academy B3
Royal Terr A5
Royal Terrace Gdns A5
Rutland Sq B2
Rutland St B2
St Andrew Sq A3
St Andrew's House A4
St Bernard's Cr A1
St Cecilia's Hall B4
St Colme St A2
St Cuthbert's B2
St Giles' † B4
St James Centre A4
St John St B5
St John's B2
St John's Hill B5
St Leonard's Hill C5
St Leonard's La C5
St Leonard's St C5
St Mary's A4
St Mary's Scottish Episcopal † B1
St Mary's St B5
St Stephen St A2
Salisbury Crags C6
Saunders St A2
Scott Monument ✦ B4
Scottish Arts Council Gallery B2
Scottish Parliament B6
Semple St C2
Shandwick Pl B2
South Bridge B4
South Charlotte St B2
South College St C4
South Learmonth Gdns A1
South St Andrew St A4
South St David St A3
Spittal St C2
Stafford St B1
Student Centre C4
TA Centre C4
Tattoo Office B4
Teviot Pl C4
The Mall B6
The Mound B3
The Royal Mile B5
Thistle St A3
Torphichen Pl C1
Torphichen St C1
Traverse Theatre B2
Tron Sq B4
Tron, The ✦ B4
Union St A4
University C4
University Library C4
Upper Grove Pl C1
Usher Hall C2
Vennel C3
Victoria St B3
Viewcraig Gdns B5
Viewcraig St B5
Walker St B1
Waterloo Pl A4
Waverley Bridge B4
Wemyss Pl A2
West Approach Rd C1
West Crosscauseway C5
West Maitland St C1
West of Nicholson St C4
West Port C3
West Princes Street Gdns B3
West Richmond St C5
West Tollcross C2
White Horse Cl B5
William St B1
Windsor St A5
York La A4
York Pl A4
Young St B2

Exeter 334

Alphington St C1
Athelstan Rd B3
Bampfylde St B2
Barnardo Rd C3
Barnfield Hill B3
Barnfield Rd B2/B3
Barnfield Theatre B2
Bartholomew St East B1
Bartholomew St West B1
Bear St B2
Beaufort Rd C1
Bedford St B2
Belgrave Rd A3
Belmont Rd A3
Blackall Rd A2
Blackboy Rd A3
Bonhay Rd B1
Bull Meadow Rd C2
Bus & Coach Sta B3
Castle St B2
Cecil Rd C1
Cheeke St A3
Church Rd C1
Chute St A3
City Industrial Estate C2
City Wall B1/B2
Civic Centre B2
Clifton Rd B3
Clifton St B3
Clock Tower A1
College Rd B3
Colleton Cr C2
Commercial Rd C1
Coombe St B2
Cowick St C1
Crown Courts B2
Custom House C2
Danes' Rd A2
Denmark Rd B3
Devon County Hall C3
Devonshire Pl A3
Dinham Rd B1
East Grove Rd C3
Edmund St C1
Elmgrove Rd A1
Exe St B1
Exeter Central Station A1
Exeter City Football Ground A3
Exeter College A1
Exeter Picture House B1
Fire Station A1
Fore St B1
Friars Walk C2
Guildhall B2
Guildhall Shopping Centre B2
Harlequins Shopping Centre B1
Haven Rd C2
Heavitree Rd B3
Hele Rd A1
High St B2
HM Prison A2
Holloway St C2
Hoopern St A2
Horseguards A2
Howell Rd A1
Information Ctr B3
Iron Bridge B1
Isca Rd C1
Jesmond Rd A3
King William St A2
King St B1
Larkbeare Rd C2
Leisure Centre C1
Library B2
Longbrook St A2
Longbrook Terr A2
Lower North St B1
Lucky La C2
Lyndhurst Rd C3
Magdalen Rd B3
Magdalen St B2
Magistrates & Crown Courts A2
Market B2
Market St B2
Marlborough Rd C3
Mary Arches St B1
Matford Ave C3
Matford La C3
Matford Rd C3
May St A3
Mol's Coffee House B2
New Bridge St B1
New North Rd A1/A2
North St B1
Northernhay St B1
Norwood Ave C3
Odeon A3
Okehampton St C1
Old Mill Cl C2
Old Tiverton Rd A3
Oxford Rd A3
Paris St B2
Parr St A3
Paul St B1
Pennsylvania Rd A2
Police HQ B3
Portland Street A3
Post Office A3/B1/B3/C1
Powderham Cr A3
Preston St B1
Princesshay Shopping Centre B2
Queen St A1
Queens Rd C1
Queen's Terr A1
Radford Rd C2
Richmond Rd A1
Roberts Rd C2
Rougemont Castle A2
Rougemont House ✦ B2
Royal Albert Memorial Mus B2
St David's Hill A1
St James' Park Station A3
St James' Rd A3
St Leonard's Rd C3
St Lukes College B3
St Mary Steps C1
St Nicholas Priory B1
St Peter's Cathedral † B2
St Thomas Station C1
Sandford Walk B3
School for the Deaf C2
School Rd C1
Sidwell St A2
Smythen St B1
South St B2
Southernhay East B2
Southernhay West B2
Spacex Gallery B1
Spicer Rd B3
Sports Centre A3
Summerland St A3
Swimming Pool B3
Sydney Rd C1
Tan La C2
The Quay C2
Thornton Hill A2
Topsham Rd C3
Tucker's Hall B1
Tudor St B1
Velwell Rd A1
Verney St A3
Water La C1/C2
Weirfield Rd C2
Well St A3
West Ave A2
West Grove Rd C3
Western Way A3/B1/B2
Wonford Rd B3/C3
York Rd A2

350 Fort William • Glasgow • Gloucester • Grimsby • Hanley • Harrogate

Fort William 335

Abrach Rd . . . A3
Achintore Rd . . . C1
Alma Rd . . . B2
Am Breun Chamas . . . A2
Ambulance Station . . . A3
An Aird . . . A2
Argyll Rd . . . C1
Argyll Terr . . . C1
Bank St . . . B2
Belford Hosp . . . B2
Belford Rd . . . B2/B3
Black Parks . . . A3
Braemore Pl . . . C2
Bruce Pl . . . C2
Bus Station . . . B2
Camanachd Cr . . . A3/B2
Cameron Rd . . . C1
Cameron Sq . . . B1
Carmichael Way . . . A2
Claggan Rd . . . B3
Connochie Rd . . . C1
Cow Hill . . . C3
Creag Dhubh . . . A2
Croft Rd . . . B3
Douglas Pl . . . B2
Dudley Rd . . . B2
Dumbarton Rd . . . C1
Earl of Inverness Rd . . . A3
Fassifern Rd . . . B1
Fort William . . . B2
Fort William (Remains) . . . B2
Glasdrum Rd . . . C1
Glen Nevis Pl . . . B3
Gordon Sq . . . B1
Grange Rd . . . C1
Heather Croft Rd . . . C1
Henderson Row . . . C2
High St . . . B1
Highland Visitor Centre . . . B3
Hill Rd . . . B2
Hospital Belhaven Annexe . . . B3
Information Ctr . . . A3
Inverlochy Ct . . . A3
Kennedy Rd . . . B2/C2
Library . . . B2
Linnhe Rd . . . B1
Lochaber College . . . A2
Lochaber Leisure Centre . . . B3
Lochiel Rd . . . A3
Lochy Rd . . . A3
Lundavra Cres . . . C1
Lundavra Rd . . . C1
Lundy Rd . . . A3
Mamore Cr . . . B2
Mary St . . . B2
Middle St . . . B1
Montrose Ave . . . A3
Moray Pl . . . C1
Morven Pl . . . C2
Moss Rd . . . B2
Nairn Cres . . . C1
Nevis Bridge . . . B3
Nevis Rd . . . A3
Nevis Sports Centre . . . A2
Nevis Terr . . . B2
North Rd . . . B3
Obelisk . . . B2
Ocean Frontier Underwater Centre . A2
Parade Rd . . . B2
Police Station . . . A3/C1
Post Office . . . A3/B2
Ross Pl . . . C1
St Andrews . . . B2
Shaw Pl . . . B2
Station Brae . . . B1
Studio . . . B1
Treig Rd . . . A3
Union Rd . . . C1
Victoria Rd . . . B2
Wades Rd . . . A3
West Highland . . . B2
Young Pl . . . B2

Glasgow 335

Admiral St . . . C2
Albert Bridge . . . C5
Albion St . . . B5
Anderston . . . B3
Anderston Centre . . . B3
Anderston Quay . . . B3
Arches . . . B4
Argyle St . . . A1/A2/B3/B4/B5
Argyle Street . . . B5
Argyll Arcade . . . B5
Arlington St . . . A3
Art Gallery & Mus . . . A1
Arts Centre . . . B3
Ashley St . . . A3
Bain St . . . C6
Baird St . . . A6
Baliol St . . . A3
Ballater St . . . C5
Barras, The (Market) . C6
Bath St . . . A3
BBC Scotland/SMG . . B1
Bell St . . . C6
Bell's Bridge . . . B1
Bentinck St . . . A2
Berkeley St . . . A3
Bishop La . . . B3
Black St . . . A6
Blackburn St . . . C2
Blackfriars St . . . B6
Blantyre St . . . A1
Blythswood Sq . . . A4
Blythswood St . . . B4
Bothwell St . . . B4
Brand St . . . C1
Breadalbane St . . . A2
Bridge St . . . C4
Bridge St (Metro Station) . . . C4
Bridgegate . . . C5
Briggait . . . C5
Broomhill Park . . . A6
Broomielaw . . . B4
Broomielaw Quay Gdns . . . B3
Brown St . . . B4
Brunswick St . . . B5
Buccleuch St . . . A3
Buchanan Bus Station . A5
Buchanan Galleries . A5
Buchanan St . . . B5
Buchanan St (Metro Station) . . . B5
Cadogan St . . . B4
Caledonian University . A5
Calgary St . . . A5
Cambridge St . . . A4
Canal St . . . A5
Candleriggs . . . B5
Carlton Pl . . . C4
Carnarvon St . . . A3
Carnoustie St . . . C3
Carrick St . . . B4
Castle St . . . B6
Cathedral Sq . . . B6
Cathedral St . . . B5
Central College of Commerce . . . B5
Centre for Contemporary Arts . A4
Centre St . . . C4
Cessnock (Metro Station) . . . C1
Cessnock St . . . C1
Charing Cross . . . A3
Charlotte St . . . C6
Cheapside St . . . B3
Citizens' Theatre . . . C5
City Chambers Complex . . . B5
City Halls . . . B5
Clairmont Gdns . . . A2
Claremont St . . . A2
Claremont Terr . . . A2
Claythorne St . . . C6
Cleveland St . . . A3
Clifford La . . . C1
Clifford St . . . C1
Clifton Pl . . . A2
Clifton St . . . A2
Clutha St . . . C1
Clyde Arc . . . B2
Clyde Auditorium . . . B2
Clyde Pl . . . C4
Clyde Place Quay . . . C4
Clyde St . . . C5
Clyde Walkway . . . C3
Clydeside Expressway . B2
Coburg St . . . C4
Cochrane St . . . B5
College of Nautical Studies . . . C5
College St . . . B6
Collins St . . . B6
Commerce St . . . C4
Cook St . . . C4
Cornwall St . . . C2
Couper St . . . A5
Cowcaddens (Metro Station) . . . A4
Cowcaddens Rd . . . A4
Crimea St . . . B3
Custom House . . . C4
Custom House Quay Gdns . . . C4
Dalhousie St . . . A4
Dental Hosp . . . A4
Derby St . . . A2
Dobbie's Loan . . . A4/A5
Dobbie's Loan Pl . . . A5
Dorset St . . . A3
Douglas St . . . B4
Doulton Fountain . . . C6
Dover St . . . A2
Drury St . . . B4
Drygate . . . B6
Duke St . . . B6
Dunaskin St . . . A1
Dunblane St . . . A4
Dundas St . . . B5
Dunlop St . . . C5
East Campbell St . . . C6
Eastvale Pl . . . A1
Eglinton St . . . C4
Elderslie St . . . A3
Elliot St . . . B2
Elmbank St . . . A3
Esmond St . . . A1
Exhibition Centre . . . B2
Exhibition Way . . . B2
Eye Infirmary . . . A2
Festival Park . . . C1
Film Theatre . . . A4
Finnieston Quay . . . B2
Finnieston Sq . . . B2
Finnieston St . . . B2
Fitzroy Pl . . . A2
Florence St . . . C5
Fox St . . . C5
Gallowgate . . . C6
Garnet St . . . A3
Garnethill St . . . A4
Garscube Rd . . . A4
George Sq . . . B5
George St . . . B5
George V Bridge . . . C4
Gilbert St . . . A1
Glasgow Bridge . . . C4
Glasgow Cathedral . . . B6
Glasgow Central . . . B4
Glasgow Green . . . C6
Glasgow Metropolitan College . . . B5/C5
Glasgow Science Centre . . . B1
Glasgow Science Centre Footbridge . . . B1
Glassford St . . . B5
Glebe St . . . A6
Gloucester St . . . C3
Gorbals Cross . . . C5
Gorbals St . . . C5
Gordon St . . . B4
Govan Rd . . . B1/C1/C2
Grace St . . . B3
Grafton Pl . . . A5
Grant St . . . A3
Granville St . . . A3
Gray St . . . A2
Greendyke St . . . C6
Harley St . . . C1
Harvie St . . . C1
Haugh Rd . . . A1
Heliport . . . B1
Henry Wood Hall . . . A2
High Court . . . C5
High St . . . B6
High Street . . . B6
Hill St . . . A3
Holland St . . . A3
Holm St . . . B4
Hope St . . . A5
Houldsworth St . . . B2
Houston Pl . . . C3
Houston St . . . C3
Howard St . . . C5
Hunter St . . . C6
Hutcheson St . . . B5
Hutchesons Hall . . . B5
Hydepark St . . . B3
Imax Cinema . . . B1
India St . . . A3
Information Ctr . . . B5
Ingram St . . . B5
Jamaica St . . . B4
James Watt St . . . B4
John Knox St . . . B6
John St . . . B5
Kelvin Hall . . . A1
Kelvin Statue . . . A2
Kelvin Way . . . A2
Kelvingrove Park . . . A2
Kelvingrove St . . . A2
Kelvinhaugh St . . . A1
Kennedy St . . . A6
Kent Rd . . . A2
Killermont St . . . A5
King St . . . B5
King's . . . A3
Kingston Bridge . . . C3
Kingston St . . . C4
Kinning Park (Metro Station) . . . C2
Kinning St . . . C3
Kyle St . . . A5
Laidlaw St . . . C3
Lancefield Quay . . . B2
Lancefield St . . . B3
Langshot St . . . C1
Lendel Pl . . . C1
Lighthouse . . . B4
Lister St . . . A6
Little St . . . B3
London Rd . . . C6
Lorne St . . . C1
Lower Harbour . . . B1
Lumsden St . . . A1
Lymburn St . . . A1
Lyndoch Cr . . . A3
Lynedoch Pl . . . A3
Lynedoch St . . . A3
Maclellan St . . . C1
Mair St . . . C2
Maitland St . . . A4
Mavisbank Gdns . . . C2
Mcalpine St . . . B3
Mcaslin St . . . A6
McLean Sq . . . C2
McLellan Gallery . . . A4
McPhater St . . . A4
Merchants' House . . . B5
Middlesex St . . . C2
Middleton St . . . C1
Midland St . . . B4
Miller St . . . B5
Millroad St . . . C6
Milnpark St . . . C2
Milton St . . . A4
Minerva St . . . B2
Mitchell Library . . . A3
Mitchell St West . . . B4
Mitchell Theatre . . . A3
Modern Art Gallery . . . B5
Moir St . . . C6
Molendinar St . . . C6
Moncur St . . . C6
Montieth Row . . . C6
Montrose St . . . B5
Morrison St . . . C3
Mosque . . . C5
Mus of Religious Life . . . B6
Nairn St . . . A1
Nelson Mandela Sq . . . B5
Nelson St . . . C4
Nelson's Monument . . . C6
New City Rd . . . A4
Newton St . . . A3
Newton Pl . . . A3
Nicholson St . . . C4
Nile St . . . B5
Norfolk Court . . . C4
Norfolk St . . . C4
North Frederick St . . . B5
North Hanover St . . . B5
North Portland St . . . B6
North St . . . A3
North Wallace St . . . A5
Odeon . . . C3
Old Dumbarton Rd . . . A1
Osborne St . . . B5/C5
Oswald St . . . B4
Overnewton St . . . A1
Oxford St . . . C4
Pacific Dr . . . B1
Paisley Rd . . . C3
Paisley Rd West . . . C1
Park Circus . . . A2
Park Gdns . . . A2
Park St South . . . A2
Park Terr . . . A2
Parkgrove Terr . . . A2
Parnie St . . . C5
Parson St . . . A6
Partick Bridge . . . A1
Passport Office . . . A5
Paterson St . . . C3
Pavilion Theatre . . . A4
Pembroke St . . . A3
People's Palace . . . C6
Pinkston Rd . . . A6
Piping Centre, The National . . . A5
Pitt St . . . A4/B4
Plantation Park . . . C1
Plantation Quay . . . B1
Police Station . . . A4/A6/B5
Port Dundas Rd . . . A5
Port St . . . B2
Portman St . . . C2
Prince's Dock . . . B1
Princes Sq . . . B5
Provand's Lordship . . . B6
Queen St . . . B5
Queen Street . . . B5
Regimental Mus . . . A3
Renfrew St . . . A3/A4
Renton St . . . A5
Richmond St . . . B5
Robertson St . . . B4
Rose St . . . A4
Rottenrow . . . B5
Royal Concert Hall . . . A5
Royal Cr . . . A2
Royal Exchange Sq . . . B5
Royal Hospital For Sick Children . . . A1
Royal Infirmary . . . B6
Royal Scottish Academy of Music & Drama . . . A4
Royal Terr . . . A2
Rutland Cr . . . C2
St Kent St . . . C6
St Andrew's (RC) . . . C5
St Andrew's . . . C6
St Andrew's St . . . C5
St Enoch (Metro Station) . . . B5
St Enoch Shopping Centre . . . B5
St Enoch Sq . . . B4
St George's Rd . . . A3
St James Rd . . . B6
St Mungo Ave . . . A5/A6
St Mungo Pl . . . A6
St Vincent Cr . . . A2
St Vincent Pl . . . B5
St Vincent St . . . B3/B4
St Vincent Street Church . . . B4
St Vincent Terr . . . B3
Saltmarket . . . C5
Sandyford Pl . . . A3
Sauchiehall St . . . A2/A4
School of Art . . . A4
Scotland St . . . C2/C3
Scott St . . . A4
Scottish Exhibition & Conference Centre . . B1
Seaward St . . . C2
Shaftesbury St . . . B3
Sheriff Court . . . C5
Shields Rd (Metro Station) . . . C3
Shuttle St . . . B6
Somerset Pl . . . A2
South Portland St . . . C4
Springburn Rd . . . A6
Springfield Quay . . . C3
Stanley St . . . C2
Stevenson St . . . C6
Stewart St . . . A4
Stirling Rd . . . B6
Stirling's Library . . . B5
Stobcross Quay . . . B1
Stobcross Rd . . . B1
Stock Exchange . . . B5
Stockwell Pl . . . C5
Stockwell St . . . B5
Stow College . . . A4
Strathclyde University B6
Sussex St . . . C2
Synagogues . . . A3/C4
Tall Ship . . . B1
Taylor Pl . . . A6
Tenement House . . . A3
Teviot St . . . A1
Theatre Royal . . . A4
Tolbooth Steeple & Mercat Cross . . . C6
Tower St . . . C2
Trades House . . . B5
Tradeston St . . . C4
Transport Mus . . . A1
Tron Steeple & Theatre . . . C5
Trongate . . . B5
Tunnel St . . . B2
Turnbull St . . . C5
UGC . . . A5
Union St . . . B4
Victoria Bridge . . . C5
Virginia St . . . B5
West Greenhill Pl . . . B2
West Regent St . . . A4
Wallace St . . . C3
Walls St . . . B6
Walmer Cr . . . C1
Warrock St . . . B3
Washington St . . . B3
Waterloo St . . . B4
Watson St . . . B6
Watt St . . . C3
Wellington St . . . B4
West Campbell St . . . B4
West George St . . . B4
West Graham St . . . A4
West Regent St . . . B4
West St . . . C4
West St (Metro Station) . . . C4
Westminster Terr . . . A2
Whitehall St . . . B3
Wilson St . . . B5
Woodlands Gate . . . A3
Woodlands Rd . . . A3
Woodlands Terr . . . A2
Woodside Cr . . . A3
Woodside Pl . . . A3
Woodside Terr . . . A3
York St . . . B4
Yorkhill Pde . . . A1
Yorkhill St . . . A1

Gloucester 335

Albion St . . . C1
Alexandra Rd . . . B3
Alfred St . . . C3
All Saints Rd . . . C2
Alvin St . . . B2
Arthur St . . . C2
Baker St . . . C1
Barton St . . . C2
Blackfriars . . . B1
Blenheim Rd . . . C2
Bristol Rd . . . C1
Brunswick Rd . . . C2
Bruton Way . . . B2
Bus Station . . . B2
Cattle Market . . . A1
City Council Offices . . B1
City Mus, Art Gall & Library . . . B2
Clarence St . . . B2
College of Art . . . C2
Commercial Rd . . . B1
Cromwell St . . . C2
Deans Way . . . A2
Denmark Rd . . . A3
Derby Rd . . . C3
Docks . . . C1
Eastgate St . . . B2
Edwy Pde . . . A2
Estcourt Cl . . . A3
Estcourt Rd . . . A3
Falkner St . . . C2
Folk Mus . . . B1
GL1 Leisure Centre . . . C2
Gloucester Cathedral . . . B1/C1
Gloucester Station . . . B2
Gloucestershire Royal Hospital (A & E) . . . B3
Goodyere St . . . C2
Gouda Way . . . A1
Great Western Rd . . . B3
Guildhall . . . B2
Heathville Rd . . . A3
Henry Rd . . . B3
Henry St . . . B2
High Orchard St . . . C1
Hinton Rd . . . A2
India Rd . . . C3
Information Ctr . . . B1
Jersey Rd . . . C3
King's . . . C2
King's Sq . . . B2
Kingsholm Rd . . . A2
Kingsholm Rugby Football Ground . . . A2
Lansdown Rd . . . A3
Library . . . C2
Llanthony Rd . . . C1
London Rd . . . B3
Longsmith St . . . B1
Malvern Rd . . . A3
Market Pde . . . B2
Merchants Rd . . . C1
Mercia Rd . . . A1
Metz Way . . . C3
Midland Rd . . . C2
Millbrook St . . . C3
Market . . . B2
Montpellier . . . C1
Napier St . . . C3
National Waterways . . . C1
Nettleton Rd . . . C2
New Inn . . . B2
New Olympus . . . C3
North Rd . . . A3
Northgate St . . . B2
Oxford Rd . . . A2
Oxford St . . . B2
Park & Ride Gloucester . . . A1
Park Rd . . . C2
Park St . . . B2
Parliament St . . . C1
Pitt St . . . B1
Police Station . . . B1
Post Office . . . B2
Quay St . . . B1
Recreation Gd . . . A1/A2
Regent St . . . C2
Robert Raikes House . . . B1
Royal Oak Rd . . . B1
Russell St . . . B2
Ryecroft St . . . C2
St Aldate St . . . B2
St Ann Way . . . C1
St Catherine St . . . A2
St Mark St . . . A2
St Mary De Crypt . . . B1
St Mary De Lode . . . B1
St Nicholas's . . . B1
St Oswald's Rd . . . A1
St Oswald's Trading Estate . . . A1
St Peter's . . . B2
Seabroke Rd . . . A3
Sebert St . . . A2
Severn Rd . . . C1
Sherborne St . . . B2
Shire Hall . . . B1
Sidney St . . . C3
Soldiers of Gloucestershire . . . B1
Southgate St . . . B1/C1
Spa Field . . . C1
Spa Rd . . . C1
Sports Ground . . . A2/B2
Station Rd . . . B2
Stratton Rd . . . C3
Stroud Rd . . . C1
Superstore . . . A1
Swan Rd . . . A2
Technical College . . . C1
The Mall . . . B1
The Park . . . C2
The Quay . . . B1
Trier Way . . . C1/C2
Union St . . . A2
Vauxhall Rd . . . C3
Victoria St . . . C2
Wellington St . . . C2
Westgate St . . . B1
Widden St . . . C2
Worcester St . . . B2

Grimsby 335

Abbey Drive East . . . C2
Abbey Drive West . . . C2
Abbey Park Rd . . . C2
Abbey Rd . . . C2
Abbey Walk . . . C2
Abbeygate Shopping Centre . . . C2
Abbotsway . . . C2
Adam Smith St . . . A1/A2
Ainslie St . . . C2
Albert St . . . A3
Alexandra Dock . . . A2/B2
Alexandra Retail Park . A2
Alexandra Rd . . . A2/B2
Annesley St . . . A2
Armstrong St . . . A1
Arthur St . . . B1
Augusta St . . . C1
Bargate . . . C1
Beeson St . . . A1
Bethlehem St . . . C2
Bodiam Way . . . B3
Bradley St . . . B3
Brighowgate . . . C1/C2
Bus Station . . . B2/C2
Canterbury Dr . . . C1
Cartergate . . . B1/C1
Catherine St . . . C3
Caxton . . . A3
Chantry La . . . B1
Charlton St . . . A1
Church La . . . C2
Church St . . . A3
Cleethorpe Rd . . . A3
College . . . A3
College St . . . C1
Compton Dr . . . C1
Corporation Bridge . . . A2
Corporation Rd . . . A1
Court . . . B3
Crescent St . . . B1
Deansgate . . . C1
Doughty Rd . . . C2
Dover St . . . B1
Duchess St . . . C2
Dudley St . . . C1
Duke of York Gardens . B1
Duncombe St . . . B3
Earl La . . . B1
East Marsh St . . . B3
East St . . . B2
Eastgate . . . B3
Eastside Rd . . . A3
Eaton Ct . . . C1
Eleanor St . . . B3
Ellis Way . . . B3
Fisherman's Chapel . . A3
Fisherman's Wharf . . . B2
Fishing Heritage Centre . . . B2
Flour Sq . . . A3
Frederick St . . . B1
Frederick Ward Way . . B2
Freeman St . . . A3/B3
Freshney Dr . . . B1
Freshney Pl . . . B2
Garden St . . . C2
Garibaldi St . . . A3
Garth La . . . B2
Grime St . . . B3
Grimsby Docks Station . . . A3
Grimsby Town Station . . . C2
Hainton Ave . . . C3
Har Way . . . B3
Hare St . . . C3
Harrison St . . . B1
Haven Ave . . . B1
Hay Croft Ave . . . B1
Hay Croft St . . . B1
Heneage Rd . . . B3/C3
Henry St . . . B1
Holme St . . . B3
Hume St . . . C1
James St . . . B1
Joseph St . . . B1
Kent St . . . A3
King Edward St . . . A3
Lambert Rd . . . C2
Library . . . B2
Lime St . . . B1
Lister St . . . B1
Littlefield La . . . C1
Lockhill . . . A3
Lord St . . . B1
Ludford St . . . C3
Macaulay St . . . B1
Mallard Mews . . . C3
Manor Ave . . . C2
Market . . . A3
Market Hall . . . B2
Market St . . . B3
Moss Rd . . . C2
Nelson St . . . A3
New St . . . B2
Osbourne St . . . B2
Pasture St . . . B3
Peaks Parkway . . . C3
Pelham Rd . . . C1
Police Station . . . A3
Post Office . . . B1/B2/C2
PS Lincoln Castle . . . B2
Pyewipe Rd . . . A1
Railway Pl . . . A3
Railway St . . . A3
Recreation Ground . . . C2
Rendel St . . . A2
Retail Park . . . B3
Richard St . . . B1
Ripon St . . . B1
Robinson St East . . . B3
Royal St . . . A3
St Hilda's Ave . . . C1
St James . . . C2
Sheepfold St . . . B3/C3
Sixhills St . . . C3
South Park . . . B2
Spring St . . . A3
Superstore . . . B3
Tasburgh St . . . C3
Tennyson St . . . B2
The Close . . . C1
Thesiger St . . . A3
Time Trap . . . C2
Town Hall . . . B2
Veal St . . . B1
Victoria Retail Park . . A3
Victoria St North . . . A2
Victoria St South . . . B2
Victoria St West . . . B2
Watkin St . . . A1
Welholme Ave . . . C2
Welholme Rd . . . C3
Wellington St . . . B3
Wellowgate . . . C2
Werneth Rd . . . B3
West Coates Rd . . . A1
Westgate . . . A2
Westminster Dr . . . C1
Willingham St . . . C3
Wintringham Rd . . . C2
Wood St . . . B3
Yarborough Dr . . . B1
Yarborough Hotel . . . C2

Hanley 335

Acton St . . . A3
Albion St . . . B2
Argyle St . . . C1
Ashbourne Gr . . . A2
Avoca St . . . A3
Baskerville Rd . . . B3
Bedford Rd . . . C1
Bedford St . . . C1
Bethesda St . . . B2
Bexley St . . . A2
Birches Head Rd . . . A3
Botteslow St . . . C3
Boundary St . . . A2
Broad St . . . C2
Broom St . . . A3
Bryan St . . . A2
Bucknall New Rd . . . B3
Bucknall Old Rd . . . B3
Bus Station . . . B3
Cannon St . . . C2
Castlefield St . . . C1
Hanley Park . . . C2
Cavendish St . . . B1
Central Forest Pk . . . A2
Charles St . . . B3
Cheapside . . . B2
Chell St . . . A3
Clarke St . . . C1
Cleveland Rd . . . C2
Clifford St . . . C3
Clough St . . . B2
Clyde St . . . C1
College Rd . . . C2
Cooper St . . . C2
Corbridge Rd . . . A1
Cutts St . . . C2
Davis St . . . C1
Denbigh St . . . A1
Derby St . . . C3
Dilke St . . . A3
Dundas St . . . A3
Dundee Rd . . . C1
Dyke St . . . B3
Eastwood Rd . . . C3
Eaton St . . . A3
Etruria Park . . . B1
Etruria Rd . . . B1
Etruria Vale Rd . . . C1
Festing St . . . A3
Fire Station . . . C2
Foundry St . . . B2
Franklyn St . . . C3
Garnet St . . . B1
Garth St . . . B3
George St . . . A3
Gilman St . . . B3
Glass St . . . B3
Goodson St . . . B3
Greyhound Way . . . A1
Grove Pl . . . C1
Hampton St . . . C3
Hanley Park . . . C2
Harding Rd . . . C2
Hassall St . . . B3
Havelock Pl . . . C1
Hazlehurst St . . . C3
Hinde St . . . C2
Hope St . . . B2
Houghton St . . . C2
Hulton St . . . A3
Hypermarket . . . A1/B2
Information Ctr . . . B3
Jasper St . . . C2
Jervis St . . . A3
John Bright St . . . A3
John St . . . B2
Keelings Rd . . . A3
Kimberley Rd . . . C1
Ladysmith Rd . . . C1
Lawrence St . . . C2
Leek Rd . . . C3
Library . . . C2
Lichfield St . . . C3
Linfield Rd . . . B3
Loftus St . . . A2
Lower Bedford St . . . C1
Lower Bryan St . . . A2
Lower Mayer St . . . A3
Lowther St . . . A1
Magistrates Court . . . C2
Malham St . . . A2
Marsh St . . . B2
Matlock St . . . C3
Mayer St . . . A3
Milton St . . . C1
Mitchell Memorial Theatre . . . B2
Morley St . . . B2
Moston St . . . A3
Mount Pleasant . . . C1
Mulgrave St . . . A1
Mynors St . . . B3
Nelson Pl . . . B3
New Century St . . . B1
New Forest Industrial Estate . . . A3
Octagon, The Shopping Park . . . B1
Ogden Rd . . . C3
Old Hall St . . . B3
Old Town Rd . . . A3
Pall Mall . . . B2
Palmerston St . . . C3
Park and Ride . . . C2
Parker St . . . B2
Pavilion Dr . . . A1
Pelham St . . . C3
Percy St . . . B2
Piccadilly . . . B2
Picton St . . . B3
Plough St . . . A3
Police Station . . . C2
Portland St . . . A1
Post Office . . . A3/B3/C3
Potteries Mus & Art Gallery . . . B2
Potteries Shopping Centre . . . B2
Potteries Way . . . C2
Powell St . . . A1
Pretoria Rd . . . C1
Quadrant Rd . . . B2
Ranelagh St . . . C2
Raymond St . . . C2
Rectory Rd . . . C1
Regent Rd . . . C2
Regent Theatre . . . B2
Richmond Terr . . . C2
Ridgehouse Dr . . . A1
Robson St . . . C2
St Ann St . . . B3
St Luke St . . . B3
Sampson St . . . B2
Shaw St . . . A1
Sheaf St . . . C2
Shearer St . . . C1
Shelton New Rd . . . C1
Shirley Rd . . . C2
Slippery La . . . B2
Snow Hill . . . C2
Sports Stadium . . . A1
Spur St . . . C3
Stafford St . . . B2
Statham St . . . B2
Stubbs La . . . C3
Sun St . . . C1
Talbot St . . . C3
The Parkway . . . C2
Town Hall . . . B2
Town Rd . . . A3
Trinity St . . . B2
Union St . . . A2
Upper Hillchurch St . . A3
Upper Huntbach St . . . B3
Victoria Hall Theatre . B3
Warner St . . . C2
Warwick St . . . C1
Waterloo Rd . . . A1
Waterloo St . . . B3
Well St . . . B3
Wellesley St . . . C2
Wellington Rd . . . B3
Wellington St . . . B3
Whitehaven Dr . . . A2
Whitmore St . . . C1
Windermere St . . . A1
Woodall St . . . A1
Yates St . . . C2
York St . . . A2

Harrogate 335

Albert St . . . C2
Alexandra Rd . . . B2
Arthington Ave . . . B2
Ashfield Rd . . . A2
Back Cheltenham Mount . . . B2
Beech Grove . . . C1
Belmont Rd . . . C1
Bilton Dr . . . A2
Bower Rd . . . B2
Bower St . . . B2
Bus Station . . . B2
Cambridge Rd . . . B2
Cambridge St . . . B2
Cemetery . . . A2
Chatsworth Pl . . . A2
Chatsworth Grove . . . A2
Chatsworth Rd . . . A2
Chelmsford Rd . . . B3
Cheltenham Cr . . . B2
Cheltenham Mt . . . B2
Cheltenham Pde . . . B2
Christ Church . . . B3
Christ Church Oval . . . B3
Chudleigh Rd . . . B3
Clarence Dr . . . B1
Claro Rd . . . A3
Claro Way . . . A3
Coach Park . . . B2
Coach Rd . . . B3
Cold Bath Rd . . . C1
Commercial St . . . B2
Coppice Ave . . . A1
Coppice Dr . . . A1
Coppice Gate . . . A1
Cornwall Rd . . . B1
Council Offices . . . B1
Court . . . C3
Crescent Gdns . . . B1
Crescent Rd . . . B1
Dawson Terr . . . A2
Devonshire Pl . . . B3
Diamond Mews . . . C1
Dixon Rd . . . A2
Dixon Terr . . . A2
Dragon Ave . . . B3
Dragon Parade . . . B2
Dragon Rd . . . B2
Duchy Rd . . . B1
East Parade . . . B2
East Park Rd . . . C3
Esplanade . . . B1
Fire Station . . . A2
Franklin Mount . . . A2
Franklin Rd . . . B2
Franklin Square . . . A2
Glebe Rd . . . C1
Grove Park Ct . . . A3
Grove Park Terr . . . A3
Grove Rd . . . A2
Hampswaite Rd . . . A1
Harcourt Dr . . . B3
Harcourt Rd . . . B3
Harrogate . . . B2
Harrogate International Centre . . . B1
Harrogate Ladies College . . . B1
Harrogate Theatre . . . B2
Heywood Rd . . . C1
Hollins Cr . . . A1
Hollins Mews . . . A1
Hollins Rd . . . A1
Homestead Rd . . . C3
Hydro Leisure Centre, The . . . A1
Information Ctr . . . B1
James St . . . B2
Jenny Field Dr . . . A1
John St . . . B2
Kent Dr . . . A1
Kent Rd . . . A1
Kings Rd . . . A2
Kingsway . . . B3
Kingsway Dr . . . B3
Lancaster Rd . . . C1
Leeds Rd . . . C2
Lime Grove . . . B3
Lime St . . . A3
Mayfield Grove . . . B2
Mayfield Pl . . . A2
Mercer . . . B1
Montpellier Hill . . . B1
Mornington Cr . . . A3
Mornington Terr . . . B3
Mowbray Sq . . . B3
North Park Rd . . . B3
Nydd Vale Rd . . . B2
Oakdale Ave . . . A1
Oatlands Dr . . . C3
Odeon . . . B2
Osborne Rd . . . A2
Otley Rd . . . C2
Oxford St . . . B2
Park Chase . . . B3
Park Parade . . . B3
Park View . . . B2
Parliament St . . . B1
Police Station . . . B3
Post Office . . . B2/C1
Providence Terr . . . A2
Queen Parade . . . C3
Queen's Rd . . . C1
Raglan St . . . C2
Regent Ave . . . A3
Regent Grove . . . A3
Regent Parade . . . A3
Regent St . . . A3
Regent Terr . . . A3
Rippon Rd . . . A1
Robert St . . . C2
Royal Baths & Turkish Baths . . . B1
Royal Pump Room . . . B1
St Luke's Mount . . . A2
St Mary's Ave . . . C1
St Mary's Walk . . . C1
Scargill Rd . . . A1
Skipton Rd . . . A3
Skipton St . . . A2
Slingsby Walk . . . C3
South Park Rd . . . C2
Spring Grove . . . A1
Springfield Ave . . . B1
Station Ave . . . B2
Station Parade . . . B2
Strawberry Dale . . . B2
Stray Rein . . . C3
Studley Rd . . . A2
Superstore . . . B2
Swan Rd . . . B1
The Parade . . . B2
The Stray . . . C2/C3
Tower St . . . C2

Trinity Rd C2
Union St B2
Valley Dr C1
Valley Gardens C1
Valley Mount C1
Victoria Ave C2
Victoria Rd C1
Victoria Shopping Centre B2
Waterloo St A2
West Park C2
West Park St C2
Wood View A1
Woodfield Ave A3
Woodfield Dr A3
Woodfield Grove A3
Woodfield Rd A3
Woodfield Square A3
Woodside B3
York Pl C3
York Rd B1

Holyhead *Caergybi* 335

Armenia St A2
Arthur St C2
Beach Rd A1
Boston St B2
Bowling Green C3
Bryn Erw Rd C3
Bryn Glas Cl C3
Bryn Glas Rd C3
Bryn Gwyn Rd C1
Bryn Marchog A1
Bryn Mor Terr A2
Bryngoleu Ave A1
Cae Braenar C3
Cambria St B1
Captain Skinner's Obelisk ✦ B2
Cecil St C2
Cemetery C1/C2
Cleveland Ave C2
Coastguard Lookout A2
Court B2
Customs House A3
Cybi Pl A2
Cyttir Rd C3
Edmund St B1
Empire B2
Ferry Terminals B2
Ffordd Beibio B3
Ffordd Feurig C3
Ffordd Hirnos C3
Ffordd Jasper C3
Ffordd Tudur B3
Fire Station C2
Garreglwyd Rd B1
Gilbert St C2
Gorsedd Circle B1
Gwelfor Ave A1
Harbour View B3
Henry St C2
High Terr C1
Hill St B2
Holborn Rd C2
Holland Park Industrial Estate C3
Holyhead Park B1
Holyhead Station B2
Information Ctr B2
King's Rd C2
Kingsland Rd C2
Lewascote C3
Library B2
Lifeboat Station A1
Llanfawr Cl C3
Llanfawr Rd C3
Lligwy St C2
Lon Deg C3
London Rd C3
Longford Rd B1
Longford Terr B1
Maes Cybi B1
Maes Hedd A1
Maes-Hyfryd Rd C1
Maes-y-Dref B1
Maes-yr-Haf A2/B1
Maes-yr-Ysgol C3
Marchog C3
Marina A1
Maritime Mus A1
Market B2
Market St B2
Mill Bank B1
Min-y-Mor Rd A1
Morawelon Industrial Estate B3
Morawelon Rd B3
Moreton Rd C1
New Park Rd B1
Newry St A2
Old Harbour Lighthouse A3
Plas Rd C1
Police Station B2
Porth-y-Felin Rd A1
Post Office A1/B1/B2/B3/C2/C3
Prince of Wales Rd A2
Priory La B3
Pump St C1
Queens Park B1
Reseifion Rd C1
Rock St B1
Roman Fort B2
St Cybi St B2
St Cybi's Church B2
St Seiriol's Cl B1
Salt Island Bridge A2
Seabourne Rd A1
South Stack Rd B1
Sports Ground B1
Stanley St B2
Station St B2
Tan-y-Bryn Rd A1
Tan-yr-Efail C2
Tara St C1
Thomas St B1
Town Hall A2
Treseifion Estate C2
Turkey Shore Rd B2
Ucheldre Arts Centre ✦ B1
Ucheldre Ave B1
Upper Baptist St B1
Victoria Rd B2
Victoria Terr B2
Vulcan St B1
Walthew Ave A1
Walthew La A1
Wian St C2

Hull 335

Adelaide St C1
Albert Dock C1
Albion St B2
Alfred Gelder St B2
Anlaby Rd B1
Beverley Rd A1
Blanket Row C2
Bond St B2
Bridlington Ave A2
Brook St B1
Brunswick Ave A1
Bus Station B1
Camilla Cl C3
Canning St B1
Cannon St A2
Cannon's C1
Caroline St A2
Carr La B2
Castle St C2
Central Library B1
Charles St A2
Citadel Way B3
City Hall B2
Clarence St B3
Cleveland St A3
Clifton St A1
Collier St B1
Colonial St B1
Court B2
Deep, The C3
Dock Office Row B3
Dock St B2
Drypool Bridge B3
Egton St A3
English St C1
Ferens Gallery B2
Ferensway B1
Francis St A2
Francis St West A2
Freehold St A1
Freetown Way A2
Garrison Rd B3
George St B2
Gibson St A2
Great Thornton St B1
Great Union St A3
Green La A2
Grey St A1
Grimston St B2
Grosvenor St A1
Guildhall B2
Guildhall Rd B2
Hands-on History B2
Harley St A1
Hessle Rd C1
High St B3
Holy Trinity B2
Hull & East Riding Mus B3
Hull Arena C1
Hull College B3
Hull (Paragon) Station B1
Hull Truck Theatre B1
Humber Dock Marina C2
Humber Dock St C2
Humber St C2
Hyperion St A3
Information Ctr B2
Jameson St B1
Jarratt St B2
Jenning St A3
King Billy Statue ✦ C2
King Edward St B2
King St A2
Kingston Retail Park C1
Kingston St C2
Library Theatre B1
Liddell St A1
Lime St A3
Lister St C1
Lockwood St A2
Maister House B3
Maritime Mus B2
Market B2
Market Place B2
Minerva Pier C2
Mulgrave St A3
Myton Bridge C3
Myton St B1
Nelson St C2
New Cleveland St A3
New George St A2
New Theatre A2
Norfolk St A1
North Bridge A3
North St B1
Odeon C1
Old Harbour C3
Osborne St B1
Paragon St B2
Park St B1
Percy St A2
Pier St C2
Police Station B1
Post Office A1/B1/B2
Porter St C1
Portland St B1
Posterngate B2
Prince's Quay B2
Prospect Centre B1
Prospect St B1
Queen's Gdns B2
Railway Dock Marina C2
Railway St C2
Reform St A2
Retail Park B1
Riverside Quay C2
Roper St B2
St James St C1
St Luke's St B1
St Mark St A3
St Mary the Virgin B3
Scott St A2
South Bridge Rd B3
Spring Bank A1
Spring St B1
Spurn Lightship C2
Spyvee St A3
Streetlife Transport Mus B3
Sykes St A2
Tidal Surge Barrier ✦ C3
Tower St B3
Trinity House B2
University B2
Vane St A1
Victoria Pier C2
Waterhouse La B2
Waterloo St A1
Waverley St C1
Wellington St C2
Wellington St West C2
West St B1
Whitefriargate B2
Wilberforce Dr B2
Wilberforce House B3
Wilberforce Monument ✦ B3
William St C1
Wincolmlee A3
Witham A3
Wright St A1

Inverness 336

Abban St A1
Academy St B2
Alexander Pl B2
Anderson St A2
Annfield Rd C3
Ardconnel St B3
Ardconnel Terr B3
Ardross Pl B2
Ardross St B2
Argyle St B3
Argyle Terr B3
Attadale Rd B1
Ballifeary La C2
Ballifeary Rd C1/C2
Balnacraig La A1
Balnain St B2
Bank St B2
Bellfield Park C2
Bellfield Terr C3
Benula Rd A1
Birnie Terr A1
Bishop's Rd C2
Bowling Green A2
Bowling Green B2
Bowling Green C2
Bridge St B2
Brown St A2
Bruce Ave C1
Bruce Gdns C1
Bruce Pk C1
Burial Ground A2
Burnett Rd A3
Bus Station B3
Caledonian Rd B1
Cameron Rd A1
Cameron Sq A1
Carse Rd A1
Carsegate Rd Sth A1
Castle (Courts) B3
Castle Rd B2
Castle St B3
Celt St B2
Chapel St A2
Charles St B3
Church St B2
Clachnacuddin Football Ground A1
College A3
Columba Rd B1/C1
Crown Ave B3
Crown Circus B3
Crown Dr B3
Crown Rd B3
Crown St B3
Culduthel Rd C3
Dalneigh Cres C1
Dalneigh Rd C1
Denny St B3
Dochfour Dr B1/C1
Douglas Row B2
Duffy Dr C3
Dunabban Rd A1
Dunain Rd B1
Duncraig St B2
Eastgate Shopping Centre B3
Eden Court C2
Fairfield Rd B1
Falcon Sq B3
Fire Station A3
Fraser St B2
Fraser St C2
Friars' Bridge A2
Friars' La B2
Friars' St A2
George St A2
Gilbert St A2
Glebe St A2
Glendoe Terr A1
Glenurquhart Rd C1
Gordon Terr B3
Gordonville Rd C2
Grant St A2
Greig St B2
HM Prison B3
Harbour Rd A3
Harrowden Rd B1
Haugh Rd C2
Heatherley Cres C3
High St B3
Highland Council HQ, The C2
Hill Park C3
Hill St B3
Huntly Pl A2
Huntly St B2
India St A2
Industrial Estate A3
Information Ctr B2
Innes St A2
Inverness B3
Inverness High School B1
Jamaica St A2
Kenneth St B2
Kilmuir Rd A1
King St B2
Kingsmills Rd B3
Laurel Ave B1/C1
Library A3
Lilac Gr B1
Lindsay Ave C1
Lochalsh Rd A1/B1
Longman Rd A3
Lotland Pl A2
Lower Kessock St A1
Madras St A2
Market Hall B3
Maxwell Dr C1
Mayfield Rd C3
Midmills College B3
Millburn Rd B3
Mitchell's La C3
Montague Row B2
Muirfield Rd C3
Muirtown St B1
Museum B2
Nelson St A2
Ness Bank C2
Ness Bridge B2
Ness Walk B2/C2
Old Edinburgh Rd C3
Old High Church B2
Park Rd C1
Paton St C2
Perceval Rd B1
Planefield Rd B2
Police Station A3
Porterfield Bank C3
Porterfield Rd C3
Portland Pl A2
Post Office A2/B1/B2/B3
Queen St B2
Queensgate B2
Railway Terr A3
Rangemore Rd B1
Reay St B3
Riverside St A2
Rose St A2
Ross Ave B1
Rowan Rd B1
Royal Northern Infirmary C2
St Andrew's Cathedral † C2
St Columba B2
St John's Ave C1
St Mary's Ave C1
Shore St A2
Smith Ave C1
Southside Pl C3
Southside Rd C3
Spectrum Centre B2
Strothers La B3
Superstore B2
TA Centre C2
Telford Gdns B1
Telford Rd A1
Telford St A1
Tomnahurich Cemetery C1
Tomnahurich St B2
Town Hall B3
Union Rd B3
Union St B3
Walker Pl A2
Walker Rd A3
War Memorial ✦ C2
Waterloo Bridge A2
Wells St B1
Young St B2

Ipswich 336

Alderman Rd B2
All Saints' Rd A1
Alpe St B2
Ancaster Rd C1
Ancient House B3
Anglesea Rd B2
Ann St B2
Arboretum A2
Austin St C2
Belstead Rd C2
Berners St B2
Bibb Way B1
Birkfield Dr C1
Black Horse La B2
Bolton La B3
Bond St C3
Bowthorpe Cl B2
Bramford La A1
Bramford Rd A1
Bridge St C2
Brookfield Rd A1
Brooks Hall Rd A1
Broomhill A2
Broomhill Rd A1
Broughton Rd A2
Bulwer Rd B1
Burrell Rd C2
Bus Station B2/C3
Butter Market B2
Butter Market Centre B3
Carr St B3
Cecil Rd B2
Cecilia St C2
Chancery Rd C2
Charles St B2
Chevallier St A1
Christchurch Mansion & Wolsey Art Gallery B3
Christchurch Park A3
Christchurch St B3
Civic Centre B2
Civic Dr B2
Clarkson St B1
Cobbold St B3
Commercial Rd C2
Constable Rd A3
Constantine Rd C1
Constitution Hill A2
Corder Rd A3
Corn Exchange B2
Cotswold Ave A2
Council Offices C2
County Hall B3
Crown Court C2
Crown St B2
Cullingham Rd B1
Cumberland St B2
Curriers La B2
Dale Hall La A2
Dales View Rd A1
Dalton Rd B2
Dillwyn St B1
Elliot St B1
Elm St B2
Elsmere Rd A3
End Quay C3
Falcon St C2
Felaw St C3
Flint Wharf C3
Fonnereau Rd B2
Fore St C3
Foundation St C3
Franciscan Way C2
Friars St C2
Gainsborough Rd A3
Gatacre Rd B1
Geneva Rd B2
Gippeswyk Ave C1
Gippeswyk Park C1
Grafton Way C2
Graham Rd A1
Grimwade St C3
Great Whip St C3
Handford Cut B1
Handford Rd B1
Henley Rd A2
Hervey St B3
High St B2
Holly Rd A2
Information Ctr B3
Ipswich School A2
Ipswich Station C2
Ipswich Town FC (Portman Road) C2
Ivry St A2
Kensington Rd A1
Kesteven Rd C1
Key St C3
Kingsfield Ave A3
Kitchener Rd A1
Magistrates Court B2
Little's Cr C2
London Rd B1
Low Brook St C3
Lower Orwell St C3
Luther Rd C2
Manor Rd A3
Mornington Ave A1
Mus & Art Gallery B2
Museum St B2
Neale St B3
New Cardinal St C2
New Cut East C3
New Cut West C3
Newson St B2
Norwich Rd A1/B1
Oban St B2
Old Customs House C3
Old Foundry Rd B3
Old Merchant's House C3
Orford St B2
Paget Rd A2
Park Rd A3
Park View Rd A2
Peter's St C2
Philip Rd C2
Pine Ave A2
Pine View Rd A2
Police Station B2
Portman Rd B2
Portman Walk C1
Post Office B2/B3
Princes St C2
Prospect St B1
Queen St B2
Ranelagh Rd C1
Recreation Ground B1
Rectory Rd C2
Regent Theatre B3
Richmond Rd A1
Rope Walk C3
Rose La C2
Russell Rd C2
St Edmund's Rd A2
St George's St B2
St Helen's St B3
Samuel Rd B3
Sherrington Rd A1
Silent St C2
Sir Alf Ramsey Way C1
Sirdar Rd B1
Soane St B3
Springfield La A1
Star La C3
Stevenson Rd B1
Suffolk College C3
Suffolk Retail Park B1
Superstore B1
Surrey Rd B1
Swimming Pool A1
Tacket St C3
Tavern St B3
The Avenue A3
Tolly Cobbold Mus C3
Tower Ramparts B2
Tower St B3
Town Hall B2
Tuddenham Rd A3
UGC C2
Upper Brook St B3
Upper Orwell St B3
Valley Rd A2
Vermont Cr B3
Vermont Rd B3
Vernon St C3
Warrington Rd A2
Waterloo Rd A1
Waterworks St C3
Wellington St B1
West End Rd B1
Westerfield Rd A3
Westgate St B2
Westholme Rd A1
Westwood Ave A1
Willoughby Rd C2
Withipoll St B3
Wolsey Theatre B2
Woodbridge Rd B3
Woodstone Ave A3
Yarmouth Rd B1

Kendal 336

Abbot Hall Art Gallery & Mus of Lakeland Life C2
Ambulance Station A2
Anchorite Fields C2
Anchorite Rd C2
Ann St A3
Appleby Rd A3
Archers Meadow C3
Ashleigh Rd A2
Aynam Rd B2
Bankfield Rd B1
Beast Banks B2
Beezon Fields A2
Beezon Rd A2
Beezon Trad Est A3
Belmont B2
Birchwood Cl C1
Blackhall Rd B2
Brewery Arts Centre B2
Bridge St B2
Brigsteer Rd C1
Burneside Rd A2
Bus Station B2
Buttery Well La C2
Canal Head North B3
Captain French La C2
Caroline St A2
Castle Hill B3
Castle Howe B2
Castle Rd B3
Castle St A3/B3
Cedar Gr C1
Council Offices B2
County Council Offices A2
Cricket Ground A3
Cricket Ground C3
Cross La C2
Dockray Hall Ind Estate A2
Dowker's La B2
Dry Ski Slope ✦ B3
East View B1
Echo Barn Hill C1
Elephant Yard Shopping Centre B2
Fairfield La A1
Finkle St B2
Fire Station A2
Fletcher Square C3
Football Ground C3
Fowling La A3
Gillinggate C2
Glebe Rd C2
Golf Course B1
Goose Holme B3
Gooseholme Bridge B3
Green St A1
Greengate C2
Greengate La C1/C2
Greenside B1
Greenwood C1
Gulfs Rd B2
High Tenterfell B1
Highgate B2
Hillswood Ave C1
Horncop La A2
Information Ctr B2
K Village and Heritage Centre ✦ C2
Kendal Business Park A3
Kendal Castle (Remains Of) B3
Kendal Fell B1
Kendal Green A1
Kendal B2
Kendal Station A3
Kent Pl B2
Kirkbarrow C2
Kirkland C2
Library B2
Library Rd B2
Little Aynam B3
Little Wood B1
Long Cl C1
Longpool A3
Lound Rd C3
Lound St C3
Low Fellside B2
Lowther St B2
Maple Dr C1
Market Pl B2
Maude St B2
Miller Bridge B2
Milnthorpe Rd C2
Mint St A3
Mintsfeet Rd A3
Mintsfeet Rd South A2
New Rd B2
Noble's Rest B2
Parish Church C2
Park Side Rd C3
Parkside Business Park C3
Parr St B3
Police Station A2
Post Office A3/B2/C2
Quaker Tapestry ✦ B2
Queen's Rd B1
Riverside Walk C2
Rydal Mount A2
Sandes Ave A2
Sandgate A3
Sandylands Rd A3
Serpentine Rd B1
Serpentine Wood B1
Shap Rd A3
South Rd C2
Stainbank Rd C1
Station Rd A3
Stramongate B2
Stramongate Bridge B2
Stricklandgate A2/B2
Sunnyside C3
Thorny Hills B3
Town Hall B2
Undercliff Rd B1
Underwood C1
Union St A2
Vicar's Fields C2
Vicarage Dr C1/C2
Wainwright Yard Shopping Centre B2
Wasdale Cl C3
Well Ings C2
Westmorland Shopping Ctr & Market Hall B2
Westwood Ave C1
Wildman St A3
Windermere Rd A1
YHA B2
YWCA B2

King's Lynn 336

Albert St A2
Albion St B2
All Saints B2
All Saints St B2
Austin Fields A2
Austin St A2
Avenue Rd B3
Bank Side B1
Beech Rd C2
Birch Tree Cl B2
Birchwood St A2
Blackfriars Rd B2
Blackfriars St B2
Boal St B1
Bridge St B2
Broad St B2
Broad Walk B3
Burkitt St A2
Bus Station A2
Carmelite Terr C2
Chapel St A2
Chase Ave C3
Checker St C2
Church St B2
Clough La B2
Coburg St B2
College of West Anglia A3
Columbia Way A3
Corn Exchange A1
County Court Rd B2
Cresswell St A2
Custom House A1
Eastgate St A2
Edma St A2
Exton's Rd C3
Ferry La B1
Ferry St A1
Framingham's Almshouses B2
Friars St C2
Gaywood Rd A3
George St A2
Gladstone Rd C2
Goodwin's Rd C3
Green Quay ✦ B1
Greyfriars' Tower ✦ B2
Guanock Terr C2
Guildhall A1
Hansa Rd C3
Hardwick Rd C2
Hextable Rd A2
High St B1
Holcombe Ave C3
Hospital Walk C2
Information Ctr B1
John Kennedy Rd A2
Kettlewell Lane A2
King George V Ave B3
King's Lynn Art Centre A1
King's Lynn Station B2
King St B1
Library B2
Littleport St A2
Loke Rd A2
London Rd B2
Lynn Mus B2
Majestic B2
Magistrates Court B1
Market La A1
Millfleet B2
Milton Ave A3
Nar Valley Walk C2
Nelson St B1
New Conduit St B2
Norfolk St A2
North St A2
Oldsunway B2
Ouse Ave C1
Page Stair Lane A1
Park Ave B3
Police Station B2
Portland Pl C1
Portland St B2
Post Office A3/B2/C2
Purfleet B1
Queen St B1
Raby Ave A3
Railway Rd A2
Red Mount Chapel B3
Regent Way B2
River Walk A1
Robert St C2
Saddlebow Rd C2
St Ann's St A1
St James' Rd B2
St James St B2
St John's Walk B3
St Margaret's B1
St Nicholas A2
St Nicholas St A1
St Peter's Rd B1
Sir Lewis St A2
Smith Ave A3
South Everard St C2
South Gate ✦ C2
South Quay B1
South St B2
Southgate St C2
Stonegate St B2
Surrey St A1
Sydney St C3
Tennyson Ave B3
Tennyson Rd B3
The Friars C2
Tower St B2
Town Hall B1
Town House & Tales of The Old Gaol House B1
Town Wall (Remains) ✦ B3
True's Yard Mus A2
Valingers Rd C2
Vancouver Ave C2
Waterloo St B2
Wellesley St B2
White Friars Rd C2
Windsor Rd C2
Winfarthing St C2
Wyatt St A2
York Rd C3

Lancaster 336

Aberdeen Rd C3
Adult College, The C3
Aldcliffe Rd C2
Alfred St B3
Ambleside Rd A3
Ambulance Sta A3
Ashfield Ave B1
Ashton Rd C2
Assembly Rooms, The B2
Balmoral Rd B3
Bath House B2
Bath Mill La B3
Bath St B3
Blades St B1
Borrowdale Rd B3
Bowerham Rd C3
Brewery La B2
Bridge La B2
Brook St C1
Bulk Rd A3
Bulk St B2
Bus Station B2
Cable St B2
Carlisle Bridge A1
Carr House La C2
Castle B1
Castle Park B1
Caton Rd A3
China St B2
Church St B2
City Mus B2
Clarence St C3
Common Gdn St B2
Coniston Rd A3
Cottage Mus B2
Council Offices B2
Court B2
Cromwell Rd C1
Dale St C3
Dallas Rd B1/C1
Dalton Rd B3
Dalton Sq B2
Damside St B2
De Vitre St B3
Dee Rd A1
Denny Ave A1
Derby Rd A2
Dukes B2
Earl St A2
East Rd B3
Eastham St C3
Edward St B3
Fairfield Rd B1
Fenton St B2
Firbank Rd A3
Fire Station B2
Friend's Meeting House B1
Garnet St B3
George St B2
Giant Axe Field B1
Gov Offices B2
Grand, The B2
Grasmere Rd B3
Greaves Rd C2
Green St A3
Gregson Centre, The B3
Gregson Rd C3
Greyhound Bridge A2
Greyhound Bridge Rd A2
High St B2
Hill Side B1
Hope St C3
Hubert Pl B1
Information Ctr B2
Judges Lodgings B2
Kelsy St B1
Kentmere Rd B3
King St B2
Kingsway A3
Kirkes Rd C3
Lancaster & Lakeland C3
Lancaster City Football Club B1
Lancaster Station B1
Langdale Rd A3
Ley Ct B1
Library B2
Lincoln Rd B1
Lindow St C2
Lodge St B2
Long Marsh La B1
Lune Rd A1
Lune St A2
Lune Valley Ramble A3
Mainway A2
Maritime Mus A1
Market St B2
Marketgate Shopping Centre B2
Meadowside C2
Meeting House La B1
Millennium Bridge A2
Moor La B2
Moorgate B3
Morecambe Rd A1/A2
Nelson St B2
North Rd B2
Orchard La C1
Owen Rd A2
Park Rd B3
Parliament St A3
Patterdale Rd A3
Penny St B2
Police Station B2
Portland St C2
Post Office A2/A3/B1/B2/B3/C3
Primrose St C3
Priory B1
Prospect St C3
Quarry Rd B3
Queen St C2
Regent St C2
Ridge La A3
Ridge St A3
Royal Lancaster Infirmary (A&E) C2
Rydal Rd B3
Ryelands Park A1
St Georges Quay A1
St John's B2
St Leonard's Gate B2
St Martin's Rd C3
St Nicholas Arcades Shopping Centre B2
St Oswald St C3
St Peter's † B3
St Peter's Rd B3
Salisbury Rd B1
Scotch Quarry Urban Park C3
Shire Hall/HM Prison B1
Sibsey St B1
Skerton Bridge A2
South Rd C2
Station Rd B1
Stirling Rd C3
Storey Ave B1
Sunnyside La C1
Sylvester St C1
Tarnsyke Rd A1
Thurnham St C2
Town Hall B2
Troutbeck Rd B3
Ulleswater Rd B3
University of Cumbria C3
Vicarage Field B1
Vue B2
West Rd B1
Westbourne Dr C1
Westbourne Rd B1
Westham St C3
Wheatfield St B1
White Cross Education Centre C2
Williamson Rd B3
Willow La B1
Windermere Rd B3
Wingate-Saul Rd B1
Wolseley St B3
Woodville St B3
Wyresdale Rd C3

Leeds 336

Aire St B3
Aireside Centre B2
Albion Pl B4
Albion St B4
Albion Way B1
Alma St A6
Arcades B4
Armley Rd B1
Back Burley Lodge Rd A1
Back Hyde Terr A2
Back Row C3
Bath Rd C3
Beckett St A6
Bedford St B3
Belgrave St A4
Belle View Rd A2
Benson St A5
Black Bull St C5
Blenheim Walk A3
Boar La B4

Llandudno • Llanelli • London 353

Walker St A6
Wapping C2
Water St B1/B2
Waterloo Rd A1
Wavertree Rd B6
West Derby Rd A6
West Derby St B5
Whitechapel B3
Whitley Gdns A5
William Brown St B3
William Henry St A4
Williamson Sq B3
Williamson St B3
Williamson's Tunnels Heritage Centre✦ C6
Women's Hosp⊞ C6
Wood St B3
World Mus, Liverpool🏛 A3
York St C3

Llandudno 337

Abbey Pl B1
Abbey Rd B1
Adelphi St B3
Alexandra Rd C2
Alice in Wonderland Centre✦ B3
Anglesey Rd A1
Argyll Rd B3
Arvon Ave A2
Atlee Cl C3
Augusta St B3
Back Madoc St B2
Bodafon St B3
Bodhyfryd Rd A2
Bodnant Cr C3
Bodnant Rd C3
Bridge Rd C2
Bryniau Rd C1
Builder St B3
Builder St West C2
Cabin Lift A2
Camera Obscura✦ A3
Caroline Rd B2
Chapel St A2
Charlton St B3
Church Cr C1
Church Walks A2
Claremont Rd B2
Clement Ave A2
Clifton Rd B2
Clonmel St B3
Coach Station B3
Conway Rd B3
Council St West C3
Cricket and Recreation Ground B2
Cwlach Rd A2
Cwlach St A1
Cwm Howard La C3
Cwm Pl C3
Cwm Rd C3
Dale Rd C1
Deganwy Ave B2
Denness Pl C2
Dinas Rd C2
Dolydd B1
Erol Pl B2
Ewloe Dr C3
Fairways C2
Ffordd Dewi C3
Ffordd Dulyn C2
Ffordd Dwyfor C3
Ffordd Elisabeth C3
Ffordd Gwynedd C3
Ffordd Las C3
Ffordd Morfa C3
Ffordd Penrhyn C3
Ffordd Tudno C3
Ffordd yr Orsedd C3
Ffordd Ysbyty C2
Fire & Ambulance Station B3
Garage St B3
George St A2
Gloddaeth Ave B1
Gloddaeth St B2
Gogarth Rd B1
Great Orme Mines✦ A1
Great Ormes Rd B1
Happy Valley A2
Happy Valley Rd A3
Haulfre Gardens✿ A1
Herkomer Cr C1
Hill Terr A2
Hospice B1
Howard Rd B3
Information Ctr⊡ B2
Invalids' Walk B1
James St B2
Jubilee St B3
King's Ave C2
King's Rd C2
Knowles Rd C2
Lees Rd C2
Library B2
Lifeboat Station B2
Llandudno🏛 A2
Llandudno (A & E)⊞ C2
Llandudno Station≠ B3
Llandudno Town Football Ground C2
Llewelyn Ave A2
Lloyd St West B1
Lloyd St B2
Llwynon Rd A1
Llys Maelgwn B1
Madoc St B2
Maelgwn Rd B2
Maesdu Bridge C2
Maesdu Rd C2/C3
Maes-y-Cwm C3
Maes-y-Orsedd C3
Marian Pl C2
Marian Rd C2
Marine Drive (Toll) A3
Market Hall A2
Market St A2
Miniature Golf Course A1
Morfa Rd B1
Mostyn🏛 B3
Mostyn Broadway B3
Mostyn St B3
Mowbray Rd C2
New St A2
Norman Rd B3
North Parade A2
North Wales Golf Links C1
Old Rd A2
Oxford Rd B3
Parc Llandudno Shopping Centre B3
Pier✦ A3
Plas Rd A2
Police Station⊡ B3
Post Office⊡ B3/C2
Promenade A3
Pyllau Rd A1
Rectory La A2
Rhuddlan Ave C3
St Andrew's Ave B2
St Andrew's Pl B2
St Beuno's Rd A1
St David's Pl B2
St David's Rd B2
St George's Pl A3
St Mary's Rd B2
St Seriol's Rd B2
Salisbury Pass B1
Salisbury Rd B2
Somerset St B3
South Parade A2
Stephen St B3
TA Centre B3
Tabor Hill A2
The Oval B1
The Parade B3
Town Hall B2
Trinity Ave B1
Trinity Cres C1
Trinity Sq B3
Tudno St A2
Ty-Coch Rd A2
Ty-Gwyn Rd A1/A2
Ty'n-y-Coed Rd A1
Vaughan St B3
Victoria Shopping Centre B3
Victoria Tram Station A2
War Memorial✦ A2
Werny Wylan C3
West Parade B1
Whiston Pass A2
Winllan Ave C2
Wyddfyd Rd A2
York Rd A2

Llanelli 337

Alban Rd B3
Albert St B1
Als St B3
Amos St C1
Andrew St A3
Ann St C2
Annesley St B2
Arfryn Ave A3
Arthur St B2
Belvedere Rd A1
Bigyn La B3
Bigyn Park Terr C3
Bigyn Rd C3
Bond Ave C3
Brettenham St A1
Bridge St B2
Bryn Pl C1
Bryn Rd C1
Bryn Terr C1
Brynhyfryd Rd A2
Brynmelyn Ave A3
Brynmor Rd B1
Bryn-More Rd C1
Burry St C1
Bus Station B2
Caersalem Terr C2
Cambrian St C1
Caswell St C3
Cedric St B3
Cemetery A2
Chapman St A1
Charles Terr C2
Church St B2
Clos Caer Elms A1
Clos Sant Paul C2
Coastal Link Rd B1/C1
Coldstream St B2
Coleshill Terr B1
College Hill B3
College Sq B3
Copperworks Rd C2
Coronation Rd C3
Corporation Ave A3
Council Offices B2
Court B2
Cowell St B2
Cradock St C2
Craig Ave C3
Cricket Ground A1
Derwent St A1
Dillwyn St C2
Druce St C1
Elizabeth St B2
Emma St C2
Erw Rd B1
Felinfoel Rd A2
Fire Station A3
Firth Rd C3
Fron Terr C3
Furnace Rugby Football Ground A1
Gelli-On B2
George St C2
Gilbert Cres A2
Gilbert Rd A2
Glanmor Rd C2
Glanmor Terr C2
Glasfryn Terr A3
Glenalla Rd B3
Glevering St B3
Goring Rd A2
Gorsedd Circle A2
Grant St C3
Graveyard C2
Great Western Cl C2
Greenway St B1
Hall St B2
Harries Ave A2
Hedley Terr A2
Heol Elli B3
Heol Goffa A3
Heol Nant-y-Felin A3
Heol Siloh B2
Hick St C2
High St C1
Indoor Bowls Centre B1
Inkerman St B2
Island Pl B2
James St B3
John St B2
King George Ave B3
Lake View Cl A2
Lakefield Pl C1
Lakefield Rd C1
Langland Rd C3
Leisure Centre B1
Library B2
Llanelli House🏛 B2
Llanelli Parish Church⛪ B2
Llanelli RUFC (Stradey Park) A1
Llanelli Station≠ C2
Llewellyn St C2
Lliedi Cres A3
Lloyd St B2
Llys Alys B3
Llys Fran A3
Llysnewedd C1
Long Row A3
Maes Gors C2
Maesyrhaf A3
Mansel St C3
Marblehall Rd B3
Marborough Rd A2
Margam St C3
Marged St C2
Marine St C1
Market B2
Market St B2
Marsh St C2
Martin Rd C3
Miles St A1
Mill La A3/B2
Mincing La B2
Murray St B2
Myn y Mor B1
Nathan St C1
Nelson Terr C1
Nevill St C2
New Dock Rd C2
New Rd A1
New Zealand St A1
Old Lodge C2
Old Rd A2
Paddock St C2
Palace Ave B3
Parc Howard A2
Parc Howard Mus & Art Gallery🏛🏛 A2
Park Cres B1
Park St B2
Parkview Terr B1
Pemberton St C2
Pembrey Rd A1
Peoples Park B1
Police Station⊡ B2
Post Office⊡ A1/A2/B2/C1/C2
Pottery Pl B3
Pottery St B3
Princess St B1
Prospect Pl A2
Pryce St A1
Queen Mary's Walk C3
Queen Victoria Rd C1
Raby St B1
Railway Terr C2
Ralph St B2
Ralph Terr C1
Regalia Terr B3
Rhydyrafon A3
Richard St B2
Robinson St B2
Roland Ave A1
Russell St C3
St David's Cl C1
St Elli Shopping Centre B2
St Margaret's Dr A1
Spowart Ave A1
Station Rd B2/C2
Stepney Pl B2
Stepney St B2
Stewart St A1
Stradey Park Ave A1
Sunny Hill A2
Swansea Rd A3
TA Centre B2
Talbot St C3
Temple St B3
The Avenue Cilfig A2
The Mariners C1
Theatr Elli♥ B2
Thomas St A2
Toft Pl A3
Town Hall B2
Traeth Ffordd C1
Trinity Rd C3
Trinity Terr C2
Tunnel Rd B3
Tyisha Rd C3
Union Blgs A2
Upper Robinson St B2
Vauxhall Rd B2
Walter's Rd B3
Waun Lanyrafon B2
Waun Rd A3
Wern Rd B3
West End A2
Y Bwthyn C3
Zion Row B3

London 338

Abbey Orchard St E3
Abchurch La D6
Abingdon St E4
Achilles Way D2
Acton St B4
Addington St E4
Air St D3
Albany St B2
Albemarle St D3
Albert Embankment F4
Aldenham St A3
Aldersgate St C6
Aldford St D2
Aldgate⊖ C7
Aldgate High St C7
Aldwych C4
Allsop Pl B1
Amwell St B5
Andrew Borde St C3
Angel⊖ A5
Appold St C7
Argyle Sq B4
Argyle St B4
Argyll St C3
Arnold Circus B7
Artillery La C7
Artillery Row E3
Ashbridge St B1
Association of Photographers Gallery🏛 B6
Baker St⊖ B1
Baker St B1
Baldwin's Gdns C5
Baltic St B6
Bank⊖ C6
Bank Mus🏛 C6
Bank of England C6
Bankside D6
Bankside Gallery🏛 D5
Banner St B6
Barbican⊖≠ C6
Barbican Gallery🏛 C6
Baroness Rd B7
Basil St E1
Bastwick St B6
Bateman's Row B7
Bath St B6
Bayley St C3
Baylis Rd E5
Beak St D3
Bedford Row C4
Bedford Sq C3
Bedford St D4
Bedford Way B3
Beech St C6
Belgrave Pl E2
Belgrave Sq E2
Bell La C7
Belvedere Rd E4
Berkeley Sq D2
Berkeley St D2
Bernard St B4
Berners Pl C3
Berners St C3
Berwick St C3
Bethnal Green Rd B7
Bevenden St B6
Bevis Marks C7
BFI London IMAX Cinema♥ D5
Bidborough St B4
Binney St C2
Birdcage Walk E3
Bishopsgate C7
Blackfriars⊖≠ D5
Blackfriars Bridge D5
Blackfriars Rd E5
Blandford St C1
Blomfield St C6
Bloomsbury St C3
Bloomsbury Way C4
Bolton St D2
Bond St⊖ C2
Boswell St C4
Bowling Green La B5
Bow St C4
Brad St D5
Bressenden Pl E3
Brewer St D3
Brick St D2
Bridge St E4
Britain at War🏛 D7
Britannia Walk B6
British Library🏛 B3
British Mus🏛 C4
Britton St B5
Broad Sanctuary E3
Broadway E3
Brook Dr F5
Brook St D2
Brown St C1
Brunswick Pl B6
Brunswick Sq B4
Brushfield St C7
Bruton St D2
Bryanston St C1
Buckingham Gate E3
Buckingham Palace🏛 E3
Buckingham Palace Rd F2
Bunhill Row B6
Byward St D7
Cabinet War Rooms & Churchill Mus🏛 E3
Cadogan La E2
Cadogan Pl E1
Cadogan Sq F1
Caledonian Rd A4
Calshot St A4
Calthorpe St B4
Calvert Ave B7
Cambridge Circus C3
Camomile St C7
Cannon St D6
Cannon St⊖≠ D6
Carey St C4
Carlisle La E4
Carlisle Pl E3
Carlton House Terr D3
Carmelite St D5
Carnaby St C3
Carter La C5
Carthusian St C6
Cartwright Gdns B4
Castle Baynard St D5
Cavendish Pl C2
Cavendish Sq C2
Caxton Hall E3
Caxton St E3
Central St B6
Chalton St B3
Chancery Lane⊖ C5
Chapel Market A5
Chapel St E2
Charing Cross⊖≠ D4
Charing Cross Rd C3
Charles II St D3
Charles Sq B6
Charles St D2
Charlotte Rd B7
Charlotte St C3
Charrington St A3
Chart St B6
Charterhouse Sq C5
Charterhouse St C5
Cheapside C6
Chenies St C3
Chesham St E2
Chester Sq F2
Chesterfield Hill D2
Chiltern St C2
Chiswell St C6
City Garden Row A5
City Rd B6
City Thameslink≠ C5
City University, The B5
Claremont Sq A5
Clarges St D2
Clerkenwell Cl B5
Clerkenwell Green B5
Clerkenwell Rd B5
Cleveland St C3
Clifford St D3
Clink Prison Mus🏛 D6
Clock Mus🏛 C6
Club Row B7
Cockspur St D3
Coleman St C6
Collier St A4
Columbia Rd B7
Commercial St C7
Compton St B5
Conduit St D2
Constitution Hill E2
Copperfield St E5
Coptic St C4
Cornhill C6
Cornwall Rd D5
Coronet St B7
Courtauld Gallery🏛 D4
Covent Garden⊖ D4
Covent Garden✦ D4
Cowcross St C5
Cowper St B6
Cranbourn St D3
Craven St D4
Crawford St C1
Creechurch La C7
Cremer St A7
Cromer St B4
Crondall St A6
Cumberland Gate D1
Cumberland Terr A2
Curtain Rd B7
Curzon St D2
Dalí Universe🏛 E4
D'arblay St C3
Davies St C2
Dean St C3
Deluxe Gallery🏛 B7
Denmark St C3
Dering St C2
Devonshire St C2
Diana, Princess of Wales Memorial Walk E3
Dingley Rd B6
Donegal St A4
Dorset St C1
Doughty St B4
Dover St D2
Downing St E4
Druid St E7
Drummond St B3
Drury La C4
Drysdale St B7
Duchess St C2
Dufferin St B6
Duke of Wellington Pl E2
Duke St C2
Duke St D3
Duke St Hill D6
Duke's Pl C7
Duncannon St D4
East Rd B6
Eastcastle St C3
Eastcheap D7
Eastman Dental Hosp⊞ B4
Eaton Pl E2
Eaton Sq E2
Eccleston Bridge F3
Eccleston St E2
Edgware Rd C1
Eldon St C6
Embankment⊖ D4
Endell St C4
Endsleigh Pl B3
Ennismore Gdns E1
Euston⊖≠ B3
Euston Rd B3
Euston Square⊖ B3
Eversholt St A3
Exmouth Market B5
Fann St B6
Farringdon⊖≠ C5
Farringdon Rd C5
Farringdon St C5
Featherstone St B6
Fenchurch St D7
Fenchurch St≠ D7
Fetter La C5
Finsbury Circus C6
Finsbury Pavement C6
Finsbury Sq B6
Fitzalan St F5
Fitzmaurice Pl D2
Fleet St C5
Floral St D4
Florence Nightingale Mus🏛 E4
Folgate St C7
Foot Hosp⊞ B3
Fore St C6
Foster La C6
Francis St F3
Frazier St E5
Freemason's Hall C4
Friday St C6
Gainsford St E7
Garden Row E5
Gee St B6
George St C1
Gerrard St D3
Giltspur St C5
Glasshouse St D3
Gloucester Pl C1
Golden Hinde⛵ D6
Golden La B6
Golden Sq D3
Goodge St⊖ C3
Goodge St C3
Gordon Sq B3
Gosset St B7
Goswell Rd B5
Gough St B4
Goulston St C7
Gower St B3
Gracechurch St D6
Grafton Way B3
Graham St A5
Gray's Inn Rd B4
Great College St E4
Great Cumberland Pl C1
Great Eastern St B7
Great Guildford St D6
Great Marlborough St C3
Great Ormond St B4
Great Ormond Street Children's Hosp⊞ B4
Great Percy St B4
Great Peter St E3
Great Portland St⊖ B2
Great Portland St C2
Great Queen St C4
Great Russell St C3
Great Scotland Yd D4
Great Smith St E3
Great Suffolk St E5
Great Titchfield St C3
Great Tower St D7
Great Windmill St D3
Greek St C3
Green Park⊖ D3
Green St D2
Greencoat Pl F3
Gresham St C6
Greville St B4/C5
Greycoat Hosp Sch E3
Greycoat Pl E3
Grosvenor Cres E2
Grosvenor Gdns E2
Grosvenor Pl E2
Grosvenor Sq D2
Grosvenor St D2
Guards Mus and Chapel🏛 E3
Guildhall Art Gallery🏛 C6
Guilford St B4
Guy's Hosp⊞ D6
Haberdasher St B6
Hackney Rd B7
Half Moon St D2
Halkin St E2
Hall St B5
Hallam St C2
Hampstead Rd B3
Hanover Sq C2
Hans Cres E1
Hanway St C3
Hardwick St B5
Harley St C2
Harrison St B4
Hastings St B4
Hatfields D5
Hayles St F5
Haymarket D3
Hayne St C5
Hay's Galleria D7
Hay's Mews D2
Hayward Gallery🏛 D4
Helmet Row B6
Herbrand St B4
Hercules Rd E4
Hertford St D2
High Holborn C4
Hill St D2
HMS Belfast⛵ D7
Hobart Pl E2
Holborn⊖ C4
Holborn C5
Holborn Viaduct C5
Holland St D5
Holmes Mus🏛 B1
Holywell La B7
Horse Guards' Rd D3
Houndsditch C7
Houses of Parliament🏛 E4
Howland St C3
Hoxton Sq B7
Hoxton St B7
Hunter St B4
Hunterian Mus🏛 C4
Hyde Park D1
Hyde Park Cnr⊖ E2
Imperial War Mus🏛 E5
Inner Circle B2
Institute of Archaeology (London Univ) B2
Ironmonger Row B6
James St C2
James St D4
Jermyn St D3
Jockey's Fields C4
John Carpenter St D5
John St B4
Judd St B4
Killick St A4
King Charles St E4
King St D3
King St C6
King William St C6
Kingley St C3
King's Cross≠ A4
King's Cross Rd B4
King's Cross St Pancras⊖ A4
King's Rd E2
Kingsland Rd B7
Kingsway C4
Kinnerton St E2
Knightsbridge⊖ E1
Lamb St C7
Lambeth Bridge F4
Lambeth High St F4
Lambeth North⊖ E5
Lambeth Palace🏛 E4
Lambeth Palace Rd E4
Lambeth Rd E5
Lambeth Walk F4
Lamb's Conduit St C4
Lancaster Pl D4
Lancaster St E5
Langham Pl C2
Leadenhall St C7
Leake St E4
Leather La C5
Leicester Sq⊖ D3
Leicester St D3
Leman St C7
Leonard St B6
Lever St B6
Lexington St D3
Lidlington Pl A3
Lime St D7
Lincoln's Inn Fields C4
Lindsey St C5
Lisle St D3
Liverpool Rd A5
Liverpool St C7
Liverpool St⊖≠ C7
Lloyd Baker St B5
Lloyd Sq B5
Lombard St C6
London Aquarium⛵ E4
London Bridge⊖≠ D6
London Bridge Hosp⊞ D6
London Canal Mus🏛 A4
London City Hall🏛 D7
London Dungeon🏛 D6
London Guildhall University C6
London Rd E5
London Transport Mus🏛 D4
London Wall C6
London-Eye✦ E4
Long Acre D4
Long La C5
Longford St B2
Lower Belgrave St E2
Lower Grosvenor Pl E2
Lower Marsh E5
Lower Thames St D6
Lowndes St E2
Ludgate Circus C5
Ludgate Hill C5
Luxborough St C2
Lyall St E2
Macclesfield Rd B6
Madame Tussaud's✦ B2
Maddox St D2
Malet St C3
Manchester Sq C2
Manchester St C2
Mandeville Pl C2
Mansell St C7
Mansion House🏛 C6
Mansion House⊖ D6
Maple St C3
Marble Arch⊖ C1
Marble Arch D1
Marchmont St B4
Margaret St C3
Margery St B5
Mark La D7
Marlborough Rd D3
Marshall St C3
Marsham St E3
Marylebone High St C2
Marylebone La C2
Marylebone Rd B2
Marylebone St C2
Mecklenburgh Sq B4
Middle Temple La C5
Middlesex St (Petticoat La) C7
Midland Rd A3
Mildmay Mission Hosp⊞ B7
Milner St F1
Minories C7
Mintern St A6
Monck St E3
Monmouth St C4
Montagu Pl C1
Montagu Sq C1
Montagu St C4
Montague Pl C3
Monument⊖ D6
Monument St D6
Monument, The✦ D6
Moor La C6
Moorfields C6
Moorfields Eye Hosp⊞ B6
Moorgate C6
Moorgate⊖≠ C6
Moreland St B5
Morley St E5
Mornington Crescent⊖ A3
Mornington Pl A3
Mortimer St C3
Mount Pleasant B5
Mount St D2
Movieum of London✦ E4
Murray Gr A6
Mus of Garden History🏛 E4
Mus of London🏛 C6
Museum St C4
Myddelton Sq B5
Myddelton St B5
National Film Theatre♥ D4
National Gallery🏛 D3
National Hosp⊞ B4
National Portrait Gallery🏛 D3
Neal St C4
Nelson's Column✦ D4
New Bond St C2/D2
New Bridge St C5
New Cavendish St C2
New Change C6
New Fetter La C5
New Inn Yard B7
New North Rd A6
New Oxford St C3
New Scotland Yard E3
New Sq C4
Newgate St C5
Newton St C4
Nile St B6
Noble St C6
Noel Rd A5
Noel St C3
North Audley St D2
North Cres C3
North Row D2
Northampton Sq B5
Northington St B4
Northumberland Ave D4
Norton Folgate C7
Nottingham Pl C2
Oakley Sq A3
Obstetric Hosp⊞ B3
Old Bailey C5
Old Broad St C6
Old Compton St C3
Old County Hall E4
Old Gloucester St C4
Old King Edward St C6
Old Nichol St B7
Old Paradise St F4
Old Spitalfields Mkt C7
Old St B6
Old St⊖≠ B6
Old Vic♥ E5
Open Air Theatre♥ B2
Operating Theatre Mus🏛 D6
Orange St D3
Orchard St C2
Ossulston St A3
Outer Circle B1
Oxford Circus⊖ C3
Oxford St C2/C3
Paddington St C2
Palace St E3
Pall Mall D3
Pall Mall East D3
Pancras Rd A3/A4
Panton St D3
Paris Gdn D5
Park Cres B2
Park La D2
Park Rd B1
Park St D2
Park St D6
Parker St C4
Parliament Sq E4
Parliament St E4
Paternoster Sq C5
Paul St B6
Pear Tree St B5
Penton Rise B4
Penton St A5
Pentonville Rd A4/A5
Percival St B5
Petticoat La (Middlesex St) C7
Petty France E3
Phoenix Pl B4
Phoenix Rd A3
Photo Gallery🏛 D3
Piccadilly D2
Piccadilly Circus⊖ D3
Pitfield St B7
Pocock St E5
Pollock's Toy Mus🏛 C3
Polygon Rd A3
Pont St E1
Portland Pl C2
Portman Mews C2
Portman Sq C2
Portman St C1
Portugal St C4
Poultry C6
Primrose St C7
Princes St C6
Procter St C4
Provost St B6
Quaker St B7
Queen Anne St C2
Queen Elizabeth Hall♥ D4
Queen Sq B4
Queen St D6
Queen Street Pl D6
Queen Victoria St D5
Queens Gallery🏛 E3
Radnor St B6
Rathbone Pl C3
Rawstorne St B5
Red Lion Sq C4
Red Lion St C4
Redchurch St B7
Redcross Way D6
Regency St F3
Regent Sq B4
Regent St C3
Regent's Park B2
Richmond Terr E4
Ridgmount St C3
Rivington St B7
Robert St B2
Rochester Row F3
Rodney St A4
Ropemaker St C6
Rosebery Ave B5
Roupell St D5
Royal Academy of Arts🏛 D3
Royal Academy of Dramatic Art B3
Royal Academy of Music B2
Royal College of Nursing C2
Royal College of Surgeons C4
Royal Festival Hall♥ D4
Royal National Theatre♥ D5
Royal National Throat, Nose and Ear Hosp⊞ B4
Royal Opera House♥ D4
Russell Sq B3
Russell Square⊖ B4
Sackville St D3
Sadlers Wells♥ B5
Saffron Hill C5
Savile Row D3
Savoy Pl D4
Savoy St D4
School of Hygiene & Tropical Medicine C3
Sclater St B7
Scrutton St B7
Sekforde St B5
Serpentine Rd D1
Seven Dials C4
Seward St B5
Seymour St C1
Shad Thames D7
Shaftesbury Ave D3
Shaftesbury St A6
Shakespeare's Globe Theatre♥ D6
Shepherd Market D2
Shepherdess Walk A6
Sherwood St D3
Shoe La C5
Shoreditch High St B7
Shorts Gdns C4
Sidmouth St B4
Silk St C6
Sir John Soane's Mus🏛 C4
Skinner St B5
Sloane St E1
Snow Hill C5
Soho Sq C3
Somerset House🏛 D4
South Audley St D2
South Carriage Dr E1
South Molton St C2
South Pl C6
South St D2
Southampton Row C4
Southampton St D4
Southwark⊖ D5
Southwark Bridge D6
Southwark Bridge Rd D6
Southwark Cath✝ D6
Southwark St D6
Speakers' Corner D1
Spencer St B5
Spital Sq C7
St Alban's St D3
St Andrew St C5
St Bartholomew's Hosp⊞ C5
St Botolph St C7
St Bride St C5
St George's Rd E5
St Giles High St C3
St James's Palace🏛 D3
St James's Park⊖ E3
St James's St D3
St John St B5
St Margaret St E4
St Mark's Hosp⊞ B5
St Martin's La D4
St Martin's Le Grand C6
St Mary Axe C7
St Pancras International≠ B4
St Paul's⊖ C6
St Paul's Cath✝ C6
St Paul's Churchyard C5
St Peter's Hosp⊞ D4
St Thomas' Hosp⊞ E4
St Thomas St D6
Stamford St D5
Stanhope St B3
Stephenson Way B3
Stock Exchange C5

354 Luton • Macclesfield • Maidstone • Manchester • Merthyr Tydfil

Stoney St D6
Strand C5
Stratton St D2
Sumner St D5
Sutton's Way B6
Swanfield St B7
Swinton St B4
Tabernacle St B6
Tate Modern D6
Tavistock Pl B4
Tavistock Sq B3
Tea & Coffee Mus D6
Temple D5
Temple Ave D5
Temple Pl D4
Terminus Pl E2
Thayer St C2
The Barbican Centre for Arts C6
The Cut E5
The Mall E3
Theobald's Rd C4
Thorney St F4
Threadneedle St C6
Throgmorton St C6
Tonbridge St B4
Tooley St D7
Torrington Pl B3
Tothill St E3
Tottenham Court Rd B3
Tottenham Court Rd C3
Tottenham St C3
Tower Bridge✦ D7
Tower Bridge App D7
Tower Bridge Rd E7
Tower Hill D7
Tower of London, The D7
Toynbee St C7
Trafalgar Square D3
Trinity Sq D7
Trocadero Centre D3
Tudor St D5
Turnmill St C5
Ufford St E5
Union St D5
University College Hosp B3
University of London C3
University of Westminster C2
University St B3
Upper Belgrave St E2
Upper Berkeley St C1
Upper Brook St D2
Upper Grosvenor St D2
Upper Ground D5
Upper Montague St C1
Upper St A5
Upper St Martin's La D4
Upper Thames St D6
Upper Wimpole St C2
Upper Woburn Pl B3
Vere St C2
Vernon Pl C4
Vestry St B6
Victoria E2
Victoria Embankment D4
Victoria Place Shopping Centre F2
Victoria St E3
Villiers St D4
Vincent Sq F3
Vinopolis City of Wine D6
Virginia Rd B7
Wakley St B5
Walbrook C6
Wallace Collection C2
Wardour St C3/D3
Warner St B5
Warren St B3
Warren St B3
Waterloo E4
Waterloo Bridge D4
Waterloo East D5
Waterloo Rd E5
Watling St C6
Webber St E5
Welbeck St C2
Wellington Arch✦ E2
Wellington Mus E2
Wells St C3
Wenlock Rd A6
Wenlock St A6
Wentworth St C7
Werrington St A3
West Smithfield C5
West Sq E5
Westminster E4
Westminster Abbey✝ E4
Westminster Bridge E4
Westminster Bridge Rd E5
Westminster Cathedral (RC)✝ E3
Westminster City Hall E3
Westminster Hall E4
Weymouth St C2
Wharf Rd A6
Wharfdale Rd A4
Wharton St B4
Whitcomb St D3
White Cube B7
White Lion Hill D5
White Lion St A5
Whitecross St B6
Whitefriars St C5
Whitehall D4
Whitehall Pl D4
Wigmore Hall C2
Wigmore St C2
William IV St D4
Wilmington Sq B5
Wilson St C6
Wilton Cres E2
Wimpole St C2
Windmill Walk D5
Woburn Pl B4
Woburn Sq B3
Women's Hosp C3
Wood St C6
Woodbridge St B5
Wootton St D5
Wormwood St C7
Worship St B6
Wren St B4
Wynford Rd A4
Wynyatt St B5
York Rd E4
York St C1
York Terrace East B2
York Terrace West B2
York Way A4

Luton 337

Adelaide St B1
Albert Rd C2
Alma St B2
Alton Rd C3
Anthony Gdns C1
Arndale Centre B2
Arthur St C2
Ashburnham Rd B1
Ashton Rd C2
Avondale Rd A1
Back St A2
Bailey St C3
Baker St C2
Biscot Rd A1
Bolton Rd B3
Boyle Cl A2
Brantwood Rd B1
Bretts Mead C1
Bridge St B2
Brook St A1
Brunswick St A3
Burr St A3
Bury Park Rd A1
Bus Station B2
Bute St B2
Buxton Rd B2
Cambridge St C3
Cardiff Grove B1
Cardiff Rd B1
Cardigan St A2
Castle St B2/C2
Chapel St C2
Charles St A3
Chase St C2
Cheapside B2
Chequer St C3
Church St B2/B3
Cinema A2
Cobden St A3
Collingdon St A1
Concorde Ave A3
Corncastle Rd C1
Cowper St C2
Crawley Green Rd B3
Crawley Rd A1
Crescent Rise A3
Crescent Rd A3
Cromwell Rd A1
Cross St A2
Crown Court B2
Cumberland St B2
Cutenhoe Rd C3
Dallow Rd B1
Downs Rd B1
Dudley St A2
Duke St A2
Dumfries St B1
Dunstable Place B2
Dunstable Rd A1/B1
Edward St A3
Elizabeth St C2
Essex Cl C3
Farley Hill C1
Flowers Way B2
Francis St A1
Frederick St A2
Galaxy Leisure Complex A2
George St B2
George St West B2
Gillam St A3
Gordon St B2
Grove Rd B1
Guildford St A2
Haddon Rd A3
Harcourt St C2
Hart Hill Drive A3
Hart Hill Lane A3
Hartley Rd A3
Hastings St B2
Hat Factory, The B2
Hatters Way A1
Havelock Rd A2
Hibbert St C2
High Town Rd A3
Highbury Rd A1
Hillary Cres C1
Hillborough Rd C1
Hitchin Rd A3
Holly St C2
Holm C1
Hucklesby Way A2
Hunts Cl C1
Information Ctr B2
Inkerman St A2
John St B2
Jubilee St A3
Kelvin Cl C2
King St B2
Kingsland Rd C3
Latimer Rd C2
Lawn Gdns C2
Lea Rd B3
Library B2
Library Rd B2
Liverpool Rd B1
London Rd C2
Luton Station A2
Lyndhurst Rd B1
Magistrates Court B2
Manchester St B2
Manor Rd B3
May St C3
Meyrick Ave C1
Midland Rd A2
Mill St A2
Milton Rd B1
Moor St A1
Moor, The A1
Moorland Gdns A2
Moulton Rise A3
Mus & Art Gallery A2
Napier Rd B1
New Bedford Rd A1
New Town St C2
North St A3
Old Bedford Rd A2
Old Orchard C2
Osbourne Rd C3
Oxen Rd A3
Park Sq B2
Park St B3/C3
Park St West B2
Park Viaduct B3
Parkland Drive C1
Police Station B1
Pomfret Ave A3
Pondwicks Rd B3
Post Office A1/A2/B2/C3
Power Court B3
Princess St B1
Red Rails C1
Regent St B2
Reginald St A2
Rothesay Rd B1
Russell Rise C1
Russell St C1
Ruthin Cl C1
St Ann's Rd B3
St George's B2
St Mary's B3
St Mary's Rd B3
St Paul's Rd C2
St Saviour's Cres C1
Salisbury Rd B1
Seymour Ave C3
Seymour Rd C3
Silver St B2
South Rd C2
Stanley St B1
Station Rd A2
Stockwood Cres C2
Stockwood Park C1
Strathmore Ave C2
Stuart St B2
Studley Rd A1
Surrey St C3
Sutherland Place C1
Tavistock St C2
Taylor St A3
Telford Way A1
Tennyson Rd C2
Tenzing Grove C1
The Cross Way C1
The Larches A2
Thistle Rd B3
Town Hall B2
Townsley Cl C2
Union St B2
University of Bedfordshire B3
Upper George St B2
Vicarage St B3
Villa Rd A2
Waldeck Rd A1
Wellington St B1/B2
Wenlock St A2
Whitby Rd A1
Whitehill Ave C1
William St A2
Wilsden Ave C1
Windmill Rd B3
Windsor St C2
Winsdon Rd B1
York St A3

Macclesfield 337

108 Steps B2
Abbey Rd A1
Alton Dr A3
Armett St C1
Athey St B1
Bank St C3
Barber St C3
Barton St C1
Beech La A2
Beswick St B1
Black La A2
Black Rd C3
Blakelow Gardens C3
Blakelow Rd C3
Bond St B1/C1
Bread St C1
Bridge St B1
Brock St A2
Brocklehurst Ave A3
Brook St B3
Brookfield La B3
Brough St West C1
Brown St C1
Brynton Rd A2
Buckley St C2
Bus Station B2
Buxton Rd B3
Byrons St C2
Canal St B3
Carlsbrook Ave A3
Castle St B2
Catherine St B1
Cemetery A1
Chadwick Terr A3
Chapel St C2
Charlotte St B2
Chester Rd B1
Chestergate B1
Churchill Way B2
Coare St A1
Commercial Rd B2
Conway Cres A3
Copper St C3
Cottage St B1
Court A2
Court B2
Crematorium A1
Crew Ave A3
Crompton Rd B1/C1
Cross St C2
Crossall St C1
Cumberland St A1/B1
Dale St B3
Duke St B2
Eastgate B3
Exchange St B2
Fence Ave B3
Fence Avenue Industrial Estate A3
Flint St B3
Foden St A2
Fountain St B3
Garden St A3
Gas Rd B2
George St B2
Glegg St B3
Golf Course C3
Goodall St B3
Grange Rd C1
Great King St B1
Green St B3
Grosvenor Shopping Centre B2
Gunco La C3
Half St C2
Hallefield Rd B3
Hatton St C1
Hawthorn Way A3
Heapy St C3
Henderson St B1
Heritage Centre & Silk Mus B2
Hibel Rd A2
High St C2
Hobson St C2
Hollins Rd C3
Hope St West B1
Horseshoe Dr B1
Hurdsfield Rd A3
Information Ctr B2
James St C2
Jodrell St B3
John St C2
Jordangate A2
King Edward St B2
King George's Field C3
King St B2
King's School A1
Knight Pool C3
Knight St C3
Lansdowne St A3
Library B2
Lime Gr B3
Little Theatre C2
Loney St B1
Longacre St B1
Lord St C2
Lowe St C2
Lowerfield Rd A3
Lyon St B1
Macclesfield Station B2
Marina B3
Market B2
Market Pl B2
Masons La A3
Mill La C2
Mill Rd C2
Mill St B2
Moran Rd C1
New Hall St A2
Newton St C1
Nicholson Ave A3
Nicholson Cl A3
Northgate Ave A2
Old Mill La C2
Paradise Mill C1
Paradise St B1
Park Green B2
Park La C1
Park Rd C1
Park St C2
Park Vale Rd C1
Parr St B1
Peel St C2
Percyvale St A3
Peter St C1
Pickford St B2
Pierce St B1
Pinfold St B1
Pitt St C2
Police Station B2
Pool St C2
Poplar Rd C2
Post Office B1/B2/B3
Pownall St A2
Prestbury Rd A1/B1
Queen Victoria St B2
Queen's Ave A3
Registrar B2
Richmond Hill C3
Riseley St B1
Roan Ct B3
Roe St B2
Rowan Way A3
Ryle St C2
Ryle's Park Rd C1
St George's St C2
St Michael's B2
Samuel St B2
Saville St C3
Shaw St B1
Slater St C1
Snow Hill C3
South Park C1
Spring Gdns A2
Statham St C2
Station St A2
Steeple St A3
Sunderland St B2
Superstore A1/A2/C2
Swettenham St B3
The Silk Rd A2/B2
Thistleton Cl C2
Thorp St B2
Town Hall B2
Townley St B2
Turnock St C3
Union Rd B3
Union St B2
Victoria Park B3
Vincent St C2
Waters Green B2
Waterside C2
West Bond St B1
West Park A1
Westbrook Dr A1
Westminster Rd A1
Whalley Hayes B1
Windmill St C3
Withyfold Dr A2
York St B3

Maidstone 340

Albion Pl B3
All Saints B2
Allen St A3
Amphitheatre✦ C2
Archbishop's Palace B2
Bank St B2
Barker Rd C2
Barton Rd C3
Beaconsfield Rd C1
Bedford Pl B1
Bentlif Art Gallery B2
Bishops Way B2
Bluett St A3
Bower La C1
Bower Mount Rd B1
Bower Pl C1
Bower St B1
Bowling Alley B3
Boxley Rd A3
Brenchley Gardens A2
Brewer St A3
Broadway B2
Brunswick St C3
Buckland Hill A1
Buckland Rd B1
Bus Station B3
Campbell Rd C3
Carriage Mus B2
Church Rd C1
Church St B3
Cinema C2
College Ave C2
College Rd C2
Collis Memorial Garden C3
Cornwallis Rd B1
Corpus Christi Hall B2
County Hall A2
County Rd A3
Crompton Gdns C3
Crown & County Courts B2
Curzon Rd A3
Dixon Cl C2
Douglas Rd C1
Earl St B2
Eccleston Rd C2
Fairmeadow B2
Fisher St A2
Florence Rd C1
Foley St A3
Foster St C3
Fremlin Walk Shopping Centre B2
Gabriel's Hill B3
George St C3
Grecian St A3
Hardy St A3
Hart St C2
Hastings Rd C3
Hayle Rd C3
Hazlitt Theatre B2
Heathorn St A3
Hedley St A3
High St B2
HM Prison A3
Holland Rd A3
Hope St A2
Information Ctr B2
James St A3
James Whatman Way A2
Jeffrey St A3
Kent County Council Offices A2
King Edward Rd C2
King St B3
Kingsley Rd C3
Knightrider St B3
Launder Way C1
Lesley Pl A1
Library B2
Little Buckland Ave A1
Lockmeadow Leisure Complex C2
London Rd B1
Lower Boxley Rd A2
Lower Fant Rd C1
Magistrates Court B3
Maidstone Barracks Station A1
Maidstone Borough Council Offices B1
Maidstone East Station A2
Maidstone Mus B2
Maidstone West Station B2
Market C2
Market Buildings B2
Marsham St B3
Medway St B2
Medway Trading Estate C2
Melville Rd C3
Mill St B2
Millennium Bridge C2
Mote Rd B3
Muir Rd C3
Old Tovil Rd C2
Palace Ave B3
Perryfield St A2
Police Station B3
Post Office A2/B2/B3/C3
Priory Rd C3
Prospect Pl C1
Pudding La B2
Queen Anne Rd B3
Queens Rd A1
Randall St A2
Rawdon Rd C3
Reginald Rd C1
Rock Pl B1
Rocky Hill B1
Romney Pl B3
Rose Yard B2
Rowland Cl C1
Royal Engineers' Rd A2
Royal Star Arcade B2
St Annes Ct B1
St Faith's St B2
St Luke's Rd A3
St Peter's Br B2
St Peter St B2
St Philip's Ave C3
Salisbury Rd A3
Sandling Rd A2
Scott St A2
Scrubs La B1
Sheal's Cres C3
Somerfield La B1
Somerfield Rd B1
Staceys St A2
Station Rd A2
Superstore A1/B2/B3
Terrace Rd B1
The Mall B3
The Somerfield Hosp A1
Tonbridge Rd C1
Tovil Rd C2
Town Hall B2
Trinity Park B3
Tufton St B3
Union St B3
Upper Fant Rd C1
Upper Stone St C3
Victoria St B1
Visitor Centre A1
Warwick Pl B1
Wat Tyler Way B3
Waterloo St C3
Waterlow Rd A3
Week St B2
Well Rd A3
Westree Rd C1
Wharf Rd C1
Whatman Park A1
Wheeler St A3
Whitchurch Cl B1
Woodville Rd C3
Wyatt St B3
Wyke Manor Rd B3

Manchester 337

Adair St B6
Addington St A5
Adelphi St A1
Air & Space Gallery B2
Albert Sq B3
Albion St C3
AMC Great Northern B3
Ancoats Gr B6
Ancoats Gr North B6
Angela St C2
Aquatic Centre C4
Ardwick Green C5
Ardwick Green North C5
Ardwick Green South C5
Arlington St A2
Arndale Centre A4
Artillery St B3
Arundel St C2
Atherton St B2
Atkinson St B3
Aytoun St B4
Back Piccadilly A4
Baird St B5
Balloon St A4
Bank Pl A1
Baring St B5
Barrack St C1
Barrow St A1
BBC TV Studios C4
Bendix St A5
Bengal St A5
Berry St C5
Blackfriars Rd A3
Blackfriars St A3
Blantyre St C2
Bloom St B4
Blossom St A5
Boad St B5
Bombay St B4
Booth St A3
Booth St B4
Bootle St B3
Brazennose St B3
Brewer St A5
Bridge St A3
Bridgewater Hall B3
Bridgewater Pl A4
Bridgewater St B2
Brook St C4
Brotherton Dr A2
Brown St A3
Brown St B4
Brunswick St C6
Brydon Ave C6
Buddhist Centre A4
Bury St A2
Bus & Coach Station B4
Bus Station B4
Butler St A6
Buxton St C5
Byrom St B3
Cable St A5
Calder St B1
Cambridge St C3/C4
Camp St B3
Canal St B4
Cannon St A1
Cannon St A4
Cardroom Rd A6
Carruthers St A6
Castle St C2
Cateaton St A3
Cathedral✝ A3
Cathedral St A3
Cavendish St C4
Chapel St A1/A3
Chapeltown St B5
Charles St C4
Charlotte St B4
Chatham St B4
Cheapside A3
Chepstow St B3
Chester Rd C1/C2
Chester St C4
Chetham's (Dept Store) A3
China La B5
Chippenham Rd A6
Chorlton Rd C2
Chorlton St B4
Church St A2
Church St A4
City Park A4
City Rd C3
Civil Justice Centre B2
Cleminson St A2
Clowes St A3
College Land A3
College of Adult Education C4
Collier St B2
Commercial St C3
Conference Centre C4
Cooper St B4
Copperas St A4
Cornbrook (Metro Station) C1
Cornell St A5
Cornerhouse C4
Corporation St A4
Cotter St C6
Cotton St A5
Cow La B1
Cross St B3
Crown Court B4
Crown St C2
Cube Gallery B4
Dalberg St C6
Dale St A4/B5
Dancehouse, The C4
Dantzic St A4
Dark La C6
Dawson St C2
Dean St A5
Deansgate A3/B3
Deansgate Station C3
Dolphin St C6
Downing St C5
Ducie St B5
Duke Pl B2
Duke St B2
Durling St C6
East Ordsall La A2/B1
Edge St A4
Egerton St C2
Ellesmere St C1
Everard St C1
Every St B6
Fairfield St B5
Faulkner St B4
Fennel St A3
Ford St A2
Ford St C6
Fountain St B4
Frederick St A2
Gartside St B2
Gaythorne St A1
George Leigh St A5
George St A1
George St B4
G-Mex (Metro Station) C3
Goadsby St A4
Gore St A2
Goulden St A5
Granada TV Studios B2
Granby Row B4
Gravel St A3
Great Ancoats St A5
Great Bridgewater St B3
Great George St A1
Great Jackson St C2
Great Marlborough St C4
Greengate A3
Green Room, The C4
Grosvenor St C5
Gun St A5
Hadrian Ave B6
Hall St B3
Hampson St B1
Hanover St A4
Hanworth Cl C5
Hardman St B3
Harkness St C6
Harrison St B6
Hart St B4
Helmet St B6
Henry St A6
Heyrod St B6
High St A4
Higher Ardwick C6
Hilton St A4/A5
Holland St A6
Hood St A5
Hope St B1
Hope St B4
Houldsworth St A5
Hoyle St C6
Hulme Hall Rd C1
Hulme St A1
Hulme St C3
Hyde Rd C6
Information Ctr B3
Irwell St A2
Islington St A2
Jackson Cr C2
Jackson's Row B3
James St A1
Jenner Cl C2
Jersey St A5
John Dalton St A1
John Dalton St B3
John Ryland's Library B3
John St A2
Kennedy St B3
Kincardine Rd C5
King St A3
King St West A3
Law Courts B3
Laystall St B5
Lever St A5
Library B3
Library Theatre B3
Linby St C2
Little Lever St A4
Liverpool Rd B2
Liverpool St B1
Lloyd St B3
Lockton Cl C5
London Rd B5
Long Millgate A3
Longacre St B6
Loom St A5
Lower Byrom St B2
Lower Mosley St B3
Lower Moss La C2
Lower Ormond St C4
Loxford La C4
Luna St A5
Major St B4
Manchester Art Gallery B4
Manchester Central B3
Manchester Metropolitan University B4/C4
Mancunian Way C3
Manor St C5
Marble St A4
Market St A2
Market St A4
Market St (Metro Station) A4
Marsden St A3
Marshall St A5
Mayan Ave A2
Medlock St C3
Middlewood St B1
Miller St A4
Minshull St B4
Mosley St A4
Mosley St (Metro Station) B4
Mount St B3
Mulberry St B3
Murray St A5
Mus of Science & Technology B2
Nathan Dr A2
National Computer Centre C4
Naval St A5
New Bailey St A2
New Elm Rd B2
New Islington A6
New Quay St B2
New Union St A6
Newgate St A4
Newton St A5
Nicholas St B4
North Western St C6
Oak St A4
Odeon A4
Old Mill St A6
Oldfield Rd A1/C1
Oldham Rd A5
Oldham St A4
Opera House B3
Ordsall La C1
Oxford Rd C4
Oxford Rd C4
Oxford St B4
Paddock St C6
Palace Theatre B4
Pall Mall A3
Palmerston St B6
Park St A1
Parker St B4
Peak St B5
Penfield Cl C5
Peoples' History Mus B2
Peru St A1
Peter St B3
Piccadilly A4
Piccadilly (Metro Station) B5
Piccadilly Gdns (Metro Station) B4
Piccadilly Station B5
Piercy St A6
Poland St A5
Police Station B3/B5
Pollard St B6
Port St A5
Portland St B4
Portugal St East B5
Post Office A1/A4/A5/B3
Potato Wharf B2
Princess St B3/C4
Pritchard St C4
Quay St A2
Quay St B2
Queen St B3
Radium St A5
Redhill St A5
Regent Rd B1
Renold Theatre A2
Retail Park A5
Rice St B2
Richmond St B4
River St C3
Roby St B5
Rodney St A6
Roman Fort B2
Rosamond St A2
Royal Exchange A3
Sackville St B4
St Andrew's St B6
St Ann St A3
St Ann's A3
St George's Ave C1
St James St B4
St John St B3
St John's Cathedral (RC)✝ A2
St Mary's B3
St Mary's Gate A3
St Mary's Parsonage A3
St Peter's Sq (Metro Station) B3
St Stephen St A2
Salford Approach A3
Salford Central A2
Sheffield St B5
Shepley St B5
Sherratt St A5
Shudehill A4
Shudehill (Metro Station) A4
Sidney St C4
Silk St A5
Silver St B4
Skerry Cl C5
Snell St B6
South King St B3
Sparkle St B5
Spear St A4
Spring Gdns A4
Stanley St A2/B2
Station Approach B5
Store St B5
Swan St A4
Tariff St B5
Tatton St C1
Temperance St B6/C6
The Triangle A4
Thirsk St C6
Thomas St A4
Thompson St A5
Tib La B3
Tib St A4
Town Hall (Manchester) B3
Town Hall (Salford) A2
Trafford St C3
Travis St B5
Trinity Way A2
Turner St A4
Union St C6
University of Manchester (Sackville Street Campus) C5
Upper Brook St C5
Upper Cleminson St A1
Upper Wharf St A1
Urbis Mus A4
Vesta St B6
Victoria (Metro Station) A4
Victoria Station A4
Victoria St A3
Wadesdon Rd C5
Water St B2
Watson St B3
West Fleet St B1
West King St A2
West Mosley St B4
West Union St B1
Weybridge Rd A6
Whitworth St B4
Whitworth St West C3
Wilburn St B1
William St A2
William St C6
Wilmott St C3
Windmill St B3
Windsor Cr A1
Withy Gr A4
Woden St C1
Wood St B3
Woodward St A6
Worrall St C1
Worsley St C2
York St B4
York St C2
York St C4

Merthyr Tydfil *Merthyr Tudful* 340

Aberdare Rd B2
Abermorlais Terr B2
Alexandra Rd A3
Alma St C3
Arfryn Pl C3
Argyle St C3
Avenue De Clichy C2
Bethesda St B2
Bishops Gr A3
Brecon Rd A1/B2
Briarmead A3
Bryn St C3
Bryntirion Rd B3/C3
Bus Station B2
Caedraw Rd C2
Cae Mari Dwn B3
Castle Sq A1
Castle St B2

Poole • Portsmouth • Preston • Reading • St Andrews • Salisbury • Scarborough • Sheffield 357

Grand Pde C1
Great Western Rd C1
Greenbank Rd A3
Greenbank Terr A3
Guildhall B2
Hampton St B3
Harwell St B1
Hill Park Cr A3
Hoe Approach B2
Hoe Rd C2
Hoegate St C2
Houndiscombe Rd A2
Information Ctr C3
James St A2
Kensington Rd A3
King St B1
Lambhay Hill C3
Leigham St C1
Library B2
Lipson Rd A3/B3
Lockyer St C2
Lockyers Quay C3
Madeira Rd C2
Marina B3
Market Ave B1
Martin St B1
Mayflower Stone & Steps C3
Mayflower St B2
Mayflower Visitor Centre C3
Merchants House B2
Millbay Rd B1
Mus & Art Gallery B2
National Marine Aquarium C3
Neswick St B1
New George St B2
New St C3
North Cross (r'about) A2
North Hill A3
North Quay B2
North Rd East A2
North Rd West A1
North St B3
Notte St B2
Octagon St B1
Pannier Market B1
Pennycomequick (r'about) A1
Pier St C1
Plymouth Pavilions B1
Plymouth Station A2
Police Station B3
Portland Sq A2
Post Office A1/B1/B2
Princess St B2
Prysten House B2
Queen Anne's Battery Seasports Centre C3
Radford Rd C1
Regent St B3
Rope Walk C3
Royal Citadel C2
Royal Pde B2
St Andrew's B2
St Andrew's Cross (r'about) B2
St Andrew's St B2
St Lawrence Rd A2
Saltash Rd A2
Smeaton's Tower C2
Southern Terr A3
Southside St C2
Stuart Rd A1
Sutherland Rd A2
Sutton Rd B3
Sydney St A1
Teats Hill Rd C3
The Crescent B1
The Hoe C2
The Octagon (r'about) B1
The Promenade C2
Theatre Royal B2
Tothill Ave B3
Union St B1
University of Plymouth A2
Vauxhall St B2/3
Victoria Park A1
West Hoe Rd C1
Western Approach B1
Whittington St A1
Wyndham St B1
YMCA B2
YWCA C2

Poole 341

Ambulance Station A3
Baiater Gdns C2
Baiter Park C3
Ballard Cl C2
Ballard Rd C2
Bay Hog La B1
Bridge Approach C1
Bus Station B2
Castle St B2
Catalina Dr B3
Chapel La B2
Church St B1
Cinnamon La B1
Colborne Cl B3
Dear Hay La B2
Denmark La A3
Denmark Rd A3
East St B2
Elizabeth Rd A3
Emerson Rd B2
Ferry Rd C1
Ferry Terminal C1
Fire Station A2
Freightliner Terminal C1
Furnell Rd B3
Garland Rd A3
Green Rd B2
Heckford La A3
Heckford Rd A3
High St B2
High St North A3
Hill St B2
Holes Bay Rd A1
Hospital (A+E) A3
Information Ctr C2
Kingland Rd B3
Kingston Rd A3
Labrador Dr C3
Lagland St B2
Lander Cl C3
Lifeboat C2
Lighthouse -Poole Centre for the Arts B3
Longfleet Rd A3
Maple Rd A3
Market Cl B2
Market St B2
Mount Pleasant Rd B3
New Harbour Rd C1
New Harbour Rd South C1
New Harbour Rd West C1
New Orchard B1
New Quay Rd C1
New St B2
Newfoundland Dr B2
North St B2
Old Orchard B2
Parish Rd A3
Park Lake Rd B3
Parkstone Rd A3
Perry Gdns B2
Pitwines Cl B2
Police Station A2
Poole Central Library B2
Poole Lifting Bridge C1
Poole Park B2
Poole Station A2
Poole Waterfront Mus C1
Post Office A2/B2
RNLI B2
St John's Rd A3
St Margaret's Rd A2
St Mary's Rd A3
Seldown Bridge B3
Seldown La B3
Seldown Rd B3
Serpentine Rd A2
Shaftesbury Rd A3
Skinner St B2
Slipway B1
Stanley Rd C2
Sterte Ave A2
Sterte Ave West A1
Sterte Cl A2
Sterte Esplanade A2
Sterte Rd A2
Strand St C2
Swimming Pool B3
Taverner Cl B3
Thames St B1
The Quay C2
Towngate Bridge B2
Vallis Cl C3
Waldren Cl B3
West Quay B1
West Quay Rd B1
West St B1
West View Rd A2
Whatleigh Cl B2
Wimborne Rd A3

Portsmouth 341

Action Stations C1
Admiralty Rd A1
Alfred Rd A2
Anglesea Rd B2
Arundel St B3
Bishop St A2
Broad St C1
Buckingham House C2
Burnaby Rd B2
Bus Station B1
Camber Dock C1
Cambridge Rd B2
Car Ferry to Isle of Wight B1
Cascades Shopping Centre A3
Castle Rd C3
Cathedral B1
Cathedral (RC) A3
City Mus & Art Gallery B2
Civic Offices B3
Clarence Pier C2
College St B1
Commercial Rd A3
Cottage Gr B3
Cross St A1
Cumberland St A2
Duisburg Way C2
Durham St A3
East St B1
Edinburgh Rd A2
Elm Gr C3
Great Southsea St C3
Green Rd B3
Greetham St B3
Grosvenor St B3
Grove Rd North C3
Grove Rd South C3
Guildhall B3
Guildhall Walk B3
Gunwharf Quays Retail Park B1
Gunwharf Rd B1
Hambrook St C2
Hampshire Terr B2
Hanover St A1
High St C2
HM Naval Base A1
HMS Nelson (Royal Naval Barracks) A2
HMS Victory A1
HMS Warrior A1
Hovercraft Terminal C2
Hyde Park Rd B3
Information Ctr A1/B3
Isambard Brunel Rd B3
Isle of Wight Car Ferry Terminal B1
Kent Rd C3
Kent St A2
King St B3
King's Rd C3
King's Terr C2
Lake Rd A3
Law Courts B3
Library B3
Long Curtain Rd C2
Market Way A3
Marmion Rd C3
Mary Rose Exhibition A1
Mary Rose Ship Hall A1
Middle St B3
Millennium Blvd B2
Millennium Promenade A1/C1
Mus Rd B2
Naval Recreation Ground C2
Nightingale Rd C3
Norfolk St B3
North St A2
Osborne Rd C3
Park Rd B2
Passenger Catamaran to Isle of Wight B1
Passenger Ferry to Gosport B1
Pelham Rd C3
Pembroke Gdns C2
Pier Rd C2
Point Battery C1
Police Station B3
Portsmouth & Southsea A3
Portsmouth Harbour B1
Post Office A2/A3/B1/B3/C3
Queen St A1
Queen's Cr C3
Round Tower C1
Royal Garrison Church C1
Royal Naval Mus A1
St Edward's Rd C3
St George's Rd B2
St George's Sq B1
St George's Way B2
St James's Rd B3
St James's St A2
St Thomas's St B2
Somers Rd B3
Southsea Common C2
Southsea Terr C2
Spinnaker Tower B1
Square Tower C1
Station St A3
Swimming Pool A2
The Hard B1
Town Fortifications C1
Unicorn Rd A2
United Services Recreation Ground B2
University of Portsmouth A2/B2
University of Portsmouth – College of Art, Design & Media B3
Upper Arundel St A3
Victoria Ave C2
Victoria Park A2
Victory Gate A1
Vue B1
Warblington St B1
Western Pde C2
White Hart Rd C1
Winston Churchill Ave B3

Preston 342

Adelphi St A2
Anchor Ct B3
Aqueduct St A1
Ardee Rd C1
Arthur St B2
Ashton St A1
Avenham La B3
Avenham Park C3
Avenham Rd B3
Avenham St B3
Bairstow St B3
Balderstone Rd C1
Beamont Dr A1
Beech St South C2
Bird St C1
Bow La B2
Brieryfield Rd A1
Broadgate C1
Brook St A2
Bus Station A3
Butler St B2
Cannon St B3
Carlton St A1
Chaddock St B3
Channel Way B1
Chapel St B3
Christ Church St B2
Christian Rd B2
Cold Bath St A2
Coleman Ct C1
Connaught Rd C2
Corn Exchange B3
Corporation St A2/B2
County Hall B2
County Records Office B2
Court A3
Court B3
Cricket Ground C2
Croft St A1
Cross St B3
Crown Court A3
Crown St A3
East Cliff C3
East Cliff Rd B3
Edward St A2
Elizabeth St A3
Euston St B1
Fishergate B2/B3
Fishergate Hill B2
Fishergate Shopping Centre B2
Fitzroy St B1
Fleetwood St A1
Friargate A3
Fylde Rd A1/A2
Gerrard St B2
Glover's Ct B3
Good St B2
Grafton St B2
Great George St A3
Great Shaw St A3
Greenbank St A2
Guild Way B1
Guildhall & Charter B3
Guildhall St B3
Harrington St A2
Harris Mus B3
Hartington Rd B1
Hasset Cl C2
Heatley St B2
Hind St C2
Information Ctr B3
Kilruddery Rd C1
Lancaster Rd A3/B3
Latham St B3
Lauderdale St C2
Lawson St A3
Leighton St A2
Leyland Rd C1
Library A1
Library B3
Liverpool Rd C1
Lodge St B2
Lune St B3
Main Sprit West B3
Maresfield Rd C1
Market St West A3
Marsh La B1/B2
Maudland Bank A2
Maudland Rd A2
Meadow Ct C2
Meath Rd C1
Mill Hill A2
Miller Arcade B3
Miller Park C3
Moor La A3
Mount St B3
North Rd A3
North St A3
Northcote Rd B1
Old Milestones B1
Old Tram Rd C3
Pedder St A1/A2
Peel St A2
Penwortham Bridge C2
Penwortham New Bridge C1
Pitt St B2
Playhouse A3
Police Station A3
Port Way B1
Post Office B3
Preston Station B2
Ribble Bank St B2
Ribble Viaduct C2
Ribblesdale Pl B3
Ringway B3
River Parade C1
Riverside C2
St Georges B3
St Georges Shopping Centre B3
St Johns B3
St Johns Shopping Centre A3
St Mark's Rd A1
St Walburges A1
Salisbury Rd B1
Sessions House B3
Snow Hill A3
South End C2
South Meadow La C2
Spa Rd B1
Sports Ground C2
Strand Rd B1
Syke St B3
Talbot Rd B1
Taylor St C1
Tithebarn St A3
Town Hall B3
Tulketh Brow A1
University of Central Lancashire A2
Valley Rd C1
Victoria St A2
Walker St A3
Walton's Parade B2
Warwick St A3
Wellfield Business Park A1
Wellfield Rd A1
Wellington St A1
West Cliff C2
West Strand A1
Winckley Rd C1
Winckley Square B3
Wolseley Rd C2

Reading 342

Abbey Ruins B2
Abbey St B2
Abbot's Walk B2
Acacia Rd C2
Addington Rd C3
Addison Rd A1
Allcroft Rd C3
Alpine St C2
Baker St B1
Berkeley Ave C1
Bridge St B1
Broad St B1
Broad Street Mall B1
Carey St B1
Castle Hill C1
Castle St B1
Caversham Rd A1
Christchurch Playing Fields A2
Civic Offices & Magistrate's Court B1
Coley Hill C1
Coley Pl C1
Craven Rd C3
Crown St C2
De Montfort Rd A1
Denmark Rd C3
Duke St B2
East St B2
Edgehill St C2
Eldon Rd B3
Eldon Terr B3
Elgar Rd C1
Erleigh Rd C3
Field Rd C1
Fire Station A1
Forbury Gdns B2
Forbury Retail Park B2
Forbury Rd B2
Francis St C1
Friar St B1
Gas Works Rd B3
George St A2
Greyfriars B1
Gun St B1
Hexagon Theatre, The B1
Hill's Meadow A2
HM Prison B2
Howard St B1
Information Ctr B1
Inner Distribution Rd B1
Katesgrove La C1
Kenavon Dr B2
Kendrick Rd C2
King's Meadow Rec Ground A2
King's Rd B2
Library B2
London Rd C3
London St B2
Lynmouth Rd A1
Market Pl B2
Mill La B2
Mill Rd A2
Minster St B1
Morgan Rd C3
Mount Pleasant C2
Mus of English Rural Life C3
Napier Rd A2
Newark St C2
Old Reading University C3
Oracle Shopping Centre, The B1
Orts Rd B3
Pell St C1
Queen Victoria St B1
Queen's Rd A2
Queen's Rd B2
Police Station B1
Post Office B2
Randolph Rd A1
Reading Bridge A2
Reading Station A1
Redlands Rd C3
Renaissance Hotel B1
Riverside Mus B3
Rose Kiln La C1
Royal Berks Hospital (A & E) C3
St Giles C2
St Laurence B2
St Mary's B1
St Mary's Butts B1
St Saviour's Rd C1
Send Rd A3
Sherman Rd C2
Sidmouth St B2
Silver St C2
South St B2
Southampton St C2
Station Hill A1
Station Rd B1
Superstore A3
Swansea Rd A1
Technical College B3
The Causeway A3
The Grove B2
Valpy St B2
Vastern Rd A1
Vue B2
Waldeck St C2
Watlington St B3
West St B1
Wolseley St C1
York Rd A1
Zinzan St B1

St Andrews 342

Abbey St B2
Abbey Walk B3
Abbotsford Cres A1
Albany Pk C3
Allan Robertson Dr C2
Ambulance Station C1
Anstruther Rd C3
Argyle St B1
Argyll Business Park C1
Auld Burn Rd B2
Bassaguard Industrial Estate B1
Bell St B2
Blackfriars Chapel (Ruins) B2
Boase Ave B2
Braid Cres C3
Brewster Pl C3
Bridge St B1
British Golf Mus A1
Broomfaulds Ave C1
Bruce Embankment A1
Bruce St C2
Bus Station A1
Byre B2
Canongate C1
Cathedral and Priory (Ruins) B3
Cemetery B3
Chamberlain St C1
Church St B2
Churchill Cres C2
City Rd A1
Claybraes C1
Cockshaugh Public Park B1
Cosmos Community Centre B3
Council Office A2
Crawford Gdns C1
Doubledykes Rd B1
Drumcarrow Rd C1
East Sands B3
East Scores A3
Fire Station C1
Forrest St C1
Fraser Ave C1
Freddie Tait St C2
Gateway Centre A1
Glebe Rd B2
Golf Pl A1
Grange Rd C3
Greenside Pl B2
Greyfriars Gdns A2
Hamilton Ave C2
Hepburn Gdns B1
Horseleys Park C1
Information Ctr B2
Irvine Cres C3
James Robb Ave C1
James St B1
John Knox Rd C1
Kennedy Gdns B1
Kilrymont Cl C3
Kilrymont Pl C3
Kilrymont Rd C3
Kinburn Park B1
Kinkell Terr C3
Kinnesburn Rd B2
Ladebraes Walk B2
Lady Buchan's Cave A3
Lamberton Pl C1
Lamond Dr C2
Langlands Rd B2
Largo Rd C1
Learmonth Pl C1
Library B2
Links Clubhouse A1
Links, The A1
Livingstone Cres B2
Long Rocks A2
Madras College B2
Market St A2
Martyr's Monument A1
Memorial Hospital (No A+E) B3
Murray Pk A2
Murray Pl A2
Nelson St B2
New Course, The A1
New Picture House A2
North Castle St A3
North St A2
Old Course, The A1
Old Station Rd A1
Pends, The B3
Pilmour Links A1
Pipeland Rd B2/C2
Police Station A2
Post Office B2
Preservation Trust B2
Priestden Pk C3
Priestden Pl C3
Priestden Rd C3
Queen's Gdns B2
Queen's Terr B2
Roundhill Rd C2
Royal & Ancient Golf Club A1
St Andrews B1
St Andrews Aquarium A2
St Andrews Botanic Gardens B1
St Andrews Castle (Ruins) & Visitor Centre A2
St Mary St B3
St Mary's College B2
St Nicholas St C3
St Rules Tower B3
St Salvator's College A2
Sandyhill Cres C2
Sandyhill Rd C2
Scooniehill Rd C2
Shields Ave C3
Shoolbraids C2
Sloan St B1
South St B2
Spottiswoode Gdns C1
Station Rd A1
Swilken Bridge A1
The Scores A2
The Shore B3
Tom Morris Dr C2
Tom Stewart La C1
Town Church B2
Town Hall B2
Union St A2
University Chapel A2
University Library A2
University of St Andrews A1
Viaduct Walk B1
War Memorial A3
Wardlaw Gdns B1
Warrack St C3
Watson Ave B2
West Port B2
West Sands A1
Westview B2
Windmill Rd A1
Winram Pl C1
Wishart Gdns C2
Woodburn Pk B3
Woodburn Pl B3
Woodburn Terr B3
Younger Hall A2

Salisbury 342

Albany Rd A2
Arts Centre A3
Ashley Rd A1
Avon Approach A2
Ayleswade Rd C2
Bedwin St A2
Belle Vue A2
Bishop's Palace C2
Bishops Walk B2
Blue Boar Row B2
Bourne Ave A3
Bourne Hill A3
Britford La C2
Broad Walk C2
Brown St B2
Bus Station B2
Castle St A2
Catherine St B2
Chapter House B2
Church House B2
Churchfields Rd B1
Churchill Way East B3
Churchill Way North A3
Churchill Way South C2
Churchill Way West A1
City Hall B2
Close Wall B2
Coldharbour La A1
College of Further Education B3
College St A3
Council House A3
Court A1
Crane Bridge Rd B2
Crane St B2
Cricket Ground C1
Culver St South B3
De Vaux Pl C2
Devizes Rd A1
Dews Rd B1
Elm Grove B3
Elm Grove Rd A3
Endless St A2
Estcourt Rd A3
Exeter St C2
Fairview Rd A3
Fire Station A1
Fisherton St A1
Folkestone Rd C1
Fowlers Hill B3
Fowlers Rd B3
Friary Estate C3
Friary La B2
Gas La A1
Gigant St B3
Greencroft B3
Greencroft St A3
Guildhall B2
Hall of John Halle B2
Hamilton Rd A2
Harnham Mill B1
Harnham Rd C1/C2
High St B2
Hosp A1
House of John A'Port B2
Information Ctr B2
Kelsey Rd A3
King's Rd A2
Laverstock Rd B3
Library B2
London Rd A3
Lower St C1
Maltings, The B2
Manor Rd A3
Marsh La A1
Medieval Hall & Discover Salisbury B2
Milford Hill B3
Milford St B3
Mill Rd B1
Millstream Approach A2
Mompesson House (NT) B2
New Bridge Rd C2
New Canal B2
New Harnham Rd C2
New St B2
North Canonry B2
North Gate B2
North Walk B2
Old Blandford Rd C1
Old Deanery B2
Park St A3
Parsonage Green C1
Playhouse Theatre A2
Post Office A2/B2/C2
Poultry Cross B2
Precinct B2
Queen Elizabeth Gdns B1
Queen's Rd A3
Rampart Rd B3
St Ann's Gate B2
St Ann St B2
St Marks Rd A3
St Martins B3
St Mary's Cathedral B2
St Nicholas Hosp B2
St Paul's A1
St Thomas B2
Salisbury & South Wiltshire Mus B2
Salisbury General Hospital (A & E) C2
Salisbury Station A1
Salt La A3
Saxon Rd C1
Scots La A2
Shady Bower B3
South Canonry C2
South Gate C2
Southampton Rd B2
Sports Ground C3
The Friary B3
Tollgate Rd B3
Town Path B1
Wain-a-Long Rd A3
Wardrobe, The B2
Wessex Rd A3
West Walk C2
Wilton Rd A1
Winchester St B3
Windsor Rd A1
Winston Churchill Gdns C3
Wyndham Rd A2
YHA B3
York Rd A1

Scarborough 342

Aberdeen Walk B2
Albert Rd A2
Albion Rd C2
Alexandra Bowling Hall A1
Alexandra Gardens A1
Auborough St B2
Belle Vue St C1
Belmont Rd C2
Brunswick Shopping Centre B2
Castle Dykes B3
Castlegate B3
Castle Holms A3
Castle Hill A3
Castle Rd B2
Castle Walls A3
Cemetery B1
Central Lift C2
Clarence Gardens A2
Coach Park B1
Columbus Ravine A1
Court B1
Cricket Ground A1
Cross St B2
Crown Terr C2
Dean Rd B1
Devonshire Dr A1
East Harbour B3
East Pier B3
Eastborough B2
Elmville Ave B1
Esplanade C2
Falconers Rd B2
Falsgrave Rd C1
Fire Station B2
Foreshore Rd B2
Friargate B2
Futurist Theatre B2
Gladstone Rd B1
Gladstone St B1
Hoxton Rd B1
Information Ctr B2/B3
King St B2
Londesborough Rd C1
Longwestgate B3
Marine Dr A3
Miniature Railway A1
Nelson St B1
Newborough B2
Nicolas St B2
North Marine Rd A1
North St B2
Northway B1
Old Harbour B3
Peasholm Park A1
Peasholm Rd A1
Plaza A1
Police Station B1
Post Office B2/C1
Princess St B3
Prospect Rd B1
Queen St B2
Queen's Parade A2
Queen's Tower (Remains) A3
Ramshill Rd C2
Roman Signal Station A3
Roscoe St C1
Rotunda Mus C2
Royal Albert Dr A2
St Martin-on-the-Hill C2
St Martin's Ave C2
St Mary's B3
St Nicholas' Lift B2
St Thomas St B2
Sandside B3
Scarborough Art Gallery and Crescent Art Studio C2
Scarborough Castle A3
Scarborough C1
Somerset Terr C2
South Cliff Lift C2
Spa, The C2
Spa Theatre, The C2
Stephen Joseph Theatre B1
Tennyson Ave B1
The Crescent C2
Tollergate B2
Town Hall B2
Trafalgar Rd B1
Trafalgar Square A1
Trafalgar St West B1
Valley Bridge Parade C2
Valley Rd C1
Vernon Rd C2
Victoria Park Mount A1
Victoria Rd B1
West Pier B3
Westbourough C1
Westover Rd C1
Westwood C1
Woodall Ave A1
York Pl B2
Yorkshire Coast College (Westwood Campus) C1

Sheffield 342

Addy Dr A2
Addy St A2
Adelphi St A3
Albert Terrace Rd A3
Albion St A2
Aldred Rd A1
Allen St A4
Alma St A4
Angel St B5
Arundel Gate B5
Arundel St C4
Ashberry Rd A2
Ashdell Rd C1
Ashgate Rd C1
Athletics Centre B2
Attercliffe Rd A6
Bailey St B4
Ball St A4
Balm Green B4
Bank St B4
Barber Rd A2
Bard St B5
Barker's Pool B4
Bates St A1
Beech Hill Rd C1
Beet St B3
Bellefield St A3
Bernard Rd A6
Bernard St B6
Birkendale A2
Birkendale Rd A2
Birkendale View A1
Bishop St C4
Blackwell Pl B6
Blake St A2
Blonk St A5
Bolsover St B2
Botanical Gdns C1
Bower Rd A1
Bradley St A1
Bramall La C4
Bramwell St A3
Bridge St A4/A5
Brighton Terrace Rd A1
Broad La B3
Broad St B6
Brocco St A3
Brook Hill B3
Broomfield Rd C1
Broomgrove Rd C2
Broomhall Pl C3
Broomhall Rd C2
Broomhall St C3
Broomspring La C2
Brown St C5
Brunswick St B3
Burgess St B4
Burlington St A2
Burns Rd A2
Bus/Coach Station B5
Cadman St A6
Cambridge St B4
Campo La B4
Carver St B4
Castle Market B5
Castle Square (tram station) B5
Castlegate A5
Cathedral (RC) B4
Cathedral (tram station) B4
Cavendish St B3
Charles St C4
Charter Row C4
Children's Hospital (A&E) B2
Church St B4
City Hall B4
City Hall (tram station) B4
City Rd C6
Claremont Cr B2
Claremont Pl B2
Clarke St C3
Clarkegrove Rd C2
Clarkehouse Rd C1
Clarkson St B2
Cobden View Rd A1
Collegiate Cr C2
Commercial St B5
Commonside A1
Conduit Rd B1
Cornish St A3
Corporation St A4
Court B4
Cricket Inn Rd B6
Cromwell St A1
Crookes Rd B1
Crookes Valley Park B2
Crookes Valley Rd B2
Crookesmoor Rd A2
Crown Court A4
Crucible Theatre B5
Cutlers Gate A6
Cutler's Hall B4
Daniel Hill A2
Dental Hosp B2
Dept for Education & Employment C4
Devonshire Green B3
Devonshire St B3
Division St B4
Dorset St C2
Dover St A3
Duchess Rd C5
Duke St B5

Duncombe St A1
Durham Rd B2
Earl St C4
Earl Way C4
Ecclesall Rd C3
Edward St B3
Effingham Rd A6
Effingham St A6
Egerton St C3
Eldon St B3
Elmore Rd B1
Exchange St B5
Eyre St C4
Fargate B4
Farm Rd C5
Fawcett St A3
Filey St B3
Fire & Police Mus A4
Fir St A1
Fitzalan Sq/Ponds Forge (tram station) B5
Fitzwater Rd C6
Fitzwilliam Gate C4
Fitzwilliam St B3
Flat St B5
Foley St A6
Foundry Climbing Centre A4
Fulton Rd A1
Furnace Hill A4
Furnival Rd A5
Furnival Sq C4
Furnival St C4
Garden St B3
Gell St B3
Gibraltar St A4
Glebe Rd B1
Glencoe Rd C6
Glossop Rd B2/B3/C1
Gloucester St C2
Granville Rd C6
Granville Rd/ Sheffield College (tram station) C5
Graves Gallery B5
Greave Rd B3
Green La A4
Hadfield St A1
Hanover St C3
Hanover Way C3
Harcourt Rd B1
Harmer La B5
Havelock St C2
Hawley St B4
Haymarket B5
Headford St C3
Heavygate Rd A1
Henry St A3
High St B4
Hodgson St C3
Holberry Gdns C2
Hollis Croft B4
Holly St B4
Hounsfield Rd B3
Howard Rd A1
Hoyle St A3
Hyde Park (tram station) A6
Infirmary Rd A3
Infirmary Rd (tram station) A3
Information Ctr B4
Jericho St A3
Johnson St A5
Kelham Island Industrial Mus A4
Lawson Rd C1
Leadmill Rd C5
Leadmill St C5
Leadmill, The C5
Leamington St A1
Leavy Rd B3
Lee Croft B4
Leopold St B4
Leveson St A6
Library A2
Library B5
Library C1
Lyceum Theatre B5
Malinda St A3
Maltravers St A5
Manor Oaks Rd B6
Mappin Art Gallery B2
Mappin St B3
Marlborough Rd B1
Mary St C4
Matilda St C4
Matlock Rd A1
Meadow St A3
Melbourn Rd A1
Melbourne Ave C1
Millennium Galleries B5
Milton St C3
Mitchell St B3
Mona Ave A1
Mona Rd A1
Montgomery Terrace Rd A3
Montgomery Theatre B4
Monument Gdns C6
Moor Oaks Rd B1
Moore St C3
Mowbray St A4
Mushroom La B2
Netherthorpe Rd B3
Netherthorpe Rd (tram station) B3
Newbould La C1
Nile St C1
Norfolk Park Rd C6
Norfolk Rd C6
Norfolk St B4
North Church St B4
Northfield Rd A1
Northumberland Rd B1
Nursery St A5
Oakholme Rd C1
Octagon B2
Odeon B5
Old St B6
Oxford St A2
Paradise St B4
Park La C2
Park Sq B5
Parker's Rd B1
Pearson Building (Univ) C2
Penistone Rd A3
Pinstone St B4
Pitt St B3
Police Station A4/B5
Pond Hill B5
Pond St B5
Ponds Forge Sports Centre B5
Portobello St B3
Post Office A1/A2/B3/B4/B5/B6/C1/C3/C4/C6
Powell St A2
Queen St B4
Queen's Rd C5
Ramsey Rd B1
Red Hill B3
Redcar Rd B1
Regent St B3
Rockingham St B4
Roebuck Rd A2
Royal Hallamshire Hosp C2
Russell St A4
Rutland Park C1
St George's Cl B3
St Mary's Gate C3
St Mary's Rd C4/C5
St Peter & St Paul Cathedral B4
St Philip's Rd A3
Savile St A5
School Rd B1
Scotland St A4
Severn Rd B1
Shalesmoor A4
Shalesmoor (tram station) A3
Sheaf St B5
Sheffield Hallam University B5
Sheffield Ice Sports Centre – Skate Central C5
Sheffield Parkway A6
Sheffield Station C5
Sheffield Station/ Sheffield Hallam University (tram station) B5
Sheffield University B2
Shepherd St A3
Shipton St A2
Shoreham St C4
Showroom, The C5
Shrewsbury Rd C5
Sidney St C4
Site Gallery C5
Slinn St A1
Smithfield A4
Snig Hill A5
Snow La A4
Solly St B3
Southbourne Rd C1
South La C4
South Street Park B5
Spital Hill A5
Spital St A5
Spring Hill B1
Spring Hill Rd B1
Springvale Rd A1
Stafford Rd C6
Stafford St B6
Stanley St A5
Suffolk Rd C5
Summer St B2
Sunny Bank C3
Surrey St B4
Sussex St A6
Sutton St B3
Sydney Rd A2
Sylvester St C4
Talbot St B5
Taptonville Rd B1
Tax Office C4
Tenter St B4
The Moor C4
Town Hall B4
Townend St A1
Townhead St B4
Trafalgar St B4
Tree Root Walk B2
Trinity St A4
Trippet La B4
Turner Mus of Glass B3
Union St B4
University Drama Studio B2
University of Sheffield (tram station) B3
Upper Allen St A3
Upper Hanover St B3
Upperthorpe Rd A2/A3
Verdon St A5
Victoria Quays B5
Victoria Rd C2
Victoria St B3
Waingate B5
Watery St A3
Watson Rd C1
Wellesley Rd B2
Wellington St C3
West Bar A4
West Bar Green A4
West One B3
West St B3
West St (tram station) B4
Westbourne Rd C1
Western Bank B2
Western Rd A1
Weston Park B2
Weston Park Hosp B2
Weston Park Mus B2
Weston St B2
Wharncliffe Rd C3
Whitham Rd B1
Wicker A5
Wilkinson St B2
William St C3
Winter Garden B4
Winter St B2
York St B4
Yorkshire Artspace C5
Young St C4

Shrewsbury 342

Abbey Church B3
Abbey Foregate B3
Abbey Lawn Business Park B3
Abbots House B2
Agricultural Show Gd A1
Albert St A2
Alma St B1
Ashley St A3
Ashton Rd C1
Avondale Dr A3
Bage Way C3
Barker St B1
Beacall's La A2
Beeches La C2
Belle Vue Gdns C2
Belle Vue Rd C2
Belmont Bank C1
Berwick Ave A1
Berwick Rd A1
Betton St C2
Bishop St C3
Bradford St B3
Bridge St B1
Bus Station B2
Butcher Row B2
Burton St A3
Butler Rd C1
Bynner St C2
Canon St B3
Canonbury C1
Castle Business Park, The A2
Castle Foregate A2
Castle Gates B2
Castle Mus B2
Castle St B2
Cathedral (RC) C1
Chester St A2
Cineworld C3
Claremont Bank B1
Claremont Hill B1
Cleveland St B3
Coleham Head B2
Coleham Pumping Station C2
College Hill B1
Corporation La A1
Coton Cres A1
Coton Hill A2
Coton Mount A1
Crescent La C1
Crewe St A2
Cross Hill B1
Darwin Centre B2
Dingle, The B1
Dogpole B2
Draper's Hall B2
English Bridge B2
Fish St B2
Frankwell B1
Gateway Centre, The A2
Gravel Hill La A1
Greyfriars Rd C2
Guildhall B1
Hampton Rd A3
Haycock Way C3
HM Prison B2
High St B1
Hills La B1
Holywell St B3
Hunter St A1
Information Ctr B1
Ireland's Mansion & Bear Steps B1
John St A3
Kennedy Rd C1
King St B3
Kingsland Bridge C1
Kingsland Bridge (toll) C1
Kingsland Rd C1
Library B2
Lime St C2
Longden Coleham C2
Longden Rd C1
Longner St B1
Luciefelde Rd C1
Mardol B1
Market B1
Monkmoor Rd B3
Moreton Cr C2
Mount St A1
Music Hall B1
New Park Cl A3
New Park Rd A2
New Park St A3
North St A2
Oakley St C1
Old Coleham C2
Old Market Hall B1
Old Potts Way C3
Parade Centre B2
Police Station B1
Post Office A2/B1/B2/B3
Pride Hill B1
Pride Hill Centre B1
Priory Rd B1
Pritchard Way C3
Queen St A3
Raby Cr C2
Rad Brook C1
Rea Brook C3
Riverside B1
Roundhill La A1
Rowley's House B1
St Alkmund's B2
St Chad's B1
St Chad's Terr B1
St John's Hill B1
St Julians Friars C2
St Mary's B2
St Mary's St B2
Scott St C3
Severn Bank A3
Severn St A2
Shrewsbury B2
Shrewsbury High School for Girls C1
Shrewsbury School C1
Shropshire Wildlife Trust B3
Smithfield Rd B1
South Hermitage C1
Swan Hill B1
Sydney Ave A3
Tankerville St B3
The Dana B2
The Quarry B1
The Square B1
Tilbrook Dr A3
Town Walls C1
Trinity St C2
Underdale Rd B3
Victoria Ave B1
Victoria Quay B1
Victoria St B2
Welsh Bridge B1
Whitehall St B3
Wood St A2
Wyle Cop B2

Southampton 342

Above Bar St A2
Albert Rd North B3
Albert Rd South C3
Anderson's Rd B3
Archaeology Mus C2
Argyle Rd A2
Arundel Tower B1
Bargate, The B2
Bargate Centre B2
BBC Regional Centre A1
Bedford Pl A1
Belvidere Rd A3
Bernard St C2
Blechynden Terr A1
Brazil Rd C3
Brinton's Rd A2
Britannia Rd A3
Briton St C2
Brunswick Pl A2
Bugle St C1
Canute Rd C3
Castle Way C2
Catchcold Tower B1
Central Bridge C3
Central Rd C2
Channel Way C3
Chapel Rd B3
Cineworld C3
City Art Gallery A1
City College B3
Civic Centre A1
Civic Centre Rd A1
Coach Station B1
Commercial Rd A1
Cumberland Pl A1
Cunard Rd C2
Derby Rd A3
Devonshire Rd A1
Dock Gate 4 C2
Dock Gate 8 B1
East Park A2
East Park Terr A2
East St B2
East St Shopping Centre B2
Endle St B3
European Way C2
Fire Station A2
Floating Bridge Rd C3
God's House Tower C2
Golden Gr A3
Graham Rd A2
Guildhall A1
Hanover Bldgs B2
Harbour Lights C3
Harbour Pde B1
Hartington Rd A3
Havelock Rd A1
Henstead Rd A1
Herbert Walker Ave B1
High St B2
Hoglands Park B2
Holy Rood (Rems), Merchant Navy Memorial B2
Hosp A2
Houndwell Park B2
Houndwell Pl B2
Hythe Ferry C2
Information Ctr A1
Isle of Wight Ferry Terminal C1
James St B3
Java Rd C2
Kingsland Market B2
Kingsway A2
Leisure World B1
Library A1
Lime St B2
London Rd A2
Marine Pde B3
Maritime C1
Marsh La B2
Mayflower Memorial C1
Mayflower Park C1
Mayflower Theatre, The A1
Medieval Merchant's House C1
Melbourne St B3
Millais A2
Morris Rd A1
Neptune Way C3
New Rd A2
Nichols Rd A3
Northam Rd A3
Ocean Dock C2
Ocean Village Marina C3
Ocean Way C3
Odeon B1
Ogle Rd B1
Old Northam Rd A2
Orchard La B2
Oxford Ave A2
Oxford St C2
Palmerston Park A2
Palmerston Rd A2
Parsonage Rd A3
Peel St A3
Platform Rd C2
Police Station A1
Portland Terr B1
Post Office A2/A3/B2
Pound Tree Rd B2
Quays Swimming & Diving Complex, The B1
Queen's Park C2
Queen's Peace Fountain A2
Queen's Terr C2
Queen's Way B2
Radcliffe Rd A3
Rochester St A3
Royal Pier C1
St Andrew's Rd A2
St Mary St A2
St Mary's B3
St Mary's Leisure Centre A2
St Mary's Pl B2
St Mary's Rd A2
St Mary's Stadium (Southampton FC) A3
St Michael's C1
Solent Sky C3
South Front B2
Southampton Central Station A1
Southampton Solent University A2
Southampton Oceanography Centre C3
SS Shieldhall C2
Terminus Terr C2
The Mall, Marlands A1
The Polygon A1
Threefield La B2
Titanic Engineers' Memorial A2
Town Quay C1
Town Walls B2
Tudor House C1
Vincent's Walk B2
West Gate C1
West Marlands Rd A1
West Park A1
West Park Rd A1
West Quay Rd B1
West Quay Retail Park B1
West Quay Shopping Centre B1
West Rd C2
Western Esplanade B1

Southend-on-Sea 343

Adventure Island C3
Albany Ave A1
Albert Rd C3
Alexandra Rd C2
Alexandra St C2
Art Gallery C1
Ashburnham Rd B2
Ave Rd B1
Avenue Terr B1
Balmoral Rd B1
Baltic Ave B3
Baxter Ave A2/B2
Bircham Rd A2
Boscombe Rd B3
Boston Ave A1/B2
Bournemouth Park Rd A3
Browning Ave A3
Bus Station C3
Byron Ave A3
Cambridge Rd C1/C2
Canewdon Rd B1
Carnarvon Rd A2
Central Ave A3
Chelmsford Ave A1
Chichester Rd B2
Church Rd C3
Civic Centre A2
Clarence Rd C2
Clarence St C2
Cliff Ave B1
Cliffs Pavilion C1
Clifftown Parade C2
Clifftown Rd C2
Colchester Rd A1
College Way B2
County Court B3
Cromer Rd B3
Crowborough Rd A2
Dryden Ave A3
East St A2
Elmer App B2
Elmer Ave B2
Gainsborough Dr A1
Gayton Rd A2
Glenhurst Rd A2
Gordon Pl B2
Gordon Rd B2
Grainger Rd A2
Greyhound Way A3
Guildford Rd B3
Hamlet Ct Rd B1
Hamlet Rd C1
Harcourt Ave A1
Hartington Rd C3
Hastings Rd B3
Herbert Gr C3
Heygate Ave C3
High St B2/C2
Information Ctr C3
Kenway A2
Kilworth Ave B3
Lancaster Gdns B3
Library B2
London Rd B1
Lucy Rd C3
MacDonald Ave A1
Magistrates Court A2
Maldon Rd A2
Marine Parade C3
Milton Rd B1
Milton St B2
Napier Ave B2
Never Never Land C2
North Ave A3
North Rd A1/B1
Odeon B2
Osborne Rd B1
Park Cres B1
Park Rd B1
Park St B1
Park Terr B1
Peter Pan's Playground C2
Pier Hill C3
Pleasant Rd C3
Police Station A2
Post Office B2/B3
Princes St B2
Queens Rd B2
Queensway B2/B3/C3
Rayleigh Ave A1
Redstock Rd A2
Rochford Ave A1
Royal Mews C2
Royal Terr C2
Royals Shopping Precinct, The C3
Ruskin Ave A3
St Ann's Rd B3
St Helen's Rd B1
St John's Rd B1
St Leonard's Rd C3
St Lukes Rd A3
St Vincent's Rd C1
Salisbury Ave A1/B1
Scratton Rd C2
Shakespeare Dr A1
Short St A2
South Ave A3
Southchurch Rd B3
South East Essex College B2
Southend Central B2
Southend Pier Railway C3
Southend United FC A1
Southend Victoria B2
Stadium Rd A2
Stanfield Rd A2
Stanley Rd C3
Sutton Rd A3/B3
Swanage Rd B3
Sweyne Ave A1
Swimming Pool B3
Sycamore Gr A3
Tennyson Ave A3
The Grove A3
Tickfield Ave A2
Tudor Rd A1
Tunbridge Rd A2
Tylers Ave B3
Tyrrel Dr B3
Vale Ave A2
Victoria Ave A2
Victoria Plaza Shopping Precinct B2
Warrior Sq B3
Wesley Rd C3
West Rd A1
West St A1
Westcliff Parade C1
Western Esplanade C1
Weston Rd C2
Whitegate Rd B3
Wilson Rd C1
Wimborne Rd B3
York Rd C3

Stirling 343

Abbey Rd A3
Abbotsford Pl A3
Abercromby Pl C1
Albert Halls B1
Albert Pl B1
Alexandra Pl A3
Allan Park C2
Ambulance Station A2
AMF Ten Pin Bowling B2
Argyll Ave A3
Argyll's Lodging B1
Back O' Hill Industrial Estate A1
Back O' Hill Rd A1
Baker St B2
Ballengeich Pass A1
Balmoral Pl B1
Barn Rd B1
Barnton St B2
Bow St B1
Bruce St A2
Burghmuir Industrial Estate C2
Burghmuir Rd A2/B2/C2
Bus Station B2
Cambuskenneth Bridge A3
Carlton C2
Castle Ct B1
Causewayhead Rd A2
Cemetery A1
Cemetery B1
Church of the Holy Rude B1
Clarendon Pl C1
Club House B1
Colquhoun St C3
Corn Exchange B2
Council Offices C2
Court B2
Cowane B2
Cowane St A2
Cowane's Hospital B1
Crawford Shopping Arcade B2
Crofthead Rd A1
Dean Cres A3
Douglas St A2
Drip Rd A1
Drummond La C1
Drummond Pl C1
Drummond Pl La C1
Dumbarton Rd C2
Eastern Access Rd B2
Edward Ave A3
Edward Rd A2
Forrest Rd A2
Fort A1
Forth Cres B2
Forth St A2
Gladstone Pl C1
Glebe Ave C1
Glebe Cres C1
Glendevon Dr A1
Golf Course C1
Goosecroft Rd B2
Gowanhill A1
Greenwood Ave B1
Harvey Wynd A1
Information Ctr A1/C2
Irvine Pl B2
James St A2
John St B1
Kerse Rd C3
King's Knot B1
King's Park C1
King's Park Rd C1
Laurencecroft Rd A2
Leisure Pool B2
Library B2
Linden Ave C2
Lovers Wk A2
Lower Back Walk B1
Lower Bridge St A2
Lower Castlehill A1
Mar Pl B1
Meadow Pl A3
Meadowforth Rd C3
Middlemuir Rd C3
Millar Pl A3
Morris Terr B2
Mote Hill A1
Murray Pl B2
Nelson Pl C2
Old Town Jail B1
Orchard House Hospital (No A+E) A2
Park Terr C1
Phoenix Industrial Estate C3
Players Rd C3
Port St C2
Princes St B2
Queen St B2
Queen's Rd B1
Queenshaugh Dr A3
Rainbow Slides B2
Ramsay Pl A2
Riverside Dr A3
Ronald Pl A1
Rosebery Pl A2
Royal Gardens B1
Royal Gdns B1
St Mary's Wynd B1
St Ninian's Rd C2
Scott St A2
Seaforth Pl B2
Shore Rd B2
Smith Art Gallery & Mus B1
Snowdon Pl C1
Snowdon Pl La C1
Spittal St B2
Springkerse Industrial Estate C3
Springkerse Rd C3
Stirling Business Centre C2
Stirling Castle A1
Stirling County Rugby Football Club A3
Stirling Enterprise Park B3
Stirling Old Bridge A2
Stirling Station B2
Superstore A2
Sutherland Ave A3
TA Centre C3
Tannery La A2
Thistle Industrial Estate C3
Thistles Shopping Centre, The B2
Tolbooth, The B1
Town Wall B1
Union St A2
Upper Back Walk B1
Upper Bridge St A1
Upper Castlehill B1
Upper Craigs C2
Victoria Pl C1
Victoria Rd B1
Victoria Sq B1/C1
Vue B2
Wallace St A2
Waverley Cres A3
Wellgreen Rd C2
Windsor Pl C1
YHA B1

Stoke 343

Ashford St A3
Avenue Rd A3
Aynsley Rd A2
Barnfield C1
Bath St C2
Beresford St A3
Bilton St C2
Boon Ave C2
Booth St C2
Boothen Rd C2/C3
Boughey St C2
Boughley Rd B3
Brighton St B1
Campbell Rd C2
Carlton Rd B3
Cauldon Rd A3
Cemetery A2
Cemetery Rd A2
Chamberlain Ave C1
Church (RC) B2
Church St C2
City Rd C3
Civic Centre B3
Cliff Vale Pk A1
College Rd A3
Convent Cl B2
Copeland St B2
Cornwallis St C3
Corporation St C2
Crowther St A3
Dominic St B1
Elenora St B2
Elgin St B2
Epworth St A3
Etruscan St A1
Fleming Rd C2
Fletcher Rd C2
Floyd St B2
Foden St C2
Frank St C2
Franklin Rd C1
Frederick Ave B1
Garden St C2
Garner St A1
Gerrard St B2
Glebe St B3
Greatbach Ave B1
Hanley Park A3
Harris St B1
Hartshill Rd B1
Hayward St A2
Hide St B2
Higson Ave B2
Hill St B2
Honeywall B2
Hunters Dr C1
Hunters Way C1
Keary St C2
Kingsway B2
Leek Rd B3
Leisure Centre C2
Library C2
Lime St C2
Liverpool Rd B2
London Rd C2
Lonsdale St C2
Lovatt St B2
Lytton St B2
Market C2
Mount School for the Deaf B1
Newcastle La C1
Newlands St A2
Norfolk St A2
North St A1/B2
North Staffordshire Royal Infirmary (A&E) B1
Northcote Ave B2
Oldmill St C3
Oriel St B1
Oxford St B1
Penkhull New Rd C1
Penkhull St C1
Police Station C2
Portmeirion Pottery C2
Post Office A3/B1/B3/C1/C2
Prince's Rd B1
Pump St B2
Quarry Ave B1
Quarry Rd B1
Queen Anne St A3
Queen's Rd C1
Queensway A1/B2/C3
Richmond St B1
Rothwell St C1
St Peter's B3
St Thomas Pl C1
Scrivenor Rd A1
Seaford St A3
Selwyn St C3
Shelton New Rd A1
Shelton Old Rd B2
Sheppard St C2
Spark St C2
Spencer Rd B3
Spode Mus & Visitor Centre B2
Spode St C2
Squires View B3
Staffordshire Univ B3
Stanley Matthews Sports Centre B3
Station Rd B3
Stoke Business Park C3
Stoke Film Theatre B3
Stoke Rd A2
Stoke-on-Trent College A3
Stoke-on-Trent Station B3
Sturgess St C2
The Villas C1
Thistley Hough C1
Thornton Rd B3
Tolkien Way B1
Trent Valley Rd C1
Vale St B2
Watford St A3
Wellesley St A3
West Ave B1
Westland St B1
Yeaman St C2
Yoxall Ave B1

Stratford-upon-Avon 343

Albany Rd B1
Alcester Rd B1
Ambulance Station B1
Arden St B2
Avenue Farm A1
Avenue Farm Industrial Estate A1
Avenue Rd A3
Avon Industrial Estate A2
Baker Ave A1
Bandstand C3
Benson Rd A3
Birmingham Rd A2
Boat Club B3
Borden Pl C1
Brass Rubbing Centre C2
Bridge St B2
Bridgetown Rd C3
Bridgeway B3
Broad St C2
Broad Walk C2
Brookvale Rd C1
Bull St C2
Bus Station B2
Butterfly Farm & Jungle Safari C3
Cemetery C1
Chapel La B2
Cherry Orchard C1
Chestnut Walk B2
Children's Playground C3
Church St C2
Civic Hall B2
Clarence Rd B1
Clopton Bridge B3
Clopton Rd A2
Coach Terminal & Park B3
College B1
College La C2
College St C2
Community Sports Centre B1
Council Offices (District) B2
Courtyard C2
Cox's Yard B3
Cricket Ground C3
Ely Gdns B2
Ely St B2
Evesham Rd C1
Fire Station B1
Foot Ferry C3
Fordham Ave A2
Gallery, The B3
Garrick Way C1
Gower Memorial B3
Great William St B2
Greenhill St B2
Grove Rd B2
Guild St B2
Guildhall & School B2
Hall's Croft C2
Hartford Rd C1
Harvard House B2
Henley St B2
High St B2
Holton St C2
Holy Trinity C2
Information Ctr B3
Jolyffe Park Rd A2
Judith Shakespeare's House B2
Kipling Rd C3
Leisure & Visitor Centre B3
Library B2
Lodge Rd B1
Maidenhead Rd A3
Mansell St B2
Masons Court B2
Masons Rd A1
Maybird Retail Park A2
Maybrook Rd A1
Mayfield Ave A2
Meer St B2
Mill La C2
Moat House Hotel B3
Narrow La C2
New Place & Nash's House B2
New St C2
Old Town C2
Orchard Way C1
Paddock La C1
Park Rd A1
Payton St B2
Percy St A2
Police Station B2
Post Office B2/B3
Recreation Ground C2
Regal Road A2
Regal Road Trading Estate A2
Rother St B2
Rowley Cr A3
Ryland St C2
Saffron Meadow C2
St Andrew's Cr B1

Sunderland • Swansea • Swindon • Taunton • Telford • Torquay • Truro 359

St Gregory's A3
St Gregory's Rd A3
St Mary's Rd A2
Sanctus Dr C2
Sanctus St C1
Sandfield Rd C2
Scholars La B2
Seven Meadows Rd C2
Shakespeare Centre B2
Shakespeare Institute C2
Shakespeare St B2
Shakespeare's Birthplace B2
Sheep St B2
Shelley Rd C3
Shipston Rd C3
Shottery Rd C1
Slingates Rd A2
Southern La C2
Station Rd B1
Stratford Healthcare B2
Stratford Hosp B2
Stratford Sports Club B1
Stratford-upon-Avon Station B1
Talbot Rd A2
The Greenway C2
The Willows B1
The Willows North B1
Tiddington Rd B3
Timothy's Bridge Rd A1
Town Hall & Council Offices B2
Town Sq B2
Tramway Bridge B3
Trinity St C2
Tyler St B2
War Memorial Gdns B3
Warwick Rd B3
Waterside B3
Welcombe Rd A3
West St C2
Western Rd A2
Wharf Rd A2
Wood St B2

Sunderland 343

Albion Pl C2
Alliance Pl B1
Argyle St C2
Ashwood St C1
Athenaeum St B2
Azalea Terr C2
Beach St A1
Bede Theatre C3
Bedford St B2
Beechwood Terr C1
Belvedere Rd C2
Blandford St B2
Borough Rd B3
Bridge Cr B2
Bridge St B2
Brooke St A2
Brougham St B2
Burdon Rd C2
Burn Park C1
Burn Park Rd C1
Burn Park Tech Park C1
Carol St B1
Charles St A3
Chester Rd C1
Chester Terr B1
Church St A3
Cineworld B2
Civic Centre C2
Cork St B3
Coronation St B3
Cowan Terr C2
Crowtree Rd B2
Dame Dorothy St A2
Deptford Rd B1
Deptford Terr A1
Derby St C2
Derwent St C2
Dock St A3
Dundas St A2
Durham Rd C1
Easington St A2
Egerton St C3
Empire Theatre B2
Farringdon Row B1
Fawcett St B2
Fox St C1
Foyle St B3
Frederick St B3
Gill Rd B2
Hanover Pl A1
Havelock Terr C1
Hay St A2
Headworth Sq B3
Hendon Rd B3
High St East B3
High St West B2/B3
Holmeside B2
Hylton Rd B1
Information Ctr B2
John St B3
Kier Hardie Way A2
Lambton St B3
Laura St C3
Lawrence St B3
Leisure Centre B2
Library & Arts Centre B3
Lily St B1
Lime St B1
Livingstone Rd B2
Low Row B2
Matamba Terr B1
Millburn St B1
Millennium Way A2
Minster B2
Monkwearmouth Station Museum A2
Mowbray Park C3
Mowbray Rd C3
Murton St C3
Museum B3
National Glass Centre A3
New Durham Rd C1
Newcastle Rd A2
Nile St B3
Norfolk St B3
North Bridge St A2
Otto Terr C1
Park La C2
Park Lane (metro station) C2
Park Rd C2
Paul's Rd B3
Peel St C3
Police Station B2
Post Office B2
Priestly Cr A1
Queen St B2
Railway Row B1
Retail Park B1
Richmond St A2
Roker Ave A2
Royalty Theatre C1
Ryhope Rd C2
St Mary's Way B2
St Michael's Way B2
St Peter's A3
St Peter's (metro station) A2
St Peter's Way A3
St Vincent St C3
Salem Rd C3
Salem St C3
Salisbury St C3
Sans St B3
Silkworth Row B1
Southwick Rd A2
Stadium of Light (Sunderland AFC) A2
Stadium Way A2
Stobart St A2
Stockton Rd C2
Suffolk St C3
Sunderland (metro station) B2
Sunderland Station B2
Sunderland St B3
Tatham St C3
Tavistock Pl B3
The Bridges B2
The Place B3
The Royalty C1
Thelma St C1
Thomas St North A2
Thornholme Rd C1
Toward Rd C3
Transport Interchange C2
Trimdon St Way B1
Tunstall Rd C2
University (metro station) C1
University Library C1
University of Sunderland (City Campus) B1
University of Sunderland (Sir Tom Cowie Campus) A3
Vaux Brewery Way A2
Villiers St B3
Villiers St South B3
Vine Pl C2
Violet St B1
Walton La B3
Waterworks Rd B1
Wearmouth Bridge B2
Wellington La A1
West Sunniside B3
West Wear St B3
Westbourne Rd B1
Western Hill C1
Wharncliffe B1
Whickham St A3
White House Rd C3
Wilson St North A2
Winter Gdns C3
Wreath Quay A1

Swansea *Abertawe* 343

Adelaide St C3
Albert Row C3
Alexandra Rd B3
Argyle St C1
Baptist Well Pl A2
Beach St C1
Belle Vue Way B3
Berw Rd A1
Berwick Terr A2
Bond St C1
Brangwyn Concert Hall C1
Bridge St A3
Brookands Terr B1
Brunswick St C1
Bryn-Syfi Terr A2
Bryn-y-Mor Rd C1
Bullins La B1
Burrows Rd C1
Bus/Rail link A3
Bus Station C2
Cadfan Rd A1
Cadrawd Rd A1
Caer St B3
Carig Cr A1
Carlton Terr B2
Carmarthen Rd A3
Castle Square B3
Castle St B3
Catherine St C1
City & County of Swansea Offices (County Hall) C2
City & County of Swansea Offices (Guildhall) C1
Clarence St C2
Colbourne Terr A2
Constitution Hill B1
Court B3
Creidiol Rd A2
Cromwell St B2
Duke St B1
Dunvant Pl C2
Dyfatty Park A3
Dyfatty St A3
Dyfed Ave A1
Dylan Thomas Ctr B3
Dylan Thomas Theatre C3
Eaton Cr C1
Eigen Cr A1
Elfed Rd A1
Emlyn Rd A1
Evans Terr A3
Fairfield Terr B1
Ffynone Dr B1
Ffynone Rd B1
Fire Station B3
Firm St A2
Fleet St C1
Francis St C1
Fullers Row B2
George St B2
Glamorgan St C2
Glyndwr Pl A1
Glynn Vivian B3
Graig Terr A3
Grand Theatre C2
Granogwen Rd A2
Guildhall Rd South C1
Gwent Rd A1
Gwynedd Ave A1
Hafod St A3
Hanover St B1
Harcourt St B2
Harries St A2
Heathfield B2
Henrietta St B1
Hewson St B2
High St A3/B3
High View A2
Hill St A2
Historic Ships Berth C3
HM Prison C2
Information Ctr C2
Islwyn Rd A1
King Edward's Rd C1
Law Courts C1
Library B3
Long Ridge A2
Madoc St C2
Mansel St B2
Maritime Quarter C3
Market B3
Mayhill Gdns B1
Mayhill Rd A1
Mega Bowl B3
Milton Terr A2
Mission Gallery C3
Montpellier Terr B1
Morfa Rd A3
Mount Pleasant B2
National Waterfront Museum C3
Nelson St C2
New Cut Rd A3
New St A3
Nicander Pde A2
Nicander Pl A2
Nicholl St B2
Norfolk St B2
North Hill Rd A2
Northampton La B2
Orchard St B3
Oxford St B2
Oystermouth Rd C1
Page St B2
Pant-y-Celyn Rd B1
Parc Tawe Link B3
Parc Tawe North B3
Parc Tawe Shopping & Leisure Centre B3
Patti Pavilion C1
Paxton St C2
Penmaen Terr B1
Pen-y-Graig Rd A1
Phillips Pde C1
Picton Terr B2
Plantasia B3
Police Station B2
Post Office A1/A2/B2/C1
Powys Ave A1
Primrose St B2
Princess Way B3
Promenade B2
Pryder Gdns A1
Quadrant Centre C2
Quay Park B3
Rhianfa La B1
Rhondda St B2
Richardson St C2
Rodney St C1
Rose Hill B1
Rosehill Terr B1
Russell St B1
St David's Sq C3
St Helen's Ave C1
St Helen's Cr C1
St Helen's Rd C1
St James Gdns B1
St James's Cr B1
St Mary's B3
Sea View Terr A3
Singleton St C2
South Dock C3
Stanley Pl B2
Strand B3
Swansea Castle B3
Swansea College Arts Centre C1
Swansea Metropolitan University B2
Swansea Mus C3
Swansea Station A3
Taliesyn Rd B1
Tan y Marian Rd A1
Tegid Rd A2
Teilo Cr A1
Terrace Rd B1/B2
The Kingsway B2
The LC C3
Tontine St A3
Tower of Eclipse C3
Townhill Rd A1
Tram Mus C3
Trawler Rd C3
Union St B2
Upper Strand A3
Vernon St A3
Victoria Quay C3
Victoria Rd B3
Vincent St C1
Walter Rd B1
Watkin St A2
Waun-Wen Rd A2
Wellington St C2
Westbury St C1
Western St C1
Westway C2
William St C2
Wind St B3
Woodlands Terr B1
YMCA B2
York St C3

Swindon 343

Albert St C3
Albion St C1
Alfred St A2
Alvescot Rd C3
Art Gallery & Mus C3
Ashford Rd C1
Aylesbury St A2
Bath Rd C2
Bathampton St B1
Bathurst Rd B3
Beatrice St A2
Beckhampton St B3
Bowood Rd C1
Bristol St B1
Broad St A3
Brunel Arcade B2
Brunel Plaza B2
Brunswick St C2
Bus Station B2
Cambria Bridge Rd B1
Cambria Place B1
Canal Walk B2
Carfax St B2
Carr St B1
Cemetery C1/C3
Chandler Cl C3
Chapel C1
Chester St B1
Christ Church C3
Church Place B1
Cirencester Way A3
Clarence St B2
Clifton St C1
Cockleberry Rdbt A2
Colbourne Rdbt A3
Colbourne St A3
College St B2
Commercial Rd B2
Corporation St A2
Council Offices B3
County Rd A3
Courts B2
Cricket Ground A3
Cricklade Street C3
Crombey St B1/C2
Cross St C2
Curtis St B1
Deacon St C1
Designer Outlet (Great Western) B1
Dixon St C2
Dover St C2
Dowling St C2
Drove Rd C3
Dryden St C1
Durham St C3
East St B1
Eastcott Hill C2
Eastcott Rd C2
Edgeware Rd B2
Elmina Rd A3
Emlyn Square B1
Euclid St B3
Exeter St B1
Fairview C1
Faringdon Rd B1
Farnsby St B1
Fire Station B3
Fleet St B2
Fleming Way B2/B3
Florence St A2
Gladstone St A3
Gooch St A2
Graham St A3
Great Western Way A1/A2
Groundwell Rd B3
Hawksworth Way A1
Haydon St A2
Henry St B2
Hillside Ave C1
Holbrook Way B2
Hunt St C3
Hydro B1
Hythe Rd C2
Information Ctr B2
Joseph St C1
Kent Rd C2
King William St C2
Kingshill Rd C1
Lansdown Rd C2
Leicester St B3
Library B2
Lincoln St B3
Little London C3
London St B1
Magic Rdbt B3
Maidstone Rd C2
Manchester Rd A3
Maxwell St B1
Milford St B2
Milton Rd B1
Morse St C2
National Monuments Record Centre B1
Newcastle St B3
Newcombe Drive A1
Newcombe Trading Estate A1
Newhall St C2
North St C2
North Star Ave A1
North Star Rdbt A1
Northampton St B3
Oasis Leisure Centre A1
Ocotal Way A3
Okus Rd C1
Old Town C3
Oxford St B1
Park Lane B1
Park Lane Rdbt B1
Pembroke St C2
Plymouth St B3
Polaris House A2
Polaris Way A2
Police Station B2
Ponting St A2
Post Office B1/B2/C1/C3
Poulton St A3
Princes St B2
Prospect Hill C2
Prospect Place C2
Queen St B2
Queen's Park C3
Radnor St C1
Read St C1
Reading St B1
Regent St B2
Retail Park A2/A3/B3
Rosebery St A3
St Mark's B1
Salisbury St A3
Savernake St C2
Shelley St C1
Sheppard St B1
South St C2
Southampton St B3
Spring Gardens B3
Stafford Street C2
Stanier St C2
Station Road A2
Steam B1
Swindon College A2
Swindon Rd C2
Swindon Station A2
Swindon Town Football Club A3
T A Centre B1
Tennyson St B1
The Lawn C3
The Nurseries C1
The Parade B2
The Park B1
Theobald St B1
Town Hall B2
Transfer Bridges Rdbt A3
Union St C2
Upham Rd C3
Victoria Rd C3
Walcot Rd B3
War Memorial B2
Wells St B3
Western St C2
Westmorland Rd B3
Whalebridge Rdbt B2
Whitehead St C1
Whitehouse Rd A2
William St C1
Wood St C3
Wyvern Theatre & Arts Centre B2
York Rd B3

Taunton 343

Addison Gr A1
Albemarle Rd A1
Alfred St B3
Alma St C2
Bath Pl C1
Belvedere Rd A1
Billet St B2
Billetfield C2
Birch Gr A1
Brewhouse Theatre B2
Bridge St B1
Bridgwater & Taunton Canal A2
Broadlands Rd C1
Burton Pl C1
Bus Station B1
Canal Rd A2
Cann St C1
Canon St B2
Castle B1
Castle St B1
Cheddon Rd A2
Chip Lane A1
Clarence St B1
Cleveland St B1
Coleridge Cres C3
Compass Hill C1
Compton Cl A2
Corporation St B1
Council Offices A1
County Walk Shopping Centre C2
Courtyard B2
Cranmer Rd B2
Critchard Way B3
Cyril St A1
Deller's Wharf B1
Duke St B2
East Reach B3
East St B3
Eastbourne Rd B2
Eastleigh Rd C3
Eaton Cres A2
Elm Gr A1
Elms Cl A1
Fons George C1
Fore St B2
Fowler St A1
French Weir Recreation Grd B1
Geoffrey Farrant Wk A2
Gray's Almshouses B2
Grays Rd B3
Greenway Ave A1
Guildford Pl C1
Hammet St B2
Haydon Rd B3
Heavitree Way A2
Herbert St A1
High St C2
Holway Ave C3
Hugo St B3
Huish's Almshouses B2
Hurdle Way C2
Information Ctr C2
Jubilee St A1
King's College C3
Kings Cl C3
Laburnum St B2
Lambrook Rd B3
Lansdowne Rd A3
Leslie Ave A1
Leycroft Rd B3
Library C2
Linden Gr A1
Livestock Market A2
Magdalene St B2
Magistrates Court B1
Malvern Terr A2
Market House B2
Mary St C2
Middle St B2
Midford Rd B3
Mitre Court B3
Mount Nebo C1
Mount St C2
Mountway C2
North St B2
Northfield Ave B1
Northfield Rd B1
Northleigh Rd C3
Obridge Allotments A3
Obridge Lane A3
Obridge Rd A3
Obridge Viaduct A3
Old Market Shopping Centre C2
Osborne Way C1
Park St C1
Paul St C2
Plais St A2
Playing Field C3
Police Station C1
Portland St B1
Post Office A1/B1/B2/C1
Priorswood Industrial Estate A3
Priorswood Rd A2
Priory Ave B2
Priory Barn Cricket Mus B2
Priory Bridge Rd B2
Priory Park A2
Priory Way A3
Queen St B3
Railway St A1
Records Office A2
Recreation Grd A1
Riverside Place B2
St Augustine St B2
St George's C2
St Georges Sq C2
St James B2
St James St B2
St John's C1
St John's Rd B1
St Josephs Field C2
St Mary Magdalene's B2
Samuels Ct A1
Shire Hall & Law Courts C1
Somerset County & Military Mus B1
Somerset County Cricket Ground B2
Somerset County Hall C1
South Rd C3
South St C3
Staplegrove Rd B1
Station Rd A1
Stephen St B2
Swimming Pool A1
Tancred St B2
Tauntfield Cl C3
Taunton Dean Cricket Club C2
Taunton Station A2
The Avenue A1
The Crescent C1
The Mount C2
Thomas St A1
Toneway A3
Tower St B1
Trevor Smith Pl C3
Trinity Rd C3
Trinity St B3
Trull Rd C1
Tudor House B2
Upper High St C1
Venture Way A3
Victoria Gate B3
Victoria Park B3
Victoria St B3
Viney St B3
Vivary Park C2
Vivary Rd C1
War Memorial C1
Wellesley St A2
Wheatley Cres A3
Whitehall A1
Wilfred Rd B3
William St A1
Wilton Church C1
Wilton Cl C1
Wilton Gr C1
Wilton St C1
Winchester St B2
Winters Field B2
Wood St B1
Yarde Pl B1

Telford 343

Alma Ave C1
Amphitheatre C2
Bowling Alley B2
Brandsfarm Way C3
Brunel Rd B1
Bus Station B2
Buxton Rd C1
Castle Trading Estate A3
Central Park A2
Civic Offices B2
Coach Central B2
Coachwell Cl B1
Colliers Way A1
Courts B2
Dale Acre Way B3
Darliston C3
Deepdale B3
Deercote B2
Dinthill C3
Doddington C3
Dodmoor Grange C3
Downemead B3
Duffryn B3
Dunsheath B3
Euston Way A3
Eyton Mound C1
Eyton Rd C1
Forge Retail Park A1
Forgegate A2
Grange Central B2
Hall Park Way B1
Hinkshay Rd C2
Hollinsworth Rd A2
Holyhead Rd A3
Housing Trust A1
Ice Rink B2
Information Ctr B2
Ironmasters Way A2
Job Centre B1
Land Registry B1
Lawn Central B2
Lawnswood C1
Library B2
Malinsgate B1
Matlock Ave C1
Moor Rd C1
Mount Rd C1
NFU Offices B1
Odeon B2
Park Lane A1
Police Station B2
Post Office B2
Priorslee Ave A3
Queen Elizabeth Ave C3
Queen Elizabeth Way B1
Queensway A2/B3
Rampart Way A2
Randlay Ave C3
Randlay Wood C3
Rhodes Ave C1
Royal Way B1
St Leonards Rd B1
St Quentin Gate B2
Shifnal Rd A3
Sixth Ave A1
Southwater Way B1
Spout Lane C1
Spout Mound B1
Spout Way C1
Stafford Court B3
Stafford Park B3
Stirchley Ave C3
Stone Row C1
Telford Bridge Retail Park A1
Telford Central Station A3
Telford Centre, The B2
Telford International Centre C2
Telford Way A3
Third Ave A2
Town Park C2
Town Park Visitor Centre B2
Town Sports Club C3
Walker House B2
Wellswood Ave A2
West Centre Way B1
Withywood Drive C1
Woodhouse Central B2
Yates Way A1

Torquay 344

Abbey Rd B2
Alexandra Rd A2
Alpine Rd B3
Ash Hill Rd A2
Babbacombe Rd B3
Bampfylde Rd B1
Barton Rd A1
Beacon Quay C2
Belgrave Rd A1/B1
Belmont Rd A3
Berea Rd A3
Braddons Hill Rd East B3
Brewery Park A3
Bronshill Rd A2
Castle Rd A2
Cavern Rd A3
Central B2
Chatsworth Rd A2
Chestnut Ave B1
Church St A1
Civic Offices A2
Coach Station A1
Corbyn Head C1
Croft Hill B1
Croft Rd B1
Daddyhole Plain C3
East St A1
Egerton Rd A3
Ellacombe Church Rd A3
Ellacombe Rd A2
Falkland Rd B1
Fleet St B2
Fleet Walk Shopping Centre B2
Grafton Rd B3
Haldon Pier C2
Hatfield Rd A2
Highbury Rd A2
Higher Warberry Rd A3
Hillesdon Rd B3
Hollywood Bowl C3
Hoxton Rd A3
Hunsdon Rd B3
Information Ctr B2
Inner Harbour C3
Kenwyn Rd A3
Laburnum St A1
Law Courts A2
Library A2
Lime Ave B1
Living Coasts C3
Lower Warberry Rd B3
Lucius St B1
Lymington Rd A1
Magdalene Rd A1
Marina C2
Market St B2
Meadfoot Lane C3
Meadfoot Rd C3
Melville St B2
Middle Warberry Rd B3
Mill Lane A1
Montpellier Rd B3
Morgan Ave A1
Museum Rd B3
Newton Rd A1
Oakhill Rd A1
Outer Harbour C2
Parkhill Rd C3
Pavilion C2
Pimlico B2
Police Station A1
Post Office A1/B2
Princes Rd A3
Princes Rd East A3
Princes Rd West A3
Princess Gdns C2
Princess Pier C2
Princess Theatre C2
Rathmore Rd B1
Recreation Grd B1
Riviera Centre International B1
Rock End Ave C3
Rock Rd B2
Rock Walk B2
Rosehill Rd A3
St Efride's Rd A1
St John's B3
St Luke's Rd B2
St Luke's Rd North B2
St Luke's Rd South B2
St Marychurch Rd A2
Scarborough Rd B1
Shedden Hill B2
South Pier C2
South St A1
Spanish Barn B1
Stitchill Rd B3
Strand B3
Sutherland Rd B3
Teignmouth Rd A1
Temperance St B2
The King's Drive B1
The Terrace B3
Thurlow Rd A1
Tor Bay B1
Tor Church Rd A1
Tor Hill Rd A1
Torbay Rd B2
Torquay Mus B3
Torquay Station C1
Torre Abbey Mansion B1
Torre Abbey Meadows B1
Torre Abbey Sands B1
Torwood Gdns B3
Torwood St C3
Union Square A2
Union St A1
Upton Hill A2
Upton Park A1
Upton Rd A1
Vanehill Rd C3
Vansittart Rd A1
Vaughan Parade C3
Victoria Parade C3
Victoria Rd A2
Warberry Rd West B2
Warren Rd B2
Windsor Rd A2/A3
Woodville Rd A3

Truro 344

Adelaide Ter B1
Agar Rd B3
Arch Hill C2
Arundell Pl C2
Avondale Rd B1
Back Quay B3
Barrack La C3
Barton Meadow A1
Benson Rd A2
Bishops Cl A2
Bosvean Gdns B1
Bosvigo Gardens B1
Bosvigo La A1
Bosvigo Rd B2
Broad St A3
Burley Cl C3
Bus Station B3
Calenick St B2
Campfield Hill B3
Carclew St B3
Carew Rd A2
Carey Park B2
Carlyon Rd A2
Carvoza Rd A3
Castle St B2
Cathedral View A2
Chainwalk Dr A2
Chapel Hill B1
Charles St B2
City Hall B3
City Rd B2
Coinage Hall B3
Comprigney Hill A1
Coosebean La A1
Copes Gdns A2
County Hall B1
Courtney Rd A2
Crescent Rd B1
Crescent Rise B1
Daniell Court C2
Daniell Rd C2
Daniell St C2
Daubuz Cl A2
Dobbs La B1
Edward St B2
Eliot Rd A2
Elm Court A3
Enys Cl A1
Enys Rd A1
Fairmantle St B3
Falmouth Rd C2
Ferris Town B2
Fire Station B1
Frances St B2
George St B2
Green Cl C2
Green La C1
Grenville Rd A2
Hall For Cornwall B3
Hendra Rd A2
Hendra Vean A1
High Cross B3
Higher Newham La C3
Higher Trehaverne A2
Hillcrest Ave B1
Hosp B2
Hunkin Cl A2
Hurland Rd C3
Infirmary Hill B2
James Pl B3
Kenwyn Church Rd A1
Kenwyn Hill A1
Kenwyn Rd A2
Kenwyn St B2
Kerris Gdns A1
King St B3
Lemon Quay B3
Lemon Street Gallery B3
Library B1/B3
Malpas Rd B3
Market B3
Memorial Gdns B3
Merrifield Close B1
Mitchell Hill A3
Moresk Cl A3
Moresk Rd A3
Morlaix Ave C3
Nancemere Rd A3
Newham Business Park C3
Newham Industrial Estate C3
Newham Rd C3
Northfield Dr C3
Oak Way A3
Pal's Terr A3
Park View C2
Pendarves Rd A2
Plaza Cinema B3
Police Station B3
Post Office B2/B3
Prince's St B3
Pydar St A2
Quay St B3
Redannick Cres C2
Redannick La B2
Richard Lander Monument C2
Richmond Hill B1
River St B2
Rosedale Rd A2
Royal Cornwall Mus B2
St Clement St B3
St George's Rd A1
School La C2
Station Rd B1
Stokes Rd A2
Strangways Terr C3
Tabernacle St B3
The Avenue A3
The Crescent B1
The Leats B2
The Spires A2
Trehaverne La A2
Tremayne Rd A2
Treseder's Gdns A3
Treworder Rd B1
Treyew Rd B1
Truro Cathedral B3
Truro Harbour Office B3
Truro Station B1
Union St B2
Upper School La C2
Victoria Gdns B2
Waterfall Gdns B2

360 Wick • Winchester • Windsor • Wolverhampton • Worcester • Wrexham • York

Wick 344

Ackergill Cres A2
Ackergill St A2
Albert St C2
Ambulance Station A2
Argyle Sq C2
Assembly Rooms C2
Bank Row C2
Bankhead B1
Barons Well B2
Barrogill St C2
Bay View B3
Bexley Terr C3
Bignold Park C2
Bowling Green C2
Breadalbane Terr C2
Bridge of Wick B1
Bridge St B2
Brown Pl C2
Burn St B2
Bus Station B1
Caithness General Hospital (A+E) B1
Cliff Rd B1
Coach Rd B2
Coastguard Station C3
Corner Cres B3
Coronation St C1
Council Offices B2
Court B2
Crane Rock C3
Dempster St C2
Dunnet Ave A2
Fire Station B2
Fish Market C3
Francis St C1
George St A1
Girnigoe St B2
Glamis Rd B2
Gowrie Pl B1
Grant St C2
Green Rd B2
Gunns Terr B3
Harbour Quay B2
Harbour Rd C3
Harbour Terr C2
Harrow Hill C2
Henrietta St A2/B2
Heritage Centre C2
High St B2
Hill Ave A2
Hillhead Rd B3
Hood St C1
Huddart St C2
Information Ctr B2
Kenneth St C1
Kinnaird St C2
Kirk Hill B1
Langwell Cres B3
Leishman Ave B3
Leith Walk A2
Library B2
Lifeboat Station C3
Lighthouse C3
Lindsay Dr B3
Lindsay Pl B3
Loch St C2
Louisburgh St B2
Lower Dunbar St C2
Macleay La B1
Macleod Rd B3
MacRae St C2
Martha Terr B2
Miller Ave B1
Miller La B1
Moray St C2
Mowat Pl B3
Murchison St C3
Newton Ave C1
Newton Rd C1
Nicolson St C3
North Highland College B2
North River Pier B3
Northcote St C2
Owen Pl A2
Police Station B1
Port Dunbar B3
Post Office B2/C2
Pulteney Distillery C2
River St B2
Robert St A1
Rutherford St C2
St John's Episcopal C2
Sandigoe Rd B3
Scalesburn B3
Seaforth Ave C1
Shore La B2
Sinclair Dr B3
Sinclair Terr C2
Smith Terr C3
South Pier C3
South Quay C3
South Rd C1
South River Pier B3
Station Rd B1
Swimming Pool B2
TA Centre C2
Telford St B2
The Shore B2
Thurso Rd B1
Thurso St B1
Town Hall B2
Union St B2
Upper Dunbar St C2
Vansittart St C3
Victoria Pl B2
War Memorial A1
Well of Cairndhuna C3
Wellington Ave C3
Wellington St C3
West Banks Ave C1
West Banks Terr C1
West Park C1
Whitehorse Park B2
Wick Harbour Bridge B2
Wick Industrial Estate A2
Wick Parish Church B1
Wick Station B1
Williamson St B2
Willowbank B2

Winchester 344

Andover Rd A2
Andover Road Retail Park A2
Archery La C2
Arthur Rd A2
Bar End Rd C3
Beaufort Rd C2
Beggar's La B3
Bereweeke Ave A1
Bereweeke Rd A1
Boscobel Rd A2
Brassey Rd A2
Broadway B3
Brooks Shopping Centre, The B3
Bus Station B3
Butter Cross B2
Canon St C2
Castle Wall C2/C3
Castle, King Arthur's Round Table B2
Cathedral C2
Cheriton Rd A1
Chesil St C3
Chesil Theatre C3
Christchurch Rd C1
City Mus B2
City Offices C3
City Rd B2
Clifton Rd B1
Clifton Terr B2
Close Wall C2/C3
Coach Park A2
Colebrook St C3
College St C2
College Walk C3
Compton Rd C2
County Council Offices B2
Cranworth Rd A2
Cromwell Rd C1
Culver Rd C2
Domum Rd C3
Durngate Pl B3
Eastgate St B3
Edgar Rd C2
Egbert Rd A2
Elm Rd B2
Fairfield Rd A1
Fire Station B3
Fordington Ave B1
Fordington Rd A1
Friarsgate B3
Gordon Rd B3
Greenhill Rd B1
Guildhall B3
HM Prison B1
Hatherley Rd A1
High St B2
Hillier Way A3
Hyde Abbey (Remains) A2
Hyde Abbey Rd B2
Hyde Cl A2
Hyde St A2
Information Ctr B3
Jane Austen's House C2
Jewry St B2
John Stripe Theatre C1
King Alfred Pl A2
Kingsgate Arch C2
Kingsgate Park C2
Kingsgate Rd C2
Kingsgate St C2
Lankhills Rd A2
Library B2
Lower Brook St B3
Magdalen Hill B3
Market La B2
Mews La B1
Middle Brook St B3
Middle Rd B1
Military Museums B2
Milland Rd C3
Milverton Rd B1
Monks Rd A3
North Hill Cl A2
North Walls B2
North Walls Rec Gnd A3
Nuns Rd A3
Oram's Arbour B1
Owen's Rd A2
Parchment St B2
Park & Ride C3
Park Ave B3
Playing Field A1
Police HQ B1
Police Station B3
Portal Rd C3
Post Office B2/C1
Quarry Rd C3
Ranelagh Rd C1
Regiment Mus B2
River Park Leisure Centre B3
Romans' Rd C2
Romsey Rd B1
Royal Hampshire County Hospital (A & E) B1
St Cross Rd C2
St George's St B2
St Giles Hill C3
St James' La B1
St James' Terr B1
St James Villas C2
St John's B3
St John's St B3
St Michael's Rd C2
St Paul's Hill B1
St Peter St B2
St Swithun St C2
St Thomas St C2
Saxon Rd A2
School of Art B3
Screen B2
Sleepers Hill Rd C1
Southgate St B2
Sparkford Rd C1
Staple Gdns B2
Station Rd B2
Step Terr B1
Stockbridge Rd A1
Stuart Cres C1
Sussex St B2
Swan Lane B2
Tanner St B3
The Square B2
The Weirs C3
The Winchester Gallery B3
Theatre Royal B2
Tower St B2
Town Hall C3
Union St B3
University of Winchester (King Alfred Campus) C1
Upper Brook St B2
Wales St B3
Water Lane B3
West End Terr B1
West Gate B2
Western Rd B1
Wharf Hill C3
Winchester College C2
Winchester Station A2
Wolvesey Castle C3
Worthy Lane A2
Worthy Rd A2

Windsor 344

Adelaide Sq C3
Albany Rd C2
Albert St B1
Alexandra Gdns B2
Alexandra Rd C2
Alma Rd B2
Ambulance Station B1
Arthur Rd B2
Bachelors Acre B3
Barry Ave B2
Beaumont Rd C2
Bexley St B1
Boat House B2
Brocas St B2
Brook St C3
Bulkeley Ave C1
Castle Hill B3
Charles St B2
Claremont Rd C2
Clarence Cr B2
Clarence Rd B1
Clewer Court Rd B1
Coach Park B2
College Cr C1
Courts C2
Cricket Ground C3
Dagmar Rd C2
Datchet Rd B3
Devereux Rd C2
Dorset Rd C2
Duke St B1
Elm Rd C1
Eton College A3
Eton Ct A2
Eton Sq A2
Eton Wick Rd A2
Fire Station C2
Farm Yard B3
Frances Rd C2
Frogmore Dr B3
Gloucester Pl C3
Goslar Way C1
Goswell Hill B2
Goswell Rd B2
Green La C1
Grove Rd C2
Guildhall B3
Helena Rd C2
Helston La B1
High St A2/B3
Holy Trinity C2
Hospital (Private) C2
Household Cavalry C2
Imperial Rd C1
Information Ctr B3
Keats La A2
King Edward Ct B2
King Edward VII Ave A3
King Edward VII Hosp C2
King George V Memorial B3
King's Rd C3
King Stable St A2
Leisure Centre & Pool B1
Library C2
Maidenhead Rd B1
Meadow La A2
Municipal Offices C3
Nell Gwynne's House B3
Osborne Rd C2
Oxford Rd B1
Park St B3
Peascod St B2
Police Station C2
Post Office A2/B2
Princess Margaret Hosp C2
Queen Victoria's Walk B3
Queen's Rd C2
River St B2
Romney Island A3
Romney Lock A3
Romney Lock Rd A3
Royal Mews Exhibition Centre B3
Russell St C2
St John's B3
St John's Chapel A2
St Leonards Rd C2
St Mark's Rd C2
Sheet St C3
South Meadow A2
South Meadow La A2
Springfield Rd C1
Stovell Rd B1
Sunbury Rd A3
Tangier La A2
Tangier St A3
Temple Rd C2
Thames St B3
The Brocas A2
The Home Park A3/C3
The Long Walk C3
Theatre Royal B3
Trinity Pl C2
Vansittart Rd B1/C1
Vansittart Rd Gdns C1
Victoria Barracks C2
Victoria St C2
Ward Royal B2
Westmead C1
White Lilies Island A1
William St B2
Windsor Arts Centre C2
Windsor Castle B3
Windsor & Eton Central B2
Windsor & Eton Riverside A3
Windsor Bridge B3
Windsor Great Park C3
Windsor Relief Rd A1
York Ave C1
York Rd C1

Wolverhampton 344

Albion St B3
Alexandra St C1
Arena B2
Art Gallery B2
Ashland St C1
Austin St A1
Badger Dr A3
Bailey St B3
Bath Ave B1
Bath Rd B1
Bell St C2
Berry St B3
Bilston Rd C3
Bilston St C3
Birmingham Canal A3
Bone Mill La A2
Brewery Rd B1
Bright St A1
Burton Cres B3
Bus Station B3
Cambridge St A3
Camp St B2
Cannock Rd A3
Castle St C2
Chapel Ash C1
Cherry St C1
Chester St A1
Church La C2
Church St C2
Civic Centre B2
Clarence Rd B2
Cleveland St C2
Clifton St C1
Coach Station B2
Compton Rd B1
Corn Hill B3
Coven St A3
Craddock St A1
Cross St North A2
Crown & County Courts C3
Crown St A2
Culwell St B3
Dale St C1
Darlington St C1
Dartmouth St C3
Devon Rd A1
Drummond St B2
Dudley Rd C2
Dudley St B2
Duke St C3
Dunkley St B1
Dunstall Ave A2
Dunstall Hill A2
Dunstall Rd A1/A2
Evans St A1
Fawdry St A1
Field St B3
Fire Station C1
Fiveways (r'about) A2
Fowler Playing Fields A3
Fox's La A2
Francis St A2
Fryer St B3
Gloucester St A1
Gordon St C3
Graiseley St C1
Grand B3
Granville St C3
Great Brickkiln St C1
Great Hampton St A1
Great Western St A2
Grimstone St B3
Harrow St A1
Hilton St A3
Horseley Fields C3
Humber Rd C1
Jack Hayward Way A2
Jameson St A1
Jenner St C3
Kennedy Rd B3
Kimberley St C1
King St B2
Laburnum St C1
Lansdowne Rd B1
Leicester St A1
Lever St C3
Library C3
Lichfield St B2
Light House B3
Little's La B3
Lock St B3
Lord St C1
Lowe St A1
Lower Stafford St A2
Magistrates Court B2
Mander Centre C2
Mander St C1
Market St B2
Market C2
Melbourne St C3
Merridale St C1
Middlecross C3
Molineux St B2
Mostyn St A1
New Hampton Rd East A1
Nine Elms La A3
North Rd A2
Oaks Cres C1
Oxley St A2
Paget St A1
Park Ave B1
Park Road East A1
Park Road West B1
Paul St C2
Pelham St C1
Penn Rd C2
Piper's Row B3
Pitt St C2
Police Station C3
Pool St C2
Poole St A3
Post Office A1/A2/B2/B2
Powlett St C3
Queen St B2
Raby St C3
Raglan St C1
Railway Dr B3
Red Hill St A2
Red Lion St B2
Retreat St C1
Ring Rd B2
Rugby St A1
Russell St C1
St Andrew's B1
St David's B3
St George's C3
St George's Pde C2
St James St C3
St John's C2
St John's C2
St John's Retail Park C2
St John's Square C2
St Mark's C1
St Marks Rd C1
St Marks St C1
St Patrick's B2
St Peter's B2
St Peter's B2
Salisbury St C1
Salop St C2
School St C2
Sherwood St A2
Smestow St A3
Snowhill C2
Springfield Rd A3
Stafford St B2
Staveley Rd A1
Steelhouse La C3
Stephenson St C1
Stewart St C2
Sun St B3
Sutherland Pl C3
Tempest St C2
Temple St C2
Tettenhall Rd B1
The Maltings B2
The Royal (Metro) C3
Thomas St C2
Thornley St B2
Tower St C2
Town Hall B2
University B2
Upper Zoar St C1
Vicarage Rd C3
Victoria St C2
Walpole St A1
Walsall St C3
Ward St C3
Warwick St C3
Water St A3
Waterloo Rd B2
Wednesfield Rd B3
West Park (not A&E) B1
West Park Swimming Pool B1
Wharf St C3
Whitmore Hill B2
Wolverhampton B3
Wolverhampton St George's (Metro) C2
Wolverhampton Wanderers Football Gnd (Molineux) B2
Worcester St C2
Wulfrun Centre C2
Yarwell Cl A3
York St C3
Zoar St C1

Worcester 344

Albany Terr A1
Alice Otley School A2
Angel Pl B2
Angel St B2
Ashcroft Rd A2
Athelstan Rd C3
Back Lane North A1
Back Lane South A1
Barbourne Rd A2
Bath Rd C2
Battenhall Rd C3
Bridge St B2
Britannia Sq A1
Broad St B2
Bromwich La C1
Bromwich Rd C1
Bromyard Rd C1
Bus Station B2
Carden St B3
Castle St A2
Cathedral C2
Cathedral Plaza B2
Charles St B3
Chequers La B1
Chestnut St A2
Chestnut Walk A2
Citizens' Advice Bureau B2
City Walls Rd B2
Cole Hill C3
College of Technology B2
College St C2
Commandery C3
County Cricket Ground C1
Cripplegate Park B1
Croft Rd B1
Cromwell St B3
Crowngate Centre B2
Deansway B2
Diglis Pde C2
Diglis Rd C2
Edgar Tower C2
Farrier St A2
Fire Station B2
Foregate St B2
Foregate Street B2
Fort Royal Hill C3
Fort Royal Park C3
Foundry St B3
Friar St C2
George St B3
Grand Stand Rd B1
Greenhill C3
Greyfriars B2
Guildhall B2
Henwick Rd B1
High St B2
Hill St B3
Huntingdon Hall B2
Hylton Rd B1
Information Ctr B2
King Charles Place Shopping Centre C1
King's School C2
King's School Playing Field C2
Kleve Walk C2
Lansdowne Cr A3
Lansdowne Rd A3
Lansdowne Walk A3
Laslett St A3
Leisure Centre A3
Library, Mus & Art Gallery A2
Little Chestnut St A2
Little London A2
London Rd C3
Lowell St A3
Lowesmoor B2
Lowesmoor Terr A3
Lowesmoor Wharf A3
Magistrates Court A2
Midland Rd B3
Mill St C2
Moors Severn Terr A1
New Rd C1
New St B2
Northfield St A2
Odeon B2
Padmore St B3
Park St C3
Pheasant St B3
Pitchcroft Racecourse A1
Police Station A2
Portland St C2
Post Office B2
Quay St B2
Queen St B2
Rainbow Hill A3
Recreation Ground A2
Reindeer Court B2
Rogers Hill A3
Sabrina Rd A1
St Dunstan's Cr C3
St John's C1
St Martin's Gate B3
St Oswald's Rd A2
St Paul's St B3
St Swithin's Church B2
St Wulstans Cr C3
Sansome Walk A2
Severn St C2
Shaw St B2
Shire Hall A2
Shrub Hill B3
Shrub Hill Retail Park B3
Shrub Hill Rd B3
Slingpool Walk C1
South Quay B2
Southfield St A2
Sports Ground A2/C1
Stanley Rd B3
Swan, The A1
Swimming Pool A2
Tallow Hill B3
Tennis Walk A2
The Avenue C1
The Butts B2
The Cross B2
The Shambles B2
The Tything A2
Tolladine Rd B3
Tudor House B2
Tybridge St B1
University of Worcester B2
Vincent Rd B3
Vue C2
Washington St A3
Woolhope Rd C3
Worcester Bridge B2
Worcester Library & History Centre B3
Worcester Porcelain Mus C2
Worcester Royal Grammar School A2
Wylds La C3

Wrexham / Wrecsam 344

Abbot St B2
Acton Rd A3
Albert St C3
Alexandra Rd C1
Aran Rd A3
Barnfield C3
Bath Rd C2
Beechley Rd C3
Belgrave Rd C2
Belle Vue Park C2
Belle Vue Rd C2
Belvedere Dr A1
Bennion's Rd C3
Berse Rd A1
Bersham Rd C1
Birch St C3
Bodhyfryd B3
Border Retail Park B3
Bradley Rd C2
Bright St B1
Bron-y-Nant C1
Brook St C2
Bryn-y-Cabanau Rd C3
Bury St C3
Bus Station B2
Butchers Market B3
Caia Rd C3
Cambrian Industrial Estate C3
Caxton Pl B2
Cemetery C1
Centenary Rd C1
Chapel St C2
Charles St B3
Chester Rd A3
Chester St B3
Cilcen Gr A3
Citizens Advice Bureau B2
Cobden Rd B1
College of Art & Design B2
Council Offices B3
County B2
Crescent Rd B3
Crispin La A2
Croesnewyth Rd B1
Cross St A2
Cunliffe St A2
Derby Rd C3
DHS B2
Dolydd Rd B1
Duke St B2
Eagles Meadow (u/c) C3
Earle St C2
East Ave A2
Edward St C2
Egerton St B2
Empress Rd C1
Erddig Rd C2
Fairy Rd C2
Fire Station B2
Foster Rd A3
Foxwood Dr C1
Garden Rd A2
General Market B3
Gerald St B2
Gibson St C1
Greenbank St C3
Greenfield A2
Grosvenor Rd B2
Grove Park B2
Grove Park Rd B3
Grove Rd A3
Guildhall B2
Haig Rd C3
Hampden Rd C2
Hazel Gr A3
Henblas St B3
High St B3
Hightown Rd C3
Hill St B2
Holt Rd B3
Holt St B3
Hope St B2
Huntroyde Ave C3
Information Ctr B3
Island Green Shopping Centre B2
Jubilee Rd B2
King St B2
Kingsmills Rd C3
Lambpit St B3
Law Courts B3
Lawson Cl A3
Lawson Rd A3
Lea Rd C2
Library & Arts Centre B2
Lilac Way B1
Llys David Lord B1
Lorne St A2
Maesgwyn Rd B1
Maesydre Rd A3
Manley Rd B3
Market St B3
Mawddy Ave A2
Mayville Ave A2
Memorial Gallery B2
Memorial Hall B3
Mold Rd A1
Mount St C3
North East Wales Institute (NEWI) A1
NEWI Sports Centre A1
Neville Cres A3
New Rd A2
North Wales Tennis Centre A1
Oak Dr A3
Park Ave A3
Park St A2
Peel St C1
Pentre Felin C2
Pen-y-Bryn C2
Penymaes Ave A3
Peoples Market B3
Percy St C2
Plas Coch Retail Park A1
Plas Coch Rd A1
Police Station B3
Poplar Rd C2
Post Office A2/B2/C2/C3
Powell Rd B3
Poyser St C2
Price's La A2
Primose Way B1
Princess St C1
Queen St B3
Queens Sq B2
Regent St B2
Rhosddu Rd A2/B2
Rhosnesni La A3
Rivulet Rd C3
Ruabon Rd C2
Ruthin Rd C1/C2
St Giles C3
St Giles Way C3
St James Ct A2
St Mary's B2
Salisbury Rd C3
Salop Rd C3
Sontley Rd C2
Spring Rd A2
Stanley St C3
Stansty Rd A2
Station Approach B2
Studio B2
Talbot Rd C2
Techniquest A2
The Beeches A3
The Pines A3
Town Hill C2
Trevor St C2
Trinity St B2
Tuttle St C3
Vale Park A1
Vernon St B2
Vicarage Hill B2
Victoria Rd C2
Walnut St A2
War Memorial B3
Waterworld Swimming Baths B3
Watery Rd B1/B2
Wellington Rd C2
Westminster Dr A3
William Aston Hall A1
Windsor Rd A1
Wrexham AFC A1
Wrexham Central B2
Wrexham General B2
Wrexham Maelor Hospital (A+E) B1
Wrexham Technology Park B1
Wynn Ave A2
Yale College B3
Yale Gr A3
Yorke St C3

York 344

Aldwark B2
Ambulance Station B3
Arc Mus, The B2
Barbican Rd C3
Barley Hall B2
Bishopgate St C2
Bishopthorpe Rd C2
Blossom St C1
Bootham A1
Bootham Cr A1
Bootham Terr A1
Bridge St B2
Brook St A2
Brownlow St A2
Burton Stone La A1
Castle Mus C2
Castlegate B2
Cemetery Rd C3
Cherry St C2
City Art Gallery A1
City Screen B2
City Wall A2/B1/C3
Clarence St A2
Clementhorpe C2
Clifford St B2
Clifford's Tower B2
Clifton A1
Coach park A2
Coney St B2
Cromwell Rd C2
Crown Court C2
Davygate B2
Deanery Gdns A2
DIG B2
Ebor Industrial Estate B3
Fairfax House B2
Fishergate C3
Foss Islands Rd B3
Fossbank A3
Fossil Island Retail Park B3
Garden St A2
George St C3
Gillygate A2
Goodramgate B2
Grand Opera House B2
Grosvenor Terr A1
Guildhall B2
Hallfield Rd A3
Heslington Rd C3
Heworth Green A3
Holy Trinity B2
Hope St C3
Huntington Rd A3
Information Ctr A2
James St B3
Jorvik Viking Centre B2
Kent St C3
Lawrence St C3
Layerthorpe A3
Leeman Rd B1
Lendal B2
Lendal Bridge B1
Library B1
Longfield Terr A1
Lord Mayor's Walk A2
Lower Eldon St A2
Lowther St A2
Margaret St C3
Marygate A1
Melbourne St C3
Merchant Adventurer's Hall B2
Merchant Taylors' Hall B2
Micklegate B1
Minster, The A2
Monkgate A2
Moss St C1
Museum Gdns B1
Museum St B1
National Railway Mus B1
Navigation Rd B3
Newton Terr C2
North Pde A1
North St B2
Nunnery La C1
Nunthorpe Rd C1
Odeon C1
Ouse Bridge B2
Paragon St C3
Park Gr A3
Park St C1
Parliament St B2
Peasholme Green B3
Penley's Grove St A2
Piccadilly B2
Police Station B2
Post Office B1/B2/C3
Priory St B1
Purey Cust Nuffield Hospital, The A2
Queen Anne's Rd A1
Regimental Mus B2
Rowntree Park C2
St Andrewgate B2
St Benedict Rd C1
St John St A2
St Olave's Rd A1
St Peter's Gr A1
St Saviourgate B2
Scarcroft Hill C1
Scarcroft Rd C1
Skeldergate C2
Skeldergate Bridge C2
Station Rd B1
Stonegate B2
Sycamore Terr A1
Terry Ave C2
The Shambles B2
The Stonebow B2
Theatre Royal B2
Thorpe St C1
Toft Green B1
Tower St C2
Townend St A2
Treasurer's House A2
Trinity La B1
Undercroft Mus A2
Union Terr A2
Victor St C2
Vine St C2
Walmgate B3
Wellington St C3
YMR Exhibition B1
York Dungeon, The B2
York Station B1
Yorkshire Mus B1
Yorkshire Wheel, The B1

Map of Britain showing county and unitary authority areas, labelled: W Isles, Moray, Highland, Aberds, Aberdeen, Perth and Kinross, Angus, Dundee, Argyll and Bute, Stirling, Fife, Glasgow, Edin, E Loth, Midloth, Borders, N Ayrs, S Lanark, E Ayrs, S Ayrs, Dumfries and Galloway, Northumberland, Tyne and Wear, Hartlepool, Redcar and Cleveland, Middlesbrough, Darlington, Stockton-on-Tees, Cumbria, Durham, North Yorkshire, York, E Yorks, IoM, Blackpool, Lancs, W Yorks, S Yorks, N Lincs, NE Lincs, Lincolnshire, Anglesey, Conwy, Flint, Denb, Ches, Wrex, Notts, Gwyn, Mers, Gtr Man, Staffs, Leics, Rutland, Norfolk, Telford, Shrops, Powys, Worcs, Warks, Northants, Cambs, Suffolk, Ceredigion, Hereford, Bedford, C Beds, Essex, Pembs, Carms, Mon, Glos, Oxon, Bucks, Herts, London, Southend, Medway, Swansea, Cardiff, Bristol, Wilts, W Berks, Surrey, Kent, Somerset, Hants, Soton, W Sus, E Sus, Devon, Dorset, IoW, Ptsmouth, Brighton, Bmouth, Poole, Torbay, Plymouth, Cornwall, Scilly.

Abbreviations used in the index

Aberdeen **Aberdeen City**
Aberds **Aberdeenshire**
Ald **Alderney**
Anglesey **Isle of Anglesey**
Angus **Angus**
Argyll **Argyll and Bute**
Bath **Bath and North East Somerset**
Bedford **Bedford**
Bl Gwent **Blaenau Gwent**
Blackburn **Blackburn with Darwen**
Blackpool **Blackpool**
Bmouth **Bournemouth**
Borders **Scottish Borders**
Brack **Bracknell**
Bridgend **Bridgend**
Brighton **City of Brighton and Hove**
Bristol **City and County of Bristol**
Bucks **Buckinghamshire**
C Beds **Central Bedfordshire**
Caerph **Caerphilly**
Cambs **Cambridgeshire**
Cardiff **Cardiff**
Carms **Carmarthenshire**
Ceredig **Ceredigion**
Ches E **Cheshire East**
Ches W **Cheshire West and Chester**
Clack **Clackmannanshire**
Conwy **Conwy**
Corn **Cornwall**
Cumb **Cumbria**
Darl **Darlington**
Denb **Denbighshire**
Derby **City of Derby**
Derbys **Derbyshire**
Devon **Devon**

Dorset **Dorset**
Dumfries **Dumfries and Galloway**
Dundee **Dundee City**
Durham **Durham**
E Ayrs **East Ayrshire**
E Dunb **East Dunbartonshire**
E Loth **East Lothian**
E Renf **East Renfrewshire**
E Sus **East Sussex**
E Yorks **East Riding of Yorkshire**
Edin **City of Edinburgh**
Essex **Essex**
Falk **Falkirk**
Fife **Fife**
Flint **Flintshire**
Glasgow **City of Glasgow**
Glos **Gloucestershire**
Gtr Man **Greater Manchester**
Guern **Guernsey**
Gwyn **Gwynedd**
Halton **Halton**
Hants **Hampshire**
Hereford **Herefordshire**
Herts **Hertfordshire**
Highld **Highland**
Hrtlpl **Hartlepool**
Hull **Hull**
IoM **Isle of Man**
IoW **Isle of Wight**
Invclyd **Inverclyde**
Jersey **Jersey**
Kent **Kent**
Lancs **Lancashire**
Leicester **City of Leicester**
Leics **Leicestershire**
Lincs **Lincolnshire**
London **Greater London**

Luton **Luton**
M Keynes **Milton Keynes**
M Tydf **Merthyr Tydfil**
Mbro **Middlesbrough**
Medway **Medway**
Mers **Merseyside**
Midloth **Midlothian**
Mon **Monmouthshire**
Moray **Moray**
N Ayrs **North Ayrshire**
N Lincs **North Lincolnshire**
N Lanark **North Lanarkshire**
N Som **North Somerset**
N Yorks **North Yorkshire**
NE Lincs **North East Lincolnshire**
Neath **Neath Port Talbot**
Newport **City and County of Newport**
Norf **Norfolk**
Northants **Northamptonshire**
Northumb **Northumberland**
Nottingham **City of Nottingham**
Notts **Nottinghamshire**
Orkney **Orkney**
Oxon **Oxfordshire**
Pboro **Peterborough**
Pembs **Pembrokeshire**

Perth **Perth and Kinross**
Plym **Plymouth**
Poole **Poole**
Powys **Powys**
Ptsmth **Portsmouth**
Reading **Reading**
Redcar **Redcar and Cleveland**
Renfs **Renfrewshire**
Rhondda **Rhondda Cynon Taff**
Rutland **Rutland**
S Ayrs **South Ayrshire**
S Glos **South Gloucestershire**
S Lanark **South Lanarkshire**
S Yorks **South Yorkshire**
Scilly **Scilly**
Shetland **Shetland**
Shrops **Shropshire**
Slough **Slough**
Som **Somerset**
Soton **Southampton**
Staffs **Staffordshire**
Southend **Southend-on-Sea**
Stirling **Stirling**
Stockton **Stockton-on-Tees**
Stoke **Stoke-on-Trent**

Suff **Suffolk**
Sur **Surrey**
Swansea **Swansea**
Swindon **Swindon**
T&W **Tyne and Wear**
Telford **Telford & Wrekin**
Thurrock **Thurrock**
Torbay **Torbay**
Torf **Torfaen**
V Glam **The Vale of Glamorgan**
W Berks **West Berkshire**
W Dunb **West Dunbartonshire**
W Isles **Western Isles**
W Loth **West Lothian**
W Mid **West Midlands**
W Sus **West Sussex**
W Yorks **West Yorkshire**
Warks **Warwickshire**
Warr **Warrington**
Wilts **Wiltshire**
Windsor **Windsor and Maidenhead**
Wokingham **Wokingham**
Worcs **Worcestershire**
Wrex **Wrexham**
York **City of York**

Index to road maps of Britain

How to use the index

Example **Blatherwycke** Northants **137 D9**
- grid square
- page number
- county or unitary authority

A

Aaron's Hill Sur 50 E3
Aaron's Town Cumb 240 E2
Ab Kettleby Leics 154 E4
Ab Lench Worcs 117 G10
Abbas Combe Som 30 C2
Abberley Worcs 116 D5
Abberton Essex 89 B8
Abberton Worcs 117 G9
Abberwick Northumb 264 G4
Abbess Roding Essex 87 C9
Abbess End Essex 87 C9
Abbey Devon 27 E10
Abbey-cwm-hir Powys 113 C11
Abbey Dore Hereford 97 E7
Abbey Field Essex 107 G9
Abbey Gate Kent 53 B9
Abbey Green Shrops 149 C10
Abbey Green Staffs 169 D7
Abbey Hey Gtr Man 184 B5
Abbey Hulton Stoke 168 F6
Abbey Mead Sur 66 F4
Abbey St Bathans Borders 272 C5
Abbey Town Cumb 238 G5
Abbey Village Lancs 194 C6
Abbey Wood London 68 D3
Abbeycwmhir Powys 113 C11
Abbeydale Glos 80 B5
Abbeydale S Yorks 186 E4
Abbeydale Park S Yorks 186 E4
Abbeyhill Edin 280 G5
Abbeystead Lancs 203 C7
Abbots Bickington Devon 24 E5
Abbots Bromley Staffs 151 E11
Abbots Langley Herts 85 E9
Abbots Leigh N Som 60 E4
Abbot's Meads W Ches 166 B5
Abbots Morton Worcs 117 F10
Abbots Ripton Cambs 122 B4
Abbots Salford Warks 117 G11
Abbots Worthy Hants 48 G3
Abbotsbury Dorset 17 D7
Abbotsford W Sus 36 C4
Abbotsham Devon 24 B6
Abbotskerswell Devon 9 B7
Abbotsleigh Devon 8 F6
Abbotsley Cambs 122 F4
Abbotstone Hants 48 G5
Abbotswood Hants 32 C5
Abbotswood Sur 50 C4
Abbotts Ann Hants 47 E10
Abbott Shrops 115 B7
Abdon Shrops 131 F11
Abdy S Yorks 186 B6
Aber Ceredig 93 B9
Aber-Arad Carms 92 D6
Aber-banc Ceredig 93 C7
Aber Cowarch Gwyn 147 F1
Aber-Giâr Carms 93 C10
Aber-gwynfi Neath 57 B11
Aber-Hirnant Gwyn 147 C9
Aber miwl = Abermule Powys 130 E3
Aber-nant Rhondda 77 E8
Aber-oer Wrex 166 F3
Aber-Rhiwlech Gwyn 147 E8
Aber-Village Powys 96 G2
Aberaeron Ceredig 111 E9
Aberaman Rhondda 77 E8
Aberangell Gwyn 146 G6
Aberarder Highld 290 E6
Aberarder House Highld 300 D6
Aberarder Lodge Highld 291 E7
Aberargie Perth 286 F5
Aberarth Ceredig 111 E9
Aberavon Neath 57 C8
Aberbargoed Caerph 77 E11
Aberbechan Powys 130 E2
Aberbeeg Bl Gwent 78 E2
Abercanaid M Tydf 77 E9
Abercarn Caerph 78 G2
Abercastle Pembs 91 E7
Abercegir Powys 128 C6
Aberchalder Highld 290 C5
Aberchirder Aberds 302 D6

Abercorn W Loth 279 F11
Abercraf Powys 76 C4
Abercregan Neath 57 B11
Abercrombie Fife 287 G9
Abercwmboi Rhondda 77 F8
Abercych Pembs 92 C4
Abercynafon Powys 77 B9
Abercynffig = Aberkenfig Bridgend 57 E11
Abercynon Rhondda 77 F9
Aberdâr = Aberdare Rhondda 77 E7
Aberdalgie Perth 286 E4
Aberdaron Gwyn 144 D3
Aberdeen Aberdeen 293 C11
Aberdesach Gwyn 162 E6
Aberdour Fife 280 D3
Aberdovey = Aberdyfi Gwyn 128 D2
Aberdulais Neath 76 E3
Aberdyfi = Aberdovey Gwyn 128 D2
Aberedw Powys 95 B11
Abereiddy Pembs 90 E5
Abererch Gwyn 145 B7
Aberfan M Tydf 77 E9
Aberfeldy Perth 286 C2
Aberffraw Anglesey 162 B5
Aberffrwd Ceredig 112 B3
Aberffrwd Mon 78 D5
Aberford W Yorks 206 F4
Aberfoyle Stirl 285 G9
Abergarw Bridgend 58 C2
Abergarwed Neath 76 E4
Abergavenny Mon 78 C3
Abergele Conwy 180 F6
Abergorlech Carms 93 E11
Abergwaun = Fishguard Pembs 91 D9
Abergwesyn Powys 113 G7
Abergwili Carms 93 G8
Abergwynant Gwyn 146 F3
Abergwynfi Neath 57 B11
Abergwyngregyn Gwyn 179 G11
Abergwynolwyn Gwyn 128 B3
Aberhosan Powys 128 D6
Aberkenfig = Abercynffig Bridgend 57 E11
Aberlady E Loth 281 E9
Aberlemno Angus 287 B9
Aberllefenni Gwyn 128 B5
Aberllydan = Broad Haven Pembs 72 C5
Aberllynfi = Three Cocks Powys 96 C3
Abermagwr Ceredig 112 C3
Abermaw = Barmouth Gwyn 146 F2
Abermeurig Ceredig 111 F11
Abermorddu Flint 166 D4
Abermule = Aber-miwl Powys 130 E3
Abernant Powys 148 E2
Abernant Carms 92 G6
Abernant Powys 130 D3
Abernethy Perth 286 F5
Abernyte Perth 286 D6
Aberogwr = Ogmore by Sea V Glam 57 F11
Aberpennar = Mountain Ash Rhondda 77 F8
Aberporth Ceredig 110 G5
Aberriw = Berriew Powys 130 C3
Abersoch Gwyn 144 D6
Abersychan Torf 78 E3
Abertawe = Swansea Swansea 56 C6
Aberteifi = Cardigan Ceredig 92 C3
Aberthin V Glam 58 D4
Abertillery Bl Gwent 78 E2
Abertridwr Caerph 58 B6
Abertridwr Powys 147 F10
Abertrinant Gwyn 128 B2
Abertysswg Caerph 77 D10
Aberuchill Castle Perth 285 E11
Aberuthven Perth 286 F3
Aberyscir Powys 95 F9

Aberystwyth Ceredig 111 A11
Abhainn Suidhe W Isles 305 H2
Abingdon Oxon 83 F7
Abinger Common Sur 50 D6
Abinger Hammer Sur 50 D5
Abington Northants 120 E5
Abington S Lnrk 259 E10
Abington Pigotts Cambs 104 C6
Abington Vale Northants 120 E5
Ablington Glos 81 D10
Ablington Wilts 47 D7
Abney Derbys 185 F11
Aboyne Aberds 293 D7
Abraham Heights Lancs 211 G9
Abram Gtr Man 194 G6
Abriachan Highld 300 F5
Abridge Essex 87 F7
Abronhill N Lnrk 278 F5
Abshot Hants 33 F8
Abson S Glos 61 E8
Abthorpe Northants 102 B2
Abune-the-Hill Orkney 314 D2
Aby Lincs 190 F6
Acaster Malbis York 207 D7
Acaster Selby N Yorks 207 E7
Accrington Lancs 195 B9
Acha Argyll 275 B8
Acha Argyll 288 D3
Acha Mor W Isles 304 F5
Achabraid Argyll 275 E9
Achachork Highld 298 E4
Achad nan Darach Highld 284 B4
Achadh an Eas Argyll 284 F5
Achadunan Argyll 284 F5
Achafolla Argyll 275 B8
Achagary Highld 308 D7
Achaglass Argyll 255 C8
Achahoish Argyll 275 F8
Achalader Perth 286 C5
Achallader Argyll 285 C7
Achalone Highld 310 D5
Ach'an Todhair Highld 290 F2
Achanalt Highld 300 C2
Achanamara Argyll 275 E8
Achandunie Highld 300 B6
Achany Highld 309 J5
Achaphubuil Highld 290 F2
Acharacle Highld 289 C8
Acharn Highld 289 D9
Acharn Perth 285 C11
Acharole Highld 310 D6
Acharossan Argyll 275 F10
Acharry Muir Highld 309 K6
Achath Aberds 293 B9
Achavanich Highld 310 E5
Achavelgin Highld 301 D9
Achavraat Highld 301 E9
Achddu Carms 74 E6
Achduart Highld 307 J5
Achentoul Highld 310 F2
Achfary Highld 306 F7
Achfrish Highld 309 H5
Achgarve Highld 307 K3
Achiemore Highld 308 C3
Achiemore Highld 310 D2
A'Chill Highld 294 E4
Achiltibuie Highld 307 J5
Achina Highld 308 C7
Achinahuagh Highld 308 C5
Achindaul Highld 290 E3
Achindown Highld 301 E8
Achinduich Highld 309 J5
Achinduin Argyll 289 F10
Achingills Highld 310 C5
Achininver Highld 308 C5
Achintee Highld 290 F3
Achintee Highld 299 E9
Achintraid Highld 295 B10
Achlaven Argyll 289 F11
Achlean Highld 291 D10
Achleck Argyll 288 E6
Achlorachan Highld 300 D3
Achluachrach Highld 290 E4
Achlyness Highld 306 D7
Achmelvich Highld 307 G5
Achmore Highld 295 B10
Achmore Stirl 285 D9

Achnaba Argyll 275 E10
Achnaba Argyll 289 F11
Achnabat Highld 300 F5
Achnabreck Argyll 275 D9
Achnacarin Highld 306 F5
Achnacarry Highld 290 E3
Achnacloich Highld 289 F11
Achnacloich Argyll 295 E7
Achnaconeran Highld 290 B6
Achnacraig Argyll 288 E6
Achnacree Argyll 289 F11
Achnacree Bay Argyll 289 F11
Achnacroish Argyll 289 E10
Achnadrish Argyll 288 D6
Achnafalnich Argyll 284 E6
Achnagarron Highld 300 C6
Achnaha Highld 288 C6
Achnahanat Highld 309 K5
Achnahannet Highld 301 G9
Achnahard Argyll 288 G5
Achnairn Highld 309 H5
Achnaluachrach Highld 309 J6
Achnandarach Highld 295 B10
Achnanellan Highld 290 E2
Achnasaul Highld 290 E3
Achnasheen Highld 299 D11
Achnashelloch Highld 275 D9
Achnavast Highld 310 C4
Achneigie Highld 299 B10
Achormlarie Highld 309 K6
Achorn Highld 310 F5
Achosnich Highld 288 C6
Achranich Highld 289 E9
Achreamie Highld 310 C4
Achriabhach Highld 290 G3
Achriesgill Highld 306 D7
Achrimsdale Highld 311 J3
Achtoty Highld 308 C6
Achurch Northants 137 G10
Achuvoldrach Highld 308 D5
Achvaich Highld 309 K7
Achvarasdal Highld 310 C3
Ackenthwaite Cumb 211 C10
Ackergill Highld 310 D7
Acklam M'bro 225 B9
Acklam N Yorks 216 G5
Ackleton Shrops 132 D5
Acklington Northumb 252 C6
Ackton W Yorks 198 C2
Ackworth Moor Top W Yorks 198 D2
Acle Norf 161 G8
Acock's Green W Mid 134 G2
Acol Kent 71 G10
Acomb Northumb 241 D10
Acomb York 207 C7
Acomb Gtr Man 196 F2
Acre Lancs 195 C9
Acre Street W Sus 21 B11
Acrefair Wrex 166 G3
Acres Nook Staffs 168 E4
Acton E Ches 167 E10
Acton London 67 C8
Acton Shrops 130 G6
Acton Staffs 168 F4
Acton Suff 107 C7
Acton Wrex 166 E4
Acton Beauchamp Hereford 116 G3
Acton Bridge W Ches 183 F10
Acton Burnell Shrops 131 C10
Acton Green Hereford 116 G3
Acton Green London 67 D8
Acton Pigott Shrops 131 C10
Acton Place Suff 107 B7
Acton Reynald Shrops 149 E10
Acton Round Shrops 132 D2
Acton Scott Shrops 131 F9
Acton Trussell Staffs 151 F8
Acton Turville S Glos 61 C10
Adabroc W Isles 304 B7
Adambrae W Loth 269 A10
Adam's Green Dorset 29 F8
Adbaston Staffs 150 D5
Adber Dorset 29 C9
Adbolton Notts 154 B2
Adderbury Oxon 101 D9
Adderley Shrops 150 B3
Adderley Green Stoke 168 G6
Adderstone Northumb 264 C4
Addiewell W Loth 269 C9

Addingham W Yorks 205 D7
Addingham Moorside W Yorks 205 D7
Addington Bucks 102 F4
Addington Corn 6 B5
Addington Kent 53 B7
Addington London 67 G11
Addinston Borders 271 E10
Addiscombe London 67 F10
Addlestone Sur 66 F5
Addlestonemoor Sur 66 F4
Addlethorpe Lincs 175 B8
Adel W Yorks 205 F11
Adeney Telford 150 F4
Adeyfield Herts 85 D9
Adfa Powys 129 C11
Adforton Hereford 115 C8
Adgestone I o W 21 D7
Adisham Kent 55 C8
Adlestrop Glos 100 F4
Adlingfleet E Yorks 199 C10
Adlington Ches 184 E6
Adlington Lancs 194 E6
Adlington Park Lancs 194 E5
Admaston Staffs 151 E10
Admaston Telford 150 G2
Admington Warks 100 B4
Adpar Ceredig 92 C6
Adsborough Som 43 F7
Adscombe Som 43 F7
Adstock Bucks 102 E4
Adstone Northants 119 G11
Adswood Gtr Man 184 D5
Adversane W Sus 35 C9
Advie Highld 301 F11
Adwalton W Yorks 197 B8
Adwell Oxon 83 F11
Adwick le Street S Yorks 198 F4
Adwick upon Dearne S Yorks 198 G3
Adziel Aberds 303 D9
Ae Dumfries 247 F11
Ae Village Dumfries 247 F11
Affetside Gtr Man 195 E9
Affleck Aberds 303 G8
Affpuddle Dorset 18 C2
Affric Lodge Highld 299 G11
Afon Eitha Wrex 166 F3
Afon-wen Flint 181 G10
Afon Wen Gwyn 145 B8
Afton I o W 20 D2
Agar Nook Leics 153 G9
Aggborough Worcs 116 B6
Agglethorpe N Yorks 213 B11
Aglionby Cumb 239 F10
Agneash I o M 192 D5
Aifft Denb 165 B10
Aigburth Mers 182 D5
Aiginis W Isles 304 E6
Aike E Yorks 209 D7
Aikenway Moray 302 E2
Aikerness Orkney 314 A4
Aikers Orkney 314 G4
Aiketgate Cumb 230 B5
Aikton Cumb 239 G7
Ailby Lincs 190 F6
Ailey Hereford 96 B6
Ailstone Warks 118 G5
Ailsworth P'boro 138 D2
Aimes Green Essex 86 E5
Ainderby Quernhow N Yorks 215 C7
Ainderby Steeple N Yorks 224 G6
Aingers Green Essex 108 G2
Ainley Top W Yorks 196 D6
Ainsdale Mers 193 E10
Ainsdale-on-Sea Mers 193 E9
Ainstable Cumb 230 B6
Ainsworth Gtr Man 195 E9
Ainthorpe N Yorks 226 D4
Aintree Mers 182 B5
Aird Argyll 275 C8
Aird Dumfries 236 C2
Aird Highld 295 B9
Aird W Isles 296 F6
Aird W Isles 304 E7
Aird a' Mhachair W Isles 297 G3
Aird a' Mhulaidh W Isles 305 G3

Aird Asaig W Isles 305 H3
Aird Dhail W Isles 304 B6
Aird Mhidhinis W Isles 297 L3
Aird Mhighe W Isles 296 C6
Aird Mhighe W Isles 305 J3
Aird Mhor W Isles 297 L3
Aird Mhòr W Isles 297 L3
Aird of Sleat Highld 295 E7
Aird Thunga W Isles 304 E6
Aird Uig W Isles 304 E2
Airdachuilinn Highld 306 E7
Airdens Highld 309 K6
Airdeny Argyll 289 G11
Airdrie N Lnrk 268 B5
Airds of Kells Dumfries 237 B8
Airdtorrisdale Highld 308 C6
Aire View N Yorks 204 D5
Airedale W Yorks 198 B3
Airidh a Bhruaich W Isles 305 G4
Airieland Dumfries 237 D9
Airinis W Isles 304 E6
Airlie Angus 287 B7
Airlies Dumfries 236 D5
Airmyn E Yorks 199 B8
Airntully Perth 286 D4
Airor Highld 295 E9
Airth Falk 279 D7
Airthrey Castle Stirl 278 B6
Airton N Yorks 204 B4
Airy Hill N Yorks 227 D7
Airyhassen Dumfries 236 E5
Airylligg Dumfries 236 C4
Aisby Lincs 155 B10
Aisby Lincs 188 C5
Aisgernis W Isles 297 J3
Aish Devon 8 C3
Aish Devon 8 D6
Aisholt Som 43 F7
Aiskew N Yorks 214 B5
Aislaby N Yorks 216 B5
Aislaby N Yorks 227 D7
Aislaby Stockton 225 C8
Aisthorpe Lincs 188 E6
Aith Orkney 314 E6
Aith Shetland 312 D8
Aith Shetland 313 H5
Aithnen Powys 148 E4
Aithsetter Shetland 313 K6
Aitkenhead S Ayrs 245 B8
Aitnoch Highld 301 F9
Akeld Northumb 263 D11
Akeley Bucks 102 D4
Akenham Suff 108 B3
Albany T & W 243 F7
Albaston Corn 12 G4
Alberbury Shrops 149 G7
Albert Town Pembs 72 B6
Albert Village Leics 152 F6
Albourne W Sus 36 D3
Albourne Green W Sus 36 D3
Albrighton Shrops 132 C6
Albrighton Shrops 149 F9
Albro Castle Ceredig 92 B3
Alburgh Norf 142 F5
Albury Herts 105 G8
Albury Sur 50 D5
Albury End Herts 105 G8
Albury Heath Sur 50 D5
Alby Hill Norf 160 C3
Albyfield Cumb 240 G2
Alcaig Highld 300 D5
Alcaston Shrops 131 F9
Alcester Dorset 30 C5
Alcester Warks 117 F11
Alcester Lane's End W Mid 133 G11
Alciston E Sus 23 D8
Alcombe Som 42 D3
Alcombe Wilts 61 F11
Alconbury Cambs 122 B3
Alconbury Weston Cambs 122 B3
Aldbar Castle Angus 287 B9
Aldborough Norf 160 C3
Aldborough N Yorks 215 F8
Aldbourne Wilts 63 D9
Aldbrough E Yorks 209 F10
Aldbrough St John N Yorks 224 C4
Aldbury Herts 85 C7
Aldcliffe Lancs 211 G9

Aldclune Perth 291 G11
Aldeburgh Suff 127 F9
Aldeby Norf 143 E8
Aldenham Herts 85 F10
Alderbury Wilts 31 B11
Aldercar Derbys 170 F6
Alderford Norf 160 F2
Alderholt Dorset 31 E10
Alderley Glos 80 G3
Alderley Edge E Ches 184 F4
Alderman's Green W Mid 135 G2
Aldermaston W Berks 64 F5
Aldermaston Soke W Berks 64 G6
Aldermaston Wharf W Berks 64 F6
Alderminster Warks 100 B4
Aldermoor Soton 32 D5
Alderney Poole 18 C6
Alder's End Hereford 98 C2
Aldersbrook London 68 C3
Aldersey Green W Ches 167 D7
Aldershawe Staffs 134 B2
Aldershot Hants 49 C11
Alderton Glos 99 E10
Alderton Northants 102 B4
Alderton Shrops 149 E9
Alderton Suff 108 C6
Alderton Wilts 61 C10
Alderton Fields Glos 99 E10
Alderwasley Derbys 170 E4
Aldfield N Yorks 214 F5
Aldford W Ches 166 D6
Aldgate Rutland 137 C9
Aldham Essex 107 F8
Aldham Suff 107 B10
Aldie Highld 309 L7
Aldingbourne W Sus 22 B6
Aldingham Cumb 210 E5
Aldington Kent 54 F5
Aldington Worcs 99 C11
Aldington Frith Kent 54 F4
Aldivalloch Moray 302 G3
Aldochlay Argyll 277 C7
Aldon Shrops 115 B8
Aldoth Cumb 229 B8
Aldreth Cambs 123 B8
Aldridge W Mid 133 C11
Aldringham Suff 127 E8
Aldsworth Glos 81 C11
Aldunie Moray 302 G3
Aldwark Derbys 170 C2
Aldwark N Yorks 215 G9
Aldwarke S Yorks 186 C6
Aldwick W Sus 22 D6
Aldwincle Northants 137 G10
Aldworth W Berks 64 D4
Ale Oak Shrops 130 G4
Alehousehill Aberds 303 E10
Alehousewells Aberds 293 B8
Alexandria W Dunb 277 F7
Aley Som 43 F7
Aley Green C Beds 85 B8
Alfardisworthy Devon 24 E3
Alfington Devon 15 B8
Alfold Sur 50 G4
Alfold Bars W Sus 50 G4
Alfold Crossways Sur 50 F4
Alford Aberds 293 B7
Alford Lincs 191 F7
Alford Som 44 G6
Alfred's Well Worcs 117 C8
Alfreton Derbys 170 D6
Alfrick Worcs 116 G4
Alfrick Pound Worcs 116 G4
Alfriston E Sus 23 E8
Algaltraig Argyll 275 F11
Algarkirk Lincs 156 B5
Alhampton Som 44 F6
Aline Lodge W Isles 305 G3
Alisary Highld 289 B9
Alkborough N Lincs 199 C11
Alkerton Glos 80 D3
Alkerton Oxon 101 C7
Alkham Kent 55 E9

Alkington Shrops 149 B10
Alkmonton Derbys 152 B3
Alkrington Garden Village Gtr Man 195 G11
All Cannings Wilts 62 G5
All Saints Devon 28 G4
All Saints South Elmham Suff 142 G6
All Stretton Shrops 131 D9
Alladale Lodge Highld 309 L4
Allaleigh Devon 8 E6
Allanaquoich Aberds 292 D3
Allanbank Borders 271 F10
Allanbank N Lnrk 268 D6
Allangrange Mains Highld 300 D6
Allanshaugh Borders 271 F8
Allanshaws Borders 271 G9
Allanton Borders 273 E7
Allanton N Lnrk 269 D7
Allanton S Lnrk 268 E4
Allardice Aberds 293 F10
Allaston Glos 79 E10
Allathasdal W Isles 297 L2
Allbrook Hants 33 C7
Allen End Warks 134 D3
Allendale Town Northum 241 F8
Allenheads Northumb 232 B3
Allens Green Herts 87 B7
Allensford Durham 242 G4
Allensmore Hereford 97 D9
Allenton Derby 153 C7
Allenwood Cumb 239 F11
Aller Devon 9 B7
Aller Devon 27 F9
Aller Dorset 30 G3
Aller Som 28 B6
Aller Park Devon 9 B7
Allerby Cumb 229 D7
Allerford Corn 27 B11
Allerford Som 42 D2
Allerston N Yorks 217 C7
Allerthorpe E Yorks 207 D11
Allerton Mers 182 D6
Allerton W Yorks 205 G8
Allerton Bywater W Yorks 198 B2
Allerton Mauleverer N Yorks 206 B4
Allesley W Mid 134 G6
Allestree Derby 152 B6
Allet Corn 4 F5
Allexton Leics 136 C6
Allgreave E Ches 169 B7
Allhallows Medway 69 D10
Allhallows-on-Sea Medway 69 D10
Alligin Shuas Highld 299 D8
Allimore Green Staffs 151 F7
Allington Kent 53 B8
Allington Lincs 172 G5
Allington Wilts 47 F8
Allington Wilts 61 D11
Allington Wilts 62 G5
Allington Bar Wilts 61 D11
Allithwaite Cumb 211 D7
Alloa Clack 279 C7
Allonby Cumb 229 C7
Allostock W Ches 184 G3
Alloway S Ayrs 257 F8
Allowenshay Som 28 E5
Allscot Shrops 132 D4
Allscott Telford 150 G2
Allt Carms 75 E9
Allt-na-giubhsaich Aberds 292 E4
Allt na h-Airbhe Highld 307 K6
Allt-nan-sùgh Highld 295 C11
Allt-yr-yn Newport 59 B9
Alltami Flint 166 B3
Alltmawr Powys 95 B11
Alltsigh Highld 290 C6
Alltwalis Carms 93 E8
Alltwen Neath 76 E2
Alltyblaca Ceredig 93 B10
Alltwood Green Suff 125 C10
Alma Notts 171 E7
Almagill Dumfries 238 B3
Almeley Hereford 114 G6

Almeley Wooton Hereford 114 G6
Almer Dorset 18 B4
Almholme S Yorks 198 F5
Almington Staffs 150 C4
Alminstone Cross Devon 24 C4
Almondbank Perth 286 E4
Almondbury W Yorks 197 D7
Almondsbury S Glos 60 C6
Almondvale W Loth 269 B11
Almshouse Green Essex 106 E5
Alne N Yorks 215 F9
Alne End Warks 118 F2
Alne Hills Warks 118 E2
Alne Station N Yorks 215 F10
Alness Highld 300 C6
Alnessferry Highld 300 C6
Alnham Northumb 263 G11
Alnmouth Northumb 264 G6
Alnwick Northumb 264 G5
Alperton London 67 C7
Alphamstone Essex 107 D7
Alpheton Suff 125 G7
Alphington Devon 14 C4
Alpington Norf 142 C5
Alport Derbys 170 C2
Alport Powys 130 D5
Alpraham E Ches 167 D9
Alresford Essex 107 G11
Alrewas Staffs 152 F3
Alsager E Ches 168 D3
Alsagers Bank Staffs 168 F4
Alscot Bucks 84 E4
Alsop en le Dale Derbys 169 D11
Alston Cumb 231 B10
Alston Devon 28 G4
Alston Sutton Som 44 C2
Alstone Glos 99 E9
Alstone Glos 99 G8
Alstone Som 43 D10
Alstonefield Staffs 169 D10
Alswear Devon 26 C2
Alt Gtr Man 196 G2
Alt Hill Gtr Man 196 G2
Altandhu Highld 307 H4
Altanduin Highld 311 G2
Altarnun Corn 11 E10
Altass Highld 309 J4
Altbough Hereford 97 E10
Altdargue Aberds 293 C7
Alterwall Highld 310 C6
Altham Lancs 203 G11
Althorne Essex 88 F6
Althorpe N Lincs 199 F10
Alticane S Ayrs 244 F6
Alticry Dumfries 236 D4
Altmore Windsor 65 D11
Altnabreac Station Highld 310 E4
Altnacealgach Hotel Highld 307 H7
Altnacraig Argyll 289 G10
Altnafeadh Highld 284 B6
Altnaharra Highld 308 F5
Altofts W Yorks 197 C11
Alton Derbys 170 C5
Alton Hants 49 F8
Alton Staffs 169 G9
Alton Wilts 47 D7
Alton Barnes Wilts 62 G6
Alton Pancras Dorset 30 G2
Alton Priors Wilts 62 G6
Altonhill E Ayrs 257 B10
Altonside Moray 302 D2
Altour Highld 290 E4
Altrincham Gtr Man 184 D3
Altrua Highld 290 E4
Altskeith Stirl 285 G8
Altyre Ho Moray 301 D10
Alum Rock W Mid 134 F2
Alva Clack 279 B7
Alvanley W Ches 183 G7
Alvaston Derby 153 C7
Alvechurch Worcs 117 C10
Alvecote Warks 134 C4
Alvediston Wilts 31 C7
Alveley Shrops 132 G5
Alverdiscott Devon 25 B8
Alverstoke Hants 21 B8
Alverstone I o W 21 D7
Alverthorpe W Yorks 197 C10
Alverton Notts 172 G3
Alves Moray 301 C11
Alvescot Oxon 82 E3
Alveston S Glos 60 B6
Alveston Warks 118 F4
Alveston Down S Glos 60 B6
Alveston Hill Warks 118 G4
Alvie Highld 291 C10
Alvingham Lincs 190 C5
Alvington Glos 79 E10
Alvington Som 29 D8
Alwalton Cambs 138 D2
Alway Newport 59 B10
Alweston Dorset 29 E11
Alwington Devon 24 C6
Alwinton Northumb 251 B10
Alwoodley W Yorks 205 E11
Alwoodley Gates W Yorks 206 E2
Alwoodley Park W Yorks 205 E11
Alyth Perth 286 C6
Am Baile W Isles 297 K3
Am Buth Argyll 289 G10
Amalebra Corn 1 B5
Amalveor Corn 1 B5
Amatnatua Highld 309 K4
Ambaston Derbys 153 C8
Amber Hill Lincs 174 F2
Ambergate Derbys 170 E4
Amberley Glos 80 E5
Amberley Hereford 97 B10
Amberley W Sus 35 E8
Amble Northumb 253 C7
Amblecote W Mid 133 F7
Ambler Thorn W Yorks 196 B5
Ambleside Cumb 221 E7
Ambleston Pembs 91 F10
Ambrosden Oxon 83 B10
Amcotts N Lincs 199 E11
Amen Corner Brack 65 F10
Amersham Bucks 85 F7
Amersham Common Bucks 85 F7
Amersham Old Town Bucks 85 F7
Amersham on the Hill Bucks 85 F7
Amerton Staffs 151 D9
Amesbury Bath 45 B7
Amesbury Wilts 47 E7
Ameysford Dorset 31 G9
Amington Staffs 134 C4
Amisfield Dumfries 247 G11
Amlwch Anglesey 178 C6
Amlwch Port Anglesey 179 C7
Ammanford = Rhydaman Carms 75 C10
Ammerham Som 28 F5
Amod Argyll 255 D8
Amotherby N Yorks 216 E4
Ampfield Hants 32 C6
Ampleforth N Yorks 215 D11
Ampney Crucis Glos 81 E9
Ampney St Mary Glos 81 E9
Ampney St Peter Glos 81 E9
Amport Hants 47 E9
Ampthill C Beds 103 D10
Ampton Suff 125 C7
Amroth Pembs 73 D11
Amulree Perth 286 D2
Amwell Herts 85 C11
An Caol Highld 298 D6
An Cnoc W Isles 304 E6
An Gleann Ur W Isles 304 E6
An Leth Meadhanach W Isles 297 K3
An t-Ob W Isles 296 C6
Anagach Highld 301 G10
Anaheilt Highld 289 C10
Anancaun Highld 299 C10
Ancarraig Highld 300 G4
Ancaster Lincs 173 G7
Anchor Shrops 130 G3
Anchor Corner Norf 141 D10
Anchor Street Norf 160 E6
Anchorage Park Ptsmth 33 G11
Anchorsholme Blkpool 202 E2
Ancoats Gtr Man 184 B5
Ancroft Northumb 273 F9
Ancroft Northmoor Northumb 273 F9
Ancrum Borders 262 E4
Ancton W Sus 35 G7
Ancumtoun Orkney 314 A7
Anderby Lincs 191 F8
Anderby Creek Lincs 191 F8
Andersea Som 43 G10
Andersfield Som 43 G8
Anderson Dorset 18 B3
Anderton Corn 7 E8
Anderton Lancs 194 E6
Anderton W Ches 183 F10
Andertons Mill Lancs 194 E4
Andover Hants 47 D11
Andover Down Hants 47 D11
Andoversford Glos 81 B8
Andreas I o M 192 C5
Andwell Hants 49 C7
Anelog Gwyn 144 D3
Anerley London 67 F10
Anfield Mers 182 C5
Angarrack Corn 2 B3
Angarrick Corn 3 B7
Angelbank Shrops 115 B11
Angersleigh Som 27 D11
Angerton Cumb 238 F6
Angle Pembs 72 E5
Angmering W Sus 35 G9
Angram N Yorks 206 D6
Angram N Yorks 223 F7
Anick Northumb 241 D11
Anie Stirl 285 F9
Ankerdine Hill Worcs 116 F4
Ankerville Highld 301 B8
Anlaby E Yorks 200 B4
Anlaby Park Hull 200 B5
Anmer Norf 158 D4
Anmore Hants 33 E11
Anna Valley Hants 47 E10
Annan Dumfries 238 D5
Annaside Cumb 210 B1
Annat Argyll 284 E4
Annat Highld 290 D5
Annat Highld 299 D8
Annbank S Ayrs 257 E10
Annesley Notts 171 E8
Annesley Woodhouse Notts 171 E7
Annfield Plain Durham 242 G5
Anniesland Glasgow 267 B10
Annifirth Shetland 313 J3
Annis Hill Suff 143 F7
Annishader Highld 298 D4
Annitsford T & W 243 C7
Ann's Hill Hants 33 G9
Annscroft Shrops 131 B9
Annwell Place Derbys 152 F6
Ansdell Lancs 193 B10
Ansells End Herts 85 B11
Ansford Som 44 G6
Ansley Warks 134 E5
Ansley Common Warks 134 E6
Anslow Staffs 152 D4
Anslow Gate Staffs 152 D3
Ansteadbrook Sur 50 G2
Anstey Herts 105 E8
Anstey Leics 135 B10
Anstruther Easter Fife 287 G9
Anstruther Wester Fife 287 G9
Ansty Hants 49 E8
Ansty W Sus 36 C3
Ansty Warks 135 G7
Ansty Wilts 31 B7
Ansty Coombe Wilts 31 B7
Ansty Cross Dorset 30 G3
Anthill Common Hants 33 E10
Anthony Corn 7 E7
Anthony's Cross Glos 98 G4
Anthorn Cumb 238 F5
Antingham Norf 160 C5
Anton's Gowt Lincs 174 F3
Antonshill Falk 279 E7
Antony Corn 7 E7
Antony Passage Corn 7 D8
Antrobus W Ches 183 F10
Anvil Green Kent 54 D6
Anvilles W Berks 63 F10
Anwick Lincs 173 E10
Anwoth Dumfries 237 D7
Aonachan Highld 290 E4
Aoradh Argyll 274 G3
Apedale Staffs 168 F4
Aperfield London 52 B2
Apes Dale Worcs 117 C9
Apes Hall Cambs 139 E11
Apethorpe Northants 137 D10
Apeton Staffs 151 F7
Apley Lincs 189 F10
Apley Forge Shrops 132 D4
Apperknowle Derbys 186 F5
Apperley Glos 99 F7
Apperley Bridge W Yorks 205 F9
Apperley Dene Northumb 242 F3
Appersett N Yorks 223 G7
Appin Argyll 289 E11
Appin House Argyll 289 E11
Appleby N Lincs 200 E3
Appleby-in-Westmorland Cumb 231 G9
Appleby Magna Leics 134 B6
Appleby Parva Leics 134 B6
Applecross Highld 299 E7
Applecross Ho Highld 299 E7
Appledore Devon 27 E9
Appledore Devon 40 G3
Appledore Kent 39 B7
Appledore Heath Kent 54 G3
Appleford Oxon 83 G8
Applegarthtown Dumfries 248 G4
Applehouse Hill Windsor 65 C10
Applemore Hants 32 F5
Appleshaw Hants 47 D10
Applethwaite Cumb 229 F11
Appleton Halton 183 D8
Appleton Oxon 82 E6
Appleton-le-Moors N Yorks 216 B4
Appleton-le-Street N Yorks 216 E4
Appleton Park Warr 183 E10
Appleton Roebuck N Yorks 207 E7
Appleton Thorn Warr 183 E10
Appleton Wiske N Yorks 225 E7
Appletreehall Borders 262 F2
Appletreewick N Yorks 213 G11
Appley I o W 21 C8
Appley Som 27 C9
Appley Bridge Lancs 194 F4
Apse Heath I o W 21 E7
Apsey Green Suff 126 E5
Apsley Herts 85 D9
Apsley End C Beds 104 E2
Apuldram W Sus 22 C4
Aqueduct Telford 132 B3
Aquhythie Aberds 293 B9
Arabella Highld 301 B8
Arbeadie Aberds 293 D8
Arberth = Narberth Pembs 73 C10
Arbirlot Angus 287 C10
Arboll Highld 311 L2
Arborfield Wokingham 65 F9
Arborfield Cross Wokingham 65 F9
Arborfield Garrison Wokingham 65 F9
Arbourthorne S Yorks 186 D5
Arbroath Angus 287 C10
Arbury Cambs 123 E8
Arbuthnott Aberds 293 F9
Archavandra Muir Highld 309 K7
Archdeacon Newton Darl 224 B5
Archenfield Hereford 96 C5
Archiestown Moray 302 E2
Archnalea Highld 289 C10
Arclid E Ches 168 C3
Arclid Green E Ches 168 C3
Ard-dhubh Highld 299 E7
Ardachu Highld 309 J6
Ardailly Argyll 255 B7
Ardalanish Argyll 274 B4
Ardallie Aberds 303 F10
Ardalum Ho Argyll 288 F6
Ardamaleish Argyll 275 G11
Ardanaiseig Argyll 284 E4
Ardaneaskan Highld 295 B10
Ardanstur Argyll 275 B9
Ardargie House Hotel Perth 286 F4
Ardarroch Highld 295 B10
Ardban Highld 295 B9
Ardbeg Argyll 254 C5
Ardbeg Argyll 276 E3
Ardcharnich Highld 307 L6
Ardchiavaig Argyll 274 B4
Ardchonnell Argyll 275 B10
Ardchronie Highld 309 L6
Ardchuilk Highld 300 F2
Ardchullarie More Stirl 285 F9
Ardchyle Stirl 285 E9
Ardclach Highld 301 E9
Arddleen Powys 148 F5
Ardechvie Highld 290 D3
Ardeley Herts 104 F6
Ardelve Highld 295 C10
Arden Argyll 277 E7
Arden E Renf 267 D10
Arden Park Gtr Man 184 C6
Ardencaple Ho Argyll 275 B8
Ardendrain Highld 300 F5
Ardens Grafton Warks 118 G2
Ardentallen Argyll 289 G10
Ardentinny Argyll 276 D3
Ardentraive Argyll 275 F11
Ardeonaig Stirl 285 D10
Ardersier Highld 301 D7
Ardery Highld 289 C9
Ardessie Highld 307 L5
Ardfern Argyll 275 C9
Ardfernal Argyll 274 F6
Ardgartan Argyll 284 G6
Ardgay Highld 309 K5
Ardglassie Aberds 303 C10
Ardgour Highld 290 G2
Ardgye Moray 301 C11
Ardheslaig Highld 299 D7
Ardiecow Moray 302 C5
Ardinamir Argyll 275 B8
Ardindrean Highld 307 L6
Ardingly W Sus 36 B4
Ardington Oxon 64 B2
Ardington Wick Oxon 64 B2
Ardintoul Highld 295 C10
Ardlair Aberds 302 G5
Ardlair Highld 299 B9
Ardlamey Argyll 255 C7
Ardlamont Ho Argyll 275 G10
Ardlawhill Aberds 303 C8
Ardleigh Essex 107 F11
Ardleigh Green London 68 B4
Ardleigh Heath Essex 107 E10
Ardler Perth 286 C6
Ardley Oxon 101 F10
Ardley End Essex 87 C8
Ardlui Argyll 285 F7
Ardlussa Argyll 275 E7
Ardmair Highld 307 K6
Ardmay Argyll 284 G6
Ardmenish Argyll 274 F6
Ardminish Argyll 255 C7
Ardmolich Highld 289 B9
Ardmore Argyll 289 G9
Ardmore Highld 306 D7
Ardmore Highld 309 L7
Ardnacross Argyll 289 E7
Ardnadam Argyll 276 E3
Ardnagowan Argyll 284 G4
Ardnagrask Highld 300 E5
Ardnarff Highld 295 B10
Ardnastang Highld 289 C10
Ardnave Argyll 274 F3
Ardneil N Ayrs 266 F3
Ardno Argyll 284 G5
Ardo Aberds 303 F8
Ardo Ho Aberds 303 G9
Ardoch Argyll 277 F7
Ardoch Perth 286 D4
Ardoch Stirl 285 F9
Ardochy House Highld 290 C4
Ardoyne Aberds 302 G6
Ardpatrick Argyll 275 G8
Ardpatrick Ho Argyll 255 B8
Ardpeaton Argyll 276 D4
Ardradnaig Perth 285 C11
Ardrishaig Argyll 275 E9
Ardross Fife 287 G9
Ardross Highld 300 B6
Ardross Castle Highld 300 B6
Ardrossan N Ayrs 266 G4
Ardshave Highld 309 K7
Ardsheal Highld 289 D11
Ardshealach Highld 289 C8
Ardskenish Argyll 274 D4
Ardsley S Yorks 197 F11
Ardslignish Highld 289 C7
Ardtalla Argyll 254 B5
Ardtalnaig Perth 285 D11
Ardtaraig Argyll 275 E11
Ardtoe Highld 289 B8
Ardtreck Highld 294 B5
Ardtrostan Perth 285 E10
Ardtur Argyll 289 E11
Arduaine Argyll 275 B8
Ardullie Highld 300 C5
Ardvannie Highld 309 L6
Ardvar Highld 306 F6
Ardvasar Highld 295 E8
Ardveich Stirl 285 E10
Ardverikie Highld 291 E7
Ardvorlich Perth 285 E10
Ardwell Dumfries 236 E3
Ardwell Moray 302 F3
Ardwell S Ayrs 244 E5
Ardwell Mains Dumfries 236 E3
Ardwick Gtr Man 184 B5
Areley Kings Worcs 116 C6
Arford Hants 49 F10
Argoed Caerph 77 F11
Argoed Powys 113 E9
Argoed Powys 130 E5
Argoed Shrops 130 G6
Argoed Shrops 148 E6
Argos Hill E Sus 37 B9
Arichamish Argyll 275 C10
Arichastlich Argyll 284 D6
Aridhglas Argyll 288 G5
Arieniskill Highld 295 G9
Arileod Argyll 288 D3
Arinacrinachd Highld 299 D7
Arinagour Argyll 288 D4
Arineckaig Highld 299 E9
Arion Orkney 314 E2
Arisaig Highld 295 G8
Ariundle Highld 289 C10
Arivegaig Highld 289 C8
Arivoichallum Argyll 254 C4
Arkendale N Yorks 215 G7
Arkesden Essex 105 E9
Arkholme Lancs 211 E11
Arkle Town N Yorks 223 E10
Arkleby Cumb 229 D8
Arkleton Dumfries 249 E9
Arkley London 86 F2
Arksey S Yorks 198 F5
Arkwright Town Derbys 186 G6
Arle Glos 99 G8
Arlebrook Glos 80 D4
Arlecdon Cumb 219 B10
Arlescote Warks 101 B7
Arlesey C Beds 104 D3
Arleston Telford 150 G3
Arley E Ches 183 E11
Arley Green E Ches 183 E11
Arlingham Glos 80 C2
Arlington Devon 40 E6
Arlington E Sus 23 D8
Arlington Glos 81 D10
Arlington Beccott Devon 40 E6
Armadale Highld 308 C7
Armadale W Loth 269 B8
Armadale Castle Highld 295 E8
Armathwaite Cumb 230 B6
Armigers Essex 105 F11
Arminghall Norf 142 C5
Armitage Staffs 151 F11
Armitage Bridge W Yorks 196 E6
Armley W Yorks 205 G11
Armscote Warks 100 C4
Armsdale Staffs 150 C5
Armshead Staffs 168 F6
Armston Northants 137 F11
Armthorpe S Yorks 198 F6
Arnabost Argyll 288 D4
Arnaby Cumb 210 C3
Arncliffe N Yorks 213 E8
Arncroach Fife 287 G9
Arndilly Ho Moray 302 E2
Arne Dorset 18 D5
Arnesby Leics 136 E2
Arngask Perth 286 F5
Arnisdale Highld 295 D10
Arnish Highld 298 E5
Arniston Midloth 270 C6
Arnol W Isles 304 D5
Arnold E Yorks 209 E8
Arnold Notts 171 F9
Arno's Vale Bristol 60 E6
Arnprior Stirl 278 C2
Arnside Cumb 211 D9
Aros Mains Argyll 289 E7
Arowry Wrex 149 B9
Arpafeelie Highld 300 D6
Arpinge Kent 55 F7
Arrad Foot Cumb 210 C6
Arram E Yorks 208 E6
Arrathorne N Yorks 224 G4
Arreton I o W 20 D6
Arrington Cambs 122 G6
Arrivain Argyll 284 D6
Arrochar Argyll 284 G6
Arrow Warks 117 F11
Arrow Green Hereford 115 F8
Arrowe Hill Mers 182 D3
Arrowfield Top Worcs 117 C10
Arrunden W Yorks 196 F6
Arscaig Highld 309 H5
Arscott Shrops 131 B8
Arthill E Ches 184 D2
Arthington W Yorks 205 E11
Arthingworth Northants 136 G5
Arthog Gwyn 146 G2
Arthrath Aberds 303 F9
Arthursdale W Yorks 206 F3
Arthurstone Perth 286 C6
Arthurville Highld 309 L7
Artington Sur 50 D3
Artrochie Aberds 303 F10
Arundel W Sus 35 F8
Arwick Orkney 314 D3
Aryhoulan Highld 290 G2
Asby Cumb 229 G7
Ascog Argyll 266 C2
Ascoil Highld 311 H2
Ascot Windsor 66 F2
Ascott Warks 100 E6
Ascott d'Oyley Oxon 82 B4
Ascott Earl Oxon 82 B3
Ascott-under-Wychwood Oxon 82 B4
Asenby N Yorks 215 D7
Asfordby Leics 154 F4
Asfordby Hill Leics 154 F4
Asgarby Lincs 173 F10
Asgarby Lincs 174 B4
Ash Devon 8 F6
Ash Dorset 30 E5
Ash Kent 55 B9
Ash Kent 68 G5
Ash Som 28 C3
Ash Som 29 C7
Ash Sur 49 C11
Ash Bank Staffs 168 F6
Ash Bullayne Devon 26 G3
Ash Green Sur 50 D2
Ash Green Warks 134 F6
Ash Grove Wrex 166 G5
Ash Hill Devon 14 G4
Ash Magna Shrops 149 B11
Ash Mill Devon 26 C3
Ash Moor Devon 26 D3
Ash Parva Shrops 149 B11
Ash Priors Som 27 B11
Ash Street Suff 107 B10
Ash Thomas Devon 27 E8
Ash Vale Sur 49 C11
Ashaig Highld 295 C8
Ashampstead W Berks 64 D5
Ashampstead Green W Berks 64 D5
Ashansworth Hants 48 B2
Ashbank Kent 53 C10
Ashbeer Som 42 F5
Ashbocking Suff 126 G3
Ashbourne Derbys 169 F11
Ashbrittle Som 27 C9
Ashbrook Shrops 131 E9
Ashburnham Forge E Sus 23 B11
Ashburton Devon 8 B5
Ashbury Devon 12 B6
Ashbury Oxon 63 C9
Ashby N Lincs 200 F2
Ashby by Partney Lincs 174 B6
Ashby cum Fenby NE Lincs 201 G9
Ashby de la Launde Lincs 173 D9
Ashby-de-la-Zouch Leics 153 F7
Ashby Folville Leics 154 G4
Ashby Hill NE Lincs 201 G8
Ashby Magna Leics 135 E11
Ashby Parva Leics 135 F10
Ashby Puerorum Lincs 190 G4
Ashby St Ledgers Northants 119 D11
Ashby St Mary Norf 142 C6
Ashchurch Glos 99 E8
Ashcombe Devon 14 F4
Ashcombe Park N Som 59 G10
Ashcott Som 44 F2
Ashcott Corner Som 44 F2
Ashculme Devon 27 E10
Ashdon Essex 105 C11
Ashe Hants 48 D4
Asheldham Essex 89 E7
Ashen Essex 106 C4
Ashendon Bucks 84 C2
Asheridge Bucks 84 E6
Ashey I o W 21 D7
Ashfield Argyll 275 E8
Ashfield Carms 94 F3
Ashfield Hants 32 D5
Ashfield Hereford 97 G11
Ashfield Shrops 148 D6
Ashfield Stirl 285 G11
Ashfield Suff 126 E4
Ashfield Cum Thorpe Suff 126 E4
Ashfield Green Suff 124 F5
Ashfield Green Suff 126 C5
Ashfields Shrops 150 D4
Ashfold Crossways W Sus 36 B2
Ashfold Side N Yorks 214 F2
Ashford Devon 8 F3
Ashford Devon 40 F4
Ashford Hants 31 E10
Ashford Kent 54 E4
Ashford Sur 66 E5
Ashford Bowdler Shrops 115 C10
Ashford Carbonell Shrops 115 C10
Ashford Common Sur 66 E5
Ashford Hill Hants 64 G5
Ashford in the Water Derbys 185 G11
Ashgate Derbys 186 G5
Ashgill S Lnrk 268 F5
Ashgrove Bath 45 B8
Ashiestiel Borders 261 B10
Ashill Devon 27 E9
Ashill Norf 141 C7
Ashill Som 28 D4
Ashingdon Essex 88 G5
Ashington Northumb 253 F7
Ashington Poole 18 B6
Ashington Som 29 C9
Ashington W Sus 35 D10
Ashington End Lincs 175 B8
Ashintully Castle Perth 292 G3
Ashkirk Borders 261 E11
Ashlett Hants 33 G7
Ashleworth Glos 98 F6
Ashley Cambs 124 E3
Ashley Devon 25 E10
Ashley Dorset 31 G10
Ashley E Ches 184 E3
Ashley Glos 80 G6
Ashley Hants 19 C11
Ashley Hants 47 G11
Ashley Kent 55 D10
Ashley Northants 136 E5
Ashley Staffs 150 B5
Ashley Wilts 61 F10
Ashley Dale Staffs 150 B5
Ashley Down Bristol 60 D5
Ashley Green Bucks 85 D7
Ashley Heath Ches 184 D3
Ashley Heath Dorset 31 G10
Ashley Heath Staffs 150 B4
Ashley Moor Hereford 115 D9
Ashley Park Sur 66 F6
Ashleyhay Derbys 170 E3
Ashmanhaugh Norf 160 E6
Ashmansworth Hants 48 B2
Ashmansworthy Devon 24 D4
Ashmead Green Glos 80 F3
Ashmill Devon 12 B3
Ashmore Dorset 30 D6
Ashmore Green W Berks 64 F4
Ashmore Lake W Mid 133 D9
Ashmore Park W Mid 133 C9
Ashnashellach Lodge Highld 299 E10
Ashopton Derbys 185 D11
Ashorne Warks 118 F6
Ashover Derbys 170 C4
Ashover Hay Derbys 170 C5
Ashow Warks 118 C6
Ashperton Hereford 98 C2
Ashprington Devon 8 D6
Ashreigney Devon 25 E10
Ashridge Court Devon 25 G11
Ashtead Sur 51 B7
Ashton Corn 2 D4
Ashton Hants 33 D9
Ashton Hereford 115 E10
Ashton Invclyd 276 F4
Ashton Northants 102 B5
Ashton Northants 137 F11
Ashton P'boro 138 B2
Ashton Som 44 D2
Ashton Common Wilts 45 B11
Ashton Gate Bristol 60 E5
Ashton Green E Sus 23 C7
Ashton Hayes W Ches 167 B8
Ashton Heath Halton 183 F9
Ashton-in-Makerfield Gtr Man 183 B9
Ashton Keynes Wilts 81 G8
Ashton under Hill Worcs 99 D9
Ashton-under-Lyne Gtr Man 184 B6
Ashton upon Mersey Gtr Man 184 C3
Ashton Vale Bristol 60 E5
Ashurst Hants 32 E4
Ashurst Kent 52 F4
Ashurst Lancs 194 F3
Ashurst W Sus 35 D11
Ashurst Bridge Hants 32 E4
Ashurst Wood W Sus 52 F2
Ashvale Bl Gwent 77 C10
Ashwater Devon 12 B3
Ashwell Devon 14 G3
Ashwell Herts 104 D5
Ashwell Rutland 155 G7
Ashwell Som 28 D5
Ashwell End Herts 104 C5
Ashwellthorpe Norf 142 D2
Ashwick Som 44 D6
Ashwicken Norf 158 F4
Ashwood Staffs 133 F7
Ashybank Borders 262 F2
Askam in Furness Cumb 210 D4
Askern S Yorks 198 E5
Askerswell Dorset 16 C6
Askerton Hill Lincs 172 F4
Askett Bucks 84 D4
Askham Cumb 230 G6
Askham Notts 188 G2
Askham Bryan York 207 D7
Askham Richard York 206 D6
Asknish Argyll 275 D10
Askrigg N Yorks 223 G8
Askwith N Yorks 205 D9
Aslackby Lincs 155 C11
Aslacton Norf 142 E3
Aslockton Notts 154 B4
Asloun Aberds 293 B7
Asney Som 44 F3
Aspall Suff 126 D3
Aspatria Cumb 229 C8
Aspenden Herts 105 F7
Asperton Lincs 156 B5
Aspley Nottingham 171 G8
Aspley Staffs 150 C6
Aspley Guise C Beds 103 D8
Aspley Heath C Beds 103 D8
Aspley Heath Warks 117 C11
Aspull Gtr Man 194 F6
Aspull Common Gtr Man 183 B10
Assater Shetland 312 F4
Asselby E Yorks 199 B8
Asserby Lincs 191 F7
Asserby Turn Lincs 191 F7
Assington Suff 107 D8
Assington Green Suff 124 G5
Assynt Ho Highld 300 C5
Astbury E Ches 168 C4
Astcote Northants 120 G3
Asterby Lincs 190 F3
Asterley Shrops 131 B7
Asterton Shrops 131 E7
Asthall Oxon 82 C3
Asthall Leigh Oxon 82 C4
Astle E Ches 184 G4
Astle Highld 309 K7
Astley Gtr Man 195 G8
Astley Shrops 149 F10
Astley Warks 134 F6
Astley Worcs 116 D5
Astley Abbotts Shrops 132 D4
Astley Bridge Gtr Man 195 E8
Astley Cross Worcs 116 D6
Astley Green Gtr Man 184 B2
Astmoor Halton 183 E8
Aston Derbys 152 C3
Aston Derbys 185 E11
Aston E Ches 167 F10
Aston Flint 166 B4
Aston Hereford 115 C9
Aston Hereford 115 E9
Aston Herts 104 G5
Aston Oxon 82 E4
Aston Powys 130 E5
Aston S Yorks 187 D7
Aston Shrops 132 E6
Aston Shrops 149 D10
Aston Staffs 151 E7
Aston Staffs 168 G3
Aston Telford 132 B2
Aston W Ches 183 F9
Aston W Mid 133 F11
Aston Wokingham 65 C9
Aston Abbotts Bucks 102 G6
Aston Bank Worcs 116 C2
Aston Botterell Shrops 132 G2
Aston-by-Stone Staffs 151 C8
Aston Cantlow Warks 118 F2
Aston Clinton Bucks 84 C5
Aston Crews Hereford 98 G3
Aston Cross Glos 99 E8
Aston End Herts 104 G5
Aston Eyre Shrops 132 E3
Aston Fields Worcs 117 D9
Aston Flamville Leics 135 E9
Aston Ingham Hereford 98 G3
Aston juxta Mondrum E Ches 167 D11
Aston le Walls Northants 119 G9
Aston Magna Glos 100 D3
Aston Munslow Shrops 131 F10
Aston on Carrant Glos 99 E8
Aston on Clun Shrops 131 G7
Aston-on-Trent Derbys 153 D8
Aston Pigott Shrops 130 B6
Aston Rogers Shrops 130 B6
Aston Rowant Oxon 84 F2
Aston Sandford Bucks 84 D3
Aston Somerville Worcs 99 D10
Aston Square Shrops 148 D6
Aston Subedge Glos 100 C2
Aston Tirrold Oxon 64 B5
Aston Upthorpe Oxon 64 B5
Astrop Northants 101 D10
Astrope Herts 84 C5
Astwick C Beds 104 D4
Astwith Derbys 170 C6
Astwood M Keynes 103 B9
Astwood Worcs 117 D8
Astwood Worcs 117 F7
Astwood Bank Worcs 117 E10
Aswarby Lincs 173 G9
Aswardby Lincs 190 G5
Atch Lench Worcs 117 G10
Atcham Shrops 131 B10
Athelhampton Dorset 17 C11
Athelington Suff 126 C4
Athelney Som 28 B4
Athelstaneford E Loth 281 F10
Atherfield Green I o W 20 F5
Atherington Devon 25 C9
Atherington W Sus 35 G8
Athersley North S Yorks 197 F11
Athersley South S Yorks 197 F11
Atherstone Som 28 D5
Atherstone Warks 134 D6
Atherstone on Stour Warks 118 G4
Atherton Gtr Man 195 G7
Athnamulloch Highld 299 G11
Athron Hall Perth 286 G4
Atley Hill N Yorks 224 E5
Atlow Derbys 170 F2
Attadale Highld 295 B11
Attadale Ho Highld 295 B11
Attenborough Notts 153 B10
Atterbury M Keynes 103 D7
Atterby Lincs 189 C7
Attercliffe S Yorks 186 D5
Atterley Shrops 132 D2
Atterton Leics 135 D7
Attleborough Norf 141 D10
Attleborough Warks 135 E7
Attlebridge Norf 160 F2
Attleton Green Suff 124 G4
Atwick E Yorks 209 C9
Atworth Wilts 61 F11
Auberrow Hereford 97 B9
Aubourn Lincs 172 C6
Auch Argyll 285 D7
Auchagallon N Ayrs 255 D9
Auchallater Aberds 292 E3
Auchareoch N Ayrs 255 E10
Aucharnie Aberds 302 E6
Auchattie Aberds 293 D8
Auchavan Angus 292 G3
Auchbreck Moray 302 G2
Auchenback E Renf 267 D10
Auchenbainzie Dumfries 247 D8
Auchenblae Aberds 293 F9
Auchenbrack Dumfries 247 D7
Auchenbreck Argyll 255 C8
Auchenbreck Argyll 275 E11
Auchencairn Dumfries 237 D9
Auchencairn Dumfries 247 G11
Auchencairn N Ayrs 256 D2
Auchencairn Ho Dumfries 237 D10
Auchencar N Ayrs 255 D9
Auchencarroch W Dunb 277 E8
Auchencrosh S Ayrs 236 B3
Auchencrow Borders 273 C7
Auchendinny Midloth 270 C5
Auchengray S Lnrk 269 E9
Auchenhalrig Moray 302 C3
Auchenharvie N Ayrs 266 G5
Auchenheath S Lnrk 268 G6
Auchenhew N Ayrs 256 E2
Auchenlaich Stirl 285 G10
Auchenleck Dumfries 237 D9
Auchenlochan Argyll 275 F10
Auchenmalg Dumfries 236 D4
Auchenreoch E Dunb 278 F3
Auchensoul S Ayrs 245 E7
Auchentibber S Lnrk 268 E3
Auchentiber N Ayrs 267 F7
Auchertyre Highld 295 C10
Auchessan Stirl 285 E8
Auchgourish Highld 291 B11
Auchinairn E Dunb 268 B2
Auchindrain Argyll 284 G4
Auchindrean Highld 307 L6
Auchininna Aberds 302 E6
Auchinleck Dumfries 236 B6
Auchinleck E Ayrs 258 E3
Auchinloch N Lnrk 278 G3
Auchinner Perth 285 F10
Auchinraith S Lnrk 268 D3
Auchinroath Moray 302 D2
Auchinstarry N Lnrk 278 F4
Auchintoul Aberds 293 B7
Auchintoul Highld 309 K5
Auchiries Aberds 303 F10
Auchlee Aberds 293 D10
Auchleeks Ho Perth 291 G9
Auchleven Aberds 302 G6
Auchlinn Aberds 303 D7
Auchlochan S Lnrk 259 B8
Auchlossan Aberds 293 C7
Auchlunachan Highld 307 L6
Auchlunies Aberds 293 D10
Auchlyne Stirl 285 E9
Auchmacoy Aberds 303 F9
Auchmair Moray 302 G3
Auchmantle Dumfries 236 C3
Auchmenzie Aberds 302 G5
Auchmillan E Ayrs 258 D2
Auchmithie Angus 287 C10
Auchmore Highld 300 D4
Auchmuirbridge Fife 286 G6
Auchmull Angus 293 F7
Auchnacraig Argyll 289 G9
Auchnacree Angus 292 G6
Auchnafree Perth 286 D2
Auchnagallin Highld 301 F10
Auchnagarron Argyll 275 E11
Auchnagatt Aberds 303 E9
Auchnaha Argyll 275 E10
Auchnahillin Highld 301 F7
Auchnarrow Moray 302 G2
Auchnashelloch Perth 285 F11
Auchnotteroch Dumfries 236 C1
Aucholzie Aberds 292 D5
Auchrannie Angus 286 B6
Auchroisk Highld 301 G10
Auchronie Angus 292 E6
Auchterarder Perth 286 F3
Auchteraw Highld 290 C5
Auchterderran Fife 280 B4
Auchterhouse Angus 287 D7
Auchtermuchty Fife 286 F6
Auchterneed Highld 300 D4
Auchtertool Fife 280 C4
Auchtertyre Moray 301 D11
Auchtertyre Stirl 285 E7
Auchtubh Stirl 285 E9
Auckengill Highld 310 C7
Auckley S Yorks 199 G7
Audenshaw Gtr Man 184 B6
Audlem E Ches 167 G11
Audley Staffs 168 E3
Audley End Essex 105 D10
Audley End Essex 106 D6
Audley End Norf 142 G2
Audley End Suff 125 G7
Auds Aberds 302 C6
Aughertree Cumb 229 D11
Aughton E Yorks 207 F10
Aughton Lancs 193 F11
Aughton Lancs 211 F10
Aughton S Yorks 187 D7
Aughton Wilts 47 B8
Aughton Park Lancs 194 F2
Aukside Durham 232 F4
Auldearn Highld 301 D9
Aulden Hereford 115 G9
Auldgirth Dumfries 247 F10
Auldhame E Loth 281 E11
Auldhouse S Lnrk 268 E2
Auldtown of Carnoustie Aberds 302 E6
Ault a'chruinn Highld 295 C11
Ault Hucknall Derbys 171 B7
Aultanrynie Highld 308 F3
Aultbea Highld 307 L3
Aultdearg Highld 300 C2
Aultgrishan Highld 307 L2
Aultguish Inn Highld 300 B3
Aultibea Highld 311 G4
Aultiphurst Highld 310 C2
Aultivullin Highld 310 C2
Aultmore Highld 301 G10
Aultmore Moray 302 D4
Aultnagoire Highld 300 G5
Aultnamain Inn Highld 309 L6
Aultnaslat Highld 290 C3
Aulton Aberds 302 G6
Aulton of Atherb Aberds 303 E9
Aultvaich Highld 300 E5
Aunby Lincs 155 G10
Aundorach Highld 291 B11
Aunk Devon 27 G8
Aunsby Lincs 155 B10
Auquhorthies Aberds 303 G8
Aust S Glos 60 B5
Austen Fen Lincs 190 C5
Austendike Lincs 156 E5
Austenwood Bucks 66 B3
Austerfield S Yorks 187 C11
Austerlands Gtr Man 196 F3
Austhorpe W Yorks 206 G3
Austrey Warks 134 B5
Austwick N Yorks 212 F5
Authorpe Lincs 190 E6
Authorpe Row Lincs 191 G8
Avebury Wilts 62 F6
Avebury Trusloe Wilts 62 F5
Aveley Thurrock 68 C5
Avening Glos 80 F5
Avening Green S Glos 80 G2
Averham Notts 172 E3
Avernish Highld 295 C10
Avery Hill London 68 E2
Aveton Gifford Devon 8 F3
Avielochan Highld 291 B11
Aviemore Highld 291 B10
Avington Hants 48 G4
Avington W Berks 63 F11
Avoch Highld 301 D7
Avon Hants 19 B8
Avon Wilts 62 D3
Avon Dassett Warks 101 B8
Avonbridge Falk 279 G8
Avoncliff Wilts 45 B10
Avonmouth Bristol 60 D4
Avonwick Devon 8 D4
Awbridge Hants 32 C4
Awhirk Dumfries 236 D2
Awkley S Glos 60 B5
Awliscombe Devon 27 G10
Awre Glos 80 D2
Awsworth Notts 171 G7
Axbridge Som 44 C2
Axford Hants 48 E6
Axford Wilts 63 F8
Axmansford Hants 64 G5
Axminster Devon 15 B11
Axmouth Devon 15 C11
Axton Flint 181 E10
Axtown Devon 7 B10
Axwell Park T & W 242 E5
Aycliff Kent 55 E10
Aycliffe Durham 233 G11
Aydon Northumb 242 D2
Aykley Heads Durham 233 C11
Aylburton Glos 79 E10
Aylburton Common Glos 79 E10
Ayle Northumb 231 B10
Aylesbeare Devon 14 C6
Aylesbury Bucks 84 C4
Aylesby NE Lincs 201 F8
Aylesford Kent 53 B8
Aylesham Kent 55 C8
Aylestone Leicester 135 C11
Aylestone Hill Hereford 97 C10
Aylestone Park Leicester 135 C11
Aylmerton Norf 160 B3
Aylsham Norf 160 D3
Aylton Hereford 98 D3
Aylworth Glos 100 G2
Aymestrey Hereford 115 D8
Aynho Northants 101 E10
Ayot Green Herts 86 C2
Ayot St Lawrence Herts 85 B11
Ayot St Peter Herts 86 B2
Ayr S Ayrs 257 E8
Ayre of Atler Shetland 313 G6
Ayres Shetland 313 H5
Ayres End Herts 85 C11
Ayres of Selivoe Shetland 313 J4
Ayres Quay T & W 243 F9
Aysgarth N Yorks 213 B10
Ayshford Devon 27 D8
Ayside Cumb 211 C7
Ayston Rutland 137 C7
Aythorpe Roding Essex 87 B9
Ayton Borders 273 C8
Ayton T & W 243 F7
Ayton Castle Borders 273 C8
Aywick Shetland 312 E7
Azerley N Yorks 214 E5

B

Babbacombe Torbay 9 B8
Babbington Notts 171 G7
Babbinswood Shrops 148 C6
Babbs Green Herts 86 B5
Babcary Som 29 B9
Babel Carms 94 D6

Babel Green Suff 106 B4
Babell Flint 181 G11
Babeny Devon 13 F9
Babingley Norf 158 D3
Babraham Cambs 123 G10
Babworth Notts 187 E11
Bac W Isles 304 D6
Bach-y-gwreiddyn Swansea 75 E10
Bachau Anglesey 178 E6
Bache Shrops 131 G9
Bache Mill Shrops 131 F10
Bacheldre Powys 130 E4
Bachelor's Bump E Sus 38 E4
Back of Keppoch Highld 295 G8
Back o' th' Brook Staffs 169 E9
Back Muir Fife 279 D11
Back Rogerton E Ayrs 258 E3
Back Street Suff 124 F4
Backaland Orkney 314 C5
Backaskaill Orkney 314 A4
Backbarrow Cumb 211 C7
Backbower Gtr Man 185 C7
Backburn Aberds 293 D10
Backe Carms 74 B3
Backfolds Aberds 303 D10
Backford W Ches 182 G6
Backford Cross W Ches 182 G5
Backhill Aberds 303 F10
Backhill Aberds 303 F7
Backhill of Clackriach Aberds 303 E9
Backhill of Fortree Aberds 303 E9
Backhill of Trustach Aberds 293 D8
Backies Highld 311 J2
Backlass Highld 310 D6
Backlass Highld 310 E4
Backwell N Som 60 F3
Backwell Common N Som 60 F3
Backwell Green N Som 60 F3
Backworth T & W 243 C8
Bacon End Essex 87 B10
Baconend Green Essex 87 B10
Bacon's End W Mid 134 F3
Baconsthorpe Norf 160 B2
Bacton Hereford 97 E7
Bacton Norf 160 C6
Bacton Suff 125 D11
Bacton Green Norf 160 C6
Bacton Green Suff 125 D10
Bacup Lancs 195 C11
Badachonacher Highld 300 B6
Badachro Highld 299 B7
Badanloch Lodge Highld 308 F7
Badarach Highld 309 K5
Badavanich Highld 299 D11
Badbea Highld 307 K5
Badbury Swindon 63 C7
Badbury Wick Swindon 63 C7
Badby Northants 119 F11
Badcall Highld 306 D7
Badcaul Highld 307 K5
Baddeley Edge Stoke 168 E6
Baddeley Green Stoke 168 E6
Baddesley Clinton Warks 118 C4
Baddesley Ensor Warks 134 D5
Baddidarach Highld 307 G5
Baddoch Aberds 292 E3
Baddock Highld 301 D7
Baddow Park Essex 88 E2
Badeach Moray 302 F2
Badenscallie Highld 307 J5
Badenscoth Aberds 303 F7
Badentoy Park Aberds 293 D11
Badenyon Aberds 292 B5
Badgall Corn 11 D10
Badgeney Cambs 139 D8
Badger Shrops 132 D5
Badger Street Som 28 D3
Badgergate Stirl 278 B5
Badger's Hill Worcs 99 B10
Badger's Mount Kent 68 G3
Badgeworth Glos 80 B6
Badgworth Som 43 C11
Badharlick Corn 11 D11
Badicaul Highld 295 C9
Badingham Suff 126 D6
Badintagairt Highld 309 H4
Badlesmere Kent 54 C4
Badlipster Highld 310 E6
Badluarach Highld 307 K4
Badminton S Glos 61 C10
Badnaban Highld 307 G5
Badnabay Highld 306 E7
Badnagie Highld 310 F5
Badninish Highld 309 K7
Badrallach Highld 307 K5
Badsey Worcs 99 C11
Badshalloch W Dunb 277 D9
Badshot Lea Sur 49 D11
Badsworth W Yorks 198 E3
Badwell Ash Suff 125 D9
Badwell Green Suff 125 D10
Badworthy Devon 8 C3
Bae Cinmel = Kinmel Bay Conwy 181 E7
Bae Colwyn = Colwyn Bay Conwy 180 F4
Bae Penrhyn = Penrhyn Bay Conwy 180 E4
Baffins Ptsmth 33 G11
Bag Enderby Lincs 190 G5
Bagber Dorset 30 E3
Bagby N Yorks 215 C9
Bagby Grange N Yorks 215 C9
Bagendon Glos 81 D8
Bagginswood Shrops 132 G3
Baggrow Cumb 229 C9
Bàgha Chàise W Isles 296 D5
Bagh a Chaisteil W Isles 297 M2
Bagh Mor W Isles 296 F4
Bagh Shiarabhagh W Isles 297 L3
Bagham Kent 54 C5
Baghasdal W Isles 297 K3
Bagillt Flint 182 F2
Baginton Warks 118 C6
Baglan Neath 57 C8
Bagley Shrops 149 D8
Bagley Som 44 D3
Bagley W Yorks 205 F10
Bagley Green Som 27 D10
Bagley Marsh Shrops 149 D7
Bagmore Hants 49 E7
Bagnall Staffs 168 E6
Bagnor W Berks 64 F3
Bagpath Glos 80 E5
Bagpath Glos 80 G4
Bagshaw Derbys 185 E9
Bagshot Sur 66 G2
Bagshot Wilts 63 F10
Bagshot Heath Sur 66 G2
Bagslate Moor Gtr Man 195 E11
Bagstone S Glos 61 B7
Bagthorpe Norf 158 C5
Bagthorpe Notts 171 E7
Baguley Gtr Man 184 D4
Bagworth Leics 135 B8
Bagwy Llydiart Hereford 97 F8
Bagwyllydiart Hereford 97 F8
Bail Ard Bhuirgh W Isles 304 C6
Bail' Iochdrach W Isles 296 F4
Bail Uachdraich W Isles 296 E4
Bail' Ur Tholastaidh W Isles 304 D7
Bailbrook Bath 61 F9
Baildon W Yorks 205 F9
Baildon Green W Yorks 205 F8
Baile W Isles 296 C5
Baile a Mhanaich W Isles 296 F3
Baile Ailein W Isles 304 F4
Baile an Truiseil W Isles 304 C5
Baile Boidheach Argyll 275 F8
Baile Gharbhaidh W Isles 297 G3
Baile Glas W Isles 296 F4
Baile Mhartainn W Isles 296 D3
Baile Mhic Phail W Isles 296 D4
Baile Mor Argyll 288 G4
Baile Mor W Isles 296 E3
Baile na Creige W Isles 297 L2
Baile nan Cailleach W Isles 296 F3
Baile Raghaill W Isles 296 D3
Bailebeag Highld 291 B7
Bailey Green Hants 33 B11
Baileyhead Cumb 240 B2
Bailiesward Aberds 302 F4
Bailiff Bridge W Yorks 196 C6
Baillieston Glasgow 268 C3
Bailrigg Lancs 202 B5
Bainbridge N Yorks 223 G8
Bainsford Falk 279 E7
Bainshole Aberds 302 F6
Bainton E Yorks 208 C5
Bainton Oxon 101 F11
Bainton P'boro 137 B11
Baintown Fife 287 G7
Bairnkine Borders 262 F5
Baker Street Thurrock 68 C6
Baker's Cross Kent 53 F9
Bakers End Herts 86 B5
Baker's Hill Glos 79 C9
Baker's Wood Bucks 66 B4
Bakesdown Corn 24 G2
Bakestone Moor Derbys 187 F8
Bakewell Derbys 170 B2
Bala = Y Bala Gwyn 147 B8
Balachroick Highld 291 C10
Balachuirn Highld 298 E5
Balance Hill Staffs 151 C11
Balavil Highld 291 C9
Balavoulin Perth 291 G10
Balbeg Highld 300 F4
Balbeg Highld 300 G4
Balbeggie Perth 286 E5
Balbegno Castle Aberds 293 F8
Balbithan Aberds 293 B9
Balbithan Ho Aberds 293 B10
Balblair Highld 300 E5
Balblair Highld 301 C7
Balblair Highld 309 K5
Balby S Yorks 198 G5
Balcherry Highld 311 L2
Balchladich Highld 306 F5
Balchraggan Highld 300 E5
Balchraggan Highld 300 F5
Balchraggan Highld 300 G5
Balchrick Highld 306 D6
Balchrystie Fife 287 G8
Balcladaich Highld 300 G2
Balcombe W Sus 51 G10
Balcombe Lane W Sus 51 G10
Balcomie Fife 287 F10
Balcraggie Lodge Highld 310 F5
Balcurvie Fife 287 G7
Baldersby N Yorks 215 D7
Baldersby St James N Yorks 215 D7
Balderstone Gtr Man 196 E2
Balderstone Lancs 203 G8
Balderton Notts 172 E4
Balderton W Ches 166 C5
Baldhu Corn 4 G5
Baldingstone Gtr Man 195 E10
Baldinnie Fife 287 F8
Baldock Herts 104 E4
Baldon Row Oxon 83 E9
Baldoon Highld 300 B6
Baldovie Dundee 287 D8
Baldrine I o M 192 D5
Baldslow E Sus 38 E3
Baldwin I o M 192 D4
Baldwinholme Cumb 239 G8
Baldwin's Gate Staffs 168 G3
Baldwins Hill W Sus 51 F11
Bale Norf 159 B10
Balearn Aberds 303 D10
Balemartine Argyll 288 E1
Balephuil Argyll 288 E1
Balerno Edin 270 B3
Balerominhor Argyll 274 D4
Balevullin Argyll 288 E1
Balfield Angus 293 G7
Balfour Orkney 314 E4
Balfour Mains Orkney 314 E4
Balfron Stirl 277 D10
Balfron Station Stirl 277 D10
Balgaveny Aberds 302 E6
Balgavies Angus 287 B9
Balgonar Fife 279 C10
Balgove Aberds 303 F8
Balgowan Highld 291 D8
Balgowan Perth 286 E3
Balgown Highld 298 C3
Balgrennie Aberds 292 C6
Balgrochan E Dunb 278 F2
Balgy Highld 299 D8
Balhaldie Stirl 286 G2
Balhalgardy Aberds 303 G7
Balham London 67 E9
Balhary Perth 286 C6
Baliasta Shetland 312 C8
Baligill Highld 310 C2
Baligortan Argyll 288 E5
Baligrundle Argyll 289 E10
Balindore Argyll 289 F11
Balinoe Argyll 288 E1
Balintore Angus 286 B6
Balintore Highld 301 B8
Balintraid Highld 301 B7
Balintuim Aberds 292 E3
Balk N Yorks 215 C9
Balk Field Notts 188 E2
Balkeerie Angus 287 C7
Balkemback Angus 287 D7
Balkholme E Yorks 199 B9
Balkissock S Ayrs 244 G4
Ball Corn 10 G6
Ball Shrops 148 D6
Ball Green Stoke 168 E5
Ball Haye Green Staffs 169 D7
Ball Hill Hants 64 G2
Ball o'Ditton Halton 183 D7
Ballabeg I o M 192 E3
Ballacannel I o M 192 D5
Ballachraggan Moray 301 E11
Ballachrochin Highld 301 F8
Ballachulish Highld 284 B4
Balladen Lancs 195 C10
Ballajora I o M 192 C5
Ballaleigh I o M 192 D4
Ballamodha I o M 192 E3
Ballantrae S Ayrs 244 G3
Ballaquine I o M 192 D5
Ballard's Ash Wilts 62 C5
Ballards Gore Essex 88 G6
Ballard's Green Warks 134 E5
Ballasalla I o M 192 C4
Ballasalla I o M 192 E3
Ballater Aberds 292 D5
Ballathie Perth 286 D5
Ballaugh I o M 192 C4
Ballaveare I o M 192 E4
Ballcorach Moray 301 G11
Ballechin Perth 286 B3
Balleich Stirl 277 B10
Balleigh Highld 309 L7
Ballencrieff E Loth 281 F9
Ballencrieff Toll W Loth 279 G9
Ballentoul Perth 291 G10
Ballhill Devon 24 C3
Ballidon Derbys 170 E2
Balliekine N Ayrs 255 D9
Balliemore Argyll 275 E11
Balliemore Argyll 289 G10
Ballikinrain Stirl 277 D11
Ballimeanoch Argyll 284 F4
Ballimore Argyll 275 E10
Ballimore Stirl 285 F9
Ballinaby Argyll 274 G3
Ballinbreich Fife 286 E6
Ballindean Perth 286 E6
Ballingdon Suff 107 C7
Ballingdon Bottom Herts 85 C8
Ballinger Bottom Bucks 84 E6
Ballinger Bottom (South) Bucks 84 E6
Ballinger Common Bucks 84 E6
Ballingham Hereford 97 E11
Ballingham Hill Hereford 97 E11
Ballingry Fife 280 B3
Ballinlick Perth 286 C3
Ballinluig Perth 286 B3
Ballintean Highld 291 C10
Ballintuim Perth 286 B5
Balliveolan Argyll 289 E10
Balloch Angus 287 B7
Balloch Highld 301 E7
Balloch N Lnrk 278 G4
Balloch W Dunb 277 E7
Ballochan Aberds 293 D7
Ballochearn Stirl 277 D11
Ballochford Moray 302 F3
Ballochmorrie S Ayrs 244 G6
Ballogie Aberds 293 D7
Balls Cross W Sus 35 B7
Balls Green E Sus 52 F3
Balls Green Essex 107 G11
Ball's Green Glos 80 F5
Balls Green W Sus 35 C10
Balls Hill W Mid 133 E9
Ballygown Argyll 288 E6
Ballygrant Argyll 274 G4
Ballygroggan Argyll 255 F7
Ballyhaugh Argyll 288 D3
Balmacara Highld 295 C10
Balmacara Square Highld 295 C10
Balmaclellan Dumfries 237 B8
Balmacneil Perth 286 B3
Balmacqueen Highld 298 B4
Balmae Dumfries 237 E8
Balmaha Stirl 277 C8
Balmalcolm Fife 287 G7
Balmalloch N Lnrk 278 F4
Balmeanach Argyll 288 F6
Balmeanach Argyll 289 E8
Balmeanach Highld 295 B7
Balmeanach Highld 298 E3
Balmeanach Highld 298 E5
Balmedie Aberds 293 B11
Balmer Shrops 149 C8
Balmer Heath Shrops 149 C8
Balmerino Fife 287 E7
Balmerlawn Hants 32 G4
Balmesh Dumfries 236 D3
Balmichael N Ayrs 255 D10
Balminnoch Dumfries 236 C4
Balmirmer Angus 287 D9
Balmoral Borders 261 B11
Balmore E Dunb 278 G2
Balmore Highld 298 E2
Balmore Highld 300 F3
Balmore Highld 301 E8
Balmore Perth 286 B3
Balmule Fife 280 D4
Balmullo Fife 287 E8
Balmungie Highld 301 D7
Balmurrie Dumfries 236 C4
Balnaboth Angus 292 G5
Balnabreich Moray 302 D3
Balnabruaich Highld 301 C7
Balnabruich Highld 311 G5
Balnacarn Highld 290 B4
Balnacoil Highld 311 H2
Balnacra Highld 299 E9
Balnacruie Highld 301 G9
Balnafoich Highld 300 F6
Balnagall Highld 311 L2
Balnagowan Aberds 293 C7
Balnagrantach Highld 300 F4
Balnaguard Perth 286 B3
Balnahanaid Perth 285 C10
Balnahard Argyll 274 D5
Balnahard Argyll 288 F6
Balnain Highld 300 F4
Balnakeil Highld 308 C3
Balnakelly Aberds 293 B7
Balnaknock Highld 298 C4
Balnamoon Aberds 303 D9
Balnamoon Angus 293 G7
Balnapaling Highld 301 C7
Balne N Yorks 198 D5
Balnoon Corn 2 B2
Balochroy Argyll 255 B8
Balole Argyll 274 G4
Balornock Glasgow 268 B2
Balquharn Perth 286 D4
Balquhidder Stirl 285 E9
Balquhidder Station Stirl 285 E9
Balquhindachy Aberds 303 E8
Balrownie Angus 293 G7
Balsall W Mid 118 B4
Balsall Common W Mid 118 B4
Balsall Heath W Mid 133 G11
Balsall Street W Mid 118 B4
Balsam Cambs 123 G11
Balscote Oxon 101 C7
Balscott Oxon 101 C7
Balsham Cambs 123 G11
Balsporran Cottages Highld 291 F8
Balstonia Thurrock 69 C7
Baltasound Shetland 312 C8
Balterley Staffs 168 E3
Balterley Green Staffs 168 E3
Balterley Heath Staffs 168 E2
Baltersan Dumfries 236 C6
Balthangie Aberds 303 D8
Balthayock Perth 286 E5
Baltonsborough Som 44 G4
Balure Argyll 289 E11
Balvaird Highld 300 D5
Balvenie Moray 302 E3
Balvicar Argyll 275 B8
Balvraid Highld 295 D10
Balvraid Highld 301 F8
Balwest Corn 2 C3
Bamber Bridge Lancs 194 B5
Bamber's Green Essex 105 G11
Bamburgh Northumb 264 C5
Bamff Perth 286 B6
Bamford Derbys 186 E2
Bamford Gtr Man 195 E11
Bamfurlong Glos 99 G8
Bamfurlong Gtr Man 194 G5
Bampton Cumb 221 B10
Bampton Devon 27 C7
Bampton Oxon 82 E4
Bampton Grange Cumb 221 B10
Banavie Highld 290 F3
Banbury Oxon 101 C9
Banc-y-Darren Ceredig 128 G3
Bancffosfelen Carms 75 C7
Banchor Highld 301 E9
Banchory Aberds 293 D8
Banchory-Devenick Aberds 293 C11
Bancycapel Carms 74 B6
Bancyfelin Carms 74 B4
Bancyffordd Carms 93 D8
Bandirran Perth 286 D6
Bandonhill London 67 G9
Bandrake Head Cumb 210 B6
Banff Aberds 302 C6
Bangor Gwyn 179 G9
Bangor is y coed = Bangor on Dee Wrex 166 F5
Bangor on Dee = Bangor-is-y-coed Wrex 166 F5
Bangor Teifi Ceredig 93 C7
Bangors Corn 11 B10
Banham Norf 141 F11
Bank Hants 32 F3
Bank End Cumb 210 B3
Bank End Cumb 228 D6
Bank Fold Blkburn 195 C8
Bank Hey Blkburn 203 G9
Bank Houses Lancs 202 C4
Bank Lane Gtr Man 195 D9
Bank Newton N Yorks 204 C4
Bank Street Worcs 116 E2
Bank Top Gtr Man 195 E8
Bank Top Lancs 194 F4
Bank Top Stoke 168 E5
Bank Top T & W 242 D4
Bank Top W Yorks 196 C6
Bank Top W Yorks 205 F9
Bank Top W Yorks 205 G8
Bankend Dumfries 238 D2
Bankfoot Perth 286 D4
Bankglen E Ayrs 258 G4
Bankhead Aberdeen 293 B10
Bankhead Aberds 293 C8
Bankhead Dumfries 236 C2
Bankhead Falk 278 E6
Bankhead S Lnrk 269 G7
Bankland Som 28 B4
Banknock Falk 278 F5
Banks Cumb 240 E3
Banks Lancs 193 C11
Banks Orkney 314 C4
Bank's Green Worcs 117 D9
Bankshead Shrops 130 F5
Bankshill Dumfries 248 G5
Bankside Falk 279 E7
Banners Gate W Mid 133 D11
Banningham Norf 160 D4
Banniskirk Ho Highld 310 D5
Banniskirk Mains Highld 310 D5
Bannister Green Essex 106 G3
Bannockburn Stirl 278 C5
Banns Corn 4 F4
Banstead Sur 51 B8
Bantam Grove W Yorks 197 B9
Bantaskin Falk 279 F7
Bantham Devon 8 G3
Banton N Lnrk 278 F5
Banwell N Som 43 B11
Banyard's Green Suff 126 C5
Bapchild Kent 70 G2
Baptist End W Mid 133 F8
Bapton Wilts 46 F3
Bar End Hants 33 B7
Bar Hill Cambs 123 E7
Bar Hill Staffs 168 G3
Bar Moor T & W 242 E4
Barabhas W Isles 304 D5
Barabhas Iarach W Isles 304 D5
Barabhas Uarach W Isles 304 C5
Barachandroman Argyll 289 G8
Baramore Highld 289 B8
Barassie S Ayrs 257 C8
Baravullin Argyll 289 F10
Barbadoes Stirl 277 B11
Barbaraville Highld 301 B7
Barbauchlaw W Loth 269 B8
Barber Booth Derbys 185 E10
Barber Green Cumb 211 C7
Barber's Moor Lancs 194 D3
Barbican Plym 7 E9
Barbieston S Ayrs 257 F10
Barbon Cumb 212 C2
Barbourne Worcs 116 F6
Barbreck Ho Argyll 275 C9
Barbridge E Ches 167 D10
Barbrook Devon 41 D8
Barby Northants 119 C10
Barby Nortoft Northants 119 C11
Barcaldine Argyll 289 E11
Barcelona Corn 6 E4
Barcheston Warks 100 D5
Barclose Cumb 239 E10
Barcombe E Sus 36 E6
Barcombe Cross E Sus 36 D6
Barcroft W Yorks 204 F6
Barden N Yorks 224 G2
Barden Park Kent 52 D5
Barden Scale N Yorks 205 B7
Bardennoch Dumfries 246 E3
Bardfield End Green Essex 106 E2
Bardfield Saling Essex 106 F3
Bardister Shetland 312 F5
Bardnabeinne Highld 309 K7
Bardney Lincs 173 B10
Bardon Leics 153 G8
Bardon Mill Northumb 241 E7
Bardowie E Dunb 277 G11
Bardown E Sus 37 B11
Bardrainney Invclyd 276 G6
Bardrishaig Argyll 275 B8
Bardsea Cumb 210 E6
Bardsey W Yorks 206 E3
Bardsley Gtr Man 196 G2
Bardwell Suff 125 C8
Bare Lancs 211 G9
Bare Ash Som 43 F9
Bareless Northumb 263 B9
Barepot Cumb 228 F6
Bareppa Corn 3 D7
Barfad Argyll 275 G9
Barfad Dumfries 236 C5
Barford Norf 142 B2
Barford Sur 49 F11
Barford Warks 118 E5
Barford St John Oxon 101 E8
Barford St Martin Wilts 46 G5
Barford St Michael Oxon 101 E8
Barfrestone Kent 55 C9
Bargaly Dumfries 236 C6
Bargarran Renfs 277 G9
Bargate Derbys 170 F5
Bargeddie N Lnrk 268 C4
Bargoed Caerph 77 F10
Bargrennan Dumfries 236 B5
Barham Cambs 122 B2
Barham Kent 55 C8
Barham Suff 126 G2
Barharrow Dumfries 237 D8
Barhill Dumfries 237 C10
Barholm Dumfries 237 D7
Barholm Lincs 155 G11
Barkby Leics 136 B2
Barkby Thorpe Leics 136 B2
Barkers Green Shrops 149 D10
Barkers Hill Wilts 30 B6
Barkestone-le-Vale Leics 154 C5
Barkham Wokingham 65 F9
Barking London 68 C2
Barking Suff 125 G11
Barking Tye Suff 125 G11
Barkingside London 68 B2
Barkisland W Yorks 196 D5
Barkla Shop Corn 4 E4
Barkston Lincs 172 G6
Barkston N Yorks 206 F5
Barkston Ash N Yorks 206 F5
Barkway Herts 105 D7
Barlake Som 45 D7
Barlanark Glasgow 268 C3
Barland Powys 114 E5
Barland Common Swansea 56 D5
Barlaston Staffs 151 B7
Barlavington W Sus 35 D7
Barlborough Derbys 187 F7
Barlby N Yorks 207 G8
Barlestone Leics 135 B8
Barley Herts 105 D7
Barley Lancs 204 E2
Barley End Bucks 85 C7
Barley Green Lancs 204 E2
Barley Mow T & W 243 G7
Barleycroft End Herts 105 F8
Barleythorpe Rutland 136 B6
Barling Essex 70 B2
Barlings Lincs 189 G9
Barlow Derbys 186 G4
Barlow N Yorks 198 B6
Barlow T & W 242 E5
Barlow Moor Gtr Man 184 C4
Barmby Moor E Yorks 207 D11
Barmby on the Marsh E Yorks 199 B7
Barmer Norf 158 C6
Barming Heath Kent 53 B8
Barmolloch Argyll 275 D9
Barmoor Castle Northumb 263 B11
Barmoor Lane End Northumb 264 B2
Barmouth = Abermaw Gwyn 146 F2
Barmpton Darl 224 B6
Barmston E Yorks 209 B9
Barmston T & W 243 F8
Barmulloch Glasgow 268 B2
Barnaby Green Suff 127 B9
Barnacabber Argyll 276 D3
Barnack P'boro 137 B11
Barnacle Warks 135 G7
Barnaline Argyll 275 B10
Barnard Castle Durham 223 B11
Barnard Gate Oxon 82 C6
Barnardiston Suff 106 B4
Barnard's Green Worcs 98 B5
Barnardtown Newport 59 B10
Barnbarroch Dumfries 237 D10
Barnbow Carr W Yorks 206 F3
Barnburgh S Yorks 198 G3
Barnby Suff 143 F9
Barnby Dun S Yorks 198 F6
Barnby in the Willows Notts 172 E5
Barnby Moor Notts 187 E11
Barncluith S Lnrk 268 E4
Barndennoch Dumfries 247 F9
Barne Barton Plym 7 D8
Barnehurst London 68 D4
Barnes London 67 D8
Barnes Cray London 68 D4
Barnes Hall S Yorks 186 B4
Barnes Street Kent 52 D6
Barnet London 86 F2
Barnet Gate London 86 F2
Barnetby le Wold N Lincs 200 F5
Barnett Brook E Ches 167 G10
Barnettbrook Worcs 117 B7
Barney Norf 159 C9
Barnfield Kent 54 D2
Barnfields Hereford 97 C9
Barnfields Staffs 169 D7
Barnham Suff 125 B7
Barnham W Sus 35 G7
Barnham Broom Norf 141 B11
Barnhead Angus 287 B10
Barnhill Dundee 287 D8
Barnhill Moray 301 D11
Barnhill W Ches 167 E7
Barnhills Dumfries 236 B1
Barningham Durham 223 C11
Barningham Suff 125 B9
Barningham Green Norf 160 C2
Barnmoor Green Warks 118 E3
Barnoldby le Beck NE Lincs 201 G8
Barnoldswick Lancs 204 D3
Barnoldswick N Yorks 212 E3
Barns Borders 260 B6
Barns Green W Sus 35 B10
Barnsbury London 67 C10
Barnsdale Rutland 137 B8
Barnside W Yorks 197 F7
Barnsley Glos 81 D9
Barnsley S Yorks 197 F10
Barnsley Shrops 132 E5
Barnsole Kent 55 B9
Barnstaple Devon 40 G5
Barnston Essex 87 B10
Barnston Mers 182 E3
Barnstone Notts 154 B4
Barnt Green Worcs 117 C10
Barnton Edin 280 F3
Barnton W Ches 183 F10
Barnwell Northants 137 G10
Barnwell All Saints Northants 137 G10
Barnwell St Andrew Northants 137 F10
Barnwood Glos 80 B5
Barochreal Argyll 289 G10
Barons Cross Hereford 115 F9
Barr Highld 289 D8
Barr S Ayrs 245 E7
Barr Som 27 C11
Barr Common W Mid 133 D11
Barra Castle Aberds 303 G7
Barrachan Dumfries 236 E5
Barrachnie Glasgow 268 C3
Barrack Aberds 303 E8
Barrack Hill Newport 59 B10
Barraer Dumfries 236 C5
Barraglom W Isles 304 E3
Barrahormid Argyll 275 E8
Barran Argyll 289 G10
Barranrioch Argyll 289 G10
Barrapol Argyll 288 E1
Barras Aberds 293 E10
Barras Cumb 222 C6
Barrasford Northumb 241 C10
Barravullin Argyll 275 C9
Barregarrow I o M 192 D4
Barrets Green E Ches 167 D9
Barrhead E Renf 267 D9
Barrhill S Ayrs 244 G6
Barrington Cambs 105 B7
Barrington Som 28 D5
Barripper Corn 2 B4
Barrmill N Ayrs 267 E7
Barrock Highld 310 B6
Barrock Ho Highld 310 C6
Barrow Glos 99 G7
Barrow Lancs 203 F10
Barrow Rutland 155 F7
Barrow S Yorks 186 B5
Barrow Shrops 132 C3
Barrow Som 44 E5
Barrow Som 45 G8
Barrow Suff 124 E5
Barrow Bridge Gtr Man 195 E7
Barrow Burn Northumb 263 G9
Barrow Common N Som 60 F4
Barrow Green Kent 70 G3
Barrow Gurney N Som 60 F4
Barrow Hann N Lincs 200 C5
Barrow Haven N Lincs 200 C5
Barrow Hill Derbys 186 F6
Barrow Hill Dorset 18 B5
Barrow-in-Furness Cumb 210 F4
Barrow Island Cumb 210 F3
Barrow Nook Lancs 194 G2
Barrow Street Wilts 45 G10
Barrow upon Humber N Lincs 200 C5
Barrow upon Soar Leics 153 F11
Barrow upon Trent Derbys 153 D7
Barrow Vale Bath 60 G6
Barrow Wake Glos 80 B6
Barroway Drove Norf 139 C11
Barrowburn Northumb 263 G9
Barrowby Lincs 155 B7
Barrowcliff N Yorks 217 B10
Barrowden Rutland 137 C8
Barrowford Lancs 204 F3
Barrowmore Estate W Ches 167 B7
Barrows Green Cumb 211 B10
Barrows Green E Ches 167 D11
Barrow's Green Mers 183 D8
Barrows Green Notts 171 E7
Barry Angus 287 D9
Barry V Glam 58 F6
Barry Dock V Glam 58 F6
Barry Island V Glam 58 F6
Barsby Leics 154 G3
Barsham Suff 143 F7
Barshare E Ayrs 258 F3
Barstable Essex 69 B8
Barston W Mid 118 B4
Bartestree Hereford 97 C11
Barthol Chapel Aberds 303 F8
Bartholomew Green Essex 106 G4
Barthomley E Ches 168 E3
Bartington W Ches 183 F10
Bartley Hants 32 E4
Bartley Green W Mid 133 G10
Bartlow Cambs 105 B11
Barton Cambs 123 F8
Barton Glos 80 B4
Barton Glos 99 F11
Barton I o W 20 D6
Barton Lancs 193 F11
Barton Lancs 202 F6
Barton N Som 43 B11
Barton N Yorks 224 D4
Barton Oxon 83 D9
Barton Torbay 9 B8
Barton W Ches 166 E6
Barton Warks 118 G2
Barton Abbey Oxon 101 G9
Barton Bendish Norf 140 B4
Barton Court Hereford 98 C4
Barton End Glos 80 F4
Barton Gate Devon 41 E7
Barton Gate Staffs 152 F3
Barton Green Staffs 152 F3
Barton Hartshorn Bucks 102 E2
Barton Hill Bristol 60 E6
Barton Hill N Yorks 216 G4
Barton in Fabis Notts 153 C10
Barton in the Beans Leics 135 B7
Barton-le-Clay C Beds 103 E11
Barton-le-Street N Yorks 216 E4
Barton-le-Willows N Yorks 216 G4
Barton Mills Suff 124 C4
Barton on Sea Hants 19 C10
Barton on the Heath Warks 100 E5
Barton St David Som 44 G4
Barton Seagrave Northants 121 B7
Barton Stacey Hants 48 E2
Barton Town Devon 41 E7
Barton Turf Norf 161 E7
Barton Turn Staffs 152 F4
Barton-under-Needwood Staffs 152 F3
Barton-upon-Humber N Lincs 200 C4
Barton Upon Irwell Gtr Man 184 B3
Barton Waterside N Lincs 200 C4
Bartonsham Hereford 97 D10
Barugh S Yorks 197 F10
Barugh Green S Yorks 197 F10
Barway Cambs 123 B10
Barwell Leics 135 D8
Barwell London 67 G7
Barwick Devon 25 F9
Barwick Herts 86 B5
Barwick Som 29 E9
Barwick in Elmet W Yorks 206 F3
Baschurch Shrops 149 E8
Bascote Warks 119 E8
Bascote Heath Warks 119 E7
Base Green Suff 125 E10
Basford Shrops 131 F7
Basford Staffs 168 F5
Basford Green Staffs 169 E7
Bashall Eaves Lancs 203 E9
Bashley Hants 19 B10
Bashley Park Hants 19 B10
Basildon Essex 69 B8
Basingstoke Hants 48 C6
Baslow Derbys 186 G3
Bason Bridge Som 43 D10
Bassaleg Newport 59 B9
Bassenthwaite Cumb 229 E10
Bassett S Yorks 186 E3
Bassett Soton 32 D6
Bassett Green Soton 32 D6
Bassingbourn Cambs 104 C6
Bassingfield Notts 154 B2
Bassingham Lincs 172 C6
Bassingthorpe Lincs 155 D9
Bassus Green Herts 104 F6
Basta Shetland 312 D7
Basted Kent 52 B6
Baston Lincs 156 G2
Bastonford Worcs 116 G6
Bastwick Norf 161 F8
Baswich Staffs 151 E8
Baswick Steer E Yorks 209 D7
Batavaime Stirl 285 D8
Batch Som 43 B10
Batchcott Shrops 115 C9
Batchfields Hereford 98 B3
Batchley Worcs 117 D10
Batchworth Herts 85 G9
Batchworth Heath Herts 85 G9
Batcombe Dorset 29 G10
Batcombe Som 45 F7
Bate Heath E Ches 183 F11
Bateman's Green Worcs 117 B11
Bateman's Hill Pembs 73 E8
Batemoor S Yorks 186 E5
Batford Herts 85 B10
Bath Bath 61 F8
Bath Side Essex 108 E5
Bath Vale E Ches 168 C5
Bathampton Bath 61 F9
Bathealton Som 27 C9
Batheaston Bath 61 F9
Bathford Bath 61 F9
Bathgate W Loth 269 B9
Bathley Notts 172 D3
Bathpool Corn 11 G11
Bathpool Som 28 B3
Bathville W Loth 269 B8
Bathway Som 44 C5
Bathwick Bath 61 F9
Batlers Green Herts 85 F11
Batley W Yorks 197 C8
Batley Carr W Yorks 197 C8
Batsford Glos 100 E3
Batson Devon 9 G9
Batsworthy Devon 26 D4
Batten's Green Som 28 D3
Battenton Green Worcs 116 D6
Battersby N Yorks 225 D11
Battersea London 67 D9
Battisborough Cross Devon 7 F11
Battisford Suff 125 G11
Battisford Tye Suff 125 G10
Battle E Sus 38 D2
Battle Powys 95 E10
Battle Hill T & W 243 D8
Battledown Glos 99 G9
Battledown Cross Devon 25 F7
Battlefield Shrops 149 F10
Battlesbridge Essex 88 G3
Battlescombe Glos 80 D6
Battlesden C Beds 103 F9
Battlesea Green Suff 126 B4
Battleton Som 26 B6
Battlies Green Suff 125 E7
Battram Leics 135 B8
Battramsley Hants 20 B2
Battramsley Cross Hants 20 B2
Batt's Corner Hants 49 E10
Battyeford W Yorks 197 C7
Batworthy Devon 13 D10
Bauds of Cullen Moray 302 C4
Baugh Argyll 288 E2
Baughton Worcs 99 C7
Baughurst Hants 48 B5
Baulking Oxon 82 G4
Baumber Lincs 190 G2
Baunton Glos 81 E8
Baverstock Wilts 46 G4
Bawburgh Norf 142 B3
Bawdeswell Norf 159 E10
Bawdrip Som 43 F10
Bawdsey Suff 108 C6
Bawsey Norf 158 F3
Bawtry S Yorks 187 C11
Baxenden Lancs 195 B9
Baxterley Warks 134 D5
Baxter's Green Suff 124 F5
Bay Dorset 30 B4
Bay Highld 298 D2
Bay Gate Lancs 203 D11
Bay Horse Lancs 202 C5
Bay View Kent 70 E4
Baybridge Hants 33 C8
Baybridge Northumb 241 G11
Baycliff Cumb 210 E5
Baydon Wilts 63 D9
Bayford Herts 86 D4
Bayford Som 30 B2
Bayles Cumb 231 C10
Bayley's Hill Kent 52 C4
Baylham Suff 126 G2
Baylis Green Worcs 117 C11
Baynard's Green Oxon 101 F10
Baynhall Worcs 99 B7
Baysham Hereford 97 F11
Bayston Hill Shrops 131 B9
Bayswater London 67 C9
Baythorne End Essex 106 C4
Baythorpe Lincs 174 G2
Bayton Worcs 116 C3
Bayton Common Worcs 116 C4
Bayworth Oxon 83 E8
Beach Highld 289 D9
Beach S Glos 61 E8
Beach Hay Worcs 116 C4
Beachampton Bucks 102 D5
Beachamwell Norf 140 B5
Beachans Moray 301 E10
Beacharr Argyll 255 C7
Beachborough Kent 55 F7
Beachlands E Sus 23 E11
Beachley Glos 79 G9
Beacon Corn 2 B5
Beacon Devon 27 F11
Beacon Devon 28 F2
Beacon Down E Sus 37 C9
Beacon End Essex 107 G9
Beacon Hill Bath 61 F9
Beacon Hill Bucks 84 G6
Beacon Hill Cumb 210 E4
Beacon Hill Dorset 18 C5
Beacon Hill Essex 88 C5
Beacon Hill Kent 53 G10
Beacon Hill Notts 172 E4
Beacon Hill Suff 108 B4
Beacon Hill Sur 49 F11
Beacon Lough T & W 243 F7
Beaconhill Northumb 243 B7
Beacon's Bottom Bucks 84 F3
Beaconsfield Bucks 66 B2
Beaconside Staffs 151 E8
Beacrabhaic W Isles 305 J3
Beadlam N Yorks 216 C3
Beadlow C Beds 104 D2
Beadnell Northumb 264 D6
Beaford Devon 25 E9
Beal N Yorks 198 B4
Beal Northumb 273 G11
Bealach Highld 289 D11
Bealach Maim Argyll 275 E10
Bealbury Corn 7 B7
Beal's Green Kent 53 G9
Bealsmill Corn 12 F3
Beam Bridge Som 27 D10
Beam Hill Staffs 152 D4
Beambridge Shrops 131 F10
Beamhurst Staffs 151 B11
Beamhurst Lane Staffs 151 B11
Beaminster Dorset 29 G7
Beamish Durham 242 G6
Beamond End Bucks 84 F6
Beamsley N Yorks 205 C7
Bean Kent 68 E5
Beanacre Wilts 62 F2
Beancross Falk 279 F8
Beanhill M Keynes 103 D7
Beanley Northumb 264 F3
Beansburn E Ayrs 257 B10
Beanthwaite Cumb 210 C4
Beaquoy Orkney 314 D3
Bear Cross Bmouth 19 B7
Beard Hill Som 44 E6
Beardly Batch Som 44 E6
Beardwood Blkburn 195 B7
Beare Devon 27 G7
Beare Green Sur 51 E7
Bearley Warks 118 E3
Bearley Cross Warks 118 E3
Bearnus Argyll 288 E5
Bearpark Durham 233 C10
Bearsbridge Northumb 241 F7
Bearsden E Dunb 277 G10
Bearsted Kent 53 B9
Bearstone Shrops 150 B4
Bearwood Hereford 115 F7
Bearwood Poole 18 B6
Bearwood W Mid 133 F10
Beasley Staffs 168 F4
Beattock Dumfries 248 C3
Beauchamp Roding Essex 87 C9
Beauchief S Yorks 186 E4
Beauclerc Northumb 242 E2
Beaudesert Warks 118 D3
Beaufort Bl Gwent 77 C11
Beaufort Castle Highld 300 E5
Beaulieu Hants 32 G5
Beaulieu Wood Dorset 30 F2
Beauly Highld 300 E5
Beaumaris Anglesey 179 F10
Beaumont Cumb 239 F8
Beaumont Essex 108 G3
Beaumont Windsor 66 E3
Beaumont Hill Darl 224 B5
Beaumont Leys Leicester 135 B11
Beausale Warks 118 C4
Beauvale Notts 171 F8
Beauworth Hants 33 B9
Beavan's Hill Hereford 98 G3
Beaworthy Devon 12 B5
Beazley End Essex 106 F4
Bebington Mers 182 E4
Bebside Northumb 253 G7
Beccles Suff 143 E8
Becconsall Lancs 194 C2
Beck Bottom Cumb 210 C5
Beck Bottom W Yorks 197 C10
Beck Foot Cumb 222 F2
Beck Foot W Yorks 205 F8
Beck Head Cumb 211 C8
Beck Hole N Yorks 226 E6
Beck Houses Cumb 221 F11
Beck Row Suff 124 B3
Beck Side Cumb 210 C4
Beck Side Cumb 211 C7
Beckbury Shrops 132 C5
Beckces Cumb 230 F4
Beckenham London 67 F11
Beckermet Cumb 219 D10
Beckermonds N Yorks 213 C7
Beckery Som 44 F3
Beckett End Norf 140 D5
Beckfoot Cumb 220 E3
Beckfoot Cumb 229 B7
Beckford Worcs 99 D9
Beckhampton Wilts 62 F5
Beckingham Lincs 172 E5

Beckingham Notts 188 D3
Beckington Som 45 C10
Beckjay Shrops 115 B7
Beckley E Sus 38 C5
Beckley Hants 19 B10
Beckley Oxon 83 C9
Beckley Furnace E Sus 38 C4
Beckside Cumb 212 B2
Beckton London 68 C2
Beckwith N Yorks 205 C11
Beckwithshaw N Yorks 205 C11
Becontree London 68 B3
Bed-y-coedwr Gwyn 146 D4
Bedale N Yorks 214 B5
Bedburn Durham 233 E8
Bedchester Dorset 30 D5
Beddau Rhondda 58 B5
Beddgelert Gwyn 163 F9
Beddingham E Sus 36 F6
Beddington London 67 G10
Beddington Corner London 67 F9
Bedfield Suff 126 D4
Bedford Beds 121 G11
Bedford Gtr Man 183 B11
Bedford Park London 67 D8
Bedgebury Cross Kent 53 G8
Bedgrove Bucks 84 C4
Bedham W Sus 35 C8
Bedhampton Hants 22 B2
Bedingfield Suff 126 D3
Bedingham Green Norf 142 E5
Bedlam N Yorks 214 G5
Bedlam Som 45 D9
Bedlam Street W Sus 36 D3
Bedlar's Green Essex 105 G10
Bedlington Northumb 253 G7
Bedlington Station Northumb 253 G7
Bedlinog M Tydf 77 E9
Bedminster Bristol 60 E5
Bedminster Down Bristol 60 F5
Bedmond Herts 85 E9
Bednall Staffs 151 F9
Bednall Head Staffs 151 F9
Bedrule Borders 262 F4
Bedstone Shrops 115 B7
Bedwas Caerph 59 B7
Bedwell Herts 104 G4
Bedwell Wrex 166 F5
Bedwellty Caerph 77 E11
Bedwellty Pits Bl Gwent 77 D11
Bedwlwyn Wrex 148 B4
Bedworth Warks 135 F7
Bedworth Heath Warks 134 F6
Bedworth Woodlands Warks 134 F6
Beeby Leics 136 B3
Beech Hants 49 F7
Beech Staffs 151 B7
Beech Hill Gtr Man 194 F5
Beech Hill W Berks 65 G7
Beech Lanes W Mid 133 F10
Beechcliff Staffs 151 B7
Beechcliffe W Yorks 205 E7
Beechen Cliff Bath 61 G9
Beechingstoke Wilts 46 B5
Beechwood Halton 183 E8
Beechwood Newport 59 B10
Beechwood W Mid 118 B5
Beechwood W Yorks 206 F2
Beecroft C Beds 103 G10
Beedon W Berks 64 D3
Beedon Hill W Berks 64 D3
Beeford E Yorks 209 C8
Beeley Derbys 170 B3
Beelsby NE Lincs 201 G8
Beenham W Berks 64 F5
Beenham Stocks W Berks 64 F5
Beenham's Heath Windsor 65 D10
Beeny Corn 11 C8
Beer Devon 15 D10
Beer Som 44 G2
Beer Hackett Dorset 29 E9
Beercrocombe Som 28 C4
Beesands Devon 8 G6
Beesby Lincs 191 E7
Beeslack Midloth 270 C4
Beeson Devon 8 G6
Beeston C Beds 104 B3
Beeston Norf 159 F8
Beeston Notts 153 B10
Beeston W Ches 167 D8
Beeston W Yorks 205 G11
Beeston Hill W Yorks 205 G11
Beeston Park Side W Yorks 197 B9
Beeston Regis Norf 177 E11
Beeston Royds W Yorks 205 G11
Beeston St Lawrence Norf 160 E6
Beeswing Dumfries 237 C10
Beetham Cumb 211 D9
Beetham Som 28 E3
Beetley Norf 159 F9
Beffcote Staffs 150 F6
Began Cardiff 59 C8
Begbroke Oxon 83 C7
Begdale Cambs 139 B9
Begelly Pembs 73 D10
Beggar Hill Essex 87 E10
Beggarington Hill W Yorks 197 C9
Beggars Ash Hereford 98 D4
Beggar's Bush Powys 114 E5
Beggars Bush W Sus 35 F11
Beggars Pound V Glam 58 F4
Beggearn Huish Som 42 F4
Beguildy Powys 114 B3
Beighton Norf 143 B7
Beighton S Yorks 186 E6
Beighton Hill Derbys 170 E3
Beili-glas Mon 78 C4
Beitearsaig W Isles 305 G1
Beith N Ayrs 266 E6
Bekesbourne Kent 55 B7
Bekesbourne Hill Kent 55 B7
Belah Cumb 239 F9
Belan Powys 130 C4
Belaugh Norf 160 F5
Belbins Hants 32 C5
Belbroughton Worcs 117 B8
Belchalwell Dorset 30 F3
Belchalwell Street Dorset 30 F3
Belchamp Otten Essex 106 C6
Belchamp St Paul Essex 106 C5
Belchamp Walter Essex 106 C6
Belcher's Bar Leics 135 B8
Belchford Lincs 190 F3
Beleybridge Fife 287 F9
Belfield Gtr Man 196 E2
Belford Northumb 264 C4
Belgrano Conwy 181 F7
Belgrave Leicester 135 B11
Belgrave Staffs 134 C4
Belgrave W Ches 166 C5
Belgravia London 67 D9
Belhaven E Loth 282 F3
Belhelvie Aberds 293 B11
Belhinnie Aberds 302 G4
Bell Bar Herts 86 D3
Bell Busk N Yorks 204 B4
Bell Common Essex 86 E6
Bell End Worcs 117 B8
Bell Green London 67 E11
Bell Green W Mid 135 G7
Bell Heath Worcs 117 B9
Bell Hill Hants 34 C2
Bell o' th' Hill W Ches 167 F8
Bellabeg Aberds 292 B5
Bellamore S Ayrs 244 F6
Bellanoch Argyll 275 D8
Bellanrigg Borders 260 B6
Bellasize E Yorks 199 B10
Bellaty Angus 286 B6
Belle Eau Park Notts 171 D11
Belle Green S Yorks 197 F11
Belle Isle W Yorks 197 B10
Belle Vale Mers 182 D6
Belle Vale W Mid 133 G9
Belle Vue Cumb 229 E8
Belle Vue Cumb 239 F9
Belle Vue Gtr Man 184 B5
Belle Vue S Yorks 198 G5
Belle Vue Shrops 149 G9
Belle Vue W Yorks 197 D10
Belleau Lincs 190 F6
Belleheiglash Moray 301 F11
Bellerby N Yorks 224 G2
Bellever Devon 13 F9
Bellevue Worcs 117 C9
Bellfield E Ayrs 257 B10
Bellfields Sur 50 C3
Belliehill Angus 293 G7
Bellingdon Bucks 84 D6
Bellingham London 67 E11
Bellingham Northumb 251 G8
Bellmount Norf 157 E10
Belloch Argyll 255 D7
Bellochantuy Argyll 255 D7
Bell's Close T & W 242 E5
Bell's Corner Suff 107 D9
Bells Yew Green E Sus 52 F6
Bellsbank E Ayrs 245 C11
Bellshill N Lnrk 268 C4
Bellshill Northumb 264 C4
Bellside N Lnrk 268 D6
Bellsmyre W Dunb 277 F8
Bellspool Borders 260 B5
Bellsquarry W Loth 269 C10
Belluton Bath 60 G6
Bellyeoman Fife 280 D2
Belmaduthy Highld 300 D6
Belmesthorpe Rutland 155 G10
Belmont Blkburn 195 D7
Belmont Durham 234 C2
Belmont E Sus 38 E4
Belmont Harrow 85 G11
Belmont London 67 G9
Belmont Oxon 63 B11
Belmont S Ayrs 257 E8
Belmont Shetland 312 C7
Belnacraig Aberds 292 B5
Belnagarrow Moray 302 E3
Belnie Lincs 156 C5
Belowda Corn 5 C9
Belper Derbys 170 F4
Belper Lane End Derbys 170 F4
Belph Derbys 187 F8
Belsay Northumb 242 B4
Belses Borders 262 D3
Belsford Devon 8 D5
Belsize Herts 85 E8
Belstead Suff 108 C2
Belston S Ayrs 257 E9
Belstone Devon 13 C8
Belstone Corner Devon 13 B8
Belthorn Blkburn 195 C8
Beltinge Kent 71 F7
Beltingham Northumb 241 E7
Beltoft N Lincs 199 F10
Belton Leics 153 E8
Belton Lincs 155 B8
Belton N Lincs 199 F9
Belton Norf 143 C9
Belton in Rutland Rutland 136 C6
Beltring Kent 53 D7
Belts of Collonach Aberds 293 D8
Belvedere London 68 D3
Belvedere W Loth 269 B9
Belvoir Leics 154 C6
Bembridge I o W 21 D8
Bemersyde Borders 262 C3
Bemerton Wilts 46 G6
Bemerton Heath Wilts 46 G6
Bempton E Yorks 218 E3
Ben Alder Lodge Highld 291 F7
Ben Armine Lodge Highld 309 H7
Ben Casgro W Isles 304 F6
Ben Rhydding W Yorks 205 D8
Benacre Suff 143 G10
Benbuie Dumfries 246 D6
Benchill Gtr Man 184 D4
Bencombe Glos 80 F3
Benderloch Argyll 289 F11
Bendish Herts 104 G3
Bendronaig Lodge Highld 299 F10
Benenden Kent 53 G10
Benfield Dumfries 236 C5
Benfieldside Durham 242 G3
Bengal Pembs 91 E9
Bengate Norf 160 D6
Bengeo Herts 86 C4
Bengeworth Worcs 99 C10
Bengrove Glos 99 E9
Benhall Glos 99 G8
Benhall Green Suff 127 E7
Benhall Street Suff 127 E7
Benhilton London 67 F9
Benholm Aberds 293 G10
Beningbrough N Yorks 206 B6
Benington Herts 104 G5
Benington Lincs 174 F5
Benington Sea End Lincs 174 F6
Benllech Anglesey 179 E8
Benmore Argyll 276 E2
Benmore Stirl 285 E8
Benmore Lodge Argyll 289 F7
Benmore Lodge Highld 309 H3
Bennacott Corn 11 C11
Bennah Devon 14 E2
Bennan N Ayrs 255 E10
Bennane Lea S Ayrs 244 F3
Bennetland E Yorks 199 B10
Bennetsfield Highld 300 D6
Bennett End Bucks 84 F3
Bennetts End Herts 85 D9
Benniworth Lincs 190 E2
Benover Kent 53 D8
Bensham T & W 242 E6
Benslie N Ayrs 266 G6
Benson Oxon 83 G10
Benston Shetland 313 H6
Bent Aberds 293 F8
Bent Gate Lancs 195 C9
Benter Som 44 D6
Bentfield Bury Essex 105 F9
Bentfield Green Essex 105 F10
Bentgate Gtr Man 196 E2
Benthall Northumb 264 D6
Benthall Shrops 132 C3
Bentham Glos 80 B6
Benthoul Aberdeen 293 C10
Bentilee Stoke 168 F6
Bentlass Pembs 73 E7
Bentlawnt Shrops 130 C6
Bentley E Yorks 208 F6
Bentley Essex 87 F9
Bentley Hants 49 E9
Bentley S Yorks 198 F5
Bentley Suff 108 D2
Bentley W Mid 133 D9
Bentley Warks 134 D5
Bentley Worcs 117 D9
Bentley Common Warks 134 D5
Bentley Heath Herts 86 F2
Bentley Heath W Mid 118 B3
Bentley Rise S Yorks 198 G5
Benton Devon 41 F7
Benton Green W Mid 118 B5
Bentpath Dumfries 249 E8
Bents W Loth 269 C9
Bents Head W Yorks 205 F7
Bentwichen Devon 41 G8
Bentworth Hants 49 E7
Benvie Dundee 287 D7
Benville Dorset 29 G8
Benwell T & W 242 E6
Benwick Cambs 138 E6
Beobridge Shrops 132 E5
Beoley Worcs 117 D11
Beoraidbeg Highld 295 F8
Bepton W Sus 34 D5
Berden Essex 105 F9
Bere Alston Devon 7 B8
Bere Ferrers Devon 7 C9
Bere Regis Dorset 18 C2
Berechurch Essex 107 G9
Berefold Aberds 303 F9
Berepper Corn 2 E5
Bergh Apton Norf 142 C6
Berghers Hill Bucks 66 B2
Berhill Som 44 F2
Berinsfield Oxon 83 F9
Berkeley Glos 79 F11
Berkeley Heath Glos 79 F11
Berkeley Road Glos 80 E2
Berkeley Towers E Ches 167 E11
Berkhamsted Herts 85 D7
Berkley Som 45 D10
Berkley Down Som 45 D9
Berkley Marsh Som 45 D10
Berkswell W Mid 118 B4
Bermondsey London 67 D10
Bermuda Warks 135 F7
Bernards Heath Herts 85 D11
Bernera Highld 295 C10
Berner's Cross Devon 25 F10
Berner's Hill E Sus 53 G8
Berners Roding Essex 87 D10
Bernice Argyll 276 C2
Bernisdale Highld 298 D4
Berrick Salome Oxon 83 G10
Berriedale Highld 311 G5
Berrier Cumb 230 F3
Berriew = Aberriw Powys 130 C3
Berrington Northumb 273 G10
Berrington Shrops 131 B10
Berrington Worcs 115 D11
Berrington Green Worcs 115 D11
Berriowbridge Corn 11 F11
Berrow Som 43 C10
Berrow Worcs 98 E5
Berrow Green Worcs 116 F4
Berry Swansea 56 D3
Berry Brow W Yorks 196 E6
Berry Cross Devon 25 E7
Berry Down Cross Devon 40 E5
Berry Hill Glos 79 C9
Berry Hill Pembs 91 C11
Berry Hill Stoke 168 F6
Berry Hill Worcs 117 E7
Berry Moor S Yorks 197 G9
Berry Pomeroy Devon 8 C6
Berryfield Wilts 61 G11
Berrygate Hill E Yorks 201 C8
Berryhillock Moray 302 C5
Berrylands London 67 F7
Berrynarbor Devon 40 D5
Berry's Green London 52 B2
Berrysbridge Devon 26 G6
Bersham Wrex 166 F4
Berstane Orkney 314 E4
Berth-ddu Flint 166 B2
Berthengam Flint 181 F10
Berwick E Sus 23 D8
Berwick Kent 54 F6
Berwick S Glos 60 C5
Berwick Bassett Wilts 62 E5
Berwick Hill Northumb 242 B5
Berwick Hills M'bro 225 B10
Berwick St James Wilts 46 F5
Berwick St John Wilts 30 C6
Berwick St Leonard Wilts 46 G2
Berwick-upon-Tweed Northumb 273 E9
Berwick Wharf Shrops 149 G10
Berwyn Denb 165 G11
Bescaby Leics 154 D6
Bescar Lancs 193 E11
Bescot W Mid 133 D10
Besford Shrops 149 E11
Besford Worcs 99 C8
Bessacarr S Yorks 198 G6
Bessels Green Kent 52 B4
Bessels Leigh Oxon 83 E7
Besses o' th' Barn Gtr Man 195 F10
Bessingby E Yorks 218 F3
Bessingham Norf 160 B3
Best Beech Hill E Sus 52 G6
Besthorpe Norf 141 D11
Besthorpe Notts 172 C4
Bestwood Nottingham 171 G9
Bestwood Village Notts 171 F9
Beswick E Yorks 208 D6
Beswick Gtr Man 184 B5
Betchcott Shrops 131 D8
Betchton Heath E Ches 168 C3
Betchworth Sur 51 D8
Bethania Ceredig 111 E11
Bethania Gwyn 163 E10
Bethania Gwyn 164 F2
Bethany Corn 6 D6
Bethel Anglesey 178 G5
Bethel Corn 5 E10
Bethel Gwyn 147 B9
Bethel Gwyn 163 B8
Bethelnie Aberds 303 F7
Bethersden Kent 54 E2
Bethesda Gwyn 163 B10
Bethesda Pembs 73 B9
Bethlehem Carms 94 F3
Bethnal Green London 67 C10
Betley Staffs 168 F3
Betley Common Staffs 168 F2
Betsham Kent 68 E6
Betteshanger Kent 55 C10
Bettiscombe Dorset 16 B3
Bettisfield Wrex 149 B9
Betton Shrops 130 C6
Betton Shrops 150 B3
Betton Strange Shrops 131 B10
Bettws Bridgend 58 B2
Bettws Mon 78 B3
Bettws Newport 78 G3
Bettws Cedewain Powys 130 D2
Bettws Gwerfil Goch Denb 165 F8
Bettws Ifan Ceredig 92 B6
Bettws Newydd Mon 78 D5
Bettws-y-crwyn Shrops 130 G4
Bettyhill Highld 308 C7
Betws Bridgend 57 D11
Betws Carms 75 C10
Betws Bledrws Ceredig 111 G11
Betws-Garmon Gwyn 163 D8
Betws Ifan Ceredig 92 B6
Betws-y-Coed Conwy 164 D4
Betws-yn-Rhos Conwy 180 G6
Beulah Ceredig 92 B5
Beulah Powys 113 G8
Bevendean Brighton 36 F4
Bevercotes Notts 187 G11
Bevere Worcs 116 F6
Beverley E Yorks 208 F6
Beverston Glos 80 G5
Bevington Glos 79 F11
Bewaldeth Cumb 229 E10
Bewbush W Sus 51 F8
Bewcastle Cumb 240 C3
Bewdley Worcs 116 B5
Bewerley N Yorks 214 G3
Bewholme E Yorks 209 C9
Bewley Common Wilts 62 F2
Bewlie Borders 262 D3
Bewlie Mains Borders 262 D3
Bewsey Warr 183 D9
Bexfield Norf 159 D10
Bexhill E Sus 38 F2
Bexley London 68 E3
Bexleyheath London 68 D3
Bexleyhill W Sus 34 B6
Bexon Kent 53 B11
Bexwell Norf 140 C2
Beyton Suff 125 E8
Beyton Green Suff 125 E8
Bhalasaigh W Isles 304 E3
Bhaltos W Isles 304 E2
Bhatarsaigh W Isles 297 M2
Bhlàraidh Highld 290 B5
Bibstone S Glos 79 G11
Bibury Glos 81 D10
Bicester Oxon 101 G11
Bickenhall Som 28 D3
Bickenhill W Mid 134 G3
Bicker Lincs 156 B4
Bicker Bar Lincs 156 B4
Bicker Gauntlet Lincs 156 B4
Bickershaw Gtr Man 194 G6
Bickerstaffe Lancs 194 G2
Bickerton Devon 9 G11
Bickerton E Ches 167 E8
Bickerton N Yorks 206 C5
Bickford Staffs 151 G7
Bickham Som 42 E3
Bickingcott Devon 26 B3
Bickington Devon 13 G11
Bickington Devon 40 G4
Bickleigh Devon 7 C10
Bickleigh Devon 26 F6
Bickleton Devon 40 G4
Bickley London 68 F2
Bickley W Ches 167 F8
Bickley Worcs 116 C2
Bickley Moss W Ches 167 F8
Bickley Town W Ches 167 F8
Bickleywood W Ches 167 F8
Bickmarsh Warks 100 B2
Bicknacre Essex 88 E3
Bicknoller Som 42 F6
Bicknor Kent 53 B11
Bickton Hants 31 E11
Bicton Hereford 115 E9
Bicton Pembs 72 D4
Bicton Shrops 130 G5
Bicton Shrops 149 F8
Bicton Heath Shrops 149 G9
Bidborough Kent 52 E5
Bidden Hants 49 D8
Biddenden Kent 53 F11
Biddenden Green Kent 53 E11
Biddenham Beds 103 B10
Biddestone Wilts 61 E11
Biddick T & W 243 F8
Biddick Hall T & W 243 E9
Biddisham Som 43 C11
Biddlesden Bucks 102 C2
Biddlestone Northumb 251 B11
Biddulph Staffs 168 D5
Biddulph Moor Staffs 168 D6
Bideford Devon 25 B7
Bidford-on-Avon Warks 118 G2
Bidlake Devon 12 D5
Bidston Mers 182 C3
Bidston Hill Mers 182 D3
Bidwell C Beds 103 G10
Bielby E Yorks 207 E11
Bieldside Aberdeen 293 C10
Bierley I o W 20 F6
Bierley W Yorks 205 G9
Bierton Bucks 84 B4
Big Mancot Flint 166 B4
Big Sand Highld 299 B7
Bigbury Devon 8 F3
Bigbury-on-Sea Devon 8 G3
Bigby Lincs 200 F5
Bigfrith Windsor 65 C11
Biggar Cumb 210 F3
Biggar S Lnrk 260 B2
Biggar Road N Lnrk 268 C5
Biggin Derbys 169 D11
Biggin Derbys 170 F3
Biggin N Yorks 206 F6
Biggin Thurrock 69 D7
Biggin Hill London 52 B2
Biggings Shetland 313 G3
Biggleswade C Beds 104 C3
Bighouse Highld 310 C2
Bighton Hants 48 G6
Biglands Cumb 239 G7
Bignall End Staffs 168 E4
Bignor W Sus 35 E7
Bigods Essex 106 G2
Bigram Stirl 285 G10
Bigrigg Cumb 219 C10
Bigswell Orkney 314 E3
Bigton Shetland 313 L5
Bilberry Corn 5 C10
Bilborough Nottingham 171 G8
Bilbrook Som 42 E4
Bilbrook Staffs 133 C7
Bilbrough N Yorks 206 D6
Bilbster Highld 310 D6
Bilby Notts 187 E10
Bildershaw Durham 233 G10
Bildeston Suff 107 B9
Bill Quay T & W 243 E7
Billacombe Plym 7 E10
Billacott Corn 11 C11
Billericay Essex 87 G11
Billesdon Leics 136 C4
Billesley W Mid 133 G11
Billesley Warks 118 F2
Billesley Common W Mid 133 G11
Billingborough Lincs 156 C2
Billinge Mers 194 G4
Billingford Norf 126 B3
Billingford Norf 159 E10
Billingham Stockton 234 G5
Billinghay Lincs 173 E11
Billingley S Yorks 198 G2
Billingshurst W Sus 35 B9
Billingsley Shrops 132 F4
Billington C Beds 103 G8
Billington Lancs 203 F10
Billington Staffs 151 E7
Billockby Norf 161 G8
Billy Mill T & W 243 D8
Billy Row Durham 233 D9
Bilmarsh Shrops 149 D9
Bilsborrow Lancs 202 F6
Bilsby Lincs 191 F7
Bilsby Field Lincs 191 F7
Bilsdon Devon 14 C2
Bilsham W Sus 35 G7
Bilsington Kent 54 G4
Bilson Green Glos 79 C11
Bilsthorpe Notts 171 C10
Bilsthorpe Moor Notts 171 D11
Bilston Midloth 270 C5
Bilston W Mid 133 D9
Bilstone Leics 135 B7
Bilting Kent 54 D5
Bilton E Yorks 209 G9
Bilton N Yorks 206 B2
Bilton Northumb 264 G6
Bilton Warks 119 C9
Bilton Haggs N Yorks 206 D5
Bilton in Ainsty N Yorks 206 D5
Bimbister Orkney 314 E3
Binbrook Lincs 190 C2
Binchester Blocks Durham 233 E10
Bincombe Dorset 17 E9
Bincombe Som 43 F7
Bindal Highld 311 L3
Bindon Som 27 C10
Binegar Som 44 D6
Bines Green W Sus 35 D11
Binfield Brack 65 E10
Binfield Heath Oxon 65 D8
Bingfield Northumb 241 C11
Bingham Edin 280 G6
Bingham Notts 154 B4
Bingley W Yorks 205 F8
Bings Heath Shrops 149 F10
Binham Norf 159 B9
Binley Hants 48 C2
Binley W Mid 119 B7
Binley Woods Warks 119 B7
Binnegar Dorset 18 D3
Binniehill Falk 279 G7
Binscombe Sur 50 D3
Binsey Oxon 83 D7
Binsoe N Yorks 214 D4
Binstead Hants 49 E9
Binstead I o W 21 C7
Binsted Hants 49 E9
Binsted W Sus 35 F7
Binton Warks 118 G2
Bintree Norf 159 E10
Binweston Shrops 130 C6
Birch Essex 88 B6
Birch Gtr Man 195 F11
Birch Acre Worcs 117 C11
Birch Berrow Worcs 116 E4
Birch Cross Staffs 152 C2
Birch Green Essex 88 B6
Birch Green Herts 86 C3
Birch Green Lancs 194 F3
Birch Green Worcs 99 B7
Birch Heath W Ches 167 C8
Birch Hill Brack 65 F11
Birch Hill W Ches 183 G8
Birch Vale Derbys 185 D8
Birchall Hereford 98 D3
Birchall Staffs 169 E7
Bircham Newton Norf 158 C5
Bircham Tofts Norf 158 C5
Birchan Coppice Worcs 116 C6
Birchanger Essex 105 G10
Birchburn N Ayrs 255 E10
Birchden E Sus 52 F4
Birchencliffe W Yorks 196 D6
Birchend Hereford 98 C3
Birchendale Staffs 151 B11
Bircher Hereford 115 D9
Birches Green W Mid 134 E2
Birches Head Stoke 168 F5
Birchett's Green E Sus 53 G7
Birchfield Highld 301 G9
Birchfield W Mid 133 E11
Birchgrove Cardiff 59 D7
Birchgrove E Sus 36 B6
Birchgrove Swansea 57 B8
Birchhall Corner Essex 107 E10
Birchill Devon 28 G4
Birchills W Mid 133 D10
Birchington Kent 71 F9
Birchley Heath Warks 134 E5
Birchmoor Warks 134 C5
Birchmoor Green C Beds 103 E8
Bircholt Forstal Kent 54 E5
Birchover Derbys 170 C2
Birchwood Herts 86 D2
Birchwood Lincs 172 B6
Birchwood Som 28 E2
Birchwood Warr 183 C10
Birchy Hill Hants 19 B11
Bircotes Notts 187 C10
Bird Street Suff 125 G10
Birdbrook Essex 106 C4
Birdbush Wilts 30 C6
Birdfield Argyll 275 D10
Birdforth N Yorks 215 D9
Birdham W Sus 22 D4
Birdholme Derbys 170 B5
Birdingbury Warks 119 D8
Birdlip Glos 80 C6
Birds Edge W Yorks 197 F8
Birds End Suff 124 E5
Birds Green Essex 87 D9
Birdsall N Yorks 216 F6
Birdsgreen Shrops 132 F5
Birdsmoorgate Dorset 28 G5
Birdston E Dunb 278 F3
Birdwell S Yorks 197 G10
Birdwood Glos 80 B2
Birgham Borders 263 B7
Birichen Highld 309 K7
Birkacre Lancs 194 D5
Birkby Cumb 229 D7
Birkby N Yorks 224 E6
Birkby W Yorks 196 D6
Birkdale Mers 193 D10
Birkenbog Aberds 302 C5
Birkenhead Mers 182 D4
Birkenhills Aberds 303 E7
Birkenshaw N Lnrk 268 C3
Birkenshaw S Lnrk 268 F5
Birkenshaw W Yorks 197 B8
Birkenshaw Bottoms W Yorks 197 B8
Birkenside Borders 271 G11
Birkett Mire Cumb 230 G2
Birkhall Aberds 292 D5
Birkhill Angus 287 D7
Birkhill Borders 260 F6
Birkhill Borders 271 G11
Birkholme Lincs 155 E9
Birkhouse W Yorks 197 C7
Birkin N Yorks 198 B4
Birks Cumb 222 G3
Birks W Yorks 197 B9
Birkshaw Northumb 241 D7
Birley Hereford 115 G9
Birley Carr S Yorks 186 C4
Birley Edge S Yorks 186 C4
Birleyhay Derbys 186 E5
Birling Kent 69 G7
Birling Northumb 252 B6
Birling Gap E Sus 23 F9
Birlingham Worcs 99 C8
Birmingham W Mid 133 F11
Birnam Perth 286 C4
Birniehill S Lnrk 268 E2
Birse Aberds 293 D7
Birsemore Aberds 293 D7
Birstall Leics 135 B11
Birstall W Yorks 197 B8
Birstall Smithies W Yorks 197 B8
Birstwith N Yorks 205 B10
Birthorpe Lincs 156 C2
Birtle Gtr Man 195 E10
Birtley Hereford 115 D7
Birtley Northumb 241 B9
Birtley Shrops 131 E9
Birtley T & W 243 F7
Birtley Green Sur 50 E4
Birts Street Worcs 98 D5
Birtsmorton Worcs 98 D6
Bisbrooke Rutland 137 D7
Biscathorpe Lincs 190 D2
Biscombe Som 27 E11
Biscot Luton 103 G11
Biscovey Corn 5 E11
Bish Mill Devon 26 B2
Bisham Windsor 65 C10
Bishampton Worcs 117 G9
Bishon Common Hereford 97 C8
Bishop Auckland Durham 233 F10
Bishop Burton E Yorks 208 F5
Bishop Kinkell Highld 300 D5
Bishop Middleham Durham 234 E2
Bishop Monkton N Yorks 214 F6
Bishop Norton Lincs 189 C7
Bishop Sutton Bath 44 B5
Bishop Thornton N Yorks 214 G5
Bishop Wilton E Yorks 207 B11
Bishopbridge Lincs 189 C8
Bishopbriggs E Dunb 278 G2
Bishopdown Wilts 47 G7
Bishopmill Moray 302 C2
Bishops Cannings Wilts 62 G4
Bishop's Castle Shrops 130 F6
Bishop's Caundle Dorset 29 E11
Bishop's Cleeve Glos 99 F9
Bishop's Down Dorset 29 E11
Bishops Frome Hereford 98 B3
Bishops Green Essex 87 B5
Bishop's Green W Berks 64 G4
Bishop's Hull Som 28 C2
Bishop's Itchington Warks 119 F7
Bishops Lydeard Som 27 B11
Bishop's Norton Glos 98 G6
Bishops Nympton Devon 26 C3
Bishop's Offley Staffs 150 D5
Bishop's Quay Corn 2 D6
Bishop's Stortford Herts 105 G9
Bishop's Sutton Hants 48 G6
Bishop's Tachbrook Warks 118 E6
Bishops Tawton Devon 40 G5
Bishop's Waltham Hants 33 D9
Bishop's Wood Staffs 132 B6
Bishopsbourne Kent 55 C7
Bishopsgarth Stockton 234 G4
Bishopsgate Sur 66 E3
Bishopsteignton Devon 14 G4
Bishopstoke Hants 33 D7
Bishopston Bristol 60 D5
Bishopston Swansea 56 D5
Bishopstone Bucks 84 C4
Bishopstone E Sus 23 E7
Bishopstone Hereford 97 C8
Bishopstone Kent 71 F8
Bishopstone Swindon 63 C8
Bishopstone Wilts 31 B9
Bishopstrow Wilts 45 E11
Bishopswood Som 28 E3
Bishopsworth Bristol 60 F5
Bishopthorpe York 207 D7
Bishopton Darl 234 G3
Bishopton Dumfries 236 E6
Bishopton N Yorks 214 E6
Bishopton Renfs 277 G8
Bishopton Warks 118 F3
Bishopwearmouth T & W 243 F9
Bishpool Newport 59 B10
Bishton Newport 59 B11
Bishton Staffs 151 E10
Bisley Glos 80 D6
Bisley Sur 50 B3
Bisley Camp Sur 50 B2
Bispham Blkpool 202 E2
Bispham Green Lancs 194 E3
Bissoe Corn 4 G5
Bissom Corn 3 C7
Bisterne Hants 31 G10
Bisterne Close Hants 32 G2
Bitchet Green Kent 52 C5
Bitchfield Lincs 155 D9
Bittadon Devon 40 E4
Bittaford Devon 8 D3
Bittering Norf 159 F8
Bitterley Shrops 115 B11
Bitterne Soton 33 E7
Bitterne Park Soton 32 E6
Bitterscote Staffs 134 C4
Bitteswell Leics 135 F10
Bittles Green Dorset 30 C5
Bitton S Glos 61 F7
Bix Oxon 65 B8
Bixter Shetland 313 H5
Blaby Leics 135 D11
Black Bank Cambs 139 F10
Black Bank Warks 135 F7
Black Banks Darl 224 C5
Black Barn Lincs 157 D8
Black Bourton Oxon 82 E3
Black Callerton T & W 242 D5
Black Carr Norf 141 D11
Black Clauchrie S Ayrs 245 G7
Black Corner W Sus 51 F9
Black Corries Lodge Highld 284 B6
Black Crofts Argyll 289 F11
Black Cross Corn 5 C8
Black Dam Hants 48 C6
Black Dog Devon 26 F4
Black Heddon Northumb 242 B3
Black Hill W Yorks 204 E6
Black Horse Drove Cambs 139 E11
Black Lake W Mid 133 E9
Black Lane Gtr Man 195 F9
Black Marsh Shrops 130 D6
Black Moor Lancs 194 E3
Black Moor W Yorks 205 F11
Black Mount Argyll 284 C6
Black Notley Essex 106 G5
Black Park Wrex 166 G4
Black Pill Swansea 56 C6
Black Pole Lancs 202 F5
Black Rock Brighton 36 G4
Black Rock Corn 2 C5
Black Street Suff 143 F10
Black Tar Pembs 73 D7
Black Torrington Devon 25 F7
Black Vein Caerph 78 G2
Blackacre Dumfries 248 E2
Blackadder West Borders 272 E6
Blackawton Devon 8 E6
Blackbeck Cumb 219 D10
Blackborough Devon 27 F9
Blackborough Norf 158 G3
Blackborough End Norf 158 G3
Blackboys E Sus 37 C8
Blackbraes Aberds 293 B10
Blackbrook Derbys 170 F4
Blackbrook Derbys 185 E9
Blackbrook Mers 183 B8
Blackbrook Staffs 150 B5
Blackbrook Sur 51 D7
Blackburn Aberds 293 B10
Blackburn Aberds 302 F5
Blackburn Blkburn 195 B7
Blackburn S Yorks 186 C5
Blackburn W Loth 269 B9
Blackcastle Midloth 271 D8
Blackchambers Aberds 293 B9
Blackcraig Dumfries 246 G6
Blackcraigs Angus 293 E7
Blackden Heath E Ches 184 G3
Blackditch Oxon 82 D6
Blackdog Aberds 293 B11
Blackdown Dorset 28 G5
Blackdown Hants 33 C8
Blackdown Warks 118 D6
Blackdyke Cumb 238 G4
Blackdykes E Loth 281 E11
Blacker Hill S Yorks 197 G11
Blacketts Kent 70 F2
Blackfell T & W 243 F7
Blackfen London 68 E3
Blackfield Hants 32 G6
Blackford Cumb 239 E9
Blackford Dumfries 248 G4
Blackford Perth 286 G2
Blackford Shrops 131 G11
Blackford Som 29 B11
Blackford Som 42 D2
Blackford Som 44 D2
Blackford Bridge Gtr Man 195 F10
Blackfordby Leics 152 F6
Blackfords Staffs 151 G9
Blackgang I o W 20 F5
Blackgate Angus 287 B8
Blackhall Aberds 293 D8
Blackhall Edin 280 G4
Blackhall Renfs 267 C9
Blackhall Colliery Durham 234 D5
Blackhall Mill T & W 242 F4
Blackhall Rocks Durham 234 D5
Blackham E Sus 52 F3
Blackhaugh Borders 261 B10
Blackheath Essex 107 G10
Blackheath London 67 D11
Blackheath Suff 127 C8
Blackheath Sur 50 D4
Blackheath W Mid 133 F9
Blackheath Park London 68 D2
Blackhill Aberds 303 D10
Blackhill Aberds 303 E10
Blackhill Aberds 303 F10
Blackhill Durham 242 G3
Blackhill Hants 32 D4
Blackhill Highld 298 D3
Blackhillock Moray 302 E4
Blackhills Highld 301 D9
Blackhills Moray 302 D2
Blackhills Swansea 56 C5
Blackhorse Devon 14 C5
Blackhorse S Glos 61 D7
Blackird Leys Oxon 83 E9
Blackjack Lincs 156 B5
Blackland Wilts 62 F4
Blacklands E Sus 38 E4
Blacklands Hereford 98 C2
Blacklaw Aberds 302 D6
Blackleach Lancs 202 G5
Blackley Gtr Man 195 G11
Blackley W Yorks 196 D6
Blacklunans Perth 292 G3
Blackmarstone Hereford 97 D10
Blackmill Bridgend 58 B2
Blackminster Worcs 99 C11
Blackmoor Bath 60 G5
Blackmoor Gtr Man 195 G7
Blackmoor Hants 49 G9
Blackmoor N Som 60 G3
Blackmoor Som 27 D11
Blackmoor Gate Devon 41 E7
Blackmoorfoot W Yorks 196 E5
Blackmore Essex 87 E10
Blackmore Shrops 130 B6
Blackmore End Essex 106 E4
Blackmore End Herts 85 B11
Blackmore End Worcs 98 C6
Blackness Aberds 293 D8
Blackness E Sus 52 G4
Blackness Falk 279 F11
Blacknest Hants 49 E9
Blacknest Windsor 66 F3
Blacknoll Dorset 18 D2
Blacko Lancs 204 E3
Blackoe Shrops 149 B10
Blackpark Dumfries 236 C5
Blackpole Worcs 117 F7
Blackpool Blkpool 202 F2
Blackpool Devon 7 E11
Blackpool Devon 9 F7
Blackpool Devon 14 G2
Blackpool Pembs 73 C9
Blackpool Gate Cumb 240 B2
Blackridge W Loth 269 B7
Blackrock Argyll 274 G4
Blackrock Bath 60 F6
Blackrock Mon 78 C2
Blackrod Gtr Man 194 E6
Blackshaw Dumfries 238 D2
Blackshaw Head W Yorks 196 B3
Blackshaw Moor Staffs 169 D8
Blacksmith's Corner Suff 108 C2
Blacksmith's Green Suff 126 D2
Blacksnape Blkburn 195 C8
Blackstone W Sus 36 D2
Blackstone Worcs 116 C5
Blackthorn Oxon 83 B10
Blackthorpe Suff 125 E8
Blacktoft E Yorks 199 C10
Blacktop Aberdeen 293 C10
Blacktown Newport 59 C9
Blackwall Derbys 170 F3
Blackwall London 67 C11
Blackwall Tunnel London 67 C11
Blackwater Corn 4 F4
Blackwater Dorset 19 B8
Blackwater Hants 49 B11
Blackwater I o W 20 D6
Blackwater Norf 159 E11
Blackwater Som 28 D3
Blackwater Lodge Moray 302 G3
Blackwaterfoot N Ayrs 255 E9
Blackweir Cardiff 59 D7
Blackwell Cumb 239 G10
Blackwell Darl 224 C5
Blackwell Derbys 170 D6
Blackwell Derbys 185 G10
Blackwell Devon 27 B8
Blackwell W Sus 51 F11
Blackwell Warks 100 C4
Blackwell Worcs 117 C9
Blackwood Caerph 77 F11
Blackwood S Lnrk 268 G5
Blackwood Warr 183 C10
Blackwood Hill Staffs 168 D6
Blacon W Ches 166 B5
Bladbean Kent 55 D7
Blades N Yorks 223 F9
Bladnoch Dumfries 236 D6
Bladon Oxon 82 C6
Blaen-Cil-Llech Ceredig 92 C6
Blaen Clydach Rhondda 77 G7
Blaen-gwynfi Neath 57 B11
Blaen-pant Ceredig 92 C5
Blaen-waun Carms 92 F4
Blaen-waun Ceredig 111 G7
Blaen-y-coed Carms 92 F6
Blaen-y-cwm Bl Gwent 77 C10
Blaen-y-Cwm Denb 147 C10
Blaen-y-cwm Gwyn 146 E4
Blaen-y-cwm Powys 147 E11
Blaenannerch Ceredig 92 B4
Blaenau Carms 75 C10
Blaenau Flint 166 D2
Blaenau Dolwyddelan Conwy 164 E2
Blaenau Ffestiniog Gwyn 164 F2
Blaenau-Gwent Bl Gwent 78 E2
Blaenavon Torf 78 D3
Blaenbedw Fawr Ceredig 111 G7
Blaencaerau Bridgend 57 C11
Blaencelyn Ceredig 111 G7
Blaencwm Rhondda 76 F6
Blaendulais = Seven Sisters Neath 76 D4
Blaenffos Pembs 92 D3
Blaengarw Bridgend 76 G6
Blaengwrach Neath 76 D5
Blaengwynfi Neath 57 B11
Blaenllechau Rhondda 77 F8
Blaenpennal Ceredig 112 E2
Blaenplwyf Ceredig 111 B11
Blaenporth Ceredig 92 B5
Blaenrhondda Rhondda 76 E6
Blaenwaun Carms 92 F4
Blaenycwm Ceredig 112 B6
Blagdon N Som 44 B4
Blagdon Torbay 9 C7
Blagdon Hill Som 28 D2
Blagill Cumb 231 B10
Blaguegate Lancs 194 F3
Blaich Highld 290 F2
Blain Highld 289 C8
Blaina Bl Gwent 78 D2
Blainacraig Ho Aberds 293 D7
Blair Fife 280 C6
Blair Atholl Perth 291 G10
Blair Drummond Stirl 278 B4
Blairbeg N Ayrs 256 C2
Blairburn Fife 279 D9
Blairdaff Aberds 293 B8
Blairdryne Aberds 293 D9
Blairglas Argyll 276 D6
Blairgowrie Perth 286 C5
Blairhall Fife 279 D10
Blairhill N Lnrk 268 B4
Blairingone Perth 279 B9
Blairland N Ayrs 266 F6
Blairlinn N Lnrk 278 G5
Blairlogie Stirl 278 B6
Blairlomond Argyll 276 B3
Blairmore Argyll 276 E3
Blairmore Highld 306 D6
Blairnamarrow Moray 292 B4
Blairquhosh Stirl 277 E10
Blair's Ferry Argyll 275 G10
Blairskaith E Dunb 277 F11
Blaisdon Glos 80 B2
Blaise Hamlet Bristol 60 D5
Blake End Essex 106 G4
Blakebrook Worcs 116 B6
Blakedown Worcs 117 B7
Blakelands M Keynes 103 C7
Blakelaw Borders 263 C7

Blakelaw T & W 242 D6
Blakeley Staffs 133 E7
Blakeley Lane Staffs 169 F7
Blakelow E Ches 167 E11
Blakemere Hereford 97 C7
Blakenall Heath W Mid 133 C10
Blakeney Glos 79 D11
Blakeney Norf 177 E8
Blakenhall E Ches 168 F2
Blakenhall W Mid 133 D8
Blakeshall Worcs 132 G6
Blakesley Northants 120 G2
Blanchland Northumb 241 G11
Bland Hill N Yorks 205 C10
Blandford Camp Dorset 30 F6
Blandford Forum Dorset 30 F5
Blandford St Mary Dorset 30 F5
Blandy Highld 308 D6
Blanefield Stirl 277 F11
Blanerne Borders 272 D6
Blank Bank Staffs 168 F4
Blankney Lincs 173 C9
Blantyre S Lnrk 268 D3
Blar a'Chaorainn Highld 290 G3
Blaran Argyll 275 B9
Blarghour Argyll 275 B10
Blarmachfoldach Highld 290 G2
Blarnalearoch Highld 307 K6
Blasford Hill Essex 88 C2
Blashford Hants 31 F11
Blaston Leics 136 D6
Blatchbridge Som 45 D9
Blatherwycke Northants 137 D9
Blawith Cumb 210 B5
Blaxhall Suff 127 F7
Blaxton S Yorks 199 G7
Blaydon T & W 242 E5
Blaydon Burn T & W 242 E5
Blaydon Haughs T & W 242 E5
Bleach Green Cumb 219 B9
Bleach Green Suff 126 B4
Bleadney Som 44 D3
Bleadon N Som 43 B10
Bleak Acre Hereford 98 B2
Bleak Hall M Keynes 103 D7
Bleak Hey Nook Gtr Man 196 F4
Bleak Hill Hants 31 E10
Blean Kent 70 G6
Bleasby Lincs 189 E10
Bleasby Notts 172 F2
Bleasby Moor Lincs 189 E10
Bleasdale Lancs 203 D7
Bleatarn Cumb 222 C4
Blebocraigs Fife 287 F8
Bleddfa Powys 114 D4
Bledington Glos 100 G4
Bledlow Bucks 84 E3
Bledlow Ridge Bucks 84 F3
Bleet Wilts 45 B11
Blegbie E Loth 271 C9
Blegbury Devon 24 B2
Blencarn Cumb 231 E8
Blencogo Cumb 229 B9
Blendworth Hants 34 E2
Blenheim Oxon 83 D9
Blenheim Oxon 83 E9
Blenheim Park Norf 158 C6
Blenkinsopp Hall Northumb 240 E5
Blennerhasset Cumb 229 C9
Blervie Castle Moray 301 D10
Bletchingdon Oxon 83 B8
Bletchingley Sur 51 C10
Bletchley M Keynes 103 E7
Bletchley Shrops 150 C2
Bletherston Pembs 91 G11
Bletsoe Beds 121 F10
Blewbury Oxon 64 B4
Bliby Kent 54 F4
Blickling Norf 160 D3
Blidworth Notts 171 D9
Blidworth Bottoms Notts 171 E9
Blidworth Dale Notts 171 E9
Blindburn Northumb 263 G8
Blindcrake Cumb 229 E8
Blindley Heath Sur 51 D11
Blindmoor Som 28 E3
Blingery Highld 310 E7
Blisland Corn 11 G8
Bliss Gate Worcs 116 C4
Blissford Hants 31 E11
Blisworth Northants 120 G4
Blithbury Staffs 151 E11
Blitterlees Cumb 238 G4
Blo' Norton Norf 125 B10
Blockley Glos 100 D3
Blofield Norf 142 B6
Blofield Heath Norf 160 G6
Bloodman's Corner Suff 143 D10
Bloomfield Bath 45 B7
Bloomfield Bath 61 G8
Bloomfield Borders 262 E3
Bloomfield W Mid 133 E9
Bloomsbury London 67 C10
Blore Staffs 150 C4
Blore Staffs 169 F10
Bloreheath Staffs 150 B4
Blossomfield W Mid 118 B2
Blount's Green Staffs 151 C11
Blowick Mers 193 D11
Blowinghouse Corn 4 E4
Bloxham Oxon 101 D8
Bloxholm Lincs 173 E9
Bloxwich W Mid 133 C9
Bloxworth Dorset 18 C3
Blubberhouses N Yorks 205 B9
Blue Anchor Corn 5 D8
Blue Anchor Som 42 E4
Blue Anchor Swansea 56 B4
Blue Bell Hill Kent 69 G8
Blue Hill Herts 104 G5
Blue Row Essex 89 C8
Blue Town Kent 70 D2
Blue Vein Wilts 61 F10
Bluebell Telford 149 G11
Bluecairn Borders 271 G10
Bluetown Kent 54 B2
Bluewater Kent 68 E5
Blughasary Highld 307 J6
Blundellsands Mers 182 B4
Blundeston Suff 143 D10
Blundies Staffs 132 F6
Blunham C Beds 122 G3
Blunsdon St Andrew Swindon 62 B6
Bluntington Worcs 117 C7
Bluntisham Cambs 123 C7
Blunts Corn 6 C6
Blunt's Green Warks 118 D2
Blurton Stoke 168 G5
Blyborough Lincs 188 C6
Blyford Suff 127 B8
Blymhill Staffs 150 G6
Blymhill Lawns Staffs 150 G6
Blyth Borders 270 F2
Blyth Northumb 253 G8
Blyth Notts 187 D10
Blyth Bridge Borders 270 F2
Blyth End Warks 134 E4
Blythburgh Suff 127 B9
Blythe Borders 271 F11
Blythe Bridge Staffs 169 G7
Blythe Marsh Staffs 169 G7
Blythswood Renfs 267 B10
Blyton Lincs 188 C5
Boarhills Fife 287 F9
Boarhunt Hants 33 F10
Boars Hill Oxon 83 E7
Boarsgreave Lancs 195 C10
Boarshead E Sus 52 G4
Boarstall Bucks 83 C10
Boasley Cross Devon 12 C5
Boat of Garten Highld 291 B11
Boath Highld 300 B5
Bobbing Kent 69 F11
Bobbington Staffs 132 E6
Bobbingworth Essex 87 D8
Bobby Hill Suff 125 C10
Boblainy Highld 300 F4
Bocaddon Corn 6 D3
Bochastle Stirl 285 G10
Bockhanger Kent 54 E4
Bocking Essex 106 G5
Bocking Churchstreet Essex 106 F5
Bocking's Elm Essex 89 B11
Bockleton Worcs 115 E11
Bockmer End Bucks 65 B10
Bocombe Devon 24 C5
Bodantionail Highld 299 B7
Boddam Aberds 303 E11
Boddam Shetland 313 M5
Bodden Som 44 E6
Boddington Glos 99 F7
Bodedern Anglesey 178 E4
Bodellick Corn 10 G5
Bodelva Corn 5 E11
Bodelwyddan Denb 181 F8
Bodenham Hereford 115 G10
Bodenham Wilts 31 B11
Bodenham Bank Hereford 98 E2
Bodenham Moor Hereford 115 G10
Bodermid Gwyn 144 D3
Bodewryd Anglesey 178 C5
Bodfari Denb 181 G9
Bodffordd Anglesey 178 F6
Bodham Norf 177 E10
Bodiam E Sus 38 B3
Bodicote Oxon 101 D9
Bodiechell Aberds 303 E7
Bodieve Corn 10 G5
Bodiggo Corn 5 D10
Bodilly Corn 2 C5
Bodinnick Corn 6 E2
Bodle Street Green E Sus 23 C11
Bodley Devon 41 D7
Bodmin Corn 5 B11
Bodmiscombe Devon 27 F10
Bodney Norf 140 D6
Bodorgan Anglesey 162 B5
Bodsham Kent 54 D6
Boduan Gwyn 144 B6
Boduel Corn 6 C4
Bodwen Corn 5 C10
Bodymoor Heath Warks 134 D4
Bofarnel Corn 6 C2
Bogallan Highld 300 D6
Bogbrae Aberds 303 F10
Bogend Borders 272 F5
Bogend Notts 171 F7
Bogend S Ayrs 257 C9
Bogentory Aberds 293 C9
Boghall Midloth 270 B4
Boghall W Loth 269 B9
Boghead Aberds 293 D8
Boghead S Lnrk 268 G5
Bogmoor Moray 302 C3
Bogniebrae Aberds 302 E5
Bogniebrae Aberds 302 E6
Bognor Regis W Sus 22 D6
Bograxie Aberds 293 B9
Bogs Aberds 302 G5
Bogs Bank Borders 270 E3
Bogside N Lnrk 268 E6
Bogthorn W Yorks 204 F6
Bogton Aberds 302 D6
Bogtown Aberds 302 C5
Bogue Dumfries 246 G4
Bohemia E Sus 38 E4
Bohemia Wilts 32 D2
Bohenie Highld 290 E4
Bohetherick Corn 7 B8
Bohortha Corn 3 C9
Bohuntine Highld 290 E4
Bohuntinville Highld 290 E4
Boirseam W Isles 296 C6
Bojewyan Corn 1 C3
Bokiddick Corn 5 C11
Bolahaul Fm Carms 74 B6
Bolam Durham 233 G9
Bolam Northumb 252 G3
Bolam West Houses Northumb 252 G3
Bolas Heath Telford 150 E3
Bolberry Devon 9 G8
Bold Heath Mers 183 D8
Boldmere W Mid 134 E2
Boldon T & W 243 E9
Boldon Colliery T & W 243 E8
Boldre Hants 20 B2
Boldron Durham 223 C10
Bole Notts 188 D3
Bole Hill Derbys 186 G4
Bolehall Staffs 134 C4
Bolehill Derbys 170 E3
Bolehill Derbys 186 G6
Bolehill S Yorks 186 E5
Boleigh Corn 1 D4
Bolenowe Corn 2 B5
Boleside Borders 261 C11
Boley Park Staffs 134 B2
Bolham Devon 27 E7
Bolham Notts 188 E2
Bolham Water Devon 27 E11
Bolholt Gtr Man 195 E9
Bolingey Corn 4 E5
Bolitho Corn 2 C5
Bollihope Durham 232 E6
Bollington E Ches 184 F6
Bollington Cross E Ches 184 F6
Bolney W Sus 36 C3
Bolnhurst Beds 121 F11
Bolnore W Sus 36 C4
Bolshan Angus 287 B10
Bolsover Derbys 187 G7
Bolsterstone S Yorks 186 B3
Bolstone Hereford 97 E11
Boltby N Yorks 215 B9
Bolter End Bucks 84 G3
Bolton Cumb 231 G8
Bolton E Loth 281 G10
Bolton E Yorks 207 C11
Bolton Gtr Man 195 F8
Bolton Northumb 264 G4
Bolton W Yorks 205 F9
Bolton Abbey N Yorks 205 C7
Bolton Bridge N Yorks 205 C7
Bolton-by-Bowland Lancs 203 D11
Bolton Green Lancs 194 D5
Bolton Houses Lancs 202 G4
Bolton-le-Sands Lancs 211 F9
Bolton Low Houses Cumb 229 C10
Bolton New Houses Cumb 229 C10
Bolton-on-Swale N Yorks 224 F5
Bolton Percy N Yorks 206 E6
Bolton Town End Lancs 211 F9
Bolton upon Dearne S Yorks 198 G3
Bolton Wood Lane Cumb 229 C11
Bolton Woods W Yorks 205 F9
Boltonfellend Cumb 239 D11
Boltongate Cumb 229 C10
Boltshope Park Durham 232 B4
Bolventor Corn 11 F9
Bomarsund Northumb 253 G7
Bombie Dumfries 237 D9
Bomby Cumb 221 B10
Bomere Heath Shrops 149 F9
Bon-y-maen Swansea 57 B7
Bonaly Edin 270 B4
Bonar Bridge Highld 309 K6
Bonawe Argyll 284 D4
Bonby N Lincs 200 D4
Boncath Pembs 92 D4
Bonchester Bridge Borders 262 G3
Bonchurch I o W 21 F7
Bond End Staffs 152 F2
Bondend Glos 80 B5
Bondleigh Devon 25 G11
Bondman Hays Leics 135 B9
Bonds Lancs 202 E5
Bondstones Devon 25 F9
Bonehill Devon 13 F10
Bonehill Staffs 134 C3
Bo'ness Falk 279 E9
Bonhill W Dunb 277 F7
Boningale Shrops 132 C6
Bonjedward Borders 262 E5
Bonkle N Lnrk 268 D6
Bonnavoulin Highld 289 D7
Bonning Gate Cumb 221 F9
Bonnington Borders 261 B7
Bonnington Edin 270 B2
Bonnington Kent 54 F5
Bonnybank Fife 287 G7
Bonnybridge Falk 278 E6
Bonnykelly Aberds 303 D8
Bonnyrigg and Lasswade Midloth 270 B6
Bonnyton Aberds 302 F6
Bonnyton Angus 287 B10
Bonnyton Angus 287 D7
Bonnyton E Ayrs 257 B10
Bonsall Derbys 170 D3
Bonskeid House Perth 291 G10
Bonson Som 43 E8
Bont Mon 78 B5
Bont-Dolgadfan Powys 129 C7
Bont Fawr Carms 94 F4
Bont goch = Elerch Ceredig 128 F3
Bont-newydd Conwy 181 G8
Bont Newydd Gwyn 146 E5
Bont Newydd Gwyn 164 G2
Bontddu Gwyn 146 F3
Bonthorpe Lincs 191 G7
Bontnewydd Ceredig 112 D2
Bontnewydd Gwyn 163 D7
Bontuchel Denb 165 D9
Bonvilston = Tresimwn V Glam 58 E5
Boode Devon 40 F4
Booker Bucks 84 G4
Bookham Dorset 30 G2
Booleybank Shrops 149 D11
Boon Borders 271 F11
Boon Hill Staffs 168 E4
Boorley Green Hants 33 E8
Boosbeck Redcar 226 B3
Boose's Green Essex 106 E6
Boot Cumb 220 E3
Boot Street Suff 108 B4
Booth Staffs 151 D10
Booth W Yorks 196 B4
Booth Bank E Ches 184 D2
Booth Bridge Lancs 204 D4
Booth Green E Ches 184 E6
Booth Wood W Yorks 196 D4
Boothby Graffoe Lincs 173 D7
Boothby Pagnell Lincs 155 C9
Boothen Stoke 168 G5
Boothferry E Yorks 199 B8
Boothgate Derbys 170 F5
Boothroyd W Yorks 197 C8
Boothsdale W Ches 167 B8
Boothstown Gtr Man 195 G8
Boothtown W Yorks 196 B5
Boothville Northants 120 E5
Bootle Cumb 210 B2
Bootle Mers 182 B4
Booton Norf 160 E2
Boots Green W Ches 184 G3
Booze N Yorks 223 E10
Boquhan Stirl 277 D10
Boquio Corn 2 C5
Boraston Shrops 116 D2
Boraston Dale Shrops 116 C2
Borden Kent 69 G11
Borden W Sus 34 C4
Border Cumb 238 G5
Bordesley W Mid 133 F11
Bordesley Green W Mid 134 F2
Bordlands Borders 270 F3
Bordley N Yorks 213 G8
Bordon Hants 49 F10
Bordon Camp Hants 49 F9
Boreham Essex 88 D3
Boreham Wilts 45 E11
Boreham Street E Sus 23 C11
Borehamwood Herts 85 F11
Boreland Dumfries 236 C5
Boreland Dumfries 248 E5
Boreland Fife 280 C6
Boreland Stirl 285 D9
Boreland of Southwick Dumfries 237 C11
Boreley Worcs 116 D6
Borestone Stirl 278 C5
Borgh W Isles 296 C5
Borgh W Isles 297 L2
Borghasdal W Isles 296 C6
Borghastan W Isles 304 D4
Borgie Highld 308 D6
Borgue Dumfries 237 E8
Borgue Highld 311 G5
Borley Essex 106 C6
Borley Green Essex 106 C6
Borley Green Suff 125 E9
Bornais W Isles 297 J3
Bornesketaig Highld 298 B3
Borness Dumfries 237 E8
Borough Scilly 1 G3
Borough Green Kent 52 B6
Borough Marsh Wokingham 65 D9
Borough Park Staffs 134 B4
Borough Post Som 28 C4
Boroughbridge N Yorks 215 F7
Borras Wrex 166 E4
Borras Head Wrex 166 E5
Borreraig Highld 296 F7
Borrobol Lodge Highld 311 G2
Borrodale Highld 297 G7
Borrohill Aberds 303 D9
Borrowash Derbys 153 C8
Borrowby N Yorks 215 B8
Borrowby N Yorks 226 B5
Borrowdale Cumb 220 C5
Borrowfield Aberds 293 D10
Borrowston Highld 310 E7
Borrowstoun Mains Falk 279 E9
Borstal Medway 69 F8
Borth = Y Borth Ceredig 128 E2
Borth-y-Gest Gwyn 145 B11
Borthwick Midloth 271 D7
Borthwickbrae Borders 261 G10
Borthwickshiels Borders 261 F10
Borve Highld 298 E4
Borve Lodge W Isles 305 J2
Borwick Lancs 211 E10
Borwick Rails Cumb 210 D3
Bosavern Corn 1 C3
Bosbury Hereford 98 C3
Boscadjack Corn 2 C5
Boscastle Corn 11 C8
Boscean Corn 1 C3
Boscombe Bmouth 19 C8
Boscombe Wilts 47 F8
Boscomoor Staffs 151 G8
Boscoppa Corn 5 E10
Boscreege Corn 2 C3
Bosham W Sus 22 C4
Bosham Hoe W Sus 22 C4
Bosherston Pembs 73 G7
Boskednan Corn 1 C4
Boskenna Corn 1 E4
Bosleake Corn 4 G3
Bosley E Ches 168 B6
Boslowick Corn 3 C7
Boslymon Corn 5 C11
Bosoughan Corn 5 C7
Bosporthennis Corn 1 B4
Bossall N Yorks 216 G4
Bossiney Corn 11 D7
Bossingham Kent 54 D6
Bossington Hants 47 G10
Bossington Kent 55 B8
Bossington Som 41 D11
Bostadh W Isles 304 D3
Bostock Green W Ches 167 B11
Boston Lincs 174 G4
Boston Long Hedges Lincs 174 F5
Boston Spa W Yorks 206 D4
Boston West Lincs 174 F3
Boswednack Corn 1 B4
Boswin Corn 2 C5
Boswinger Corn 5 G9
Boswyn Corn 2 B5
Botallack Corn 1 C3
Botany Bay London 86 F3
Botany Bay Mon 79 E8
Botcherby Cumb 239 F10
Botcheston Leics 135 B9
Botesdale Suff 125 B10
Bothal Northumb 252 F6
Bothampstead W Berks 64 D4
Bothamsall Notts 187 G11
Bothel Cumb 229 D9
Bothenhampton Dorset 16 C5
Bothwell S Lnrk 268 D4
Bothy Highld 290 F4
Botley Bucks 85 E7
Botley Hants 33 E8
Botley Oxon 83 D7
Botloe's Green Glos 98 F4
Botolph Claydon Bucks 102 G4
Botolphs W Sus 35 F11
Botstacks Highld 300 C4
Botternell Corn 11 G11
Bottesford Leics 154 B6
Bottesford N Lincs 199 F11
Bottisham Cambs 123 E10
Bottlesford Wilts 46 B6
Bottom Boat W Yorks 197 C11
Bottom House Staffs 169 E8
Bottom o' th' Moor Gtr Man 195 E7
Bottom of Hutton Lancs 194 B3
Bottom Pond Kent 53 B11
Bottomcraig Fife 287 E7
Bottomley W Yorks 196 D5
Bottoms Corn 1 E3
Botreaux Mill Devon 26 B4
Botts Green Warks 134 E4
Botusfleming Corn 7 C8
Botwnnog Gwyn 144 C5
Bough Beech Kent 52 D3
Boughrood Powys 96 D2
Boughrood Brest Powys 96 D2
Boughspring Glos 79 F9
Boughton Lincs 173 F10
Boughton Norf 140 C3
Boughton Northants 120 D5
Boughton Notts 171 B11
Boughton W Ches 166 B6
Boughton Aluph Kent 54 D4
Boughton Corner Kent 54 D4
Boughton Green Kent 53 C9
Boughton Heath W Ches 166 B6
Boughton Lees Kent 54 D4
Boughton Malherbe Kent 53 D11
Boughton Monchelsea Kent 53 C9
Boughton Street Kent 54 B5
Bougton End C Beds 103 D9
Boulby Redcar 226 B5
Bould Oxon 100 G4
Boulden Shrops 131 F10
Boulder Clough W Yorks 196 C4
Bouldnor I o W 20 D3
Bouldon Shrops 131 F10
Boulmer Northumb 265 G7
Boulsdon Glos 98 G4
Boulston Pembs 73 C7
Boultenstone Aberds 292 B6
Boultham Lincs 173 B7
Boultham Moor Lincs 173 B7
Boulton Derbys 153 C7
Boulton Moor Derbys 153 C7
Boundary Leics 152 F6
Boundary Staffs 169 G7
Boundstone Sur 49 E10
Bountis Thorne Devon 24 D5
Bourn Cambs 122 F6
Bournbrook W Mid 133 G10
Bourne Lincs 155 E11
Bourne N Som 44 B3
Bourne End Beds 121 F10
Bourne End Bucks 65 B11
Bourne End C Beds 103 C9
Bourne End Herts 85 D8
Bourne Vale W Mid 133 D11
Bourne Valley Poole 19 C7
Bournemouth Bmouth 19 C7
Bournes Green Glos 80 E6
Bournes Green Sthend 70 B2
Bournes Green Worcs 117 C8
Bournheath Worcs 117 C9
Bournmoor Durham 243 G8
Bournside Glos 99 G8
Bournstream Glos 80 G2
Bournville W Mid 133 G10
Bourton Bucks 102 E4
Bourton Dorset 45 G9
Bourton N Som 59 G11
Bourton Oxon 63 B8
Bourton Shrops 131 D11
Bourton Wilts 62 G4
Bourton on Dunsmore Warks 119 C8
Bourton-on-the-Hill Glos 100 E3
Bourton-on-the-Water Glos 100 G3
Bourtreehill N Ayrs 257 B8
Bousd Argyll 288 C4
Bousta Shetland 313 H4
Boustead Hill Cumb 239 F7
Bouth Cumb 210 B6
Bouthwaite N Yorks 214 E2
Bouts Worcs 117 F10
Bovain Stirl 285 D9
Boveney Bucks 66 D2
Boveridge Dorset 31 E9
Boverton V Glam 58 F3
Bovey Tracey Devon 14 F2
Bovingdon Herts 85 E8
Bovingdon Green Bucks 65 B10
Bovingdon Green Herts 85 E8
Bovinger Essex 87 D8
Bovington Camp Dorset 18 D2
Bow Borders 271 G9
Bow Devon 8 D6
Bow Devon 26 G2
Bow Orkney 314 G3
Bow Oxon 82 G4
Bow Brickhill M Keynes 103 E8
Bow Broom S Yorks 187 B7
Bow Common London 67 C11
Bow of Fife Fife 287 F7
Bow Street Ceredig 128 G2
Bow Street Norf 141 D10
Bowbank Durham 232 G4
Bowbeck Suff 125 B8
Bowbridge Glos 80 E5
Bowbrook Shrops 149 G9
Bowburn Durham 234 D2
Bowcombe I o W 20 D5
Bowd Devon 15 C8
Bowden Borders 262 C3
Bowden Devon 8 F6
Bowden Dorset 30 C3
Bowden Hill Wilts 62 F2
Bowderdale Cumb 222 E3
Bowdon Gtr Man 184 D3
Bower Highld 310 C6
Bower Northumb 251 G7
Bower Ashton Bristol 60 E5
Bower Heath Herts 85 B10
Bower Hinton Som 29 D7
Bower House Tye Suff 107 C9
Bowerchalke Wilts 31 C8
Bowerhill Wilts 62 G2
Bowerhope Borders 261 E7
Bowermadden Highld 310 C6
Bowers Staffs 150 B6
Bowers Gifford Essex 69 B9
Bowershall Fife 279 C11
Bowertower Highld 310 C6
Bowes Durham 223 C9
Bowes Park London 86 G4
Bowgreave Lancs 202 E5
Bowgreen Gtr Man 184 D3
Bowhill Borders 261 D10
Bowhill Fife 280 B4
Bowhouse Dumfries 238 D2
Bowhousebog or Liquo N Lnrk 269 D7
Bowing Park Mers 182 D6
Bowismiln Borders 262 E2
Bowithick Corn 11 E9
Bowker's Green Lancs 194 G2
Bowland Bridge Cumb 211 B8
Bowldown Wilts 62 D2
Bowlee Gtr Man 195 F10
Bowlees Durham 232 F4
Bowler's Town E Sus 38 C6
Bowley Hereford 115 G10
Bowley Lane Hereford 98 C3
Bowley Town Hereford 115 G10
Bowlhead Green Sur 50 F2
Bowling W Dunb 277 G9
Bowling W Yorks 205 G9
Bowling Alley Hants 49 D9
Bowling Bank Wrex 166 F5
Bowling Green Corn 5 D10
Bowling Green Corn 12 G3
Bowling Green Glos 81 E8
Bowling Green Hants 19 B11
Bowling Green Shrops 150 D2
Bowling Green W Mid 133 F8
Bowling Green Worcs 116 G6
Bowlish Som 44 E6
Bowmans Kent 68 E4
Bowmanstead Cumb 220 F6
Bowmore Argyll 254 B4
Bowness-on-Solway Cumb 238 E6
Bowness-on-Windermere Cumb 221 F8
Bowridge Hill Dorset 30 B4
Bowrie-fauld Angus 287 C9
Bowsden Northumb 273 G9
Bowsey Hill Windsor 65 C10
Bowshank Borders 271 G9
Bowside Lodge Highld 310 C2
Bowston Cumb 221 F9
Bowthorpe Norf 142 B3
Bowyer's Common Hants 34 B3
Box Glos 80 E5
Box Wilts 61 F10
Box End Beds 103 B10
Box Hill Sur 51 C7
Box Hill Wilts 61 F10
Box Trees W Mid 118 C2
Boxbush Glos 80 C2
Boxbush Glos 98 G3
Boxford Suff 107 C9
Boxford W Berks 64 E2
Boxgrove W Sus 22 B6
Boxley Kent 53 B9
Boxmoor Herts 85 D9
Box's Shop Corn 24 G2
Boxted Essex 107 E9
Boxted Suff 124 G6
Boxted Cross Essex 107 E10
Boxted Heath Essex 107 E10
Boxwell Glos 80 G4
Boxworth Cambs 122 E6
Boxworth End Cambs 123 D7
Boyatt Wood Hants 32 C6
Boyden End Suff 124 F4
Boyden Gate Kent 71 F8
Boyland Common Norf 141 G11
Boylestone Derbys 152 B3
Boylestonfield Derbys 152 B3
Boyn Hill Windsor 65 C11
Boyndie Aberds 302 C6
Boynton E Yorks 218 F2
Boys Hill Dorset 29 E11
Boys Village V Glam 58 F4
Boysack Angus 287 C10
Boysack Angus 287 C9
Boythorpe Derbys 186 G5
Boyton Corn 12 C2
Boyton Suff 109 B7
Boyton Wilts 46 F3
Boyton Cross Essex 87 D10
Boyton End Essex 106 E2
Boyton End Suff 106 C4
Bozeat Northants 121 F8
Bozen Green Herts 105 F8
Brù W Isles 304 D5
Braaid I o M 192 E4
Braal Castle Highld 310 C5
Brabling Green Suff 126 E5
Brabourne Kent 54 E5
Brabourne Lees Kent 54 E5
Brabster Highld 310 C7
Bracadale Highld 294 B5
Bracara Highld 295 F9
Braceborough Lincs 155 G11
Bracebridge Lincs 173 B7
Bracebridge Heath Lincs 173 B7
Bracebridge Low Fields Lincs 173 B7
Braceby Lincs 155 B10
Bracewell Lancs 204 D3
Bracken Bank W Yorks 204 F6
Bracken Hill W Yorks 197 C7
Bracken Park W Yorks 206 E3
Brackenber Cumb 222 B4
Brackenbottom N Yorks 212 E6
Brackenfield Derbys 170 D5
Brackenhall W Yorks 197 D7
Brackenlands Cumb 229 B11
Brackenthwaite Cumb 229 B11
Brackenthwaite Cumb 229 G9
Brackenthwaite N Yorks 205 C11
Brackla = Bragle Bridgend 58 D2
Bracklamore Aberds 303 D8
Bracklesham W Sus 22 D4
Brackletter Highld 290 E3
Brackley Argyll 255 C8
Brackley Northants 101 D11
Brackloch Highld 307 G6
Bracknell Brack 65 F11
Braco Perth 286 G2
Braco Castle Perth 286 F2
Braco Park Aberds 303 C9
Bracobrae Moray 302 D5
Bracon N Lincs 199 F9
Bracon Ash Norf 142 D3
Bracorina Highld 295 F9
Bradaford Devon 12 C3
Bradbourne Derbys 170 E2
Bradbury Durham 234 F2
Bradda I o M 192 F2
Bradden Northants 102 B2
Braddock Corn 6 C3
Braddocks Hay Staffs 168 D5
Bradeley Stoke 168 E5
Bradeley Green E Ches 167 G8
Bradenham Bucks 84 F4
Bradenham Norf 141 B8
Bradenstoke Wilts 62 D4
Brades Village W Mid 133 E9
Bradfield Devon 27 F9
Bradfield Essex 108 E2
Bradfield Norf 160 C5
Bradfield W Berks 64 E6
Bradfield Combust Suff 125 F7
Bradfield Green E Ches 167 D11
Bradfield Heath Essex 108 F2
Bradfield St Clare Suff 125 F8
Bradfield St George Suff 125 E8
Bradford Corn 11 F8
Bradford Derbys 170 C2
Bradford Devon 24 F6
Bradford Gtr Man 184 B5
Bradford Northumb 264 C5
Bradford W Yorks 205 G9
Bradford Abbas Dorset 29 E9
Bradford Leigh Wilts 61 G10
Bradford-on-Avon Wilts 61 G10
Bradford-on-Tone Som 27 C11
Bradford Peverell Dorset 17 C9
Bradgate S Yorks 186 C6
Bradiford Devon 40 G5
Brading I o W 21 D8
Bradley Derbys 170 F2
Bradley Glos 80 G3
Bradley Hants 48 E6
Bradley NE Lincs 201 F8
Bradley Staffs 151 F7
Bradley W Mid 133 D8
Bradley W Yorks 197 C7
Bradley Wrex 166 E4
Bradley Cross Som 44 C3
Bradley Fold Gtr Man 195 F9
Bradley Green Glos 80 G2
Bradley Green Som 43 F9
Bradley Green W Ches 167 F8
Bradley Green Warks 134 C5
Bradley Green Worcs 117 E9
Bradley in the Moors Staffs 169 G9
Bradley Mills W Yorks 197 D7
Bradley Mount E Ches 184 F6
Bradley Stoke S Glos 60 C6
Bradlow Hereford 98 D4
Bradmore Notts 153 C11
Bradmore W Mid 133 D7
Bradney Shrops 132 D5
Bradney Som 43 F10
Bradninch Devon 27 G8
Bradnocks Marsh W Mid 118 B4
Bradnop Staffs 169 D8
Bradnor Green Hereford 114 F5
Bradpole Dorset 16 C5
Bradshaw Gtr Man 195 E8
Bradshaw Staffs 168 D6
Bradshaw W Yorks 196 E5
Bradshaw W Yorks 205 G7
Bradstone Devon 12 E3
Bradville M Keynes 102 C6
Bradwall Green E Ches 168 C3
Bradway S Yorks 186 E4
Bradwell Derbys 185 E11
Bradwell Devon 40 E3
Bradwell Essex 106 G6
Bradwell M Keynes 102 D6
Bradwell Norf 143 C10
Bradwell Staffs 168 F4
Bradwell Common M Keynes 102 D6
Bradwell Grove Oxon 82 D2
Bradwell Hills Derbys 185 E11
Bradwell on Sea Essex 89 D8
Bradwell Waterside Essex 89 D7
Bradworthy Devon 24 E4
Bradworthy Cross Devon 24 E4
Brae Dumfries 237 B10
Brae Highld 307 L3
Brae Highld 309 J4
Brae Shetland 312 G5
Brae of Achnahaird Highld 307 H5
Brae of Boquhapple Stirl 285 G10
Brae Roy Lodge Highld 290 D5
Braeantra Highld 300 B5
Braebuster Orkney 314 F5
Braedownie Angus 292 F4
Braeface Falk 278 E5
Braefield Highld 300 F4
Braefindon Highld 300 D6
Braegrum Perth 286 E4
Braehead Dumfries 236 D6
Braehead Orkney 314 B4
Braehead Orkney 314 F5
Braehead S Ayrs 257 E8
Braehead S Lnrk 259 C8
Braehead S Lnrk 267 D11
Braehead S Lnrk 269 E9
Braehead Stirl 278 C6
Braehead of Lunan Angus 287 B10
Braehoulland Shetland 312 F4
Braehour Highld 310 D4
Braehungie Highld 310 F5
Braeintra Highld 295 B10
Braelangwell Lodge Highld 309 K5
Braemar Aberds 292 D3
Braemore Highld 299 B11
Braemore Highld 310 F4
Braepark Edin 280 F3
Braes of Enzie Moray 302 D3
Braes of Ullapool Highld 307 K6
Braeside Invclyd 276 F4
Braeswick Orkney 314 C6
Braevallich Argyll 275 C10
Braewick Shetland 312 F4
Braewick Shetland 313 H5
Brafferton Darl 233 G11
Brafferton N Yorks 215 E8
Brafield-on-the-Green Northants 120 F6
Bragar W Isles 304 D4
Bragbury End Herts 104 G5
Bragenham Bucks 103 F8
Bragle = Brackla Bridgend 58 D2
Bragleenmore Argyll 289 G11
Braichmelyn Gwyn 163 B10
Braichyfedw Powys 129 E7
Braid Edin 280 G4
Braides Lancs 202 C4
Braidfauld Glasgow 268 C2
Braidley N Yorks 213 C10
Braids Argyll 255 C8
Braidwood S Lnrk 268 F6
Braigh Chalasaigh W Isles 296 D5
Braigo Argyll 274 G3
Brailsford Derbys 170 G3
Brailsford Green Derbys 170 G3
Braingortan Argyll 275 F11
Brain's Green Glos 79 D11
Brainshaugh Northumb 252 C6
Braintree Essex 106 G5
Braiseworth Suff 126 C2
Braishfield Hants 32 B5
Braiswick Essex 107 F9
Braithwaite Cumb 229 G10
Braithwaite S Yorks 198 E6
Braithwaite W Yorks 204 E6
Braithwell S Yorks 187 C8
Brakefield Green Norf 141 B10
Brakenhill W Yorks 198 D2
Bramber W Sus 35 E11
Bramblecombe Dorset 30 G3
Brambridge Hants 33 C7
Bramcote Notts 153 B10
Bramcote Warks 135 F8
Bramcote Hills Notts 153 B10
Bramcote Mains Warks 135 F8
Bramdean Hants 33 B10
Bramerton Norf 142 C5
Bramfield Herts 86 B3
Bramfield Suff 127 C7
Bramford Suff 108 B2
Bramford W Mid 133 E8
Bramhall Gtr Man 184 D5
Bramhall Moor Gtr Man 184 D6
Bramhall Park Gtr Man 184 D5
Bramham W Yorks 206 E4
Bramhope W Yorks 205 E11
Bramley Derbys 186 F6
Bramley Hants 48 B6
Bramley S Yorks 187 C7
Bramley Sur 50 D4
Bramley W Yorks 205 F10
Bramley Corner Hants 48 B6
Bramley Green Hants 49 B7
Bramley Head N Yorks 205 B8
Bramley Vale Derbys 171 B7
Bramling Kent 55 B8
Brampford Speke Devon 14 B4
Brampton Cambs 122 C4
Brampton Cumb 231 G9
Brampton Cumb 240 E2
Brampton Derbys 186 G5
Brampton Hereford 97 D8
Brampton Lincs 188 F4
Brampton Norf 160 E4
Brampton S Yorks 198 G2
Brampton Suff 143 G8
Brampton Abbotts Hereford 98 F2
Brampton Ash Northants 136 F5
Brampton Bryan Hereford 115 C7
Brampton en le Morthen S Yorks 187 D7
Brampton Park Cambs 122 C4
Brampton Street Suff 143 G8
Bramshall Staffs 151 C11
Bramshaw Hants 32 D3
Bramshill Hants 65 G8
Bramshott Hants 49 G10
Bramwell Som 28 B6
Bran End Essex 106 F3
Branatwatt Shetland 313 H4
Branault Highld 289 C7
Branbridges Kent 53 D7
Brancaster Norf 176 E3
Brancaster Staithe Norf 176 E3
Brancepeth Durham 233 D10
Branch End Northumb 242 E3
Branchill Moray 301 D10
Branchton Invclyd 276 F4
Brand End Lincs 174 F5
Brand Green Glos 98 F4
Brand Green Hereford 98 C5
Branderburgh Moray 302 B2
Brandesburton E Yorks 209 D8
Brandeston Suff 126 E4
Brandhill Shrops 115 B8
Brandis Corner Devon 24 G6
Brandish Street Som 42 D2
Brandiston Norf 160 E2
Brandlingill Cumb 229 F8
Brandon Durham 233 D10
Brandon Lincs 172 F6
Brandon Northumb 264 F2
Brandon Suff 140 F5
Brandon Warks 119 B8
Brandon Bank Cambs 140 F2
Brandon Creek Norf 140 E2
Brandon Parva Norf 141 B11
Brands Hill Windsor 66 D4
Brandsby N Yorks 215 E11
Brandwood Shrops 149 D9
Brandwood End W Mid 117 B11
Brandy Carr W Yorks 197 C10
Brandy Hole Essex 88 F4
Brandy Wharf Lincs 189 B8
Brandyquoy Orkney 314 G4
Brane Corn 1 D4
Branksome Darl 224 B5
Branksome Poole 18 C6
Branksome Park Poole 19 C7
Bransbury Hants 48 E2
Bransby Lincs 188 F5
Branscombe Devon 15 D9
Bransford Worcs 116 G5
Bransgore Hants 19 B9
Branshill Clack 279 C7
Bransholme Hull 209 G8
Branson's Cross Worcs 117 C11
Branston Leics 154 D6
Branston Lincs 173 B8
Branston Staffs 152 E4
Branston Booths Lincs 173 B9
Branstone I o W 21 E7
Bransty Cumb 219 B9
Brant Broughton Lincs 172 E6
Brantham Suff 108 E2
Branthwaite Cumb 229 D11
Branthwaite Cumb 229 G7
Branthwaite Edge Cumb 229 G7
Brantingham E Yorks 200 B2
Branton Northumb 264 F2
Branton S Yorks 198 G6
Branton Green N Yorks 215 G8
Branxholm Park Borders 261 G11
Branxholme Borders 261 G11
Branxton Northumb 263 B9
Brascote Leics 135 C8
Brassey Green W Ches 167 C8
Brassington Derbys 170 E2
Brasted Kent 52 C3
Brasted Chart Kent 52 C3
Brathens Aberds 293 D8
Bratoft Lincs 175 B7
Brattle Kent 54 G2
Brattleby Lincs 188 E6
Bratton Som 42 D2
Bratton Telford 150 G2
Bratton Wilts 46 C2
Bratton Clovelly Devon 12 C5
Bratton Fleming Devon 40 F6
Bratton Seymour Som 29 B11
Braughing Herts 105 F7
Braughing Friars Herts 105 G8
Braulen Lodge Highld 300 F2
Braunston Northants 119 D10
Braunston-in-Rutland Rutland 136 B6
Braunstone Leics 135 C11
Braunstone Town Leicester 135 C11
Braunton Devon 40 F3
Brawby N Yorks 216 D4
Brawith N Yorks 225 D10
Brawl Highld 310 C2
Brawlbin Highld 310 D4
Bray Windsor 66 D2
Bray Shop Corn 12 G2
Bray Wick Windsor 65 D11
Braybrooke Northants 136 G5
Braydon Side Wilts 62 B4
Brayford Devon 41 G7
Brayfordhill Devon 41 G7
Brays Grove Essex 87 D7
Braystones Cumb 219 D10
Brayswick Worcs 98 B6
Braythorn N Yorks 205 D10
Brayton N Yorks 207 G8
Braytown Dorset 18 D2
Braywoodside Windsor 65 D11
Brazacott Corn 11 C11
Brazenhill Staffs 151 E7
Brea Corn 4 G3
Breach Bath 60 G6
Breach Kent 69 F10
Breach W Sus 22 B3
Breachacha Castle Argyll 288 D3
Breachwood Green Herts 104 G2
Breacleit W Isles 304 E3
Bread Street Glos 80 D4
Breaden Heath Shrops 149 B8
Breadsall Derbys 153 B7
Breadsall Hilltop Derby 153 B7
Breadstone Glos 80 E2
Breage Corn 2 D4
Breakachy Highld 300 E4
Brealeys Devon 25 D8
Bream Glos 79 D10
Breamore Hants 31 D11
Bream's Meend Glos 79 D9
Brean Som 43 B9
Breanais W Isles 304 F1
Brearley W Yorks 196 B4
Brearton N Yorks 214 G6
Breascleit W Isles 304 E4
Breaston Derbys 153 C9
Brechfa Carms 93 E10
Brechin Angus 293 G7
Breck of Cruan Orkney 314 E3
Breckan Orkney 314 F2
Breckles Norf 141 E9
Breckrey Highld 298 C5
Brecks S Yorks 187 C7
Brecon Powys 95 F10
Bredbury Gtr Man 184 C6
Bredbury Green Gtr Man 184 C6
Brede E Sus 38 D4
Bredenbury Hereford 116 F2
Bredfield Suff 126 G5
Bredgar Kent 69 G11

Bredhurst Kent 69 G9
Bredicot Worcs 117 G8
Bredon Worcs 99 D8
Bredon's Hardwick
 Worcs 99 D8
Bredon's Norton Worcs 99 D8
Bredwardine Hereford 96 C6
Breedon on the Hill
 Leics 153 E8
Breeds Essex 87 C11
Breedy Butts Lancs 202 E2
Breibhig W Isles 297 M2
Breibhig W Isles 304 E6
Breich W Loth 269 C9
Breightmet Gtr Man 195 F8
Breighton E Yorks 207 G10
Breinton Hereford 97 D9
Breinton Common
 Hereford 97 C9
Breiwick Shetland 313 J6
Brelston Green
 Hereford 97 C11
Bremhill Wilts 62 E3
Bremhill Wick Wilts 62 E3
Bremirehoull Shetland 313 L6
Brenachoile Lodge
 Stirl 285 G8
Brenchley Kent 53 E7
Brenchoillie Argyll 284 G4
Brendon Devon 24 C5
Brendon Devon 24 F5
Brendon Devon 41 D9
Brenkley T & W 242 B6
Brent Corn 6 I4
Brent Eleigh Suff 107 B8
Brent Knoll Som 43 C10
Brent Mill Devon 8 D3
Brent Pelham Herts 105 E8
Brentford London 67 D7
Brentford End London 67 D7
Brentingby Leics 154 F5
Brentry Bristol 60 D5
Brentwood Essex 87 G9
Brenzett Kent 39 B8
Brenzett Green Kent 39 B8
Brereton Staffs 151 F11
Brereton Cross Staffs 151 F11
Brereton Green
 E Ches 168 C3
Brereton Heath E Ches 168 C4
Breretonhill Staffs 151 F11
Bressingham Norf 141 G11
Bressingham
 Common Norf 141 G11
Bretby Derbys 152 E5
Bretford Warks 119 B8
Bretforton Worcs 99 C11
Bretherdale Head
 Cumb 221 E11
Bretherton Lancs 194 C3
Brettabister Shetland 313 H6
Brettenham Norf 141 G8
Brettenham Suff 125 G9
Bretton Derbys 186 F2
Bretton Flint 166 C5
Bretton P'boro 138 C3
Brewer Street Sur 51 C10
Brewer's End Essex 105 G11
Brewers Green Norf 142 G2
Brewlands Bridge
 Angus 292 G3
Brewood Staffs 133 B7
Briach Moray 301 D10
Briants Puddle Dorset 18 C2
Briar Hill Northants 120 F4
Brick End Essex 105 F11
Brick House End Essex 105 F9
Brick Houses S Yorks 186 E4
Brick-kiln End Notts 171 D9
Brickendon Herts 86 D4
Bricket Wood Herts 85 E10
Brickfields Worcs 117 F7
Brickhill Beds 121 G11
Brickhouses E Ches 168 C3
Brickkiln Green Essex 106 E4
Bricklehampton Worcs 99 C9
Bride I o M 192 B5
Bridekirk Cumb 229 E8
Bridell Pembs 92 C3
Bridestowe Devon 12 D6
Brideswell Aberds 302 F5
Bridford Devon 14 D2
Bridfordmills Devon 14 D2
Bridge Corn 2 D6
Bridge Corn 4 G3
Bridge Kent 55 C7
Bridge Som 28 F5
Bridge Ball Devon 41 D8
Bridge End Beds 121 G10
Bridge End Cumb 230 B3
Bridge End Devon 8 F3
Bridge End Durham 232 D6
Bridge End Essex 106 E3
Bridge End Flint 166 D4
Bridge End Hereford 98 B2
Bridge End Lincs 173 G8
Bridge End Northumb 241 D10
Bridge End Northumb 241 E10
Bridge End Warks 118 E5
Brelston Green Shetland 313 K5
Bridge-End Shetland 313 K5
Bridge End Sur 50 B5
Bridge End Warks 118 E5
Bridge End Works 98 E6
Bridge Green Essex 105 D9
Bridge Green Norf 142 G2
Bridge Hewick N Yorks 214 E6
Bridge Ho W Loth 254 B4
Bridge of Alford Aberds 293 B7
Bridge of Allan Stirl 278 B5
Bridge of Avon Moray 301 G11
Bridge of Avon Moray 301 G11
Bridge of Awe Argyll 284 E4
Bridge of Balgie Perth 285 C9
Bridge of Cally Perth 286 B5
Bridge of Canny Aberds 293 D8
Bridge of Craigisla
 Angus 286 B6
Bridge of Dee Dumfries 237 D9
Bridge of Don
 Aberdeen 293 B11
Bridge of Dun Angus 287 B10
Bridge of Dye Aberds 293 E8
Bridge of Earn Perth 286 F5
Bridge of Ericht Perth 285 B8
Bridge of Feugh Aberds 293 D9
Bridge of Forss Highld 310 C4
Bridge of Gairn Aberds 292 D5
Bridge of Gaur Perth 285 B9
Bridge of Lyon Perth 285 C10
Bridge of Muchalls
 Aberds 293 D10
Bridge of Muick Aberds 292 D5
Bridge of Oich Highld 290 C5
Bridge of Orchy Argyll 284 D6
Bridge of Waith Orkney 314 E2
Bridge of Walls
 Shetland 313 H4
Bridge of Weir Renfs 267 B7

Bridge Reeve Devon 25 E11
Bridge Sollers Hereford 97 C8
Bridge Street Suff 107 B7
Bridge Town Warks 118 G4
Bridge Trafford W Ches 183 G7
Bridge Yate S Glos 61 E7
Bridgefoot Aberds 292 C6
Bridgefoot Angus 287 D7
Bridgefoot Cumb 229 F7
Bridgehampton Som 29 C9
Bridgehill Durham 242 G3
Bridgeholm Green
 Derbys 185 E8
Bridgehouse Gate
 N Yorks 214 F3
Bridgelands Borders 261 C11
Bridgemary Hants 33 G9
Bridgemere E Ches 168 F2
Bridgemont Derbys 185 E8
Bridgend Aberds 293 B7
Bridgend Aberds 302 F5
Bridgend Angus 293 G7
Bridgend Argyll 255 D8
Bridgend Argyll 274 G4
Bridgend Argyll 275 D9
Bridgend Corn 6 D2
Bridgend Cumb 221 C7
Bridgend Devon 7 F11
Bridgend Fife 287 F7
Bridgend Glos 80 E4
Bridgend Highld 300 D3
Bridgend Invclyd 276 F5
Bridgend Moray 302 F3
Bridgend N Lnrk 278 G3
Bridgend Pembs 92 B3
Bridgend W Loth 279 F11
Bridgend =
 Pen-y-Bont ar-ogwr
 Bridgend 58 C2
Bridgend of Lintrathen
 Angus 286 B6
Bridgeness Falk 279 E11
Bridgerule Devon 24 G3
Bridges Corn 5 D10
Bridges Shrops 131 D7
Bridgeton Glasgow 268 C2
Bridgetown Corn 12 D2
Bridgetown Devon 8 C6
Bridgetown Som 42 G2
Bridgetown Staffs 133 B9
Bridgham Norf 141 F9
Bridgnorth Shrops 132 E4
Bridgtown Staffs 133 B9
Bridgwater Som 43 F10
Bridlington E Yorks 218 F3
Bridport Dorset 16 C5
Bridstow Hereford 97 G11
Brierfield Lancs 204 F2
Brierholme Carr
 S Yorks 199 E7
Brierley Glos 79 B10
Brierley Hereford 115 F9
Brierley S Yorks 198 E2
Brierley W Yorks 197 D8
Brierton Hrtlpl 234 E5
Briery Cumb 229 G11
Briery Hill Bl Gwent 77 D11
Briestfield W Yorks 197 D8
Brig o'Turk Stirl 285 G9
Brigflatts Cumb 222 G2
Brigg N Lincs 200 F3
Brigg N Lincs 200 F4
Briggate Norf 160 D6
Briggswath N Yorks 227 D7
Brigham Cumb 229 E7
Brigham Cumb 229 G11
Brigham E Yorks 209 C7
Brighouse W Yorks 196 C6
Brighstone I o W 20 E4
Brightgate Derbys 170 C3
Brighthampton Oxon 82 E5
Brightholmlee S Yorks 186 C3
Brightley Devon 13 B7
Brightling E Sus 37 C11
Brightlingsea Essex 89 B9
Brighton Brighton 36 G4
Brighton Corn 5 E8
Brighton Hill Hants 48 D6
Brighton le Sands Mers 182 B4
Brightons Falk 279 F8
Brightside S Yorks 186 D5
Brightwalton W Berks 64 D2
Brightwalton Green
 W Berks 64 D2
Brightwalton Holt
 W Berks 64 D2
Brightwell Suff 108 C4
Brightwell Baldwin
 Oxon 83 F11
Brightwell cum Sotwell
 Oxon 83 G9
Brigmerston Wilts 47 D7
Brignall Durham 223 C11
Brigsley NE Lincs 201 G9
Brigsteer Cumb 211 B9
Brigstock Northants 137 F8
Brill Bucks 83 C11
Brill Corn 2 D6
Brilley Hereford 96 B5
Brilley Mountain Powys 114 G5
Brimaston Pembs 91 G8
Brimfield Hereford 115 D10
Brimington Derbys 186 G6
Brimington Common
 Derbys 186 G6
Brimley Devon 13 F11
Brimley Devon 28 G4
Brimps Hill Glos 79 B11
Brimpsfield Glos 80 C6
Brimpton W Berks 64 G5
Brimpton Common
 W Berks 64 G5
Brims Orkney 314 H2
Brims Castle Highld 310 B4
Brimscombe Glos 80 E5
Brimsdown London 86 F5
Brimstage Mers 182 E4
Brinacorry Highld 295 P9
Brincliffe S Yorks 186 D4
Brind E Yorks 207 G10
Brindham Som 44 E4
Brindister Shetland 313 H4
Brindister Shetland 313 K6
Brindle Lancs 194 C6
Brindle Heath Gtr Man 195 G10
Brindley E Ches 167 E9
Brindley Ford Stoke 168 E5
Brindwoodgate Derbys 186 F4
Brineton Staffs 150 G6
Bringewood Forge
 Hereford 115 C9
Bringhurst Leics 136 E6
Bringsty Common
 Hereford 116 F4
Brington Cambs 121 B11
Brinian Orkney 314 D4
Briningham Norf 159 C10
Brinkhill Lincs 190 G5
Brinkley Cambs 124 G2
Brinkley Notts 172 E2
Brinkley Hill Hereford 97 E11
Brinklow M Keynes 103 D8

Brinklow Warks 119 B8
Brinkworth Wilts 62 C4
Brinmore Highld 300 G5
Brinnington Gtr Man 184 C6
Brinscall Lancs 194 C6
Brinsea N Som 60 G2
Brinsford Staffs 133 B8
Brinsley Notts 171 F7
Brinsop Hereford 97 C8
Brinsop Common
 Hereford 97 C8
Brinsworth S Yorks 186 D6
Brinsworthy Devon 41 G9
Brinton Norf 159 B10
Brisco Cumb 239 G10
Briscoe Cumb 219 C10
Briscoerigg N Yorks 205 C11
Brisley Norf 159 E8
Brislington Bristol 60 E6
Brissenden Green Kent 54 F2
Bristnall Fields W Mid 133 F9
Bristol Bristol 60 E5
Briston Norf 159 C11
Britford Wilts 31 B11
Brithdir Caerph 77 E11
Brithdir Ceredig 92 B6
Brithdir Gwyn 146 F5
Brithem Bottom Devon 27 E8
British Torf 78 E3
Briton Ferry =
 Llansawel Neath 57 C8
Britten's Bath 45 B7
Britwell Slough 66 C3
Britwell Salome Oxon 83 G11
Brixham Torbay 9 D8
Brixton Devon 7 E11
Brixton London 67 D10
Brixton Deverill Wilts 45 F11
Brixworth Northants 120 C4
Brize Norton Oxon 82 D4
Broad Alley Worcs 117 D7
Broad Blunsdon
 Swindon 81 G11
Broad Campden Glos 100 D3
Broad Carr W Yorks 196 D5
Broad Chalke Wilts 31 B8
Broad Clough Lancs 195 C11
Broad Colney Herts 85 E11
Broad Common Worcs 117 D7
Broad Ford Kent 53 F8
Broad Green C Beds 103 C8
Broad Green Cambs 124 F3
Broad Green Essex 105 G8
Broad Green Essex 107 G7
Broad Green London 67 F10
Broad Green Mers 182 C6
Broad Green Suff 124 F5
Broad Green Suff 125 F11
Broad Green Worcs 116 F5
Broad Green Worcs 117 C9
Broad Haven =
 Aberllydan Pembs 72 C5
Broad Heath Powys 114 C6
Broad Heath Staffs 151 D7
Broad Heath Worcs 116 D3
Broad Hill Cambs 123 B11
Broad Hinton Wilts 62 D6
Broad Ings E Yorks 208 C2
Broad Lane Corn 4 G3
Broad Lanes Shrops 132 F5
Broad Laying Hants 64 G2
Broad Layings Hants 64 G2
Broad Marston Worcs 100 B2
Broad Meadow Staffs 168 F4
Broad Oak Carms 93 G11
Broad Oak Cumb 220 G2
Broad Oak Dorset 30 E3
Broad Oak E Sus 37 C10
Broad Oak E Sus 38 D4
Broad Oak E Sus 49 C9
Broad Oak Hereford 97 G9
Broad Oak Kent 54 F4
Broad Oak Kent 71 G7
Broad Oak Mers 183 B8
Broad Oak Shrops 132 F5
Broad Parkham Devon 24 C5
Broad Street E Sus 38 D5
Broad Street Kent 53 B10
Broad Street Kent 54 C6
Broad Street Kent 55 C7
Broad Street Medway 69 E9
Broad Street Suff 107 C9
Broad Street Wilts 46 B6
Broad Street Green
 Essex 88 D5
Broad Tenterden Kent 53 G11
Broad Town Wilts 62 D5
Broadbottom Gtr Man 185 C7
Broadbridge W Sus 22 B4
Broadbridge Heath
 W Sus 50 G6
Broadbury Devon 12 B5
Broadbush Swindon 81 G11
Broadclyst Devon 14 B5
Broadfield Gtr Man 195 E10
Broadfield Inclyd 276 G6
Broadfield Lancs 194 C4
Broadfield Lancs 195 B8
Broadfield Pembs 73 E10
Broadfield W Sus 51 G9
Broadford Highld 295 C8
Broadford Sur 50 D3
Broadford Bridge W Sus 35 C9
Broadgate Hants 32 C6
Broadgrass Green Suff 125 E9
Broadgreen Wood
 Herts 86 D4
Broadhalgh Gtr Man 195 E11
Broadham Green Sur 51 C11
Broadhaugh Borders 249 G11
Broadhaven Highld 310 D7
Broadheath Gtr Man 184 D3
Broadheath Worcs 116 D3
Broadhembury Devon 27 G9
Broadhempston Devon 8 B6
Broadholm Derbys 170 F4
Broadholme Derbys 170 F5
Broadholme Lincs 188 G5
Broadland Row E Sus 38 D4
Broadlands Devon 14 G3
Broadlane Corn 2 C4
Broadley Carms 74 D5
Broadley Lancs 195 D11
Broadley Moray 302 C4
Broadley Common Essex 86 D6
Broadmayne Dorset 17 D10
Broadmeadows
 Borders 261 C10
Broadmere Hants 48 D6
Broadmoor Pembs 73 D9
Broadmoor Som 50 D6
Broadmoor Common
 Hereford 98 D2
Broadmore Green
 Worcs 116 G6
Broadoak Dorset 16 B4
Broadoak Glos 80 C2
Broadoak Hants 33 B8
Broadoak Shrops 149 F9
Broadoak Wrex 166 D5

Broadoak End Herts 86 C4
Broadoak Park Gtr Man 195 G9
Broadplat Oxon 65 C8
Broadrashes Moray 302 D4
Broadrock Glos 79 F8
Broad's Green Essex 87 C11
Broad's Green Wilts 62 F3
Broadsands Torbay 9 D7
Broadsea Aberds 303 C9
Broadshard Som 28 E6
Broadstairs Kent 71 F11
Broadstone Kent 53 D11
Broadstone Mon 79 E8
Broadstone Poole 18 B6
Broadstone Shrops 131 F10
Broadstreet Common
 Newport 59 C11
Broadwas Worcs 116 F5
Broadwater Herts 104 G4
Broadwater W Sus 35 G11
Broadwater Down Kent 52 F5
Broadwaters Worcs 116 B6
Broadwath Cumb 239 F11
Broadway Carms 74 D3
Broadway Carms 74 D5
Broadway Pembs 72 C5
Broadway Som 28 D4
Broadway Suff 127 B7
Broadway Worcs 99 D11
Broadway Lands
 Hereford 97 C11
Broadwell Glos 79 C9
Broadwell Glos 100 F4
Broadwell Oxon 82 E3
Broadwell Warks 119 D9
Broadwell Ho Northumb 241 G9
Broadwey Dorset 17 E9
Broadwindsor Dorset 28 G5
Broadwood Kelly Devon 25 F10
Broadwoodwidger
 Devon 12 D4
Brobury Hereford 96 C6
Brochel Highld 298 E5
Brochloch Argyll 284 D4
Brochroy Argyll 284 D4
Brock Lancs 202 E6
Brock Hill Essex 88 F2
Brockamin Worcs 116 G5
Brockbridge Hants 33 D10
Brockdish Norf 126 B4
Brockencote Worcs 117 D7
Brockenhurst Hants 32 G4
Brocketsbrae S Lnrk 259 B8
Brockfield Devon 14 B5
Brockford Green Suff 126 D2
Brockford Street Suff 126 D2
Brockhall Northants 120 E2
Brockhall Village
 Lancs 203 F10
Brockham Sur 51 D7
Brockham End Bath 61 F8
Brockham Park Sur 51 D8
Brockhampton Glos 99 G9
Brockhampton Glos 99 G11
Brockhampton Hants 22 B2
Brockhampton Hereford 97 D11
Brockhampton Green
 Dorset 30 F2
Brockhill Borders 261 E9
Brockholes W Yorks 197 E7
Brockhollands Glos 79 D10
Brockhurst Derbys 170 C4
Brockhurst Hants 33 G10
Brockhurst Warks 135 G9
Brocklebank Cumb 230 C2
Brocklebirst Dumfries 238 C3
Brocklesby Lincs 200 E6
Brockley London 67 E11
Brockley N Som 60 F3
Brockley Corner Suff 124 C6
Brockley Green Suff 106 B4
Brockley Green Suff 124 G6
Brockleymoor Cumb 230 D5
Brockloch Dumfries 246 D2
Brockmanton Hereford 115 F11
Brockmoor W Mid 133 F8
Brock's Green Hants 64 G4
Brock's Watering Norf 142 E2
Brockscombe Devon 12 C5
Brockton Shrops 130 C6
Brockton Shrops 130 F6
Brockton Shrops 131 E11
Brockton Shrops 132 C4
Brockton Shrops 132 E5
Brockton Staffs 150 B5
Brockton Telford 150 H4
Brockweir Glos 79 E8
Brockwell Som 42 E2
Brockworth Glos 80 B4
Brockworth Powys 35 G9
Brocton Corn 6 C3
Brocton Staffs 151 F9
Brodie Moray 301 D9
Brodiesord Aberds 302 C5
Brodsworth S Yorks 198 F4
Brogaig Highld 298 C4
Brogborough C Beds 103 D9
Broke Hall Suff 108 C3
Broken Cross E Ches 184 G6
Broken Cross W Ches 183 G11
Broken Green Herts 105 G8
Brokenborough Wilts 62 B2
Brokerswood Wilts 45 C11
Brokes N Yorks 224 F3
Bromborough Mers 182 E4
Bromborough Pool
 Mers 182 E4
Bromdon Shrops 132 G2
Brome Suff 126 B2
Brome Street Suff 126 B3
Bromeswell Suff 126 G6
Bromfield Cumb 229 C9
Bromfield Shrops 115 B9
Bromford W Mid 134 E2
Bromham Beds 121 G10
Bromham Wilts 62 F3
Bromley Herts 105 E8
Bromley London 67 F11
Bromley London 68 F2
Bromley S Yorks 186 B4
Bromley Shrops 132 C4
Bromley Shrops 149 D8
Bromley W Mid 133 F8
Bromley Common
 London 68 F2
Bromley Cross Essex 107 F11
Bromley Cross Gtr Man 195 E8
Bromley Green Kent 54 G3
Bromley Hall Staffs 150 C5
Bromley Heath S Glos 61 D7
Bromley Park London 67 F11
Bromley Wood Staffs 152 E2
Bromlow Shrops 130 C6
Brompton London 67 D9
Brompton Medway 69 E9
Brompton N Yorks 217 D8
Brompton N Yorks 225 F7
Brompton Shrops 131 B10
Brompton-by-Sawdon
 N Yorks 217 C8

Brompton-on-Swale
 N Yorks 224 F4
Brompton Ralph Som 42 G5
Brompton Regis Som 42 G3
Bromsash Hereford 98 G2
Bromsberrow Glos 98 E4
Bromsberrow Heath Glos 98 E4
Bromsgrove Worcs 117 C9
Bromstead Common
 Staffs 150 F6
Bromstead Heath Staffs 150 F6
Bromstone Kent 71 F11
Bromyard Hereford 116 F3
Bromyard Downs
 Hereford 116 F3
Bronaber Gwyn 146 C4
Broncroft Shrops 131 F10
Brondesbury Park
 London 67 C8
Broneirion Powys 129 F10
Brongest Ceredig 92 B6
Brongwyn Ceredig 92 C5
Bronington Wrex 149 B9
Bronllys Powys 96 D2
Bronnant Ceredig 112 C2
Bronwydd Carms 93 G7
Bronwydd Arms Carms 93 G8
Bronydd Powys 96 B4
Bronygarth Shrops 148 B5
Brook Carms 74 D3
Brook Devon 12 C5
Brook Devon 14 C2
Brook Hants 32 C3
Brook Hants 32 E3
Brook I o W 20 E3
Brook Kent 54 E5
Brook Sur 50 E3
Brook Sur 50 F2
Brook Bottom Gtr Man 185 D7
Brook Bottom Gtr Man 196 G3
Brook Bottom Lancs 202 E6
Brook End Beds 121 E11
Brook End C Beds 104 B3
Brook End Cambs 121 C11
Brook End Herts 104 F6
Brook End M Keynes 103 C8
Brook End Worcs 99 B7
Brook Green London 67 D8
Brook Hill Hants 32 E3
Brook Hill Hants 153 C11
Brook Place Sur 66 G3
Brook Street Kent 52 D5
Brook Street Kent 54 G2
Brook Street Suff 106 B6
Brook Street W Sus 36 B4
Brook Waters Wilts 30 C6
Brooke Rutland 137 B7
Brooke Norf 142 D5
Brookenby Lincs 190 B2
Brookend Glos 79 E11
Brookend Glos 79 F9
Brookend Oxon 100 G6
Brookfield Derbys 185 B8
Brookfield Lancs 203 G7
Brookfield M'bro 225 B9
Brookfield Renfs 267 C8
Brookfoot W Yorks 196 C6
Brookhampton Oxon 83 F10
Brookhampton Shrops 131 E11
Brookhouse Blkburn 195 B7
Brookhouse Denb 165 B9
Brookhouse E Ches 184 F6
Brookhouse Lancs 211 G10
Brookhouse S Yorks 187 D8
Brookhouse W Yorks 196 B5
Brookhouse Green
 E Ches 168 C4
Brookhouses Derbys 185 D8
Brookhouses Derbys 169 G7
Brookhurst Mers 182 E4
Brookland Kent 39 B7
Brooklands Dumfries 237 B10
Brooklands Gtr Man 184 C3
Brooklands Shrops 167 G8
Brooklands Sur 66 G5
Brookleigh Devon 14 B5
Brookmans Park Herts 86 E2
Brookpits W Sus 35 G8
Brookrow Shrops 116 C2
Brooks Powys 130 D2
Brooks End Kent 71 F9
Brooks Green W Sus 35 C10
Brooksbottoms Gtr Man 195 D9
Brooksby Leics 154 F3
Brookside Telford 132 C3
Brookthorpe Glos 80 C4
Brookvale Mers 183 E8
Brookville Norf 140 D5
Brookwood Sur 50 B2
Broom C Beds 104 C3
Broom Cumb 231 G9
Broom Devon 27 F11
Broom E Renf 267 D10
Broom Pembs 73 D10
Broom S Yorks 186 C5
Broom Warks 117 G11
Broom Green Norf 159 E9
Broom Hill Bristol 60 E6
Broom Hill Dorset 31 G8
Broom Hill Durham 242 G4
Broom Hill London 68 F3
Broom Hill Suff 108 B4
Broom Hill Worcs 117 B8
Broom Street Kent 70 G4
Broome Norf 143 E7
Broome Shrops 131 G10
Broome Shrops 131 B11
Broome Worcs 117 B7
Broome Park Northumb 264 G4
Broomedge Warr 184 D2
Broomer's Corner
 W Sus 35 D11
Broomershill W Sus 35 D9
Broomfield Aberds 303 F9
Broomfield Cumb 230 B2
Broomfield Essex 88 C2
Broomfield Kent 53 C10
Broomfield Kent 70 G2
Broomfield Som 43 G8
Broomfield Wilts 62 D5
Broomfields Shrops 149 F8
Broomfleet E Yorks 199 B11
Broomhall Windsor 66 F3
Broomhall Green
 E Ches 167 F10
Broomhaugh Northumb 242 E2
Broomhill Bristol 60 D6
Broomhill Borders 261 D11
Broomhill Highld 301 G9
Broomhill Kent 55 B8

Broomhill Norf 140 C2
Broomhill Northumb 252 C6
Broomhill Notts 171 E8
Broomhill S Yorks 198 G2
Broomhill W Ches 167 B7
Broomhill Bank Kent 52 E5
Broomholm Norf 160 C6
Broomhouse Glasgow 268 C3
Broomlands N Ayrs 267 B8
Bromley N Ayrs 242 G2
Broompark Durham 233 C10
Broom's Barn Suff 124 D5
Broom's Green Glos 98 E4
Broomsgrove E Sus 38 E4
Broomsthorpe Norf 158 D6
Broomton Highld 301 B8
Broomy Hill Hereford 97 C9
Broomy Lodge Hants 32 E2
Broomyshaw Staffs 169 F9
Brora Highld 311 J3
Broseley Shrops 132 C3
Brotherhouse Bar Lincs 156 G5
Brotheridge Green
 Worcs 98 C6
Brotherlee Durham 232 D4
Brotherstone Borders 262 B4
Brothertoft Lincs 174 F3
Brotherton N Yorks 198 B3
Brotton Redcar 226 B3
Broubster Highld 310 C4
Brough Cumb 222 C5
Brough Derbys 185 E11
Brough E Yorks 200 B2
Brough Highld 310 B6
Brough Notts 172 D4
Brough Orkney 314 E3
Brough Orkney 314 H4
Brough Shetland 312 C7
Brough Shetland 312 F6
Brough Shetland 313 H6
Brough Shetland 313 J7
Brough Lodge Shetland 312 D7
Brough Sowerby Cumb 222 C5
Broughall Shrops 167 G9
Broughton Borders 260 B4
Broughton Bucks 84 C4
Broughton Cambs 122 B5
Broughton Edin 280 F5
Broughton Flint 166 C4
Broughton Hants 47 G10
Broughton Lancs 202 F6
Broughton M Keynes 103 C7
Broughton N Lincs 200 F3
Broughton N Yorks 204 C4
Broughton N Yorks 216 E5
Broughton Northants 120 B6
Broughton Orkney 314 B4
Broughton Oxon 101 D8
Broughton Shrops 132 E6
Broughton Shrops 149 D9
Broughton Staffs 150 C5
Broughton V Glam 58 E2
Broughton Astley Leics 135 E10
Broughton Beck Cumb 210 C5
Broughton Common
 Wilts 61 G11
Broughton Cross Cumb 229 E7
Broughton Gifford
 Wilts 61 G11
Broughton Green Worcs 117 E9
Broughton Hackett
 Worcs 117 G8
Broughton in Furness
 Cumb 210 B4
Broughton Lodges Leics 154 E4
Broughton Mills Cumb 220 G4
Broughton Moor Cumb 228 E6
Broughton Park
 Gtr Man 195 G10
Broughton Poggs Oxon 82 E2
Broughtown Orkney 314 B6
Broughty Ferry Dundee 287 D8
Brow Edge Cumb 211 C7
Browhouses Dumfries 239 D7
Browland Shetland 313 H4
Brown Bank N Yorks 205 C10
Brown Candover Hants 48 F5
Brown Edge E Ches 183 G8
Brown Edge Lancs 193 E11
Brown Edge Mers 183 E8
Brown Edge Staffs 168 E6
Brown Heath E Ches 167 B7
Brown Heath W Ches 167 B7
Brown Knowl W Ches 167 E7
Brown Lees W Ches 168 D5
Brown Moor W Yorks 206 G4
Brown Street Lincs 125 D11
Brownber Cumb 222 D4
Brownbread Street
 E Sus 23 B1
Brownedge E Ches 168 C3
Brownheath Devon 27 G10
Brownheath Shrops 149 D9
Brownheath Common
 Worcs 117 E7
Brownhill Aberds 302 E6
Brownhill Aberds 303 E8
Brownhill Blkburn 203 G9
Brownhill Shrops 149 E8
Brownhills Fife 287 F9
Brownhills W Mid 133 B10
Browninghill Green
 Hants 48 B5
Brownlow E Ches 168 C4
Brownlow Mers 194 G4
Brownlow Fold Gtr Man 195 E8
Brownmuir Aberds 293 F9
Brownsover Warks 119 B10
Brownston Devon 8 E3
Brownsbank Dumfries 268 C5
Browston Green Norf 143 D9
Browtop Cumb 229 G2
Broxa N Yorks 227 G9
Broxbourne Herts 86 D5
Broxburn E Loth 282 F3
Broxburn W Loth 279 G11
Broxfield Northumb 264 F6
Broxholme Lincs 188 F5
Broxted Essex 105 F11
Broxton W Ches 167 E7
Broxtowe Nottingham 171 G8
Broxwood Hereford 115 G8
Broyle Side E Sus 23 C7
Bruairnis W Isles 297 L3
Bruan Highld 310 F7
Bruar Lodge Perth 291 G10
Brucefield Fife 280 D2

Brucehill W Dunb 277 F7
Bruchag Argyll 266 D2
Brucklebog Aberds 293 D9
Bruera W Ches 166 C6
Bruern Abbey Oxon 100 G5
Bruichladdich Argyll 274 G3
Bruisyard Suff 126 D6
Brumby N Lincs 199 F11
Brund Staffs 169 C10
Brundall Norf 142 A6
Brundish Norf 143 D7
Brundish Suff 126 D5
Brundish Street Suff 126 C5
Brunery Highld 289 B9
Brunnion Corn 2 B2
Brunshaw Lancs 204 G3
Brunstane Edin 280 G6
Brunstock Cumb 239 F10
Brunswick Village
 T & W 242 C6
Brunt Hamersland
 Shetland 313 H6
Bruntcliffe W Yorks 197 B8
Brunthwaite W Yorks 205 D7
Bruntingthorpe Leics 136 F2
Brunton Fife 287 E7
Brunton Northumb 264 E6
Brunton Wilts 47 B8
Brushes Gtr Man 185 B7
Brushford Devon 25 F11
Brushford Som 42 G3
Bruton Som 45 G7
Bryans Midloth 270 C6
Bryan's Green Worcs 117 D7
Bryanston Dorset 30 F5
Bryanstown Dorset 30 C3
Brydekirk Dumfries 238 C5
Bryher Scilly 1 G3
Brymbo Conwy 180 G4
Brymbo Wrex 166 E3
Brympton D'Evercy
 Som 29 D8
Bryn Caerph 77 F11
Bryn Carms 75 E8
Bryn Gtr Man 194 G5
Bryn Gwyn 179 G8
Bryn Neath 57 C10
Bryn Powys 130 D3
Bryn Rhondda 76 D6
Bryn Shrops 130 F5
Bryn Swansea 56 C4
Bryn W Berks 64 E4
Bryn-coch Neath 57 B8
Bryn Common Flint 166 D3
Bryn Du Anglesey 178 G4
Bryn Dulas Conwy 180 F6
Bryn Eglwys Gwyn 163 B10
Bryn Gates Gtr Man 194 G5
Bryn Golau Rhondda 58 B4
Bryn-henllan Pembs 91 D10
Bryn-Iwan Carms 92 G6
Bryn Mawr Powys 148 F5
Bryn Myrddin Carms 93 G8
Bryn-nantllech Conwy 164 B6
Bryn-newydd Denb 165 G11
Bryn Pen-y-lan Wrex 166 G4
Bryn-penarth Powys 130 C2
Bryn Pydew Conwy 180 F4
Bryn Rhyd-yr-Arian
 Conwy 165 B7
Bryn Saith Marchog
 Denb 165 D9
Bryn Sion Gwyn 147 F7
Bryn Tanat Powys 148 E4
Bryn-y-cochin Shrops 149 B7
Bryn-y-gwenin Mon 78 B4
Bryn-y-maen Conwy 180 F4
Bryn-yr-Eos Wrex 166 F3
Bryn-yr-eryr Gwyn 162 F5
Bryn-yr-ogof Denb 165 D11
Brynafan Ceredig 112 C4
Brynamman Carms 76 C2
Brynawel Caerph 77 F11
Brynbanc Ceredig 92 D5
Bryncae Rhondda 58 C3
Bryncethin Bridgend 58 C2
Bryncir Gwyn 163 F7
Bryncroes Gwyn 144 C4
Bryncrug Gwyn 128 C2
Bryndu Carms 75 D8
Brynderwen Powys 130 D3
Bryndyffryn Powys 148 F5
Bryneglwys Denb 165 E11
Brynford Flint 181 G11
Bryngwran Anglesey 178 F4
Bryngwyn Ceredig 92 B5
Bryngwyn Mon 78 D5
Bryngwyn Powys 96 B3
Brynhenllan Pembs 91 D10
Brynheulog Bridgend 57 C11
Brynhoffnant Ceredig 110 G6
Bryniau Denb 181 E9
Bryning Lancs 194 B2
Brynithel Bl Gwent 78 E2
Brynllywarch Powys 130 F3
Brynmawr Bl Gwent 77 C11
Brynmawr Gwyn 144 C5
Brynmenyn Bridgend 58 C2
Brynmill Swansea 56 C6
Brynmorfudd Conwy 164 C6
Brynna Rhondda 58 C3
Brynnau Gwynion
 Rhondda 58 C3
Brynore Shrops 149 B7
Brynrefail Anglesey 179 D7
Brynrefail Gwyn 163 C9
Brynsadler Rhondda 58 C3
Brynsiencyn Anglesey 163 B7
Brynteg Anglesey 179 E7
Brynteg Wrex 166 E4
Bryntirion Bridgend 57 E11
Buaile nam Bodach
 W Isles 297 L3
Bualintur Highld 294 C6
Bualnaluib Highld 307 K3
Buarthmeini Gwyn 146 C6
Bubbenhall Warks 119 C7
Bubnell Derbys 186 G2
Bubwith E Yorks 207 F10
Buccleuch Borders 261 G9

Buchan Hill W Sus 51 G9
Buchanan Smithy Stirl 277 D9
Buchanhaven Aberds 303 E11
Buchanty Perth 286 E3
Buchley E Dunb 277 G11
Buchlyvie Stirl 277 C11
Buck Hill Wilts 62 E3
Buckabank Cumb 230 B3
Buckbury Worcs 98 E6
Buckden Cambs 122 D3
Buckden N Yorks 213 D8
Buckenham Norf 143 B7
Buckerell Devon 27 G9
Bucket Corner Hants 32 C5
Buckfast Devon 8 B4
Buckfastleigh Devon 8 B4
Buckhaven Fife 281 B7
Buckholm Borders 261 B11
Buckholt Mon 79 B8
Buckhorn Devon 12 B3
Buckhorn Weston
 Dorset 30 C3
Buckhurst Kent 52 E5
Buckhurst Hill Essex 86 G6
Buckie Moray 302 C4
Buckies Highld 310 C5
Buckingham Bucks 102 E3
Buckland Bucks 84 C4
Buckland Devon 8 G3
Buckland Devon 14 G3
Buckland Glos 99 D11
Buckland Hants 20 B2
Buckland Herts 105 E7
Buckland Kent 55 E10
Buckland Oxon 82 G4
Buckland Som 45 G7
Buckland Sur 51 C8
Buckland Brewer Devon 24 C6
Buckland Common
 Bucks 84 D6
Buckland Dinham Som 45 C9
Buckland Down Som 45 C9
Buckland End W Mid 134 F2
Buckland Filleigh Devon 25 F7
Buckland in the Moor
 Devon 13 G10
Buckland Marsh Oxon 82 F4
Buckland Monachorum
 Devon 7 B9
Buckland Newton
 Dorset 29 F11
Buckland Ripers Dorset 17 E8
Buckland St Mary Som 28 E3
Buckland Valley Kent 55 E10
Bucklands Borders 262 F2
Bucklebury W Berks 64 E5
Bucklebury Alley
 W Berks 64 E4
Bucklegate Lincs 156 B6
Buckleigh Devon 24 B6
Bucklerheads Angus 287 D8
Bucklers Hard Hants 20 B4
Bucklesham Suff 108 C4
Buckley = Bwcle Flint 166 C3
Buckley Green Warks 118 D3
Buckley Hill Mers 182 B4
Bucklow Hill E Ches 184 E2
Buckminster Leics 155 E7
Bucknall Lincs 173 B11
Bucknall Stoke 168 F6
Bucknell Oxon 101 F11
Bucknell Shrops 115 C7
Buckoak W Ches 183 G8
Buckover S Glos 79 G11
Buckpool Moray 302 C4
Buckpool W Mid 133 F7
Buckridge Worcs 116 C4
Buck's Cross Devon 24 C4
Bucks Green W Sus 50 G5
Bucks Hill Herts 85 E9
Bucks Horn Oak Hants 49 E10
Buck's Mills Devon 24 C4
Bucksburn Aberdeen 293 C10
Buckskin Hants 48 C6
Buckton E Yorks 218 E3
Buckton Hereford 115 C7
Buckton Northumb 264 B3
Buckton Vale Gtr Man 196 G3
Buckworth Cambs 122 B2
Buddbrooke Warks 118 D5
Buddileigh Staffs 168 E3
Buddon Angus 287 D9
Budds' Common E Sus 37 C7
Budock Water Corn 3 C7
Budworth Heath
 W Ches 183 F11
Buersill Head Gtr Man 196 E2
Buerton E Ches 167 G11
Buffler's Holt Bucks 102 D3
Bufton Leics 135 B8
Bugbrooke Northants 120 F3
Bugford Devon 40 E6
Bughtlin Edin 280 G3
Buglawton E Ches 168 C5
Bugle Corn 5 D10
Bugley Dorset 30 C3
Bugthorpe E Yorks 207 B11
Buildwas Shrops 132 C2
Builth Road Powys 113 G10
Builth Wells Powys 113 G10
Buirgh W Isles 305 J2
Bulbourne Herts 84 C6
Bulby Lincs 155 D11
Bulcote Notts 171 G11
Buldoo Highld 310 C3
Bulford Wilts 47 E7
Bulford Camp Wilts 47 E7
Bulkeley E Ches 167 E8
Bulkeley Hall Shrops 168 G2
Bulkington Warks 135 F7
Bulkington Wilts 46 B3
Bulkworthy Devon 24 E5
Bull Bay =
 Porthllechog Anglesey 178 C6
Bull Hill Hants 20 B2
Bullamoor N Yorks 225 G7
Bullbridge Derbys 170 E5
Bullbrook Brack 65 E11
Bullen's Green Herts 86 D2
Bulley Glos 80 B2
Bullgill Cumb 229 D7
Bullhurst Hill Derbys 170 G4
Bullinghope Hereford 97 D10
Bullington Hants 48 E3
Bullington Lincs 189 F9

Carnhedryn Pembs 90 F6
Carnhedryn Uchaf Pembs 90 F5
Carnhell Green Corn 2 B4
Carnhot Corn 4 F4
Carnkie Corn 2 B5
Carnkie Corn 2 C6
Carnkief Corn 4 E5
Carno Powys 129 D9
Carnoch Highld 300 D2
Carnoch Highld 300 F3
Carnock Fife 279 D10
Carnon Downs Corn 4 G5
Carnousie Aberds 302 D6
Carnoustie Angus 287 D9
Carnsmerry Corn 5 D10
Carntyne Glasgow 268 B2
Carnwadric E Renf 267 D10
Carnwath S Lnrk 269 F9
Carnyorth Corn 1 C3
Caroe Corn 11 C9
Carol Green W Mid 118 B5
Carpalla Corn 5 E9
Carpenders Park Herts 85 G10
Carpenter's Hill Worcs 117 C11
Carperby N Yorks 213 B10
Carpley Green N Yorks 213 B8
Carr Gtr Man 195 D9
Carr S Yorks 187 C8
Carr Bank Cumb 211 D9
Carr Cross Lancs 193 E11
Carr Gate W Yorks 197 C10
Carr Green Gtr Man 184 D2
Carr Hill T & W 243 E7
Carr Houses Mers 193 G10
Carr Vale Derbys 171 B7
Carradale Argyll 255 D9
Carragraich W Isles 305 J3
Carrbridge Highld 301 G9
Carrbrook Gtr Man 196 G3
Carreg-wen Pembs 92 C4
Carreg y Garth Gwyn 163 B9
Carreglefn Anglesey 178 D5
Carrhouse Devon 26 F3
Carrick Argyll 275 E10
Carrick Dumfries 237 D7
Carrick Fife 287 E8
Carrick Castle Argyll 276 C3
Carrick Ho Orkney 314 C5
Carriden Falk 279 E10
Carrington Gtr Man 184 C2
Carrington Lincs 174 E4
Carrington Midloth 270 C6
Carrington Nottingham 171 G9
Carroch Dumfries 246 E5
Carrog Conwy 164 F3
Carrog Denb 165 G10
Carroglen Perth 285 E11
Carrol Highld 311 J2
Carron Falk 279 E7
Carron Moray 302 E2
Carron Bridge Stirl 278 E4
Carronbridge Dumfries 247 D9
Carronshore Falk 279 E7
Carrot Angus 287 C8
Carrow Hill Mon 78 G6
Carroway Head Staffs 134 D3
Carrshield Northumb 232 B2
Carrutherstown Dumfries 238 C4
Carrville Durham 234 C2
Carry Argyll 275 G10
Carsaig Argyll 275 E8
Carsaig Argyll 289 G7
Carscreugh Dumfries 236 D4
Carse Gray Angus 287 B8
Carse Ho Argyll 275 G8
Carsegowan Dumfries 236 D6
Carseriggan Dumfries 236 C5
Carsethorn Dumfries 237 D11
Carshalton London 67 G9
Carshalton Beeches London 67 G9
Carshalton on the Hill London 67 G9
Carsington Derbys 170 E3
Carskiey Argyll 255 G7
Carsluith Dumfries 236 D6
Carsphairn Dumfries 246 E3
Carstairs S Lnrk 269 F8
Carstairs Junction S Lnrk 269 F9
Carswell Marsh Oxon 82 F4
Cartbridge Sur 50 B4
Carter Knowle S Yorks 186 E4
Carterhaugh Borders 261 D10
Carter's Clay Hants 32 C4
Carter's Green Essex 87 C8
Carter's Hill Wokingham 65 F9
Carterspiece Glos 79 C9
Carterton Oxon 82 D3
Carterway Heads Northumb 242 G2
Carthamartha Corn 12 F3
Carthew Corn 2 B5
Carthew Corn 5 D10
Carthorpe N Yorks 214 C6
Cartington Northumb 252 C2
Cartland S Lnrk 269 F7
Cartledge Derbys 186 F4
Cartmel Cumb 211 D7
Cartmel Fell Cumb 211 B8
Cartsdyke Invclyd 276 F5
Cartworth W Yorks 196 F6
Carty Port Dumfries 236 C6
Carway Carms 75 D7
Carwinley Cumb 239 C10
Carwynnen Corn 2 B5
Cary Fitzpaine Som 29 B9
Carzantic Corn 12 E3
Carzield Dumfries 247 G11
Carzise Corn 2 C3
Cas Mael = Puncheston Pembs 91 F10
Cascob Powys 114 D4
Cashes Green Glos 80 D4
Cashlie Perth 285 C8
Cashmoor Dorset 31 E7
Cassey Compton Glos 81 C9
Cassington Oxon 83 C7
Cassop Durham 234 D2
Castallack Corn 1 D5
Castell Conwy 164 B3
Castell Denb 165 B10
Castell-Howell Ceredig 93 B8
Castell nedd = Neath Neath 57 B8
Castell Newydd Emlyn = Newcastle Emlyn Carms 92 C6
Castell-y-bwch Torf 78 G3
Castell-y-rhingyll Carms 75 C9
Castellau Rhondda 58 B5
Casterton Cumb 212 D2
Castle Devon 28 G4
Castle Som 27 B9
Castle Acre Norf 158 F6
Castle Ashby Northants 121 F7
Castle Bolton N Yorks 223 G10
Castle Bromwich W Mid 134 F2
Castle Bytham Lincs 155 F9
Castle Caereinion Powys 130 B3
Castle Camps Cambs 106 C2
Castle Carlton Lincs 190 E5
Castle Carrock Cumb 240 F2
Castle Cary Som 44 G6
Castle Combe Wilts 61 D10
Castle Donington Leics 153 D8
Castle Douglas Dumfries 237 C9
Castle Eaton Swindon 81 F10
Castle Eden Durham 234 D4
Castle End P'boro 138 B2
Castle Fields Shrops 149 G10
Castle Forbes Aberds 293 B8
Castle Frome Hereford 98 B3
Castle Gate Corn 1 C5
Castle Green London 68 C3
Castle Green S Yorks 197 G9
Castle Green Sur 66 G3
Castle Gresley Derbys 152 F5
Castle Heaton Northumb 273 G8
Castle Hedingham Essex 106 D5
Castle Hill E Sus 37 B9
Castle Hill Gtr Man 184 C6
Castle Hill Kent 53 E7
Castle Hill Suff 108 B3
Castle Hill Worcs 116 F5
Castle Huntly Perth 287 E7
Castle Kennedy Dumfries 236 D3
Castle O'er Dumfries 248 E6
Castle Rising Norf 158 E3
Castle Street W Yorks 196 C3
Castle Stuart Highld 301 E7
Castle Toward Argyll 266 B2
Castle Town W Sus 36 E2
Castle-upon-Alun V Glam 58 E2
Castle Vale W Mid 134 E2
Castlebythe Pembs 91 F10
Castlecary N Lnrk 278 F5
Castle Craig Borders 270 G2
Castlecraig Highld 301 C8
Castlecroft Staffs 133 D7
Castlefairn Dumfries 246 F6
Castlefields Halton 183 E8
Castleford W Yorks 198 B2
Castlegreen Shrops 130 F6
Castlehead Renfs 267 C9
Castlehill Argyll 254 B4
Castlehill Borders 260 B6
Castlehill Highld 310 C5
Castlehill S Ayrs 257 E9
Castlehill W Dunb 277 F7
Castlemaddy Dumfries 246 F3
Castlemartin Pembs 72 F6
Castlemilk Dumfries 238 B5
Castlemilk Glasgow 268 D2
Castlemorris Pembs 91 E8
Castlemorton Worcs 98 D5
Castlerigg Cumb 229 G11
Castleside Durham 233 B7
Castlethorpe M Keynes 102 C6
Castlethorpe N Lincs 200 F3
Castleton Angus 287 C7
Castleton Argyll 275 E9
Castleton Derbys 185 E11
Castleton Gtr Man 195 E11
Castleton Moray 301 G11
Castleton N Yorks 226 D3
Castleton Newport 59 C9
Castleton Village Highld 300 E6
Castletown Cumb 230 E6
Castletown Dorset 17 G9
Castletown Highld 301 E7
Castletown Highld 310 C5
Castletown I o M 192 F3
Castletown Staffs 151 E8
Castletown T & W 243 F9
Castletown W Ches 166 E6
Castletump Glos 98 F4
Castleweary Borders 249 C10
Castlewigg Dumfries 236 E6
Castley N Yorks 205 D11
Castling's Heath Suff 107 C9
Caston Norf 141 D9
Castor P'boro 138 D2
Caswell Swansea 56 D5
Cat Bank Cumb 220 F6
Cat Hill S Yorks 197 F8
Catacol N Ayrs 255 C10
Catbrain S Glos 60 C5
Catbrook Mon 79 E8
Catch Flint 182 G2
Catchall Corn 1 D4
Catchems Corner W Mid 118 B4
Catchems End Worcs 116 B5
Catchgate Durham 242 G5
Catchory Highld 310 D6
Catcleugh Northumb 250 C6
Catcliffe S Yorks 186 D6
Catcomb Wilts 62 D4
Catcott Som 43 F11
Caterham Sur 51 B10
Catfield Norf 161 E7
Catfirth Shetland 313 H6
Catford London 67 E11
Catforth Lancs 202 F5
Cathays Cardiff 59 D7
Cathays Park Cardiff 59 D7
Cathcart Glasgow 267 C11
Cathedine Powys 96 F2
Catherine-de-Barnes W Mid 134 G3
Catherine Slack W Yorks 196 B5
Catherington Hants 33 E11
Catherton Shrops 116 B3
Cathiron Warks 119 B9
Catholes Cumb 222 G3
Cathpair Borders 271 F9
Catisfield Hants 33 F8
Catley Lane Head Gtr Man 195 D11
Catley Southfield Hereford 98 C3
Catlodge Highld 291 D8
Catlowdy Cumb 239 B11
Catmere End Essex 105 D9
Catmore W Berks 64 C3
Caton Devon 13 G11
Caton Lancs 211 G10
Caton Green Lancs 211 F10
Catrine E Ayrs 258 D2
Cat's Ash Newport 78 G5
Cat's Common Norf 160 E6
Cats Edge Staffs 169 E7
Cat's Hill Cross Staffs 150 C6
Catsfield E Sus 38 E2
Catsfield Stream E Sus 38 E2
Catsgore Som 29 B8
Catsham Som 44 G5
Catshaw S Yorks 197 G8
Catshill W Mid 133 B11
Catshill Worcs 117 C9
Catslackburn Borders 261 D8
Catslip Oxon 65 B8
Catstree Shrops 132 D4
Cattadale Argyll 274 G4
Cattal N Yorks 206 C4
Cattawade Suff 108 E2
Cattedown Plym 7 E9
Catterall Lancs 202 E5
Catterick N Yorks 224 F4
Catterick Bridge N Yorks 224 F4
Catterick Garrison N Yorks 224 F3
Catterlen Cumb 230 E5
Catterline Aberds 293 F10
Catterton N Yorks 206 D6
Catteshall Sur 50 E3
Catthorpe Leics 119 B11
Cattistock Dorset 17 B7
Cattle End Northants 102 C3
Catton N Yorks 215 D7
Catton Northumb 241 F8
Catwick E Yorks 209 D8
Catworth Cambs 121 C11
Caudle Green Glos 80 C6
Caudlesprings Norf 141 C8
Caulcott C Beds 103 C9
Caulcott Oxon 101 G10
Cauld Borders 261 G11
Cauldcoats Holdings Falk 279 F10
Cauldcots Angus 287 C10
Cauldhame Stirl 278 C2
Cauldmill Borders 262 G2
Cauldon Staffs 169 F9
Cauldon Lowe Staffs 169 F9
Cauldwells Aberds 303 D7
Caulkerbush Dumfries 237 D11
Caulside Dumfries 249 G10
Caundle Marsh Dorset 29 E11
Caunsall Worcs 132 G6
Caunton Notts 172 D2
Causeway Hants 33 E11
Causeway Hants 34 C2
Causeway Mon 60 B2
Causeway End Cumb 210 C6
Causeway End Cumb 211 B9
Causeway End Dumfries 236 C6
Causeway End Essex 87 B11
Causeway End Wilts 62 C4
Causeway Foot W Yorks 197 E7
Causeway Foot W Yorks 205 G7
Causeway Green W Mid 133 F9
Causewayend S Lnrk 260 B2
Causewayhead Cumb 238 G4
Causewayhead Stirl 278 B6
Causewaywood Shrops 131 D10
Causey Durham 242 F6
Causey Park Bridge Northumb 252 E5
Causeyend Aberds 293 B11
Causeyton Aberds 293 B8
Caute Devon 24 E6
Cautley Cumb 222 G3
Cavendish Suff 106 B6
Cavendish Bridge Leics 153 D8
Cavenham Suff 124 D5
Cavers Carre Borders 262 D3
Caversfield Oxon 101 F11
Caversham Reading 65 E8
Caversham Heights Reading 65 D8
Caverswall Staffs 169 G7
Cavil E Yorks 207 G11
Cawdor Highld 301 D8
Cawkeld E Yorks 208 C5
Cawkwell Lincs 190 F3
Cawood N Yorks 207 F7
Cawsand Corn 7 E8
Cawston Norf 160 E2
Cawston Warks 119 C9
Cawthorne N Yorks 216 B5
Cawthorne S Yorks 197 F9
Cawthorpe Lincs 155 E11
Cawton N Yorks 216 D2
Caxton Cambs 122 F6
Caynham Shrops 115 C11
Caythorpe Lincs 172 F6
Caythorpe Notts 171 F11
Cayton N Yorks 217 C11
Ceallan W Isles 296 F4
Ceann a Bhàigh W Isles 305 J4
Ceann a Bhaigh W Isles 296 E3
Ceann a Deas Loch Baghasdail W Isles 297 K3
Ceann Shiphoirt W Isles 305 G4
Ceann Tarabhaigh W Isles 305 G4
Ceannacroc Lodge Highld 290 B4
Cearsiadair W Isles 304 F5
Ceathramh Meadhanach W Isles 296 D4
Cefn Newport 59 B9
Cefn Powys 148 G5
Cefn Berain Conwy 165 B7
Cefn-brith Conwy 164 E6
Cefn-bryn-brain Carms 76 C2
Cefn-bychan Swansea 56 B4
Cefn-bychan Wrex 166 G3
Cefn Canol Powys 148 C4
Cefn-coch Conwy 164 B5
Cefn Coch Powys 129 C10
Cefn Coch Powys 148 D2
Cefn-coed-y-cymmer M Tydf 77 D9f
Cefn Cribbwr Bridgend 57 E11
Cefn Cross Bridgend 57 E11
Cefn-ddwysarn Gwyn 147 B9
Cefn Einion Shrops 130 F5
Cefn-eurgain Flint 166 B2
Cefn Fforest Caerph 77 F11
Cefn Glas Bridgend 57 E11
Cefn Golau Bl Gwent 77 D10
Cefn-gorwydd Powys 95 B8
Cefn Hengoed Caerph 77 F10
Cefn-hengoed Swansea 57 B7
Cefn Llwyd Ceredig 128 G2
Cefn-mawr Wrex 166 G3
Cefn Rhigos Rhondda 76 D6
Cefn-y-bedd Flint 166 D4
Cefn-y-Crib Torf 78 F2
Cefn-y-Garth Swansea 76 E2
Cefn-y-pant Carms 92 F3
Cefncaeau Carms 56 B4
Cefneithin Carms 75 C9
Cefnpennar Rhondda 77 E8
Cegidfa = Guilsfield Powys 148 G4
Cei-bach Ceredig 111 F8
Ceinewydd = New Quay Ceredig 111 F7
Ceint Anglesey 179 F7
Ceinws Powys 128 B5
Cellan Ceredig 94 B2
Cellarhead Staffs 169 F7
Cellarhill Kent 70 G3
Celyn-Mali Flint 165 B11
Cemaes Anglesey 178 C5
Cemmaes Powys 128 B6
Cemmaes Road = Glantwymyn Powys 128 C6
Cenarth Carms 92 C5
Cenin Gwyn 163 F7
Central Invclyd 276 F5
Central Milton Keynes M Keynes 102 D6
Ceos W Isles 304 F5
Ceres Fife 287 F8
Ceri = Kerry Powys 130 F2
Cerne Abbas Dorset 29 G11
Cerney Wick Glos 81 F9
Cerrig Llwydion Neath 57 C9
Cerrig-mân Anglesey 179 C7
Cerrigceinwen Anglesey 178 G6
Cerrigydrudion Conwy 165 F7
Cess Norf 161 F8
Cessford Borders 262 E6
Ceunant Gwyn 163 C8
Chaceley Glos 99 E7
Chaceley Hole Glos 98 E6
Chaceley Stock Glos 99 F7
Chacewater Corn 4 G4
Chackmore Bucks 102 D3
Chacombe Northants 101 C9
Chad Valley W Mid 133 F10
Chadbury Worcs 99 B10
Chadderton Gtr Man 196 F2
Chadderton Fold Gtr Man 195 F11
Chaddesden Derby 153 B7
Chaddesley Corbett Worcs 117 C7
Chaddlehanger Devon 12 F5
Chaddlewood Plym 7 D11
Chaddleworth W Berks 64 D2
Chadkirk Gtr Man 184 D6
Chadlington Oxon 100 G6
Chadshunt Warks 118 G6
Chadsmoor Staffs 151 G9
Chadstone Northants 121 F7
Chadwell Leics 154 E5
Chadwell Shrops 150 G5
Chadwell End Beds 121 D11
Chadwell Heath London 68 B3
Chadwell St Mary Thurrock 68 D6
Chadwick Worcs 116 D6
Chadwick End W Mid 118 C4
Chadwick Green Mers 183 B8
Chaffcombe Som 28 E5
Chafford Hundred Thurrock 68 D5
Chagford Devon 13 D10
Chailey E Sus 36 D5
Chain Bridge Lincs 174 G4
Chainbridge Cambs 139 C8
Chainhurst Kent 53 D8
Chalbury Dorset 31 F8
Chalbury Common Dorset 31 F8
Chaldon Sur 51 B10
Chaldon Herring or East Chaldon Dorset 17 E11
Chale I o W 20 F5
Chale Green I o W 20 F5
Chalfont Common Bucks 85 G8
Chalfont Grove Bucks 85 G7
Chalfont St Giles Bucks 85 G7
Chalfont St Peter Bucks 85 G8
Chalford Glos 80 E5
Chalford Oxon 84 E2
Chalford Wilts 45 C11
Chalford Hill Glos 80 E5
Chalgrave C Beds 103 F10
Chalgrove Oxon 83 F10
Chalk Kent 69 E7
Chalk End Essex 87 C10
Chalkfoot Cumb 230 B2
Chalkhill Norf 141 C7
Chalkhouse Green Oxon 65 D8
Chalkshire Bucks 84 D4
Chalksole Kent 55 E9
Chalkway Som 28 F5
Chalkwell Kent 69 G11
Chalkwell Sthend 69 B11
Challaborough Devon 8 G3
Challacombe Devon 41 E7
Challister Shetland 312 G7
Challoch Dumfries 236 C5
Challock Kent 54 C4
Chalmington Dorset 29 G9
Chalton C Beds 103 F10
Chalton Hants 34 D2
Chalvedon Essex 69 B8
Chalvey Slough 66 D3
Chalvington E Sus 23 D8
Chambercombe Devon 40 D4
Chamber's Green Kent 54 E2
Champson Devon 26 B4
Chance Inn Fife 287 F7
Chancery = Rhydgaled Ceredig 111 B11
Chance's Pitch Hereford 98 C4
Chandler's Cross Herts 85 F9
Chandler's Cross Worcs 98 D5
Chandler's Ford Hants 32 C6
Chandlers Green Hants 49 B8
Channel Tunnel Kent 55 F7
Channel's End Beds 122 F2
Channerwick Shetland 313 L6
Chantry Devon 25 C9
Chantry Som 45 D8
Chantry Suff 108 C2
Chapel Corn 4 C6
Chapel Cumb 229 E10
Chapel Fife 280 C5
Chapel Allerton Som 44 C2
Chapel Allerton W Yorks 206 F2
Chapel Amble Corn 10 F5
Chapel Brampton Northants 120 D4
Chapel Chorlton Staffs 150 B6
Chapel Cleeve Som 42 E4
Chapel Cross E Sus 37 C10
Chapel-en-le-Frith Derbys 185 E9
Chapel End Beds 103 B11
Chapel End Beds 122 F2
Chapel End C Beds 103 C11
Chapel End Cambs 138 G2
Chapel End E Ches 167 G11
Chapel End Essex 105 G11
Chapel End Northants 138 F2
Chapel End Warks 134 E6
Chapel Field Gtr Man 195 F9
Chapel Field Norf 161 E7
Chapel Fields W Mid 118 B6
Chapel Fields York 207 C7
Chapel Green Herts 104 D6
Chapel Green Warks 119 E9
Chapel Green Warks 134 F5
Chapel Haddlesey N Yorks 198 B5
Chapel Head Cambs 138 G6
Chapel Hill Aberds 303 F10
Chapel Hill Glos 79 E10
Chapel Hill Lincs 174 E2
Chapel Hill Mon 79 F8
Chapel Hill N Yorks 206 D2
Chapel House Lancs 194 F3
Chapel Knapp Wilts 61 F11
Chapel Lawn Shrops 114 B6
Chapel-le-Dale N Yorks 212 D4
Chapel Leigh Som 27 B10
Chapel Mains Borders 271 G11
Chapel Milton Derbys 185 E9
Chapel of Garioch Aberds 303 G7
Chapel of Stoneywood Aberdeen 293 B10
Chapel on Leader Borders 271 G11
Chapel Outon Dumfries 236 E6
Chapel Plaister Wilts 61 F10
Chapel Row E Sus 23 C10
Chapel Row Essex 88 E3
Chapel Row W Berks 64 F5
Chapel St Leonards Lincs 191 G9
Chapel Stile Cumb 220 D6
Chapel Town Corn 5 D7
Chapelgate Lincs 157 E8
Chapelhall N Lnrk 268 C5
Chapelhill Dumfries 248 E3
Chapelhill Highld 301 B8
Chapelhill N Ayrs 266 G4
Chapelhill Perth 286 D4
Chapelhill Perth 286 E3
Chapelhill Perth 286 E6
Chapelknowe Dumfries 239 C8
Chapels Blkburn 195 C7
Chapels Cumb 210 C4
Chapelthorpe W Yorks 197 D10
Chapelton Angus 287 C10
Chapelton Devon 25 B9
Chapelton Highld 291 B11
Chapelton S Lnrk 268 F3
Chapelton Row Dumfries 237 E8
Chapeltown Blkburn 195 D8
Chapeltown Moray 302 G2
Chapeltown S Yorks 186 B5
Chapeltown W Yorks 206 F2
Chapman's Hill Worcs 117 B9
Chapman's Town E Sus 23 B10
Chapmans Well Devon 12 C3
Chapmanslade Wilts 45 D10
Chapmore End Herts 86 B4
Chappel Essex 107 F7
Charaton Cross Corn 6 B6
Charcott Kent 52 D4
Chard Som 28 F4
Chard Junction Dorset 28 G4
Chardleigh Green Som 28 E4
Chardstock Devon 28 G4
Charfield S Glos 80 G2
Charfield Green S Glos 80 G2
Charfield Hill S Glos 80 G2
Charford Worcs 117 D9
Chargrove Glos 80 B6
Charing Kent 54 D3
Charing Cross Dorset 31 E10
Charing Heath Kent 54 D2
Charing Hill Kent 54 C3
Charingworth Glos 100 D4
Charlbury Oxon 82 B5
Charlcombe Bath 61 F8
Charlcutt Wilts 62 D3
Charlecote Warks 118 F5
Charlemont W Mid 133 E10
Charles Devon 41 G7
Charles Bottom Devon 41 G7
Charles Tye Suff 125 G10
Charlesfield Borders 262 D3
Charlesfield Dumfries 238 D5
Charleshill Sur 49 E11
Charleston Angus 287 C7
Charleston Renfs 267 C9
Charlestown Aberdeen 293 C11
Charlestown Corn 5 E10
Charlestown Derbys 185 C8
Charlestown Dorset 17 F9
Charlestown Fife 279 E11
Charlestown Gtr Man 195 G10
Charlestown Gtr Man 195 G11
Charlestown Highld 299 B8
Charlestown Highld 300 E6
Charlestown W Yorks 196 B3
Charlestown W Yorks 205 F9
Charlestown of Aberlour Moray 302 E2
Charlesworth Derbys 185 C8
Charleton Devon 8 G5
Charlinch Som 43 F8
Charlottetown Fife 286 F6
Charlton Hants 47 D11
Charlton Herts 104 F3
Charlton London 68 D2
Charlton Northants 101 D10
Charlton Northumb 251 F8
Charlton Oxon 64 B2
Charlton Redcar 226 B2
Charlton Som 28 B3
Charlton Som 44 E6
Charlton Som 45 C7
Charlton Sur 66 F5
Charlton Telford 149 G11
Charlton W Sus 34 E5
Charlton Wilts 30 C6
Charlton Wilts 46 B6
Charlton Wilts 62 B3
Charlton Worcs 99 B10
Charlton Worcs 116 C6
Charlton Abbots Glos 99 G10
Charlton Adam Som 29 B8
Charlton-All-Saints Wilts 31 C11
Charlton Down Dorset 17 C9
Charlton Horethorne Som 29 C11
Charlton Kings Glos 99 G9
Charlton Mackrell Som 29 B8
Charlton Marshall Dorset 30 G5
Charlton Musgrove Som 30 B2
Charlton on Otmoor Oxon 83 B9
Charlton on the Hill Dorset 30 G5
Charlton Park Glos 99 G9
Charlton St Peter Wilts 46 B6
Charltonbrook S Yorks 186 B4
Charlwood E Sus 51 G11
Charlwood Hants 49 G7
Charlwood Sur 51 E8
Charlynch Som 43 F8
Charminster Bmouth 19 C8
Charminster Dorset 17 C9
Charmouth Dorset 16 C3
Charnage Wilts 45 G10
Charndon Bucks 102 G3
Charnes Staffs 150 C5
Charney Bassett Oxon 82 G5
Charnock Green Lancs 194 D5
Charnock Hall S Yorks 186 E5
Charnock Richard Lancs 194 D5
Charsfield Suff 126 F5
Chart Corner Kent 53 C9
Chart Hill Kent 53 D9
Chart Sutton Kent 53 D10
Charter Alley Hants 48 B5
Charterhouse Som 44 B3
Chartershall Stirl 278 C6
Charterville Allotments Oxon 82 C4
Chartham Kent 54 C6
Chartham Hatch Kent 54 B6
Chartridge Bucks 84 E6
Charvil Wokingham 65 D9
Charwelton Northants 119 F10
Chase Cross London 87 G8
Chase End Street Worcs 98 D5
Chase Hill S Glos 61 B8
Chase Terrace Staffs 133 B10
Chasetown Staffs 133 B10
Chastleton Oxon 100 F4
Chasty Devon 24 G4
Chat Hill W Yorks 205 G8
Chatburn Lancs 203 E11
Chatcull Staffs 150 C5
Chatford Shrops 131 B9
Chatham Caerph 59 B8
Chatham Medway 69 F9
Chatham Green Essex 88 B2
Chathill Northumb 264 D5
Chatley Worcs 117 E7
Chattenden Medway 69 E9
Chatter End Essex 105 F9
Chatteris Cambs 139 F7
Chatterley Staffs 168 E4
Chattern Hill Sur 66 E5
Chatterton Lancs 195 D9
Chattisham Suff 107 C11
Chattle Hill Warks 134 E3
Chatto Borders 263 F7
Chatton Northumb 264 D3
Chaul End C Beds 103 G11
Chaulden Herts 85 D8
Chavel Shrops 149 G8
Chavenage Green Glos 80 F5
Chavey Down Brack 65 F11
Chawleigh Devon 26 E2
Chawley Oxon 83 E7
Chawson Worcs 117 E7
Chawston Beds 122 F3
Chawton Hants 49 F8
Chaxhill Glos 80 C2
Chazey Heath Oxon 65 D7
Cheadle Gtr Man 184 D5
Cheadle Staffs 169 G8
Cheadle Heath Gtr Man 184 D5
Cheadle Hulme Gtr Man 184 D5
Cheadle Park Staffs 169 G8
Cheam London 67 G8
Cheapside Herts 105 E8
Cheapside Sur 50 B4
Cheapside Windsor 66 F2
Chearsley Bucks 84 C2
Chebsey Staffs 151 D7
Checkendon Oxon 65 C7
Checkley E Ches 168 F2
Checkley Hereford 97 D11
Checkley Staffs 151 B10
Checkley Green E Ches 168 F2
Chedburgh Suff 124 F5
Cheddar Som 44 C3
Cheddington Bucks 84 B6
Cheddleton Staffs 169 E7
Cheddleton Heath Staffs 169 E7
Cheddon Fitzpaine Som 28 B2
Chedglow Wilts 80 G6
Chedgrave Norf 143 D7
Chedington Dorset 29 F7
Chediston Suff 127 B7
Chediston Green Suff 127 B7
Chedworth Glos 81 C9
Chedworth Laines Glos 81 C8
Chedzoy Som 43 F10
Cheeklaw Borders 272 E5
Cheeseman's Green Kent 54 F4
Cheetam Hill Gtr Man 195 G10
Cheglinch Devon 40 E4
Chegworth Kent 53 C10
Cheldon Devon 26 E2
Chelfham Devon 40 F6
Chelford E Ches 184 G4
Chell Heath Stoke 168 E5
Chellaston Derby 153 C7
Chellington Beds 121 F9
Chells Herts 104 F5
Chelmarsh Shrops 132 F4
Chelmer Village Essex 88 D2
Chelmick Shrops 131 E9
Chelmondiston Suff 108 D4
Chelmorton Derbys 169 B10
Chelmsford Essex 88 D2
Chelmsine Som 27 D11
Chelmsley Wood W Mid 134 F3
Chelsea London 67 D9
Chelsfield London 68 G3
Chelsham Sur 51 B11
Chelston Som 27 C11
Chelston Torbay 9 C7
Chelston Heathfield Som 27 C11
Chelsworth Suff 107 B9
Chelsworth Common Suff 107 B9
Cheltenham Glos 99 G8
Chelveston Northants 121 D9
Chelvey N Som 60 F3
Chelvey Batch N Som 60 F3
Chelwood Bath 60 G6
Chelwood Common E Sus 36 B6
Chelwood Gate E Sus 36 B6
Chelworth Wilts 81 G7
Chelworth Lower Green Wilts 81 G9
Chelworth Upper Green Wilts 81 G9
Chelynch Som 45 E7
Chemistry Shrops 167 G8
Cheney Longville Shrops 131 G8
Chenhalls Corn 2 B3
Chenies Bucks 85 F8
Cheny Longville Shrops 131 G8
Chepstow Mon 79 G8
Chequerbent Gtr Man 195 F7
Chequerfield W Yorks 198 C3
Chequers Corner Norf 139 B9
Chequertree Kent 54 F4
Cherhill Wilts 62 E4
Cherington Glos 80 F6
Cherington Warks 100 D5
Cheristow Devon 24 B3
Cheriton Devon 41 D8
Cheriton Hants 33 B9
Cheriton Kent 55 F7
Cheriton Swansea 56 C3
Cheriton Bishop Devon 13 C11
Cheriton Cross Devon 13 C11
Cheriton Fitzpaine Devon 26 F5
Cheriton or Stackpole Elidor Pembs 73 F7
Cherrington Telford 150 E3
Cherry Burton E Yorks 208 E5
Cherry Green Essex 105 F11
Cherry Green Herts 105 F7
Cherry Hinton Cambs 123 F9
Cherry Orchard Shrops 149 G9
Cherry Orchard Worcs 117 G7
Cherry Tree Blkburn 195 B7
Cherry Tree Gtr Man 185 C7
Cherry Willingham Lincs 189 G8
Cherrybank Perth 286 E5
Cherrytree Hill Derby 153 B7
Chertsey Sur 66 F4
Chertsey Meads Sur 66 F5
Cheselbourne Dorset 17 B11
Chesham Bucks 85 E7
Chesham Gtr Man 195 E10
Chesham Bois Bucks 85 F7
Cheshunt Herts 86 E5
Chesley Kent 69 G11
Cheslyn Hay Staffs 133 B9
Chessetts Wood Warks 118 C3
Chessington London 67 G7
Chessmount Bucks 85 E7
Chestall Staffs 151 G11
Chester W Ches 166 B6
Chester-le-Street Durham 243 G7
Chester Moor Durham 233 B11
Chesterblade Som 45 E7
Chesterfield Derbys 186 G5
Chesterfield Staffs 134 B2
Chesterhill Midloth 271 B7
Chesterhope Northumb 251 F9
Chesterknowes Borders 262 D2
Chesters Borders 262 E4
Chesters Borders 262 G4
Chesterton Cambs 123 E9
Chesterton Cambs 138 D2
Chesterton Glos 81 E8
Chesterton Oxon 101 G11
Chesterton Shrops 132 D5
Chesterton Staffs 168 F4
Chesterton Warks 118 F6
Chesterton Green Warks 118 F6
Chesterwood Northumb 241 D8
Chestfield Kent 70 F6
Chestnut Hill Cumb 229 G11
Chestnut Street Kent 69 G11
Cheston Devon 8 D3
Cheswardine Shrops 150 D4
Cheswell Telford 150 F4
Cheswick Northumb 273 F10
Cheswick Buildings Northumb 273 F10
Cheswick Green W Mid 118 B2
Chetnole Dorset 29 F10
Chettiscombe Devon 27 E7
Chettisham Cambs 139 G10
Chettle Dorset 31 E7
Chetton Shrops 132 E3
Chetwode Bucks 102 F2
Chetwynd Aston Telford 150 F5
Cheveley Cambs 124 E3
Chevening Kent 52 B3
Cheverell's Green Herts 85 B9
Chevin End W Yorks 205 E9
Chevington Suff 124 F5
Chevithorne Devon 27 D7
Chew Magna Bath 60 G5
Chew Moor Gtr Man 195 F7
Chew Stoke Bath 60 G5
Chewton Keynsham Bath 61 F7
Chewton Mendip Som 44 C5
Cheylesmore W Mid 118 B6
Chichacott Devon 13 B8
Chicheley M Keynes 103 B8
Chichester W Sus 22 C5
Chickenley W Yorks 197 C9
Chickerell Dorset 17 E8
Chicklade Wilts 46 G2
Chickney Essex 105 F11
Chicksands C Beds 104 D2
Chicksgrove Wilts 46 G3
Chickward Hereford 114 G5
Chidden Hants 33 D11
Chiddingfold Sur 50 F3
Chiddingly E Sus 23 C8
Chiddingstone Kent 52 D3
Chiddingstone Causeway Kent 52 D4
Chiddingstone Hoath Kent 52 E3
Chideock Dorset 16 C4
Chidgley Som 42 F4
Chidham W Sus 22 C3
Chidswell W Yorks 197 C9
Chieveley W Berks 64 E3
Chignall St James Essex 87 D11
Chignall Smealy Essex 87 C11
Chigwell Essex 86 G6
Chigwell Row Essex 87 G7
Chilbolton Hants 47 F11
Chilbolton Down Hants 48 F2
Chilbridge Dorset 31 G7
Chilcomb Hants 33 B8
Chilcombe Dorset 16 C6
Chilcombe Som 42 F6
Chilcompton Som 44 C6
Chilcote Leics 152 G5
Child Okeford Dorset 30 E4
Childer Thornton W Ches 182 F5
Childerditch Essex 68 B6
Childerley Gate Cambs 123 F7
Childrey Oxon 63 B11
Child's Ercall Shrops 150 E3
Child's Hill London 67 B8
Childsbridge Kent 52 B5
Childswickham Worcs 99 D11
Childwall Mers 182 D6
Childwick Bury Herts 85 C10
Childwick Green Herts 85 C10
Chilfrome Dorset 17 B7
Chilgrove W Sus 34 E4
Chilham Kent 54 C5
Chilhampton Wilts 46 G5
Chilla Devon 24 G6
Chillaton Devon 12 E4
Chillenden Kent 55 C9
Chillerton I o W 20 E5
Chillesford Suff 127 G7
Chillingham Northumb 264 D3
Chillington Devon 8 G5
Chillington Som 28 E5
Chillmill Kent 53 E7
Chilmark Wilts 46 G3
Chilmington Green Kent 54 E3
Chilsham E Sus 23 C10
Chilson Oxon 82 B4
Chilson Som 28 G4
Chilson Common Som 28 G4
Chilsworthy Corn 12 G4
Chilsworthy Devon 24 F4
Chiltern Green Beds 85 B10
Chilthorne Domer Som 29 D8
Chiltington E Sus 36 D5
Chilton Bucks 83 C11
Chilton Durham 233 F11
Chilton Kent 71 G11
Chilton Oxon 64 B3
Chilton Suff 107 C7
Chilton Candover Hants 48 E5
Chilton Cantelo Som 29 C9
Chilton Foliat Wilts 63 E10
Chilton Lane Durham 234 E2
Chilton Moor T & W 234 B2
Chilton Polden Som 43 F11
Chilton Street Suff 106 B5
Chilton Trinity Som 43 F9
Chilvers Coton Warks 135 E7
Chilwell Notts 153 B10
Chilworth Hants 32 D6
Chilworth Sur 50 D4
Chilworth Old Village Hants 32 D6
Chimney Oxon 82 E5
Chimney-end Oxon 82 B4
Chimney Street Suff 106 B4
Chineham Hants 49 C7
Chingford London 86 G5
Chingford Green London 86 G5
Chingford Hatch London 86 G5
Chinley Derbys 185 E8
Chinley Head Derbys 185 E9
Chinnor Oxon 84 E3
Chipley Som 27 C10
Chipmans Platt Glos 80 D3
Chipnall Shrops 150 C4
Chippenhall Green Suff 126 B5
Chippenham Cambs 124 D3
Chippenham Wilts 62 E2
Chipperfield Herts 85 E8
Chipping Herts 105 E7
Chipping Lancs 203 E8
Chipping Barnet London 86 F2
Chipping Campden Glos 100 D3
Chipping Hill Essex 88 B4
Chipping Norton Oxon 100 F6
Chipping Ongar Essex 87 E8
Chipping Sodbury S Glos 61 C8
Chipping Warden Northants 101 B9
Chipstable Som 27 B8
Chipstead Kent 52 B3
Chipstead Sur 51 B9
Chirbury Shrops 130 D5
Chirk = Y Waun Wrex 148 B5
Chirk Bank Shrops 148 B5
Chirk Green Wrex 148 B5
Chirmorrie S Ayrs 236 B4
Chirnside Borders 273 D7
Chirnsidebridge Borders 273 D7
Chirton T & W 243 D8
Chirton Wilts 46 B5
Chisbridge Cross Bucks 65 B10
Chisbury Wilts 63 F9
Chiselborough Som 29 E7
Chiseldon Swindon 63 D7
Chiserley W Yorks 196 B4
Chislehampton Oxon 83 F9
Chislehurst London 68 E2
Chislehurst West London 68 E2
Chislet Kent 71 G8
Chislet Forstal Kent 71 G8
Chiswell Dorset 17 G9
Chiswell Green Herts 85 E10
Chiswick London 67 D8
Chiswick End Cambs 105 B7
Chisworth Derbys 185 C7
Chitcombe E Sus 38 C4
Chithurst W Sus 34 C4
Chittering Cambs 123 C9
Chitterley Devon 26 G6
Chitterne Wilts 46 E3
Chittlehamholt Devon 25 C11
Chittlehampton Devon 25 B10
Chittoe Wilts 62 F3
Chitts Hills Essex 107 F9
Chitty Kent 71 G8
Chivelstone Devon 9 G10
Chivenor Devon 40 G4
Chivery Bucks 84 D6
Chobham Sur 66 G3
Choicelee Borders 272 E4
Cholderton Wilts 47 E8
Cholesbury Bucks 84 D6
Chollerford Northumb 241 C10
Chollerton Northumb 241 C10
Cholmondeston E Ches 167 C10
Cholsey Oxon 64 B5
Cholstrey Hereford 115 F9
Cholwell Bath 44 B6
Chop Gate N Yorks 225 F11
Choppington Northumb 253 G7
Chopwell T & W 242 F4
Chorley E Ches 167 E9
Chorley Lancs 194 D5
Chorley Shrops 132 G3
Chorley Staffs 151 G11
Chorley Common W Sus 34 B4
Chorleywood Herts 85 F8
Chorleywood Bottom Herts 85 F8
Chorleywood West Herts 85 F8
Chorlton E Ches 168 E2
Chorlton-cum-Hardy Gtr Man 184 C4
Chorlton Lane W Ches 167 F7
Choulton Shrops 131 F7
Chowdene T & W 243 F7
Chowley W Ches 167 D7
Chownes Mead W Sus 36 C4
Chreagain Highld 289 C10
Chrishall Essex 105 D8
Christchurch Cambs 139 D9
Christchurch Dorset 19 C9
Christchurch Glos 79 C9
Christchurch Newport 59 B10
Christian Malford Wilts 62 D3
Christleton W Ches 166 B6
Christmas Common Oxon 84 G2
Christon N Som 43 B11
Christon Bank Northumb 264 E6
Christow Devon 14 D2
Chryston N Lnrk 278 G3
Chub Tor Devon 7 B10
Chuck Hatch E Sus 52 G3
Chudleigh Devon 14 F3
Chudleigh Knighton Devon 14 F2
Chulmleigh Devon 25 E11

Chunal Derbys 185 C8
Church Lancs 195 B8
Church Aston Telford 150 F4
Church Brampton Northants 120 D4
Church Brough Cumb 222 C5
Church Broughton Derbys 152 C4
Church Charwelton Northants 119 F10
Church Clough Lancs 204 F3
Church Common Hants 34 B2
Church Coombe Corn 4 G3
Church Cove Corn 2 G6
Church Crookham Hants 49 C10
Church Eaton Staffs 150 F6
Church End Beds 122 F2
Church End Bucks 84 B6
Church End Bucks 84 D2
Church End C Beds 85 B8
Church End C Beds 103 E9
Church End C Beds 103 G9
Church End C Beds 104 D3
Church End C Beds 122 G3
Church End Cambs 121 C11
Church End Cambs 123 C7
Church End Cambs 123 D7
Church End Cambs 138 G4
Church End Cambs 139 B7
Church End E Yorks 209 C7
Church End Essex 88 B2
Church End Essex 105 C11
Church End Essex 105 F11
Church End Essex 106 F4
Church End Glos 80 D2
Church End Glos 99 D7
Church End Hants 49 B7
Church End Herts 85 C10
Church End Herts 85 F8
Church End Herts 104 E5
Church End Herts 105 G8
Church End Lincs 156 C4
Church End Lincs 190 B6
Church End London 67 C8
Church End London 86 G2
Church End Norf 157 F10
Church End Oxon 82 D5
Church End Oxon 100 E6
Church End Suff 108 D4
Church End Sur 50 B5
Church End W Mid 119 B7
Church End Warks 134 E4
Church End Warks 134 E5
Church End Wilts 62 D4
Church End Worcs 98 C6
Church Enstone Oxon 101 G7
Church Fenton N Yorks 206 F6
Church Green Devon 15 B9
Church Green Norf 141 E11
Church Gresley Derbys 152 F5
Church Hanborough Oxon 82 C6
Church Hill Pembs 73 C7
Church Hill Staffs 151 G10
Church Hill W Ches 167 C10
Church Hill W Mid 133 D9
Church Hill Worcs 117 D11
Church Hougham Kent 55 E9
Church Houses N Yorks 226 F3
Church Knowle Dorset 18 E4
Church Laneham Notts 188 F4
Church Langton Leics 136 E4
Church Lawford Warks 119 B8
Church Lawton E Ches 168 D4
Church Leigh Staffs 151 B10
Church Lench Worcs 117 G10
Church Mayfield Staffs 169 G11
Church Minshull E Ches 167 C11
Church Norton W Sus 22 D5
Church Oakley Hants 48 C5
Church Preen Shrops 131 D10
Church Pulverbatch Shrops 131 C8
Church Stowe Northants 120 F2
Church Street Essex 106 C5
Church Street Kent 69 E8
Church Stretton Shrops 131 E9
Church Town Corn 4 G3
Church Town Leics 153 F7
Church Town N Lincs 199 F9
Church Town Sur 51 C11
Church Village Rhondda 58 B5
Church Warsop Notts 171 B9
Church Westcote Glos 100 G4
Church Whitfield Kent 55 D10
Church Wilne Derbys 153 C8
Churcham Glos 80 B3
Churchbank Shrops 114 B6
Churchbridge Corn 6 D4
Churchbridge Staffs 133 B9
Churchdown Glos 80 B5
Churchend Essex 89 G8
Churchend Essex 106 G2
Churchend Glos 80 D3
Churchend Reading 65 E7
Churchend S Glos 80 G2
Churches Green E Sus 23 B10
Churchfield Hereford 98 B4
Churchfield W Mid 133 E10
Churchfields Wilts 31 B10
Churchgate Herts 86 E4
Churchgate Street Essex 87 C7
Churchill Devon 28 G4
Churchill Devon 40 E5
Churchill N Som 44 B2
Churchill Oxon 100 G5
Churchill Worcs 117 B7
Churchill Worcs 117 G8
Churchill Green N Som 60 G2
Churchinford Som 28 E2
Churchmoor Rough Shrops 131 F8
Churchover Warks 135 G10
Churchstanton Som 27 E11
Churchstoke Powys 130 E5
Churchstow Devon 8 F4
Churchton Pembs 73 D10
Churchtown Corn 11 F7
Churchtown Cumb 230 C3
Churchtown Derbys 170 C3
Churchtown Devon 24 G3
Churchtown Devon 41 E7
Churchtown I o M 192 C5
Churchtown Lancs 202 E5
Churchtown Mers 193 D11
Churchtown Shrops 130 F5
Churchtown Som 42 F3
Churchwood W Sus 35 D8
Churnet Grange Staffs 169 E7
Churnsike Lodge Northumb 240 B5
Churscombe Torbay 9 C7
Churston Ferrers Torbay 9 D8
Churt Sur 49 F11
Churton W Ches 166 D6
Churwell W Yorks 197 B9
Chute Cadley Wilts 47 C10
Chute Standen Wilts 47 C10
Chwefforddd Conwy 180 G4
Chwilog Gwyn 145 B8
Chwitffordd = Whitford Flint 181 F10
Chyandour Corn 1 C5
Chyanvounder Corn 2 E5
Chycoose Corn 3 B8
Chynhale Corn 2 C4
Chynoweth Corn 2 C2
Chyvarloe Corn 2 E5
Cicelyford Mon 79 E8
Cil y coed = Caldicot Mon 60 B3
Cilan Uchaf Gwyn 144 E5
Cilau Pembs 91 D8
Cilcain Flint 165 B11
Cilcennin Ceredig 111 E10
Cilcewydd Powys 130 C4
Cilfor Gwyn 146 B2
Cilfrew Neath 76 E3
Cilfynydd Rhondda 77 G9
Cilgerran Pembs 92 C3
Cilgwyn Carms 94 F4
Cilgwyn Ceredig 92 C6
Cilgwyn Gwyn 163 E7
Cilgwyn Pembs 91 D11
Ciliau Aeron Ceredig 111 F9
Cill Amhlaidh W Isles 297 G3
Cill Donnain W Isles 297 J3
Cill Eireabhagh W Isles 297 G4
Cille Bhrighde W Isles 297 K3
Cille Pheadair W Isles 297 K3
Cilmaengwyn Neath 76 D2
Cilmery Powys 113 G10
Cilsan Carms 93 G11
Ciltalgarth Gwyn 164 G5
Ciltwrch Powys 96 C3
Cilwendeg Pembs 92 D4
Cilybebyll Neath 76 E2
Cilycwm Carms 94 D5
Cimla Neath 57 B9
Cinder Hill Gtr Man 195 F9
Cinder Hill Kent 52 D4
Cinder Hill W Mid 133 E8
Cinder Hill W Sus 36 B5
Cinderford Glos 79 C11
Cinderhill Derbys 170 F5
Cinderhill Nottingham 171 G8
Cinnamon Brow Warr 183 C10
Cippenham Slough 66 C2
Cippyn Pembs 92 B2
Circebost W Isles 304 E3
Cirencester Glos 81 E8
Ciribhig W Isles 304 D3
City London 67 C10
City Powys 130 F4
City V Glam 58 D3
City Dulas Anglesey 179 D7
Clabhach Argyll 288 D3
Clachaig Argyll 276 E2
Clachaig Highld 292 B2
Clachaig N Ayrs 255 E10
Clachan Argyll 255 B8
Clachan Argyll 275 B8
Clachan Argyll 284 F5
Clachan Argyll 289 E10
Clachan Highld 295 B7
Clachan Highld 298 C4
Clachan Highld 307 L6
Clachan W Isles 297 G3
Clachan na Luib W Isles 296 E4
Clachan of Campsie E Dunb 278 F2
Clachan of Glendaruel Argyll 275 E10
Clachan-Seil Argyll 275 B8
Clachan Strachur Argyll 284 G4
Clachaneasy Dumfries 236 B5
Clachanmore Dumfries 236 E2
Clachbreck Argyll 275 F8
Clachnabrain Angus 292 G5
Clachtoll Highld 307 G5
Clackmannan Clack 279 C8
Clackmarras Moray 302 D2
Clacton-on-Sea Essex 89 B11
Cladach N Ayrs 256 B2
Cladach Chairinis W Isles 296 F4
Cladach Chireboist W Isles 296 E3
Claddach Argyll 254 B2
Claddach-knockline W Isles 296 E3
Cladich Argyll 284 E4
Cladich Steading Argyll 284 E4
Cladswell Worcs 117 F10
Claggan Highld 289 E8
Claggan Highld 290 F3
Claggan Perth 285 D11
Claigan Highld 298 D2
Claines Worcs 117 F7
Clandown Bath 45 B7
Clanfield Hants 33 D11
Clanfield Oxon 82 E3
Clanking Bucks 84 D4
Clanville Hants 47 D10
Clanville Som 44 G6
Clanville Wilts 62 D2
Claonaig Argyll 255 B9
Claonel Highld 309 J5
Clap Hill Kent 54 F5
Clapgate Dorset 31 G8
Clapgate Herts 105 G8
Clapham Beds 121 G10
Clapham Devon 14 D3
Clapham London 67 D9
Clapham N Yorks 212 F4
Clapham W Sus 35 F9
Clapham Green Beds 121 G10
Clapham Green N Yorks 205 B10
Clapham Hill Kent 70 G6
Clapham Park London 67 E9
Clapper Corn 10 G6
Clapper Hill Kent 53 F10
Clappers Borders 273 D8
Clappersgate Cumb 221 E7
Clapphoull Shetland 313 L6
Clapton Som 28 F6
Clapton Som 44 C6
Clapton W Berks 63 E11
Clapton in Gordano N Som 60 E3
Clapton-on-the-Hill Glos 81 B11
Clapton Park London 67 B11
Clapworthy Devon 25 C11
Clara Vale T & W 242 E4
Clarach Ceredig 128 G2
Clarack Aberds 292 D6
Clarbeston Pembs 91 G10
Clarbeston Road Pembs 91 G10
Clarborough Notts 188 E2
Clardon Highld 310 C5
Clare Oxon 83 F11
Clare Suff 106 B5
Clarebrand Dumfries 237 C9
Claregate W Mid 133 C7
Claremont Park Sur 66 G6
Claremount W Yorks 196 B5
Clarence Park N Som 59 G10
Clarencefield Dumfries 238 D3
Clarendon Park Leicester 135 C11
Clareston Pembs 73 C7
Clarilaw Borders 262 D3
Clarilaw Borders 262 F2
Clark Green E Ches 184 F6
Clarken Green Hants 48 C5
Clark's Green Sur 51 F7
Clark's Hill Lincs 157 E7
Clarksfield Gtr Man 196 G2
Clarkston E Renf 267 D11
Clarkston N Lnrk 268 B5
Clase Swansea 57 B7
Clashandorran Highld 300 E5
Clashcoig Highld 309 K6
Clasheddy Highld 308 C6
Clashgour Argyll 284 C6
Clashindarroch Aberds 302 F4
Clashmore Highld 306 F5
Clashmore Highld 309 L7
Clashnessie Highld 306 F5
Clashnoir Moray 302 G2
Clate Shetland 313 G7
Clatford Wilts 63 F7
Clatford Oakcuts Hants 47 F10
Clathy Perth 286 F3
Clatt Aberds 302 G5
Clatter Powys 129 E9
Clatterford I o W 20 D5
Clatterford End Essex 87 C10
Clatterford End Essex 87 D9
Clatterford End Essex 87 E8
Clatterin Bridge Aberds 293 F8
Clatto Fife 287 F8
Clatworthy Som 42 G5
Clauchlands N Ayrs 256 C2
Claughton Lancs 202 E6
Claughton Lancs 211 F11
Claughton Mers 182 D4
Clavelshay Som 43 G9
Claverdon Warks 118 E3
Claverham N Som 60 F2
Claverhambury Essex 86 E6
Clavering Essex 105 E9
Claverley Shrops 132 E5
Claverton Bath 61 G9
Claverton Down Bath 61 G9
Clawdd-côch V Glam 58 D5
Clawdd-newydd Denb 165 E9
Clawdd Poncen Denb 165 G9
Clawthorpe Cumb 211 D10
Clawton Devon 12 B3
Claxby Lincs 189 C10
Claxby Lincs 191 G7
Claxby St Andrew Lincs 191 G7
Claxton N Yorks 216 G3
Claxton Norf 142 C6
Clay Common Suff 143 G9
Clay Coton Northants 119 B11
Clay Cross Derbys 170 C5
Clay End Herts 104 F6
Clay Hill Bristol 60 E6
Clay Hill London 86 F4
Clay Hill W Berks 64 E5
Clay Lake Lincs 156 E5
Clay Mills Derbys 152 D5
Claybokie Aberds 292 D2
Claybrooke Magna Leics 135 F9
Claybrooke Parva Leics 135 F9
Claydon Glos 99 E8
Claydon Oxon 119 G9
Claydon Suff 126 G2
Claygate Dumfries 239 B9
Claygate Kent 52 C6
Claygate Kent 53 E8
Claygate Sur 67 G7
Claygate Cross Kent 52 B6
Clayhall Hants 21 B8
Clayhall London 86 G6
Clayhanger Devon 27 C8
Clayhanger Som 28 E4
Clayhanger W Mid 133 C10
Clayhidon Devon 27 D11
Clayhill E Sus 38 C4
Clayhill Hants 32 F4
Clayhithe Cambs 123 E10
Clayholes Angus 287 D9
Clayland Stirl 277 D11
Clayock Highld 310 D5
Claypit Hill Cambs 123 G7
Claypits Devon 27 B7
Claypits Glos 80 D3
Claypits Kent 55 B9
Claypits Suff 140 G4
Claypole Lincs 172 F5
Clays End Bath 61 G8
Claythorpe Lincs 190 F6
Clayton Gtr Man 184 B5
Clayton S Yorks 198 F3
Clayton Staffs 168 G5
Clayton W Sus 36 E3
Clayton W Yorks 205 G8
Clayton Brook Lancs 194 C5
Clayton Green Lancs 194 C5
Clayton Heights W Yorks 205 G8
Clayton-le-Dale Lancs 203 G9
Clayton-le-Moors Lancs 203 G10
Clayton-le-Woods Lancs 194 C5
Clayton West W Yorks 197 E9
Clayworth Notts 188 D2
Cleadale Highld 294 G6
Cleadon T & W 243 E9
Cleadon Park T & W 243 E9
Clearbrook Devon 7 B10
Clearwell Glos 79 D9
Clearwell Newport 59 B9
Clearwood Wilts 45 D10
Cleasby N Yorks 224 C5
Cleat Orkney 314 B4
Cleat Orkney 314 H4
Cleatlam Durham 224 B2
Cleator Cumb 219 C10
Cleator Moor Cumb 219 B10
Cleave Devon 28 G2
Clebrig Highld 308 F5
Cleckheaton W Yorks 197 B7
Cleddon Mon 79 E8
Clee St Margaret Shrops 131 G11
Cleedownton Shrops 131 G11
Cleehill Shrops 115 B11
Cleekhimin N Lnrk 268 D5
Cleemarsh Shrops 131 G11
Cleestanton Shrops 115 B11
Cleethorpes NE Lincs 201 F10
Cleeton St Mary Shrops 116 B2
Cleeve Glos 80 C2
Cleeve N Som 60 F3
Cleeve Oxon 64 C6
Cleeve Hill Glos 99 F9
Cleeve Prior Worcs 99 B11
Cleghorn S Lnrk 269 F8
Clegyrnant Powys 129 B8
Clehonger Hereford 97 D9
Cleirwy = Clyro Powys 96 C4
Cleish Perth 279 B11
Cleland N Lnrk 268 D5
Clement Street Kent 68 E4
Clement's End C Beds 85 B8
Clements End Glos 79 D9
Clench Wilts 63 G7
Clench Common Wilts 63 F7
Clencher's Mill Hereford 98 D4
Clenchwarton Norf 157 E11
Clennell Northumb 251 B10
Clent Worcs 117 B8
Cleobury Mortimer Shrops 116 B3
Cleobury North Shrops 132 F2
Cleongart Argyll 255 D7
Clephanton Highld 301 D8
Clerk Green W Yorks 197 C8
Clerkenwater Corn 5 B11
Clerkenwell London 67 C10
Clerklands Borders 262 E2
Clermiston Edin 280 G3
Clestrain Orkney 314 F3
Cleuch Head Borders 262 G3
Cleughbrae Dumfries 238 C3
Clevancy Wilts 62 D5
Clevans Renfs 267 B7
Clevedon N Som 60 E2
Cleveley Oxon 101 G7
Cleveleys Lancs 202 E2
Cleverton Wilts 62 B3
Clevis Bridgend 57 F10
Clewer Som 44 C2
Clewer Green Windsor 66 D2
Clewer New Town Windsor 66 D3
Clewer Village Windsor 66 D3
Cley next the Sea Norf 177 E8
Cliaid W Isles 297 L2
Cliasmol W Isles 305 H2
Cliburn Cumb 231 G7
Click Mill Orkney 314 D3
Cliddesden Hants 48 D6
Cliff Derbys 185 D8
Cliff Warks 134 D4
Cliff End E Sus 38 E5
Cliff End W Yorks 196 D6
Cliffburn Angus 287 C10
Cliffe Lancs 203 G10
Cliffe Medway 69 D8
Cliffe N Yorks 207 G9
Cliffe N Yorks 224 B4
Cliffe Woods Medway 69 E8
Clifford Devon 24 C4
Clifford Hereford 96 B4
Clifford W Yorks 206 E4
Clifford Chambers Warks 118 G3
Clifford's Mesne Glos 98 G4
Cliffs End Kent 71 G10
Clifftown Sthend 69 B11
Clifton Bristol 60 E5
Clifton C Beds 104 D3
Clifton Cumb 230 F6
Clifton Derbys 169 G11
Clifton Devon 40 E5
Clifton Gtr Man 195 G9
Clifton Lancs 202 G5
Clifton N Yorks 205 D9
Clifton Northumb 252 G6
Clifton Nottingham 153 C11
Clifton Oxon 101 E9
Clifton S Yorks 186 C6
Clifton S Yorks 187 B8
Clifton Stirl 285 D7
Clifton W Ches 183 F8
Clifton W Yorks 197 C7
Clifton Worcs 98 B6
Clifton York 207 C7
Clifton Campville Staffs 152 G5
Clifton Green Gtr Man 195 G9
Clifton Hampden Oxon 83 F8
Clifton Junction Gtr Man 195 G9
Clifton Maybank Dorset 29 E9
Clifton Moor York 207 B7
Clifton Reynes M Keynes 121 G8
Clifton upon Dunsmore Warks 119 B10
Clifton upon Teme Worcs 116 E4
Cliftoncote Borders 263 E8
Cliftonville Kent 71 E11
Cliftonville N Lnrk 268 B4
Cliftonville Norf 160 B6
Climping W Sus 35 G8
Climpy S Lnrk 269 D8
Clink Som 45 D9
Clinkham Wood Mers 183 B8
Clint N Yorks 205 B11
Clint Green Norf 159 G10
Clintmains Borders 262 C4
Clints N Yorks 224 E2
Cliobh W Isles 304 E2
Clipiau Gwyn 146 G6
Clippesby Norf 161 G8
Clippings Green Norf 159 G10
Clipsham Rutland 155 F9
Clipston Northants 136 G4
Clipston Notts 154 C2
Clipstone C Beds 103 F8
Clitheroe Lancs 203 E10
Cliton Manor C Beds 104 D3
Cliuthar W Isles 305 J3
Clive Shrops 149 E10
Clive W Ches 167 B11
Clive Green W Ches 167 C11
Clive Vale E Sus 38 E4
Clivocast Shetland 312 C8
Clixby Lincs 200 G6
Cloatley Wilts 81 G7
Cloatley End Wilts 81 G7
Clocaenog Denb 165 E9
Clochan Aberds 303 E9
Clochan Moray 302 C4
Clock Face Mers 183 C8
Clock House London 67 G9
Clock Mills Hereford 96 B5
Clockmill Borders 272 E5
Cloddiau Powys 130 B4
Cloddymoss Moray 301 D9
Clodock Hereford 96 F6
Cloford Som 45 E8
Cloford Common Som 45 E8
Cloigyn Carms 74 C6
Clola Aberds 303 E10
Clophill C Beds 103 D11
Clopton Northants 137 G11
Clopton Suff 126 G4
Clopton Corner Suff 126 G4
Clopton Green Suff 124 G5
Clopton Green Suff 125 E9
Close Clark I o M 192 E3
Close House Durham 233 F10
Closeburn Dumfries 247 E9
Closworth Som 29 E9
Clothall Herts 104 E5
Clothall Common Herts 104 E5
Clotton W Ches 167 C8
Clotton Common W Ches 167 C8
Cloud Side Staffs 168 C6
Cloudesley Bush Warks 135 F9
Clouds Hereford 97 D11
Clough Gtr Man 196 D2
Clough Gtr Man 196 F2
Clough W Yorks 196 E5
Clough Dene Durham 242 F5
Clough Foot W Yorks 196 C2
Clough Hall Staffs 168 E4
Clough Head W Yorks 196 C5
Cloughfold Lancs 195 C10
Cloughton N Yorks 227 G10
Cloughton Newlands N Yorks 227 F10
Clounlaid Highld 289 D9
Clousta Shetland 313 H5
Clouston Orkney 314 E2
Clova Aberds 302 G4
Clova Angus 292 F5
Clove Lodge Durham 223 B8
Clovelly Devon 24 C4
Clovenfords Borders 261 B10
Clovenstone Aberds 293 B9
Cloves Moray 301 C11
Clovullin Highld 290 G2
Clow Bridge Lancs 195 B10
Clowance Wood Corn 2 C4
Clowne Derbys 187 F7
Clows Top Worcs 116 C4
Cloy Wrex 166 G5
Cluanie Inn Highld 290 B2
Cluanie Lodge Highld 290 B2
Clubmoor Mers 182 C5
Clubworthy Corn 11 C11
Cluddley Telford 150 G2
Clun Shrops 130 G6
Clunbury Shrops 131 G7
Clunderwen Carms 73 B10
Clune Highld 301 D9
Clune Highld 301 G7
Clunes Highld 290 E4
Clungunford Shrops 115 B7
Clunie Aberds 302 D6
Clunie Perth 286 C5
Clunton Shrops 130 G6
Cluny Fife 280 B4
Cluny Castle Aberds 293 B8
Cluny Castle Highld 291 D8
Clutton Bath 44 B6
Clutton W Ches 167 E7
Clutton Hill Bath 44 B6
Clwt-grugoer Conwy 165 C7
Clwt-y-bont Gwyn 163 C9
Clwydyfagwyr M Tydf 77 D8
Clydach Mon 78 C2
Clydach Swansea 75 E11
Clydach Terrace Powys 77 C11
Clydach Vale Rhondda 77 G7
Clydebank W Dunb 277 G9
Clyffe Pypard Wilts 62 D5
Clynder Argyll 276 E4
Clyne Neath 76 E4
Clynelish Highld 311 J2
Clynnog-fawr Gwyn 162 F6
Clyro = Cleirwy Powys 96 C4
Clyst Honiton Devon 14 C5
Clyst Hydon Devon 27 G8
Clyst St George Devon 14 D5
Clyst St Lawrence Devon 27 G8
Clyst St Mary Devon 14 C5
Cnìp W Isles 304 E2
Cnoc Amhlaigh W Isles 304 E7
Cnoc an t-Solais W Isles 304 D6
Cnoc Fhionn Highld 295 D10
Cnoc Màiri W Isles 304 E6
Cnoc Rolum W Isles 296 F3
Cnocbreac Argyll 274 F5
Cnwch-coch Ceredig 112 B3
Coachford Aberds 302 E4
Coad's Green Corn 11 F11
Coal Aston Derbys 186 F5
Coal Bank Darl 234 G3
Coal Pool W Mid 133 C10
Coalbrookdale Telford 132 C3
Coalbrookvale Bl Gwent 77 D11
Coalburn S Lnrk 259 C8
Coalburns T & W 242 E4
Coalcleugh Northumb 232 B2
Coaley Glos 80 E3
Coaley Peak Glos 80 E3
Coalford Aberds 293 D10
Coalhall E Ayrs 257 F10
Coalhill Essex 88 F3
Coalmoor Telford 132 B3
Coalpit Field Warks 135 F7
Coalpit Heath S Glos 61 C7
Coalpit Hill Staffs 168 E4
Coalport Telford 132 C3
Coalsnaughton Clack 279 B8
Coaltown of Balgonie Fife 280 B5
Coaltown of Wemyss Fife 280 B6
Coalville Leics 153 G8
Coalway Glos 79 C9
Coanwood Northumb 240 F5
Coarsewell Devon 8 E4
Coat Som 29 C7
Coatbridge N Lnrk 268 C4
Coatdyke N Lnrk 268 C5
Coate Swindon 63 C7
Coate Wilts 62 G4
Coates Cambs 138 D6
Coates Glos 81 E7
Coates Lancs 204 D3
Coates Lincs 188 E6
Coates Midloth 270 C4
Coates Notts 188 E4
Coates W Sus 35 D7
Coatham Redcar 235 F7
Coatham Mundeville Darl 233 G11
Coatsgate Dumfries 248 B3
Cobairdy Aberds 302 E5
Cobbaton Devon 25 B10
Cobbler's Corner Worcs 116 F5
Cobbler's Green Norf 142 E5
Cobbler's Plain Mon 79 E7
Cobbs Warr 183 D10
Cobb's Cross Glos 98 E5
Cobbs Fenn Essex 106 E5
Cobby Syke N Yorks 205 B9
Coberley Glos 81 B7
Cobhall Common Hereford 97 D9
Cobham Kent 69 F7
Cobham Sur 66 G6
Cobleland Stirl 277 B10
Cobler's Green Essex 87 B11
Cobley Dorset 31 C8
Cobley Hill Worcs 117 C10
Cobnash Hereford 115 E9
Cobridge Stoke 168 F5
Cobscot Shrops 150 B3
Coburty Aberds 303 C9
Cock and End Suff 124 G4
Cock Alley Derbys 186 G6
Cock Bank Wrex 166 F5
Cock Bevington Warks 117 G11
Cock Bridge Aberds 292 C4
Cock Clarks Essex 88 E4
Cock Gate Hereford 115 D9
Cock Green Essex 87 B11
Cock Hill N Yorks 206 B6
Cock Marling E Sus 38 D5
Cock Street Kent 53 C9
Cock Street Suff 107 D9
Cockadilly Glos 80 E4
Cockayne N Yorks 226 F2
Cockburnspath Borders 282 G5
Cockden Lancs 204 G3
Cockenzie and Port Seton E Loth 281 F8
Cocker Bar Lancs 194 C4
Cockerham Lancs 202 C5
Cockermouth Cumb 229 E8
Cockernhoe Herts 104 G2
Cockernhoe Green Herts 104 G2
Cockersdale W Yorks 197 B8
Cockerton Darl 224 B5
Cockett Swansea 56 C6
Cocketty Aberds 293 F9
Cockfield Durham 233 G8
Cockfield Suff 125 G8
Cockfosters London 86 F3
Cockhill Som 44 G6
Cocking W Sus 34 D5
Cocking Causeway W Sus 34 D5
Cockington Torbay 9 C7
Cocklake Som 44 D2
Cocklaw Northumb 241 C10
Cockleford Glos 81 C7
Cockley Beck Cumb 220 E4
Cockley Cley Norf 140 C5
Cockley Hill W Yorks 197 D7
Cocknowle Dorset 18 E4
Cockpole Green Wokingham 65 C9
Cocks Corn 4 E5
Cocks Green Suff 125 F7
Cockshead Ceredig 112 F2
Cockshoot Hereford 97 D11
Cockshutford Shrops 131 F11
Cockshutt Shrops 132 G4
Cockshutt Shrops 149 D8
Cockthorpe Norf 177 E7
Cockwells Corn 2 C2
Cockwood Devon 14 E5
Cockwood Som 43 E8
Cockyard Derbys 185 F8
Cockyard Hereford 97 E8
Codda Corn 11 F9
Coddenham Suff 126 G2
Coddenham Green Suff 126 F2
Coddington Hereford 98 C4
Coddington Notts 172 E4
Coddington W Ches 167 D7
Codford St Mary Wilts 46 F3
Codford St Peter Wilts 46 F3
Codicote Herts 86 B2
Codicote Bottom Herts 86 B2
Codmore Bucks 85 E7
Codmore Hill W Sus 35 C9
Codnor Derbys 170 F6
Codnor Breach Derbys 170 F6
Codnor Gate Derbys 170 E6
Codnor Park Derbys 170 E6
Codrington S Glos 61 D8
Codsall Staffs 133 C7
Codsall Wood Staffs 132 B6
Codsend Som 41 F11
Coed Cwnwr Mon 78 F6
Coed Eva Torf 78 G3
Coed Llai = Leeswood Flint 166 D3
Coed Mawr Gwyn 179 G9
Coed Morgan Mon 78 C5
Coed-Talon Flint 166 D3
Coed-y-bryn Ceredig 93 C7
Coed-y-caerau Newport 78 G5
Coed-y-fedw Mon 78 D6
Coed y Garth Ceredig 128 E3
Coed y go Shrops 148 D5
Coed-y-paen Mon 78 F4
Coed-y-parc Gwyn 163 B10
Coed-y-wlad Powys 130 B4
Coed-yr-ynys Powys 96 G3
Coed Ystumgwern Gwyn 145 E11
Coedcae Bl Gwent 77 D11
Coedcae Torf 78 D3
Coedely Rhondda 58 B4
Coedkernew Newport 59 C9
Coedpoeth Wrex 166 E3
Coedway Powys 148 G6
Coelbren Powys 76 C4
Coffee Hall M Keynes 103 D7
Coffinswell Devon 9 B7
Cofton Devon 14 E5
Cofton Common W Mid 117 B10
Cofton Hackett Worcs 117 B10
Cog V Glam 59 F7
Cogan V Glam 59 E7
Cogenhoe Northants 120 E6
Cogges Oxon 82 D5
Coggeshall Essex 106 G6
Coggeshall Hamlet Essex 107 G7
Coggins Mill E Sus 37 B9
Coig Peighinnean W Isles 304 B7
Coig Peighinnean Bhuirgh W Isles 304 C6
Coignafearn Lodge Highld 291 B8
Coignascallan Highld 291 B9
Coilacriech Aberds 292 D5
Coilantogle Stirl 285 G9
Coilessan Argyll 284 G6
Coilleag W Isles 297 K3
Coillemore Highld 300 B6
Coillore Highld 294 B5
Coirea-chrombe Stirl 285 G9
Coisley Hill S Yorks 186 E6
Coity Bridgend 58 C2
Cokenach Herts 105 D7
Cokhay Green Derbys 152 D5
Col W Isles 304 D6
Col Uarach W Isles 304 E6
Colaboll Highld 309 H5
Colan Corn 5 C7
Colaton Raleigh Devon 15 D7
Colbost Highld 298 E2
Colburn N Yorks 224 F3
Colby Cumb 231 G9
Colby I o M 192 E3
Colby Norf 160 C4
Colchester Essex 107 F10
Colchester Green Suff 125 F8
Colcot V Glam 58 F6
Cold Ash W Berks 64 F4
Cold Ash Hill Hants 49 G10
Cold Ashby Northants 120 B3
Cold Ashton S Glos 61 E9
Cold Aston Glos 81 B10
Cold Blow Pembs 73 C10
Cold Brayfield M Keynes 121 G8
Cold Christmas Herts 86 B5
Cold Cotes N Yorks 212 E4
Cold Elm Glos 98 E6
Cold Hanworth Lincs 189 E8
Cold Harbour Dorset 18 D4
Cold Harbour Herts 85 B10
Cold Harbour Kent 69 G11
Cold Harbour Lincs 155 C9
Cold Harbour Oxon 64 D6
Cold Harbour Wilts 45 B11
Cold Harbour Wilts 45 D11
Cold Harbour Windsor 65 D10
Cold Hatton Telford 150 E2
Cold Hatton Heath Telford 150 E2
Cold Hesledon Durham 234 B4
Cold Hiendley W Yorks 197 E11
Cold Higham Northants 120 G3
Cold Inn Pembs 73 D10
Cold Kirby N Yorks 215 C10
Cold Moss Heath E Ches 168 C3
Cold Newton Leics 136 B4
Cold Northcott Corn 11 D10
Cold Norton Essex 88 E4
Cold Overton Leics 154 G6
Cold Row Lancs 202 E3
Cold Well Staffs 151 G11
Coldbackie Highld 308 D6
Coldbeck Cumb 222 E4
Coldblow London 68 E4
Coldbrook Powys 96 D3
Coldean Brighton 36 F4
Coldeast Devon 14 G2
Coldeaton Derbys 169 D10
Colden W Yorks 196 B3
Colden Common Hants 33 C7
Coldfair Green Suff 127 E8
Coldham Cambs 139 C8
Coldham Staffs 133 B7
Coldham's Common Cambs 123 F9
Coldharbour Corn 4 F5
Coldharbour Devon 27 E9
Coldharbour Dorset 17 E9
Coldharbour Glos 79 E9
Coldharbour Kent 52 C5
Coldharbour London 68 D4
Coldharbour Sur 50 E6
Coldingham Borders 273 B8
Coldmeece Staffs 151 C7
Coldoch Stirl 278 B3
Coldra Newport 59 B11
Coldrain Perth 286 G4
Coldred Kent 55 D9
Coldridge Devon 25 F11
Coldstream Angus 287 D7
Coldstream Borders 263 B8
Coldvreath Corn 5 D9
Coldwaltham W Sus 35 D8
Coldwells Aberds 303 E11
Coldwells Croft Aberds 302 G5
Cole Som 45 G7
Cole End Essex 105 D11
Cole End Warks 134 F3
Cole Green Herts 86 C3
Cole Green Herts 105 E8
Cole Henley Hants 48 C3
Cole Park London 67 E7
Colebatch Shrops 130 F6
Colebrook Devon 27 F8
Colebrooke Devon 13 B11
Coleburn Moray 302 D2
Coleby Lincs 173 C7
Coleby N Lincs 199 D11
Coleford Devon 26 G3
Coleford Glos 79 C9
Coleford Som 45 D7
Coleford Water Som 42 G6
Colegate End Norf 142 F3
Colehall W Mid 134 F2
Colehill Dorset 31 G8
Coleman Green Herts 85 C11
Coleman's Hatch E Sus 52 G3
Colemere Shrops 149 C8
Colemore Hants 49 G8
Colemore Green Shrops 132 D4
Coleorton Leics 153 F8
Coleorton Moor Leics 153 F8
Colerne Wilts 61 E10
Cole's Cross Dorset 28 G5
Coles Green Suff 107 C11
Cole's Green Suff 126 E5
Coles Green Worcs 116 G5
Coles Meads Sur 51 C9
Colesbourne Glos 81 C7
Colesbrook Dorset 30 B4
Colesden Beds 122 F2
Coleshill Bucks 85 F7
Coleshill Oxon 82 G2
Coleshill Warks 134 F4
Colestocks Devon 27 G9
Colethrop Glos 80 C4
Coley Bath 44 B5
Coley Reading 65 E8
Coley W Yorks 196 B6
Colfin Dumfries 236 D2
Colgate W Sus 51 G8
Colgrain Argyll 276 E6
Colham Green London 66 C5
Colindale London 67 B8
Colinsburgh Fife 287 G8
Colinton Edin 270 B4
Colintraive Argyll 275 F11
Colkirk Norf 159 D8
Collace Perth 286 D6
Collafield Glos 79 C11
Collafirth Shetland 312 G6
Collam W Isles 305 J3
Collamoor Head Corn 11 C9
Collaton Devon 9 G9
Collaton St Mary Torbay 9 D7
College Milton S Lnrk 268 D2
College of Roseisle Moray 301 C11
College Park London 67 C8
College Town Brack 65 G11
Collennan S Ayrs 257 C8
Collessie Fife 286 F6
Colleton Mills Devon 25 D11
Collett's Br Norf 139 B9
Collett's Green Worcs 116 G6
Collier Row London 87 G8
Collier Street Kent 53 D8
Collier's End Herts 105 G7
Collier's Green E Sus 38 C3
Collier's Green Kent 53 F9
Colliers Hatch Essex 87 E8
Collier's Wood London 67 E9
Colliery Row T & W 234 B2
Collieston Aberds 303 G10
Collin Dumfries 238 B2
Collingbourne Ducis Wilts 47 C8
Collingbourne Kingston Wilts 47 B8
Collingham Notts 172 C4
Collingham W Yorks 206 D3
Collington Hereford 116 E2
Collingtree Northants 120 F5
Collingwood Northumb 243 B7
Collins End Oxon 65 D7
Collins Green Warr 183 C9
Collins Green Worcs 116 F4
Collipriest Devon 27 E7
Colliston Angus 287 C10
Colliton Devon 27 G9
Collycroft Warks 135 F7
Collyhurst Gtr Man 195 G11
Collynie Aberds 303 F8
Collyweston Northants 137 C9
Colmonell S Ayrs 244 F4
Colmslie Borders 262 B2
Colmsliehill Borders 271 G10
Colmworth Beds 122 F2
Coln Rogers Glos 81 D9
Coln St Aldwyns Glos 81 D10
Coln St Dennis Glos 81 C9
Colnabaichin Aberds 292 C4
Colnbrook Slough 66 D4
Colne Cambs 123 B7
Colne Lancs 204 E3
Colne Bridge W Yorks 197 C7
Colne Edge Lancs 204 E3
Colne Engaine Essex 107 E7
Colnefields Cambs 123 B7
Colney Norf 142 B3
Colney Hatch London 86 G3
Colney Heath Herts 86 D2
Colney Street Herts 85 E11
Cologin Argyll 289 G10
Colpitts Grange Northumb 241 F11
Colpy Aberds 302 F6
Colquhar Borders 270 G6
Colscott Devon 24 E5
Colshaw Staffs 169 B8
Colsterdale N Yorks 214 C2
Colsterworth Lincs 155 E8
Colston E Dunb 268 B2
Colston Pembs 91 F9
Colston Bassett Notts 154 C3
Colstrope Bucks 65 B9
Colt Hill Hants 49 C8
Colt Park Cumb 210 E5
Coltfield Moray 301 C11
Colthouse Cumb 221 F7
Colthrop W Berks 64 F4
Coltishall Norf 160 F5
Coltness N Lnrk 268 D6
Colton Cumb 210 B6
Colton N Yorks 206 E6
Colton Norf 142 B2
Colton Staffs 151 E11
Colton Suff 125 D7
Colton W Yorks 206 G3
Colton Hills Staffs 133 D8
Colt's Green S Glos 61 C8
Colt's Hill Kent 52 E6
Columbia T & W 243 F8
Columbjohn Devon 14 B5
Colva Powys 114 G4
Colvend Dumfries 237 D10
Colvister Shetland 312 D7
Colwall Hereford 98 C4
Colwall Green Hereford 98 C4
Colwall Stone Hereford 98 C5
Colwell I o W 20 D2
Colwell Northumb 241 B11
Colwich Staffs 151 E10
Colwick Notts 171 G10
Colwinston = Tregolwyn V Glam 58 D2
Colworth W Sus 22 C6
Colwyn Bay = Bae Colwyn Conwy 180 F4
Colychurch Bridgend 58 D2
Colyford Devon 15 C10
Colyton Devon 15 C10
Colzie Fife 286 F6
Combe Devon 7 E10
Combe Devon 8 B4
Combe Devon 9 G9
Combe E Sus 37 B10
Combe Hereford 114 E6
Combe Oxon 82 B6
Combe Som 28 B6
Combe W Berks 63 G11
Combe Almer Dorset 18 B5
Combe Common Sur 50 F3
Combe Down Bath 61 G9
Combe Fishacre Devon 8 C6
Combe Florey Som 43 G7
Combe Hay Bath 45 B8
Combe Martin Devon 40 D5
Combe Moor Hereford 115 E7
Combe Pafford Torbay 9 B8
Combe Raleigh Devon 27 G11
Combe St Nicholas Som 28 E4
Combe Throop Som 30 C2
Combebow Devon 12 D5
Combeinteignhead Devon 14 G4
Comberbach W Ches 183 F10
Comberford Staffs 134 B3
Comberton Cambs 123 F7
Comberton Hereford 115 D9
Combpyne Devon 15 C11
Combrew Devon 40 G4
Combridge Staffs 151 B11
Combrook Warks 118 G6
Combs Derbys 185 F8
Combs Suff 125 F10
Combs W Yorks 197 D8
Combs Ford Suff 125 F11
Combwich Som 43 E9
Come-to-Good Corn 4 G6
Comers Aberds 293 C8
Comeytrowe Som 28 C2
Comford Corn 2 B6
Comfort Corn 2 D6
Comhampton Worcs 116 D6
Comins Coch Ceredig 128 G2
Comiston Edin 270 B4
Comley Shrops 131 D9
Commercial End Cambs 123 E11
Commins Denb 165 C10
Commins Capel Betws Ceredig 112 F2
Commins Coch Powys 128 C6
Common Cefn-llwyn Mon 78 G4
Common Edge Blkpool 202 G2
Common End Cumb 228 G6
Common End Derbys 170 C6
Common Hill Hereford 97 E11
Common Moor Corn 6 B4
Common Platt Wilts 62 B6
Common Side Derbys 170 F6
Common Side Derbys 186 F4
Common Side W Ches 167 B9
Common-y-coed Mon 60 B2

Commondale N Yorks 226 C3
Commonmoor Corn 6 B4
Commonside Derbys 170 G2
Commonside Notts 171 D7
Commonside W Ches 183 G8
Commonwood Herts 85 E8
Commonwood Shrops 149 D9
Commonwood Wrex 166 E5
Comp Kent 52 B6
Compass Som 43 G9
Compstall Gtr Man 185 C7
Compton Derbys 169 F11
Compton Devon 9 C7
Compton Hants 32 B4
Compton Hants 33 B7
Compton Plym 7 D9
Compton Staffs 132 G6
Compton Sur 49 D11
Compton Sur 50 D3
Compton W Berks 64 D4
Compton W Mid 133 D7
Compton W Sus 34 E3
Compton W Yorks 206 E3
Compton Wilts 46 C6
Compton Abbas Dorset 30 D5
Compton Abdale Glos 81 B9
Compton Bassett Wilts 62 E4
Compton Beauchamp Oxon 63 B9
Compton Bishop Som 43 B11
Compton Chamberlayne Wilts 31 B8
Compton Common Bath 60 G6
Compton Dando Bath 60 G6
Compton Dundon Som 44 G3
Compton Durville Som 28 D6
Compton End Hants 33 B7
Compton Green Glos 98 F4
Compton Greenfield S Glos 60 C5
Compton Martin Bath 44 B4
Compton Pauncefoot Som 29 B10
Compton Valence Dorset 17 C7
Comrie Fife 279 D10
Comrie Highld 300 D4
Comrie Perth 285 C11
Comrie Perth 285 E11
Comrue Dumfries 248 F3
Conaglen House Highld 290 G2
Conanby S Yorks 187 B7
Conchra Argyll 275 E11
Conchra Highld 295 C10
Concord T & W 243 F8
Concraig Perth 286 F2
Concraigie Perth 286 C5
Conder Green Lancs 202 B5
Conderton Worcs 99 D9
Condicote Glos 100 F3
Condorrat N Lnrk 278 G4
Condover Shrops 131 B9
Coney Hall London 67 G11
Coney Hill Glos 80 B5
Coney Weston Suff 125 B9
Coneyhurst W Sus 35 C10
Coneysthorpe N Yorks 216 E4
Coneythorpe N Yorks 206 B3
Conford Hants 49 G10
Congash Highld 301 G10
Congdon's Shop Corn 11 F11
Congeith Dumfries 237 C10
Congelow Kent 53 D7
Congerstone Leics 135 B7
Congham Norf 158 E4
Congl-y-wal Gwyn 164 G2
Congleton E Ches 168 C5
Congleton Edge E Ches 168 C5
Congresbury N Som 60 G2
Congreve Staffs 151 G8
Conham Bristol 60 E6
Conicavel Moray 301 D9
Coningsby Lincs 174 D2
Conington Cambs 122 D6
Conington Cambs 138 F3
Conisbrough S Yorks 187 B8
Conisby Argyll 274 G3
Conisholme Lincs 190 B6
Coniston Cumb 220 F6
Coniston E Yorks 209 F9
Coniston Cold N Yorks 204 B4
Conistone N Yorks 213 F9
Conkwell Wilts 61 G9
Connage Moray 302 C4
Connah's Quay Flint 166 B3
Connel Argyll 289 F11
Connel Park E Ayrs 258 G4
Conniburrow M Keynes 103 D7
Connista Highld 298 B4
Connon Corn 6 C3
Connor Downs Corn 2 B3
Conock Wilts 46 B5
Conon Bridge Highld 300 D5
Conon House Highld 300 D5
Cononish Stirl 285 E7
Cononley N Yorks 204 D5
Cononley Woodside N Yorks 204 D5
Cononsyth Angus 287 C9
Conordan Highld 295 B7
Conquermoor Heath Telford 150 F3
Consall Staffs 169 F7
Consett Durham 242 G4
Constable Burton N Yorks 224 G3
Constable Lee Lancs 195 C10
Constantine Corn 2 D6
Constantine Bay Corn 10 G3
Contin Highld 300 D4
Contlaw Aberdeen 293 C10
Conwy Conwy 180 F3
Conyer Kent 70 G3
Conyers Green Suff 125 D7
Cooden E Sus 38 F2
Cooil I o M 192 E4
Cookbury Devon 24 F6
Cookbury Wick Devon 24 F5
Cookham Windsor 65 B11
Cookham Dean Windsor 65 C11
Cookham Rise Windsor 65 C11
Cookhill Worcs 117 F11
Cookley Suff 126 B6
Cookley Worcs 132 G6
Cookley Green Oxon 83 G11
Cookney Aberds 293 D10
Cookridge W Yorks 205 E11
Cook's Green Essex 89 B11
Cook's Green Suff 125 G9
Cooksbridge E Sus 36 E6
Cooksey Corner Worcs 117 D8
Cooksey Green Worcs 117 D8
Cookshill Staffs 168 G6
Cooksland Corn 5 B11
Cooksmill Green Essex 87 D10
Cooksongreen W Ches 183 G9
Coolham W Sus 35 C10
Cooling Medway 69 D9
Cooling Street Medway 69 E8
Coolinge Kent 55 F8
Coomb Hill Kent 69 G7
Coombe Bucks 84 D4
Coombe Corn 4 G2
Coombe Corn 4 G5
Coombe Corn 4 G6
Coombe Corn 5 E9
Coombe Corn 6 C4
Coombe Corn 24 E2
Coombe Devon 14 G4
Coombe Devon 27 D8
Coombe Glos 80 G3
Coombe Hants 33 C11
Coombe Kent 55 B9
Coombe London 67 E8
Coombe Som 28 B3
Coombe Som 28 F6
Coombe Wilts 30 C5
Coombe Wilts 47 C7
Coombe Bissett Wilts 31 B10
Coombe Dingle Bristol 60 D5
Coombe Hill Glos 99 F7
Coombe Keynes Dorset 18 E2
Coombes W Sus 35 F11
Coombesdale Staffs 150 B6
Coombeswood W Mid 133 F9
Coombs End S Glos 61 C9
Coombses Som 28 F4
Cooper Street Kent 55 B10
Cooper Turning Gtr Man 194 F6
Cooper's Corner Kent 52 D3
Cooper's Green E Sus 37 C7
Cooper's Green Herts 85 D11
Cooper's Hill C Beds 103 D10
Cooper's Hill Sur 66 E3
Coopersale Common Essex 87 E7
Coopersale Street Essex 87 E7
Cootham W Sus 35 E9
Cop Street Kent 55 B9
Copcut Worcs 117 F7
Copdock Suff 108 C2
Coped Hall Wilts 62 C5
Copenhagen Denb 165 B8
Copford Essex 107 G8
Copford Green Essex 107 G8
Copgrove N Yorks 214 G6
Copister Shetland 312 F6
Cople Beds 104 B2
Copley Durham 233 F7
Copley Gtr Man 185 B7
Copley W Yorks 196 C5
Copley Hill W Yorks 197 B8
Coplow Dale Derbys 185 F11
Copmanthorpe York 207 D7
Copmere End Staffs 150 D6
Copnor Ptsmth 33 G11
Copp Lancs 202 F4
Coppathorne Corn 24 G2
Coppenhall E Ches 168 D2
Coppenhall Staffs 151 F8
Coppenhall Moss E Ches 168 D2
Copperhouse Corn 2 B3
Coppice Gtr Man 196 G2
Coppicegate Shrops 132 G4
Coppingford Cambs 138 G3
Coppins Corner Kent 54 D2
Coppleham Som 42 G2
Copplestone Devon 26 G3
Coppull Lancs 194 E5
Coppull Moor Lancs 194 E5
Copsale W Sus 35 C11
Copse Hill London 67 E8
Copster Green Lancs 203 G9
Copster Hill Gtr Man 196 G2
Copston Magna Warks 135 F9
Copt Green Warks 118 D3
Copt Heath W Mid 118 B3
Copt Hewick N Yorks 214 E6
Copt Oak Leics 153 G9
Copthall Green Essex 86 E6
Copthill Durham 232 C3
Copthorne Corn 11 C11
Copthorne E Ches 167 G11
Copthorne Shrops 149 G9
Copthorne Sur 51 F10
Coptiviney Shrops 149 B8
Copton Kent 54 B4
Copy's Green Norf 159 B8
Copythorne Hants 32 E4
Corbets Tey London 68 B5
Corbridge Northumb 241 E11
Corbriggs Derbys 170 B6
Corby Northants 137 F7
Corby Glen Lincs 155 E9
Corby Hill Cumb 239 F11
Cordon N Ayrs 256 C2
Cordwell Norf 142 E2
Coreley Shrops 116 C2
Cores End Bucks 66 B2
Corfe Som 28 D2
Corfe Castle Dorset 18 E5
Corfe Mullen Dorset 18 B5
Corfton Shrops 131 F9
Corfton Bache Shrops 131 F9
Corgarff Aberds 292 C4
Corgee Corn 5 C10
Corhampton Hants 33 C10
Corlae Dumfries 246 D5
Corlannau Neath 57 C9
Corley Warks 134 F6
Corley Ash Warks 134 F5
Corley Moor Warks 134 F5
Cornaa I o M 192 D5
Cornabus Argyll 254 C4
Cornaigbeg Argyll 288 E1
Cornaigmore Argyll 288 C4
Cornaigmore Argyll 288 E1
Cornard Tye Suff 107 C8
Cornbank Midloth 270 C4
Cornbrook Shrops 116 B2
Corncatterach Aberds 302 F5
Cornel Conwy 164 C2
Corner Row Lancs 202 F4
Cornett Hereford 97 B11
Corney Cumb 220 G2
Cornforth Durham 234 E2
Cornharrow Dumfries 246 E5
Cornhill Aberds 302 D5
Cornhill Powys 96 C2
Cornhill Stoke 168 E5
Cornhill-on-Tweed Northumb 263 B9
Cornholme W Yorks 196 B2
Cornish Hall End Essex 106 D3
Cornquoy Orkney 314 G5
Cornriggs Durham 232 C2
Cornsay Durham 233 C8
Cornsay Colliery Durham 233 C9
Cornton Stirl 278 B5
Corntown Highld 300 D5
Corntown V Glam 58 D2
Cornwell Oxon 100 F5
Cornwood Devon 8 D2
Cornworthy Devon 8 D6
Corpach Highld 290 F2
Corpusty Norf 160 C2
Corran Highld 290 G2
Corran Highld 295 E10
Corran a Chan Uachdaraich Highld 295 C7
Corranbuie Argyll 275 G9
Corrany I o M 192 D5
Corrichoich Highld 311 G4
Corrie N Ayrs 255 C11
Corrie Common Dumfries 248 F6
Corriecravie N Ayrs 255 E10
Corriecravie Moor N Ayrs 255 E10
Corriedoo Dumfries 246 G5
Corriegarth Lodge Highld 291 B7
Corriemoillie Highld 300 C3
Corriemulzie Lodge Highld 309 K3
Corrievarkie Lodge Perth 291 F7
Corrievorrie Highld 301 G7
Corrigall Orkney 314 E3
Corrimony Highld 300 F3
Corringham Lincs 188 C5
Corringham Thurrock 69 C8
Corris Gwyn 128 B5
Corris Uchaf Gwyn 128 B4
Corrour Highld 290 G5
Corrour Shooting Lodge Highld 290 G6
Corrow Argyll 284 G5
Corry Highld 295 C8
Corry of Ardnagrask Highld 300 E5
Corrybrough Highld 301 G8
Corrydon Perth 292 G3
Corryghoil Argyll 284 E5
Corrykinloch Highld 309 G3
Corrylach Argyll 255 D8
Corrymuckloch Perth 286 D2
Corrynachenchy Argyll 289 E8
Cors-y-Gedol Gwyn 145 E11
Corsback Highld 310 B6
Corscombe Dorset 29 F8
Corse Aberds 302 E6
Corse Glos 98 F5
Corse Lawn Worcs 98 E6
Corse of Kinnoir Aberds 302 E5
Corsewall Dumfries 236 C2
Corsham Wilts 61 E11
Corsindae Aberds 293 C8
Corsley Wilts 45 D10
Corsley Heath Wilts 45 D10
Corsock Dumfries 237 B9
Corston Bath 61 F7
Corston Orkney 314 E3
Corston Wilts 62 C2
Corstorphine Edin 280 G3
Cortachy Angus 287 B7
Corton Suff 143 D10
Corton Wilts 46 E2
Corton Denham Som 29 C10
Cortworth S Yorks 186 B6
Coruanan Lodge Highld 290 G2
Corunna W Isles 296 E4
Corvast Highld 309 K5
Corwen Denb 165 G9
Cory Devon 24 D5
Coryates Dorset 17 D8
Coryton Cardiff 58 C6
Coryton Devon 12 E5
Coryton Thurrock 69 C8
Còsag Highld 295 D10
Cosby Leics 135 E10
Coscote Oxon 64 B4
Coseley W Mid 133 E8
Cosford Warks 119 B9
Cosgrove Northants 102 C5
Cosham Ptsmth 33 F11
Cosheston Pembs 73 E8
Cosmeston V Glam 59 F7
Cosmore Dorset 29 F11
Cossall Notts 171 G7
Cossall Marsh Notts 171 G7
Cosses S Ayrs 244 G4
Cossington Leics 154 G2
Cossington Som 43 E11
Costa Orkney 314 D3
Costessey Norf 160 G3
Costessey Park Norf 160 G3
Costhorpe Notts 187 D9
Costislost Corn 10 G6
Costock Notts 153 D11
Coston Leics 154 E6
Coston Norf 141 B11
Coswinsawsin Corn 2 B4
Cote Oxon 82 E4
Cote Som 43 E10
Cote W Sus 35 F10
Cotebrook W Ches 167 B9
Cotehill Cumb 239 G11
Cotes Cumb 211 B9
Cotes Leics 153 E11
Cotes Staffs 150 C6
Cotes Heath Staffs 150 C6
Cotes Park Derbys 170 E6
Cotesbach Leics 135 G10
Cotford St Lukes Som 27 B11
Cotgrave Notts 154 B2
Cothall Aberds 293 B10
Cotham Bristol 60 E5
Cotham Notts 172 F3
Cothelstone Som 43 G7
Cotheridge Worcs 116 G5
Cotherstone Durham 223 B10
Cothill Oxon 83 F7
Cotland Mon 79 E8
Cotleigh Devon 28 G2
Cotmanhay Derbys 171 G7
Cotmarsh Wilts 62 D5
Cotmaton Devon 15 D8
Coton Cambs 123 F8
Coton Northants 120 C3
Coton Shrops 149 C10
Coton Staffs 134 B3
Coton Staffs 150 E6
Coton Staffs 151 C9
Coton Clanford Staffs 151 E7
Coton Hayes Staffs 151 C9
Coton Hill Shrops 149 G9
Coton Hill Staffs 151 C9
Coton in the Clay Staffs 152 D3
Coton in the Elms Derbys 152 F4
Coton Park Derbys 152 F5
Cotonwood Shrops 149 B10
Cotonwood Staffs 150 E6
Cotswold Community Wilts 81 F8
Cott Devon 8 C5
Cottam E Yorks 217 F9
Cottam Lancs 202 G6
Cottam Notts 188 F4
Cottartown Highld 301 F10
Cottenham Cambs 123 D8
Cottenham Park London 67 F8
Cotterdale N Yorks 222 G6
Cottered Herts 104 F6
Cotterhill Woods S Yorks 187 E9
Cotteridge W Mid 117 B10
Cotterstock Northants 137 E10
Cottesbrooke Northants 120 C4
Cottesmore Rutland 155 G8
Cotteylands Devon 26 E6
Cottingham E Yorks 208 G6
Cottingham Northants 136 E6
Cottingley W Yorks 205 F8
Cottisford Oxon 101 E11
Cotton Staffs 169 F9
Cotton Suff 125 D11
Cotton End Beds 103 B11
Cotton End Northants 120 F5
Cotton Stones W Yorks 196 C4
Cotton Tree Lancs 204 F4
Cottonworth Hants 47 F11
Cottown Aberds 293 B9
Cottown Aberds 302 G5
Cottown Aberds 303 E8
Cotts Devon 7 B8
Cottwood Devon 25 E10
Cotwall Telford 150 F2
Cotwalton Staffs 151 B8
Coubister Orkney 314 E3
Couch Green Hants 48 G4
Couch's Mill Corn 6 D2
Coughton Hereford 97 G11
Coughton Warks 117 E11
Coughton Fields Warks 117 F11
Cougie Highld 300 G2
Coulaghailtro Argyll 275 G8
Coulags Highld 299 E9
Coulby Newham M'bro 225 B10
Coulderton Cumb 219 D9
Couldoran Highld 299 E8
Couligartan Stirl 285 G8
Coulin Highld 299 D10
Coulin Lodge Highld 299 D10
Coull Aberds 293 C7
Coull Argyll 274 G3
Coulmony Ho Highld 301 E9
Coulport Argyll 276 D4
Coulsdon London 51 B9
Coulshill Perth 286 G3
Coulston Wilts 46 C3
Coulter S Lnrk 260 C2
Coultings Som 43 E8
Coulton N Yorks 216 E2
Coultra Fife 287 E7
Cound Shrops 131 C11
Coundlane Shrops 131 B11
Coundmoor Shrops 131 C11
Coundon Durham 233 F10
Coundon W Mid 134 G6
Coundon Grange Durham 233 F10
Coundongate Durham 233 F10
Counters End Herts 85 D8
Countersett N Yorks 213 B8
Countess Wilts 47 E7
Countess Cross Essex 107 E7
Countess Wear Devon 14 D4
Countesthorpe Leics 135 D11
Countisbury Devon 41 D8
County Oak W Sus 51 F9
Coup Green Lancs 194 B5
Coupar Angus Perth 286 C6
Coupland Cumb 222 B4
Coupland Northumb 263 C10
Cour Argyll 255 C9
Courance Dumfries 248 E3
Coursley Som 42 G6
Court-at-Street Kent 54 F5
Court Barton Devon 14 D2
Court Colman Bridgend 57 E11
Court Corner Hants 48 B6
Court Henry Carms 93 G11
Court House Green W Mid 135 G7
Courteenhall Northants 120 G5
Courthill Perth 286 C5
Courtsend Essex 89 G8
Courtway Som 43 G8
Cousland Midloth 271 B7
Cousley Wood E Sus 53 G7
Couston Argyll 275 F11
Cova Shetland 313 J5
Cove Argyll 276 E4
Cove Borders 282 G5
Cove Devon 27 D7
Cove Hants 49 B11
Cove Highld 307 K3
Cove Bay Aberdeen 293 C11
Cove Bottom Suff 127 B9
Covehithe Suff 143 G10
Coven Staffs 133 B8
Coven Heath Staffs 133 C8
Coven Lawn Staffs 133 B8
Covender Hereford 98 C2
Coveney Cambs 139 G9
Covenham St Bartholomew Lincs 190 C4
Covenham St Mary Lincs 190 C4
Coventry W Mid 118 B6
Coverack Corn 3 F7
Coverack Bridges Corn 2 C5
Coverham N Yorks 214 B2
Covesea Moray 301 B11
Covingham Swindon 63 B7
Covington Cambs 121 C11
Covington S Lnrk 259 B11
Cow Ark Lancs 203 D9
Cow Green Suff 125 D11
Cow Hill Lancs 203 G7
Cow Roast Herts 85 C7
Cowan Bridge Lancs 212 D2
Cowan Head Cumb 221 F9
Cowbar Redcar 226 B5
Cowbeech E Sus 23 C10
Cowbeech Hill E Sus 23 C10
Cowbit Lincs 156 F5
Cowbog Aberds 303 D8
Cowbridge Lincs 174 F4
Cowbridge Som 42 E3
Cowbridge = Y Bont-Faen V Glam 58 E3
Cowcliffe W Yorks 196 D6
Cowdale Derbys 185 G9
Cowden Kent 52 E3
Cowdenbeath Fife 280 C3
Cowdenburn Borders 270 E4
Cowen Head Cumb 221 F9
Cowers Lane Derbys 170 F4
Cowes I o W 20 B5
Cowesby N Yorks 215 B9
Cowesfield Green Wilts 32 C3
Cowfold W Sus 36 C2
Cowgill Cumb 212 B5
Cowgrove Dorset 18 B5
Cowhill Derbys 170 F5
Cowhill S Glos 79 G10
Cowhorn Hill S Glos 61 E7
Cowie Aberds 293 E10
Cowie Stirl 278 D6
Cowlands Corn 4 G6
Cowleaze Corner Oxon 82 E4
Cowley Derbys 186 F4
Cowley Devon 14 B4
Cowley Glos 81 C7
Cowley London 66 C5
Cowley Oxon 83 E8
Cowley Peachy London 66 C5
Cowleymoor Devon 27 E7
Cowling Lancs 194 D5
Cowling N Yorks 204 E5
Cowling N Yorks 214 B4
Cowlinge Suff 124 G4
Cowlow Derbys 185 G9
Cowmes W Yorks 197 D7
Cowpe Lancs 195 C10
Cowpen Northumb 253 G7
Cowpen Bewley Stockton 234 G5
Cowplain Hants 33 E11
Cowshill Durham 232 C3
Cowslip Green N Som 60 G3
Cowstrandburn Fife 279 C10
Cowthorpe N Yorks 206 C4
Cox Common Suff 143 G8
Cox Green Gtr Man 195 E8
Cox Green Sur 50 G5
Cox Green Windsor 65 D11
Cox Hill Corn 4 G4
Cox Moor Notts 171 D8
Coxall Hereford 115 C7
Coxbank E Ches 167 G11
Coxbench Derbys 170 G5
Coxbridge Som 44 F4
Coxford Corn 11 B9
Coxford Norf 158 D6
Coxford Soton 32 D5
Coxgreen Staffs 132 F6
Coxheath Kent 53 C8
Coxhill Kent 55 D8
Coxhoe Durham 234 D2
Coxley Som 44 E4
Coxley W Yorks 197 D9
Coxley Wick Som 44 E4
Coxlodge T & W 242 D6
Coxpark Corn 12 G4
Coxtie Green Essex 87 F9
Coxwold N Yorks 215 D10
Coychurch Bridgend 58 D2
Coylton S Ayrs 257 E10
Coylumbridge Highld 291 B11
Coynach Aberds 292 C6
Coynachie Aberds 302 F4
Coytrahen Bridgend 57 D11
Coytrahën Bridgend 57 D11
Crab Orchard Dorset 31 F9
Crabadon Devon 8 E5
Crabbet Park W Sus 51 F10
Crabble Kent 55 E9
Crabbs Cross Worcs 117 E10
Crabbs Green Herts 105 F9
Crabgate Norf 159 D11
Crabtree Plym 7 D10
Crabtree W Sus 36 B2
Crabtree Green Wrex 166 G4
Crackaig Argyll 274 G6
Crackenedge W Yorks 197 C8
Crackenthorpe Cumb 231 G9
Crackington Haven Corn 11 B8
Crackley Staffs 168 E4
Crackley Warks 118 C5
Crackleybank Shrops 150 G5
Crackpot N Yorks 223 F9
Crackthorn Corner Suff 125 B10
Cracoe N Yorks 213 G9
Cracow Moss E Ches 168 F2
Cracow Moss Staffs 168 F3
Craddock Devon 27 E9
Cradhlastadh W Isles 304 E2
Cradle Edge W Yorks 205 F7
Cradle End Herts 105 G9
Cradley Hereford 98 B4
Cradley W Mid 133 G8
Cradley Heath W Mid 133 F8
Cradoc Powys 95 E10
Crafthole Corn 7 E7
Crafton Bucks 84 B5
Crag Bank Lancs 211 E9
Crag Foot Lancs 211 E9
Cragg Hill W Yorks 205 F10
Cragg Vale W Yorks 196 C4
Craggan Highld 301 G10
Craggan Moray 301 F11
Craggan Stirl 285 E9
Cragganvallie Highld 300 F5
Craggenmore Moray 301 F11
Craggie Highld 301 F7
Craggie Highld 311 H2
Craggiemore Highld 309 J7
Craghead Durham 242 G6
Crahan Corn 2 C5
Crai Powys 95 G7
Craibstone Moray 302 D4
Craichie Angus 287 C9
Craig Dumfries 237 B8
Craig Dumfries 237 C8
Craig Highld 299 E10
Craig Berthlwyd M Tydf 77 F9
Craig Castle Aberds 302 G4
Craig-cefn-parc Swansea 75 E11
Craig Douglas Borders 261 E7
Craig Llangiwg Neath 76 D2
Craig-llwyn Shrops 148 D4
Craig Lodge Argyll 275 G10
Craig-moston Aberds 293 F8
Craig Penllyn V Glam 58 D3
Craig-y-don Conwy 180 E3
Craig-y-Duke Swansea 76 E2
Craig-y-nos Powys 76 B4
Craig-y-penrhyn Ceredig 128 E3
Craig-y-Rhacca Caerph 59 B7
Craiganor Lodge Perth 285 B10
Craigdallie Perth 286 E6
Craigdam Aberds 303 F8
Craigdarroch Dumfries 246 E6
Craigdarroch Highld 300 D4
Craigdhu Highld 300 E4
Craigearn Aberds 293 B9
Craigellachie Moray 302 E2
Craigencallie Ho Dumfries 237 B7
Craigencross Dumfries 236 C2
Craigend Borders 271 F9
Craigend Glasgow 268 B3
Craigend Perth 286 E3
Craigend Perth 286 E5
Craigend Stirl 278 D5
Craigendive Argyll 275 E11
Craigendoran Argyll 276 E6
Craigendowie Angus 293 G7
Craigends Renfs 267 B8
Craigens Argyll 274 G3
Craigens E Ayrs 258 F3
Craigentinny Edin 280 G5
Craigerne Borders 261 B7
Craighall Perth 286 C5
Craighat Stirl 277 E9
Craighead Fife 287 G10
Craighead Highld 301 C7
Craighill Aberds 303 E7
Craighlaw Mains Dumfries 236 C5
Craighouse Argyll 274 G6
Craigie Aberds 293 B11
Craigie Dundee 287 D8
Craigie Perth 286 C5
Craigie Perth 286 E5
Craigie S Ayrs 257 C10
Craigie S Ayrs 257 E8
Craigiefield Orkney 314 E4
Craigiehall Edin 280 F3
Craigielaw E Loth 281 F9
Craigierig Borders 260 E6
Craigleith Edin 280 G4
Craiglockhart Edin 280 G4
Craigmalloch E Ayrs 245 E11
Craigmaud Aberds 303 D8
Craigmill Stirl 278 B6
Craigmillar Edin 280 G5
Craigmore Argyll 266 B2
Craignant Shrops 148 B5
Craignell Dumfries 237 B7
Craigneuk N Lnrk 268 C5
Craigneuk N Lnrk 268 D5
Craignish Castle Argyll 275 C8
Craignure Argyll 289 F9
Craigo Angus 293 G8
Craigow Perth 286 G4
Craigrory Highld 300 E6
Craigrothie Fife 287 F7
Craigroy Moray 301 D11
Craigruie Stirl 285 E8
Craig's End Essex 106 D4
Craigsford Mains Borders 262 B3
Craigshill W Loth 269 B11
Craigside Durham 233 D8
Craigston Castle Aberds 303 D7
Craigton Aberdeen 293 C10
Craigton Angus 287 B7
Craigton Angus 287 D9
Craigton Glasgow 267 C10
Craigton Highld 300 E6
Craigton Highld 309 H6
Craigton Highld 309 K6
Craigtown Highld 310 D2
Craik Borders 249 B8
Crail Fife 287 G10
Crailing Borders 262 E5
Crailinghall Borders 262 E5
Crakaig Highld 311 H3
Crakehill N Yorks 215 E8
Crakemarsh Staffs 151 B11
Crambe N Yorks 216 G4
Crambeck N Yorks 216 F4
Cramhurst Sur 50 E2
Cramlington Northumb 243 B7
Cramond Edin 280 F3
Cramond Bridge Edin 280 F3
Crampmoor Hants 32 C5
Cranage E Ches 168 B3
Cranberry Staffs 150 B6
Cranborne Dorset 31 E9
Cranbourne Brack 66 E2
Cranbourne Hants 48 C6
Cranbrook Kent 53 F9
Cranbrook London 68 B2
Cranbrook Common Kent 53 F9
Crane Moor S Yorks 197 G10
Crane's Corner Norf 159 G8
Cranfield C Beds 103 C9
Cranford Devon 24 C4
Cranford London 66 D6
Cranford St Andrew Northants 121 B8
Cranford St John Northants 121 B8
Cranham Glos 80 C5
Cranham London 68 B5
Cranhill Glasgow 268 B2
Cranhill Warks 118 G2
Crank Mers 183 B8
Crank Wood Gtr Man 194 G6
Crankwood Gtr Man 194 G6
Cranleigh Sur 50 F5
Cranley Suff 126 C3
Cranley Gardens London 67 B9
Cranmer Green Suff 125 C10
Cranmore I o W 20 D3
Cranmore Som 45 E7
Cranna Aberds 302 D6
Crannich Argyll 289 E7
Crannoch Moray 302 D4
Cranoe Leics 136 D5
Cransford Suff 126 E6
Cranshaws Borders 272 C3
Cranstal I o M 192 B5
Cranswick E Yorks 208 C6
Crantock Corn 4 C5
Cranwell Lincs 173 F8
Cranwich Norf 140 E5
Cranworth Norf 141 C9
Craobh Haven Argyll 275 C8
Crapstone Devon 7 B10
Crarae Argyll 275 D10
Crask Highld 308 C7
Crask Inn Highld 309 G5
Crask of Aigas Highld 300 E4
Craskins Aberds 293 C7
Craster Northumb 265 F7
Craswall Hereford 96 D5
Crateford Shrops 132 F4
Crateford Staffs 133 B8
Cratfield Suff 126 B6
Crathes Aberds 293 D9
Crathie Aberds 292 D4
Crathie Highld 291 D7
Crathorne N Yorks 225 D8
Craven Arms Shrops 131 G8
Crawcrook T & W 242 E4
Crawford Lancs 194 G3
Crawford S Lnrk 259 E11
Crawforddyke S Lnrk 269 F7
Crawfordjohn S Lnrk 259 E9
Crawick Dumfries 259 G7
Crawley Devon 28 F3
Crawley Hants 48 G2
Crawley Oxon 82 C4
Crawley W Sus 51 F9
Crawley Down W Sus 51 F10
Crawley End Essex 105 C8
Crawley Hill Sur 65 G11
Crawleyside Durham 232 C5
Crawshaw W Yorks 197 E8
Crawshawbooth Lancs 195 B10
Crawton Aberds 293 F10
Cray N Yorks 213 D8
Cray Perth 292 G3
Crayford London 68 E4
Crayke N Yorks 215 E11
Craymere Beck Norf 159 C11
Crays Hill Essex 88 G2
Cray's Pond Oxon 64 C6
Crazies Hill Wokingham 65 C9
Creacombe Devon 26 D4
Creag Aoil Highld 290 F3
Creag Ghoraidh W Isles 297 G3
Creagan Argyll 289 E11
Creagan Sithe Argyll 284 G6
Creagastrom W Isles 297 G4
Creaguaineach Lodge Highld 290 G5
Creaksea Essex 88 F6
Creamore Bank Shrops 149 C10
Crean Corn 1 E3
Creaton Northants 120 C4
Creca Dumfries 238 C6
Credenhill Hereford 97 C9
Crediton Devon 26 G4
Creebridge Dumfries 236 C6
Creech Dorset 18 E4
Creech Bottom Dorset 18 E4
Creech Heathfield Som 28 B3
Creech St Michael Som 28 B3
Creed Corn 5 F8
Creediknowe Shetland 312 G7
Creegbrawse Corn 4 G4
Creekmoor Poole 18 C6
Creekmouth London 68 C3
Creeksea Essex 88 F6
Creeting Bottoms Suff 126 F2
Creeting St Mary Suff 125 F11
Creeton Lincs 155 E10
Creetown Dumfries 236 D6
Creg-ny-Baa I o M 192 D4
Creggans Argyll 284 G4
Cregneash I o M 192 F2
Cregrina Powys 114 G2
Creich Fife 287 E7
Creigau Mon 79 F7
Creighton Staffs 151 B11
Creigiau Cardiff 58 C5
Crelly Corn 2 C5
Cremyll Corn 7 E9
Crendell Dorset 31 E9
Crepkill Highld 298 E4
Creslow Bucks 102 G6
Cress Green Glos 80 E3
Cressage Shrops 131 C11
Cressbrook Derbys 185 G11
Cresselly Pembs 73 D9
Cressex Bucks 84 G4
Cressing Essex 106 G5
Cresswell Northumb 253 E7
Cresswell Staffs 151 B9
Cresswell Quay Pembs 73 D9
Creswell Derbys 187 G8
Creswell Staffs 151 D7
Creswell Staffs 151 D8
Creswell Green Staffs 151 G11
Cretingham Suff 126 E4
Cretshengan Argyll 275 G8
Creunant = Crynant Neath 76 E3
Crewe E Ches 168 D2
Crewe W Ches 166 E6
Crewe-by-Farndon W Ches 166 E6
Crewgarth Cumb 231 E8
Crewgreen Powys 148 F6
Crewkerne Som 28 F6
Crews Hill London 86 F4
Crew's Hole Bristol 60 E6
Crewton Derby 153 C7
Crianlarich Stirl 285 E7
Cribbs Causeway S Glos 60 C5
Cribden Side Lancs 195 C9
Cribyn Ceredig 111 G10
Criccieth Gwyn 145 B9
Crich Derbys 170 E5
Crich Carr Derbys 170 E4
Crichie Aberds 303 E9
Crichton Midloth 271 C7
Crick Mon 79 G7
Crick Northants 119 C11
Crickadarn Powys 95 C11
Cricket Hill Hants 65 G10
Cricket Malherbie Som 28 E5
Cricket St Thomas Som 28 F5
Crickham Som 44 D2
Crickheath Shrops 148 E5
Crickheath Wharf Shrops 148 E5
Crickhowell Powys 78 B2
Cricklade Wilts 81 G10
Cricklewood London 67 B8
Crickmery Shrops 150 D3
Crick's Green Hereford 116 G2
Criddlestyle Hants 31 E11
Cridling Stubbs N Yorks 198 C4
Cridmore I o W 20 E5
Crieff Perth 286 E2
Criggan Corn 5 C10
Criggion Powys 148 F5
Crigglestone W Yorks 197 D10
Crimble Gtr Man 195 E11
Crimchard Som 28 F4
Crimdon Park Durham 234 D5
Crimond Aberds 303 D10
Crimonmogate Aberds 303 D10
Crimp Corn 24 D3
Crimplesham Norf 140 C3
Crimscote Warks 100 B4
Crinan Argyll 275 D8
Crinan Ferry Argyll 275 D8
Crindau Newport 59 B10
Crindledyke N Lnrk 268 D6
Cringleford Norf 142 B3
Cringles W Yorks 204 D6
Cringletie Borders 270 G4
Crinow Pembs 73 C10
Cripple Corner Essex 107 E7
Cripplesease Corn 2 B2
Cripplestyle Dorset 31 E9
Cripp's Corner E Sus 38 C3
Crispie Argyll 275 F10
Crist Derbys 185 E8
Crit Hall Kent 53 G9
Critchell's Green Hants 32 B3
Critchill Som 45 D9
Critchmere Sur 49 G11
Crizeley Hereford 97 E8
Croanford Corn 10 G6
Croasdale Cumb 219 B11
Crock Street Som 28 E4
Crockenhill Kent 68 F4
Crocker End Oxon 65 B8
Crockerhill Hants 33 F9
Crockerhill W Sus 22 B6
Crockernwell Devon 13 C11
Crockers Devon 40 F5
Crocker's Ash Hereford 79 B8
Crockerton Wilts 45 E11
Crockerton Green Wilts 45 E11
Crocketford or Ninemile Bar Dumfries 237 B10
Crockey Hill York 207 D8
Crockham Heath W Berks 64 G2
Crockham Hill Kent 52 C2
Crockhurst Street Kent 52 E6
Crockleford Heath Essex 107 F10
Crockleford Hill Essex 107 F10
Crockness Orkney 314 G3
Croes-goch Pembs 87 E11
Croes-Hywel Mon 78 C4
Croes-lan Ceredig 93 C7
Croes Llanfair Mon 78 D4
Croes-wian Flint 181 G10
Croes-y-mwyalch Torf 78 G4
Croes y pant Mon 78 E4
Croesau Bach Shrops 148 D4
Croeserw Neath 57 B11
Croesor Gwyn 163 G10
Croespenmaen Caerph 77 F11
Croesyceiliog Carms 74 B6
Croesyceiliog Torf 78 F4
Croesywaun Gwyn 163 D8
Croft Hereford 115 D9
Croft Leics 135 D10
Croft Lincs 175 C8
Croft Pembs 92 C3
Croft Warr 183 C10
Croft Mitchell Corn 2 B5
Croft of Tillymaud Aberds 303 F11
Croft-on-Tees N Yorks 224 D5
Croftamie Stirl 277 D9
Croftfoot S Lnrk 268 C2
Crofthandy Corn 4 G4
Croftlands Cumb 210 D5
Croftmalloch W Loth 269 C8
Croftmoraig Perth 285 C11
Crofton Cumb 239 G8
Crofton London 68 F2
Crofton W Yorks 197 D11
Crofton Wilts 63 G9
Crofts Dumfries 237 B9
Crofts Bank Gtr Man 184 B3
Crofts of Benachielt Highld 310 F5
Crofts of Haddo Aberds 303 F8
Crofts of Inverthernie Aberds 303 E7
Crofts of Meikle Ardo Aberds 303 E8
Crofty Swansea 56 B4
Croggan Argyll 289 G9
Croglin Cumb 231 B7
Croich Highld 309 K4
Croick Highld 310 D2
Croig Argyll 288 D6
Crois Dughaill W Isles 297 J3
Cromarty Highld 301 C7
Cromasaig Highld 299 C10
Crombie Fife 279 D10
Crombie Castle Aberds 302 D5
Cromblet Aberds 303 F7
Cromdale Highld 301 G10
Cromer Herts 104 F5
Cromer Norf 160 A4
Cromer-Hyde Herts 86 C2
Cromford Derbys 170 D3
Cromhall S Glos 79 G11
Cromhall Common S Glos 61 B7
Cromor W Isles 304 F6
Crompton Fold Gtr Man 196 F2
Cromra Highld 291 D7
Cromwell Notts 172 C3
Cromwell Bottom W Yorks 196 C6
Cronberry E Ayrs 258 E4
Crondall Hants 49 D9
Cronk-y-Voddy I o M 192 D4
Cronton Mers 183 D7
Crook Cumb 221 G9
Crook Devon 27 G11
Crook Durham 233 D9
Crook of Devon Perth 286 G4
Crookdake Cumb 229 C9
Crooke Gtr Man 194 F5
Crooked Billet London 67 E8
Crooked Soley Wilts 63 E10
Crooked Withies Dorset 31 F9
Crookedholm E Ayrs 257 B11
Crookes S Yorks 186 D4
Crookesmoor S Yorks 186 D4
Crookfur E Renf 267 D10
Crookgate Bank Durham 242 F5
Crookhall Durham 242 G4
Crookham Northumb 263 B10
Crookham W Berks 64 G4
Crookham Village Hants 49 C9
Crookhaugh Borders 260 D4
Crookhill T & W 242 E5
Crookhouse Borders 263 D7
Crooklands Cumb 211 C10
Crookston Glasgow 267 C10
Cropredy Oxon 101 B9
Cropston Leics 153 G11
Cropthorne Worcs 99 C9
Cropton N Yorks 216 B5
Cropwell Bishop Notts 154 B3
Cropwell Butler Notts 154 B3
Cros W Isles 304 B7
Crosben Highld 289 D9
Crosbost W Isles 304 F5
Crosby Cumb 229 D7
Crosby I o M 192 E4
Crosby Mers 182 B4
Crosby N Lincs 199 E11
Crosby Court N Yorks 225 G7
Crosby Garrett Cumb 222 D4
Crosby-on-Eden Cumb 239 F11
Crosby Ravensworth Cumb 222 C2
Crosby Villa Cumb 229 D7
Croscombe Som 44 E5
Crosemere Shrops 149 D8
Crosland Edge W Yorks 196 E6
Crosland Hill W Yorks 196 E6
Crosland Moor W Yorks 196 D6
Croslands Park Cumb 210 E4
Cross Devon 40 F3
Cross Devon 40 G6
Cross Shrops 149 B7
Cross Som 44 C2
Cross Ash Mon 78 B6
Cross-at-Hand Kent 53 D9
Cross Bank Worcs 116 C4
Cross Coombe Corn 4 E4
Cross End Beds 121 F11
Cross End Essex 107 E7
Cross End M Keynes 103 D8
Cross Gate W Sus 35 E8
Cross Gates W Yorks 206 F3
Cross Gates W Yorks 206 G3
Cross Green Devon 12 D3
Cross Green Staffs 133 B8
Cross Green Suff 124 G6
Cross Green Suff 125 F7
Cross Green Suff 125 G9
Cross Green Telford 150 G2
Cross Green W Yorks 206 G2
Cross Green Warks 119 F7
Cross Hands Carms 75 C9
Cross-hands Carms 92 G3
Cross Hands Pembs 73 C9
Cross Heath Staffs 168 F4
Cross Hill Corn 10 G6
Cross Hill Derbys 170 F6
Cross Hill Glos 79 F9
Cross Hills N Yorks 204 E6
Cross Holme N Yorks 225 F11
Cross Houses Shrops 131 B10
Cross Houses Shrops 132 E3
Cross in Hand E Sus 37 C9
Cross in Hand Leics 135 G10
Cross Inn Carms 74 C3
Cross Inn Ceredig 111 E10
Cross Inn Ceredig 111 F7
Cross Inn Rhondda 58 C5
Cross Keys Kent 52 C4
Cross Keys Wilts 61 E11
Cross Lane E Ches 167 C11
Cross Lane Head Shrops 132 D4
Cross Lanes Corn 2 E5
Cross Lanes Dorset 30 G3
Cross Lanes N Yorks 215 F10
Cross Lanes Oxon 65 D7

Cross Lanes Wrex 166 F5
Cross Llyde Hereford 97 F8
Cross o' th' hands Derbys 170 F3
Cross o' th' Hill W Ches 167 F7
Cross Oak Powys 96 G2
Cross of Jackston Aberds 303 F7
Cross Roads Devon 12 D5
Cross Roads W Yorks 204 F6
Cross Stone Aberds 303 G9
Cross Street Suff 126 B3
Cross Town E Ches 184 F3
Crossaig Argyll 255 B9
Crossal Highld 294 B6
Crossapol Argyll 288 E1
Crossbrae Aberds 302 D6
Crossburn Falk 279 G7
Crossbush W Sus 35 F8
Crosscanonby Cumb 229 D7
Crosscrake Cumb 211 B10
Crossdale Street Norf 160 B4
Crossens Mers 193 D11
Crossflatts W Yorks 205 E8
Crossford Fife 279 D11
Crossford S Lnrk 268 F6
Crossgate Lincs 156 D4
Crossgate Orkney 314 E4
Crossgate Staffs 151 B8
Crossgatehall E Loth 271 B7
Crossgates Cumb 229 G7
Crossgates Fife 280 D2
Crossgates N Yorks 217 C10
Crossgates Powys 113 E11
Crossgill Cumb 231 C10
Crossgill Lancs 211 G11
Crossgreen Shrops 149 F9
Crosshands Carms 92 G3
Crosshill E Ayrs 257 E11
Crosshill Fife 280 B3
Crosshill S Ayrs 245 B8
Crosshouse E Ayrs 257 B9
Crossings Cumb 240 B2
Crosskeys Caerph 78 G2
Crosskirk Highld 310 B4
Crosslands Cumb 210 B6
Crosslanes Shrops 148 F6
Crosslee Borders 261 F8
Crosslee Renfs 267 B8
Crossley Hall W Yorks 205 G8
Crossmichael Dumfries 237 C9
Crossmill E Renf 267 D10
Crossmoor Lancs 202 F4
Crossmount Perth 285 B11
Crosspost W Sus 36 C3
Crossroads Aberds 293 D9
Crossroads E Ayrs 257 C11
Crossroads Fife 281 B7
Crosston Angus 287 B9
Crosstown Corn 24 D2
Crosstown V Glam 58 F4
Crosswater Sur 49 F11
Crossway Hereford 98 E2
Crossway Mon 78 B6
Crossway Powys 113 F11
Crossway Green Mon 79 G8
Crossway Green Worcs 116 D6
Crossways Dorset 17 D11
Crossways Kent 68 D5
Crossways Mon 96 G6
Crossways S Glos 79 G11
Crossways Sur 49 F11
Crosswell = Ffynnongroes Pembs 92 D2
Crosswood Ceredig 112 C3
Crosthwaite Cumb 221 G8
Croston Lancs 194 D3
Crostwick Norf 160 F5
Crostwight Norf 160 D6
Crothair W Isles 304 E3
Crouch Kent 52 B6
Crouch Kent 54 B5
Crouch End London 67 B9
Crouch Hill Dorset 30 E2
Crouch House Green Kent 52 D2
Crouchers W Sus 22 C4
Croucheston Wilts 31 B9
Croughly Moray 301 G11
Croughton Northants 101 E10
Crovie Aberds 303 C8
Crow Hants 31 G11
Crow Edge S Yorks 197 G7
Crow Green Essex 87 F9
Crow Hill Hereford 98 F2
Crow Nest W Yorks 205 F8
Crow Wood Halton 183 D8
Crowan Corn 2 C4
Crowborough E Sus 52 G4
Crowborough Staffs 168 D6
Crowborough Warren E Sus 52 G4
Crowcombe Som 42 F6
Crowcroft Worcs 116 G5
Crowden Derbys 185 B9
Crowden Devon 12 B5
Crowder Park Devon 8 D4
Crowdhill Hants 33 C7
Crowdicote Derbys 169 B10
Crowdleham Kent 52 B5
Crowdon N Yorks 227 F9
Crowell Oxon 84 F2
Crowell Hill Oxon 84 F3
Crowfield Northants 102 C2
Crowfield Suff 126 F2
Crowgate Street Norf 160 E6
Crowgreaves Shrops 132 D4
Crowhill Gtr Man 184 B6
Crowhill M Keynes 102 D6
Crowhole Derbys 186 F4
Crowhurst E Sus 38 E3
Crowhurst Sur 51 D11
Crowhurst Lane End Sur 51 D11
Crowland Lincs 156 G4
Crowlas Corn 2 C2
Crowle N Lincs 199 E9
Crowle Worcs 117 F8
Crowle Green Worcs 117 F8
Crowle Hill N Lincs 199 E9
Crowle Park N Lincs 199 E9
Crowmarsh Gifford Oxon 64 B6
Crown Corner Suff 126 C5
Crown East Worcs 116 G6
Crown Hills Leicester 136 C2
Crown Wood Brack 65 F11
Crownfield Bucks 84 F4
Crownhill Plym 7 D9
Crownland Suff 125 D10
Crownpits Sur 50 E3
Crownthorpe Norf 141 C11
Crowntown Corn 2 C4
Crows-an-wra Corn 1 D3
Crow's Green Essex 106 F3
Crow's Nest Corn 6 B5
Crowshill Norf 141 B8
Crowsley Oxon 65 D8
Crowsnest Shrops 131 C7
Crowther's Pool Powys 96 B4
Crowthorne Brack 65 G10
Crowton W Ches 183 G9
Croxall Staffs 152 G3
Croxby Lincs 189 B11
Croxby Top Lincs 189 B11
Croxdale Durham 233 D11
Croxden Staffs 151 B11
Croxley Green Herts 85 F9
Croxteth Mers 182 B6
Croxton Cambs 122 E4
Croxton N Lincs 200 E5
Croxton Norf 141 F7
Croxton Norf 159 C9
Croxton Staffs 150 C5
Croxton Green E Ches 167 E8
Croxton Kerrial Leics 154 D6
Croxtonbank Staffs 150 C5
Croy Highld 301 E7
Croy N Lnrk 278 F4
Croyde Devon 40 F2
Croyde Bay Devon 40 F2
Croydon Cambs 104 B6
Croydon London 67 F10
Crozen Hereford 97 B11
Crubenbeg Highld 291 D8
Crubenmore Lodge Highld 291 D8
Cruckmeole Shrops 131 B8
Cruckton Shrops 149 G8
Cruden Bay Aberds 303 F10
Crudgington Telford 150 F2
Crudie Aberds 303 D7
Crudwell Wilts 81 G7
Crug Powys 114 C3
Crugmeer Corn 10 F4
Crugybar Carms 94 D3
Cruise Hill Worcs 117 E10
Crulabhig W Isles 304 E3
Crumlin Caerph 78 F2
Crumplehorn Corn 6 E4
Crumpsall Gtr Man 195 G10
Crumpsbrook Shrops 116 B2
Crumpton Hill Worcs 98 B5
Crundale Kent 54 D5
Crundale Pembs 73 B7
Cruwys Morchard Devon 26 E5
Crux Easton Hants 48 B2
Cruxton Dorset 17 B8
Crwbin Carms 75 C7
Crya Orkney 314 F3
Cryers Hill Bucks 84 F5
Crymlyn Gwyn 179 G10
Crymych Pembs 92 E3
Crynant = Creunant Neath 76 E3
Crynfryn Ceredig 111 E11
Cuaich Highld 291 E8
Cuaig Highld 299 D7
Cuan Argyll 275 B8
Cubbington Warks 118 D6
Cubeck N Yorks 213 B9
Cubert Corn 4 D5
Cubitt Town London 67 D11
Cubley S Yorks 197 G8
Cubley Common Derbys 152 B3
Cublington Bucks 102 G6
Cublington Hereford 97 D8
Cuckfield W Sus 36 B4
Cucklington Som 30 B3
Cuckney Notts 187 G9
Cuckold's Green Suff 143 G9
Cuckold's Green Wilts 46 B3
Cuckoo Green Suff 143 D10
Cuckoo Hill Notts 188 C2
Cuckoo Tye Suff 107 C7
Cuckoo's Corner Hants 49 E8
Cuckoo's Corner Wilts 46 B4
Cuckoo's Knob Wilts 63 G7
Cuckron Shetland 313 H6
Cucumber Corner Norf 143 B7
Cuddesdon Oxon 83 E10
Cuddington Bucks 84 C2
Cuddington W Ches 183 G10
Cuddington Heath W Ches 167 F7
Cuddy Hill Lancs 202 F5
Cudham London 52 B2
Cudlipptown Devon 12 F6
Cudliptown Devon 12 F6
Cudworth S Yorks 197 F11
Cudworth Som 28 E5
Cudworth Sur 51 E8
Cudworth Common S Yorks 197 F11
Cuerden Green Lancs 194 C5
Cuerdley Cross Warr 183 D8
Cufaude Hants 48 B6
Cuffern Pembs 91 G7
Cuffley Herts 86 E4
Cuiashader W Isles 304 C7
Cuidhir W Isles 297 L2
Cuidhtinis W Isles 296 C6
Cuiken Midloth 270 C4
Cuilcheanna Ho Highld 290 G2
Cuin Argyll 288 D6
Cul na h-Aird W Isles 305 H3
Cùl Doirlinn Highld 289 B8
Culbo Highld 300 C6
Culbokie Highld 300 D6
Culburnie Highld 300 E4
Culcabock Highld 300 E6
Culcairn Highld 300 C6
Culcharry Highld 301 D8
Culcheth Warr 183 B11
Culcronchie Dumfries 237 C7
Culdrain Aberds 302 F5
Culduie Highld 299 E7
Culeave Highld 309 K5
Culford Suff 124 D6
Culfordheath Suff 125 C7
Culfosie Aberds 293 C9
Culgaith Cumb 231 F8
Culham Oxon 83 F8
Culkein Highld 306 F5
Culkein Drumbeg Highld 306 F6
Culkerton Glos 80 F6
Cullachie Highld 301 G9
Cullen Moray 302 C5
Cullercoats T & W 243 C9
Cullicudden Highld 300 C6
Cullingworth W Yorks 205 F7
Cullipool Argyll 275 B8
Cullivoe Shetland 312 C7
Culloch Perth 285 F11
Culloden Highld 301 E7
Cullompton Devon 27 F8
Culm Davy Devon 27 D10
Culmaily Highld 311 K2
Culmazie Dumfries 236 D5
Culmer Sur 50 F2
Culmers Kent 70 G5
Culmington Shrops 131 G9
Culmore Stirl 278 B3
Culmstock Devon 27 E10
Culnacraig Highld 307 J5
Culnaightrie Dumfries 237 D9
Culnaknock Highld 298 C5
Culnaneam Highld 294 C6
Culpho Suff 108 B4
Culra Lodge Highld 291 F7
Culrain Highld 309 K5
Culross Fife 279 D9
Culroy S Ayrs 257 G8
Culscadden Dumfries 236 E6
Culsh Aberds 292 D5
Culsh Aberds 303 E8
Culshabbin Dumfries 236 D5
Culswick Shetland 313 J4
Cultercullen Aberds 303 G9
Cults Aberdeen 293 C10
Cults Aberds 302 F5
Cults Dumfries 236 E6
Cults Fife 287 G7
Culverlane Devon 8 C4
Culverstone Green Kent 68 G6
Culverthorpe Lincs 173 G8
Culworth Northants 101 B10
Culzie Lodge Highld 300 B5
Cumberlow Green Herts 104 E6
Cumbernauld N Lnrk 278 G5
Cumbernauld Village N Lnrk 278 F5
Cumber's Bank Wrex 149 B8
Cumberworth Lincs 191 G8
Cumdivock Cumb 230 B2
Cumeragh Village Lancs 203 F7
Cuminestown Aberds 303 D8
Cumledge Borders 272 D5
Cumlewick Shetland 313 L6
Cumlodden Argyll 275 D11
Cumlodden Dumfries 236 C6
Cummersdale Cumb 239 G9
Cummerton Aberds 303 C8
Cummertrees Dumfries 238 D4
Cummingston Moray 301 C11
Cumnock E Ayrs 258 E3
Cumnor Oxon 83 E7
Cumnor Hill Oxon 83 D7
Cumrew Cumb 240 G2
Cumwhinton Cumb 239 G10
Cumwhitton Cumb 240 G2
Cundall N Yorks 215 E8
Cundy Cross S Yorks 197 F11
Cundy Hos S Yorks 186 B4
Cunninghamhead N Ayrs 267 G7
Cunnister Shetland 312 D7
Cupar Fife 287 F7
Cupar Muir Fife 287 F7
Cupernham Hants 32 C5
Cupid Green Herts 85 D9
Cupid's Hill Mon 97 F8
Curbar Derbys 186 G3
Curborough Staffs 152 G2
Curbridge Hants 33 E8
Curbridge Oxon 82 D4
Curdridge Hants 33 E8
Curdworth Warks 134 E3
Curgurrell Corn 3 B9
Curin Highld 300 D3
Curland Som 28 D3
Curland Common Som 28 D3
Curlew Green Suff 127 D7
Curling Tye Green Essex 88 D4
Curload Som 28 B4
Currarie S Ayrs 244 E5
Currian Vale Corn 5 D9
Curridge W Berks 64 E3
Currie Edin 270 B3
Currock Cumb 239 G10
Curry Lane Corn 11 C11
Curry Mallet Som 28 C4
Curry Rivel Som 28 B5
Cursiter Orkney 314 E3
Curteis' Corner Kent 53 F11
Curtisden Green Kent 53 E8
Curtisknowle Devon 8 E4
Curtismill Green Essex 87 F8
Cury Corn 2 E5
Cusbay Orkney 314 C5
Cusgarne Corn 4 G5
Cushnie Aberds 303 C7
Cushuish Som 43 G7
Cusop Hereford 96 C4
Custards Hants 32 F3
Custom House London 68 C2
Cusveorth Coombe Corn 4 G5
Cusworth S Yorks 198 G4
Cutcloy Dumfries 236 F6
Cutcombe Som 42 F2
Cutgate Gtr Man 195 E11
Cuthill E Loth 281 G7
Cutiau Gwyn 146 F2
Cutlers Green Essex 105 E11
Cutler's Green Som 44 C5
Cutmadoc Corn 5 C11
Cutmere Corn 6 C6
Cutnall Green Worcs 117 D7
Cutsdean Glos 99 E11
Cutsyke W Yorks 198 C2
Cutteslowe Oxon 83 C8
Cutthorpe Derbys 186 G4
Cuttiford's Door Som 28 E4
Cutts Shetland 313 K6
Cuttybridge Pembs 72 B6
Cuttyhill Aberds 303 D10
Cuxham Oxon 83 F11
Cuxton Medway 69 F8
Cuxwold Lincs 201 G7
Cwm Bl Gwent 77 D11
Cwm Denb 181 F9
Cwm Neath 57 C10
Cwm Powys 129 D11
Cwm Powys 130 E5
Cwm Shrops 114 B6
Cwm Swansea 57 B7
Cwm-byr Carms 94 E2
Cwm Capel Carms 75 E7
Cwm-celyn Bl Gwent 78 D2
Cwm-Cewydd Gwyn 147 G7
Cwm-cou Ceredig 92 C5
Cwm Dows Caerph 78 F2
Cwm-Dulais Swansea 75 E10
Cwm felin fach Caerph 77 G11
Cwm Ffrwd-oer Torf 78 E3
Cwm-Fields Torf 78 E3
Cwm Gelli Caerph 77 F11
Cwm Gwyn Swansea 56 C6
Cwm Head Shrops 131 F8
Cwm-hesgen Gwyn 146 D5
Cwm-hwnt Rhondda 76 D6
Cwm Irfon Powys 95 B7
Cwm-Llinau Powys 128 B6
Cwm-mawr Carms 75 C8
Cwm-miles Carms 92 G3
Cwm Nant-gam Bl Gwent 78 C2
Cwm-parc Rhondda 77 F7
Cwm Penmachno Conwy 164 F3
Cwm Plysgog Ceredig 92 C3
Cwm-twrch Isaf Powys 76 C3
Cwm-twrch Uchaf Powys 76 C3
Cwm-y-glo Carms 75 C9
Cwm-y-glo Gwyn 163 C8
Cwmafan Neath 57 C9
Cwmaman Rhondda 77 F8
Cwmann Carms 93 B11
Cwmavon Torf 78 D3
Cwmbach Carms 75 E7
Cwmbach Carms 92 F5
Cwmbach Powys 96 D3
Cwmbach Rhondda 77 E8
Cwmbach Llechrhyd Powys 113 G10
Cwmbelan Powys 129 G8
Cwmbran Torf 78 G3
Cwmbrwyno Ceredig 128 G4
Cwmcarn Caerph 78 G2
Cwmcarvan Mon 79 D7
Cwmcoednerth Ceredig 92 B6
Cwmcrawnon Powys 77 B10
Cwmcych Carms 92 D5
Cwmdare Rhondda 77 E7
Cwmdu Carms 94 E2
Cwmdu Powys 96 G3
Cwmdu Swansea 56 C6
Cwmduad Carms 93 E7
Cwmdwr Carms 94 E4
Cwmerfyn Ceredig 128 G3
Cwmfelin Bridgend 57 D11
Cwmfelin M Tydf 77 E9
Cwmfelin Boeth Carms 73 B11
Cwmfelin Mynach Carms 92 G4
Cwmffrwd Carms 74 B6
Cwmgiedd Powys 76 C3
Cwmgors Neath 76 C2
Cwmgwili Carms 75 C9
Cwmgwrach Neath 76 E5
Cwmhiraeth Carms 92 D6
Cwmifor Carms 94 F3
Cwmisfael Carms 75 B7
Cwmllynfell Neath 76 C2
Cwmnantyrodyn Caerph 77 F11
Cwmorgan Pembs 92 E5
Cwmparc Rhondda 77 F7
Cwmpengraig Carms 92 D6
Cwmpennar Rhondda 77 E8
Cwmrhos Powys 96 G3
Cwmrhydyceirw Swansea 57 B7
Cwmsychpant Ceredig 93 B9
Cwmsyfiog Caerph 77 E11
Cwmsymlog Ceredig 128 G4
Cwmtillery Bl Gwent 78 D2
Cwmwdig Water Pembs 90 E6
Cwmwysg Powys 95 F7
Cwmynyscoy Torf 78 F3
Cwmyoy Mon 96 G5
Cwmystwyth Ceredig 112 C5
Cwrt Gwyn 128 C3
Cwrt-newydd Ceredig 93 B9
Cwrt-y-cadno Carms 94 C3
Cwrt-y-gollen Powys 78 B2
Cydweli = Kidwelly Carms 74 D6
Cyffordd Llandudno = Llandudno Junction Conwy 180 F3
Cyffylliog Denb 165 D9
Cyfronydd Powys 130 B2
Cymau Flint 166 D3
Cymdda Bridgend 58 C2
Cymer Neath 57 B11
Cymmer Rhondda 77 G8
Cyncoed Cardiff 59 C7
Cynghordy Carms 94 C6
Cynheidre Carms 75 D7
Cynonville Neath 57 B10
Cyntwell Cardiff 58 D6
Cynwyd Denb 165 G9
Cynwyl Elfed Carms 93 F7
Cywarch Gwyn 147 F7

D

Daccombe Devon 9 B8
Dacre Cumb 230 F5
Dacre N Yorks 214 G3
Dacre Banks N Yorks 214 G3
Daddry Shield Durham 232 D3
Dadford Bucks 102 D3
Dadlington Leics 135 D8
Dafarn Faig Gwyn 163 F7
Dafen Carms 75 E8
Daffy Green Norf 141 B9
Dagdale Staffs 151 C11
Dagenham London 68 C3
Daggons Dorset 31 E10
Daglingworth Glos 81 D7
Dagnall Bucks 85 B7
Dagtail End Worcs 117 E10
Dagworth Suff 125 E10
Dail Beag W Isles 304 D4
Dail bho Dheas W Isles 304 B6
Dail bho Thuath W Isles 304 B6
Dail Mor W Isles 304 D4
Daill Argyll 274 G4
Dailly S Ayrs 245 C7
Dainton Devon 9 B7
Dairsie or Osnaburgh Fife 287 F8
Daisy Green Suff 125 D10
Daisy Green Suff 125 D11
Daisy Hill Gtr Man 195 G7
Daisy Hill W Yorks 197 B9
Daisy Hill W Yorks 205 G8
Daisy Nook Gtr Man 196 G2
Dalabrog W Isles 297 J3
Dalavich Argyll 275 B10
Dalbeattie Dumfries 237 C10
Dalbeg Highld 291 B8
Dalblair E Ayrs 258 F4
Dalbog Angus 293 F7
Dalbrack Stirl 285 G11
Dalbury Derbys 152 C5
Dalby I o M 192 E3
Dalby Lincs 190 G6
Dalby N Yorks 216 E2
Dalchalloch Perth 291 G9
Dalchalm Highld 311 J3
Dalchenna Argyll 284 G4
Dalchirach Moray 301 F11
Dalchonzie Perth 285 E11
Dalchork Highld 309 H5
Dalchreichart Highld 290 B4
Dalchruin Perth 285 F11
Dalderby Lincs 174 B2
Dale Cumb 230 C6
Dale Gtr Man 196 F3
Dale Pembs 72 D4
Dale Shetland 312 G6
Dale Abbey Derbys 153 B8
Dale Bottom Cumb 229 G11
Dale Brow E Ches 184 F6
Dale End Derbys 170 C2
Dale End N Yorks 204 D5
Dale Head Cumb 221 B8
Dale Hill E Sus 53 G7
Dale Hill E Sus 53 G8
Dale Moor Derbys 153 B8
Dale of Walls Shetland 313 H3
Dalebank Derbys 170 C5
Dalelia Highld 289 C9
Dales Brow Gtr Man 195 G9
Dales Green Staffs 168 D5
Daless Highld 301 F8
Dalestie Moray 292 B3
Dalestorth Notts 171 C8
Dalfaber Highld 291 B11
Dalfoil Stirl 277 D11
Dalganachan Highld 310 E4
Dalgarven N Ayrs 266 F5
Dalgety Bay Fife 280 E3
Dalginross Perth 285 E11
Dalguise Perth 286 C3
Dalhalvaig Highld 310 D2
Dalham Suff 124 E4
Dalhastnie Angus 293 F7
Dalhenzean Perth 292 G3
Dalinlongart Argyll 276 E2
Dalkeith Midloth 270 B6
Dallam Warr 183 C9
Dallas Moray 301 D11
Dallas Lodge Moray 301 D11
Dallcharn Highld 308 D6
Dalleagles E Ayrs 258 G3
Dallicott Shrops 132 E5
Dallimores I o W 20 C6
Dallinghoo Suff 126 G5
Dallington E Sus 23 B11
Dallington Northants 120 E4
Dallow N Yorks 214 E3
Dalmadilly Aberds 293 B9
Dalmally Argyll 284 E5
Dalmarnock Glasgow 268 C2
Dalmarnock Perth 286 C3
Dalmary Stirl 277 B10
Dalmellington E Ayrs 245 B11
Dalmeny Edin 280 F2
Dalmigavie Highld 291 B9
Dalmigavie Lodge Highld 301 G7
Dalmilling S Ayrs 257 E9
Dalmore Highld 300 C6
Dalmuir W Dunb 277 G9
Dalnabreck Highld 289 C8
Dalnacardoch Lodge Perth 291 F9
Dalnacroich Highld 300 D3
Dalnaglar Castle Perth 292 G3
Dalnahaitnach Highld 301 G8
Dalnamein Lodge Perth 291 G9
Dalnarrow Argyll 289 F9
Dalnaspidal Lodge Perth 291 F8
Dalnavaid Perth 292 G2
Dalnavie Highld 300 B6
Dalnaw Dumfries 236 B5
Dalnawillan Lodge Highld 310 E4
Dalness Highld 284 B5
Dalnessie Highld 309 H6
Dalphaid Highld 309 H3
Dalqueich Perth 286 G4
Dalrannoch Argyll 289 E11
Dalreavoch Highld 309 J7
Dalriach Highld 301 F10
Dalrigh Stirl 285 E7
Dalry Edin 280 G4
Dalry N Ayrs 266 F5
Dalrymple E Ayrs 257 G9
Dalscote Northants 120 G3
Dalserf S Lnrk 268 E6
Dalshannon N Lnrk 278 G4
Dalston Cumb 239 G9
Dalston London 67 C10
Dalswinton Dumfries 247 F10
Dalton Cumb 211 D10
Dalton Dumfries 238 C4
Dalton Lancs 194 F3
Dalton N Yorks 215 D8
Dalton N Yorks 224 D2
Dalton Northumb 241 F10
Dalton Northumb 242 C4
Dalton S Lnrk 268 D3
Dalton S Yorks 187 C7
Dalton W Yorks 197 D7
Dalton-in-Furness Cumb 210 E4
Dalton-le-Dale Durham 234 B4
Dalton Magna S Yorks 187 C7
Dalton-on-Tees N Yorks 224 D5
Dalton Parva S Yorks 187 C7
Dalton Piercy Hrtlpl 234 E5
Dalveallan Highld 300 F6
Dalveich Stirl 285 E10
Dalvina Lo Highld 308 E6
Dalwey Telford 132 B3
Dalwhinnie Highld 291 E8
Dalwood Devon 28 G3
Dalwyne S Ayrs 245 D8
Dam Green Norf 141 F11
Dam Head W Yorks 196 B6
Dam Mill Staffs 133 C7
Dam of Quoiggs Perth 286 G2
Dam Side Lancs 202 D4
Damask Green Herts 104 F5
Damems W Yorks 204 F6
Damerham Hants 31 D10
Damery Glos 80 G2
Damgate Norf 143 B8
Damgate Norf 161 F9
Damhead Moray 301 D10
Damhead Holdings Midloth 270 B5
Damnaglaur Dumfries 236 F3
Damside Borders 270 F3
Dan Caerlan Rhondda 58 C5
Danaway Kent 69 G11
Danbury Essex 88 E3
Danbury Common Essex 88 E3
Danby N Yorks 226 D4
Danby Wiske N Yorks 224 F6
Dancers Hill Herts 86 F2
Dancing Green Hereford 98 G2
Dandaleith Moray 302 E2
Danderhall Midloth 270 B6
Dandy Corner Suff 125 D11
Dane Bank Gtr Man 184 B6
Dane End Herts 104 G6
Dane in Shaw E Ches 168 C5
Dane Street Kent 54 C5
Danebank E Ches 185 E7
Danebridge E Ches 169 B7
Danegate E Sus 52 G5
Danehill E Sus 36 B6
Danemoor Green Norf 141 B11
Danes Moss E Ches 184 G6
Danesbury Herts 86 B2
Danesfield Bucks 65 C10
Danesford Shrops 132 E4
Daneshill Hants 49 C7
Danesmoor Derbys 170 C6
Daneway Glos 80 E6
Dangerous Corner Gtr Man 195 G7
Dangerous Corner Lancs 194 E4
Daniel's Water Kent 54 E3
Danna na Cloiche Argyll 275 F7
Dannonchapel Corn 10 E6
Danskine E Loth 271 B11
Danthorpe E Yorks 209 G10
Danygraig Caerph 78 G2
Danzey Green Warks 118 D2
Dapple Heath Staffs 151 D10
Darby End W Mid 133 F9
Darby Green Hants 65 G10
Darbys Green Worcs 116 F4
Darby's Hill W Mid 133 F9
Darcy Lever Gtr Man 195 F8
Dardy Powys 78 B2
Darenth Kent 68 E5
Daresbury Halton 183 E9
Daresbury Delph Halton 183 E9
Darfield S Yorks 198 G2
Darfoulds Notts 187 F9
Dargate Kent 70 G5
Dargate Common Kent 70 G5
Darite Corn 6 B5
Darkland Moray 302 C2
Darland Wrex 166 D5
Darlaston W Mid 133 D9
Darlaston Green W Mid 133 D9
Darley N Yorks 205 B10
Darley Shrops 132 D3
Darley Abbey Derby 153 B7
Darley Bridge Derbys 170 C3
Darley Dale Derbys 170 C3
Darley Green Warks 118 C3
Darley Head N Yorks 205 B9
Darley Hillside Derbys 170 C3
Darleyford Corn 11 G11
Darleyhall Herts 104 G2
Darlingscott Warks 100 C4
Darlington Darl 224 C5
Darliston Shrops 149 C11
Darlton Notts 188 G3
Darmsden Suff 125 G11
Darn Hill Gtr Man 195 E10
Darnall S Yorks 186 D5
Darnaway Castle Moray 301 D9
Darnford Staffs 134 B2
Darnhall W Ches 167 C10
Darnhall Mains Borders 270 F4
Darnick Borders 262 C2
Darowen Powys 128 C6
Darra Aberds 303 E7
Darracott Devon 24 D2
Darracott Devon 40 F3
Darras Hall Northumb 242 C5
Darrington W Yorks 198 D3
Darrow Green Norf 142 F5
Darsham Suff 127 D8
Darshill Som 44 E6
Dartford Kent 68 E4
Dartford Crossing Kent 68 D5
Dartington Devon 8 C5
Dartmeet Devon 13 G9
Dartmouth Devon 9 E7
Darton S Yorks 197 F10
Darvel E Ayrs 258 B3
Darvillshill Bucks 84 F4
Darwell Hole E Sus 23 B11
Darwen Blkburn 195 C7
Dassels Herts 105 F7
Datchet Windsor 66 D3
Datchet Common Windsor 66 D3
Datchworth Herts 86 B3
Datchworth Green Herts 86 B3
Daubhill Gtr Man 195 F8
Daugh of Kinermony Moray 302 E2
Dauntsey Wilts 62 C3
Dauntsey Lock Wilts 62 C3
Dava Moray 301 F10
Davenham W Ches 183 G11
Davenport E Ches 168 B4
Davenport Gtr Man 184 D5
Davenport Green E Ches 184 F4
Davenport Green Gtr Man 184 D4
Daventry Northants 119 E11
David Street Kent 68 G6
David's Well Powys 113 B11
Davidson's Mains Edin 280 F4
Davidston Highld 301 C7
Davidstow Corn 11 D9
Davington Dumfries 248 C6
Davington Kent 70 G4
Daviot Aberds 303 G7
Daviot Highld 301 F7
Davis's Town E Sus 23 B8
Davoch of Grange Moray 302 D4
Davyhulme Gtr Man 184 B3
Daw Cross N Yorks 205 C11
Daw End W Mid 133 C10
Dawdon Durham 234 B4
Dawesgreen Sur 51 D8
Dawker Hill N Yorks 207 F7
Dawley Telford 132 B3
Dawley Bank Telford 132 B3
Dawlish Devon 14 F5
Dawlish Warren Devon 14 F5
Dawn Conwy 180 G5
Daw's Cross Essex 107 E7
Daw's Green Som 27 C11
Daws Heath Essex 69 B10
Daw's House Corn 12 E2
Dawshill Worcs 116 G6
Dawsmere Lincs 157 C8
Day Green E Ches 168 D3
Daybrook Notts 171 F9
Dayhills Staffs 151 C9
Dayhouse Bank Worcs 117 B9
Daylesford Glos 100 F4
Daywall Shrops 148 C5
Ddol Flint 181 G10
Ddôl Cownwy Powys 147 F10
Ddrydwy Anglesey 178 G5
De Beauvoir Town London 67 C10
Deacons Hill Herts 85 F11
Deadman's Cross C Beds 104 C2
Deadman's Green Staffs 151 B10
Deadwater Hants 49 F10
Deadwater Northumb 250 D4
Deaf Hill Durham 234 D3
Deal Hall Kent 55 C11
Deal Hall Essex 89 F8
Dean Cumb 229 F7
Dean Devon 8 C4
Dean Devon 40 D6
Dean Devon 40 E4
Dean Devon 41 D8
Dean Dorset 31 D7
Dean Edin 280 G4
Dean Hants 33 D9
Dean Hants 48 G2
Dean Lancs 195 B11
Dean Oxon 100 G6
Dean Som 45 E7
Dean Bank Durham 233 E11
Dean Court Oxon 83 D7
Dean Cross Devon 40 E4
Dean Head S Yorks 197 G9
Dean Lane Head W Yorks 205 G7
Dean Park Renfs 267 B10
Dean Prior Devon 8 C4
Dean Row E Ches 184 E5
Dean Street Kent 53 C8
Deanburnhaugh Borders 261 G9
Deane Gtr Man 195 F7
Deane Hants 48 C4
Deanend Dorset 31 D7
Deanich Lodge Highld 309 L3
Deanland Dorset 31 D7
Deanlane End W Sus 34 E2
Deans W Loth 269 B10
Deans Bottom Kent 69 G11
Dean's Green Warks 118 D2
Deans Hill Kent 69 G11
Deanscales Cumb 229 F7
Deansgreen E Ches 183 D11
Deanshanger Northants 102 D5
Deanston Stirl 285 G11
Dearham Cumb 229 D7
Dearnley Gtr Man 196 D2
Debach Suff 126 G4
Debdale Gtr Man 184 B5
Debden Essex 86 F6
Debden Essex 105 E11
Debden Cross Essex 105 E11
Debden Green Essex 86 F6
Debden Green Essex 105 E11
Debenham Suff 126 E3
Deblin's Green Worcs 98 B6
Dechmont W Loth 279 G10
Deckham T & W 243 E7
Deddington Oxon 101 E9
Dedham Essex 107 E11
Dedham Heath Essex 107 E11
Dedridge W Loth 269 B11
Dedworth Windsor 66 D2
Deebank Aberds 293 D8
Deecastle Aberds 292 D6
Deene Northants 137 E8
Deenethorpe Northants 137 E9
Deepcar S Yorks 186 B3
Deepclough Derbys 185 B8
Deepcut Sur 50 B2
Deepdale C Beds 104 B4
Deepdale Cumb 212 C4
Deepdale N Yorks 213 D7
Deepdene Sur 51 D7
Deepfields W Mid 133 E8
Deeping Gate Lincs 138 B2
Deeping St James Lincs 138 B3
Deeping St Nicholas Lincs 156 F4
Deepthwaite Cumb 211 C10
Deepweir Mon 60 B3
Deerhill Moray 302 D4
Deerhurst Glos 99 F7
Deerhurst Walton Glos 99 F7
Deerland Pembs 73 C7
Deerness Orkney 314 F5
Deer's Green Essex 105 E9
Deerstones N Yorks 205 C7
Deerton Street Kent 70 G3
Defford Worcs 99 C8
Defynnog Powys 95 F8
Deganwy Conwy 180 F3
Degar V Glam 58 D4
Degibna Corn 2 D5
Deighton N Yorks 225 E7
Deighton W Yorks 197 D7
Deighton York 207 E8
Deiniolen Gwyn 163 C9
Deishar Highld 291 B11
Delabole Corn 11 E7
Delamere W Ches 167 B9
Delfour Highld 291 C10
Delfrigs Aberds 303 G9
Dell Lodge Highld 292 B2
Dell Quay W Sus 22 C4
Delliefure Highld 301 F10
Delly End Oxon 82 C5
Delnabo Moray 292 B3
Delnadamph Aberds 292 C4
Delnamer Angus 292 G3
Delph Gtr Man 196 F3
Delves Durham 233 B8
Delvin End Essex 106 D5
Delvine Perth 286 C5
Dembleby Lincs 155 B10
Demelza Corn 5 C9
Denaby Main S Yorks 187 B7
Denbeath Fife 281 B7
Denbigh Denb 165 B9
Denbury Devon 8 B6
Denby Derbys 170 F5
Denby Bottles Derbys 170 F5
Denby Common Derbys 170 F6
Denby Dale W Yorks 197 F8
Denchworth Oxon 82 G5
Dendron Cumb 210 E4
Dene Park Kent 52 C5
Deneend C Beds 103 D10
Denend Aberds 302 F6
Deneside Durham 234 B4
Denford Northants 121 B9
Denford Staffs 169 E7
Dengie Essex 89 E7
Denham Bucks 66 B4
Denham Bucks 102 G5
Denham Suff 124 E5
Denham Suff 126 C3
Denham Corner Suff 126 C3
Denham End Suff 124 E5
Denham Green Bucks 66 B4
Denham Street Suff 126 C3
Denhead Aberds 303 D9
Denhead Fife 287 F8
Denhead of Arbilot Angus 287 C9
Denhead of Gray Dundee 287 D7
Denholm Borders 262 F3
Denholme W Yorks 205 G7
Denholme Clough W Yorks 205 G7
Denholme Edge W Yorks 205 G7
Denholme Gate W Yorks 205 G7
Denholmhill Borders 262 F3
Denio Gwyn 145 B7
Denmead Hants 33 E11
Denmore Aberdeen 293 B11
Denmoss Aberds 302 E6
Dennington Suff 126 D5
Dennington Corner Suff 126 D5
Dennington Hall Suff 126 D5
Denny Falk 278 E6
Denny Bottom Kent 52 F5
Denny End Cambs 123 D9
Denny Lodge Hants 32 F4
Dennyloanhead Falk 278 E6
Denshaw Gtr Man 196 E3
Denside Aberds 293 D10
Densole Kent 55 E8
Denston Suff 124 G5
Denstone Staffs 169 G9
Denstroude Kent 70 G6
Dent Cumb 212 B4
Dent Bank Durham 232 F4
Denton Cambs 138 F2
Denton Darl 224 B4
Denton E Sus 23 E7
Denton Gtr Man 184 B6
Denton Kent 55 D8
Denton Kent 69 E7
Denton Lincs 155 C7
Denton N Yorks 205 D8
Denton Norf 142 F5
Denton Northants 120 F6
Denton Oxon 83 E9
Denton Burn T & W 242 D6
Denton Holme Cumb 239 G10
Denton's Green Mers 183 B7
Denver Norf 140 C2
Denvilles Hants 22 B2
Denwick Northumb 264 G6
Deopham Norf 141 C11
Deopham Green Norf 141 D10
Deopham Stalland Norf 141 D10
Depden Suff 124 F5
Depden Green Suff 124 F5
Deppers Bridge Warks 119 F7
Deptford London 67 D11
Deptford T & W 243 F9
Deptford Wilts 46 F4
Derby Derbys 153 B7
Derby Devon 40 G5
Derbyhaven I o M 192 F3
Derbyshire Hill Mers 183 C8
Dereham Norf 159 G9
Dergoals Dumfries 236 D4
Deri Caerph 77 E10
Derriford Plym 7 D9
Derril Devon 24 G4
Derringstone Kent 55 D8
Derrington Shrops 132 E2
Derrington Staffs 151 E7
Derriton Devon 24 G4
Derry Stirl 285 E10
Derry Downs London 68 F3
Derry Fields Wilts 81 G8
Derry Hill Wilts 62 E3
Derry Lodge Aberds 292 D2
Derrydaroch Stirl 285 E7
Derryguaig Argyll 288 F6
Derrythorpe N Lincs 199 F10
Dersingham Norf 158 C3
Dertfords Wilts 45 D10
Dervaig Argyll 288 D6
Derwen Bridgend 58 C2
Derwen Denb 165 E9
Derwenlas Powys 128 D4
Desborough Northants 136 G6
Desford Leics 135 C9
Deskryshiel Aberds 292 B6
Detchant Northumb 264 B3
Detling Kent 53 B9
Deuchar Angus 292 G6
Deuddwr Powys 148 F4
Deuxhill Shrops 132 F3
Devauden Mon 79 F7
Deveral Corn 2 B3
Devil's Bridge = Pontarfynach Ceredig 112 B4
Devitts Green Warks 134 E5
Devizes Wilts 62 G4
Devol Invclyd 276 G6
Devon Village Clack 279 B8
Devonport Plym 7 E9
Devonside Clack 279 B8
Devoran Corn 3 B7
Dewar Borders 270 F6
Dewartown Midloth 271 C7
Dewes Green Essex 105 E9
Dewlands Common Dorset 31 F9
Dewlish Dorset 17 B11
Dewsbury W Yorks 197 C8
Dewsbury Moor W Yorks 197 C8
Dewshall Court Hereford 97 E9
Dhoon I o M 192 D5
Dhoor I o M 192 C5
Dhowin I o M 192 B5
Dhustone Shrops 115 B11
Dial Green W Sus 34 B6
Dial Post W Sus 35 D11
Dibberford Dorset 29 G7
Dibden Hants 32 F6
Dibden Purlieu Hants 32 F6
Dickens Heath W Mid 118 B2
Dickleburgh Norf 142 G3
Dickleburgh Moor Norf 142 G3
Dickon Hills Lincs 174 D6
Didbrook Glos 99 E11
Didcot Oxon 64 B4
Diddington Cambs 122 D3
Diddlebury Shrops 131 F10
Diddywell Devon 25 B7
Didley Hereford 97 E9
Didling W Sus 34 D4
Didlington Norf 140 D5
Didmarton Glos 61 B10
Didsbury Gtr Man 184 C4
Didworthy Devon 8 C3
Diebidale Highld 309 L4
Digbeth W Mid 133 F11
Digby Lincs 173 E9
Digg Highld 298 C4
Diggle Gtr Man 196 F4
Diglis Worcs 116 G6
Digmoor Lancs 194 F3
Digswell Herts 86 B3
Digswell Park Herts 86 C2
Digswell Water Herts 86 C3
Dihewyd Ceredig 111 F9
Dilham Norf 160 D6
Dilhorne Staffs 169 G7
Dill Hall Lancs 195 B8
Dillarburn S Lnrk 268 G6
Dillington Cambs 122 D2
Dillington Som 28 D5
Dilston Northumb 241 E11
Dilton Marsh Wilts 45 D11
Dilwyn Hereford 115 G8
Dimlands V Glam 58 F3
Dimmer Som 44 G6
Dimple Derbys 170 C3
Dimple Gtr Man 195 D8
Dimsdale Staffs 168 F4
Dimson Corn 12 G4
Dinas Carms 92 E5
Dinas Corn 10 G4
Dinas Gwyn 144 B5
Dinas Gwyn 163 D7
Dinas Cross Pembs 91 D10
Dinas Dinlle Gwyn 162 D6
Dinas-Mawddwy Gwyn 147 G7
Dinas Mawr Conwy 164 E4
Dinas Powys V Glam 59 E7
Dinbych y Pysgod = Tenby Pembs 73 E10
Dinckley Lancs 203 F9
Dinder Som 44 E5
Dinedor Hereford 97 D10
Dinedor Cross Hereford 97 D10
Dines Green Worcs 116 F6
Dingestow Mon 79 C7
Dinghurst N Som 44 B2
Dingle Mers 182 D5
Dingleden Kent 53 G10
Dingleton Borders 262 C2
Dingley Northants 136 F5
Dingwall Highld 300 D5
Dinlabyre Borders 250 E2
Dinmael Conwy 165 G8
Dinnet Aberds 292 D6
Dinnington S Yorks 187 D8
Dinnington Som 28 E6
Dinnington T & W 242 C6
Dinorwic Gwyn 163 C9
Dinton Bucks 84 C3
Dinton Wilts 46 G4
Dinwoodie Mains Dumfries 248 E4

East Hoathly E Sus 23 B8
East Hogaland Shetland 313 K5
East Holme Dorset 18 D3
East Holton Dorset 18 C5
East Holywell Northumb 243 C8
East Horndon Essex 68 B6
East Horrington Som 44 D5
East Horsley Sur 50 C5
East Horton Northumb 264 C2
East Howdon T & W 243 D8
East Howe Bmouth 19 B7
East Huntspill Som 43 E10
East Hyde C Beds 85 B10
East Ilkerton Devon 41 D8
East Ilsley W Berks 64 C3
East Keal Lincs 174 C5
East Kennett Wilts 62 F6
East Keswick W Yorks 206 E3
East Kilbride S Lnrk 268 E2
East Kimber Devon 12 B5
East Kingston W Sus 35 G9
East Kirkby Lincs 174 C4
East Knapton N Yorks 217 D7
East Knighton Dorset 18 D2
East Knowstone Devon 26 C4
East Knoyle Wilts 45 G11
East Kyloe Northumb 264 B3
East Kyo Durham 242 G5
East Lambrook Som 28 D6
East Lamington Highld 301 B7
East Langdon Kent 55 D10
East Langton Leics 136 E4
East Langwell Highld 309 J7
East Lavant W Sus 22 B5
East Lavington W Sus 34 D6
East Law Northumb 242 G3
East Layton N Yorks 224 D3
East Leake Notts 153 D11
East Learmouth
Northumb 263 B9
East Leigh Devon 8 E3
East Leigh Devon 25 F11
East Lexham Norf 159 F7
East Lilburn Northumb 264 E2
East Linton E Loth 281 F11
East Liss Hants 34 B3
East Lockinge Oxon 64 B2
East Loftus Redcar 226 B4
East Looe Corn 6 E5
East Lound N Lincs 188 B3
East Lulworth Dorset 18 E3
East Lutton N Yorks 217 F8
East Lydeard Som 27 B11
East Lydford Som 44 G5
East Lyng Som 28 B4
East Mains Aberds 293 D8
East Mains Borders 271 F11
East Mains S Lnrk 268 E2
East Malling Kent 53 B8
East Malling Heath Kent 53 B7
East March Angus 287 D8
East Marden W Sus 34 E4
East Markham Notts 188 G2
East Marsh NE Lincs 201 E9
East Martin Hants 31 D9
East Marton N Yorks 204 C4
East Melbury Dorset 30 C5
East Meon Hants 33 C11
East Mere Devon 27 D7
East Mersea Essex 89 C9
East Mey Highld 310 B7
East Molesey Sur 67 F7
East Moor W Yorks 197 C10
East Moors Cardiff 59 D8
East Morden Dorset 18 B4
East Morton W Yorks 205 E7
East Moulsecoomb
Brighton 36 F4
East Ness N Yorks 216 D3
East Newton E Yorks 209 F11
East Newton N Yorks 216 D2
East Norton Leics 136 C5
East Nynehead Som 27 C11
East Oakley Hants 48 C5
East Ogwell Devon 14 G2
East Orchard Dorset 30 D4
East Ord Northumb 273 E9
East Panson Devon 12 C3
East Parley Dorset 19 B8
East Peckham Kent 53 D7
East Pennard Som 44 F5
East Perry Cambs 122 D3
East Portholland Corn 5 G9
East Portlemouth Devon 9 G9
East Prawle Devon 9 G10
East Preston W Sus 35 G9
East Pulham Dorset 30 F2
East Putford Devon 24 D5
East Quantoxhead Som 42 E6
East Rainton T & W 234 B2
East Ravendale NE Lincs 190 B2
East Raynham Norf 159 D7
East Rhidorroch Lodge
Highld 307 K7
East Rigton W Yorks 206 E3
East Rolstone N Som 59 G11
East Rounton N Yorks 225 E8
East Row N Yorks 227 C7
East Rudham Norf 158 D6
East Runton Norf 177 E11
East Ruston Norf 160 D6
East Saltoun E Loth 271 B9
East Sheen London 67 D8
East Skelston Dumfries 247 F8
East Sleekburn
Northumb 253 G7
East Somerton Norf 161 F9
East Stanley Durham 242 G6
East Stockwith Lincs 188 C3
East Stoke Dorset 18 D3
East Stoke Notts 172 F3
East Stoke Som 29 D7
East Stour Dorset 30 C4
East Stour Common
Dorset 30 C4
East Stourmouth Kent 71 G9
East Stowford Devon 25 B10
East Stratton Hants 48 F4
East Street Kent 55 B10
East Street Som 44 F4
East Studdal Kent 55 D10
East Suisnish Highld 295 B7
East Taphouse Corn 6 C3
East-the-Water Devon 25 B7
East Third Borders 262 B4
East Thirston Northumb 252 D5
East Tilbury Thurrock 69 D7
East Tisted Hants 49 G8
East Torrington Lincs 189 E10
East Town Som 42 G6
East Town Som 44 E6
East Town Wilts 45 B11
East Trewent Pembs 73 F8
East Tuddenham Norf 159 G11
East Tuelmenna Corn 6 B4
East Tytherley Hants 32 B3
East Tytherton Wilts 62 E3
East Village Devon 26 F4
East Village V Glam 58 E3
East Wall Shrops 131 E10
East Walton Norf 158 F4
East Water Som 44 C4
East Week Devon 13 C9
East Wellow Hants 32 C4
East Wemyss Fife 280 B6
East Whitburn W Loth 269 B9
East Wickham London 68 D3
East Williamston Pembs 73 E9
East Winch Norf 158 F3
East Winterslow Wilts 47 G8
East Wittering W Sus 21 B11
East Witton N Yorks 214 B2
East Woodburn
Northumb 251 F10
East Woodhay Hants 64 G2
East Woodlands Som 45 E9
East Worldham Hants 49 F8
East Worlington Devon 26 E3
East Worthing W Sus 35 G11
East Wretham Norf 141 E8
East Youlstone Devon 24 D3
Eastacombe Devon 25 B8
Eastacombe Devon 25 C9
Eastacott Devon 25 C10
Eastbourne Darl 224 C6
Eastbourne E Sus 23 F10
Eastbridge Suff 127 D9
Eastbrook Som 28 C2
Eastbrook V Glam 59 E7
Eastburn E Yorks 208 B5
Eastburn W Yorks 204 E6
Eastburn Br W Yorks 204 E6
Eastbury London 85 G9
Eastbury W Berks 63 D10
Eastby N Yorks 204 C6
Eastchurch Kent 70 E3
Eastcombe Glos 80 E5
Eastcote London 66 B6
Eastcote Northants 120 G3
Eastcote W Mid 118 B3
Eastcote Village London 66 B6
Eastcott Corn 24 D3
Eastcott Wilts 46 B4
Eastcotts Beds 103 B11
Eastcourt Wilts 63 G8
Eastcourt Wilts 81 G7
Eastdon Devon 14 F5
Eastdown Devon 8 F6
Eastend Essex 86 C6
Eastend Oxon 100 G6
Easter Aberchalder
Highld 291 B7
Easter Ardross Highld 300 B6
Easter Balgedie Perth 286 G5
Easter Balmoral Aberds 292 D4
Easter Boleskine Highld 300 G5
Easter Brackland Stirl 285 G10
Easter Brae Highld 300 C6
Easter Cardno Aberds 303 C9
Easter Compton S Glos 60 C5
Easter Cringate Stirl 278 D4
Easter Culfosie Aberds 293 C9
Easter Davoch Aberds 292 C6
Easter Earshaig
Dumfries 248 C2
Easter Ellister Argyll 254 B3
Easter Fearn Highld 309 L6
Easter Galcantray
Highld 301 E8
Easter Housebyres
Borders 262 B2
Easter Howgate Midloth 270 C4
Easter Howlaws
Borders 272 G4
Easter Kinkell Highld 300 D5
Easter Knox Angus 287 D9
Easter Langlee Borders 262 B2
Easter Lednathie Angus 292 G5
Easter Milton Highld 301 D9
Easter Moniack Highld 300 E5
Easter Ord Aberdeen 293 C10
Easter Quarff Shetland 313 K6
Easter Rhynd Perth 286 F5
Easter Row Stirl 278 B5
Easter Silverford
Aberds 303 C7
Easter Skeld Shetland 313 J5
Easter Softlaw Borders 263 C7
Easter Tulloch Highld 291 B11
Easter Whyntie Aberds 302 C6
Eastergate W Sus 22 B6
Easterhouse Glasgow 268 B3
Eastern Green W Mid 134 G5
Easterside M'bro 225 B10
Easterton Wilts 46 C4
Easterton of Lenabo
Aberds 303 E10
Easterton Sands Wilts 46 B4
Eastertown Som 43 C10
Eastertown of
Auchleuchries Aberds 303 F10
Eastfield Borders 262 D2
Eastfield Bristol 60 D5
Eastfield N Lnrk 269 C7
Eastfield N Lnrk 278 G4
Eastfield N Yorks 217 C10
Eastfield Northumb 243 B7
Eastfield P'boro 138 D4
Eastfield S Lnrk 268 C2
Eastfield S Yorks 197 G9
Eastfield Hall Northumb 252 B6
Eastgate Durham 232 D5
Eastgate Norf 160 E2
Eastgate P'boro 138 D4
Easthall Herts 104 G3
Eastham Mers 182 E5
Eastham Worcs 116 D3
Eastham Ferry Mers 182 E5
Easthampstead Brack 65 F11
Easthampton Hereford 115 E8
Easthaugh Norf 159 F11
Eastheath Wokingham 65 F10
Easthope Shrops 131 D11
Easthopewood Shrops 131 D11
Easthorpe Essex 107 G8
Easthorpe Leics 154 B6
Easthorpe Notts 172 E2
Easthouse Shetland 313 J5
Easthouses Midloth 270 B6
Easting Orkney 314 A7
Eastington Devon 26 F2
Eastington Glos 80 D3
Eastington Glos 81 C10
Eastland Gate Hants 33 E11
Eastleach Martin Glos 82 D2
Eastleach Turville Glos 81 D11
Eastleigh Devon 25 B7
Eastleigh Hants 32 D6
Eastling Kent 54 B3
Eastmoor Derbys 186 G4
Eastmoor Norf 140 C4
Eastney Ptsmth 21 B9
Eastnor Hereford 98 D4
Eastoft N Lincs 199 D10
Eastoke Hants 21 B10
Easton Bristol 60 E6
Easton Cambs 122 C2
Easton Cumb 239 C10
Easton Cumb 239 F7
Easton Devon 8 F3
Easton Devon 13 D10
Easton Dorset 17 G9
Easton Hants 48 G4
Easton I o W 20 D2
Easton Lincs 155 D8
Easton Norf 160 G2
Easton Som 44 D4
Easton Suff 126 F5
Easton W Berks 64 E2
Easton Wilts 61 E11
Easton Grey Wilts 61 B11
Easton in Gordano
N Som 60 D4
Easton Maudit Northants 121 F7
Easton on the Hill
Northants 137 C10
Easton Royal Wilts 63 G8
Easton Town Som 44 G5
Easton Town Wilts 61 B11
Eastover Som 43 F10
Eastpark Dumfries 238 D2
Eastrea Cambs 138 D5
Eastriggs Dumfries 238 D6
Eastrington E Yorks 199 B9
Eastrip Wilts 61 E10
Eastrop Hants 48 C6
Eastry Kent 55 C10
Eastville Bristol 60 E6
Eastville Lincs 174 D6
Eastwell Leics 154 D5
Eastwell Park Kent 54 D4
Eastwick Herts 86 C6
Eastwick Shetland 312 F5
Eastwood Hereford 98 C2
Eastwood Notts 171 F7
Eastwood S Yorks 186 C6
Eastwood Sthend 69 B10
Eastwood W Yorks 196 B3
Eastwood End Cambs 139 E8
Eastwood Hall Notts 171 F7
Eathorpe Warks 119 D7
Eaton E Ches 168 B5
Eaton Hereford 115 F10
Eaton Leics 154 D5
Eaton Norf 142 B4
Eaton Notts 188 F2
Eaton Oxon 82 E6
Eaton Shrops 131 F10
Eaton Shrops 131 F7
Eaton W Ches 167 C9
Eaton Bishop Hereford 97 D8
Eaton Bray C Beds 103 G9
Eaton Constantine
Shrops 131 B11
Eaton Ford Cambs 122 E3
Eaton Green C Beds 103 G9
Eaton Hastings Oxon 82 F3
Eaton Mascott Shrops 131 B10
Eaton on Tern Shrops 150 E3
Eaton Socon Cambs 122 F3
Eaton upon Tern Shrops 150 E3
Eau Brink Norf 157 F11
Eau Withington
Hereford 97 C10
Eaves Green W Mid 134 G5
Eavestone N Yorks 214 F4
Ebberly Hill Devon 25 D9
Ebberston N Yorks 217 C7
Ebbesbourne Wake
Wilts 31 C7
Ebblake Hants 31 F10
Ebbw Vale Bl Gwent 77 D11
Ebchester Durham 242 F4
Ebdon N Som 59 G11
Ebernoe W Sus 35 B7
Ebford Devon 14 D5
Ebley Glos 80 D4
Ebnal W Ches 167 F7
Ebnall Hereford 115 F9
Ebreywood Shrops 149 F10
Ebrington Glos 100 C3
Ecchinswell Hants 48 B4
Ecclaw Borders 272 B5
Eccle Riggs Cumb 210 B4
Ecclefechan Dumfries 238 C5
Eccles Borders 272 G5
Eccles Gtr Man 184 B3
Eccles Kent 69 G8
Eccles on Sea Norf 161 D8
Eccles Road Norf 141 E10
Ecclesall S Yorks 186 E4
Ecclesfield S Yorks 186 C5
Ecclesgreig Aberds 293 G9
Eccleshall Staffs 150 D6
Eccleshill W Yorks 205 F9
Ecclesmachan
W Loth 279 G11
Eccleston Lancs 194 D4
Eccleston Mers 183 B7
Eccleston W Ches 166 C6
Eccleston Park Mers 183 C7
Eccliffe Dorset 30 B3
Eccup W Yorks 205 E11
Echt Aberds 293 C9
Eckford Borders 262 D6
Eckfordmoss Borders 262 D6
Eckington Derbys 186 F6
Eckington Worcs 99 C8
Eckington Corner E Sus 23 D8
Ecklands S Yorks 197 G8
Eckworthy Devon 24 D6
Ecton Northants 120 E6
Ecton Staffs 169 D9
Ecton Brook Northants 120 E6
Edale Derbys 185 D10
Edale End Derbys 185 D11
Edbrook Som 43 E8
Edburton W Sus 36 E2
Edderside Cumb 229 B7
Edderton Highld 309 L7
Eddington Kent 71 F7
Eddington W Berks 63 F10
Eddistone Devon 24 C3
Eddleston Borders 270 F4
Eddlewood S Lnrk 268 E4
Eden Mount Cumb 211 D8
Eden Park London 67 F11
Eden Vale Durham 234 D4
Eden Vale Wilts 45 C11
Edenbridge Kent 52 D2
Edenfield Lancs 195 D9
Edenhall Cumb 231 E7
Edenham Lincs 155 E11
Edensor Derbys 170 B2
Edentaggart Argyll 276 C6
Edenthorpe S Yorks 198 F6
Edentown Cumb 239 F9
Ederline Argyll 275 C9
Edern Gwyn 144 B5
Edford Som 45 D7
Edgarley Som 44 F4
Edgbaston W Mid 133 G11
Edgcote Northants 101 B10
Edgcott Bucks 102 G3
Edgcott Som 41 F10
Edgcumbe Corn 2 C6
Edge Glos 80 D4
Edge Shrops 131 B7
Edge End Glos 79 C9
Edge End Lancs 203 G10
Edge Fold Blkburn 195 D8
Edge Fold Gtr Man 195 F8
Edge Green Gtr Man 183 B9
Edge Green Norf 141 F10
Edge Green W Ches 167 E7
Edge Hill Mers 182 C5
Edge Hill Warks 134 D4
Edge Mount S Yorks 186 C3
Edgebolton Shrops 149 E11
Edgefield Norf 159 C11
Edgefield Street Norf 159 C11
Edgehill Warks 101 B7
Edgeley Gtr Man 184 D5
Edgerley Shrops 148 F6
Edgerston Borders 262 G5
Edgerton W Yorks 196 D6
Edgeside Lancs 195 C10
Edgeworth Glos 80 D6
Edginswell Devon 9 B7
Edgiock Worcs 117 E10
Edgmond Telford 150 F4
Edgmond Marsh Telford 150 E4
Edgton Shrops 131 F7
Edgware London 85 G11
Edgwick W Mid 134 G6
Edgworth Blkburn 195 D8
Edham Borders 262 B6
Edial Staffs 133 B11
Edinample Stirl 285 E9
Edinbane Highld 298 D3
Edinburgh Edin 280 G5
Edinchip Stirl 285 E9
Edingale Staffs 152 G4
Edingight Ho Moray 302 D5
Edinglassie Ho Aberds 292 B5
Edingley Notts 171 D11
Edingthorpe Norf 160 C6
Edingthorpe Green
Norf 160 C6
Edington Som 43 E11
Edington Wilts 46 C2
Edingworth Som 43 C11
Edintore Moray 302 E4
Edistone Devon 24 C2
Edith Weston Rutland 137 B8
Edithmead Som 43 D10
Edlaston Derbys 169 G11
Edlesborough Bucks 85 B7
Edlingham Northumb 252 B4
Edlington Lincs 190 G2
Edmondsham Dorset 31 E9
Edmondsley Durham 233 B10
Edmondstown Rhondda 77 G8
Edmondthorpe Leics 155 F7
Edmonston S Lnrk 269 G11
Edmonstone Orkney 314 D5
Edmonton Corn 10 G5
Edmonton London 86 G4
Edmundbyers Durham 242 G2
Ednam Borders 262 B6
Ednaston Derbys 170 G2
Edney Common Essex 87 E11
Edradynate Perth 286 B2
Edrom Borders 272 D6
Edstaston Shrops 149 C10
Edstone Warks 118 E3
Edvin Loach Hereford 116 F3
Edwalton Notts 153 B11
Edwardstone Suff 107 C8
Edwardsville M Tydf 77 F9
Edwinsford Carms 94 E2
Edwinstowe Notts 171 B10
Edworth C Beds 104 C4
Edwyn Ralph Hereford 116 F2
Edzell Angus 293 G7
Efail-fôch Neath 57 B9
Efail Isaf Rhondda 58 C5
Efailnewydd Gwyn 145 B7
Efailwen Carms 92 F2
Efenechtyd Denb 165 D10
Effingham Sur 50 C6
Effirth Shetland 313 H5
Effledge Borders 262 F3
Efflinch Staffs 152 F3
Efford Devon 26 G5
Efford Plym 7 D10
Egbury Hants 48 C2
Egdon Worcs 117 G8
Egerton Gtr Man 195 E8
Egerton Kent 54 D2
Egerton Forstal Kent 53 D11
Egerton Green E Ches 167 E8
Egford Som 45 D9
Eggbeare Corn 12 D2
Eggborough N Yorks 198 C5
Eggbuckland Plym 7 D10
Eggesford Station
Devon 25 E11
Eggington C Beds 103 F9
Egginton Derbys 152 D5
Egginton Common
Derbys 152 D5
Egglesburn Durham 232 G5
Egglescliffe Stockton 225 C8
Eggleston Durham 232 G5
Egham Sur 66 E4
Egham Hythe Sur 66 E4
Egham Wick Sur 66 E3
Egleton Rutland 137 B7
Eglingham Northumb 264 F4
Egloshayle Corn 10 G5
Egloskerry Corn 11 D11
Eglwys-Brewis V Glam 58 F4
Eglwys Cross Wrex 167 G7
Eglwys Fach Ceredig 128 D3
Eglwysbach Conwy 180 G4
Eglwyswen Pembs 92 D3
Eglwyswrw Pembs 92 D2
Egmanton Notts 172 B2
Egmere Norf 159 B8
Egremont Cumb 219 C10
Egremont Mers 182 C4
Egton N Yorks 226 D6
Egton Bridge N Yorks 226 D6
Egypt Bucks 66 B3
Egypt Hants 48 E3
Egypt W Berks 64 D2
Egypt W Yorks 205 G7
Eiden Highld 309 J7
Eight Ash Green Essex 107 F8
Eighton Banks T & W 243 F7
Eign Hill Hereford 97 D10
Eignaig Highld 289 E9
Eil Highld 291 B10
Eilanreach Highld 295 D10
Eildon Borders 262 C3
Eilean Anabaich
W Isles 305 H4
Eilean Darach Highld 307 L6
Eilean Shona Ho Highld 289 B8
Eileanach Lodge Highld 300 C5
Einacleite W Isles 304 F3
Einsiob = Evenjobb
Powys 114 E5
Eisgean W Isles 305 G5
Eisingrug Gwyn 146 C2
Elan Village Powys 113 D8
Eland Green Northumb 242 C5
Elberton S Glos 60 B6
Elborough N Som 43 B11
Elbridge Shrops 149 E7
Elbridge W Sus 22 C6
Elburton Plym 7 E10
Elcho Perth 286 E5
Elcock's Brook Worcs 117 E10
Elcombe Glos 80 F3
Elcombe Swindon 62 C6
Elcot W Berks 63 F11
Eldene Swindon 63 C7
Elder Street Essex 105 E11
Eldernell Cambs 138 D6
Eldersfield Worcs 98 E6
Elderslie Renfs 267 C8
Eldon Durham 233 F10
Eldon Lane Durham 233 F10
Eldrick S Ayrs 245 G7
Eldroth N Yorks 212 F5
Eldwick W Yorks 205 E8
Elemore Vale T & W 234 B3
Elerch = Bont-goch
Ceredig 128 F3
Elfhowe Cumb 221 F9
Elford Northumb 264 C5
Elford Staffs 152 G3
Elford Closes Cambs 123 C10
Elgin Moray 302 C2
Elgol Highld 295 D7
Elham Kent 55 E7
Eliburn W Loth 269 B10
Elie Fife 287 G8
Elim Anglesey 178 D5
Eling Hants 32 E5
Eling W Berks 64 D4
Elishader Highld 298 C5
Elishaw Northumb 251 D9
Elizafield Dumfries 238 C2
Elkesley Notts 187 F11
Elkington Northants 120 B2
Elkins Green Essex 87 E10
Elkstone Glos 81 C7
Ellacombe Torbay 9 C8
Ellan Highld 301 G8
Elland W Yorks 196 C6
Elland Lower Edge
W Yorks 196 C6
Elland Upper Edge
W Yorks 196 C6
Ellary Argyll 275 F8
Ellastone Staffs 169 G10
Ellel Lancs 202 B5
Ellemford Borders 272 C4
Ellenborough Cumb 228 D6
Ellenbrook Herts 86 D2
Ellenbrook I o M 192 E4
Ellenglaze Corn 4 D5
Ellenhall Staffs 150 D6
Ellen's Green Sur 50 F5
Ellerbeck N Yorks 225 F8
Ellerburn N Yorks 216 C6
Ellerby N Yorks 226 C5
Ellerdine Telford 150 E2
Ellerdine Heath Telford 150 E2
Ellerhayes Devon 27 G7
Elleric Argyll 284 C4
Ellerker E Yorks 200 B2
Ellerton E Yorks 207 F10
Ellerton N Yorks 224 F5
Ellerton Shrops 150 D4
Ellesborough Bucks 84 D4
Ellesmere Shrops 149 C8
Ellesmere Park Gtr Man 184 B3
Ellesmere Port W Ches 182 F6
Ellicombe Som 42 E3
Ellingham Hants 31 F10
Ellingham Norf 143 E7
Ellingham Northumb 264 D5
Ellingstring N Yorks 214 C3
Ellington Cambs 122 C3
Ellington Northumb 253 E7
Ellington Thorpe Cambs 122 C3
Elliot Angus 287 D10
Elliots Green Som 45 D9
Elliot's Town Caerph 77 E10
Ellisfield Hants 48 D6
Elliston Borders 262 D3
Ellistown Leics 153 G8
Ellon Aberds 303 F9
Ellonby Cumb 230 D4
Ellough Suff 143 F8
Elloughton E Yorks 200 B2
Ellwood Glos 79 D9
Elm Cambs 139 B9
Elm Corner Sur 50 B5
Elm Cross Wilts 62 D6
Elm Hill Dorset 30 B4
Elm Park London 68 B4
Elmbridge Glos 80 B5
Elmbridge Worcs 117 D8
Elmdon Essex 105 D9
Elmdon W Mid 134 G3
Elmdon Heath W Mid 134 G3
Elmer W Sus 35 G7
Elmers End London 67 F11
Elmers Green Lancs 194 F3
Elmers Marsh W Sus 34 B5
Elmesthorpe Leics 135 D9
Elmfield I o W 21 C8
Elmhurst Bucks 84 B4
Elmhurst Staffs 152 G2
Elmley Castle Worcs 99 C9
Elmley Lovett Worcs 117 D7
Elmore Glos 80 B3
Elmore Back Glos 80 B3
Elms Green Hereford 115 F10
Elms Green Worcs 116 D4
Elmscott Devon 24 C2
Elmsett Suff 107 B11
Elmslack Lancs 211 D9
Elmstead Essex 107 F11
Elmstead London 68 E2
Elmstead Heath Essex 107 G11
Elmstead Market
Essex 107 G11
Elmsted Kent 54 E6
Elmsthorpe Leics 135 D9
Elmstone Kent 71 G9
Elmstone Hardwicke
Glos 99 F8
Elmswell E Yorks 208 B5
Elmswell Suff 125 E9
Elmton Derbys 187 G8
Elness Orkney 314 C6
Elphin Highld 307 H7
Elphinstone E Loth 281 G7
Elrick Aberds 293 C10
Elrig Dumfries 236 E5
Elrigbeag Argyll 284 F5
Elrington Northumb 241 E9
Elscar S Yorks 197 G11
Elsdon Hereford 114 G6
Elsdon Northumb 251 E10
Elsecar S Yorks 186 B5
Elsecar S Yorks 197 G11
Elsenham Essex 105 F10
Elsenham Sta Essex 105 F10
Elsfield Oxon 83 C8
Elsham N Lincs 200 E4
Elsing Norf 159 F11
Elslack N Yorks 204 D4
Elson Hants 33 G10
Elson Shrops 149 B7
Elsrickle S Lnrk 269 G11
Elstead Sur 50 E2
Elsted W Sus 34 D4
Elsthorpe Lincs 155 E11
Elstob Durham 234 G2
Elston Devon 26 G3
Elston Notts 172 F3
Elston Wilts 46 E5
Elstone Devon 25 D11
Elstow Beds 103 B11
Elstree Herts 85 F11
Elstronwick E Yorks 209 G10
Elswick Lancs 202 F4
Elswick T & W 242 E6
Elswick Leys Lancs 202 F4
Elsworth Cambs 122 E6
Elterwater Cumb 220 E6
Eltham London 68 E2
Eltisley Cambs 122 F5
Elton Cambs 137 E11
Elton Derbys 170 C2
Elton Glos 80 C2
Elton Gtr Man 195 E9
Elton Hereford 115 C9
Elton Notts 154 B5
Elton Stockton 225 B8
Elton W Ches 183 F7
Elton Green W Ches 183 G7
Elton's Marsh Hereford 97 C9
Eltringham Northumb 242 E3
Elvanfoot S Lnrk 259 F11
Elvaston Derbys 153 C8
Elveden Suff 124 B6
Elvet Hill Durham 233 C11
Elvingston E Loth 281 G9
Elvington Kent 55 C9
Elvington York 207 D9
Elwell Devon 41 G7
Elwell Dorset 17 E9
Elwick Hrtlpl 234 E5
Elwick Northumb 264 B4
Elworth E Ches 168 C2
Elworthy Som 42 G5
Ely Cambs 139 G10
Ely Cardiff 58 D6
Emberton M Keynes 103 B7
Embleton Cumb 229 E9
Embleton Durham 234 F4
Embleton Northumb 264 E6
Embo Highld 311 K2
Embo Street Highld 311 K2
Emborough Som 44 C6
Embsay N Yorks 204 C6
Emerson Park London 68 B4
Emerson Valley
M Keynes 102 E6
Emerson's Green S Glos 61 D7
Emery Down Hants 32 F3
Emley W Yorks 197 E8
Emmbrook Wokingham 65 F9
Emmer Green Reading 65 D8
Emmett Carr Derbys 187 F7
Emmington Oxon 84 E2
Emneth Norf 139 B9
Emneth Hungate Norf 139 B10
Emorsgate Norf 157 E10
Empingham Rutland 137 B8
Empshott Hants 49 G9
Empshott Green Hants 49 G8
Emscote Warks 118 D5
Emstrey Shrops 149 G10
Emsworth Hants 22 B2
Enborne W Berks 64 F2
Enborne Row W Berks 64 G2
Enchmarsh Shrops 131 D10
Enderby Leics 135 D10
Endmoor Cumb 211 C10
Endon Staffs 168 E6
Endon Bank Staffs 168 E6
Energlyn Caerph 58 B6
Enfield London 86 F4
Enfield Worcs 117 D10
Enfield Highway London 86 F5
Enfield Lock London 86 F5
Enfield Town London 86 F4
Enfield Wash London 86 F5
Enford Wilts 46 C6
Engamoor Shetland 313 H4
Engedi Anglesey 178 F5
Engine Common S Glos 61 C7
Englefield W Berks 64 E6
Englefield Green Sur 66 E3
Englesea-brook E Ches 168 E3
English Bicknor Glos 79 B9
English Frankton
Shrops 149 D9
Englishcombe Bath 61 G8
Engollan Corn 10 G3
Enham Alamein Hants 47 D11
Enis Devon 25 B9
Enisfirth Shetland 312 F5
Enmore Som 43 G8
Enmore Field Hereford 115 E9
Enmore Green Dorset 30 C5
Ennerdale Bridge
Cumb 219 B11
Enniscaven Corn 5 D9
Enoch Dumfries 247 C9
Enochdhu Perth 292 G2
Ensay Argyll 288 E5
Ensbury Bmouth 19 B7
Ensbury Park Bmouth 19 C7
Ensdon Shrops 149 F8
Ensis Devon 25 B9
Enslow Oxon 83 B7
Enstone Oxon 101 G7
Enterkinfoot Dumfries 247 C9
Enterpen N Yorks 225 D9
Enton Green Sur 50 E3
Enville Staffs 132 F6
Eolaigearraidh W Isles 297 L3
Eorabus Argyll 288 G5
Eòropaidh W Isles 304 B7
Epney Glos 80 C3
Epperstone Notts 171 F11
Epping Essex 87 E7
Epping Green Essex 86 D6
Epping Green Herts 86 D3
Epping Upland Essex 86 E6
Eppleby N Yorks 224 C3
Eppleworth E Yorks 208 G6
Epsom Sur 67 G8
Epwell Oxon 101 C7
Epworth N Lincs 199 G9
Epworth Turbary N Lincs 199 G9
Erbistock Wrex 166 G5
Erbusaig Highld 295 C9
Erchless Castle Highld 300 E4
Erdington W Mid 134 E2
Eredine Argyll 275 C10
Eriboll Highld 308 D4
Ericstane Dumfries 260 G3
Eridge Green E Sus 52 F5
Erines Argyll 275 F9
Eriswell Suff 124 B4
Erith London 68 D4
Erlestoke Wilts 46 C3
Ermine Lincs 189 G7
Ermington Devon 8 E2
Ernesettle Plym 7 D8
Erpingham Norf 160 C3
Erriottwood Kent 54 B2
Errogie Highld 300 G5
Errol Perth 286 E6
Errol Station Perth 286 E6
Erskine Renfs 277 G9
Erskine Bridge Renfs 277 G9
Ervie Dumfries 236 C2
Erwarton Suff 108 E4
Erwood Powys 95 C11
Eryholme N Yorks 224 D6
Eryrys Denb 166 D2
Escomb Durham 233 E9
Escott Som 42 F5
Escrick N Yorks 207 E8
Esgairdawe Carms 94 C2
Esgairgeiliog Powys 128 B5
Esgyryn Conwy 180 F4
Esh Durham 233 C9
Esh Winning Durham 233 C9
Esher Sur 66 G6
Eshiels Borders 261 B7
Esholt W Yorks 205 E9
Eshott Northumb 252 D6
Eshton N Yorks 204 B4
Esk Valley N Yorks 226 E6
Eskadale Highld 300 F4
Eskbank Midloth 270 B6
Eskdale Green Cumb 220 E2
Eskdalemuir Dumfries 249 D7
Eske E Yorks 209 E7
Eskham Lincs 190 B5
Eskholme S Yorks 198 D6
Esknish Argyll 274 G4
Eslington Park
Northumb 264 G2
Esperley Lane Ends
Durham 233 G8
Esprick Lancs 202 F4
Essendine Rutland 155 G10
Essendon Herts 86 D3
Essich Highld 300 F6
Essington Staffs 133 C9
Esslemont Aberds 303 G9
Eston Redcar 225 B11
Estover Plym 7 D10
Eswick Shetland 313 H6
Etal Northumb 263 B10
Etchilhampton Wilts 62 G4
Etchingham E Sus 38 B2
Etchinghill Kent 55 F7
Etchinghill Staffs 151 F10
Etchingwood E Sus 37 C8
Etherley Dene Durham 233 F9
Ethie Castle Angus 287 C10
Ethie Mains Angus 287 C10
Etling Green Norf 159 G10
Etloe Glos 79 D11
Eton Windsor 66 D3
Eton Wick Windsor 66 D2
Etruria Stoke 168 F5
Etsell Shrops 131 C7
Etterby Cumb 239 F9
Etteridge Highld 291 D8
Ettersgill Durham 232 F3
Ettiley Heath E Ches 168 C2
Ettingshall W Mid 133 D8
Ettingshall Park W Mid 133 D8
Ettington Warks 100 B5
Etton E Yorks 208 E5
Etton P'boro 138 B2
Ettrick Borders 261 G7
Ettrickbridge Borders 261 E9
Ettrickdale Argyll 275 G11
Ettrickhill Borders 261 G7
Etwall Derbys 152 C5
Etwall Common Derbys 152 C5
Eudon Burnell Shrops 132 F3
Eudon George Shrops 132 F3
Euston Suff 125 B7
Euximoor Drove Cambs 139 D9
Euxton Lancs 194 D5
Evanstown Bridgend 58 B3
Evanton Highld 300 C6
Eve Hill W Mid 133 E8
Evedon Lincs 173 F9
Evelix Highld 309 K7
Even Pits Hereford 97 D11
Even Swindon Swindon 62 B6
Evendine Hereford 98 C5
Evenjobb = Einsiob
Powys 114 E5
Evenley Northants 101 E11
Evenlode Glos 100 F4
Evenwood Durham 233 G9
Evenwood Gate Durham 233 G9
Everbay Orkney 314 D6
Evercreech Som 44 F6
Everdon Northants 119 F11
Everingham E Yorks 208 E2
Everland Shetland 312 D8
Everleigh Wilts 47 C8
Everley N Yorks 217 B9
Eversholt C Beds 103 E9
Evershot Dorset 29 G9
Eversley Essex 69 B8
Eversley Hants 65 G9
Eversley Centre Hants 65 G9
Eversley Cross Hants 65 G9
Everthorpe E Yorks 208 G4
Everton C Beds 122 G4
Everton Hants 19 C11
Everton Mers 182 C5
Everton Notts 187 C11
Evertown Dumfries 239 B9
Evesbatch Hereford 98 B3
Evesham Worcs 99 C10
Evington Kent 54 D6
Evington Leicester 136 C2
Ewanrigg Cumb 228 D6
Ewden Village S Yorks 186 B3
Ewell Sur 67 G8
Ewell Minnis Kent 55 E9
Ewelme Oxon 83 G10
Ewen Glos 81 F8
Ewenny V Glam 58 D2
Ewerby Lincs 173 F10
Ewerby Thorpe Lincs 173 F10
Ewes Dumfries 249 E9
Ewesley Northumb 252 E3
Ewhurst Sur 50 E5
Ewhurst Green E Sus 38 C3
Ewhurst Green Sur 50 F5
Ewloe Flint 166 B4
Ewloe Green Flint 166 B3
Ewood Blkburn 195 B7
Ewood Bridge Lancs 195 C9
Eworthy Devon 12 C5
Ewshot Hants 49 D10
Ewyas Harold Hereford 97 F7
Exbourne Devon 25 G10
Exbury Hants 20 B4
Exceat E Sus 23 F8
Exebridge Devon 26 C6
Exelby N Yorks 214 B5
Exeter Devon 14 C4
Exford Som 41 F11
Exfords Green Shrops 131 B9
Exhall Warks 118 F2
Exhall Warks 135 F7
Exlade Street Oxon 65 C7
Exley W Yorks 196 C5
Exley Head W Yorks 204 F6
Exminster Devon 14 D4
Exmouth Devon 14 E6
Exnaboe Shetland 313 M5
Exning Suff 124 D2
Exted Kent 55 E7
Exton Devon 14 D5
Exton Hants 33 C10
Exton Rutland 155 G8
Exton Som 42 G2
Exwick Devon 14 C4
Eyam Derbys 186 F2
Eydon Northants 119 G10
Eye Hereford 115 E9
Eye P'boro 138 C4
Eye Suff 126 C2
Eye Green P'boro 138 C4
Eyemouth Borders 273 C8
Eyeworth C Beds 104 B4
Eyhorne Street Kent 53 C10
Eyke Suff 126 G6
Eynesbury Cambs 122 F3
Eynort Highld 294 C5
Eynsford Kent 68 F4
Eynsham Oxon 82 D6
Eype Dorset 16 C5
Eyre Highld 295 B7
Eyre Highld 298 D4
Eyres Monsell Leicester 135 D11
Eythorne Kent 55 D9
Eyton Hereford 115 E9
Eyton Shrops 131 F7
Eyton Shrops 149 G7
Eyton Wrex 166 G4
Eyton on Severn
Shrops 131 B11
Eyton upon the Weald
Moors Telford 150 G3

F

Faberstown Wilts 47 C9
Faccombe Hants 47 B11
Faceby N Yorks 225 E9
Fachell Gwyn 163 B8
Fachwen Gwyn 163 C9
Facit Lancs 195 D11
Fackley Notts 171 C7
Faddiley E Ches 167 E9
Faddonch Highld 295 C11
Fadmoor N Yorks 216 B3
Faerdre Swansea 75 E11
Fagley W Yorks 205 G9
Fagwyr Swansea 75 E11
Faichem Highld 290 C4
Faifley W Dunb 277 G10
Failand N Som 60 E4
Failford S Ayrs 257 D11
Failsworth Gtr Man 195 G11
Fain Highld 299 B11
Faindouran Lodge
Moray 292 C2
Fair Cross London 68 B3
Fair Green Norf 158 F3
Fair Hill Cumb 230 E6
Fair Moor Northumb 252 F5
Fair Oak Hants 33 D7
Fair Oak Hants 64 G5
Fair Oak Lancs 203 D8
Fair Oak Green Hants 65 G7
Fairbourne Gwyn 146 G2
Fairbourne Heath Kent 53 C11
Fairburn N Yorks 198 B3
Fairburn House Highld 300 D4
Fairfield Clack 279 C7
Fairfield Derbys 185 G9
Fairfield Gtr Man 184 B6
Fairfield Gtr Man 195 E10
Fairfield Kent 39 B7
Fairfield Mers 182 C5
Fairfield Stockton 225 B8
Fairfield Worcs 99 C10
Fairfield Worcs 117 B8
Fairfield Park Bath 61 F9
Fairfields Glos 98 E4
Fairford Glos 81 E11
Fairhaven Lancs 193 B10
Fairhaven N Ayrs 255 C10
Fairhill S Lnrk 268 E4
Fairlands Sur 50 C3
Fairlee I o W 20 C6
Fairlie N Ayrs 266 D4
Fairlight E Sus 38 E5
Fairlight Cove E Sus 38 E5
Fairlop London 87 G7
Fairmile Devon 15 B7
Fairmile Dorset 19 C9
Fairmile Sur 66 G6
Fairmilehead Edin 270 B4
Fairoak Caerph 77 F11
Fairoak Staffs 150 C5
Fairseat Kent 68 G6
Fairstead Essex 88 B3
Fairstead Norf 158 F2
Fairview Glos 99 G9
Fairwarp E Sus 37 B7
Fairwater Cardiff 58 D6
Fairwater Torf 78 G3
Fairwood Wilts 45 C10
Fairy Cottage I o M 192 D5
Fairy Cross Devon 24 C6
Fakenham Norf 159 D8
Fakenham Magna Suff 125 B8
Fala Midloth 271 C8
Fala Dam Midloth 271 C8
Falahill Borders 271 D7
Falcon Hereford 98 E2
Falcon Lodge W Mid 134 D2
Falconwood London 68 D3
Falcutt Northants 101 C11
Faldingworth Lincs 189 E9
Faldonside Borders 262 C2
Falfield Fife 287 G8
Falfield S Glos 79 G11
Falkenham Suff 108 D5
Falkenham Sink Suff 108 D5
Falkirk Falk 279 F7
Falkland Fife 286 G6
Falla Borders 262 G6
Fallgate Derbys 170 C5
Fallin Stirl 278 C6
Fallinge Derbys 170 B3
Fallings Heath W Mid 133 D9
Fallowfield Gtr Man 184 C5
Fallside N Lnrk 268 C4
Falmer E Sus 36 F4
Falmouth Corn 3 C8
Falnash Borders 249 B9
Falsgrave N Yorks 217 B10
Falside W Loth 269 B9
Falsidehill Borders 272 G3
Falstone Northumb 250 F6
Fanagmore Highld 306 E6
Fancott C Beds 103 F10
Fangdale Beck N Yorks 225 G11
Fangfoss E Yorks 207 C11
Fanich Highld 311 J2
Fankerton Falk 278 E5
Fanmore Argyll 288 E6
Fanner's Green Essex 87 C11
Fannich Lodge Highld 300 C2
Fans Borders 272 G2
Fanshowe E Ches 184 G5
Fant Kent 53 B8
Faoilean Highld 295 C7
Far Arnside Cumb 211 D8
Far Bank S Yorks 198 E6
Far Banks Lancs 194 C2
Far Bletchley M Keynes 103 E7

Far Coton Leics 135 C7
Far Cotton Northants 120 F4
Far End Cumb 220 F6
Far Forest Worcs 116 C4
Far Green Glos 80 E3
Far Hoarcross Staffs 152 E2
Far Laund Derbys 170 F5
Far Ley Staffs 132 D5
Far Moor Gtr Man 194 G4
Far Oakridge Glos 80 E6
Far Royds W Yorks 205 G11
Far Sawrey Cumb 221 F7
Far Thrupp Glos 80 E5
Farcet Cambs 138 E4
Farden Shrops 115 B11
Fareham Hants 33 F9
Farewell Staffs 151 G11
Farforth Lincs 190 F4
Farhill Derbys 170 C5
Faringdon Oxon 82 F3
Farington Lancs 194 B4
Farington Moss Lancs 194 C4
Farlam Cumb 240 F3
Farlands Booth Derbys 185 D9
Farlary Highld 309 J7
Farleigh N Som 60 F3
Farleigh Sur 67 G11
Farleigh Court Sur 67 G11
Farleigh Green Kent 53 C8
Farleigh Hungerford Som 45 B10
Farleigh Wallop Hants 48 D6
Farleigh Wick Wilts 61 G10
Farlesthorpe Lincs 191 G7
Farleton Cumb 211 C10
Farleton Lancs 211 F11
Farley Bristol 60 E2
Farley Derbys 170 C3
Farley Shrops 131 B7
Farley Shrops 132 C2
Farley Staffs 169 G9
Farley Wilts 32 B2
Farley Green Suff 124 G4
Farley Green Sur 50 D5
Farley Hill Luton 103 G11
Farley Hill Wokingham 65 G8
Farleys End Glos 80 B3
Farlington N Yorks 216 F2
Farlington Ptsmth 33 F11
Farlow Shrops 132 G2
Farm Town Leics 153 F7
Farmborough Bath 61 G7
Farmbridge End Essex 87 C10
Farmcote Glos 99 F11
Farmcote Shrops 132 E5
Farmington Glos 81 B10
Farmoor Oxon 82 D6
Farms Common Corn 2 C5
Farmtown Moray 302 D5
Farnah Green Derbys 170 F4
Farnborough Hants 49 C11
Farnborough London 68 G2
Farnborough W Berks 64 C2
Farnborough Warks 101 B8
Farnborough Green Hants 49 B11
Farnborough Park Hants 49 B11
Farnborough Street Hants 49 B11
Farncombe Sur 50 E3
Farndish Beds 121 E8
Farndon Notts 172 E3
Farndon W Ches 166 E6
Farnell Angus 287 B10
Farnham Dorset 31 D7
Farnham Essex 105 G9
Farnham N Yorks 215 G7
Farnham Suff 127 E7
Farnham Sur 49 D10
Farnham Common Bucks 66 C3
Farnham Green Essex 105 F9
Farnham Park Bucks 66 C3
Farnham Royal Bucks 66 C3
Farnhill N Yorks 204 D6
Farningham Kent 68 F4
Farnley N Yorks 205 D10
Farnley W Yorks 205 G11
Farnley Bank W Yorks 197 E7
Farnley Tyas W Yorks 197 E7
Farnsfield Notts 171 D10
Farnworth Gtr Man 195 F8
Farnworth Halton 183 D8
Farr Highld 291 C10
Farr Highld 300 F6
Farr Highld 308 C7
Farr House Highld 300 F6
Farraline Highld 300 G5
Farringdon Devon 14 C6
Farringdon T & W 243 G9
Farrington Dorset 30 D4
Farrington Gurney Bath 44 B6
Farsley W Yorks 205 F10
Farsley Beck Bottom W Yorks 205 F10
Farther Howegreen Essex 88 E4
Farthing Corner Medway 69 G10
Farthing Green Kent 53 D10
Farthinghoe Northants 101 D10
Farthingloe Kent 55 E9
Farthingstone Northants 120 F2
Fartown W Yorks 196 D6
Farway Devon 15 B9
Farway Marsh Devon 28 G4
Fasach Highld 297 G7
Fasag Highld 299 D8
Fascadale Highld 289 B7
Faslane Port Argyll 276 D4
Fasnacloich Argyll 284 C4
Fasnakyle Ho Highld 300 G3
Fassfern Highld 290 F2
Fatfield T & W 243 G8
Fattahead Aberds 302 D6
Faucheldean W Loth 279 G11
Faugh Cumb 240 G2
Faughill Borders 262 C2
Fauld Staffs 152 D3
Fauldhouse W Loth 269 C8
Fauldiehill Angus 287 D9
Fauldshope Borders 261 D10
Faulkbourne Essex 88 B3
Faulkland Som 45 C8
Fauls Shrops 149 C11
Faverdale Darl 224 B5
Faversham Kent 70 G4
Favillar Moray 302 F2
Fawdington N Yorks 215 E8
Fawdon Northumb 264 F2
Fawdon T & W 242 D6
Fawfieldhead Staffs 169 C9
Fawkham Green Kent 68 F5
Fawler Oxon 63 B10
Fawler Oxon 82 B5
Fawley Bucks 65 B9
Fawley Hants 33 G7
Fawley W Berks 63 C11
Fawley Bottom Bucks 65 B8
Fawley Chapel Hereford 97 F11
Faxfleet E Yorks 199 C11
Faygate W Sus 51 G8
Fazakerley Mers 182 B5
Fazeley Staffs 134 C4
Feagour Highld 291 D7
Fearby N Yorks 214 C3
Fearn Highld 301 B8
Fearn Lodge Highld 309 L6
Fearn Station Highld 301 B8
Fearnan Perth 285 C11
Fearnbeg Highld 299 D7
Fearnhead Warr 183 C10
Fearnmore Highld 299 C7
Fearnville W Yorks 206 F2
Featherstone Staffs 133 B8
Featherstone W Yorks 198 C2
Featherwood Northumb 251 C8
Feckenham Worcs 117 E10
Fedw Fawr Anglesey 179 E10
Feering Essex 107 G7
Feetham N Yorks 223 F9
Fegg Hayes Stoke 168 E5
Fèith Mhor Highld 301 G8
Feizor N Yorks 212 F5
Felbridge Sur 51 F11
Felbrigg Norf 160 B4
Felcourt Sur 51 E11
Felden Herts 85 E8
Felderland Kent 55 B10
Feldy E Ches 183 F11
Felhampton Shrops 131 F8
Felin-Crai Powys 95 G7
Felin Newydd Carms 94 D3
Felin-newydd Powys 96 D2
Felin Newydd = New Mills Powys 129 C11
Felin Puleston Wrex 166 F4
Felin-Wnda Ceredig 92 B6
Felindre Carms 75 C7
Felindre Carms 93 D7
Felindre Carms 93 G11
Felindre Carms 94 E3
Felindre Carms 94 F4
Felindre Ceredig 111 F10
Felindre Powys 96 D3
Felindre Powys 96 G3
Felindre Powys 130 C3
Felindre Powys 130 G3
Felindre Rhondda 58 C3
Felindre Swansea 75 E10
Felindre Farchog Pembs 92 D2
Felinfach Ceredig 111 F10
Felinfach Powys 95 E11
Felinfoel Carms 75 E8
Felingwmisaf Carms 93 G10
Felingwmuchaf Carms 93 G10
Felinwynt Ceredig 110 G4
Felixkirk N Yorks 215 C9
Felixstowe Suff 108 E5
Felixstowe Ferry Suff 108 D6
Felkington Northumb 273 G8
Felkirk W Yorks 197 E11
Fell End Cumb 222 F4
Fell Lane W Yorks 204 E6
Fell Side Cumb 230 D2
Felldyke Cumb 219 B11
Fellgate T & W 243 E8
Felling T & W 243 E7
Felling Shore T & W 243 E7
Fellside T & W 242 E5
Felmersham Beds 121 F9
Felmingham Norf 160 D5
Felmore Essex 69 B8
Felpham W Sus 35 H7
Felsham Suff 125 F8
Felsted Essex 106 G3
Feltham London 66 E6
Feltham Som 28 D2
Felthamhill London 66 E5
Felthorpe Norf 160 F3
Felton Hereford 97 B11
Felton N Som 60 F4
Felton Northumb 252 C5
Felton Butler Shrops 149 F7
Feltwell Norf 140 E4
Fen Ditton Cambs 123 E9
Fen Drayton Cambs 122 D6
Fen End Lincs 156 E4
Fen End W Mid 118 B4
Fen Side Lincs 174 D4
Fen Street Norf 141 G11
Fen Street Suff 125 B11
Fen Street Suff 125 B9
Fenay Bridge W Yorks 197 D7
Fence Lancs 204 F2
Fence Houses T & W 243 G8
Fencott Oxon 83 B9
Fengate Norf 160 E3
Fengate P'boro 138 D4
Fenham Northumb 273 G11
Fenham T & W 242 D6
Fenhouses Lincs 174 G3
Feniscliffe Blkburn 195 B7
Feniscowles Blkburn 194 B6
Feniton Devon 15 B8
Fenlake Beds 103 B11
Fenn Green Shrops 132 G5
Fenn Street Medway 69 D9
Fennington Som 27 B11
Fenn's Bank Wrex 149 B10
Fenny Bentley Derbys 169 E11
Fenny Bridges Devon 15 B8
Fenny Castle Som 44 E4
Fenny Compton Warks 119 G8
Fenny Drayton Leics 134 D6
Fenny Stratford M Keynes 103 E7
Fenrother Northumb 252 E5
Fenstanton Cambs 122 D6
Fenstead End Suff 124 G6
Fenton Cambs 122 B6
Fenton Cumb 240 F2
Fenton Lincs 172 E5
Fenton Lincs 188 F4
Fenton Northumb 263 C11
Fenton Stoke 168 G5
Fenton Barns E Loth 281 E10
Fenton Low Stoke 168 F5
Fenton Pits Corn 5 C11
Fenton Town Northumb 263 C11
Fentonadle Corn 11 F7
Fenwick E Ayrs 267 G9
Fenwick Northumb 242 C3
Fenwick Northumb 273 G11
Fenwick S Yorks 198 D5
Feochaig Argyll 255 F8
Feock Corn 3 B8
Feolin Ferry Argyll 274 G5
Ferguslie Park Renfs 267 C9
Ferindonald Highld 295 E8
Feriniquarrie Highld 296 F7
Ferlochan Argyll 289 E11
Fern Angus 292 G6
Fern Bucks 65 B11
Fern Bank Gtr Man 185 B7
Fern Hill Suff 106 B6
Ferndale Kent 52 E5
Ferndale Rhondda 77 F7
Ferndown Dorset 31 G9
Ferne Wilts 30 C6
Ferness Highld 301 E9
Ferney Green Cumb 221 F8
Fernham Oxon 82 G3
Fernhill Gtr Man 195 E10
Fernhill Rhondda 77 F8
Fernhill W Sus 51 E10
Fernhill Gate Gtr Man 195 F7
Fernhill Heath Worcs 117 F7
Fernhurst W Sus 34 B5
Fernie Fife 287 F7
Ferniebrae Aberds 303 D9
Ferniegair S Lnrk 268 E4
Ferniehirst Borders 271 G8
Fernilea Highld 294 B5
Fernilee Derbys 185 F8
Fernsplatt Corn 4 G5
Ferrensby N Yorks 215 G7
Ferring W Sus 35 G9
Ferry Hill Cambs 139 G7
Ferry Point Highld 309 L7
Ferrybridge W Yorks 198 C3
Ferryden Angus 287 B11
Ferryhill Aberdeen 293 C11
Ferryhill Durham 233 E11
Ferryhill Station Durham 234 E2
Ferryside = Glan-y-Ffer Carms 74 C5
Ferryton Highld 300 C6
Fersfield Norf 141 G11
Fersit Highld 290 F5
Feshiebridge Highld 291 C10
Fetcham Sur 50 B6
Fetterangus Aberds 303 D9
Fettercairn Aberds 293 F8
Fetterdale Fife 287 E8
Fettes Highld 300 D5
Fewcott Oxon 101 F10
Fewston N Yorks 205 C9
Fewston Bents N Yorks 205 C9
Ffair-Rhos Ceredig 112 D4
Ffairfach Carms 94 G2
Ffaldybrenin Carms 94 C2
Ffarmers Carms 94 C3
Ffawyddog Powys 78 B2
Ffodun = Forden Powys 130 C4
Ffont y gari = Font y gary V Glam 58 F5
Ffordd-las Denb 165 C10
Ffordd-y-Gyfraith Bridgend 57 E11
Fforddlas Powys 96 D4
Fforest Carms 75 E9
Fforest-fach Swansea 56 B6
Fforest Gôch Neath 76 E2
Ffos-y-ffin Ceredig 111 E8
Ffos-y-go Wrex 166 E4
Ffostrasol Ceredig 93 B7
Ffridd Powys 130 D3
Ffrith Wrex 166 D3
Ffrwd Gwyn 163 D7
Ffwl y mwn = Fonmon V Glam 58 F4
Ffynnon Carms 74 B5
Ffynnon ddrain Carms 93 G8
Ffynnon Gron Pembs 91 F8
Ffynnon Gynydd Powys 96 C3
Ffynnon-oer Ceredig 111 G10
Ffynnongroes = Crosswell Pembs 92 D2
Ffynnongroyw Flint 181 E10
Fickleshole Sur 67 G11
Fidden Argyll 288 G5
Fiddes Aberds 293 E10
Fiddington Glos 99 E8
Fiddington Som 43 E8
Fiddington Sands Wilts 46 C4
Fiddleford Dorset 30 E4
Fiddler' Green Norf 141 D10
Fiddler's Ferry Mers 193 C11
Fiddler's Ferry Warr 183 D9
Fiddler's Green Glos 99 G8
Fiddler's Green Hereford 97 D11
Fiddlers Hamlet Essex 87 E7
Field Hereford 114 G6
Field Som 44 E6
Field Staffs 151 C10
Field Assarts Oxon 82 C4
Field Broughton Cumb 211 C7
Field Common Sur 66 F6
Field Dalling Norf 159 B10
Field Green Kent 38 B3
Field Head Leics 135 B9
Fields End Herts 85 D8
Field's Place Hereford 115 G8
Fife Keith Moray 302 D4
Fifehead Magdalen Dorset 30 C3
Fifehead Neville Dorset 30 E3
Fifehead St Quintin Dorset 30 E3
Fifield Oxon 82 B2
Fifield Wilts 46 C6
Fifield Windsor 66 D2
Fifield Bavant Wilts 31 B8
Figheldean Wilts 47 D7
Filands Wilts 62 B2
Filby Norf 161 G9
Filby Heath Norf 161 G9
Filchampstead Oxon 83 D7
Filey N Yorks 218 C2
Filgrave M Keynes 103 B7
Filham Devon 8 D2
Filkins Oxon 82 E2
Filleigh Devon 25 B11
Filleigh Devon 26 E2
Fillingham Lincs 188 D6
Fillongley Warks 134 F5
Filmore Hill Hants 33 B11
Filton S Glos 60 D6
Filwood Park Bristol 60 F5
Fimber E Yorks 217 G7
Finavon Angus 287 B8
Fincastle Ho Perth 291 G10
Finchairn Argyll 275 C10
Fincham Mers 182 C6
Fincham Norf 140 B3
Finchampstead Wokingham 65 G9
Finchdean Hants 34 E2
Finchingfield Essex 106 E3
Finchley London 86 G3
Findern Derbys 152 C6
Findhorn Moray 301 C10
Findhorn Bridge Highld 301 G8
Findo Gask Perth 286 E4
Findochty Moray 302 C4
Findon Aberds 293 D11
Findon W Sus 35 F10
Findon Mains Highld 300 C6
Findon Valley W Sus 35 F10
Findrack Ho Aberds 293 C8
Fine Street Hereford 96 D6
Finedon Northants 121 C8
Fineglen Argyll 275 B10
Fingal Street Suff 126 D4
Fingask Aberds 303 G7
Fingerpost Worcs 116 C4
Fingest Bucks 84 G3
Finghall N Yorks 214 B3
Fingland Cumb 239 F7
Fingland Dumfries 259 F7
Finglesham Kent 55 C10
Fingringhoe Essex 107 G10
Finham W Mid 118 B6
Finkle Street S Yorks 186 B4
Finlarig Stirl 285 D9
Finmere Oxon 102 E2
Finnart Perth 285 B9
Finney Green E Ches 184 E5
Finney Green Staffs 168 F3
Finningham Suff 125 D11
Finningley S Yorks 187 B11
Finnygaud Aberds 302 D5
Finsbury London 67 C10
Finsbury Park London 67 B10
Finstall Worcs 117 D9
Finsthwaite Cumb 211 B7
Finstock Oxon 82 B5
Finstown Orkney 314 E3
Fintry Aberds 303 D7
Fintry Dundee 287 D8
Fintry Stirl 278 D2
Finwood Warks 118 D3
Finzean Aberds 293 D8
Finzean Ho Aberds 293 D7
Fionnphort Argyll 288 G5
Fionnsbhagh W Isles 296 C6
Fir Toll Kent 54 E2
Fir Tree Durham 233 E8
Fir Vale S Yorks 186 C5
Firbank Cumb 222 G2
Firbeck S Yorks 187 D9
Firby N Yorks 214 B5
Firby N Yorks 216 F4
Firemore Highld 307 L3
Firgrove Gtr Man 196 E2
Firkin Argyll 285 G7
Firle E Sus 23 D7
Firs Lane Gtr Man 194 G6
First Coast Highld 307 K4
Firsby Lincs 175 C7
Firsdown Wilts 47 G8
Firswood Gtr Man 184 B4
Firth Borders 262 E2
Firth Moor Darl 224 C6
Firth Park S Yorks 186 C5
Firwood Fold Gtr Man 195 E8
Fishbourne I o W 21 C7
Fishbourne W Sus 22 C4
Fishburn Durham 234 E3
Fishcross Clack 279 B7
Fisher Place Cumb 220 B6
Fisherford Aberds 302 F6
Fishermead M Keynes 103 D7
Fisherrow E Loth 280 G6
Fishers Green Herts 104 F4
Fisher's Pond Hants 33 C7
Fishersgate Brighton 36 F3
Fisherstreet W Sus 50 G3
Fisherton Highld 301 D7
Fisherton S Ayrs 257 F7
Fisherton de la Mere Wilts 46 F4
Fisherwick Staffs 134 B3
Fishery Windsor 65 C11
Fishguard = Abergwaun Pembs 91 D9
Fishlake S Yorks 199 E7
Fishleigh Devon 25 F8
Fishleigh Barton Devon 25 C9
Fishleigh Castle Devon 25 F8
Fishley Norf 161 G8
Fishley W Mid 133 C10
Fishmere End Lincs 156 B5
Fishponds Bristol 60 D6
Fishpool Glos 98 F3
Fishpool Gtr Man 195 F10
Fishpool N Yorks 205 D10
Fishpools Powys 114 D3
Fishtoft Lincs 174 G5
Fishtoft Drove Lincs 174 F4
Fishtown of Usan Angus 287 B11
Fishwick Borders 273 E8
Fishwick Lancs 194 B5
Fiskavaig Highld 294 B5
Fiskerton Lincs 189 G8
Fiskerton Notts 172 E2
Fitling E Yorks 209 G11
Fittleton Wilts 46 D6
Fittleworth W Sus 35 D8
Fitton End Cambs 157 G8
Fitton Hill Gtr Man 196 G2
Fitz Shrops 149 F8
Fitzhead Som 27 B10
Fitzwilliam W Yorks 198 D2
Fiunary Highld 289 E8
Five Acres Glos 79 C9
Five Ash Down E Sus 37 C7
Five Ashes E Sus 37 C9
Five Bells Som 42 E5
Five Bridges Hereford 98 B3
Five Houses I o W 20 D4
Five Lane Ends Lancs 202 C6
Five Lanes Mon 78 G6
Five Oak Green Kent 52 D6
Five Oaks W Sus 35 B9
Five Roads Carms 75 D7
Five Ways Warks 118 D4
Five Wents Kent 53 C10
Fivecrosses W Ches 183 F8
Fivehead Som 28 C5
Fivelanes Corn 11 E10
Fixby W Yorks 196 C6
Flackley Ash E Sus 38 C5
Flack's Green Essex 88 B3
Flackwell Heath Bucks 65 B11
Fladbury Worcs 99 B9
Fladbury Cross Worcs 99 B9
Fladda Shetland 312 E5
Fladdabister Shetland 313 K6
Flagg Derbys 169 B10
Flaggoners Green Hereford 116 G2
Flamborough E Yorks 218 E4
Flamstead Herts 85 C9
Flamstead End Herts 86 E4
Flansham W Sus 35 G7
Flanshaw W Yorks 197 C10
Flappit Spring W Yorks 205 F7
Flasby N Yorks 204 B4
Flash Staffs 169 B8
Flashader Highld 298 D3
Flask Inn N Yorks 227 E8
Flathurst W Sus 35 C7
Flaunden Herts 85 E8
Flawborough Notts 172 G3
Flawith N Yorks 215 F9
Flax Bourton N Som 60 F4
Flax Moss Lancs 195 C9
Flaxby N Yorks 206 B3
Flaxholme Derbys 170 G4
Flaxlands Norf 142 E2
Flaxley Glos 79 B11
Flaxpool Som 42 F6
Flaxton N Yorks 216 G3
Fleckney Leics 136 E2
Flecknoe Warks 119 E10
Fledborough Notts 188 G4
Fleet Dorset 17 E8
Fleet Hants 22 C2
Fleet Hants 49 C10
Fleet Lincs 157 E7
Fleet Downs Kent 68 E5
Fleet Hargate Lincs 157 E7
Fleetend Hants 33 F8
Fleetlands Hants 33 G9
Fleets N Yorks 213 G9
Fleetville Herts 85 D11
Fleetwood Lancs 202 D2
Fleggburgh = Burgh St Margaret Norf 161 G8
Fleming Field Durham 234 C3
Flemings Kent 55 B9
Flemingston V Glam 58 E4
Flemington S Lnrk 268 D3
Flemington S Lnrk 268 G4
Flempton Suff 124 D6
Fleoideabhagh W Isles 296 C6
Fletcher's Green Kent 52 C4
Fletchersbridge Corn 6 B2
Fletchertown Cumb 229 C10
Fletching E Sus 36 C6
Fletching Common E Sus 36 C6
Fleuchary Highld 309 K7
Fleuchlang Dumfries 237 D8
Fleur-de-lis Caerph 77 F11
Flexbury Corn 24 F2
Flexford Hants 32 C6
Flexford Sur 50 D2
Flimby Cumb 228 E6
Flimwell E Sus 53 G8
Flint Flint 182 G2
Flint Cross Cambs 105 C8
Flint Hill Durham 242 G5
Flint Mountain = Mynydd Fflint Flint 182 G2
Flintham Notts 172 F2
Flinton E Yorks 209 F10
Flint's Green W Mid 134 G5
Flintsham Hereford 114 F6
Flishinghurst Kent 53 F9
Flitcham Norf 158 D4
Flitholme Cumb 222 B5
Flitton C Beds 103 D11
Flitwick C Beds 103 D10
Flixborough N Lincs 199 D11
Flixborough Stather N Lincs 199 E11
Flixton Gtr Man 184 C2
Flixton N Yorks 217 D10
Flixton Suff 142 F6
Flockton W Yorks 197 E8
Flockton Green W Yorks 197 D8
Flockton Moor W Yorks 197 E8
Flodaigh W Isles 296 F4
Flodden Northumb 263 B10
Flodigarry Highld 298 B4
Flood Street Hants 31 D10
Floodgates Hereford 114 F5
Flood's Ferry Cambs 139 E7
Flookburgh Cumb 211 D7
Flordon Norf 142 D3
Flore Northants 120 E2
Florence Stoke 168 G6
Flotterton Northumb 251 C11
Flowers Bottom Bucks 84 F4
Flowers Green E Sus 23 C10
Flowery Field Gtr Man 184 B6
Flowton Suff 107 B11
Fluchter E Dunb 277 G11
Flugarth Shetland 313 G6
Flush House W Yorks 196 F6
Flushdyke W Yorks 197 C9
Flushing Aberds 303 E10
Flushing Corn 3 C8
Flushing Corn 3 D7
Flyford Flavell Worcs 117 G9
Foals Green Suff 126 C5
Fobbing Thurrock 69 C8
Fochabers Moray 302 D3
Fochriw Caerph 77 D10
Fockerby N Lincs 199 D10
Fodderletter Moray 301 G11
Fodderstone Gap Norf 140 B3
Fodderty Highld 300 D5
Foddington Som 29 B9
Foel Powys 147 G9
Foel-gastell Carms 75 C8
Foffarty Angus 287 C8
Foggathorpe E Yorks 207 F11
Foggbrook Gtr Man 184 D6
Fogo Borders 272 F5
Fogorig Borders 272 F5
Fogrigarth Shetland 313 H4
Fogwatt Moray 302 D2
Foindle Highld 306 E6
Fold Head Lancs 195 D11
Fold Hill Lincs 175 E7
Folda Angus 292 G3
Foldrings S Yorks 186 C3
Fole Staffs 151 B10
Foleshill W Mid 135 G7
Foley Park Worcs 116 B6
Folke Dorset 29 E11
Folkestone Kent 55 F8
Folkingham Lincs 155 C11
Folkington E Sus 23 E9
Folksworth Cambs 138 F2
Folkton N Yorks 217 D11
Folla Rule Aberds 303 F7
Folley Shrops 132 D5
Follifoot N Yorks 206 C2
Follingsby T & W 243 E8
Folly Dorset 30 G2
Folly Pembs 91 G8
Folly Cross Devon 25 F7
Folly Gate Devon 13 B7
Folly Green Essex 106 F6
Fonmon = Ffwl-y-mwn V Glam 58 F4
Fonston Corn 11 C10
Font-y-gary = Ffont-y-gari V Glam 58 F5
Fonthill Bishop Wilts 46 G2
Fonthill Gifford Wilts 46 G2
Fontmell Magna Dorset 30 D5
Fontmell Parva Dorset 30 E4
Fontwell W Sus 35 F7
Foodieash Fife 287 F7
Foolow Derbys 185 F11
Footbridge Glos 99 F10
Footherley Staffs 134 C2
Footrid Worcs 116 C3
Foots Cray London 68 E3
Forbestown Aberds 292 B5
Force Forge Cumb 220 G6
Force Green Kent 52 B2
Force Mills Cumb 220 G6
Forcett N Yorks 224 C3
Ford Argyll 275 C9
Ford Bucks 84 D3
Ford Derbys 186 E6
Ford Devon 8 E2
Ford Devon 8 G5
Ford Devon 24 C6
Ford Devon 28 G2
Ford Glos 99 F11
Ford Hereford 115 F10
Ford Kent 71 F8
Ford Mers 182 B4
Ford Northumb 263 B10
Ford Pembs 91 F9
Ford Plym 7 D9
Ford Shrops 149 G8
Ford Som 27 B9
Ford Som 44 C5
Ford Staffs 169 E9
Ford W Sus 35 G7
Ford Wilts 47 G7
Ford Wilts 61 E10
Ford End Essex 87 B11
Ford End Essex 105 E9
Ford Forge Northumb 263 B10
Ford Green Lancs 202 D5
Ford Green Stoke 168 E5
Ford Heath Shrops 149 G8
Ford Hill Northumb 263 B11
Ford Street Som 27 D11
Forda Devon 12 C6
Forda Devon 40 F3
Fordbridge W Mid 134 F3
Fordcombe Kent 52 E4
Fordell Fife 280 D3
Forden = Ffodun Powys 130 C4
Forder Corn 7 D8
Forder Green Devon 8 B5
Fordgate Som 43 G10
Fordham Cambs 124 C2
Fordham Essex 107 F8
Fordham Norf 140 D2
Fordham Heath Essex 107 F8
Fordhouses W Mid 133 C8
Fordingbridge Hants 31 E10
Fordington Lincs 190 G6
Fordley T & W 243 C7
Fordon E Yorks 217 D10
Fordoun Aberds 293 F9
Ford's Green E Sus 36 B6
Ford's Green Suff 125 D11
Fordstreet Essex 107 F8
Fordton Devon 14 B2
Fordwater Devon 28 G4
Fordwells Oxon 82 C4
Fordwich Kent 55 B7
Fordyce Aberds 302 C5
Forebridge Staffs 151 E8
Foredale N Yorks 212 F6
Forehill S Ayrs 257 E8
Foreland Fields I o W 21 D9
Foreland Ho Argyll 274 G3
Foremark Derbys 152 D6
Forest Lodge Argyll 284 C6
Forest Lodge Highld 292 B2
Forest Lodge Perth 291 F11
Forest Becks Lancs 203 C11
Forest Coal Pit Mon 96 G5
Forest Gate Hants 33 E10
Forest Gate London 68 C2
Forest Green Glos 80 E4
Forest Green Sur 50 E6
Forest Hall Cumb 221 E10
Forest Hall T & W 243 D7
Forest Head Cumb 240 F3
Forest Hill London 67 E11
Forest Hill Oxon 83 D9
Forest Hill Wilts 63 F8
Forest Holme Lancs 195 B10
Forest-in-Teesdale Durham 232 F3
Forest Lane Head N Yorks 206 B2
Forest Mill Clack 279 C9
Forest Moor N Yorks 206 B2
Forest Row E Sus 52 G2
Forest Side I o W 20 D5
Forest Town Notts 171 C9
Forestburn Gate Northumb 252 D3
Forestdale London 67 G11
Foresterseat Moray 301 D11
Forestreet Devon 24 E5
Forestside W Sus 34 E3
Forewoods Common Wilts 61 G10
Forfar Angus 287 B8
Forgandenny Perth 286 F4
Forge Corn 4 F3
Forge Powys 128 D5
Forge Hammer Torf 78 F3
Forge Side Torf 78 D2
Forgewood N Lnrk 268 D4
Forgie Moray 302 D3
Forglen Ho Aberds 302 D6
Forgue Aberds 302 E6
Forhill Worcs 117 B11
Formby Mers 193 F10
Forncett End Norf 142 E2
Forncett St Mary Norf 142 E3
Forncett St Peter Norf 142 E3
Forneth Perth 286 C4
Fornham All Saints Suff 124 D6
Fornham St Genevieve Suff 124 D6
Fornham St Martin Suff 125 D7
Fornighty Highld 301 D9
Forrabury Corn 11 C7
Forres Moray 301 D10
Forrest Lodge Dumfries 246 F3
Forrestfield N Lnrk 269 B7
Forry's Green Essex 106 E5
Forsbrook Staffs 169 G7
Forse Highld 310 F6
Forse Ho Highld 310 F6
Forsinain Highld 310 E3
Forsinard Highld 310 E2
Forsinard Station Highld 310 E2
Forstal Kent 53 B8
Forston Dorset 17 B9
Fort Augustus Highld 290 C5
Fort George Highld 301 D7
Fort Matilda Invclyd 276 F5
Fort William Highld 290 F3
Forteviot Perth 286 F4
Forth S Lnrk 269 E8
Forth Road Bridge Edin 280 F2
Forthampton Glos 99 E7
Forthay Glos 80 F2
Fortingall Perth 285 C11
Fortis Green London 67 B9
Forton Hants 33 G10
Forton Hants 48 E2
Forton Lancs 202 C5
Forton Shrops 149 F8
Forton Som 28 F4
Forton Staffs 150 E5
Forton Heath Shrops 149 F8
Fortrie Aberds 302 E6
Fortrie Aberds 303 D7
Fortrose Highld 301 D7
Fortuneswell Dorset 17 G9
Forty Green Bucks 84 E3
Forty Green Bucks 84 G6
Forty Hill London 86 F4
Forward Green Suff 125 F11
Forwood Glos 80 E5
Fosbury Wilts 47 B10
Foscot Oxon 100 G4
Foscote Bucks 102 D4
Foscote Northants 102 B3
Foscote Wilts 61 D11
Fosdyke Lincs 156 C6
Fosdyke Bridge Lincs 156 C6
Foss Perth 285 B11
Foss Cross Glos 81 D9
Fossebridge Glos 81 C9
Fostall Kent 70 G5
Fosten Green Kent 53 F10
Foster Street Essex 87 D7
Fosterhouses S Yorks 199 E7
Foster's Booth Northants 120 G3
Foster's Green Worcs 117 D9
Foston Derbys 152 C3
Foston Leics 136 D2
Foston Lincs 172 G5
Foston N Yorks 216 F3
Foston on the Wolds E Yorks 209 B8
Fotherby Lincs 190 C4
Fothergill Cumb 228 E6
Fotheringhay Northants 137 E11
Foubister Orkney 314 F5
Foul Anchor Cambs 157 F9
Foul End Warks 134 E4
Foul Mile E Sus 23 B10
Foulbridge Cumb 230 B4
Foulby W Yorks 197 D11
Foulden Borders 273 D8
Foulden Norf 140 D5
Foulford Hants 31 F11
Foulis Castle Highld 300 C5
Foulride Green E Sus 23 E9
Foulridge Lancs 204 E3
Foulsham Norf 159 E10
Foundry Corn 2 B3
Foundry Hill Norf 159 D11
Fountain Bridgend 57 E11
Fountainhall Borders 271 F8
Four Ashes Bucks 84 F5
Four Ashes Staffs 132 F6
Four Ashes Staffs 133 B8
Four Ashes Suff 125 C10
Four Ashes W Mid 118 B3
Four Crosses Powys 129 B11
Four Crosses Powys 148 F5
Four Crosses Staffs 133 B9
Four Crosses Wrex 166 E3
Four Elms Devon 28 F3
Four Elms Kent 52 D3
Four Foot Som 44 G5
Four Forks Som 43 F8
Four Gates Gtr Man 194 F6
Four Gotes Cambs 157 F9
Four Houses Corner W Berks 64 F6
Four Lane End S Yorks 197 G9
Four Lane Ends Blkburn 195 B7
Four Lane Ends Gtr Man 195 E9
Four Lane Ends W Ches 167 C9
Four Lane Ends W Yorks 205 G8
Four Lanes Corn 2 B5
Four Marks Hants 49 G7
Four Mile Bridge Anglesey 178 F3
Four Mile Elm Glos 80 C4
Four Oaks E Sus 38 C5
Four Oaks Glos 98 F3
Four Oaks Kent 70 G3
Four Oaks W Mid 134 D2
Four Oaks W Mid 134 G4
Four Oaks Park W Mid 134 D2
Four Points W Berks 64 D5
Four Pools Worcs 99 C10
Four Roads Carms 74 D6
Four Roads I o M 192 F3
Four Throws Kent 38 B3
Four Wantz Essex 87 C10
Four Wents Kent 53 F9
Fourlane Ends Derbys 170 D5
Fourlanes End E Ches 168 D4
Fourpenny Highld 311 K2
Fourstones Northumb 241 D9
Fovant Wilts 31 B8
Foveran Aberds 303 G9
Fowey Corn 6 E2
Fowler's Plot Som 43 F10
Fowley Common Warr 183 B11
Fowlis Angus 287 D7
Fowlis Wester Perth 286 E3
Fowlmere Cambs 105 B8
Fownhope Hereford 97 E11
Fox Corner C Beds 103 F8
Fox Corner Sur 50 C3
Fox Hatch Essex 87 F9
Fox Hill Bath 61 G9
Fox Hill Hereford 98 B3
Fox Hole Swansea 56 D5
Fox Holes Wilts 45 E11
Fox Lane Hants 49 B11
Fox Royd W Yorks 197 D8
Fox Street Essex 107 F10
Foxash Estate Essex 107 E11
Foxbar Renfs 267 C9
Foxbury London 68 E2
Foxcombe Hill Oxon 83 E7
Foxcote Glos 81 B8
Foxcote Som 45 B8
Foxdale I o M 192 E3
Foxdown Hants 48 C4
Foxearth Essex 106 C6
Foxendown Kent 69 F7
Foxfield Cumb 210 B4
Foxford W Mid 135 G7
Foxham Wilts 62 D3
Foxhills Hants 32 E4
Foxhole Corn 5 E9
Foxhole Norf 142 D4
Foxhole Swansea 57 C7
Foxholes N Yorks 217 E10
Foxhunt Green E Sus 23 B8
Foxley Hereford 97 B8
Foxley Norf 159 E10
Foxley Staffs 168 E3
Foxley Wilts 61 B11
Foxlydiate Worcs 117 D10
Fox's Cross Kent 70 G6
Foxt Staffs 169 F8
Foxton Cambs 105 B8
Foxton Durham 234 F3
Foxton Leics 136 E4
Foxton N Yorks 225 F8
Foxup N Yorks 213 D7
Foxwist Green W Ches 167 B10
Foxwood Shrops 116 B2
Foy Hereford 97 F11
Foyers Highld 300 G4
Foynesfield Highld 301 D8
Fraddam Corn 2 C3
Fraddon Corn 5 D8
Fradley Staffs 152 G3
Fradley Junction Staffs 152 G2
Fradswell Staffs 151 C9
Fraisthorpe E Yorks 218 G3
Framfield E Sus 37 C7
Framingham Earl Norf 142 C5
Framingham Pigot Norf 142 C5
Framlingham Suff 126 E5
Frampton Dorset 17 B8
Frampton Lincs 156 B6
Frampton Cotterell S Glos 61 C7
Frampton Court Glos 99 E10
Frampton End S Glos 61 C7
Frampton Mansell Glos 80 E6
Frampton on Severn Glos 80 D2
Frampton West End Lincs 174 G3
Framsden Suff 126 F3
Framwellgate Moor Durham 233 C11
France Lynch Glos 80 E6
Franche Worcs 116 B6
Frandley W Ches 183 F10
Frankby Mers 182 D2
Frankfort Norf 160 E6
Franklands Gate Hereford 97 B10
Frankley Worcs 133 G9
Frankley Green Worcs 133 G9
Frankley Hill Worcs 117 B9
Frank's Bridge Powys 114 F2
Frankton Warks 119 C8
Frankwell Shrops 149 G9
Frans Green Norf 160 G2
Frant E Sus 52 F5
Fraserburgh Aberds 303 C9
Frating Essex 107 G11
Frating Green Essex 107 G11
Fratton Ptsmth 21 B9
Freasley Warks 134 D4
Freathy Corn 7 E8
Frecheville S Yorks 186 E5
Freckenham Suff 124 C3
Freckleton Lancs 194 B2
Fredley Sur 51 C7
Free Town Gtr Man 195 E10
Freebirch Derbys 186 G4
Freeby Leics 154 E6
Freefolk Hants 48 D3
Freehay Staffs 169 G8
Freeland Oxon 82 C6
Freeland Renfs 267 B9
Freeland Corner Norf 160 F3
Freemantle Soton 32 E6
Freeport Village W Loth 269 C10
Freester Shetland 313 H6
Freethorpe Norf 143 B8
Freezy Water London 86 F5
Freiston Lincs 174 G5
Freiston Shore Lincs 174 G5
Fremington Devon 40 G4
Fremington N Yorks 223 F10
French Street Kent 52 C3
Frenchay S Glos 60 D6
Frenchbeer Devon 13 D9
Frenches Green Essex 106 G4
Frenchmoor Hants 32 B3
Frenchwood Lancs 194 B4
Frenich Stirl 285 G8
Frensham Sur 49 E10
Frenze Norf 142 G2
Fresgoe Highld 310 C3
Freshbrook Swindon 62 C6
Freshfield Mers 193 F9
Freshford Bath 61 G9
Freshwater I o W 20 D2
Freshwater Bay I o W 20 D2
Freshwater East Pembs 73 F8
Fressingfield Suff 126 B5
Freston Suff 108 D3
Freswick Highld 310 C7
Fretherne Glos 80 D2
Frettenham Norf 160 F4
Freuchie Fife 286 G6
Freuchies Angus 292 G4
Freystrop Pembs 73 C7
Friar Park W Mid 133 E10
Friarn Som 43 F7
Friar's Cliff Dorset 19 C9
Friar's Gate E Sus 52 G3
Friar's Hill E Sus 38 E5
Friarton Perth 286 E5
Friday Bridge Cambs 139 C9
Friday Hill London 86 G5
Friday Street E Sus 23 E10
Friday Street Suff 126 G6
Friday Street Suff 127 E7
Friday Street Sur 50 D6
Fridaythorpe E Yorks 208 B3
Friendly W Yorks 196 C5
Friern Barnet London 86 G3
Friesland Argyll 288 D3
Friesthorpe Lincs 189 E9
Frieston Lincs 172 F6
Frieth Bucks 84 G3
Frieze Hill Som 28 B2
Friezeland Notts 171 E7
Frilford Oxon 82 F6
Frilford Heath Oxon 82 F6
Frilsham W Berks 64 E4
Frimley Sur 49 B11
Frimley Green Sur 49 B11
Frimley Ridge Sur 49 B11
Frindsbury Medway 69 E8
Fring Norf 158 C4
Fringford Oxon 102 F2
Friningham Kent 53 B10
Frinkle Green Essex 106 C4
Frinsted Kent 53 B11
Frinton-on-Sea Essex 108 G4
Friockheim Angus 287 C9
Friog Gwyn 146 G2
Frisby Leics 136 C4
Frisby on the Wreake Leics 154 F3
Friskney Lincs 175 D7
Friskney Eaudyke Lincs 175 D7
Friskney Tofts Lincs 175 E7
Friston E Sus 23 F8
Friston Suff 127 E8
Fritchley Derbys 170 E5
Frith Kent 54 B2
Frith Bank Lincs 174 F4
Frith Common Worcs 116 D3
Frith-hill Bucks 84 E6
Frith Hill Sur 50 E3
Fritham Hants 32 E2
Frithelstock Devon 25 D7
Frithelstock Stone Devon 25 D7
Frithend Hants 49 F10
Frithsden Herts 85 D8
Frithville Lincs 174 E4
Frittenden Kent 53 E10
Frittiscombe Devon 8 G6
Fritton Norf 142 E4
Fritton Norf 143 C9
Fritton Norf 161 F8
Fritwell Oxon 101 F10
Frizinghall W Yorks 205 F8
Frizington Cumb 219 B10
Frobost W Isles 297 J3
Frocester Glos 80 E3
Frochas Powys 148 G5
Frodesley Shrops 131 C10
Frodingham N Lincs 199 E11
Frodsham W Ches 183 F8
Frog End Cambs 123 F10
Frog End Cambs 123 G8
Frog Moor Swansea 56 C3
Frog Pool Worcs 116 D5
Frogden Borders 263 D7
Froggatt Derbys 186 F2

Froghall Staffs 169 F8
Frogham Hants 31 E11
Frogham Kent 55 C9
Froghole Kent 52 C2
Frogholt Kent 55 F7
Frogland Cross S Glos 60 C6
Frogmore Devon 8 G5
Frogmore Hants 33 C11
Frogmore Hants 49 B10
Frogmore Herts 85 E11
Frognal S Ayrs 257 D8
Frognall Lincs 156 G3
Frogpool Corn 4 G5
Frogs' Green Essex 105 D11
Frogshail Norf 160 B5
Frogwell Corn 6 B6
Frolesworth Leics 135 E10
Frome St Quintin Dorset 29 G9
Fromebridge Glos 80 D3
Fromefield Som 45 D9
Fromes Hill Hereford 98 B3
Fromington Hereford 97 B10
Fron Denb 165 B9
Fron Gwyn 145 B7
Fron Gwyn 163 D8
Fron Powys 113 D11
Fron Powys 129 C8
Fron Powys 130 C4
Fron Powys 130 D3
Fron Shrops 148 B5
Fron-Bache Denb 166 G2
Fron-dêg Wrex 166 F3
Fron Isaf Wrex 166 G3
Froncysyllte Wrex 166 G3
Frongoch Gwyn 147 B8
Frost Devon 26 F3
Frost Hill N Som 60 G2
Frost Row Norf 141 C10
Frostenden Suff 143 G9
Frostenden Corner Suff 143 G9
Frosterley Durham 232 D6
Frostlane Hants 32 F6
Frotoft Orkney 314 D4
Froxfield C Beds 103 E9
Froxfield Wilts 63 F9
Froxfield Green Hants 34 B2
Froyle Hants 49 E9
Fryern Hill Hants 32 C6
Fryerning Essex 87 E10
Fryerns Essex 69 B8
Fryton N Yorks 216 E3
Fugglestone St Peter Wilts 46 G6
Fulbeck Lincs 172 E6
Fulbeck Northumb 252 F5
Fulbourn Cambs 123 F10
Fulbrook Oxon 82 C3
Fulflood Hants 33 B7
Fulford Som 28 B2
Fulford Staffs 151 B9
Fulford York 207 D8
Fulham London 67 D8
Fulking W Sus 36 E2
Full Sutton E Yorks 207 B10
Fullabrook Devon 40 E4
Fullarton Glasgow 268 C2
Fullarton N Ayrs 257 B8
Fuller Street Essex 88 B2
Fuller's End Essex 105 F10
Fuller's Moor W Ches 167 E7
Fullerton Hants 47 F11
Fulletby Lincs 190 G3
Fullshaw S Yorks 197 G8
Fullwell Cross London 86 G6
Fullwood E Ayrs 267 E8
Fullwood Gtr Man 196 F2
Fulmer Bucks 66 B3
Fulmodestone Norf 159 C9
Fulneck W Yorks 205 G10
Fulnetby Lincs 189 F9
Fulney Lincs 156 E5
Fulready Warks 100 B5
Fulshaw Park E Ches 184 E4
Fulstone W Yorks 197 F7
Fulstow Lincs 190 B4
Fulthorpe Stockton 234 G4
Fulwell Oxon 101 G7
Fulwell T & W 243 F9
Fulwood Lancs 202 G6
Fulwood S Yorks 186 D4
Fulwood Som 28 C2
Fundenhall Norf 142 D3
Fundenhall Street Norf 142 D2
Funtington W Sus 22 B3
Funtley Hants 33 F9
Funtullich Perth 285 E11
Funzie Shetland 312 D8
Furley Devon 28 G3
Furnace Argyll 284 G4
Furnace Carms 74 E6
Furnace Carms 75 E8
Furnace Ceredig 128 D3
Furnace Highld 299 B9
Furnace End Warks 134 E4
Furnace Green W Sus 51 F9
Furnace Wood W Sus 51 F11
Furneaux Pelham Herts 105 F8
Furner's Green E Sus 36 B6
Furness Vale Derbys 185 E8
Furneux Pelham Herts 105 F8
Furnham Som 28 F4
Further Ford End Essex 105 E9
Further Quarter Kent 53 F11
Furtho Northants 102 C5
Furze Devon 25 B10
Furze Hill Hants 31 E11
Furze Platt Windsor 65 C11
Furzebrook Dorset 18 E4
Furzedown Hants 32 B5
Furzedown London 67 E9
Furzehill Devon 41 D8
Furzehill Dorset 31 G8
Furzeley Corner Hants 33 E11
Furzey Lodge Hants 32 G5
Furzley Hants 32 D3
Furzton M Keynes 102 D6
Fyfett Som 28 E2
Fyfield Essex 87 D9
Fyfield Glos 82 E2
Fyfield Hants 47 D9
Fyfield Oxon 82 F6
Fyfield Wilts 63 F7
Fyfield Wilts 63 G7
Fylingthorpe N Yorks 227 D8
Fyning W Sus 34 C4
Fyvie Aberds 303 F7

G

Gabalfa Cardiff 59 D7
Gabhsann bho Dheas W Isles 304 C6
Gabhsann bho Thuath W Isles 304 C6
Gable Head Hants 21 B10
Gablon Highld 309 K7
Gabroc Hill E Ayrs 267 E9
Gadbrook Sur 51 D8
Gaddesby Leics 154 G3
Gadebridge Herts 85 D8
Gadfa Anglesey 179 D7
Gadfield Elm Worcs 98 E5
Gadlas Shrops 149 B7
Gadlys Rhondda 77 E7
Gadshill Kent 69 E8
Gaer Newport 59 B9
Gaer Powys 96 G3
Gaer-fawr Mon 78 F6
Gaerllwyd Mon 78 F6
Gaerwen Anglesey 179 G7
Gagingwell Oxon 101 F8
Gaick Lodge Highld 291 E9
Gailey Staffs 151 G8
Gailey Wharf Staffs 151 G8
Gain Hill Kent 53 D8
Gainfield Oxon 82 F4
Gainford Durham 224 B3
Gainsborough Lincs 188 C4
Gainsborough Suff 108 C3
Gainsford End Essex 106 D4
Gairletter Argyll 276 E3
Gairloch Highld 299 B8
Gairlochy Highld 290 E3
Gairney Bank Perth 280 B2
Gairnshiel Lodge Aberds 292 C4
Gaisgill Cumb 222 D2
Gaitsgill Cumb 230 B3
Galadean Borders 271 G11
Galashiels Borders 261 B11
Galdlys Flint 182 G2
Gale Gtr Man 196 D2
Galgate Lancs 202 B5
Galhampton Som 29 B10
Gallaberry Dumfries 247 G11
Gallachoille Argyll 275 E8
Gallanach Argyll 288 C4
Gallanach Argyll 289 G10
Gallanach Highld 294 G6
Gallantry Bank E Ches 167 E8
Gallatown Fife 280 C5
Galley Common Warks 134 E6
Galley Hill Cambs 122 D6
Galley Hill Lincs 190 F6
Galleyend Essex 88 E2
Galleywood Essex 88 E2
Galligill Cumb 231 B11
Gallin Perth 285 C9
Gallovie Highld 291 E7
Gallowfauld Angus 287 C8
Gallowhill Glasgow 267 D11
Gallowhill Renfs 267 B9
Gallowhills Aberds 303 D10
Gallows Corner London 87 G8
Gallows Green Essex 106 F2
Gallows Green Essex 107 F8
Gallows Green Staffs 169 G9
Gallows Green Worcs 117 E8
Gallows Inn Derbys 171 G7
Gallowsgreen Torf 78 D3
Gallowstree Common Oxon 65 C7
Gallt Melyd = Meliden Denb 181 E9
Gallt-y-foel Gwyn 163 C9
Galltair Highld 295 C10
Galltegfa Denb 165 D10
Gallypot Street E Sus 52 F3
Galmington Som 28 C2
Galmisdale Highld 294 G6
Galmpton Devon 8 G3
Galmpton Torbay 9 D7
Galon Uchaf M Tydf 77 D9
Galphay N Yorks 214 E5
Galston E Ayrs 258 B2
Galtrigill Highld 296 F7
Gam Corn 11 F7
Gamble Hill W Yorks 205 G11
Gamble's Green Essex 88 C3
Gamblesby Cumb 231 D8
Gamelsby Cumb 239 G7
Gamesley Derbys 185 C8
Gamlingay Cambs 122 G4
Gamlingay Cinques Cambs 122 G4
Gamlinghay Great Heath Cambs 122 G4
Gammaton Devon 25 B7
Gammaton Moor Devon 25 C7
Gammersgill N Yorks 213 C11
Gamston Notts 154 B2
Gamston Notts 188 F2
Ganarew Hereford 79 B8
Ganavan Argyll 289 F10
Ganders Green Glos 98 G4
Gang Corn 6 B6
Ganllwyd Gwyn 146 E4
Gannetts Dorset 30 D3
Gannochy Angus 293 F7
Gannochy Perth 286 E5
Gansclet Highld 310 E7
Ganstead E Yorks 209 G9
Ganthorpe N Yorks 216 E3
Ganton N Yorks 217 D9
Gants Hill London 68 B2
Ganwick Corner Herts 86 F3
Gaodhail Argyll 289 F8
Gappah Devon 14 F3
Garafad Highld 298 C4
Garamor Highld 295 F8
Garbat Highld 300 C4
Garbhallt Argyll 275 D11
Garboldisham Norf 141 G10
Garbole Highld 301 G7
Garden City Bl Gwent 77 D11
Garden City Flint 166 B4
Garden Village S Yorks 186 B3
Garden Village Swansea 56 B5
Garden Village W Yorks 206 G4
Garden Village Wrex 166 E4
Gardeners Green Wokingham 65 F10
Gardenstown Aberds 303 C7
Garderhouse Shetland 313 J5
Gardham E Yorks 208 E5
Gardie Shetland 312 D7
Gardin Shetland 312 G6
Gare Hill Som 45 E9
Garelochhead Argyll 276 C4
Garford Oxon 82 F6
Garforth W Yorks 206 G4
Gargrave N Yorks 204 C4
Gargunnock Stirl 278 C4
Garizim Conwy 179 F11
Garker Corn 5 E10
Garlandhayes Devon 27 E11
Garlands Cumb 239 G10
Garleffin S Ayrs 244 G3
Garlic Street Norf 142 G4
Garlieston Dumfries 236 E6
Garliford Devon 26 B3
Garlinge Kent 71 F10
Garlinge Green Kent 54 C6
Garlogie Aberds 293 C9
Garmelow Staffs 150 D5
Garmond Aberds 303 D8
Garmondsway Durham 234 E2
Garmony Argyll 289 E8
Garmouth Moray 302 C3
Garmston Shrops 132 B2
Garn Powys 130 G2
Garn-swllt Swansea 75 D10
Garn-yr-erw Torf 78 C2
Garnant Carms 75 C11
Garndiffaith Torf 78 E3
Garndolbenmaen Gwyn 163 G7
Garnedd Conwy 164 E2
Garnett Bridge Cumb 221 F10
Garnetts Essex 87 B10
Garnfadryn Gwyn 144 C5
Garnkirk N Lnrk 268 B3
Garnlydan Bl Gwent 77 C11
Garnsgate Lincs 157 E8
Garnswllt Swansea 75 D10
Garra Eallabus Argyll 274 F3
Garrabost W Isles 304 E7
Garrachra Argyll 275 E11
Garralburn Moray 302 D4
Garraron Argyll 275 C9
Garras Corn 2 E6
Garreg Flint 181 F10
Garreg Gwyn 163 G10
Garrets Green W Mid 134 F2
Garrick Perth 286 F2
Garrigill Cumb 231 C10
Garrison Stirl 285 G7
Garriston N Yorks 224 G3
Garroch Dumfries 246 G3
Garrogie Lodge Highld 291 B7
Garros Highld 298 C4
Garrow Perth 286 C2
Garrowhill Glasgow 268 C3
Garrygualach Highld 290 C3
Garryhorn Dumfries 246 E2
Garsdale Cumb 212 B4
Garsdale Head Cumb 222 G5
Garsdon Wilts 62 B3
Garshall Green Staffs 151 C9
Garsington Oxon 83 E9
Garstang Lancs 202 D5
Garston Herts 85 F10
Garston Mers 182 E6
Garswood Mers 183 B9
Gartachoil Stirl 277 C10
Gartbreck Argyll 254 B3
Gartcosh N Lnrk 268 B3
Garth Bridgend 57 C11
Garth Ceredig 128 G2
Garth Flint 181 E10
Garth Gwyn 179 G9
Garth Newport 59 B9
Garth Newport 78 G4
Garth Perth 285 B11
Garth Powys 95 B9
Garth Powys 114 C5
Garth Shetland 313 H4
Garth Shetland 313 H6
Garth Wrex 166 G3
Garth Owen Powys 130 E2
Garth Row Cumb 221 F10
Garth Trevor Wrex 166 G3
Garthamlock Glasgow 268 B3
Garthbeg Highld 291 B7
Garthbrengy Powys 95 E10
Garthdee Aberdeen 293 C11
Gartheli Ceredig 111 F11
Garthmyl Powys 130 D3
Garthorpe Leics 154 E6
Garthorpe N Lincs 199 D11
Gartlea N Lnrk 268 C5
Gartloch Glasgow 268 B3
Gartly Aberds 302 F5
Gartmore Stirl 277 B10
Gartmore Ho Stirl 277 B10
Gartnagrenach Argyll 255 B8
Gartness N Lnrk 268 C5
Gartness Stirl 277 D10
Gartocharn W Dunb 277 D8
Garton E Yorks 209 F11
Garton-on-the-Wolds E Yorks 208 B5
Gartsherrie N Lnrk 268 B4
Gartur Stirl 277 B11
Gartymore Highld 311 H4
Garvald E Loth 281 G11
Garvamore Highld 291 D7
Garvard Argyll 274 D4
Garvault Hotel Highld 308 F7
Garve Highld 300 C3
Garvestone Norf 141 B10
Garvock Aberds 293 F9
Garvock Invclyd 276 G5
Garvock Hill Fife 280 D2
Garway Hereford 97 G9
Garway Hill Hereford 97 F8
Gaskan Highld 289 B9
Gasper Wilts 45 G9
Gastard Wilts 61 F11
Gasthorpe Norf 141 G9
Gaston Green Essex 87 B7
Gatacre Park Shrops 132 F5
Gatcombe I o W 20 D5
Gate Burton Lincs 188 E4
Gate Helmsley N Yorks 207 B9
Gateacre Mers 182 D6
Gatebeck Cumb 211 B10
Gateford Notts 187 E9
Gateford Common Notts 187 E9
Gateforth N Yorks 198 B5
Gatehead E Ayrs 257 B9
Gatehouse Northumb 251 F7
Gatehouse of Fleet Dumfries 237 D8
Gatelawbridge Dumfries 247 D10
Gateley Norf 159 E9
Gatenby N Yorks 214 B6
Gatesgarth Cumb 220 B3
Gateshead T & W 243 E7
Gatesheath W Ches 167 C7
Gateside Aberds 293 B8
Gateside Angus 287 C8
Gateside Dumfries 248 E4
Gateside E Renf 267 D9
Gateside Fife 286 G5
Gateside N Ayrs 267 E7
Gateside Shetland 312 F4
Gatewen Wrex 166 E4
Gatherley Devon 12 E3
Gathurst Gtr Man 194 F4
Gatlas Newport 78 G4
Gatley End Gtr Man 184 D4
Gatley End Cambs 104 C5
Gatton Sur 51 C9
Gattonside Borders 262 B2
Gatwick Glos 80 C2
Gatwick Airport W Sus 51 E9
Gaufron Powys 113 D9
Gaulby Leics 136 C3
Gauldry Fife 287 E7
Gauntons Bank E Ches 167 F9
Gaunt's Common Dorset 31 F8
Gaunt's Earthcott S Glos 60 C6
Gaunt's End Essex 105 F10
Gautby Lincs 189 G11
Gavinton Borders 272 E5
Gawber S Yorks 197 F10
Gawcott Bucks 102 E3
Gawsworth E Ches 168 B5
Gawthorpe W Yorks 197 C9
Gawthorpe W Yorks 197 D7
Gawthrop Cumb 212 B3
Gawthwaite Cumb 210 C5
Gay Bowers Essex 88 E3
Gay Street W Sus 35 C9
Gaydon Warks 119 G7
Gayfield Orkney 314 A4
Gayhurst M Keynes 103 B7
Gayle N Yorks 213 B7
Gayles N Yorks 224 D2
Gayton Mers 182 E3
Gayton Norf 158 F4
Gayton Northants 120 G4
Gayton Staffs 151 D9
Gayton Engine Lincs 191 D7
Gayton le Marsh Lincs 190 E6
Gayton le Wold Lincs 190 D2
Gayton Thorpe Norf 158 F4
Gaywood Norf 158 E2
Gaza Shetland 312 F5
Gazeley Suff 124 E4
Geàrraidh Sheilidh W Isles 297 J3
Geanies House Highld 301 B8
Gearraidh Bhailteas W Isles 297 J3
Gearraidh Bhaird W Isles 304 F5
Gearraidh Dubh W Isles 296 F4
Gearraidh na h-Aibhne W Isles 304 E4
Gearraidh na Monadh W Isles 297 K3
Geary Highld 298 C2
Geat Wolford Warks 100 E4
Geddes House Highld 301 D8
Gedding Suff 125 F9
Geddington Northants 137 G7
Gedgrave Hall Suff 109 B8
Gedintailor Highld 295 B7
Gedling Notts 171 G10
Gedney Lincs 157 E8
Gedney Broadgate Lincs 157 E8
Gedney Drove End Lincs 157 D9
Gedney Dyke Lincs 157 D8
Gedney Hill Lincs 156 G6
Gee Cross Gtr Man 185 C7
Geeston Rutland 137 C9
Gegin Wrex 166 E3
Geilston Argyll 276 F6
Geinas Denb 165 B9
Geirinis W Isles 297 G3
Geise Highld 310 C5
Geisiadar W Isles 304 E3
Geldeston Norf 143 E7
Gell Conwy 164 B5
Gelli Pembs 73 B9
Gelli Rhondda 77 G7
Gelli-gaer Neath 57 C9
Gelli-hôf Caerph 77 F11
Gellideg M Tydf 77 D8
Gellifor Denb 165 C10
Gelligaer Caerph 77 F10
Gelligroes Caerph 77 G11
Gellilydan Gwyn 146 B3
Gellinud Neath 76 E2
Gellinudd Neath 76 E2
Gellyburn Perth 286 D4
Gellygron Neath 76 E2
Gellywen Carms 92 G5
Gelsmoor Leics 153 F8
Gelston Dumfries 237 D9
Gelston Lincs 172 G6
Gembling E Yorks 209 B8
Gemini Warr 183 C9
Gendros Swansea 56 B6
Genesis Green Suff 124 F4
Gentleshaw Staffs 151 G11
Geocrab W Isles 305 J3
George Green Bucks 66 C4
George Nympton Devon 26 C2
Georgefield Dumfries 249 E7
Georgeham Devon 40 F3
Georgetown Bl Gwent 77 D10
Georgia Corn 1 B5
Gergask Highld 291 D8
Gerlan Gwyn 163 B10
Germansweek Devon 12 C4
Germiston Glasgow 268 B2
Germoe Corn 2 D3
Gernon Bushes Essex 87 E7
Gerrans Corn 3 B9
Gerrard's Bromley Staffs 150 C5
Gerrards Cross Bucks 66 B4
Gerrick Redcar 226 C4
Geseilfa Powys 129 E8
Gestingthorpe Essex 106 D6
Gesto Ho Highld 294 B5
Geuffordd Powys 148 G4
Geufron Denb 166 G2
Gib Heath W Mid 133 F11
Gibb Hill W Ches 183 F10
Gibbet Hill W Mid 118 C6
Gibbet Hill Warks 135 G10
Gibbshill Dumfries 237 B9
Gibraltar Beds 103 B10
Gibraltar Bucks 84 C3
Gibraltar Kent 55 F8
Gibralter Oxon 83 B7
Gibshill Invclyd 276 G6
Gibsmere Notts 172 F2
Giddeahall Wilts 61 E11
Giddy Green Dorset 18 D2
Gidea Park London 68 B4
Gidleigh Devon 13 D9
Giffard Park M Keynes 103 C7
Giffnock E Renf 267 D11
Gifford E Loth 271 B10
Giffordland N Ayrs 266 F5
Giffordtown Fife 286 F6
Gigg Gtr Man 195 F10
Giggetty Staffs 133 E7
Giggleswick N Yorks 212 G6
Giggshill Sur 67 F7
Gignog Pembs 91 G7
Gilberdyke E Yorks 199 B10
Gilbert Street Hants 49 G7
Gilbert's Coombe Corn 4 G3
Gilbert's End Worcs 98 C6
Gilbert's Green Warks 118 C2
Gilbertstone W Mid 134 G2
Gilchriston E Loth 271 B9
Gilcrux Cumb 229 D8
Gildersome W Yorks 197 B8
Gildersome Street W Yorks 197 B8
Gildingwells S Yorks 187 D9
Gilesgate Durham 233 C11
Gilesgate Moor Durham 233 C11
Gileston V Glam 58 F4
Gilfach Caerph 77 F11
Gilfach Hereford 96 E6
Gilfach Goch Rhondda 58 B3
Gilfachrheda Ceredig 111 F8
Gilgarran Cumb 228 G6
Gill N Yorks 204 E5
Gillamoor N Yorks 216 B3
Gillan Corn 3 E7
Gillar's Green Mers 183 B7
Gillbank Cumb 221 F7
Gillbent Gtr Man 184 E5
Gillen Highld 298 D2
Gillesbie Dumfries 248 E5
Gilling East N Yorks 216 D2
Gilling West N Yorks 224 D3
Gillingham Dorset 30 B4
Gillingham Medway 69 F9
Gillingham Norf 143 E8
Gillmoss Mers 182 B6
Gillock Highld 310 D6
Gillow Heath Staffs 168 D5
Gills Highld 310 B7
Gill's Green Kent 53 G9
Gillway Staffs 134 C4
Gilmanscleuch Borders 261 E8
Gilmerton Edin 270 B5
Gilmerton Perth 286 E2
Gilmonby Durham 223 C9
Gilmorton Leics 135 F11
Gilmourton S Lnrk 268 G3
Gilnow Gtr Man 195 F8
Gilroyd S Yorks 197 G10
Gilsland Northumb 240 D4
Gilsland Spa Cumb 240 D4
Gilson Warks 134 E3
Gilstead W Yorks 205 F8
Gilston Borders 271 D8
Gilston Herts 86 C6
Gilston Park Herts 86 C6
Giltbrook Notts 171 F7
Gilver's Lane Worcs 98 C6
Gilwell Park Essex 86 F5
Gilwern Mon 78 C2
Gimingham Norf 160 B5
Ginclough E Ches 185 F7
Ginger's Green E Sus 23 C10
Giosla W Isles 304 F3
Gipping Suff 125 E11
Gipsey Bridge Lincs 174 F3
Gipsy Row Suff 107 D11
Gipsyville Hull 200 B5
Gipton W Yorks 206 F2
Gipton Wood W Yorks 206 F2
Girdle Toll N Ayrs 266 G6
Girlington W Yorks 205 G8
Girlsta Shetland 313 H6
Girsby Lincs 190 D2
Girsby N Yorks 225 D7
Girt Som 29 C10
Girtford C Beds 104 B3
Girtford C Beds 122 G3
Girthon Dumfries 237 D8
Girton Cambs 123 E8
Girton Notts 172 B4
Girvan S Ayrs 244 D5
Gisburn Lancs 204 D2
Gisleham Suff 143 F10
Gislingham Suff 125 C11
Gissing Norf 142 F2
Gittisham Devon 15 B8
Givons Grove Sur 51 C7
Glachavoil Argyll 275 F11
Glack of Midthird Moray 302 E3
Glackmore Highld 300 D6
Gladestry Powys 114 F4
Gladsmuir E Loth 281 G9
Glaichbea Highld 300 F5
Glais Swansea 76 E2
Glaisdale N Yorks 226 D5
Glame Highld 298 E5
Glamis Angus 287 C7
Glan Adda Gwyn 179 G9
Glan-Conwy Conwy 164 E4
Glan-Duar Carms 93 C10
Glan-Dwyfach Gwyn 163 G7
Glan Gors Anglesey 179 F7
Glan-rhyd Gwyn 163 D7
Glan-rhyd Powys 76 D3
Glan-traeth Anglesey 178 F3
Glan-y-don Flint 181 F11
Glan y Ffer = Ferryside Carms 74 C5
Glan-y-llyn Rhondda 58 C6
Glan-y-môr Carms 74 C4
Glan-y-nant Caerph 77 F10
Glan-y-nant Powys 129 F9
Glan-y-wern Gwyn 146 C2
Glan-yr-afon Anglesey 179 E10
Glan-yr-afon Flint 181 F10
Glan-yr-afon Gwyn 164 G6
Glan-yr-afon Gwyn 165 G8
Glan-yr-afon Shrops 148 E4
Glanafon Pembs 73 B7
Glanaman Carms 75 C11
Glandford Norf 177 E8
Glandwr Caerph 78 E2
Glandwr Pembs 92 F3
Glandy Cross Carms 92 F2
Glandyfi Ceredig 128 D3
Glangrwyney Powys 78 B2
Glanhanog Powys 129 D8
Glanmule Powys 130 E3
Glanrafon Ceredig 128 G2
Glanrhyd Gwyn 144 B5
Glanrhyd Pembs 92 C2
Glantlees Northumb 252 B4
Glanton Northumb 264 G3
Glanton Pike Northumb 264 G3
Glantwymyn = Cemmaes Road Powys 128 C6
Glanvilles Wootton Dorset 29 F11
Glanwern Ceredig 128 F2
Glanwydden Conwy 180 E4
Glapthorn Northants 137 E10
Glapwell Derbys 171 B7
Glas-allt Shiel Aberds 292 E4
Glasbury Powys 96 D3
Glaschoil Highld 301 F10
Glascoed Denb 181 G7
Glascoed Mon 78 E4
Glascoed Powys 129 F11
Glascoed Powys 148 G2
Glascoed Wrex 166 E3
Glascorrie Aberds 292 D5
Glascorrie Perth 286 E2
Glascote Staffs 134 C4
Glascwm Powys 114 G3
Glasdir Flint 181 E10
Glasdrum Argyll 284 C4
Glasfryn Conwy 164 E6
Glasgoed Ceredig 92 B6
Glasgoforest Aberds 293 B10
Glasgow Glasgow 267 B11
Glashvin Highld 298 C4
Glasinfryn Gwyn 163 B9
Glasllwch Newport 59 B9
Glasnacardoch Highld 295 F8
Glasnakille Highld 295 D7
Glasphein Highld 297 G7
Glaspwll Powys 128 D4
Glass Houghton W Yorks 198 C2
Glassburn Highld 300 F3
Glassenbury Kent 53 F8
Glasserton Dumfries 236 F6
Glassford S Lnrk 268 F4
Glassgreen Moray 302 C2
Glasshouse Glos 98 G4
Glasshouse Hill Glos 98 G4
Glasshouses N Yorks 214 G3
Glasslie Fife 286 G6
Glasson Cumb 228 D6
Glasson Cumb 239 E7
Glasson Lancs 202 B4
Glassonby Cumb 231 D7
Glasterlaw Angus 287 B9
Glaston Rutland 137 C7
Glastonbury Som 44 F4
Glatton Cambs 138 F3
Glazebrook Warr 183 C11
Glazebury Warr 183 B11
Glazeley Shrops 132 F4
Gleadless S Yorks 186 E5
Gleadless Valley S Yorks 186 E5
Gleadmoss E Ches 168 B4
Gleadsmoss E Ches 168 B4
Gleanhead Dumfries 245 G10
Gleann Tholàstaidh W Isles 304 D7
Gleaston Cumb 210 E5
Glebe Hants 33 D9
Glebe Shetland 313 J6
Glebe T & W 243 F8
Glecknabae Argyll 275 G11
Gledhow W Yorks 206 F2
Gledrid Shrops 148 B5
Gleiniant Powys 129 E9
Glemsford Suff 106 B6
Glen Dumfries 237 B10
Glen Dumfries 237 D7
Glen Auldyn I o M 192 C5
Glen Bernisdale Highld 298 E4
Glen Ho Borders 261 C7
Glen Mona I o M 192 D5
Glen Mor Highld 295 B10
Glen Nevis House Highld 290 F3
Glen of Newmill Moray 302 D4
Glen Parva Leics 135 D11
Glen Sluain Argyll 275 D11
Glen Tanar House Aberds 292 D6
Glen Trool Lodge Dumfries 245 G10
Glen Vic Askil Highld 298 E3
Glen Village Falk 279 F7
Glen Vine I o M 192 E4
Glenallachie Moray 302 E2
Glenalmond College Perth 286 E3
Glenalmond Ho Perth 286 E3
Glenamachrie Argyll 289 G11
Glenample Stirl 285 E9
Glenancross Highld 295 F8
Glenapp Castle S Ayrs 244 G3
Glenaros Ho Argyll 289 E7
Glenbarr Argyll 255 D7
Glenbeg Highld 289 C7
Glenbeg Highld 301 G10
Glenbervie Aberds 293 E9
Glenboig N Lnrk 268 B4
Glenborrodale Highld 289 C8
Glenbranter Argyll 276 B2
Glenbreck Borders 260 E3
Glenbrein Lodge Highld 290 B6
Glenbrittle House Highld 294 C6
Glenbrook Edin 270 B2
Glenbuchat Castle Aberds 292 B5
Glenbuchat Lodge Aberds 292 B5
Glenbuck E Ayrs 259 D7
Glenburn Renfs 267 C9
Glenbyre Argyll 289 G7
Glencalvie Lodge Highld 309 L4
Glencanisp Lodge Highld 307 G6
Glencaple Dumfries 237 C11
Glencarron Lodge Highld 299 D10
Glencarse Perth 286 E5
Glencassley Castle Highld 309 J4
Glencat Aberds 293 D7
Glenceitlein Highld 284 C5
Glencoe Highld 284 B4
Glencraig Fife 280 B3
Glencripesdale Highld 289 D8
Glencrosh Dumfries 247 F7
Glendavan Ho Aberds 292 C6
Glendearg Borders 262 B2
Glendevon Perth 286 G3
Glendoe Lodge Highld 290 C6
Glendoebeg Highld 290 C6
Glendoick Perth 286 E6
Glendoll Lodge Angus 292 F4
Glendoune S Ayrs 244 D5
Glenduckie Fife 286 F6
Glendye Lodge Aberds 293 E8
Gleneagles Hotel Perth 286 F3
Gleneagles House Perth 286 G3
Glenearn Perth 286 F5
Glenegedale Argyll 254 B4
Glenelg Highld 295 D10
Glenernie Moray 301 E10
Glenfarg Perth 286 F5
Glenfarquhar Lodge Aberds 293 E9
Glenferness House Highld 301 E9
Glenfeshie Lodge Highld 291 D10
Glenfiddich Lodge Moray 302 F3
Glenfield Leics 135 B10
Glenfinnan Highld 295 G10
Glenfinnan Lodge Highld 295 G11
Glenfintaig Ho Highld 290 E4
Glenfoot Perth 286 F5
Glenfyne Lodge Argyll 284 F6
Glengap Dumfries 237 D8
Glengarnock N Ayrs 266 E6
Glengolly Highld 310 C5
Glengorm Castle Argyll 288 D6
Glengoulandie Perth 285 B11
Glengrasco Highld 298 E4
Glenhead Farm Angus 292 G4
Glenholt Plym 7 C10
Glenhoul Dumfries 246 F4
Glenhurich Highld 289 C10
Glenkerry Borders 261 G7
Glenkiln Dumfries 237 B10
Glenkindie Aberds 292 B6
Glenlair Dumfries 237 B9
Glenlatterach Moray 301 D11
Glenlee Dumfries 246 G4
Glenleigh Park E Sus 38 F2
Glenleraig Highld 306 F6
Glenlichorn Perth 285 F11
Glenlicht Ho Highld 290 B2
Glenlivet Moray 301 G11
Glenlochar Dumfries 237 C9
Glenlochsie Perth 292 F2
Glenlocksie Lodge Perth 292 F2
Glenloig N Ayrs 255 D10
Glenlomond Perth 286 G5
Glenluce Dumfries 236 D4
Glenlussa Ho Argyll 255 E8
Glenmallan Argyll 276 B5
Glenmark Angus 292 E6
Glenmarkie Lodge Angus 292 G4
Glenmarksie Highld 300 D3
Glenmavis N Lnrk 268 B4
Glenmavis W Loth 269 B9
Glenmaye I o M 192 E3
Glenmayne Borders 261 C11
Glenmeanie Highld 300 D2
Glenmidge Dumfries 247 F9
Glenmoidart Ho Highld 289 B9
Glenmore Argyll 275 B9
Glenmore Argyll 275 G11
Glenmore Highld 298 E4
Glenmore Lodge Highld 291 C11
Glenmoy Angus 292 G6
Glennoe Argyll 284 D4
Glenogil Angus 292 G6
Glenowen Pembs 73 D7
Glenprosen Lodge Angus 292 G4
Glenprosen Village Angus 292 G5
Glenquaich Lodge Perth 286 D2
Glenquiech Angus 292 G6
Glenquithlie Aberds 303 C8
Glenrath Borders 260 C6
Glenrazie Dumfries 236 C5
Glenreasdell Mains Argyll 255 B9
Glenree N Ayrs 255 E10
Glenridding Cumb 221 B7
Glenrosa N Ayrs 256 B2
Glenrossal Highld 309 J4
Glenrothes Fife 286 G6
Glensanda Highld 289 E10
Glensaugh Aberds 293 F8
Glensburgh Falk 279 E8
Glenshero Lodge Highld 291 D7
Glenshoe Lodge Perth 292 G3
Glenstockadale Dumfries 236 C2
Glenstriven Argyll 275 F11
Glentaggart S Lnrk 259 D8
Glentarkie Perth 286 F5
Glenternie Borders 260 B6
Glentham Lincs 189 C8
Glentirranmuir Stirl 278 C3
Glenton Aberds 302 G6
Glentress Borders 261 B7
Glentromie Lodge Highld 291 D9
Glentrool Village Dumfries 236 B5
Glentruan I o M 192 B5
Glentruim House Highld 291 D8
Glentworth Lincs 188 D6
Glenuaig Lodge Highld 299 E11
Glenuig Highld 289 B8
Glenure Argyll 284 C4
Glenurquhart Highld 301 C7
Glenview Argyll 284 E5
Glespin S Lnrk 259 D8
Gletness Shetland 313 H6
Glewstone Hereford 97 G11
Glinton P'boro 138 B3
Globe Town London 67 C11
Glodwick Gtr Man 196 G2
Glogue Pembs 92 E4
Glooston Leics 136 D4
Glororum Northumb 264 C5
Glossop Derbys 185 C8
Gloster Hill Northumb 253 C7
Gloucester Glos 80 B4
Gloup Shetland 312 C7
Gloweth Corn 4 G5
Glusburn N Yorks 204 E6
Glutt Lodge Highld 310 F3
Glutton Bridge Staffs 169 B9
Gluvian Corn 5 C8
Glympton Oxon 101 G8
Glyn Mon 79 F7
Glyn Powys 129 F8
Glyn Castle Neath 76 E4
Glyn-Ceiriog Wrex 148 B4
Glyn-cywarch Gwyn 146 C2
Glyn Etwy Bl Gwent 77 D11
Glyn-neath = Glynedd Neath 76 D5
Glynarthen Ceredig 92 B6
Glynbrochan Powys 129 G8
Glyncoch Rhondda 77 G9
Glyncoed Bl Gwent 77 C11
Glyncorrwg Neath 57 B11
Glynde E Sus 23 D7
Glyndebourne E Sus 23 C7
Glyndyfrdwy Denb 165 G10
Glyne Gap E Sus 38 F3
Glynedd = Glyn neath Neath 76 D5
Glynhafren Powys 129 G7
Glynllan Bridgend 58 B2
Glynmorlas Shrops 148 B6
Glynogwr Bridgend 58 B3
Glyntaff Rhondda 58 B5
Glyntawe Powys 76 B4
Gnosall Staffs 150 E6
Gnosall Heath Staffs 150 E6
Goadby Leics 136 D4
Goadby Marwood Leics 154 D5
Goat Lees Kent 54 D4
Goatacre Wilts 62 D4
Goatham Green E Sus 38 C4
Goathill Dorset 29 D11
Goathland N Yorks 226 E6
Goathurst Som 43 G9
Goathurst Common Kent 52 C3
Gobernuisgach Lodge Highld 308 E4
Gobernuisgeach Highld 310 F3
Gobhaig W Isles 305 H2
Gobley Hole Hants 48 D6
Gobowen Shrops 148 C6
Godalming Sur 50 E3
Goddards Bucks 84 G3
Goddard's Corner Suff 126 D5
Goddard's Green Kent 53 G10
Goddard's Green W Berks 65 F7
Goddards' Green W Sus 36 C3
Godden Green Kent 52 B5
Goddington London 68 F3
Godley Gtr Man 185 B7
Godley Hill Gtr Man 185 C7
Godleybrook Staffs 169 G7
Godleys Green E Sus 36 D5
Godmanchester Cambs 122 C4
Godmanstone Dorset 17 B9
Godmersham Kent 54 C5
Godney Som 44 E3
Godolphin Cross Corn 2 C4
Godre'r-graig Neath 76 D3
God's Blessing Green Dorset 31 G8
Godshill Hants 31 E11
Godshill I o W 20 E6
Godstone Sur 51 C10
Godswinscroft Hants 19 B9
Godwell Devon 8 D2
Godwick Norf 159 E8
Godwinscroft Hants 19 B9
Goetre Mon 78 D4
Goferydd Anglesey 178 E2
Goff's Oak Herts 86 E4
Gogar Edin 280 G3
Goginan Ceredig 128 G3
Goirtean a'Chladaich Highld 290 F2
Golan Gwyn 163 G8
Golant Corn 6 E2
Golberdon Corn 12 G2
Golborne Gtr Man 183 B10
Golcar W Yorks 196 D6
Golch Flint 181 F11
Gold Hill Dorset 30 E4
Gold Hill Norf 139 E10
Goldcliff Newport 59 C11
Golden Balls Oxon 83 F9
Golden Cross E Sus 23 C10
Golden Cross E Sus 23 C8
Golden Green Kent 52 D6
Golden Grove Carms 75 B9
Golden Hill Bristol 60 D5
Golden Hill Hants 19 B11
Golden Hill Pembs 73 E7
Golden Hill Pembs 91 G9
Golden Park Devon 24 C2
Golden Pot Hants 49 E8
Golden Valley Derbys 170 E6
Golden Valley Glos 99 G8
Golden Valley Hereford 98 B3
Goldenhill Stoke 168 E5
Golder Field Hereford 115 E11
Golders Green London 67 B9
Goldfinch Bottom W Berks 64 G4
Goldhanger Essex 88 D6
Golding Shrops 131 C10
Goldington Beds 121 G11
Gold's Cross Bath 60 G5
Golds Green W Mid 133 E9
Goldsborough N Yorks 206 B3
Goldsborough N Yorks 226 C6
Goldsithney Corn 2 C2
Goldstone Shrops 150 D4
Goldthorn Park W Mid 133 D8
Goldthorpe S Yorks 198 G3
Goldworthy Devon 24 C5
Golford Kent 53 F9
Golftyn Flint 182 G3
Golgotha Kent 55 D9
Gollanfield Highld 301 D8
Gollawater Corn 4 E5
Gollinglith Foot N Yorks 214 C3
Golly Wrex 166 D4
Golsoncott Som 42 F4
Golspie Highld 311 J2
Golval Highld 310 C2
Golynos Torf 78 E3
Gomeldon Wilts 47 F7
Gomersal W Yorks 197 B8
Gometra Ho Argyll 288 E5
Gomshall Sur 50 D5
Gonalston Notts 171 F11
Gonamena Corn 11 G11
Gonerby Hill Foot Lincs 155 B8
Gonfirth Shetland 313 G5
Good Easter Essex 87 C10
Gooderstone Norf 140 C5
Goodleigh Devon 40 G6
Goodley Stock Kent 52 C2
Goodmanham E Yorks 208 E3
Goodmayes London 68 B3
Goodnestone Kent 55 C9
Goodnestone Kent 70 G4
Goodrich Hereford 79 B9
Goodrington Torbay 9 D7
Good's Green Worcs 132 G5
Goodshaw Lancs 195 B10
Goodshaw Chapel Lancs 195 B10
Goodshaw Fold Lancs 195 B10
Goodstone Devon 13 G11
Goodwick = Wdig Pembs 91 D8
Goodworth Clatford Hants 47 E11
Goodyers End Warks 134 F6
Goodyhills Cumb 229 B8
Goom's Hill Worcs 117 G10
Goon Gumpas Corn 4 G4
Goon Piper Corn 3 B8
Goonabarn Corn 5 E9
Goonbell Corn 4 F4
Goonhavern Corn 4 E5
Goonhusband Corn 2 D5
Goonlaze Corn 2 B6
Goonown Corn 4 E4
Goonvrea Corn 4 F4
Goose Eye W Yorks 204 E6
Goose Green Cumb 211 C10
Goose Green Essex 108 F2
Goose Green Gtr Man 194 G5
Goose Green Hants 32 F4
Goose Green Herts 86 D5
Goose Green Kent 52 C6
Goose Green Kent 53 F10
Goose Green Lancs 194 C3
Goose Green Norf 142 F2
Goose Green S Glos 61 C8
Goose Green W Sus 34 C3
Goose Green W Sus 35 D10
Goose Hill Hants 64 G4
Goose Pool Hereford 97 D9
Gooseberry Green Essex 87 F11
Gooseford Devon 13 C9
Gooseham Mill Devon 24 D2
Goosehill W Yorks 197 C11
Goosehill Green Worcs 117 E8
Goosemoor Staffs 150 F6
Goosemoor Green Staffs 151 G11
Goosenford Som 28 B2
Goosewell Devon 40 D5
Goosey Oxon 82 G5
Goosnargh Lancs 203 F7
Goostrey E Ches 184 G3
Gorbals Glasgow 267 C11
Gorcott Hill Warks 117 D11
Gord Shetland 313 L6
Gorddinog Conwy 179 G11
Gordon Borders 272 G2
Gordonbush Highld 311 J2
Gordonsburgh Moray 302 C4
Gordonstoun Moray 301 C11
Gordonstown Aberds 302 D5
Gordonstown Aberds 303 F7
Gore Dorset 29 D9
Gore Kent 55 B10
Gore Cross Wilts 46 C4
Gore End Hants 64 G2
Gore Pit Essex 88 B5
Gore Street Kent 71 F9
Gorebridge Midloth 270 C6
Gorefield Cambs 157 G8
Gorehill W Sus 35 C7
Gorgie Edin 280 G4

376 Gor – Hai

Gorhambury Herts 85 D10
Goring Oxon 64 C6
Goring-by-Sea W Sus 35 G10
Goring Heath Oxon 65 D7
Gorleston-on-Sea Norf 143 C10
Gornalwood W Mid 133 E8
Gorrachie Aberds 303 D7
Gorran Churchtown Corn 5 G9
Gorran Haven Corn 5 G10
Gorran High Lanes Corn 5 G9
Gorrenberry Borders 249 D11
Gorrig Ceredig 93 C8
Gorse Covert Warr 183 C11
Gorse Hill Gtr Man 184 B4
Gorse Hill Swindon 63 B7
Gorsedd Flint 181 F11
Gorseinon Swansea 56 B5
Gorseness Orkney 314 E4
Gorsethorpe Notts 171 B9
Gorseybank Derbys 170 E3
Gorsgoch Ceredig 111 G9
Gorslas Carms 75 C9
Gorsley Glos 98 F3
Gorsley Common Hereford 98 F3
Gorsley Ley Staffs 133 B11
Gorst Hill Worcs 116 C4
Gorstage W Ches 183 G10
Gorstan Highld 300 C3
Gorstanvorran Highld 289 B10
Gorstella W Ches 166 C5
Gorsteyhill E Ches 168 E2
Gorsty Hill Staffs 151 D11
Gorstyhill Staffs 168 E2
Gortan Argyll 274 G3
Gortantaoid Argyll 274 F4
Gortenacullish Highld 295 G8
Gorteneorn Highld 289 C8
Gortenfern Highld 289 C8
Gortinanane Argyll 255 C8
Gorton Gtr Man 184 B5
Gortonallister N Ayrs 256 D2
Gosbeck Suff 126 F3
Gosberton Lincs 156 C4
Gosberton Cheal Lincs 156 D4
Gosberton Clough Lincs 156 D3
Goscote W Mid 133 C10
Goseley Dale Derbys 152 E6
Gosfield Essex 106 F5
Gosford Hereford 115 D10
Gosford Oxon 83 C7
Gosford Green W Mid 118 B6
Gosforth Cumb 219 E11
Gosforth T & W 242 D6
Gosforth Valley Derbys 186 F4
Gosland Green Suff 124 G5
Gosling Green Suff 107 C9
Gosmere Kent 54 B4
Gosmore Herts 104 F3
Gospel Ash Staffs 132 E6
Gospel End Village Staffs 133 E7
Gospel Green W Sus 50 G2
Gospel Oak London 67 B9
Gosport Hants 21 B8
Gosport Hants 32 C5
Gossabrough Shetland 312 E7
Gossard's Green C Beds 103 C9
Gossington Glos 80 E2
Gossops Green W Sus 51 F9
Goswick Northumb 273 F11
Gotham Dorset 31 E9
Gotham E Sus 38 F2
Gotham Notts 153 C10
Gothelney Green Som 43 F9
Gotherington Glos 99 F9
Gothers Corn 5 D9
Gott Argyll 288 E2
Gott Shetland 313 J6
Gotton Som 28 B2
Goudhurst Kent 53 F8
Goukstone Moray 302 D4
Goulceby Lincs 190 F3
Goulton N Yorks 225 E9
Gourdas Aberds 303 E7
Gourdon Aberds 293 F10
Gourock Invclyd 276 F4
Govan Glasgow 267 B11
Govanhill Glasgow 267 C11
Gover Hill Kent 52 C6
Goverton Notts 172 E2
Goveton Devon 8 F5
Govilon Mon 78 C3
Gowanhill Aberds 303 C10
Gowanwell Aberds 303 E8
Gowdall E Yorks 198 C6
Gowerton = Tre-Gwyr Swansea 56 B5
Gowhole Derbys 185 E8
Gowkhall Fife 279 D11
Gowkthrapple N Lnrk 268 E5
Gowthorpe E Yorks 207 C11
Goxhill E Yorks 209 E9
Goxhill N Lincs 200 C6
Goxhill Haven N Lincs 200 B6
Goybre Neath 57 D9
Goytre Neath 57 D9
Gozzard's Ford Oxon 83 F7
Grabhair W Isles 305 G5
Graby Lincs 155 D11
Gracca Corn 5 D10
Gracemount Edin 270 B5
Grade Corn 2 G6
Graffham W Sus 34 D6
Grafham Cambs 122 D3
Grafham Sur 50 E4
Grafton Hereford 97 D9
Grafton N Yorks 215 G8
Grafton Oxon 82 E3
Grafton Shrops 149 F8
Grafton Worcs 99 D9
Grafton Worcs 115 E11
Grafton Flyford Worcs 117 F9
Grafton Regis Northants 102 B5
Grafton Underwood Northants 137 G8
Grafty Green Kent 53 D11
Grahamston Falk 279 E7
Graianrhyd Denb 166 D2
Graig Carms 74 E6
Graig Conwy 180 G4
Graig Denb 181 G9
Graig Rhondda 58 B5
Graig Wrex 148 B4
Graig-Fawr Swansea 75 E10
Graig-fechan Denb 165 E10
Graig Felen Swansea 75 E11
Graig Penllyn V Glam 58 D3
Graig Trewyddfa Swansea 57 B7
Grain Medway 69 D11
Grains Bar Gtr Man 196 F3
Grainsby Lincs 190 B3
Grainthorpe Lincs 190 B5
Grainthorpe Fen Lincs 190 B5
Graiselound N Lincs 188 B3
Grampound Corn 5 F8
Grampound Road Corn 5 E8
Gramsdal W Isles 296 F4
Granborough Bucks 102 F5
Granby Notts 154 B5
Grandborough Warks 119 D9
Grandpont Oxon 83 D8
Grandtully Perth 286 B3
Grange Cumb 220 B5
Grange Dorset 31 G8
Grange E Ayrs 257 B10
Grange Fife 287 G8
Grange Halton 183 E8
Grange Lancs 203 G7
Grange Medway 69 F9
Grange Mers 182 D2
Grange N Yorks 223 G8
Grange NE Lincs 201 F9
Grange Perth 286 E6
Grange Warr 183 C10
Grange Crossroads Moray 302 D4
Grange Estate Dorset 31 G10
Grange Hall Moray 301 C10
Grange Hill Durham 233 F10
Grange Hill Essex 86 G6
Grange Moor W Yorks 197 D8
Grange of Cree Dumfries 236 D6
Grange of Lindores Fife 286 F6
Grange-over-Sands Cumb 211 D8
Grange Park London 86 F4
Grange Park Mers 183 C7
Grange Park Northants 120 F5
Grange Park Swindon 62 C6
Grange Villa Durham 242 G6
Grange Village Glos 79 C11
Grangemill Derbys 170 D2
Grangemouth Falk 279 E8
Grangemuir Fife 287 G9
Grangepans Falk 279 E10
Grangetown Cardiff 59 E7
Grangetown Redcar 235 G7
Grangetown T & W 243 G10
Granish Highld 291 B11
Gransmoor E Yorks 209 B8
Gransmore Green Essex 106 G3
Granston = Treopert Pembs 91 E7
Grant Thorold NE Lincs 201 F9
Grantchester Cambs 123 F8
Grantham Lincs 155 B8
Grantley N Yorks 214 F4
Grantley Hall N Yorks 214 F4
Grantlodge Aberds 293 B9
Granton Dumfries 248 B3
Granton Edin 280 F4
Grantown Aberds 302 D5
Grantown-on-Spey Highld 301 G10
Grantsfield Hereford 115 E10
Grantshouse Borders 272 B6
Graplin Dumfries 237 E8
Grappenhall Warr 183 D10
Grasby Lincs 200 G5
Grasmere Cumb 220 D6
Grass Green Essex 106 D4
Grasscroft Gtr Man 196 G3
Grassendale Mers 182 D5
Grassgarth Cumb 221 F8
Grassgarth Cumb 230 C2
Grassholme Durham 232 G4
Grassington N Yorks 213 G10
Grassmoor Derbys 170 B6
Grassthorpe Notts 172 B3
Grasswell T & W 243 G8
Grateley Hants 47 E9
Gratton Devon 24 E5
Gratwich Staffs 151 C10
Gravel W Ches 167 B11
Gravel Castle Kent 55 D8
Gravel Hill Bucks 85 G8
Gravel Hole Gtr Man 196 F2
Gravel Hole Shrops 149 B7
Graveley Cambs 122 E4
Graveley Herts 104 F4
Gravelhill Shrops 149 G9
Gravelly Hill W Mid 134 E2
Gravels Shrops 130 D6
Gravelsbank Shrops 130 C6
Graven Shetland 312 F6
Graveney Kent 70 G5
Gravenhunger Moss Shrops 168 G2
Gravesend Herts 105 F8
Gravesend Kent 68 E6
Grayingham Lincs 188 B6
Grayrigg Cumb 221 F11
Grays Thurrock 68 D6
Grayshott Hants 49 F11
Grayson Green Cumb 228 F5
Grayswood Sur 50 G2
Graythorp Hrtlpl 234 F6
Grazeley Wokingham 65 F7
Grazeley Green W Berks 65 F7
Greagdhubh Lodge Highld 291 D8
Greamchary Highld 310 F2
Greasbrough S Yorks 186 B6
Greasby Mers 182 D3
Greasley Notts 171 F7
Great Abington Cambs 105 B10
Great Addington Northants 121 B9
Great Alne Warks 118 F2
Great Altcar Lancs 193 F10
Great Amwell Herts 86 C5
Great Asby Cumb 222 C3
Great Ashfield Suff 125 D9
Great Ashley Wilts 61 G10
Great Ayton N Yorks 225 C11
Great Baddow Essex 88 E2
Great Bardfield Essex 106 E3
Great Barford Beds 122 G2
Great Barrington Glos 82 C2
Great Barrow W Ches 167 B7
Great Barton Suff 125 D7
Great Barugh N Yorks 216 D4
Great Bavington Northumb 251 G11
Great Bealings Suff 108 B4
Great Bedwyn Wilts 63 G9
Great Bentley Essex 108 G2
Great Berry Essex 69 B7
Great Billing Northants 120 E6
Great Bircham Norf 158 C5
Great Blakenham Suff 126 G2
Great Blencow Cumb 230 E5
Great Bolas Telford 150 E2
Great Bookham Sur 50 C6
Great Bosullow Corn 1 C4
Great Bourton Oxon 101 B9
Great Bowden Leics 136 F4
Great Bower Kent 54 C4
Great Bradley Suff 124 G3
Great Braxted Essex 88 C5
Great Bricett Suff 125 G10
Great Brickhill Bucks 103 E8
Great Bridge W Mid 133 E9
Great Bridgeford Staffs 151 D7
Great Brington Northants 120 D3
Great Bromley Essex 107 F11
Great Broughton Cumb 229 E7
Great Broughton N Yorks 225 D10
Great Buckland Kent 69 G7
Great Budworth W Ches 183 F11
Great Burdon Darl 224 B6
Great Burgh Sur 51 B8
Great Burstead Essex 87 G11
Great Busby N Yorks 225 D10
Great Canfield Essex 87 B9
Great Carlton Lincs 190 D6
Great Casterton Rutland 137 B10
Great Chalfield Wilts 61 G11
Great Chart Kent 54 E3
Great Chatwell Staffs 150 G5
Great Chell Stoke 168 E5
Great Chesterford Essex 105 C10
Great Cheveney Kent 53 E8
Great Cheverell Wilts 46 C3
Great Chilton Durham 233 E11
Great Chishill Cambs 105 D8
Great Clacton Essex 89 B11
Great Claydons Essex 88 E3
Great Cliff W Yorks 197 D10
Great Clifton Cumb 228 F6
Great Coates NE Lincs 201 F8
Great Comberton Worcs 99 C9
Great Common Suff 143 F7
Great Common W Sus 35 B8
Great Corby Cumb 239 G11
Great Cornard Suff 107 C7
Great Cowden E Yorks 209 E10
Great Coxwell Oxon 82 G3
Great Crakehall N Yorks 224 G4
Great Cransley Northants 120 B6
Great Cressingham Norf 141 C7
Great Crosby Mers 182 B4
Great Crosthwaite Cumb 229 G11
Great Cubley Derbys 152 B3
Great Dalby Leics 154 G4
Great Denham Beds 103 B10
Great Doddington Northants 121 E7
Great Doward Hereford 79 B9
Great Dunham Norf 159 G7
Great Dunmow Essex 106 G2
Great Durnford Wilts 46 F6
Great Easton Essex 106 F2
Great Easton Leics 136 E6
Great Eccleston Lancs 202 E4
Great Edstone N Yorks 216 C4
Great Ellingham Norf 141 D10
Great Elm Som 45 D8
Great Eppleton T & W 234 B3
Great Eversden Cambs 123 G7
Great Fencote N Yorks 224 G5
Great Finborough Suff 125 F10
Great Fransham Norf 159 G7
Great Gaddesden Herts 85 C8
Great Gate Staffs 169 G9
Great Gidding Cambs 138 G2
Great Givendale E Yorks 208 C2
Great Glemham Suff 126 E6
Great Glen Leics 136 D3
Great Gonerby Lincs 155 B7
Great Gransden Cambs 122 F5
Great Green Cambs 104 C5
Great Green Norf 142 F5
Great Green Suff 125 B11
Great Green Suff 125 F8
Great Green Suff 126 B2
Great Habton N Yorks 216 D5
Great Hale Lincs 173 G10
Great Hallingbury Essex 87 B8
Great Hampden Bucks 84 E4
Great Harrowden Northants 121 C7
Great Harwood Lancs 203 G10
Great Haseley Oxon 83 E10
Great Hatfield E Yorks 209 E9
Great Haywood Staffs 151 E10
Great Haywood Staffs 151 E9
Great Heath W Mid 134 G6
Great Heck N Yorks 198 C5
Great Henny Essex 107 D7
Great Hinton Wilts 46 B2
Great Hivings Bucks 85 E7
Great Hockham Norf 141 E9
Great Holcombe Oxon 83 F10
Great Holland Essex 89 B12
Great Hollands Brack 65 F11
Great Holm M Keynes 102 D6
Great Honeyborough Pembs 73 D7
Great Horkesley Essex 107 E9
Great Hormead Herts 105 F7
Great Horton W Yorks 205 G8
Great Horwood Bucks 102 E5
Great Houghton Northants 120 F5
Great Houghton S Yorks 198 F2
Great Howarth Gtr Man 196 D2
Great Hucklow Derbys 185 F11
Great Job's Cross Kent 38 B4
Great Kelk E Yorks 209 B8
Great Kendale E Yorks 217 G10
Great Kimble Bucks 84 D4
Great Kingshill Bucks 84 F5
Great Langton N Yorks 224 F5
Great Lea Common Reading 65 F8
Great Leighs Essex 88 B2
Great Lever Gtr Man 195 F8
Great Limber Lincs 200 F6
Great Linford M Keynes 103 C7
Great Livermere Suff 125 C7
Great Longstone Derbys 186 G2
Great Lumley Durham 233 B11
Great Lyth Shrops 131 B9
Great Malgraves Thurrock 69 C7
Great Malvern Worcs 98 B5
Great Maplestead Essex 106 E6
Great Marton Blkpool 202 F2
Great Marton Moss Blkpool 202 G2
Great Massingham Norf 158 E5
Great Melton Norf 142 B2
Great Milton Oxon 83 E10
Great Missenden Bucks 84 E5
Great Mitton Lancs 203 F10
Great Mongeham Kent 55 C10
Great Moor Gtr Man 184 D6
Great Moor Staffs 132 D6
Great Moulton Norf 142 E3
Great Munden Herts 105 G7
Great Musgrave Cumb 222 C5
Great Ness Shrops 149 F7
Great Notley Essex 106 G4
Great Oak Mon 78 D5
Great Oakley Essex 108 F3
Great Oakley Northants 137 F7
Great Offley Herts 104 F2
Great Ormside Cumb 222 B4
Great Orton Cumb 239 G8
Great Ouseburn N Yorks 215 G8
Great Oxendon Northants 136 G4
Great Oxney Green Essex 87 D11
Great Palgrave Norf 158 G6
Great Parndon Essex 86 D6
Great Pattenden Kent 53 E8
Great Paxton Cambs 122 E4
Great Plumpton Lancs 202 G3
Great Plumstead Norf 160 G6
Great Ponton Lincs 155 C8
Great Preston W Yorks 198 B2
Great Purston Northants 101 D10
Great Raveley Cambs 138 G5
Great Rissington Glos 81 B11
Great Rollright Oxon 100 E6
Great Ryburgh Norf 159 D9
Great Ryle Northumb 264 G2
Great Ryton Shrops 131 C9
Great Saling Essex 106 F4
Great Salkeld Cumb 231 D7
Great Sampford Essex 106 D2
Great Sankey Warr 183 D9
Great Saredon Staffs 133 B9
Great Saxham Suff 124 E5
Great Shefford W Berks 63 E11
Great Shelford Cambs 123 G9
Great Shoddesden Hants 47 D9
Great Smeaton N Yorks 224 E6
Great Snoring Norf 159 C8
Great Somerford Wilts 62 C3
Great Stainton Darl 234 G2
Great Stambridge Essex 88 G5
Great Staughton Cambs 122 E2
Great Steeping Lincs 174 C6
Great Stoke S Glos 60 C6
Great Stonar Kent 55 B10
Great Stretton Leics 136 C3
Great Strickland Cumb 231 G7
Great Stukeley Cambs 122 C4
Great Sturton Lincs 190 F2
Great Sutton Shrops 131 G10
Great Sutton W Ches 182 F5
Great Swinburne Northumb 241 B10
Great Tew Oxon 101 F7
Great Tey Essex 107 F7
Great Thirkleby N Yorks 215 D9
Great Thurlow Suff 124 G3
Great Torrington Devon 25 D7
Great Tosson Northumb 252 C2
Great Totham Essex 88 C5
Great Tows Lincs 190 C2
Great Tree Corn 6 D5
Great Urswick Cumb 210 E5
Great Wakering Essex 70 B2
Great Waldingfield Suff 107 C8
Great Walsingham Norf 159 B8
Great Waltham Essex 87 C11
Great Warley Essex 87 G9
Great Washbourne Glos 99 E9
Great Weeke Devon 13 D10
Great Weldon Northants 137 F8
Great Welnetham Suff 125 F7
Great Wenham Suff 107 D11
Great Whittington Northumb 242 C2
Great Wigborough Essex 89 C7
Great Wilbraham Cambs 123 F10
Great Wilne Derbys 153 C8
Great Wishford Wilts 46 F5
Great Witchingham Norf 160 E2
Great Witcombe Glos 80 C6
Great Witley Worcs 116 D5
Great Wolford Warks 100 E4
Great Wratting Suff 106 B3
Great Wymondley Herts 104 F4
Great Wyrley Staffs 133 B9
Great Wytheford Shrops 149 F11
Great Yarmouth Norf 143 B10
Great Yeldham Essex 106 D5
Greater Doward Hereford 79 B9
Greatfield Wilts 62 B5
Greatford Lincs 155 G11
Greatgap Bucks 84 B6
Greatgate Staffs 169 G9
Greatham Hants 49 G9
Greatham Hrtlpl 234 F5
Greatham W Sus 35 D8
Greatmoor Bucks 102 G4
Greatness Kent 52 B4
Greatstone-on-Sea Kent 39 C9
Greatworth Northants 101 C11
Greave Gtr Man 184 C6
Greave Lancs 195 C11
Grebby Lincs 174 B6
Greeba I o M 192 D4
Green Denb 165 B9
Green Pembs 73 E7
Green Powys 130 E5
Green Bank Cumb 211 C7
Green Bottom Corn 4 F5
Green Bottom Glos 79 B11
Green Close N Yorks 212 F4
Green Clough W Yorks 205 G7
Green Crize Hereford 97 D10
Green Cross Sur 49 F11
Green Down Devon 28 G3
Green End Beds 103 B10
Green End Beds 121 E11
Green End Beds 122 E2
Green End Beds 122 G2
Green End Bucks 84 F4
Green End Bucks 103 E8
Green End C Beds 103 D11
Green End Cambs 122 C4
Green End Cambs 123 F7
Green End Herts 85 D8
Green End Herts 104 E5
Green End Herts 104 E6
Green End Herts 104 G6
Green End Herts 105 F7
Green End Lancs 204 D4
Green End N Yorks 226 E6
Green End Warks 134 F5
Green Gate Devon 27 D8
Green Hailey Bucks 84 E4
Green Hammerton N Yorks 206 B5
Green Haworth Lancs 195 B9
Green Head Cumb 230 B3
Green Heath Staffs 151 G9
Green Hill Kent 53 C9
Green Hill Lincs 155 B8
Green Hill W Yorks 206 F4
Green Hill Wilts 62 B5
Green Lane Devon 13 F11
Green Lane Hereford 98 B2
Green Lane Powys 130 D3
Green Lane Warks 117 E11
Green Lane Warks 118 B6
Green Moor S Yorks 186 B3
Green Ore Som 44 C5
Green Parlour Bath 45 C8
Green Quarter Cumb 221 E9
Green St Green London 68 G3
Green Side W Yorks 197 E7
Green Side W Yorks 205 G11
Green Street E Sus 38 E3
Green Street Essex 87 F10
Green Street Glos 80 B5
Green Street Glos 80 E3
Green Street Herts 85 F11
Green Street Herts 105 G9
Green Street W Sus 35 C10
Green Street Worcs 99 B7
Green Street Worcs 99 C7
Green Street Green Kent 68 E5
Green Street Green London 68 G3
Green Tye Herts 86 B6
Greenacres Gtr Man 196 F2
Greenan Argyll 275 G11
Greenbank Falk 279 F7
Greenbank Shetland 312 C7
Greenbank W Ches 183 G10
Greenburn W Loth 269 C8
Greencroft Durham 242 G5
Greendale E Ches 184 F5
Greendikes Northumb 264 D3
Greendown Som 44 C5
Greendykes Northumb 264 D3
Greenend N Lnrk 268 C4
Greenend Oxon 100 G6
Greenfaulds N Lnrk 278 G5
Greenfield C Beds 103 E11
Greenfield Glasgow 268 C2
Greenfield Gtr Man 196 G3
Greenfield Highld 289 D11
Greenfield Highld 290 C4
Greenfield Oxon 84 G2
Greenfield = Maes-Glas Flint 181 F11
Greenfoot N Lnrk 268 B4
Greenford London 66 C6
Greengairs N Lnrk 278 G5
Greengarth Hall Cumb 219 E11
Greengate Gtr Man 196 D2
Greengate Norf 159 F10
Greengates W Yorks 205 F9
Greengill Cumb 229 D8
Greenhalgh Lancs 202 F4
Greenhall S Lnrk 268 D3
Greenham Dorset 28 G6
Greenham Som 27 C9
Greenham W Berks 64 F3
Greenhaugh Northumb 251 F7
Greenhead Borders 261 D11
Greenhead Dumfries 247 D9
Greenhead N Lnrk 268 E6
Greenhead Northumb 240 D5
Greenhead Staffs 169 F7
Greenheys Gtr Man 195 G8
Greenhill Dumfries 238 B4
Greenhill Durham 234 B3
Greenhill Falk 278 F6
Greenhill Hereford 98 B4
Greenhill Kent 71 F7
Greenhill Leics 153 G8
Greenhill London 67 B7
Greenhill S Yorks 186 E4
Greenhill Worcs 99 B10
Greenhill Worcs 116 B6
Greenhill Bank Shrops 149 B7
Greenhillocks Derbys 170 F6
Greenhills N Ayrs 267 E7
Greenhills S Lnrk 268 E2
Greenhithe Kent 68 E5
Greenholm E Ayrs 258 B2
Greenholme Cumb 221 D11
Greenhouse Borders 262 E3
Greenhow N Yorks 214 G2
Greenhow Hill N Yorks 214 G2
Greenigoe Orkney 314 F4
Greenland Highld 310 C6
Greenland S Yorks 186 D5
Greenland Mains Highld 310 C6
Greenlands Bucks 65 B9
Greenlands Worcs 117 D11
Greenlaw Aberds 302 D6
Greenlaw Borders 272 F4
Greenlaw Mains Midloth 270 C4
Greenlea Dumfries 238 B2
Greenley M Keynes 102 C6
Greenloaning Perth 286 G2
Greenlooms W Ches 167 C7
Greenman's Lane Wilts 62 C3
Greenmeadow Swindon 62 B6
Greenmeadow Torf 78 F3
Greenmount Gtr Man 195 E9
Greenmow Shetland 313 L6
Greenoak E Yorks 199 B10
Greenock Invclyd 276 F5
Greenock West Invclyd 276 F5
Greenodd Cumb 210 C6
Greenrigg W Loth 269 C8
Greenrow Cumb 238 G4
Greens Borders 249 F11
Greens Norton Northants 102 B3
Greensforge Staffs 133 F7
Greensgate Norf 160 F2
Greenside Cumb 222 E4
Greenside Derbys 186 F5
Greenside Gtr Man 184 B6
Greenside T & W 242 E4
Greenside W Yorks 197 D7
Greensidehill Northumb 263 F11
Greensplat Corn 5 D9
Greenstead Essex 107 F10
Greenstead Green Essex 106 F6
Greensted Essex 87 E8
Greensted Green Essex 87 E8
Greenstreet Green Suff 107 B10
Greenway Hereford 98 E4
Greenway Pembs 91 E11
Greenway Som 27 B11
Greenway V Glam 58 E5
Greenway Worcs 116 C4
Greenwell Cumb 240 F2
Greenwells Borders 262 C3
Greenwich London 67 D11
Greenwich Suff 108 C3
Greenwich Wilts 46 G2
Greenwith Common Corn 4 G5
Greenwoods Essex 87 F11
Greeny Orkney 314 D2
Greep Highld 298 E2
Greet Glos 99 E10
Greet Kent 54 B2
Greete Shrops 115 C11
Greetham Lincs 190 G4
Greetham Rutland 155 G8
Greetland W Yorks 196 C5
Greetland Wall Nook W Yorks 196 C5
Greetwell N Lincs 200 G2
Gregg Hall Cumb 221 G9
Gregson Lane Lancs 194 B5
Gregynog Powys 129 D11
Greinetobht W Isles 296 D4
Grèin W Isles 297 L2
Greinton Som 44 F2
Gremista Shetland 313 J6
Grenaby I o M 192 E3
Grendon Northants 121 E7
Grendon Warks 134 C5
Grendon Bishop Hereford 115 F11
Grendon Common Warks 134 D5
Grendon Green Hereford 115 F11
Grendon Underwood Bucks 102 G3
Grenofen Devon 12 G5
Grenoside S Yorks 186 C4
Greosabhagh W Isles 305 J3
Gresford Wrex 166 E5
Gresham Norf 160 B3
Greshornish Highld 298 D3
Gressenhall Norf 159 F9
Gressingham Lancs 211 F11
Gresty Green E Ches 168 E2
Greta Bridge Durham 223 C11
Gretna Dumfries 239 D8
Gretna Green Dumfries 239 D8
Gretton Glos 99 E10
Gretton Northants 137 E7
Gretton Shrops 131 D10
Gretton Fields Glos 99 E10
Grewelthorpe N Yorks 214 D4
Grey Green N Lincs 199 F9
Greyfield Bath 44 B6
Greygarth N Yorks 214 E3
Greylake Som 43 G11
Greylake Fosse Som 44 F2
Greynor Carms 75 D9
Greynor-isaf Carms 75 D9
Greyrigg Dumfries 248 F3
Greys Green Oxon 65 C8
Greysouthen Cumb 229 F7
Greystead Northumb 251 F7
Greystoke Cumb 230 E4
Greystoke Gill Cumb 230 F4
Greystone Aberds 292 D6
Greystone Aberds 302 F6
Greystone Angus 287 C9
Greystone Cumb 211 D10
Greystone Dumfries 237 B11
Greystonegill N Yorks 212 F3
Greystones S Yorks 186 D4
Greystones Warks 99 B11
Greytree Hereford 97 F11
Greywell Hants 49 C8
Griais W Isles 304 D6
Grianan W Isles 304 E6
Gribb Dorset 28 G5
Gribthorpe E Yorks 207 F11
Gridley Corner Devon 12 C3
Griff Warks 135 F7
Griffins Hill W Mid 133 G10
Griffithstown Torf 78 F3
Griffydam Leics 153 F8
Grigg Kent 53 E11
Griggs Green Hants 49 G10
Grillis Corn 2 B5
Grilstone Devon 26 C2
Grimbister Orkney 314 E3
Grimblethorpe Lincs 190 D2
Grimeford Village Lancs 194 E6
Grimes Hill Worcs 117 B11
Grimesthorpe S Yorks 186 C5
Grimethorpe S Yorks 198 F2
Griminis W Isles 296 D3
Griminis W Isles 296 F3
Grimister Shetland 312 D6
Grimley Worcs 116 E6
Grimness Orkney 314 G4
Grimoldby Lincs 190 D5
Grimpo Shrops 149 D7
Grimsargh Lancs 203 G7
Grimsbury Oxon 101 C9
Grimsby NE Lincs 201 E9
Grimscote Northants 120 G3
Grimscott Corn 24 F3
Grimshaw Blkburn 195 C8
Grimshaw Green Lancs 194 E3
Grimsthorpe Lincs 155 E10
Grimston E Yorks 209 F11
Grimston Leics 154 E3
Grimston Norf 158 E4
Grimston York 207 C8
Grimstone Dorset 17 C8
Grimstone End Suff 125 D8
Grinacombe Moor Devon 12 C4
Grindale E Yorks 218 E2
Grindigar Orkney 314 F5
Grindiscol Shetland 313 K6
Grindle Shrops 132 C5
Grindleford Derbys 186 F2
Grindleton Lancs 203 D11
Grindley Staffs 151 D10
Grindley Brook Shrops 167 G8
Grindlow Derbys 185 F11
Grindon Northumb 273 G8
Grindon Staffs 169 E9
Grindon Stockton 234 F3
Grindon T & W 243 G9
Grindonmoor Gate Staffs 169 E9
Grindsbrook Booth Derbys 185 D10
Gringley on the Hill Notts 188 C2
Grinsdale Cumb 239 F9
Grinshill Shrops 149 E10
Grinstead Hill Suff 125 G11
Grinton N Yorks 223 F10
Griomasaigh W Isles 297 G4
Griomsidar W Isles 304 F5
Grisdale Cumb 222 G5
Grishipoll Argyll 288 D3
Grisling Common E Sus 36 C6
Gristhorpe N Yorks 217 C11
Griston Norf 141 D8
Gritley Orkney 314 F5
Grittenham Wilts 62 C4
Grittlesend Hereford 98 B4
Grittleton Wilts 61 C11
Grizebeck Cumb 210 C4
Grizedale Cumb 220 G6
Groam Highld 300 E5
Grobister Orkney 314 D6
Grobsness Shetland 313 G5
Groby Leics 135 B10
Groes Conwy 165 C8
Groes Neath 57 D9
Groes Efa Denb 165 B10
Groes-faen Rhondda 58 C5
Groes-fawr Denb 165 B10
Groes-lwyd Mon 96 G6
Groes-lwyd Powys 148 G4
Groes-wen Caerph 58 B6
Groesffordd Gwyn 144 B5
Groesffordd Powys 95 F11
Groesffordd Marli Denb 181 G8
Groeslon Gwyn 163 C8
Groeslon Gwyn 163 D7
Groespluan Powys 130 B4
Grogport Argyll 255 C9
Gromford Suff 127 F7
Gronant Flint 181 E9
Gronwen Shrops 148 D5
Groombridge E Sus 52 F4
Grosmont Mon 97 G8
Grosmont N Yorks 226 D6
Gross Green Warks 119 F7
Grotaig Highld 300 G4
Groton Suff 107 C9
Grotton Gtr Man 196 G3
Grougfoot Falk 279 F10
Grove Bucks 103 G8
Grove Dorset 17 G10
Grove Hereford 98 C2
Grove Kent 71 G8
Grove Notts 188 F2
Grove Oxon 82 G6
Grove Pembs 73 E7
Grove End Kent 69 G11
Grove End Warks 134 D3
Grove Green Kent 53 B9
Grove Hill E Sus 23 C10
Grove Hill Kent 71 G8
Grove Park London 67 D8
Grove Park London 68 E2
Grove Town W Yorks 198 C3
Grove Vale W Mid 133 E10
Grovehill E Yorks 208 F6
Grovehill Herts 85 D9
Groves Kent 55 B9
Grovesend Swansea 75 E9
Grub Street Staffs 150 D5
Grubb Street Kent 68 F5
Grudie Highld 300 C3
Gruids Highld 309 J5
Gruinard House Highld 307 K4
Gruinards Highld 309 K5
Grula Highld 294 C5
Gruline Argyll 289 E7
Gruline Ho Argyll 289 F7
Grumbeg Highld 308 F6
Grumbla Corn 1 D4
Grunasound Shetland 313 K5
Grundisburgh Suff 126 G4
Grunsagill Lancs 203 C11
Gruting Shetland 313 J4
Grutness Shetland 313 N6
Gryn Goch Gwyn 162 F6
Gualachulain Highld 284 C5
Gualin Ho Highld 308 D3
Guard House W Yorks 204 E6
Guardbridge Fife 287 F8
Guarlford Worcs 98 B6
Guay Perth 286 C4
Gubbion's Green Essex 88 B2
Gubblecote Herts 84 C6
Guesachan Highld 289 B10
Guestling Green E Sus 38 E5
Guestling Thorn E Sus 38 D4
Guestwick Norf 159 D11
Guestwick Green Norf 159 D11
Guide Blkburn 195 B8
Guide Bridge Gtr Man 184 B6
Guide Post Northumb 253 G7
Guilden Morden Cambs 104 C5
Guilden Sutton W Ches 166 B6
Guildford Sur 50 D3
Guildford Park Sur 50 D3
Guildiehaugh W Loth 269 B9
Guildtown Perth 286 D5
Guilford Pembs 73 D7
Guilsborough Northants 120 C3
Guilsfield = Cegidfa Powys 148 G4
Guilthwaite S Yorks 187 D7
Guilton Kent 55 B9
Guineaford Devon 40 F5
Guisachan Highld 300 G3
Guisborough Redcar 226 B2
Guiseley W Yorks 205 E9
Guist Norf 159 D9
Guith Orkney 314 C5
Guiting Power Glos 99 G11
Gulberwick Shetland 313 K6
Gullane E Loth 281 E9
Guller's End Worcs 99 D7
Gulling Green Suff 124 F6
Gulval Corn 1 C5
Gulworthy Devon 12 G4
Gumfreston Pembs 73 E10
Gumley Leics 136 E3
Gummow's Shop Corn 5 D7
Gun Green Kent 53 G9
Gun Hill E Sus 23 C9
Gunby E Yorks 207 F10
Gunby Lincs 155 E8
Gunby Lincs 175 B7
Gundenham Som 27 C10
Gundleton Hants 48 G6
Gunn Devon 40 G6
Gunnersbury London 67 D7
Gunnerside N Yorks 223 F9
Gunnerton Northumb 241 C10
Gunness N Lincs 199 E10
Gunnislake Corn 12 G4
Gunnista Shetland 313 J7
Gunstone Staffs 133 C7
Gunter's Bridge W Sus 35 C7
Gunthorpe Lincs 188 B4
Gunthorpe Norf 159 C10
Gunthorpe Notts 171 G11
Gunthorpe P'boro 138 C3
Gunthorpe Rutland 137 B7
Gunton Suff 143 D10
Gunville I o W 20 D5
Gunwalloe Corn 2 E5
Gunwalloe Fishing Cove Corn 2 E5
Gupworthy Som 42 F3
Gurnard I o W 20 B5
Gurnett E Ches 184 G6
Gurney Slade Som 44 D6
Gurnos M Tydf 77 D8
Gurnos Powys 76 D3
Gushmere Kent 54 B4
Gussage All Saints Dorset 31 E8
Gussage St Andrew Dorset 31 E7
Gussage St Michael Dorset 31 E7
Gustard Wood Herts 85 B11
Guston Kent 55 E10
Gutcher Shetland 312 D7
Guthram Gowt Lincs 156 E3
Guthrie Angus 287 B9
Guyhirn Cambs 139 C7
Guyhirn Gull Cambs 139 C7
Guy's Cliffe Warks 118 D5
Guy's Head Lincs 157 D9
Guy's Marsh Dorset 30 C4
Guyzance Northumb 252 C6
Gwaelod-y-garth Cardiff 58 C6
Gwaenysgor Flint 181 E9
Gwalchmai Anglesey 178 F5
Gwalchmai Uchaf Anglesey 178 F5
Gwallon Corn 2 C2
Gwastad Pembs 91 G10
Gwastadgoed Gwyn 145 G11
Gwastadnant Gwyn 163 D10
Gwaun-Cae-Gurwen Neath 76 C2
Gwaun-Leision Neath 76 C2
Gwavas Corn 2 D5
Gwavas Corn 2 G6
Gwbert Ceredig 92 B3
Gwedna Corn 2 C4
Gweek Corn 2 D6
Gwehelog Mon 78 E5
Gwenddwr Powys 95 C11
Gwennap Corn 2 B6
Gwenter Corn 2 F6
Gwern y brenin Shrops 148 D6
Gwern-y-Steeple V Glam 58 D5
Gwernaffield-y-Waun Flint 166 C2
Gwernafon Powys 129 E8
Gwerneirin Powys 129 F10
Gwerneirin Powys 130 G3
Gwernesney Mon 78 E6
Gwernogle Carms 93 E10
Gwernol Denb 166 E2
Gwernydd Powys 129 C11
Gwernymynydd Flint 166 C2
Gwersyllt Wrex 166 E4
Gwespyr Flint 181 E10
Gwills Corn 4 D6
Gwinear Corn 2 B3
Gwinear Downs Corn 2 C4
Gwithian Corn 2 A3
Gwredog Anglesey 178 D6
Gwrhay Caerph 77 F11
Gwyddelwern Denb 165 F9
Gwyddgrug Carms 93 D9
Gwynfryn Wrex 166 E3
Gwystre Powys 113 D11
Gwytherin Conwy 164 C5
Gyfelia Wrex 166 F4
Gyffin Conwy 180 F3
Gylen Park Argyll 289 G10
Gyre Orkney 314 F3
Gyrn Denb 165 D11
Gyrn-goch Gwyn 162 F6

H

Habberley Shrops 131 C7
Habberley Worcs 116 B6
Habergham Lancs 204 G2
Habertoft Lincs 175 B8
Habin W Sus 34 C4
Habrough NE Lincs 200 E6
Haccombe Devon 14 G3
Haceby Lincs 155 B10
Hacheston Suff 126 F6
Hack Green E Ches 167 F10
Hackbridge London 67 F9
Hackenthorpe S Yorks 186 E6
Hackford Norf 141 C11
Hackforth N Yorks 224 G4
Hackland Orkney 314 D3
Hackleton Northants 120 F6
Hacklinge Kent 55 C10
Hackman's Gate Worcs 117 B7
Hackness N Yorks 227 G9
Hackness Orkney 314 G3
Hackness Som 43 D10
Hackney London 67 C10
Hackney Wick London 67 C11
Hackthorn Lincs 189 E7
Hackthorn Wilts 47 D7
Hackthorpe Cumb 230 G6
Haclait W Isles 297 G4
Haconby Lincs 156 D2
Hacton London 68 B4
Haddacott Devon 25 C8
Hadden Borders 263 B7
Haddenham Bucks 84 D2
Haddenham Cambs 123 B9
Haddenham End Field Cambs 123 B9
Haddington E Loth 281 G10
Haddington Lincs 172 C6
Haddiscoe Norf 143 D8
Haddoch Aberds 302 E5
Haddon Cambs 138 E2
Haddon E Ches 169 B7
Hade Edge W Yorks 196 F6
Hademore Staffs 134 B3
Haden Cross W Mid 133 F9
Hadfield Derbys 185 B8
Hadham Cross Herts 86 B6
Hadham Ford Herts 105 G8
Hadleigh Essex 69 B10
Hadleigh Suff 107 C10
Hadleigh Heath Suff 107 C9
Hadley London 86 F2
Hadley Telford 150 G3
Hadley Worcs 117 E7
Hadley Castle Telford 150 G3
Hadley End Staffs 152 E2
Hadley Wood London 86 F3
Hadlow Kent 52 D6
Hadlow Down E Sus 37 C8
Hadlow Stair Kent 52 D6
Hadnall Shrops 149 F10
Hadspen Som 45 G7
Hadstock Essex 105 C11
Hadston Northumb 253 D7
Hady Derbys 186 G5
Hadzor Worcs 117 E8
Haffenden Quarter Kent 53 E11
Hafod Swansea 57 C7
Hafod-Dinbych Conwy 164 E5
Hafod Grove Pembs 92 C2
Hafod-lom Conwy 180 G5
Hafod-y-Green Denb 181 G8
Hafodiwan Ceredig 111 G7
Hafodyrynys Bl Gwent 78 F2
Hag Fold Gtr Man 195 G7
Haggate Gtr Man 196 F2
Haggate Lancs 204 F3
Haggbeck Cumb 239 C11
Haggersta Shetland 313 J5
Haggerston London 67 C10
Haggerston Northumb 273 G10
Haggington Hill Devon 40 D5
Haggrister Shetland 312 F5
Haggs Falk 278 F5
Haghill Glasgow 268 B2
Hagley Hereford 97 C11
Hagley Worcs 133 G8
Hagloe Glos 79 D11
Hagmore Green Suff 107 D9
Hagnaby Lincs 174 C4
Hagnaby Lincs 191 F7
Hagnaby Lock Lincs 174 D4
Hague Bar Derbys 185 D7
Hagworthingham Lincs 174 B4
Haigh Gtr Man 194 F6
Haigh S Yorks 197 E9
Haigh Moor W Yorks 197 C9
Haighton Green Lancs 203 G7
Haighton Top Lancs 203 G7
Hail Weston Cambs 122 E3
Haile Cumb 219 D10
Hailes Glos 99 E10
Hailey Herts 86 C5
Hailey Oxon 64 B6
Hailey Oxon 82 C5
Hailsham E Sus 23 D9
Hailstone Hill Wilts 81 G9
Haimer Highld 310 C5
Haimwood Powys 148 F6
Hainault London 87 G7
Haine Kent 71 F11
Hainford Norf 160 F4

Hains Dorset 30 D3
Hainton Lincs 189 E11
Hainworth W Yorks 205 F7
Hainworth Shaw W Yorks 205 F7
Hairmyres S Lnrk 268 E2
Haisthorpe E Yorks 218 G2
Hakeford Devon 40 F6
Hakin Pembs 72 D5
Halabezack Corn 2 C6
Halam Notts 171 E11
Halamanning Corn 2 C3
Halbeath Fife 280 D2
Halberton Devon 27 E8
Halcon Som 28 B2
Halcro Highld 310 C6
Haldens Herts 86 C2
Hale Cumb 211 D10
Hale Gtr Man 184 D3
Hale Halton 183 E7
Hale Hants 31 D11
Hale Kent 71 F9
Hale Medway 69 F9
Hale Som 30 B3
Hale Sur 49 D10
Hale Bank Halton 183 E7
Hale Barns Gtr Man 184 D3
Hale Coombe N Som 44 B2
Hale End London 86 G5
Hale Green E Sus 23 C9
Hale Mills Corn 4 G5
Hale Nook Lancs 202 E3
Hale Street Kent 53 D7
Halecommon W Sus 34 C4
Hales Norf 143 D7
Hales Staffs 150 C4
Hales Bank Hereford 116 G2
Hales Green Derbys 169 G11
Hales Green Norf 143 D10
Hales Park Worcs 116 B5
Hales Place Kent 54 B6
Hales Street Norf 142 F3
Hales Wood Hereford 98 E2
Halesfield Telford 132 C4
Halesgate Lincs 156 D6
Halesowen W Mid 133 G9
Halesworth Suff 127 B7
Halewood Mers 183 D7
Half Moon Village Devon 14 B3
Halford Shrops 131 G8
Halford Warks 100 B5
Halfpenny Cumb 211 B10
Halfpenny Furze Carms 74 C3
Halfpenny Green Staffs 132 E6
Halfway Carms 75 E8
Halfway Carms 94 E2
Halfway Carms 94 E6
Halfway S Yorks 186 E6
Halfway W Berks 64 F2
Halfway Wilts 45 D11
Halfway Bridge W Sus 34 C6
Halfway House Shrops 148 G6
Halfway Houses Gtr Man 195 F9
Halfway Houses Kent 70 E2
Halfway Street Kent 55 D9
Halgabron Corn 11 D7
Halifax W Yorks 196 B5
Halkburn Borders 271 G9
Halket E Ayrs 267 E8
Halkirk Highld 310 D5
Halkyn = Helygain Flint 182 G2
Halkyn Mountain Flint 182 G2
Hall Bower W Yorks 196 E6
Hall Broom S Yorks 186 D3
Hall Cross Lancs 202 G4
Hall Dunnerdale Cumb 220 F4
Hall End Beds 103 B10
Hall End C Beds 103 D11
Hall End Lincs 174 E6
Hall End S Glos 61 B8
Hall End Warks 134 C5
Hall Flat Worcs 117 C9
Hall Garth York 207 C9
Hall Green Ches E 168 D4
Hall Green Essex 106 D5
Hall Green Lancs 194 C3
Hall Green Lancs 194 F4
Hall Green W Mid 133 E10
Hall Green W Mid 134 G2
Hall Green W Mid 135 G7
Hall Green W Yorks 197 D10
Hall Green Wrex 167 G7
Hall Grove Herts 89 C8
Hall i' th' Wood Gtr Man 195 E8
Hall of Clestrain Orkney 314 F2
Hall of Tankerness Orkney 314 F5
Hall of the Forest Shrops 130 G4
Hall Santon Cumb 220 E2
Hall Waberthwaite Cumb 220 F2
Hallam Fields Derbys 153 B9
Halland E Sus 23 B8
Hallaton Leics 136 D5
Hallatrow Bath 44 B6
Hallbankgate Cumb 240 F3
Halleaths Dumfries 248 G3
Hallen S Glos 60 C5
Hallend Warks 118 D2
Hallew Corn 5 D10
Hallfield Gate Derbys 170 D5
Hallgarth Durham 234 C2
Hallglen Falk 279 F7
Halliburton Borders 261 B11
Halliburton Borders 272 F3
Hallin Highld 298 D2
Halling Medway 69 G8
Hallingbury Street Essex 87 B8
Hallington Lincs 190 D4
Hallington Northumb 241 B11
Halliwell Gtr Man 195 E8
Hallon Shrops 132 D5
Hallonsford Shrops 132 D5
Halloughton Notts 171 E11
Hallow Worcs 116 F6
Hallow Heath Worcs 116 F6
Hallowes Derbys 186 F5
Hallowsgate W Ches 167 B8
Hallrule Borders 262 G3
Halls E Loth 282 G3
Hall's Cross E Sus 23 D11
Halls Green Essex 86 D6
Hall's Green Herts 104 F5
Hall's Green Kent 52 D4
Hallsands Devon 9 G11
Hallsford Bridge Essex 87 E9
Hallspill Devon 25 C7
Hallthwaites Cumb 210 B3
Hallwood Green Glos 98 E3
Hallworthy Corn 11 D9
Hallyards Borders 260 B6
Hallyburton House Perth 286 D6
Hallyne Borders 270 G3
Halmer End Staffs 168 F3
Halmond's Frome Hereford 98 B3
Halmore Glos 79 E11
Halmyre Mains Borders 270 F3
Halnaker W Sus 22 B6
Halsall Lancs 193 E11
Halse Northants 101 C11
Halse Som 27 B10
Halsetown Corn 2 B2
Halsfordwood Devon 14 C3
Halsham E Yorks 201 B9
Halsinger Devon 40 F4
Halstead Essex 106 E6
Halstead Kent 68 G3
Halstead Leics 136 B4
Halstock Dorset 29 F8
Halsway Som 42 F6
Haltcliff Bridge Cumb 230 D3
Halterworth Hants 32 C5
Haltham Lincs 174 C2
Haltoft End Lincs 174 F5
Halton Bucks 84 C5
Halton Halton 183 E8
Halton Lancs 211 G10
Halton Northumb 241 D11
Halton W Yorks 206 G2
Halton Wrex 148 B6
Halton Barton Corn 7 B8
Halton Brook Halton 183 E8
Halton East N Yorks 204 C6
Halton Fenside Lincs 174 C6
Halton Gill N Yorks 213 D7
Halton Green Lancs 211 F10
Halton Holegate Lincs 174 B6
Halton Lea Gate Northumb 240 F5
Halton Moor W Yorks 206 G2
Halton Shields Northumb 242 D2
Halton View Halton 183 D8
Halton West N Yorks 204 C2
Haltwhistle Northumb 240 E6
Halvergate Norf 143 B8
Halvosso Corn 2 C6
Halwell Devon 8 E5
Halwill Devon 12 B4
Halwill Junction Devon 24 G6
Halwin Corn 2 C5
Ham Devon 28 G2
Ham Glos 79 F11
Ham Glos 99 G9
Ham Highld 310 B6
Ham Kent 55 C10
Ham London 67 E7
Ham Plym 7 D9
Ham Shetland 313 K1
Ham Som 27 C11
Ham Som 28 B3
Ham Som 28 E3
Ham Som 45 D7
Ham Wilts 63 G10
Ham Common Dorset 30 B4
Ham Green Bucks 83 B11
Ham Green Hants 48 G2
Ham Green Hereford 98 C4
Ham Green Kent 38 B5
Ham Green Kent 69 F10
Ham Green N Som 60 D4
Ham Green Wilts 61 G11
Ham Green Worcs 117 E10
Ham Hill Kent 69 G8
Ham Moor Sur 66 G5
Ham Street Som 44 G5
Hamar Shetland 312 F5
Hamarhill Orkney 314 C5
Hamars Shetland 313 G6
Hamble-le-Rice Hants 33 F7
Hambleden Bucks 65 B9
Hambledon Hants 33 E10
Hambledon Sur 50 F3
Hambleton Lancs 202 E3
Hambleton N Yorks 205 C7
Hambleton N Yorks 207 G7
Hambleton Moss Side Lancs 202 E3
Hambridge Som 28 C5
Hambrook S Glos 60 D6
Hambrook W Sus 22 B3
Hameringham Lincs 174 B4
Hamerton Cambs 122 B2
Hametoun Shetland 313 K1
Hamilton S Lnrk 268 D3
Hamister Shetland 313 G7
Hamlet Dorset 29 F9
Hammer W Sus 49 G11
Hammer Bottom Hants 49 G11
Hammerfield Herts 85 D8
Hammerpot W Sus 35 F9
Hammersmith Derbys 170 E5
Hammersmith London 67 D8
Hammerwich Staffs 133 B11
Hammerwood E Sus 52 F2
Hammill Kent 55 B9
Hammond Street Herts 86 E4
Hammoon Dorset 30 E4
Hamnavoe Shetland 312 E4
Hamnavoe Shetland 312 F6
Hamnavoe Shetland 312 F6
Hamnavoe Shetland 313 K5
Hamnish Clifford Hereford 115 F10
Hamp Som 43 F10
Hampden Park E Sus 23 E10
Hampen Glos 81 B9
Hamperden End Essex 105 E11
Hamperley Shrops 131 F8
Hampers Green W Sus 35 C7
Hampeth Northumb 252 B5
Hampnett Glos 81 B10
Hampole S Yorks 198 E4
Hampreston Dorset 19 B7
Hampsfield Cumb 211 C8
Hampson Green Lancs 202 C5
Hampstead London 67 B9
Hampstead Garden Suburb London 67 B9
Hampstead Norreys W Berks 64 D4
Hampsthwaite N Yorks 205 B11
Hampton Kent 71 F7
Hampton London 66 F6
Hampton Shrops 132 F4
Hampton Swindon 81 G11
Hampton Worcs 99 C10
Hampton Bank Shrops 149 C9
Hampton Beech Shrops 130 B6
Hampton Bishop Hereford 97 D11
Hampton Fields Glos 80 F5
Hampton Gay Oxon 83 B7
Hampton Green Glos 80 E5
Hampton Green W Ches 167 F8
Hampton Hargate P'boro 138 E3
Hampton Heath W Ches 167 F7
Hampton Hill London 66 E6
Hampton in Arden W Mid 134 G4
Hampton Loade Shrops 132 F5
Hampton Lovett Worcs 117 D7
Hampton Lucy Warks 118 F5
Hampton Magna Warks 118 D5
Hampton on the Hill Warks 118 E5
Hampton Park Hereford 97 D10
Hampton Park Soton 32 D6
Hampton Poyle Oxon 83 B8
Hampton Wick London 67 F7
Hamptons Kent 52 C6
Hamptworth Wilts 32 D2
Hamrow Norf 159 E8
Hamsey E Sus 36 E6
Hamsey Green London 51 B10
Hamshill Glos 80 E3
Hamstall Ridware Staffs 152 F2
Hamstead I o W 20 C4
Hamstead W Mid 133 E10
Hamstead Marshall W Berks 64 F2
Hamsterley Durham 233 E8
Hamsterley Durham 242 F4
Hamstreet Kent 54 G4
Hamworthy Poole 18 C5
Hanbury Staffs 152 D3
Hanbury Worcs 117 E9
Hanbury Woodend Staffs 152 D3
Hanby Lincs 155 C10
Hanchett Village Suff 106 B3
Hanchurch Staffs 168 G4
Hand Green W Ches 167 C8
Handbridge W Ches 166 B6
Handcross W Sus 36 B3
Handforth E Ches 184 E5
Handless Shrops 131 E7
Handley Derbys 170 C5
Handley W Ches 167 D7
Handley Green Essex 87 E11
Handsacre Staffs 151 F11
Handside Herts 86 C2
Handsworth S Yorks 186 D6
Handsworth W Mid 133 E10
Handsworth Wood W Mid 133 E11
Handy Cross Bucks 84 G5
Handy Cross Devon 24 B6
Handy Cross Som 42 G6
Hanford Dorset 30 E4
Hanford Stoke 168 G5
Hangersley Hants 31 F11
Hanging Bank Kent 52 C3
Hanging Heaton W Yorks 197 C9
Hanging Houghton Northants 120 C5
Hanging Langford Wilts 46 F4
Hangingshaw Borders 261 C9
Hangingshaw Dumfries 248 F4
Hangleton Brighton 36 F3
Hangleton W Sus 35 G9
Hangsman Hill S Yorks 199 E7
Hanham S Glos 60 E6
Hanham Green S Glos 60 E6
Hankelow E Ches 167 F11
Hankerton Wilts 81 G7
Hankham E Sus 23 D10
Hanley Stoke 168 F5
Hanley Castle Worcs 98 C6
Hanley Child Worcs 116 E3
Hanley Swan Worcs 98 C6
Hanley William Worcs 116 D3
Hanlith N Yorks 213 G8
Hanmer Wrex 149 B9
Hannaford Devon 25 B10
Hannafore Corn 6 E5
Hannah Lincs 191 F8
Hanningfields Green Suff 125 G7
Hannington Hants 48 B4
Hannington Northants 120 C6
Hannington Swindon 81 G11
Hannington Wick Swindon 81 F11
Hanscombe End C Beds 104 E2
Hansel Devon 8 F6
Hansel Village S Ayrs 257 C9
Hansley Cross Staffs 169 G9
Hanslope M Keynes 102 B6
Hanthorpe Lincs 155 E11
Hanwell London 67 C7
Hanwell Oxon 101 C8
Hanwood Shrops 131 B8
Hanwood Bank Shrops 149 G8
Hanworth Brack 65 F11
Hanworth London 66 E6
Hanworth Norf 160 B3
Happendon S Lnrk 259 C9
Happisburgh Norf 161 C7
Happisburgh Common Norf 161 D7
Hapsford Som 45 D9
Hapsford W Ches 183 G7
Hapton Lancs 203 G11
Hapton Norf 142 D3
Hararden = Penarlëg Flint 166 B4
Harberton Devon 8 D5
Harbertonford Devon 8 D5
Harbledown Kent 54 B6
Harborne W Mid 133 G10
Harborough Magna Warks 119 B9
Harborough Parva Warks 119 B9
Harbottle Northumb 251 C10
Harbour Heights E Sus 36 G6
Harbour Village Pembs 91 D8
Harbourland Kent 53 B9
Harbourneford Devon 8 C4
Harbours Hill Worcs 117 D9
Harbridge Hants 31 E10
Harbridge Green Hants 31 E10
Harburn W Loth 269 C10
Harbury Warks 119 F7
Harby Leics 154 C4
Harby Notts 188 G5
Harcombe Devon 14 E3
Harcombe Devon 15 C9
Harcombe Bottom Devon 16 B2
Harcourt Corn 3 B8
Harcourt Hill Oxon 83 E7
Hardbreck Orkney 314 F4
Hardeicke Glos 80 C4
Harden S Yorks 197 G7
Harden W Mid 133 C10
Harden W Yorks 205 F7
Harden Park E Ches 184 F4
Hardendale Cumb 221 C11
Hardenhuish Wilts 62 E2
Hardgate Aberds 293 C9
Hardgate Dumfries 237 C10
Hardgate N Yorks 214 G5
Hardgate W Dunb 277 G10
Hardham W Sus 35 D8
Hardhorn Lancs 202 F3
Hardingham Norf 141 C10
Hardings Booth Staffs 169 C9
Hardings Wood Staffs 168 E4
Hardingstone Northants 120 F5
Hardington Som 45 C8
Hardington Mandeville Som 29 E8
Hardington Marsh Som 29 F8
Hardington Moor Som 29 E8
Hardiston Perth 279 B11
Hardisworthy Devon 24 C2
Hardley Hants 32 G6
Hardley Street Norf 143 C7
Hardmead M Keynes 103 B8
Hardrow N Yorks 223 G7
Hardstoft Derbys 170 C6
Hardstoft Common Derbys 170 C6
Hardway Hants 33 G10
Hardway Som 45 G8
Hardwick Bucks 84 B4
Hardwick Cambs 122 D3
Hardwick Cambs 123 F7
Hardwick Norf 142 F4
Hardwick Norf 158 F2
Hardwick Northants 121 D7
Hardwick Oxon 82 D5
Hardwick Oxon 101 C8
Hardwick Oxon 101 F11
Hardwick S Yorks 187 D7
Hardwick Shrops 131 E7
Hardwick Stockton 234 G4
Hardwick W Mid 133 D11
Hardwick Green Worcs 98 E6
Hardwick Village Notts 187 F10
Hardwicke Glos 80 C3
Hardwicke Glos 99 F8
Hardwicke Hereford 96 C5
Hardy's Green Essex 107 G8
Hare Som 28 D3
Hare Appletree Lancs 202 B6
Hare Edge Derbys 186 G4
Hare Green Essex 107 G11
Hare Hatch Wokingham 65 D10
Hare Street Essex 86 D6
Hare Street Herts 104 F6
Hare Street Herts 105 F7
Hareby Lincs 174 B4
Harecroft W Yorks 205 F7
Hareden Lancs 203 C8
Harefield London 85 G9
Harefield Soton 33 E7
Harefield Grove London 85 G9
Haregate Staffs 169 D7
Harehill Derbys 152 B3
Harehills W Yorks 206 G2
Harehope Borders 270 G4
Harehope Northumb 264 E3
Harelaw Durham 242 G5
Hareleeshill S Lnrk 268 E5
Hareplain Kent 53 F10
Haresceugh Cumb 231 C8
Harescombe Glos 80 C4
Haresfield Glos 80 C4
Haresfield Swindon 82 G2
Haresfinch Mers 183 B8
Hareshaw N Lnrk 268 C6
Hareshaw Head Northumb 251 F9
Harestanes E Dunb 278 G3
Harestock Hants 48 G3
Harewood W Yorks 206 D2
Harewood End Hereford 97 F10
Harewood Hill W Yorks 204 F6
Harford Carms 94 C2
Harford Devon 8 D2
Harford Devon 40 G6
Hargate Norf 142 E2
Hargate Hill Derbys 185 C8
Hargatewall Derbys 185 F10
Hargrave Northants 121 C10
Hargrave Suff 124 F5
Hargrave W Ches 167 C7
Harker Cumb 239 E9
Harker Marsh Cumb 229 E7
Harkland Shetland 312 E6
Harknett's Gate Essex 86 D6
Harkstead Suff 108 E3
Harlaston Staffs 152 G4
Harlaw Ho Aberds 303 G7
Harlaxton Lincs 155 C7
Harle Syke Lancs 204 F3
Harlech Gwyn 145 C11
Harlequin Notts 154 B3
Harlescott Shrops 149 F10
Harlesden London 67 C8
Harlesthorpe Derbys 187 F7
Harleston Devon 8 F5
Harleston Norf 142 G4
Harleston Suff 125 E10
Harlestone Northants 120 E4
Harley S Yorks 186 B5
Harley Shrops 131 C11
Harley Shute E Sus 38 F3
Harleyholm S Lnrk 259 B10
Harleywood Glos 80 F4
Harling Road Norf 141 F9
Harlington C Beds 103 E10
Harlington London 66 D5
Harlington S Yorks 198 G3
Harlosh Highld 298 E2
Harlow Essex 86 C6
Harlow Carr N Yorks 205 C11
Harlow Green T & W 243 F7
Harlow Hill N Yorks 205 C11
Harlow Hill Northumb 242 D3
Harlthorpe E Yorks 207 F10
Harlton Cambs 123 G7
Harlyn Corn 10 F3
Harman's Corner Kent 69 G11
Harman's Cross Dorset 18 E5
Harmans Water Brack 65 F11
Harmby N Yorks 214 B2
Harmer Green Herts 86 B3
Harmer Hill Shrops 149 E9
Harmondsworth London 66 D5
Harmston Lincs 173 C7
Harnage Shrops 131 C11
Harnham Northumb 242 B3
Harnham Wilts 31 B10
Harnham Wilts 31 B11
Harnhill Glos 81 E9
Harold Hill London 87 G8
Harold Park London 87 G9
Harold Wood London 87 G8
Haroldston West Pembs 72 B5
Haroldswick Shetland 312 B8
Harome N Yorks 216 C2
Harpenden Herts 85 C10
Harpenden Common Herts 85 C10
Harper Green Gtr Man 195 F8
Harperley Durham 242 G5
Harper's Gate Staffs 169 D7
Harper's Green Norf 159 E8
Harpford Devon 15 C7
Harpham E Yorks 217 G11
Harpley Norf 158 D5
Harpley Worcs 116 E3
Harpole Northants 120 E3
Harpsdale Highld 310 D5
Harpsden Oxon 65 C9
Harpsden Bottom Oxon 65 C9
Harpswell Lincs 188 D6
Harpton Powys 114 F4
Harpur Hill Derbys 185 G9
Harpurhey Gtr Man 195 G11
Harraby Cumb 239 G10
Harracott Devon 25 B9
Harrapool Highld 295 C8
Harras Cumb 219 B9
Harraton T & W 243 G7
Harrier Shetland 313 J1
Harrietfield Perth 286 E3
Harrietsham Kent 53 C11
Harringay London 67 B10
Harrington Cumb 228 F5
Harrington Lincs 190 G5
Harrington Northants 136 G5
Harringworth Northants 137 D8
Harris Highld 294 F5
Harriseahead Staffs 168 D5
Harriston Cumb 229 C9
Harrogate N Yorks 206 C2
Harrold Beds 121 F8
Harrop Dale Gtr Man 196 F4
Harrow Highld 310 B6
Harrow London 67 B7
Harrow Green Suff 125 G7
Harrow Hill Glos 79 B10
Harrow on the Hill London 67 B7
Harrow Street Suff 107 D9
Harrow Weald London 85 G11
Harrowbarrow Corn 7 B7
Harrowbeer Devon 7 B10
Harrowby Lincs 155 B8
Harrowden Beds 103 B11
Harrowgate Hill Darl 224 B5
Harrowgate Village Darl 224 B5
Harry Stoke S Glos 60 D6
Harston Cambs 123 G8
Harston Leics 154 C6
Harswell E Yorks 208 E2
Hart Hrtlpl 234 E5
Hart Common Gtr Man 194 F6
Hart Hill Luton 104 G2
Hart Station Hrtlpl 234 D5
Hartbarrow Cumb 221 G8
Hartburn Northumb 252 F3
Hartburn Stockton 225 B8
Hartcliffe Bristol 60 F5
Hartest Suff 124 G6
Hartest Hill Suff 124 G6
Hartfield E Sus 52 F3
Hartfield Highld 299 E7
Hartford Cambs 122 C5
Hartford Som 27 B7
Hartford W Ches 183 G10
Hartford End Essex 87 B11
Hartfordbeach W Ches 183 G10
Hartfordbridge Hants 49 B9
Hartforth N Yorks 224 D3
Hartgrove Dorset 30 D4
Hartham Herts 86 C4
Harthill N Lnrk 269 C8
Harthill S Yorks 187 E7
Harthill W Ches 167 D8
Hartington Derbys 169 C10
Hartland Devon 24 C3
Hartland Quay Devon 24 C2
Hartle Worcs 117 B8
Hartlebury Shrops 132 D4
Hartlebury Worcs 116 C6
Hartlebury Common Worcs 116 C6
Hartlepool Hrtlpl 234 E6
Hartley Cumb 222 D5
Hartley Kent 53 G9
Hartley Kent 68 F6
Hartley Northumb 243 B8
Hartley Plym 7 D9
Hartley Green Kent 68 F6
Hartley Green Staffs 151 D9
Hartley Mauditt Hants 49 F8
Hartley Westpall Hants 49 B7
Hartley Wintney Hants 49 B9
Hartlington N Yorks 213 G10
Hartlip Kent 69 G10
Hartmoor Dorset 30 C3
Hartmount Highld 301 B7
Hartoft End N Yorks 226 G5
Harton N Yorks 216 G4
Harton Shrops 131 F9
Harton T & W 243 E9
Hartpury Glos 98 F5
Hart's Green Suff 125 F7
Hart's Hill W Mid 133 F8
Hartsgreen Shrops 132 G5
Hartshead W Yorks 197 C7
Hartshead Green Gtr Man 196 G3
Hartshead Moor Side W Yorks 197 C7
Hartshead Moor Top W Yorks 197 B7
Hartshead Pike Gtr Man 196 G3
Hartshill Stoke 168 F5
Hartshill Warks 134 E6
Hartshill Green Warks 134 E6
Hartshorne Derbys 152 E6
Hartsop Cumb 221 C8
Hartswell Som 27 B9
Hartwell Northants 120 G5
Hartwell Staffs 151 B8
Hartwith N Yorks 214 G4
Hartwood Lancs 194 D5
Hartwood N Lnrk 268 D6
Hartwoodburn Borders 261 D11
Harvel Kent 68 G6
Harvest Hill W Mid 134 G5
Harvieston Stirl 277 D11
Harvills Hawthorn W Mid 133 E9
Harvington Worcs 99 B11
Harvington Worcs 117 C7
Harvington Cross Worcs 99 B11
Harvington Hill Worcs 99 B10
Harwell Notts 187 C11
Harwell Oxon 64 B3
Harwich Essex 108 E5
Harwood Durham 232 E2
Harwood Gtr Man 195 E8
Harwood Dale N Yorks 227 F9
Harwood Lee Gtr Man 195 E8
Harwood on Teviot Borders 249 B10
Harworth Notts 187 C10
Hasbury W Mid 133 G9
Hascombe Sur 50 E3
Haselbech Northants 120 B4
Haselbury Plucknett Som 29 E7
Haseley Warks 118 D4
Haseley Green Warks 118 D4
Haseley Knob Warks 118 C4
Haselor Warks 118 F2
Hasfield Glos 98 F6
Hasguard Pembs 72 D5
Haskayne Lancs 193 F11
Hasketon Suff 126 G4
Hasland Derbys 170 B5
Haslemere Sur 50 G2
Haslingbourne W Sus 35 C7
Haslingden Lancs 195 C9
Haslingfield Cambs 123 G8
Haslington E Ches 168 D2
Hasluck's Green W Mid 118 B2
Hassall E Ches 168 D3
Hassall Green E Ches 168 D3
Hassell Street Kent 54 D5
Hassendean Borders 262 E2
Hassingham Norf 143 B7
Hassocks W Sus 36 D3
Hassop Derbys 186 G2
Haster Highld 310 D7
Hasthorpe Lincs 175 B7
Hastigrow Highld 310 C6
Hasting Hill T & W 243 G9
Hastingleigh Kent 54 E5
Hastings E Sus 38 F4
Hastings Som 28 D4
Hastingwood Essex 87 D7
Hastoe Herts 84 D6
Haston Shrops 149 E10
Haswell Durham 234 C3
Haswell Moor Durham 234 C3
Haswell Plough Durham 234 C3
Haswellsykes Borders 260 B6
Hatch C Beds 104 B3
Hatch Devon 8 F4
Hatch Hants 49 C7
Hatch Wilts 30 B6
Hatch Beauchamp Som 28 C4
Hatch Bottom Hants 33 E7
Hatch End Beds 121 E11
Hatch End London 85 G10
Hatch Farm Hill W Sus 34 B6
Hatch Green Som 28 D4
Hatch Warren Hants 48 D6
Hatchet Gate Hants 32 G5
Hatchet Green Hants 31 D11
Hatching Green Herts 85 C10
Hatchmere W Ches 183 G9
Hatcliffe NE Lincs 201 G8
Hateley Heath W Mid 133 E10
Hatfield Hereford 115 F11
Hatfield Herts 86 D2
Hatfield S Yorks 199 F7
Hatfield Worcs 117 G7
Hatfield Broad Oak Essex 87 B8
Hatfield Chase S Yorks 199 E8
Hatfield Garden Village Herts 86 D2
Hatfield Heath Essex 87 B8
Hatfield Hyde Herts 86 C2
Hatfield Peverel Essex 88 C3
Hatfield Woodhouse S Yorks 199 F7
Hatford Oxon 82 G4
Hatherden Hants 47 C10
Hatherleigh Devon 25 G8
Hatherley Glos 99 G8
Hathern Leics 153 E9
Hatherop Glos 81 D11
Hathersage Derbys 186 E2
Hathersage Booths Derbys 186 E2
Hathershaw Gtr Man 196 G2
Hatherton E Ches 167 F11
Hatherton Staffs 151 G9
Hatley St George Cambs 122 G5
Hatston Orkney 314 E4
Hatt Corn 7 C7
Hatt Hill Hants 32 B4
Hattersley Gtr Man 185 C7
Hattingley Hants 48 F6
Hatton Aberds 303 F10
Hatton Angus 287 D9
Hatton Derbys 152 D4
Hatton Lincs 189 F11
Hatton London 66 D5
Hatton Moray 301 D11
Hatton Shrops 131 E9
Hatton Warks 118 D4
Hatton Warr 183 E9
Hatton Castle Aberds 303 E7
Hatton Grange Shrops 132 C5
Hatton Heath W Ches 167 C7
Hatton Hill Sur 66 G2
Hatton of Fintray Aberds 293 B10
Hatton Park Northants 121 D7
Hattonburn Aberds 293 C9
Hattoncrook Aberds 303 G8
Hattonknowe Borders 270 F4
Haugh E Ayrs 257 D11
Haugh Gtr Man 196 E2
Haugh Lincs 190 F6
Haugh-head Borders 261 B8
Haugh Head Northumb 264 D2
Haugh of Glass Moray 302 F4
Haugh of Kilnmaichlie Moray 301 F11
Haugh of Urr Dumfries 237 C10
Haugham Lincs 190 E4
Haughland Orkney 314 E5
Haughley Suff 125 E10
Haughley Green Suff 125 E10
Haughley New Street Suff 125 E10
Haughs of Clinterty Aberdeen 293 B10
Haughton E Ches 167 D9
Haughton Notts 187 G11
Haughton Powys 148 F6
Haughton Shrops 132 B4
Haughton Shrops 132 D3
Haughton Shrops 149 D7
Haughton Shrops 149 F11
Haughton Staffs 151 E7
Haughton Castle Northumb 241 C10
Haughton Green Gtr Man 184 C6
Haughton Le Skerne Darl 224 B6
Haughurst Hill W Berks 64 G5
Haulkerton Aberds 293 F9
Haultwick Herts 104 G6
Haunn Argyll 288 E5
Haunn W Isles 297 K3
Haunton Staffs 152 G4
Hauxton Cambs 123 G8
Havannah E Ches 168 C5
Havant Hants 22 B2
Haven Hereford 115 G8
Haven Hereford 97 B11
Haven Bank Lincs 174 E2
Haven Side E Yorks 201 B7
Havenstreet I o W 21 C7
Havercroft W Yorks 197 E11
Haverfordwest = Hwlffordd Pembs 73 B7
Haverhill Suff 106 B3
Haverigg Cumb 210 D3
Havering-atte-Bower London 87 G8
Haveringland Norf 160 E3
Haversham M Keynes 102 C6
Haverthwaite Cumb 210 C6
Haverton Hill Stockton 234 G5
Haviker Street Kent 53 D8
Havyatt Som 44 F4
Havyatt Green N Som 60 G3
Hawarden = Penarläg Flint 166 B4
Hawbridge Worcs 99 B8
Hawbush Green Essex 106 G5
Hawcoat Cumb 210 E4
Hawcross Glos 98 E5
Hawddamor Gwyn 146 F3
Hawen Ceredig 92 B6
Hawes N Yorks 213 B7
Hawes' Green Norf 142 D4
Hawes Side Blkpool 202 G2
Hawford Worcs 116 E6
Hawgreen Shrops 150 D2
Hawick Borders 262 F2
Hawk Green Gtr Man 185 D7
Hawk Hill Cumb 228 F6
Hawkchurch Devon 28 G4
Hawkcombe Som 41 D11
Hawkedon Suff 124 G5
Hawkenbury Kent 52 F5
Hawkenbury Kent 53 E10
Hawkeridge Wilts 45 C11
Hawkerland Devon 15 D7
Hawkersland Cross Hereford 97 B10
Hawkes End W Mid 134 G6
Hawkesbury S Glos 61 B9
Hawkesbury Warks 135 G7
Hawkesbury Upton S Glos 61 B9
Hawkesley W Mid 117 B10
Hawkhill Northumb 264 G6
Hawkhope Northumb 250 F6
Hawkhurst Kent 53 G9
Hawkhurst Common E Sus 23 B8
Hawkinge Kent 55 F8
Hawkin's Hill Essex 106 E3
Hawkley Gtr Man 194 G5
Hawkley Hants 34 B2
Hawkridge Som 41 G11
Hawks Green Staffs 151 G9
Hawks Hill Bucks 66 B2
Hawk's Hill Sur 51 B7
Hawks Stones W Yorks 196 B2
Hawksdale Cumb 230 B3
Hawkshaw Blkburn 195 D9
Hawkshead Cumb 221 F7
Hawkshead Hill Cumb 220 F6
Hawksland S Lnrk 259 B8
Hawkspur Green Essex 106 E3
Hawkswick N Yorks 213 E9
Hawksworth Notts 172 G3
Hawksworth W Yorks 205 E9
Hawksworth W Yorks 205 F11
Hawkwell Essex 88 G4
Hawley Hants 49 B11
Hawley Kent 68 E4
Hawley Bottom Devon 28 G2
Hawley Lane Hants 49 B11
Hawling Glos 99 G11
Hawn Orkney 314 D4
Hawnby N Yorks 215 B10
Hawne W Mid 133 G9
Haworth W Yorks 204 F6
Haws Bank Cumb 220 F6
Hawstead Suff 125 F7
Hawstead Green Suff 125 F7
Hawthorn Durham 234 B4
Hawthorn Hants 49 G7
Hawthorn Rhondda 58 B6
Hawthorn Wilts 61 F11
Hawthorn Corner Kent 71 F8
Hawthorn Hill Brack 65 E11
Hawthorn Hill Lincs 174 D2
Hawthorns Staffs 168 F4
Hawthorpe Lincs 155 D10
Hawton Notts 172 E3
Haxby York 207 B8
Haxey N Lincs 188 B3
Haxey N Lincs 199 G9
Haxey Carr N Lincs 199 G9
Haxted Sur 52 D2
Haxton Wilts 46 D6
Hay Corn 10 G5
Hay Field S Yorks 187 B10
Hay Green Essex 87 E10
Hay Green Herts 104 D6
Hay Green Norf 157 F10
Hay Mills W Mid 134 G2
Hay-on-Wye Powys 96 C4
Hay Street Herts 105 F7
Haybridge Shrops 116 C2
Haybridge Som 44 D4
Haybridge Telford 150 G3
Hayden Glos 99 G8
Haydock Mers 183 B9
Haydon Bath 45 C7
Haydon Dorset 29 D11
Haydon Som 28 C3
Haydon Som 44 D5
Haydon Swindon 62 B6
Haydon Bridge Northumb 241 E8
Haydon Wick Swindon 62 B6
Haye Corn 7 B7
Haye Fm Corn 6 B6
Hayes London 66 C6
Hayes London 68 F2
Hayes Staffs 169 C9
Hayes End London 66 C5
Hayes Knoll Wilts 81 G10
Hayes Town London 66 C6
Hayfield Derbys 185 D8
Hayfield Fife 280 C5
Hayfield Green S Yorks 187 B11
Haygate Telford 150 G2
Haygrass Som 28 C2
Hayhill E Ayrs 257 F11
Hayhillock Angus 287 C9
Haylands I o W 21 C7
Hayle Corn 2 B3
Hayley Green W Mid 133 G8
Haymoor End Som 28 B4
Haymoor Green E Ches 167 E11
Hayne Devon 26 F5
Haynes C Beds 103 C11
Haynes Church End C Beds 103 C11
Haynes West End C Beds 103 C11
Hayscastle Pembs 91 F7
Hayscastle Cross Pembs 91 G8
Haysford Pembs 91 G8
Hayshead Angus 287 C10
Hayston E Dunb 278 G2
Haystoun Borders 261 B7
Haythorne Dorset 31 F8
Hayton Aberdeen 293 C11
Hayton Cumb 229 C8
Hayton Cumb 240 F2
Hayton E Yorks 208 D2
Hayton Notts 188 E2
Hayton's Bent Shrops 131 G10
Haytor Vale Devon 13 F11
Haytown Devon 24 E5
Haywards Heath W Sus 36 C4
Haywood S Lnrk 269 E9
Haywood S Yorks 198 E5
Haywood Oaks Notts 171 D10
Hazard's Green E Sus 23 C11
Hazel End Essex 105 G9
Hazel Grove Gtr Man 184 D6
Hazel Street Kent 53 B11
Hazel Street Kent 53 F7
Hazel Stub Suff 106 C3
Hazelbank S Lnrk 268 F6
Hazelbeach Pembs 72 E6
Hazelbury Bryan Dorset 30 F2
Hazeleigh Essex 88 E4
Hazeley Hants 49 B8
Hazeley Bottom Hants 49 B9
Hazeley Heath Hants 49 B9
Hazeley Lea Hants 49 B8
Hazelgrove Notts 171 F8
Hazelhurst Gtr Man 195 D9
Hazelhurst Gtr Man 195 G9
Hazelhurst Gtr Man 196 G3
Hazelslack Cumb 211 D9
Hazelslade Staffs 151 G10
Hazelton Glos 81 B9
Hazelton Walls Fife 287 E7
Hazelwood Derbys 170 F4
Hazelwood Devon 8 E4
Hazelwood London 68 G2
Hazlehead S Yorks 197 G7
Hazlemere Bucks 84 F5
Hazler Shrops 131 E9
Hazlerigg T & W 242 C6
Hazles Staffs 169 F8
Hazlescross Staffs 169 F8
Hazleton Glos 81 B9
Hazlewood N Yorks 205 C7
Hazon Northumb 252 C5
Heacham Norf 158 B3
Head of Muir Falk 278 E6
Headbourne Worthy Hants 48 G3
Headbrook Hereford 114 F6
Headcorn Kent 53 E10
Headingley W Yorks 205 F11
Headington Oxon 83 D8
Headington Hill Oxon 83 D8
Headlam Durham 224 B3
Headless Cross Cumb 211 D7
Headless Cross Worcs 117 D10
Headley Hants 49 F10
Headley Hants 64 G4
Headley Sur 51 C8
Headley Down Hants 49 F10
Headley Heath Worcs 117 B11
Headley Park Bristol 60 F5
Headon Devon 24 G5
Headon Notts 188 F2
Heads S Lnrk 268 F4
Heads Nook Cumb 239 F11
Headshaw Borders 261 E11
Headstone London 66 B6
Headwell Fife 279 D11
Heady Hill Gtr Man 195 E10
Heage Derbys 170 E5
Healaugh N Yorks 206 D5
Healaugh N Yorks 223 F10
Heald Green Gtr Man 184 D4
Healds Green Gtr Man 195 F11
Heale Devon 40 D6
Heale Som 28 B5
Heale Som 28 D5
Heale Som 45 E7
Healey Gtr Man 195 D11
Healey N Yorks 214 C3
Healey Northumb 242 F2
Healey W Yorks 197 C8
Healey W Yorks 197 D9
Healey Cote Northumb 252 C4
Healey Hall Northumb 242 F2
Healeyfield Durham 233 B7
Healing NE Lincs 201 E8
Heamoor Corn 1 C5
Heaning Cumb 221 F8
Heanish Argyll 288 E2
Heanor Derbys 170 F6
Heanor Gate Derbys 170 F6
Heanton Punchardon Devon 40 F4
Heap Bridge Gtr Man 195 E10
Heapham Lincs 188 D5
Hearn Hants 49 F10
Hearnden Green Kent 53 D10
Hearthstane Borders 260 D4
Hearthstone Derbys 170 D4
Hearts Delight Kent 69 G11
Heasley Mill Devon 41 G8
Heast Highld 295 D8
Heath Cardiff 59 D7
Heath Derbys 170 B6
Heath Halton 183 E8
Heath and Reach C Beds 103 F8
Heath Charnock Lancs 194 E5
Heath Common W Sus 35 E10
Heath Common W Yorks 197 D11
Heath Cross Devon 13 B10
Heath Cross Devon 14 C2
Heath End Bucks 84 F5
Heath End Derbys 153 E7
Heath End Hants 64 G2
Heath End Hants 64 G5
Heath End S Glos 61 B7
Heath End Sur 49 D10
Heath End W Mid 133 C10
Heath End W Sus 35 D7
Heath End Warks 118 E4
Heath Green Hants 48 F6
Heath Green Worcs 117 C11
Heath Hayes Staffs 151 G10
Heath Hill Shrops 150 G5
Heath House Som 44 D2
Heath Lanes Telford 150 E2
Heath Park London 68 B4
Heath Side Kent 68 E4
Heath Town W Mid 133 D8
Heathcot Aberds 293 C10
Heathcote Derbys 169 C10
Heathcote Shrops 150 D3
Heathcote Warks 118 E6
Heather Leics 153 G7
Heather Row Hants 49 C8
Heathercombe Devon 13 E10
Heatherfield Highld 298 E4
Heatherside Sur 50 B2
Heatherwood Park Highld 311 K2
Heatherybanks Aberds 303 E7
Heathfield Cambs 105 B9
Heathfield Devon 14 F2
Heathfield E Sus 37 C9
Heathfield Glos 80 F2
Heathfield Hants 33 F9
Heathfield Lincs 189 C10
Heathfield N Yorks 214 F2
Heathfield S Ayrs 257 E9
Heathfield Som 27 B11
Heathfield Som 43 G7
Heathfield Village Oxon 83 B8
Heathhall Dumfries 237 B11
Heathlands Wokingham 65 F10
Heathrow Airport London 66 D5
Heathstock Devon 28 G2
Heathton Shrops 132 E6
Heathtop Derbys 152 C4
Heathwaite Cumb 221 F8
Heathwaite N Yorks 225 E9
Heatley Staffs 151 D11
Heatley Warr 184 D2
Heaton Gtr Man 195 F7
Heaton Lancs 211 G8
Heaton Staffs 169 C7
Heaton T & W 243 D7
Heaton W Yorks 205 F8
Heaton Chapel Gtr Man 184 C5

Heaton Mersey Gtr Man 184 C5
Heaton Moor Gtr Man 184 C5
Heaton Norris Gtr Man 184 C5
Heaton Royds W Yorks 205 F8
Heaton Shay W Yorks 205 F8
Heaton's Bridge Lancs 194 E2
Heaven's Door Som 29 C10
Heaverham Kent 52 B5
Heaviley Gtr Man 184 D6
Heavitree Devon 14 C4
Hebburn T & W 243 E8
Hebburn Colliery T & W 243 D8
Hebburn New Town T & W 243 E8
Hebden N Yorks 213 G10
Hebden Bridge W Yorks 196 B3
Hebden Green W Ches 167 B10
Hebing End Herts 104 G6
Hebron Anglesey 179 E7
Hebron Carms 92 F3
Hebron Northumb 252 F5
Heck Dumfries 248 G3
Heckdyke N Lincs 188 B3
Heckfield Hants 65 G8
Heckfield Green Suff 126 B3
Heckfordbridge Essex 107 G8
Heckingham Norf 143 D7
Heckington Lincs 173 G10
Heckmondwike W Yorks 197 C8
Heddington Wilts 62 F3
Heddington Wick Wilts 62 F3
Heddle Orkney 314 E3
Heddon Devon 25 B11
Heddon-on-the-Wall Northumb 242 D4
Hedenham Norf 142 E6
Hedge End Dorset 30 F4
Hedge End Hants 33 E7
Hedgehog Bridge Lincs 174 F3
Hedgerley Bucks 66 B3
Hedgerley Green Bucks 66 B3
Hedgerley Hill Bucks 66 B3
Hedging Som 28 B4
Hedley Hill Durham 233 C9
Hedley on the Hill Northumb 242 F3
Hednesford Staffs 151 G9
Hedon E Yorks 201 B7
Hedsor Bucks 66 B2
Hedworth T & W 243 E8
Heelands M Keynes 102 D6
Heeley S Yorks 186 E5
Hegdon Hill Hereford 115 G11
Heggerscales Cumb 222 C6
Heggle Lane Cumb 230 D3
Heglibister Shetland 313 H5
Heighington Darl 233 G11
Heighington Lincs 173 B8
Heighley Staffs 168 F3
Height End Lancs 195 C9
Heightington Worcs 116 C5
Heights Gtr Man 196 F3
Heights of Brae Highld 300 C5
Heights of Kinlochewe Highld 299 C10
Heilam Highld 308 C4
Heiton Borders 262 C6
Helbeck Cumb 222 B5
Hele Devon 12 C2
Hele Devon 13 G10
Hele Devon 27 G7
Hele Devon 40 D4
Hele Som 27 C11
Hele Torbay 9 B8
Helebridge Corn 24 G2
Helensburgh Argyll 276 E5
Helford Corn 3 D7
Helford Passage Corn 3 D7
Helham Green Herts 86 B5
Helhoughton Norf 159 D7
Helions Bumpstead Essex 106 C3
Hell Corner W Berks 63 G11
Hellaby S Yorks 187 C8
Helland Corn 11 G7
Helland Som 28 C4
Hellandbridge Corn 11 G7
Hellesdon Norf 160 G4
Hellesveor Corn 2 A2
Hellidon Northants 119 F10
Hellifield N Yorks 204 B3
Hellifield Green N Yorks 204 B3
Hellingly E Sus 23 C9
Hellington Norf 142 C6
Hellister Shetland 313 J5
Hellman's Cross Essex 87 B9
Helm N Yorks 223 G8
Helm Northumb 252 D5
Helmburn Borders 261 E9
Helmdon Northants 101 C11
Helme W Yorks 196 E5
Helmingham Suff 126 F3
Helmington Row Durham 233 D9
Helmsdale Highld 311 H4
Helmshore Lancs 195 C9
Helmside Cumb 212 B3
Helmsley N Yorks 216 C2
Helperby N Yorks 215 F8
Helperthorpe N Yorks 217 E9
Helpringham Lincs 173 G10
Helpston P'boro 138 B2
Helsby W Ches 183 F7
Helscott Corn 24 G2
Helsey Lincs 191 G8
Helston Corn 2 D5
Helston Water Corn 4 G5
Helstone Corn 11 E7
Helton Cumb 230 G6
Helwith Bridge N Yorks 212 F6
Helygain = Halkyn Flint 182 G2
Hem Heath Stoke 168 G5
Hemblington Norf 160 G6
Hemblington Corner Norf 160 G6
Hembridge Som 44 F5
Hemel Hempstead Herts 85 D9
Hemerdon Devon 7 D11
Hemford Shrops 130 C6
Hemingbrough N Yorks 207 G9
Hemingby Lincs 190 G2
Hemingfield S Yorks 197 G11
Hemingford Abbots Cambs 122 C5
Hemingford Grey Cambs 122 C5
Hemingstone Suff 126 G3
Hemington Leics 153 D9
Hemington Northants 137 F11
Hemington Som 45 C8
Hemley Suff 108 C5
Hemlington M'bro 225 C10
Hemp Green Suff 127 D7
Hempholme E Yorks 209 C7
Hempnall Norf 142 E4
Hempnall Green Norf 142 E4
Hempriggs House Highld 310 E7
Hemp's Green Essex 107 F8
Hempshill Vale Notts 171 G8
Hempstead Essex 106 D2
Hempstead Medway 69 G9
Hempstead Norf 160 B2
Hempstead Norf 161 D8
Hempsted Glos 80 B4
Hempton Norf 159 D8
Hempton Oxon 101 E8
Hempton Wainhill Oxon 84 E3
Hemsby Norf 161 F9
Hemsted Kent 54 E6
Hemswell Lincs 188 C6
Hemswell Cliff Lincs 188 D6
Hemsworth Dorset 31 F7
Hemsworth S Yorks 186 E5
Hemsworth W Yorks 198 E2
Hemyock Devon 27 E10
Hen Bentref Llandegfan Anglesey 179 G9
Hên-efail Denb 165 C9
Hen-feddau fawr Pembs 92 E4
Henaford Devon 24 D2
Henbrook Worcs 117 D8
Henbury Bristol 60 D5
Henbury Dorset 18 B5
Henbury E Ches 184 G5
Hendomen Powys 130 D4
Hendon London 67 B8
Hendon T & W 243 F10
Hendra Corn 2 B6
Hendra Corn 2 C5
Hendra Corn 2 D3
Hendra Corn 2 F6
Hendra Corn 5 C9
Hendra Corn 5 D9
Hendra Corn 11 E7
Hendra Croft Corn 4 D5
Hendrabridge Corn 6 B5
Hendraburnick Corn 11 D8
Hendre Flint 165 B11
Hendre Gwyn 110 B2
Hendre Powys 129 D9
Hendre-ddu Conwy 164 B5
Hendredenny Park Caerph 58 B6
Hendreforgan Rhondda 58 B3
Hendrerwydd Denb 165 C10
Hendrewen Swansea 75 D10
Hendy Carms 75 E9
Hendy-Gwyn Carms 74 B2
Hendy Gwyn = Whitland Carms 73 B11
Heneglwys Anglesey 178 F6
Henfield S Glos 61 D7
Henfield W Sus 36 D2
Henford Devon 12 C3
Henfords Marsh Wilts 45 E11
Henghurst Kent 54 F3
Hengoed Caerph 77 F10
Hengoed Denb 165 D9
Hengoed Powys 114 G4
Hengoed Shrops 148 C5
Hengrave Norf 160 F2
Hengrave Suff 124 D6
Hengrove Bristol 60 F6
Hengrove Park Bristol 60 F5
Henham Essex 105 F10
Heniarth Powys 130 B2
Henlade Som 28 C3
Henleaze Bristol 60 D5
Henley Dorset 29 G11
Henley Glos 80 B6
Henley Shrops 115 B10
Henley Shrops 131 F9
Henley Som 44 G2
Henley Suff 126 G3
Henley W Sus 34 B5
Henley Wilts 47 B10
Henley Wilts 61 F10
Henley Common W Sus 34 B5
Henley Green W Mid 135 G7
Henley-in-Arden Warks 118 D3
Henley-on-Thames Oxon 65 C9
Henley Street Kent 69 F7
Henley's Down E Sus 38 E2
Henllan Ceredig 93 C7
Henllan Denb 165 B8
Henllan Amgoed Carms 92 G3
Henlle Shrops 148 C6
Henllys Torf 78 G3
Henllys Vale Torf 78 G3
Henlow C Beds 104 D3
Hennock Devon 14 E2
Henny Street Essex 107 D7
Henryd Conwy 180 G3
Henry's Moat Pembs 91 F10
Hensall N Yorks 198 C5
Henshaw Northumb 241 E7
Henshaw W Yorks 205 E10
Hensingham Cumb 219 B9
Hensington Oxon 83 B7
Henstead Suff 143 F9
Hensting Hants 33 C7
Henstridge Devon 40 E5
Henstridge Som 30 D2
Henstridge Ash Som 30 C2
Henstridge Bowden Som 29 C11
Henstridge Marsh Som 30 C2
Henton Oxon 84 E3
Henton Som 44 D3
Henwood Corn 11 G11
Henwood Oxon 83 E7
Henwood Green Kent 52 E6
Heogan Shetland 313 J6
Heol-ddu Carms 75 E7
Heol-ddu Swansea 56 B6
Heol-laethog Bridgend 58 C2
Heol-las Bridgend 58 C2
Heol-las Swansea 57 B7
Heol Senni Powys 95 G8
Heol-y-gaer Powys 96 D3
Heol-y-mynydd V Glam 57 G11
Heolgerrig M Tydf 77 D8
Hepburn Northumb 264 E3
Hepple Northumb 251 C11
Hepscott Northumb 252 G6
Hepthorne Lane Derbys 170 C6
Heptonstall W Yorks 196 B3
Hepworth Suff 125 C9
Hepworth W Yorks 197 F7
Herbrandston Pembs 72 D5
Hereford Hereford 97 C10
Heribusta Highld 298 B4
Heriot Borders 271 E7
Hermiston Edin 280 G3
Hermit Hill S Yorks 197 G10
Hermit Hole W Yorks 205 F7
Hermitage Borders 250 D2
Hermitage Dorset 29 F10
Hermitage W Berks 64 E4
Hermitage W Sus 22 B3
Hermitage Green Mers 183 C10
Hermon Anglesey 162 B5
Hermon Carms 93 E7
Hermon Carms 94 F3
Hermon Pembs 92 E4
Herne Kent 71 F7
Herne Bay Kent 71 F7
Herne Common Kent 71 F7
Herne Hill London 67 E10
Herne Pound Kent 53 C7
Herner Devon 25 B9
Hernhill Kent 70 G5
Herniss Corn 2 C6
Herodsfoot Corn 6 C4
Heron Cross Stoke 168 G5
Heronden Kent 55 C9
Herongate Essex 87 G10
Heron's Ghyll E Sus 37 B7
Herons Green Bath 44 B5
Heronsford S Ayrs 244 G4
Heronsgate Herts 85 G8
Heronston Bridgend 58 D2
Herra Shetland 312 D8
Herriard Hants 49 D7
Herringfleet Suff 143 D9
Herring's Green Beds 103 C11
Herringswell Suff 124 C4
Herringthorpe S Yorks 186 C6
Hersden Kent 71 G8
Hersham Corn 24 F3
Hersham Sur 66 G6
Herstmonceux E Sus 23 C10
Herston Dorset 18 F6
Herston Orkney 314 G4
Hertford Herts 86 C4
Hertford Heath Herts 86 C4
Hertingfordbury Herts 86 C4
Hesket Newmarket Cumb 230 D2
Hesketh Bank Lancs 194 C2
Hesketh Lane Lancs 203 E8
Hesketh Moss Lancs 194 C2
Heskin Green Lancs 194 D4
Hesleden Durham 234 D4
Hesleyside Northumb 251 G8
Heslington York 207 C8
Hessay York 206 C6
Hessenford Corn 6 D6
Hessett Suff 125 E8
Hessle E Yorks 200 B4
Hessle W Yorks 198 D2
Hest Bank Lancs 211 F9
Hester's Way Glos 99 G8
Hestinsetter Shetland 313 J4
Heston London 66 D6
Hestwall Orkney 314 E2
Heswall Mers 182 E3
Hethe Oxon 101 F11
Hethel Norf 142 C3
Hethelpit Cross Glos 98 F5
Hethersett Norf 142 C3
Hethersgill Cumb 239 D11
Hetherside Cumb 239 D10
Hetherson Green W Ches 167 F8
Hethpool Northumb 263 D9
Hett Durham 233 D11
Hetton N Yorks 204 B5
Hetton Downs T & W 234 B3
Hetton-le-Hill T & W 234 B3
Hetton-le-Hole T & W 234 B3
Hetton Steads Northumb 264 B2
Heugh Northumb 242 C3
Heugh-head Aberds 292 B5
Heveningham Suff 126 C6
Hever Kent 52 E3
Heversham Cumb 211 C9
Hevingham Norf 160 E3
Hew Green N Yorks 205 B10
Hewas Water Corn 5 F9
Hewelsfield Glos 79 E9
Hewelsfield Common Glos 79 E8
Hewer Hill Cumb 230 D3
Hewish N Som 60 G2
Hewish Som 28 F6
Hewood Dorset 28 G5
Heworth T & W 243 E7
Heworth York 207 C8
Hexham Northumb 241 E10
Hextable Kent 68 E4
Hexthorpe S Yorks 198 G5
Hexton Herts 104 E2
Hexworthy Devon 13 G9
Hey Lancs 204 E3
Hey Green W Yorks 196 E4
Hey Houses Lancs 193 B10
Heybridge Essex 88 D5
Heybridge Essex 87 F10
Heybridge Basin Essex 88 D5
Heybrook Bay Devon 7 F10
Heydon Cambs 105 C8
Heydon Norf 160 D2
Heydour Lincs 155 B10
Heyheads Gtr Man 196 G3
Heylipol Argyll 288 E1
Heylor Shetland 312 E4
Heyope Powys 114 C4
Heyrod Gtr Man 185 B7
Heysham Lancs 211 G8
Heyshaw N Yorks 214 G3
Heyshott W Sus 34 D5
Heyshott Green W Sus 34 D5
Heyside Gtr Man 196 F2
Heytesbury Wilts 46 E2
Heythrop Oxon 101 F7
Heywood Gtr Man 195 E11
Heywood Wilts 45 C11
Hibaldstow N Lincs 200 G3
Hibb's Green Suff 125 G7
Hickford Hill Essex 106 C5
Hickleton S Yorks 198 F3
Hickling Norf 161 E8
Hickling Notts 154 D3
Hickling Green Norf 161 E8
Hickling Heath Norf 161 E8
Hickling Pastures Notts 154 D3
Hickmans Green Kent 54 B5
Hicks Forstal Kent 71 G7
Hicks Gate Bath 60 F6
Hick's Mill Corn 4 G5
Hickstead W Sus 36 C3
Hidcote Bartrim Glos 100 C3
Hidcote Boyce Glos 100 C3
Hifnal Shrops 132 D4
Higginshaw Gtr Man 196 F2
High Ackworth W Yorks 198 D2
High Angerton Northumb 252 F3
High Bankhill Cumb 231 C7
High Banton N Lnrk 278 E4
High Barn Lincs 174 C5
High Barnes T & W 243 F9
High Barnet London 86 F2
High Beach Essex 86 F6
High Bentham N Yorks 212 F3
High Bickington Devon 25 C10
High Biggins Cumb 212 D2
High Birkwith N Yorks 212 D5
High Birstwith N Yorks 205 B10
High Blantyre S Lnrk 268 D3
High Bonnybridge Falk 278 F6
High Bradfield S Yorks 186 C3
High Bradley N Yorks 204 D6
High Bray Devon 41 G7
High Brooms Kent 52 E5
High Brotheridge Glos 80 C5
High Bullen Devon 25 C8
High Buston Northumb 252 B6
High Callerton Northumb 242 C5
High Cark Cumb 211 C7
High Casterton Cumb 212 D2
High Catton E Yorks 207 C10
High Church Northumb 252 F5
High Cogges Oxon 82 D5
High Common Norf 141 B9
High Coniscliffe Darl 224 B4
High Crompton Gtr Man 196 F2
High Cross Cambs 123 F8
High Cross Corn 2 D6
High Cross E Sus 37 B9
High Cross Hants 34 B2
High Cross Herts 85 F10
High Cross Herts 86 B5
High Cross Newport 59 B9
High Cross W Sus 36 D2
High Cross Warks 118 D3
High Crosshill S Lnrk 268 C2
High Cunsey Cumb 221 G7
High Dubmire T & W 234 B2
High Dyke Durham 232 F5
High Easter Essex 87 C10
High Eggborough N Yorks 198 C5
High Eldrig Dumfries 236 C4
High Ellington N Yorks 214 C3
High Ercall Telford 149 F11
High Etherley Durham 233 F9
High Ferry Lincs 174 F5
High Field Lancs 203 C10
High Flatts W Yorks 197 F8
High Forge Durham 242 G6
High Friarside Durham 242 F5
High Gallowhill E Dunb 278 G2
High Garrett Essex 106 F5
High Grange Durham 233 E9
High Grantley N Yorks 214 F4
High Green Cumb 221 E8
High Green Norf 141 B8
High Green Norf 142 B2
High Green Norf 159 G8
High Green S Yorks 186 B4
High Green Shrops 132 G4
High Green Suff 125 E7
High Green W Yorks 197 E7
High Green Worcs 99 B7
High Halden Kent 53 F11
High Halstow Medway 69 D9
High Ham Som 44 G2
High Handenhold Durham 242 G6
High Harrington Cumb 228 F6
High Harrogate N Yorks 206 B2
High Haswell Durham 234 C3
High Hatton Shrops 150 E2
High Hauxley Northumb 253 C7
High Hawsker N Yorks 227 D8
High Heath Shrops 150 D3
High Heath W Mid 133 C10
High Hesket Cumb 230 C5
High Hesleden Durham 234 D5
High Hill Cumb 229 G11
High Houses Essex 87 C11
High Hoyland S Yorks 197 E9
High Hunsley E Yorks 208 F4
High Hurstwood E Sus 37 B7
High Hutton N Yorks 216 F5
High Ireby Cumb 229 D10
High Kelling Norf 177 E10
High Kilburn N Yorks 215 D10
High Lands Durham 233 F8
High Lane Gtr Man 185 D7
High Lane Worcs 116 E3
High Lanes Corn 2 B3
High Laver Essex 87 D8
High Legh E Ches 184 E2
High Leven Stockton 225 C8
High Littleton Bath 44 B6
High Longthwaite Cumb 229 B11
High Lorton Cumb 229 F9
High Marishes N Yorks 216 D6
High Marnham Notts 188 G4
High Melton S Yorks 198 G4
High Mickley Northumb 242 E3
High Mindork Dumfries 236 D5
High Moor Derbys 187 E7
High Moor Lancs 194 E4
High Moorsley T & W 234 B2
High Nash Glos 79 C9
High Newton Cumb 211 C8
High Newton-by-the-Sea Northumb 264 D6
High Nibthwaite Cumb 210 B5
High Oaks Cumb 222 G2
High Offley Staffs 150 D5
High Ongar Essex 87 E9
High Onn Staffs 150 F6
High Onn Wharf Staffs 150 F6
High Park Cumb 221 G10
High Park Mers 193 D11
High Risby N Lincs 200 E2
High Roding Essex 87 B10
High Rougham Suff 125 E8
High Row Cumb 230 D3
High Row Cumb 230 G3
High Salvington W Sus 35 F10
High Scales Cumb 229 B9
High Sellafield Cumb 219 E10
High Shaw N Yorks 223 G7
High Shields T & W 243 D9
High Shincliffe Durham 233 C11
High Side Cumb 229 E10
High Southwick T & W 243 F9
High Spen T & W 242 F4
High Stakesby N Yorks 227 C7
High Stoop Durham 233 C8
High Street Corn 5 E9
High Street Kent 53 G8
High Street Pembs 73 B11
High Street Suff 107 B7
High Street Suff 127 C8
High Street Suff 127 F8
High Street Suff 143 G7
High Street Green Suff 125 F10
High Sunderland Borders 261 C11
High Throston Hrtlpl 234 E5
High Tirfergus Argyll 255 F7
High Town Luton 103 G11
High Town Shrops 132 E4
High Town Staffs 151 G9
High Toynton Lincs 174 B3
High Trewhitt Northumb 252 B2
High Urpeth Durham 242 G6
High Valleyfield Fife 279 D10
High Walton Cumb 219 C9
High Warden Northumb 241 D10
High Water Head Cumb 220 F6
High Westwood Durham 242 F4
High Whinnow Cumb 239 G8
High Woolaston Glos 79 F9
High Worsall N Yorks 225 D7
High Wray Cumb 221 F7
High Wych Herts 87 C7
High Wycombe Bucks 84 G5
Higham Derbys 170 D5
Higham Fife 286 F6
Higham Kent 69 E8
Higham Lancs 204 F2
Higham S Yorks 197 F10
Higham Suff 107 D10
Higham Suff 124 E4
Higham Common S Yorks 197 F10
Higham Dykes Northumb 242 B4
Higham Ferrers Northants 121 D9
Higham Gobion C Beds 104 E2
Higham Hill London 86 G5
Higham on the Hill Leics 135 D7
Higham Wood Kent 52 D5
Highampton Devon 25 G7
Highams Park London 86 G5
Highbridge Cumb 230 C3
Highbridge Hants 33 C7
Highbridge Highld 290 E3
Highbridge Som 43 D10
Highbridge W Mid 133 C10
Highbrook W Sus 51 G11
Highburton W Yorks 197 E7
Highbury London 67 B10
Highbury Ptsmth 33 G11
Highbury Som 45 D7
Highbury Vale Nottingham 171 G8
Highclere Hants 64 G2
Highcliffe Derbys 186 F2
Highcliffe Dorset 19 C10
Higher Alham Som 45 E7
Higher Ansty Dorset 30 G3
Higher Ashton Devon 14 E3
Higher Audley Blkburn 195 B7
Higher Bal Corn 4 E4
Higher Ballam Lancs 202 G3
Higher Bartle Lancs 202 G6
Higher Bebington Mers 182 D4
Higher Berry End C Beds 103 E9
Higher Blackley Gtr Man 195 G10
Higher Boarshaw Gtr Man 195 F11
Higher Bockhampton Dorset 17 C10
Higher Bojewyan Corn 1 C3
Higher Boscaswell Corn 1 C3
Higher Brixham Torbay 9 D8
Higher Broughton Gtr Man 195 G10
Higher Burrow Som 28 C6
Higher Burwardsley W Ches 167 D8
Higher Chalmington Dorset 29 G9
Higher Cheriton Devon 27 G10
Higher Chillington Som 28 E5
Higher Chisworth Derbys 185 C7
Higher Clovelly Devon 24 C4
Higher Condurrow Corn 2 B5
Higher Crackington Corn 11 B9
Higher Cransworth Corn 5 B9
Higher Croft Blkburn 195 B7
Higher Denham Bucks 66 B4
Higher Dinting Derbys 185 C8
Higher Disley E Ches 185 E7
Higher Downs Corn 2 C3
Higher Durston Som 28 B3
Higher End Gtr Man 194 G4
Higher Folds Gtr Man 195 G7
Higher Gabwell Torbay 9 B8
Higher Green Gtr Man 195 G8
Higher Halstock Leigh Dorset 29 F8
Higher Heysham Lancs 211 G8
Higher Hogshead Lancs 195 C11
Higher Holton Som 29 B11
Higher Hurdsfield E Ches 184 G6
Higher Kingcombe Dorset 16 B6
Higher Kinnerton Flint 166 C4
Higher Land Corn 12 G3
Higher Marsh Som 30 C2
Higher Melcombe Dorset 30 G2
Higher Menadew Corn 5 D10
Higher Molland Devon 41 G8
Higher Muddiford Devon 40 F5
Higher Nyland Dorset 30 C2
Higher Penwortham Lancs 194 B4
Higher Pertwood Wilts 45 F11
Higher Porthpean Corn 5 E10
Higher Poynton E Ches 184 E6
Higher Prestacott Devon 12 B3
Higher Rads End C Beds 103 E9
Higher Ridge Shrops 149 C7
Higher Rocombe Barton Devon 9 B8
Higher Row Dorset 31 G8
Higher Runcorn Halton 183 E8
Higher Sandford Dorset 29 C10
Higher Shotton Flint 166 B4
Higher Shurlach W Ches 183 G11
Higher Slade Devon 40 D4
Higher Street Som 42 E6
Higher Tale Devon 27 G9
Higher Tolcarne Corn 5 B7
Higher Totnell Dorset 29 F10
Higher Town Corn 5 C10
Higher Town Scilly 1 F4
Higher Town Som 42 D3
Higher Tremarcoombe Corn 6 B5
Higher Vexford Som 42 F6
Higher Walreddon Devon 12 G5
Higher Walton Lancs 194 B5
Higher Walton Warr 183 D9
Higher Wambrook Som 28 F3
Higher Warcombe Devon 40 D3
Higher Weaver Devon 27 G9
Higher Whatcombe Dorset 30 G4
Higher Wheelton Lancs 194 C6
Higher Whitley W Ches 183 E10
Higher Wincham W Ches 183 F11
Higher Woodsford Dorset 17 D11
Higher Wraxall Dorset 29 G9
Higher Wych W Ches 167 G7
Highercliff Corn 6 D4
Higherford Lancs 204 E3
Highertown Corn 4 G6
Highertown Corn 11 E8
Highfield E Yorks 207 F10
Highfield Glos 79 E10
Highfield Gtr Man 194 G5
Highfield Gtr Man 195 F8
Highfield Herts 85 D9
Highfield N Ayrs 266 E6
Highfield Oxon 101 G11
Highfield S Yorks 186 D5
Highfield Soton 32 E6
Highfield T & W 242 F4
Highfields Cambs 123 F7
Highfields Derbys 170 B6
Highfields Essex 88 B5
Highfields Glos 80 F3
Highfields Leicester 136 C2
Highfields Northumb 273 E9
Highfields S Yorks 198 F4
Highfields Staffs 151 E8
Highgate E Sus 52 G2
Highgate Kent 53 G9
Highgate London 67 B9
Highgate Powys 130 D2
Highgate S Yorks 198 G3
Highgate W Mid 133 F11
Highlane Derbys 186 E6
Highlane E Ches 168 B5
Highlanes Corn 10 G4
Highlanes Staffs 150 C5
Highlaws Cumb 229 B8
Highleadon Glos 98 G5
Highleigh W Sus 22 D4
Highley Shrops 132 G4
Highmoor Cumb 229 B11
Highmoor Oxon 65 B8
Highmoor Cross Oxon 65 C8
Highmoor Hill Mon 60 B3
Highnam Glos 80 B3
Highnam Green Glos 98 G5
Highoak Norf 141 C11
Highridge Bristol 60 F5
Highroad Well Moor W Yorks 196 B5
Highstead Kent 71 F8
Highsted Kent 70 G2
Highstreet Kent 70 G5
Highstreet Green Essex 106 E5
Highstreet Green Sur 50 F3
Hightae Dumfries 238 B3
Highter's Heath W Mid 117 B11
Hightown E Ches 168 C5
Hightown Hants 31 G11
Hightown Mers 193 G10
Hightown Soton 33 E7
Hightown W Yorks 197 C7
Hightown Wrex 166 F4
Hightown Green Suff 125 F9
Hightown Heights W Yorks 197 C7
Highway Corn 4 G4
Highway Hereford 97 B9
Highway Som 29 C7
Highway Wilts 62 E4
Highway Windsor 65 C11
Highweek Devon 14 G2
Highwood Devon 27 F10
Highwood Dorset 18 D3
Highwood Essex 87 E10
Highwood Hants 31 F11
Highwood Worcs 116 D3
Highwood Hill London 86 G2
Highworth Swindon 82 G2
Highworthy Devon 24 F6
Hilborough Norf 140 C6
Hilborough Ho Norf 140 C6
Hilcot Glos 81 B7
Hilcot End Glos 81 E9
Hilcote Derbys 171 D7
Hilcott Wilts 46 B6
Hilden Park Kent 52 D5
Hildenborough Kent 52 D5
Hildersham Cambs 105 B10
Hildersley Hereford 98 G2
Hilderstone Staffs 151 C8
Hilderthorpe E Yorks 218 F3
Hilfield Dorset 29 F10
Hilgay Norf 140 D2
Hill S Glos 79 G10
Hill W Mid 134 D2
Hill Warks 119 D9
Hill Bottom Oxon 64 D6
Hill Brow W Sus 34 B3
Hill Chorlton Staffs 150 B5
Hill Common Norf 161 E8
Hill Corner Som 45 D10
Hill Croome Worcs 99 C7
Hill Dale Lancs 194 E3
Hill Deverill Wilts 45 E11
Hill Dyke Lincs 174 F4
Hill End Durham 232 D6
Hill End Fife 279 B10
Hill End Glos 99 D8
Hill End London 85 G8
Hill End N Yorks 205 C7
Hill End Som 29 E8
Hill End Worcs 117 E8
Hill Furze Worcs 99 B9
Hill Gate Hereford 97 F9
Hill Green Essex 105 E9
Hill Green Kent 69 G10
Hill Head Hants 33 G8
Hill Head Northumb 241 D10
Hill Hoath Kent 52 E3
Hill Hook W Mid 134 C2
Hill Houses Shrops 116 B2
Hill Mountain Pembs 73 D7
Hill of Beath Fife 280 C3
Hill of Drip Stirl 278 B5
Hill of Fearn Highld 301 B8
Hill of Keillor Angus 286 C6
Hill of Mountblairy Aberds 302 D6
Hill of Overbrae Aberds 303 C8
Hill Park Hants 33 F9
Hill Park Kent 52 B2
Hill Ridware Staffs 151 F11
Hill Side Hants 34 B3
Hill Side S Yorks 197 G8
Hill Side W Yorks 197 D7
Hill Side Worcs 116 E5
Hill Somersal Derbys 152 C2
Hill Street Kent 54 D6
Hill Top Derbys 186 F5
Hill Top Durham 232 G5
Hill Top Durham 233 C10
Hill Top Durham 242 G5
Hill Top Gtr Man 195 G8
Hill Top Hants 32 G6
Hill Top N Yorks 214 G3
Hill Top N Yorks 214 G5
Hill Top Notts 171 F7
Hill Top S Yorks 186 C5
Hill Top S Yorks 186 D3
Hill Top S Yorks 187 B7
Hill Top S Yorks 197 F9
Hill Top Staffs 133 B7
Hill Top W Mid 133 E9
Hill Top W Sus 34 C5
Hill Top W Yorks 196 E5
Hill Top W Yorks 197 D10
Hill Top W Yorks 205 G11
Hill Top W Yorks 205 G7
Hill Top Warks 134 E5
Hill Top Warks 135 F7
Hill View Dorset 18 B5
Hill Wood W Mid 134 C2
Hill Wootton Warks 118 D6
Hillam N Yorks 198 B4
Hillbeck Cumb 222 B5
Hillblock Pembs 73 B8
Hillborough Kent 71 F8
Hillbourne Poole 18 C6
Hillbrae Aberds 302 E6
Hillbrae Aberds 303 G7
Hillbutts Dorset 31 G7
Hillcliffe Warr 183 D10
Hillcliftlane Derbys 170 F3
Hillcommon Som 27 B11
Hillcross Derbys 152 C6
Hilldyke Lincs 174 F4
Hillend Fife 280 E2
Hillend N Lnrk 268 B6
Hillend N Som 43 B11
Hillend Shrops 132 E6
Hillend Swansea 56 C2
Hillend Green Glos 98 F4
Hillersland Glos 79 C9
Hillerton Devon 13 B10
Hillesden Bucks 102 F3
Hillesden Hamlet Bucks 102 E3
Hillesley Glos 61 B9
Hillfarance Som 27 C11
Hillfarrance Som 27 C11
Hillfield Devon 8 E6
Hillfield W Mid 118 B2
Hillfields S Glos 60 D6
Hillfields W Mid 118 B6
Hillfoot Aberds 303 D9
Hillfoot W Yorks 205 G10
Hillfoot End C Beds 104 E2
Hillgreen W Berks 64 D3
Hillgrove W Sus 34 B6
Hillhampton Hereford 97 B11
Hillhead Aberds 302 F5
Hillhead Aberds 303 G8
Hillhead Corn 5 C11
Hillhead Devon 9 E8
Hillhead E Ayrs 257 B10
Hillhead S Ayrs 257 F10
Hillhead of Auchentumb Aberds 303 D9
Hillhead of Blairy Aberds 302 D6
Hillhead of Cocklaw Aberds 303 E10
Hillhouse Borders 271 D10
Hilliard's Cross Staffs 152 G3
Hilliclay Highld 310 C5
Hillingdon London 66 C5
Hillingdon Heath London 66 C5
Hillington Glasgow 267 C10
Hillington Norf 158 D4
Hillis Corner I o W 20 C5
Hillmoor Devon 27 E10
Hillmorton Warks 119 C10
Hillock Vale Lancs 195 B9
Hillockhead Aberds 292 B6
Hillockhead Aberds 292 C5
Hillpool Worcs 117 B7
Hillpound Hants 33 D9
Hills Town Derbys 171 B7
Hillsborough S Yorks 186 C4
Hillside Aberds 293 D11
Hillside Angus 293 G9
Hillside Devon 8 C4
Hillside Devon 27 F11
Hillside Hants 49 C9
Hillside Mers 193 E10
Hillside Orkney 314 G4
Hillside Orkney 314 D3
Hillside Shetland 313 G6
Hillside Shrops 131 F11
Hillside Wilts 81 G9
Hillstreet Hants 32 D4
Hillswick Shetland 312 F4
Hilltop Bl Gwent 77 D11
Hilltop Bucks 85 E7
Hilltop Derbys 170 C4
Hillview T & W 243 G9
Hillway I o W 21 D8
Hillwell Shetland 313 M5
Hillyfields Hants 32 D5
Hilmarton Wilts 62 D4
Hilperton Wilts 45 B11
Hilperton Marsh Wilts 45 B11
Hilsea Ptsmth 33 G11
Hilston E Yorks 209 G11
Hiltingbury Hants 32 C6
Hilton Aberds 303 F9
Hilton Borders 273 E7
Hilton Cambs 122 D5
Hilton Cumb 231 G10
Hilton Derbys 152 C4
Hilton Dorset 30 G3
Hilton Durham 233 G9
Hilton Highld 309 L7
Hilton Highld 311 L3
Hilton Shrops 132 D5
Hilton Staffs 133 B11
Hilton Stockton 225 C9
Hilton House Gtr Man 194 F6
Hilton Lodge Highld 300 G2
Hilton of Cadboll Highld 301 B8
Hilton Park Gtr Man 195 G10
Himbleton Worcs 117 F8
Himley Staffs 133 E7
Hincaster Cumb 211 C10
Hinchley Wood Sur 67 F7
Hinchliffe Mill W Yorks 196 F6
Hinchwick Glos 100 E2
Hinckley Leics 135 E8
Hinderclay Suff 125 B10
Hinderton W Ches 182 F4
Hinderwell N Yorks 226 B5
Hindford Shrops 148 C6
Hindhead Sur 49 F11
Hindle Fold Lancs 203 G10
Hindley Gtr Man 194 G6
Hindley Northumb 242 F2
Hindley Green Gtr Man 194 G6
Hindlip Worcs 117 F7
Hindolveston Norf 159 D10
Hindon Wilts 46 G2
Hindpool Cumb 210 F3
Hindringham Norf 159 B9
Hindsford Gtr Man 195 G7
Hingham Norf 141 C10
Hinstock Shrops 150 D3
Hintlesham Suff 107 C11
Hinton Glos 79 E11
Hinton Hants 19 B10
Hinton Hereford 96 D6
Hinton Northants 119 G10
Hinton S Glos 61 D8
Hinton Shrops 131 B8
Hinton Som 29 C9
Hinton Ampner Hants 33 B9
Hinton Blewett Bath 44 B5
Hinton Charterhouse Bath 45 B9
Hinton Cross Worcs 99 C10
Hinton-in-the-Hedges Northants 101 D11
Hinton Martell Dorset 31 F8
Hinton on the Green Worcs 99 C10
Hinton Parva Dorset 31 G7
Hinton Parva Swindon 63 C8
Hinton St George Som 28 E6
Hinton St Mary Dorset 30 D3
Hinton Waldrist Oxon 82 F5
Hints Shrops 116 C2
Hints Staffs 134 C3
Hinwick Beds 121 E8
Hinwood Shrops 131 B7
Hinxhill Kent 54 E5
Hinxton Cambs 105 B9
Hinxworth Herts 104 C4
Hipperholme W Yorks 196 B6
Hipplecote Worcs 116 F4
Hipsburn Northumb 264 G6
Hipswell N Yorks 224 F3
Hirael Gwyn 179 G9
Hiraeth Carms 92 G3
Hirn Aberds 293 C9
Hirnant Powys 147 E11
Hirst N Lnrk 269 C7
Hirst Northumb 253 F7
Hirst Courtney N Yorks 198 C6
Hirwaen Denb 165 C10
Hirwaun Rhondda 77 D7
Hirwaun Common Bridgend 58 C2
Hiscott Devon 25 B8
Hislop Borders 249 C9
Hisomley Wilts 45 D11
Histon Cambs 123 E8
Hitcham Suff 125 G9
Hitchill Dumfries 238 D4
Hitchin Herts 104 F3
Hitchin Hill Herts 104 F3
Hitcombe Bottom Wilts 45 E10
Hither Green London 67 E11
Hittisleigh Devon 13 C10
Hittisleigh Barton Devon 13 B10
Hive E Yorks 208 G2
Hixon Staffs 151 D10
Hoaden Kent 55 B9
Hoar Cross Staffs 152 E2
Hoarwithy Hereford 97 F10
Hoath Kent 71 G8
Hoath Corner Kent 52 E3
Hob Hill W Ches 167 E7
Hobarris Shrops 114 B6
Hobbister Orkney 314 F3
Hobble End Staffs 133 B10
Hobbles Green Suff 124 G4
Hobbs Cross Essex 87 C7
Hobbs Cross Essex 87 F7
Hobbs Wall Bath 61 G7
Hobkirk Borders 262 G3
Hobroyd Derbys 185 C8
Hobson Durham 242 F5
Hoby Leics 154 F3
Hoccombe Som 27 B10
Hockenden London 68 F3
Hockerill Herts 105 G9
Hockering Norf 159 G11
Hockering Heath Norf 159 G11
Hockerton Notts 172 D2
Hockholler Som 27 C11
Hockholler Green Som 27 C11
Hockley E Ches 184 E6
Hockley Essex 88 G4
Hockley Kent 54 B3
Hockley Staffs 134 C4
Hockley W Mid 118 B5
Hockley Heath W Mid 118 C3
Hockliffe C Beds 103 F9
Hockwold cum Wilton Norf 140 F4
Hockworthy Devon 27 D8
Hocombe Hants 32 C6
Hoddesdon Herts 86 D5
Hoddlesden Blkburn 195 C8
Hoddom Mains Dumfries 238 C5
Hoddomcross Dumfries 238 C5
Hoden Worcs 99 B11
Hodgefield Staffs 168 E6
Hodgehill E Ches 168 B4
Hodgehill W Mid 134 F2
Hodgeston Pembs 73 F8
Hodley Powys 130 E3
Hodnet Shrops 150 D2
Hodnetheath Shrops 150 D2
Hodsock Notts 187 D10
Hodsoll Street Kent 68 G6
Hodson Swindon 63 C7
Hodthorpe Derbys 187 F8
Hoe Hants 33 D9
Hoe Norf 159 F9
Hoe Sur 50 D5
Hoe Benham W Berks 64 F2
Hoe Gate Hants 33 E10
Hoff Cumb 222 B3
Hoffleet Stow Lincs 156 B4
Hog Hatch Sur 49 D10
Hogaland Shetland 312 F5
Hogben's Hill Kent 54 B4
Hogganfield Glasgow 268 B2
Hoggard's Green Suff 125 F7
Hoggeston Bucks 102 G6
Hoggington Wilts 45 B10
Hoggrill's End Warks 134 E4
Hogha Gearraidh W Isles 296 D3
Hoghton Lancs 194 B6
Hoghton Bottoms Lancs 194 B6
Hogley Green W Yorks 196 F6
Hognaston Derbys 170 E2
Hogpits Bottom Herts 85 E8
Hogsthorpe Lincs 191 G8
Hogstock Dorset 31 F7
Holbeach Lincs 157 E7
Holbeach Bank Lincs 157 D7
Holbeach Clough Lincs 156 D6
Holbeach Drove Lincs 156 G6
Holbeach Hurn Lincs 157 D7
Holbeach St Johns Lincs 156 F6
Holbeach St Marks Lincs 157 C7
Holbeach St Matthew Lincs 157 C8
Holbeache Worcs 116 B5
Holbeck Notts 187 G8
Holbeck W Yorks 205 G11
Holbeck Woodhouse Notts 187 G8
Holberrow Green Worcs 117 F10
Holbeton Devon 8 E2
Holborn London 67 C10
Holborough Kent 69 G8
Holbrook Derbys 170 G5
Holbrook S Yorks 186 E6
Holbrook Suff 108 D3
Holbrook Common S Glos 61 E7
Holbrook Moor Derbys 170 F5
Holbrooks W Mid 134 G6
Holburn Northumb 264 B2
Holbury Hants 32 G6
Holcombe Devon 14 G5
Holcombe Gtr Man 195 D9
Holcombe Som 45 D7
Holcombe Brook Gtr Man 195 E9
Holcombe Rogus Devon 27 D9
Holcot Northants 120 D5
Holdbrook London 86 F5
Holden Lancs 203 D11
Holden Fold Gtr Man 196 F2
Holdenby Northants 120 D3
Holdenhurst Bmouth 19 B8
Holder's Green Essex 106 F2
Holders Hill London 86 G2
Holdfast Worcs 99 D7
Holdgate Shrops 131 F11
Holdingham Lincs 173 F9

Insch Aberds 302 E3
Insh Highld 291 C10
Inshegra Highld 306 D7
Inshore Highld 308 C3
Inskip Lancs 202 F5
Inskip Moss Side Lancs 202 F5
Instoneville S Yorks 198 E5
Instow Devon 40 G3
Intack Blkburn 195 B8
Intake S Yorks 186 F6
Intake S Yorks 198 G5
Intake W Yorks 205 F10
Interfield Worcs 98 B5
Intwood Norf 142 C3
Isel Cumb 229 E9
Inver Cumb 292 D4
Inver Highld 311 L2
Inver Perth 286 C4
Inver Mallie Highld 290 E3
Inverailort Highld 295 C9
Inveraldie Angus 287 D8
Inveralligin Highld 299 D8
Inverallochy Aberds 303 C10
Inveran Highld 299 B8
Inveran Highld 309 K5
Inveraray Argyll 284 G4
Inverarish Highld 295 B7
Inverarity Angus 287 C8
Inverarnan Stirl 285 E7
Inverasdale Highld 307 L3
Inverawe Ho Argyll 284 D4
Inverbeg Argyll 276 B6
Inverbervie Aberds 293 F10
Inverboyndie Aberds 302 C6
Inverbroom Highld 307 L6
Invercarron Mains Highld 309 K5
Invercassley Highld 309 J4
Invercauld House Aberds 292 D3
Inverchaolain Argyll 275 F11
Invercharnan Highld 284 C5
Inverchoran Highld 300 D2
Invercreran Argyll 284 C4
Inverdruie Highld 291 B11
Inverebrie Aberds 303 F9
Invereck Argyll 276 E3
Inverenran Ho Argyll 292 B5
Invereshie House Highld 291 C10
Inveresk E Loth 280 G6
Inverey Aberds 292 E2
Inverfarigaig Highld 300 G5
Invergarry Highld 290 C5
Invergelder Aberds 292 D4
Invergeldie Perth 285 E11
Invergordon Highld 301 C7
Invergowrie Perth 287 D7
Inverguseran Highld 295 E9
Inverhadden Perth 285 B10
Inverhaggernie Stirl 285 E7
Inverharroch Moray 302 F3
Inverherive Stirl 285 E7
Inverie Highld 295 F9
Inverinan Argyll 275 B10
Inverinate Highld 295 C11
Inverkeilor Angus 287 C10
Inverkeithing Fife 280 E2
Inverkeithny Aberds 302 E6
Inverkip Invclyd 276 G4
Inverkirkaig Highld 307 H5
Inverlael Highld 307 L6
Inverleith Edin 280 F4
Inverliever Lodge Argyll 275 C9
Inverliver Argyll 284 D4
Inverlochlarig Stirl 285 F8
Inverlochy Argyll 284 E5
Inverlochy Highld 290 F3
Inverlussa Argyll 275 E7
Invermark Lodge Angus 292 E6
Invermoidart Highld 289 B8
Invermoriston Highld 290 B6
Invernaver Highld 308 C7
Inverneill Argyll 275 E7
Inverness Highld 300 E6
Invernettie Aberds 303 E11
Invernoaden Argyll 276 B2
Inveroran Hotel Argyll 284 C6
Inverpolly Lodge Highld 307 H5
Inverquharity Angus 287 B8
Inverquhomery Aberds 303 E10
Inverroy Highld 290 E4
Inversanda Highld 289 D11
Invershiel Highld 295 D11
Invershin Highld 309 K5
Invershore Highld 310 F6
Inversnaid Hotel Stirl 285 D7
Invertrossachs Stirl 285 G9
Inveruglas Aberds 303 E11
Inveruglas Argyll 285 D7
Inveruglass Highld 291 C10
Inverurie Aberds 303 G7
Invervar Perth 285 C10
Inverythan Aberds 303 E7
Inwardleigh Devon 13 B7
Inwood Shrops 131 D9
Inworth Essex 88 B5
Iochdar W Isles 297 G3
Iping W Sus 34 C5
Ipplepen Devon 8 B6
Ipsden Oxon 64 B6
Ipsley Worcs 117 D11
Ipstones Staffs 169 F8
Ipswich Suff 108 C3
Irby Mers 182 E3
Irby in the Marsh Lincs 175 C7
Irby upon Humber NE Lincs 201 G7
Irchester Northants 121 D8
Ireby Cumb 229 D10
Ireby Lancs 212 D3
Ireland C Beds 104 C2
Ireland Orkney 314 F3
Ireland Shetland 313 L5
Ireland W Isles 45 C10
Ireland Wood W Yorks 205 F10
Ireland's Cross Shrops 168 G2
Ireleth Cumb 210 D4
Ireshopeburn Durham 232 D3
Ireton Wood Derbys 170 F4
Irlam Gtr Man 184 C2
Irlams o' th' Height Gtr Man 195 G9
Irnham Lincs 155 D10
Iron Acton S Glos 61 C7
Iron Bridge Cambs 139 D9
Iron Cross Warks 117 G11
Iron Lo Highld 299 G10
Ironbridge Telford 132 C3
Irongray Dumfries 237 B11
Ironmacannie Dumfries 237 B8

Irons Bottom Sur 51 D9
Ironside Aberds 303 D8
Ironville Derbys 170 E6
Irstead Norf 161 F7
Irstead Street Norf 161 F7
Irthington Cumb 239 E11
Irthlingborough Northants 121 C8
Irton N Yorks 217 C10
Irvine N Ayrs 257 B8
Irwell Vale Lancs 195 C9
Isabella Pit Northumb 253 G8
Isallt Bach Anglesey 178 F3
Isauld Highld 310 C3
Isbister Orkney 314 E3
Isbister Orkney 314 D2
Isbister Shetland 312 D5
Isbister Shetland 313 F5
Isel Cumb 229 E9
Isfield E Sus 36 D6
Isham Northants 121 C7
Ishriff Argyll 289 F8
Isington Hants 49 E9
Island Carr N Lincs 200 F3
Islands Common Cambs 122 E3
Islay Ho Argyll 274 G4
Isle Abbotts Som 28 C5
Isle Brewers Som 28 C5
Isle of Axholme N Lincs 199 F9
Isle of Dogs London 67 D11
Isle of Man Dumfries 238 B2
Isle of Whithorn Dumfries 236 F6
Isleham Cambs 124 C2
Isleornsay Highld 295 D9
Islesburgh Shetland 312 G5
Islesteps Dumfries 237 B11
Isleworth London 67 D7
Isley Walton Leics 153 D8
Islibhig W Isles 304 F1
Islington London 67 C10
Islington Telford 150 E4
Islip Oxon 83 C8
Islip Northants 121 B9
Isombridge Telford 150 G2
Istead Rise Kent 68 F6
Isycoed Wrex 166 E6
Itchen Soton 32 E6
Itchen Abbas Hants 48 G4
Itchen Stoke Hants 48 G5
Itchingfield W Sus 35 B10
Itchington S Glos 61 B7
Itteringham Norf 160 C2
Itteringham Common Norf 160 D3
Itton Devon 13 B9
Itton Mon 79 F7
Itton Common Mon 79 F7
Ivegill Cumb 230 C4
Ivelet N Yorks 223 F8
Iver Bucks 66 C4
Iver Heath Bucks 66 C4
Iverley Staffs 133 G7
Iveston Durham 242 G4
Ivinghoe Bucks 84 B6
Ivinghoe Aston Bucks 85 B7
Ivington Hereford 115 F9
Ivington Green Hereford 115 F9
Ivy Chimneys Essex 86 E6
Ivy Cross Dorset 30 C5
Ivy Hatch Kent 52 C5
Ivy Todd Norf 141 B7
Ivybridge Devon 8 D2
Ivychurch Kent 39 B8
Iwade Kent 69 F11
Iwerne Courtney or Shroton Dorset 30 E5
Iwerne Minster Dorset 30 E5
Ixworth Suff 125 C8
Ixworth Thorpe Suff 125 C8

J

Jack Green Lancs 194 B5
Jack Hayes Staffs 168 F6
Jack Hill N Yorks 205 C10
Jack in the Green Devon 14 B6
Jackfield Telford 132 C3
Jack's Green Essex 105 G11
Jack's Green Glos 80 D5
Jack's Hatch Essex 86 D6
Jacksdale Notts 170 E6
Jackson Bridge W Yorks 197 F7
Jackstown Aberds 303 F7
Jacobs Well Sur 50 C3
Jacobstow Corn 11 B9
Jacobstowe Devon 25 G9
Jagger Green W Yorks 196 D5
Jameston Pembs 73 F9
Jamestown Dumfries 249 D8
Jamestown Highld 300 D4
Jamestown W Dunb 277 E7
Jamphlars Fife 280 B4
Janetstown Highld 310 C5
Janke's Green Essex 107 F8
Jarrow T & W 243 D8
Jarvis Brook E Sus 37 B8
Jasper's Green Essex 106 F4
Java Argyll 289 F9
Jaw Hill W Yorks 197 C9
Jawcraig Falk 278 F6
Jaywick Essex 89 C11
Jealott's Hill Brack 65 E11
Jeaniefield Borders 271 G10
Jedburgh Borders 262 E5
Jedurgh Borders 262 F5
Jeffreyston Pembs 73 E9
Jellyhill E Dunb 278 G2
Jemimaville Highld 301 C7
Jennetts Hill W Berks 64 E5
Jennyfield N Yorks 205 B11
Jericho Gtr Man 195 E10
Jersey Farm Herts 85 D11
Jersey Marine Neath 57 C8
Jesmond T & W 243 D7
Jevington E Sus 23 E9
Jewell's Cross Corn 24 G3
Jingle Street Mon 79 C7
Jockey End Herts 85 C8
Jodrell Bank E Ches 184 G3
Jodrell Bank Bath 61 F8
John O'Gaunts W Yorks 197 B11
John o'Groats Highld 310 B7
Johnby Cumb 230 E4
John's Cross E Sus 38 C2
Johnshaven Aberds 293 G9
Johnson Fold Gtr Man 195 E7
Johnson Street Norf 161 F7
Johnson's Hillock Lancs 194 C5
Johnston Pembs 72 C6
Johnstone Renfs 267 C8
Johnstone Mains Aberds 293 F9
Johnstonebridge Dumfries 248 E3
Johnstown Carms 74 B6

Johnstown Wrex 166 F4
Jolly's Bottom Corn 4 F5
Joppa Corn 2 B3
Joppa Edin 280 G6
Joppa S Ayrs 257 F10
Jordan Green Norf 159 E11
Jordanhill Glasgow 267 B10
Jordans Bucks 85 G7
Jordanston Pembs 91 E8
Jordanthorpe S Yorks 186 E5
Jordon S Yorks 186 C6
Joyford Glos 79 B10
Joy's Green Glos 79 B10
Jubilee Gtr Man 196 E2
Jubilee N Som 60 E3
Jugbank Staffs 150 B5
Jump S Yorks 197 G11
Jumpers Common Dorset 19 C8
Jumpers Green Dorset 19 C8
Jumper's Town E Sus 52 G3
Junction N Yorks 204 D6
Juniper Northumb 241 F10
Juniper Green Edin 270 B3
Jurby East I o M 192 C4
Jurby West I o M 192 C4
Jurston Devon 13 G11
Jury's Gap E Sus 39 D7

K

Kaber Cumb 222 C5
Kaimend S Lnrk 269 F9
Kaimes Edin 270 B5
Kaimrig End Borders 269 G11
Kalemouth Borders 262 D6
Kame Fife 287 G7
Kames Argyll 275 F10
Kames Argyll 289 F8
Kames S Ayrs 258 D5
Kates Hill W Mid 133 F9
Kea Corn 4 G6
Keadby N Lincs 199 E10
Keal Cotes Lincs 174 C5
Kearby Town End N Yorks 206 D2
Kearnsey Kent 55 E9
Kearsley Gtr Man 195 F9
Kearstwick Cumb 212 C2
Kearton N Yorks 223 F9
Kearvaig Highld 306 B7
Keasden N Yorks 212 F4
Kebroyd W Yorks 196 C4
Keckwick Halton 183 E9
Keddington Lincs 190 D4
Keddington Corner Lincs 190 D5
Kedington Suff 106 B4
Kedleston Derbys 170 G4
Kedslie Borders 271 G11
Keekle Cumb 219 B10
Keelars Tye Essex 107 G11
Keelby Lincs 201 E7
Keele Staffs 168 F4
Keeley Green Beds 103 B10
Keeston Pembs 72 B6
Keevil Wilts 46 B2
Kegworth Leics 153 D9
Kehelland Corn 4 G2
Keig Aberds 293 B8
Keighley W Yorks 205 E7
Keil Highld 289 D11
Keilarsbrae Clack 279 C7
Keilhill Aberds 303 D7
Keillmore Argyll 275 E7
Keillor Perth 286 C6
Keillour Perth 286 E3
Keills Argyll 274 G5
Keils Argyll 274 G6
Keinton Mandeville Som 44 G4
Keir Mill Dumfries 247 E9
Keisby Lincs 155 D10
Keiss Highld 310 C7
Keistle Highld 298 D4
Keith Moray 302 D4
Keith Hall Aberds 303 G7
Keith Inch Aberds 303 E11
Keithock Angus 293 G8
Kelbrook Lancs 204 E4
Kelby Lincs 173 G8
Kelcliffe W Yorks 205 E9
Keld Cumb 221 C11
Keld N Yorks 223 E7
Keld Houses N Yorks 205 B8
Keldholme N Yorks 216 B4
Kelfield N Lincs 199 G10
Kelfield N Yorks 207 F7
Kelham Notts 172 D3
Kelhurn Argyll 276 F6
Kellacott Devon 12 D4
Kellamergh Lancs 194 B2
Kellan Argyll 289 E7
Kellas Angus 287 D8
Kellas Moray 301 D11
Kellaton Devon 9 G11
Kellaways Wilts 62 D3
Kelleth Cumb 222 D3
Kelleythorpe E Yorks 208 B5
Kelleythorpe E Yorks 208 B5
Kelling Norf 177 E9
Kellingley N Yorks 198 C5
Kellington N Yorks 198 C5
Kelloe Durham 234 D2
Kelloholm Dumfries 258 G6
Kells Cumb 219 B9
Kelly Corn 10 G6
Kelly Devon 12 E3
Kelly Bray Corn 12 G3
Kelmarsh Northants 120 H4
Kelmscot Oxon 82 F3
Kelsale Suff 127 D7
Kelsall W Ches 167 B8
Kelsall Hill W Ches 167 B8
Kelsay Argyll 254 B2
Kelshall Herts 104 D6
Kelsick Cumb 238 G5
Kelso Borders 262 C6
Kelstedge Derbys 170 C4
Kelstern Lincs 190 C3
Kelsterton Flint 182 G3
Kelston Bath 61 F8
Keltneyburn Perth 285 C11
Kelton Dumfries 237 B11
Kelton Durham 232 G4
Kelty Fife 280 B2
Keltybridge Perth 280 B2
Kelvedon Essex 88 B5
Kelvedon Hatch Essex 87 F9
Kelvin S Lnrk 268 D2
Kelvindale Glasgow 267 B11
Kelvinside Glasgow 267 B11
Kelynack Corn 1 D3
Kemacott Devon 41 D7
Kemback Fife 287 F8
Kemberton Shrops 132 C4
Kemble Glos 81 F7
Kemble Wick Glos 81 F7

Kemerton Worcs 99 D8
Kemeys Commander Mon 78 E4
Kemincham E Ches 168 B4
Kemnay Aberds 293 B9
Kemp Town Brighton 36 G4
Kempe's Corner Kent 54 D4
Kempie Highld 308 D4
Kempley Glos 98 F3
Kempley Green Glos 98 F3
Kemps Green Warks 118 C2
Kempsey Worcs 99 B7
Kempsford Glos 81 F11
Kempshott Hants 48 C6
Kempston Beds 103 B10
Kempston Church End Beds 103 B10
Kempston Hardwick Beds 103 C10
Kempston West End Beds 103 B9
Kempton Shrops 131 G2
Kemsing Kent 52 B5
Kemsley Kent 70 F2
Kemsley Street Kent 69 G10
Kenardington Kent 54 G3
Kenchester Hereford 97 C8
Kencot Oxon 82 E3
Kendal Cumb 221 G10
Kendal End Worcs 117 C10
Kendleshire S Glos 61 D7
Kendon Caerph 77 F11
Kendray S Yorks 197 G11
Kenfig Bridgend 57 E10
Kenfig Hill Bridgend 57 E10
Kengharair Argyll 288 E6
Kenilworth Warks 118 C5
Kenknock Stirl 285 D8
Kenley London 51 B10
Kenley Shrops 131 C11
Kenmore Argyll 284 C4
Kenmore Highld 299 D7
Kenmore Perth 285 C11
Kenn Devon 14 D4
Kenn N Som 59 G10
Kenn Moor Gate N Som 60 F2
Kennacley W Isles 305 J3
Kennacraig Argyll 275 G8
Kennards House Corn 11 E11
Kenneggy Corn 2 D3
Kenneggy Downs Corn 2 D3
Kennerleigh Devon 26 F4
Kenneggy Clack 279 C8
Kennet End Suff 124 D3
Kennethmont Aberds 302 G5
Kennett Cambs 124 D3
Kennford Devon 14 D4
Kenninghall Norf 141 F10
Kenninghall Heath Norf 141 G10
Kennington Kent 54 E4
Kennington London 67 D10
Kennington Oxon 83 E8
Kennoway Fife 287 G7
Kenny Som 28 D4
Kenny Hill Suff 124 B3
Kennythorpe N Yorks 216 F5
Kenovay Argyll 288 E1
Kensal Green London 67 C8
Kensal Rise London 67 C8
Kensal Town London 67 C8
Kensaleyre Highld 298 D4
Kensary Highld 310 E6
Kensington London 67 D9
Kensington Mers 182 C5
Kensworth C Beds 85 B8
Kensworth Common C Beds 85 B8
Kent Street E Sus 38 D3
Kent Street Kent 53 C7
Kent Street W Sus 36 C2
Kentallen Highld 284 B4
Kentford Suff 124 D4
Kentisbeare Devon 27 F9
Kentisbury Devon 40 E6
Kentisbury Ford Devon 40 E6
Kentish Town London 67 C9
Kentmere Cumb 221 E9
Kenton Devon 14 E5
Kenton London 67 B7
Kenton Suff 126 D3
Kenton T & W 242 D6
Kenton Bankfoot T & W 242 D6
Kenton Bar T & W 242 D6
Kenton Corner Suff 126 D4
Kenton Green Glos 80 C3
Kentra Highld 289 C8
Kentrigg Cumb 221 G10
Kents Corn 11 B9
Kents Bank Cumb 211 D7
Kents Hill M Keynes 103 D7
Kent's Green Glos 98 G4
Kents Hill M Keynes 103 D7
Kent's Oak Hants 32 C4
Kenwick Shrops 149 C8
Kenwick Park Shrops 149 D8
Kenwyn Corn 4 F6
Kenyon Warr 183 B10
Keoldale Highld 308 C3
Keonchulish Ho Highld 307 K6
Kepdowrie Stirl 277 C11
Kepnal Wilts 63 G7
Keppanach Highld 290 G2
Keppoch Highld 295 C11
Keprigan Argyll 255 F7
Kepwick N Yorks 225 G9
Kerchesters Borders 263 B7
Kerdiston Norf 159 E11
Keresforth Hill S Yorks 197 G10
Keresley Warks 134 G6
Keresley Newlands Warks 134 G6
Kerfield Borders 270 G5
Kerley Downs Corn 4 G5
Kernborough Devon 8 G5
Kerne Bridge Hereford 79 B9
Kernsary Highld 299 B8
Kerridge E Ches 184 F6
Kerridge-end E Ches 184 F6
Kerris Corn 1 D4
Kerry = Ceri Powys 130 F2
Kerry Hill Staffs 168 F5
Kerrycroy Argyll 266 C2
Kerry's Gate Hereford 97 E7
Kerrysdale Highld 299 B8
Kersal Gtr Man 195 G10
Kersall Notts 172 C2
Kersbrook Cross Corn 12 F2
Kerscott Devon 25 B10
Kersey Suff 107 C10
Kersey Tye Suff 107 C9
Kersey Upland Suff 107 C9
Kershopefoot Cumb 249 G11
Kersoe Worcs 99 D9
Kerswell Devon 27 F9
Kerswell Green Worcs 99 B7
Kerthen Wood Corn 2 C3
Kesgrave Suff 108 C4
Kessingland Suff 143 F10

Kessingland Beach Suff 143 F10
Kessington E Dunb 277 G11
Kestle Corn 5 F9
Kestle Mill Corn 5 D7
Keston London 68 G2
Keston Mark London 68 F2
Keswick Cumb 229 G11
Keswick Norf 142 C4
Keswick Norf 161 C7
Kete Pembs 72 E4
Ketford Glos 98 E4
Ketley Telford 150 G3
Ketley Bank Telford 150 G3
Ketsby Lincs 190 F5
Kettering Northants 121 B7
Ketteringham Norf 142 C3
Kettins Perth 286 D6
Kettlebaston Suff 125 G9
Kettlebridge Fife 287 G7
Kettlebrook Staffs 134 C4
Kettleburgh Suff 126 E5
Kettlehill Fife 287 G7
Kettleholm Dumfries 238 B4
Kettleness N Yorks 226 B5
Kettlesing N Yorks 205 B10
Kettlesing Bottom N Yorks 205 B10
Kettlesing Head N Yorks 205 B10
Kettlestone Norf 159 C7
Kettlethorpe Lincs 188 F4
Kettletoft Orkney 314 C6
Kettlewell N Yorks 213 E10
Ketton Rutland 137 C9
Kevingtown London 68 F3
Kew London 67 D7
Kew Bridge London 67 D7
Keward Som 44 E4
Kewstoke N Som 59 G10
Kexbrough S Yorks 197 F9
Kexby Lincs 188 D5
Kexby York 207 C10
Key Green E Ches 168 C5
Key Green N Yorks 226 D6
Key Street Kent 69 G10
Keybridge Corn 11 G7
Keyford Som 45 D9
Keyham Leics 136 B3
Keyhaven Hants 20 C2
Keyingham E Yorks 201 B8
Keymer W Sus 36 D4
Keynsham Bath 61 F7
Keysers Estate Essex 86 D5
Keysoe Beds 121 D11
Keysoe Row Beds 121 D11
Keyston Beds 121 B10
Keyworth Notts 154 C2
Khantore Aberds 292 D4
Kibblesworth T & W 242 F6
Kibworth Beauchamp Leics 136 E3
Kibworth Harcourt Leics 136 E3
Kidbrooke London 68 D2
Kidburngill Cumb 229 G7
Kiddal Lane End W Yorks 206 F4
Kiddemore Green Staffs 133 B7
Kidderminster Worcs 116 B6
Kiddington Oxon 101 G8
Kidd's Moor Norf 142 C2
Kidlington Oxon 83 C7
Kidmore End Oxon 65 D7
Kidsdale Dumfries 236 F6
Kidsgrove Staffs 168 E4
Kidstones N Yorks 213 C9
Kidwelly = Cydweli Carms 74 D6
Kiel Crofts Argyll 289 F11
Kielder Northumb 250 E4
Kierfiold Ho Orkney 314 E2
Kiff Green W Berks 64 F5
Kilbagie Clack 279 D8
Kilbarchan Renfs 267 C8
Kilbeg Highld 295 E8
Kilberry Argyll 275 G8
Kilbirnie N Ayrs 266 E6
Kilbride W Dunb 277 G10
Kilbraur Highld 311 H2
Kilbride Argyll 254 C4
Kilbride Argyll 275 D9
Kilbride Argyll 289 G10
Kilbridemore Argyll 275 D11
Kilburn Angus 292 G5
Kilburn Derbys 170 F5
Kilburn London 67 C9
Kilburn N Yorks 215 D10
Kilby Leics 136 D2
Kilby Bridge Leics 136 D2
Kilchattan Argyll 274 D4
Kilchattan Bay Argyll 266 E2
Kilchenzie Argyll 255 E7
Kilcheran Argyll 289 F10
Kilchenan Argyll 284 E4
Kilchiaran Argyll 274 G3
Kilchoan Argyll 275 B8
Kilchoan Highld 288 C5
Kilchoman Argyll 274 G3
Kilchrenan Argyll 284 E4
Kilconquhar Fife 287 G8
Kilcot Glos 98 F3
Kilcoy Highld 300 D5
Kilcreggan Argyll 276 E4
Kildale N Yorks 226 D2
Kildalloig Argyll 255 F8
Kildary Highld 301 B7
Kildavanan Argyll 275 G11
Kildermorie Lodge Highld 300 B5
Kildonan Dumfries 236 E2
Kildonan Highld 298 D3
Kildonan N Ayrs 256 E2
Kildonan Lodge Highld 311 G3
Kildonnan Highld 294 G6
Kildrummy Aberds 292 B6
Kildwick N Yorks 204 D6
Kilfinan Argyll 275 F10
Kilfinnan Highld 290 D4
Kilgetty Pembs 73 D10
Kilgour Fife 286 G6
Kilgrammie S Ayrs 245 C7
Kilgwrrwg Common Mon 79 F7
Kilham E Yorks 217 G11
Kilham Northumb 263 C8
Kilkeddan Argyll 255 E8
Kilkenneth Argyll 288 E1
Kilkenny Glos 81 B8
Kilkerran Argyll 255 F8
Kilkhampton Corn 24 E3
Killamarsh Derbys 187 E7
Killay Swansea 56 C6
Killbeg Argyll 289 E8
Killean Argyll 255 C7
Killearn Stirl 277 D10
Killellan Argyll 255 F7
Killen Highld 300 D6
Killerby Darl 224 B3
Killichonan Perth 285 B9
Killiechonate Highld 290 E4
Killiecrankie Perth 291 G11
Killiehuntly Highld 291 D9
Killiemor Argyll 288 F6
Killilan Highld 295 B11
Killimster Highld 310 D7
Killin Stirl 285 D9
Killin Lodge Highld 291 C7
Killinallan Argyll 274 F4
Killinghall N Yorks 205 B11
Killingbeck W Yorks 206 G2
Killingholme Lincs 201 E7
Killingthorpe Lincs 188 F4
Killington Cumb 212 B3
Killingworth T & W 243 C7
Killingworth Moor T & W 243 C7
Killingworth Village T & W 243 C7
Killivose Corn 2 B4
Killmahumaig Argyll 275 D8
Killochyett Borders 271 F9
Killocraw Argyll 255 D7
Killundine Highld 289 E7
Kilmacolm Invclyd 267 B7
Kilmaha Argyll 275 C10
Kilmahog Stirl 285 G10
Kilmalieu Highld 289 D10
Kilmaluag Highld 298 B4
Kilmany Fife 287 E7
Kilmarie Highld 295 D7
Kilmarnock E Ayrs 257 B10
Kilmaron Castle Fife 287 F7
Kilmartin Argyll 275 D9
Kilmaurs E Ayrs 267 G8
Kilmelford Argyll 275 B9
Kilmeny Argyll 274 G4
Kilmersdon Som 45 C7
Kilmeston Hants 33 B9
Kilmichael Argyll 255 E7
Kilmichael Glassary Argyll 275 D9
Kilmichael of Inverlussa Argyll 275 D8
Kilmington Wilts 45 G9
Kilmington Devon 28 G2
Kilmonivaig Highld 290 E3
Kilmorack Highld 300 E4
Kilmore Argyll 289 G10
Kilmore Highld 295 E8
Kilmory Argyll 275 F8
Kilmory Highld 289 B7
Kilmory Highld 294 C4
Kilmory N Ayrs 255 E10
Kilmory Lodge Argyll 275 C8
Kilmote Highld 311 H3
Kilmuir Highld 298 E3
Kilmuir Highld 300 E6
Kilmuir Highld 301 B7
Kilmuir Highld 301 B7
Kilmun Argyll 275 E10
Kilmun Argyll 276 E3
Kiln Green Hereford 98 G3
Kiln Green Wokingham 65 D10
Kiln Pit Hill Northumb 242 G3
Kilnave Argyll 274 F3
Kilncadzow S Lnrk 269 F7
Kilndown Kent 53 G8
Kilnhill Cumb 229 E10
Kilnhurst S Yorks 187 B7
Kilninian Argyll 288 E5
Kilninver Argyll 289 G10
Kilnsea E Yorks 201 D12
Kilnsey N Yorks 213 F9
Kilnwick E Yorks 208 D5
Kilnwick Percy E Yorks 208 C2
Kiloran Argyll 274 D4
Kilpatrick N Ayrs 255 E10
Kilpeck Hereford 97 E8
Kilphedir Highld 311 H3
Kilpin E Yorks 199 B8
Kilpin Pike E Yorks 199 B8
Kilrenny Fife 287 G9
Kilsby Northants 119 C11
Kilspindie Perth 286 E6
Kilsyth N Lnrk 278 F4
Kiltarlity Highld 300 E5
Kilton Notts 187 F9
Kilton Redcar 226 B4
Kilton Som 43 E7
Kilton Thorpe Redcar 226 B4
Kiltyrie Perth 285 D10
Kilvaxter Highld 298 C3
Kilve Som 43 E7
Kilvington Notts 172 G3
Kilwinning N Ayrs 266 G6
Kimberley Norf 141 C11
Kimberley Notts 171 G8
Kimberworth S Yorks 186 C6
Kimberworth Park S Yorks 186 C6
Kimble Wick Bucks 84 D4
Kimblesworth Durham 233 B11
Kimbolton Cambs 121 D11
Kimbolton Hereford 115 E10
Kimbridge Hants 32 B4
Kimcote Leics 135 F11
Kimmeridge Dorset 18 F4
Kimmerston Northumb 263 B11
Kimpton Hants 47 D9
Kimpton Herts 85 B11
Kimworthy Devon 24 E4
Kinabus Argyll 254 C3
Kinbeachie Highld 300 C6
Kinbrace Highld 310 F2
Kinbuck Stirl 285 G11
Kincaidston S Ayrs 257 F9
Kincaple Fife 287 F8
Kincardine Fife 279 D8
Kincardine Highld 309 L6
Kincardine Bridge Falk 279 D8
Kincardine O'Neil Aberds 293 D7
Kinclaven Perth 286 D5
Kincorth Aberdeen 293 C11
Kincorth Ho Moray 301 C10
Kincraig Highld 291 C10
Kincraigie Perth 286 C3
Kindallachan Perth 286 C3
Kineton Glos 99 F11
Kineton Warks 118 G6

Kineton Warks 118 G6
Kineton Green W Mid 134 G2
Kinfauns Perth 286 E5
King Edward Aberds 303 D7
King Sterndale Derbys 185 G9
Kingairloch Highld 289 D10
Kingarth Argyll 266 E2
Kingcoed Mon 78 D6
Kingdown N Som 60 G4
Kingerby Lincs 189 C9
Kingham Oxon 100 G5
Kinghay Wilts 30 B5
Kingholm Quay Dumfries 237 B11
Kinghorn Fife 280 D5
Kingie Highld 290 C3
Kinglassie Fife 280 B4
Kingledores Borders 260 D4
Kingoodie Perth 287 E7
King's Acre Hereford 97 C9
King's Bromley Staffs 152 F2
King's Caple Hereford 97 F11
King's Cliffe Northants 137 D10
Kings Clipstone Notts 171 C10
King's Coughton Warks 117 F11
King's Dyke Cambs 138 D4
King's End Worcs 116 G6
King's Furlong Hants 48 C6
King's Green Glos 98 E5
King's Green Worcs 116 E5
King's Heath W Mid 133 G11
Kings Hedges Cambs 123 E9
King's Hill Glos 80 G2
King's Hill W Mid 133 D9
King's Hill Kent 53 C7
Kings Langley Herts 85 E9
King's Lynn Norf 158 E2
King's Meaburn Cumb 231 G8
King's Mills Derbys 153 D8
King's Mills Wrex 166 F4
Kings Moss Mers 194 G4
King's Newnham Warks 119 B9
King's Newton Derbys 153 D7
King's Norton Leics 136 C3
King's Norton W Mid 117 B11
King's Nympton Devon 25 D11
King's Pyon Hereford 115 G8
King's Ripton Cambs 122 B5
King's Somborne Hants 47 G11
King's Stag Dorset 30 E2
King's Stanley Glos 80 E4
King's Sutton Northants 101 D9
King's Tamerton Plym 7 D9
King's Thorn Hereford 97 E10
King's Walden Herts 104 G3
Kings Walden Hants 48 G3
King's Worthy Hants 48 G3
Kingsand Corn 7 E8
Kingsash Bucks 84 D5
Kingsbarns Fife 287 F9
Kingsbridge Som 42 F3
Kingsbridge Devon 8 G4
Kingsburgh Highld 298 D3
Kingsbury London 67 B8
Kingsbury Warks 134 E4
Kingsbury Episcopi Som 28 C6
Kingsbury Regis Som 29 D7
Kingscausway Highld 301 B7
Kingscavil W Loth 279 F10
Kingsclere Hants 48 B4
Kingsclere Woodlands Hants 64 G4
Kingscote Glos 80 F4
Kingscott Devon 25 D8
Kingscourt Glos 80 E4
Kingscross N Ayrs 256 D2
Kingsditch Glos 99 G8
Kingsdon Som 29 C7
Kingsdown Kent 54 E2
Kingsdown Kent 55 D11
Kingsdown Swindon 63 C7
Kingsdown Wilts 61 G10
Kingseat Fife 280 C2
Kingseathill Fife 280 D2
Kingsett Devon 12 E6
Kingsey Bucks 84 D2
Kingsfold W Sus 51 F7
Kingsfold Lancs 194 B4
Kingsford Aberds 293 B8
Kingsford E Ayrs 267 G8
Kingsford Worcs 132 G6
Kingsforth Lincs 200 D5
Kingsgate Kent 71 E11
Kingshall Street Suff 125 E8
Kingsheanton Devon 40 F4
Kingshouse Stirl 285 E10
Kingshouse Hotel Highld 284 B6
Kingshurst W Mid 134 F3
Kingside Hill Cumb 238 G5
Kingskerswell Devon 9 B7
Kingskettle Fife 287 G7
Kingsland Anglesey 178 E2
Kingsland Hereford 115 E8
Kingsland Shrops 149 G7
Kingsland W Ches 183 G7
Kingsley Ches 183 F9
Kingsley Hants 49 F8
Kingsley Staffs 169 F8
Kingsley Green W Sus 49 G11
Kingsley Holt Staffs 169 F8
Kingsley Moor Staffs 169 G7
Kingsley Park Northants 120 E5
Kingslow Shrops 132 D5
Kingsmead Hants 33 E8
Kingsmoor Essex 86 D6
Kingsmuir Angus 287 C8
Kingsmuir Fife 287 G9
Kingsnorth Kent 54 F4
Kingstanding W Mid 133 E11
Kingsteignton Devon 14 G3
Kingsteps Highld 301 D9
Kingsthorpe Northants 120 E5
Kingsthorpe Hollow Northants 120 E5
Kingston Cambs 122 F6
Kingston Devon 8 F2
Kingston Devon 14 G5
Kingston Dorset 18 E5
Kingston Dorset 30 E3
Kingston E Loth 281 E9
Kingston Gtr Man 184 B6
Kingston Hants 31 F11
Kingston I o W 20 E5
Kingston Kent 55 C7

Kingston M Keynes 103 D8
Kingston Moray 302 C3
Kingston Ptsmth 33 G11
Kingston Bagpuize Oxon 82 F6
Kingston Blount Oxon 84 F2
Kingston by Sea W Sus 36 G2
Kingston Deverill Wilts 45 F10
Kingston Gorse W Sus 35 G9
Kingston Lisle Oxon 63 B10
Kingston Maurward Dorset 17 C10
Kingston near Lewes E Sus 36 F5
Kingston on Soar Notts 153 D10
Kingston Russell Dorset 17 C7
Kingston St Mary Som 28 B2
Kingston Seymour N Som 60 F2
Kingston Stert Oxon 84 E2
Kingston upon Hull Hull 200 B5
Kingston upon Thames London 67 F7
Kingston Vale London 67 E8
Kingstone Hereford 97 D8
Kingstone Hereford 98 G2
Kingstone S Yorks 197 F10
Kingstone Som 28 E5
Kingstone Staffs 151 D11
Kingstone Winslow Oxon 63 B9
Kingstown Cumb 239 F9
Kingsway Bath 61 G8
Kingsway Halton 183 D8
Kingswear Devon 9 E7
Kingswells Aberds 293 C10
Kingswinford W Mid 133 F7
Kingswood Bucks 83 B11
Kingswood Essex 69 B8
Kingswood Glos 80 G2
Kingswood Hereford 114 G5
Kingswood Herts 85 B10
Kingswood Kent 53 C10
Kingswood Powys 130 C4
Kingswood S Glos 60 E6
Kingswood Som 42 F6
Kingswood Sur 51 B8
Kingswood Warks 118 C3
Kingswood Warr 183 C10
Kingswood Brook Warks 118 C3
Kingswood Common Staffs 132 C6
Kingswood Common Worcs 116 F4
Kingthorpe Lincs 189 F10
Kington Hereford 114 F5
Kington S Glos 79 G10
Kington Worcs 117 F9
Kington Langley Wilts 62 D2
Kington Magna Dorset 30 C3
Kington St Michael Wilts 62 D2
Kingussie Highld 291 C9
Kingweston Som 44 G4
Kinharrachie Aberds 303 F9
Kinharvie Dumfries 237 C11
Kinhrive Ho Moray 302 E3
Kinkell Bridge Perth 286 F3
Kinknockie Aberds 303 E10
Kinkry Hill Cumb 240 B2
Kinlet Shrops 132 G4
Kinloch Fife 286 F6
Kinloch Highld 289 G8
Kinloch Highld 294 G5
Kinloch Highld 295 G8
Kinloch Highld 308 D5
Kinloch Perth 286 C5
Kinloch Perth 286 C6
Kinloch Damph Highld 299 E8
Kinloch Hourn Highld 295 E11
Kinloch Laggan Highld 291 E7
Kinloch Lodge Highld 308 D5
Kinloch Rannoch Perth 285 B9
Kinlochan Highld 289 C10
Kinlochard Stirl 285 G8
Kinlochbeoraid Highld 295 G10
Kinlochbervie Highld 306 D7
Kinlocheil Highld 289 B11
Kinlochewe Highld 299 C10
Kinlochleven Highld 290 G3
Kinlochmoidart Highld 289 B9
Kinlochmorar Highld 295 F10
Kinlochmore Highld 290 G3
Kinlochspelve Argyll 289 G8
Kinloid Highld 295 G8
Kinloss Moray 301 C10
Kinmel Bay = Bae Cinmel Conwy 181 E7
Kinmuck Aberds 293 B10
Kinmundy Aberds 293 B10
Kinnadie Aberds 303 E9
Kinnaird Perth 286 E6
Kinnaird Castle Angus 287 B10
Kinnauld Highld 309 J7
Kinneff Aberds 293 F10
Kinnelhead Dumfries 248 C2
Kinnell Angus 287 C10
Kinnerley Shrops 148 E6
Kinnernie Aberds 293 B9
Kinnersley Hereford 96 B6
Kinnersley Worcs 99 C7
Kinnerton Powys 114 E4
Kinnerton Green Flint 166 C4
Kinnesswood Perth 286 G5
Kinninvie Durham 233 G7
Kinnordy Angus 287 B7
Kinoulton Notts 154 C2
Kinross Perth 286 G5
Kinrossie Perth 286 E6
Kinsbourne Green Herts 85 B10
Kinsey Heath E Ches 167 G11
Kinsham Hereford 115 D7
Kinsham Worcs 99 D8
Kinsley W Yorks 198 E2
Kinson Bmouth 19 B7
Kintallan Argyll 275 E8
Kintbury W Berks 63 F11
Kintessack Moray 301 C9
Kintillo Perth 286 F5
Kintocher Aberds 293 C7
Kinton Hereford 115 C8
Kinton Shrops 149 F7
Kintore Aberds 293 B10
Kintour Argyll 254 B5
Kintra Argyll 254 C3
Kintra Argyll 288 G5
Kintradwell Highld 311 J3
Kintraw Argyll 275 C9
Kinuachdrachd Argyll 275 C7
Kinveachy Highld 291 B11
Kinver Staffs 132 G6
Kinwalsey Warks 134 F4
Kip Hill Durham 242 G6
Kiplin N Yorks 224 F4
Kiplingcotes E Yorks 208 D4
Kippax W Yorks 206 G4
Kippen Stirl 278 C3
Kippford or Scaur Dumfries 237 D10

Kippilaw Borders 262 D2
Kippilaw Mains Borders 262 D2
Kipping's Cross Kent 52 F6
Kippington Kent 52 C4
Kirbister Orkney 314 E2
Kirbister Orkney 314 D6
Kirbister Orkney 314 F3
Kirbuster Orkney 314 D2
Kirby Bedon Norf 142 B5
Kirby Bellars Leics 154 F4
Kirby Cane Norf 143 E7
Kirby Corner W Mid 118 B5
Kirby Cross Essex 108 G4
Kirby Fields Leics 135 C10
Kirby Green Norf 143 E7
Kirby Grindalythe N Yorks 217 F8
Kirby Hill N Yorks 215 F7
Kirby Hill N Yorks 224 D2
Kirby Knowle N Yorks 215 B9
Kirby-le-Soken Essex 108 G4
Kirby Misperton N Yorks 216 D5
Kirby Moor Cumb 240 E2
Kirby Muxloe Leics 135 C10
Kirby Row Norf 143 E7
Kirby Sigston N Yorks 225 G8
Kirby Underdale E Yorks 208 B2
Kirby Wiske N Yorks 215 C7
Kirdford W Sus 35 B8
Kirk Highld 310 D6
Kirk Bramwith S Yorks 198 E6
Kirk Deighton N Yorks 206 C3
Kirk Ella E Yorks 200 B4
Kirk Hallam Derbys 171 G7
Kirk Hammerton N Yorks 206 B5
Kirk Ireton Derbys 170 E3
Kirk Langley Derbys 152 B5
Kirk Merrington Durham 233 E11
Kirk Michael I o M 192 C4
Kirk of Shotts N Lnrk 268 C6
Kirk Sandall S Yorks 198 F6
Kirk Smeaton N Yorks 198 D4
Kirk Yetholm Borders 263 D8
Kirkabister Shetland 312 G6
Kirkabister Shetland 313 K6
Kirkandrews Dumfries 237 E8
Kirkandrews-on-Eden Cumb 239 F9
Kirkapol Argyll 288 E2
Kirkbampton Cumb 239 F8
Kirkbean Dumfries 237 D11
Kirkborough Cumb 229 D7
Kirkbrae Orkney 314 B4
Kirkbride Cumb 238 F6
Kirkbridge N Yorks 224 G5
Kirkbuddo Angus 287 C9
Kirkburn Borders 261 B7
Kirkburn E Yorks 208 B5
Kirkburton W Yorks 197 E7
Kirkby Lincs 189 C9
Kirkby Mers 182 B6
Kirkby N Yorks 225 D10
Kirkby Fenside Lincs 174 C4
Kirkby Fleetham N Yorks 224 G5
Kirkby Green Lincs 173 D9
Kirkby Hill N Yorks 215 F7
Kirkby in Ashfield Notts 171 D8
Kirkby-in-Furness Cumb 210 C4
Kirkby la Thorpe Lincs 173 F10
Kirkby Lonsdale Cumb 212 D2
Kirkby Malham N Yorks 213 G7
Kirkby Mallory Leics 135 C9
Kirkby Malzeard N Yorks 214 E4
Kirkby Mills N Yorks 216 B4
Kirkby on Bain Lincs 174 C2
Kirkby Overblow N Yorks 206 D2
Kirkby Stephen Cumb 222 D5
Kirkby Thore Cumb 231 F8
Kirkby Underwood Lincs 155 D11
Kirkby Wharfe N Yorks 206 E6
Kirkby Woodhouse Notts 171 E7
Kirkbymoorside N Yorks 216 B3
Kirkcaldy Fife 280 C5
Kirkcambeck Cumb 240 D2
Kirkcarswell Dumfries 237 E9
Kirkcolm Dumfries 236 C2
Kirkconnel Dumfries 258 G6
Kirkconnell Dumfries 237 C11
Kirkcowan Dumfries 236 C5
Kirkcudbright Dumfries 237 D8
Kirkdale Mers 182 C4
Kirkfieldbank S Lnrk 269 G7
Kirkforthar Feus Fife 286 G6
Kirkgunzeon Dumfries 237 C10
Kirkham Lancs 202 G4
Kirkham N Yorks 216 F4
Kirkhamgate W Yorks 197 C9
Kirkhams Gtr Man 195 F10
Kirkharle Northumb 252 G2
Kirkheaton Northumb 242 B2
Kirkheaton W Yorks 197 D7
Kirkhill Angus 293 G8
Kirkhill E Renf 267 D11
Kirkhill Highld 300 E5
Kirkhill Midloth 270 C4
Kirkhill Moray 302 E2
Kirkhill W Loth 279 G11
Kirkholt Gtr Man 195 E11
Kirkhope Borders 261 E9
Kirkhouse Borders 261 C8
Kirkhouse Cumb 240 F3
Kirkiboll Highld 308 D5
Kirkibost Highld 295 D7
Kirkinch Angus 287 C7
Kirkinner Dumfries 236 D6
Kirkintilloch E Dunb 278 G3
Kirkland Cumb 219 B11
Kirkland Cumb 229 B11
Kirkland Cumb 231 E8
Kirkland Dumfries 247 E8
Kirkland Dumfries 258 G6
Kirkland S Ayrs 244 E6
Kirkland Guards Cumb 229 C9
Kirkleatham Redcar 235 G7
Kirklees Gtr Man 195 E9
Kirklevington Stockton 225 D8
Kirkley Suff 143 E10
Kirklington N Yorks 214 C6
Kirklington Notts 171 D11
Kirklinton Cumb 239 D10
Kirkliston Edin 280 G2
Kirkmaiden Dumfries 236 F3
Kirkmichael Perth 286 B4
Kirkmichael S Ayrs 245 B8
Kirkmichael Mains Dumfries 248 F2
Kirkmuirhill S Lnrk 268 G5
Kirknewton Northumb 263 C10
Kirknewton W Loth 270 B2
Kirkney Aberds 302 F5
Kirkoswald Cumb 231 C7
Kirkoswald S Ayrs 244 B6
Kirkpatrick Dumfries 247 E10
Kirkpatrick Durham Dumfries 237 B9
Kirkpatrick-Fleming Dumfries 239 C7
Kirksanton Cumb 210 C2
Kirkshaw N Lnrk 268 C4
Kirkstall W Yorks 205 F11
Kirkstead Borders 261 E7
Kirkstead Lincs 173 C11
Kirkstile Aberds 302 F5
Kirkstyle Highld 310 B7
Kirkthorpe W Yorks 197 C11
Kirkton Aberds 302 E6
Kirkton Aberds 302 G6
Kirkton Angus 286 C6
Kirkton Angus 287 C8
Kirkton Angus 287 D8
Kirkton Argyll 275 C8
Kirkton Borders 262 G3
Kirkton Dumfries 247 G11
Kirkton Fife 280 D4
Kirkton Fife 287 E7
Kirkton Highld 295 C10
Kirkton Highld 299 E9
Kirkton Highld 301 D7
Kirkton Highld 309 K7
Kirkton Perth 286 F3
Kirkton S Lnrk 259 E10
Kirkton Stirl 285 G9
Kirkton W Loth 269 B10
Kirkton Manor Borders 260 B6
Kirkton of Airlie Angus 287 B7
Kirkton of Auchterhouse Angus 287 D7
Kirkton of Auchterless Aberds 303 E7
Kirkton of Barevan Highld 301 E8
Kirkton of Bourtie Aberds 303 G8
Kirkton of Collace Perth 286 D5
Kirkton of Craig Angus 287 B11
Kirkton of Culsalmond Aberds 302 F6
Kirkton of Durris Aberds 293 D9
Kirkton of Glenbuchat Aberds 292 B5
Kirkton of Glenisla Angus 292 G4
Kirkton of Kingoldrum Angus 287 B7
Kirkton of Largo Fife 287 G8
Kirkton of Lethendy Perth 286 C5
Kirkton of Logie Buchan Aberds 303 G9
Kirkton of Maryculter Aberds 293 D10
Kirkton of Menmuir Angus 293 G7
Kirkton of Monikie Angus 287 D9
Kirkton of Oyne Aberds 302 G6
Kirkton of Rayne Aberds 302 G6
Kirkton of Skene Aberds 293 C10
Kirkton of Tough Aberds 293 B8
Kirktonhill Borders 271 E9
Kirktonhill W Dunb 277 G7
Kirktoun E Ayrs 267 G8
Kirktown Aberds 303 D10
Kirktown of Alvah Aberds 302 C6
Kirktown of Deskford Moray 302 C5
Kirktown of Fetteresso Aberds 293 E10
Kirktown of Mortlach Moray 302 F3
Kirktown of Slains Aberds 303 G10
Kirkurd Borders 270 G2
Kirkwall Orkney 314 E4
Kirkwhelpington Northumb 251 G11
Kirkwood Dumfries 238 B4
Kirkwood N Lnrk 268 C4
Kirmington N Lincs 200 E6
Kirmond le Mire Lincs 189 C11
Kirn Argyll 276 F3
Kirriemuir Angus 287 B7
Kirstead Green Norf 142 D5
Kirtlebridge Dumfries 238 C6
Kirtleton Dumfries 249 G7
Kirtling Cambs 124 F3
Kirtling Green Cambs 124 F3
Kirtlington Oxon 83 B7
Kirtomy Highld 308 C7
Kirton Lincs 156 B6
Kirton Notts 171 B11
Kirton Suff 108 D5
Kirton Campus W Loth 269 B10
Kirton End Lincs 174 G3
Kirton Holme Lincs 174 G3
Kirton in Lindsey N Lincs 188 B6
Kiskin Cumb 210 B1
Kislingbury Northants 120 F3
Kit Hill Dorset 30 D4
Kitbridge Devon 28 G4
Kitchenroyd W Yorks 197 F8
Kite Green Warks 118 D3
Kite Hill I o W 21 C7
Kitebrook Warks 100 E4
Kites Hardwick Warks 119 D9
Kitlye Glos 80 E5
Kit's Coty Kent 69 G8
Kitt Green Gtr Man 194 F5
Kittisford Som 27 C9
Kittle Swansea 56 D5
Kitts End Herts 86 F2
Kitt's Green W Mid 134 F3
Kitt's Moss Gtr Man 184 E5
Kittwhistle Dorset 28 G5
Kittybrewster Aberdeen 293 C11
Kitwell W Mid 133 G9
Kitwood Hants 49 G7
Kivernoll Hereford 97 E9
Kiveton Park S Yorks 187 E7
Knaith Lincs 188 E4
Knaith Park Lincs 188 D4
Knap Corner Dorset 30 C4
Knaphill Sur 50 B3
Knapp Hants 32 C6
Knapp Perth 286 D6
Knapp Som 28 B4
Knapp Wilts 31 B8
Knapp Hill Wilts 30 B5
Knapthorpe Notts 172 D2
Knaptoft Leics 136 F2
Knapton Norf 160 C6
Knapton York 207 C7
Knapton Green Hereford 115 G8
Knapwell Cambs 122 E6
Knaresborough N Yorks 206 B3
Knarsdale Northumb 240 G5
Knatts Valley Kent 68 G5
Knauchland Moray 302 D5
Knaven Aberds 303 E8
Knave's Ash Kent 71 G7
Knaves Green Suff 126 D2
Knavesmire York 207 D7
Knayton N Yorks 215 B8
Knebworth Herts 104 G5
Knedlington E Yorks 199 B8
Kneesall Notts 172 C2
Kneesworth Cambs 104 C6
Kneeton Notts 172 F2
Knelston Swansea 56 D3
Knenhall Staffs 151 B8
Knettishall Suff 141 G9
Knightacott Devon 41 F7
Knightcote Warks 119 G7
Knightcott N Som 43 B11
Knightley Staffs 150 D6
Knightley Dale Staffs 150 E6
Knighton Devon 7 F10
Knighton Dorset 29 E10
Knighton Leicester 135 C11
Knighton Oxon 63 B9
Knighton Poole 18 B6
Knighton Som 43 E7
Knighton Staffs 150 D4
Knighton Staffs 168 G2
Knighton Wilts 63 E9
Knighton Worcs 117 F10
Knighton = Tref-y-Clawdd Powys 114 C5
Knighton Fields Leicester 135 C11
Knighton on Teme Worcs 116 C2
Knightor Corn 5 D10
Knight's End Cambs 139 E8
Knights Enham Hants 47 D11
Knight's Hill London 67 E10
Knightsbridge Glos 99 F7
Knightsbridge London 67 D9
Knightsmill Corn 11 E7
Knightswood Glasgow 267 B10
Knightwick Worcs 116 F4
Knill Hereford 114 E5
Knipe Fold Cumb 220 F6
Knipoch Argyll 289 G10
Knipton Leics 154 C6
Knitsley Durham 233 B8
Kniveton Derbys 170 E2
Knocharthur Highld 309 J7
Knock Argyll 289 F7
Knock Cumb 231 F9
Knock Moray 302 D5
Knockally Highld 311 G5
Knockan Highld 307 H7
Knockandhu Moray 302 G2
Knockando Moray 301 E11
Knockando Ho Moray 302 E2
Knockandoo Highld 301 G7
Knockbain Highld 300 D6
Knockbreck Highld 298 C2
Knockbrex Dumfries 237 E7
Knockcarrach Highld 290 B6
Knockdee Highld 310 C5
Knockdolian S Ayrs 244 F4
Knockdow Argyll 276 G2
Knockdown Glos 61 B10
Knockenbaird Aberds 302 G6
Knockenkelly N Ayrs 256 D2
Knockentiber E Ayrs 257 B9
Knockerdown Derbys 170 E2
Knockespock Ho Aberds 302 G5
Knockfarrel Highld 300 D5
Knockglass Dumfries 236 D2
Knockhall Kent 68 E5
Knockhall Castle Aberds 303 G9
Knockholt Kent 52 B3
Knockholt Pound Kent 52 B3
Knockie Lodge Highld 290 B6
Knockin Shrops 148 E6
Knockinlaw E Ayrs 257 B10
Knockinnon Highld 310 F5
Knocklaw Northumb 252 C3
Knocklearn Dumfries 237 B9
Knocklearoch Argyll 274 G4
Knockmill Kent 68 G5
Knocknaha Argyll 255 F7
Knocknain Dumfries 236 C1
Knockothie Aberds 303 F9
Knockrome Argyll 274 F6
Knocksharry I o M 192 D3
Knockstapplemore Argyll 255 F7
Knockvologan Argyll 274 B4
Knodishall Suff 127 E8
Knokan Argyll 288 G6
Knole Som 29 B7
Knoll Green Som 43 F8
Knoll Top N Yorks 214 F3
Knollbury Mon 60 B2
Knolls Green E Ches 184 F4
Knolton Wrex 149 B7
Knolton Bryn Wrex 149 B7
Knook Wilts 46 E2
Knossington Leics 136 B6
Knotbury Staffs 169 B8
Knott End-on-Sea Lancs 202 D3
Knott Lanes Gtr Man 196 G2
Knott Oak Som 28 E5
Knotting Beds 121 E10
Knotting Green Beds 121 E10
Knottingley W Yorks 198 C4
Knotts Cumb 230 G4
Knotts Lancs 203 C11
Knotty Ash Mers 182 C6
Knotty Corner Devon 24 B6
Knotty Green Bucks 84 G6
Knowbury Shrops 115 C11
Knowe Dumfries 236 B5
Knowe Shetland 313 G5
Knowefield Cumb 239 F10
Knowehead Aberds 293 C7
Knowehead Aberds 302 D5
Knowehead Dumfries 246 E4
Knowes E Loth 282 F2
Knowes of Elrick Aberds 302 D6
Knowesgate Northumb 251 F11
Knoweton N Lnrk 268 D5
Knowetop N Lnrk 268 D5
Knowhead Aberds 303 D9
Knowl Bank Staffs 168 F3
Knowl Green Essex 106 C5
Knowl Hill Windsor 65 D10
Knowl Wall Staffs 151 B7
Knowl Wood W Yorks 196 C2
Knowle Bristol 60 E6
Knowle Devon 15 E7
Knowle Devon 26 G3
Knowle Devon 27 F8
Knowle Devon 40 F3
Knowle Hants 33 F9
Knowle Shrops 115 C11
Knowle Som 43 F10
Knowle W Mid 118 B3
Knowle Wilts 63 G7
Knowle Fields Worcs 117 F10
Knowle Green Lancs 203 F8
Knowle Green Sur 66 E4
Knowle Grove W Mid 118 B3
Knowle Hill Sur 66 F3
Knowle Park W Yorks 205 E7
Knowle St Giles Som 28 E4
Knowlegate Shrops 115 C11
Knowles Hill Devon 14 G3
Knowlesands Shrops 132 E4
Knowlton Dorset 31 E8
Knowlton Kent 55 C9
Knowsley Mers 182 B6
Knowsthorpe W Yorks 206 G2
Knowstone Devon 26 C4
Knox Bridge Kent 53 E9
Knucklas Powys 114 C5
Knuston Northants 121 D8
Knutsford E Ches 184 F3
Knutton Staffs 168 F4
Knuzden Brook Lancs 195 B8
Knypersley Staffs 168 D5
Kraiknish Highld 294 C5
Krumlin W Yorks 196 D5
Kuggar Corn 2 F6
Kyle of Lochalsh Highld 295 C9
Kyleakin Highld 295 C9
Kylepark N Lnrk 268 C3
Kylerhea Highld 295 C9
Kylesknoydart Highld 295 F10
Kylesku Highld 306 F7
Kylesmorar Highld 295 F10
Kylestrome Highld 306 F7
Kyllachy House Highld 301 G7
Kymin Hereford 97 B11
Kymin Mon 79 C8
Kynaston Hereford 97 F10
Kynaston Shrops 149 E7
Kynnersley Telford 150 F3
Kyre Worcs 116 E2
Kyre Green Worcs 116 E2
Kyre Magna Worcs 116 E2
Kyre Park Worcs 116 E2
Kyrewood Worcs 116 D2

L

Labost W Isles 304 D4
Lacasaidh W Isles 304 F5
Lacasdal W Isles 304 E6
Laceby NE Lincs 201 F8
Laceby Acres NE Lincs 201 F8
Lacey Green Bucks 84 F4
Lacey Green E Ches 184 E4
Lach Dennis W Ches 184 G2
Lache W Ches 166 C5
Lackenby Redcar 225 B11
Lackford Suff 124 C5
Lacock Wilts 62 F2
Ladbroke Warks 119 F8
Laddenvean Corn 3 E7
Laddingford Kent 53 D7
Lade Kent 39 C9
Lade Bank Lincs 174 E5
Ladies Riggs N Yorks 214 G2
Ladmanlow Derbys 185 G8
Ladock Corn 5 E7
Ladwell Hants 32 C6
Lady Orkney 314 B6
Lady Green Mers 193 G10
Lady Hall Cumb 210 B3
Lady Halton Shrops 115 B9
Lady House Gtr Man 196 E2
Lady Park T & W 242 F6
Lady Wood W Yorks 206 F2
Ladybank Fife 287 F7
Ladybrook Notts 171 C8
Ladyburn Invclyd 276 F6
Ladycross Corn 12 D2
Ladyes Hill Warks 118 C5
Ladykirk Borders 273 F7
Ladyoak Shrops 131 C7
Ladyridge Hereford 97 E11
Lady's Green Suff 124 F5
Ladysford Aberds 303 C9
Ladywell London 67 E11
Ladywell Shrops 149 C9
Ladywell W Loth 269 B10
Ladywood Telford 132 C3
Ladywood W Mid 133 F11
Ladywood Worcs 117 E7
Laffak Mers 183 B8
Laga Highld 289 C8
Lagafater Lodge Dumfries 236 B3
Lagalochan Argyll 275 B9
Lagavulin Argyll 254 C5
Lagg Argyll 274 F6
Lagg N Ayrs 255 E10
Laggan Argyll 254 B3
Laggan Highld 289 B9
Laggan Highld 290 D4
Laggan Highld 291 D8
Laggan S Ayrs 245 G7
Laggan Lodge Argyll 289 G8
Lagganlia Highld 291 C10
Lagganmullan Dumfries 237 D7
Lagganulva Argyll 288 E6
Lagness W Sus 22 C5
Laide Highld 307 K3
Laig Highld 294 G6
Laigh Carnduff S Lnrk 268 F3
Laigh Fenwick E Ayrs 267 G9
Laigh Glengall S Ayrs 257 F8
Laighmuir E Ayrs 267 F9
Laighstonehall S Lnrk 268 E4
Laindon Essex 69 B7
Lair Highld 299 E10
Lair Perth 292 G3
Laira Plym 7 D10
Lairg Highld 309 J5
Lairg Lodge Highld 309 J5
Lairg Muir Highld 309 J5
Lairgmore Highld 300 F5
Laisterdyke W Yorks 205 G9
Laithes Cumb 230 E5
Laithkirk Durham 232 G5
Laity Moor Corn 4 F3
Lake Devon 12 D6
Lake Devon 24 F6
Lake Devon 40 G5
Lake I o W 21 E7
Lake Poole 18 C5
Lake Wilts 46 F6
Lake End Bucks 66 D2
Lakenham Norf 142 B4
Lakenheath Suff 140 G4
Laker's Green Sur 50 F4
Lakesend Norf 139 D10
Lakeside Cumb 211 B7
Lakeside Thurrock 68 D5
Lakeside Worcs 117 D11
Laleham Sur 66 F5
Laleston = Trelales Bridgend 57 F11
Lamanva Corn 3 C7
Lamarsh Essex 107 D7
Lamas Norf 160 E4
Lamb Corner Essex 107 E10
Lambden Borders 272 G4
Lamberden Kent 38 B4
Lamberhead Green Gtr Man 194 G4
Lamberhurst Kent 53 F7
Lamberhurst Quarter Kent 53 F7
Lamberton Borders 273 D9
Lambert's End W Mid 133 E9
Lambeth London 67 D10
Lambfair Green Suff 124 G4
Lambfoot Cumb 229 E9
Lambhill Glasgow 267 B11
Lambley Northumb 240 F5
Lambley Notts 171 F10
Lambourn W Berks 63 D10
Lambourn Woodlands W Berks 63 D10
Lambourne Corn 4 E5
Lambourne Essex 87 F7
Lambourne End Essex 87 G7
Lambridge Bath 61 F9
Lamb's Cross Kent 53 D9
Lambs' Green Dorset 18 B5
Lambs Green W Sus 51 F8
Lambston Pembs 72 B6
Lambton T & W 243 G7
Lamellion Corn 6 C4
Lamerton Devon 12 F5
Lamesley T & W 243 F7
Laminess Orkney 314 C6
Lamington Highld 301 B7
Lamington S Lnrk 259 C11
Lamlash N Ayrs 256 C2
Lamledra Corn 5 G10
Lamloch Dumfries 246 D2
Lammack Blkburn 195 B7
Lamonby Cumb 230 D4
Lamorick Corn 5 C10
Lamorna Corn 1 E4
Lamorran Corn 5 G7
Lampardbrook Suff 126 E5
Lampeter = Llanbedr Pont Steffan Ceredig 93 B11
Lampeter Velfrey Pembs 73 C11
Lamphey Pembs 73 E8
Lamplugh Cumb 229 G7
Lamport Northants 120 C5
Lampton London 66 D6
Lamyatt Som 45 F7
Lana Devon 12 B2
Lana Devon 24 F4
Lanark S Lnrk 269 G7
Lancaster Lancs 211 G9
Lanchester Durham 233 B9
Lancing W Sus 35 G11
Land Gate Gtr Man 194 G5
Landbeach Cambs 123 D9
Landcross Devon 25 C7
Landerberry Aberds 293 C9
Landewednack Corn 2 G6
Landford Wilts 32 D3
Landford Manor Wilts 32 C3
Landfordwood Wilts 32 C3
Landguard Manor I o W 21 E7
Landhill Devon 12 B4
Landican Mers 182 D3
Landimore Swansea 56 C3
Landkey Devon 40 G5
Landkey Newland Devon 40 G5
Landore Swansea 57 B7
Landport E Sus 36 E6
Landport Ptsmth 33 G10
Landrake Corn 7 C7
Landscove Devon 8 B5
Landshipping Pembs 73 C8
Landshipping Quay Pembs 73 C8
Landslow Green Gtr Man 185 B7
Landulph Corn 7 C8
Landwade Suff 124 D2
Landywood Staffs 133 B9
Lane Corn 4 C6
Lane Bottom Lancs 204 F3
Lane Bottom W Yorks 205 F7
Lane End Bucks 84 G4
Lane-end Corn 5 B10
Lane End Cumb 220 G2
Lane End Derbys 170 C6
Lane End Devon 24 G6
Lane End Dorset 18 C3
Lane End Flint 166 C3
Lane End Glos 79 B10
Lane End Hants 33 B11
Lane End Hants 33 B9
Lane End I o W 21 D9
Lane End Kent 68 E5
Lane End Lancs 204 D3
Lane End S Yorks 186 B5
Lane End Sur 49 E10
Lane End W Yorks 204 F6
Lane End Wilts 45 D10
Lane Ends Cumb 210 C6
Lane Ends Derbys 152 C4
Lane Ends E Ches 168 D2
Lane Ends E Ches 185 E7
Lane Ends Gtr Man 185 C7
Lane Ends Gtr Man 194 D6
Lane Ends Lancs 203 C11
Lane Ends Lancs 203 G11
Lane Ends N Yorks 204 E5
Lane Ends Stoke 168 E5
Lane Ends W Yorks 205 F10
Lane Green Staffs 133 C7
Lane Head Derbys 185 F11
Lane Head Durham 224 C2
Lane Head Gtr Man 183 B10
Lane Head Pembs 73 E8
Lane Head W Mid 133 C9
Lane Head W Yorks 197 F7
Lane Heads Lancs 202 F4
Lane Side Lancs 195 C9
Laneast Corn 11 E10
Laneham Notts 188 F4
Lanehead Durham 232 C2
Lanehead Northumb 251 F7
Lanehouse Dorset 17 F9
Lanercost Cumb 240 E3
Lanes End Bucks 84 D6
Lane's End Shrops 132 G2
Lanescot Corn 5 D11
Lanesend Pembs 73 D9
Lanesfield W Mid 133 D8
Laneshaw Bridge Lancs 204 E4
Laney Green Staffs 133 B9
Lanfach Caerph 78 F2
Langaford Devon 12 B4
Langage Devon 7 E11
Langal Highld 289 C9
Langaller Som 28 B3
Langar Notts 154 C4
Langbank Renfs 277 G7
Langbar N Yorks 205 C7
Langbaurgh N Yorks 225 C11
Langburnshiels Borders 250 C2
Langcliffe N Yorks 212 G6
Langdale Highld 308 E6
Langdale End N Yorks 227 G8
Langdon Corn 12 D2
Langdon Beck Durham 232 E3
Langdon Hills Essex 69 B7
Langdown Hants 32 F6
Langdyke Dumfries 238 C3
Langdyke Fife 287 G7
Langenhoe Essex 89 B8
Langford C Beds 104 C3
Langford Devon 14 B4
Langford Devon 27 G8
Langford Essex 88 D4
Langford Notts 172 D4
Langford Oxon 82 E2
Langford Som 28 B2
Langford Budville Som 27 C10
Langford Green Devon 27 G8
Langford Green N Som 44 B3
Langham Dorset 30 B3
Langham Essex 107 E10
Langham Norf 177 E8
Langham Rutland 154 G6
Langham Som 28 E4
Langham Suff 125 D9
Langhaugh Borders 260 C6
Langho Lancs 203 G10
Langholm Dumfries 249 G9
Langholme N Lincs 188 B3
Langhope Borders 261 E10
Langland Swansea 56 D6
Langlee Borders 262 B2
Langlee Mains Borders 262 B2
Langleeford Northumb 263 E10
Langlees Falk 279 E7
Langley Derbys 170 F6
Langley E Ches 184 G6
Langley Essex 105 D8
Langley Glos 99 F10
Langley Gtr Man 195 F11
Langley Hants 32 G6
Langley Herts 104 G4
Langley Kent 53 C10
Langley Northumb 241 E8
Langley Oxon 82 B4
Langley Slough 66 D4
Langley Som 27 B9
Langley W Mid 133 F9
Langley W Sus 34 B4
Langley Warks 118 E3
Langley Burrell Wilts 62 D2
Langley Common Derbys 152 B5
Langley Common Wokingham 65 F9
Langley Corner Bucks 66 C4
Langley Green Derbys 152 B5
Langley Green Essex 107 G7
Langley Green W Mid 133 F9
Langley Green W Sus 51 F9
Langley Green Warks 118 E3
Langley Heath Kent 53 C10
Langley Marsh Som 27 B9
Langley Mill Derbys 170 F6
Langley Moor Durham 233 C11
Langley Park Durham 233 C10
Langley Street Norf 143 C7
Langley Vale Sur 51 B8
Langleybury Herts 85 E9
Langloan N Lnrk 268 C4
Langney E Sus 23 E10
Langold Notts 187 D9
Langore Corn 12 D2
Langport Som 28 B6
Langrick Lincs 174 F3
Langrick Bridge Lincs 174 F3
Langridge Bath 61 F8
Langridge Ford Devon 25 C9
Langrigg Cumb 222 C5
Langrigg Cumb 229 B9
Langrish Hants 34 C2
Langsett S Yorks 197 G8
Langshaw Borders 262 B2
Langside Glasgow 267 C11
Langside Perth 285 F11
Langskaill Orkney 314 B4
Langstone Devon 13 E10
Langstone Hants 22 C2
Langstone Newport 78 G5
Langthorne N Yorks 224 G5
Langthorpe N Yorks 215 F7
Langthwaite N Yorks 223 E10
Langtoft E Yorks 217 F10
Langtoft Lincs 156 G2
Langton Durham 224 B3
Langton Lincs 174 B2
Langton Lincs 190 G5
Langton N Yorks 216 F5
Langton by Wragby Lincs 189 F11
Langton Green Kent 52 F4
Langton Green Suff 126 C2
Langton Herring Dorset 17 E8
Langton Long Blandford Dorset 30 F5
Langton Matravers Dorset 18 F6
Langtree Devon 25 D7
Langtree Week Devon 25 D7
Langwathby Cumb 231 E7
Langwell Ho Highld 311 G5
Langwell Lodge Highld 307 J6
Langwith Derbys 171 B8
Langwith Junction Derbys 171 B8
Langworth Lincs 189 F9
Lanham Green Essex 106 G5
Lanivet Corn 5 C10
Lanjeth Corn 5 E9
Lanjew Corn 5 C9
Lank Corn 11 F7
Lanlivery Corn 5 D11
Lanner Corn 2 B6
Lanreath Corn 6 D3
Lanrick Stirl 285 G10
Lansallos Corn 6 E3
Lansbury Park Caerph 59 B7
Lansdown Bath 61 F8
Lansdown Glos 99 G8
Lanstephan Corn 12 D2
Lanteglos Corn 11 E7
Lanteglos Highway Corn 6 E3
Lanton Borders 262 E4
Lanton Northumb 263 C10
Lantuel Corn 5 B9
Lantyan Corn 6 D2
Lapal W Mid 133 G9
Lapford Devon 26 F2
Lapford Cross Devon 26 F2
Laphroaig Argyll 254 C4
Lapley Staffs 151 G7
Lapworth Warks 118 C3
Larachbeg Highld 289 E8
Larbert Falk 279 E7
Larbreck Lancs 202 E4
Larches Lancs 202 G6
Larden Green E Ches 167 E9
Larg Highld 292 B2
Largie Aberds 302 F6
Largiebaan Argyll 255 F7
Largiemore Argyll 275 E10
Largoward Fife 287 G8
Largs N Ayrs 266 D4
Largue Aberds 302 E6
Largybeg N Ayrs 256 E3
Largymeanoch N Ayrs 256 E2
Largymore N Ayrs 256 E2
Lark Hill Gtr Man 195 G7
Larkfield Invclyd 276 F4
Larkfield Kent 53 B8
Larkfield W Yorks 205 F10
Larkhall Bath 61 F9
Larkhall S Lnrk 268 E5
Larkhill Wilts 46 E6
Larklands Derbys 171 G7
Larks' Hill Suff 108 B3
Larling Norf 141 F9
Larport Hereford 97 D11
Larrick Corn 12 F2
Larriston Borders 250 E2
Lartington Durham 223 B10
Lary Aberds 292 C5
Lasborough Glos 80 G4
Lasham Hants 49 E7
Lashenden Kent 53 E10
Lask Edge Staffs 168 D6
Lassington Glos 98 G5
Lassodie Fife 280 C2
Lastingham N Yorks 226 G4
Latcham Som 44 D2
Latchbrook Corn 7 D8
Latchford Herts 105 G7
Latchford Oxon 83 E11
Latchford Warr 183 D10
Latchingdon Essex 88 E5
Latchley Corn 12 G4
Latchmere Green Hants 64 G6
Latchmore Bank Essex 87 B7
Lately Common Warr 183 B11
Lathallan Mill Fife 287 G8
Lathbury M Keynes 103 B7
Latheron Highld 310 F5
Latheronwheel Highld 310 F5
Latheronwheel Ho Highld 310 F5
Lathom Lancs 194 E3
Lathones Fife 287 G8
Latimer Bucks 85 F8
Latteridge S Glos 61 C7
Lattiford Som 29 B11
Lattinford Hill Suff 107 D11
Latton Wilts 81 F9
Latton Bush Essex 87 D7
Lauchintilly Aberds 293 B9
Laudale Ho Highld 289 D9
Lauder Borders 271 F10
Lauder Barns Borders 271 F10
Laugharne = Talacharn Carms 74 C4
Laughern Hill Worcs 116 F5
Laughterton Lincs 188 F4
Laughton E Sus 23 C8
Laughton Leics 136 F3
Laughton Lincs 155 C11
Laughton Lincs 188 B4
Laughton Common E Sus 23 C7
Laughton Common S Yorks 187 D8
Laughton en le Morthen S Yorks 187 D8
Launcells Corn 24 F2
Launcells Cross Corn 24 F3
Launceston Corn 12 D2
Launcherley Som 44 E4
Laund Lancs 195 C10
Launton Oxon 102 G2
Laurencekirk Aberds 293 F9
Laurieston Dumfries 237 C8
Laurieston Falk 279 F8
Lavendon M Keynes 121 G8
Lavenham Suff 107 B8
Laverackloch Moray 301 C11
Laverhay Dumfries 248 D4
Laverlaw Borders 261 B7
Laverley Som 44 F5
Lavernock V Glam 59 F7
Laversdale Cumb 239 E11
Laverstock Wilts 47 G7
Laverstoke Hants 48 D3
Laverton Glos 99 D11
Laverton N Yorks 214 E4
Laverton Som 45 C9
Lavington Sands Wilts 46 B4
Lavister Wrex 166 D5
Lavrean Corn 5 D10
Law Hill S Lnrk 268 E6
Lawers Perth 285 D10
Lawers Perth 285 E11
Lawford Essex 107 E11
Lawford Som 42 F6
Lawford Heath Warks 119 C9
Lawhill Perth 286 F3
Lawhitton Corn 12 E3
Lawkland N Yorks 212 F5
Lawkland Green N Yorks 212 F5
Lawley Telford 132 B3
Lawn Swindon 63 C7
Lawnhead Staffs 150 E6
Lawns W Yorks 197 C10
Lawnswood W Yorks 205 F11
Lawnt Denb 165 B8
Lawrence Hill Newport 59 B10
Lawrence Weston Bristol 60 D4
Lawrenny Pembs 73 D8
Lawrenny Quay Pembs 73 D8
Lawshall Suff 125 G7
Lawshall Green Suff 125 G7
Lawton Hereford 115 F8
Lawton Shrops 131 G10
Lawton-gate E Ches 168 D4
Lawton Heath End E Ches 168 D3
Laxey I o M 192 D5
Laxfield Suff 126 C5
Laxfirth Shetland 313 H6
Laxfirth Shetland 313 J6
Laxford Bridge Highld 306 E7
Laxo Shetland 313 G6
Laxobigging Shetland 312 F6
Laxton E Yorks 199 B9
Laxton Northants 137 D8
Laxton Notts 172 B2
Laycock W Yorks 204 E6
Layer Breton Essex 88 B6
Layer de la Haye Essex 89 B7
Layer Marney Essex 88 B6
Layerthorpe York 207 C8
Layham Suff 107 C10
Laymore Dorset 28 G5
Layters Green Bucks 85 G7
Laytham E Yorks 207 F10
Layton Blkpool 202 F2
Lazenby Redcar 225 B11
Lazonby Cumb 230 D6
Le Skerne Haughton Darl 224 B6
Lea Derbys 170 D4
Lea Hereford 98 G3
Lea Lancs 202 G5
Lea Lincs 188 D4
Lea Shrops 131 B8
Lea Shrops 131 F7
Lea Wilts 62 B3
Lea Bridge London 67 B11
Lea by Backford W Ches 182 G5
Lea End Worcs 117 B10
Lea Forge E Ches 168 F2
Lea Green Mers 183 C8
Lea Hall W Mid 134 F2
Lea Heath Staffs 151 D10
Lea Line Hereford 98 G3
Lea Marston Warks 134 E4
Lea Town Lancs 202 G5
Lea Valley Herts 85 B11
Lea Yeat Cumb 212 B5
Leabrooks Derbys 170 E6
Leac a Li W Isles 305 J3
Leacainn W Isles 305 H3
Leachkin Highld 300 E6
Leacnasaide Highld 299 B7
Leadburn Midloth 270 D4
Leaden Roding Essex 87 C9
Leadendale Staffs 151 B8
Leadenham Lincs 173 E7
Leadgate Cumb 231 C10
Leadgate Durham 242 G4
Leadgate T & W 242 F4
Leadhills S Lnrk 259 G9
Leadingcross Green Kent 53 C11
Leadmill Derbys 186 E2
Leadmill Flint 166 C2
Leafield Oxon 82 B4
Leafield Wilts 61 F11
Leagrave Luton 103 G10
Leagreen Hants 19 C11
Leake Lincs 174 F6
Leake N Yorks 225 G8
Leake Commonside Lincs 174 E5
Leake Fold Hill Lincs 174 E6
Lealholm N Yorks 226 D5
Lealholm Side N Yorks 226 D5
Lealt Argyll 275 D7
Lealt Highld 298 C5
Leam Derbys 186 F2
Leamington Hastings Warks 119 D8
Leamoor Common Shrops 131 F8
Leamore W Mid 133 C9
Leamside Durham 234 B2
Leanach Argyll 275 D11
Leanachan Highld 290 F4
Leanaig Highld 300 D5
Leapgate Worcs 116 C6
Leargybreck Argyll 274 F6
Lease Rigg N Yorks 226 E6
Leasey Bridge Herts 85 C11
Leasgill Cumb 211 C9
Leasingham Lincs 173 F9
Leasingthorne Durham 233 F11
Leason Swansea 56 C3
Leasowe Mers 182 C3
Leatherhead Sur 51 B7
Leatherhead Common Sur 51 B7
Leathern Bottle Glos 80 E2
Leathley N Yorks 205 D10
Leaths Dumfries 237 C9
Leaton Shrops 149 F9
Leaton Telford 150 G2
Leaton Heath Shrops 149 F9
Leaveland Kent 54 C4
Leavenheath Suff 107 D9
Leavening N Yorks 216 G5
Leaves Green London 68 G2
Leavesden Green Herts 85 E9
Leazes Durham 242 F5
Lebberston N Yorks 217 C11
Leburnick Corn 12 E3
Lechlade-on-Thames Glos 82 F2
Leck Lancs 212 D2
Leckford Hants 47 F11
Leckfurin Highld 308 D7
Leckgruinart Argyll 274 G3
Leckhampstead Bucks 102 D4
Leckhampstead W Berks 64 D2
Leckhampstead Thicket W Berks 64 D2
Leckhampton Glos 80 B6
Leckie Highld 299 C10
Leckmelm Highld 307 K6
Leckuary Argyll 275 D9
Leckwith V Glam 59 E7
Leconfield E Yorks 208 E6
Ledaig Argyll 289 F11
Ledburn Bucks 103 G8
Ledbury Hereford 98 D4
Ledcharrie Stirl 285 E9
Leddington Glos 98 E3
Ledgemoor Hereford 115 G8
Ledgowan Highld 299 D11
Ledicot Hereford 115 E8
Ledmore Angus 293 G7
Ledmore Highld 307 H7
Lednagullin Highld 308 C7
Ledsham W Ches 182 G5
Ledsham W Yorks 198 B3
Ledston W Yorks 198 B2
Ledston Luck W Yorks 206 G4
Ledstone Devon 8 F4
Ledwell Oxon 101 F8
Lee Argyll 288 G6
Lee Devon 40 D3
Lee Devon 40 D5
Lee Hants 32 D5
Lee Lancs 203 B7
Lee London 67 E11
Lee Northumb 241 F10
Lee Shrops 149 C8
Lee Bank W Mid 133 F11
Lee Brockhurst Shrops 149 D10
Lee Chapel Essex 69 B7
Lee Clump Bucks 84 E6
Lee Common Bucks 84 E6
Lee Gate Bucks 84 D5
Lee Ground Hants 33 F8
Lee Head Derbys 185 C8
Lee Mill Devon 8 D2
Lee Moor Devon 7 C11
Lee Moor W Yorks 197 B10
Lee-on-the-Solent Hants 33 G9
Lee-over-Sands Essex 89 C10
Leeans Shetland 313 J5
Leebotten Shetland 313 L6
Leebotwood Shrops 131 D9
Leece Cumb 210 F4
Leechpool Mon 60 B4
Leechpool Pembs 73 B7
Leeds Kent 53 C10
Leeds W Yorks 205 G11
Leedstown Corn 2 C4
Leeford Devon 41 D9
Leegomery Telford 150 G3
Leeholme Durham 233 E10
Leek Staffs 169 D7
Leek Wootton Warks 118 D5
Leekbrook Staffs 169 E7
Leeming N Yorks 214 B5
Leeming W Yorks 204 G6
Leeming Bar N Yorks 224 G5
Leemings Lancs 203 D10
Lees Derbys 152 B5
Lees Gtr Man 196 G3

382 Lee – Lla

Lees W Yorks 204 F6
Leesthorpe Leics 154 G5
Leeswood = Coed-Llai Flint 166 D3
Leetown Perth 286 E6
Leftwich W Ches 183 G11
Legar Powys 78 B2
Legbourne Lincs 190 E5
Legburthwaite Cumb 220 B6
Legerwood Borders 271 G11
Leggatt Hill W Sus 34 C6
Legsby Lincs 189 D10
Leicester Leicester 135 C11
Leicester Forest East Leics 135 C10
Leicester Grange Warks 135 E8
Leigh Devon 26 E2
Leigh Dorset 18 B6
Leigh Dorset 29 F10
Leigh Dorset 30 F3
Leigh Glos 99 F7
Leigh Gtr Man 195 G7
Leigh Kent 52 D4
Leigh Shrops 130 C6
Leigh Sur 51 D8
Leigh Wilts 81 G9
Leigh Worcs 116 G5
Leigh Beck Essex 69 C10
Leigh Common Som 30 B2
Leigh Delamere Wilts 61 D11
Leigh Green Kent 54 G2
Leigh-on-Sea Sthend 69 B10
Leigh Park Hants 22 B2
Leigh Sinton Worcs 116 G5
Leigh upon Mendip Som 45 D7
Leigh Woods N Som 60 E5
Leigham Plym 7 D10
Leighland Chapel Som 42 F4
Leighswood W Mid 133 C11
Leighterton Glos 80 G4
Leighton N Yorks 214 D3
Leighton Shrops 132 B2
Leighton Som 45 E8
Leighton = Tre'r llai Powys 130 B4
Leighton Bromswold Cambs 122 B2
Leighton Buzzard C Beds 103 F8
Leinthall Earls Hereford 115 D8
Leinthall Starkes Hereford 115 D8
Leintwardine Hereford 115 C8
Leire Leics 135 E10
Leirinmore Highld 308 C4
Leiston Suff 127 E8
Leitfie Perth 286 C6
Leith Edin 280 F5
Leithenhall Dumfries 248 D4
Leitholm Borders 272 G5
Lelant Corn 2 B2
Lelant Downs Corn 2 B2
Lelley E Yorks 209 G10
Lem Hill Worcs 116 C4
Lemington T & W 242 E5
Lemmington Hall Northumb 264 G4
Lempitlaw Borders 263 C7
Lemsford Herts 86 C2
Lenacre Cumb 212 B3
Lenborough Bucks 102 E3
Lenchwick Worcs 99 B10
Lendalfoot S Ayrs 244 F4
Lendrick Lodge Stirl 285 G9
Lenham Kent 53 C11
Lenham Forstal Kent 54 C2
Lenham Heath Kent 54 D2
Lennel Borders 273 G7
Lennoxtown E Dunb 278 F2
Lent Bucks 66 C2
Lent Rise Bucks 66 C2
Lenten Pool Denb 165 B8
Lenton Lincs 155 C10
Lenton Nottingham 153 B11
Lenton Abbey Nottingham 153 B10
Lentran Highld 300 E5
Lenwade Norf 159 F11
Leny Ho Stirl 285 G10
Lenzie E Dunb 278 G3
Lenziemill N Lnrk 278 G5
Leoch Angus 287 D7
Leochel-Cushnie Aberds 293 B7
Leominster Hereford 115 F9
Leomonsley Staffs 134 B2
Leonard Stanley Glos 80 E4
Leonardston Pembs 72 D6
Leorin Argyll 254 C4
Lepe Hants 20 B5
Lephin Highld 297 G7
Lephinchapel Argyll 275 D10
Lephinmore Argyll 275 D10
Leppington N Yorks 216 G5
Lepton W Yorks 197 D8
Lepton Edge W Yorks 197 D8
Lerigoligan Argyll 275 C9
Lerrocks Stirl 285 G11
Lerryn Corn 6 D2
Lerwick Shetland 313 J6
Lesbury Northumb 264 G6
Leschangie Aberds 293 B9
Leslie Aberds 302 G5
Leslie Fife 286 G6
Lesmahagow S Lnrk 259 B8
Lesnewth Corn 11 C8
Lessendrum Aberds 302 E5
Lessingham Norf 161 D7
Lessness Heath London 68 D3
Lessonhall Cumb 238 G6
Leswalt Dumfries 236 C2
Letchmore Heath Herts 85 F11
Letchworth Herts 104 E4
Letcombe Bassett Oxon 63 B11
Letcombe Regis Oxon 63 B11
Letham Angus 287 C9
Letham Falk 279 D7
Letham Fife 287 F7
Letham Perth 286 E4
Letham Grange Angus 287 C10
Lethem Borders 250 B5
Lethen Ho Highld 301 D9
Lethenty Aberds 303 E8
Lethenty Aberds 303 G7
Letheringham Suff 126 F5
Letheringsett Norf 159 B11
Lettaford Devon 13 E10
Lettan Orkney 314 B7
Letter Aberds 293 B9
Letterewe Highld 299 B9
Letterfearn Highld 295 C10
Letterfinlay Highld 290 D4
Lettermay Argyll 284 G5
Lettermorar Highld 295 G9
Lettermore Argyll 288 E6
Letters Highld 307 L6
Letterston = Treletert Pembs 91 F8
Lettoch Highld 292 B2
Lettoch Highld 301 F10
Lettoch Moray 302 F3
Lettoch Perth 291 G11
Letton Hereford 96 B6
Letton Hereford 115 C7
Letton Green Norf 141 B9
Lett's Green Kent 52 B3
Letty Brongu Bridgend 57 D11
Letty Green Herts 86 C3
Letwell S Yorks 187 D9
Leuchars Fife 287 E8
Leuchars Ho Moray 302 C2
Leumrabhagh W Isles 305 G5
Levalsa Meor Corn 5 F10
Levan Invclyd 276 F4
Levaneap Shetland 313 G6
Levedale Staffs 151 F7
Level of Mendalgief Newport 59 B10
Level's Green Essex 105 G9
Leven E Yorks 209 D8
Leven Fife 287 G7
Leven Seat W Loth 269 D8
Levencorroch N Ayrs 256 E2
Levenhall E Loth 281 G7
Levens Cumb 211 B9
Levens Green Herts 105 G7
Levenshulme Gtr Man 184 C5
Leventhorpe W Yorks 205 G8
Levenwick Shetland 313 L6
Lever-Edge Gtr Man 195 F8
Leverington Cambs 157 G8
Leverington Common Cambs 157 G8
Leverstock Green Herts 85 D9
Leverton Lincs 174 F6
Leverton W Berks 63 E10
Leverton Highgate Lincs 174 F6
Leverton Lucasgate Lincs 174 F6
Leverton Outgate Lincs 174 F6
Levington Suff 108 D4
Levisham N Yorks 226 G6
Levishie Highld 290 B6
Lew Oxon 82 D4
Lewannick Corn 11 E11
Lewcombe Dorset 29 F9
Lewdown Devon 12 D4
Lewes E Sus 36 E6
Leweston Pembs 91 G8
Lewisham London 67 D11
Lewiston Highld 300 G5
Lewistown Bridgend 58 B2
Lewknor Oxon 84 F2
Leworthy Devon 24 G4
Leworthy Devon 41 F7
Lewson Street Kent 70 G3
Lewth Lancs 202 F5
Lewthorn Cross Devon 13 F11
Lewtrenchard Devon 12 D5
Lexden Essex 107 G9
Ley Aberds 293 B7
Ley Corn 6 B3
Ley Som 41 F10
Ley Green Herts 104 G3
Ley Hey Park Gtr Man 185 D7
Ley Hill W Mid 134 D2
Leybourne Kent 53 B7
Leyburn N Yorks 224 G2
Leycett Staffs 168 F3
Leyfields Staffs 134 B4
Leyhill Bucks 85 E7
Leyhill S Glos 79 G11
Leyland Lancs 194 C4
Leylodge Aberds 293 B9
Leymoor W Yorks 196 D6
Leys Aberds 292 C6
Leys Aberds 303 D10
Leys Cumb 219 B11
Leys Perth 286 D6
Leys Staffs 169 G8
Leys Castle Highld 300 E6
Leys Hill Hereford 79 B9
Leys of Cossans Angus 287 C7
Leysdown-on-Sea Kent 70 E4
Leysmill Angus 287 C10
Leysters Hereford 115 E11
Leysters Pole Hereford 115 E11
Leyton London 67 B11
Leytonstone London 67 B11
Lezant Corn 12 F2
Lezerea Corn 2 C5
Leziate Norf 158 F3
Lhanbryde Moray 302 C2
Liatrie Highld 300 F2
Libanus Powys 95 F9
Libberton S Lnrk 269 G9
Libbery Worcs 117 F9
Liberton Edin 270 B5
Liceasto W Isles 305 J3
Lichfield Staffs 134 B2
Lick Perth 286 B2
Lickey Worcs 117 B9
Lickey End Worcs 117 C9
Lickfold W Sus 34 B6
Lickhill Worcs 116 C6
Lickleyhead Castle Aberds 302 G6
Liddaton Devon 12 E5
Liddel Orkney 314 H4
Liddesdale Highld 289 D9
Liddeston Pembs 72 D5
Liddington Swindon 63 C8
Liden Swindon 63 C7
Lidgate Suff 124 F4
Lidget S Yorks 199 G7
Lidget Green W Yorks 205 G8
Lidgett Notts 171 B10
Lidgett Park W Yorks 206 F2
Lidham Hill E Sus 38 D4
Lidlington C Beds 103 D9
Lidsey W Sus 22 C6
Lidsing Kent 69 G9
Lidstone Oxon 101 G7
Lieurary Highld 310 C4
Liff Angus 287 D7
Lifford W Mid 117 B11
Lifton Devon 12 D3
Liftondown Devon 12 D3
Light Oaks Staffs 168 E6
Lightcliffe W Yorks 196 B6
Lighteach Shrops 149 C10
Lightfoot Green Lancs 202 G6
Lighthorne Warks 118 F6
Lighthorne Heath Warks 119 F7
Lighthorne Rough Warks 118 F6
Lightmoor Telford 132 B3
Lightpill Glos 80 E4
Lightwater Sur 66 G2
Lightwood S Yorks 186 E5
Lightwood Shrops 132 E2
Lightwood Shrops 150 D3
Lightwood Staffs 169 G8
Lightwood Stoke 168 G6
Lightwood Green E Ches 167 G10
Lightwood Green Wrex 166 G5
Liglartrie S Ayrs 244 F6
Lilbourne Northants 119 B11
Lilburn Tower Northumb 264 E2
Lilford Gtr Man 195 G7
Lillesdon Som 28 C4
Lilleshall Telford 150 F4
Lilley Herts 104 F2
Lilley W Berks 64 D2
Lilliesleaf Borders 262 E2
Lillingstone Dayrell Bucks 102 D4
Lillingstone Lovell Bucks 102 C4
Lillington Dorset 29 E10
Lillington Warks 118 D6
Lilliput Poole 18 C6
Lilstock Som 43 E7
Lilybank Invclyd 276 G6
Lilyhurst Shrops 150 G4
Lilyvale Kent 54 F5
Limbrick Lancs 194 D6
Limbury Luton 103 G11
Lime Side Gtr Man 196 G2
Lime Street Worcs 98 E6
Lime Tree Park W Mid 118 B5
Limebrook Hereford 115 D7
Limefield Gtr Man 195 E10
Limehouse London 67 C11
Limehurst Gtr Man 196 G2
Limekiln Field Derbys 187 G7
Limekilnburn S Lnrk 268 E4
Limekilns Fife 279 E11
Limerigg Falk 279 G7
Limerstone I o W 20 E4
Limestone Brae Northumb 231 B11
Limington Som 29 C8
Limpenhoe Norf 143 C7
Limpenhoe Hill Norf 143 C8
Limpers Hill Wilts 45 G10
Limpley Stoke Wilts 61 G9
Limpsfield Sur 52 C2
Limpsfield Chart Sur 52 C2
Limpsfield Common Sur 52 C2
Linbriggs Northumb 251 B9
Linburn W Loth 270 B2
Linby Notts 171 E8
Linchmere W Sus 49 G11
Lincluden Dumfries 237 B11
Lincoln Lincs 189 G7
Lincomb Worcs 116 D6
Lincombe Devon 8 D4
Lincombe Devon 40 D3
Lindal in Furness Cumb 210 D5
Lindale Cumb 211 C8
Lindean Borders 261 C11
Linden Glos 80 B4
Lindfield W Sus 36 B4
Lindford Hants 49 F10
Lindifferon Fife 287 F7
Lindley N Yorks 205 D10
Lindley W Yorks 196 D6
Lindley Green N Yorks 205 D10
Lindores Fife 286 F6
Lindow End E Ches 184 F4
Lindrick Dale S Yorks 187 E8
Lindridge Worcs 116 D3
Lindsell Essex 106 F2
Lindsey Suff 107 C9
Lindsey Tye Suff 107 B9
Lindwell W Yorks 196 C5
Lineholt Worcs 116 D6
Lineholt Common Worcs 116 D6
Liney Som 43 F11
Linfitts Gtr Man 196 F3
Linford Hants 31 F11
Linford Thurrock 69 D7
Lingague I o M 192 E3
Lingards Wood W Yorks 196 E5
Lingbob W Yorks 205 F7
Lingdale Redcar 226 B3
Lingen Hereford 115 D7
Lingfield Darl 224 C6
Lingfield Sur 51 E11
Lingfield Common Sur 51 E11
Lingley Green Warr 183 D9
Lingley Mere Warr 183 D10
Lingreabhagh W Isles 296 C6
Lingwood Norf 143 B7
Linhope Borders 249 C10
Linhope Northumb 263 F11
Linicro Highld 298 C3
Link N Som 44 B3
Linkend Worcs 98 E6
Linkenholt Hants 47 B11
Linkhill Kent 38 B4
Linkinhorne Corn 12 G2
Linklater Orkney 314 H4
Linklet Orkney 314 A7
Linksness Orkney 314 E5
Linksness Orkney 314 F2
Linktown Fife 280 C5
Linley Shrops 131 E7
Linley Shrops 132 D3
Linley Brook Shrops 132 D3
Linley Green Hereford 116 G3
Linleygreen Shrops 132 D3
Linlithgow W Loth 279 F10
Linlithgow Bridge W Loth 279 F9
Linndhu Ho Argyll 289 D7
Linneraineach Highld 307 J6
Linns Angus 292 F3
Linnyshaw Gtr Man 195 G8
Linshiels Northumb 251 B9
Linsiadar W Isles 304 E4
Linsidemore Highld 309 K5
Linslade C Beds 103 F8
Linstead Parva Suff 126 B6
Linstock Cumb 239 F10
Linthorpe M'bro 225 B9
Linthurst Worcs 117 C9
Linthwaite W Yorks 196 E6
Lintlaw Borders 272 D6
Lintmill Moray 302 C5
Linton Borders 263 D7
Linton Cambs 105 B11
Linton Derbys 152 F5
Linton Hereford 98 F3
Linton Kent 53 D9
Linton N Yorks 213 G9
Linton Northumb 253 E7
Linton W Yorks 206 D3
Linton Heath Derbys 152 F5
Linton Hill Hereford 98 G3
Linton-on-Ouse N Yorks 215 G9
Lintridge Glos 98 E4
Lintz Durham 242 F5
Lintzford T & W 242 F4
Lintzgarth Durham 232 C4
Linwood Hants 31 F11
Linwood Lincs 189 D10
Linwood Renfs 267 C8
Lionacleit W Isles 297 G3
Lional W Isles 304 B7
Lions Green E Sus 23 B9
Liphook Hants 49 G10
Lipley Shrops 150 C4
Lippitts Hill Essex 86 F5
Liquo or Bowhousebog N Lnrk 269 D7
Liscard Mers 182 C4
Liscombe Som 41 G11
Liskeard Corn 6 C5
Liss Hants 34 B3
Liss Forest Hants 34 B3
Lissett E Yorks 209 B8
Lissington Lincs 189 E10
Lisson Grove London 67 C9
Listerdale S Yorks 187 C7
Listock Som 28 C4
Listoft Lincs 191 G8
Liston Essex 107 C7
Liston Garden Essex 106 B6
Lisvane Cardiff 59 C7
Liswerry Newport 59 B10
Litcham Norf 159 F7
Litchard Bridgend 58 C2
Litchborough Northants 120 G2
Litchfield Hants 48 C3
Litchurch Derbys 153 B7
Litherland Mers 182 B4
Litlington Cambs 104 C6
Litlington E Sus 23 E8
Litmarsh Hereford 97 B10
Little Abington Cambs 105 B10
Little Addington Northants 121 C9
Little Airmyn E Yorks 199 B8
Little Almshoe Herts 104 F3
Little Alne Warks 118 E2
Little Altcar Mers 193 F10
Little Ann Hants 47 E10
Little Arowry Wrex 167 G7
Little Asby Cumb 222 D3
Little Ashley Wilts 61 G10
Little Assynt Highld 307 G6
Little Aston Staffs 133 C11
Little Atherfield I o W 20 E5
Little Ayre Orkney 314 G3
Little-ayre Shetland 313 G5
Little Ayton N Yorks 225 C11
Little Baddow Essex 88 D3
Little Badminton S Glos 61 C10
Little Ballinluig Perth 286 B3
Little Bampton Cumb 239 F7
Little Bardfield Essex 106 E3
Little Barford Beds 122 F3
Little Barningham Norf 160 C2
Little Barrington Glos 82 C2
Little Barrow W Ches 183 G7
Little Barugh N Yorks 216 D5
Little Bavington Northumb 241 B11
Little Bayham E Sus 52 F6
Little Bealings Suff 108 B4
Little Beckford Glos 99 E9
Little Bedwyn Wilts 63 F9
Little Bentley Essex 108 F2
Little Berkhamsted Herts 86 D3
Little Billing Northants 120 E6
Little Billington C Beds 103 G8
Little Birch Hereford 97 E10
Little Bispham Blkpool 202 E2
Little Blakenham Suff 108 B2
Little Blencow Cumb 230 E5
Little Bloxwich W Mid 133 C10
Little Bognor W Sus 35 C8
Little Bolehill Derbys 170 E3
Little Bollington E Ches 184 D2
Little Bolton Gtr Man 184 B3
Little Bookham Sur 50 C6
Little Bosullow Corn 1 C4
Little Bourton Oxon 101 C9
Little Bowden Leics 136 F4
Little Boys Heath Bucks 84 F6
Little Bradley Suff 124 G3
Little Braithwaite Cumb 229 G10
Little Brampton Shrops 131 G7
Little Braxted Essex 88 C4
Little Bray Devon 41 F7
Little Brechin Angus 293 G7
Little Brickhill M Keynes 103 E8
Little Bridgeford Staffs 151 D7
Little Brington Northants 120 E3
Little Bristol S Glos 80 G2
Little Britain Warks 118 G2
Little Bromley Essex 107 F11
Little Bromwich W Mid 134 F2
Little Broughton Cumb 229 E7
Little Budworth W Ches 167 B9
Little Burstead Essex 87 G11
Little Bytham Lincs 155 F10
Little Cambridge Essex 106 F2
Little Canfield Essex 105 G11
Little Canford Poole 18 B6
Little Carleton Lancs 202 F2
Little Carlton Lincs 190 D5
Little Carlton Notts 172 D3
Little Casterton Rutland 137 B10
Little Catwick E Yorks 209 E8
Little Catworth Cambs 122 C2
Little Cawthorpe Lincs 190 E5
Little Chalfield Wilts 61 G11
Little Chalfont Bucks 85 F7
Little Chart Kent 54 D2
Little Chart Forstal Kent 54 D3
Little Chell Stoke 168 E5
Little Chester Derby 153 B7
Little Chesterford Essex 105 C10
Little Chesterton Oxon 101 G11
Little Cheverell Wilts 46 C3
Little Chishill Cambs 105 D8
Little Clacton Essex 89 B11
Little Clanfield Oxon 82 E3
Little Clegg Gtr Man 196 E2
Little Clifton Cumb 229 F7
Little Coates NE Lincs 201 F8
Little Colp Aberds 303 E7
Little Comberton Worcs 99 C9
Little Comfort Corn 12 E2
Little Common E Sus 38 F2
Little Common Lincs 156 D7
Little Common Shrops 115 B7
Little Common W Sus 34 C6
Little Compton Warks 100 E5
Little Corby Cumb 239 F11
Little Cornard Suff 107 D7
Little Cowarne Hereford 116 G2
Little Coxwell Oxon 82 G3
Little Crakehall N Yorks 224 G4
Little Cransley Northants 120 B6
Little Crawley M Keynes 103 B8
Little Creaton Northants 120 C4
Little Creich Highld 309 L6
Little Cressingham Norf 141 D7
Little Crosby Mers 193 G10
Little Cubley Derbys 152 B3
Little Dalby Leics 154 G5
Little Dawley Telford 132 B3
Little Dens Aberds 303 E10
Little Dewchurch Hereford 97 E10
Little Ditton Cambs 124 F3
Little Doward Hereford 79 B8
Little Downham Cambs 139 G10
Little Drayton Shrops 150 C3
Little Driffield E Yorks 208 B6
Little Drybrook Glos 79 D9
Little Dunham Norf 159 G7
Little Dunkeld Perth 286 C4
Little Dunmow Essex 106 G3
Little Durnford Wilts 46 G6
Little Eastbury Worcs 116 F6
Little Easton Essex 106 G2
Little Eaton Derbys 170 G5
Little Eccleston Lancs 202 E4
Little Ellingham Norf 141 D10
Little End Cambs 122 F3
Little End E Yorks 208 F2
Little End Essex 87 E8
Little Everdon Northants 119 F11
Little Eversden Cambs 123 G7
Little Faringdon Oxon 82 E2
Little Fencote N Yorks 224 G5
Little Fenton N Yorks 206 F6
Little Finborough Suff 125 G10
Little Fransham Norf 159 G8
Little Frith Kent 54 B2
Little Gaddesden Herts 85 C7
Little Gidding Cambs 138 G2
Little Gight Aberds 303 F8
Little Glemham Suff 126 F6
Little Glenshee Perth 286 D3
Little Gorsley Glos 98 F3
Little Gransden Cambs 122 F5
Little Green Cambs 104 B5
Little Green Notts 172 G2
Little Green Som 45 D8
Little Green Suff 125 C11
Little Green Wrex 167 G7
Little Grimsby Lincs 190 C4
Little Gringley Notts 188 E2
Little Gruinard Highld 307 L4
Little Habton N Yorks 216 D4
Little Hadham Herts 105 G8
Little Hale Lincs 173 G10
Little Hale Norf 141 B8
Little Hallam Derbys 171 G7
Little Hallingbury Essex 87 B7
Little Hampden Bucks 84 E5
Little Haresfield Glos 80 D4
Little Harrowden Northants 121 C7
Little Harwood Blkburn 195 B7
Little Haseley Oxon 83 E10
Little Hatfield E Yorks 209 E9
Little Hautbois Norf 160 E5
Little Haven Pembs 72 C5
Little Haven W Sus 51 G7
Little Hay Staffs 134 C2
Little Hayfield Derbys 185 D8
Little Haywood Staffs 151 E10
Little Heath E Ches 167 G11
Little Heath Herts 85 D8
Little Heath Herts 86 E3
Little Heath London 68 B3
Little Heath Staffs 151 F8
Little Heath Sur 66 G6
Little Heath W Berks 65 E7
Little Heath W Ches 166 B6
Little Heath W Mid 134 G6
Little Heck N Yorks 198 C5
Little Henham Essex 105 E10
Little Henny Essex 107 D7
Little Herbert's Glos 81 B7
Little Hereford Hereford 115 D11
Little Hill Hereford 97 F9
Little Hill Som 28 E3
Little Holbury Hants 32 G6
Little Honeyborough Pembs 73 D7
Little Hoole Moss Houses Lancs 194 C3
Little Horkesley Essex 107 E9
Little Hormead Herts 105 F8
Little Horsted E Sus 23 B7
Little Horton W Yorks 205 G9
Little Horton Wilts 62 G4
Little Horwood Bucks 102 E5
Little Houghton Northants 120 F6
Little Houghton S Yorks 198 G2
Little Hucklow Derbys 185 F11
Little Hulton Gtr Man 195 G8
Little Humber E Yorks 201 C8
Little Hungerford W Berks 64 E4
Little Ilford London 68 B2
Little Ingestre Staffs 151 E9
Little Inkberrow Worcs 117 F10
Little Irchester Northants 121 D8
Little Keyford Som 45 D9
Little Kimble Bucks 84 D4
Little Kineton Warks 118 G6
Little Kingshill Bucks 84 F5
Little Knowles Green Suff 124 F5
Little Langdale Cumb 220 E6
Little Langford Wilts 46 F4
Little Laver Essex 87 D8
Little Lawford Warks 119 B9
Little Layton Blkpool 202 F2
Little Leigh W Ches 183 F10
Little Leighs Essex 88 B2
Little Lepton W Yorks 197 E8
Little Leven E Yorks 209 D8
Little Lever Gtr Man 195 F9
Little Limber Lincs 200 E6
Little Linford M Keynes 102 C6
Little Load Som 29 C7
Little London Bucks 83 C10
Little London Bucks 84 D5
Little London Cambs 139 D8
Little London E Sus 23 B9
Little London Essex 105 F9
Little London Essex 106 D3
Little London Glos 80 B2
Little London Hants 47 D11
Little London Hants 48 B6
Little London Lincs 156 E4
Little London Lincs 157 E8
Little London Lincs 189 D10
Little London Lincs 190 F4
Little London Norf 140 D2
Little London Norf 160 C2
Little London Norf 160 E3
Little London Oxon 83 E8
Little London Powys 129 F10
Little London Shrops 131 F10
Little London Som 44 D6
Little London Suff 125 F10
Little London W Yorks 205 F10
Little London Worcs 116 C2
Little Longstone Derbys 185 G11
Little Lynturk Aberds 293 B7
Little Lyth Shrops 131 B9
Little Madeley Staffs 168 F3
Little Malvern Worcs 98 C5
Little Mancot Flint 166 B4
Little Maplestead Essex 106 E6
Little Marcle Hereford 98 D3
Little Marlow Bucks 65 B11
Little Marsden Lancs 204 F3
Little Marsh Bucks 102 G3
Little Marsh Norf 159 B10
Little Marsh Wilts 45 B11
Little Marton Blkpool 202 G3
Little Mascalls Essex 88 E2
Little Massingham Norf 158 E5
Little Melton Norf 142 B3
Little Merthyr Hereford 96 B5
Little Milford Pembs 73 C7
Little Mill Kent 53 D7
Little Mill Mon 78 E4
Little Milton Newport 59 B11
Little Milton Oxon 83 E10
Little Minster Oxon 82 C4
Little Missenden Bucks 84 F6
Little Mongeham Kent 55 C10
Little Moor Gtr Man 184 D6
Little Moor Lancs 203 E10
Little Moor End Lancs 195 B8
Little Morrell Warks 118 F6
Little Mountain Flint 166 C3
Little Musgrave Cumb 222 C5
Little Ness Shrops 149 F8
Little Neston W Ches 182 F3
Little Newcastle Pembs 91 F9
Little Newsham Durham 224 B2
Little Norlington E Sus 23 C7
Little Norton Som 29 D7
Little Oakley Essex 108 F4
Little Oakley Northants 137 F7
Little Odell Beds 121 F9
Little Offley Herts 104 F2
Little Onn Staffs 150 F6
Little Ormside Cumb 222 B4
Little Orton Cumb 239 F9
Little Orton Leics 134 B6
Little Ouse Norf 140 F2
Little Ouseburn N Yorks 215 G8
Little Overton Wrex 166 G5
Little Oxney Green Essex 87 D11
Little Packington Warks 134 G4
Little Parndon Essex 86 C6
Little Paxton Cambs 122 E3
Little Petherick Corn 10 G4
Little Pitlurg Moray 302 E4
Little Plumpton Lancs 202 G3
Little Plumstead Norf 160 G6
Little Ponton Lincs 155 C8
Little Posbrook Hants 33 G8
Little Poulton Lancs 202 F3
Little Preston Kent 53 B8
Little Preston W Yorks 206 G3
Little Raveley Cambs 122 B5
Little Reedness E Yorks 199 C10
Little Reynoldston Swansea 56 D3
Little Ribston N Yorks 206 C3
Little Rissington Glos 81 B11
Little Rogart Highld 309 J7
Little Rollright Oxon 100 E5
Little Ryburgh Norf 159 D9
Little Ryle Northumb 264 G2
Little Ryton Shrops 131 C9
Little Salisbury Wilts 63 G7
Little Salkeld Cumb 231 D7
Little Sampford Essex 106 E3
Little Sandhurst Brack 65 G10
Little Saredon Staffs 133 B8
Little Saxham Suff 124 E5
Little Scatwell Highld 300 D3
Little Scotland Gtr Man 194 E6
Little Sessay N Yorks 215 E9
Little Shelford Cambs 123 G9
Little Shoddesden Hants 47 D9
Little Shrewley Warks 118 D4
Little Shurdington Glos 80 B6
Little Silver Devon 26 F6
Little Silver Devon 40 E4
Little Singleton Lancs 202 F3
Little Skillymarno Aberds 303 D9
Little Skipwith N Yorks 207 F9
Little Smeaton N Yorks 198 D4
Little Smeaton N Yorks 224 E6
Little Snoring Norf 159 C9
Little Sodbury S Glos 61 C9
Little Sodbury End S Glos 61 C8
Little Somborne Hants 47 G11
Little Somerford Wilts 62 C3
Little Soudley Shrops 150 D4
Little Stainforth N Yorks 212 F6
Little Stainton Darl 234 G2
Little Stanmore London 85 G11
Little Stanney W Ches 182 G6
Little Staughton Beds 122 E2
Little Steeping Lincs 174 C6
Little Stoke S Glos 60 C6
Little Stoke Staffs 151 C8
Little Stonham Suff 126 E2
Little Stretton Leics 136 C3
Little Stretton Shrops 131 E8
Little Strickland Cumb 221 B11
Little Studley N Yorks 214 E6
Little Stukeley Cambs 122 B4
Little Sugnall Staffs 150 C6
Little Sutton Lincs 157 E9
Little Sutton Shrops 131 G10
Little Sutton W Ches 182 F5
Little Swinburne Northumb 241 B10
Little Tarrington Hereford 98 C2
Little Tew Oxon 101 F7
Little Tey Essex 107 G7
Little Thetford Cambs 123 B10
Little Thirkleby N Yorks 215 D9
Little Thornage Norf 159 B11
Little Thornton Lancs 202 E3
Little Thorpe Durham 234 C4
Little Thorpe W Yorks 197 C7
Little Thurlow Suff 124 G3
Little Thurlow Green Suff 124 G3
Little Thurrock Thurrock 68 D6
Little Torboll Highld 309 K7
Little Torrington Devon 25 D7
Little Totham Essex 88 C5
Little Toux Aberds 302 D5
Little Town Cumb 220 B4
Little Town Lancs 203 F9
Little Town Warr 183 C10
Little Tring Herts 84 C6
Little Twycross Leics 134 B6
Little Urswick Cumb 210 E5
Little Vantage W Loth 270 C2
Little Wakering Essex 70 B2
Little Walden Essex 105 C10
Little Waldingfield Suff 107 B8
Little Walsingham Norf 159 B8
Little Waltham Essex 88 C2
Little Walton Warks 135 G9
Little Warley Essex 87 G10
Little Warton Warks 134 C5
Little Washbourne Glos 99 E9
Little Weighton E Yorks 208 G5
Little Weldon Northants 137 F8
Little Welland Worcs 98 D6
Little Welnetham Suff 125 E7
Little Welton Lincs 190 D4
Little Wenham Suff 107 D11
Little Wenlock Telford 132 B2
Little Weston Som 29 B10
Little Whitehouse I o W 20 C5
Little Whittingham Green Suff 126 B5
Little Wigborough Essex 89 B7
Little Wilbraham Cambs 123 F10
Little Wisbeach Lincs 156 C2
Little Wishford Wilts 46 F5
Little Witcombe Glos 80 B6
Little Witley Worcs 116 E5
Little Wittenham Oxon 83 G9
Little Wolford Warks 100 D5
Little Wood Corner Bucks 84 E6
Little Woodcote London 67 G9
Little Woolgarston Dorset 18 E5
Little Worthen Shrops 130 B6
Little Wratting Suff 106 B3
Little Wymington Beds 121 D9
Little Wymondley Herts 104 F4
Little Wyrley Staffs 133 B10
Little Wytheford Shrops 149 F11
Little Yeldham Essex 106 D5
Littlebeck N Yorks 227 D7
Littleborough Devon 26 E4
Littleborough Gtr Man 196 D2
Littleborough Notts 188 E4
Littlebourne Kent 55 B8
Littlebredy Dorset 17 D7
Littlebury Essex 105 D10
Littlebury Green Essex 105 D9
Littlecote Bucks 102 G6
Littlecott Wilts 46 C6
Littledean Glos 79 C11
Littledean Hill Glos 79 C11
Littledown Bmouth 19 C8
Littledown Hants 47 B10
Littleferry Highld 311 K2
Littlefield NE Lincs 201 F9
Littlefield Common Sur 50 C3
Littlefield Green Windsor 65 D11
Littlegain Shrops 132 D5
Littleham Devon 14 E6
Littleham Devon 24 C6
Littlehampton W Sus 35 G8
Littlehempston Devon 8 C6
Littlehoughton Northumb 264 F6
Littlemill Aberds 292 D5
Littlemill E Ayrs 257 F11
Littlemill Highld 301 D9
Littlemill Northumb 264 F6
Littlemoor Derbys 170 C5
Littlemoor Dorset 17 E9
Littlemore Oxon 83 E8
Littlemoss Gtr Man 184 B6
Littleover Derby 152 C6
Littleport Cambs 139 F11
Littler W Ches 167 B10
Littlestead Green Oxon 65 D8
Littlestone-on-Sea Kent 39 C9
Littlethorpe Leics 135 D10
Littlethorpe N Yorks 214 F6
Littleton Bath 60 G5
Littleton Dorset 30 G5
Littleton Hants 48 G3
Littleton Perth 286 D6
Littleton Som 44 G3
Littleton Sur 50 D3
Littleton Sur 66 F5
Littleton W Ches 166 B6
Littleton Wilts 62 G2
Littleton Common Sur 66 E5
Littleton Drew Wilts 61 C10
Littleton-on-Severn S Glos 60 B5
Littleton Panell Wilts 46 C4
Littleton-upon-Severn S Glos 79 G9
Littletown Durham 234 C2
Littletown I o W 20 C6
Littletown W Yorks 197 C8
Littlewick Green Windsor 65 D10
Littlewindsor Dorset 28 G6
Littlewood Staffs 133 B9
Littlewood Green Warks 117 E11
Littleworth Beds 103 C11
Littleworth Glos 80 E4
Littleworth Glos 100 D2
Littleworth Oxon 82 F4
Littleworth Oxon 83 D9
Littleworth Oxon 83 G10
Littleworth S Yorks 187 B10
Littleworth Staffs 151 E8
Littleworth Staffs 151 G10
Littleworth W Sus 35 C11
Littleworth Warks 118 E4
Littleworth Wilts 63 G7
Littleworth Worcs 117 E9
Littleworth Worcs 117 G7
Littleworth Common Bucks 66 B2
Littleworth End Warks 134 D3
Littley Green Essex 87 B11
Litton Derbys 185 F11
Litton N Yorks 213 E8
Litton Som 44 C5
Litton Cheney Dorset 17 C7
Litton Mill Derbys 185 G11
Liurbost W Isles 304 F5
Livermead Torbay 9 C8
Liverpool Mers 182 C4
Liverpool Airport Mers 182 E6
Liversedge W Yorks 197 C8
Liverton Devon 14 F2
Liverton Redcar 226 B4
Liverton Mines Redcar 226 B4
Liverton Street Kent 53 C11
Livesey Street Kent 53 C8
Livingshayes Devon 27 G7
Livingston W Loth 269 B11
Livingston Village W Loth 269 B10
Lix Toll Stirl 285 D9
Lixwm Flint 181 G11
Lizard Corn 2 G6
Llaingoch Anglesey 178 E2
Llaithddu Powys 129 G11
Llampha V Glam 58 D2
Llan Powys 129 C7
Llan eurgain = Northop Flint 166 B2
Llan Ffestiniog Gwyn 164 G2
Llan-mill Pembs 73 C10
Llan-non = Llanon Ceredig 111 D10
Llan-y-pwll Wrex 166 E5
Llanaber Gwyn 146 F2
Llanaelhaearn Gwyn 162 G5
Llanafan Ceredig 112 C3
Llanafan-fawr Powys 113 F9
Llanallgo Anglesey 179 D7
Llananno Powys 113 C11
Llanarmon Gwyn 145 B8
Llanarmon Dyffryn Ceiriog Wrex 148 C3
Llanarmon Mynydd-mawr Powys 148 D2
Llanarmon-yn-Ial Denb 165 D11
Llanarth Ceredig 111 F8
Llanarth Mon 78 C5
Llanarthne Carms 93 G10
Llanasa Flint 181 E10
Llanbabo Anglesey 178 D5
Llanbad Rhondda 58 C3
Llanbadarn Fawr Ceredig 128 G2
Llanbadarn Fynydd Powys 114 B2
Llanbadarn-y-Garreg Powys 96 B2
Llanbadoc Mon 78 E5
Llanbadrig Anglesey 178 C5
Llanbeder Newport 78 G5
Llanbedr Gwyn 145 D11
Llanbedr Powys 96 B2
Llanbedr Powys 96 G4
Llanbedr-Dyffryn-Clwyd Denb 165 D10
Llanbedr Pont Steffan = Lampeter Ceredig 93 B11
Llanbedr-y-cennin Conwy 164 B3
Llanbedrgoch Anglesey 179 E8
Llanbedrog Gwyn 144 C6
Llanberis Gwyn 163 C9
Llanbethery V Glam 58 F4
Llanbister Powys 114 C2
Llanblethian = Llanfleiddan V Glam 58 E3
Llanboidy Carms 92 G4
Llanbradach Caerph 77 G10
Llanbrynmair Powys 129 C7
Llancadle = Llancatal V Glam 58 F4
Llancaiach Caerph 77 F10
Llancarfan V Glam 58 E5
Llancatal = Llancadle V Glam 58 F4
Llancayo Mon 78 E5
Llancloudy Hereford 97 G9
Llancowrid Powys 130 E3
Llancynfelyn Ceredig 128 E2
Llandaff Cardiff 59 D7
Llandaff North Cardiff 59 D7
Llandanwg Gwyn 145 D11
Llandarcy Neath 57 B8
Llandawke Carms 74 C3
Llanddaniel Fab Anglesey 179 G7
Llanddarog Carms 75 B8
Llanddeiniol Ceredig 111 C11
Llanddeiniolen Gwyn 163 B8
Llandderfel Gwyn 147 B9
Llanddeusant Anglesey 178 D4
Llanddeusant Carms 94 G5
Llanddew Powys 95 E11
Llanddewi Swansea 56 D3
Llanddewi-Brefi Ceredig 112 F3
Llanddewi Fach Mon 78 F4
Llanddewi Rhydderch Mon 78 C5
Llanddewi Skirrid Mon 78 B4
Llanddewi Velfrey Pembs 73 B10
Llanddewi Ystradenni Powys 114 D2
Llanddewi'r Cwm Powys 95 B10
Llanddoged Conwy 164 C4
Llanddona Anglesey 179 F9
Llanddowror Carms 74 C3
Llanddulas Conwy 180 F6
Llanddwywe Gwyn 145 E11
Llanddyfynan Anglesey 179 F8
Llandecwyn Gwyn 146 B2
Llandefaelog Powys 95 E10
Llandefaelog Fach Powys 95 E10
Llandefaelog-tre'r-graig Powys 96 F2
Llandefalle Powys 96 D2
Llandegai Gwyn 179 G9
Llandegfan Anglesey 179 G9
Llandegla Denb 165 E11
Llandegley Powys 114 E2
Llandegveth Mon 78 F4
Llandegwning Gwyn 144 C5
Llandeilo Carms 94 G2
Llandeilo Graban Powys 95 C11
Llandeilo'r Fan Powys 95 E7
Llandeloy Pembs 91 F7
Llandenny Mon 78 E6
Llandenny Walks Mon 78 E5
Llandevaud Newport 78 G6
Llandevenny Mon 60 B2
Llandewi Ystradenny Powys 114 D2
Llandilo Pembs 92 F2
Llandilo-yr-ynys Carms 93 G9
Llandinabo Hereford 97 F10
Llandinam Powys 129 F10
Llandissilio Pembs 92 G2
Llandogo Mon 79 E8
Llandough V Glam 58 E3
Llandough V Glam 59 E7
Llandovery = Llanymddyfri Carms 94 E5
Llandow = Llandw V Glam 58 E2
Llandre Carms 94 C3
Llandre Ceredig 128 F2
Llandrillo Denb 147 B10
Llandrillo-yn-Rhôs Conwy 180 E4
Llandrindod Wells Powys 113 E11
Llandrinio Powys 148 F5
Llandruidion Pembs 90 G5
Llandudno Conwy 180 E3
Llandudno Junction = Cyffordd Llandudno Conwy 180 F3
Llandudoch = St Dogmaels Pembs 92 B3
Llandw = Llandow V Glam 58 E2
Llandwrog Gwyn 163 D7
Llandybie Carms 75 B10
Llandyfaelog Carms 74 C6
Llandyfan Carms 75 B10
Llandyfriog Ceredig 92 C6
Llandyfrydog Anglesey 178 D6
Llandygwydd Ceredig 92 C4
Llandynan Denb 165 F11
Llandyrnog Denb 165 B10
Llandysilio Powys 148 F5
Llandyssil Powys 130 D3
Llandysul Ceredig 93 C8

Llanedeyrn Cardiff 59 C8
Llanedi Carms 75 D9
Llanedwen Anglesey 163 B8
Llaneglwys Powys 95 D11
Llanegryn Gwyn 110 B2
Llanegwad Carms 93 G10
Llaneilian Anglesey 179 C7
Llanelian yn-Rhôs Conwy 180 F5
Llanelidan Denb 165 E10
Llanelieu Powys 96 E3
Llanellen Mon 78 C4
Llanelli Carms 56 B4
Llanelltyd Gwyn 146 F4
Llanelly Mon 78 C2
Llanelly Hill Mon 78 C2
Llanelwedd Powys 113 G10
Llanelwy = St Asaph Denb 181 G8
Llanenddwyn Gwyn 145 E11
Llanengan Gwyn 144 D5
Llanerch Powys 130 E6
Llanerch Emrys Powys 148 E4
Llanerchymedd Anglesey 178 E6
Llanerfyl Powys 129 B10
Llaneuddog Anglesey 179 D7
Llanfabon Caerph 77 G10
Llanfachraeth Anglesey 178 E4
Llanfachreth Gwyn 146 E5
Llanfaelog Anglesey 178 G4
Llanfaelrhys Gwyn 144 D4
Llanfaenor Mon 78 B6
Llanfaes Anglesey 179 F10
Llanfaes Powys 95 F10
Llanfaethlu Anglesey 178 D4
Llanfaglan Gwyn 163 C7
Llanfair Gwyn 145 D11
Llanfair Caereinion Powys 130 B2
Llanfair Clydogau Ceredig 112 G2
Llanfair-Dyffryn-Clwyd Denb 165 D10
Llanfair Kilgeddin Mon 78 D4
Llanfair Kilgheddin Mon 78 D4
Llanfair-Nant-Gwyn Pembs 92 D3
Llanfair Talhaiarn Conwy 180 G6
Llanfair Waterdine Shrops 114 B4
Llanfairfechan Conwy 179 F11
Llanfairpwll-gwyngyll Anglesey 179 G8
Llanfairyneubwll Anglesey 178 F3
Llanfairynghornwy Anglesey 178 C4
Llanfallteg Carms 73 B11
Llanfallteg West Carms 73 B10
Llanfaredd Powys 113 G11
Llanfarian Ceredig 111 B11
Llanfechain Powys 148 E3
Llanfechan Powys 113 G9
Llanfechell Anglesey 178 C5
Llanferres Denb 165 C11
Llanfflewyn Anglesey 178 D5
Llanfigael Anglesey 178 E4
Llanfihangel-ar-arth Carms 93 D9
Llanfihangel-Crucorney Mon 96 G6
Llanfihangel Glyn Myfyr Conwy 165 F7
Llanfihangel-helygen Powys 113 E10
Llanfihangel Nant Bran Powys 95 E8
Llanfihangel-nant-Melan Powys 114 F3
Llanfihangel Rhydithon Powys 114 D3
Llanfihangel Rogiet Mon 60 B2
Llanfihangel Tal-y-llyn Powys 96 F2
Llanfihangel Tor y Mynydd Mon 79 E7
Llanfihangel-uwch-Gwili Carms 93 G9
Llanfihangel-y-Creuddyn Ceredig 112 B3
Llanfihangel-y-pennant Gwyn 128 B3
Llanfihangel-y-pennant Gwyn 163 F8
Llanfihangel-yng-Ngwynfa Powys 147 F11
Llanfihangel yn Nhowyn Anglesey 178 F4
Llanfilo Powys 96 E2
Llanfleiddan = Llanblethian V Glam 58 E3
Llanfoist Mon 78 C3
Llanfor Gwyn 147 B8
Llanfrechfa Torf 78 G4
Llanfrothen Gwyn 163 G10
Llanfrynach Powys 95 F11
Llanfwrog Anglesey 178 E4
Llanfwrog Denb 165 D10
Llanfyllin Powys 148 F2
Llanfynydd Carms 93 F11
Llanfynydd Flint 166 D3
Llanfyrnach Pembs 92 E4
Llangadfan Powys 147 G10
Llangadog Carms 74 D6
Llangadog Carms 94 F4
Llangadwaladr Anglesey 162 B5
Llangadwaladr Powys 148 C3
Llangaffo Anglesey 162 B6
Llangain Carms 74 B5
Llangammarch Wells Powys 95 B8
Llangan V Glam 58 D3
Llangarron Hereford 97 G10
Llangasty Talyllyn Powys 96 F2
Llangathen Carms 93 G11
Llangattock Powys 78 B2
Llangattock Lingoed Mon 97 G7
Llangattock nigh Usk Mon 78 D4
Llangattock-Vibon-Avel Mon 79 B7
Llangedwyn Powys 148 E3
Llangefni Anglesey 179 F7
Llangeinor Bridgend 58 B2
Llangeitho Ceredig 112 F2
Llangeler Carms 93 D7
Llangendeirne Carms 75 C7
Llangennech Carms 75 E9
Llangennith Swansea 56 C2
Llangenny Powys 78 B2
Llangernyw Conwy 164 B5
Llangeview Mon 78 E5
Llangewydd Court Bridgend 57 E11
Llangian Gwyn 144 D5
Llangloffan Pembs 91 E8
Llanglydwen Carms 92 F3
Llangoed Anglesey 179 F10
Llangoedmor Ceredig 92 B3
Llangollen Denb 166 G2
Llangolman Pembs 92 F2
Llangors Powys 96 F2
Llangorwen Ceredig 128 G2
Llangovan Mon 79 D7
Llangower Gwyn 147 C8
Llangrannog Ceredig 110 G6
Llangristiolus Anglesey 178 G6
Llangrove Hereford 79 B8
Llangua Mon 97 F7
Llangunllo Powys 114 C4
Llangunnor Carms 74 B6
Llangurig Powys 113 B8
Llangwm Conwy 165 G7
Llangwm Mon 78 E6
Llangwm Pembs 73 D7
Llangwnnadl Gwyn 144 C4
Llangwyfan Denb 165 B10
Llangwyfan-isaf Anglesey 162 B4
Llangwyllog Anglesey 178 F6
Llangwyryfon Ceredig 111 C11
Llangybi Ceredig 112 G2
Llangybi Gwyn 162 G6
Llangybi Mon 78 F5
Llangyfelach Swansea 56 B6
Llangyndeyrn Carms 75 C7
Llangynhafal Denb 165 C10
Llangynidr Powys 77 B11
Llangyniew Powys 130 B2
Llangynin Carms 74 B2
Llangynog Carms 74 B4
Llangynog Powys 147 D11
Llangynwyd Bridgend 57 D11
Llanhamlach Powys 95 F11
Llanharan Rhondda 58 C4
Llanharry Rhondda 58 C4
Llanhennock Mon 78 G5
Llanhiledd = Llanhilleth Bl Gwent 78 E2
Llanhowel Pembs 90 F6
Llanidloes Powys 129 G9
Llaniestyn Gwyn 144 C5
Llanifyny Powys 129 G7
Llanigon Powys 96 D4
Llanilar Ceredig 112 C2
Llanilid Rhondda 58 C3
Llanilltud Fawr = Llantwit Major V Glam 58 F3
Llanio Ceredig 112 F2
Llanion Pembs 73 E7
Llanishen Cardiff 59 C7
Llanishen Mon 79 E7
Llanllawddog Carms 93 F9
Llanllechid Gwyn 163 B10
Llanllowell Mon 78 F5
Llanllugan Powys 129 C11
Llanllwch Carms 74 B5
Llanllwchaiarn Powys 130 E2
Llanllwni Carms 93 D9
Llanllwyd Shrops 130 G3
Llanllyfni Gwyn 163 E7
Llanmadoc Swansea 56 C2
Llanmaes Cardiff 58 D6
Llanmaes V Glam 58 F3
Llanmartin Newport 59 B11
Llanmerwig Powys 130 E3
Llanmihangel V Glam 58 E3
Llanmiloe Carms 74 D3
Llanmorlais Swansea 56 C4
Llannefydd Conwy 181 G7
Llannerch-y-môr Flint 181 F11
Llannon Carms 75 D8
Llannor Gwyn 145 B7
Llanon Pembs 90 E6
Llanon = Llan-non Ceredig 111 D10
Llanover Mon 78 D4
Llanpumsaint Carms 93 F8
Llanreath Pembs 73 E7
Llanreithan Pembs 91 F7
Llanrhaeadr Denb 165 C9
Llanrhaeadr-ym-Mochnant Powys 148 D2
Llanrhian Pembs 90 E6
Llanrhidian Swansea 56 C3
Llanrhos Conwy 180 E3
Llanrhyddlad Anglesey 178 D4
Llanrhystud Ceredig 111 D10
Llanrosser Hereford 96 D5
Llanrothal Hereford 79 B7
Llanrug Gwyn 163 C8
Llanrumney Cardiff 59 C8
Llanrwst Conwy 164 C4
Llansadurnen Carms 74 C3
Llansadwrn Anglesey 179 F9
Llansadwrn Carms 94 E3
Llansaint Carms 74 D5
Llansamlet Swansea 57 B7
Llansanffraid Glan Conwy Conwy 180 F4
Llansannan Conwy 164 B6
Llansannor V Glam 58 D3
Llansantffraed Ceredig 111 D10
Llansantffraed Powys 96 G2
Llansantffraed Cwmdeuddwr Powys 113 D9
Llansantffraed-in-Elwel Powys 113 G11
Llansantffraid-ym-Mechain Powys 148 E4
Llansawel Carms 94 D2
Llansawel = Briton Ferry Neath 57 C8
Llansilin Powys 148 D4
Llansoy Mon 78 E6
Llanspyddid Powys 95 F10
Llanstadwell Pembs 72 D6
Llansteffan Carms 74 C5
Llanstephan Powys 96 C2
Llantarnam Torf 78 G4
Llanteems Mon 96 G6
Llanteg Pembs 73 C11
Llanthony Mon 96 F5
Llantilio Crossenny Mon 78 C5
Llantilio Pertholey Mon 78 B4
Llantood Pembs 92 C3
Llantrisant Anglesey 178 E5
Llantrisant Mon 78 F5
Llantrisant Rhondda 58 C4
Llantrithyd V Glam 58 E4
Llantwit Neath 57 B9
Llantwit Fardre Rhondda 58 B5
Llantwit Major = Llanilltud Fawr V Glam 58 F3
Llanuwchllyn Gwyn 147 C7
Llanvaches Newport 78 G6
Llanvair Discoed Mon 78 G6
Llanvapley Mon 78 C5
Llanvetherine Mon 78 B5
Llanveynoe Hereford 96 E6
Llanvihangel Crucorney Mon 96 G6
Llanvihangel Gobion Mon 78 D4
Llanvihangel-Ystern-Llewern Mon 78 C6
Llanwarne Hereford 97 F10
Llanwddyn Powys 147 F10
Llanwenarth Mon 78 C3
Llanwenog Ceredig 93 B9
Llanwern Newport 59 B11
Llanwinio Carms 92 F5
Llanwnda Gwyn 163 D7
Llanwnda Pembs 91 D8
Llanwnnen Ceredig 93 B10
Llanwnog Powys 129 E10
Llanwrda Carms 94 E4
Llanwrin Powys 128 C5
Llanwrthwl Powys 113 E9
Llanwrtud = Llanwrtyd Wells Powys 95 B7
Llanwrtyd Powys 95 B7
Llanwrtyd Wells = Llanwrtud Powys 95 B7
Llanwyddelan Powys 129 C11
Llanyblodwel Shrops 148 E4
Llanybri Carms 74 C4
Llanybydder Carms 93 C10
Llanycefn Pembs 91 G11
Llanychaer Pembs 91 D9
Llanycil Gwyn 147 C8
Llanycrwys Carms 94 B2
Llanymawddwy Gwyn 147 F8
Llanymddyfri = Llandovery Carms 94 E5
Llanymynech Powys 148 E5
Llanynghenedl Anglesey 178 E4
Llanynys Denb 165 C10
Llanyrafon Torf 78 G4
Llanyre Powys 113 E10
Llanystumdwy Gwyn 145 B9
Llanywern Powys 96 F2
Llawhaden Pembs 73 B9
Llawnt Shrops 148 C5
Llawrdref Bellaf Gwyn 144 D5
Llawr-y-glyn Powys 129 E8
Llay Wrex 166 D4
Llechcynfarwy Anglesey 178 E5
Llecheiddior Gwyn 163 G7
Llechfaen Powys 95 F11
Llechfraith Gwyn 146 F3
Llechryd Caerph 77 D10
Llechryd Ceredig 92 C4
Llechrydau Powys 148 C4
Lledrod Ceredig 112 C2
Llenmerewig Powys 130 E3
Llethrid Swansea 56 C4
Llettyrychen Carms 75 E7
Llidiad Nenog Carms 93 D10
Llidiardau Gwyn 147 B7
Llidiart-y-parc Denb 165 G10
Llithfaen Gwyn 162 G5
Lloc Flint 181 F10
Llong Flint 166 C3
Llowes Powys 96 C3
Lloyney Powys 114 B4
Llugwy Powys 128 D4
Llundain-fach Ceredig 111 F11
Llwydarth Bridgend 57 C11
Llwydcoed Rhondda 77 E7
Llwyn Denb 165 C9
Llwyn Shrops 130 G5
Llwyn-derw Powys 129 G8
Llwyn-du Mon 78 B3
Llwyn-hendy Carms 56 B4
Llwyn-on Village M Tydf 77 C8
Llwyn-tg Carms 75 D9
Llwyn-y-brain Carms 73 C11
Llwyn-y-go Shrops 148 E5
Llwyn-y-groes Ceredig 111 F11
Llwyn-yr-hwrdd Pembs 92 E4
Llwyncelyn Ceredig 111 F8
Llwyndafydd Ceredig 111 F7
Llwynderw Powys 130 C4
Llwynduris Ceredig 92 C4
Llwyndyrys Gwyn 162 G5
Llwyneinion Wrex 166 F3
Llwyngwril Gwyn 110 B2
Llwynhendy Carms 56 B4
Llwynmawr Wrex 148 B4
Llwynygog Powys 129 E7
Llwynypia Rhondda 77 G7
Llynclys Shrops 148 E5
Llynfaes Anglesey 178 F6
Llys-y-frôn Pembs 91 G10
Llysfaen Conwy 180 F5
Llyswen Powys 96 D2
Llysworney V Glam 58 E3
Llywel Powys 95 E7
Llywernog Ceredig 128 G4
Load Brook S Yorks 186 D3
Loan Falk 279 F9
Loandhu Highld 301 B8
Loanend Northumb 273 E8
Loanhead Aberds 302 D6
Loanhead Midloth 270 B5
Loanhead Perth 286 D5
Loanreoch Highld 300 B6
Loans S Ayrs 257 C8
Loans of Tullich Highld 301 B8
Loansdean Northumb 252 G5
Lobb Devon 40 F3
Lobhillcross Devon 12 D5
Lobley Hill T & W 242 E6
Lobthorpe Lincs 155 E9
Loch a Charnain W Isles 297 G4
Loch a' Ghainmhich W Isles 304 F4
Loch Baghasdail W Isles 297 K3
Loch Choire Lodge Highld 308 F6
Loch Eil Highld 290 F2
Loch Euphoirt W Isles 296 E4
Loch Head Dumfries 236 E5
Loch Head Dumfries 245 E11
Loch Loyal Lodge Highld 308 E6
Loch nam Madadh W Isles 296 E5
Loch Sgioport W Isles 297 H4
Lochailort Highld 295 G9
Lochaline Highld 289 E8
Lochanhully Highld 301 G9
Lochans Dumfries 236 D2
Locharbriggs Dumfries 247 G11
Lochassynt Lodge Highld 307 G6
Lochavich Ho Argyll 275 B10
Lochawe Argyll 284 E5
Lochbuie Argyll 289 G8
Lochbuie Ho Argyll 289 G8
Lochcallater Lodge Aberds 292 E3
Lochcarron Highld 295 B10
Lochdhu Highld 310 E4
Lochdochart House Stirl 285 E8
Lochdon Argyll 289 F9
Lochdrum Highld 300 B2
Lochead Argyll 275 E11
Lochead Argyll 275 F8
Lochearnhead Stirl 285 E9
Lochee Dundee 287 D7
Lochend Edin 280 G5
Lochend Highld 300 F5
Lochend Highld 310 C6
Lochend Ho Stirl 277 B11
Locherben Dumfries 247 D11
Lochetive Ho Highld 284 C5
Lochfoot Dumfries 237 B10
Lochgair Argyll 275 D10
Lochgarthside Highld 291 B7
Lochgelly Fife 280 C3
Lochgilphead Argyll 275 E9
Lochgoilhead Argyll 284 G6
Lochhill Moray 302 C2
Lochhussie Highld 300 D4
Lochinch Castle Dumfries 236 C3
Lochindorb Lodge Highld 301 F9
Lochinver Highld 307 G5
Lochlane Perth 286 E2
Lochletter Highld 300 G4
Lochluichart Highld 300 C3
Lochmaben Dumfries 248 G3
Lochmore Cottage Highld 310 E4
Lochmore Lodge Highld 306 F7
Lochnell Ho Argyll 289 F10
Lochore Fife 280 B3
Lochorodale Argyll 255 F7
Lochportain W Isles 296 D5
Lochran Perth 280 B2
Lochranza N Ayrs 255 B10
Lochs Crofts Moray 302 C3
Lochside Aberds 293 G9
Lochside Highld 301 D8
Lochside Highld 308 D4
Lochside Highld 310 F2
Lochside S Ayrs 257 E8
Lochslin Highld 311 L2
Lochstack Lodge Highld 306 E7
Lochton Aberds 293 D9
Lochty Angus 293 G7
Lochty Fife 287 G9
Lochty Perth 286 E4
Lochuisge Highld 289 D9
Lochurr Dumfries 247 F7
Lochwinnoch Renfs 267 D7
Lochwood Dumfries 248 D3
Lochwood Glasgow 268 B3
Lochyside Highld 290 F3
Lockengate Corn 5 C10
Lockerbie Dumfries 248 G4
Lockeridge Wilts 62 F6
Lockeridge Dene Wilts 62 F6
Lockerley Hants 32 B3
Lockhills Cumb 230 B6
Locking N Som 43 B11
Locking Stumps Warr 183 C10
Lockinge Oxon 64 B2
Lockington E Yorks 208 D5
Lockington Leics 153 D9
Lockleaze Bristol 60 D6
Lockleywood Shrops 150 D3
Locks Heath Hants 33 F8
Locksbottom London 68 F2
Locksbrook Bath 61 G8
Locksgreen I o W 20 C4
Lockton N Yorks 226 G6
Lockwood W Yorks 196 D6
Loddington Leics 136 C5
Loddington Northants 120 B6
Loddiswell Devon 8 F4
Loddon Norf 143 D7
Loddon Ingloss Norf 142 D6
Lode Cambs 123 E10
Lode Heath W Mid 134 G3
Loders Dorset 16 C5
Lodge Green N Yorks 223 F9
Lodge Green W Mid 134 G5
Lodge Hill Corn 6 C4
Lodge Hill W Mid 133 G10
Lodge Hill W Yorks 197 C9
Lodge Lees Kent 55 D8
Lodge Moor S Yorks 186 D3
Lodge Park Worcs 117 D10
Lodgebank Shrops 149 D11
Lodsworth W Sus 34 C6
Lodsworth Common W Sus 34 C6
Lodway Bristol 60 D4
Lofthouse N Yorks 214 E2
Lofthouse W Yorks 197 B10
Lofthouse Gate W Yorks 197 C10
Loftus Redcar 226 B4
Logan E Ayrs 258 E3
Logan Mains Dumfries 236 E2
Loganlea W Loth 269 C9
Loggerheads Denb 165 C11
Loggerheads Staffs 150 B4
Logie Angus 293 G8
Logie Fife 287 E8
Logie Moray 301 D10
Logie Coldstone Aberds 292 C6
Logie Hill Highld 301 B7
Logie Newton Aberds 302 F6
Logie Pert Angus 293 G8
Logiealmond Lodge Perth 286 D3
Logierait Perth 286 B3
Login Carms 92 G3
Logmore Green Sur 50 D6
Loidse Mhorsgail W Isles 304 F3
Lolworth Cambs 123 E7
Lomeshaye Lancs 204 F2
Lôn Gwyn 147 C7
Lon-las Swansea 57 B8
Lonbain Highld 298 D6
Londesborough E Yorks 208 D3
London Apprentice Corn 5 E10
London Beach Kent 53 F11
London Colney Herts 85 E11
London End Cambs 121 D11
London Fields W Mid 133 E8
London Minstead Hants 32 E3
Londonderry N Yorks 214 B6
Londonderry W Mid 133 F10
Londonthorpe Lincs 155 B9
Londubh Highld 307 L3
Lonemore Highld 299 B7
Lonemore Highld 309 L7
Long Ashton N Som 60 E5
Long Bank Worcs 116 C5
Long Bennington Lincs 172 G4
Long Bredy Dorset 17 C7
Long Buckby Northants 120 D2
Long Buckby Wharf Northants 120 D2
Long Clawson Leics 154 D4
Long Common Hants 33 E8
Long Compton Staffs 151 E7
Long Compton Warks 100 E5
Long Crendon Bucks 83 D11
Long Crichel Dorset 31 E7
Long Cross Wilts 45 G9
Long Dean Wilts 61 D11
Long Ditton Sur 67 F7
Long Drax N Yorks 199 B7
Long Duckmanton Derbys 186 G6
Long Eaton Derbys 153 C9
Long Gardens Essex 106 D6
Long Green Suff 125 B11
Long Green W Ches 183 G7
Long Green Worcs 98 E6
Long Hanborough Oxon 82 C6
Long Itchington Warks 119 D8
Long John's Hill Norf 142 B4
Long Lane Telford 150 F2
Long Lawford Warks 119 B9
Long Lee W Yorks 205 E7
Long Load Som 29 C7
Long Marston Herts 84 B5
Long Marston N Yorks 206 C6
Long Marston Warks 100 B3
Long Marton Cumb 231 G9
Long Meadow Cambs 123 E10
Long Meadowend Shrops 131 G8
Long Melford Suff 107 B7
Long Newnton Glos 80 G6
Long Newton E Loth 271 C10
Long Oak Shrops 149 E7
Long Park Hants 48 G2
Long Preston N Yorks 204 B2
Long Riston E Yorks 209 E8
Long Sandall S Yorks 198 F6
Long Sight Gtr Man 196 F2
Long Stratton Norf 142 E3
Long Street M Keynes 102 B5
Long Sutton Hants 49 D8
Long Sutton Lincs 157 E8
Long Sutton Som 29 B7
Long Thurlow Suff 125 D10
Long Whatton Leics 153 E9
Long Wittenham Oxon 83 G8
Longbar N Ayrs 266 E6
Longbarn Warr 183 C10
Longbenton T & W 243 D7
Longborough Glos 100 F3
Longbridge Plym 7 D10
Longbridge W Mid 117 B10
Longbridge Warks 118 E5
Longbridge Deverill Wilts 45 E11
Longbridge Hayes Stoke 168 E5
Longbridgemuir Dumfries 238 D3
Longburgh Cumb 239 F8
Longburton Dorset 29 E11
Longcause Devon 8 C5
Longcliffe Derbys 170 D2
Longcot Oxon 82 G3
Longcroft Cumb 238 F6
Longcroft Falk 278 F5
Longcross Devon 12 F4
Longcross Sur 66 F3
Longdale Cumb 222 D2
Longdales Cumb 230 C6
Longden Shrops 131 B8
Longden Common Shrops 131 C8
Longdon Staffs 151 G11
Longdon Worcs 98 D6
Longdon Green Staffs 151 G11
Longdon Heath Worcs 98 D6
Longdon Hill End Worcs 98 D6
Longdon on Tern Telford 150 F2
Longdown Devon 14 C3
Longdowns Corn 2 C6
Longdrum Angus 292 G4
Longfield Kent 68 F6
Longfield Shetland 313 M5
Longfield Wilts 45 B11
Longfield Hill Kent 68 F6
Longfleet Poole 18 C6
Longford Derbys 152 B4
Longford Glos 98 G6
Longford Kent 52 B4
Longford London 66 D4
Longford Shrops 150 C2
Longford Telford 150 F4
Longford W Mid 135 G7
Longford Warr 183 C10
Longfordlane Derbys 152 B4
Longforgan Perth 287 E7
Longformacus Borders 272 D3
Longframlington Northumb 252 C4
Longham Dorset 19 B7
Longham Norf 159 F8
Longhaven Aberds 303 F11
Longhedge Wilts 45 E10
Longhill Aberds 303 D9
Longhirst Northumb 252 F6
Longhope Glos 79 B11
Longhope Orkney 314 G3
Longhorsley Northumb 252 E4
Longhoughton Northumb 264 G6
Longhouse Bath 61 G8
Longlands Cumb 229 D11
Longlands London 68 E2
Longlane Derbys 152 B5
Longlane W Berks 64 E3
Longlevens Glos 99 G7
Longley W Yorks 196 C5
Longley W Yorks 196 E6
Longley Estate S Yorks 186 C5
Longley Green Worcs 116 G4
Longleys Perth 286 C6
Longmanhill Aberds 303 C7
Longmoor Camp Hants 49 G9
Longmorn Moray 302 D2
Longmoss E Ches 184 G5
Longnewton Borders 262 D3
Longnewton Stockton 225 B7
Longney Glos 80 C3
Longniddry E Loth 281 F8
Longnor Shrops 131 C9
Longnor Staffs 151 G7
Longnor Staffs 169 C9
Longnor Park Shrops 131 C9
Longparish Hants 48 E2
Longpark Cumb 239 E10
Longpark E Ayrs 257 B10
Longport Stoke 168 F5
Longridge Glos 80 D5
Longridge Lancs 203 F8
Longridge Staffs 151 F8
Longridge W Loth 269 C9
Longridge End Glos 98 G6
Longrigg N Lnrk 278 G6
Longriggend N Lnrk 278 G6
Longrock Corn 1 C5
Longscales N Yorks 205 B10
Longsdon Staffs 169 E7
Longshaw Gtr Man 194 G4
Longshaw Staffs 169 F9
Longside Aberds 303 E10
Longsight Gtr Man 184 B5
Longslow Shrops 150 B3
Longsowerby Cumb 239 G9
Longstanton Cambs 123 D7
Longstock Hants 47 F11
Longstone Corn 2 B2
Longstone Corn 11 G7
Longstone Edin 280 G4
Longstone Pembs 73 D10
Longstone Som 28 B5
Longstowe Cambs 122 G6
Longstreet Wilts 46 C6
Longthorpe P'boro 138 D3
Longthwaite Cumb 230 G4
Longton Lancs 194 B3
Longton Stoke 168 G6
Longtown Cumb 239 D9
Longtown Hereford 96 F6
Longtownmail Orkney 314 F4
Longview Mers 182 C6
Longville in the Dale Shrops 131 E10
Longway Bank Derbys 170 E4
Longwell Green S Glos 61 E7
Longwick Bucks 84 D3
Longwitton Northumb 252 F3
Longwood Shrops 132 B2
Longwood W Yorks 196 D6
Longwood Edge W Yorks 196 D6
Longworth Oxon 82 F5
Longyester E Loth 271 B10
Lonmay Aberds 303 D10
Lonmore Highld 298 E2
Looe Corn 6 E5
Looe Mills Corn 6 C4
Loose Kent 53 C9
Loose Hill Kent 53 C9
Loosegate Lincs 156 D6
Loosley Row Bucks 84 E4
Lopcombe Corner Wilts 47 F9
Lopen Som 28 E6
Lopen Head Som 28 E6
Loppergarth Cumb 210 D5
Loppington Shrops 149 D9
Lopwell Devon 7 C9
Lorbottle Northumb 252 B2
Lorbottle Hall Northumb 252 B2
Lord's Hill Soton 32 D5
Lords Wood Medway 69 G9
Lordsbridge Norf 157 G11
Lordshill Common Sur 50 E4
Lordswood Soton 32 D6
Lornty Perth 286 C5
Loscoe Derbys 170 F6
Loscoe W Yorks 198 C2
Loscombe Dorset 16 B6
Losgaintir W Isles 305 J2
Lossiemouth Moray 302 B2
Lossit Argyll 254 B2
Lossit Lodge Argyll 274 G5
Lostford Shrops 150 C2
Lostock Gtr Man 195 F7
Lostock Gralam W Ches 183 F11
Lostock Green W Ches 183 G11
Lostock Hall Lancs 194 B4
Lostock Junction Gtr Man 195 F7
Lostwithiel Corn 6 D2
Loth Orkney 314 C6
Lothbeg Highld 311 H3
Lothersdale N Yorks 204 D5
Lothianbridge Midloth 270 C6
Lothmore Highld 311 H3
Lottisham Som 44 G5
Loudwater Bucks 84 G6
Loudwater Herts 85 F9
Loughborough Leics 153 F10
Loughor Swansea 56 B5
Loughton Essex 86 F6
Loughton M Keynes 102 D6
Loughton Shrops 132 G2
Lound Lincs 155 F11
Lound Notts 187 D11
Lound Suff 143 D10
Loundsley Green Derbys 186 G5
Lount Leics 153 F7
Lour Angus 287 C8
Louth Lincs 190 D4
Lovat Highld 300 E5
Lovaton Devon 7 B10
Love Clough Lancs 195 B10
Love Green Bucks 66 C4
Lovedean Hants 33 E11
Lover Wilts 32 C2
Loversall S Yorks 187 B9
Loves Green Essex 87 E10
Lovesome Hill N Yorks 225 F7
Loveston Pembs 73 D9
Lovington Som 44 G5
Low Ackworth W Yorks 198 D3
Low Alwinton Northumb 251 B10
Low Angerton Northumb 252 G3
Low Barlings Lincs 189 G9
Low Barugh S Yorks 197 F10
Low Bentham N Yorks 212 F2
Low Biggins Cumb 212 D2
Low Blantyre S Lnrk 268 D3
Low Borrowbridge Cumb 222 E2
Low Bradfield S Yorks 186 C3
Low Bradley N Yorks 204 D6
Low Braithwaite Cumb 230 C4
Low Bridge Wilts 62 E3
Low Brunton Northumb 241 C10
Low Burnham N Lincs 199 G9
Low Burton N Yorks 214 C4
Low Buston Northumb 252 B6
Low Catton E Yorks 207 C10
Low Clanyard Dumfries 236 F3
Low Common Norf 142 E2
Low Compton Gtr Man 196 F2
Low Coniscliffe Darl 224 C5
Low Cotehill Cumb 239 G11
Low Coylton S Ayrs 257 F10
Low Crosby Cumb 239 F10
Low Dalby N Yorks 217 B7
Low Dinsdale Darl 224 C6
Low Eighton T & W 243 F7
Low Ellington N Yorks 214 C4
Low Etherley Durham 233 F9
Low Fell T & W 243 F7
Low Fold W Yorks 205 F10
Low Fulney Lincs 156 E5
Low Garth N Yorks 226 D4
Low Gate Northumb 241 E10
Low Geltbridge Cumb 240 F2
Low Grantley N Yorks 214 E4
Low Green N Yorks 205 B10
Low Green Suff 125 E7
Low Green W Yorks 205 F10
Low Greenside T & W 242 E4
Low Habberley Worcs 116 B6
Low Ham Som 28 B6
Low Hauxley Northumb 253 C7
Low Hawsker N Yorks 227 D8
Low Hesket Cumb 230 B5
Low Hesleyhurst Northumb 252 D3
Low Hill W Mid 133 C8
Low Hutton N Yorks 216 F5
Low Knipe Cumb 230 G6
Low Laithe N Yorks 214 G3
Low Laithes S Yorks 197 G11
Low Leighton Derbys 185 D8
Low Lorton Cumb 229 F9
Low Marishes N Yorks 216 D6
Low Marnham Notts 172 B4
Low Mill N Yorks 226 F3
Low Moor Lancs 203 E10
Low Moor W Yorks 197 B7
Low Moorsley T & W 234 B2
Low Moresby Cumb 228 G5
Low Newton Cumb 211 C8
Low Newton-by-the-Sea Northumb 264 E6
Low Prudhoe Northumb 242 E4
Low Risby N Lincs 200 E2
Low Row Cumb 229 C9
Low Row Cumb 240 E3
Low Row N Yorks 223 F9
Low Salchrie Dumfries 236 C2
Low Smerby Argyll 255 E8
Low Snaygill N Yorks 204 D5
Low Street Norf 141 B10
Low Street Thurrock 69 D7
Low Tharston Norf 142 D3
Low Thornley T & W 242 E5
Low Torry Fife 279 D10
Low Town Shrops 132 E4
Low Toynton Lincs 190 G3
Low Valley S Yorks 198 G2
Low Valleyfield Fife 279 D10
Low Walton Cumb 219 C9
Low Waters S Lnrk 268 E4
Low Westwood Durham 242 F4
Low Whinnow Cumb 239 G8
Low Whita N Yorks 223 F10
Low Wood Cumb 210 C6
Low Worsall N Yorks 225 C7
Low Wray Cumb 221 E7
Lowbands Glos 98 E5
Lowbridge House Cumb 221 E10
Lowca Cumb 228 G5
Lowcross Hill W Ches 167 E7
Lowdham Notts 171 F11
Lowe Shrops 149 C10
Lowe Hill Staffs 169 D7
Lowedges S Yorks 186 E4
Lower Achachenna Argyll 284 E4
Lower Aisholt Som 43 F8
Lower Allscot Shrops 132 D4
Lower Altofts W Yorks 197 C11
Lower Amble Corn 10 G5
Lower Ansty Dorset 30 G3
Lower Ardtun Argyll 288 G5
Lower Arncott Oxon 83 B10
Lower Ashtead Sur 51 B7
Lower Ashton Devon 14 E2
Lower Assendon Oxon 65 C8
Lower Badcall Highld 306 E6
Lower Ballam Lancs 202 G3
Lower Bartle Lancs 202 G5
Lower Basildon W Berks 64 D6
Lower Bassingthorpe Lincs 155 D9
Lower Bearwood Hereford 115 F7
Lower Bebington Mers 182 E4
Lower Beeding W Sus 36 B2
Lower Benefield Northants 137 F9
Lower Bentley Worcs 117 D9
Lower Beobridge Shrops 132 E5
Lower Berry Hill Glos 79 C9
Lower Binton Warks 118 G2
Lower Birchwood Derbys 170 E6
Lower Bitchet Kent 52 C5
Lower Blandford St Mary Dorset 30 F5
Lower Blunsdon Swindon 81 G10
Lower Bobbingworth Green Essex 87 E8
Lower Bockhampton Dorset 17 C10
Lower Boddington Northants 119 G9
Lower Bodham Norf 160 B2
Lower Bodinnar Corn 1 C4
Lower Bois Bucks 85 E7
Lower Bordean Hants 33 C11
Lower Boscaswell Corn 1 C3
Lower Bourne Sur 49 E10
Lower Bradley W Mid 133 D9
Lower Brailes Warks 100 D6
Lower Breakish Highld 295 C8
Lower Bredbury Gtr Man 184 C6
Lower Breinton Hereford 97 D9
Lower Broadheath Worcs 116 F6
Lower Brook Hants 32 B4
Lower Broughton Gtr Man 184 B4
Lower Brynamman Neath 76 C2
Lower Brynn Corn 5 C9
Lower Buckenhill Hereford 98 E2
Lower Buckland Hants 20 B2
Lower Bullingham Hereford 97 D10
Lower Bullington Hants 48 E3
Lower Bunbury E Ches 167 D9
Lower Burgate Hants 31 D11
Lower Burrow Som 28 C6
Lower Burton Hereford 115 F8
Lower Bush Medway 69 F7
Lower Cadsden Bucks 84 E4
Lower Caldecote C Beds 104 B3
Lower Cam Glos 80 E2
Lower Canada N Som 43 B11
Lower Carden W Ches 167 E7
Lower Catesby Northants 119 F10
Lower Cator Devon 13 F9
Lower Caversham Reading 65 E8
Lower Chapel Powys 95 D10
Lower Chedworth Glos 81 C9
Lower Cheriton Devon 27 G10
Lower Chicksgrove Wilts 46 G3
Lower Chute Wilts 47 C10
Lower Clapton London 67 B11
Lower Clent Worcs 117 B8
Lower Clicker Corn 6 C5
Lower Clopton Warks 118 F3
Lower Common Hants 48 E6
Lower Common Hants 65 G9
Lower Common Mon 78 B2
Lower Common Mon 78 E4
Lower Common Shrops 131 B9
Lower Copthurst Lancs 194 C5
Lower Cotburn Aberds 303 D7
Lower Cousley Wood E Sus 53 G7
Lower Cox Street Kent 69 G10
Lower Cragabus Argyll 254 C4
Lower Creedy Devon 26 G4
Lower Croan Corn 10 G6
Lower Crossings Derbys 185 E8
Lower Cumberworth W Yorks 197 F8
Lower Cwm-twrch Powys 76 C3
Lower Daggons Hants 31 E9
Lower Darwen Blkburn 195 B7
Lower Dean Beds 121 D11
Lower Dean Devon 8 C4
Lower Dell Highld 292 B2
Lower Denby W Yorks 197 F8
Lower Denzell Corn 5 B7
Lower Deuchries Aberds 302 D6
Lower Diabaig Highld 299 C7
Lower Dicker E Sus 23 C9
Lower Dinchope Shrops 131 G9
Lower Dowdeswell Glos 81 B8
Lower Down Shrops 130 G6
Lower Drift Corn 1 D4
Lower Dunsforth N Yorks 215 G8
Lower Durston Som 28 B3
Lower Earley Wokingham 65 E9
Lower East Carleton Norf 142 C3
Lower Eastern Green W Mid 118 B5
Lower Edmonton London 86 G4
Lower Egleton Hereford 98 B2
Lower Elkstone Staffs 169 D9
Lower Ellastone Staffs 169 G10
Lower End Bucks 83 D11
Lower End Bucks 102 E4
Lower End C Beds 103 D8
Lower End C Beds 103 G9
Lower End Glos 81 E7
Lower End Northants 120 F6
Lower End Northants 120 G5
Lower End Northants 121 E7
Lower End Oxon 82 B4
Lower Everleigh Wilts 47 C7
Lower Eythorne Kent 55 D9
Lower Failand N Som 60 E4
Lower Faintree Shrops 132 F3
Lower Falkenham Suff 108 D5
Lower Farringdon Hants 49 F8
Lower Feltham London 66 E5
Lower Fittleworth W Sus 35 D8
Lower Forge Shrops 132 F4
Lower Foxdale I o M 192 E3
Lower Frankton Shrops 149 C7
Lower Freystrop Pembs 73 C7
Lower Froyle Hants 49 E9
Lower Gabwell Devon 9 B8
Lower Gledfield Highld 309 K5
Lower Godney Som 44 E3
Lower Goldstone Kent 71 G9
Lower Gornal W Mid 133 E8
Lower Grange W Yorks 205 G8
Lower Gravenhurst C Beds 104 D2
Lower Green Essex 88 E2
Lower Green Essex 105 E8
Lower Green Essex 106 E4
Lower Green Gtr Man 184 B2
Lower Green Herts 104 E3
Lower Green Kent 52 E5
Lower Green Kent 52 E6
Lower Green Norf 159 B9
Lower Green Staffs 133 B8
Lower Green Suff 124 D4
Lower Green Sur 66 F6
Lower Green W Berks 63 G11
Lower Green Warks 119 D10
Lower Grove Common Hereford 97 F11
Lower Hacheston Suff 126 F6
Lower Halistra Highld 298 D2
Lower Halliford Sur 66 F5
Lower Halstock Leigh Dorset 29 F8
Lower Halstow Kent 69 F11
Lower Hamswell S Glos 61 E8
Lower Hamworthy Poole 18 C6
Lower Hardres Kent 55 C7
Lower Hardwick Hereford 115 F8
Lower Harpton Powys 114 E5
Lower Hartlip Kent 69 G10
Lower Hartshay Derbys 170 E5
Lower Hartwell Bucks 84 C3
Lower Hatton Staffs 150 B6
Lower Hawthwaite Cumb 210 B4
Lower Haysden Kent 52 D5
Lower Hayton Shrops 131 G10
Lower Hazel S Glos 60 B6
Lower Heath E Ches 168 C5
Lower Hempriggs Moray 301 C11
Lower Heppington Kent 54 C6
Lower Hergest Hereford 114 F5
Lower Herne Kent 71 F7
Lower Heyford Oxon 101 G9
Lower Heysham Lancs 211 G8
Lower Higham Kent 69 E8
Lower Highmoor Oxon 65 B8
Lower Holbrook Suff 108 E3
Lower Holditch Dorset 28 G4
Lower Holloway London 67 B10
Lower Holwell Dorset 31 E9
Lower Hook Worcs 98 C6
Lower Hookner Devon 13 E10
Lower Hopton Shrops 149 E7
Lower Hopton W Yorks 197 D7
Lower Hordley Shrops 149 D7
Lower Horncroft W Sus 35 D8
Lower Horsebridge E Sus 23 C9
Lower House Halton 183 D8
Lower Houses W Yorks 197 D7
Lower Howsell Worcs 98 B5
Lower Illey Worcs 133 G9
Lower Island Kent 70 F6
Lower Kersal Gtr Man 195 G10
Lower Kilburn Derbys 170 F5
Lower Kilcott Glos 61 B9
Lower Killeyan Argyll 254 C3
Lower Kingcombe Dorset 17 B7
Lower Kingswood Sur 51 C8
Lower Kinnerton W Ches 166 C4
Lower Kinsham Hereford 115 E7
Lower Knapp Som 28 B4
Lower Knightley Staffs 150 E6
Lower Knowle Bristol 60 E5
Lower Langford N Som 60 G3
Lower Largo Fife 287 G8
Lower Layham Suff 107 C10
Lower Ledwyche Shrops 115 C10
Lower Leigh Staffs 151 B10
Lower Lemington Glos 100 E4
Lower Lenie Highld 300 G5
Lower Lode Glos 99 E7
Lower Lovacott Devon 25 B8
Lower Loxhore Devon 40 F6
Lower Lydbrook Glos 79 B9
Lower Lye Hereford 115 D8
Lower Machen Newport 59 B8
Lower Maes-coed Hereford 96 E6
Lower Mains Clack 279 B9
Lower Mannington Dorset 31 F9
Lower Marsh Som 30 C2
Lower Marston Som 45 E9
Lower Meend Glos 79 E9

Lower Menadue Corn 5 D10
Lower Merridge Som 43 G8
Lower Mickletown W Yorks 198 B2
Lower Middleton Cheney Northants 101 C10
Lower Midway Derbys 152 E6
Lower Mill Corn 3 B10
Lower Milovaig Highld 296 F7
Lower Milton Som 44 D4
Lower Moor Wilts 81 G8
Lower Moor Worcs 99 B9
Lower Morton S Glos 79 G10
Lower Mountain Flint 166 D4
Lower Nazeing Essex 86 D5
Lower Netchwood Shrops 132 E2
Lower Netherton Devon 14 G3
Lower New Inn Torf 78 F4
Lower Ninnes Corn 1 C5
Lower Nobut Staffs 151 C10
Lower North Dean Bucks 84 F5
Lower Norton Warks 118 E4
Lower Nyland Dorset 30 C2
Lower Ochrwyth Caerph 59 B8
Lower Odcombe Som 29 D8
Lower Oddington Glos 100 F4
Lower Ollach Highld 295 B7
Lower Padworth W Berks 64 F6
Lower Penarth V Glam 59 F7
Lower Penn Staffs 133 D7
Lower Pennington Hants 20 C2
Lower Penwortham Lancs 194 B4
Lower Peover W Ches 184 G2
Lower Pexhill E Ches 184 G5
Lower Pilsley Derbys 170 C6
Lower Pitkerrie Highld 311 L2
Lower Place Gtr Man 196 E2
Lower Place London 67 C8
Lower Pollicot Bucks 84 C2
Lower Porthkerry V Glam 58 F5
Lower Porthpean Corn 5 E10
Lower Quinton Warks 100 B3
Lower Rabber Hereford 114 G5
Lower Race Torf 78 E3
Lower Radley Oxon 83 F8
Lower Rainham Medway 69 F10
Lower Ratley Hants 32 C4
Lower Raydon Suff 107 D10
Lower Rea Glos 80 B4
Lower Ridge Devon 28 G2
Lower Ridge Shrops 148 C6
Lower Roadwater Som 42 F4
Lower Rochford Worcs 116 D2
Lower Rose Corn 4 E5
Lower Row Dorset 31 G8
Lower Sapey Worcs 116 E3
Lower Seagry Wilts 62 C3
Lower Sheering Essex 87 C7
Lower Shelton C Beds 103 C9
Lower Shiplake Oxon 65 D9
Lower Shuckburgh Warks 119 E9
Lower Skelty Swansea 56 C6
Lower Slackstead Hants 32 B5
Lower Slade Devon 40 D4
Lower Slaughter Glos 100 G3
Lower Solva Pembs 87 G11
Lower Southill W Yorks 197 C9
Lower Soudley Glos 79 D11
Lower Southfield Hereford 98 C3
Lower Stanton St Quintin Wilts 62 C2
Lower Stoke Medway 69 D10
Lower Stoke W Mid 119 B7
Lower Stondon C Beds 104 D3
Lower Stone Glos 79 G11
Lower Stonnall Staffs 133 C11
Lower Stow Bedon Norf 141 E9
Lower Stratton Som 28 D6
Lower Stratton Swindon 63 B7
Lower Street E Sus 38 E2
Lower Street Norf 160 B5
Lower Street Norf 160 C3
Lower Street Norf 160 F6
Lower Street Suff 108 E3
Lower Street Suff 124 G5
Lower Strensham Worcs 99 C8
Lower Stretton Warr 183 E10
Lower Studley Wilts 45 B11
Lower Sundon C Beds 103 F10
Lower Swainswick Bath 61 F9
Lower Swanwick Hants 33 F7
Lower Swell Glos 100 F3
Lower Sydenham London 67 E11
Lower Tadmarton Oxon 101 D8
Lower Tale Devon 27 G9
Lower Tasburgh Norf 142 D3
Lower Tean Staffs 151 B10
Lower Thorpe Northants 101 B10
Lower Threapwood Wrex 166 G6
Lower Thurlton Norf 143 D8
Lower Thurnham Lancs 202 C5
Lower Thurvaston Derbys 152 B4
Lower Todding Hereford 115 B8
Lower Tote Highld 298 C5
Lower Town Devon 27 E8
Lower Town Hereford 98 C2
Lower Town Pembs 91 D9
Lower Town W Yorks 204 G6
Lower Town Worcs 117 F7
Lower Trebullett Corn 12 F2
Lower Tregunnon Corn 11 E10
Lower Treworrick Corn 6 B4
Lower Tuffley Glos 80 C4
Lower Turmer Hants 31 F10
Lower Twitchen Devon 24 D5
Lower Twydall Medway 69 F10
Lower Tysoe Warks 100 B6
Lower Upham Hants 33 D8
Lower Upnor Medway 69 E9
Lower Vexford Som 42 F6
Lower Wainhill Oxon 84 E3
Lower Walton Warr 183 D10
Lower Wanborough Swindon 63 C8
Lower Weacombe Som 42 E6
Lower Weald M Keynes 102 D5
Lower Wear Devon 14 D4
Lower Weare Som 44 C2
Lower Weedon Northants 120 F2
Lower Welson Hereford 114 G5
Lower Westholme Som 44 E5
Lower Westhouse N Yorks 212 E3
Lower Westmancote Worcs 99 D8
Lower Weston Bath 61 F8
Lower Whatcombe Dorset 30 G4
Lower Whatley Som 45 D8
Lower Whitley W Ches 183 F10
Lower Wick Glos 80 F2
Lower Wick Worcs 116 G6
Lower Wield Hants 48 E6
Lower Willingdon E Sus 23 E9
Lower Winchendon or Nether Winchendon Bucks 84 C2
Lower Withington E Ches 168 B4
Lower Wolverton Worcs 117 G8
Lower Woodend Aberds 293 B8
Lower Woodend Bucks 65 B10
Lower Woodford Wilts 46 G6
Lower Woodley Corn 5 B10
Lower Woodside Herts 86 D2
Lower Woolston Som 29 B11
Lower Woon Corn 5 C10
Lower Wraxall Dorset 29 G9
Lower Wraxall Som 44 F6
Lower Wraxall Wilts 61 G10
Lower Wych W Ches 167 G7
Lower Wyche Worcs 98 C5
Lower Wyke W Yorks 197 B7
Lower Yelland Devon 40 G3
Lower Zeals Wilts 45 G9
Lowerford Lancs 204 F3
Lowerhouse E Ches 184 F6
Lowerhouse Lancs 204 G2
Lowertown Corn 2 D5
Lowertown Corn 5 C11
Lowertown Devon 12 E5
Lowes Barn Durham 233 C11
Lowesby Leics 136 B4
Lowestoft Suff 143 E10
Loweswater Cumb 229 G8
Lowfield S Yorks 186 D5
Lowfield Heath W Sus 51 E9
Lowford Hants 33 E7
Lowgill Cumb 222 F2
Lowgill Lancs 212 G3
Lowick Cumb 210 B5
Lowick Northants 137 G9
Lowick Northumb 264 B2
Lowick Bridge Cumb 210 B5
Lowick Green Cumb 210 B5
Lowlands Torf 78 F3
Lowmoor Row Cumb 231 F8
Lowna N Yorks 226 G3
Lownie Moor Angus 287 C8
Lowood Borders 262 B2
Lowsonford Warks 118 D3
Lowther Cumb 230 G6
Lowthertown Dumfries 238 D6
Lowtherville I o W 21 F7
Lowthorpe E Yorks 217 G11
Lowton Gtr Man 183 B10
Lowton Som 27 D11
Lowton Common Gtr Man 183 B10
Lowton Heath Gtr Man 183 B10
Lowton St Mary's Gtr Man 183 B10
Loxbeare Devon 26 D6
Loxford London 68 B2
Loxhill Sur 50 F4
Loxhore Devon 40 F6
Loxhore Cott Devon 40 F6
Loxley S Yorks 186 D4
Loxley Warks 118 G5
Loxley Green Staffs 151 C11
Loxter Hereford 98 C4
Loxton N Som 43 B11
Loxwood W Sus 50 G4
Loyter's Green Essex 87 C8
Loyterton Kent 70 G3
Lozells W Mid 133 F11
Lubachlaggan Highld 300 B3
Lubachoinnich Highld 309 K4
Lubberland Shrops 116 B2
Lubcroy Highld 309 J3
Lubenham Leics 136 F4
Lubinvullin Highld 308 C5
Lucas End Herts 86 E4
Lucas Green Lancs 194 C5
Lucas Green Sur 50 B2
Luccombe Som 42 E2
Luccombe Village I o W 21 F7
Lucker Northumb 264 C5
Luckett Corn 12 G3
Lucking Street Essex 106 E6
Luckington Wilts 61 C10
Lucklawhill Fife 287 E8
Luckwell Bridge Som 42 F2
Lucton Hereford 115 E8
Ludag W Isles 297 K3
Ludborough Lincs 190 B3
Ludbrook Devon 8 E3
Ludchurch Pembs 73 C10
Luddenden W Yorks 196 B4
Luddenden Foot W Yorks 196 C4
Ludderburn Cumb 221 G8
Luddesdown Kent 69 F7
Luddington N Lincs 199 D10
Luddington Warks 118 G3
Luddington in the Brook Northants 138 G2
Lude House Perth 291 G10
Ludford Lincs 190 D2
Ludford Shrops 115 C10
Ludgershall Bucks 83 B11
Ludgershall Wilts 47 C9
Ludgvan Corn 2 C2
Ludham Norf 161 F7
Ludlow Shrops 115 C10
Ludney Lincs 190 B5
Ludney Som 28 E5
Ludstock Hereford 98 D3
Ludstone Shrops 132 E6
Ludwell Wilts 30 C6
Ludworth Durham 234 C3
Luffenhall Herts 104 F5
Luffincott Devon 12 B2
Lufton Som 29 D8
Lugar E Ayrs 258 E3
Lugate Borders 271 G8
Lugg Green Hereford 115 E9
Luggate Burn E Loth 282 G2
Luggiebank N Lnrk 278 G5
Lugsdale Halton 183 D8
Lugton E Ayrs 267 E8
Lugwardine Hereford 97 C11
Luib Highld 295 C7
Luibeilt Highld 290 G4
Lulham Hereford 97 C8
Lullenden Sur 52 E2
Lullington Derbys 152 G5
Lullington Som 45 C9
Lulsgate Bottom N Som 60 F4
Lulsley Worcs 116 F4
Lulworth Camp Dorset 18 E2
Lumb Lancs 195 C10
Lumb Lancs 195 D9
Lumb W Yorks 196 C4
Lumb W Yorks 197 E7
Lumb Foot W Yorks 204 F6
Lumburn Devon 12 G5
Lumbutts W Yorks 196 C3
Lumby N Yorks 206 G5
Lumley W Sus 22 B3
Lumley Thicks Durham 243 G8
Lumloch E Dunb 268 B2
Lumphanan Aberds 293 C7
Lumphinnans Fife 280 C3
Lumsdaine Borders 273 B7
Lumsden Aberds 302 G4
Lunan Angus 287 B10
Lunanhead Angus 287 B8
Luncarty Perth 286 E4
Lund E Yorks 208 D5
Lund N Yorks 207 G9
Lund Shetland 312 C7
Lundal W Isles 304 E3
Lundavra Highld 290 G2
Lunderton Aberds 303 E11
Lundie Angus 286 D6
Lundie Highld 290 B3
Lundin Links Fife 287 G8
Lundwood S Yorks 197 F11
Lundy Green Norf 142 E4
Lunga Argyll 275 C8
Lunna Shetland 312 G6
Lunning Shetland 312 G7
Lunnister Shetland 312 F5
Lunnon Swansea 56 D4
Lunsford Kent 53 B7
Lunsford's Cross E Sus 38 E2
Lunt Mers 193 G10
Luntley Hereford 115 F7
Lunts Heath Halton 183 D8
Lupin Staffs 152 F2
Luppitt Devon 27 F11
Lupridge Devon 8 E4
Lupset W Yorks 197 D10
Lupton Cumb 211 C11
Lurg Aberds 293 C8
Lurgashall W Sus 34 B6
Lurignich Argyll 289 D11
Lurley Devon 26 E6
Lusby Lincs 174 B4
Lushcott Shrops 131 D11
Luson Devon 8 F2
Luss Argyll 277 C7
Lussagiven Argyll 275 E7
Lusta Highld 298 D2
Lustleigh Devon 13 E11
Lustleigh Cleave Devon 13 E11
Luston Hereford 115 E9
Lusty Som 45 G7
Luthermuir Aberds 293 G8
Luthrie Fife 287 F7
Lutley W Mid 133 G8
Luton Devon 14 F4
Luton Devon 27 G9
Luton Luton 103 G11
Luton Medway 69 F9
Lutsford Devon 24 D3
Lutterworth Leics 135 G10
Lutton Devon 7 D11
Lutton Devon 8 C3
Lutton Lincs 157 D8
Lutton Northants 138 F2
Lutton Gowts Lincs 157 E8
Lutworthy Devon 26 D3
Luxborough Som 42 F3
Luxley Glos 98 G3
Luxted London 68 G2
Luxton Devon 28 E2
Luxulyan Corn 5 D11
Luzley Gtr Man 196 G3
Luzley Brook Gtr Man 196 F2
Lyatts Som 29 E8
Lybster Highld 310 F6
Lydbury North Shrops 131 F7
Lydcott Devon 41 F7
Lydd Kent 39 C8
Lydd on Sea Kent 39 C9
Lydden Kent 55 D9
Lydden Kent 71 F11
Lyddington Rutland 137 D7
Lyde Orkney 314 E3
Lyde Shrops 130 C6
Lyde Cross Hereford 97 C10
Lyde Green Hants 49 B8
Lyde Green S Glos 61 D7
Lydeard St Lawrence Som 42 G6
Lydford Devon 12 E6
Lydford Fair Place Som 44 G5
Lydford-on-Fosse Som 44 G5
Lydgate Derbys 186 F4
Lydgate Gtr Man 196 G3
Lydgate W Yorks 196 B2
Lydham Shrops 130 E6
Lydiard Green Wilts 62 B5
Lydiard Millicent Wilts 62 B5
Lydiard Plain Wilts 62 B5
Lydiard Tregoze Swindon 62 C6
Lydiate Mers 193 G11
Lydiate Ash Worcs 117 B9
Lydlinch Dorset 30 E2
Lydmarsh Som 28 F5
Lydney Glos 79 E10
Lydstep Pembs 73 F9
Lye W Mid 133 G8
Lye Cross N Som 60 G3
Lye Green Bucks 85 E7
Lye Green E Sus 52 G4
Lye Green Warks 118 D3
Lye Green Wilts 45 B10
Lye Head Worcs 116 C5
Lye Hole N Som 60 G4
Lyewood Common E Sus 52 F4
Lyford Oxon 82 G5
Lymbridge Green Kent 54 E6
Lyme Green E Ches 184 G6
Lyme Regis Dorset 16 C2
Lymiecleuch Borders 249 C9
Lyminge Kent 55 E7
Lymington Hants 20 B2
Lyminster W Sus 35 G8
Lymm Warr 183 D11
Lymore Hants 19 C11
Lympne Kent 54 F6
Lympsham Som 43 C10
Lympstone Devon 14 E5
Lynbridge Devon 41 D8
Lynch Hants 48 D4
Lynch Som 42 D2
Lynch Hill Hants 48 D3
Lynch Hill Slough 66 C2
Lynchat Highld 291 C9
Lynchgate Shrops 131 F7
Lyndale Ho Highld 298 D3
Lyndhurst Hants 32 F4
Lyndon Rutland 137 C8
Lyndon Green W Mid 134 F2
Lyne Borders 270 G4
Lyne Sur 66 F4
Lyne Down Hereford 98 E2
Lyne of Gorthleck Highld 300 G5
Lyne of Skene Aberds 293 B9
Lyne Station Borders 260 B6
Lyneal Shrops 149 C9
Lyneal Mill Shrops 149 C9
Lyneal Wood Shrops 149 C9
Lyneham Oxon 100 G5
Lyneham Wilts 62 D4
Lynemore Highld 301 G10
Lynemouth Northumb 253 E7
Lyness Orkney 314 G3
Lynford Norf 140 E6
Lyng Norf 159 F11
Lyng Som 28 B4
Lyngate Norf 160 C5
Lyngford Som 28 B2
Lynmore Highld 301 F10
Lynmouth Devon 41 D8
Lynn Staffs 133 C11
Lynn Telford 150 F5
Lynnwood Borders 261 G11
Lynsore Bottom Kent 55 D7
Lynsted Kent 70 G2
Lynstone Corn 24 F2
Lynton Devon 41 D8
Lynwilg Highld 291 B10
Lynworth Glos 99 G9
Lyons T & W 234 B3
Lyon's Gate Dorset 29 F11
Lyon's Green Norf 159 G8
Lyonshall Hereford 114 F6
Lypiatt Glos 80 D6
Lyrabus Argyll 274 G3
Lytchett Matravers Dorset 18 B4
Lytchett Minster Dorset 18 C5
Lyth Highld 310 C6
Lytham Lancs 193 B11
Lytham St Anne's Lancs 193 B10
Lythbank Shrops 131 B9
Lythe N Yorks 226 C6
Lythes Orkney 314 H4
Lythmore Highld 310 C4

M

Maam Argyll 284 F5
Mabe Burnthouse Corn 3 C7
Mabie Dumfries 237 B11
Mableden Kent 52 E5
Mablethorpe Lincs 191 D8
Macclesfield E Ches 184 G6
Macclesfield Forest E Ches 185 G7
Macduff Aberds 303 C7
Mace Green Suff 108 C2
Machan S Lnrk 268 E5
Macharioch Argyll 255 G8
Machen Caerph 59 B8
Machrie N Ayrs 255 D9
Machrie Hotel Argyll 254 C4
Machrihanish Argyll 255 E7
Machroes Gwyn 144 D6
Machynlleth Powys 128 C4
Machynys Carms 56 B4
Mackerel's Common W Sus 35 B8
Mackerye End Herts 85 B11
Mackham Devon 27 F11
Mackney Oxon 64 B5
Mackside Borders 262 G4
Mackworth Derbys 152 B6
Macmerry E Loth 281 G8
Madderty Perth 286 E3
Maddington Wilts 46 E5
Maddiston Falk 279 F8
Maddox Moor Pembs 73 C7
Madehurst W Sus 35 E7
Madeley Staffs 168 G3
Madeley Telford 132 C3
Madeley Heath Staffs 168 F3
Madeley Heath Worcs 117 B9
Madeley Park Staffs 168 G3
Madeleywood Telford 132 C3
Maders Corn 12 G2
Madford Devon 27 E10
Madingley Cambs 123 E7
Madjeston Dorset 30 B4
Madley Hereford 97 D8
Madresfield Worcs 98 B6
Madron Corn 1 C5
Maen-y-groes Ceredig 111 F7
Maenaddwyn Anglesey 179 E7
Maenclochog Pembs 91 F11
Maendy V Glam 58 D4
Maenporth Corn 3 D7
Maentwrog Gwyn 163 G11
Maer Corn 24 F2
Maer Staffs 150 B5
Maerdy Carms 94 G2
Maerdy Conwy 165 G8
Maerdy Rhondda 77 F7
Maes-bangor Ceredig 128 G3
Maes-glas Newport 59 B9
Maes Glas = Greenfield Flint 181 F11
Maes Llyn Ceredig 93 C7
Maes Pennant Flint 181 F11
Maes-Treylow Powys 114 D5
Maes-y-dre Flint 166 C2
Maesbrook Shrops 148 E5
Maesbury Shrops 148 D6
Maesbury Marsh Shrops 148 D6
Maesgeirchen Gwyn 179 G9
Maesgwyn-Isaf Powys 148 G3
Maesgwynne Carms 92 G4
Maeshafn Denb 166 C2
Maesllyn Ceredig 93 C7
Maesmynis Powys 95 B10
Maesteg Bridgend 57 C10
Maesybont Carms 75 B9
Maesycoed Rhondda 58 B5
Maesycrugiau Carms 93 C9
Maesycwmmer Caerph 77 G11
Maesygwartha Mon 78 C2
Maesymeillion Ceredig 93 B8
Maesypandy Powys 129 D9
Maesyrhandir Powys 129 E11
Magdalen Laver Essex 87 D8
Maggieknockater Moray 302 E3
Maggots End Essex 105 F9
Magham Down E Sus 23 C10
Maghull Mers 193 G11
Magor Mon 60 B2
Magpie Green Suff 125 B11
Mahaar Dumfries 236 B2
Maida Vale London 67 C9
Maiden Bradley Wilts 45 F10
Maiden Head N Som 60 F5
Maiden Law Durham 233 B9
Maiden Newton Dorset 17 B7
Maiden Wells Pembs 73 F7
Maidenbower W Sus 51 F9
Maidencombe Torbay 9 B8
Maidenhall Suff 108 C3
Maidenhead Windsor 65 C11
Maidenhead Court Windsor 66 C2
Maidenpark Falk 279 E9
Maidens S Ayrs 244 B6
Maiden's Green Brack 65 E11
Maiden's Hall Northumb 252 D6
Maidensgrave Suff 108 B5
Maidensgrove Oxon 65 B8
Maidenwell Corn 11 G8
Maidenwell Lincs 190 F4
Maidford Northants 120 G2
Maids Moreton Bucks 102 D4
Maidstone Kent 53 B9
Maidwell Northants 120 B4
Mail Shetland 313 L6
Mailand Shetland 312 C8
Mailingsland Borders 270 G4
Main Powys 148 F3
Maindee Newport 59 B10
Maindy Cardiff 59 D7
Mainholm S Ayrs 257 E9
Mains Cumb 229 G7
Mains of Airies Dumfries 236 C1
Mains of Allardice Aberds 293 F10
Mains of Annochie Aberds 303 E9
Mains of Ardestie Angus 287 D9
Mains of Arnage Aberds 303 F9
Mains of Auchoynanie Moray 302 E4
Mains of Baldoon Dumfries 236 D6
Mains of Balhall Angus 293 G7
Mains of Ballindarg Angus 287 B8
Mains of Balnakettle Aberds 293 F8
Mains of Birness Aberds 303 F9
Mains of Blackhall Aberds 303 G7
Mains of Burgie Moray 301 D10
Mains of Cairnbrogie Aberds 303 G8
Mains of Cairnty Moray 302 D3
Mains of Clunas Highld 301 E8
Mains of Crichie Aberds 303 E9
Mains of Daltulich Highld 301 E7
Mains of Dalvey Highld 301 F11
Mains of Dellavaird Aberds 293 E9
Mains of Drum Aberds 293 D10
Mains of Edingight Moray 302 D5
Mains of Fedderate Aberds 303 E8
Mains of Flichity Highld 300 G6
Mains of Hatton Aberds 303 D9
Mains of Hatton Aberds 303 E7
Mains of Inkhorn Aberds 303 F9
Mains of Innerpeffray Perth 286 F3
Mains of Kirktonhill Aberds 293 G8
Mains of Laithers Aberds 302 E6
Mains of Mayen Moray 302 E5
Mains of Melgund Angus 287 B9
Mains of Taymouth Perth 285 C11
Mains of Thornton Aberds 293 F8
Mains of Towie Aberds 303 E7
Mains of Ulbster Highld 310 E7
Mains of Watten Highld 310 D6
Mainsforth Durham 234 E2
Mainsriddle Dumfries 237 D11
Mainstone Shrops 130 F5
Maisemore Glos 98 G6
Maitland Park London 67 C9
Major's Green W Mid 118 B2
Makeney Derbys 170 G5
Malacleit W Isles 296 D3
Malborough Devon 9 G9
Malcoff Derbys 185 E9
Malden Rushett London 67 G7
Maldon Essex 88 D4
Malehurst Shrops 131 B7
Malham N Yorks 213 G8
Maligar Highld 298 C4
Malinbridge S Yorks 186 D4
Malinslee Telford 132 B3
Malkin's Bank E Ches 168 D3
Mallaig Highld 295 F8
Mallaig Bheag Highld 295 F8
Malleny Mills Edin 270 B3
Malling Stirl 285 G9
Mallows Green Essex 105 F9
Malltraeth Anglesey 162 B6
Mallwyd Gwyn 147 G7
Malmesbury Wilts 62 B2
Malmsmead Devon 41 D9
Malpas Corn 4 G6
Malpas Newport 78 G4
Malpas W Berks 64 E6
Malpas W Ches 167 F7
Malswick Glos 98 F4
Maltby Lincs 190 E4
Maltby S Yorks 187 C8
Maltby Stockton 225 C9
Maltby le Marsh Lincs 191 E7
Malting End Suff 124 G4
Malting Green Essex 107 G9
Maltings Angus 293 G9
Maltman's Hill Kent 54 E2
Malton N Yorks 216 E5
Malvern Common Worcs 98 C5
Malvern Link Worcs 98 B5
Malvern Wells Worcs 98 C5
Mambeg Argyll 276 D4
Mamble Worcs 116 C3
Mamhilad Mon 78 E4
Man-moel Caerph 77 E11
Manaccan Corn 3 E7
Manadon Plym 7 D9
Manafon Powys 130 C2
Manais W Isles 296 C7
Manar Ho Aberds 303 G7
Manaton Devon 13 E11
Manby Lincs 190 D5
Mancetter Warks 134 D6
Manchester Gtr Man 184 B4
Manchester Airport Gtr Man 184 D4
Mancot Flint 166 B4
Mancot Royal Flint 166 B4
Mandally Highld 290 C4
Manea Cambs 139 F9
Maney W Mid 134 D2
Manfield N Yorks 224 C4
Mangaster Shetland 312 F5
Mangotsfield S Glos 61 D7
Mangrove Green Herts 104 G2
Mangurstadh W Isles 304 E2
Manhay Corn 2 C5
Manian-fawr Pembs 92 B3
Mankinholes W Yorks 196 C3
Manley Devon 27 E7
Manley W Ches 183 G8
Manley Common W Ches 183 G8
Manmoel Caerph 77 E11
Mannal Argyll 288 E1
Mannamead Plym 7 D9
Mannerston W Loth 279 F10
Manningford Abbots Wilts 46 B6
Manningford Bohune Wilts 46 B6
Manningford Bruce Wilts 46 B6
Manningham W Yorks 205 G9
Mannings Heath W Sus 36 B2
Mannington Dorset 31 F9
Manningtree Essex 107 E11
Mannofield Aberdeen 293 C11
Manor London 68 B2
Manor Bourne Devon 7 F9
Manor Estate S Yorks 186 D5
Manor Hill Corner Lincs 157 F8
Manor House W Mid 135 G7
Manor Park Bucks 84 C4
Manor Park E Sus 37 C7
Manor Park London 68 B2
Manor Park Notts 153 C11
Manor Park S Yorks 186 D5
Manor Park Slough 66 C3
Manor Park W Ches 167 B11
Manor Park W Yorks 205 D9
Manor Parsley Corn 4 F4
Manor Royal W Sus 51 F9
Manorbier Pembs 73 F9
Manorbier Newton Pembs 73 F8
Manordeilo Carms 94 F3
Manorhill Borders 262 C5
Manorowen Pembs 91 D8
Man's Cross Essex 106 D5
Mansegate Dumfries 247 G9
Mansel Lacy Hereford 97 B8
Manselfield Swansea 56 D5
Mansell Gamage Hereford 97 C7
Manselton Swansea 57 B7
Mansergh Cumb 212 C2
Mansewood Glasgow 267 C11
Mansfield E Ayrs 258 G4
Mansfield Notts 171 C8
Mansfield Woodhouse Notts 171 C8
Manson Green Norf 141 C10
Mansriggs Cumb 210 C5
Manston Dorset 30 D4
Manston Kent 71 F10
Manston W Yorks 206 F3
Manthorpe Lincs 155 B8
Manthorpe Lincs 155 F11
Mantles Green Bucks 85 F7
Manton N Lincs 200 G2
Manton Notts 187 F9
Manton Rutland 137 C7
Manton Wilts 63 F7
Manton Warren N Lincs 200 F2
Manuden Essex 105 F9
Manwood Green Essex 87 C8
Manywells Height W Yorks 205 F7
Maperton Som 29 B11
Maple Cross Herts 85 G8
Maple End Essex 105 D11
Maplebeck Notts 172 C2
Mapledurham Oxon 65 D7
Mapledurwell Hants 49 C7
Maplehurst W Sus 35 C11
Maplescombe Kent 68 G5
Mapleton Derbys 169 F11
Mapperley Derbys 170 G6
Mapperley Nottingham 171 G9
Mapperley Park Nottingham 171 G9
Mapperton Dorset 16 B6
Mapperton Dorset 18 B4
Mappleborough Green Warks 117 D11
Mappleton E Yorks 209 E10
Mapplewell S Yorks 197 F10
Mappowder Dorset 30 F2
Mar Lodge Aberds 292 D2
Maraig W Isles 305 H3
Marazanvose Corn 4 E6
Marazion Corn 2 C2
Marbhig W Isles 305 G6
Marbrack Dumfries 246 E3
Marbury E Ches 167 F9
March Cambs 139 D8
March S Lnrk 259 G11
Marcham Oxon 83 F7
Marchamley Shrops 149 D11
Marchamley Wood Shrops 149 C11
Marchington Staffs 152 C2
Marchington Woodlands Staffs 152 D2
Marchroes Gwyn 144 D6
Marchwiel Wrex 166 F5
Marchwood Hants 32 E5
Marcross V Glam 58 F2
Marden Hereford 97 B10
Marden Kent 53 E8
Marden T & W 243 C9
Marden Wilts 46 B5
Marden Ash Essex 87 E9
Marden Beech Kent 53 E8
Marden Thorn Kent 53 E9
Marden's Hill E Sus 52 G3
Mardleybury Herts 86 B3
Mardu Shrops 130 G5
Mardy Mon 78 B4
Mardy Shrops 148 C5
Marefield Leics 136 B4
Mareham le Fen Lincs 174 C3
Mareham on the Hill Lincs 174 B3
Marehay Derbys 170 F5
Marehill W Sus 35 D9
Maresfield E Sus 37 C7
Maresfield Park E Sus 37 C7
Marfleet Hull 200 B6
Marford Wrex 166 D5
Margam Neath 57 D9
Margaret Marsh Dorset 30 D4
Margaret Roding Essex 87 C9
Margaretting Essex 87 E11
Margaretting Tye Essex 87 E11
Margate Kent 71 E11
Margery Sur 51 C9
Margnaheglish N Ayrs 256 C2
Margreig Dumfries 237 B10
Margrove Park Redcar 226 B3
Marham Norf 158 G4
Marhamchurch Corn 24 G2
Marholm P'boro 138 C2
Marian Flint 181 F9
Marian Cwm Denb 181 F9
Marian-glas Anglesey 179 E8
Marian y de = South Beach Gwyn 145 C7
Marian y mor = West End Gwyn 145 C7
Mariandyrys Anglesey 179 E10
Marianglas Anglesey 179 E8
Mariansleigh Devon 26 C2
Marine Town Kent 70 E2
Marionburgh Aberds 293 C9
Marishader Highld 298 C4
Marjoriebanks Dumfries 248 G3
Mark Dumfries 236 D3
Mark Dumfries 237 C7
Mark S Ayrs 236 B2
Mark Som 43 D11
Mark Causeway Som 43 D11
Mark Cross E Sus 23 C7
Mark Cross E Sus 52 G5
Mark Hall North Essex 87 C7
Mark Hall South Essex 87 C7
Markbeech Kent 52 E3
Markby Lincs 191 F7
Markeaton Derbys 152 B6
Market Bosworth Leics 135 C8
Market Deeping Lincs 138 B2
Market Drayton Shrops 150 C3
Market Harborough Leics 136 F4
Market Lavington Wilts 46 C4
Market Overton Rutland 155 F7
Market Rasen Lincs 189 D10
Market Stainton Lincs 190 F2
Market Warsop Notts 171 B9
Market Weighton E Yorks 208 E3
Market Weston Suff 125 B9
Markethill Perth 286 D6
Markfield Leics 153 G9
Markham Caerph 77 E11
Markham Moor Notts 188 G2
Markinch Fife 286 G6
Markington N Yorks 214 F5
Markland Hill Gtr Man 195 F7
Markle E Loth 281 F11
Mark's Corner I o W 20 C5
Marks Gate London 87 G7
Marks Tey Essex 107 G8
Marksbury Bath 61 G7
Markyate Herts 85 B9
Marl Bank Worcs 98 C5
Marland Gtr Man 195 E11
Marlas Hereford 97 F8
Marlborough Wilts 63 F7
Marlbrook Hereford 115 G10
Marlbrook Worcs 117 C9
Marlcliff Warks 117 G11
Marldon Devon 9 C7
Marle Green E Sus 23 B9
Marle Hill Glos 99 G9
Marlesford Suff 126 F6
Marley Kent 55 C10
Marley Kent 55 C7
Marley Green E Ches 167 F9
Marley Heights W Sus 49 G11
Marley Hill T & W 242 F6
Marley Pots T & W 243 F9
Marlingford Norf 142 B2
Marloes Pembs 72 D3
Marlow Bucks 65 B10
Marlow Hereford 115 B8
Marlow Bottom Bucks 65 B11
Marlow Common Bucks 65 B10
Marlpit Hill Kent 52 D2
Marlpits E Sus 38 E2
Marlpool Derbys 170 F6
Marnhull Dorset 30 D3
Marnoch Aberds 302 D5
Marnock N Lnrk 268 B4
Marple Gtr Man 185 D7
Marple Bridge Gtr Man 185 D7
Marpleridge Gtr Man 185 D7
Marr S Yorks 198 F4
Marr Green Wilts 63 G8
Marrel Highld 311 H4
Marrick N Yorks 223 F11
Marrister Shetland 313 G7
Marros Carms 74 D2
Marsden T & W 243 E9
Marsden W Yorks 196 E4
Marsden Height Lancs 204 F3
Marsett N Yorks 213 B8
Marsh Bucks 84 D4
Marsh Devon 28 E3
Marsh W Yorks 196 D6
Marsh W Yorks 204 F6
Marsh Baldon Oxon 83 F9
Marsh Benham W Berks 64 F2
Marsh Common S Glos 60 C5
Marsh End Worcs 98 D6
Marsh Gate W Berks 63 F10
Marsh Gibbon Bucks 102 G2
Marsh Green Devon 14 C6
Marsh Green Gtr Man 194 F5
Marsh Green Kent 52 E2
Marsh Green Staffs 168 D5
Marsh Green Telford 150 G2
Marsh Green W Ches 183 F8
Marsh Houses Lancs 202 C5
Marsh Lane Derbys 186 F6
Marsh Lane Glos 79 D9
Marsh Mills Som 43 F7
Marsh Side Norf 176 E3
Marsh Street Som 42 E3
Marshall Meadows Northumb 273 D9
Marshall's Cross Mers 183 C8
Marshall's Elm Som 44 G3
Marshall's Heath Herts 85 B11
Marshalsea Dorset 28 G5
Marshalswick Herts 85 D11
Marsham Norf 160 E3
Marshaw Lancs 203 C7
Marshborough Kent 55 B10
Marshbrook Shrops 131 F8
Marshchapel Lincs 190 B5
Marshfield Newport 59 C9
Marshfield S Glos 61 E9
Marshfield Bank E Ches 167 D11
Marshgate Corn 11 C9
Marshland St James Norf 139 B10
Marshmoor Herts 86 D2
Marshside Kent 71 F8
Marshside Mers 193 D11
Marshwood Dorset 16 B3
Marske N Yorks 224 E2
Marske-by-the-Sea Redcar 235 G8
Marston Hereford 115 F7
Marston Lincs 172 G5
Marston Oxon 83 D8
Marston Staffs 150 G6
Marston Staffs 151 D8
Marston W Ches 183 F11
Marston Warks 119 B8
Marston Warks 134 E4
Marston Wilts 46 B3
Marston Bigot Som 45 E9
Marston Doles Warks 119 F9
Marston Gate Som 45 D9
Marston Green W Mid 134 F3
Marston Hill Glos 81 F10
Marston Jabbett Warks 135 F7
Marston Magna Som 29 C9
Marston Meysey Wilts 81 F10
Marston Montgomery Derbys 152 B2
Marston Moretaine C Beds 103 C9
Marston on Dove Derbys 152 D4
Marston St Lawrence Northants 101 C10
Marston Stannett Hereford 115 F11
Marston Trussell Northants 136 F3
Marstow Hereford 79 B9
Marsworth Bucks 84 C6
Marten Wilts 47 B9
Marthall E Ches 184 F4
Martham Norf 161 F9
Marthwaite Cumb 222 G2
Martin Hants 31 D9
Martin Kent 55 D10
Martin Lincs 173 D10
Martin Lincs 174 B2
Martin Dales Lincs 173 C11
Martin Drove End Hants 31 C9
Martin Hussingtree Worcs 117 E7
Martin Mill Kent 55 D10
Martin Moor Lincs 174 C2
Martindale Cumb 221 B8
Martinhoe Devon 41 D7
Martinhoe Cross Devon 41 D7
Martin's Moss E Ches 168 C4
Martinscroft Warr 183 D11
Martinstown Dorset 17 D8
Martinstown or Winterbourne St Martin Dorset 17 D8
Martlesham Suff 108 B4
Martlesham Heath Suff 108 B4
Martletwy Pembs 73 C8
Martley Worcs 116 E5
Martock Som 29 D7
Marton Cumb 210 D4
Marton E Ches 168 B5
Marton E Yorks 209 F9
Marton Lincs 188 E4
Marton M'bro 225 B10
Marton N Yorks 215 G8
Marton N Yorks 216 C4
Marton Shrops 130 C5
Marton Shrops 149 E8
Marton W Ches 167 B10
Marton Warks 119 D8
Marton Green W Ches 167 B10
Marton Grove M'bro 225 B9
Marton-in-the-Forest N Yorks 215 F11
Marton-le-Moor N Yorks 215 E7
Marton Moor Warks 119 D8
Marton Moss Side Blkpool 202 G2
Martyr Worthy Hants 48 G4
Martyr's Green Sur 50 B5
Marwick Orkney 314 D2
Marwood Devon 40 F4
Mary Tavy Devon 12 F6
Marybank Highld 300 D4
Marybank Highld 301 B7
Maryburgh Highld 300 D5
Maryfield Aberds 293 D7
Maryfield Corn 7 D8
Maryhill Glasgow 267 B11
Marykirk Aberds 293 G8
Maryland Mon 79 D8
Marylebone Gtr Man 194 F5
Marypark Moray 301 F11
Maryport Cumb 228 D6
Maryport Dumfries 236 F3
Maryton Angus 287 B10
Maryton Angus 287 B7
Marywell Aberds 293 D11
Marywell Aberds 293 D7
Marywell Angus 287 C10
Masbrough S Yorks 186 C6
Mascle Bridge Pembs 73 D7
Masham N Yorks 214 C4
Mashbury Essex 87 C11
Masongill N Yorks 212 D3
Masonhill S Ayrs 257 E9
Mastin Moor Derbys 187 F7
Mastrick Aberdeen 293 C10
Matchborough Worcs 117 D11
Matching Essex 87 C8
Matching Green Essex 87 C8
Matching Tye Essex 87 C8
Matfen Northumb 242 C2
Matfield Kent 53 E7
Mathern Mon 79 G8
Mathon Hereford 98 B4
Mathry Pembs 91 E7
Matlaske Norf 160 C3
Matley Gtr Man 185 B7
Matlock Derbys 170 C3
Matlock Bank Derbys 170 C3
Matlock Bath Derbys 170 D3
Matlock Bridge Derbys 170 D3
Matlock Cliff Derbys 170 D4
Matlock Dale Derbys 170 D3
Matshead Lancs 202 E6
Matson Glos 80 B4
Matterdale End Cumb 230 G3
Mattersey Notts 187 D11
Mattersey Thorpe Notts 187 D11
Matthewsgreen Wokingham 65 F10
Mattingley Hants 49 B8
Mattishall Norf 159 G11
Mattishall Burgh Norf 159 G11
Mauchline E Ayrs 257 D11
Maud Aberds 303 E9
Maudlin Corn 5 C11
Maudlin Dorset 28 F5
Maudlin W Sus 22 B5
Maudlin Cross Dorset 28 F5
Maugersbury Glos 100 F4
Maughold I o M 192 C5
Mauld Highld 300 F4
Maulden C Beds 103 D11
Maulds Meaburn Cumb 222 B2
Maunby N Yorks 215 B7
Maund Bryan Hereford 115 G11
Maundown Som 27 B9
Mauricewood Midloth 270 C4
Mautby Norf 161 G9
Mavesyn Ridware Staffs 151 F11
Mavis Enderby Lincs 174 B5
Maviston Highld 301 D9
Maw Green E Ches 168 D2
Mawbray Cumb 229 B7
Mawdesley Lancs 194 E3
Mawdlam Bridgend 57 E10
Mawgan Corn 2 D6
Mawgan Porth Corn 5 B7
Mawla Corn 4 F4
Mawnan Corn 3 D7
Mawnan Smith Corn 3 D7
Mawsley Northants 120 B6
Mawson Green S Yorks 198 D6
Mawthorpe Lincs 191 G7
Maxey P'boro 138 B2
Maxstoke Warks 134 F4

Maxted Street Kent 54 E6
Maxton Borders 262 C4
Maxton Kent 55 E10
Maxwellheugh Borders 262 C6
Maxwelltown Dumfries 237 B11
Maxworthy Corn 11 C11
May Bank Staffs 168 F5
May Hill Mon 79 C8
May Hill Village Glos 98 G4
Mayals Swansea 56 C6
Maybole S Ayrs 257 G8
Maybury Sur 50 B4
Maybush Soton 32 E6
Mayer's Green W Mid 133 E10
Mayes Green Sur 50 F6
Mayeston Pembs 73 E8
Mayfair London 67 C9
Mayfield E Sus 37 B9
Mayfield Midloth 271 C7
Mayfield Northumb 243 B7
Mayfield Staffs 169 F11
Mayfield W Loth 269 B8
Mayford Sur 50 B3
Mayhill Swansea 56 C6
Mayland Essex 88 E6
Maylandsea Essex 88 E6
Maynard's Green E Sus 23 B9
Mayne Ho Moray 302 C2
Mayon Corn 1 D3
Maypole Kent 68 E4
Maypole Kent 68 G3
Maypole Kent 71 G8
Maypole Mon 79 B7
Maypole Scilly 1 G4
Maypole Green Essex 107 G9
Maypole Green Norf 143 D8
Maypole Green Suff 125 F8
Maypole Green Suff 126 D5
May's Green N Som 59 G11
Mays Green Oxon 65 C8
May's Green Sur 50 B5
Mayshill S Glos 61 C7
Maythorn S Yorks 197 F7
Maythorne Notts 171 D11
Maywick Shetland 313 L5
Mead Devon 13 G11
Mead Devon 24 D2
Mead End Hants 19 B11
Mead End Hants 33 E11
Mead End Wilts 31 C8
Mead Vale Sur 51 D9
Meadgate Bath 45 B7
Meadle Bucks 84 D4
Meadow Green Hereford 116 F4
Meadow Hall S Yorks 186 C5
Meadow Head S Yorks 186 E4
Meadowbank Edin 280 G5
Meadowbank W Ches 167 B11
Meadowend Essex 106 C4
Meadowfield Durham 233 D10
Meadowfoot N Ayrs 266 F4
Meadowley Shrops 132 E3
Meadowmill E Loth 281 G8
Meadows Nottingham 153 B11
Meadowtown Shrops 130 C6
Meads E Sus 23 F10
Meadside Oxon 83 G9
Meadwell Devon 12 E4
Meaford Staffs 151 B7
Meagill N Yorks 205 B9
Meal Bank Cumb 221 F10
Meal Hill W Yorks 197 F7
Mealabost Bhuirgh W Isles 304 C6
Mealabost W Isles 304 E6
Mealasta W Isles 304 F1
Mealrigg Cumb 229 B8
Mealsgate Cumb 229 C10
Meanwood W Yorks 205 F11
Mearbeck N Yorks 212 G6
Meare Som 44 E3
Meare Green Som 28 B4
Meare Green Som 28 C3
Mearns Bath 45 B8
Mearns E Renf 267 D10
Mears Ashby Northants 120 D6
Measborough Dike S Yorks 197 F11
Measham Leics 152 G6
Meath Green Sur 51 E9
Meathop Cumb 211 C8
Meaux E Yorks 209 F7
Meaver Corn 2 F5
Meavy Devon 7 B10
Medbourne Leics 136 E5
Medbourne M Keynes 102 D6
Medburn Northumb 242 C4
Meddon Devon 24 D3
Meden Vale Notts 171 B9
Medhurst Row Kent 52 D3
Medlam Lincs 174 D4
Medlar Lancs 202 F4
Medlicott Shrops 131 E8
Medlyn Corn 2 C6
Medmenham Bucks 65 C10
Medomsley Durham 242 G4
Medstead Hants 49 F7
Meer Common Hereford 115 G7
Meer End W Mid 118 C4
Meerbrook Staffs 169 C7
Meerhay Dorset 29 G7
Meers Bridge Lincs 191 D7
Meersbrook S Yorks 186 E5
Meesden Herts 105 E8
Meeson Telford 150 E3
Meeson Heath Telford 150 E3
Meeth Devon 25 F8
Meethe Devon 25 C11
Meeting Green Suff 124 F4
Meeting House Hill Norf 160 D6
Meggernie Castle Perth 285 C9
Meggethead Borders 260 E5
Meidrim Carms 92 G5
Meifod Denb 165 D8
Meifod Powys 148 G3
Meigle N Ayrs 266 B3
Meigle Perth 286 C6
Meikle Earnock S Lnrk 268 E4
Meikle Ferry Highld 309 L7
Meikle Forter Angus 292 G3
Meikle Gluich Highld 309 L6
Meikle Obney Perth 286 D4
Meikle Pinkerton E Loth 282 F4
Meikle Strath Aberds 293 F8
Meikle Tarty Aberds 303 G9
Meikle Wartle Aberds 303 F7
Meikleour Perth 286 D5
Meinciau Carms 75 C7
Meir Stoke 168 G6
Meir Heath Staffs 168 G6
Melbourn Cambs 105 C7
Melbourne Derbys 153 D7
Melbourne E Yorks 207 E11
Melbourne S Lnrk 269 G11
Melbury Abbas Dorset 30 D5
Melbury Bubb Dorset 29 F9
Melbury Osmond Dorset 29 F9
Melbury Sampford Dorset 29 F9
Melby Shetland 313 H3
Melchbourne Beds 121 D10
Melcombe Som 43 G9
Melcombe Bingham Dorset 30 G3
Melcombe Regis Dorset 17 E9
Meldon Devon 13 C7
Meldon Northumb 252 G4
Meldreth Cambs 105 B7
Meldrum Ho Aberds 303 G8
Melfort Argyll 275 B9
Melgarve Highld 290 D6
Meliden = Gallt Melyd Denb 181 E9
Melin Caiach Caerph 77 F10
Melin-y-coed Conwy 164 C4
Melin-y-ddôl Powys 129 B11
Melin-y-grug Powys 129 B11
Melin-y-Wig Denb 165 F8
Melinbyrhedyn Powys 128 D6
Melincourt Neath 76 E4
Melincryddan Neath 57 B8
Melinsey Corn 3 B10
Melkington Northumb 273 G7
Melkinthorpe Cumb 231 F7
Melkridge Northumb 240 E6
Melksham Wilts 62 G2
Melksham Forest Wilts 62 G2
Mell Green W Berks 64 D3
Mellangaun Highld 307 L3
Mellangoose Corn 2 D5
Melldalloch Argyll 275 F10
Mellguards Cumb 230 B4
Melling Lancs 211 E11
Melling Mers 193 G11
Melling Mount Mers 194 G2
Mellingey Corn 10 G4
Mellis Suff 126 C2
Mellis Green Suff 125 C11
Mellon Charles Highld 307 K3
Mellon Udrigle Highld 307 K3
Mellor Gtr Man 185 D7
Mellor Lancs 203 G9
Mellor Brook Lancs 203 G8
Mells Som 45 D8
Mells Suff 127 B8
Mells Green Som 45 D8
Melmerby Cumb 231 D8
Melmerby N Yorks 213 B11
Melmerby N Yorks 214 D6
Melon Green Suff 124 F6
Melplash Dorset 16 B5
Melrose Borders 262 C2
Melsetter Orkney 314 H2
Melsonby N Yorks 224 D3
Meltham W Yorks 196 E6
Meltham Mills W Yorks 196 E6
Melton E Yorks 200 B3
Melton Suff 126 G5
Melton Constable Norf 159 C10
Melton Mowbray Leics 154 F5
Melton Ross N Lincs 200 E5
Meltonby E Yorks 207 C11
Melvaig Highld 307 L2
Melverley Shrops 148 F6
Melverley Green Shrops 148 F6
Melvich Highld 310 C2
Membland Devon 7 F11
Membury Devon 28 G3
Memsie Aberds 303 C9
Memus Angus 287 B8
Mena Corn 5 C10
Menabilly Corn 5 E11
Menadarva Corn 4 G2
Menagissey Corn 4 F4
Menai Bridge = Porthaethwy Anglesey 179 G9
Mendham Suff 142 G5
Mendlesham Suff 126 D2
Mendlesham Green Suff 125 E11
Menethorpe N Yorks 216 F5
Mengham Hants 21 B10
Menheniot Corn 6 C5
Menherion Corn 2 B6
Menithwood Worcs 116 D4
Menna Corn 5 E8
Mennock Dumfries 247 B8
Menston W Yorks 205 E9
Menstrie Clack 278 B6
Mentmore Bucks 84 B6
Menzion Borders 260 E3
Meoble Highld 295 G9
Meole Brace Shrops 149 G9
Meols Mers 182 C2
Meon Hants 33 G8
Meonstoke Hants 33 D10
Meopham Kent 68 F6
Meopham Green Kent 68 F6
Meopham Station Kent 68 F6
Mepal Cambs 139 G8
Meppershall C Beds 104 D2
Merbach Hereford 96 B6
Mercaton Derbys 170 G3
Merchant Fields W Yorks 197 B7
Merchiston Edin 280 G4
Mere E Ches 184 E2
Mere Wilts 45 G10
Mere Brow Lancs 194 D2
Mere Green W Mid 134 D2
Mere Green Worcs 117 E9
Mere Heath W Ches 183 G11
Mereclough Lancs 204 G3
Merehead Wrex 149 B9
Meresborough Medway 69 G10
Mereside Blkpool 202 G2
Meretown Staffs 150 E5
Mereworth Kent 53 C7
Mergie Aberds 293 E9
Meriden Herts 85 F10
Meriden W Mid 134 G4
Merkadale Highld 294 B5
Merkland Dumfries 237 B9
Merkland N Ayrs 256 B2
Merkland S Ayrs 244 E6
Merkland Lodge Highld 309 G4
Merle Common Sur 52 D2
Merley Poole 18 B6
Merlin's Bridge Pembs 72 C6
Merlin's Cross Pembs 73 E7
Merridale W Mid 133 D7
Merridge Som 43 G8
Merrie Gardens I o W 21 E7
Merrifield Devon 8 F6
Merrifield Devon 24 G3
Merrington Shrops 149 E9
Merrion Pembs 72 F6
Merriott Dorset 16 B6
Merriott Som 28 E6
Merriottsford Som 28 E6
Merritown Dorset 19 B8
Merrivale Devon 12 F6
Merrivale Hereford 98 E2
Merrow Sur 50 C4
Merry Field Hill Dorset 31 G8
Merry Hill Herts 85 G10
Merry Hill W Mid 133 D7
Merry Lees Leics 135 B9
Merry Meeting Corn 11 G7
Merry Oak Soton 32 E6
Merrybent Darl 224 C4
Merryhill Green Wokingham 65 E9
Merrylee E Renf 267 D11
Merrymeet Corn 6 B5
Mersham Kent 54 F5
Merstham Sur 51 C9
Merston W Sus 22 C5
Merstone I o W 20 E6
Merther Corn 5 G7
Merther Lane Corn 5 G7
Merthyr Carms 93 G7
Merthyr Cynog Powys 95 D9
Merthyr-Dyfan V Glam 58 F6
Merthyr Mawr Bridgend 57 F11
Merthyr Tydfil M Tydf 77 D8
Merthyr Vale M Tydf 77 F9
Merton Devon 25 E8
Merton London 67 E9
Merton Norf 141 D8
Merton Oxon 83 B9
Merton Park London 67 F9
Mervinslaw Borders 262 G5
Meshaw Devon 26 D3
Messing Essex 88 B5
Messingham N Lincs 199 G11
Mesty Croft W Mid 133 E9
Mesur-y-dorth Pembs 87 E11
Metal Bridge Durham 233 E11
Metfield Suff 142 G5
Metherell Corn 7 B8
Metheringham Lincs 173 C9
Methersgate Suff 108 B5
Methil Fife 281 B7
Methilhill Fife 281 B7
Methlem Gwyn 144 C3
Methley W Yorks 197 B11
Methley Junction W Yorks 197 B11
Methley Lanes W Yorks 197 B11
Methlick Aberds 303 F8
Methven Perth 286 E4
Methwold Norf 140 E4
Methwold Hythe Norf 140 E4
Mettingham Suff 143 F7
Metton Norf 160 B3
Mevagissey Corn 5 G10
Mewith Head N Yorks 212 F4
Mexborough S Yorks 187 B7
Mey Highld 310 B6
Meyrick Park Bmouth 19 C7
Meysey Hampton Glos 81 F10
Miabhag W Isles 305 H2
Miabhag W Isles 305 J3
Miabhig W Isles 304 E2
Mial Highld 299 B7
Michaelchurch Hereford 97 F10
Michaelchurch Escley Hereford 96 E6
Michaelchurch on Arrow Powys 114 G4
Michaelston-le-Pit V Glam 59 E7
Michaelston-y-Fedw Newport 59 C8
Michaelstow Corn 11 F7
Michealston-super-Ely Cardiff 58 D6
Michelcombe Devon 8 B3
Micheldever Hants 48 F4
Michelmersh Hants 32 B4
Mickfield Suff 126 E2
Mickle Trafford W Ches 166 B6
Micklebring S Yorks 187 C8
Mickleby N Yorks 226 C6
Micklefield Bucks 84 G5
Micklefield W Yorks 206 G4
Micklefield Green Herts 85 F8
Mickleham Sur 51 C7
Micklehurst Gtr Man 196 G3
Mickleover Derby 152 C6
Micklethwaite Cumb 239 G7
Micklethwaite W Yorks 205 E8
Mickleton Durham 232 G5
Mickleton Glos 100 C3
Mickletown W Yorks 197 B11
Mickley Derbys 186 F4
Mickley N Yorks 214 D5
Mickley Shrops 150 C2
Mickley Green Suff 124 F6
Mickley Square Northumb 242 E3
Mid Ardlaw Aberds 303 C9
Mid Auchinleck Invclyd 276 G6
Mid Beltie Aberds 293 C8
Mid Calder W Loth 269 B11
Mid Cloch Forbie Aberds 303 D7
Mid Clyth Highld 310 F6
Mid Garrary Dumfries 237 B7
Mid Holmwood Sur 51 D7
Mid Lambrook Som 28 D6
Mid Lavant W Sus 22 B5
Mid Letter Argyll 284 G4
Mid Main Highld 300 F4
Mid Murthat Dumfries 248 D3
Mid Urchany Highld 301 E8
Mid Walls Shetland 313 H4
Mid Yell Shetland 312 D7
Midanbury Hants 33 E7
Midbea Orkney 314 B4
Middle Assendon Oxon 65 B8
Middle Aston Oxon 101 F9
Middle Balnald Perth 286 B4
Middle Barton Oxon 101 F8
Middle Bickenhill W Mid 134 G4
Middle Bockhampton Dorset 19 B9
Middle Bourne Sur 49 E10
Middle Bridge N Som 60 D3
Middle Burnham Som 43 D10
Middle Cairncake Aberds 303 E8
Middle Chinnock Som 29 E7
Middle Claydon Bucks 102 F4
Middle Cliff Staffs 169 E8
Middle Crackington Corn 11 B9
Middle Drums Angus 287 B9
Middle Duntisbourne Glos 81 D7
Middle Green Bucks 66 C4
Middle Green Som 27 D10
Middle Green Suff 124 D4
Middle Handley Derbys 186 F6
Middle Harling Norf 141 F9
Middle Herrington T & W 243 G9
Middle Hill Pembs 73 C7
Middle Hill Staffs 133 B9
Middle Kames Argyll 275 E10
Middle Littleton Worcs 99 B11
Middle Luxton Devon 28 E2
Middle Madeley Staffs 168 F3
Middle Maes-coed Hereford 96 E6
Middle Marwood Devon 40 F4
Middle Mayfield Staffs 169 G10
Middle Mill Pembs 87 F11
Middle Quarter Kent 53 F11
Middle Rainton T & W 234 B2
Middle Rasen Lincs 189 D9
Middle Rigg Perth 286 G4
Middle Rocombe Devon 9 B8
Middle Side Durham 232 F4
Middle Stoford Som 27 C11
Middle Stoke Devon 13 G9
Middle Stoke Medway 69 D10
Middle Stoke W Mid 119 B7
Middle Stoughton Som 44 D2
Middle Strath W Loth 279 G8
Middle Street Glos 80 E3
Middle Taphouse Corn 6 C3
Middle Town Scilly 1 F4
Middle Tysoe Warks 100 C6
Middle Wallop Hants 47 F9
Middle Weald M Keynes 102 D5
Middle Wick Glos 80 F2
Middle Winterslow Wilts 47 G8
Middle Woodford Wilts 46 F6
Middlebie Dumfries 238 B6
Middlecave N Yorks 216 E5
Middlecliffe S Yorks 198 F2
Middlecott Devon 13 D10
Middlecott Devon 24 F6
Middlecott Devon 26 F3
Middlecroft Derbys 186 G6
Middlefield Falk 279 E7
Middleforth Green Lancs 194 B4
Middleham N Yorks 214 B2
Middlehill Corn 6 B5
Middlehill Wilts 61 F10
Middlehope Shrops 131 F9
Middlemarsh Dorset 29 F11
Middlemoor Devon 12 G5
Middlemuir Aberds 303 D9
Middlemuir Aberds 303 E8
Middlemuir Aberds 303 G9
Middleport Stoke 168 F5
Middlerig Falk 279 F8
Middlesbrough M'bro 234 G5
Middlesceugh Cumb 230 C4
Middleshaw Cumb 211 B11
Middlesmoor N Yorks 213 E11
Middlestone Durham 233 E11
Middlestone Moor Durham 233 E10
Middlestown W Yorks 197 D9
Middlethird Borders 272 G3
Middlethorpe York 207 D7
Middleton Aberds 293 B10
Middleton Argyll 288 E1
Middleton Cumb 212 B2
Middleton Derbys 169 C11
Middleton Derbys 170 D3
Middleton Essex 107 D7
Middleton Gtr Man 195 F11
Middleton Hants 48 E2
Middleton Hereford 115 D10
Middleton Hrtlpl 234 E6
Middleton I o W 20 D2
Middleton Lancs 202 B4
Middleton Midloth 271 D7
Middleton N Yorks 204 E5
Middleton N Yorks 205 D8
Middleton N Yorks 216 B5
Middleton Norf 158 F3
Middleton Northants 136 F6
Middleton Northumb 252 F3
Middleton Northumb 264 B4
Middleton Perth 286 C5
Middleton Perth 286 F2
Middleton Perth 286 G5
Middleton Shrops 115 B10
Middleton Shrops 130 D5
Middleton Shrops 148 D6
Middleton Suff 127 D8
Middleton Swansea 56 D2
Middleton W Yorks 197 B10
Middleton Warks 134 D3
Middleton Baggot Shrops 132 E2
Middleton Cheney Northants 101 C9
Middleton Green Staffs 151 B9
Middleton Hall Northumb 263 D11
Middleton-in-Teesdale Durham 232 F4
Middleton Junction Gtr Man 195 G11
Middleton Moor Suff 127 D8
Middleton of Rora Aberds 303 E10
Middleton-on-Leven N Yorks 225 D9
Middleton-on-Sea W Sus 35 G7
Middleton on the Hill Hereford 115 E10
Middleton-on-the-Wolds E Yorks 208 D4
Middleton One Row Darl 225 C7
Middleton Place Cumb 219 G11
Middleton Priors Shrops 132 E2
Middleton Quernhow N Yorks 214 D6
Middleton St George Darl 224 C6
Middleton Scriven Shrops 132 F3
Middleton Stoney Oxon 101 G10
Middleton Tyas N Yorks 224 D4
Middletown Cumb 219 D9
Middletown N Som 60 E3
Middletown Powys 148 G6
Middletown Warks 117 E11
Middlewich E Ches 167 B11
Middlewick Wilts 61 E11
Middlewood Corn 11 F11
Middlewood E Ches 184 E6
Middlewood S Yorks 186 C4
Middlewood Green Suff 125 E11
Middleyard Glos 80 E4
Middlezoy Som 43 G11
Middridge Durham 233 F11
Midelney Som 28 C6
Midfield Highld 308 C5
Midford Bath 45 B8
Midgard Borders 262 F3
Midge Hall Lancs 194 C4
Midgehole W Yorks 196 B3
Midgeholme Cumb 240 F4
Midgham W Berks 64 F5
Midgham Green W Berks 64 F5
Midgley W Yorks 196 B4
Midgley W Yorks 197 E9
Midhopestones S Yorks 186 B2
Midhurst W Sus 34 C5
Midland Orkney 314 F3
Midlem Borders 262 D2
Midlock S Lnrk 259 E11
Midmar Aberds 293 C8
Midmuir Argyll 289 G11
Midpark Argyll 255 B11
Midplaugh Aberds 302 E5
Midsomer Norton Bath 45 C7
Midton Invclyd 276 F4
Midtown Highld 307 L3
Midtown Highld 308 C5
Midtown of Buchromb Moray 302 E3
Midtown of Glass Aberds 302 E4
Midville Lincs 174 D5
Midway E Ches 184 E6
Midway Som 45 D7
Miekle Toux Aberds 302 D5
Migdale Highld 309 K6
Migvie Aberds 292 C6
Milarrochy Stirl 277 C8
Milber Devon 14 G3
Milborne Port Som 29 D11
Milborne St Andrew Dorset 18 B2
Milborne Wick Som 29 C11
Milbourne Northumb 242 B4
Milbourne Wilts 62 B2
Milburn Aberds 302 E5
Milburn Aberds 302 F6
Milburn Cumb 231 F9
Milbury Heath S Glos 79 G11
Milby N Yorks 215 F8
Milch Hill Essex 106 G4
Milcombe Corn 6 D4
Milcombe Oxon 101 E8
Milden Suff 107 B9
Mildenhall Suff 124 C4
Mildenhall Wilts 63 F8
Mile Cross Norf 160 G4
Mile Elm Wilts 62 F3
Mile End Cambs 140 G2
Mile End Devon 14 G2
Mile End Essex 107 F9
Mile End Glos 79 C9
Mile End London 67 C11
Mile End Suff 124 G6
Mile Oak Brighton 36 F2
Mile Oak Kent 53 E7
Mile Oak Shrops 148 D6
Mile Oak Staffs 134 C3
Mile Town Kent 70 E2
Milebrook Powys 114 C6
Milebush Kent 53 D9
Mileham Norf 159 F8
Miles Green Staffs 168 F4
Miles Green Sur 50 B3
Miles Hill W Yorks 205 F11
Miles Platting Gtr Man 184 B5
Milesmark Fife 279 D11
Miles's Green W Berks 64 F4
Milfield Northumb 263 C10
Milford Derbys 170 F5
Milford Devon 24 C2
Milford Powys 129 E11
Milford Shrops 149 E8
Milford Staffs 151 E9
Milford Sur 50 E2
Milford Wilts 31 B11
Milford Haven Pembs 72 D6
Milford on Sea Hants 19 C11
Milkhouse Water Wilts 63 G7
Milkieston Borders 270 F4
Milkwall Glos 79 D9
Milkwell Wilts 30 C6
Mill Bank W Yorks 196 C4
Mill Brow Gtr Man 185 D7
Mill Common Norf 142 C6
Mill Common Suff 143 G8
Mill Corner E Sus 38 C4
Mill Dam N Yorks 212 F3
Mill End Bucks 65 C9
Mill End Cambs 124 F3
Mill End Glos 81 C10
Mill End Herts 85 G8
Mill End Herts 104 E6
Mill End Green Essex 106 F2
Mill Farm Aberds 303 C8
Mill Green Cambs 106 B2
Mill Green Essex 87 E10
Mill Green Hants 64 G4
Mill Green Herts 86 D2
Mill Green Norf 142 G2
Mill Green Shrops 150 D3
Mill Green Suff 107 C9
Mill Green Suff 125 F9
Mill Green Suff 126 E2
Mill Green W Mid 133 C11
Mill Hall Dumfries 237 E8
Mill Hill Blkburn 195 B7
Mill Hill E Sus 23 D10
Mill Hill Essex 88 G4
Mill Hill Glos 79 D10
Mill Hill Gtr Man 195 F8
Mill Hill Kent 55 C11
Mill Hill Lincs 175 B8
Mill Hill London 86 G2
Mill Hill Suff 125 G7
Mill Hills Suff 108 B5
Mill Hirst N Yorks 214 G3
Mill Lane Hants 49 C9
Mill Meads London 67 C11
Mill of Brydock Aberds 302 D6
Mill of Chon Stirl 285 G8
Mill of Haldane W Dunb 277 E8
Mill of Kingoodie Aberds 303 G8
Mill of Lynebain Aberds 302 F4
Mill of Muiresk Aberds 302 E6
Mill of Rango Orkney 314 E2
Mill of Sterin Aberds 292 D5
Mill of Uras Aberds 293 E10
Mill Park Argyll 255 G8
Mill Place N Lincs 200 F3
Mill Shaw W Yorks 205 G11
Mill Side Cumb 211 C8
Mill Street Kent 53 B7
Mill Street Norf 159 F11
Mill Street Suff 107 D9
Mill Throop Bmouth 19 B8
Milland W Sus 34 B4
Millarston Renfs 267 C9
Millbank Aberds 303 E11
Millbank Highld 310 C5
Millbank Kent 71 F8
Millbeck Cumb 229 F11
Millbounds Orkney 314 C5
Millbreck Aberds 303 E10
Millbridge Sur 49 E10
Millbrook C Beds 103 D10
Millbrook Corn 7 E8
Millbrook Devon 41 G9
Millbrook Gtr Man 185 B7
Millbrook Soton 32 E5
Millburn S Ayrs 257 D10
Millcombe Devon 8 F6
Milldale Staffs 169 E10
Millden Lodge Angus 293 F7
Milldens Angus 287 B9
Millend Glos 80 D3
Millend Glos 80 F3
Millendreath Corn 6 E5
Millerhill Midloth 270 B6
Miller's Dale Derbys 185 G10
Miller's Green Derbys 170 E3
Miller's Green Essex 87 D9
Millersneuk E Dunb 278 G3
Millerston Glasgow 268 B2
Millgate Lancs 195 D11
Millgate Norf 160 D3
Millgillhead Cumb 229 G7
Millhalf Hereford 96 B5
Millhall Kent 53 B8
Millhayes Devon 27 E10
Millhayes Devon 28 G2
Millhead Lancs 211 E9
Millheugh S Lnrk 268 E5
Millhill Devon 12 G5
Millholme Cumb 221 G11
Millhouse Argyll 275 F10
Millhouse Cumb 230 D3
Millhouse Green S Yorks 197 G8
Millhousebridge Dumfries 248 F4
Millhouses S Yorks 186 E4
Millhouses S Yorks 198 G2
Millikenpark Renfs 267 C8
Millin Cross Pembs 73 C7
Millington E Yorks 208 C2
Millington Green Derbys 170 F3
Millmeece Staffs 150 C6
Millmoor Devon 27 E10
Millness Cumb 211 C10
Millom Cumb 210 C3
Millook Corn 11 B9
Millow C Beds 104 C4
Millpool Corn 2 C3
Millpool Corn 11 G8
Millport N Ayrs 266 E3
Millquarter Dumfries 246 G4
Milltack Aberds 303 D7
Millthorpe Derbys 186 F4
Millthorpe Lincs 156 C2
Millthrop Cumb 222 G3
Milltimber Aberdeen 293 C10
Milltown Aberds 292 C4
Milltown Corn 6 B2
Milltown Corn 6 D2
Milltown Derbys 170 C5
Milltown Devon 40 F5
Milltown Highld 301 E9
Milltown of Aberdalgie Perth 286 E4
Milltown of Auchindoun Moray 302 E3
Milltown of Craigston Aberds 303 D7
Milltown of Edinvillie Moray 302 E2
Milltown of Kildrummy Aberds 292 B6
Milltown of Rothiemay Moray 302 E5
Milltown of Towie Aberds 292 B6
Millwall London 67 D11
Milnathort Perth 286 G5
Milner's Heath W Ches 167 C7
Milngavie E Dunb 277 G11
Milnquarter Falk 278 F6
Milnrow Gtr Man 196 E2
Milnsbridge W Yorks 196 D6
Milnshaw Lancs 195 B9
Milnthorpe Cumb 211 C9
Milnthorpe W Yorks 197 D10
Milnwood N Lnrk 268 D4
Milo Carms 75 B9
Milson Shrops 116 C2
Milstead Kent 54 B2
Milston Wilts 47 D7
Milthorpe Northants 101 B11
Milton Angus 287 C7
Milton Angus 292 E6
Milton Cambs 123 E9
Milton Cumb 211 C10
Milton Cumb 240 E3
Milton Derbys 152 D6
Milton Dumfries 236 D4
Milton Dumfries 237 B10
Milton Dumfries 247 G8
Milton Fife 287 E8
Milton Glasgow 267 B11
Milton Highld 299 E7
Milton Highld 300 D3
Milton Highld 300 E5
Milton Highld 300 F4
Milton Highld 301 B7
Milton Highld 301 E7
Milton Highld 310 D7
Milton Kent 69 E7
Milton Moray 292 B3
Milton Moray 302 C5
Milton N Som 59 G10
Milton Notts 188 G2
Milton Oxon 83 G7
Milton Oxon 101 E8
Milton Pembs 73 E8
Milton Perth 286 F3
Milton Powys 114 G4
Milton Ptsmth 21 B9
Milton S Yorks 197 G11
Milton Som 29 C7
Milton Stirl 285 G9
Milton Stoke 168 E6
Milton W Dunb 277 G8
Milton Wilts 45 G11
Milton Abbas Dorset 30 G4
Milton Bridge Midloth 270 C4
Milton Bryan C Beds 103 E9
Milton Clevedon Som 45 F7
Milton Coldwells Aberds 303 F9
Milton Combe Devon 7 B9
Milton Common Oxon 83 E11
Milton Coombe Devon 7 B9
Milton Damerel Devon 24 E5
Milton End Glos 80 C2
Milton End Glos 81 E10
Milton Ernest Beds 121 F10
Milton Green Devon 12 F4
Milton Green W Ches 167 D7
Milton Heights Oxon 83 G7
Milton Hill Devon 14 F4
Milton Hill Oxon 83 G7
Milton Keynes M Keynes 103 D7
Milton Keynes Village M Keynes 103 D7
Milton Lilbourne Wilts 63 G7
Milton Malsor Northants 120 F4
Milton Morenish Perth 285 D10
Milton of Auchinhove Aberds 293 C7
Milton of Balgonie Fife 287 G7
Milton of Buchanan Stirl 277 C8
Milton of Campfield Aberds 293 C8
Milton of Campsie E Dunb 278 F3
Milton of Corsindae Aberds 293 C8
Milton of Cullerlie Aberds 293 C9
Milton of Cultoquhey Perth 286 E2
Milton of Cushnie Aberds 293 B7
Milton of Dalcapon Perth 286 B3
Milton of Drimmie Perth 286 B5
Milton of Edradour Perth 286 B3
Milton of Gollanfield Highld 301 D7
Milton of Lesmore Aberds 302 G4
Milton of Logie Aberds 292 C6
Milton of Machany Perth 286 F3
Milton of Mathers Aberds 293 G9
Milton of Murtle Aberdeen 293 C10
Milton of Noth Aberds 302 G5
Milton of Tullich Aberds 292 D5
Milton on Stour Dorset 30 B3
Milton Regis Kent 70 F2
Milton Street E Sus 23 E8
Milton under Wychwood Oxon 82 B3
Miltonduff Moray 301 C11
Miltonhill Moray 301 C10
Miltonise Dumfries 236 B3
Milverton Som 27 B10
Milverton Warks 118 D6
Milwich Staffs 151 C9
Milwr Flint 181 G11
Mimbridge Sur 66 G3
Minard Argyll 275 D10
Minard Castle Argyll 275 D10
Minchington Dorset 31 E7
Minchinhampton Glos 80 E5
Mindrum Northumb 263 C8
Minehead Som 42 D3
Minera Wrex 166 E3
Mineshope Corn 11 B9
Minety Wilts 81 G8
Minffordd Gwyn 145 B11
Minffordd Gwyn 146 G4
Minffordd Gwyn 179 G9
Mingarrypark Highld 289 C8
Mingoose Corn 4 F4
Miningsby Lincs 174 C4
Minions Corn 11 G11
Minishant S Ayrs 257 G8
Minllyn Gwyn 147 G7
Minnes Aberds 303 G9
Minngearraidh W Isles 297 J3
Minnigaff Dumfries 236 C6
Minnonie Aberds 303 C7
Minnow End Essex 88 C2
Minnygap Dumfries 248 D2
Minshull Vernon E Ches 167 C11
Minskip N Yorks 215 G7
Minstead Hants 32 E3
Minsted W Sus 34 C5
Minster Kent 70 E3
Minster Kent 71 G10
Minster Lovell Oxon 82 C4
Minsterley Shrops 131 C7
Minsterworth Glos 80 B3
Minterne Magna Dorset 29 G11
Minterne Parva Dorset 29 G11
Minting Lincs 189 G11
Mintlaw Aberds 303 E10
Minto Borders 262 E3
Minto Kames Borders 262 E3
Minton Shrops 131 E8
Mintsfeet Cumb 221 G10
Minwear Pembs 73 C8
Minworth W Mid 134 E3
Mirbister Orkney 314 E2
Mirehouse Cumb 219 B9
Mireland Highld 310 C7
Mirfield W Yorks 197 D8
Miserden Glos 80 D6
Misery Corner Norf 142 F5
Miskin Rhondda 58 C4
Miskin Rhondda 77 F8
Misselfore Wilts 31 C8
Misson Notts 187 C11
Misterton Leics 135 G11
Misterton Notts 188 C3
Misterton Som 29 F7
Misterton Soss Notts 188 B3
Mistley Essex 108 E2
Mistley Heath Essex 108 E2
Mitcham London 67 F9
Mitchel Troy Mon 79 C7
Mitcheldean Glos 79 B11
Mitchell Corn 5 E7
Mitchell Hill Borders 260 C3
Mitchellslacks Dumfries 247 D11
Mitchelston Borders 271 F9
Mitcheltroy Common Mon 79 D7
Mite Houses Cumb 219 F11
Mitford Northumb 252 F5
Mithian Corn 4 E4
Mithian Downs Corn 4 F4
Mitton Staffs 151 F7
Mitton Worcs 99 E8
Mixbury Oxon 102 E2
Mixenden W Yorks 196 B5
Mixtow Corn 6 E2
Moat Cumb 239 C10
Moats Tye Suff 125 F10
Mobberley E Ches 184 F3
Mobberley Staffs 169 G8
Moblake E Ches 167 G11
Mobwell Bucks 84 E5
Moccas Hereford 97 C7
Mochdre Conwy 180 F4
Mochdre Powys 129 F11
Mochrum Dumfries 236 E5
Mockbeggar Hants 31 F11
Mockbeggar Kent 54 E6
Mockbeggar Medway 69 E8
Mockerkin Cumb 229 G7
Moclett Orkney 314 B4
Modbury Devon 8 E3
Moddershall Staffs 151 B8
Model Village Derbys 187 G8
Model Village Warks 119 E8
Modest Corner Kent 52 E5
Moel Tryfan Gwyn 163 D8
Moel-y-crio Flint 165 B11
Moelfre Anglesey 179 D8
Moelfre Conwy 181 G7
Moelfre Powys 148 D3
Moffat Dumfries 248 B3
Moffat Mills N Lnrk 268 C5
Mogador Sur 51 C8
Moggerhanger C Beds 104 B2
Mogworthy Devon 26 D5
Moira Leics 152 F6
Moity Powys 96 C3
Mol-chlach Highld 294 D6
Molash Kent 54 C4
Mold Flint 166 C2
Moldgreen W Yorks 197 D7
Molehill Green Essex 105 G11
Molehill Green Essex 106 G4
Molescroft E Yorks 208 E6
Molesden Northumb 252 G4
Molesworth Cambs 121 B11
Molinnis Corn 5 D10
Moll Highld 295 B7
Molland Devon 26 B4
Mollington Oxon 101 B8
Mollington W Ches 182 G5
Mollinsburn N Lnrk 278 G4
Monachty Ceredig 111 E10
Monachylemore Stirl 285 F8
Monar Lodge Highld 300 E2
Monaughty Powys 114 D4
Monboddo House Aberds 293 F9
Mondaytown Shrops 130 B6
Mondynes Aberds 293 F9
Monemore Stirl 285 D9
Monevechadan Argyll 284 G5
Monewden Suff 126 F4
Money Hill Leics 153 F7
Moneyacres E Ayrs 267 E8
Moneydie Perth 286 E4
Moneyhill Herts 85 G8
Moneyrow Green Windsor 65 D11
Moneystone Staffs 169 F9
Mongleath Corn 3 C7
Moniaive Dumfries 247 E7
Monifieth Angus 287 D8
Monikie Angus 287 D8
Monimail Fife 286 F6
Monington Pembs 92 C2
Monk Bretton S Yorks 197 F11
Monk End N Yorks 224 D5
Monk Fryston N Yorks 198 B4
Monk Hesleden Durham 234 D5
Monk Sherborne Hants 48 B6
Monk Soham Suff 126 D4
Monk Street Essex 106 F2
Monken Hadley London 86 F3
Monkerton Devon 14 C5
Monkhide Hereford 98 C2
Monkhill Cumb 239 F8
Monkhill W Yorks 198 C3
Monkhopton Shrops 132 E2
Monkland Hereford 115 F9
Monkleigh Devon 25 C7
Monkmoor Shrops 149 G10
Monknash V Glam 58 E2
Monkokehampton Devon 25 F9
Monks Eleigh Suff 107 B9
Monk's Gate W Sus 36 B2
Monks Heath E Ches 184 G4
Monks Hill Kent 53 E11
Monks Kirby Warks 135 G9
Monks Orchard London 67 F11
Monk's Park Wilts 61 F11
Monks Risborough Bucks 84 E4
Monkscross Corn 12 G3
Monkseaton T & W 243 C8
Monkshill Aberds 303 E7
Monksilver Som 42 F5
Monkspath W Mid 118 B2
Monksthorpe Lincs 174 B6
Monkston Park M Keynes 103 D7
Monkswood Midloth 270 C6
Monkswood Mon 78 E4
Monkswood W Yorks 206 F2
Monkton Devon 27 G11
Monkton Kent 71 G9
Monkton Pembs 73 E7
Monkton S Ayrs 257 D9
Monkton T & W 243 E8
Monkton V Glam 58 E2
Monkton Combe Bath 61 G9
Monkton Deverill Wilts 45 F11
Monkton Farleigh Wilts 61 F10
Monkton Heathfield Som 28 B3
Monkton Up Wimborne Dorset 31 E8
Monktonhall E Loth 280 G6
Monkwearmouth T & W 243 F9
Monkwood Hants 49 G7
Monkwood Green Worcs 116 E6
Monmarsh Hereford 97 B10
Monmore Green W Mid 133 D8
Monmouth Mon 79 C8
Monmouth Cap Mon 97 F7
Monnington on Wye Hereford 97 C7
Monreith Dumfries 236 E5
Monreith Mains Dumfries 236 E5
Montacute Som 29 D7
Montcliffe Gtr Man 195 E7
Montcoffer Ho Aberds 302 C6
Montford Argyll 266 C2
Montford Shrops 149 G8
Montford Bridge Shrops 149 F8
Montgarrie Aberds 293 B7
Montgomery Powys 130 D4
Montgomery Lines Hants 49 C11
Monton Gtr Man 184 B3
Montpelier Bristol 60 E5
Montrave Fife 287 G7
Montrose Angus 287 B11
Montsale Essex 89 F8
Monwode Lea Warks 134 E5
Monxton Hants 47 E10
Monyash Derbys 169 B11
Monymusk Aberds 293 B8
Monzie Perth 286 E2
Monzie Castle Perth 286 E2
Moodiesburn N Lnrk 278 G3
Moolham Som 28 E5
Moon's Green Kent 38 B5
Moon's Moat Worcs 117 D11
Moonzie Fife 287 F7
Moor Som 28 D6
Moor Allerton W Yorks 205 F11
Moor Common Bucks 84 G4
Moor Crichel Dorset 31 F7
Moor Cross Devon 8 D2
Moor Edge W Yorks 205 F7
Moor End Bucks 84 G4
Moor End C Beds 103 G9
Moor End Cambs 105 B7
Moor End Durham 234 C2
Moor End E Yorks 208 F2
Moor End Glos 99 G9
Moor End Lancs 202 E3
Moor End N Yorks 207 F7
Moor End N Yorks 215 G7
Moor End S Yorks 197 G9
Moor End W Yorks 196 B5
Moor End W Yorks 206 D4
Moor End Worcs 117 F8
Moor End York 207 B9
Moor End Field N Yorks 215 F8
Moor Green Herts 104 F6
Moor Green Staffs 169 G7
Moor Green W Mid 133 G11
Moor Green Wilts 61 F11
Moor Hall W Mid 134 D2
Moor Head W Yorks 197 B8
Moor Head W Yorks 197 E8
Moor Monkton N Yorks 206 B6
Moor Monkton Moor N Yorks 206 B6

New Parks Leicester 135 B11
New Passage S Glos 60 B4
New Pitsligo Aberds 303 D8
New Polzeath Corn 10 F4
New Quay = Ceinewydd Ceredig 111 F7
New Rackheath Norf 160 G5
New Radnor Powys 114 E4
New Rent Cumb 230 D5
New Ridley Northumb 242 F3
New Road Side N Yorks 204 E5
New Road Side W Yorks 197 B7
New Romney Kent 39 C9
New Rossington S Yorks 187 B10
New Row Ceredig 112 C4
New Row Lancs 203 F8
New Row N Yorks 226 C2
New Sarum Wilts 46 G6
New Sawley Derbys 153 C9
New Scarbro W Yorks 205 G10
New Sharlston W Yorks 197 C11
New Silksworth T & W 243 G9
New Skelton Redcar 226 B3
New Smithy Derbys 185 E9
New Southgate London 86 G3
New Springs Gtr Man 194 F6
New Sprowston Norf 160 G4
New Stanton Derbys 153 B9
New Stevenston N Lnrk 268 D5
New Street Kent 68 G6
New Street Staffs 169 E9
New Swanage Dorset 18 E6
New Swannington Leics 153 F8
New Thirsk N Yorks 215 C8
New Thundersley Essex 69 B9
New Totley S Yorks 186 F4
New Town Bath 45 B9
New Town Bath 60 G5
New Town Dorset 30 C3
New Town Dorset 30 D6
New Town Dorset 31 D7
New Town Dorset 31 F7
New Town E Loth 281 G8
New Town E Sus 37 C7
New Town Edin 280 G4
New Town Edin 280 G5
New Town Glos 99 E10
New Town Kent 53 B7
New Town Kent 68 E4
New Town Lancs 203 F8
New Town Luton 103 G11
New Town Medway 69 G8
New Town Oxon 100 F5
New Town Reading 65 E8
New Town Shetland 312 E6
New Town Som 29 D11
New Town Som 29 D9
New Town Som 44 D3
New Town Soton 33 E7
New Town Swindon 63 C7
New Town T & W 234 B2
New Town T & W 243 E8
New Town W Berks 64 D6
New Town W Mid 133 B11
New Town W Mid 133 E9
New Town W Sus 35 B11
New Town W Yorks 198 C3
New Town Wilts 46 C6
New Town Wilts 63 E9
New Tredegar Caerph 77 E10
New Trows S Lnrk 259 B8
New Ulva Argyll 275 E8
New Village E Yorks 209 G7
New Village S Yorks 198 F5
New Walsoken Cambs 139 B9
New Waltham NE Lincs 201 G9
New Well Powys 113 B11
New Wells Powys 130 D3
New Whittington Derbys 186 F5
New Wimpole Cambs 104 B6
New Winton E Loth 281 G8
New Woodhouses Shrops 167 G9
New Works Telford 132 B3
New Wortley W Yorks 205 G11
New Yatt Oxon 82 C5
New York Lincs 174 D2
New York N Yorks 214 G3
New York T & W 243 C8
New Zealand Wilts 62 D4
Newall W Yorks 205 D10
Newall Green Gtr Man 184 D4
Newark Orkney 314 B7
Newark P'boro 138 C4
Newark-on-Trent Notts 172 E3
Newarthill N Lnrk 268 D5
Newball Lincs 189 F9
Newbarn Kent 55 F7
Newbarns Cumb 210 E4
Newbattle Midloth 270 B6
Newbie Dumfries 238 D5
Newbiggin Cumb 210 F5
Newbiggin Cumb 211 D11
Newbiggin Cumb 219 G11
Newbiggin Cumb 230 F5
Newbiggin Cumb 231 B7
Newbiggin Cumb 231 F8
Newbiggin Durham 232 B5
Newbiggin Durham 232 F4
Newbiggin Durham 233 B8
Newbiggin N Yorks 213 B9
Newbiggin N Yorks 223 G9
Newbiggin-by-the-Sea Northumb 253 F8
Newbiggin Hall Estate T & W 242 D6
Newbiggin-on-Lune Cumb 222 D4
Newbigging Aberds 303 G7
Newbigging Angus 287 D8
Newbigging Borders 262 F6
Newbigging Edin 280 F2
Newbigging S Lnrk 269 F10
Newbiggings Orkney 314 B6
Newbold Derbys 186 G5
Newbold Gtr Man 196 E2
Newbold Leics 136 B5
Newbold Leics 153 F8
Newbold Heath Leics 135 B8
Newbold on Avon Warks 119 B9
Newbold on Stour Warks 100 B4
Newbold Pacey Warks 118 F5
Newbold Verdon Leics 135 C8
Newbolds W Mid 133 C8
Newborough P'boro 138 B4
Newborough Staffs 152 D2
Newbottle Northants 101 D10
Newbottle T & W 243 G8
Newbourne Suff 108 C5
Newbridge Bath 61 F8
Newbridge Caerph 78 F2
Newbridge Ceredig 111 F10
Newbridge Corn 1 C4
Newbridge Corn 4 G5
Newbridge Corn 7 B7
Newbridge Dumfries 237 B11
Newbridge E Sus 52 G3
Newbridge Edin 280 G2
Newbridge Hants 32 D3
Newbridge I o W 20 D4
Newbridge Lancs 204 F3
Newbridge N Yorks 216 B6
Newbridge Oxon 82 E6
Newbridge Pembs 91 E8
Newbridge Shrops 148 D6
Newbridge W Mid 133 D7
Newbridge Wrex 166 G3
Newbridge Green Worcs 98 D6
Newbridge-on-Usk Mon 78 G5
Newbridge-on-Wye Powys 113 F10
Newbrough Northumb 241 D9
Newbuildings Devon 26 G3
Newburgh Aberds 303 D9
Newburgh Aberds 303 G9
Newburgh Borders 261 F8
Newburgh Fife 286 F6
Newburgh Lancs 194 E3
Newburn T & W 242 D5
Newbury Kent 54 B2
Newbury W Berks 64 F3
Newbury Wilts 45 E10
Newbury Park London 68 B2
Newby Cumb 231 G7
Newby Lancs 204 D2
Newby N Yorks 205 D11
Newby N Yorks 212 E4
Newby N Yorks 215 F7
Newby N Yorks 225 C10
Newby N Yorks 227 G10
Newby Bridge Cumb 211 B7
Newby Cote N Yorks 212 E4
Newby East Cumb 239 F11
Newby Head Cumb 231 G7
Newby West Cumb 239 G9
Newby Wiske N Yorks 215 B7
Newcastle Bridgend 58 D2
Newcastle Mon 78 B6
Newcastle Shrops 130 G4
Newcastle Emlyn = Castell Newydd Emlyn Carms 92 C6
Newcastle-under-Lyme Staffs 168 F4
Newcastle upon Tyne T & W 242 E6
Newcastleton or Copshaw Holm Borders 249 F11
Newchapel Powys 129 G9
Newchapel Staffs 168 E5
Newchapel Sur 51 E11
Newchapel = Capel Newydd Pembs 92 D4
Newchurch Bl Gwent 77 C11
Newchurch Carms 93 G7
Newchurch Hereford 115 G7
Newchurch I o W 21 D7
Newchurch Kent 54 G5
Newchurch Lancs 195 C10
Newchurch Mon 79 F7
Newchurch Powys 114 G4
Newchurch Staffs 152 E2
Newchurch in Pendle Lancs 204 F2
Newcott Devon 28 F2
Newcraighall Edin 280 G6
Newdigate Sur 51 E7
Newell Green Brack 65 E11
Newenden Kent 38 B4
Newent Glos 98 F4
Newerne Glos 79 E10
Newfield Durham 233 E10
Newfield Durham 242 G6
Newfield Highld 301 B7
Newfield Stoke 168 E6
Newford Scilly 1 G4
Newfound Hants 48 C5
Newgale Pembs 90 G6
Newgarth Orkney 314 E2
Newgate Lancs 194 F4
Newgate Norf 177 E9
Newgate Corner Norf 161 G8
Newgate Street Herts 86 D4
Newgrounds Hants 31 E11
Newhailes Edin 280 G6
Newhall Derbys 152 E5
Newhall E Ches 167 F10
Newhall Green Warks 134 F5
Newhall House Highld 300 C6
Newhall Point Highld 301 C7
Newham Lincs 174 E3
Newham Northumb 264 D5
Newhaven Derbys 169 C11
Newhaven Devon 24 C5
Newhaven E Sus 36 G6
Newhaven Edin 280 F5
Newhay N Yorks 207 G9
Newhey Gtr Man 196 E2
Newhill Fife 286 F6
Newhill Perth 286 G5
Newhill S Yorks 186 B6
Newhills Aberdeen 293 C10
Newholm N Yorks 227 C7
Newhouse Borders 262 E2
Newhouse N Lnrk 268 C5
Newhouse Shetland 313 G6
Newhouses Borders 271 G10
Newick E Sus 36 C6
Newingreen Kent 54 F6
Newington Edin 280 G5
Newington Kent 55 F7
Newington Kent 69 G11
Newington Kent 71 F11
Newington London 67 D10
Newington Notts 187 C11
Newington Oxon 83 F10
Newington Shrops 131 G8
Newington Bagpath Glos 80 G4
Newland Cumb 210 D6
Newland E Yorks 199 B10
Newland Glos 79 D9
Newland Hull 209 G7
Newland N Yorks 199 C7
Newland Oxon 82 C5
Newland Worcs 98 B5
Newland Bottom Cumb 210 B5
Newland Common Worcs 117 E8
Newland Green Kent 54 D2
Newlandrig Midloth 271 C7
Newlands Borders 250 E2
Newlands Borders 262 E2
Newlands Cumb 229 G10
Newlands Cumb 230 D2
Newlands Derbys 170 F6
Newlands Dumfries 247 F11
Newlands Glasgow 267 C11
Newlands Highld 301 E7
Newlands Moray 302 D3
Newlands Northumb 242 F3
Newlands Notts 171 C9
Newlands Staffs 151 E11
Newlands Corner Sur 50 D4
Newlands of Geise Highld 310 C4
Newlands of Tynet Moray 302 C3
Newlands Park Anglesey 178 E3
Newlandsmuir S Lnrk 268 E2
Newliston Edin 280 G2
Newliston Fife 280 C5
Newlot Orkney 314 E5
Newlyn Corn 1 D5
Newmachar Aberds 293 B10
Newmains N Lnrk 268 D6
Newman's End Essex 87 C8
Newman's Green Suff 107 C7
Newman's Place Hereford 96 B5
Newmarket Glos 80 F4
Newmarket Suff 124 E2
Newmarket W Isles 304 E6
Newmill Borders 261 G11
Newmill Corn 1 C5
Newmill Moray 302 D4
Newmill of Inshewan Angus 292 G6
Newmillerdam W Yorks 197 D10
Newmills Corn 11 D11
Newmills Fife 279 D10
Newmills Highld 300 C6
Newmills of Boyne Aberds 302 D5
Newmiln Perth 286 D5
Newmilns E Ayrs 258 B2
Newmore Highld 300 B6
Newmore Highld 300 D5
Newnes Shrops 149 C7
Newney Green Essex 87 D11
Newnham Cambs 123 F8
Newnham Glos 79 C11
Newnham Hants 49 C8
Newnham Herts 104 D4
Newnham Kent 54 B3
Newnham Northants 119 F11
Newnham Warks 118 E3
Newnham Bridge Worcs 116 D2
Newpark Fife 287 F8
Newpool Staffs 168 D5
Newport Corn 12 D2
Newport Devon 40 G5
Newport Dorset 18 C3
Newport E Yorks 208 G3
Newport Essex 105 E10
Newport Glos 79 F11
Newport Highld 311 G5
Newport I o W 20 D6
Newport Newport 59 B10
Newport Norf 161 F10
Newport Som 28 C4
Newport Telford 150 F4
Newport = Trefdraeth Pembs 91 D11
Newport-on-Tay Fife 287 E8
Newport Pagnell M Keynes 103 C7
Newpound Common W Sus 35 B9
Newquay Corn 4 C6
Newsam Green W Yorks 206 G3
Newsbank E Ches 168 B4
Newseat Aberds 303 E10
Newseat Aberds 303 F7
Newsells Herts 105 D7
Newsham Lancs 202 F6
Newsham N Yorks 215 C7
Newsham N Yorks 224 C2
Newsham Northumb 243 B8
Newsholme E Yorks 199 B8
Newsholme Lancs 204 C2
Newsholme W Yorks 204 F6
Newsome W Yorks 196 E6
Newstead Borders 262 C3
Newstead Northumb 264 D5
Newstead Notts 171 E8
Newstead Staffs 168 G5
Newstead W Yorks 197 E11
Newstreet Lane Shrops 150 B2
Newtake Devon 14 G3
Newthorpe N Yorks 206 G5
Newthorpe Notts 171 F7
Newthorpe Common Notts 171 F7
Newtoft Lincs 189 D8
Newton Argyll 275 D11
Newton Borders 262 E3
Newton Borders 262 F2
Newton Bridgend 57 F10
Newton C Beds 104 C4
Newton Cambs 105 B8
Newton Cambs 157 G8
Newton Cardiff 59 D8
Newton Corn 5 C11
Newton Cumb 210 E4
Newton Derbys 170 D6
Newton Dorset 30 E3
Newton Dumfries 239 C7
Newton Dumfries 248 E4
Newton Gtr Man 185 B7
Newton Hereford 96 C5
Newton Hereford 96 E6
Newton Hereford 115 D7
Newton Hereford 115 G10
Newton Highld 301 C7
Newton Highld 301 E7
Newton Highld 306 F7
Newton Highld 310 E7
Newton Lancs 202 F2
Newton Lancs 202 G4
Newton Lancs 203 C9
Newton Lancs 211 E11
Newton Lincs 155 B10
Newton Mers 182 D2
Newton Moray 301 C11
Newton Norf 158 F6
Newton Northants 137 G7
Newton Northumb 242 E2
Newton Notts 171 G11
Newton Perth 286 D2
Newton S Glos 79 G10
Newton S Lnrk 259 C10
Newton S Lnrk 268 C3
Newton S Yorks 198 G5
Newton Shetland 312 E5
Newton Shetland 313 K5
Newton Shrops 132 D4
Newton Shrops 149 C8
Newton Som 42 F6
Newton Staffs 151 D10
Newton Suff 107 C8
Newton Swansea 56 D6
Newton W Ches 166 B6
Newton W Ches 167 D8
Newton W Ches 183 F8
Newton W Loth 279 F11
Newton W Mid 133 E10
Newton Warks 119 B10
Newton Wilts 32 C2
Newton Abbot Devon 14 G3
Newton Arlosh Cumb 238 G5
Newton Aycliffe Durham 233 G11
Newton Bewley Hrtlpl 234 F5
Newton Blossomville M Keynes 121 G8
Newton Bromswold Northants 121 D9
Newton Burgoland Leics 135 B7
Newton by Toft Lincs 189 D9
Newton Cross Pembs 91 F7
Newton Ferrers Devon 7 F10
Newton Flotman Norf 142 D4
Newton Green Mon 79 G8
Newton Hall Durham 233 B11
Newton Hall Northumb 242 D2
Newton Harcourt Leics 136 D2
Newton Heath Gtr Man 184 B5
Newton Hill W Yorks 197 C10
Newton Ho Aberds 302 G6
Newton Hurst Staffs 151 D11
Newton Ketton Darl 234 G2
Newton Kyme N Yorks 206 E5
Newton-le-Willows Mers 183 B9
Newton-le-Willows N Yorks 214 B4
Newton Longville Bucks 102 E6
Newton Mearns E Renf 267 D10
Newton Morrell N Yorks 224 D4
Newton Morrell Oxon 102 F2
Newton Mulgrave N Yorks 226 B5
Newton of Ardtoe Highld 289 B8
Newton of Balcanquhal Perth 286 F5
Newton of Balcormo Fife 287 G9
Newton of Falkland Fife 286 G6
Newton of Mountblairy Aberds 302 D6
Newton of Pitcairns Perth 286 F4
Newton on Ayr S Ayrs 257 E8
Newton on Ouse N Yorks 206 B6
Newton-on-Rawcliffe N Yorks 226 G6
Newton on the Hill Shrops 149 E9
Newton on the Moor Northumb 252 B5
Newton on Trent Lincs 188 G4
Newton Park Argyll 266 B4
Newton Park Mers 183 C9
Newton Peveril Dorset 18 B4
Newton Poppleford Devon 15 D7
Newton Purcell Oxon 102 E2
Newton Regis Warks 134 B5
Newton Reigny Cumb 230 E5
Newton Rigg Cumb 230 E5
Newton St Boswells Borders 262 C3
Newton St Cyres Devon 14 B3
Newton St Faith Norf 160 F4
Newton St Loe Bath 61 G8
Newton St Petrock Devon 24 E6
Newton Solney Derbys 152 D5
Newton Stacey Hants 48 E2
Newton Stewart Dumfries 236 C6
Newton Tony Wilts 47 E8
Newton Tracey Devon 25 B8
Newton under Roseberry Redcar 225 C11
Newton Underwood Northumb 252 F4
Newton upon Derwent E Yorks 207 D10
Newton Valence Hants 49 G8
Newton with Scales Lancs 202 G4
Newton Wood Gtr Man 184 B6
Newtonairds Dumfries 247 G9
Newtongrange Midloth 270 C6
Newtonhill Aberds 293 D11
Newtonhill Highld 300 E5
Newtonia E Ches 167 B11
Newtonmill Angus 293 G8
Newtonmore Highld 291 D9
Newtown Argyll 284 G4
Newtown Bl Gwent 77 C11
Newtown Bucks 85 E7
Newtown Caerph 78 G2
Newtown Cambs 121 D11
Newtown Corn 2 D3
Newtown Corn 11 F11
Newtown Cumb 229 B7
Newtown Cumb 239 F9
Newtown Cumb 240 E2
Newtown Derbys 185 E7
Newtown Devon 26 B3
Newtown Dorset 29 G7
Newtown E Ches 184 E6
Newtown Falk 279 E9
Newtown Glos 79 E11
Newtown Glos 80 D3
Newtown Glos 99 E8
Newtown Gtr Man 194 F5
Newtown Gtr Man 195 G9
Newtown Hants 21 B8
Newtown Hants 32 C4
Newtown Hants 32 E3
Newtown Hants 33 D8
Newtown Hants 33 E10
Newtown Hants 33 F7
Newtown Hants 49 F8
Newtown Hants 49 G10
Newtown Hants 64 G3
Newtown Hereford 97 E10
Newtown Hereford 98 C2
Newtown Highld 290 C5
Newtown I o W 20 C4
Newtown I o M 192 E4
Newtown Mers 183 B7
Newtown Norf 143 B10
Newtown Northumb 252 C2
Newtown Northumb 263 C11
Newtown Northumb 264 D2
Newtown Oxon 65 C9
Newtown Poole 18 C6
Newtown Powys 130 E2
Newtown Rhondda 77 F9
Newtown Shrops 132 C2
Newtown Shrops 149 C9
Newtown Shrops 149 E8
Newtown Som 28 E3
Newtown Som 43 F9
Newtown Staffs 133 C9
Newtown Staffs 168 C6
Newtown Staffs 169 C9
Newtown W Ches 183 F8
Newtown W Mid 133 F11
Newtown Wilts 30 B6
Newtown Wilts 63 G10
Newtown Worcs 116 F5
Newtown Worcs 117 E7
Newtown-in-St Martin Corn 2 E6
Newtown Linford Leics 135 B10
Newtown St Boswells Borders 262 C3
Newtown Unthank Leics 135 C9
Newtyle Angus 286 C6
Newyears Green London 66 B5
Nextend Hereford 114 F6
Neyland Pembs 73 D7
Niarbyl I o M 192 E3
Nib Heath Shrops 149 F8
Nibley Glos 79 D11
Nibley S Glos 61 C7
Nibley Green Glos 80 F2
Nibon Shetland 312 F5
Nicholashayne Devon 27 D10
Nicholaston Swansea 56 D4
Nidd N Yorks 214 G6
Niddrie Edin 280 G5
Nigg Aberdeen 293 C11
Nigg Highld 301 B8
Nigg Ferry Highld 301 C7
Nightcott Som 26 B5
Nilig Denb 165 D8
Nimble Nook Gtr Man 196 G2
Nimlet S Glos 61 E8
Nimmer Som 28 E4
Nine Ashes Essex 87 E9
Nine Elms London 67 D9
Nine Elms Swindon 62 B6
Nine Maidens Downs Corn 2 B5
Nine Mile Burn Midloth 270 D3
Nine Wells Pembs 90 G5
Ninebanks Northumb 241 G7
Nineveh Worcs 116 C3
Nineveh Worcs 116 E2
Ninewells Glos 79 C9
Ninfield E Sus 38 E2
Ningwood I o W 20 D3
Ningwood Common I o W 20 D3
Ninnes Bridge Corn 2 B2
Nisbet Borders 262 D5
Nisthouse Orkney 314 E3
Nisthouse Shetland 313 G7
Nithbank Dumfries 247 D9
Niton I o W 20 F6
Nitshill Glasgow 267 C10
No Man's Heath W Ches 167 F8
No Man's Heath Warks 134 B5
No Man's Land Corn 6 D5
No Man's Land Hants 33 B8
Noah's Arks Kent 52 B5
Noah's Green Worcs 117 E10
Noak Bridge Essex 87 G11
Noak Hill Essex 87 G11
Noak Hill London 87 G8
Nob End Gtr Man 195 F9
Nobland Green Herts 86 B5
Noblethorpe S Yorks 197 F9
Nobold Shrops 149 G9
Nobottle Northants 120 E3
Nob's Crook Hants 33 C7
Nocton Lincs 173 C9
Noctorum Mers 182 D3
Nodmore W Berks 64 D2
Noel Park London 86 G4
Nog Tow Lancs 202 G6
Nogdam End Norf 143 C7
Noke Oxon 83 C8
Noke Street Medway 69 E8
Nolton Pembs 72 B5
Nolton Haven Pembs 72 B5
Nomansland Devon 26 E4
Nomansland Herts 85 C11
Nomansland Wilts 32 D3
Noneley Shrops 149 D9
Noness Shetland 313 L6
Nonikiln Highld 300 B6
Nonington Kent 55 C9
Nook Cumb 211 C10
Noon Nick W Yorks 205 F8
Noonsbrough Shetland 313 H4
Noonsun E Ches 184 F4
Noonvares Corn 2 C3
Noranside Angus 292 G6
Norbiton London 67 F7
Norbreck Blkpool 202 E2
Norbridge Hereford 98 C4
Norbury Derbys 169 G10
Norbury E Ches 167 F9
Norbury London 67 F10
Norbury Shrops 131 E7
Norbury Staffs 150 E5
Norbury Common E Ches 167 F9
Norbury Junction Staffs 150 E5
Norbury Moor Gtr Man 184 D6
Norby N Yorks 215 C8
Norby Shetland 313 H3
Norchard Worcs 116 D6
Norcote Glos 81 E8
Norcott Brook W Ches 183 E10
Norcross Blkpool 202 E2
Nordelph Norf 139 C11
Nordelph Corner Norf 141 C10
Norden Dorset 18 E4
Norden Gtr Man 195 E11
Norden Heath Dorset 18 E4
Nordley Shrops 132 D3
Norham Northumb 273 F8
Norham West Mains Northumb 273 F8
Nork Sur 51 B8
Nork Sur 67 G8
Norland Town W Yorks 196 C5
Norleaze Wilts 45 C11
Norley Devon 25 G8
Norley W Ches 183 G9
Norley Common Sur 50 E4
Norleywood Hants 20 B3
Norlington E Sus 36 E6
Normacot Stoke 168 G6
Norman Cross Cambs 138 E3
Norman Hill Glos 80 F3
Normanby N Lincs 199 D11
Normanby N Yorks 216 C4
Normanby Redcar 225 B10
Normanby-by-Spital Lincs 189 D7
Normanby by Stow Lincs 188 E5
Normanby le Wold Lincs 189 B10
Normandy Sur 50 C2
Norman's Bay E Sus 23 D11
Norman's Green Devon 27 G9
Normanston Suff 143 E10
Normanton Derby 152 C6
Normanton Leics 172 G4
Normanton Lincs 172 F6
Normanton Notts 172 E2
Normanton Rutland 137 B8
Normanton W Yorks 197 C11
Normanton Wilts 46 E6
Normanton le Heath Leics 153 G7
Normanton on Soar Notts 153 E10
Normanton-on-the-Wolds Notts 154 C2
Normanton on Trent Notts 172 B3
Normanton Spring S Yorks 186 E6
Normanton Turville Leics 135 D9
Normoss Lancs 202 F2
Norney Sur 50 E2
Norr W Yorks 205 F7
Norrington Common Wilts 61 G11
Norris Green Corn 7 B8
Norris Green Mers 182 C5
Norris Hill Leics 152 F6
Norristhorpe W Yorks 197 C8
Norseman Orkney 314 E3
North Acton London 67 C8
North Anston S Yorks 187 E8
North Ascot Brack 66 F2
North Aston Oxon 101 F9
North Ayre Shetland 312 F6
North Baddesley Hants 32 D5
North Ballachulish Highld 290 G2
North Barrow Som 29 B10
North Barsham Norf 159 C8
North Batsom Som 41 G10
North Beer Corn 12 C2
North Benfleet Essex 69 B9
North Bersted W Sus 22 C6
North Berwick E Loth 281 D11
North Bitchburn Durham 233 E9
North Blyth Northumb 253 G8
North Boarhunt Hants 33 E10
North Bockhampton Dorset 19 B9
North Bovey Devon 13 E10
North Bradley Wilts 45 C11
North Brentor Devon 12 E5
North Brewham Som 45 F8
North Brook End Cambs 104 C5
North Broomage Falk 279 E7
North Buckland Devon 40 E3
North Burlingham Norf 161 G7
North Cadbury Som 29 B10
North Cairn Dumfries 236 B1
North Camp Hants 49 C11
North Carlton Lincs 188 F6
North Carlton Notts 187 E9
North Carrine Argyll 255 G7
North Cave E Yorks 208 G3
North Cerney Glos 81 D8
North Chailey E Sus 36 C5
North Charford Wilts 31 D11
North Charlton Northumb 264 E5
North Cheam London 67 F8
North Cheriton Som 29 B11
North Cliff E Yorks 209 D10
North Cliffe E Yorks 208 F3
North Clifton Notts 188 G4
North Close Durham 233 E11
North Cockerington Lincs 190 C5
North Coker Som 29 E8
North Collafirth Shetland 312 E5
North Common S Glos 61 E7
North Common Suff 125 B9
North Connel Argyll 289 F11
North Cornelly Bridgend 57 E10
North Corner Corn 3 F7
North Corner S Glos 61 C7
North Corriegills N Ayrs 256 C2
North Corry Highld 289 D10
North Cotes Lincs 201 G11
North Country Corn 4 G3
North Court Som 41 F11
North Cove Suff 143 F9
North Cowton N Yorks 224 E5
North Craigo Angus 293 G8
North Crawley M Keynes 103 C8
North Cray London 68 E3
North Creake Norf 159 B7
North Curry Som 28 B4
North Dalton E Yorks 208 C4
North Darley Corn 11 G11
North Dawn Orkney 314 F4
North Deighton N Yorks 206 C3
North Denes Norf 161 G10
North Dronley Angus 287 D7
North Drumachter Lodge Highld 291 F8
North Duffield N Yorks 207 F9
North Dykes Cumb 230 D6
North Eastling Kent 54 B3
North Elham Kent 55 E7
North Elkington Lincs 190 C3
North Elmham Norf 159 E9
North Elmsall W Yorks 198 E3
North Elmshall W Yorks 198 E3
North Elphinestone E Loth 281 G7
North End Bath 60 G6
North End Beds 103 B9
North End Beds 121 F10
North End Bucks 102 F4
North End Bucks 102 F6
North End Cumb 239 F8
North End Devon 27 D10
North End Dorset 30 B4
North End Durham 233 C11
North End E Yorks 209 C9
North End E Yorks 209 F9
North End E Yorks 209 G11
North End Essex 87 B11
North End Essex 106 D5
North End Hants 31 D10
North End Hants 33 B9
North End Hants 64 G2
North End Leics 153 F11
North End Lincs 174 G2
North End Lincs 189 B8
North End Lincs 190 C5
North End Lincs 190 D6
North End Lincs 191 D7
North End Lincs 201 G10
North End London 67 B9
North End London 68 D4
North End N Lincs 200 C6
North End N Som 60 F2
North End Norf 141 E10
North End Northumb 252 C4
North End Ptsmth 33 G11
North End Som 28 B3
North End W Sus 35 F10
North End W Sus 35 G7
North End W Sus 51 F11
North End Wilts 81 G8
North Erradale Highld 307 L2
North Evington Leicester 136 C2
North Ewster N Lincs 199 G10
North Fambridge Essex 88 F5
North Fearns Highld 295 B7
North Featherstone W Yorks 198 C2
North Feltham London 66 E6
North Feorline N Ayrs 255 E10
North Ferriby E Yorks 200 B3
North Finchley London 86 G3
North Flobbets Aberds 303 F7
North Frodingham E Yorks 209 C8
North Gluss Shetland 312 F5
North Gorley Hants 31 E11
North Green Norf 141 B10
North Green Norf 142 F4
North Green Suff 126 B6
North Green Suff 126 E6
North Green Suff 127 D7
North Greetwell Lincs 189 G8
North Grimston N Yorks 216 F6
North Halley Orkney 314 F5
North Halling Medway 69 F8
North Harrow London 66 B6
North Hayling Hants 22 C2
North Hazelrigg Northumb 264 C3
North Heasley Devon 41 G8
North Heath W Berks 64 E3
North Heath W Sus 35 C9
North Hill Corn 11 F11
North Hillingdon London 66 C5
North Hinksey Oxon 83 D7
North Hinksey Village Oxon 83 D7
North Ho Shetland 313 J5
North Holmwood Sur 51 D7
North Houghton Hants 47 G10
North Howden E Yorks 207 G11
North Huish Devon 8 D4
North Hyde London 66 D6
North Hykeham Lincs 172 B6
North Hylton T & W 243 F8
North Kelsey Lincs 200 G4
North Kelsey Moor Lincs 200 G5
North Kensington London 67 C8
North Kessock Highld 300 E6
North Killingholme N Lincs 200 D6
North Kilvington N Yorks 215 B8
North Kilworth Leics 136 G2
North Kingston Hants 31 G11
North Kirkton Aberds 303 D11
North Kiscadale N Ayrs 256 D2
North Kyme Lincs 173 E11
North Laggan Highld 290 D4
North Lancing W Sus 35 F11
North Landing E Yorks 218 E4
North Lee Bucks 84 D4
North Lees N Yorks 214 E6
North Leigh Kent 54 D6
North Leigh Oxon 82 C5
North Leverton with Habblesthorpe Notts 188 E3
North Littleton Worcs 99 B11
North Looe Sur 67 G8
North Lopham Norf 141 G10
North Luffenham Rutland 137 C8
North Marden W Sus 34 D4
North Marston Bucks 102 G5
North Middleton Midloth 271 D7
North Middleton Northumb 264 E2
North Millbrex Aberds 303 E8
North Molton Devon 26 B2
North Moreton Oxon 64 B5
North Mosstown Aberds 303 D10
North Motherwell N Lnrk 268 D4
North Moulsecoomb Brighton 36 F4
North Mundham W Sus 22 C5
North Muskham Notts 172 D3
North Newbald E Yorks 208 F4
North Newington Oxon 101 D8
North Newnton Wilts 46 B6
North Newton Som 43 G9
North Nibley Glos 80 F2
North Oakley Hants 48 C4
North Ockendon London 68 C5
North Ormesby M'bro 234 G6
North Ormsby Lincs 190 C3
North Otterington N Yorks 215 B7
North Owersby Lincs 189 C9
North Perrott Som 29 F7
North Petherton Som 43 G9
North Petherwin Corn 11 D11
North Pickenham Norf 141 B7
North Piddle Worcs 117 G9
North Poorton Dorset 16 B6
North Port Argyll 284 E4
North Poulner Hants 31 F11
North Queensferry Fife 280 E2
North Radworthy Devon 41 G9
North Rauceby Lincs 173 F8
North Reddish Gtr Man 184 C5
North Reston Lincs 190 E5
North Rigton N Yorks 205 D11
North Ripley Hants 19 B9
North Rode E Ches 168 B5
North Roe Shetland 312 E5
North Row Cumb 229 E10
North Runcton Norf 158 F2
North Sandwick Shetland 312 D7
North Scale Cumb 210 F3
North Scarle Lincs 172 B5
North Seaton Northumb 253 F7
North Seaton Colliery Northumb 253 F7
North Sheen London 67 D7
North Shian Argyll 289 E11
North Shields T & W 243 D9
North Shoebury Sthend 70 B2
North Shore Blkpool 202 F2
North Side Cumb 228 F6
North Side P'boro 138 D5
North Skelmanae Aberds 303 D9
North Skelton Redcar 226 B3
North Somercotes Lincs 190 B6
North Stainley N Yorks 214 D5
North Stainmore Cumb 222 B6
North Stifford Thurrock 68 C6
North Stoke Bath 61 F8
North Stoke Oxon 64 B6
North Stoke W Sus 35 E8
North Stoneham Hants 32 D6
North Street Hants 31 D11
North Street Hants 48 G6
North Street Kent 54 B4
North Street Medway 69 E10
North Street W Berks 64 E6
North Sunderland Northumb 264 C6
North Synton Borders 261 E11
North Tamerton Corn 12 B2
North Tawton Devon 25 G11
North Thoresby Lincs 190 B3
North Tidworth Wilts 47 D8
North Togston Northumb 252 C6
North Town Devon 25 F8
North Town Hants 49 C11
North Town Som 29 B10
North Town Som 44 E5
North Town Windsor 65 C11
North Tuddenham Norf 159 G10
North Walbottle T & W 242 D5
North Walney Cumb 210 F3
North Walsham Norf 160 C5
North Waltham Hants 48 D5
North Warnborough Hants 49 C8
North Water Bridge Angus 293 G8
North Waterhayne Devon 28 F3
North Watford Herts 85 F10
North Watten Highld 310 D6
North Weald Bassett Essex 87 E7
North Weirs Hants 32 G3
North Wembley London 67 B7
North Weston N Som 60 D3
North Weston Oxon 83 D11
North Wheatley Notts 188 D3
North Whilborough Devon 9 B7
North Whiteley Moray 302 E4
North Wick Bath 60 F5
North Widcombe Bath 44 B5
North Willingham Lincs 189 D11
North Wingfield Derbys 170 B6
North Witham Lincs 155 E8
North Woolwich London 68 D2
North Wootton Dorset 29 E11
North Wootton Norf 158 E2
North Wootton Som 44 E5
North Wraxall Wilts 61 D10
North Wroughton Swindon 63 C7
Northacre Norf 141 D9
Northall Bucks 103 G9
Northall Green Norf 159 G9
Northallerton N Yorks 225 G7
Northam Devon 24 B6
Northam Soton 32 E6
Northampton Northants 120 E5
Northaw Herts 86 E3
Northay Devon 28 G5
Northay Som 28 E3
Northbeck Lincs 173 G9
Northborough P'boro 138 B3
Northbourne Bmouth 19 B7
Northbourne Kent 55 C10
Northbridge Street E Sus 38 C2
Northbrook Dorset 17 C11
Northbrook Hants 33 D9
Northbrook Hants 48 F4
Northbrook Oxon 101 G9
Northbrook Wilts 46 C4
Northchapel W Sus 35 B7
Northchurch Herts 85 D7
Northcote Devon 27 G11
Northcott Corn 24 F2
Northcott Devon 12 C2
Northcott Devon 27 E9
Northcott Devon 27 F10
Northcourt Oxon 83 F8
Northdown Kent 71 E11
Northdyke Orkney 314 D2
Northedge Derbys 170 B5
Northend Bath 61 F9
Northend Bucks 84 G2
Northend Essex 89 E7
Northend Essex 105 D10
Northend Warks 119 G7
Northenden Gtr Man 184 C4
Northern Moor Gtr Man 184 C4
Northfield Aberdeen 293 C11
Northfield Borders 262 D3
Northfield Borders 273 B8
Northfield E Yorks 200 B4
Northfield Edin 280 G5
Northfield Highld 301 B7
Northfield M Keynes 103 C7
Northfield Northants 137 E7
Northfield Som 43 F9
Northfield W Mid 117 B10
Northfields Hants 33 B7
Northfields Lincs 137 B10
Northfleet Kent 68 E6
Northfleet Green Kent 68 E6
Northgate Lincs 156 D3
Northgate Som 27 B9
Northgate W Sus 51 F9
Northhouse Borders 249 B10
Northiam E Sus 38 B4
Northill C Beds 104 B2
Northington Glos 80 D2
Northington Hants 48 F5
Northlands Lincs 174 E4
Northlea Durham 243 G10
Northleach Glos 81 C10
Northleigh Devon 15 B9
Northleigh Devon 40 G6
Northlew Devon 12 B6
Northmoor Devon 24 D4
Northmoor Oxon 82 E6
Northmoor Corner Som 43 G10
Northmoor Green or Moorland Som 43 G10
Northmuir Angus 287 B7
Northney Hants 22 C2
Northolt London 66 C6
Northop = Llan-eurgain Flint 166 B2
Northop Hall Flint 166 B3
Northorpe Lincs 155 F11
Northorpe Lincs 156 B4
Northorpe Lincs 188 B5
Northorpe W Yorks 197 C8
Northover Som 29 C8
Northover Som 44 F3
Northowram W Yorks 196 B6
Northpark Argyll 275 G11
Northport Dorset 18 D4
Northpunds Shetland 313 L6
Northrepps Norf 160 B4
Northside Aberds 303 D8
Northside Orkney 314 D2
Northtown Aberds 293 C9
Northtown Orkney 314 G4
Northtown Shetland 313 M5
Northumberland Heath London 68 D4
Northville Torf 78 F3
Northway Devon 24 C5
Northway Glos 99 E8
Northway Som 27 B10
Northway Swansea 56 D5
Northwich W Ches 183 G11
Northwick S Glos 60 B5
Northwick Som 43 D11
Northwick Worcs 116 F6
Northwold Norf 140 D5
Northwood Derbys 170 C3
Northwood I o W 20 C5
Northwood Kent 71 F11
Northwood London 85 G9
Northwood Mers 182 B6
Northwood Shrops 149 C9
Northwood Staffs 168 G5
Northwood Stoke 168 F5
Northwood Green Glos 80 B2
Northwood Hills London 85 G9
Norton Devon 9 E7
Norton Devon 24 B3
Norton E Sus 23 E7
Norton Glos 99 G7
Norton Halton 183 E9
Norton Herts 104 E4
Norton I o W 20 D2

Norton Mon 78 B6
Norton N Som 59 G10
Norton Northants 120 E2
Norton Notts 187 G9
Norton Powys 114 D6
Norton S Yorks 186 E5
Norton S Yorks 198 D4
Norton Shrops 131 B11
Norton Shrops 131 G9
Norton Shrops 132 C4
Norton Stockton 234 G4
Norton Suff 125 D9
Norton Swansea 56 D3
Norton Swansea 56 D6
Norton W Mid 133 G7
Norton W Sus 22 B6
Norton W Sus 22 D5
Norton Wilts 61 C11
Norton Worcs 99 B10
Norton Worcs 117 G7
Norton Ash Kent 70 G3
Norton Bavant Wilts 46 E2
Norton Bridge Staffs 151 C7
Norton Canes Staffs 133 B10
Norton Canon Hereford 97 B7
Norton Corner Norf 159 D11
Norton Disney Lincs 172 D5
Norton East Staffs 133 B10
Norton Ferris Wilts 45 F9
Norton Fitzwarren Som 27 B11
Norton Green Herts 104 G4
Norton Green I o W 20 D2
Norton Green Staffs 168 E6
Norton Green W Mid 118 C3
Norton Hawkfield Bath 60 G5
Norton Heath Essex 87 E10
Norton in Hales Shrops 150 B4
Norton-in-the-Moors Stoke 168 E5
Norton-Juxta-Twycross Leics 134 B6
Norton-le-Clay N Yorks 215 E8
Norton Lindsey Warks 118 E4
Norton Little Green Suff 125 D9
Norton Malreward Bath 60 F6
Norton Mandeville Essex 87 E9
Norton-on-Derwent N Yorks 216 E5
Norton St Philip Som 45 B9
Norton sub Hamdon Som 29 D7
Norton Subcourse Norf 143 D8
Norton Woodseats S Yorks 186 E5
Norton's Wood N Som 60 E2
Norwell Notts 172 C3
Norwell Woodhouse Notts 172 C2
Norwich Norf 142 B4
Norwick Shetland 312 B8
Norwood Derbys 187 E7
Norwood Dorset 29 F8
Norwood End Essex 87 D9
Norwood Green London 66 D6
Norwood Green W Yorks 196 B6
Norwood Hill Sur 51 E8
Norwood New Town London 67 E10
Norwoodside Cambs 139 D8
Noseley Leics 136 D4
Noss Highld 310 D7
Noss Shetland 313 M5
Noss Mayo Devon 7 F11
Nosterfield N Yorks 214 C5
Nosterfield End Cambs 106 C2
Nostie Highld 295 C10
Notgrove Glos 100 G2
Nottage Bridgend 57 F10
Notter Corn 7 C7
Notting Hill London 67 C8
Nottingham Nottingham 153 B11
Nottington Dorset 17 E9
Notton W Yorks 197 E10
Notton Wilts 62 F2
Nounsley Essex 88 C3
Noutard's Green Worcs 116 D5
Nova Scotia W Ches 167 B10
Novar House Highld 300 C6
Novers Park Bristol 60 F5
Noverton Glos 99 G9
Nowton Suff 125 E7
Nox Shrops 149 G8
Noyadd Trefawr Ceredig 92 B5
Noyadd Wilym Ceredig 92 C5
Nuffield Oxon 65 B7
Nun Appleton N Yorks 207 F7
Nun Hills Lancs 195 C11
Nun Monkton N Yorks 206 B6
Nunburnholme E Yorks 208 D2
Nuncargate Notts 171 E8
Nunclose Cumb 230 B5
Nuneaton Warks 135 E7
Nuneham Courtenay Oxon 83 F9
Nuney Green Oxon 65 D7
Nunhead London 67 D11
Nunney Som 45 D8
Nunney Catch Som 45 E8
Nunnington N Yorks 216 D3
Nunnykirk Northumb 252 E3
Nunsthorpe NE Lincs 201 F9
Nunthorpe M'bro 225 C10
Nunthorpe York 207 C8
Nunton Wilts 31 B11
Nunwick N Yorks 214 E6
Nup End Bucks 84 B5
Nup End Herts 86 B2
Nupdown S Glos 79 F10
Nupend Glos 80 D3
Nupend Glos 80 F4
Nuper's Hatch Essex 87 G8
Nuppend Glos 79 E10
Nuptown Brack 65 E11
Nursling Hants 32 D5
Nursted Hants 34 C3
Nursteed Wilts 62 G4
Nurston V Glam 58 F5
Nurton Staffs 132 D6
Nurton Hill Staffs 132 D6
Nut Grove Mers 183 C7
Nutbourne W Sus 22 B3
Nutbourne W Sus 35 D9
Nutbourne Common W Sus 35 D9
Nutburn Hants 32 C5
Nutcombe Sur 49 G11
Nutfield Sur 51 C10
Nuthall Notts 171 G8
Nuthampstead Herts 105 E8
Nuthurst W Sus 35 B11
Nuthurst Warks 118 C3
Nutley E Sus 36 B6
Nutley Hants 48 E6
Nuttall Gtr Man 195 D9
Nutwell S Yorks 198 G6
Nybster Highld 310 C7
Nye N Som 60 G2
Nyetimber W Sus 22 D5
Nyewood W Sus 34 C4
Nyland Som 44 C3
Nymet Rowland Devon 26 F2
Nymet Tracey Devon 26 G2
Nympsfield Glos 80 E4
Nynehead Som 27 C10
Nythe Som 44 G2
Nythe Swindon 63 B7
Nyton W Sus 22 B6

O

Oad Street Kent 69 G11
Oadby Leics 136 C2
Oak Bank Gtr Man 195 F10
Oak Cross Devon 12 B6
Oak Hill Stoke 168 G5
Oak Hill Suff 109 B7
Oak Tree Darl 225 C7
Oakall Green Worcs 116 E6
Oakamoor Staffs 169 G9
Oakbank W Loth 269 B11
Oakdale Caerph 77 F11
Oakdale N Yorks 205 B11
Oakdale Poole 18 C6
Oake Som 27 B11
Oake Green Som 27 B11
Oaken Staffs 133 C7
Oakenclough Lancs 202 D6
Oakengates Telford 150 G4
Oakenholt Flint 182 G3
Oakenshaw Durham 233 D10
Oakenshaw Lancs 203 G10
Oakenshaw W Yorks 197 B7
Oakerthorpe Derbys 170 E5
Oakes W Yorks 196 D6
Oakfield Herts 104 F3
Oakfield I o W 21 C7
Oakfield Torf 78 G4
Oakford Ceredig 111 F9
Oakford Devon 26 C6
Oakfordbridge Devon 26 C6
Oakgrove E Ches 168 B6
Oakgrove M Keynes 103 D7
Oakham Rutland 137 B7
Oakham W Mid 133 F9
Oakhanger E Ches 168 E3
Oakhanger Hants 49 F9
Oakhill Som 44 D6
Oakhill W Sus 51 G7
Oakhurst Kent 52 C4
Oakington Cambs 123 E8
Oaklands Carms 74 B6
Oaklands Herts 86 B2
Oaklands Powys 113 G10
Oakle Street Glos 80 B3
Oakleigh Park London 86 G3
Oakley Beds 121 G10
Oakley Bucks 83 C10
Oakley Fife 279 D10
Oakley Glos 99 G9
Oakley Hants 48 C5
Oakley Oxon 84 E3
Oakley Poole 18 B6
Oakley Staffs 150 B4
Oakley Suff 126 B3
Oakley Court Oxon 64 B6
Oakley Green Windsor 66 D2
Oakley Park Powys 129 F9
Oakley Park Suff 126 B3
Oakley Wood Oxon 64 B6
Oakmere W Ches 167 B9
Oakridge Glos 80 E6
Oakridge Hants 48 C6
Oakridge Lynch Glos 80 E6
Oaks Shrops 131 C8
Oaks Green Derbys 152 C3
Oaks in Charnwood Leics 153 F9
Oaksey Wilts 81 G7
Oakshaw Ford Cumb 240 B2
Oakshott Hants 34 B2
Oakthorpe Leics 152 G6
Oakwell W Yorks 197 B8
Oakwood Derby 153 B7
Oakwood London 86 F3
Oakwood Northumb 241 D10
Oakwood W Yorks 206 F2
Oakwood Warr 183 C11
Oakwoodhill Sur 50 F6
Oakworth W Yorks 204 F6
Oape Highld 309 J4
Oare Kent 70 G4
Oare Som 41 D10
Oare W Berks 64 E4
Oare Wilts 63 G7
Oareford Som 41 D10
Oasby Lincs 155 B10
Oath Som 28 B5
Oathill Dorset 28 F6
Oathlaw Angus 287 B8
Oatlands Glasgow 267 C11
Oatlands N Yorks 205 C11
Oatlands Park Sur 66 G5
Oban Argyll 289 G10
Oban Highld 295 G10
Oban W Isles 305 H3
Obley Shrops 114 B6
Oborne Dorset 29 D11
Obthorpe Lincs 155 F11
Obthorpe Lodge Lincs 156 F2
Occlestone Green W Ches 167 C11
Occold Suff 126 C3
Ocean Village Soton 32 E6
Ochiltree E Ayrs 258 E2
Ochr-y-foel Denb 181 F9
Ochtermuthill Perth 286 F2
Ochtertyre Perth 286 E2
Ochtow Highld 309 J4
Ockbrook Derbys 153 B8
Ocker Hill W Mid 133 E9
Ockeridge Worcs 116 E5
Ockford Ridge Sur 50 E3
Ockham Sur 50 B5
Ockle Highld 289 B7
Ockley Sur 50 F6
Ocle Pychard Hereford 97 B11
Octon E Yorks 217 F10
Octon Cross Roads E Yorks 217 F10
Odam Barton Devon 26 D2
Odcombe Som 29 D8
Odd Down Bath 61 G8
Oddendale Cumb 221 C11
Odder Lincs 188 G6
Oddingley Worcs 117 F8
Oddington Glos 100 F4
Oddington Oxon 83 C9
Odell Beds 121 F9
Odham Devon 25 G7
Odie Orkney 314 D6
Odiham Hants 49 C8
Odsal W Yorks 197 B7
Odsey Cambs 104 D5
Odstock Wilts 31 B10
Odstone Leics 135 B7
Offchurch Warks 119 D7
Offenham Worcs 99 B11
Offenham Cross Worcs 99 B11
Offerton Gtr Man 184 D6
Offerton T & W 243 F8
Offerton Green Gtr Man 184 D6
Offham E Sus 36 E5
Offham Kent 53 B7
Offham W Sus 35 F8
Offleyhay Staffs 150 D5
Offleymarsh Staffs 150 D5
Offleyrock Staffs 150 D5
Offord Cluny Cambs 122 D4
Offord D'Arcy Cambs 122 D4
Offton Suff 107 B11
Offwell Devon 15 B9
Ogbourne Maizey Wilts 63 E7
Ogbourne St Andrew Wilts 63 E7
Ogbourne St George Wilts 63 E8
Ogden W Yorks 205 G7
Ogdens Hants 31 E11
Ogil Angus 292 G6
Ogle Northumb 242 B4
Ogmore V Glam 57 F11
Ogmore-by-Sea = Aberogwr V Glam 57 F11
Ogmore Vale Bridgend 76 G6
Okeford Fitzpaine Dorset 30 E4
Okehampton Devon 13 B7
Okehampton Camp Devon 13 C7
Oker Derbys 170 C3
Okewood Hill Sur 50 F6
Okle Green Glos 98 F5
Okraquoy Shetland 313 K6
Okus Swindon 62 C6
Olchard Devon 14 F3
Old Northants 120 C5
Old Aberdeen Aberdeen 293 C11
Old Alresford Hants 48 G5
Old Arley Warks 134 E5
Old Balornock Glasgow 268 B2
Old Basford Nottingham 171 G8
Old Basing Hants 49 C7
Old Belses Borders 262 E3
Old Bewick Northumb 264 E3
Old Bexley London 68 E3
Old Blair Perth 291 G10
Old Bolingbroke Lincs 174 B4
Old Boston Mers 183 B9
Old Bramhope W Yorks 205 E10
Old Brampton Derbys 186 G4
Old Bridge of Tilt Perth 291 G10
Old Bridge of Urr Dumfries 237 C9
Old Buckenham Norf 141 E11
Old Burdon T & W 243 G9
Old Burghclere Hants 48 B3
Old Byland N Yorks 215 B11
Old Cambus Borders 272 B6
Old Cardinham Castle Corn 6 B2
Old Carlisle Cumb 229 B11
Old Cassop Durham 234 D2
Old Castleton Borders 250 E2
Old Catton Norf 160 G4
Old Chalford Oxon 100 F6
Old Church Stoke Powys 130 E5
Old Clee NE Lincs 201 F9
Old Cleeve Som 42 E4
Old Colwyn Conwy 180 F5
Old Coppice Shrops 131 B9
Old Corry Highld 295 C8
Old Coulsdon London 51 B10
Old Country Hereford 98 C4
Old Craig Aberds 303 G9
Old Craig Angus 292 G4
Old Crombie Aberds 302 D5
Old Cryals Kent 53 E7
Old Cullen Moray 302 C5
Old Dailly S Ayrs 244 D6
Old Dalby Leics 154 E3
Old Dam Derbys 185 F10
Old Deer Aberds 303 E9
Old Denaby S Yorks 187 B7
Old Ditch Som 44 D4
Old Dolphin W Yorks 205 G8
Old Down S Glos 60 B6
Old Duffus Moray 301 C11
Old Edlington S Yorks 187 B8
Old Eldon Durham 233 F10
Old Ellerby E Yorks 209 F9
Old Fallings W Mid 133 C8
Old Farm Park M Keynes 103 D8
Old Felixstowe Suff 108 D6
Old Field Shrops 115 B9
Old Fletton P'boro 138 D3
Old Fold T & W 243 E7
Old Ford London 67 C11
Old Forge Hereford 79 B9
Old Furnace Torf 78 E3
Old Gate Lincs 157 E8
Old Glossop Derbys 185 C8
Old Goginan Ceredig 128 G3
Old Goole E Yorks 199 C8
Old Gore Hereford 98 F2
Old Graitney Dumfries 239 D8
Old Grimsby Scilly 1 F3
Old Hall Powys 129 G8
Old Hall Green Herts 105 G7
Old Hall Street Norf 160 C6
Old Harlow Essex 87 C7
Old Hatfield Herts 86 D2
Old Heath Essex 107 G10
Old Heathfield E Sus 37 C9
Old Hill W Mid 133 F9
Old Hills Worcs 98 B6
Old Hunstanton Norf 175 G11
Old Hurst Cambs 122 B5
Old Hutton Cumb 211 B11
Old Johnstone Dumfries 248 D6
Old Kea Corn 4 G6
Old Kilpatrick W Dunb 277 G9
Old Kinnernie Aberds 293 C9
Old Knebworth Herts 104 G4
Old Langho Lancs 203 F10
Old Laxey I o M 192 D5
Old Leake Lincs 174 E6
Old Leckie Stirl 278 C3
Old Lindley W Yorks 196 D5
Old Linslade C Beds 103 F8
Old Llanberis = Nant Peris Gwyn 163 D10
Old Malden London 67 F8
Old Malton N Yorks 216 E5
Old Marton Shrops 148 C6
Old Mead Essex 105 F10
Old Micklefield W Yorks 206 G4
Old Mill Corn 12 G3
Old Milton Hants 19 C10
Old Milverton Warks 118 D5
Old Monkland N Lnrk 268 C4
Old Nenthorn Borders 262 B5
Old Netley Hants 33 F7
Old Neuadd Powys 129 F11
Old Newton Suff 125 E11
Old Oak Common London 67 C8
Old Park Corn 6 B4
Old Park Telford 132 B3
Old Passage S Glos 60 B5
Old Perton Staffs 133 D7
Old Philpstoun W Loth 279 F11
Old Polmont Falk 279 F8
Old Portsmouth Ptsmth 21 B8
Old Quarrington Durham 234 D2
Old Radnor Powys 114 F5
Old Rattray Aberds 303 D10
Old Rayne Aberds 302 G6
Old Romney Kent 39 B8
Old Shirley Soton 32 E5
Old Shoreham W Sus 36 F2
Old Snydale W Yorks 198 C2
Old Sodbury S Glos 61 C9
Old Somerby Lincs 155 C9
Old Stillington Stockton 234 G3
Old Storridge Common Worcs 116 G4
Old Stratford Northants 102 C5
Old Struan Perth 291 G10
Old Swan Mers 182 C5
Old Swarland Northumb 252 C5
Old Swinford W Mid 133 G8
Old Tame Gtr Man 196 F3
Old Tebay Cumb 222 D2
Old Thirsk N Yorks 215 C8
Old Tinnis Borders 261 D9
Old Toll S Ayrs 257 E9
Old Town Cumb 211 C11
Old Town Cumb 230 C5
Old Town E Sus 23 F9
Old Town E Sus 38 F2
Old Town E Sus 38 F4
Old Town E Yorks 218 F3
Old Town Edin 280 G5
Old Town Herts 104 F4
Old Town Scilly 1 G4
Old Town Swindon 63 C7
Old Town W Yorks 196 B3
Old Trafford Gtr Man 184 B4
Old Tree Kent 71 G8
Old Tupton Derbys 170 B5
Old Warden C Beds 104 C2
Old Warren Flint 166 C4
Old Way Som 28 D5
Old Weston Cambs 121 B11
Old Wharf Hereford 98 D4
Old Whittington Derbys 186 G5
Old Wick Highld 310 D7
Old Wimpole Cambs 122 G6
Old Windsor Windsor 66 E3
Old Wingate Durham 234 D3
Old Wives Lees Kent 54 C5
Old Woking Sur 50 B4
Old Wolverton M Keynes 102 C6
Old Woodhall Lincs 174 B2
Old Woodhouses Shrops 167 G9
Old Woodstock Oxon 82 B6
Oldany Highld 306 F6
Oldberrow Warks 118 D2
Oldborough Devon 26 F3
Oldbrook M Keynes 103 D7
Oldbury Kent 52 B5
Oldbury Shrops 132 E4
Oldbury W Mid 133 F9
Oldbury Warks 134 E6
Oldbury Naite S Glos 79 G10
Oldbury-on-Severn S Glos 79 G10
Oldbury on the Hill Glos 61 B10
Oldcastle Mon 96 G6
Oldcastle Heath W Ches 167 F7
Oldcotes Notts 187 D9
Oldcroft Glos 79 D10
Oldend Glos 80 D3
Oldfallow Staffs 151 G9
Oldfield Cumb 229 F7
Oldfield Shrops 132 F3
Oldfield W Yorks 196 E6
Oldfield W Yorks 204 F6
Oldfield Worcs 116 E6
Oldfield Brow Gtr Man 184 D3
Oldfield Park Bath 61 G8
Oldford Som 45 C9
Oldfurnace Staffs 169 G8
Oldhall Renfs 267 C10
Oldhall Green Suff 125 F7
Oldhall Ho Highld 310 D6
Oldham Gtr Man 196 F2
Oldham Edge Gtr Man 196 F2
Oldhamstocks E Loth 282 G4
Oldhurst Cambs 122 B6
Oldington Shrops 132 D4
Oldland S Glos 61 E7
Oldland Common S Glos 61 E7
Oldmeldrum Aberds 303 G8
Oldmixon N Som 43 B10
Oldshore Beg Highld 306 D6
Oldshoremore Highld 306 D7
Oldstead N Yorks 215 C10
Oldtown Aberds 293 C7
Oldtown Aberds 302 G5
Oldtown Highld 309 L5
Oldtown of Ord Aberds 302 D6
Oldwalls Swansea 56 C3
Oldway Swansea 56 D5
Oldway Torbay 9 C7
Oldways End Devon 26 B5
Oldwhat Aberds 303 D8
Oldwich Lane W Mid 118 C4
Oldwood Worcs 115 D11
Olgrinmore Highld 310 D4
Olive Green Staffs 152 F2
Oliver's Battery Hants 33 B7
Ollaberry Shetland 312 E5
Ollag W Isles 297 G3
Ollerbrook Booth Derbys 185 D10
Ollerton E Ches 184 F3
Ollerton Notts 171 B11
Ollerton Shrops 150 D2
Ollerton Fold Lancs 194 C6
Ollerton Lane Shrops 150 D3
Olmarch Ceredig 112 F2
Olmstead Green Essex 106 C2
Olney M Keynes 121 G7
Olrig Ho Highld 310 C5
Olton W Mid 134 G2
Olveston S Glos 60 B6
Olwen Ceredig 93 B11
Ombersley Worcs 116 E6
Ompton Notts 171 B11
Omunsgarth Shetland 313 J5
Onchan I o M 192 E4
Onecote Staffs 169 D9
Onehouse Suff 125 F10
Onen Mon 78 C6
Onesacre S Yorks 186 C3
Ongar Hill Norf 157 E11
Ongar Street Hereford 115 D7
Onibury Shrops 115 B9
Onich Highld 290 G2
Onllwyn Neath 76 C4
Onneley Staffs 168 G3
Onslow Village Sur 50 D3
Onthank E Ayrs 267 G8
Onziebust Orkney 314 D4
Openshaw Gtr Man 184 B5
Openwoodgate Derbys 170 F5
Opinan Highld 299 B7
Opinan Highld 307 K3
Orange Lane Borders 272 G5
Orange Row Norf 157 E10
Orasaigh W Isles 305 G5
Orbiston N Lnrk 268 D4
Orbliston Moray 302 D3
Orbost Highld 298 E2
Orby Lincs 175 B7
Orchard Hill Devon 24 B6
Orchard Leigh Bucks 85 E7
Orchard Portman Som 28 C2
Orcheston Wilts 46 D5
Orcop Hereford 97 F9
Orcop Hill Hereford 97 F9
Ord Highld 295 D8
Ordale Shetland 312 C8
Ordhead Aberds 293 B8
Ordie Aberds 292 C6
Ordiequish Moray 302 D3
Ordiqhill Aberds 302 D5
Ordley Northumb 241 F10
Ordsall Gtr Man 184 B4
Ordsall Notts 187 E11
Ore E Sus 38 E4
Oreston Plym 7 E10
Oreton Shrops 132 G3
Orford Suff 109 B8
Orford Warr 183 C10
Organford Dorset 18 C4
Orgreave S Yorks 186 D6
Orgreave Staffs 152 F3
Oridge Street Glos 98 F5
Orlandon Pembs 72 D4
Orlestone Kent 54 G3
Orleton Hereford 115 D9
Orleton Worcs 116 D3
Orleton Common Hereford 115 D9
Orlingbury Northants 121 C7
Ormacleit W Isles 297 H3
Ormathwaite Cumb 229 F11
Ormesby Redcar 225 B10
Ormesby St Margaret Norf 161 G9
Ormesby St Michael Norf 161 G9
Ormiclate Castle W Isles 297 H3
Ormidale Lodge Argyll 275 F11
Ormiscaig Highld 307 K3
Ormiston Borders 262 G2
Ormiston E Loth 271 B8
Ormsaigbeg Highld 288 C6
Ormsaigmore Highld 288 C6
Ormsary Argyll 275 F8
Ormsgill Cumb 210 E3
Ormskirk Lancs 194 F2
Ornsby Hill Durham 233 B9
Orpington London 68 F3
Orrell Gtr Man 194 F4
Orrell Mers 182 B4
Orrell Post Gtr Man 194 G4
Orrisdale I o M 192 C4
Orrock Fife 280 D4
Orroland Dumfries 237 E9
Orsett Thurrock 68 C6
Orsett Heath Thurrock 68 D6
Orslow Staffs 150 F6
Orston Notts 172 G3
Orthwaite Cumb 229 E11
Ortner Lancs 202 C6
Orton Cumb 222 D2
Orton Northants 120 B6
Orton Staffs 133 D7
Orton Brimbles P'boro 138 D3
Orton Goldhay P'boro 138 D3
Orton Longueville P'boro 138 D3
Orton Malborne P'boro 138 D3
Orton-on-the-Hill Leics 134 C6
Orton Rigg Cumb 239 G8
Orton Southgate P'boro 138 E2
Orton Waterville P'boro 138 D3
Orton Wistow P'boro 138 D2
Orwell Cambs 123 G7
Osbaldeston Lancs 203 G8
Osbaldeston Green Lancs 203 G8
Osbaldwick York 207 C8
Osbaston Leics 135 C8
Osbaston Shrops 148 E6
Osbaston Telford 149 F11
Osbaston Hollow Leics 135 B8
Osbournby Lincs 155 B11
Oscroft W Ches 167 B8
Ose Highld 298 E3
Osea Island Essex 88 D6
Osehill Green Dorset 29 F11
Osgathorpe Leics 153 F8
Osgodby Lincs 189 C9
Osgodby N Yorks 207 G8
Osgodby N Yorks 217 C11
Osgodby Common N Yorks 207 F8
Osidge London 86 G3
Oskaig Highld 295 B7
Oskamull Argyll 288 E6
Osleston Derbys 152 B4
Osmaston Derby 153 C7
Osmaston Derbys 170 G2
Osmington Dorset 17 E10
Osmington Mills Dorset 17 E10
Osmondthorpe W Yorks 206 G2
Osmotherley N Yorks 225 F9
Osney Oxon 83 D8
Ospisdale Highld 309 L7
Ospringe Kent 70 G4
Ossaborough Devon 40 E3
Ossemsley Hants 19 B10
Osset Spa W Yorks 197 D9
Ossett W Yorks 197 C9
Ossett Street Side W Yorks 197 C9
Ossington Notts 172 C3
Ostend Essex 88 F6
Ostend Norf 161 C7
Osterley London 66 D6
Oswaldkirk N Yorks 216 D2
Oswaldtwistle Lancs 195 B8
Oswestry Shrops 148 D5
Otby Lincs 189 C10
Otford Kent 52 B4
Otham Kent 53 C9
Otham Hole Kent 53 C10
Otherton Staffs 151 G8
Othery Som 43 G11
Otley Suff 126 F4
Otley W Yorks 205 D10
Otter Ferry Argyll 275 E10
Otter Ho Argyll 275 F10
Otterbourne Hants 33 C7
Otterburn N Yorks 204 B3
Otterburn Northumb 251 E9
Otterburn Camp Northumb 251 D9
Otterden Place Kent 54 C2
Otterford Som 28 E2
Otterham Corn 11 C9
Otterham Quay Kent 69 F10
Otterham Station Corn 11 D9
Otterhampton Som 43 E8
Ottershaw Sur 66 G4
Otterspool Mers 182 D5
Otterswick Shetland 312 E7
Otterton Devon 15 D7
Otterwood Hants 32 G6
Ottery St Mary Devon 15 B8
Ottinge Kent 55 E7
Ottringham E Yorks 201 C9
Oughterby Cumb 239 F7
Oughtershaw N Yorks 213 C7
Oughterside Cumb 229 C8
Oughtibridge S Yorks 186 C4
Oughtrington Warr 183 D11
Oulston N Yorks 215 E10
Oulton Cumb 238 G6
Oulton Norf 160 D2
Oulton Staffs 150 E5
Oulton Staffs 151 B8
Oulton Suff 143 D10
Oulton W Yorks 197 B11
Oulton Broad Suff 143 E10
Oulton Grange Staffs 151 B8
Oulton Heath Staffs 151 B8
Oulton Street Norf 160 D3
Oultoncross Staffs 151 C8
Oundle Northants 137 F10
Ousby Cumb 231 E8
Ousdale Highld 311 G4
Ousden Suff 124 F4
Ousefleet E Yorks 199 C10
Ousel Hole W Yorks 205 E8
Ouston Durham 243 G7
Ouston Northumb 241 G7
Ouston Northumb 242 C3
Out Elmstead Kent 55 C8
Out Newton E Yorks 201 C11
Out Rawcliffe Lancs 202 E4
Outcast Cumb 210 D6
Outer Hope Devon 8 G3
Outertown Orkney 314 E2
Outgate Cumb 221 F7
Outhgill Cumb 222 E5
Outhill Warks 118 D2
Outhills Aberds 303 D10
Outlands Staffs 150 C5
Outlane W Yorks 196 D5
Outlane Moor W Yorks 196 D5
Outlet Village W Ches 182 G6
Outmarsh Wilts 61 G11
Outwell Norf 139 C10
Outwick Hants 31 D10
Outwood Gtr Man 195 F9
Outwood Som 28 B4
Outwood Sur 51 D10
Outwood W Yorks 197 C10
Outwoods Leics 153 F8
Outwoods Staffs 150 F5
Outwoods Staffs 152 E4
Outwoods Warks 134 G4
Ouzlewell Green W Yorks 197 B10
Ovenden W Yorks 196 B5
Ovenscloss Borders 261 C11
Over Cambs 123 C7
Over Glos 80 B4
Over S Glos 60 C5
Over W Ches 167 B10
Over Burrow Lancs 212 D2
Over Burrows Derbys 152 B5
Over Compton Dorset 29 D9
Over End Cambs 137 E11
Over End Derbys 186 G3
Over Green W Mid 134 E3
Over Haddon Derbys 170 B2
Over Hulton Gtr Man 195 F7
Over Kellet Lancs 211 E10
Over Kiddington Oxon 101 G8
Over Knutsford E Ches 184 F3
Over Langshaw Borders 271 G10
Over Monnow Mon 79 C8
Over Norton Oxon 100 F6
Over Peover E Ches 184 G3
Over Silton N Yorks 225 G9
Over Stowey Som 43 F7
Over Stratton Som 28 D6
Over Tabley E Ches 184 E2
Over Town Lancs 195 B11
Over Wallop Hants 47 F9
Over Whitacre Warks 134 E5
Over Worton Oxon 101 F8
Overa Farm Stud Norf 141 F9
Overbister Orkney 314 B6
Overbury Worcs 99 D9
Overcombe Dorset 17 E9
Overend W Mid 133 G9
Overgreen Derbys 186 G4
Overleigh Som 44 F3
Overley Staffs 152 F3
Overley Green Warks 117 F11
Overmoor Staffs 169 F7
Overpool W Ches 182 F5
Overs Shrops 131 D7
Overscaig Hotel Highld 309 G4
Overseal Derbys 152 F5
Overslade Warks 119 C9
Oversland Kent 54 B5
Oversley Green Warks 117 F11
Overstone Northants 120 D6
Overstrand Norf 160 A4
Overthorpe Northants 101 C9
Overthorpe W Yorks 197 D8
Overton Aberdeen 293 B10
Overton Aberds 293 B9
Overton Dumfries 237 C11
Overton Glos 80 C2
Overton Hants 48 D4
Overton Invclyd 276 G5
Overton Lancs 202 B4
Overton N Yorks 207 B7
Overton Shrops 115 C10
Overton Staffs 151 B10
Overton Swansea 56 D3
Overton W Ches 183 F8
Overton W Yorks 197 D9
Overton = Owrtyn Wrex 166 G5
Overton Bridge Wrex 166 G5
Overtown Lancs 212 D2
Overtown N Lnrk 268 E6
Overtown Swindon 63 D7
Overtown W Yorks 197 D11
Oving Bucks 102 G5
Oving W Sus 22 C6
Ovingdean Brighton 36 G5
Ovingham Northumb 242 E3
Ovington Durham 224 C2
Ovington Essex 106 C5
Ovington Hants 48 G5
Ovington Norf 141 C8
Ovington Northumb 242 E3
Owen's Bank Staffs 152 D4
Ower Hants 32 B4
Owermoigne Dorset 17 D11
Owl End Cambs 122 B4
Owlbury Shrops 130 E6
Owlcotes Derbys 170 B6
Owler Bar Derbys 186 F3
Owlerton S Yorks 186 D4
Owlet W Yorks 205 F9
Owlpen Glos 80 F4
Owl's Green Suff 126 D5
Owlsmoor Brack 65 G11
Owlswick Bucks 84 D3
Owlthorpe S Yorks 186 E6
Owmby Lincs 200 G5
Owmby-by-Spital Lincs 189 D8
Ownham W Berks 64 E2
Owrtyn = Overton Wrex 166 G5
Owslebury Hants 33 C8
Owston Leics 136 B5
Owston S Yorks 198 E5
Owston Ferry N Lincs 199 G10
Owstwick E Yorks 209 G11
Owthorne E Yorks 201 B10
Owthorpe Notts 154 C3
Owton Manor Hrtlpl 234 F5
Oxborough Norf 140 C4
Oxclose S Yorks 186 E6
Oxclose T & W 243 F7
Oxcombe Lincs 190 F4
Oxcroft Derbys 187 G7
Oxcroft Estate Derbys 187 G7
Oxen End Essex 106 F3
Oxen Park Cumb 210 B6
Oxenhall Glos 98 F4
Oxenholme Cumb 211 B10
Oxenhope W Yorks 204 F6
Oxenpill Som 44 E2
Oxenton Glos 99 E9
Oxenwood Wilts 47 B10
Oxford Oxon 83 D8
Oxford Stoke 168 E5
Oxgang E Dunb 278 G3
Oxgangs Edin 270 B4
Oxhey Herts 85 F10
Oxhill Durham 242 G5
Oxhill Warks 100 B6
Oxlease Herts 86 D2
Oxley W Mid 133 C8
Oxley Green Essex 88 C6
Oxley's Green E Sus 37 C11
Oxlode Cambs 139 F9
Oxnam Borders 262 F5
Oxnead Norf 160 E4
Oxshott Sur 66 G6
Oxspring S Yorks 197 G9
Oxted Sur 51 C11
Oxton Borders 271 E9
Oxton Mers 182 D3
Oxton N Yorks 206 E6
Oxton Notts 171 E10
Oxton Rakes Derbys 186 G4
Oxwich Swansea 56 D3
Oxwich Green Swansea 56 D3
Oxwick Norf 159 D8
Oykel Bridge Highld 309 J3
Oyne Aberds 302 G6
Oystermouth Swansea 56 D6
Ozleworth Glos 80 G3

P

Pabail Iarach W Isles 304 E7
Pabail Uarach W Isles 304 E7
Pabo Conwy 180 F4
Pace Gate N Yorks 205 C8
Pachesham Park Sur 51 B7
Packers Hill Dorset 30 E2
Packington Leics 153 G7
Packmoor Staffs 168 E5
Packmores Warks 118 D5
Packwood W Mid 118 C3
Packwood Gullet W Mid 118 C3
Padanaram Angus 287 B8
Padbury Bucks 102 E4
Paddington London 67 C9
Paddington Warr 183 D10
Paddlesworth Kent 55 F7
Paddlesworth Kent 69 G7
Paddock Kent 54 C3
Paddock W Yorks 196 D6
Paddock Wood Kent 53 E7
Paddockhaugh Moray 302 D2
Paddockhill E Ches 184 F4
Paddockhole Dumfries 248 G6
Paddolgreen Shrops 149 C10
Padfield Derbys 185 B8
Padgate Warr 183 D10
Padham's Green Essex 87 F10
Padiham Lancs 203 G11
Padney Cambs 123 C10
Padog Conwy 164 E4
Padside N Yorks 205 B9
Padside Green N Yorks 205 B9
Padson Devon 13 B7
Padstow Corn 10 F4
Padworth W Berks 64 F6
Padworth Common Hants 64 G6
Paganhill Glos 80 D4
Page Bank Durham 233 D10
Page Moss Mers 182 C6
Pagelsham Eastend Essex 88 G6
Page's Green Suff 126 D2
Pagham W Sus 22 D5
Paglesham Churchend Essex 88 G6
Paglesham Eastend Essex 88 G6
Paibeil W Isles 296 E3
Paible W Isles 305 J2
Paignton Torbay 9 C7
Pailton Warks 135 G9
Painleyhill Staffs 151 C10
Pains Hill Sur 52 C2
Painscastle Powys 96 B3
Painshawfield Northumb 242 E3
Painsthorpe E Yorks 208 B2
Painswick Glos 80 D5
Painter's Forstal Kent 54 B3
Painter's Green Herts 86 B3
Painters Green Wrex 167 G8
Painthorpe W Yorks 197 D10
Paintmoor Som 28 F4
Pairc Shiaboist W Isles 304 D4
Paisley Renfs 267 C9
Pakefield Suff 143 E10
Pakenham Suff 125 D8
Pale Gwyn 147 B9
Pale Green Essex 106 C3
Palehouse Common E Sus 23 B7
Palestine Hants 47 E9
Paley Street Windsor 65 D11
Palfrey W Mid 133 D10
Palgowan Dumfries 245 G9
Palgrave Suff 126 B2
Pallaflat Cumb 219 C9
Pallington Dorset 17 C11
Pallion T & W 243 F9
Pallister M'bro 225 B10
Palmarsh Kent 54 G6
Palmer Moor Derbys 152 C2
Palmers Cross Staffs 133 C7
Palmers Cross Sur 50 E4
Palmer's Flat Glos 79 D9
Palmer's Green Kent 53 E7
Palmers Green London 86 G4
Palmersbridge Corn 11 F9
Palmerstown V Glam 58 F6
Palmersville T & W 243 C7
Palmstead Kent 55 D7
Palnackie Dumfries 237 D10
Palnure Dumfries 236 C6
Palterton Derbys 171 B7
Pamber End Hants 48 B6
Pamber Green Hants 48 B6
Pamber Heath Hants 64 G6
Pamington Glos 99 E8
Pamphill Dorset 31 G7
Pampisford Cambs 105 B9
Pan I o W 20 D6
Pan Orkney 314 G3
Panborough Som 44 D3
Panbride Angus 287 D9
Pancakehill Glos 81 C9
Pancrasweek Devon 24 F3
Pancross V Glam 58 F4
Pandy Gwyn 128 C2
Pandy Gwyn 146 F4
Pandy Gwyn 147 D7
Pandy Mon 96 G6
Pandy Powys 129 C8
Pandy Wrex 148 B3
Pandy Wrex 166 G6
Pandy Tudur Conwy 164 C5
Pandy'r Capel Denb 165 E9
Panfield Essex 106 F4
Pangbourne W Berks 64 D6
Panhall Fife 280 C6
Panks Bridge Hereford 98 B2
Pannal N Yorks 206 C2
Pannal Ash N Yorks 205 C11
Pannel's Ash Essex 106 C5
Panpunton Powys 114 C5
Panshanger Herts 86 C3
Pant Denb 166 E2
Pant Flint 181 G10
Pant Gwyn 144 C4
Pant M Tydf 77 D9
Pant Powys 129 C11
Pant Shrops 148 E5
Pant Wrex 166 D5
Pant Wrex 166 F3
Pant-glâs Powys 128 D5
Pant-glas Gwyn 163 F7
Pant-glas Shrops 148 C5
Pant-lasau Swansea 57 B7
Pant Mawr Powys 129 G7
Pant-pastynog Denb 165 C8
Pant-teg Carms 93 F9
Pant-y-Caws Carms 92 F3
Pant-y-crûg Ceredig 112 B3
Pant-y-dwr Powys 113 B9
Pant-y-dwr Powys 113 C9
Pant-y-ffridd Powys 130 C3
Pant-y-pyllau Bridgend 58 C2
Pant-y-Wacco Flint 181 F10
Pant-yr-awel Bridgend 58 B2
Pantasaph Flint 181 F11
Pantdu Neath 57 C9
Panteg Ceredig 111 E9
Panteg Torf 78 F4
Pantersbridge Corn 6 B3
Pantgwyn Carms 93 F11
Pantgwyn Ceredig 92 B4
Pantmawr Cardiff 58 C6
Panton Lincs 189 F11
Pantperthog Gwyn 128 C4
Pantside Caerph 78 F2
Pantyffynnon Carms 75 C10
Pantygasseg Torf 78 F3
Pantymwyn Flint 165 C11
Panxworth Norf 161 G7
Papcastle Cumb 229 E8
Papermill Bank Shrops 149 D11
Papigoe Highld 310 D7
Papil Shetland 313 K5
Papley Northants 138 F2
Papley Orkney 314 G4
Papple E Loth 281 G11
Papplewick Notts 171 E8
Papworth Everard Cambs 122 E5
Papworth St Agnes Cambs 122 E5
Papworth Village Settlement Cambs 122 E5
Par Corn 5 E11
Paradise Glos 80 C5
Paradise Green Hereford 97 B10
Paramoor Corn 5 F9
Paramour Street Kent 71 G9
Parbold Lancs 194 E3
Parbrook Som 44 F5
Parbrook W Sus 35 B9
Parc Gwyn 147 C7
Parc Erissey Corn 4 G3
Parc-hendy Swansea 56 B4
Parc Mawr Caerph 77 G10
Parc-Seymour Newport 78 G6
Parc-y-rhôs Carms 93 B11
Parchey Som 43 F10
Parciau Anglesey 179 E7
Parcllyn Ceredig 110 G4
Pardown Hants 48 D5
Pardshaw Cumb 229 G7
Pardshaw Hall Cumb 229 F8
Parham Suff 126 E6
Park Corn 10 G6
Park Devon 14 B2
Park Dumfries 247 E10
Park Som 44 G3
Park Swindon 63 C7
Park Barn Sur 50 C3
Park Bottom Corn 4 G3
Park Bridge Gtr Man 196 G2
Park Broom Cumb 239 F10
Park Close Lancs 204 E3
Park Corner Bath 45 B9
Park Corner E Sus 23 C8
Park Corner E Sus 52 F4
Park Corner Oxon 65 B7
Park Corner Windsor 65 C11
Park End Beds 121 G9
Park End Cambs 123 E11
Park End M'bro 225 B10
Park End Northumb 241 B9
Park End Som 43 G7
Park End Staffs 168 E3
Park End Worcs 116 C5
Park Gate Dorset 30 F2
Park Gate Hants 33 F8
Park Gate Kent 55 D7
Park Gate Suff 124 F4
Park Gate W Yorks 197 E8
Park Gate Worcs 117 C8
Park Green Essex 105 F9
Park Hall Shrops 148 C6
Park Head Cumb 231 C7
Park Head Derbys 170 E5
Park Head W Yorks 197 F7
Park Hill Glos 79 F9
Park Hill Kent 54 G3
Park Hill Mers 194 G3
Park Hill N Yorks 214 F6
Park Hill Notts 171 E11
Park Hill S Yorks 186 D5
Park Lane Staffs 133 B7
Park Lane Wrex 149 B8
Park Langley London 67 F11

Plympton Plym 7 D10
Plymstock Plym 7 E10
Plymtree Devon 27 G9
Pobgreen Gtr Man 196 F4
Pochin Houses Caerph 77 E11
Pocket Nook Gtr Man 183 B10
Pockley N Yorks 216 B2
Pocklington E Yorks 208 D2
Pockthorpe Norf 141 D8
Pockthorpe Norf 158 D6
Pockthorpe Norf 159 E10
Pockthorpe Norf 159 F11
Pode Hole Lincs 156 E4
Podimore Som 29 C8
Podington Beds 121 E8
Podmoor Worcs 117 C7
Podmore Norf 159 G9
Podmore Staffs 150 B5
Podsmead Glos 80 B4
Poffley End Oxon 82 C5
Pogmoor S Yorks 197 F10
Point Corn 3 B8
Point Clear Essex 89 C9
Pointon Lincs 156 C2
Pokesdown Bmouth 19 C8
Pol a Charra W Isles 297 K3
Polbae Dumfries 236 B4
Polbain Highld 307 H4
Polbathic Corn 7 D7
Polbeth W Loth 269 C10
Polborder Corn 7 C7
Polbrock Corn 5 B10
Polchar Highld 291 C10
Pole Elm Worcs 98 B6
Pole Moor W Yorks 196 D5
Polebrook Northants 137 F11
Polegate E Sus 23 D9
Poles Highld 309 K7
Pole's Hole Wilts 45 C10
Polesden Lacey Sur 50 C6
Poleshill Som 27 C9
Polesworth Warks 134 C5
Polgear Corn 2 B5
Polgigga Corn 1 E3
Polglass Highld 307 J5
Polgooth Corn 5 E9
Poling W Sus 35 G8
Poling Corner W Sus 35 F8
Polkerris Corn 5 E11
Poll Hill Mers 182 E3
Polla Highld 308 D3
Polladras Corn 2 C4
Pollard Street Norf 160 C6
Pollhill Kent 53 C11
Pollie Highld 309 H7
Pollington E Yorks 198 D6
Polliwilline Argyll 255 G8
Polloch Highld 289 C9
Pollok Glasgow 267 C10
Pollokshields Glasgow 267 C11
Polmadie Glasgow 267 C11
Polmarth Corn 2 B6
Polmassick Corn 5 F9
Polmear Corn 5 E11
Polmont Falk 279 F8
Polmorla Corn 10 G5
Polnessan E Ayrs 257 G10
Polnish Highld 295 G9
Polopit Northants 121 B10
Polpenwith Corn 2 D6
Polpeor Corn 2 B2
Polperro Corn 6 E4
Polruan Corn 6 E2
Polsham Som 44 E4
Polsloe Devon 14 C4
Polstead Suff 107 D9
Polstead Heath Suff 107 C9
Poltalloch Argyll 275 D9
Poltesco Corn 2 F6
Poltimore Devon 14 B5
Polton Midloth 270 C5
Polwarth Borders 272 E4
Polwheveral Corn 2 D6
Polyphant Corn 11 E11
Polzeath Corn 10 F4
Pomeroy Derbys 169 B10
Pomphlett Plym 7 E10
Ponciau Wrex 166 F3
Pond Close Som 27 B10
Pond Park Bucks 85 E7
Pond Street Essex 105 D9
Ponde Powys 96 D2
Ponders End London 86 F5
Pondersbridge Cambs 138 E5
Pondtail Hants 49 C10
Pondwell I o W 21 C8
Poniou Corn 1 B4
Ponjeravah Corn 2 D6
Ponsanooth Corn 3 B7
Ponsford Devon 27 F8
Ponsonby Cumb 219 D11
Ponsongath Corn 3 F7
Ponsworthy Devon 13 G10
Pont Corn 6 E2
Pont Aber Carms 94 G4
Pont Aber-Geirw Gwyn 146 D5
Pont-ar-gothi Carms 93 G10
Pont ar Hydfer Powys 95 F7
Pont-ar-llechau Carms 94 G4
Pont Cyfyng Conwy 164 D2
Pont Cysyllte Wrex 166 G3
Pont Dolydd Prysor Gwyn 146 B4
Pont-faen Powys 95 E9
Pont-Faen Shrops 148 B5
Pont Fronwydd Gwyn 146 E6
Pont-gareg Pembs 92 C2
Pont-Henri Carms 75 D7
Pont Hwfa Anglesey 178 E2
Pont iets = Pontyates Carms 75 D7
Pont-Llogel Powys 147 F10
Pont-newydd Carms 74 D6
Pont-newydd Flint 165 B11
Pont Pen-y-benglog Gwyn 163 C10
Pont Rhyd-goch Conwy 163 C11
Pont-Rhyd-sarn Gwyn 147 D7
Pont Rhyd-y-berry Powys 95 D9
Pont Rhyd-y-cyff Bridgend 57 D11
Pont-rhyd-y-groes Ceredig 112 C4
Pont Rhydgaled Powys 128 G6
Pont-Rhythallt Gwyn 163 C8
Pont-rug Gwyn 163 C8
Pont Senni = Sennybridge Powys 95 F8
Pont Siôn Norton Rhondda 77 G9
Pont-siôn Ceredig 93 B8
Pont-Walby Neath 76 D5
Pont-y-blew Shrops 148 B6
Pont-y-gwaith Rhondda 77 G8
Pont-y-pant Conwy 164 E3
Pont y Pennant Gwyn 147 E8
Pont-y-rhyl Bridgend 58 B2
Pont-y-wal Powys 96 D2
Pont yr Afon-Gam Gwyn 164 G2
Pont-yr-hafod Pembs 91 F8
Pont-Ystrad Denb 165 C9
Pontamman Carms 75 C10
Pontantwn Carms 74 C6
Pontardawe Neath 76 E2
Pontarddulais Swansea 75 E9
Pontarfynach = Devils Bridge Ceredig 112 B4
Pontarsais Carms 93 F8
Pontblyddyn Flint 166 C3
Pontbren Araeth Carms 94 G3
Pontbren Llwyd Rhondda 76 D6
Pontcanna Cardiff 59 D7
Pontdolgoch Powys 129 E10
Pontefract W Yorks 198 C3
Ponteland Northumb 242 C5
Ponterwyd Ceredig 128 G4
Pontesbury Shrops 131 B7
Pontesbury Hill Shrops 131 B7
Pontesford Shrops 131 B8
Pontfadog Wrex 148 B4
Pontfaen Pembs 91 E10
Pontgarreg Ceredig 110 G6
Ponthen Shrops 148 F6
Ponthir Torf 78 G4
Ponthirwaun Ceredig 92 B5
Pontiago Pembs 91 D8
Pontithel Powys 96 D3
Pontllanfraith Caerph 77 F11
Pontlliw Swansea 75 E10
Pontllyfni Gwyn 162 E6
Pontlottyn Caerph 77 D10
Pontneddfechan Powys 76 D6
Pontnewydd Torf 78 F3
Pontnewynydd Torf 78 E3
Pontrhydfendigaid Ceredig 112 D4
Pontrhydyfen Neath 57 C9
Pontrhydyrun Torf 78 F3
Pontrilas Hereford 97 F7
Pontrobert Powys 148 G2
Ponts Green E Sus 23 B11
Pontshill Hereford 98 G2
Pontsticill M Tydf 77 C9
Pontwgan Conwy 180 G3
Pontyates = Pont-iets Carms 75 D7
Pontyberem Carms 75 C8
Pontyclun Rhondda 58 C4
Pontycymer Bridgend 76 G6
Pontyglasier Pembs 92 D2
Pontymister Caerph 78 G2
Pontymoel Torf 78 E3
Pontypool Torf 78 E3
Pontypridd Rhondda 58 B5
Pontywaun Caerph 78 G2
Pooksgreen Hants 32 E5
Pool Corn 4 G3
Pool W Yorks 205 D10
Pool Head Hereford 115 G11
Pool Hey Lancs 193 D11
Pool o' Muckhart Clack 286 G4
Pool Quay Powys 148 G5
Poolbrook Worcs 98 C5
Poole N Yorks 198 B3
Poole Poole 18 C6
Poole Som 27 C10
Poole Keynes Glos 81 F8
Poolend Staffs 169 D7
Poolestown Dorset 30 D2
Poolewe Highld 307 L3
Pooley Bridge Cumb 230 G5
Pooley Street Norf 141 G11
Poolfold Staffs 168 D5
Poolhead Shrops 149 C9
Poolhill Glos 98 F4
Poolmill Hereford 97 G11
Poolsbrook Derbys 186 G6
Poolside Moray 302 E4
Poolstock Gtr Man 194 G5
Pooltown Som 42 F3
Pootings Kent 52 D3
Pope Hill Pembs 72 C6
Pope's Hill Glos 79 C11
Popeswood Brack 65 F10
Popham Devon 41 G8
Popham Hants 48 E5
Poplar London 67 C11
Poplar Grove Lincs 190 B6
Poplars Herts 104 G5
Popley Hants 48 C6
Porchester Nottingham 171 G9
Porchfield I o W 20 C4
Porin Highld 300 D3
Poringland Norf 142 C5
Porkellis Corn 2 C5
Porlock Som 41 D11
Porlock Weir Som 41 D11
Porlockford Som 41 D11
Port Allen Perth 286 E6
Port Ann Argyll 275 E10
Port Appin Argyll 289 E11
Port Arthur Shetland 313 K5
Port Askaig Argyll 274 G5
Port Bannatyne Argyll 275 G11
Port Brae Fife 280 C5
Port Bridge Devon 9 D7
Port Carlisle Cumb 238 E6
Port Charlotte Argyll 254 B3
Port Clarence Stockton 234 G5
Port Dinorwic = Y Felinheli Gwyn 163 B8
Port Driseach Argyll 275 F10
Port Dundas Glasgow 267 B11
Port e Vullen I o M 192 C5
Port Edgar Edin 280 F2
Port Ellen Argyll 254 C4
Port Elphinstone Aberds 293 B9
Port Erin I o M 192 F2
Port Erroll Aberds 303 F10
Port-Eynon Swansea 56 D3
Port Gaverne Corn 10 E6
Port Glasgow Invclyd 276 G6
Port Henderson Highld 299 B7
Port Hill Oxon 65 B7
Port Isaac Corn 10 E5
Port Lamont Argyll 275 F11
Port Lion Pembs 73 D7
Port Logan Dumfries 236 E2
Port Mead Swansea 56 B6
Port Mholair W Isles 304 E7
Port Mor Highld 288 B6
Port Mulgrave N Yorks 226 B5
Port Nan Giùran W Isles 304 E7
Port nan Long W Isles 296 D4
Port Nis W Isles 304 B7
Port of Menteith Stirl 285 G9
Port Quin Corn 10 E5
Port Ramsay Argyll 289 E10
Port St Mary I o M 192 F3
Port Solent Ptsmth 33 F10
Port Sunlight Mers 182 E4
Port Sutton Bridge Lincs 157 E9
Port Talbot Neath 57 D9
Port Tennant Swansea 57 C7
Port Wemyss Argyll 254 B2
Port William Dumfries 236 E5
Portachoillan Argyll 255 B8
Portash Wilts 46 G3
Portavadie Argyll 275 G10
Portbury N Som 60 D4
Portchester Hants 33 F10
Portclair Highld 290 B6
Porteath Corn 10 F5
Portencalzie Dumfries 236 B2
Portencross N Ayrs 266 F3
Porterfield Renfs 267 B9
Porter's End Herts 85 B11
Portesham Dorset 17 D8
Portessie Moray 302 C4
Portfield Argyll 289 G9
Portfield Som 28 B6
Portfield W Sus 22 B5
Portfield Gate Pembs 72 B6
Portgate Devon 12 D4
Portgordon Moray 302 C3
Portgower Highld 311 H4
Porth Corn 4 C6
Porth Rhondda 77 G8
Porth Colmon Gwyn 144 C3
Porth Kea Corn 4 G6
Porth Navas Corn 3 D7
Porth Tywyn = Burry Port Carms 74 E6
Porth-y-felin Anglesey 178 E2
Porth-y-waen Shrops 148 E5
Porthallow Corn 3 E7
Porthallow Corn 6 E4
Porthcawl Bridgend 57 F10
Porthcothan Corn 10 G3
Porthcurno Corn 1 E3
Portheiddy Pembs 90 E6
Porthgain Pembs 90 E6
Porthgwarra Corn 1 E3
Porthhallow Corn 3 E7
Porthill Shrops 149 G9
Porthill Staffs 168 F5
Porthilly Corn 10 F4
Porthkerry V Glam 58 F5
Porthleven Corn 2 D4
Porthllechog = Bull Bay Anglesey 178 C6
Porthloo Scilly 1 G4
Porthmadog Gwyn 145 B11
Porthmeor Corn 1 B4
Porthoustock Corn 3 E8
Porthpean Corn 5 E10
Porthtowan Corn 4 F3
Porthyrhyd Carms 75 B8
Porthyrhyd Carms 94 D4
Portico Mers 183 C7
Portincaple Argyll 276 C4
Portington Devon 12 F4
Portington E Yorks 207 G11
Portinnisherrich Argyll 275 B10
Portinscale Cumb 229 G11
Portishead N Som 60 D3
Portkil Argyll 276 E5
Portknockie Moray 302 C4
Portland Som 44 F3
Portlethen Aberds 293 D11
Portlethen Village Aberds 293 D11
Portlevorchy Highld 306 D7
Portling Dumfries 237 D10
Portloe Corn 3 B10
Portlooe Corn 6 E4
Portmahomack Highld 311 L3
Portmeirion Gwyn 145 B11
Portmellon Corn 5 G10
Portmore Hants 20 B2
Portnacroish Argyll 289 E11
Portnahaven Argyll 254 B2
Portnalong Highld 294 B5
Portnaluchaig Highld 295 G8
Portnancon Highld 308 C4
Portnellan Stirl 285 E8
Portnellan Stirl 285 F8
Portobello Edin 280 G6
Portobello T & W 243 F7
Portobello W Mid 133 D9
Portobello W Yorks 197 D10
Porton Wilts 47 F7
Portpatrick Dumfries 236 D2
Portrack Stockton 225 B9
Portreath Corn 4 F3
Portree Highld 298 E4
Portscatho Corn 3 B9
Portsea Ptsmth 33 G10
Portsea Island Ptsmth 33 G11
Portskerra Highld 310 C2
Portskewett Mon 60 B4
Portslade Brighton 36 F3
Portslade-by-Sea Brighton 36 G3
Portslade Village Brighton 36 F3
Portsmouth Ptsmth 21 B9
Portsmouth W Yorks 196 B2
Portsonachan Argyll 284 E4
Portsoy Aberds 302 C5
Portswood Soton 32 E6
Porttanachy Moray 302 C3
Portuairk Highld 288 C6
Portvasgo Highld 308 C5
Portway Dorset 18 D2
Portway Glos 98 E5
Portway Hereford 97 B9
Portway Hereford 97 D9
Portway Som 28 B6
Portway Som 44 F3
Portway W Mid 133 F9
Portway Worcs 117 C11
Portwood Gtr Man 184 C6
Portwrinkle Corn 7 E7
Posenhall Shrops 132 C3
Poslingford Suff 106 B5
Posso Borders 260 C6
Post Green Dorset 18 C5
Post Mawr = Synod Inn Ceredig 111 G8
Postbridge Devon 13 F9
Postcombe Oxon 84 F2
Postling Kent 54 F6
Postlip Glos 99 F10
Postwick Norf 142 B5
Pot Common Sur 50 E2
Potarch Aberds 293 D8
Potash Suff 108 D2
Potbridge Hants 49 C8
Potholm Dumfries 249 F9
Potmaily Highld 300 F4
Potman's Heath Kent 38 B5
Potsgrove C Beds 103 F9
Pott Row Norf 158 E4
Pott Shrigley E Ches 184 F6
Potten End Herts 85 D8
Potten Street Kent 71 F9
Potter Brompton N Yorks 217 D9
Potter Heigham Norf 161 F8
Potter Hill Leics 154 E4
Potter Hill S Yorks 186 B4
Potter Somersal Derbys 152 B2
Potter Street Essex 87 D7
Pottergate Street Norf 142 E3
Potterhanworth Lincs 173 B9
Potterhanworth Booths Lincs 173 B9
Potterne Wilts 46 B3
Potterne Wick Wilts 46 B4
Potternewton W Yorks 206 F2
Potters Bar Herts 86 E3
Potters Brook Lancs 202 C5
Potters Corner Kent 54 E3
Potter's Cross Staffs 132 G6
Potters Crouch Herts 85 D10
Potter's Forstal Kent 53 D11
Potter's Green E Sus 37 C8
Potter's Green W Mid 135 G7
Potters Hill N Som 60 F4
Potters Marston Leics 135 D9
Pottersheath Herts 86 B2
Pottersbury Northants 102 C5
Potterton Aberds 293 B11
Potterton W Yorks 206 F4
Pottery Field W Yorks 206 G2
Potthorpe Norf 159 E8
Pottington Devon 40 G5
Potto N Yorks 225 E9
Potton C Beds 104 B4
Pouchen End Herts 85 D8
Poughill Corn 24 F2
Poughill Devon 26 F5
Poulner Hants 31 F11
Poulshot Wilts 46 B3
Poulton Glos 81 E10
Poulton Mers 182 C4
Poulton Mers 182 E4
Poulton W Ches 166 D5
Poulton-le-Fylde Lancs 202 F2
Pound Som 28 D6
Pound Bank Worcs 98 B5
Pound Bank Worcs 116 C4
Pound Green E Sus 37 C8
Pound Green Hants 48 B5
Pound Green I o W 20 D2
Pound Green Suff 124 G4
Pound Green Worcs 116 B5
Pound Hill W Sus 51 F9
Pound Street Hants 64 G3
Poundbury Dorset 17 C9
Poundffald Swansea 56 C5
Poundfield E Sus 52 G4
Poundford E Sus 37 C9
Poundgate E Sus 37 B7
Poundgreen Wokingham 65 F7
Poundland S Ayrs 244 F5
Poundon Bucks 102 F2
Poundsbridge Kent 52 E4
Poundsgate Devon 13 G10
Poundstock Corn 11 B10
Pounsley E Sus 37 C8
Pour Bridge Hants 68 F3
Povey Cross Sur 51 E9
Pow Green Hereford 98 C4
Powburn Northumb 264 F3
Powder Mills Kent 52 D5
Powderham Devon 14 E5
Powers Hall End Essex 88 B4
Powerstock Dorset 16 B6
Powfoot Dumfries 238 D4
Powhill Cumb 238 F6
Powick Worcs 116 G6
Powler's Piece Devon 24 D5
Powmill Perth 279 B10
Pownall Park E Ches 184 E4
Powntley Copse Hants 49 E8
Poxwell Dorset 17 E10
Poyle Slough 66 D4
Poynings W Sus 36 E3
Poyntington Dorset 29 D11
Poynton E Ches 184 E6
Poynton Telford 149 F11
Poynton Green Telford 149 F11
Poyntzfield Highld 301 C7
Poyston Pembs 73 B7
Poyston Cross Pembs 73 B7
Poystreet Green Suff 125 F9
Praa Sands Corn 2 D3
Pratling Street Kent 53 B8
Pratt's Bottom London 68 G3
Praze Corn 2 B3
Praze-an-Beeble Corn 2 B4
Predannack Wollas Corn 2 F5
Prees Shrops 149 C11
Prees Green Shrops 149 C11
Prees Heath Shrops 149 B11
Prees Higher Heath Shrops 149 B11
Prees Lower Heath Shrops 149 C11
Prees Wood Shrops 149 C11
Preesall Lancs 202 D3
Preesall Park Lancs 202 D3
Preesgweene Shrops 148 B5
Preeshenlle Shrops 148 C6
Pren-gwyn Ceredig 93 C8
Prenbrigog Flint 166 C3
Prendergast Pembs 73 B7
Prendergast Pembs 90 G6
Prendergust Borders 273 D8
Prendwick Northumb 264 G2
Prenteg Gwyn 163 G9
Prenton Mers 182 D4
Prescot Mers 183 C7
Prescott Devon 27 E9
Prescott Glos 99 F9
Prescott Shrops 132 G3
Prescott Shrops 149 E8
Presdales Herts 86 C5
Preshome Moray 302 C4
Press Derbys 170 B5
Pressen Northumb 263 B8
Prestatyn Denb 181 E9
Prestbury E Ches 184 F6
Prestbury Glos 99 G9
Presteigne Powys 114 E6
Prestholpe Shrops 131 D11
Prestleigh Som 44 E6
Prestolee Gtr Man 195 F9
Preston Borders 272 D5
Preston Brighton 36 F4
Preston Devon 14 G3
Preston Dorset 17 E10
Preston E Loth 281 F11
Preston E Loth 281 G7
Preston E Yorks 209 G9
Preston Glos 81 E8
Preston Glos 98 E3
Preston Herts 104 G3
Preston Kent 70 G4
Preston Kent 71 G8
Preston Lancs 194 B4
Preston London 67 B7
Preston Northumb 264 D5
Preston Rutland 137 C7
Preston Shrops 149 G10
Preston T & W 243 D8
Preston Torbay 9 C7
Preston Wilts 62 D4
Preston Wilts 63 E9
Preston Bagot Warks 118 D3
Preston Bissett Bucks 102 F3
Preston Bowyer Som 27 B10
Preston Brockhurst Shrops 149 E10
Preston Brook Halton 183 E9
Preston Candover Hants 48 E6
Preston Capes Northants 119 G11
Preston Crowmarsh Oxon 83 G10
Preston Deanery Northants 120 F5
Preston Fields Warks 118 D3
Preston Grange T & W 243 C8
Preston Green Warks 118 D3
Preston Gubbals Shrops 149 F9
Preston-le-Skerne Durham 234 G2
Preston Marsh Hereford 97 B11
Preston Montford Shrops 149 G8
Preston on Stour Warks 118 G4
Preston-on-Tees Stockton 225 B8
Preston on the Hill Halton 183 E9
Preston on Wye Hereford 97 C7
Preston Pastures Worcs 100 B3
Preston Plucknett Som 29 D8
Preston St Mary Suff 125 G8
Preston-under-Scar N Yorks 223 G11
Preston upon the Weald Moors Telford 150 F3
Preston Wynne Hereford 97 B11
Prestonfield Edin 280 G5
Prestonmill Dumfries 237 D11
Prestonpans E Loth 281 G7
Prestwich Gtr Man 195 G10
Prestwick Northumb 242 C5
Prestwick S Ayrs 257 D9
Prestwold Leics 153 E11
Prestwood Bucks 84 E5
Prestwood Staffs 133 F7
Prestwood Staffs 169 G10
Prey Heath Sur 50 B3
Price Town Bridgend 76 G6
Prickwillow Cambs 139 G11
Priddy Som 44 C4
Pride Park Derbys 153 B7
Priest Down Bath 60 G6
Priest Hutton Lancs 211 E10
Priest Weston Shrops 130 D5
Priestacott Devon 24 F6
Priestcliffe Derbys 185 G10
Priestcliffe Ditch Derbys 185 G10
Priestfield W Mid 133 D8
Priestfield Worcs 98 C6
Priesthaugh Borders 249 C11
Priesthill Glasgow 267 C10
Priesthorpe W Yorks 205 F10
Priestley Green W Yorks 196 B6
Prieston Borders 262 D2
Priestside Dumfries 238 D4
Priestthorpe W Yorks 205 F8
Priestwood Brack 65 F11
Priestwood Kent 69 G7
Priestwood Green Kent 69 G7
Primethorpe Leics 135 E10
Primrose T & W 243 E8
Primrose Corner Norf 160 G6
Primrose Green Norf 159 F11
Primrose Hill Bath 61 F8
Primrose Hill Lancs 193 F11
Primrose Hill London 67 C9
Primrose Hill W Mid 133 F8
Primrose Valley N Yorks 218 D2
Primrosehill Herts 85 E9
Primsland Worcs 117 E8
Prince Hill E Ches 168 G2
Prince Royd W Yorks 196 D6
Princes End W Mid 133 E9
Princes Gate Pembs 73 C10
Prince's Marsh Hants 34 B3
Princes Park Mers 182 D5
Princes Risborough Bucks 84 E4
Princethorpe Warks 119 C8
Princetown Caerph 77 C10
Princetown Devon 13 G7
Prinsted W Sus 22 B3
Printstile Kent 52 E5
Prion Denb 165 C9
Prior Muir Fife 287 F9
Prior Park Northumb 273 E9
Prior Rigg Cumb 239 D11
Priors Frome Hereford 97 D11
Priors Halton Shrops 115 B9
Priors Hardwick Warks 119 F9
Priors Marston Warks 119 F9
Prior's Norton Glos 99 G7
Priors Park Glos 99 E7
Priorslee Telford 150 G4
Priorswood Som 28 B2
Priory Pembs 72 D6
Priory Green Suff 107 C8
Priory Heath Suff 108 C3
Priory Wood Hereford 96 B5
Prisk V Glam 58 D4
Pristacott Devon 25 B8
Priston Bath 61 G7
Pristow Green Norf 142 F2
Prittlewell Sthend 69 B11
Privett Hants 21 B7
Privett Hants 33 B11
Prixford Devon 40 F4
Probus Corn 5 F7
Proncy Highld 309 K7
Prospect Cumb 229 C8
Prospect Village Staffs 151 G10
Prospidnick Corn 2 C4
Provanmill Glasgow 268 B2
Prowse Devon 26 F4
Prudhoe Northumb 242 E3
Prussia Cove Corn 2 D3
Ptarmigan Lodge Stirl 285 G7
Pubil Perth 285 C8
Publow Bath 60 G6
Puckeridge Herts 105 G7
Puckington Som 28 D5
Pucklechurch S Glos 61 D7
Pucknall Hants 32 B5
Puckrup Glos 99 D7
Puckshole Glos 80 D4
Puddaven Devon 8 C5
Pudding Pie Nook Lancs 202 F6
Puddinglake W Ches 168 B2
Puddington Devon 26 E4
Puddington W Ches 182 G4
Puddle Corn 5 D11
Puddlebridge Som 28 E4
Puddledock Kent 52 C3
Puddledock Kent 68 E4
Puddledock Norf 141 E11
Puddletown Dorset 17 C11
Puddleigh Som 28 E4
Pudleston Hereford 115 F11
Pudsey W Yorks 196 B2
Pudsey W Yorks 205 G10
Pulborough W Sus 35 D8
Pulcree Dumfries 237 D7
Pule Hill W Yorks 196 B5
Puleston Telford 150 E4
Pulford W Ches 166 D5
Pulham Dorset 30 F2
Pulham Market Norf 142 F3
Pulham St Mary Norf 142 F4
Pullens Green S Glos 79 G10
Pulley Shrops 131 B9
Pullington Kent 53 G10
Pulloxhill C Beds 103 E11
Pulverbatch Shrops 131 C8
Pumpherston W Loth 269 B11
Pumsaint Carms 94 C3
Puncheston = Cas-Mael Pembs 91 F10
Puncknowle Dorset 16 D6
Punnett's Town E Sus 37 C10
Purbrook Hants 33 F11
Purewell Dorset 19 C9
Purfleet Thurrock 68 D5
Puriton Som 43 E10
Purleigh Essex 88 E4
Purley London 67 G10
Purley on Thames W Berks 65 D7
Purlogue Shrops 114 B5
Purlpit Wilts 61 F11
Purls Bridge Cambs 139 F9
Purn N Som 43 B10
Purse Caundle Dorset 29 D11
Purslow Shrops 131 G7
Purston Jaglin W Yorks 198 D2
Purtington Som 28 F5
Purton Glos 79 E11
Purton W Berks 64 D3
Purton Wilts 62 B5
Purton Common Wilts 62 B5
Purton Stoke Wilts 81 G9
Purwell Herts 104 F4
Pury End Northants 102 B4
Pusey Oxon 82 F5
Putley Hereford 98 D2
Putley Common Hereford 98 D2
Putley Green Hereford 98 D3
Putloe Glos 80 D3
Putney London 67 D8
Putney Heath London 67 E8
Putney Vale London 67 E8
Putnoe Beds 121 G11
Putsborough Devon 40 E3
Putson Hereford 97 D10
Puttenham Herts 84 C5
Puttenham Sur 50 D2
Puttock End Essex 106 C6
Puttock's End Essex 87 B9
Putton Dorset 17 E9
Puxey Dorset 30 E3
Puxley Northants 102 C5
Puxton N Som 60 G2
Pwll Carms 75 E7
Pwll Powys 130 C3
Pwll-clai Flint 181 G11
Pwll-glas Denb 165 E10
Pwll-Mawr Cardiff 59 D8
Pwll-melyn Flint 181 G11
Pwll-trap Carms 74 B3
Pwll-y-glaw Neath 57 C9
Pwllcrochan Pembs 72 E6
Pwllgloyw Powys 95 E10
Pwllheli Gwyn 145 B7
Pwllmeyric Mon 79 G8
Pwllypant Caerph 59 B7
Pye Bridge Derbys 170 E6
Pye Corner Devon 14 B4
Pye Corner Kent 53 D11
Pye Corner Newport 59 B9
Pye Corner S Glos 60 D6
Pye Green Staffs 151 G9
Pye Hill Notts 170 E6
Pyecombe W Sus 36 E3
Pyewipe NE Lincs 201 E9
Pyle I o W 20 F5
Pyle Swansea 56 D5
Pyle = Y Pîl Bridgend 57 E10
Pyle Hill Sur 50 B3
Pylehill Hants 33 D7
Pyleigh Som 42 G6
Pylle Som 44 F6
Pymore or Pymoor Cambs 139 F9
Pype Hayes W Mid 134 E2
Pyrford Sur 50 B4
Pyrford Green Sur 50 B4
Pyrford Village Sur 50 B4
Pyrland Som 28 B2
Pyrton Oxon 83 F11
Pytchley Northants 121 C7
Pyworthy Devon 24 G4

Q

Quabbs Shrops 130 G4
Quabrook E Sus 52 G2
Quadring Lincs 156 C4
Quadring Eaudike Lincs 156 C4
Quags Corner W Sus 34 C5
Quainton Bucks 84 B2
Quaker's Yard M Tydf 77 F9
Quaking Houses Durham 242 G5
Quality Corner Cumb 219 B9
Quarhouse Glos 80 E5
Quarley Hants 47 E9
Quarmby W Yorks 196 D6
Quarndon Derbys 170 G4
Quarndon Common Derbys 170 G4
Quarr Hill I o W 21 C7
Quarrelton Renfs 267 C8
Quarrendon Bucks 84 B4
Quarriers Village Invclyd 267 B7
Quarrington Lincs 173 G9
Quarrington Hill Durham 234 D2
Quarry Bank W Mid 133 F8
Quarry Heath Staffs 151 G8
Quarry Hill Staffs 134 C4
Quarrybank W Ches 167 B8
Quarryford E Loth 271 B11
Quarryhead Aberds 303 C9
Quarryhill Highld 309 L7
Quarrywood Moray 301 C11
Quarter S Lnrk 268 E4
Quartley Devon 27 B7
Quatford Shrops 132 E4
Quatquoy Orkney 314 E3
Quatt Shrops 132 F5
Quebec Durham 233 C9
Quebec W Sus 34 C3
Quedgeley Glos 80 C4
Queen Adelaide Cambs 139 G11
Queen Camel Som 29 C9
Queen Charlton Bath 60 F6
Queen Dart Devon 26 D4
Queen Oak Dorset 45 G9
Queen Street Kent 53 D7
Queen Street Wilts 62 B4
Queenborough Kent 70 E2
Queenhill Worcs 99 D7
Queen's Bower I o W 21 E7
Queen's Corner W Sus 34 B5
Queen's Head Shrops 148 D6
Queen's Park Beds 103 B10
Queen's Park Blkburn 195 B7
Queen's Park Essex 87 F11
Queen's Park Northants 120 E5
Queen's Park W Ches 166 B6
Queensbury London 67 B7
Queensbury W Yorks 205 G8
Queensferry Edin 280 F2
Queensferry Flint 166 B4
Queenslie Glasgow 268 B3
Queenstown Blkpool 202 F2
Queensville Staffs 151 E8
Queenzieburn N Lnrk 278 F3
Quemerford Wilts 62 F4
Quendale Shetland 313 M5
Quendon Essex 105 E10
Queniborough Leics 154 G2
Quenington Glos 81 E10
Quernmore Lancs 202 B6
Queslett W Mid 133 E11
Quethiock Corn 6 C6
Quhamm Shetland 312 G6
Quholm Orkney 314 E2
Quick Gtr Man 196 G3
Quick Edge Gtr Man 196 G3
Quicks Green W Berks 64 D5
Quidenham Norf 141 F10
Quidhampton Hants 48 C4
Quidhampton Wilts 46 G6
Quilquox Aberds 303 F9
Quina Brook Shrops 149 C10
Quinbury End Northants 120 G2
Quindry Orkney 314 G4
Quinton Northants 120 G5
Quinton W Mid 133 G9
Quintrell Downs Corn 5 C7
Quixhill Staffs 169 G10
Quoditch Devon 12 B4
Quoig Perth 286 E2
Quoisley E Ches 167 F8
Quoit Corn 5 C8
Quorndon or Quorn Leics 153 F11
Quothquan S Lnrk 259 B11
Quoyloo Orkney 314 D2
Quoynee Highld 310 D6
Quoyness Orkney 314 F2
Quoys Shetland 312 B8
Quoys Shetland 313 G6

R

Raasay Ho Highld 295 B7
Rabbit's Cross Kent 53 D9
Rableyheath Herts 86 B2
Raby Cumb 238 G5
Raby Mers 182 F4
Racecourse Suff 108 C3
Racedown Hants 47 E9
Rachan Mill Borders 260 C4
Rachub Gwyn 163 B10
Rack End Oxon 82 E6
Rackenford Devon 26 D5
Rackham W Sus 35 E9
Rackheath Norf 160 G5
Rackley Som 43 C11
Racks Dumfries 238 C2
Rackwick Orkney 314 B4
Rackwick Orkney 314 G2
Radbourne Derbys 152 B5
Radcliffe Gtr Man 195 F9
Radcliffe Northumb 253 C7
Radcliffe on Trent Notts 154 B2
Radclive Bucks 102 E3
Radcot Oxon 82 F3
Raddery Highld 301 D7
Raddington Som 27 B8
Raddon Devon 26 G6
Radernie Fife 287 G8
Radfall Kent 70 G6
Radford Bath 45 B7
Radford Nottingham 171 G9
Radford Oxon 101 G8
Radford W Mid 134 G6
Radford Worcs 117 F10
Radford Semele Warks 118 E6
Radfordbridge Oxon 101 G8
Radipole Dorset 17 E9
Radlet Som 43 F8
Radlett Herts 85 F11
Radley Oxon 83 F8
Radley Green Essex 87 D10
Radley Park Oxon 83 F8
Radlith Shrops 131 B8
Radmanthwaite Notts 171 C8
Radmoor Shrops 150 E2
Radmore Green E Ches 167 D9
Radmore Wood Staffs 151 D11
Radnage Bucks 84 F3
Radnor Corn 4 G4
Radnor Park W Dunb 277 G9
Radstock Bath 45 C7
Radstone Northants 101 C11
Radway Warks 101 B7
Radway Green E Ches 168 E3
Radwell Beds 121 F10
Radwell Herts 104 D4
Radwinter Essex 106 D2
Radwinter End Essex 106 D2
Radyr Cardiff 58 C6
Raehills Dumfries 248 E3
Raera Argyll 289 G10
Rafborough Hants 49 B11
Rafford Moray 301 D10
Raga Shetland 312 D6
Ragdale Leics 154 F3
Ragdon Shrops 131 E9
Raggalds W Yorks 205 G7
Ragged Appleshaw Hants 47 D10
Ragginis Corn 1 D5
Raglan Mon 78 D6
Ragmere Norf 141 E11
Ragnal Wilts 63 E10
Ragnall Notts 188 G4
Rahane Argyll 276 D4
Rahoy Highld 289 D8
Raigbeg Highld 301 G8
Rails S Yorks 186 D3
Rain Shore Gtr Man 195 D11
Rainbow Hill Worcs 117 F7
Rainford Mers 194 G3
Rainford Junction Mers 194 G3
Rainham London 68 C4
Rainham Medway 69 F10
Rainhill Mers 183 C7
Rainhill Stoops Mers 183 C8
Rainow E Ches 185 F7
Rainowlow E Ches 185 F7
Rainsough Gtr Man 195 G10
Rainton Dumfries 237 D8
Rainton N Yorks 215 D7
Rainton Bridge T & W 234 B2
Rainton Gate Durham 234 B2
Rainworth Notts 171 D9
Raisbeck Cumb 222 D2
Raise Cumb 231 B10
Rait Perth 286 E6
Raithby Lincs 190 E4
Raithby by Spilsby Lincs 174 B5
Rake W Sus 34 B4
Rake Common Hants 34 B3
Rake End Staffs 151 F11
Rake Head Lancs 195 C10
Rakes Dale Staffs 169 G9
Rakeway Staffs 169 G8
Rakewood Gtr Man 196 E2
Raleigh Devon 40 G5
Ralia Lodge Highld 291 D9
Rallt Swansea 56 C4
Ram Carms 93 B11
Ram Alley Wilts 63 G8
Ram Hill S Glos 61 D7
Ram Lane Kent 54 D3
Ramasaig Highld 297 G7
Rame Corn 2 C6
Rame Corn 7 F8
Rameldry Mill Bank Fife 287 G7
Ramnageo Shetland 312 C8
Rampisham Dorset 29 G9
Rampside Cumb 210 F4
Rampton Cambs 123 D8
Rampton Notts 188 F3
Ramsbottom Gtr Man 195 D9
Ramsburn Moray 302 D5
Ramsbury Wilts 63 E9
Ramscraigs Highld 311 G5
Ramsdean Hants 34 C2
Ramsdell Hants 48 B5
Ramsden London 68 F3
Ramsden Oxon 82 B5
Ramsden Worcs 99 B8
Ramsden Bellhouse Essex 88 G2
Ramsden Heath Essex 88 F2
Ramsden Wood W Yorks 196 C2
Ramsey Cambs 138 F5
Ramsey Essex 108 E4
Ramsey I o M 192 C5
Ramsey Forty Foot Cambs 138 F6
Ramsey Heights Cambs 138 F5
Ramsey Island Essex 89 D7
Ramsey Mereside Cambs 138 F5
Ramsey St Mary's Cambs 138 F5
Ramseycleuch Borders 261 G7
Ramsgate Kent 71 G11
Ramsgill N Yorks 214 E2
Ramshaw Durham 232 B5
Ramshaw Durham 233 F8
Ramsholt Suff 108 C6
Ramshorn Staffs 169 F9
Ramsley Devon 13 C8
Ramslye Kent 52 F5
Ramsnest Common Sur 50 G2
Ranais W Isles 304 F6
Ranby Lincs 190 F2
Ranby Notts 187 E11
Rand Lincs 189 F10
Randwick Glos 80 D4
Ranfurly Renfs 267 C7
Rangag Highld 310 E5
Rangemore Staffs 152 E3
Rangeworthy S Glos 61 B7
Rankinston E Ayrs 257 G11
Rank's Green Essex 88 B3
Ranmoor S Yorks 186 D4
Ranmore Common Sur 50 C6
Rannerdale Cumb 220 B3
Rannoch Lodge Perth 285 B9
Rannoch Station Perth 285 B8
Ranochan Highld 295 G10
Ranskill Notts 187 D11
Ranton Staffs 151 E7
Ranton Green Staffs 150 E6
Ranworth Norf 161 G7
Rapkyns W Sus 50 G6
Raploch Stirl 278 C5
Rapness Orkney 314 B5
Rapps Som 28 D4
Rascal Moor E Yorks 208 F2
Rascarrel Dumfries 237 E9
Rashielee Renfs 277 G9
Rashiereive Aberds 303 G9
Rashwood Worcs 117 D8
Raskelf N Yorks 215 E9
Rassal Highld 299 E8
Rassau Bl Gwent 77 C11
Rastrick W Yorks 196 C6
Ratagan Highld 295 D11
Ratby Leics 135 B10
Ratcliff London 67 C11
Ratcliffe Culey Leics 134 D6
Ratcliffe on Soar Leics 153 D9
Ratcliffe on the Wreake Leics 154 G2
Ratford Wilts 62 E3
Ratfyn Wilts 47 E7
Rathen Aberds 303 C10
Rathillet Fife 287 E7
Rathmell N Yorks 204 B2
Ratho Edin 280 G2
Ratho Station Edin 280 G2
Rathven Moray 302 C4
Ratlake Hants 32 C6
Ratley Warks 101 B7
Ratling Kent 55 C8
Ratlinghope Shrops 131 D8
Ratsloe Devon 14 B5
Rattar Highld 310 B6
Ratten Row Cumb 230 B3
Ratten Row Cumb 230 C2
Ratten Row Lancs 202 E4
Ratten Row Norf 157 G10
Rattery Devon 8 C4
Rattlesden Suff 125 F9
Rattray Perth 286 C5
Raughton Cumb 230 B3
Raughton Head Cumb 230 B3
Raunds Northants 121 C9
Ravelston Edin 280 G4
Ravenfield S Yorks 187 B7
Ravenglass Cumb 219 F11
Ravenhead Mers 183 C8
Ravenhills Green Worcs 116 G4
Raveningham Norf 143 D7
Raven's Green Essex 108 G2
Ravenscar N Yorks 227 E9
Ravenscliffe Stoke 168 E4
Ravenscliffe W Yorks 205 F9
Ravenscraig Invclyd 276 F5
Ravensdale I o M 192 C4
Ravensden Beds 121 G11
Ravenseat N Yorks 223 E7
Ravenshall Staffs 168 F3
Ravenshead Notts 171 E9
Ravensmoor E Ches 167 E10
Ravensthorpe Northants 120 C3
Ravensthorpe P'boro 138 C3
Ravensthorpe W Yorks 197 C8
Ravenstone Leics 153 G8
Ravenstone M Keynes 120 G6
Ravenstonedale Cumb 222 E4
Ravenstown Cumb 211 D7
Ravenstruther S Lnrk 269 F8
Ravenswood Village Settlement Wokingham 65 G10
Ravensworth N Yorks 224 D2
Raw N Yorks 227 D8
Raw Green S Yorks 197 F9

Rawcliffe E Yorks 199 C7
Rawcliffe York 207 C7
Rawcliffe Bridge E Yorks 199 C7
Rawdon W Yorks 205 F10
Rawdon Carrs W Yorks 205 F10
Rawfolds W Yorks 197 C7
Rawgreen Northumb 241 F10
Rawmarsh S Yorks 186 B6
Rawnsley Staffs 151 G10
Rawreth Essex 88 G3
Rawreth Shot Essex 88 G3
Rawridge Devon 28 F2
Rawson Green Derbys 170 F5
Rawtenstall Lancs 195 C10
Rawthorpe W Yorks 197 D7
Rawyards N Lnrk 268 B5
Raxton Aberds 303 F8
Raydon Suff 107 D11
Raygill N Yorks 204 D4
Raylees Northumb 251 E10
Rayleigh Essex 88 G4
Rayne Essex 106 G4
Rayners Lane London 66 B6
Raynes Park London 67 F8
Reabrook Shrops 131 C7
Reach Cambs 123 D11
Read Lancs 203 G11
Reader's Corner Essex 88 E2
Reading Reading 65 E8
Reading Street Kent 54 G2
Reading Street Kent 71 F11
Readings Glos 79 B10
Ready Token Glos 81 E10
Readymoney Corn 6 E2
Reagill Cumb 222 B2
Rearquhar Highld 309 K7
Rearsby Leics 154 G3
Reasby Lincs 189 F9
Rease Heath E Ches 167 E10
Reaster Highld 310 C6
Reaulay Highld 299 D7
Reawick Shetland 313 J5
Reawla Corn 2 B4
Reay Highld 310 C3
Rechullin Highld 299 D8
Reculver Kent 71 F8
Red Ball Devon 27 D9
Red Bridge Lancs 211 D9
Red Bull E Ches 168 D4
Red Bull Staffs 150 B4
Red Dial Cumb 229 B11
Red Hill Bmouth 19 B7
Red Hill Hants 34 E2
Red Hill Hereford 97 D10
Red Hill Kent 53 C7
Red Hill Leics 135 D10
Red Hill Pembs 72 B6
Red Hill W Yorks 198 B2
Red Hill Warks 118 F2
Red Hill Worcs 117 G7
Red House Common E Sus 36 C5
Red Lake Telford 150 G3
Red Lodge Suff 124 C3
Red Lumb Gtr Man 195 D10
Red Pits Norf 159 D11
Red Post Corn 24 F3
Red Rail Hereford 97 F10
Red Rice Hants 47 E10
Red Rock Gtr Man 194 F5
Red Roses Carms 74 C2
Red Row Northumb 253 D7
Red Scar Lancs 203 G7
Red Street Staffs 168 E4
Red Wharf Bay Anglesey 179 E8
Redberth Pembs 73 E9
Redbourn Herts 85 C10
Redbournbury Herts 85 C10
Redbourne N Lincs 189 B7
Redbourne N Lincs 200 G3
Redbridge Dorset 17 D11
Redbridge London 68 B2
Redbridge Soton 32 E5
Redbrook Mon 79 C8
Redbrook Wrex 167 G8
Redburn Highld 300 C5
Redburn Highld 301 E9
Redburn Northumb 241 E7
Redcar Redcar 235 G8
Redcastle Angus 287 B10
Redcastle Highld 300 E5
Redcliff Bay N Som 60 D2
Redcroft Dumfries 237 B9
Redcross Worcs 117 C7
Reddicap Heath W Mid 134 D2
Redding Falk 279 F8
Reddingmuirhead Falk 279 F8
Reddish Gtr Man 184 C5
Reddish Warr 183 D11
Redditch Worcs 117 D10
Rede Suff 124 F6
Redenhall Norf 142 G5
Redenham Hants 47 D10
Redesdale Camp Northumb 251 D8
Redesmouth Northumb 251 G9
Redford Aberds 293 F9
Redford Angus 287 C9
Redford Dorset 29 F10
Redford Durham 233 E7
Redford W Sus 34 B5
Redfordgreen Borders 261 F9
Redgorton Perth 286 E4
Redgrave Suff 125 B10
Redheugh Angus 292 G6
Redhill Aberds 293 C9
Redhill Aberds 302 F6
Redhill Herts 104 E6
Redhill N Som 60 G4
Redhill Notts 171 F9
Redhill Shrops 131 B9
Redhill Shrops 150 G4
Redhill Staffs 150 D6
Redhill Sur 51 C9
Redhill Telford 150 G4
Redhills Cumb 230 F6
Redhills Devon 14 C4
Redhouse Argyll 275 G9
Redhouses Argyll 274 G4
Redisham Suff 143 G8
Redland Bristol 60 D5
Redland Orkney 314 D3
Redland End Bucks 84 E4
Redlands Dorset 17 E9
Redlands Som 44 G3
Redlands Swindon 81 G11
Redlane Som 28 E2
Redlingfield Suff 126 C3
Redlynch Som 45 G8
Redlynch Wilts 32 C2
Redmain Cumb 229 E8
Redmarley D'Abitot Glos 98 E5
Redmarshall Stockton 234 G3
Redmile Leics 154 B5
Redmire N Yorks 223 G10
Redmonsford Devon 24 D4
Redmoor Corn 5 C11
Redmoss Aberds 303 F8
Rednal Shrops 149 D7
Rednal W Mid 117 B10
Redpath Borders 262 B3
Redpoint Highld 299 C7
Redruth Corn 4 G3
Redscarhead Borders 270 G4
Redstocks Wilts 62 G2
Redtye Corn 5 C10
Redvales Gtr Man 195 F10
Redwick Newport 60 C2
Redwick S Glos 60 B4
Redwith Shrops 148 E6
Redworth Darl 233 G10
Reed Herts 105 D7
Reed End Herts 104 D6
Reed Point Lincs 174 E2
Reedham Lincs 174 D2
Reedham Norf 143 C8
Reedley Lancs 204 F2
Reedness E Yorks 199 C9
Reeds Beck Lincs 174 B2
Reeds Holme Lancs 195 C10
Reedsford Northumb 263 C9
Reedy Devon 14 D2
Reen Manor Corn 4 E5
Reepham Lincs 189 G8
Reepham Norf 159 E11
Reeth N Yorks 223 F10
Reeves Green W Mid 118 B5
Refail Powys 130 C3
Regaby I o M 192 C5
Regil Bath 60 G4
Regoul Highld 301 D8
Reiff Highld 307 H4
Reigate Sur 51 C9
Reigate Heath Sur 51 C8
Reighton N Yorks 218 D2
Reighton Gap N Yorks 218 D2
Reinigeadal W Isles 305 H4
Reisque Aberds 293 B10
Reiss Highld 310 D7
Rejerrah Corn 4 D5
Releath Corn 2 C5
Relubbus Corn 2 C3
Relugas Moray 301 E9
Remenham Wokingham 65 C9
Remenham Hill Wokingham 65 C9
Remony Perth 285 C11
Rempstone Notts 153 E11
Remusaig Highld 309 J7
Rendcomb Glos 81 D8
Rendham Suff 126 E6
Rendlesham Suff 126 G6
Renfrew Renfs 267 B10
Renhold Beds 121 G11
Renishaw Derbys 186 F6
Renmure Angus 287 B10
Rennington Northumb 264 F6
Renshaw Wood Shrops 132 B6
Renton W Dunb 277 F7
Renwick Cumb 231 C7
Repps Norf 161 F8
Repton Derbys 152 D6
Reraig Highld 295 C10
Reraig Cot Highld 295 B10
Rerwick Shetland 313 M5
Rescassa Corn 5 G9
Rescobie Angus 287 B9
Rescorla Corn 5 D10
Resipole Highld 289 C9
Reskadinnick Corn 4 G2
Resolfen = Resolven Neath 76 E4
Resolis Highld 300 C6
Resolven = Resolfen Neath 76 E4
Restalrig Edin 280 G5
Reston Borders 273 C7
Reston Cumb 221 F9
Restronguet Passage Corn 3 B8
Restrop Wilts 62 B5
Resugga Green Corn 5 D10
Reswallie Angus 287 B9
Retallack Corn 5 B8
Retew Corn 5 D8
Retford Notts 188 E2
Retire Corn 5 C10
Rettendon Essex 88 F3
Rettendon Place Essex 88 F3
Revesby Lincs 174 C3
Revesby Bridge Lincs 174 C4
Revidge Blkburn 195 B7
Rew Devon 9 G9
Rew Devon 13 G11
Rew Devon 29 F11
Rew Street I o W 20 C5
Rewe Devon 14 B4
Rexon Devon 12 D4
Rexon Cross Devon 12 D4
Reybridge Wilts 62 F2
Reydon Suff 127 B9
Reydon Smear Suff 127 B9
Reymerston Norf 141 B10
Reynalton Pembs 73 D9
Reynoldston Swansea 56 C3
Rezare Corn 12 F3
Rhadyr Mon 78 E5
Rhaeadr Gwy = Rhayader Powys 113 D9
Rhandir Conwy 180 G4
Rhandirmwyn Carms 94 C5
Rhayader = Rhaeadr Gwy Powys 113 D9
Rhedyn Gwyn 144 C5
Rhegreanoch Highld 307 H5
Rhemore Highld 289 D7
Rhencullen I o M 192 C4
Rhenetra Highld 298 D4
Rhes-y-cae Flint 181 G11
Rhewl Denb 165 C10
Rhewl Denb 165 F11
Rhewl Shrops 148 C6
Rhewl Wrex 149 B7
Rhewl-fawr Flint 181 E10
Rhewl-Mostyn Flint 181 E11
Rhian Highld 309 H5
Rhicarn Highld 307 G5
Rhiconich Highld 306 D7
Rhicullen Highld 300 B6
Rhidorroch Ho Highld 307 K6
Rhiews Shrops 150 B2
Rhifail Highld 308 E7
Rhigolter Highld 308 D3
Rhigos Rhondda 76 D6
Rhilochan Highld 309 J7
Rhippinllwyd Ceredig 92 C5
Rhippinllwyd Ceredig 110 G6
Rhiroy Highld 307 L6
Rhitongue Highld 308 D6
Rhivichie Highld 306 D7
Rhiw Gwyn 144 D4
Rhiwabon = Ruabon Wrex 166 G4
Rhiwbebyll Denb 165 B10
Rhiwbina Cardiff 59 C7
Rhiwbryfdir Gwyn 163 F11
Rhiwceiliog Bridgend 58 C3
Rhiwderin Newport 59 B9
Rhiwen Gwyn 163 C9
Rhiwfawr Neath 76 C2
Rhiwinder Rhondda 58 B4
Rhiwlas Gwyn 147 B8
Rhiwlas Gwyn 163 B9
Rhiwlas Powys 148 C3
Rhode Som 43 G9
Rhode Common Kent 54 B5
Rhodes Gtr Man 195 F11
Rhodes Minnis Kent 55 E7
Rhodesia Notts 187 F9
Rhodiad Pembs 90 F5
Rhonadale Argyll 255 D8
Rhondda Rhondda 77 F7
Rhonehouse or Kelton Hill Dumfries 237 D9
Rhoose V Glam 58 F5
Rhos Carms 93 D7
Rhôs Neath 76 E2
Rhôs Denb 165 C10
Rhos Powys 148 F5
Rhos Common Powys 148 F5
Rhos-ddû Gwyn 144 B5
Rhos-fawr Gwyn 145 B7
Rhos-goch Powys 96 B3
Rhos Haminiog Ceredig 111 E10
Rhos-hill Pembs 92 C3
Rhos Isaf Gwyn 163 D7
Rhos Lligwy Anglesey 179 D7
Rhôs-on-Sea Conwy 180 E4
Rhos-y-brithdir Powys 148 E2
Rhos-y-garth Ceredig 112 C2
Rhos-y-gwaliau Gwyn 147 C8
Rhos-y-llan Gwyn 144 B4
Rhos-y-Madoc Wrex 166 G4
Rhos-y-meirch Powys 114 D5
Rhosaman Carms 76 C2
Rhosbeirio Anglesey 178 C5
Rhoscefnhir Anglesey 179 F8
Rhoscolyn Anglesey 178 F3
Rhoscrowther Pembs 72 E6
Rhosddu Wrex 166 E4
Rhosdylluan Gwyn 147 D7
Rhosesmor Flint 166 B2
Rhosfach Pembs 92 F2
Rhosgadfan Gwyn 163 D8
Rhosgoch Anglesey 178 D6
Rhosgoch Powys 96 B3
Rhosgyll Gwyn 163 G7
Rhoshirwaun Gwyn 144 D3
Rhoslan Gwyn 163 G7
Rhoslefain Gwyn 110 B2
Rhosllanerchrugog Wrex 166 F3
Rhosmaen Carms 94 G2
Rhosmeirch Anglesey 179 F7
Rhosneigr Anglesey 178 G4
Rhosnesni Wrex 166 E5
Rhosrobin Wrex 166 E4
Rhossili Swansea 56 D2
Rhosson Pembs 90 F4
Rhostrehwfa Anglesey 178 G6
Rhostryfan Gwyn 163 D7
Rhostyllen Wrex 166 F4
Rhoswiel Shrops 148 B5
Rhosybol Anglesey 178 D6
Rhosycaerau Pembs 91 D8
Rhosygadair Newydd Ceredig 92 B4
Rhosygadfa Shrops 148 C6
Rhosygilwen Pembs 92 C4
Rhosymedre Wrex 166 G3
Rhosyn-coch Carms 92 G5
Rhu Argyll 275 G9
Rhu Argyll 276 E5
Rhualit Denb 181 F9
Rhubodach Argyll 275 F11
Rhuddall Heath W Ches 167 C9
Rhuddlan Ceredig 93 C9
Rhuddlan Denb 181 F8
Rhue Highld 307 K5
Rhulen Powys 96 B2
Rhunahaorine Argyll 255 C8
Rhyd Ceredig 92 C5
Rhyd Gwyn 163 G10
Rhyd Powys 129 C9
Rhyd-Ddu Gwyn 163 E9
Rhyd-Rosser Ceredig 111 D11
Rhyd-uchaf Gwyn 147 B8
Rhyd-y-Brown Pembs 91 G11
Rhyd-y-clafdy Gwyn 144 B6
Rhyd-y-cwm Shrops 130 G3
Rhyd-y-foel Conwy 180 F6
Rhyd-y-fro Neath 76 D2
Rhyd-y-gwin Swansea 75 E11
Rhyd-y-gwystl Gwyn 145 B8
Rhyd-y-meirch Mon 78 D4
Rhyd-y-meudwy Denb 165 E10
Rhyd-y-pandy Swansea 75 E11
Rhyd-y-sarn Gwyn 163 G11
Rhyd-yr-onen Gwyn 128 C2
Rhydaman = Ammanford Carms 75 C10
Rhydargaeau Carms 93 F8
Rhydcymerau Carms 93 D11
Rhydd Worcs 98 B6
Rhydd Green Worcs 98 B6
Rhydding Neath 57 B8
Rhydfudr Ceredig 111 D11
Rhydgaled Conwy 165 C7
Rhydgaled = Chancery Ceredig 111 B11
Rhydlewis Ceredig 92 B6
Rhydlios Gwyn 144 C3
Rhydlydan Conwy 164 E5
Rhydlydan Powys 129 E11
Rhydmoelddu Powys 113 B11
Rhydness Powys 96 C2
Rhydowen Carms 92 F3
Rhydowen Ceredig 93 B8
Rhydspence Hereford 96 B4
Rhydtalog Flint 166 D2
Rhydwen Gwyn 146 F4
Rhydwyn Anglesey 178 D4
Rhydycroesau Powys 148 C4
Rhydyfelin Carms 92 D5
Rhydyfelin Ceredig 111 B11
Rhydyfelin Powys 129 E11
Rhydyfelin Rhondda 58 B5
Rhydygele Pembs 91 G7
Rhydymain Gwyn 146 E6
Rhydymwyn Flint 166 B2
Rhydywrach Carms 73 B11
Rhyl Denb 181 E8
Rhymney Caerph 77 D10
Rhyn Wrex 148 B6
Rhynd Fife 287 E8
Rhynd Perth 286 E5
Rhynie Aberds 302 G4
Rhynie Highld 301 B8
Ribbesford Worcs 116 C5
Ribble Head N Yorks 212 D5
Ribblehead N Yorks 212 D5
Ribbleton Lancs 203 G7
Ribby Lancs 202 G4
Ribchester Lancs 203 F8
Riber Derbys 170 D4
Ribigill Highld 308 D5
Riby Lincs 201 F7
Riby Cross Roads Lincs 201 F7
Riccall N Yorks 207 F8
Riccarton E Ayrs 257 B10
Richards Castle Hereford 115 D9
Richborough Port Kent 71 G10
Richings Park Bucks 66 D4
Richmond London 67 E7
Richmond N Yorks 224 E3
Richmond S Yorks 186 D6
Richmond Hill W Yorks 206 G2
Richmond's Green Essex 106 F2
Rich's Holford Som 42 G6
Rickard's Down Devon 24 B6
Rickarton Aberds 293 E10
Rickerby Cumb 239 F10
Rickerscote Staffs 151 E8
Rickford N Som 44 B3
Rickinghall Suff 125 B10
Rickleton T & W 243 G7
Rickling Essex 105 E9
Rickling Green Essex 105 F10
Rickmansworth Herts 85 G9
Rickney E Sus 23 D10
Riddell Borders 262 E2
Riddings Derbys 170 E6
Riddlecombe Devon 25 E10
Riddlesden W Yorks 205 E7
Riddrie Glasgow 268 B2
Ridgacre W Mid 133 G10
Ridge Bath 44 B5
Ridge Dorset 18 D4
Ridge Hants 32 D4
Ridge Herts 86 E2
Ridge Lancs 211 G9
Ridge Som 28 F3
Ridge Wilts 46 G3
Ridge Common Hants 34 C2
Ridge Green Sur 51 D10
Ridge Hill Gtr Man 185 B7
Ridge Lane Warks 134 E5
Ridge Row Kent 55 E8
Ridgebourne Powys 113 E11
Ridgehill N Som 60 G4
Ridgemarsh Herts 85 G8
Ridgeway Bristol 60 D6
Ridgeway Derbys 170 E5
Ridgeway Derbys 186 E6
Ridgeway Kent 54 E5
Ridgeway Newport 59 B9
Ridgeway Pembs 73 D10
Ridgeway Som 45 D8
Ridgeway Staffs 168 E5
Ridgeway Cross Hereford 98 B4
Ridgeway Moor Derbys 186 E6
Ridgewell Essex 106 C4
Ridgewood E Sus 23 B7
Ridgmont C Beds 103 D9
Ridgway Shrops 131 F7
Ridgway Sur 50 B4
Riding Gate Som 30 B2
Riding Mill Northumb 242 E2
Ridley Kent 68 G6
Ridley Northumb 241 E7
Ridley Stokoe Northumb 250 F6
Ridleywood Wrex 166 E6
Ridlington Norf 160 C6
Ridlington Rutland 136 C6
Ridlington Street Norf 160 C6
Ridsdale Northumb 251 G10
Riechip Perth 286 C4
Riemore Perth 286 C4
Rienachait Highld 306 F5
Rievaulx N Yorks 215 B11
Rift Orkney 314 E4
Riffin Aberds 303 E7
Rifle Green Torf 78 D3
Rift House Hrtlpl 234 E5
Rigg Dumfries 239 D7
Riggend N Lnrk 278 G5
Rigsby Lincs 190 F6
Rigside S Lnrk 259 B9
Riley Green Lancs 194 B6
Rileyhill Staffs 152 F2
Rilla Mill Corn 11 G11
Rillaton Corn 11 G11
Rillington N Yorks 217 E7
Rimac Lincs 191 C7
Rimington Lancs 204 D2
Rimpton Som 29 C10
Rimswell E Yorks 201 B10
Rimswell Valley E Yorks 201 B10
Rinaston Pembs 91 F9
Rindleford Shrops 132 D4
Ring o' Bells Lancs 194 E3
Ringasta Shetland 313 M5
Ringford Dumfries 237 D8
Ringing Hill Leics 153 F9
Ringinglow S Yorks 186 E3
Ringland Newport 59 B11
Ringland Norf 160 G2
Ringles Cross E Sus 37 C7
Ringlestone Kent 53 B11
Ringlestone Kent 53 B9
Ringley Gtr Man 195 F9
Ringmer E Sus 36 E6
Ringmore Devon 8 F3
Ringorm Moray 302 E2
Ring's End Cambs 139 C7
Ringsfield Suff 143 F8
Ringsfield Corner Suff 143 F8
Ringshall Herts 85 C7
Ringshall Suff 125 G10
Ringshall Stocks Suff 125 G10
Ringstead Norf 176 E2
Ringstead Northants 121 B9
Ringtail Green Essex 87 B11
Ringwood Hants 31 F11
Ringwould Kent 55 D11
Rinmore Aberds 292 B6
Rinnigill Orkney 314 G3
Rinsey Corn 2 D3
Rinsey Croft Corn 2 D4
Riof W Isles 304 E3
Ripe E Sus 23 C8
Ripley Derbys 170 E5
Ripley Hants 19 B9
Ripley N Yorks 214 G5
Ripley Sur 50 B5
Riplingham E Yorks 208 G5
Ripon N Yorks 214 E6
Ripper's Cross Kent 54 E3
Rippingale Lincs 155 D11
Ripple Kent 55 D10
Ripple Worcs 99 D7
Ripponden W Yorks 196 D4
Rireavach Highld 307 K5
Risabus Argyll 254 C4
Risbury Hereford 115 G10
Risby E Yorks 208 G6
Risby Lincs 189 C10
Risby Suff 124 D5
Risca Caerph 78 G2
Rise E Yorks 209 E9
Rise Carr Darl 224 B5
Rise End Derbys 170 D3
Rise Park London 87 G8
Rise Park Nottingham 171 F9
Riseden E Sus 52 G6
Riseden Kent 53 F8
Risegate Lincs 156 D4
Riseholme Lincs 189 F7
Risehow Cumb 228 E6
Riseley Beds 121 E10
Riseley Wokingham 65 G8
Rishangles Suff 126 D3
Rishton Lancs 203 G10
Rishworth W Yorks 196 D4
Rising Bridge Lancs 195 B9
Rising Sun Corn 12 G3
Risingbrook Staffs 151 E8
Risinghurst Oxon 83 D9
Risley Derbys 153 B9
Risley Warr 183 C10
Risplith N Yorks 214 F4
Rispond Highld 308 C4
Rivar Wilts 63 G10
Rivenhall Essex 88 B4
Rivenhall End Essex 88 B4
River Kent 55 E9
River W Sus 34 C6
River Bank Cambs 123 D10
Riverhead Kent 52 B4
Rivers' Corner Dorset 30 E3
Riverside Cardiff 59 D7
Riverside Plym 7 D8
Riverside Stirl 278 C6
Riverside Worcs 117 D10
Riverside Docklands Lancs 194 B4
Riverton Devon 40 G6
Riverview Park Kent 69 E7
Rivington Lancs 194 E6
Rixon Dorset 30 E3
Rixton Warr 183 C11
Roa Island Cumb 210 G4
Roach Bridge Lancs 194 B5
Roaches Gtr Man 196 G3
Roachill Devon 26 C4
Road Green Norf 142 E5
Road Weedon Northants 120 F2
Roade Northants 120 G5
Roadhead Cumb 240 C2
Roadmeetings S Lnrk 269 F7
Roadside Highld 310 C5
Roadside of Catterline Aberds 293 F10
Roadside of Kinneff Aberds 293 F10
Roadwater Som 42 F4
Roag Highld 298 E2
Roast Green Essex 105 E9
Roath Cardiff 59 D7
Roath Park Cardiff 59 D7
Rob Roy's House Argyll 284 F5
Roberton Borders 261 G10
Roberton S Lnrk 259 D10
Robertsbridge E Sus 38 C2
Robertstown Moray 302 E2
Robertstown Rhondda 77 E8
Roberttown W Yorks 197 C7
Robeston Back Pembs 73 B9
Robeston Cross Pembs 72 D5
Robeston Wathen Pembs 73 B9
Robeston West Pembs 72 D5
Robhurst Kent 54 G2
Robin Hill Staffs 168 D6
Robin Hood Derbys 186 G3
Robin Hood Lancs 194 E4
Robin Hood W Yorks 197 B10
Robin Hood's Bay N Yorks 227 D9
Robinhood End Essex 106 D4
Robins W Sus 34 B4
Robinson's End Warks 134 E6
Roborough Devon 7 C10
Roborough Devon 25 D9
Robroyston Glasgow 268 B2
Roby Mers 182 C6
Roby Mill Lancs 194 F4
Rocester Staffs 152 B2
Roch Pembs 91 G7
Roch Gate Pembs 91 G7
Rochdale Gtr Man 195 E11
Roche Corn 5 C9
Roche Grange Staffs 169 C7
Rochester Medway 69 F8
Rochester Northumb 251 D8
Rochford Essex 88 G5
Rochford Worcs 116 D2
Rock Caerph 77 F11
Rock Corn 10 F4
Rock Devon 28 G3
Rock Neath 57 C9
Rock Northumb 264 E6
Rock Som 28 C4
Rock W Sus 35 E10
Rock Worcs 116 C4
Rock End Staffs 168 D5
Rock Ferry Mers 182 D4
Rockbeare Devon 14 C6
Rockbourne Hants 31 D10
Rockcliffe Cumb 239 E9
Rockcliffe Dumfries 237 D10
Rockcliffe Flint 182 G3
Rockcliffe Lancs 195 C11
Rockcliffe Cross Cumb 239 E8
Rockfield Highld 311 L3
Rockfield Mon 79 C7
Rockford Devon 41 D9
Rockford Hants 31 F11
Rockgreen Shrops 115 B10
Rockhampton S Glos 79 G11
Rockhead Corn 11 E7
Rockhill Shrops 114 B5
Rockingham Northants 137 E7
Rockland All Saints Norf 141 D9
Rockland St Mary Norf 142 C6
Rockland St Peter Norf 141 D9
Rockley Notts 188 G2
Rockley Wilts 63 E7
Rockley Ford Som 45 C8
Rockness Glos 80 F4
Rockrobin E Sus 52 G6
Rocks Park E Sus 37 C7
Rocksavage Halton 183 E8
Rockstowes Glos 80 F3
Rockville Argyll 276 C4
Rockwell End Bucks 65 B9
Rockwell Green Som 27 C10
Rocky Hill Scilly 1 G4
Rodbaston Staffs 151 G8
Rodborough Glos 80 E4
Rodbourne Swindon 62 C6
Rodbourne Wilts 62 C2
Rodbourne Bottom Wilts 62 C2
Rodbourne Cheney Swindon 62 B6
Rodbridge Corner Essex 107 C7
Rodd Hereford 114 E6
Rodd Hurst Hereford 114 E6
Roddam Northumb 264 E2
Rodden Dorset 17 E8
Roddymoor Durham 233 D9
Rode Som 45 C10
Rode Heath E Ches 168 D3
Rode Hill Som 45 C10
Rodeheath E Ches 168 B5
Roden Telford 149 F11
Rodford S Glos 61 C7
Rodgrove Som 30 C2
Rodhuish Som 42 F4
Rodington Telford 149 G11
Rodington Heath Telford 149 G11
Rodley Glos 80 C2
Rodley W Yorks 205 F10
Rodmarton Glos 80 F6
Rodmell E Sus 36 F6
Rodmer Clough W Yorks 196 B3
Rodmersham Kent 70 G2
Rodmersham Green Kent 70 G2
Rodney Stoke Som 44 C3
Rodsley Derbys 170 G2
Rodway Som 43 F9
Rodway Telford 150 F3
Rodwell Dorset 17 F9
Roe Cross Gtr Man 185 B7
Roe End Herts 85 B8
Roe Green Gtr Man 195 G9
Roe Green Herts 86 D2
Roe Green Herts 104 E6
Roe Lee Blkburn 203 G9
Roebuck Low Gtr Man 196 F3
Roecliffe N Yorks 215 F7
Roedean Brighton 36 G4
Roehampton London 67 E8
Roesound Shetland 312 G5
Roestock Herts 86 D2
Roffey W Sus 51 G7
Rogart Highld 309 J7
Rogart Station Highld 309 J7
Rogate W Sus 34 C4
Roger Ground Cumb 221 F7
Rogerstone Newport 59 B9
Rogerton S Lnrk 268 D2
Roghadal W Isles 296 C6
Rogiet Mon 60 B3
Rogue's Alley Cambs 139 B7
Roke Oxon 83 G10
Rokemarsh Oxon 83 G10
Roker T & W 243 F10
Rollesby Norf 161 F8
Rolleston Leics 136 C4
Rolleston Notts 172 E2
Rolleston-on-Dove Staffs 152 D4
Rollestone S Yorks 186 E5
Rollestone Wilts 46 E5
Rollestone Camp Wilts 46 E5
Rolls Mill Dorset 30 E3
Rolston E Yorks 209 D10
Rolstone N Som 59 G11
Rolvenden Kent 53 G10
Rolvenden Layne Kent 53 G11
Romaldkirk Durham 232 G5
Roman Hill Suff 143 E10
Romanby N Yorks 225 G7
Romannobridge Borders 270 F3
Romansleigh Devon 26 C2
Rome Angus 293 G7
Romesdal Highld 298 D4
Romford Dorset 31 F9
Romford Kent 52 E6
Romford London 68 B4
Romiley Gtr Man 184 C6
Romney Street Kent 68 G4
Rompa Shetland 313 L6
Romsey Hants 32 C5
Romsey Town Cambs 123 F9
Romsley Shrops 132 G5
Romsley Worcs 117 B9
Romsley Hill Worcs 117 B9
Ronachan Ho Argyll 255 B8
Ronague I o M 192 E3
Rondlay Telford 132 B4
Ronkswood Worcs 117 G7
Rood End W Mid 133 F10
Rook End Essex 105 E11
Rook Street Wilts 45 G10
Rookby Cumb 222 C6
Rookhope Durham 232 C4
Rooking Cumb 221 B8
Rookley I o W 20 E6
Rookley Green I o W 20 E6
Rooks Bridge Som 43 C11
Rooks Hill Kent 52 C5
Rook's Nest Som 42 G5
Rooksey Green Suff 125 G8
Rooksmoor Glos 80 E4
Rookwith N Yorks 214 B4
Rookwood W Sus 21 B11
Roos E Yorks 209 G11
Roose Cumb 210 F4
Roosebeck Cumb 210 F5
Roosecote Cumb 210 F4
Roost End Essex 106 C4
Rootham's Green Beds 122 F2
Rooting Street Kent 54 D3
Rootpark S Lnrk 269 E9
Ropley Hants 48 G6
Ropley Dean Hants 48 G6
Ropley Soke Hants 49 G7
Ropsley Lincs 155 C9
Rora Aberds 303 D10
Rorandle Aberds 293 B8
Rorrington Shrops 130 C5
Rosarie Moray 302 E3
Roscroggan Corn 4 G3
Rose Corn 4 E5
Rose-an-Grouse Corn 2 B2
Rose Ash Devon 26 C3
Rose Green Essex 107 F8
Rose Green Suff 107 C9
Rose Green Suff 107 D8
Rose Green W Sus 22 D6
Rose Grove Lancs 204 G2
Rose Hill Bucks 66 C2
Rose Hill Derbys 153 B7
Rose Hill E Sus 23 B7
Rose Hill Gtr Man 195 F8
Rose Hill Lancs 204 G2
Rose Hill Oxon 83 E8
Rose Hill Suff 108 C3
Rose Hill Sur 51 D7
Rose Valley Pembs 73 E8
Roseacre Kent 53 B9
Roseacre Lancs 202 F4
Rosebank E Dunb 278 G3
Rosebank S Lnrk 268 F6
Rosebery Midloth 270 D6
Rosebrae Moray 301 C11
Rosebrough Northumb 264 D4
Rosebush Pembs 91 F11
Rosecare Corn 11 B9
Rosedale Herts 86 E4
Rosedale Abbey N Yorks 226 F4
Roseden Northumb 264 E2
Rosedinnick Corn 5 B8
Rosedown Devon 24 C3
Rosefield Highld 301 D8
Rosehall Highld 309 J4
Rosehall N Lnrk 268 C4
Rosehaugh Mains Highld 300 D6
Rosehearty Aberds 303 C9
Rosehill Blkburn 195 C8
Rosehill Corn 4 E5
Rosehill Corn 5 C10
Rosehill Gtr Man 184 D3
Rosehill London 67 F9
Rosehill Pembs 72 B5
Rosehill Shrops 150 C3
Rosehill T & W 243 D8
Roseisle Moray 301 C11
Roseland Corn 6 C5
Roselands E Sus 23 E10
Rosemarket Pembs 73 D7
Rosemarkie Highld 301 D7
Rosemary Lane Devon 27 E11
Rosemelling Corn 5 D10
Rosemergy Corn 1 B4
Rosemount Perth 286 C5
Rosenannon Corn 5 B9
Rosenithon Corn 3 E8
Roser's Cross E Sus 37 C9
Rosevean Corn 5 D10
Rosevear Corn 2 E5
Roseville W Mid 133 E8
Rosevine Corn 3 B9
Rosewarne Corn 2 B4
Rosewarne Corn 4 G2
Rosewell Midloth 270 C5
Roseworth Stockton 234 G4
Roseworthy Corn 2 B4
Roseworthy Corn 4 F5
Roseworthy Barton Corn 2 B4
Rosgill Cumb 221 B10
Rosherville Kent 68 E6
Roshven Highld 289 B9
Roskear Croft Corn 4 G3
Roskhill Highld 298 E2
Roskill House Highld 300 D6
Roskorwell Corn 3 E7
Rosley Cumb 230 B2
Roslin Midloth 270 C5
Rosliston Derbys 152 F4
Rosneath Argyll 276 E5
Ross Borders 273 C9
Ross Dumfries 237 E8
Ross Northumb 264 B4
Ross Perth 285 E11
Ross Green Worcs 116 E5
Ross-on-Wye Hereford 98 G2
Rossett Wrex 166 D5
Rossett Green N Yorks 206 C2
Rossie Ochill Perth 286 F4
Rossie Priory Perth 286 D6
Rossington S Yorks 187 B10
Rosskeen Highld 300 C6
Rossland Renfs 277 G8
Rossmore Poole 19 C7
Roster Highld 310 F6
Rostherne E Ches 184 E2
Rostholme S Yorks 198 F5
Rosthwaite Cumb 220 C5
Rosthwaite Cumb 220 G4
Roston Derbys 169 G10
Rosudgeon Corn 2 D3
Rosyth Fife 280 E2
Rotchfords Essex 107 E8
Rotcombe Bath 44 B6
Rothbury Northumb 252 C3
Rotherbridge W Sus 35 C7
Rotherby Leics 154 F3
Rotherfield E Sus 37 B9
Rotherfield Greys Oxon 65 C8
Rotherfield Peppard Oxon 65 C8
Rotherham S Yorks 186 C6
Rotherhithe London 67 D11
Rothersthorpe Northants 120 F4
Rotherwas Hereford 97 D10
Rotherwick Hants 49 B8
Rothes Moray 302 E2
Rothesay Argyll 275 G11
Rothiebrisbane Aberds 303 F7
Rothiemay Crossroads Moray 302 E5
Rothiemurchus Lodge Highld 291 C11
Rothienorman Aberds 303 F7
Rothiesholm Orkney 314 D6
Rothley Leics 153 G11
Rothley Northumb 252 F2
Rothley Plain Leics 153 G11
Rothley Shield East Northumb 252 E2
Rothmaise Aberds 302 F6
Rothwell Lincs 189 B11
Rothwell Northants 136 G6
Rothwell W Yorks 197 B10
Rothwell Haigh W Yorks 197 B10
Rotsea E Yorks 209 C7
Rottal Angus 292 G5
Rotten End Essex 106 F4
Rotten End Suff 127 D7
Rotten Green Hants 49 B9
Rotten Row W Berks 64 E5
Rotten Row W Mid 118 B3
Rottingdean Brighton 36 G5
Rottington Cumb 219 C9
Rotton Park W Mid 133 F10
Roud I o W 20 E6
Rough Bank Gtr Man 196 E2
Rough Close Staffs 151 B8
Rough Common Kent 54 B6
Rough Haugh Highld 308 E7
Rough Hay Staffs 152 E4
Roughan Norf 158 E6
Rougham Suff 125 E8
Rougham Green Suff 125 E8
Roughbirchworth S Yorks 197 G9
Roughburn Highld 290 E5
Roughcote Staffs 168 G6
Roughlee Lancs 204 E2
Roughley W Mid 134 D2
Roughmoor Som 28 B2
Roughmoor Swindon 62 B6
Roughrigg N Lnrk 278 G6
Roughsike Cumb 240 B2
Roughton Lincs 174 C2
Roughton Norf 160 B4
Roughton Shrops 132 E5
Roughton Moor Lincs 174 C2
Roughway Kent 52 C6
Round Bush Herts 85 F10
Round Green Luton 103 G11
Round Maple Suff 107 C9
Round Oak Shrops 131 G7
Round Oak W Mid 133 F8
Round Spinney Northants 120 D5
Round Street Kent 69 F7
Roundbush Essex 88 E5
Roundbush Green Essex 87 C9
Roundham Som 28 F6
Roundhay W Yorks 206 F2
Round's Green W Mid 133 F9
Roundshaw London 67 G10
Roundstonefoot Dumfries 248 B4
Roundstreet Common W Sus 35 B9
Roundswell Devon 40 G4
Roundthorn Gtr Man 184 D4
Roundthwaite Cumb 222 E2
Roundway Wilts 62 G4
Roundyhill Angus 287 B7
Rous Lench Worcs 117 G10
Rousdon Devon 15 C11
Rousham Oxon 101 G9
Routenburn N Ayrs 266 C3
Routh E Yorks 209 E7
Rout's Green Bucks 84 F3
Row Corn 11 F7
Row Cumb 211 B8
Row Cumb 231 E8
Row Ash Hants 33 E8
Row Brow Cumb 229 D7
Row Green Essex 106 G4
Row Heath Essex 89 B10
Row-of-trees E Ches 184 F4
Row Town Sur 66 G4
Rowanburn Dumfries 239 B10
Rowanfield Glos 99 G8
Rowardennan Stirl 277 B7
Rowarth Derbys 185 D8
Rowbarton Som 28 B2
Rowberrow Som 44 B3
Rowde Wilts 62 G3
Rowden Devon 13 B8
Rowden N Yorks 205 B11
Rowe Head Cumb 210 D5
Rowen Conwy 180 G3
Rowfoot Northumb 240 E5
Rowford Som 28 B2
Rowhedge Essex 107 G10
Rowhill Sur 66 G4
Rowhook W Sus 50 G6
Rowington Warks 118 D4
Rowington Green Warks 118 D4
Rowland Derbys 186 G2
Rowlands Castle Hants 34 E2
Rowlands Gill T & W 242 F5
Rowland's Green Hereford 98 D3
Rowledge Sur 49 E10
Rowlestone Hereford 97 F7
Rowley E Yorks 208 G5
Rowley Shrops 130 B6
Rowley Green London 86 F2
Rowley Hill W Yorks 197 E7
Rowley Park Staffs 151 E8
Rowley Regis W Mid 133 F9
Rowley's Green W Mid 134 G6
Rowling Kent 55 C9
Rowly Sur 50 E4
Rownall Staffs 169 F7
Rowner Hants 33 G9
Rowney Green Worcs 117 C10
Rownhams Hants 32 D5
Rowrah Cumb 219 B11
Rowsham Bucks 84 B4
Rowsley Derbys 170 B3
Rowstock Oxon 64 B3
Rowston Lincs 173 D9
Rowthorne Derbys 171 C7
Rowton Shrops 149 G7
Rowton Telford 150 F2
Rowton W Ches 166 C6
Rowton Moor W Ches 166 C6
Roxburgh Borders 262 C5
Roxburgh Mains Borders 262 D5
Roxby N Lincs 200 D2
Roxby N Yorks 226 B5
Roxeth London 66 B6
Roxton Beds 122 G3
Roxwell Essex 87 D10
Royal British Legion Village Kent 53 B8
Royal Leamington Spa Warks 118 D6
Royal Oak Darl 233 G10
Royal Oak Lancs 194 G2
Royal Oak N Yorks 218 D2
Royal Tunbridge Wells = Tunbridge Wells Kent 52 F5
Royal's Green E Ches 167 G10
Roybridge Highld 290 E4
Royd S Yorks 197 G8
Royd Moor S Yorks 197 G8
Royd Moor W Yorks 198 E2
Roydhouse W Yorks 197 E8
Roydon Essex 86 D6
Roydon Norf 141 G11
Roydon Norf 158 E4
Roydon Hamlet Essex 86 D6
Royds Green W Yorks 197 B11
Royston Glasgow 268 B2
Royston Herts 105 C7
Royston S Yorks 197 E11
Royston Water Som 28 E2
Royton Gtr Man 196 F2
Ruabon = Rhiwabon Wrex 166 G4
Ruaig Argyll 288 E2
Ruan High Lanes Corn 3 B10
Ruan Lanihorne Corn 5 G7
Ruan Major Corn 2 F6
Ruan Minor Corn 2 F6
Ruarach Highld 295 C11
Ruardean Glos 79 B10
Ruardean Hill Glos 79 B10
Ruardean Woodside Glos 79 B10
Rubery Worcs 117 B9
Rubha Ghaisinis W Isles 297 G4
Rubha Stoer Highld 306 F5
Ruchazie Glasgow 268 B3
Ruchill Glasgow 267 B11
Ruckcroft Cumb 230 C6
Ruckhall Hereford 97 D9
Ruckinge Kent 54 G4
Ruckland Lincs 190 F4
Rucklers Lane Herts 85 E9
Ruckley Shrops 131 C10
Rudbaxton Pembs 91 G9
Rudby N Yorks 225 D9
Ruddington Notts 153 C11
Ruddle Glos 79 C11
Rudford Glos 98 G5
Rudge Shrops 132 D6
Rudge Som 45 C10
Rudge Heath Shrops 132 D5
Rudgeway S Glos 60 B6
Rudgwick W Sus 50 G5
Rudhall Hereford 98 F2
Rudheath W Ches 183 G11
Rudheath Woods W Ches 184 G2
Rudhja Garbh Argyll 289 E11
Rudley Green Essex 88 E4
Rudloe Wilts 61 E10
Rudry Caerph 59 B7
Rudston E Yorks 217 F11
Rudyard Staffs 169 D7
Ruewood Shrops 149 D9
Rufford Lancs 194 D3
Rufforth York 206 C6
Ruffs Notts 171 F8
Rugby Warks 119 B10
Rugeley Staffs 151 F10
Ruggin Som 27 D11
Ruglen S Ayrs 245 C7
Rugley Northumb 264 G5
Ruilick Highld 300 E5
Ruishton Som 28 C3
Ruisigearraidh W Isles 296 C5
Ruislip London 66 B5
Ruislip Common London 66 B5
Ruislip Gardens London 66 B5
Ruislip Manor London 66 B6
Ruiton W Mid 133 E8
Ruloe W Ches 183 G9
Rumach Highld 295 G8

Rumbling Bridge Perth 279 B10
Rumbow Cottages Worcs 117 B8
Rumburgh Suff 142 G6
Rumbush W Mid 118 B2
Rumer Hill Staffs 133 B9
Rumford Corn 10 G3
Rumford Falk 279 F8
Rumney Cardiff 59 D8
Rumsam Devon 40 G5
Rumwell Som 27 C11
Runcorn Halton 183 E8
Runcton W Sus 22 C5
Runcton Holme Norf 140 B2
Rundlestone Devon 13 G7
Runfold Sur 49 D11
Runhall Norf 141 B11
Runham Norf 143 B10
Runham Norf 161 G9
Runham Vauxhall Norf 143 B10
Running Hill Head Gtr Man 196 F4
Running Waters Durham 234 C2
Runnington Som 27 C10
Runsell Green Essex 88 D3
Runshaw Moor Lancs 194 D4
Runswick Bay N Yorks 226 B6
Runwell Essex 88 G2
Ruscombe Glos 80 D4
Ruscombe Wokingham 65 D9
Ruscote Oxon 101 C8
Rush Green Essex 89 B11
Rush Green Herts 86 C5
Rush Green Herts 104 G4
Rush Green London 68 B4
Rush Green Norf 141 B11
Rush-head Aberds 303 E8
Rush Hill Bath 61 G8
Rushall Hereford 98 E2
Rushall Norf 142 G3
Rushall W Mid 133 C10
Rushall Wilts 46 B6
Rushbrooke Suff 125 E7
Rushbury Shrops 131 E10
Rushcombe Bottom Poole 18 B5
Rushden Herts 104 E6
Rushden Northants 121 D9
Rushenden Kent 70 E2
Rusher's Cross E Sus 37 B10
Rushey Mead Leicester 136 B2
Rushford Devon 12 F4
Rushford Norf 141 G8
Rushgreen Warr 183 D11
Rushington Hants 32 E5
Rushlake Green E Sus 23 B10
Rushland Cross Cumb 210 B6
Rushley Green Essex 106 D5
Rushmere C Beds 103 F8
Rushmere Suff 143 F9
Rushmere St Andrew Suff 108 B4
Rushmere Street Suff 108 B4
Rushmoor Sur 49 E11
Rushmoor Telford 150 G2
Rushmore Hants 33 E11
Rushmore Hill London 68 G3
Rushock Hereford 114 F6
Rushock Worcs 117 C7
Rusholme Gtr Man 184 B5
Rushton Dorset 18 D3
Rushton N Yorks 217 C9
Rushton Northants 136 G6
Rushton Shrops 132 B2
Rushton W Ches 167 C9
Rushton Spencer Staffs 168 C6
Rushwick Worcs 116 G6
Rushy Green E Sus 23 C7
Rushyford Durham 233 F11
Ruskie Stirl 285 G10
Ruskington Lincs 173 E9
Rusland Cumb 210 B6
Rusling End Herts 104 G4
Rusper W Sus 51 F8
Ruspidge Glos 79 C11
Russ Hill Sur 51 E8
Russel Highld 299 E8
Russell Hill London 67 G10
Russell's Green E Sus 38 E2
Russell's Hall W Mid 133 F8
Russell's Water Oxon 65 B8
Russel's Green Suff 126 C5
Rusthall Kent 52 F5
Rustington W Sus 35 G9
Ruston N Yorks 217 C9
Ruston Parva E Yorks 217 G11
Ruswarp N Yorks 227 D7
Ruthall Shrops 131 F11
Rutherford Borders 262 C4
Rutherglen S Lnrk 268 C2
Ruthernbridge Corn 5 B10
Ruthin Denb 165 D10
Ruthin V Glam 58 D3
Ruthrieston Aberdeen 293 C11
Ruthven Aberds 302 E5
Ruthven Angus 286 C6
Ruthven Highld 291 D9
Ruthven Highld 301 F8
Ruthven House Angus 287 C7
Ruthvoes Corn 5 C8
Ruthwaite Cumb 229 D10
Ruthwell Dumfries 238 D3
Ruxley London 68 E3
Ruxton Hereford 97 F11
Ruxton Green Hereford 79 B8
Ruyton-XI-Towns Shrops 149 E7
Ryal Northumb 242 C2
Ryal Fold Blkburn 195 C7
Ryall Dorset 16 C4
Ryall Worcs 99 C7
Ryarsh Kent 53 B7
Rychraggan Highld 300 F4
Rydal Cumb 221 D7
Ryde I o W 21 C7
Rydens Sur 66 F6
Rydeshill Sur 50 C3
Rydon Devon 14 G3
Rye E Sus 38 C6
Rye Common Hants 49 C9
Rye Foreign E Sus 38 C5
Rye Harbour E Sus 38 D6
Rye Park Herts 86 C5
Rye Street Worcs 98 D5
Ryebank Shrops 149 C10
Ryecroft S Yorks 186 B6
Ryecroft W Yorks 205 F7
Ryecroft Gate Staffs 168 C6
Ryeford Glos 80 E4
Ryehill E Yorks 201 B8
Ryeish Green Wokingham 65 F8
Ryelands Hereford 115 F9
Ryeworth Glos 99 G9
Ryhall Rutland 155 G10
Ryhill W Yorks 197 E11
Ryhope T & W 243 G10
Rylah Derbys 171 B7
Rylands Notts 153 B10
Rylstone N Yorks 204 B5
Ryme Intrinseca Dorset 29 E9
Ryther N Yorks 207 F7
Ryton Glos 98 E4
Ryton N Yorks 216 D5
Ryton Shrops 132 C5
Ryton T & W 242 E5
Ryton Warks 135 F7
Ryton-on-Dunsmore Warks 119 C7
Ryton Woodside T & W 242 E4

S

Sabden Lancs 203 F11
Sabine's Green Essex 87 F8
Sackers Green Suff 107 D8
Sacombe Herts 86 B4
Sacombe Green Herts 86 B4
Sacriston Durham 233 B10
Sadberge Darl 224 B6
Saddell Argyll 255 D8
Saddell Ho Argyll 255 D8
Saddington Leics 136 E3
Saddle Bow Norf 158 F2
Saddle Street Dorset 28 G5
Saddlescombe W Sus 36 E3
Sadgill Cumb 221 D9
Saffron Walden Essex 105 D10
Saffron's Cross Hereford 115 G10
Sageston Pembs 73 E9
Saham Hills Norf 141 C8
Saham Toney Norf 141 C8
Saighdinis W Isles 296 E4
Saighton W Ches 166 C6
Sain Dunwyd = St Donats V Glam 58 F2
Sain Tathon = St Athan V Glam 58 F4
St Abbs Borders 273 B8
St Abb's Haven Borders 273 B8
St Agnes Corn 4 E4
St Agnes Scilly 1 H3
St Albans Herts 85 D10
St Allen Corn 4 E6
St Andrews Fife 287 F9
St Andrew's Major V Glam 58 E6
St Andrew's Wood Devon 27 F9
St Annes Lancs 193 B10
St Anne's Park Bristol 60 E6
St Ann's Dumfries 248 E3
St Ann's Nottingham 171 G9
St Ann's Chapel Corn 12 G4
St Ann's Chapel Devon 8 F3
St Anthony Corn 3 C9
St Anthony-in-Meneage Corn 3 D7
St Anthony's T & W 243 E7
St Anthony's Hill E Sus 23 E10
St Arvans Mon 79 F8
St Asaph = Llanelwy Denb 181 G8
St Athan = Sain Tathon V Glam 58 F4
St Augustine's Kent 54 C6
St Austell Corn 5 E10
St Austins Hants 20 B2
St Bees Cumb 219 C9
St Blazey Corn 5 E11
St Blazey Gate Corn 5 E11
St Boswells Borders 262 C3
St Breock Corn 10 G5
St Breward Corn 11 F7
St Briavels Glos 79 E9
St Briavels Common Glos 79 E8
St Bride's Pembs 72 C4
St Brides Major = Saint-y-Brid V Glam 57 G11
St Bride's Netherwent Mon 60 B2
St Brides-super-Ely V Glam 58 D5
St Brides Wentlooge Newport 59 C9
St Budeaux Plym 7 D8
St Buryan Corn 1 D4
St Catherine Bath 61 E9
St Catherine's Argyll 284 G5
St Catherine's Hill Dorset 19 B8
St Chloe Glos 80 E4
St Clears = Sanclêr Carms 74 B3
St Cleer Corn 6 B5
St Clement Corn 4 G6
St Clether Corn 11 E10
St Colmac Argyll 275 G11
St Columb Major Corn 5 C8
St Columb Minor Corn 4 C6
St Columb Road Corn 5 D8
St Combs Aberds 303 C10
St Cross Hants 33 B7
St Cross South Elmham Suff 142 G5
St Cyrus Aberds 293 G9
St David's Perth 286 E3
St David's = Tyddewi Pembs 90 F5
St Day Corn 4 G4
St Decumans Som 42 E5
St Dennis Corn 5 D9
St Denys Soton 32 E6
St Devereux Hereford 97 E8
St Dials Torf 78 G3
St Dogmaels = Llandudoch Pembs 92 B3
St Dominick Corn 7 B8
St Donat's = Sain Dunwyd V Glam 58 F2
St Edith's Wilts 62 G3
St Endellion Corn 10 F5
St Enoder Corn 5 D7
St Erme Corn 4 E6
St Erney Corn 7 D7
St Erth Corn 2 B3
St Erth Praze Corn 2 B3
St Ervan Corn 10 G3
St Eval Corn 5 B7
St Ewe Corn 5 F9
St Fagans Cardiff 58 D6
St Fergus Aberds 303 D10
St Fillans Perth 285 E10
St Florence Pembs 73 E9
St Gennys Corn 11 B8
St George Bristol 60 E6
St George Conwy 181 F7
St George in the East London 67 C10
St George's Gtr Man 184 B4
St Georges N Som 59 G11
St George's Telford 150 G4
St George's V Glam 58 D5
St George's Hill Sur 66 G5
St George's Well Devon 27 F8
St Germans Corn 7 D7
St Giles Lincs 189 G7
St Giles London 67 C10
St Giles in the Wood Devon 25 D8
St Giles on the Heath Devon 12 C3
St Giles's Hill Hants 33 B7
St Gluvias Corn 3 C7
St Godwalds Worcs 117 D9
St Harmon Powys 113 C9
St Helen Auckland Durham 233 F9
St Helena Warks 134 C5
St Helens Cumb 228 E6
St Helen's E Sus 38 E4
St Helens I o W 21 D8
St Helens Mers 183 B8
St Helen's S Yorks 197 F11
St Helen's Wood E Sus 38 E4
St Helier London 67 F9
St Hilary Corn 2 C3
St Hilary V Glam 58 E4
St Ibbs Herts 104 F3
St Illtyd Bl Gwent 78 E2
St Ippollytts Herts 104 F3
St Ishmael's Pembs 72 D4
St Issey Corn 10 G4
St Ive Corn 6 B6
St Ive Cross Corn 6 B6
St Ives Cambs 122 C6
St Ives Corn 2 A2
St Ives Dorset 31 G10
St James Dorset 30 C5
St James London 67 C9
St James Norf 160 E5
St James South Elmham Suff 142 G6
St James's End Northants 120 E4
St Jidgey Corn 5 B8
St John Corn 7 E8
St John's E Sus 52 G4
St John's I o M 192 D3
St John's Kent 52 B4
St John's Kent 52 E5
St Johns London 67 D11
St John's Sur 50 B3
St John's W Yorks 206 F4
St Johns Warks 118 C5
St John's Worcs 116 G6
St John's Chapel Devon 25 B8
St John's Chapel Durham 232 D3
St John's Fen End Norf 157 G10
St John's Highway Norf 157 G10
St John's Park I o W 21 C8
St John's Town of Dalry Dumfries 246 G4
St John's Wells Aberds 303 F7
St John's Wood London 67 C9
St Judes I o M 192 C4
St Julians Herts 85 D10
St Julians Newport 59 B10
St Just in Roseland Corn 3 B9
St Just Corn 1 C3
St Justinian Pembs 90 F4
St Katharines Wilts 63 G9
St Katherine's Aberds 303 F7
St Keverne Corn 3 E7
St Kew Corn 10 F6
St Kew Highway Corn 10 F6
St Keyne Corn 6 C4
St Lawrence Corn 5 B10
St Lawrence Essex 89 E7
St Lawrence I o W 20 F6
St Lawrence Kent 71 F11
St Leonard's Bucks 84 D6
St Leonards Dorset 31 G10
St Leonards E Sus 38 F3
St Leonards S Lnrk 268 E2
St Leonard's Street Kent 53 B7
St Levan Corn 1 E3
St Luke's Derby 152 B6
St Luke's London 67 C10
St Lythans V Glam 58 E6
St Mabyn Corn 10 G6
St Madoes Perth 286 E5
St Margaret South Elmham Suff 142 G6
St Margaret's Hereford 97 E7
St Margarets Herts 86 C5
St Margarets London 67 E7
St Margaret's at Cliffe Kent 55 E11
St Margaret's Hope Orkney 314 G4
St Mark's Glos 99 G8
St Mark's I o M 192 E3
St Martin Corn 2 E6
St Martin Corn 6 E5
St Martins Perth 286 D5
St Martin's Shrops 148 B6
St Martin's Moor Shrops 148 B6
St Mary Bourne Hants 48 C2
St Mary Church V Glam 58 E4
St Mary Cray London 68 F3
St Mary Hill V Glam 58 D3
St Mary Hoo Medway 69 D10
St Mary in the Marsh Kent 39 B9
St Marychurch Torbay 9 B8
St Mary's Orkney 314 F4
St Mary's Bay Kent 39 B9
St Maughans Mon 79 B7
St Maughans Green Mon 79 B7
St Mawes Corn 3 C8
St Mawgan Corn 5 B7
St Mellion Corn 7 B7
St Mellons Cardiff 59 C8
St Merryn Corn 10 G3
St Mewan Corn 5 E9
St Michael Caerhays Corn 5 G9
St Michael Church Som 43 G10
St Michael Penkevil Corn 5 G7
St Michael South Elmham Suff 142 G6
St Michaels Kent 53 F11
St Michaels Torbay 9 C7
St Michaels Worcs 115 D11
St Michael's Hamlet Mers 182 D5
St Michael's on Wyre Lancs 202 E5
St Minver Corn 10 F5
St Monans Fife 287 G9
St Neot Corn 6 B3
St Neots Cambs 122 E3
St Newlyn East Corn 4 D6
St Nicholas Herts 104 F5
St Nicholas Pembs 91 D7
St Nicholas V Glam 58 E5
St Nicholas at Wade Kent 71 F9
St Nicholas South Elmham Suff 142 G6
St Nicolas Park Warks 135 E7
St Ninians Stirl 278 C5
St Olaves Norf 143 D9
St Osyth Essex 89 B10
St Osyth Heath Essex 89 B10
St Owens Cross Hereford 97 G10
St Pancras London 67 C10
St Paul's Glos 80 B4
St Paul's Cray London 68 F3
St Paul's Walden Herts 104 G3
St Peter South Elmham Suff 142 G6
St Peter The Great Worcs 117 G7
St Peter's Glos 99 G8
St Peters Kent 71 F11
St Peter's T & W 243 E7
St Petrox Pembs 73 F7
St Pinnock Corn 6 C4
St Quivox S Ayrs 257 E9
St Ruan Corn 2 F6
St Stephen Corn 5 E8
St Stephens Corn 7 D8
St Stephen's Corn 12 D2
St Stephens Herts 85 D10
St Teath Corn 11 E7
St Thomas Devon 14 C4
St Thomas Swansea 57 C7
St Tudy Corn 11 F7
St Twynnells Pembs 73 F7
St Veep Corn 6 E2
St Vigeans Angus 287 C10
St Vincent's Hamlet Essex 87 G9
St Wenn Corn 5 C9
St Weonards Hereford 97 G9
St Winnow Corn 6 D2
St y-Nyll V Glam 58 D5
Saint Hill Devon 27 F9
Saint Hill W Sus 51 F11
Saint y Brid = St Brides Major V Glam 57 G11
Saintbridge Glos 80 B5
Saintbury Glos 100 D2
Saint's Hill Kent 52 E4
Saith ffynnon Flint 181 F11
Salcombe Devon 9 G9
Salcombe Regis Devon 15 D9
Salcott-cum-Virley Essex 88 C6
Salden Bucks 102 F6
Sale Gtr Man 184 C3
Sale Green Worcs 117 F8
Saleby Lincs 191 F7
Salehurst E Sus 38 C2
Salem Carms 94 F2
Salem Ceredig 128 G3
Salem Corn 4 G4
Salen Argyll 289 E7
Salen Highld 289 C8
Salendine Nook W Yorks 196 D6
Salenside Borders 261 E11
Salesbury Lancs 203 G9
Saleway Worcs 117 F8
Salford C Beds 103 D8
Salford Gtr Man 184 B4
Salford Oxon 100 F5
Salford Ford C Beds 103 D8
Salford Priors Warks 117 G11
Salfords Sur 51 D9
Salhouse Norf 160 G6
Saligo Argyll 274 G3
Salisbury Wilts 31 B10
Salkeld Dykes Cumb 230 D6
Sallachan Highld 289 C11
Sallachy Highld 295 B11
Sallachy Highld 309 J5
Salle Norf 160 E2
Salmans Kent 52 E4
Salmonby Lincs 190 G4
Salmond's Muir Angus 287 D9
Salmonhutch Devon 14 B2
Salperton Glos 99 G11
Salperton Park Glos 81 B9
Salph End Beds 121 G11
Salsburgh N Lnrk 268 C6
Salt Staffs 151 D9
Salt Coates Cumb 238 G5
Salt End E Yorks 201 B7
Salt Hill Slough 66 C3
Salta Cumb 229 B7
Saltaire W Yorks 205 F8
Saltash Corn 7 D8
Saltburn Highld 301 C7
Saltburn-by-the-Sea Redcar 235 G9
Saltby Leics 155 D7
Saltcoats Cumb 219 F11
Saltcoats E Loth 281 E9
Saltcoats N Ayrs 266 G4
Saltcotes Lancs 193 B11
Saltdean Brighton 36 G5
Salter Lancs 212 G2
Salter Street W Mid 118 C2
Salterbeck Cumb 228 F5
Salterforth Lancs 204 D3
Salters Heath Hants 48 B6
Salters Lode Norf 139 C11
Saltershill Shrops 150 D2
Salterswall W Ches 167 B10
Salterton Wilts 46 F6
Saltfleet Lincs 191 C7
Saltfleetby All Saints Lincs 191 C7
Saltfleetby St Clement Lincs 191 C7
Saltfleetby St Peter Lincs 190 D6
Saltford Bath 61 F7
Salthouse Cumb 210 F4
Salthouse Norf 177 E9
Saltley W Mid 133 F11
Saltmarsh Newport 59 C11
Saltmarshe E Yorks 199 C9
Saltness Orkney 314 G2
Saltness Shetland 313 J4
Saltney Flint 166 B5
Salton N Yorks 216 D4
Saltrens Devon 25 C7
Saltwell T & W 243 E7
Saltwick Northumb 242 B5
Saltwood Kent 55 F7
Salum Argyll 288 E2
Salvington W Sus 35 F10
Salwarpe Worcs 117 E7
Salwayash Dorset 16 B5
Sambourne Warks 117 E11
Sambourne Wilts 45 E11
Sambrook Telford 150 E4
Samhla W Isles 296 E3
Samlesbury Lancs 203 G7
Samlesbury Bottoms Lancs 194 B6
Sampford Arundel Som 27 D10
Sampford Brett Som 42 E5
Sampford Chapple Devon 25 G10
Sampford Courtenay Devon 25 G10
Sampford Moor Som 27 D10
Sampford Peverell Devon 27 E8
Sampford Spiney Devon 12 G6
Sampool Bridge Cumb 211 B9
Samuel's Corner Essex 70 B3
Samuelston E Loth 281 G9
Sanachan Highld 299 E8
Sanaigmore Argyll 274 F3
Sanclêr = St Clears Carms 74 B3
Sancreed Corn 1 D4
Sancton E Yorks 208 F4
Sand Highld 307 K4
Sand Shetland 313 J5
Sand Som 44 D2
Sand Gate Cumb 211 D7
Sand Hole E Yorks 208 F2
Sand Hutton N Yorks 207 B9
Sand Side Cumb 210 C4
Sand Side Lancs 202 C4
Sandaig Highld 295 E9
Sandal W Yorks 197 D10
Sandal Magna W Yorks 197 D10
Sandale Cumb 229 C10
Sandavore Highld 294 G6
Sandbach E Ches 168 C3
Sandbach Heath E Ches 168 C3
Sandbank Argyll 276 E3
Sandbanks Kent 70 G4
Sandbanks Poole 18 D6
Sandborough Staffs 152 F2
Sandbraes Lincs 200 G6
Sandend Aberds 302 C5
Sanderstead London 67 G10
Sandfields Glos 99 G8
Sandfields Neath 57 C8
Sandfields Staffs 134 B2
Sandford Cumb 222 B4
Sandford Devon 26 G4
Sandford Dorset 18 D4
Sandford Hants 31 G11
Sandford I o W 20 E6
Sandford N Som 44 B2
Sandford S Lnrk 268 G4
Sandford Shrops 148 E6
Sandford Shrops 149 C11
Sandford W Yorks 205 F11
Sandford Worcs 99 B7
Sandford Batch N Som 44 B2
Sandford Hill Stoke 168 G6
Sandford on Thames Oxon 83 E8
Sandford Orcas Dorset 29 C10
Sandford St Martin Oxon 101 F8
Sandfordhill Aberds 303 E11
Sandgate Kent 55 G7
Sandgreen Dumfries 237 D7
Sandhaven Aberds 303 C9
Sandhaven Argyll 276 E3
Sandhead Dumfries 236 E2
Sandhill Bucks 102 F4
Sandhill Cambs 139 F11
Sandhill S Yorks 198 F2
Sandhills Dorset 29 E11
Sandhills Dorset 29 G9
Sandhills Mers 182 C4
Sandhills Oxon 83 D9
Sandhills Sur 50 F2
Sandhills W Yorks 206 F3
Sandhoe Northumb 241 D11
Sandhole Argyll 275 D11
Sandholme E Yorks 208 G2
Sandholme Lincs 156 B6
Sandhurst Brack 65 G10
Sandhurst Glos 98 G6
Sandhurst Kent 38 B3
Sandhurst Cross Kent 38 B3
Sandhutton N Yorks 215 C7
Sandiacre Derbys 153 B9
Sandilands Lincs 191 E8
Sandilands S Lnrk 259 B9
Sandiway W Ches 183 G10
Sandleheath Hants 31 E10
Sandling Kent 53 B9
Sandlow Green E Ches 168 B3
Sandness Shetland 313 H3
Sandon Essex 88 E2
Sandon Herts 104 E6
Sandon Staffs 151 C8
Sandonbank Staffs 151 D8
Sandown I o W 21 E7
Sandown Park Kent 52 E6
Sandpit Dorset 28 G6
Sandpits Glos 98 F6
Sandplace Corn 6 D5
Sandridge Herts 85 C11
Sandridge Wilts 62 F2
Sandringham Norf 158 D3
Sands Bucks 84 G4
Sands End London 67 D9
Sandsend N Yorks 227 C7
Sandside Cumb 210 D6
Sandside Cumb 211 C9
Sandside Orkney 314 F2
Sandside Ho Highld 310 C3
Sandsound Shetland 313 J5
Sandtoft N Lincs 199 F8
Sandvoe Shetland 312 D5
Sandway Kent 53 C11
Sandwell W Mid 133 F10
Sandwich Kent 55 B10
Sandwich Bay Estate Kent 55 B11
Sandwick Cumb 221 B8
Sandwick Orkney 314 H4
Sandwick Shetland 313 L6
Sandwith Cumb 219 C9
Sandwith Newtown Cumb 219 C9
Sandy C Beds 104 B3
Sandy Carms 75 E7
Sandy Bank Lincs 174 E3
Sandy Carrs Durham 234 C3
Sandy Cross E Sus 37 C9
Sandy Cross Sur 49 D11
Sandy Down Hants 20 B2
Sandy Gate Devon 14 C5
Sandy Haven Pembs 72 D5
Sandy Lane W Yorks 205 F8
Sandy Lane Wilts 62 F3
Sandy Lane Wrex 166 G5
Sandy Way I o W 20 E5
Sandybank Orkney 314 C5
Sandycroft Flint 166 B4
Sandyford Dumfries 248 E6
Sandyford Stoke 168 E5
Sandygate Devon 14 G3
Sandygate I o M 192 C4
Sandygate S Yorks 186 D4
Sandyhills Dumfries 237 D10
Sandylake Corn 6 C2
Sandylands Lancs 211 G8
Sandylands Som 27 C10
Sandylane Swansea 56 D5
Sandypark Devon 13 D10
Sandysike Cumb 239 D9
Sangobeg Highld 308 C4
Sangomore Highld 308 C4
Sanham Green W Berks 63 F10
Sankey Bridges Warr 183 D9
Sankyns Green Worcs 116 E5
Sanna Highld 288 C6
Sanndabhaig W Isles 297 G4
Sanndabhaig W Isles 304 E6
Sannox N Ayrs 255 C11
Sanquhar Dumfries 247 B7
Sansaw Heath Shrops 149 E10
Santon Cumb 220 E2
Santon N Lincs 200 E2
Santon Bridge Cumb 220 E2
Santon Downham Suff 140 F6
Sapcote Leics 135 E9
Sapey Bridge Worcs 116 F4
Sapey Common Hereford 116 E4
Sapiston Suff 125 B8
Sapley Cambs 122 C4
Sapperton Derbys 152 C3
Sapperton Glos 80 E6
Sapperton Lincs 155 C10
Saracen's Head Lincs 156 D6
Sarclet Highld 310 E7
Sardis Carms 75 D9
Sardis Pembs 73 D10
Sarisbury Hants 33 F8
Sarn Bridgend 58 C2
Sarn Flint 181 F10
Sarn Powys 130 E4
Sarn Bach Gwyn 144 D6
Sarn Meyllteyrn Gwyn 144 C4
Sarnau Carms 74 B4
Sarnau Ceredig 110 G6
Sarnau Gwyn 147 B9
Sarnau Powys 95 E10
Sarnau Powys 148 F4
Sarnesfield Hereford 115 G7
Saron Carms 75 C10
Saron Carms 93 D7
Saron Denb 165 C8
Saron Gwyn 163 B8
Saron Gwyn 163 D7
Sarratt Herts 85 F8
Sarratt Bottom Herts 85 F8
Sarre Kent 71 G9
Sarsden Oxon 100 G5
Sarsden Halt Oxon 100 G5
Sarsgrum Highld 308 C3
Sasaig Highld 295 E8
Sascott Shrops 149 G8
Satley Durham 233 C8
Satmar Kent 55 F9
Satran Highld 294 B6
Satron N Yorks 223 F8
Satterleigh Devon 25 C11
Satterthwaite Cumb 220 G6
Satwell Oxon 65 C8
Sauchen Aberds 293 B8
Saucher Perth 286 D5
Sauchie Clack 279 C7
Sauchieburn Aberds 293 G8
Saughall W Ches 182 G5
Saughall Massie Mers 182 D3
Saughton Edin 280 G4
Saughtree Borders 250 D3
Saul Glos 80 D2
Saundby Notts 188 D3
Saundersfoot Pembs 73 E10
Saunderton Bucks 84 E3
Saunderton Lee Bucks 84 F4
Saunton Devon 40 F3
Sausthorpe Lincs 174 B5
Saval Highld 309 J5
Savary Highld 289 E8
Saveock Corn 4 F5
Saverley Green Staffs 151 B9
Savile Park W Yorks 196 C5
Savile Town W Yorks 197 C8
Sawbridge Warks 119 D10
Sawbridgeworth Herts 87 B7
Sawdon N Yorks 217 B8
Sawley Derbys 153 C9
Sawley Lancs 203 D11
Sawley N Yorks 214 F4
Sawood W Yorks 204 G6
Sawston Cambs 105 B9
Sawtry Cambs 138 G3
Sawyer's Hill Som 27 C11
Sawyers Hill Wilts 81 G8
Saxby Leics 154 F6
Saxby Lincs 189 D8
Saxby W Sus 35 G7
Saxby All Saints N Lincs 200 D3
Saxelbye Leics 154 E4
Saxham Street Suff 125 E11
Saxilby Lincs 188 F5
Saxlingham Norf 159 B10
Saxlingham Green Norf 142 D4
Saxlingham Nethergate Norf 142 D4
Saxlingham Thorpe Norf 142 D4
Saxmundham Suff 127 E7
Saxon Street Cambs 124 F3
Saxondale Notts 154 B3
Saxtead Suff 126 D5
Saxtead Green Suff 126 E5
Saxtead Little Green Suff 126 D5
Saxthorpe Norf 160 C2
Saxton N Yorks 206 F5
Sayers Common W Sus 36 D3
Scackleton N Yorks 216 E2
Scadabhagh W Isles 305 J3
Scaftworth Notts 187 C11
Scagglethorpe N Yorks 216 E6
Scaitcliffe Lancs 195 B9
Scaladal W Isles 305 G3
Scalan Moray 292 B4
Scalasaig Argyll 274 D4
Scalby E Yorks 199 B10
Scalby N Yorks 227 G10
Scald End Beds 121 F10
Scaldwell Northants 120 C5
Scale Hall Lancs 211 G9
Scale Houses Cumb 231 B7
Scaleby Cumb 239 E11
Scalebyhill Cumb 239 E10
Scales Cumb 210 E5
Scales Cumb 230 F2
Scales Cumb 231 C7
Scales Lancs 202 G5
Scalford Leics 154 E5
Scaling Redcar 226 C4
Scaliscro W Isles 304 F3
Scallasaig Highld 295 D10
Scallastle Argyll 289 F8
Scalloway Shetland 313 K6
Scalpay W Isles 305 J4
Scalpay Ho Highld 295 C8
Scalpsie Argyll 255 B11
Scamadale Highld 295 F9
Scamblesby Lincs 190 F3
Scamland E Yorks 207 E11
Scammadale Argyll 289 G10
Scamodale Highld 289 B10
Scampston N Yorks 217 D7
Scampton Lincs 189 F7
Scaniport Highld 300 F6
Scapa Orkney 314 F4
Scapegoat Hill W Yorks 196 D5
Scar Orkney 314 B6
Scar Head Cumb 220 G5
Scarborough N Yorks 217 B10
Scarcewater Corn 5 E8
Scarcliffe Derbys 171 B7
Scarcroft W Yorks 206 E3
Scarcroft Hill W Yorks 206 E3
Scardroy Highld 300 D2
Scarff Shetland 312 E4
Scarfskerry Highld 310 B6
Scargill Durham 223 C11
Scarinish Argyll 288 E2
Scarisbrick Lancs 193 E11
Scarness Cumb 229 E10
Scarning Norf 159 G9
Scarrington Notts 172 G2
Scarth Hill Lancs 194 F2
Scarthingwell N Yorks 206 F5
Scartho NE Lincs 201 F9
Scarvister Shetland 313 J5
Scarwell Orkney 314 D2
Scatness Shetland 313 M5
Scatraig Highld 301 F7
Scatwell Ho Highld 300 D3
Scawby N Lincs 200 F3
Scawsby S Yorks 198 G5
Scawthorpe S Yorks 198 F5
Scawton N Yorks 215 C10
Scayne's Hill W Sus 36 C5
Scethrog Powys 96 F2
Scholar Green E Ches 168 D4
Scholemoor W Yorks 205 G8
Scholes Gtr Man 194 F5
Scholes S Yorks 186 B5
Scholes W Yorks 197 B7
Scholes W Yorks 197 F7
Scholes W Yorks 204 F6
Scholes W Yorks 206 F3
Scholey Hill W Yorks 197 B11
School Aycliffe Durham 233 G11
School Green Essex 106 E4
School Green I o W 20 D2
School Green W Ches 167 C10
School Green W Yorks 205 G8
School House Dorset 28 G5
Schoolgreen Wokingham 65 F8
Schoolhill Aberds 293 D11
Sciberscross Highld 309 H7
Scilly Bank Cumb 219 B9
Scissett W Yorks 197 E8
Scleddau Pembs 91 E8
Sco Ruston Norf 160 E5
Scofton Notts 187 E10
Scole Norf 126 B2
Scole Common Norf 142 G2
Scolpaig W Isles 296 D3
Scone Perth 286 E5
Sconser Highld 295 B7
Scoonie Fife 287 G7
Scoor Argyll 274 B5
Scopwick Lincs 173 D9
Scoraig Highld 307 K5
Scorborough E Yorks 208 D6
Scorrier Corn 4 G4
Scorriton Devon 8 B4
Scorton Lancs 202 D6
Scorton N Yorks 224 E5
Scot Hay Staffs 168 F4
Scot Lane End Gtr Man 194 F6
Scotbheinn W Isles 296 F4
Scotby Cumb 239 G10
Scotch Corner N Yorks 224 E4
Scotches Derbys 170 F4
Scotforth Lancs 202 B5
Scotgate W Yorks 196 E6
Scothern Lincs 189 F8
Scotland Leics 136 D3
Scotland Leics 153 E7
Scotland Lincs 155 C10
Scotland W Berks 64 F5
Scotland End Oxon 100 E6
Scotland Gate Northumb 253 G7
Scotland Street Suff 107 D9
Scotlands W Mid 133 C8
Scotlandwell Perth 286 G5
Scots' Gap Northumb 252 F2
Scotsburn Highld 301 B7
Scotscalder Station Highld 310 D4
Scotscraig Fife 287 E8
Scotston Aberds 293 F9
Scotston Perth 286 C3
Scotstoun Glasgow 267 B10
Scotstown Highld 289 C10
Scotswood T & W 242 E5
Scotswood Windsor 66 F2
Scott Willoughby Lincs 155 B11
Scottas Highld 295 E9
Scotter Lincs 199 G11
Scotterthorpe Lincs 199 G11
Scottlethorpe Lincs 155 E11
Scotton Lincs 188 B5
Scotton N Yorks 206 B2
Scotton N Yorks 224 F3
Scottow Norf 160 E5
Scoughall E Loth 282 E2
Scoulag Argyll 266 D2
Scoulton Norf 141 C9
Scounslow Green Staffs 151 D11
Scourie Highld 306 E6
Scourie More Highld 306 E6
Scousburgh Shetland 313 M5
Scout Dike S Yorks 197 G8
Scout Green Cumb 221 D11
Scouthead Gtr Man 196 F3
Scowles Glos 79 C9
Scrabster Highld 310 B4
Scraesburgh Borders 262 F5
Scrafield Lincs 174 B4
Scragged Oak Kent 69 G10
Scrainwood Northumb 251 B11
Scrane End Lincs 174 G5
Scrapsgate Kent 70 E2
Scraptoft Leics 136 B2
Scrapton Som 28 E3
Scratby Norf 161 F10
Scrayingham N Yorks 216 G4
Scredda Corn 5 E10
Scredington Lincs 173 G9
Screedy Som 27 B9
Scremby Lincs 174 B6
Scremerston Northumb 273 F10
Screveton Notts 172 G2
Scrivelsby Lincs 174 B3
Scriven N Yorks 206 B2
Scronkey Lancs 202 D4
Scrooby Notts 187 C11
Scropton Derbys 152 C3
Scrub Hill Lincs 174 D2
Scruton N Yorks 224 G5
Scrwgan Powys 148 E3
Scuddaborg Highld 298 C3
Scuggate Cumb 239 C10
Sculcoates Hull 209 G7
Sculthorpe Norf 159 C7
Scunthorpe N Lincs 199 E11
Scurlage Swansea 56 D3
Sea Som 28 E4
Sea Mill Cumb 210 F5
Sea Mills Bristol 60 D5
Sea Mills Corn 10 G4
Sea Palling Norf 161 D8
Seaborough Dorset 28 F6
Seabridge Staffs 168 G4
Seabrook Kent 55 G7
Seaburn T & W 243 F10
Seacombe Mers 182 C4
Seacox Heath Kent 53 G8
Seacroft Lincs 175 C9
Seacroft W Yorks 206 F3
Seadyke Lincs 156 B6
Seafar N Lnrk 278 G5
Seafield Highld 311 L3
Seafield Midloth 270 C5
Seafield S Ayrs 257 E8
Seafield W Loth 269 B10
Seaford E Sus 23 F7
Seaforth Mers 182 B4
Seagrave Leics 154 F2
Seagry Heath Wilts 62 C3
Seaham Durham 234 B4
Seahouses Northumb 264 C6
Seal Kent 52 B4
Sealand Flint 166 B5
Seale Sur 49 D11
Seamer N Yorks 217 C10
Seamer N Yorks 225 C9
Seamill N Ayrs 266 F4
Searby Lincs 200 F5
Seasalter Kent 70 F5
Seascale Cumb 219 E10
Seathorne Lincs 175 B9
Seathwaite Cumb 220 C4
Seathwaite Cumb 220 F4
Seatle Cumb 211 C7
Seatoller Cumb 220 C4
Seaton Corn 6 E6
Seaton Cumb 228 E6
Seaton Devon 15 C10
Seaton Durham 243 G9
Seaton E Yorks 209 D9
Seaton Kent 55 B8
Seaton Northumb 243 B8
Seaton Rutland 137 D8
Seaton Burn T & W 242 C6
Seaton Carew Hrtlpl 234 F6
Seaton Delaval Northumb 243 B8
Seaton Ross E Yorks 207 E11
Seaton Sluice Northumb 243 B8
Seatown Aberds 302 C5
Seatown Aberds 303 D11
Seatown Dorset 16 C4
Seaureaugh Moor Corn 2 B6
Seave Green N Yorks 225 E11
Seaview I o W 21 C8
Seaville Cumb 238 G5
Seavington St Mary Som 28 E6
Seavington St Michael Som 28 D6
Seawick Essex 89 C10
Sebastopol Torf 78 F3
Sebay Orkney 314 F5
Sebergham Cumb 230 C3
Sebiston Velzian Orkney 314 D2
Seckington Warks 134 B5
Second Coast Highld 307 K4
Second Drove Cambs 139 F10
Sedbergh Cumb 222 G3
Sedbury Glos 79 G8
Sedbusk N Yorks 223 G7
Seddington C Beds 104 B3
Sedgeberrow Worcs 99 D10
Sedgebrook Lincs 155 B7
Sedgefield Durham 234 F3
Sedgeford Norf 158 B4
Sedgehill Wilts 30 B5
Sedgemere W Mid 118 B4
Sedgley W Mid 133 E8
Sedgley Park Gtr Man 195 G10
Sedgwick Cumb 211 B10
Sedlescombe E Sus 38 D3
Sedlescombe Street E Sus 38 D3
Sedrup Bucks 84 C3
Seed Kent 54 B2
Seed Lee Lancs 194 C5
Seedley Gtr Man 184 B4
Seend Wilts 62 G2
Seend Cleeve Wilts 62 G2
Seend Head Wilts 62 G2
Seer Green Bucks 85 G7
Seething Norf 142 D6
Seething Wells London 67 F7
Sefton Mers 193 G11
Segensworth Hants 33 F8
Seggat Aberds 303 E7
Seghill Northumb 243 C7
Seifton Shrops 131 G9
Seighford Staffs 151 D7
Seilebost W Isles 305 J2
Seion Gwyn 163 B8
Seisdon Staffs 132 E6
Seisiadar W Isles 304 E7
Selattyn Shrops 148 C5
Selborne Hants 49 G8
Selby N Yorks 207 G8
Selgrove Kent 54 B4
Selham W Sus 34 C6
Selhurst London 67 F10
Selkirk Borders 261 D11
Sellack Hereford 97 F11
Sellack Boat Hereford 97 F11
Sellafirth Shetland 312 D7
Sellan Corn 1 C4
Sellibister Orkney 314 B7
Sellick's Green Som 28 D2
Sellindge Kent 54 F6
Selling Kent 54 B4
Sells Green Wilts 62 G3
Selly Hill N Yorks 227 D7
Selly Oak W Mid 133 G10
Selly Park W Mid 133 G11
Selmeston E Sus 23 D8
Selsdon London 67 G10
Selsey W Sus 22 E5
Selsfield Common W Sus 51 G10
Selside Cumb 221 F10
Selside N Yorks 212 D5
Selsley Glos 80 E4
Selsmore Hants 21 B10
Selson Kent 55 B10
Selsted Kent 55 E8
Selston Notts 171 E7
Selston Common Notts 171 E7
Selston Green Notts 171 E7
Selwick Orkney 314 F2
Selworthy Som 42 D2
Sem Hill Wilts 30 B5
Semblister Shetland 313 H5
Semer Suff 107 B9
Semington Wilts 61 G11
Semley Wilts 30 B5
Sempringham Lincs 156 C2
Send Sur 50 B4
Send Grove Sur 50 C4
Send Marsh Sur 50 B4
Senghenydd Caerph 77 G10
Sennen Corn 1 D3
Sennen Cove Corn 1 D3

Sennybridge = Pont Senni Powys 95 F8
Serlby Notts 187 D10
Serrington Wilts 46 F5
Sessay N Yorks 215 D9
Setchey Norf 158 G2
Setley Hants 32 G4
Seton E Loth 281 G8
Seton Mains E Loth 281 F8
Setter Shetland 312 E6
Setter Shetland 313 H5
Setter Shetland 313 J7
Setter Shetland 313 L6
Settiscarth Orkney 314 E3
Settle N Yorks 212 G6
Settrington N Yorks 216 E6
Seven Ash Som 43 G7
Seven Kings London 68 B3
Seven Sisters = Blaendulais Neath 76 D4
Seven Springs Glos 81 B7
Seven Star Green Essex 107 F8
Sevenhampton Glos 99 G10
Sevenhampton Swindon 82 G2
Sevenoaks Kent 52 C4
Sevenoaks Common Kent 52 C4
Sevenoaks Weald Kent 52 C4
Severn Beach S Glos 60 B4
Severn Stoke Worcs 99 C7
Severnhampton Swindon 82 G2
Sevick End Beds 121 G11
Sevington Kent 54 E4
Sewards End Essex 105 D11
Sewardstone Essex 86 F5
Sewardstonebury Essex 86 F5
Sewell C Beds 103 G9
Sewerby E Yorks 218 F3
Seworgan Corn 2 C6
Sewstern Leics 155 E7
Sexhow N Yorks 225 D9
Sezincote Glos 100 E3
Sgarasta Mhor W Isles 305 J2
Sgiogarstaigh W Isles 304 B7
Sgiwen = Skewen Neath 57 B8
Shab Hill Glos 80 B6
Shabbington Bucks 83 D11
Shackerley Shrops 132 B6
Shackerstone Leics 135 B7
Shacklecross Derbys 153 C8
Shackleford Sur 50 D2
Shackleton W Yorks 196 B3
Shacklewell London 67 B10
Shackloford Sur 50 D2
Shade W Yorks 196 C2
Shadforth Durham 234 C2
Shadingfield Suff 143 G8
Shadoxhurst Kent 54 F3
Shadsworth Blkburn 195 B8
Shadwell Glos 80 F3
Shadwell London 67 C11
Shadwell Norf 141 G8
Shadwell W Yorks 206 F2
Shaffalong Staffs 169 E7
Shaftenhoe End Herts 105 D8
Shaftesbury Dorset 30 C5
Shafton S Yorks 197 E11
Shafton Two Gates S Yorks 197 E11
Shaggs Dorset 18 E3
Shakeford Shrops 150 D3
Shakerley Gtr Man 195 G7
Shakesfield Glos 98 E3
Shalbourne Wilts 63 G10
Shalcombe I o W 20 D3
Shalden Hants 49 E7
Shalden Green Hants 49 E7
Shaldon Devon 14 G4
Shalfleet I o W 20 D4
Shalford Essex 106 F4
Shalford Som 45 G8
Shalford Sur 50 D4
Shalford Green Essex 106 F4
Shalloch Moray 302 D3
Shallowford Devon 25 B11
Shallowford Devon 41 E8
Shallowford Staffs 151 D7
Shalmsford Street Kent 54 C5
Shalstone Bucks 102 D2
Shamley Green Sur 50 E4
Shandon Argyll 276 D5
Shandwick Highld 301 B8
Shangton Leics 136 D4
Shankhouse Northumb 243 B7
Shanklin I o W 21 E7
Shannochie N Ayrs 255 E10
Shannochill Stirl 277 B10
Shanquhar Aberds 302 F5
Shanwell Fife 287 E8
Shanzie Perth 286 B6
Shap Cumb 221 B11
Shapridge Glos 79 B11
Shapwick Dorset 30 G6
Shapwick Som 44 F2
Sharcott Wilts 46 B6
Shard End W Mid 134 F3
Shardlow Derbys 153 C8
Shareshill Staffs 133 B8
Sharlston W Yorks 197 D11
Sharlston Common W Yorks 197 D11
Sharmans Cross W Mid 118 B2
Sharnal Street Medway 69 E9
Sharnbrook Beds 121 F9
Sharneyford Lancs 195 C11
Sharnford Leics 135 E9
Sharnhill Green Dorset 30 F2
Sharoe Green Lancs 202 G6
Sharow N Yorks 214 E6
Sharp Street Norf 161 E7
Sharpenhoe C Beds 103 E11
Sharperton Northumb 251 C11
Sharples Gtr Man 195 E8
Sharpley Heath Staffs 151 B9
Sharpness Glos 79 E11
Sharp's Corner E Sus 23 B9
Sharpsbridge E Sus 36 C6
Sharpstone Bath 45 B9
Sharpthorne W Sus 51 G11
Sharptor Corn 11 G11
Sharpway Gate Worcs 117 D9
Sharrington Norf 159 B10
Sharrow S Yorks 186 D4
Sharston Gtr Man 184 D4
Shatterford Worcs 132 G5
Shatterling Kent 55 B9
Shatton Derbys 185 E11
Shaugh Prior Devon 7 C10
Shavington E Ches 168 E2
Shaw Gtr Man 196 F2
Shaw Swindon 62 B6
Shaw W Berks 64 F3
Shaw W Yorks 204 F6
Shaw Wilts 61 F11
Shaw Common Glos 98 F3
Shaw Green Herts 104 E5
Shaw Green Lancs 194 D4
Shaw Green N Yorks 205 C11
Shaw Heath E Ches 184 F3
Shaw Heath Gtr Man 184 D5
Shaw Lands S Yorks 197 F10
Shaw Mills N Yorks 214 G5
Shaw Side Gtr Man 196 F2
Shawbank Shrops 131 G9
Shawbirch Telford 150 G2
Shawbury Shrops 149 E11
Shawclough Gtr Man 195 E11
Shawdon Hall Northumb 264 G3
Shawell Leics 135 G10
Shawfield Gtr Man 195 E11
Shawfield Staffs 169 C9
Shawfield Head N Yorks 205 C11
Shawford Hants 33 C7
Shawford Som 45 C9
Shawforth Lancs 195 C11
Shawhead Dumfries 237 B10
Shawhead N Lnrk 268 C4
Shawhill Dumfries 238 D6
Shawlands Glasgow 267 C11
Shawsburn S Lnrk 268 E5
Shawton S Lnrk 268 F3
Shawtonhill S Lnrk 268 F3
Shay Gate W Yorks 205 F8
Sheandow Moray 302 F2
Shear Cross Wilts 45 E11
Shearington Dumfries 238 D2
Shearsby Leics 136 E2
Shearston Som 43 G9
Shebbear Devon 24 F6
Shebdon Staffs 150 D5
Shebster Highld 310 C4
Sheddens E Renf 267 D11
Shedfield Hants 33 E9
Sheen Staffs 169 C10
Sheep Hill Durham 242 F5
Sheepbridge Derbys 186 G5
Sheepdrove W Berks 63 D10
Sheeplane C Beds 103 E8
Sheepridge Bucks 65 B11
Sheepridge W Yorks 197 D7
Sheepscar W Yorks 206 G2
Sheepscombe Glos 80 C5
Sheepstor Devon 7 B11
Sheepwash Devon 25 F7
Sheepwash Northumb 253 F7
Sheepway N Som 60 D3
Sheepy Magna Leics 134 C6
Sheepy Parva Leics 134 C6
Sheering Essex 87 C8
Sheerness Kent 70 E2
Sheerwater Sur 66 G4
Sheet Hants 34 C3
Sheet Shrops 115 C10
Sheets Heath Sur 50 B2
Sheffield Corn 1 D5
Sheffield S Yorks 186 D5
Sheffield Bottom W Berks 65 F7
Sheffield Green E Sus 36 C6
Sheffield Park S Yorks 186 D5
Shefford C Beds 104 D2
Shefford Woodlands W Berks 63 E11
Sheigra Highld 306 C6
Sheildmuir N Lnrk 268 D5
Sheinton Shrops 132 C2
Shelderton Shrops 115 B8
Sheldon Derbys 169 B11
Sheldon Devon 27 F10
Sheldon W Mid 134 G3
Sheldwich Kent 54 B4
Sheldwich Lees Kent 54 B4
Shelf Bridgend 58 C2
Shelf W Yorks 196 B6
Shelfanger Norf 142 G2
Shelfield W Mid 133 C10
Shelfield Warks 118 E2
Shelfield Green Warks 118 E2
Shelfleys Northants 120 F4
Shelford Notts 171 G11
Shelford Warks 135 F8
Shell Worcs 117 F9
Shell Green Halton 183 D8
Shelland Suff 125 E10
Shellbrook Leics 152 F6
Shelley Essex 87 E9
Shelley Suff 107 D10
Shelley W Yorks 197 E8
Shelley Woodhouse W Yorks 197 E8
Shellingford Oxon 82 G4
Shellow Bowells Essex 87 D10
Shellwood Cross Sur 51 D8
Shelsley Beauchamp Worcs 116 E4
Shelsley Walsh Worcs 116 E4
Shelthorpe Leics 153 F10
Shelton Beds 121 D10
Shelton Norf 142 E4
Shelton Notts 172 G3
Shelton Shrops 149 G9
Shelton Stoke 168 F5
Shelton Green Norf 142 E4
Shelton Lock Derby 153 C7
Shelton under Harley Staffs 150 B6
Shelve Shrops 130 D6
Shelvin Devon 27 G11
Shelvingford Kent 71 F8
Shelwick Hereford 97 C10
Shelwick Green Hereford 97 C10
Shenfield Essex 87 G10
Shenington Oxon 101 C7
Shenley Herts 85 E11
Shenley Brook End M Keynes 102 D6
Shenley Church End M Keynes 102 D6
Shenley Fields W Mid 133 G10
Shenley Lodge M Keynes 102 D6
Shenley Wood M Keynes 102 D6
Shenleybury Herts 85 E11
Shenmore Hereford 97 D7
Shennanton Dumfries 236 C5
Shennanton Ho Dumfries 236 C5
Shenstone Staffs 134 C2
Shenstone Worcs 117 C7
Shenstone Woodend Staffs 134 C2
Shenton Leics 135 C7
Shenval Highld 300 G4
Shenval Moray 302 G2
Shenvault Moray 301 E10
Shepeau Stow Lincs 156 G6
Shephall Herts 104 G5
Shepherd Hill W Yorks 197 C9
Shepherd's Bush London 67 C8
Shepherd's Gate Norf 157 F11
Shepherd's Green Oxon 65 C8
Shepherd's Hill Sur 50 G2
Shepherd's Patch Glos 80 E2
Shepherd's Port Norf 158 C3
Shepherdswell or Sibertswold Kent 55 D9
Shepley W Yorks 197 F7
Shepperdine S Glos 79 F10
Shepperton Sur 66 F5
Shepperton Green Sur 66 F5
Shepreth Cambs 105 B7
Shepshed Leics 153 F9
Shepton Beauchamp Som 28 D6
Shepton Mallet Som 44 E6
Shepton Montague Som 45 G7
Shepway Kent 53 C9
Sheraton Durham 234 D4
Sherberton Devon 13 G8
Sherborne Bath 44 B5
Sherborne Dorset 29 D10
Sherborne Glos 81 C11
Sherborne St John Hants 48 B6
Sherbourne Warks 118 E5
Sherbourne Street Suff 107 C9
Sherburn Durham 234 C2
Sherburn N Yorks 217 D9
Sherburn Grange Durham 234 C2
Sherburn Hill Durham 234 C2
Sherburn in Elmet N Yorks 206 G5
Shere Sur 50 D5
Shereford Norf 159 D7
Sherfield English Hants 32 C3
Sherfield on Loddon Hants 49 B7
Sherfin Lancs 195 B9
Sherford Devon 8 G5
Sherford Dorset 18 C4
Sherford Som 28 C2
Sheriff Hill T & W 243 E7
Sheriff Hutton N Yorks 216 F3
Sheriffhales Shrops 150 G5
Sheriff's Lench Worcs 99 B10
Sheringham Norf 177 E11
Sherington M Keynes 103 B7
Sheringwood Norf 177 E11
Shermanbury W Sus 36 D2
Shernal Green Worcs 117 E8
Shernborne Norf 158 C4
Sherrard's Green Worcs 98 B5
Sherrardspark Herts 86 C2
Sherriffhales Shrops 150 G5
Sherrington Wilts 46 F3
Sherston Wilts 61 B11
Sherwood Nottingham 171 G9
Sherwood Green Devon 25 C9
Sherwood Park Kent 52 E6
Shettleston Glasgow 268 C2
Shevington Gtr Man 194 F4
Shevington Moor Gtr Man 194 E4
Shevington Vale Gtr Man 194 F4
Sheviock Corn 7 D7
Shewalton N Ayrs 257 B8
Shibden Head W Yorks 196 B5
Shide I o W 20 D5
Shiel Aberds 292 B4
Shiel Bridge Highld 295 D11
Shield Row Durham 242 G6
Shieldaig Highld 299 B8
Shieldaig Highld 299 D8
Shieldhall Glasgow 267 B10
Shieldhill Dumfries 248 F2
Shieldhill Falk 279 F7
Shieldhill S Lnrk 269 G10
Shielfoot Highld 289 C8
Shielhill Angus 287 B8
Shielhill Invclyd 276 G4
Shifford Oxon 82 E5
Shifnal Shrops 132 B4
Shilbottle Northumb 252 B5
Shilbottle Grange Northumb 252 B6
Shildon Durham 233 F10
Shillford E Renf 267 D8
Shillingford Devon 27 C7
Shillingford Oxon 83 G9
Shillingford Abbot Devon 14 D4
Shillingford St George Devon 14 D4
Shillingstone Dorset 30 E4
Shillington C Beds 104 E2
Shillmoor Northumb 251 B9
Shilton Oxon 82 D3
Shilton Warks 135 G8
Shilvington Northumb 252 G5
Shimpling Norf 142 G3
Shimpling Suff 125 G7
Shimpling Street Suff 125 G7
Shincliffe Durham 233 C11
Shiney Row T & W 243 G8
Shinfield Wokingham 65 F8
Shingay Cambs 104 B6
Shingham Norf 140 C5
Shingle Street Suff 109 C7
Shinner's Bridge Devon 8 C5
Shinness Highld 309 H5
Shipbourne Kent 52 C5
Shipdham Norf 141 B9
Shipdham Airfield Norf 141 B9
Shipham Som 44 B2
Shiphay Torbay 9 B7
Shiplake Oxon 65 D9
Shiplake Bottom Oxon 65 C8
Shiplake Row Oxon 65 D9
Shiplate N Som 43 B11
Shiplaw Borders 270 F4
Shipley Derbys 170 G6
Shipley Northumb 264 F4
Shipley Shrops 132 D6
Shipley W Sus 35 C10
Shipley W Yorks 205 F8
Shipley Bridge Sur 51 E10
Shipley Common Derbys 171 G7
Shipley Shiels Northumb 251 E7
Shipmeadow Suff 143 F7
Shipping Pembs 73 D10
Shippon Oxon 83 F7
Shipston-on-Stour Warks 100 C5
Shipton Bucks 102 F5
Shipton Glos 81 B8
Shipton N Yorks 207 B7
Shipton Shrops 131 E11
Shipton Bellinger Hants 47 D8
Shipton Gorge Dorset 16 C5
Shipton Green W Sus 22 C4
Shipton Lee Bucks 102 G4
Shipton Moyne Glos 61 B11
Shipton Oliffe Glos 81 B8
Shipton on Cherwell Oxon 83 B7
Shipton Solers Glos 81 B8
Shipton-under-Wychwood Oxon 82 B3
Shiptonthorpe E Yorks 208 E3
Shirburn Oxon 83 F11
Shirdley Hill Lancs 193 E11
Shire Oak W Mid 133 C11
Shirebrook Derbys 171 B8
Shirecliffe S Yorks 186 C4
Shiregreen S Yorks 186 C5
Shirehampton Bristol 60 D4
Shiremoor T & W 243 C8
Shirenewton Mon 79 G7
Shireoaks Derbys 185 E9
Shireoaks Notts 187 E9
Shires Mill Fife 279 D10
Shirkoak Kent 54 F2
Shirl Heath Hereford 115 F8
Shirland Derbys 170 D6
Shirlett Shrops 132 D3
Shirley Derbys 170 G2
Shirley Hants 19 B9
Shirley London 67 F11
Shirley Soton 32 E6
Shirley W Mid 118 B2
Shirley Heath W Mid 118 B2
Shirley holms Hants 19 B11
Shirley Warren Soton 32 E5
Shirrell Heath Hants 33 E9
Shirwell Devon 40 F5
Shirwell Cross Devon 40 F5
Shiskine N Ayrs 255 E10
Shitterton Dorset 18 C2
Shobdon Hereford 115 E8
Shobley Hants 31 F11
Shobnall Staffs 152 E4
Shobrooke Devon 26 G5
Shoby Leics 154 F3
Shocklach W Ches 166 F6
Shocklach Green W Ches 166 F6
Shoeburyness Sthend 70 C2
Sholden Kent 55 C11
Sholing Soton 33 E7
Sholing Common Soton 33 E7
Sholver Gtr Man 196 F3
Shoot Hill Shrops 149 G8
Shootash Hants 32 C4
Shooters Hill London 68 D2
Shootersway Herts 85 D7
Shop Corn 10 G3
Shop Corn 24 E2
Shop Devon 24 E5
Shop Corner Suff 108 E4
Shopford Cumb 240 C3
Shopnoller Som 43 G7
Shopp Hill W Sus 34 B6
Shopwyke W Sus 22 B5
Shore Gtr Man 196 D2
Shore W Yorks 196 B2
Shore Bottom Devon 28 G2
Shore Mill Highld 301 C7
Shoreditch London 67 C10
Shoreditch Som 28 C2
Shoregill Cumb 222 E5
Shoreham Kent 68 G4
Shoreham Beach W Sus 36 G2
Shoreham-by-Sea W Sus 36 F2
Shores Green Oxon 82 D5
Shoresdean Northumb 273 F9
Shoreside Shetland 313 J4
Shoreswood Northumb 273 F8
Shoreton Highld 300 C6
Shorley Hants 33 B9
Shorncliffe Camp Kent 55 F7
Shorncote Glos 81 F8
Shorne Kent 69 E7
Shorne Ridgeway Kent 69 E7
Shorne West Kent 69 E7
Short Cross W Mid 133 G9
Short Green Norf 141 F11
Short Heath Derbys 152 G6
Short Heath W Mid 133 C9
Short Heath W Mid 133 E11
Short Street Wilts 45 D10
Shortacombe Devon 12 D6
Shortacross Corn 6 D5
Shortbridge E Sus 37 C7
Shortfield Common Sur 49 E10
Shortgate E Sus 23 B7
Shorthampton Oxon 100 G6
Shortheath Hants 49 F9
Shortheath Sur 49 E10
Shorthill Shrops 131 B8
Shortlands London 67 F11
Shortlanesend Corn 4 F6
Shortlees E Ayrs 257 B10
Shortmoor Devon 28 G2
Shortmoor Dorset 29 G7
Shorton Torbay 9 C7
Shortroods Renfs 267 B9
Shortstanding Glos 79 C9
Shortstown Beds 103 B11
Shortwood Glos 80 F4
Shortwood S Glos 61 D7
Shorwell I o W 20 E5
Shoscombe Bath 45 B8
Shoscombe Vale Bath 45 B8
Shotatton Shrops 149 E7
Shotesham Norf 142 D5
Shotgate Essex 88 G3
Shotley Northants 137 D8
Shotley Suff 108 D4
Shotley Bridge Durham 242 G3
Shotley Gate Suff 108 E4
Shotleyfield Northumb 242 G3
Shottenden Kent 54 C4
Shottermill Sur 49 G11
Shottery Warks 118 G3
Shotteswell Warks 101 B8
Shottisham Suff 108 C6
Shottle Derbys 170 F4
Shottlegate Derbys 170 F4
Shotton Durham 234 D4
Shotton Durham 234 F3
Shotton Flint 166 B4
Shotton Northumb 242 B6
Shotton Northumb 263 C8
Shotton Colliery Durham 234 C3
Shotts N Lnrk 269 C7
Shotwick W Ches 182 G4
Shouldham Norf 140 B3
Shouldham Thorpe Norf 140 B3
Shoulton Worcs 116 F6
Shover's Green E Sus 53 G7
Shraleybrook Staffs 168 F3
Shrawardine Shrops 149 F8
Shrawley Worcs 116 E6
Shreding Green Bucks 66 C4
Shrewley Warks 118 D4
Shrewley Common Warks 118 D4
Shrewsbury Shrops 149 G9
Shrewton Wilts 46 E5
Shripney W Sus 22 C6
Shrivenham Oxon 63 B8
Shropham Norf 141 E9
Shroton or Iwerne Courtney Dorset 30 E5
Shrub End Essex 107 G9
Shrubs Hill Sur 66 F3
Shruthertill S Lnrk 268 F5
Shucknall Hereford 97 C11
Shudy Camps Cambs 106 C2
Shulishadermor Highld 298 E4
Shulista Highld 298 B4
Shuna Ho Argyll 275 C8
Shurdington Glos 80 B6
Shurlock Row Windsor 65 E10
Shurnock Worcs 117 E10
Shurrery Highld 310 D4
Shurrery Lodge Highld 310 D4
Shurton Som 43 E8
Shustoke Warks 134 E4
Shut Heath Staffs 151 E7
Shute Devon 15 B11
Shute Devon 26 G5
Shute End Wilts 31 B11
Shutford Oxon 101 C7
Shuthonger Glos 99 D7
Shutlanger Northants 120 G4
Shutt Green Staffs 133 B7
Shutta Corn 6 E5
Shuttington Warks 134 B5
Shuttlesfield Kent 55 E7
Shuttlewood Derbys 187 G7
Shuttleworth Gtr Man 195 D10
Shutton Hereford 98 F3
Shwt Bridgend 57 D11
Siabost bho Dheas W Isles 304 D4
Siabost bho Thuath W Isles 304 D4
Siadar W Isles 304 C5
Siadar Iarach W Isles 304 C5
Siadar Uarach W Isles 304 C5
Sibbaldbie Dumfries 248 F4
Sibbertoft Northants 136 G3
Sibdon Carwood Shrops 131 G8
Sibford Ferris Oxon 101 D7
Sibford Gower Oxon 101 D7
Sible Hedingham Essex 106 E5
Sibley's Green Essex 106 F2
Sibsey Lincs 174 E5
Sibsey Fen Side Lincs 174 E4
Sibson Cambs 137 D11
Sibson Leics 135 C7
Sibster Highld 310 D7
Sibthorpe Notts 172 F3
Sibthorpe Notts 188 G2
Sibton Suff 127 D7
Sibton Green Suff 127 C7
Sicklesmere Suff 125 E7
Sicklinghall N Yorks 206 D3
Sid Devon 15 D8
Sidbrook Som 28 B3
Sidbury Devon 15 C8
Sidbury Shrops 132 F3
Sidcot N Som 44 B2
Sidcup London 68 E3
Siddal W Yorks 196 C6
Siddick Cumb 228 E6
Siddington E Ches 184 G4
Siddington Glos 81 F8
Siddington Heath E Ches 184 G4
Side of the Moor Gtr Man 195 E8
Sidemoor Worcs 117 C9
Sidestrand Norf 160 B5
Sideway Stoke 168 G5
Sidford Devon 15 C8
Sidlesham W Sus 22 D5
Sidlesham Common W Sus 22 C5
Sidley E Sus 38 F2
Sidlow Sur 51 D9
Sidmouth Devon 15 D8
Sidway Staffs 150 B5
Sigford Devon 13 G11
Sigglesthorne E Yorks 209 D9
Sighthill Edin 280 G3
Sighthill Glasgow 268 B2
Sigingstone = Tresigin V Glam 58 E3
Signet Oxon 82 C2
Sigwells Som 29 C10
Silchester Hants 64 G6
Sildinis W Isles 305 G4
Sileby Leics 153 F11
Silecroft Cumb 210 C2
Silfield Norf 142 D2
Silford Devon 24 B6
Silian Ceredig 111 G11
Silk Willoughby Lincs 173 G9
Silkstead Hants 32 C6
Silkstone S Yorks 197 F9
Silkstone Common S Yorks 197 G9
Silloth Cumb 238 G4
Sills Northumb 251 C8
Sillyearn Moray 302 D5
Siloh Carms 94 D4
Silpho N Yorks 227 G9
Silsden W Yorks 204 D6
Silsoe C Beds 103 D11
Silton Dorset 30 B3
Silver End Essex 88 B4
Silver End W Mid 133 F8
Silver Green Norf 142 E5
Silver Hill E Sus 38 B2
Silver Knap Som 29 C11
Silver Street Glos 80 E3
Silver Street Kent 69 G11
Silver Street Som 27 C11
Silver Street Som 44 G4
Silver Street Worcs 117 B11
Silverburn Midloth 270 C4
Silverdale Lancs 211 E9
Silverdale Staffs 168 F4
Silverdale Green Lancs 211 E9
Silvergate Norf 160 D3
Silverhill E Sus 38 E3
Silverhill Park E Sus 38 E4
Silverknowes Edin 280 F4
Silverley's Green Suff 126 B5
Silvermuir S Lnrk 269 F8
Silverstone Northants 102 C3
Silverton Devon 27 G7
Silverton W Dunb 277 F8
Silvertonhill S Lnrk 268 E4
Silvertown London 68 D2
Silverwell Corn 4 F4
Silvington Shrops 116 B2
Silwick Shetland 313 J4
Sim Hill S Yorks 197 G9
Simister Gtr Man 195 F10
Simmondley Derbys 185 C8
Simm's Cross Halton 183 D8
Simm's Lane End Mers 194 G4
Simonburn Northumb 241 C9
Simonsbath Som 41 F9
Simonsburrow Devon 27 D10
Simonside T & W 243 E8
Simonstone Lancs 203 G11
Simonstone N Yorks 223 G7
Simprim Borders 272 F6
Simpson M Keynes 103 D7
Simpson Pembs 72 B5
Simpson Cross Pembs 72 B5
Simpson Green W Yorks 205 F9
Sinclair's Hill Borders 272 E6
Sinclairston E Ayrs 257 F11
Sinclairtown Fife 280 C5
Sinderby N Yorks 214 C6
Sinderhope Northumb 241 G8
Sinderland Green Gtr Man 184 C2
Sindlesham Wokingham 65 F9
Sinfin Derby 152 C6
Sinfin Moor Derby 153 C7
Singdean Borders 250 C3
Single Hill Bath 45 B8
Singleborough Bucks 102 E5
Singleton Lancs 202 F3
Singleton W Sus 34 E5
Singlewell Kent 69 E7
Singret Wrex 166 D4
Sinkhurst Green Kent 53 E10
Sinnahard Aberds 292 B6
Sinnington N Yorks 216 B4
Sinton Worcs 116 E6
Sinton Green Worcs 116 E6
Sion Hill Bath 61 F8
Sipson London 66 D5
Sirhowy Bl Gwent 77 C11
Sisland Norf 142 D6
Sissinghurst Kent 53 F9
Sisterpath Borders 272 F5
Siston S Glos 61 D7
Sithney Corn 2 D4
Sithney Common Corn 2 D4
Sithney Green Corn 2 D4
Sittingbourne Kent 70 G2
Six Ashes Staffs 132 F5
Six Bells Bl Gwent 78 E2
Six Hills Leics 154 E2
Six Mile Bottom Cambs 123 F11
Sixhills Lincs 189 D11
Sixmile Kent 54 E6
Sixpenny Handley Dorset 31 D7
Sizewell Suff 127 E9
Skaigh Devon 13 C8
Skail Highld 308 E7
Skaill Orkney 314 F5
Skaill Orkney 314 C4
Skaill Orkney 314 E2
Skares E Ayrs 258 F2
Skateraw E Loth 282 F4
Skaw Shetland 312 B8
Skaw Shetland 312 G7
Skeabost Highld 298 E4
Skeabrae Orkney 314 D2
Skeeby N Yorks 224 E4
Skeete Kent 54 E6
Skeffington Leics 136 C4
Skeffling E Yorks 201 D11
Skegby Notts 171 C7
Skegby Notts 188 G3
Skegness Lincs 175 C9
Skelberry Shetland 313 G6
Skelberry Shetland 313 M5
Skelbo Highld 309 K7
Skelbo Street Highld 309 K7
Skelbrooke S Yorks 198 E4
Skeldyke Lincs 156 B6
Skelfhill Borders 249 C11
Skellingthorpe Lincs 188 G6
Skellister Shetland 313 H6
Skellorn Green E Ches 184 E6
Skellow S Yorks 198 E4
Skelmanthorpe W Yorks 197 E8
Skelmersdale Lancs 194 F3
Skelmonae Aberds 303 F8
Skelmorlie N Ayrs 266 B3
Skelmuir Aberds 303 E9
Skelpick Highld 308 D7
Skelton Cumb 230 D4
Skelton E Yorks 199 B9
Skelton N Yorks 223 E11
Skelton Redcar 226 B3
Skelton York 207 B7
Skelton-on-Ure N Yorks 215 F7
Skelwick Orkney 314 B4
Skelwith Bridge Cumb 220 E6
Skendleby Lincs 174 B6
Skendleby Psalter Lincs 190 G6
Skene Ho Aberds 293 C9
Skenfrith Mon 97 G9
Skerne E Yorks 208 B6
Skerne Park Darl 224 C5
Skeroblingarry Argyll 255 E8
Skerray Highld 308 C6
Skerricha Highld 306 D7
Skerryford Pembs 72 C6
Skerton Lancs 211 G9
Sketchley Leics 135 E8
Sketty Swansea 56 C6
Skewen = Sgiwen Neath 57 B8
Skewes Corn 5 B9
Skewsby N Yorks 216 E2
Skeyton Norf 160 D4
Skeyton Corner Norf 160 D5
Skiag Bridge Highld 307 G7
Skibo Castle Highld 309 L7
Skidbrooke Lincs 190 C6
Skidbrooke North End Lincs 190 B6
Skidby E Yorks 208 G6
Skilgate Som 27 B7
Skillington Lincs 155 D7
Skinburness Cumb 238 F4
Skinflats Falk 279 E8
Skinidin Highld 298 E2
Skinner's Bottom Corn 4 F4
Skinners Green W Berks 64 F2
Skinnet Highld 308 C5
Skinningrove Redcar 226 B4
Skipness Argyll 255 B9
Skippool Lancs 202 E3
Skiprigg Cumb 230 B3
Skipsea E Yorks 209 B9
Skipsea Brough E Yorks 209 C9
Skipton N Yorks 204 C5
Skipton-on-Swale N Yorks 215 D7
Skipwith N Yorks 207 F9
Skirbeck Lincs 174 G4
Skirbeck Quarter Lincs 174 G4
Skirethorns N Yorks 213 G9
Skirlaugh E Yorks 209 F8
Skirling Borders 260 B3
Skirmett Bucks 65 B9
Skirpenbeck E Yorks 207 B10
Skirwith Cumb 231 E8
Skirza Highld 310 C7
Skitby Cumb 239 D10
Skitham Lancs 202 E4
Skittle Green Bucks 84 E3
Skulamus Highld 295 C8
Skullomie Highld 308 C6
Skyborry Green Shrops 114 C5
Skye Green Essex 107 G7
Skye of Curr Highld 301 G9
Skyfog Pembs 90 F6
Skyreholme N Yorks 213 G11
Slack Derbys 170 C4
Slack W Yorks 196 B3
Slack W Yorks 196 D5
Slack Head Cumb 211 D9
Slackcote Gtr Man 196 F3
Slackhall Derbys 185 E9
Slackhead Moray 302 C4
Slackholme End Lincs 191 G8
Slacks of Cairnbanno Aberds 303 E8
Slad Glos 80 D5
Sladbrook Glos 98 F5
Slade Devon 27 F10
Slade Devon 40 D4
Slade Kent 54 C2
Slade Pembs 72 B6
Slade End Oxon 83 G9
Slade Green London 68 D4
Slade Heath Staffs 133 B8
Slade Hooton S Yorks 187 D8
Sladen Green Hants 48 C2
Slades Green Worcs 99 E7
Sladesbridge Corn 10 G6
Slaggyford Northumb 240 G5
Slaidburn Lancs 203 C10
Slaithwaite W Yorks 196 E5
Slaley Derbys 170 D3
Slaley Northumb 241 F11
Slamannan Falk 279 G7
Slape Cross Som 43 F10
Slapewath Redcar 226 B2
Slapton Bucks 103 G8
Slapton Devon 8 G6
Slapton Northants 102 B2
Slate Haugh Moray 302 C4
Slateford Edin 280 G4
Slatepit Dale Derbys 170 B4
Slattocks Gtr Man 195 F11
Slaugham W Sus 36 B3
Slaughter Hill E Ches 168 D2
Slaughterbridge Corn 11 D8
Slaughterford Wilts 61 E10
Slawston Leics 136 E5
Slay Pits S Yorks 199 F7
Sleaford Hants 49 F10
Sleaford Lincs 173 F9
Sleagill Cumb 221 B11
Sleap Shrops 149 D9
Sleapford Telford 150 F2
Sleapshyde Herts 86 D2
Sleastary Highld 309 K6
Slebech Pembs 73 B8
Sledge Green Worcs 98 E6
Sledmere E Yorks 217 G8
Sleeches Cross E Sus 52 G5
Sleepers Hill Hants 33 B7
Sleet Moor Derbys 170 E6
Sleetbeck Cumb 240 B2
Sleight Dorset 18 B5
Sleights N Yorks 227 D7
Slepe Dorset 18 C4
Sliabhna h-Airde W Isles 296 F3
Slickly Highld 310 C6
Sliddery N Ayrs 255 E10
Slideslow Worcs 117 C9
Sligachan Hotel Highld 294 C6
Sligneach Argyll 288 G4
Sligrachan Argyll 276 C3
Slimbridge Glos 80 E2
Slindon Staffs 150 C6
Slindon W Sus 35 F7
Slinfold W Sus 50 G6
Sling Glos 79 D9
Sling Gwyn 163 B10
Slingsby N Yorks 216 E3
Slioch Aberds 302 F5
Slip End C Beds 85 B9
Slip End Herts 104 D5
Slippery Ford W Yorks 204 E6
Slipton Northants 121 B9
Slitting Mill Staffs 151 F10
Slochd Highld 301 G8
Slockavullin Argyll 275 D9
Slogan Moray 302 E3
Sloley Norf 160 E5
Sloncombe Devon 13 D10
Sloothby Lincs 191 G7
Slough Slough 66 D3
Slough Green Som 28 C3
Slough Green W Sus 36 B3
Slough Hill Suff 125 G7
Sluggan Highld 301 G8
Sluggans Highld 298 E4
Slumbay Highld 295 B10
Sly Corner Kent 54 G3
Slyfield Sur 50 C3
Slyne Lancs 211 F9
Smailholm Borders 262 B4
Small Dole W Sus 36 E2
Small End Lincs 174 D6
Small Heath W Mid 134 F2
Small Hythe Kent 53 G11
Small Way Som 44 G6
Smallbridge Gtr Man 196 D2
Smallbrook Devon 14 B3
Smallbrook Glos 79 E9
Smallburgh Norf 160 E6
Smallburn Aberds 303 E10
Smallburn E Ayrs 258 D5
Smalldale Derbys 185 E11
Smalldale Derbys 185 F9
Smalley Derbys 170 G6
Smalley Common Derbys 170 G6
Smalley Green Derbys 170 G6
Smallfield Sur 51 E10
Smallford Herts 85 D11
Smallholm Dumfries 238 B4
Smallmarsh Devon 25 C10
Smallrice Staffs 151 C9
Smallridge Devon 28 G4
Smallshaw Gtr Man 196 G2
Smallthorne Stoke 168 E5
Smallwood E Ches 168 C4
Smallwood Worcs 117 D10
Smallwood Green Suff 125 F8
Smallwood Hey Lancs 202 D3
Smallworth Norf 141 G10
Smannell Hants 47 D11
Smardale Cumb 222 D4
Smarden Kent 53 E11
Smarden Bell Kent 53 E11
Smart's Hill Kent 52 E4
Smaull Argyll 274 G3
Smeatharpe Devon 27 E11
Smeaton Fife 280 C5
Smeeth Kent 54 F5
Smeeton Westerby Leics 136 E3
Smelthouses N Yorks 214 G3
Smercleit W Isles 297 K3
Smerral Highld 310 F5
Smestow Staffs 133 E7
Smethcott Shrops 131 D9
Smethwick W Mid 133 F10
Smethwick Green E Ches 168 C4
Smirisary Highld 289 B8
Smisby Derbys 152 F6
Smite Hill Worcs 117 F7
Smith End Green Worcs 116 G5
Smith Green Lancs 202 C5
Smithaleigh Devon 7 D11
Smithbrook W Sus 34 C6
Smithfield Cumb 239 D10
Smithies S Yorks 197 F11
Smithincott Devon 27 E9
Smithley S Yorks 197 G11
Smith's End Herts 105 D8
Smith's Green E Ches 168 E3
Smiths Green E Ches 184 G4
Smith's Green Essex 105 G11
Smith's Green Essex 106 C3
Smithston Aberds 302 G5
Smithstown Highld 299 B7
Smithton Highld 301 E7
Smithwood Green Suff 125 G8
Smithy Bridge Gtr Man 196 D2
Smithy Gate Flint 181 F11
Smithy Green E Ches 184 G2
Smithy Green Gtr Man 184 D5
Smithy Houses Derbys 170 F5
Smithy Lane Ends Lancs 194 E2
Smock Alley W Sus 35 D9
Smockington Leics 135 F9
Smoky Row Bucks 84 D4
Smoogro Orkney 314 F3
Smug Oak Herts 85 E10
Smyrton S Ayrs 244 G4
Smythe's Green Essex 88 B6
Snagshall E Sus 38 C3
Snaigow House Perth 286 C4
Snailbeach Shrops 131 C7
Snails Hill Som 29 E7
Snailswell Herts 104 E3
Snailwell Cambs 124 D2
Snainton N Yorks 217 C8
Snaisgill Durham 232 F5
Snaith E Yorks 198 C6
Snape N Yorks 214 C5
Snape Suff 127 F7
Snape Green Lancs 193 E11
Snape Hill Derbys 186 F5
Snape Hill S Yorks 198 G2
Snapper Devon 40 G5
Snaresbrook London 67 B11
Snarestone Leics 134 B6
Snarford Lincs 189 E9
Snargate Kent 39 B7
Snarraness Shetland 313 H4
Snatchwood Torf 78 E3
Snave Kent 39 B8
Sneachill Worcs 117 G8
Snead Powys 130 E6
Snead Common Worcs 116 D4
Sneads Green Worcs 117 D7
Sneath Common Norf 142 F3
Sneaton N Yorks 227 D7
Sneatonthorpe N Yorks 227 D8
Snedshill Telford 132 B4
Sneinton Nottingham 153 B11
Snelland Lincs 189 E9
Snelston Derbys 169 G11
Snetterton Norf 141 E9
Snettisham Norf 158 C3
Sneyd Green Stoke 168 F5
Sneyd Park Bristol 60 D5
Snibston Leics 153 G8
Snig's End Glos 98 F5
Snipeshill Kent 70 G2
Sniseabhal W Isles 297 H3
Snitter Northumb 252 C2
Snitterby Lincs 189 C7
Snitterfield Warks 118 F4
Snitterton Derbys 170 C3
Snitton Shrops 115 B11
Snittongate Shrops 115 B11
Snodhill Hereford 96 C6
Snodland Kent 69 G7
Snods Edge Northumb 242 G3
Snow End Herts 105 E8
Snow Hill E Ches 167 E10
Snow Hill W Yorks 197 C10
Snow Lea W Yorks 196 D5
Snow Street Norf 141 G11
Snowden Hill S Yorks 197 G9
Snowdown Kent 55 C8
Snowshill Glos 99 E11
Snydale W Yorks 198 D2
Soake Hants 33 E11
Soar Anglesey 178 G5
Soar Carms 94 F2
Soar Devon 9 G9
Soar Gwyn 146 B2
Soar Powys 95 E9
Soar-y-Mynydd Ceredig 112 G5
Soberton Hants 33 D10
Soberton Heath Hants 33 E10
Sockbridge Cumb 230 F6
Sockburn Darl 224 D6
Socketty Dorset 29 F7
Sodom Denb 181 G9
Sodom Shetland 313 G7
Sodom Wilts 62 C4
Sodylt Bank Shrops 148 B6
Soham Cambs 123 C11
Soham Cotes Cambs 123 B11
Soho London 67 C9
Soho Som 45 D7
Soho W Mid 133 F10
Solas W Isles 296 D4
Soldon Cross Devon 24 E4
Soldridge Hants 49 G7
Sole Street Kent 54 D5
Sole Street Kent 69 F7
Solfach = Solva Pembs 90 G5
Solihull W Mid 118 B2
Solihull Lodge W Mid 117 B11
Sollers Dilwyn Hereford 115 F8
Sollers Hope Hereford 98 E2
Sollom Lancs 194 D3
Solva = Solfach Pembs 90 G5
Somerby Leics 154 G5
Somerby Lincs 200 F5
Somercotes Derbys 170 E6
Somerdale Bath 61 F7
Somerford Dorset 19 C9
Somerford E Ches 168 B4
Somerford Staffs 133 B7
Somerford Keynes Glos 81 G8
Somerley W Sus 22 D4
Somerleyton Suff 143 D9
Somers Town London 67 C9
Somers Town Ptsmth 21 B8
Somersal Herbert Derbys 152 B2
Somersby Lincs 190 G4
Somersham Cambs 123 B7
Somersham Suff 107 B11
Somerton Newport 59 B10
Somerton Oxon 101 F9
Somerton Som 29 B7
Somerton Suff 124 G6
Somerton Hill Som 29 B7
Somerwood Shrops 149 G11
Sompting W Sus 35 G11
Sompting Abbotts W Sus 35 F11
Sonning Wokingham 65 D9
Sonning Common Oxon 65 C8
Sonning Eye Oxon 65 D9
Sontley Wrex 166 F4
Sookholme Notts 171 B8
Sopley Hants 19 B9
Sopwell Herts 85 D11
Sopworth Wilts 61 B10
Sorbie Dumfries 236 E6
Sordale Highld 310 C5
Sorisdale Argyll 288 C4
Sorley Devon 8 F4
Sorn E Ayrs 258 D3
Sornhill E Ayrs 258 C2
Sortat Highld 310 C6
Sotby Lincs 190 F2
Sothall S Yorks 186 E6
Sots Hole Lincs 173 C10
Sotterley Suff 143 G9
Soudley Shrops 131 E9
Soudley Shrops 150 D4
Soughley S Yorks 197 G7
Soughton = Sychdyn Flint 166 B2
Soulbury Bucks 103 F7

394 Sou – Sto

Soulby Cumb 222 C4
Soulby Cumb 230 F5
Souldern Oxon 101 E10
Souldrop Beds 121 E9
Sound E Ches 167 F10
Sound Shetland 313 H5
Sound Shetland 313 J6
Sound Heath E Ches 167 F10
Soundwell S Glos 60 D6
Sour Nook Cumb 230 C3
Sourhope Borders 263 E8
Sourin Orkney 314 C4
Sourlie N Ayrs 266 G6
Sourton Devon 12 C6
Soutergate Cumb 210 C4
South Acre Norf 158 G6
South Acton London 67 D7
South Alkham Kent 55 E8
South Allington Devon 9 G10
South Alloa Falk 279 C7
South Ambersham W Sus 34 C6
South Anston S Yorks 187 E8
South Ascot Windsor 66 F2
South Ashford Kent 54 E4
South Auchmachar Aberds 303 E9
South Baddesley Hants 20 B3
South Ballachulish Highld 284 B4
South Balloch S Ayrs 245 D8
South Bank Redcar 234 G6
South Bank York 207 C7
South Barrow Som 29 B10
South Beach Northumb 243 B8
South Beach = Marian-y-de Gwyn 145 C7
South Beddington London 67 G9
South Benfleet Essex 69 B9
South Bents T & W 243 E10
South Bersted W Sus 22 C6
South Blainslie Borders 271 G10
South Bockhampton Dorset 19 B9
South Bramwith S Yorks 198 E6
South Brent Devon 8 D3
South Brewham Som 45 F8
South Bromley London 67 C11
South Broomage Falk 279 E7
South Broomhill Northumb 252 D6
South Burlingham Norf 143 B7
South Cadbury Som 29 B10
South Cairn Dumfries 236 C1
South Carlton Lincs 189 F7
South Carlton Notts 187 E9
South Carne Corn 11 E10
South Cave E Yorks 208 G4
South Cerney Glos 81 F8
South Chailey E Sus 36 D5
South Chard Som 28 F4
South Charlton Northumb 264 E5
South Cheriton Som 29 C11
South Church Durham 233 F10
South Cliffe E Yorks 208 F3
South Clifton Notts 188 G4
South Clunes Highld 300 E5
South Cockerington Lincs 190 D5
South Common Devon 28 G4
South Cornelly Bridgend 57 E10
South Corriegills N Ayrs 256 C2
South Corrielaw Dumfries 248 G5
South Cove Suff 143 G9
South Creagan Argyll 289 E11
South Creake Norf 159 B7
South Crosland W Yorks 196 E6
South Croxton Leics 154 G3
South Croydon London 67 G10
South Cuil Highld 298 C3
South Dalton E Yorks 208 D5
South Darenth Kent 68 F5
South Denes Norf 143 C10
South Down Hants 33 C7
South Down Som 28 E2
South Duffield N Yorks 207 G9
South Dunn Highld 310 D5
South Earlswood Sur 51 D9
South Elkington Lincs 190 D3
South Elmsall W Yorks 198 E3
South Elphinstone E Loth 281 G7
South End Beds 103 B10
South End Bucks 103 F7
South End Cumb 210 G4
South End E Yorks 209 E9
South End Hants 31 D10
South-end Herts 86 B6
South End N Lincs 200 C6
South End Norf 141 E9
South Erradale Highld 299 B7
South Fambridge Essex 88 G5
South Farnborough Hants 49 C11
South Fawley W Berks 63 C11
South Ferriby N Lincs 200 C3
South Field E Yorks 200 B4
South Field Windsor 66 D3
South Flobbets Aberds 303 F7
South Garth Shetland 312 D7
South Garvan Highld 289 B11
South Glendale W Isles 297 K3
South Gluss Shetland 312 F5
South Godstone Sur 51 D11
South Gorley Hants 31 E11
South Gosforth T & W 242 D6
South Green Essex 89 B8
South Green Essex 87 G11
South Green Kent 69 G11
South Green Norf 157 F10
South Green Norf 159 G11
South Green Suff 126 B3
South Gyle Edin 280 G3
South-haa Shetland 312 E5
South Hackney London 67 C11
South Ham Hants 48 C6
South Hampstead London 67 C9
South Hanningfield Essex 88 F2
South Harefield London 66 B5
South Harrow London 66 B6
South Harting W Sus 34 D3
South Hatfield Herts 86 D2
South Hayling Hants 21 B10
South Hazelrigg Northumb 264 C3
South Heath Bucks 84 E6
South Heath Essex 89 B10
South Heighton E Sus 23 E7
South-heog Shetland 312 E5
South Hetton Durham 234 B3
South Hiendley W Yorks 197 E11
South Hill Corn 12 G2
South Hill N Som 43 B10
South Hill Pembs 72 C4
South Hinksey Oxon 83 E8
South Hole Devon 24 C2
South Holme N Yorks 216 D3
South Holmwood Sur 51 D7
South Hornchurch London 68 C4
South Huish Devon 8 G3
South Hykeham Lincs 172 C6
South Hylton T & W 243 F9
South Kelsey Lincs 189 B8
South Kensington London 67 D9
South Kessock Highld 300 E6
South Killingholme N Lincs 201 D7
South Kilvington N Yorks 215 C8
South Kilworth Leics 136 G2
South Kirkby W Yorks 198 E2
South Kirkton Aberds 293 C9
South Kiscadale N Ayrs 256 D2
South Knighton Devon 14 G2
South Knighton Leicester 136 C2
South Kyme Lincs 173 F11
South Lambeth London 67 D10
South Lancing W Sus 35 G11
South Lane S Yorks 197 F9
South Leigh Oxon 82 D5
South Leverton Notts 188 E3
South Littleton Worcs 99 B11
South Lopham Norf 141 G10
South Luffenham Rutland 137 C8
South Malling E Sus 36 E6
South Marston Swindon 63 B7
South Merstham Sur 51 C9
South Middleton Northumb 263 E11
South Milford N Yorks 206 G5
South Millbrex Aberds 303 E8
South Milton Devon 8 G4
South Mimms Herts 86 E2
South Molton Devon 26 B2
South Moor Durham 242 G5
South Moreton Oxon 64 B5
South Mundham W Sus 22 C5
South Muskham Notts 172 D3
South Newbald E Yorks 208 F4
South Newbarns Cumb 210 F4
South Newington Oxon 101 E8
South Newsham Northumb 243 B8
South Newton Wilts 46 G5
South Normanton Derbys 170 D6
South Norwood London 67 F10
South Nutfield Sur 51 D10
South Ockendon Thurrock 68 C5
South Ormsby Lincs 190 F5
South Ossett W Yorks 197 D9
South Otterington N Yorks 215 B7
South Owersby Lincs 189 C9
South Oxhey Herts 85 G10
South Park Sur 51 D8
South Pelaw Durham 243 G7
South Perrott Dorset 29 F7
South Petherton Som 28 D6
South Petherwin Corn 12 E2
South Pickenham Norf 141 C7
South Pill Corn 7 D8
South Pool Devon 8 G5
South Poorton Dorset 16 B6
South Port Argyll 284 E4
South Quilquox Aberds 303 F8
South Radworthy Devon 41 G9
South Rauceby Lincs 173 F8
South Raynham Norf 159 E7
South Reddish Gtr Man 184 C5
South Reston Lincs 190 E6
South Ruislip London 66 B6
South Runcton Norf 140 B2
South Scarle Notts 172 C4
South Shian Argyll 289 E11
South Shields T & W 243 D9
South Shore Blkpool 202 G2
South Side Durham 233 F8
South Side Orkney 314 D5
South Somercotes Lincs 190 C6
South Stainley N Yorks 214 G6
South Stainmore Cumb 222 C6
South Stanley Durham 242 G5
South Stifford Thurrock 68 D6
South Stoke Oxon 64 C6
South Stoke W Sus 35 F8
South Stour Kent 54 F4
South Street E Sus 36 D5
South Street Kent 54 B5
South Street Kent 68 G6
South Street Kent 69 G10
South Street Kent 70 F6
South Street London 52 B2
South Tawton Devon 13 C9
South Tehidy Corn 4 G3
South Thoresby Lincs 190 F6
South Tidworth Wilts 47 D8
South Tottenham London 67 B10
South Town Devon 14 E5
South Town Hants 49 F7
South Twerton Bath 61 G8
South Ulverston Cumb 210 D6
South View Hants 48 C6
South Voxter Shetland 313 G5
South Walsham Norf 161 G7
South Warnborough Hants 49 D8
South Weald Essex 87 G9
South Weirs Hants 32 G3
South Weston Oxon 84 F2
South Wheatley Corn 11 C10
South Wheatley Notts 188 D3
South Whiteness Shetland 313 J5
South Widcombe Bath 44 B5
South Wigston Leics 135 D11
South Willesborough Kent 54 E4
South Willingham Lincs 189 E11
South Wimbledon London 67 E9
South Wingate Durham 234 E4
South Wingfield Derbys 170 D5
South Witham Lincs 155 F8
South Wonston Hants 48 F3
South Woodford London 86 G6
South Woodham Ferrers Essex 88 F4
South Wootton Norf 158 E2
South Wraxall Wilts 61 G10
South Yardley W Mid 134 G2
South Yarrows Highld 310 E7
South Yeo Devon 25 G8
South Zeal Devon 13 C9
Southall London 66 C6
Southam Cumb 219 C9
Southam Glos 99 F9
Southam Warks 119 E8
Southampton Soton 32 E6
Southay Som 28 D6
Southborough Kent 52 E5
Southborough London 67 F7
Southborough London 68 F2
Southbourne Bmouth 19 C8
Southbourne W Sus 22 B3
Southbrook Wilts 45 G10
Southburgh Norf 141 C9
Southburn E Yorks 208 C5
Southchurch Sthend 70 B2
Southcoombe Oxon 100 F6
Southcote Reading 65 E7
Southcott Corn 11 B9
Southcott Devon 24 D6
Southcott Wilts 47 B7
Southcourt Bucks 84 C4
Southcrest Worcs 117 D10
Southdean Borders 250 B4
Southdene Mers 182 B6
Southdown Bath 61 G8
Southdown Corn 7 E8
Southease E Sus 36 F6
Southend Argyll 255 G7
Southend Bucks 65 B9
Southend Glos 80 F2
Southend London 67 E11
Southend Oxon 83 E9
Southend W Berks 64 D2
Southend W Berks 64 E5
Southend Wilts 63 E7
Southend-on-Sea Sthend 69 B11
Southerhouse Shetland 313 K5
Southerly Devon 12 D6
Southern Cross Brighton 36 F3
Southern Green Herts 104 E6
Southernby Cumb 230 D3
Southernden Kent 53 D11
Southerndown V Glam 57 G11
Southerness Dumfries 237 D11
Southery Norf 140 E2
Southey Green Essex 106 E5
Southfield Northumb 243 B7
Southfields London 67 E9
Southfields Thurrock 69 C7
Southfleet Kent 68 E6
Southford I o W 20 F6
Southgate Ceredig 111 B11
Southgate London 86 G3
Southgate Norf 159 C7
Southgate Norf 160 E2
Southgate Swansea 56 D5
Southgate W Sus 51 F9
Southill C Beds 104 C3
Southill Dorset 17 E9
Southington Hants 48 D4
Southlands Dorset 17 F9
Southleigh Devon 15 C10
Southmarsh Som 45 G8
Southmead Bristol 60 D5
Southminster Essex 89 F7
Southmoor Oxon 82 F5
Southoe Cambs 122 E3
Southolt Suff 126 D3
Southorpe P'boro 137 C11
Southover Dorset 17 C8
Southover E Sus 36 F6
Southover E Sus 37 B11
Southowram W Yorks 196 C6
Southport Mers 193 D10
Southpunds Shetland 313 L6
Southrepps Norf 160 B5
Southrey Lincs 173 B10
Southrop Glos 81 E11
Southrop Oxon 101 E7
Southrope Hants 49 E7
Southsea Ptsmth 21 B8
Southsea Wrex 166 E4
Southstoke Bath 61 G8
Southtown Norf 143 B10
Southtown Orkney 314 G4
Southtown Som 28 D4
Southtown Som 44 F5
Southville Devon 8 G4
Southville Torf 78 F3
Southwaite Cumb 230 C4
Southwark London 67 D10
Southwater W Sus 35 B11
Southwater Street W Sus 35 B11
Southway Plym 7 C9
Southway Som 44 E4
Southwell Dorset 17 G9
Southwell Notts 172 E2
Southwick Hants 33 F10
Southwick Northants 137 E10
Southwick Som 43 D11
Southwick T & W 243 F9
Southwick W Sus 36 F2
Southwick Wilts 45 B10
Southwold Suff 127 B10
Southwood Derbys 153 E7
Southwood Hants 49 B10
Southwood Norf 143 B7
Southwood Som 44 G5
Southwood Worcs 116 E4
Soval Lodge W Isles 304 F5
Sowber Gate N Yorks 215 B7
Sower Carr Lancs 202 E3
Sowerby N Yorks 215 C8
Sowerby W Yorks 196 C4
Sowerby Bridge W Yorks 196 C5
Sowerby Row Cumb 230 D3
Sowley Green Suff 124 G4
Sowood W Yorks 196 D5
Sowood Green W Yorks 196 D5
Sowton Devon 14 C5
Sowton Barton Devon 14 D2
Soyal Highld 309 K5
Soyland Town W Yorks 196 C4
Spa Common Norf 160 C5
Spacey Houses N Yorks 206 C2
Spalding Lincs 156 E4
Spaldington E Yorks 207 G11
Spaldwick Cambs 122 C2
Spalford Notts 172 B4
Spanby Lincs 155 B11
Spango Invclyd 276 G4
Spanish Green Hants 49 B7
Sparham Norf 159 F11
Sparhamhill Norf 159 F11
Spark Bridge Cumb 210 C6
Sparkbrook W Mid 133 G11
Sparkford Som 29 B10
Sparkhill W Mid 133 G11
Sparkwell Devon 7 D11
Sparl Shetland 312 G5
Sparnon Corn 1 E3
Sparnon Gate Corn 4 G3
Sparrow Green Norf 159 G9
Sparrow Hill Som 44 C2
Sparrowpit Derbys 185 E9
Sparrow's Green E Sus 52 G6
Sparsholt Hants 48 G2
Sparsholt Oxon 63 B10
Spartylea Northumb 232 B3
Spath Staffs 151 B11
Spaunton N Yorks 226 G4
Spaxton Som 43 F8
Spean Bridge Highld 290 E4
Spear Hill W Sus 35 D10
Spearywell Hants 32 B4
Speckington Som 29 C9
Speed Gate Kent 68 F5
Speedwell Bristol 60 E6
Speen Bucks 84 F4
Speen W Berks 64 F3
Speeton N Yorks 218 E2
Speke Mers 182 E6
Speldhurst Kent 52 E5
Spellbrook Herts 87 B7
Spelsbury Oxon 101 G7
Spelter Bridgend 57 C11
Spen W Yorks 197 B7
Spen Green E Ches 168 C4
Spencers Wood Wokingham 65 F8
Spennells Worcs 116 C6
Spennithorne N Yorks 214 B2
Spennymoor Durham 233 E11
Spernall Warks 117 E11
Spetchley Worcs 117 G7
Spetisbury Dorset 30 G6
Spexhall Suff 143 G7
Spey Bay Moray 302 C3
Speybank Highld 291 C10
Speybridge Highld 301 G10
Speyview Moray 302 E2
Spillardsford Aberds 303 D10
Spilsby Lincs 174 B6
Spindlestone Northumb 264 C5
Spinkhill Derbys 187 F7
Spinney Hill Northants 120 E5
Spinney Hills Leicester 136 C2
Spinningdale Highld 309 L6
Spion Kop Notts 171 B9
Spirthill Wilts 62 D3
Spital Mers 182 E4
Spital Windsor 66 D3
Spital Hill S Yorks 187 C10
Spital in the Street Lincs 189 D7
Spital Tongues T & W 242 D6
Spitalbrook Herts 86 D5
Spitalfields London 67 C10
Spitalhill Derbys 169 F11
Spithurst E Sus 36 D6
Spittal Dumfries 236 D5
Spittal E Loth 281 F9
Spittal E Yorks 207 C11
Spittal Highld 310 D5
Spittal Northumb 273 E10
Spittal Pembs 91 G9
Spittal Stirl 277 D10
Spittal Houses S Yorks 186 B5
Spittal of Glenmuick Aberds 292 E5
Spittal of Glenshee Perth 292 F3
Spittalfield Perth 286 C5
Spittlegate Lincs 155 C8
Spixworth Norf 160 F4
Splatt Corn 10 F4
Splatt Corn 11 D10
Splatt Devon 25 F10
Splatt Som 43 F8
Splayne's Green E Sus 36 C6
Splott Cardiff 59 D7
Spofforth N Yorks 206 C3
Spon End W Mid 118 B6
Spon Green Flint 166 C3
Spondon Derby 153 B8
Spooner Row Norf 141 D11
Spoonleygate Shrops 132 D6
Sporle Norf 158 G6
Spotland Bridge Gtr Man 195 E11
Spott E Loth 282 F3
Spratton Northants 120 C4
Spreakley Sur 49 E10
Spreyton Devon 13 B9
Spriddlestone Devon 7 E10
Spridlington Lincs 189 E8
Sprig's Alley Oxon 84 F3
Spring Bank Cumb 229 G10
Spring Cottage Leics 152 F6
Spring End N Yorks 223 F9
Spring Gardens Som 45 D9
Spring Green Lancs 204 E4
Spring Grove London 67 D7
Spring Hill Gtr Man 196 F2
Spring Hill Lancs 195 B8
Spring Hill W Mid 133 D7
Spring Park London 67 F11
Spring Vale S Yorks 197 G9
Spring Valley I o M 192 E4
Springbank Glos 99 G8
Springboig Glasgow 268 C3
Springbourne Bmouth 19 C8
Springburn Glasgow 268 B2
Springfield Argyll 275 F11
Springfield Caerph 77 F11
Springfield Dumfries 239 D8
Springfield Essex 88 D2
Springfield Fife 287 F7
Springfield Gtr Man 194 F5
Springfield Highld 300 C6
Springfield M Keynes 103 D7
Springfield Moray 301 D10
Springfield W Mid 133 D8
Springfield W Mid 133 F9
Springfield W Mid 133 G11
Springfields Stoke 168 G5
Springhead Gtr Man 196 G3
Springhill E Renf 267 D10
Springhill I o W 20 B6
Springhill N Lnrk 269 D7
Springhill Staffs 133 B11
Springhill Staffs 133 C9
Springholm Dumfries 237 C10
Springkell Dumfries 239 B7
Springside N Ayrs 257 B9
Springthorpe Lincs 188 D5
Springwell Essex 105 C10
Springwell T & W 243 F7
Springwell T & W 243 F9
Springwells Dumfries 248 E3
Sproatley E Yorks 209 G9
Sproston Green W Ches 168 B2
Sprotbrough S Yorks 198 G4
Sproughton Suff 108 C2
Sprouston Borders 263 B7
Sprowston Norf 160 G4
Sproxton Leics 155 E7
Sproxton N Yorks 216 C2
Sprunston Cumb 230 B3
Spunhill Shrops 149 C8
Spurlands End Bucks 84 F5
Spurstow E Ches 167 D9
Spurtree Shrops 116 D2
Spynie Moray 302 C2
Spyway Dorset 16 C6
Square and Compass Pembs 91 E7
Squires Gate Blkpool 202 G2
Sraid Ruadh Argyll 288 E1
Srannda W Isles 296 C6
Sronphadruig Lodge Perth 291 F9
Stableford Shrops 132 D5
Stableford Staffs 150 B6
Stacey Bank S Yorks 186 C3
Stackhouse N Yorks 212 F6
Stackpole Pembs 73 F7
Stackpole Quay Pembs 73 F7
Stacksford Norf 141 E11
Stacksteads Lancs 195 C10
Stackyard Green Suff 107 B9
Staddiscombe Plym 7 E10
Staddlethorpe E Yorks 199 B10
Staddon Devon 24 C3
Staddon Devon 24 G5
Staden Derbys 185 G9
Stadhampton Oxon 83 F10
Stadhlaigearraidh W Isles 297 H3
Stadmorslow Staffs 168 D5
Staffield Cumb 230 C6
Staffin Highld 298 C4
Stafford Staffs 151 E8
Stafford Park Telford 132 B4
Stafford's Corner Essex 89 B7
Stafford's Green Dorset 29 C10
Stagbatch Hereford 115 F9
Stagden Cross Essex 87 C10
Stagehall Borders 271 G9
Stag's Head Devon 25 B11
Stagsden Beds 103 B9
Stagsden West End Beds 103 B9
Stain Highld 310 C7
Stainburn Cumb 228 F6
Stainburn N Yorks 205 D10
Stainby Lincs 155 E8
Staincliffe W Yorks 197 C8
Staincross S Yorks 197 E10
Staindrop Durham 233 G8
Staines Sur 66 E4
Staines Green Herts 86 C3
Stainfield Lincs 155 D11
Stainfield Lincs 189 G10
Stainforth N Yorks 212 F6
Stainforth S Yorks 198 E6
Staining Lancs 202 F3
Stainland W Yorks 196 D5
Stainsacre N Yorks 227 D8
Stainsby Derbys 170 B6
Stainsby Lincs 190 G4
Stainton Cumb 211 B10
Stainton Cumb 230 F5
Stainton Cumb 239 F9
Stainton Durham 223 B11
Stainton M'bro 225 C9
Stainton N Yorks 224 F2
Stainton S Yorks 187 C9
Stainton by Langworth Lincs 189 F9
Stainton le Vale Lincs 189 C11
Stainton with Adgarley Cumb 210 E5
Staintondale N Yorks 227 F9
Stair Cumb 229 G10
Stair E Ayrs 257 E10
Stairfoot S Yorks 197 F11
Stairhaven Dumfries 236 D4
Staithes N Yorks 226 B5
Stake Hill Gtr Man 195 F11
Stake Pool Lancs 202 D4
Stakeford Northumb 253 F7
Stakenbridge Worcs 117 B7
Stalbridge Dorset 30 D2
Stalbridge Weston Dorset 30 D2
Stalham Norf 161 D7
Stalham Green Norf 161 E7
Stalisfield Green Kent 54 C3
Stallen Dorset 29 D10
Stalling Busk N Yorks 213 B8
Stallingborough NE Lincs 201 E7
Stallington Staffs 151 B8
Stalmine Lancs 202 D3
Stalmine Moss Side Lancs 202 D3
Stalybridge Gtr Man 185 B7
Stambermill W Mid 133 G8
Stamborough Som 42 F4
Stambourne Essex 106 D4
Stambourne Green Essex 106 D4
Stamford Lincs 137 B10
Stamford Bridge E Yorks 207 B10
Stamford Bridge W Ches 167 B7
Stamford Hill London 67 B10
Stamfordham Northumb 242 C3
Stamperland E Renf 267 D11
Stamshaw Ptsmth 33 G10
Stanah Cumb 220 B6
Stanah Lancs 202 E3
Stanborough Herts 86 C2
Stanbridge C Beds 103 G9
Stanbridge Dorset 31 G8
Stanbridgeford C Beds 103 G9
Stanbrook Essex 106 F2
Stanbrook Worcs 98 B6
Stanbury W Yorks 204 F6
Stand Gtr Man 195 F9
Stand N Lnrk 268 B5
Standburn Falk 279 G8
Standeford Staffs 133 B8
Standen Kent 53 E11
Standen Hall Lancs 203 E10
Standen Street Kent 53 G10
Standerwick Som 45 C10
Standford Hants 49 G10
Standford Bridge Telford 150 E4
Standingstone Cumb 229 B11
Standingstone Cumb 229 E7
Standish Glos 80 D4
Standish Gtr Man 194 E5
Standish Lower Ground Gtr Man 194 F5
Standlake Oxon 82 E5
Standon Hants 32 B6
Standon Herts 105 G7
Standon Staffs 150 B6
Standon Green End Herts 86 B5
Stane N Lnrk 269 D7
Stanecastle N Ayrs 257 B8
Stanfield Norf 159 E8
Stanfield Stoke 168 E5
Stanford C Beds 104 C3
Stanford Kent 54 F6
Stanford Norf 141 E7
Stanford Shrops 148 G6
Stanford Bishop Hereford 116 G3
Stanford Bridge Worcs 116 D4
Stanford Dingley W Berks 64 E5
Stanford End Wokingham 65 G8
Stanford Hills Notts 153 E10
Stanford in the Vale Oxon 82 G4
Stanford-le-Hope Thurrock 69 C7
Stanford on Avon Northants 119 B11
Stanford on Soar Notts 153 E10
Stanford on Teme Worcs 116 D4
Stanford Rivers Essex 87 E8
Stanfree Derbys 187 G7
Stanground P'boro 138 D4
Stanhill Lancs 195 B8
Stanhoe Norf 158 B6
Stanhope Borders 260 D4
Stanhope Durham 232 D5
Stanhope Kent 54 E3
Stanion Northants 137 F8
Stank Cumb 210 E4
Stanklyn Worcs 117 C7
Stanks W Yorks 206 F3
Stanley Derbys 170 G6
Stanley Durham 242 G5
Stanley Lancs 194 F3
Stanley Notts 171 C7
Stanley Perth 286 D5
Stanley Shrops 132 G3
Stanley Shrops 132 G5
Stanley Staffs 168 E6
Stanley W Yorks 197 C10
Stanley Wilts 62 E3
Stanley Common Derbys 170 G6
Stanley Crook Durham 233 D9
Stanley Downton Glos 80 E4
Stanley Ferry W Yorks 197 C11
Stanley Gate Lancs 194 G2
Stanley Green E Ches 184 E5
Stanley Green Poole 18 C6
Stanley Green Shrops 149 B10
Stanley Hill Hereford 98 C3
Stanley Moor Staffs 168 E6
Stanley Pontlarge Glos 99 E9
Stanleytown Rhondda 77 G8
Stanlow Staffs 132 D5
Stanlow W Ches 182 F6
Stanmer Brighton 36 F4
Stanmore Hants 33 B7
Stanmore London 85 G11
Stanmore Shrops 132 E4
Stanmore W Berks 64 D3
Stanner Powys 114 F5
Stannergate Dundee 287 D8
Stanners Hill Sur 66 G3
Stannersburn Northumb 250 F6
Stanningfield Suff 125 F7
Stanningley W Yorks 205 G10
Stannington Northumb 242 B6
Stannington S Yorks 186 D4
Stanpit Dorset 19 C9
Stansbatch Hereford 114 E6
Stansfield Suff 124 G5
Stanshope Staffs 169 E10
Stanstead Suff 106 B6
Stanstead Abbotts Herts 86 C5
Stansted Kent 68 G6
Stansted Airport Essex 105 G11
Stansted Mountfitchet Essex 105 F10
Stanthorne W Ches 167 B11
Stanton Glos 99 E11
Stanton Mon 96 G6
Stanton Northumb 252 F4
Stanton Staffs 169 F10
Stanton Suff 125 C9
Stanton by Bridge Derbys 153 D7
Stanton-by-Dale Derbys 153 B9
Stanton Chare Suff 125 C9
Stanton Drew Bath 60 G5
Stanton Fitzwarren Swindon 81 G11
Stanton Gate Notts 153 B9
Stanton Harcourt Oxon 82 D6
Stanton Hill Notts 171 C7
Stanton in Peak Derbys 170 C2
Stanton Lacy Shrops 115 B9
Stanton Lees Derbys 170 C3
Stanton Long Shrops 131 E11
Stanton-on-the-Wolds Notts 154 C2
Stanton Prior Bath 61 G7
Stanton St Bernard Wilts 62 G5
Stanton St John Oxon 83 D9
Stanton St Quintin Wilts 62 D2
Stanton Street Suff 125 D9
Stanton under Bardon Leics 153 G9
Stanton upon Hine Heath Shrops 149 E11
Stanton Wick Bath 60 G6
Stantonbury M Keynes 102 C6
Stantway Glos 80 C2
Stanwardine in the Fields Shrops 149 E8
Stanwardine in the Wood Shrops 149 D8
Stanway Essex 107 G8
Stanway Glos 99 E11
Stanway Green Essex 107 G9
Stanway Green Suff 126 C4
Stanwell Sur 66 E5
Stanwell Moor Sur 66 E4
Stanwick Northants 121 C9
Stanwick-St-John N Yorks 224 C3
Stanwix Cumb 239 F10
Stanycliffe Gtr Man 195 F11
Stanydale Shetland 313 H4
Staoinebrig W Isles 297 H3
Stape N Yorks 226 G5
Stapehill Dorset 31 G9
Stapeley E Ches 167 F11
Stapenhill Staffs 152 E5
Staple Kent 55 B9
Staple Som 42 E6
Staple Cross Devon 27 C8
Staple Fitzpaine Som 28 D3
Staple Hill S Glos 61 D7
Staple Hill Worcs 117 C9
Staple Lawns Som 28 D3
Staplecross E Sus 38 C3
Staplefield W Sus 36 B3
Stapleford Cambs 123 G9
Stapleford Herts 86 B4
Stapleford Leics 154 F6
Stapleford Lincs 172 D5
Stapleford Notts 153 B9
Stapleford Wilts 46 F5
Stapleford Abbotts Essex 87 G8
Stapleford Tawney Essex 87 F8
Staplegrove Som 28 B2
Staplehay Som 28 C2
Staplehurst Kent 53 E9
Staplers I o W 20 D6
Staples Hill W Sus 35 B8
Staplestreet Kent 70 G5
Stapleton Bristol 60 D6
Stapleton Cumb 240 C2
Stapleton Hereford 114 D6
Stapleton Leics 135 D8
Stapleton N Yorks 198 D4
Stapleton N Yorks 224 C5
Stapleton Shrops 131 C9
Stapleton Som 29 C7
Stapley Som 27 E11
Staploe Beds 122 E2
Staplow Hereford 98 C3
Stapness Shetland 313 J4
Star Fife 287 G7
Star Pembs 92 E4
Star Som 44 B2
Star Hill Mon 79 E7
Stara Orkney 314 D2
Starbeck N Yorks 206 B2
Starbotton N Yorks 213 E9
Starcross Devon 14 E5
Stareton Warks 118 C6
Stargate T & W 242 E5
Starkholmes Derbys 170 D4
Starling Gtr Man 195 E9
Starlings Green Essex 105 E9
Starr's Green E Sus 38 D3
Starston Norf 142 G4
Start Devon 8 G6
Start Hill Essex 105 G10
Startforth Durham 223 B10
Startley Wilts 62 C2
Startop's End Bucks 84 C6
Starveall S Glos 61 B9
Starvecrow Kent 52 D5
Statenborough Kent 55 B10
Statford St Andrew Suff 127 E7
Statham Warr 183 D11
Stathe Som 28 B5
Stathern Leics 154 C5
Station Hill Cumb 229 B11
Station Town Durham 234 D4
Statland Common Norf 141 D10
Staughton Green Cambs 122 D2
Staughton Highway Cambs 122 E2
Staughton Moor Beds 122 E2
Staunton Glos 79 C8
Staunton Glos 98 F5
Staunton in the Vale Notts 172 G4
Staunton on Arrow Hereford 115 E7
Staunton on Wye Hereford 97 B7
Staupes N Yorks 205 B10
Staveley Cumb 211 B7
Staveley Cumb 221 F9
Staveley Derbys 186 G6
Staveley N Yorks 215 G7
Staveley-in-Cartmel Cumb 211 B7
Staverton Devon 8 C5
Staverton Glos 99 G7
Staverton Northants 119 E10
Staverton Wilts 61 G11
Staverton Bridge Glos 99 G7
Stawell Som 43 F11
Stawley Som 27 C9
Staxigoe Highld 310 D7
Staxton N Yorks 217 D10
Staylittle Ceredig 128 F2
Staylittle = Penffordd-Lâs Powys 129 E7
Staynall Lancs 202 E3
Staythorpe Notts 172 E3
Stead W Yorks 205 D8
Steam Mills Glos 79 B10
Stean N Yorks 213 E11
Steanbow Som 44 F5
Stearsby N Yorks 216 E2
Steart Som 29 B9
Steart Som 43 D9
Stebbing Essex 106 G3
Stebbing Green Essex 106 G3
Stechford W Mid 134 F2
Stede Quarter Kent 53 F11
Stedham W Sus 34 C5
Steel Northumb 241 F10
Steel Northumb 251 G9
Steel Bank S Yorks 186 D4
Steel Cross E Sus 52 G4
Steel Green Cumb 210 D3
Steel Heath Shrops 149 B10
Steele Road Borders 250 E2
Steelend Fife 279 C10
Steeleroad-end Borders 250 E2
Steen's Bridge Hereford 115 F10
Steep Hants 34 B2
Steep Lane W Yorks 196 C4
Steep Marsh Hants 34 B3
Steephill I o W 21 F7
Steeple Dorset 18 E4
Steeple Essex 88 E6
Steeple Ashton Wilts 46 B2
Steeple Aston Oxon 101 F9
Steeple Barton Oxon 101 G8
Steeple Bumpstead Essex 106 C3
Steeple Claydon Bucks 102 F3
Steeple Gidding Cambs 138 G2
Steeple Langford Wilts 46 F4
Steeple Morden Cambs 104 C5
Steeraway Telford 132 B3
Steeton W Yorks 204 E6
Stein Highld 298 D2
Steinmanhill Aberds 303 E7
Stella T & W 242 E5
Stelling Minnis Kent 54 D6
Stelvio Newport 59 B9
Stembridge Som 28 C6
Stembridge Swansea 56 C3
Stemster Highld 310 C5
Stemster Ho Highld 310 C5
Stenalees Corn 5 D10
Stenaquoy Orkney 314 C5
Stencoose Corn 4 F4
Stenhill Devon 27 E9
Stenhouse Dumfries 247 E8
Stenhouse Edin 280 G4
Stenhousemuir Falk 279 E7
Stenigot Lincs 190 E3
Stennack Corn 2 B5
Stenness Shetland 312 F4
Stenscholl Highld 298 C4
Stenso Orkney 314 D3
Stenson Derbys 152 D6
Stenton E Loth 282 G2
Stenton Fife 280 B5
Stentwood Devon 27 F10
Stenwith Lincs 154 B6
Stepaside Corn 5 F9
Stepaside Pembs 73 D10
Stepaside Powys 129 F11
Stepping Hill Gtr Man 184 D6
Steppingley C Beds 103 D10
Stepps N Lnrk 268 B3
Sterndale Moor Derbys 169 B10
Sternfield Suff 127 E7
Sterridge Devon 40 D5
Stert Wilts 46 B4
Sterte Poole 18 C6
Stetchworth Cambs 124 F2
Stevenage Herts 104 G4
Steven's Crouch E Sus 38 D2
Stevenston N Ayrs 266 G5
Stevenstone Devon 25 D8
Steventon Hants 48 D4
Steventon Oxon 83 G7
Steventon Shrops 115 C10
Steventon End Essex 105 C11
Stevington Beds 121 G9
Stewards Essex 87 D7
Steward's Green Essex 87 E7
Stewartby Beds 103 C10
Stewarton Argyll 255 F7
Stewarton E Ayrs 267 F8
Stewkley Bucks 103 F7
Stewkley Dean Bucks 102 F6
Stewley Som 28 D4
Stewton Lincs 190 D5
Steyne Cross I o W 21 D8
Steyning W Sus 35 E11
Steynton Pembs 72 D6
Stibb Corn 24 E2
Stibb Cross Devon 24 E6
Stibb Green Wilts 63 G8
Stibbard Norf 159 D9
Stibbington Cambs 137 D11
Stichill Borders 262 B6
Stick Hill Kent 52 E3
Sticker Corn 5 E9
Stickford Lincs 174 D5
Sticklepath Devon 13 C8
Sticklepath Devon 40 G5
Sticklepath Som 28 E4
Sticklepath Som 42 F4
Sticklinch Som 44 F5
Stickling Green Essex 105 E9
Stickney Lincs 174 D4
Stiff Street Kent 69 G11
Stiffkey Norf 177 E7
Stifford's Bridge Hereford 98 B4
Stileway Som 44 E3
Stillingfleet N Yorks 207 E7
Stillington N Yorks 215 F11
Stillington Stockton 234 G3
Stilton Cambs 138 F3
Stinchcombe Glos 80 F2
Stinsford Dorset 17 C10
Stiperstones Shrops 131 C7
Stirchley Telford 132 B4
Stirchley W Mid 133 G11
Stirkoke Ho Highld 310 D7
Stirling Aberds 303 E11
Stirling Stirl 278 C5
Stirtloe Cambs 122 D3
Stirton N Yorks 204 C5
Stisted Essex 106 G5
Stitchcombe Wilts 63 F8
Stitchin's Hill Worcs 116 G5
Stithians Corn 2 B6
Stittenham Highld 300 B6
Stivichall W Mid 118 B6
Stixwould Lincs 173 B11
Stoak W Ches 182 G6
Stobhill Northumb 252 G6
Stobhillgate Northumb 252 F6
Stobieside S Lnrk 258 B4
Stobo Borders 260 B5
Stoborough Dorset 18 D4
Stoborough Green Dorset 18 D4
Stobs Castle Borders 250 B2
Stobshiel E Loth 271 C9
Stobswood Northumb 252 E6
Stock Essex 87 F11
Stock Lancs 204 D3
Stock N Som 60 G3
Stock Green Worcs 117 F9
Stock Hill Suff 125 D9
Stock Wood Worcs 117 F10
Stockbridge Hants 47 G11
Stockbridge S Yorks 198 F5
Stockbridge W Sus 22 C5
Stockbridge W Yorks 205 E7
Stockbridge Village Mers 182 C6
Stockbury Kent 69 G10
Stockcross W Berks 64 F2
Stockend Glos 80 D4
Stocker's Head Kent 54 C3
Stockerston Leics 136 D6
Stockfield W Mid 134 G2
Stockheath Hants 22 B2
Stockholes Turbary N Lincs 199 F9
Stockiemuir Stirl 277 E10
Stocking Hereford 98 E2
Stocking Green Essex 105 D11
Stocking Pelham Herts 105 F9
Stockingford Warks 134 E6
Stockland Devon 28 G2
Stockland Bristol Som 43 E8
Stockland Green Kent 52 E5
Stockland Green W Mid 133 E11
Stockleigh English Devon 26 F5
Stockleigh Pomeroy Devon 26 G5
Stockley Wilts 62 F4
Stocklinch Som 28 D5
Stockport Gtr Man 184 C5
Stocks Green Kent 52 D5
Stocksbridge S Yorks 186 B3
Stocksfield Northumb 242 E3
Stockstreet Essex 106 G6
Stockton Hereford 115 E10
Stockton Norf 143 E7
Stockton Shrops 130 C5
Stockton Shrops 132 D4
Stockton Telford 150 F5
Stockton Warks 119 E8
Stockton Wilts 46 F3
Stockton Brook Staffs 168 E6
Stockton Heath Warr 183 D10
Stockton-on-Tees Stockton 225 B8
Stockton on Teme Worcs 116 D4
Stockton on the Forest York 207 B9
Stocktonwood Shrops 130 C5
Stockwell Devon 27 G7
Stockwell Glos 80 C6
Stockwell London 67 D10
Stockwell End W Mid 133 D7
Stockwell Heath Staffs 151 E11
Stockwitch Cross Som 29 C9
Stockwood Bristol 60 F6
Stockwood Dorset 29 F9
Stockwood Vale Bath 60 F6
Stodday Lancs 202 B5
Stodmarsh Kent 71 G8
Stody Norf 159 C11
Stoer Highld 307 G5
Stoford Som 29 E9
Stoford Wilts 46 F5
Stoford Water Devon 27 F9
Stogumber Som 42 F5

Stogursey Som 43 E8
Stoke Devon 24 C2
Stoke Hants 22 C2
Stoke Hants 48 C2
Stoke Medway 69 D10
Stoke Plym 7 D9
Stoke Suff 108 C3
Stoke W Mid 119 B7
Stoke Abbott Dorset 29 G7
Stoke Albany Northants 136 F6
Stoke Aldermoor W Mid 119 B7
Stoke Ash Suff 126 C2
Stoke Bardolph Notts 171 G10
Stoke Bishop Bristol 60 D5
Stoke Bliss Worcs 116 E3
Stoke Bruerne Northants 102 B4
Stoke by Clare Suff 106 C4
Stoke-by-Nayland Suff 107 D9
Stoke Canon Devon 14 B4
Stoke Charity Hants 48 F3
Stoke Climsland Corn 12 G3
Stoke Common Hants 33 C7
Stoke Cross Hereford 116 G2
Stoke D'Abernon Sur 50 B6
Stoke Doyle Northants 137 F10
Stoke Dry Rutland 137 D7
Stoke Edith Hereford 98 C2
Stoke End Warks 134 D3
Stoke Farthing Wilts 31 B9
Stoke Ferry Norf 140 D4
Stoke Fleming Devon 9 F7
Stoke Gabriel Devon 8 D6
Stoke Gifford S Glos 60 D6
Stoke Golding Leics 135 D7
Stoke Goldington M Keynes 102 B6
Stoke Green Bucks 66 C3
Stoke Hammond Bucks 103 F7
Stoke Heath Shrops 150 D3
Stoke Heath W Mid 135 G7
Stoke Heath Worcs 117 D8
Stoke Hill Devon 14 C4
Stoke Hill Hereford 98 B2
Stoke Holy Cross Norf 142 C4
Stoke Lacy Hereford 98 B2
Stoke Lane Hereford 116 G2
Stoke Lyne Oxon 101 F11
Stoke Mandeville Bucks 84 C4
Stoke Newington London 67 B10
Stoke on Tern Shrops 150 D2
Stoke-on-Trent Stoke 168 F5
Stoke Orchard Glos 99 F8
Stoke Park Suff 108 C3
Stoke Poges Bucks 66 C3
Stoke Pound Worcs 117 D9
Stoke Prior Hereford 115 F10
Stoke Prior Worcs 117 D8
Stoke Rivers Devon 40 F6
Stoke Rochford Lincs 155 D8
Stoke Row Oxon 65 C7
Stoke St Gregory Som 28 B4
Stoke St Mary Som 28 C3
Stoke St Michael Som 45 D7
Stoke St Milborough Shrops 131 G11
Stoke sub Hamdon Som 29 D7
Stoke Talmage Oxon 83 F11
Stoke Trister Som 30 B2
Stoke Wake Dorset 30 F3
Stoke Water Dorset 29 G7
Stoke Wharf Worcs 117 D9
Stokeford Dorset 18 D3
Stokegorse Shrops 131 G11
Stokeham Notts 188 F3
Stokeinteignhead Devon 14 G4
Stokenchurch Bucks 84 F3
Stokenham Devon 8 G6
Stokesay Shrops 131 G8
Stokesby Norf 161 G8
Stokesley N Yorks 225 D10
Stokoe Northumb 250 F6
Stolford Som 43 D8
Ston Easton Som 44 C6
Stondon Massey Essex 87 E9
Stone Bucks 84 C3
Stone Glos 79 F11
Stone Kent 38 B6
Stone Kent 68 E5
Stone S Yorks 187 D9
Stone Som 44 G5
Stone Staffs 151 C8
Stone Worcs 117 B7
Stone Allerton Som 44 C2
Stone Bridge Corner P'boro 138 C5
Stone Chair W Yorks 196 B6
Stone Cross E Sus 23 E10
Stone Cross E Sus 37 B8
Stone Cross E Sus 52 G6
Stone Cross Kent 52 F4
Stone Cross Kent 54 F4
Stone Cross Kent 55 B10
Stone Cross W Mid 133 E10
Stone-edge Batch N Som 60 E3
Stone Head N Yorks 204 E4
Stone Heath Staffs 151 B9
Stone Hill Kent 54 D2
Stone Hill Kent 54 F5
Stone Hill S Glos 60 E6
Stone Hill S Yorks 199 F7
Stone House Cumb 212 B5
Stone in Oxney Kent 38 B6
Stone Raise Cumb 230 B4
Stone Street Kent 52 C5
Stone Street Suff 107 D9
Stone Street Suff 143 G7
Stonea Cambs 139 E9
Stoneacton Shrops 131 E10
Stonebow Worcs 99 B8
Stonebridge Essex 70 B2
Stonebridge London 67 C8
Stonebridge N Som 43 B11
Stonebridge Norf 141 E8
Stonebridge Sur 51 D7
Stonebridge W Mid 134 G4
Stonebridge Green Kent 54 D2
Stonebroom Derbys 170 D6
Stonebyres Holdings S Lnrk 268 G6
Stoneclough Gtr Man 195 F9
Stonecombe Devon 40 E6
Stonecrouch Kent 53 G7
Stonedge Borders 250 B3
Stoneferry Hull 209 G8
Stonefield Argyll 289 F11
Stonefield S Lnrk 268 D3
Stonefield Staffs 151 C7
Stonefield Castle Hotel Argyll 275 F9
Stonegate E Sus 37 B11
Stonegate N Yorks 226 D5
Stonegrave N Yorks 216 D3
Stonegravels Derbys 186 G5
Stonehall Kent 55 D9
Stonehall Worcs 99 B7
Stonehaugh Northumb 241 B7
Stonehaven Aberds 293 E10
Stonehill Sur 66 G4
Stonehills Hants 33 G7
Stonehouse Aberds 303 F8
Stonehouse Glos 80 D4
Stonehouse Northumb 240 F5
Stonehouse Plym 7 E9
Stonehouse S Lnrk 268 F5
Stonehouses Staffs 169 G7
Stoneleigh London 67 G8
Stoneleigh Warks 118 C6
Stoneley Green E Ches 167 E10
Stonely Cambs 122 D2
Stonepits Worcs 117 F10
Stonequarry W Sus 52 F2
Stoner Hill Hants 34 B2
Stones Green Essex 108 F3
Stonesby Leics 154 E6
Stonesfield Oxon 82 B5
Stonestreet Green Kent 54 F5
Stonethwaite Cumb 220 C5
Stoneton Warks 119 G9
Stonewells Moray 302 C2
Stonewood Kent 68 E5
Stoney Cross Hants 32 E3
Stoney Hill Worcs 117 C9
Stoney Middleton Derbys 186 F2
Stoney Royd W Yorks 196 C5
Stoney Stanton Leics 135 E9
Stoney Stoke Som 45 G8
Stoney Stratton Som 45 F7
Stoney Stretton Shrops 131 B7
Stoneyard Green Hereford 98 C4
Stoneybank E Loth 280 G6
Stoneybreck Shetland 313 N2
Stoneyburn W Loth 269 C9
Stoneycombe Devon 9 B7
Stoneycroft Mers 182 C5
Stoneyfield Gtr Man 195 E11
Stoneyfield Moray 301 D11
Stoneyford Derbys 170 F6
Stoneyford Devon 27 F8
Stoneygate Aberds 303 F10
Stoneygate Leicester 136 C2
Stoneyhills Essex 88 F6
Stoneykirk Dumfries 236 D2
Stoneylane Shrops 115 B11
Stoneywood Aberdeen 293 B10
Stoneywood Falk 278 E5
Stonganess Shetland 312 C7
Stonham Aspal Suff 126 F2
Stonnall Staffs 133 C11
Stonor Oxon 65 B8
Stonton Wyville Leics 136 D4
Stony Batter Hants 32 B3
Stony Cross Devon 25 B8
Stony Cross Hereford 98 B4
Stony Cross Hereford 115 D10
Stony Dale Notts 172 G2
Stony Gate T & W 243 G9
Stony Green Bucks 84 F5
Stony Heap Durham 242 G4
Stony Heath Hants 48 B5
Stony Houghton Derbys 171 B7
Stony Knaps Dorset 28 G5
Stony Littleton Bath 45 B8
Stony Stratford M Keynes 102 C5
Stonyfield Highld 300 B6
Stonyford Hants 32 D4
Stonyland Devon 25 B8
Stonymarsh Hants 32 B4
Stoodleigh Devon 26 D6
Stop-and-Call Pembs 91 D8
Stopes S Yorks 186 D3
Stopgate Devon 28 F2
Stopham W Sus 35 D8
Stopper Lane Lancs 204 D2
Stopsley Luton 104 G2
Stoptide Corn 10 F4
Stores Corner Suff 109 B7
Storeton Mers 182 E4
Storiths N Yorks 205 C7
Stormontfield Perth 286 E5
Stormore Wilts 45 D10
Stornoway W Isles 304 E6
Storridge Hereford 98 B4
Storrington W Sus 35 E9
Storrs Cumb 221 G7
Storrs S Yorks 186 D3
Storth Cumb 211 C9
Storwood E Yorks 207 E10
Stotfield Moray 302 B2
Stotfold C Beds 104 D4
Stottesdon Shrops 132 G3
Stoughton Leics 136 C2
Stoughton Sur 50 C3
Stoughton W Sus 34 E4
Stoughton Cross Som 44 D2
Stoul Highld 295 F9
Stoulton Worcs 99 B8
Stour Provost Dorset 30 C3
Stour Row Dorset 30 C4
Stourbridge W Mid 133 G8
Stourpaine Dorset 30 F5
Stourport on Severn Worcs 116 C6
Stourton Staffs 133 F7
Stourton W Yorks 206 G2
Stourton Warks 100 D5
Stourton Wilts 45 G9
Stourton Caundle Dorset 30 D2
Stourton Hill Warks 100 D6
Stout Som 44 G2
Stove Orkney 314 C6
Stove Shetland 313 L6
Stoven Suff 143 G8
Stow Borders 271 G9
Stow Lincs 155 B11
Stow Lincs 188 E5
Stow Bardolph Norf 140 B2
Stow Bedon Norf 141 D9
Stow cum Quy Cambs 123 E10
Stow Lawn W Mid 133 D8
Stow Longa Cambs 122 C2
Stow Maries Essex 88 F4
Stow-on-the-Wold Glos 100 F3
Stow Park Newport 59 B10
Stowbridge Norf 140 B2
Stowe Glos 79 D9
Stowe Hereford 96 B5
Stowe Lincs 156 G2
Stowe Shrops 114 C6
Stowe Staffs 152 G2
Stowe-by-Chartley Staffs 151 D10
Stowe Green Glos 79 D9
Stowell Glos 81 C9
Stowell Som 29 C11
Stowey Bath 44 B5
Stowfield Hereford 79 B9
Stowford Devon 12 B4
Stowford Devon 12 D4
Stowford Devon 24 E3
Stowford Devon 25 B10
Stowford Devon 41 E7
Stowgate Lincs 156 G3
Stowlangtoft Suff 125 D9
Stowmarket Suff 125 F10
Stowting Kent 54 E6
Stowting Common Kent 54 E6
Stowting Court Kent 54 E6
Stowupland Suff 125 F11
Straad Argyll 275 G11
Strachan Aberds 293 D8
Strachurmore Argyll 284 G5
Stradbroke Suff 126 C4
Stradishall Suff 124 G4
Stradsett Norf 140 C3
Stragglethorpe Lincs 172 E6
Straid S Ayrs 244 E4
Straight Soley Wilts 63 E10
Straith Dumfries 247 F8
Straiton Edin 270 B5
Straiton S Ayrs 245 C9
Straloch Aberds 303 G8
Straloch Perth 292 G2
Stramshall Staffs 151 B11
Strand Glos 80 C2
Strand London 67 C10
Strands Cumb 210 C3
Strang I o M 192 E4
Strangeways Gtr Man 184 B4
Strangford Hereford 97 F11
Stranghow Redcar 226 B3
Strangways Wilts 46 E6
Stranog Aberds 293 D10
Stranraer Dumfries 236 C2
Strata Florida Ceredig 112 D4
Stratfield Mortimer W Berks 65 G7
Stratfield Saye Hants 65 G7
Stratfield Turgis Hants 49 B7
Stratford C Beds 104 B3
Stratford Glos 99 D7
Stratford London 67 C11
Stratford Marsh London 67 C11
Stratford New Town London 67 C11
Stratford St Andrew Suff 127 E7
Stratford St Mary Suff 107 E10
Stratford Sub Castle Wilts 46 G6
Stratford Tony Wilts 31 B9
Stratford-upon-Avon Warks 118 F3
Strath Highld 299 B7
Strath Highld 310 D6
Strathallan Castle Perth 286 F3
Strathan Highld 295 F11
Strathan Highld 307 G5
Strathan Highld 308 C5
Strathan Skerray Highld 308 C6
Strathaven S Lnrk 268 G4
Strathavon Lo Moray 301 G11
Strathblane Stirl 277 F11
Strathcanaird Highld 307 J6
Strathcarron Highld 299 E9
Strathcoil Argyll 289 F8
Strathcoul Highld 310 D5
Strathdon Aberds 292 B5
Strathellie Aberds 303 C10
Strathgarve Lodge Highld 300 C4
Strathkinness Fife 287 F8
Strathmashie House Highld 291 D7
Strathmiglo Fife 286 F6
Strathmore Lodge Highld 310 E5
Strathpeffer Highld 300 D4
Strathrannoch Highld 300 B3
Strathtay Perth 286 B3
Strathvaich Lodge Highld 300 B3
Strathwhillan N Ayrs 256 B2
Strathy Highld 300 B6
Strathy Highld 310 C2
Strathyre Stirl 285 F9
Stratton Corn 24 F2
Stratton Dorset 17 C9
Stratton Glos 81 E8
Stratton Audley Oxon 102 F2
Stratton Chase Bucks 85 G7
Stratton-on-the-Fosse Som 45 C7
Stratton St Margaret Swindon 63 B7
Stratton St Michael Norf 142 E4
Stratton Strawless Norf 160 E4
Stravithie Fife 287 F9
Strawberry Bank Cumb 211 B8
Strawberry Hill E Sus 52 F5
Strawberry Hill London 67 E7
Strawberry Hill W Yorks 198 C2
Streat E Sus 36 D5
Streatham London 67 E10
Streatham Hill London 67 E10
Streatham Park London 67 E9
Streatham Vale London 67 E9
Streatley C Beds 103 F11
Streatley W Berks 64 C5
Street Cumb 222 D2
Street Lancs 202 C6
Street N Yorks 226 E4
Street Som 28 F5
Street Som 44 F3
Street Ash Som 28 E3
Street Ashton Warks 135 G9
Street Dinas Shrops 148 B6
Street End Hants 33 D9
Street End Kent 54 C6
Street End W Sus 22 D5
Street Gate T & W 242 F6
Street Houses N Yorks 206 D6
Street Lane Derbys 170 F5
Street Lydan Wrex 149 B8
Street of Kincardine Highld 291 B11
Street on the Fosse Som 44 F6
Streethay Staffs 152 G2
Streethouse W Yorks 197 C11
Streetlam N Yorks 224 F6
Streetly W Mid 133 D11
Streetly End Cambs 106 B2
Strefford Shrops 131 F8
Strelley Notts 171 G8
Strensall York 216 G2
Strensham Worcs 99 C8
Stretch Down Devon 26 E4
Stretcholt Som 43 E9
Strete Devon 8 F6
Stretford Gtr Man 184 C4
Stretford Hereford 115 F10
Stretford Court Hereford 115 F8
Strethall Essex 105 D9
Stretham Cambs 123 C10
Strettington W Sus 22 B5
Stretton Derbys 170 C5
Stretton Rutland 155 F8
Stretton Staffs 151 G7
Stretton Staffs 152 D5
Stretton W Ches 166 E6
Stretton Warr 183 E10
Stretton en le Field Leics 152 G6
Stretton Grandison Hereford 98 C2
Stretton-on-Dunsmore Warks 119 C8
Stretton-on-Fosse Warks 100 D4
Stretton Sugwas Hereford 97 C9
Stretton under Fosse Warks 135 G8
Stretton Westwood Shrops 131 D11
Strichen Aberds 303 D9
Strines Gtr Man 185 D7
Stringston Som 43 E7
Strixton Northants 121 E8
Stroat Glos 79 F9
Strode N Som 60 G4
Strom Shetland 313 J5
Stromeferry Highld 295 B10
Stromemore Highld 295 B10
Stromness Orkney 314 F2
Stronaba Highld 290 E4
Stronachlachar Stirl 285 F8
Stronachullin Lodge Argyll 275 F9
Stronchreggan Highld 290 F2
Stronchrubie Highld 307 H7
Strone Argyll 255 F7
Strone Argyll 274 G6
Strone Argyll 276 E3
Strone Highld 290 E3
Strone Highld 291 D9
Strone Highld 300 G5
Strone Invclyd 276 G5
Stronelairg Lodge Highld 291 C7
Stroneskar Argyll 275 C9
Stronmachair Stirl 285 G8
Stronmilchan Argyll 284 E5
Stronord Dumfries 236 C6
Stronsaul Argyll 276 F2
Strontian Highld 289 C10
Stronvar Stirl 285 E9
Strood Kent 53 G11
Strood Medway 69 F8
Strood Green Sur 51 D8
Strood Green W Sus 35 C8
Strood Green W Sus 50 G6
Strothers Dale Northumb 241 F11
Stroud Glos 80 D4
Stroud Hants 34 C2
Stroud Sur 50 F2
Stroud Green Essex 88 G5
Stroud Green Glos 80 D4
Stroud Green London 67 B10
Stroude Sur 66 F4
Strouden Bmouth 19 C8
Stroul Argyll 276 E4
Stroupster Highld 310 C7
Stroxton Lincs 155 C8
Stroxworthy Devon 24 D4
Struan Highld 294 B5
Struan Perth 291 G10
Strubby Lincs 191 E7
Structon's Heath Worcs 116 D5
Strugg's Hill Lincs 156 B5
Strumpshaw Norf 142 B6
Strutherhill S Lnrk 268 F5
Struthers Fife 287 G7
Struy Highld 300 F3
Stryd Anglesey 178 E2
Stryd y Facsen Anglesey 178 E4
Stryt-issa Wrex 166 F3
Stuartfield Aberds 303 E9
Stub Place Cumb 219 G11
Stubb Norf 161 E8
Stubbermere W Sus 22 B3
Stubber's Green W Mid 133 C10
Stubbings Windsor 65 C10
Stubbing's Green Suff 125 C11
Stubbington Hants 33 G9
Stubbins Lancs 195 D9
Stubbins Lancs 202 E6
Stubble Green Cumb 219 F11
Stubbles W Berks 64 D5
Stubbs Cross Kent 54 F3
Stubb's Green Norf 142 D5
Stubbs Green Norf 143 D7
Stubhampton Dorset 30 E6
Stubshaw Cross Gtr Man 194 G5
Stubton Lincs 172 F5
Stubwood Staffs 151 B11
Stuckgowan Argyll 285 G7
Stuckton Hants 31 E11
Stud Green E Ches 168 C2
Stud Green Windsor 65 D11
Studd Hill Kent 71 F7
Studdal Kent 55 D10
Studfold N Yorks 212 E6
Studham C Beds 85 B8
Studland Dorset 18 E6
Studley Warks 117 E11
Studley Wilts 62 E3
Studley Green Bucks 84 F3
Studley Green Wilts 45 B10
Studley Roger N Yorks 214 E5
Studley Royal N Yorks 214 E5
Stump Cross Essex 105 C10
Stumps Cross Glos 99 E11
Stuntney Cambs 123 B11
Stunts Green E Sus 23 C10
Sturbridge Staffs 150 C6
Sturford Wilts 45 E10
Sturgate Lincs 188 D5
Sturmer Essex 106 C3
Sturminster Common Dorset 30 E3
Sturminster Marshall Dorset 31 G7
Sturminster Newton Dorset 30 E3
Sturry Kent 71 G7
Stursdon Corn 24 E2
Sturton N Lincs 200 G3
Sturton by Stow Lincs 188 E5
Sturton le Steeple Notts 188 E3
Stuston Suff 126 B2
Stutton N Yorks 206 E5
Stutton Suff 108 E3
Styal E Ches 184 E4
Styants Bottom Kent 52 B5
Stydd Lancs 203 F9
Styrrup Notts 187 C10
Suainebost W Isles 304 B7
Suardail W Isles 304 E6
Succoth Aberds 302 F4
Succoth Argyll 284 G6
Suckley Worcs 116 G4
Suckley Green Worcs 116 G4
Suckley Knowl Worcs 116 G4
Suckquoy Orkney 314 H4
Sucksted Green Essex 105 F11
Sudborough Northants 137 G9
Sudbourne Suff 127 G8
Sudbrook Lincs 173 G7
Sudbrook Mon 60 B4
Sudbrooke Lincs 189 F8
Sudbury Derbys 152 C3
Sudbury London 67 C7
Sudbury Suff 107 C7
Sudden Gtr Man 195 E11
Suddie Highld 300 D6
Sudgrove Glos 80 D6
Suffield N Yorks 227 G9
Suffield Norf 160 C4
Sugnall Staffs 150 C5
Sugwas Pool Hereford 97 C9
Suisnish Highld 295 D7
Suladale Highld 298 D3
Sulaisiadar W Isles 304 E7
Sulby I o M 192 C4
Sulgrave Northants 101 B11
Sulgrave T & W 243 F8
Sulham W Berks 64 E6
Sulhampstead W Berks 64 F6
Sulhampstead Abbots W Berks 64 F6
Sulhampstead Bannister Upper End W Berks 64 F6
Sulhamstead W Berks 64 F6
Sulland Orkney 314 B5
Sullington W Sus 35 E9
Sullington Warren W Sus 35 E9
Sullom Shetland 312 F5
Sullom Voe Oil Terminal Shetland 312 F5
Sully V Glam 59 F7
Sumburgh Shetland 313 N6
Summer Bridge N Yorks 214 G4
Summer Heath Bucks 84 G2
Summer Hill E Sus 23 D9
Summer Hill W Mid 133 E9
Summerbridge N Yorks 214 G4
Summercourt Corn 5 D7
Summerfield Kent 55 B9
Summerfield Norf 158 B5
Summerfield Worcs 116 C6
Summerfield Park W Mid 133 F10
Summergangs Hull 209 G8
Summerhill Newport 59 B10
Summerhill Pembs 73 D11
Summerhill Staffs 133 B11
Summerhill Telford 150 F4
Summerhill Worcs 116 B6
Summerhill Wrex 166 E4
Summerhouse Darl 224 B4
Summerlands Cumb 211 B10
Summerlands Som 29 D8
Summerleaze Mon 60 B2
Summerley Derbys 186 F5
Summerscales N Yorks 205 C8
Summersdale W Sus 22 B5
Summerseat Gtr Man 195 E9
Summerston Glasgow 277 G11
Summerstown Bucks 102 G3
Summerstown London 67 E9
Summertown Oxon 83 D8
Summit Gtr Man 195 E10
Summit Gtr Man 196 D2
Summit Gtr Man 196 F2
Sun Green Gtr Man 185 B7
Sunbrick Cumb 210 E5
Sunbury Common Sur 66 E5
Sunbury-on-Thames Sur 66 F6
Sundayshill S Glos 79 G11
Sundaywell Dumfries 247 G8
Sunderland Argyll 274 G3
Sunderland Cumb 229 D9
Sunderland Lancs 202 B4
Sunderland T & W 243 F9
Sunderland Bridge Durham 233 D11
Sundhope Borders 261 D8
Sundon Park Luton 103 F11
Sundridge Kent 52 B3
Sundridge London 68 E2
Sunhill Glos 81 E10
Sunipol Argyll 288 D5
Sunk Island E Yorks 201 D9
Sunken Marsh Essex 69 C10
Sunningdale Windsor 66 F3
Sunninghill Windsor 66 F2
Sunningwell Oxon 83 E7
Sunniside Durham 233 D8
Sunniside T & W 242 F6
Sunniside T & W 243 G8
Sunny Bank Gtr Man 195 F10
Sunny Bower Lancs 203 G10
Sunny Hill Derby 152 C6
Sunnybrow Durham 233 E9
Sunnyfields S Yorks 198 F4
Sunnyhurst Blkburn 195 C7
Sunnylaw Stirl 278 B5
Sunnymead Oxon 83 D8
Sunnymeads Windsor 66 D4
Sunnymede Essex 87 G11
Sunnyside S Yorks 187 C7
Sunnyside W Sus 51 F11
Sunset Hereford 114 F6
Sunton Wilts 47 C8
Surbiton London 67 F7
Surby I o M 192 E3
Surfleet Lincs 156 D5
Surfleet Seas End Lincs 156 D5
Surlingham Norf 142 B6
Surrex Essex 107 G7
Suspension Bridge Norf 139 E10
Sustead Norf 160 B3
Susworth Lincs 199 G10
Sutcombe Devon 24 E4
Sutcombemill Devon 24 E4
Sutherland Grove Argyll 289 E11
Suton Norf 141 D11
Sutors of Cromarty Highld 301 C8
Sutterby Lincs 190 G5
Sutterton Lincs 156 B5
Sutterton Dowdyke Lincs 156 C5
Sutton Bucks 66 D4
Sutton C Beds 104 B4
Sutton Cambs 123 B8
Sutton Devon 8 G4
Sutton E Sus 23 F7
Sutton Kent 55 D10
Sutton Lincs 172 E5
Sutton London 67 G9
Sutton Mers 183 C8
Sutton N Yorks 198 B3
Sutton Norf 161 E7
Sutton Notts 154 B5
Sutton Notts 187 E11
Sutton Oxon 82 D6
Sutton P'boro 137 D11
Sutton Pembs 72 B6
Sutton S Yorks 198 E5
Sutton Shrops 132 F4
Sutton Shrops 149 D7
Sutton Shrops 149 G10
Sutton Shrops 150 C3
Sutton Som 44 G6
Sutton Staffs 150 E5
Sutton Suff 108 B6
Sutton Sur 50 D5
Sutton W Sus 35 D7
Sutton Abinger Sur 50 D6
Sutton at Hone Kent 68 E5
Sutton Bassett Northants 136 E5
Sutton Benger Wilts 62 D2
Sutton Bingham Som 29 E8
Sutton Bonington Notts 153 E10
Sutton Bridge Lincs 157 E9
Sutton Cheney Leics 135 C8
Sutton Coldfield W Mid 134 D2
Sutton Corner Lincs 157 D8
Sutton Courtenay Oxon 83 G8
Sutton Crosses Lincs 157 E8
Sutton Cum Lound Notts 187 E11
Sutton End W Sus 35 D7
Sutton Forest Side Notts 171 D8
Sutton Gault Cambs 123 B8
Sutton Green Sur 50 C4
Sutton Green W Ches 182 F5
Sutton Green Wrex 166 F6
Sutton Hall Shrops 132 C4
Sutton Heath Mers 183 C8
Sutton Hill Telford 132 C4
Sutton Holms Dorset 31 F9
Sutton Howgrave N Yorks 214 D6
Sutton in Ashfield Notts 171 D7
Sutton-in-Craven N Yorks 204 E6
Sutton in the Elms Leics 135 E10
Sutton Ings Hull 209 G8
Sutton Lakes Hereford 97 B10
Sutton Lane Ends E Ches 184 G6
Sutton Leach Mers 183 C8
Sutton Maddock Shrops 132 C4
Sutton Mallet Som 43 F11
Sutton Mandeville Wilts 31 B7
Sutton Manor Mers 183 C8
Sutton Marsh Hereford 97 C10
Sutton Mill N Yorks 204 E6
Sutton Montis Som 29 C10
Sutton on Hull Hull 209 G8
Sutton on Sea Lincs 191 E8
Sutton-on-the-Forest N Yorks 215 G11
Sutton on the Hill Derbys 152 C4
Sutton on Trent Notts 172 B3
Sutton Poyntz Dorset 17 E10
Sutton Row Wilts 31 B7
Sutton St Edmund Lincs 157 G7
Sutton St James Lincs 157 F7
Sutton St Michael Hereford 97 B10
Sutton St Nicholas Hereford 97 B10
Sutton Scarsdale Derbys 170 B6
Sutton Scotney Hants 48 F3
Sutton Street Suff 108 C6
Sutton under Brailes Warks 100 D6
Sutton-under-Whitestonecliffe N Yorks 215 C9
Sutton upon Derwent E Yorks 207 D10
Sutton Valence Kent 53 D10
Sutton Veny Wilts 45 E11
Sutton Waldron Dorset 30 D5
Sutton Weaver W Ches 183 F8
Sutton Wick Bath 44 B5
Sutton Wick Oxon 83 G7
Swaby Lincs 190 F5
Swadlincote Derbys 152 F6
Swaffham Norf 140 B6
Swaffham Bulbeck Cambs 123 E11
Swaffham Prior Cambs 123 E11
Swafield Norf 160 C5
Swaile's Green E Sus 38 C3
Swain House W Yorks 205 F9
Swainby N Yorks 225 E9
Swainshill Hereford 97 C9
Swainsthorpe Norf 142 C4
Swainswick Bath 61 F9
Swaithe S Yorks 197 G11
Swalcliffe Oxon 101 D7
Swalecliffe Kent 70 F6
Swallow Lincs 201 G7
Swallow Beck Lincs 173 B7
Swallowcliffe Wilts 31 B7
Swallowfield Wokingham 65 G8
Swallowfields Devon 8 C5
Swallowhurst Cumb 220 G2
Swallownest S Yorks 187 E7
Swallows Cross Essex 87 F10
Swalwell T & W 242 E6
Swampton Hants 48 C2
Swan Bottom Bucks 84 D6
Swan Green Suff 126 C5
Swan Green W Ches 184 G2
Swan Street Essex 107 F7
Swan Village W Mid 133 E9
Swanage Dorset 18 F6
Swanbach E Ches 167 G11
Swanbister Orkney 314 F3
Swanborough Swindon 81 G11
Swanbourne Bucks 102 F6
Swanbridge V Glam 59 F7
Swanland E Yorks 200 B3
Swanley Glos 80 F2
Swanley Kent 68 F4
Swanley Bar Herts 86 E3
Swanley Village Kent 68 F4
Swanmore Hants 33 D9
Swanmore I o W 21 C7
Swannay Orkney 314 D2
Swannington Leics 153 F8
Swannington Norf 160 F2
Swanpool Lincs 189 G7
Swanscombe Kent 68 E6
Swansea = Abertawe Swansea 56 C6
Swanside Mers 182 C6
Swanston Edin 270 B4
Swanton Abbott Norf 160 D5
Swanton Hill Norf 160 D5
Swanton Morley Norf 159 F10
Swanton Novers Norf 159 C10
Swanton Street Kent 53 B11
Swanwick Derbys 170 E6
Swanwick Hants 33 F8
Swanwick Green E Ches 167 F9
Swarby Lincs 173 G8
Swarcliffe W Yorks 206 F3
Swardeston Norf 142 C4
Swarister Shetland 312 E7
Swarkestone Derbys 153 D7
Swarland Northumb 252 C5
Swarraton Hants 48 F5
Swartha W Yorks 205 D7
Swarthmoor Cumb 210 D5
Swartland Orkney 314 D2
Swathwick Derbys 170 B5
Swaton Lincs 156 B2
Swavesey Cambs 123 D7
Sway Hants 19 B11
Swayfield Lincs 155 E9
Swaythling Soton 32 D6
Sweet Green Worcs 116 E2
Sweetham Devon 14 B3
Sweethaws E Sus 37 B8
Sweethay Som 28 C2
Sweetholme Cumb 221 B11
Sweethouse Corn 5 C11
Sweets Corn 11 B9
Sweetshouse Corn 5 C11
Swefling Suff 126 E6
Swell Som 28 C5
Swelling Hill Hants 49 G7
Swepstone Leics 153 G7
Swerford Oxon 101 E7
Swettenham E Ches 168 B4
Swetton N Yorks 214 E3
Swffryd Caerph 78 F2
Swift's Green Kent 53 E11
Swiftsden E Sus 38 B2
Swilland Suff 126 G3
Swillbrook Lancs 202 G5
Swillington W Yorks 206 G3
Swillington Common W Yorks 206 G3
Swimbridge Devon 25 B10
Swimbridge Newland Devon 40 G6
Swinbrook Oxon 82 C3
Swincliffe N Yorks 205 B10
Swincliffe W Yorks 197 B8
Swincombe Devon 41 E7
Swinden N Yorks 204 C3
Swinderby Lincs 172 C5
Swindon Glos 99 G8
Swindon Staffs 133 E7
Swindon Swindon 63 C7
Swine E Yorks 209 F8
Swinefleet E Yorks 199 C9
Swineford S Glos 61 F7
Swineshead Beds 121 D11
Swineshead Lincs 174 G2
Swineshead Bridge Lincs 174 G2
Swinethorpe Lincs 172 B5
Swiney Highld 310 F6
Swinford Leics 119 B11
Swinford Oxon 82 D6
Swingate Notts 171 G8
Swingbrow Cambs 139 F7
Swingfield Minnis Kent 55 E8
Swingfield Street Kent 55 E8
Swingleton Green Suff 107 B9
Swinhoe Northumb 264 D6
Swinhope Lincs 190 B2
Swining Shetland 312 G6
Swinister Shetland 312 E5
Swinister Shetland 313 L6
Swinithwaite N Yorks 213 B10
Swinmore Common Hereford 98 C3
Swinnie Borders 262 F4
Swinnow Moor W Yorks 205 G10
Swinscoe Staffs 169 F10
Swinside Cumb 229 G10
Swinside Townfoot Borders 262 F6
Swinstead Lincs 155 E10
Swinton Borders 272 F6
Swinton Glasgow 268 C3
Swinton Gtr Man 195 G9
Swinton N Yorks 214 D4
Swinton N Yorks 216 E5
Swinton S Yorks 186 B6
Swinton Bridge S Yorks 187 B7
Swinton Hill Borders 272 F6
Swinton Park Gtr Man 195 G9
Swintonmill Borders 272 F6
Swiss Valley Carms 75 E8
Swithland Leics 153 G10
Swordale Highld 300 C5
Swordale Highld 309 K6
Swordland Highld 295 F9
Swordly Highld 308 C7
Sworton Heath E Ches 183 E11
Swyddffynnon Ceredig 112 D3
Swynnerton Staffs 151 B7
Swyre Dorset 16 D6
Sycamore Devon 28 F3
Sychdyn = Soughton Flint 166 B2
Sychtyn Powys 129 B9
Sydallt Wrex 166 D4
Syde Glos 81 C7
Sydenham London 67 E11
Sydenham Oxon 84 E2
Sydenham Som 43 F10
Sydenham Damerel Devon 12 F4
Syderstone Norf 158 C6
Sydling St Nicholas Dorset 17 B8
Sydmonton Hants 48 B3
Sydney E Ches 168 D2
Syerston Notts 172 F2
Syke Gtr Man 195 D11
Sykehouse S Yorks 198 D6
Sykes Lancs 203 C8
Syleham Suff 126 B4
Sylen Carms 75 D8
Symbister Shetland 313 G7
Symington Borders 271 F8
Symington S Ayrs 257 C9
Symington S Lnrk 259 B11
Symonds Green Herts 104 F4
Symonds Yat Hereford 79 B9
Symondsbury Dorset 16 C4
Synderford Dorset 28 G5
Synod Inn = Post Mawr Ceredig 111 G8
Synton Borders 261 E11
Synton Mains Borders 261 E11
Synwell Glos 80 G3
Syre Highld 308 E6
Syreford Glos 99 G10
Syresham Northants 102 C2
Syster Highld 310 C6
Syston Leics 154 G2
Syston Lincs 172 G6
Sytch Ho Green Shrops 132 E5
Sytch Lane Telford 150 E2
Sytchampton Worcs 116 D6
Sywell Northants 120 D6

T

Taagan Highld 299 C10
Tabley Hill E Ches 184 F2
Tabor Gwyn 146 F5
Tabost W Isles 305 G5
Tàbost W Isles 304 B7
Tachbrook Mallory Warks 118 E6
Tacker Street Som 42 F4
Tackley Oxon 101 G9
Tacleit W Isles 304 E3
Tacolneston Norf 142 D2
Tadcaster N Yorks 206 E5
Tadden Dorset 31 G7
Taddington Derbys 185 G10
Taddington Glos 99 E11
Taddiport Devon 25 D7
Tadhill Som 45 D7
Tadley Hants 64 G6
Tadley Oxon 64 B4
Tadlow Beds 104 B5
Tadlow C Beds 104 B5
Tadmarton Oxon 101 D7
Tadnoll Dorset 17 D11
Tadwick Bath 61 E8
Tadworth Sur 51 B8
Tafarn-y-bwlch Pembs 91 E11
Tafarn-y-gelyn Denb 165 C11
Tafarnau-bach Bl Gwent 77 C10
Taff Merthyr Garden Village M Tydf 77 F10
Taff's Well Rhondda 58 C6
Tafolwern Powys 129 C7
Tai Conwy 164 C3
Tai-bach Powys 148 D3
Tai-mawr Conwy 165 G7
Tai-morfa Gwyn 144 D5
Tai-nant Wrex 166 F3
Tai-Ucha Denb 165 D8
Taibach Neath 57 D9
Taigh a Ghearraidh W Isles 296 D3
Taigh Bhalaigh W Isles 296 D3
Tain Highld 309 L7
Tain Highld 310 C6
Tainlon Gwyn 162 E6
Tai'r-Bull Powys 95 F9
Tai'r-heol Caerph 77 G10
Tai'r-ysgol Swansea 57 B7
Tairbeart W Isles 305 H3
Tairgwaith Neath 76 C2
Takeley Essex 105 G11
Takeley Street Essex 105 G10
Tal-sarn Ceredig 111 F10
Tal-y-Bont Ceredig 128 F3
Tal-y-Bont Conwy 164 B3
Tal-y-bont Gwyn 145 E11
Tal-y-bont Gwyn 179 G10
Tal-y-cafn Conwy 180 G3
Tal-y-coed Mon 78 B6
Tal-y-llyn Gwyn 128 B4
Tal-y-waenydd Gwyn 163 F11
Tal-y-wern Powys 128 C6
Talacharn = Laugharne Carms 74 C4
Talachddu Powys 95 E11
Talacre Flint 181 E10
Talardd Gwyn 147 D7
Talaton Devon 15 B7
Talbenny Pembs 72 C4
Talbot Green Rhondda 58 C4
Talbot Heath Poole 19 C7
Talbot Village Poole 19 C7
Talbot Woods Bmouth 19 C7
Talbot's End S Glos 80 G2
Tale Devon 27 G9
Talerddig Powys 129 C8
Talgarreg Ceredig 111 G8
Talgarth Powys 96 E3
Talgarth's Well Swansea 56 D2
Talisker Highld 294 B5
Talke Staffs 168 E4
Talke Pits Staffs 168 E4
Talkin Cumb 240 F3
Talla Linnfoots Borders 260 E4
Talladale Highld 299 B9
Tallaminnoch S Ayrs 245 D10
Talland Corn 6 E4
Tallarn Green Wrex 166 G6
Tallentire Cumb 229 D8
Talley Carms 94 E2
Tallington Lincs 137 B11
Talmine Highld 308 C5
Talog Carms 92 F6
Talsarn Carms 94 F5
Talsarnau Gwyn 146 B2
Talskiddy Corn 5 B8
Talwrn Anglesey 179 F7
Talwrn Wrex 166 F3
Talybont-on-Usk Powys 96 G2
Talygarn Rhondda 58 C4
Talyllyn Powys 96 F2
Talysarn Gwyn 163 E7
Talywain Torf 78 E3
Tamanabhagh W Isles 304 F2
Tame Bridge N Yorks 225 D10
Tame Water Gtr Man 196 F3
Tamer Lane End Gtr Man 194 G6
Tamerton Foliot Plym 7 C9
Tamfourhill Falk 279 E7
Tamworth Staffs 134 C4
Tamworth Green Lincs 174 G5
Tan Hills Durham 233 B11
Tan Hinon Powys 129 F7
Tan-lan Conwy 164 C3
Tan-lan Gwyn 163 G10
Tan Office Suff 126 E2
Tan Office Green Suff 124 F5
Tan-y-bwlch Gwyn 163 G11
Tan-y-fron Conwy 165 C7
Tan-y-graig Anglesey 179 F8
Tan-y-graig Gwyn 144 B6
Tan-y-groes Ceredig 92 B5
Tan-y-mynydd Gwyn 144 C6
Tan-y-pistyll Powys 147 D11
Tan-yr-allt Denb 181 E9
Tan-yr-allt Gwyn 163 E7
Tancred N Yorks 206 B5
Tandem W Yorks 197 D7
Tanden Kent 54 F2
Tandlehill Renfs 267 C8
Tandridge Sur 51 C11
Tanerdy Carms 93 G8
Tanfield Durham 242 F5
Tanfield Lea Durham 242 G5
Tang N Yorks 205 B10
Tang Hall York 207 C8
Tangasdal W Isles 297 M2
Tangiers Pembs 73 B7
Tangley Hants 47 C10
Tanglwst Carms 92 E6
Tangmere W Sus 22 B6
Tangwick Shetland 312 F4
Tangy Argyll 255 E7
Tanhouse Lancs 194 F3
Tanis Wilts 62 G3
Tankersley S Yorks 197 G10
Tankerton Kent 70 F6
Tanlan Flint 181 E10
Tanlan Banks Flint 181 E10
Tannach Highld 310 E7
Tannachie Aberds 293 E9
Tannadice Angus 287 B8
Tanner's Green Worcs 117 C11
Tannington Suff 126 D4
Tannington Place Suff 126 D4
Tannochside N Lnrk 268 C4
Tansley Derbys 170 D4
Tansley Hill W Mid 133 F9

396 Tan – Tix

Tansley Knoll Derbys 170 C4
Tansor Northants 137 E11
Tanterton Lancs 202 G6
Tantobie Durham 242 G5
Tanton N Yorks 225 C10
Tanwood Worcs 117 C8
Tanworth-in-Arden Warks 118 C2
Tanyfron Wrex 166 E3
Tanygrisiau Gwyn 163 F11
Tanyrhydiau Ceredig 112 D4
Tanysgafell Gwyn 163 B10
Taobh a Chaolais W Isles 297 K3
Taobh a' Ghlinne W Isles 305 G5
Taobh a Thuath Loch Aineort W Isles 297 J3
Taobh a Tuath Loch Baghasdail W Isles 297 J3
Taobh Siar W Isles 305 H3
Taobh Tuath W Isles 296 C5
Taplow Bucks 66 C2
Tapnage Hants 33 E9
Tapton Derbys 186 G5
Tapton Hill S Yorks 186 D4
Tarbat Ho Highld 301 B7
Tarbert Argyll 255 B7
Tarbert Argyll 275 E7
Tarbert Argyll 275 G9
Tarbet Argyll 285 G7
Tarbet Highld 295 F9
Tarbet Highld 306 E6
Tarbock Green Mers 183 D7
Tarbolton S Ayrs 257 D10
Tarbrax S Lnrk 269 D10
Tardebigge Worcs 117 D10
Tardy Gate Lancs 194 B4
Tarfside Angus 292 F6
Tarland Aberds 292 C6
Tarleton Lancs 194 C3
Tarleton Moss Lancs 194 C2
Tarlogie Highld 309 L7
Tarlscough Lancs 194 E2
Tarlton Glos 81 F7
Tarn W Yorks 205 F9
Tarnbrook Lancs 203 B7
Tarnock Som 43 C11
Tarns Cumb 229 B8
Tarnside Cumb 221 G8
Tarporley W Ches 167 C9
Tarpots Essex 69 B9
Tarr Som 42 G6
Tarraby Cumb 239 F10
Tarrant Crawford Dorset 30 G6
Tarrant Gunville Dorset 30 E6
Tarrant Hinton Dorset 30 E6
Tarrant Keyneston Dorset 30 G6
Tarrant Launceston Dorset 30 F6
Tarrant Monkton Dorset 30 F6
Tarrant Rawston Dorset 30 F6
Tarrant Rushton Dorset 30 F6
Tarrel Highld 311 L2
Tarring Neville E Sus 36 G6
Tarrington Hereford 98 C2
Tarrington Common Hereford 98 D2
Tarryblake Ho Moray 302 E5
Tarsappie Perth 286 E5
Tarskavaig Highld 295 E7
Tarts Hill Shrops 149 B8
Tarves Aberds 303 F8
Tarvie Highld 300 D4
Tarvie Perth 292 G2
Tarvin W Ches 167 B7
Tarvin Sands W Ches 167 B7
Tasburgh Norf 142 D4
Tasley Shrops 132 E3
Taston Oxon 101 G7
Tat Bank W Mid 133 F9
Tatenhill Staffs 152 E4
Tatenhill Common Staffs 152 E3
Tathall End M Keynes 102 B6
Tatham Lancs 212 F2
Tathwell Lincs 190 E4
Tatling End Bucks 66 B4
Tatsfield Sur 52 B2
Tattenhall W Ches 167 D7
Tattenhoe M Keynes 102 E6
Tatterford Norf 159 D7
Tattersett Norf 158 C6
Tattershall Lincs 174 D2
Tattershall Bridge Lincs 173 D11
Tattershall Thorpe Lincs 174 D2
Tattingstone Suff 108 D2
Tattingstone White Horse Suff 108 D2
Tattle Bank Warks 118 E3
Tatton Dale E Ches 184 E2
Tatworth Som 28 F4
Taunton Gtr Man 196 G2
Taunton Som 28 C2
Taverham Norf 160 G3
Taverners Green Essex 87 B9
Tavernspite Pembs 73 C11
Tavistock Devon 12 G5
Taw Green Devon 13 B9
Tawstock Devon 25 B9
Taxal Derbys 185 F8
Tay Bridge Dundee 287 E8
Tayinloan Argyll 255 C7
Taymouth Castle Perth 285 C11
Taynish Argyll 275 E8
Taynton Glos 98 G4
Taynton Oxon 82 C2
Taynuilt Argyll 284 D4
Tayport Fife 287 E8
Tayvallich Argyll 275 E8
Tea Green Herts 104 G2
Tealby Lincs 189 C11
Tealing Angus 287 D8
Team Valley T & W 242 E6
Teams T & W 242 E6
Teanford Staffs 169 G8
Teangue Highld 295 E8
Teanna Mhachair W Isles 296 E3
Teasley Mead E Sus 52 F4
Tebay Cumb 222 E2
Tebworth C Beds 103 F9
Tedburn St Mary Devon 14 C2
Teddington Glos 99 E9
Teddington London 67 E7
Teddington Hands Worcs 99 E9
Tedsmore Shrops 149 D7
Tedstone Delamere Hereford 116 F3
Tedstone Wafer Hereford 116 F3
Teesville Redcar 225 B10
Teeton Northants 120 C3
Teffont Evias Wilts 46 G3
Teffont Magna Wilts 46 G3
Tegryn Pembs 92 E4
Teigh Rutland 155 F7
Teign Village Devon 14 E2
Teigncombe Devon 13 D9
Teigngrace Devon 14 G2
Teignmouth Devon 14 G4
Telford Telford 132 B3
Telham E Sus 38 E3
Tellisford Som 45 B10
Telscombe E Sus 36 G6
Telscombe Cliffs E Sus 36 G5
Templand Dumfries 248 F3
Temple Corn 11 G8
Temple Glasgow 267 B10
Temple Midloth 270 D6
Temple Wilts 45 E10
Temple Windsor 65 C10
Temple Balsall W Mid 118 B4
Temple Bar Carms 75 B9
Temple Bar Ceredig 111 G10
Temple Bar W Sus 22 B5
Temple Cloud Bath 44 B6
Temple Cowley Oxon 83 E8
Temple End Essex 106 C6
Temple End Suff 124 G3
Temple Ewell Kent 55 E9
Temple Fields Essex 87 C7
Temple Grafton Warks 118 G2
Temple Guiting Glos 99 F11
Temple Herdewyke Warks 119 G7
Temple Hill Kent 68 D5
Temple Hirst N Yorks 198 C6
Temple Normanton Derbys 170 B6
Temple Sowerby Cumb 231 F8
Templeborough S Yorks 186 C6
Templecombe Som 30 C2
Templehall Fife 280 C5
Templeman's Ash Dorset 28 G6
Templeton Devon 26 E5
Templeton Pembs 73 C10
Templeton W Berks 63 F11
Templeton Bridge Devon 26 E5
Templetown Durham 242 G4
Tempsford C Beds 122 G3
Ten Acres W Mid 133 G11
Ten Mile Bank Norf 140 D2
Tenandry Perth 291 G11
Tenbury Wells Worcs 115 D11
Tenby = Dinbych-y-Pysgod Pembs 73 E10
Tencreek Corn 6 E4
Tendring Essex 108 G2
Tendring Green Essex 108 F2
Tendring Heath Essex 108 F2
Tenston Orkney 314 E2
Tenterden Kent 53 G11
Terfyn Conwy 180 F6
Terfyn Gwyn 163 C9
Terhill Som 43 G7
Terling Essex 88 B3
Ternhill Shrops 150 C2
Terpersie Castle Aberds 302 G5
Terras Corn 5 E8
Terregles Banks Dumfries 237 B11
Terrible Down E Sus 23 B7
Terrick Bucks 84 D4
Terriers Bucks 84 G5
Terrington N Yorks 216 E3
Terrington St Clement Norf 157 E10
Terrington St John Norf 157 G10
Terryhorn Aberds 302 F4
Terry's Green Warks 118 C2
Terwick Common W Sus 34 C4
Teston Kent 53 C8
Testwood Hants 32 E5
Tetbury Glos 80 G5
Tetbury Upton Glos 80 F5
Tetchill Shrops 149 C7
Tetchwick Bucks 83 B11
Tetcott Devon 12 B2
Tetford Lincs 190 G4
Tetley N Lincs 199 E9
Tetney Lincs 201 G10
Tetney Lock Lincs 201 G10
Tetsworth Oxon 83 E11
Tettenhall W Mid 133 D7
Tettenhall Wood W Mid 133 D7
Tetworth Cambs 122 G4
Teuchan Aberds 303 F10
Teversal Notts 171 C7
Teversham Cambs 123 F9
Teviothead Borders 249 B10
Tewel Aberds 293 E10
Tewin Herts 86 C3
Tewin Wood Herts 86 B3
Tewitfield Lancs 211 E10
Tewkesbury Glos 99 E7
Teynham Kent 70 G3
Teynham Street Kent 70 G3
Thackley W Yorks 205 F9
Thackley End W Yorks 205 F9
Thackthwaite Cumb 229 G8
Thainston Aberds 293 F8
Thakeham W Sus 35 D10
Thame Oxon 84 D2
Thames Ditton Sur 67 F7
Thames Haven Thurrock 69 C8
Thames Head Glos 81 F7
Thamesmead London 68 C3
Thanington Kent 54 B6
Thankerton S Lnrk 259 B11
Tharston Norf 142 E3
Thatcham W Berks 64 F4
Thatto Heath Mers 183 C8
Thaxted Essex 106 E2
The Aird Highld 298 D4
The Alders Staffs 134 C3
The Arms Norf 141 D7
The Bage Hereford 96 C5
The Balloch Perth 286 F2
The Bank E Ches 168 D4
The Banks Gtr Man 185 D7
The Banks Wilts 62 D4
The Barony E Ches 167 E11
The Barony Orkney 314 D2
The Barton Wilts 62 D5
The Batch S Glos 61 E7
The Beeches Glos 81 E8
The Bell Gtr Man 194 F4
The Bents Staffs 151 C10
The Blythe Staffs 151 D10
The Bog Shrops 131 D7
The Borough Dorset 30 E2
The Borough London 67 D10
The Bourne Sur 49 E10
The Bourne Worcs 117 F9
The Bows Stirl 285 G11
The Braes Highld 295 B7
The Brampton Staffs 168 F4
The Brand Leics 153 G10
The Bratch Staffs 133 E7
The Breck Orkney 314 F3
The Brents Kent 70 G4
The Bridge Dorset 30 E3
The Broad Hereford 115 E9
The Brook Suff 125 B11
The Brushes Derbys 186 F5
The Bryn Mon 78 D4
The Burf Worcs 116 D6
The Butts Hants 49 F8
The Butts Som 45 D9
The Camp Glos 80 D6
The Camp Herts 85 D11
The Cape Warks 118 D5
The Chart Kent 52 C3
The Chequer Wrex 167 G7
The Chuckery W Mid 133 D10
The City Bucks 84 F3
The Cleaver Hereford 97 F10
The Close W Sus 22 C5
The Colony Oxon 100 D6
The Common Bath 60 G6
The Common Bucks 102 E5
The Common Dorset 30 E3
The Common Shrops 150 D3
The Common Suff 108 B2
The Common Swansea 56 C4
The Common W Sus 51 G7
The Common Wilts 47 G8
The Common Wilts 61 G11
The Common Wilts 62 C4
The Corner Kent 53 E8
The Corner Shrops 131 F8
The Cot Mon 79 F8
The Craigs Highld 309 K4
The Crofts E Yorks 218 E4
The Cronk I o M 192 C4
The Cross Hands Leics 134 C6
The Cwm Mon 79 G7
The Dell Suff 143 D9
The Delves W Mid 133 D10
The Den N Ayrs 266 E6
The Dene Durham 242 G4
The Dene Hants 47 C11
The Down Kent 53 F7
The Down Shrops 132 E3
The Downs Sur 50 F3
The Dunks Wrex 166 E4
The Eals Northumb 251 F7
The Eaves Glos 79 D10
The Fall W Yorks 197 B10
The Fence Glos 79 D8
The Flat Glos 80 B3
The Flatt Cumb 240 B3
The Flourish Derbys 153 B8
The Folly Herts 85 C11
The Folly S Glos 61 E8
The Fording Hereford 98 F3
The Forge Hereford 114 F6
The Forstal Kent 54 F4
The Forties Derbys 152 F6
The Four Alls Shrops 150 C3
The Fox Wilts 62 B6
The Foxholes Shrops 132 G2
The Frenches Hants 32 C4
The Frythe Herts 86 C2
The Garths Shetland 312 B8
The Gibb Wilts 61 D10
The Glack Borders 260 B6
The Gore Shrops 131 G11
The Grange N Yorks 225 F11
The Grange Norf 160 E2
The Green C Beds 85 B8
The Green Cambs 122 D5
The Green Cumb 210 C3
The Green Cumb 211 D7
The Green Essex 88 B3
The Green Hants 32 B3
The Green M Keynes 103 C7
The Green Norf 141 C11
The Green Norf 159 B11
The Green Northants 102 C5
The Green Oxon 101 F9
The Green S Yorks 197 G8
The Green Shrops 130 G6
The Green Warks 118 F4
The Green Wilts 45 G11
The Grove Dumfries 237 B11
The Grove Durham 242 G3
The Grove Herts 85 F9
The Grove Shrops 131 B7
The Grove Shrops 131 G8
The Grove Worcs 99 C7
The Gutter Derbys 170 F5
The Gutter Worcs 117 B9
The Hacket S Glos 61 B7
The Hague Derbys 185 C8
The Hall Shetland 312 D8
The Hallands N Lincs 200 C5
The Ham Wilts 45 C11
The Handfords Staffs 151 E7
The Harbour Kent 53 D10
The Haven W Sus 50 G5
The Headland Hrtlpl 234 E6
The Heath Norf 159 D8
The Heath Norf 160 E3
The Heath Norf 160 E4
The Heath Staffs 151 C11
The Heath Suff 108 D2
The Hem Shrops 132 B4
The Hendre Mon 79 C7
The Herberts V Glam 58 E3
The Hermitage Cambs 123 C7
The High Essex 86 C6
The Highlands E Sus 38 F2
The Hill Cumb 210 C3
The Hobbins Shrops 132 E4
The Hollands Staffs 168 D6
The Hollies Notts 172 E4
The Holmes Derbys 153 B7
The Holt Wokingham 65 D10
The Hook Worcs 98 C6
The Hope Shrops 115 B10
The Howe Cumb 211 B9
The Howe I o M 192 F2
The Humbers Telford 150 G3
The Hundred Hereford 115 E10
The Hyde London 67 B8
The Hyde Worcs 98 C6
The Hythe Essex 107 G10
The Inch Edin 280 G5
The Knab Swansea 56 D6
The Knap V Glam 58 F5
The Knapp Hereford 116 G3
The Knapp S Glos 79 G11
The Knowle W Mid 133 F9
The Laches Staffs 133 B8
The Lake Dumfries 237 E8
The Lakes Worcs 116 B5
The Lawe T & W 243 D9
The Lawns E Yorks 208 G6
The Leacon Kent 54 G3
The Leath Shrops 131 F11
The Lee Bucks 84 E6
The Lees Kent 54 C4
The Leigh Glos 99 F7
The Leys Staffs 134 C4
The Lhen I o M 192 B4
The Ling Norf 142 D6
The Lings Norf 141 B10
The Lings S Yorks 199 F7
The Linleys Wilts 61 F11
The Lunt W Mid 133 D9
The Manor W Sus 22 C4
The Marsh E Ches 168 C4
The Marsh Hereford 115 F9
The Marsh Powys 130 D6
The Marsh Shrops 150 D3
The Marsh Staffs 150 D6
The Marsh Suff 125 B11
The Marsh Suff 126 B2
The Marsh Wilts 62 C5
The Middles Durham 242 G6
The Mint Hants 34 B3
The Moor Flint 166 B4
The Moor Kent 38 B3
The Moors Hereford 97 E10
The Mount Hants 64 G2
The Mount Reading 65 E8
The Mumbles = Y Mwmbwls Swansea 56 D6
The Murray S Lnrk 268 E2
The Mythe Glos 99 E7
The Nant Wrex 166 E3
The Narth Mon 79 D8
The Neuk Aberds 293 D9
The Node Herts 104 G4
The Nook Shrops 149 C11
The Nook Shrops 150 E3
The North Mon 79 D8
The Oval Bath 61 G8
The Park Glos 99 G8
The Parks S Yorks 198 F6
The Pitts Wilts 31 B9
The Platt Oxon 83 E9
The Pludds Glos 79 B10
The Point Devon 14 E5
The Pole of Itlaw Aberds 302 D6
The Port of Felixstowe Suff 108 E5
The Potteries Stoke 168 F5
The Pound Glos 98 E4
The Quarry Glos 80 F2
The Quarry Shrops 149 G9
The Quarter Kent 53 E11
The Quarter Kent 53 G11
The Rampings Worcs 99 E7
The Rectory Lincs 156 G2
The Reddings Glos 99 G8
The Rhos Pembs 73 C8
The Rhydd Hereford 97 E9
The Riddle Hereford 115 E9
The Ridge Wilts 61 F11
The Ridges Wokingham 65 G10
The Ridgeway Herts 86 E3
The Riding Northumb 241 D10
The Riggs Borders 261 C8
The Rink Borders 261 C11
The Rise Windsor 66 F2
The Rock Telford 132 B3
The Rocks Kent 53 B8
The Rocks S Glos 61 C8
The Roe Denb 181 G8
The Rookery Herts 85 G10
The Rookery Staffs 168 D5
The Row Lancs 211 D9
The Rowe Staffs 150 B6
The Ryde Herts 86 D2
The Sands Sur 49 D11
The Scarr Glos 98 F4
The Shoe Wilts 61 E10
The Shruggs Staffs 151 C8
The Slack Durham 233 F8
The Slade W Berks 64 F4
The Smeeth Norf 157 G10
The Smithies Shrops 132 D3
The Spa Wilts 62 G2
The Spring Warks 118 C5
The Square Torf 78 F3
The Stocks Kent 38 B6
The Stocks Wilts 62 G2
The Straits Hants 49 F9
The Straits W Mid 133 E8
The Strand Wilts 46 B2
The Swillett Herts 85 F8
The Sydnall Shrops 150 C3
The Thrift Cambs 104 D6
The Throat Wokingham 65 F10
The Toft Staffs 151 F8
The Towans Corn 2 B3
The Town Scilly 1 F3
The Twittocks Glos 99 D7
The Tynings Glos 80 B6
The Vale W Mid 133 G11
The Valley E Ches 167 D11
The Valley Kent 54 C3
The Valley Leics 154 F4
The Valley Pembs 73 D10
The Vauld Hereford 97 B10
The Village Newport 78 G4
The Village W Mid 133 F7
The Village Windsor 66 E3
The Walshes Worcs 116 C6
The Warren Kent 54 E3
The Warren Wilts 63 F8
The Waterwheel Shrops 131 C7
The Weaven Hereford 97 E10
The Wells Sur 67 G7
The Wern Wrex 166 E3
The Willows NE Lincs 201 F8
The Wood Shrops 148 E6
The Wood Shrops 149 D9
The Woodlands Leics 136 D3
The Woodlands Suff 107 C11
The Woodlands Suff 108 D3
The Woods W Mid 133 D10
The Wrangle Bath 44 B4
The Wrythe London 67 F9
The Wyke Shrops 132 B4
The Wymm Hereford 97 B10
The Yeld Shrops 131 G11
Theakston N Yorks 214 B6
Thealby N Lincs 199 D11
Theale Som 44 D3
Theale W Berks 64 E6
Thearne E Yorks 209 F7
Theberton Suff 127 D8
Theddingworth Leics 136 F3
Theddlethorpe All Saints Lincs 191 D7
Theddlethorpe St Helen Lincs 191 D7
Thelbridge Barton Devon 26 E3
Thelnetham Suff 125 B10
Thelveton Norf 142 G3
Thelwall Warr 183 D10
Themelthorpe Norf 159 E11
Thenford Northants 101 C10
Theobald's Green Wilts 62 F4
Therfield Herts 104 D6
Thetford Lincs 156 F2
Thetford Norf 141 G7
Theydon Bois Essex 86 F6
Theydon Garnon Essex 87 F7
Theydon Mount Essex 87 F7
Thick Hollins W Yorks 196 F6
Thicket Mead Bath 45 B7
Thickthorn Hall Norf 142 B3
Thickwood Wilts 61 E10
Thimble End W Mid 134 E2
Thimbleby Lincs 190 G2
Thimbleby N Yorks 225 F9
Thinford Durham 233 E11
Thingley Wilts 61 E11
Thingwall Mers 182 E3
Thirdpart N Ayrs 266 F3
Thirlby N Yorks 215 C9
Thirlestane Borders 271 F11
Thirn N Yorks 214 B4
Thirsk N Yorks 215 C8
Thirtleby E Yorks 209 G9
Thistleton Lancs 202 F4
Thistleton Rutland 155 F8
Thistley Green Essex 88 B2
Thistley Green Suff 124 B3
Thixendale N Yorks 216 G6
Thockrington Northumb 241 B11
Tholomas Drove Cambs 139 B7
Tholthorpe N Yorks 215 F9
Thomas Chapel Pembs 73 D10
Thomas Close Cumb 230 C4
Thomastown Aberds 302 F5
Thomastown Rhondda 58 B4
Thompson Norf 141 D8
Thomshill Moray 302 D2
Thong Kent 69 E7
Thongsbridge W Yorks 196 F6
Thoralby N Yorks 213 B10
Thoresby Notts 187 G10
Thoresthorpe Lincs 191 F7
Thoresway Lincs 189 B11
Thorganby Lincs 190 B2
Thorganby N Yorks 207 E9
Thorgill N Yorks 226 F4
Thorington Suff 127 C8
Thorington Street Suff 107 D10
Thorlby N Yorks 204 C5
Thorley Herts 87 B7
Thorley I o W 20 D3
Thorley Houses Herts 105 G9
Thorley Street Herts 87 B7
Thorley Street I o W 20 D3
Thormanby N Yorks 215 E9
Thorn Devon 13 D9
Thorn Powys 114 E5
Thorn Hill S Yorks 186 C6
Thornaby on Tees Stockton 225 B9
Thornage Norf 159 B11
Thornborough Bucks 102 E4
Thornborough N Yorks 214 D5
Thornbury Devon 24 F6
Thornbury Hereford 116 F2
Thornbury S Glos 79 G10
Thornbury W Yorks 205 G9
Thornby Cumb 239 G7
Thornby Northants 120 B3
Thorncliff W Yorks 197 E8
Thorncliffe Staffs 169 D8
Thorncombe Dorset 28 G5
Thorncombe Dorset 30 G5
Thorncombe Street Sur 50 E4
Thorncote Green C Beds 104 B3
Thorncross I o W 20 E4
Thorndon Suff 126 D2
Thorndon Cross Devon 12 C6
Thorne Corn 24 G2
Thorne S Yorks 199 E7
Thorne Coffin Som 29 D8
Thorne Moor Devon 12 D3
Thorne St Margaret Som 27 C9
Thornehillhead Devon 24 D6
Thornend Wilts 62 D3
Thorner W Yorks 206 E3
Thornes Staffs 133 C11
Thornes W Yorks 197 D10
Thorney Bucks 66 D4
Thorney Notts 188 G5
Thorney P'boro 138 C5
Thorney Som 28 C6
Thorney Close T & W 243 G9
Thorney Crofts E Yorks 201 C8
Thorney Green Suff 125 E11
Thorney Hill Hants 19 B9
Thorney Island W Sus 22 C3
Thorney Toll P'boro 138 C6
Thorneywood Notts 171 G9
Thornfalcon Som 28 C3
Thornford Dorset 29 E10
Thorngrafton Northumb 241 D7
Thorngrove Som 43 G11
Thorngumbald E Yorks 201 B8
Thornham Norf 176 E2
Thornham Fold Gtr Man 195 F11
Thornham Magna Suff 126 C2
Thornham Parva Suff 126 C2
Thornhaugh P'boro 137 C11
Thornhill Cardiff 59 C7
Thornhill Cumb 219 D10
Thornhill Derbys 185 E11
Thornhill Dumfries 247 D9
Thornhill Soton 33 E7
Thornhill Stirl 278 B3
Thornhill Torf 78 F3
Thornhill W Yorks 197 D9
Thornhill Wilts 62 D5
Thornhill Edge W Yorks 197 D8
Thornhill Lees W Yorks 197 D8
Thornhill Park Hants 33 E7
Thornhills W Yorks 197 C7
Thornholme E Yorks 218 G2
Thornicombe Dorset 30 G5
Thornielee Borders 261 B10
Thornley Durham 233 D8
Thornley Durham 234 D3
Thornliebank E Renf 267 D10
Thornly Park Renfs 267 C9
Thornroan Aberds 303 F8
Thorns N Yorks 223 E7
Thorns Suff 124 F4
Thorns Green E Ches 184 E3
Thornseat S Yorks 186 C2
Thornsett Derbys 185 D8
Thornthwaite Cumb 229 F10
Thornthwaite N Yorks 205 B9
Thornton Angus 287 C7
Thornton Bucks 102 D5
Thornton E Yorks 207 D11
Thornton Fife 280 B5
Thornton Lancs 202 E2
Thornton Leics 135 B9
Thornton Lincs 174 B2
Thornton M'bro 225 C9
Thornton Mers 193 G10
Thornton Northumb 273 F9
Thornton Pembs 72 D6
Thornton W Yorks 205 G8
Thornton Curtis N Lincs 200 D5
Thornton Heath London 67 F10
Thornton Hough Mers 182 E4
Thornton in Craven N Yorks 204 D4
Thornton in Lonsdale N Yorks 212 E3
Thornton-le-Beans N Yorks 225 G7
Thornton-le-Clay N Yorks 216 F3
Thornton-le-Dale N Yorks 216 C6
Thornton le Moor Lincs 189 B9
Thornton-le-Moor N Yorks 215 B7
Thornton-le-Moors W Ches 182 G6
Thornton-le-Street N Yorks 215 B8
Thornton Rust N Yorks 213 B9
Thornton Steward N Yorks 214 B3
Thornton Watlass N Yorks 214 B4
Thorntonhall S Lnrk 267 D11
Thorntonloch E Loth 282 G4
Thornton Park Northumb 273 F8
Thornwood Common Essex 87 D7
Thornydykes Borders 272 F2
Thoroton Notts 172 G3
Thorp Gtr Man 196 F2
Thorp Arch W Yorks 206 D4
Thorpe Cumb 230 F5
Thorpe Derbys 169 E11
Thorpe E Yorks 208 D5
Thorpe Lincs 191 E7
Thorpe N Yorks 213 G10
Thorpe Norf 143 D8
Thorpe Notts 172 F3
Thorpe Sur 66 F4
Thorpe Abbotts Norf 126 B3
Thorpe Acre Leics 153 E10
Thorpe Arnold Leics 154 E5
Thorpe Audlin W Yorks 198 D3
Thorpe Bassett N Yorks 217 E7
Thorpe Bay Sthend 70 B2
Thorpe by Water Rutland 137 D7
Thorpe Common Suff 108 D5
Thorpe Constantine Staffs 134 B5
Thorpe Culvert Lincs 175 C7
Thorpe Edge W Yorks 205 F9
Thorpe End Norf 160 G5
Thorpe Fendykes Lincs 175 C7
Thorpe Green Essex 108 G3
Thorpe Green Lancs 194 C5
Thorpe Green Suff 125 G8
Thorpe Green Sur 66 F4
Thorpe Hamlet Norf 142 B4
Thorpe Hesley S Yorks 186 B5
Thorpe in Balne S Yorks 198 E5
Thorpe in the Fallows Lincs 188 E6
Thorpe Langton Leics 136 E4
Thorpe Larches Durham 234 F3
Thorpe Latimer Lincs 156 B2
Thorpe-le-Soken Essex 108 G3
Thorpe le Street E Yorks 208 E2
Thorpe le Vale Lincs 190 C2
Thorpe Lea Sur 66 E4
Thorpe Malsor Northants 120 B6
Thorpe Mandeville Northants 101 B10
Thorpe Market Norf 160 B4
Thorpe Marriot Norf 160 F3
Thorpe Morieux Suff 125 G8
Thorpe on the Hill Lincs 172 B6
Thorpe on The Hill W Yorks 197 B10
Thorpe Row Norf 141 B9
Thorpe St Andrew Norf 142 B5
Thorpe St Peter Lincs 175 C7
Thorpe Salvin S Yorks 187 E8
Thorpe Satchville Leics 154 G4
Thorpe Street Suff 125 B10
Thorpe Thewles Stockton 234 G4
Thorpe Tilney Lincs 173 D10
Thorpe Underwood N Yorks 206 B5
Thorpe Underwood Northants 136 G5
Thorpe Waterville Northants 137 G10
Thorpe Willoughby N Yorks 207 G7
Thorpe Wood N Yorks 207 G7
Thorpeness Suff 127 F9
Thorpland Norf 140 B2
Thorrington Essex 89 B9
Thorverton Devon 26 G6
Thoulstone Wilts 45 D10
Thrandeston Suff 126 B2
Thrapston Northants 121 B9
Thrashbush N Lnrk 268 B5
Threapland Cumb 229 D9
Threapland N Yorks 213 G9
Threapwood Staffs 169 G8
Threapwood W Ches 166 F6
Three Ashes Hants 64 G6
Three Ashes Hereford 97 G10
Three Ashes Shrops 115 B7
Three Ashes Som 45 D7
Three Bridges Argyll 284 F4
Three Bridges Lincs 190 D6
Three Bridges W Sus 51 F9
Three Burrows Corn 4 F4
Three Chimneys Kent 53 F10
Three Cocked Hat Norf 143 D8
Three Cocks = Aberllynfi Powys 96 D3
Three Crosses Swansea 56 C5
Three Cups Corner E Sus 37 C10
Three Fingers Wrex 167 G7
Three Gates Dorset 29 F10
Three Hammers Corn 11 D10
Three Holes Norf 139 C10
Three Holes Cross Corn 10 G6
Three Leg Cross E Sus 53 G7
Three Legged Cross Dorset 31 F9
Three Maypoles W Mid 118 B2
Three Mile Cross Wokingham 65 F8
Three Oaks E Sus 38 E4
Three Sisters Denb 165 C9
Threehammer Common Norf 160 E6
Threekingham Lincs 155 B11
Threelows Staffs 169 F9
Threemile Cross Wokingham 65 F8
Threemilestone Corn 4 G5
Threemiletown W Loth 279 F11
Threepwood Borders 271 G10
Threewaters Corn 5 B10
Threlkeld Cumb 230 F2
Threshers Bush Essex 87 D7
Threshfield N Yorks 213 G9
Thrigby Norf 161 G9
Thringarth Durham 232 G4
Thringstone Leics 153 F8
Thrintoft N Yorks 224 G6
Thriplow Cambs 105 B8
Throapham S Yorks 187 D8
Throckenholt Lincs 139 B7
Throcking Herts 104 E6
Throckley T & W 242 D5
Throckmorton Worcs 99 B9
Throop Dorset 18 C2
Throphill Northumb 252 F4
Thropton Northumb 252 C2
Throsk Stirl 279 C7
Througham Glos 80 D6
Throughgate Dumfries 247 G9
Throwleigh Devon 13 C9
Throwley Kent 54 B3
Throwley Forstal Kent 54 C3
Throxenby N Yorks 217 B10
Thrumpton Notts 153 C10
Thrumpton Notts 188 E2
Thrumster Highld 310 E7
Thrunton Northumb 264 G3
Thrupe Som 44 D6
Thrupp Glos 80 E5
Thrupp Oxon 82 F3
Thrupp Oxon 83 B7
Thruscross N Yorks 205 B9
Thrushelton Devon 12 D4
Thrussington Leics 154 F2
Thruxton Hants 47 D9
Thruxton Hereford 97 E8
Thrybergh S Yorks 187 B7
Thulston Derbys 153 C8
Thunder Bridge W Yorks 197 E7
Thunder Hill Norf 161 F8
Thundergay N Ayrs 255 C9
Thunder's Hill E Sus 23 C9
Thundersley Essex 69 B9
Thundridge Herts 86 B5
Thurcaston Leics 153 G11
Thurcroft S Yorks 187 D7
Thurdon Corn 24 E3
Thurgarton Norf 160 C3
Thurgarton Notts 171 F11
Thurgoland S Yorks 197 G9
Thurlaston Leics 135 D10
Thurlaston Warks 119 C9
Thurlbear Som 28 C3
Thurlby Lincs 156 F2
Thurlby Lincs 172 C6
Thurlby Lincs 191 F7
Thurleigh Beds 121 F11
Thurlestone Devon 8 G3
Thurloxton Som 43 G9
Thurlstone S Yorks 197 G8
Thurlton Norf 143 D8
Thurlton Links Norf 143 D8
Thurlwood E Ches 168 D4
Thurmaston Leics 136 B2
Thurnby Leics 136 C2
Thurne Norf 161 F8
Thurnham Kent 53 B10
Thurnham Lancs 202 C5
Thurning Norf 159 D11
Thurning Northants 137 G11
Thurnscoe S Yorks 198 F3
Thurnscoe East S Yorks 198 F3
Thursby Cumb 239 G8
Thursford Norf 159 C9
Thursford Green Norf 159 C9
Thursley Sur 50 F2
Thurso Highld 310 C5
Thurso East Highld 310 C5
Thurstaston Mers 182 E2
Thurston Suff 125 D8
Thurston Clough Gtr Man 196 F3
Thurston End Suff 124 G5
Thurstonfield Cumb 239 F8
Thurstonland W Yorks 197 E7
Thurton Norf 142 C6
Thurvaston Derbys 152 B2
Thurvaston Derbys 152 B4
Thuxton Norf 141 B10
Thwaite N Yorks 223 F7
Thwaite Suff 126 D2
Thwaite Flat Cumb 210 E4
Thwaite Head Cumb 220 G6
Thwaite St Mary Norf 142 E6
Thwaites W Yorks 205 E7
Thwaites Brow W Yorks 205 E7
Thwing E Yorks 217 E11
Tibbermore Perth 286 E4
Tibberton Glos 98 G5
Tibberton Telford 150 E3
Tibberton Worcs 117 F8
Tibenham Norf 142 F2
Tibshelf Derbys 170 C6
Tibshelf Wharf Notts 171 C7
Tibthorpe E Yorks 208 B5
Ticehurst E Sus 53 G7
Tichborne Hants 48 G5
Tickencote Rutland 137 B9
Tickenham N Som 60 E3
Ticket Wood Devon 8 G4
Tickford End M Keynes 103 C7
Tickhill S Yorks 187 C9
Tickleback Row Brack 65 E11
Ticklerton Shrops 131 E9
Tickmorend Glos 80 F4
Ticknall Derbys 153 E7
Tickton E Yorks 209 E7
Tidbury Green W Mid 117 B11
Tidcombe Wilts 47 B9
Tiddington Oxon 83 E11
Tiddington Warks 118 F4
Tidebrook E Sus 37 B10
Tideford Corn 6 D6
Tideford Cross Corn 6 C6
Tidenham Glos 79 F9
Tidenham Chase Glos 79 F9
Tideswell Derbys 185 F11
Tidmarsh W Berks 64 E6
Tidmington Warks 100 D5
Tidnor Hereford 97 D11
Tidpit Hants 31 D9
Tidworth Wilts 47 D8
Tiers Cross Pembs 72 C6
Tiffield Northants 120 G3
Tifty Aberds 303 E7
Tigerton Angus 293 G7
Tigh-na-Blair Perth 285 F11
Tighnabruaich Argyll 275 F10
Tighnacachla Argyll 274 G3
Tighnafiline Highld 307 L3
Tighness Argyll 284 G6
Tigley Devon 8 C5
Tilbrook Cambs 121 D11
Tilbury Thurrock 68 D6
Tilbury Green Essex 106 C4
Tilbury Juxta Clare Essex 106 C5
Tile Cross W Mid 134 F3
Tile Hill W Mid 118 B5
Tilegate Green Essex 87 D8
Tilehouse Green W Mid 118 B3
Tilehurst Reading 65 E7
Tilekiln Green Essex 105 G10
Tiley Dorset 29 F11
Tilford Sur 49 E11
Tilford Common Sur 49 E11
Tilford Reeds Sur 49 E11
Tilgate W Sus 51 G9
Tilgate Forest Row W Sus 51 G9
Tilkey Essex 106 G6
Tilland Corn 6 C6
Tillathrowie Aberds 302 F4
Tillers' Green Glos 98 E3
Tilley Shrops 149 D10
Tilley Green Shrops 149 D10
Tillicoultry Clack 279 B8
Tillietudlem S Lnrk 268 F6
Tillingham Essex 89 E7
Tillington Hereford 97 B9
Tillington Staffs 151 E8
Tillington W Sus 35 C7
Tillington Common Hereford 97 B9
Tillislow Devon 12 C3
Tillworth Devon 28 G4
Tilly Down Hants 47 D10
Tilly Lo Aberds 293 C7
Tillyarblet Angus 293 G7
Tillybirloch Aberds 293 C8
Tillycorthie Aberds 303 G9
Tillydrine Aberds 293 D8
Tillyfour Aberds 293 B7
Tillyfourie Aberds 293 B8
Tillygarmond Aberds 293 D8
Tillygreig Aberds 303 G8
Tillykerrie Aberds 303 G8
Tillynaught Aberds 302 C5
Tilmanstone Kent 55 C10
Tilney All Saints Norf 157 F11
Tilney cum Islington Norf 157 G11
Tilney Fen End Norf 157 G10
Tilney High End Norf 157 F11
Tilney St Lawrence Norf 157 G10
Tilsdown Glos 80 F2
Tilshead Wilts 46 D4
Tilsmore E Sus 37 C9
Tilsop Shrops 116 C2
Tilstock Shrops 149 B10
Tilston W Ches 167 E7
Tilstone Bank W Ches 167 D9
Tilstone Fearnall W Ches 167 C9
Tilsworth C Beds 103 G9
Tilton on the Hill Leics 136 B4
Tilts S Yorks 198 F5
Tiltups End Glos 80 F4
Tilty Essex 105 F11
Timberden Bottom Kent 68 G4
Timberhonger Worcs 117 C8
Timberland Lincs 173 D10
Timbersbrook E Ches 168 C5
Timberscombe Som 42 E3
Timble N Yorks 205 C9
Timbold Hill Kent 54 B2
Timbrelham Corn 12 E3
Timperley Gtr Man 184 D3
Timsbury Bath 45 B7
Timsbury Hants 32 C4
Timsgearraidh W Isles 304 E2
Timworth Suff 125 D7
Timworth Green Suff 125 D7
Tincleton Dorset 17 C11
Tindale Cumb 240 F4
Tindale Crescent Durham 233 F9
Tindon End Essex 106 E2
Tingewick Bucks 102 E3
Tingley W Yorks 197 B9
Tingon Shetland 312 E4
Tingrith C Beds 103 E10
Tingwall Orkney 314 D3
Tinhay Devon 12 E3
Tinkers End Bucks 102 F5
Tinshill W Yorks 205 F11
Tinsley S Yorks 186 C6
Tinsley Green W Sus 51 F9
Tintagel Corn 11 D7
Tintern Parva Mon 79 E8
Tintinhull Som 29 D8
Tintwistle Derbys 185 B8
Tinwald Dumfries 248 G2
Tinwell Rutland 137 B10
Tipner Ptsmth 33 G10
Tippacott Devon 41 D9
Tipper's Hill Warks 134 F5
Tipperty Aberds 302 C6
Tipperty Aberds 303 G9
Tipple Cross Devon 12 D3
Tipps End Norf 139 D10
Tip's Cross Essex 87 E9
Tiptoe Hants 19 B11
Tipton W Mid 133 E8
Tipton Green W Mid 133 E9
Tipton St John Devon 15 C7
Tiptree Essex 88 B5
Tiptree Heath Essex 88 B5
Tir-y-berth Caerph 77 F11
Tir-y-dail Carms 75 C10
Tirabad Powys 95 C7
Tiraghoil Argyll 288 G5
Tircanol Swansea 57 B7
Tirdeunaw Swansea 57 B7
Tirinie Perth 291 G10
Tirley Glos 98 F6
Tirley Knowle Glos 98 F6
Tiroran Argyll 288 G6
Tirphil Caerph 77 E10
Tirril Cumb 230 F6
Tirryside Highld 309 H5
Tisbury Wilts 30 B6
Tisman's Common W Sus 50 G5
Tissington Derbys 169 E11
Titchberry Devon 24 B2
Titchfield Hants 33 F8
Titchfield Common Hants 33 F8
Titchfield Park Hants 33 F8
Titchmarsh Northants 121 B10
Titchwell Norf 176 E3
Titcomb W Berks 63 F11
Tithby Notts 154 B3
Tithe Barn Hillock Mers 183 B9
Tithebarn Staffs 169 G9
Titley Hereford 114 E6
Titlington Northumb 264 F4
Titmore Green Herts 104 F4
Titsey Sur 52 C2
Titson Corn 24 G2
Tittenhurst Windsor 66 F3
Tittensor Staffs 151 B7
Titterhill Shrops 131 G10
Tittle Row Windsor 65 C11
Tittleshall Norf 159 E7
Titton Worcs 116 D6
Titty Hill W Sus 34 B5
Tiverton Devon 27 E7
Tiverton W Ches 167 C9
Tivetshall St Margaret Norf 142 F3
Tivetshall St Mary Norf 142 F3
Tividale W Mid 133 E9
Tivington Som 42 D2
Tivington Knowle Som 42 E2
Tivoli Cumb 228 G5
Tivy Dale S Yorks 197 F9
Tixall Staffs 151 E9

Name	County	Page	Grid
Tixover	Rutland	137	C9
Toab	Orkney	314	F5
Toab	Shetland	313	M5
Toad Row	Suff	143	F10
Toadmoor	Derbys	170	E4
Tobermory	Argyll	289	D7
Toberonochy	Argyll	275	C8
Tobha Beag	W Isles	296	D5
Tobha Mor	W Isles	297	H3
Tobhtarol	W Isles	304	E3
Tobson	W Isles	304	E3
Toby's Hill	Lincs	191	C7
Tocher	Aberds	302	F6
Tockenham	Wilts	62	C4
Tockenham Wick	Wilts	62	C4
Tockholes	Blkburn	195	C7
Tockington	S Glos	60	B6
Tockwith	N Yorks	206	C5
Todber	Dorset	30	C4
Todding	Hereford	115	B8
Toddington	C Beds	103	F10
Toddington	Glos	99	E10
Toddington	W Sus	35	G8
Toddlehills	Aberds	303	E10
Todenham	Glos	100	E4
Todhill	Angus	287	D8
Todhills	Cumb	239	E9
Todhills	Durham	233	E10
Todlachie	Aberds	293	B8
Todmorden	W Yorks	196	C2
Todpool	Corn	4	G4
Todrig	Borders	261	F10
Todwick	S Yorks	187	E7
Toft	Cambs	123	F7
Toft	Lincs	155	F11
Toft	Shetland	312	F6
Toft Hill	Durham	233	F9
Toft Hill	Lincs	174	C2
Toft Monks	Norf	143	E8
Toft next Newton	Lincs	189	D8
Toftrees	Norf	159	D7
Tofts	Highld	310	C7
Toftshaw	W Yorks	197	B7
Toftwood	Norf	159	G9
Togston	Northumb	252	C6
Tokavaig	Highld	295	D8
Tokers Green	Oxon	65	D8
Tokyngton	London	67	C7
Tolastadh a Chaolais	W Isles	304	E3
Tolastadh bho Thuath	W Isles	304	D7
Tolborough	Corn	11	F9
Tolcarne	Corn	2	B5
Tolcarne	Corn	2	C5
Tolcarne Wartha	Corn	2	B5
Toldish	Corn	5	D8
Tolgus Mount	Corn	4	G3
Tolhurst	E Sus	53	G7
Toll Bar	Mers	183	C7
Toll Bar	Rutland	137	B10
Toll Bar	S Yorks	198	F5
Toll End	W Mid	133	E9
Toll of Birness	Aberds	303	F10
Tolladine	Worcs	117	F7
Tolland	Som	42	G6
Tollard Farnham	Dorset	30	D6
Tollard Royal	Wilts	30	D6
Tollbar End	W Mid	119	B7
Toller Fratrum	Dorset	17	B7
Toller Porcorum	Dorset	17	B7
Toller Whelme	Dorset	29	G8
Tollerford	Dorset	17	B7
Tollerton	N Yorks	215	G10
Tollerton	Notts	154	C2
Tollesbury	Essex	89	C7
Tollesby	M'bro	225	B10
Tolleshunt D'Arcy	Essex	88	C6
Tolleshunt Knights	Essex	88	C6
Tolleshunt Major	Essex	88	C6
Tollie	Highld	300	D5
Tolm	W Isles	304	E6
Tolmers	Herts	86	E4
Tolpuddle	Dorset	17	C11
Tolvaddon Downs	Corn	4	G3
Tolvah	Highld	291	D10
Tolworth	London	67	F7
Tom an Fhuadain	W Isles	305	G5
Tomakneock	Perth	286	E2
Tomatin	Highld	301	G8
Tombreck	Highld	300	F6
Tombui	Perth	286	B2
Tomchrasky	Highld	290	B4
Tomdoun	Highld	290	C3
Tomich	Highld	300	B6
Tomich	Highld	300	F5
Tomich House	Highld	300	D5
Tomintoul	Aberds	292	B3
Tomintoul	Moray	292	B3
Tomlow	Warks	119	E9
Tomnamoon	Moray	302	E2
Tomnavoulin	Moray	302	G2
Tomperrow	Corn	4	G5
Tompkin	Staffs	168	E6
Tompset's Bank	E Sus	52	G2
Tomsleibhe	Argyll	289	F8
Tomthorn	Derbys	185	F9
Ton	Mon	57	B10
Ton Breigam	V Glam	58	D3
Ton-Pentre	Rhondda	76	E5
Ton-teg	Rhondda	58	B5
Ton-y-pistyll	Caerph	77	F11
Tonbridge	Kent	52	D5
Tonderghie	Dumfries	236	F6
Tondu	Bridgend	57	E11
Tone	Som	27	C10
Tone Green	Som	27	C11
Tonedale	Som	27	C10
Tong	Kent	53	D10
Tong	Shrops	132	B5
Tong	W Yorks	205	G10
Tong Forge	Shrops	132	B5
Tong Green	Kent	54	C3
Tong Norton	Shrops	132	B5
Tong Park	W Yorks	205	F9
Tong Street	W Yorks	205	G9
Tonge	Leics	153	E8
Tonge Corner	Kent	70	F2
Tonge Fold	Gtr Man	195	F8
Tonge Moor	Gtr Man	195	E8
Tongham	Sur	49	D11
Tongland	Dumfries	237	D8
Tongue	Highld	308	D5
Tongue End	Lincs	156	F3
Tongwell	M Keynes	103	C7
Tongwynlais	Cardiff	58	C6
Tonmawr	Neath	57	B10
Tonna = Tonnau	Neath	57	B9
Tonnau = Tonna	Neath	57	B9
Tontine	Lancs	194	D4
Tonwell	Herts	86	B4
Tonypandy	Rhondda	77	G7
Tonyrefail	Rhondda	58	B4
Toot Baldon	Oxon	83	E9
Toot Hill	Essex	87	E8
Toot Hill	Staffs	169	G9
Toothill	Hants	32	D5
Toothill	Swindon	62	C6
Toothill	W Yorks	196	C6
Tooting Graveney	London	67	E9
Top End	Beds	121	E10
Top Green	Notts	172	E3
Top Lock	Gtr Man	194	F6
Top o' th' Lane	Lancs	194	C5
Top o' th' Meadows	Gtr Man	196	F3
Top of Hebers	Gtr Man	195	F11
Top Valley	Nottingham	171	F9
Topcliffe	N Yorks	215	D8
Topcliffe	W Yorks	197	B9
Topcroft	Norf	142	E5
Topcroft Street	Norf	142	E5
Topham	S Yorks	198	D5
Topleigh	W Sus	34	D6
Toppesfield	Essex	106	D4
Toppings	Gtr Man	195	E8
Toprow	Norf	142	D3
Topsham	Devon	14	D5
Torbeg	N Ayrs	255	E10
Torboll Farm	Highld	309	K7
Torbothie	N Lnrk	269	D7
Torbreck	Highld	309	J7
Torbrex	Stirl	278	C5
Torbryan	Devon	8	B6
Torbush	N Lnrk	268	D6
Torcross	Devon	8	G6
Torcroy	Highld	291	D9
Tore	Highld	300	D6
Torfrey	Corn	6	E2
Torgyle	Highld	290	B5
Torinturk	Argyll	275	G9
Torkington	Gtr Man	184	D6
Torksey	Lincs	188	F4
Torlum	W Isles	296	F3
Torlundy	Highld	290	F3
Tormarton	S Glos	61	D9
Tormisdale	Argyll	254	B2
Tormitchell	S Ayrs	244	E6
Tormore	Highld	295	E8
Tormore	N Ayrs	255	D9
Tornagrain	Highld	301	E7
Tornahaish	Aberds	292	C4
Tornapress	Highld	299	E8
Tornaveen	Aberds	293	C8
Torness	Highld	300	G5
Toronto	Durham	233	E9
Torpenhow	Cumb	229	D10
Torphichen	W Loth	279	G9
Torphin	Edin	270	B4
Torphins	Aberds	293	C8
Torpoint	Corn	7	D8
Torquay	Torbay	9	C8
Torquhan	Borders	271	F8
Torr	Devon	7	E11
Torr	Corn	8	C2
Torra	Argyll	254	B4
Torran	Argyll	275	C9
Torran	Highld	298	E5
Torran	Highld	301	B7
Torrance	E Dunb	278	B2
Torrans	Argyll	288	G6
Torranyard	N Ayrs	267	G7
Torre	Som	42	E4
Torre	Torbay	9	C8
Torridon	Highld	299	D9
Torridon Ho	Highld	299	D8
Torries	Aberds	293	B8
Torrin	Highld	295	C7
Torrisdale	Highld	308	C7
Torrisdale Castle	Argyll	255	D8
Torrisdale-Square	Argyll	255	D8
Torrish	Highld	311	H3
Torrisholme	Lancs	211	G9
Torroble	Highld	309	J5
Torroy	Highld	309	K5
Torrpark	Corn	11	D10
Torry	Aberdeen	293	C11
Torry	Aberds	302	F4
Torryburn	Fife	279	D10
Torsonce	Borders	271	G9
Torsonce Mains	Borders	271	G9
Torterston	Aberds	303	E10
Torthorwald	Dumfries	238	B2
Tortington	W Sus	35	F8
Torton	Worcs	116	C6
Tortworth	S Glos	80	G2
Torver	Cumb	220	G5
Torwood	Falk	278	E6
Torwoodlee Mains	Borders	261	B11
Torworth	Notts	187	D11
Tosberry	Devon	24	C3
Toscaig	Highld	295	B9
Toseland	Cambs	122	E4
Tosside	N Yorks	203	B11
Tostock	Suff	125	E9
Tot Hill	Hants	64	G3
Totaig	Highld	295	C10
Totaig	Highld	298	D2
Totardor	Highld	294	B5
Tote	Highld	298	E4
Tote Hill	Hants	34	C4
Tote Hill	W Sus	34	C5
Totegan	Highld	310	C2
Totford	Hants	48	F5
Totham Hill	Essex	88	C5
Totham Plains	Essex	88	C5
Tothill	Lincs	190	E6
Totland	I o W	20	D2
Totley	S Yorks	186	F4
Totley Brook	S Yorks	186	F4
Totley Rise	S Yorks	186	F4
Totmonslow	Staffs	151	B9
Totnell	Dorset	29	F10
Totnes	Devon	8	C6
Totnor	Hereford	97	E11
Toton	Notts	153	C10
Totronald	Argyll	288	D3
Totscore	Highld	298	C3
Tottenham	London	86	G4
Tottenhill	Norf	158	G2
Tottenhill Row	Norf	158	G2
Totteridge	Bucks	84	G5
Totteridge	London	67	B10
Totternhoe	C Beds	103	G9
Totteroak	S Glos	61	C7
Tottington	Gtr Man	195	E9
Tottington	Norf	141	D7
Tottleback	Cumb	210	C6
Tottleworth	Lancs	203	G10
Totton	Hants	32	E5
Touchen End	Windsor	65	D11
Toulston	N Yorks	206	E5
Toulton	Som	43	G7
Toulvaddie	Highld	311	L2
Tournaig	Highld	307	L3
Toux	Aberds	303	D9
Tovil	Kent	53	D9
Tow House	Northumb	241	E7
Tow Law	Durham	233	D8
Towan	Corn	10	G3
Towan Cross	Corn	4	F4
Toward	Argyll	266	B2
Towcester	Northants	102	B3
Townednack	Corn	1	B5
Tower End	Norf	158	F3
Tower Hamlets	London	67	C11
Tower Hill	Devon	12	C3
Tower Hill	E Ches	184	F6
Tower Hill	Essex	108	E5
Tower Hill	Herts	85	E8
Tower Hill	Mers	194	G2
Tower Hill	Sur	51	D7
Tower Hill	W Mid	133	E11
Tower Hill	W Sus	35	B11
Towerage	Bucks	84	G4
Towerhead	N Som	44	B2
Towersey	Oxon	84	D2
Towie	Aberds	292	B6
Towie	Aberds	302	C5
Towie	Aberds	303	D8
Towiemore	Moray	302	E3
Town Barton	Devon	14	C2
Town End	Bucks	84	F3
Town End	Cambs	139	D8
Town End	Cumb	211	B7
Town End	Cumb	211	C8
Town End	Cumb	212	C2
Town End	Cumb	220	D6
Town End	Cumb	221	G8
Town End	Cumb	221	F7
Town End	Cumb	231	F8
Town End	E Yorks	207	C10
Town End	Mers	183	D7
Town End	W Yorks	196	D5
Town Fields	W Ches	167	B10
Town Green	Gtr Man	183	B9
Town Green	Lancs	194	F2
Town Green	Norf	161	G7
Town Head	Cumb	220	D6
Town Head	Cumb	221	E8
Town Head	Cumb	222	C2
Town Head	Cumb	222	C3
Town Head	Cumb	231	F7
Town Head	Derbys	185	F11
Town Head	N Yorks	204	B2
Town Head	N Yorks	212	F5
Town Head	Staffs	169	F8
Town Head	W Yorks	204	D6
Town Kelloe	Durham	234	D3
Town Lane	Gtr Man	183	B11
Town Littleworth	E Sus	36	D6
Town of Lowton	Mers	183	B10
Town Park	Telford	132	B3
Town Row	E Sus	52	G5
Town Street	Glos	98	F6
Town Yetholm	Borders	263	D8
Townend	Derbys	185	E9
Townend	Staffs	151	B9
Townend	W Dunb	277	F8
Townfield	Durham	232	B5
Towngate	Cumb	230	B6
Towngate	Lincs	156	G2
Townhead	Argyll	275	G11
Townhead	Cumb	229	D7
Townhead	Cumb	230	D6
Townhead	Cumb	231	B8
Townhead	Dumfries	237	E8
Townhead	S Ayrs	244	G6
Townhead	S Yorks	186	F4
Townhead	S Yorks	197	G7
Townhead of Greenlaw	Dumfries	237	C9
Townhill	Fife	280	D2
Townhill	Swansea	56	C6
Townhill Park	Hants	33	E7
Townlake	Devon	12	G4
Townland Green	Kent	54	G2
Town's End	Bucks	102	G2
Town's End	Dorset	18	B3
Town's End	Dorset	18	E5
Town's End	Dorset	29	F7
Town's End	Hants	48	B5
Towns End	Som	30	D2
Towns End	Som	44	D4
Town's End	Som	45	D7
Townsend	Bath	45	B7
Townsend	Bath	44	C6
Townsend	Bucks	84	D2
Townsend	Herts	85	D10
Townsend	Oxon	63	B11
Townsend	Pembs	72	D4
Townsend	Som	44	C4
Townsend	Stoke	168	F6
Townsend	Wilts	46	B3
Townsend	Wilts	46	B4
Townsend Fold	Lancs	195	C10
Townshend	Corn	2	C3
Townthorpe	E Yorks	217	G8
Towthorpe	W Yorks	207	B8
Towton	N Yorks	206	F5
Towyn	Conwy	181	F7
Toxteth	Mers	182	D5
Toynton All Saints	Lincs	174	C5
Toynton Fen Side	Lincs	174	C5
Toynton St Peter	Lincs	174	C6
Toy's Hill	Kent	52	C3
Trabboch	E Ayrs	257	E10
Traboe	Corn	2	E6
Trabrown	Borders	271	F11
Tracebridge	Som	27	C9
Tradespark	Orkney	314	H4
Tradespark	Highld	301	D8
Trafford Park	Gtr Man	184	B3
Traigh Ho	Highld	295	F8
Trallong	Powys	95	F9
Trallwn	Rhondda	77	G9
Trallwn	Swansea	57	B7
Tram Inn	Hereford	97	E9
Tramagenna	Corn	11	E7
Tranch	Torf	78	E3
Tranent	E Loth	281	G8
Tranmere	Mers	182	D4
Trantlebeg	Highld	310	D2
Trantlemore	Highld	310	D2
Tranwell	Northumb	252	G5
Trapp	Carms	75	B11
Traprain	E Loth	281	F11
Trapshill	W Berks	63	G11
Traquair	Borders	261	C8
Trash Green	W Berks	65	F7
Travellers' Rest	Carms	75	F7
Trawden	Lancs	204	F4
Trawscoed	Powys	95	F11
Trawsfynydd	Gwyn	146	B4
Trawsnant	Ceredig	111	D11
Tre-Aubrey	V Glam	58	E4
Tre-Beferad	V Glam	58	F3
Tre-boeth	Swansea	57	B7
Tre-derwen	Powys	148	F4
Tre-Gibbon	Rhondda	77	E7
Tre Gwyr = Gowerton	Swansea	56	B5
Tre-gynwr	Carms	74	B6
Tre-hill	V Glam	58	E5
Tre-Ifor	Rhondda	77	D7
Tre-Ian	Flint	165	B11
Tre-Mostyn	Flint	181	F10
Tre-pit	V Glam	58	E2
Tre-Taliesin	Ceredig	128	E3
Tre-wyn	Mon	96	G6
Treadam	Mon	78	B5
Treaddow	Hereford	97	G10
Treal	Corn	2	F6
Trealaw	Rhondda	77	G8
Treales	Lancs	202	G4
Trearddur	Anglesey	178	F3
Treaslane	Highld	298	D3
Treath	Corn	3	D7
Treator	Corn	10	F4
Trebanog	Rhondda	77	G8
Trebanos	Neath	76	E2
Trebarber	Corn	5	C7
Trebartha	Corn	11	F11
Trebarwith	Corn	11	D7
Trebarwith Strand	Corn	11	D11
Trebeath	Corn	11	D11
Trebell Green	Corn	5	C11
Treberfydd	Powys	96	F2
Trebetherick	Corn	10	F4
Treborough	Som	42	F4
Trebudannon	Corn	5	C7
Trebullett	Corn	12	F2
Treburgett	Corn	11	F7
Treburgie	Corn	6	C4
Treburley	Corn	12	F3
Treburrick	Corn	10	G4
Trebyan	Corn	5	C11
Trecastle	Powys	95	F8
Trecenydd	Caerph	58	B6
Trecott	Devon	25	G10
Trecwn	Pembs	91	E9
Trecynon	Rhondda	77	E7
Tredaule	Corn	11	E10
Tredavoe	Corn	1	D5
Treddiog	Pembs	91	F7
Tredegar	Bl Gwent	77	D10
Trederwen	Powys	148	F5
Tredethy	Corn	11	G7
Tredington	Glos	99	F8
Tredington	Warks	100	C5
Tredinnick	Corn	5	D10
Tredinnick	Corn	6	D4
Tredinnick	Corn	6	D3
Tredinnick	Corn	11	G8
Tredogan	V Glam	58	F5
Tredomen	Caerph	77	G10
Tredomen	Powys	96	E2
Tredown	Devon	24	D2
Tredrizzick	Corn	10	F5
Tredunnock	Mon	78	G5
Tredustan	Powys	96	E2
Tredworth	Glos	80	B4
Treen	Corn	1	B4
Treen	Corn	1	E3
Treesmill	Corn	5	D11
Treeton	S Yorks	186	D6
Tref y Clawdd = Knighton	Powys	114	C5
Trefasser	Pembs	91	D7
Trefdraeth	Anglesey	178	G6
Trefdraeth = Newport	Pembs	91	D11
Trefecca	Powys	96	E2
Trefechan	Ceredig	111	A11
Trefechan	M Tydf	77	D8
Trefechan	Wrex	166	F3
Trefeglwys	Powys	129	E9
Trefeitha	Powys	96	E2
Trefenter	Ceredig	112	D2
Treffgarne	Pembs	91	G9
Treffynnon	Pembs	90	F6
Treffynnon = Holywell	Flint	181	F11
Trefgarn Owen	Pembs	91	G7
Trefil	Bl Gwent	77	C10
Trefilan	Ceredig	111	F11
Trefin = Trevine	Pembs	90	E6
Treflach	Shrops	148	D5
Trefnanney	Powys	148	F5
Trefnant	Denb	181	G9
Trefonen	Shrops	148	D5
Trefor	Anglesey	178	E5
Trefor	Gwyn	162	F5
Treforda	Corn	11	E7
Treforest	Rhondda	58	B5
Treforgan	Ceredig	92	B4
Trefriw	Conwy	164	C3
Trefrize	Corn	12	F2
Tregada	Corn	12	E2
Tregadgwith	Corn	1	D4
Tregadillett	Corn	12	E2
Tregaian	Anglesey	178	F6
Tregajorran	Corn	4	G3
Tregamere	Corn	5	C8
Tregardock	Corn	10	E6
Tregare	Mon	78	C6
Tregarland Bridge	Corn	6	E4
Tregarne	Corn	3	E7
Tregaron	Ceredig	112	F3
Tregarrick Mill	Corn	6	D4
Tregarth	Gwyn	163	B10
Tregatta	Corn	11	D7
Tregatillian	Corn	5	C8
Tregavarah	Corn	1	D4
Tregeare	Corn	11	D10
Tregeiriog	Wrex	148	C3
Tregele	Anglesey	178	C5
Tregellist	Corn	11	F7
Tregeseal	Corn	1	C3
Tregew	Corn	3	C8
Tregidden	Corn	3	E7
Treginnis	Pembs	90	G4
Treglemais	Pembs	90	F6
Tregole	Corn	11	B9
Tregolls	Corn	3	B7
Tregolwyn = Colwinston	V Glam	58	D2
Tregona	Corn	5	B7
Tregonce	Corn	10	G5
Tregonetha	Corn	5	C9
Tregonning	Corn	5	D7
Tregony	Corn	5	F9
Tregoodwell	Corn	11	E8
Tregorden	Corn	10	G6
Tregorrick	Corn	5	E10
Tregoss	Corn	5	C9
Tregowris	Corn	3	E7
Tregoyd	Powys	96	D4
Tregoyd Mill	Powys	96	D3
Tregrehan Mills	Corn	5	E10
Tregroes	Ceredig	93	C8
Tregullon	Corn	5	C11
Tregunna	Corn	10	G5
Tregunnon	Corn	5	B7
Tregurrian	Corn	5	B7
Tregurtha Downs	Corn	2	C2
Tregynon	Powys	129	D11
Trehafod	Rhondda	77	G8
Trehafren	Powys	129	E11
Trehan	Corn	7	D8
Treharris	M Tydf	77	F9
Trehemborne	Corn	10	G3
Treherbert	Rhondda	76	F6
Trehunist	Corn	6	C6
Trekeivesteps	Corn	11	G10
Trekenner	Corn	12	F2
Trekenning	Corn	5	C8
Treknow	Corn	11	D7
Trelales = Laleston	Bridgend	57	F11
Trelan	Corn	2	F6
Trelash	Corn	11	C9
Trelassick	Corn	5	E7
Trelawnyd	Flint	181	F9
Trelech	Carms	92	E5
Treleddyd-fawr	Pembs	90	F5
Treleigh	Corn	4	G4
Treletert = Letterston	Pembs	91	F8
Trelew	Corn	11	D7
Trelewis	M Tydf	77	F10
Treligga	Corn	11	E7
Trelights	Corn	10	F5
Trelill	Corn	10	F6
Trelion	Corn	5	E8
Treliske	Corn	4	F6
Trelissick	Corn	3	B8
Treliver	Corn	5	C8
Trellech	Mon	79	D8
Trelleck Grange	Mon	79	E7
Trelogan	Flint	181	E10
Treloquithack	Corn	2	D5
Trelowia	Corn	6	D5
Trelowth	Corn	5	E9
Trelystan	Powys	130	C5
Tremadog	Gwyn	163	G9
Tremail	Corn	11	D9
Tremain	Ceredig	92	B4
Tremaine	Corn	11	D10
Tremains	Bridgend	58	D2
Tremar	Corn	6	B5
Trematon	Corn	7	D7
Trematon Castle	Corn	7	D7
Tremayne	Corn	2	B4
Trembraze	Corn	6	B5
Tremedda	Corn	1	B5
Tremeirchion	Denb	181	G9
Tremethick Cross	Corn	1	C4
Tremore	Corn	5	C10
Tremorebridge	Corn	5	C10
Tremorfa	Cardiff	59	D8
Trenance	Corn	4	C6
Trenance	Corn	5	B7
Trenance	Corn	5	C9
Trenance	Corn	10	G4
Trenance	Corn	10	G5
Trenant	Corn	5	E9
Trenarren	Corn	5	F10
Trenay	Corn	6	B4
Trench	Telford	150	G3
Trench Green	Oxon	65	D7
Trench Wood	Kent	52	D5
Trencreek	Corn	4	C6
Trencrom	Corn	2	B2
Trendeal	Corn	5	E7
Trenear	Corn	2	C5
Treneglos	Corn	11	D10
Trenerth	Corn	2	C3
Trenewan	Corn	6	E3
Trengune	Corn	11	B9
Trenhorne	Corn	11	E11
Treningle	Corn	5	C10
Treninnick	Corn	4	C6
Trenoon	Corn	2	F5
Trenoweth	Corn	3	C7
Trent	Dorset	29	D9
Trent Vale	Stoke	168	G5
Trentham	Stoke	168	G5
Trentishoe	Devon	40	D6
Trentlock	Derbys	153	C9
Trenwheal	Corn	2	C4
Treoes	V Glam	58	D2
Treopert = Granston	Pembs	91	E7
Treorchy = Treorci	Rhondda	77	F7
Treorci = Treorchy	Rhondda	77	F7
Treowen	Caerph	78	F2
Treowen	Powys	130	E2
Trequite	Corn	10	F6
Tre'r-ddôl	Ceredig	128	E3
Trerhyngyll	V Glam	58	D4
Trerise	Corn	2	F6
Trerose	Corn	3	D7
Trerulefoot	Corn	6	D6
Tresaith	Ceredig	110	G5
Tresamble	Corn	3	B7
Tresarrett	Corn	11	G7
Tresavean	Corn	2	B6
Tresawle	Corn	5	F7
Tresawsen	Corn	4	F5
Trescoll	Corn	5	C10
Trescott	Staffs	132	D6
Trescowe	Corn	2	C3
Tresean	Corn	4	D4
Tresevern Croft	Corn	2	B6
Tresham	Glos	80	G3
Tresigin = Sigingstone	V Glam	58	E3
Tresillian	Corn	5	F7
Tresimwn = Bonvilston	V Glam	58	E5
Tresinney	Corn	11	E8
Tresinwen	Pembs	91	C7
Treskerby	Corn	4	G4
Treskillard	Corn	2	B5
Treskilling	Corn	5	D10
Treskinnick Cross	Corn	11	B10
Treslothan	Corn	2	B5
Tresmeer	Corn	11	D10
Tresoweshill	Corn	2	D3
Tresowes Green	Corn	2	D3
Tresparrett	Corn	11	C8
Tresparrett Posts	Corn	11	C8
Tressady	Highld	309	J6
Tressait	Perth	291	G10
Tresta	Shetland	312	D8
Tresta	Shetland	313	H5
Treswell	Notts	188	F3
Treswithian	Corn	2	B4
Treswithian Downs	Corn	4	G2
Trethellan Water	Corn	2	B6
Trethevy	Corn	11	D7
Trethewell	Corn	3	B9
Trethewey	Corn	1	E3
Trethillick	Corn	10	F4
Trethomas	Caerph	59	B7
Trethosa	Corn	5	E8
Trethowel	Corn	5	E10
Trethurgy	Corn	5	D10
Tretio	Pembs	90	F5
Tretire	Hereford	97	G10
Tretower	Powys	96	G3
Treuddyn	Flint	166	D3
Trevadlock	Corn	11	F11
Trevail	Corn	4	D5
Trevalga	Corn	11	D7
Trevalyn	Wrex	166	D5
Trevance	Corn	10	G5
Trevanger	Corn	10	F5
Trevanson	Corn	10	G5
Trevarrack	Corn	1	C5
Trevarren	Corn	5	C8
Trevarrian	Corn	4	B6
Trevarrick	Corn	5	G9
Trevarth	Corn	4	G4
Trevaughan	Carms	73	B11
Trevaughan	Carms	93	G7
Trevaylor	Corn	1	A5
Treveal	Corn	1	D3
Treveighan	Corn	11	F7
Trevellas	Corn	4	E4
Trevelmond	Corn	6	C4
Trevelver	Corn	10	G5
Trevemper	Corn	4	D6
Treven	Corn	11	D7
Trevena	Corn	2	D5
Trevenen Bal	Corn	2	D5
Trevenning	Corn	11	F7
Treveor	Corn	5	G9
Treverbyn	Corn	5	D10
Treverbyn	Corn	6	B4
Treverva	Corn	3	C7
Trevescan	Corn	1	E3
Trevethin	Torf	78	E3
Trevia	Corn	11	E7
Trevigro	Corn	6	B6
Trevilder	Corn	10	G6
Trevilla	Corn	3	B8
Trevilson	Corn	4	D6
Trevine	Corn	11	D7
Trevine = Trefin	Pembs	90	E6
Treviscoe	Corn	5	D8
Treviskey	Corn	2	B6
Trevivian	Corn	11	D9
Trevoll	Corn	4	D6
Trevone	Corn	10	F4
Trevor	Wrex	166	G3
Trevor Uchaf	Denb	166	G2
Trevorrick	Corn	10	G4
Trevowah	Corn	4	D5
Trevowhan	Corn	1	B4
Trew	Corn	2	D4
Trewalder	Corn	11	E7
Trewarmett	Corn	11	D7
Trewartha	Corn	2	B2
Trewartha	Corn	3	B10
Trewassa	Corn	11	D8
Treween	Corn	11	E10
Trewellard	Corn	1	C3
Trewen	Corn	11	D7
Trewen	Corn	11	E11
Trewen	Hereford	79	B9
Trewennack	Corn	2	D5
Trewennan	Corn	11	E7
Trewent	Corn	11	E7
Trewern	Powys	148	F5
Trewethen	Corn	10	F6
Trewethern	Corn	10	F6
Trewey	Corn	1	B5
Trewidland	Corn	6	D5
Trewindle	Corn	6	C2
Trewint	Corn	11	C9
Trewint	Corn	11	D11
Trewint	Corn	11	B9
Trewithian	Corn	3	C8
Trewoodloe	Corn	12	G2
Trewoofe	Corn	1	D4
Trewoon	Corn	2	F5
Trewoon	Corn	5	E9
Treworga	Corn	5	G7
Treworgan Common	Mon	78	D6
Treworlas	Corn	3	B9
Treworld	Corn	11	C8
Treworrick	Corn	6	C5
Treworthal	Corn	3	B9
Trewyddel = Moylgrove	Pembs	92	C2
Trewyn	Devon	24	G4
Treyarnon	Corn	10	G3
Treyford	W Sus	34	D4
Trezaise	Corn	5	D9
Trezelah	Corn	1	C5
Triangle	Glos	79	E8
Triangle	Staffs	133	B11
Triangle	W Yorks	196	C5
Trickett's Cross	Dorset	31	G9
Triffleton	Pembs	91	G9
Trillacott	Corn	11	D11
Trimdon	Durham	234	D3
Trimdon Colliery	Durham	234	D3
Trimdon Grange	Durham	234	D3
Trimingham	Norf	160	B5
Trimley Lower Street	Suff	108	D5
Trimley St Martin	Suff	108	D5
Trimley St Mary	Suff	108	D5
Trimpley	Worcs	116	B5
Trims Green	Herts	87	B7
Trimsaran	Carms	75	D7
Trimstone	Devon	40	E3
Trinafour	Perth	291	G9
Trinant	Caerph	78	E2
Tring	Herts	84	C6
Tring Wharf	Herts	84	C6
Tringford	Herts	84	C6
Trinity	Angus	293	G8
Trinity	Devon	27	F7
Trinity	Edin	280	F4
Trinity Fields	Staffs	151	D8
Trisant	Ceredig	112	B4
Triscombe	Som	43	F7
Trislaig	Highld	290	F2
Trispen	Corn	4	E6
Tritlington	Northumb	252	E6
Troan	Corn	5	D8
Trochry	Perth	286	C3
Trodigal	Argyll	255	F7
Troedrhiwdalar	Powys	113	G9
Troedrhiwfuwch	Caerph	77	E10
Troedrhiwfelen	Ceredig	93	C8
Troedyraur	Ceredig	92	B6
Troedyrhiw	M Tydf	77	F9
Trofarth	Conwy	180	G5
Troon	S Ayrs	257	C8
Trooper's Inn	Pembs	73	C7
Trosaraidh	W Isles	297	K3
Trossachs Hotel	Stirl	285	G8
Troston	Suff	125	C7
Trostre	Carms	56	B4
Trostrey Common	Mon	78	E5
Troswell	Corn	11	C11
Trotshill	Worcs	117	F7
Trotsholme	S Lnrk	259	B8
Trotten Marsh	W Sus	34	B4
Trottiscliffe	Kent	68	G6
Trotton	W Sus	34	C4
Trough Gate	Lancs	195	C11
Troustan	Argyll	275	E11
Troutbeck	Cumb	221	B8
Troutbeck	Cumb	230	F3
Troutbeck Bridge	Cumb	221	F8
Trow Green	Glos	79	D9
Troway	Derbys	186	F5
Trowbridge	Cardiff	59	C8
Trowbridge	Wilts	45	B11
Trowell	Notts	153	B9
Trowle Common	Wilts	45	B11
Trowley Bottom	Herts	85	C9
Trows	Borders	262	C5
Trowse Newton	Norf	142	B4
Troy Town	Kent	52	D2
Troy Town	Kent	54	E5
Troy Town	Medway	69	F8
Troydale	W Yorks	205	G10
Truas	Highld	11	D7
Trub	Gtr Man	195	F11
Trudoxhill	Som	45	E8
True Street	Devon	8	C6
Trueman's Heath	Worcs	117	B11
Trull	Som	28	C2
Trumaisgearraidh	W Isles	296	D4
Trumfleet	S Yorks	198	E6
Trumpan	Highld	298	C2
Trumpet	Hereford	98	D3
Trumpington	Cambs	123	F8
Trumpsgreen	Sur	66	F3
Trunch	Norf	160	C5
Trunnah	Lancs	202	E2
Truro	Corn	4	F6
Truscott	Corn	12	D2
Trusham	Devon	14	E3
Trusley	Derbys	152	B5
Trussall	Corn	2	D5
Trussell	Corn	11	D10
Trusthorpe	Lincs	191	E8
Truthan	Corn	4	E6
Truthwall	Corn	2	C2
Trwstllewelyn	Powys	130	D3
Tryfil	Anglesey	178	E6
Trysull	Staffs	133	E7
Trythogga	Corn	1	C5
Tubbs Mill	Corn	5	G9
Tubney	Oxon	82	F6
Tubslake	Kent	53	G9
Tuckenhay	Devon	8	D6
Tuckermarsh	Devon	7	B8
Tuckerton	Som	28	B3
Tuckhill	Shrops	132	F5
Tucking Mill	Bath	61	G9
Tuckingmill	Corn	4	G3
Tuckingmill	Corn	11	F7
Tuckingmill	Wilts	30	B6
Tuckton	Bmouth	19	C8
Tuddenham	Suff	108	B3
Tuddenham	Suff	124	C4
Tuddenham St Martin	Suff	108	B3
Tudeley	Kent	52	D6
Tudeley Hale	Kent	52	D6
Tudhay	Devon	28	G4
Tudhoe	Durham	233	D11
Tudhoe Grange	Durham	233	E11
Tudor Hill	W Mid	134	D2
Tudorville	Hereford	97	G11
Tudweiliog	Gwyn	144	B4
Tuebrook	Mers	182	C5
Tuesley	Sur	50	E3
Tuesnoad	Kent	54	E3
Tuffley	Glos	80	C4
Tufton	Hants	48	D3
Tufton	Pembs	91	F10
Tugby	Leics	136	C5
Tugford	Shrops	131	F11
Tughall	Northumb	264	D6
Tulchan Lodge	Angus	292	F3
Tullecombe	W Sus	34	B4
Tullibardine	Perth	286	F3
Tullibody	Clack	279	B7
Tullich	Argyll	284	F4
Tullich	Highld	299	C9
Tullich	Highld	301	B7
Tullich	Perth	286	C4
Tullich Muir	Highld	301	B7
Tulliemet	Perth	286	B3
Tulloch	Aberds	293	F9
Tulloch	Aberds	303	E8
Tulloch	Perth	286	E4
Tulloch Castle	Highld	300	C5
Tulloch-gribban	Highld	301	G9
Tullochbeg	Aberds	293	G7
Tullochgorm	Argyll	275	D10
Tullochroisk	Perth	285	B11
Tullochvenus	Aberds	293	C7
Tulloes	Angus	287	C9
Tullybannocher	Perth	285	E11
Tullybelton	Perth	286	D4
Tullyfergus	Perth	286	C6
Tullymurdoch	Perth	286	B5
Tullynessle	Aberds	293	B7
Tumble = Y Tymbl	Carms	75	C8
Tumbler's Green	Essex	106	F6
Tumby	Lincs	174	D2
Tumby Woodside	Lincs	174	D3
Tummel Bridge	Perth	285	B11
Tumpy Green	Glos	80	E2
Tumpy Lakes	Hereford	97	B10
Tunbridge Hill	Medway	69	E10
Tunbridge Wells = Royal Tunbridge Wells	Kent	52	F5
Tunga	W Isles	304	E6
Tungate	Norf	160	D5
Tunley	Bath	45	B7
Tunley	Glos	80	E6
Tunnel Hill	Worcs	98	C6
Tunnel Pits	N Lincs	199	G8
Tunshill	Gtr Man	196	F2
Tunstall	E Yorks	209	G12
Tunstall	Kent	69	G11
Tunstall	Lancs	212	D2
Tunstall	N Yorks	224	F4
Tunstall	Norf	143	B8
Tunstall	Staffs	150	D5
Tunstall	Stoke	168	E5
Tunstall	Suff	108	B5
Tunstall	T & W	243	G9
Tunstead	Derbys	185	G8
Tunstead	Gtr Man	196	C4
Tunstead	Norf	160	E5
Tunstead Milton	Derbys	185	E8
Tunworth	Hants	49	D7
Tupholme	Lincs	173	C10
Tupsley	Hereford	97	C10
Tupton	Derbys	170	B5
Tur Langton	Leics	136	E4
Turbary Common	Poole	19	C7
Turf Hill	Gtr Man	196	E2
Turfdown	Corn	5	B11
Turfholm	S Lnrk	259	B8
Turfmoor	Devon	28	G3
Turfmoor	Shrops	149	F7
Turgis Green	Hants	49	B7
Turin	Angus	287	B9
Turkdean	Glos	81	B10
Turkey Island	Hants	33	E9
Turkey Island	W Sus	34	D3
Turkey Tump	Hereford	97	F10
Turleigh	Wilts	61	G10
Turleygreen	Shrops	132	F5
Turlin Moor	Poole	18	C5
Turmer	Hants	31	F10
Turn	Lancs	195	D10
Turnalt	Argyll	275	C9
Turnastone	Hereford	97	D7
Turnberry	S Ayrs	244	B6
Turnchapel	Plym	7	E9
Turnditch	Derbys	170	F3
Turner Green	Lancs	203	G8
Turner's Green	E Sus	52	G6
Turner's Green	W Berks	64	F4
Turner's Green	Warks	118	D3
Turners Hill	W Sus	51	F10
Turners Puddle	Dorset	18	C2
Turnerwood	S Yorks	187	E8
Turnford	Herts	86	E5
Turnhouse	Edin	280	G3
Turnhurst	Stoke	168	E5
Turnstead Milton	Derbys	185	E8
Turnworth	Dorset	30	F4
Turriff	Aberds	303	D7
Tursdale	Durham	234	D2
Turton Bottoms	Blkburn	195	D8
Turves	Cambs	138	D6
Turves Green	W Mid	117	B10
Turvey	Beds	121	G8
Turville	Bucks	84	G3
Turville Heath	Bucks	84	G2
Turweston	Bucks	102	D2
Tushielaw	Borders	261	F8
Tutbury	Staffs	152	D4
Tutnall	Worcs	117	C9
Tutshill	Glos	79	G8
Tutt Hill	Kent	54	E3
Tuttington	Norf	160	D4
Tutts Clump	W Berks	64	E5
Tutwell	Corn	12	F3
Tuxford	Notts	188	G2
Twatt	Orkney	314	D2
Twatt	Shetland	313	H5
Twechar	E Dunb	278	F4
Tweedale	Telford	132	C4
Tweeddaleburn	Borders	270	E5
Tweedmouth	Northumb	273	E9
Tweedsmuir	Borders	260	E3
Twelve Heads	Corn	4	G5
Twelve Oaks	E Sus	37	C11
Twelvewoods	Corn	6	B4
Twemlow Green	E Ches	168	B3
Twenties	Kent	71	F10
Twenty	Lincs	156	E3
Twerton	Bath	61	G8
Twickenham	London	67	E7
Twigworth	Glos	98	G6
Twineham	W Sus	36	C3
Twineham Green	W Sus	36	C3
Twinhoe	Bath	45	B8
Twinstead	Essex	107	D7
Twinstead Green	Essex	106	D6
Twiss Green	Warr	183	B11
Twiston	Lancs	204	E2
Twitchen	Devon	41	G9
Twitchen	Shrops	115	B7
Twitchen Mill	Devon	41	G9
Twitham	Kent	55	B9
Twitton	Kent	52	B4
Two Bridges	Glos	79	E10
Two Burrows	Corn	4	F4
Two Dales	Derbys	170	C3
Two Gates	Staffs	134	C4
Two Mile Ash	M Keynes	102	D6
Two Mile Ash	W Sus	35	B10
Two Mile Hill	Bristol	60	E6
Two Mile Oak Cross	Devon	8	B6
Two Mills	Ches	182	G5
Two Pots	Devon	40	E4
Two Waters	Herts	85	D9
Twr	Anglesey	178	E2
Twycross	Leics	134	C6
Twydall	Medway	69	F10
Twyford	Bucks	102	F2
Twyford	Derbys	152	D6
Twyford	Dorset	30	D5
Twyford	Hants	33	C7
Twyford	Leics	154	G4
Twyford	Lincs	155	E8
Twyford	Norf	159	E10
Twyford	Oxon	101	D7
Twyford	Shrops	148	D5
Twyford	Wokingham	65	D10
Twyford	Worcs	99	B7
Twyford Common	Hereford	97	D10
Twyn-Allws	Mon	78	C3
Twyn Shôn-Ifan	Caerph	77	G10
Twyn-y-Sheriff	Mon	78	D6
Twyn-yr-odyn	V Glam	58	D6
Twynholm	Dumfries	237	D8
Twyning	Glos	99	D7
Twyning Green	Glos	99	D8
Twynllanan	Carms	94	G5
Twynmynydd	Carms	75	C11
Twynrodyn	M Tydf	77	E9
Twywell	Northants	121	B9
Ty-croes	Swansea	56	C6
Ty-draw	Conwy	164	G5
Ty-draw	Swansea	57	B7
Ty-fry	Mon	78	F6
Ty-hen	Carms	92	G6
Ty-hen	Gwyn	144	C3
Ty-isaf	Carms	56	B4
Ty Llwyn	Bl Gwent	77	D11
Ty Mawr	Carms	93	C10
Ty Mawr Cwm	Conwy	164	F5
Ty-nant	Conwy	147	D8
Ty-nant	Gwyn	147	D8
Ty-Newydd	Ceredig	111	D10
Ty Rhiw	Rhondda	58	C5
Ty-Sign	Caerph	78	G2
Ty-uchaf	Powys	147	E10
Tyberton	Hereford	97	D7
Tyburn	W Mid	134	E2

Tyby Norf 159 D11
Tycroes Carms 75 C10
Tycrwyn Powys 148 F2
Tydd Gote Lincs 157 F9
Tydd St Giles Cambs 157 F8
Tydd St Mary Lincs 157 F8
Tyddewi = St Davids Pembs 90 F5
Tyddyn Powys 129 F9
Tyddyn Angharad Denb 165 F9
Tyddyn Dai Anglesey 178 C6
Tyddyn-mawr Gwyn 163 G9
Tye Hants 22 C2
Tye Common Essex 87 G11
Tye Green Essex 87 C10
Tye Green Essex 87 D7
Tye Green Essex 87 F11
Tye Green Essex 105 D11
Tye Green Essex 105 G10
Tye Green Essex 106 G5
Tyegate Green Norf 161 G7
Tyersal W Yorks 205 G9
Tyganol V Glam 58 E4
Tyla Mon 78 C2
Tylagwyn Bridgend 58 B2
Tyldesley Gtr Man 195 G7
Tyle Carms 94 F3
Tyle-garw Rhondda 58 C4
Tyler Hill Kent 70 G6
Tylers Causeway Herts 86 D3
Tylers Green Bucks 84 G6
Tyler's Green Essex 87 D8
Tyler's Green Sur 51 C11
Tyler's Hill Bucks 85 E7
Tylorstown Rhondda 77 F8
Tylwch Powys 129 G9
Tyn-Ion Gwyn 163 D7
Ty'n-y-bryn Rhondda 58 B4
Tyn-y-celyn Wrex 148 B3
Tyn-y-coed Shrops 148 D4
Ty'n-y-coedcae Caerph 59 B7
Tyn-y-cwm Swansea 75 E10
Ty'n-y-fedwen Powys 148 D2
Ty'n-y-ffordd Denb 181 G8
Tyn-y-ffridd Powys 148 C2
Ty'n-y-garn Bridgend 57 E11
Tyn-y-graig Powys 113 G10
Ty'n-y-groes Conwy 180 G3
Ty'n-y-maes Gwyn 163 C10
Tyn-y-pwll Anglesey 178 D6
Ty'n-yr-eithin Ceredig 112 E3
Tynant Rhondda 58 B5
Tyncelyn Ceredig 112 E2
Tyndrum Stirl 285 D7
Tyne Dock T & W 243 D9
Tyne Tunnel T & W 243 D8
Tyneham Dorset 18 E3
Tynehead Midloth 271 D7
Tynemouth T & W 243 D9
Tynewydd Ceredig 92 B4
Tynewydd Neath 76 D4
Tynewydd Rhondda 76 F6
Tyning Bath 45 B7
Tyninghame E Loth 282 F2
Tynron Dumfries 247 E8
Tyntesfield N Som 60 E4
Tyntetown Rhondda 77 F9
Tynyfedw Conwy 165 B7
Tynygongl Anglesey 179 E8
Tynygraig Ceredig 112 D3
Tynyrwtra Powys 129 F7
Tŷ'r-felin-isaf Conwy 164 C5
Tyrells End C Beds 103 E9
Tyrell's Wood Sur 51 B7
Tyrie Aberds 303 C9
Tyringham M Keynes 103 B7
Tyseley W Mid 134 G2
Tythecott Devon 24 D6
Tythegston Bridgend 57 F11
Tytherington E Ches 184 F6
Tytherington S Glos 61 B7
Tytherington Som 45 D9
Tytherington Wilts 46 E2
Tytherleigh Devon 28 G4
Tytherton Lucas Wilts 62 E2
Tyttenhanger Herts 85 D11
Tywardreath Corn 5 E11
Tywardreath Highway Corn 5 D11
Tywyn Conwy 180 F3
Tywyn Gwyn 110 C2

U

Uachdar W Isles 296 F3
Uags Highld 295 B9
Ubberley Stoke 168 F6
Ubbeston Green Suff 126 C6
Ubley Bath 44 B4
Uckerby N Yorks 224 E4
Uckfield E Sus 37 C7
Uckinghall Worcs 99 D7
Uckington Glos 99 G8
Uckington Shrops 131 B11
Uddingston S Lnrk 268 C3
Uddington S Lnrk 259 C9
Udimore E Sus 38 D5
Udley N Som 60 G3
Udny Green Aberds 303 G8
Udny Station Aberds 303 G9
Udston S Lnrk 268 D3
Udstonhead S Lnrk 268 F4
Uffcott Wilts 62 D6
Uffculme Devon 27 E9
Uffington Lincs 137 B11
Uffington Oxon 63 B10
Uffington Shrops 149 G10
Ufford P'boro 137 C11
Ufford Suff 126 G5
Ufton Warks 119 E7
Ufton Green W Berks 64 F6
Ufton Nervet W Berks 64 F6
Ugadale Argyll 255 E8
Ugborough Devon 8 D3
Ugford Wilts 46 G5
Uggeshall Suff 143 G8
Ugglebarnby N Yorks 227 D7
Ughill S Yorks 186 C3
Ugley Essex 105 F10
Ugley Green Essex 105 F10
Ugthorpe N Yorks 226 C5
Uidh W Isles 297 M2
Uig Argyll 276 E2
Uig Argyll 288 D3
Uig Highld 296 F7
Uig Highld 298 C3
Uigen W Isles 304 E2
Uigshader Highld 298 E4
Uisken Argyll 274 B4
Ulaw Aberds 303 G9
Ulbster Highld 310 E7
Ulcat Row Cumb 230 G4
Ulceby Lincs 190 G6
Ulceby N Lincs 200 E6
Ulceby Skitter N Lincs 200 E6
Ulcombe Kent 53 D10
Uldale Cumb 229 D10
Uley Glos 80 F3
Ulgham Northumb 252 E6
Ullapool Highld 307 K6
Ullcombe Devon 28 F2
Ullenhall Warks 118 D2
Ullenwood Glos 80 B6
Ulleskelf N Yorks 206 E6
Ullesthorpe Leics 135 F10
Ulley S Yorks 187 D7
Ullingswick Hereford 97 B11
Ullington Worcs 100 B2
Ullinish Highld 294 B5
Ullock Cumb 229 G10
Ullock Cumb 229 G7
Ulnes Walton Lancs 194 D4
Ulpha Cumb 220 G3
Ulrome E Yorks 209 B9
Ulshaw N Yorks 214 B2
Ulsta Shetland 312 E6
Ulva House Argyll 288 F6
Ulverley Green W Mid 134 G2
Ulverston Cumb 210 D5
Ulwell Dorset 18 E6
Umberleigh Devon 25 C10
Unapool Highld 306 F7
Unasary W Isles 297 J3
Under Bank W Yorks 196 F6
Under the Wood Kent 71 F8
Under Tofts S Yorks 186 D4
Underbarrow Cumb 221 G9
Undercliffe W Yorks 205 G9
Underdale Shrops 149 G10
Underdown Devon 14 D3
Underhill London 86 F3
Underhill Wilts 45 G11
Underhoull Shetland 312 C7
Underling Green Kent 53 D9
Underriver Kent 52 C5
Underriver Ho Kent 52 C5
Underton Shrops 132 E3
Underwood Newport 59 B11
Underwood Notts 171 E7
Underwood Pembs 73 C7
Underwood Plym 7 D10
Undley Suff 140 G3
Undy Mon 60 B2
Ungisiadar W Isles 304 F3
Unifirth Shetland 313 H4
Union Cottage Aberds 293 D10
Union Mills I o M 192 E4
Union Street E Sus 53 G8
United Downs Corn 4 G4
Unstone Derbys 186 F5
Unstone Green Derbys 186 F5
Unsworth Gtr Man 195 F10
Unthank Cumb 230 B3
Unthank Cumb 230 D5
Unthank Cumb 231 C8
Unthank Derbys 186 F4
Unthank End Cumb 230 E5
Up Cerne Dorset 29 G11
Up End M Keynes 103 B8
Up Exe Devon 26 G6
Up Green Hants 65 G9
Up Hatherley Glos 99 G8
Up Holland Lancs 194 F4
Up Marden W Sus 34 E3
Up Mudford Som 29 D9
Up Nately Hants 49 C7
Up Somborne Hants 47 G11
Up Sydling Dorset 29 G10
Upavon Wilts 46 C6
Upchurch Kent 69 F10
Upcott Devon 24 D2
Upcott Devon 25 F11
Upcott Devon 25 F9
Upcott Devon 40 F3
Upcott Hereford 114 G6
Upcott Som 27 C11
Upend Cambs 124 F3
Upgate Norf 160 F2
Upgate Street Norf 141 E11
Upgate Street Norf 142 E5
Uphall Dorset 29 G9
Uphall W Loth 279 G11
Uphall Station W Loth 279 G11
Upham Devon 26 F5
Upham Hants 33 C8
Uphampton Hereford 115 E7
Uphampton Worcs 116 E6
Uphempston Devon 8 C6
Uphill N Som 43 B10
Uphill Manor N Som 43 B10
Uplands Glos 80 D5
Uplands Swansea 56 C6
Uplawmoor E Renf 267 D8
Upleadon Glos 98 F5
Upleadon Court Glos 98 F5
Upleatham Redcar 226 B2
Uplees Kent 70 G3
Uploders Dorset 16 C6
Uplowman Devon 27 D8
Uplyme Devon 16 C2
Upminster London 68 B5
Upnor Medway 69 E9
Upottery Devon 28 F2
Uppacott Devon 25 B9
Uppat Highld 311 J2
Uppend Essex 105 F9
Upper Affcot Shrops 131 F8
Upper Ardchronie Highld 309 L6
Upper Ardgrain Aberds 303 F9
Upper Ardroscadale Argyll 275 G11
Upper Arley Worcs 132 G5
Upper Armley W Yorks 205 G11
Upper Arncott Oxon 83 B10
Upper Astley Shrops 149 F10
Upper Aston Shrops 132 E6
Upper Astrop Northants 101 D10
Upper Badcall Highld 306 E6
Upper Bangor Gwyn 179 G9
Upper Basildon W Berks 64 D5
Upper Batley W Yorks 197 B8
Upper Battlefield Shrops 149 F10
Upper Beeding W Sus 35 E11
Upper Benefield Northants 137 F9
Upper Bentley Worcs 117 D9
Upper Bighouse Highld 310 D2
Upper Birchwood Derbys 170 E6
Upper Blainslie Borders 271 G10
Upper Boat Rhondda 58 B6
Upper Boddam Aberds 302 F6
Upper Boddington Northants 119 G9
Upper Bogrow Highld 309 L7
Upper Bogside Moray 302 D2
Upper Bonchurch I o W 21 F7
Upper Booth Derbys 185 D10
Upper Borth Ceredig 128 F2
Upper Boyndlie Aberds 303 C9
Upper Brailes Warks 100 D6
Upper Brandon Parva Norf 141 B10
Upper Breakish Highld 295 C8
Upper Breinton Hereford 97 C9
Upper Broadheath Worcs 116 F6
Upper Brockholes W Yorks 196 B5
Upper Broughton Notts 154 D3
Upper Broxwood Hereford 115 G7
Upper Bruntingthorpe Leics 136 F2
Upper Brynamman Carms 76 C2
Upper Buckenhill Hereford 97 E11
Upper Bucklebury W Berks 64 F4
Upper Bullington Hants 48 E3
Upper Burgate Hants 31 D11
Upper Burnhaugh Aberds 293 D10
Upper Bush Medway 69 F7
Upper Caldecote C Beds 104 B3
Upper Cam Glos 80 F3
Upper Canada N Som 43 B11
Upper Canterton Hants 32 E3
Upper Catesby Northants 119 F10
Upper Catshill Worcs 117 C9
Upper Chapel Powys 95 C10
Upper Cheddon Som 28 B2
Upper Chicksgrove Wilts 31 B7
Upper Church Village Rhondda 58 B5
Upper Chute Wilts 47 C9
Upper Clapton London 67 B10
Upper Clatford Hants 47 E11
Upper Coberley Glos 81 B7
Upper College Shrops 149 C11
Upper Colwall Hereford 98 C5
Upper Common Hants 48 D6
Upper Cotburn Aberds 303 D7
Upper Cotton Staffs 169 F9
Upper Coullie Aberds 293 B9
Upper Cound Shrops 131 C11
Upper Croxley Som 44 E4
Upper Cudworth S Yorks 197 F11
Upper Culphin Aberds 302 D6
Upper Cumberworth W Yorks 197 F8
Upper Cwm-twrch Powys 76 C3
Upper Cwmbran Torf 78 F3
Upper Dallachy Moray 302 C3
Upper Deal Kent 55 C11
Upper Dean Beds 121 D10
Upper Dean Devon 8 C4
Upper Denby W Yorks 197 D8
Upper Denby W Yorks 197 F8
Upper Denton Cumb 240 D4
Upper Derraid Highld 301 F10
Upper Diabaig Highld 299 C8
Upper Dicker E Sus 23 D9
Upper Dinchope Shrops 131 G9
Upper Dormington Hereford 97 D11
Upper Dounreay Highld 310 C4
Upper Dovercourt Essex 108 E4
Upper Dowdeswell Glos 81 B8
Upper Druimfin Argyll 289 D7
Upper Dunsforth N Yorks 215 G8
Upper Dunsley Herts 84 C6
Upper Eashing Sur 50 E3
Upper Eastern Green W Mid 134 G5
Upper Eathie Highld 301 C7
Upper Edmonton London 86 G4
Upper Egleton Hereford 98 C2
Upper Elkstone Staffs 169 D9
Upper Ellastone Staffs 169 G10
Upper Elmers End London 67 F11
Upper End Derbys 185 F9
Upper End Glos 81 C10
Upper End Glos 81 D8
Upper End Leics 154 G4
Upper Enham Hants 47 D11
Upper Farmcote Shrops 132 E5
Upper Farringdon Hants 49 F8
Upper Feorlig Highld 298 E2
Upper Fivehead Som 28 C4
Upper Forge Shrops 132 F4
Upper Framilode Glos 80 C3
Upper Froyle Hants 49 E9
Upper Gambolds Worcs 117 D9
Upper Gills Highld 310 B7
Upper Glenfintaig Highld 290 E4
Upper Godney Som 44 E3
Upper Goldstone Kent 71 G9
Upper Gornal W Mid 133 E8
Upper Gravenhurst C Beds 104 D2
Upper Green Essex 105 E8
Upper Green Mon 78 B5
Upper Green Suff 124 E4
Upper Green W Berks 63 G11
Upper Green W Yorks 197 B9
Upper Grove Common Hereford 97 F11
Upper Guist Norf 159 D10
Upper Hackney Derbys 170 C3
Upper Hale Sur 49 D10
Upper Halistra Highld 298 D2
Upper Halliford Sur 66 F5
Upper Halling Medway 69 G7
Upper Ham Worcs 99 D7
Upper Hambleton Rutland 137 B8
Upper Hamnish Hereford 115 F10
Upper Harbledown Kent 54 B6
Upper Hardres Court Kent 55 C7
Upper Hardwick Hereford 115 F8
Upper Hartfield E Sus 52 G3
Upper Hartshay Derbys 170 E5
Upper Haselor Worcs 99 C10
Upper Hatton Staffs 150 B6
Upper Haugh S Yorks 186 B6
Upper Hawkhillock Aberds 303 F10
Upper Hayesden Kent 52 E5
Upper Hayton Shrops 131 G10
Upper Heath Shrops 131 F11
Upper Heaton W Yorks 197 D7
Upper Hellesdon Norf 160 G4
Upper Helmsley N Yorks 207 B9
Upper Hengoed Shrops 148 C5
Upper Hergest Hereford 114 G5
Upper Heyford Northants 120 F3
Upper Heyford Oxon 101 F9
Upper Hill Glos 79 F11
Upper Hill Hereford 115 G9
Upper Hindhope Borders 251 B7
Upper Holloway London 67 B9
Upper Holton Suff 127 B8
Upper Hopton W Yorks 197 D7
Upper Horsebridge E Sus 23 C9
Upper Howsell Worcs 98 B5
Upper Hoyland S Yorks 197 G11
Upper Hulme Staffs 169 C8
Upper Hyde I o W 21 E7
Upper Ifold Sur 50 G4
Upper Inglesham Swindon 82 F2
Upper Inverbrough Highld 301 F8
Upper Kergord Shetland 313 H6
Upper Kidston Borders 270 G4
Upper Kilcott Glos 61 B9
Upper Killay Swansea 56 C5
Upper Killeyan Argyll 254 C3
Upper Kinsham Hereford 115 D7
Upper Knockando Moray 301 E11
Upper Lambourn W Berks 63 C10
Upper Landywood Staffs 133 B9
Upper Langford N Som 44 B3
Upper Langwith Derbys 171 B8
Upper Layham Suff 107 C10
Upper Leigh Staffs 151 B10
Upper Lenie Highld 300 G5
Upper Littleton N Som 60 G5
Upper Loads Derbys 170 B4
Upper Lochton Aberds 293 D8
Upper Lode Worcs 99 E7
Upper Longdon Staffs 151 G11
Upper Longwood Shrops 132 B2
Upper Ludstone Shrops 132 D6
Upper Lybster Highld 310 F6
Upper Lydbrook Glos 79 B10
Upper Lyde Hereford 97 C9
Upper Lye Hereford 115 D7
Upper Maes-coed Hereford 96 D6
Upper Marsh W Yorks 204 F6
Upper Midhope S Yorks 186 B2
Upper Midway Derbys 152 E5
Upper Milovaig Highld 297 G7
Upper Milton Oxon 82 B3
Upper Milton Som 44 D4
Upper Minety Wilts 81 G8
Upper Mitton Worcs 116 C6
Upper Moor Worcs 99 B9
Upper Moor Side W Yorks 205 G10
Upper Morton S Glos 79 G11
Upper Nash Pembs 73 E8
Upper Netchwood Shrops 132 E2
Upper Newbold Derbys 186 G5
Upper Nobut Staffs 151 B10
Upper North Dean Bucks 84 F4
Upper Norwood London 67 F10
Upper Norwood W Sus 34 D6
Upper Obney Perth 286 D4
Upper Ochrwyth Caerph 59 B8
Upper Oddington Glos 100 F4
Upper Ollach Highld 295 B7
Upper Padley Derbys 186 F2
Upper Pickwick Wilts 61 E11
Upper Pollicott Bucks 84 C2
Upper Poppleton York 207 C7
Upper Port Highld 301 G10
Upper Postern Kent 52 D6
Upper Quinton Warks 100 B3
Upper Race Torf 78 F3
Upper Ratley Hants 32 C4
Upper Ridinghill Aberds 303 D10
Upper Rissington Glos 82 B2
Upper Rochford Worcs 116 D2
Upper Rodmersham Kent 70 G2
Upper Sandaig Highld 295 D9
Upper Sanday Orkney 314 F5
Upper Sapey Hereford 116 E3
Upper Saxondale Notts 154 B3
Upper Seagry Wilts 62 C2
Upper Shelton C Beds 103 C9
Upper Sheringham Norf 177 E10
Upper Shirley London 67 G11
Upper Shirley Soton 32 E6
Upper Siddington Glos 81 F8
Upper Skelmorlie N Ayrs 266 B4
Upper Slackstead Hants 32 B5
Upper Slaughter Glos 100 G3
Upper Solva Pembs 90 G5
Upper Soudley Glos 79 C11
Upper Stanton Drew Bath 60 G6
Upper Staploe Beds 122 F2
Upper Stoke Norf 142 C5
Upper Stoke W Mid 135 G7
Upper Stondon C Beds 104 D2
Upper Stowe Northants 120 F2
Upper Stratton Swindon 63 B7
Upper Street Hants 31 D11
Upper Street Norf 142 G3
Upper Street Norf 160 B5
Upper Street Norf 160 E6
Upper Street Norf 160 F6
Upper Street Norf 161 F7
Upper Street Suff 108 E2
Upper Street Suff 124 G5
Upper Street Suff 126 G2
Upper Strensham Worcs 99 D8
Upper Studley Wilts 45 B10
Upper Sundon C Beds 103 F10
Upper Swainswick Bath 61 F9
Upper Swanmore Hants 33 D9
Upper Swell Glos 100 F3
Upper Sydenham London 67 E10
Upper Tankersley S Yorks 186 B4
Upper Tean Staffs 151 B10
Upper Threapwood W Ches 166 F6
Upper Thurnham Lancs 202 C5
Upper Tillyrie Perth 286 G5
Upper Tooting London 67 E9
Upper Tote Highld 298 D5
Upper Town Derbys 170 D3
Upper Town Derbys 170 E2
Upper Town Durham 233 D7
Upper Town Hereford 97 B11
Upper Town N Som 60 F4
Upper Town Suff 125 D8
Upper Town W Yorks 204 G6
Upper Town Wilts 62 D3
Upper Treverward Shrops 114 B5
Upper Tysoe Warks 100 C6
Upper Up Glos 81 F8
Upper Upham Wilts 63 D8
Upper Upnor Medway 69 E9
Upper Vobster Som 45 D8
Upper Walthamstow London 67 B11
Upper Wardington Oxon 101 B9
Upper Wardley W Sus 34 B4
Upper Weald M Keynes 102 D5
Upper Weedon Northants 120 F2
Upper Welland Worcs 98 C5
Upper Wellingham E Sus 36 E6
Upper Welson Hereford 114 G5
Upper Westholme Som 44 E5
Upper Weston Bath 61 F8
Upper Weybread Suff 126 B4
Upper Whiston S Yorks 187 D7
Upper Wick Glos 80 F2
Upper Wick Worcs 116 G6
Upper Wield Hants 48 F6
Upper Wigginton Shrops 148 B6
Upper Winchendon Bucks 84 C2
Upper Witton W Mid 133 E11
Upper Wolvercote Oxon 83 D7
Upper Wolverton Worcs 117 G8
Upper Woodend Aberds 293 B8
Upper Woodford Wilts 46 F6
Upper Woolhampton W Berks 64 F5
Upper Wootton Hants 48 C5
Upper Wraxall Wilts 61 E10
Upper Wyche Hereford 98 C5
Upperby Cumb 239 G10
Upperdale Derbys 185 G11
Uppermill Gtr Man 196 F3
Uppersound Shetland 313 J6
Upperthong W Yorks 196 F6
Upperthorpe Derbys 187 E7
Upperthorpe N Lincs 199 G9
Upperton E Sus 23 E10
Upperton Oxon 83 G11
Upperton W Sus 35 C7
Uppertown Derbys 170 C4
Uppertown Highld 300 F4
Uppertown Highld 310 B7
Uppertown Northumb 241 C9
Uppertown Orkney 314 G4
Upperwood Derbys 170 D3
Uppincott Devon 26 G5
Uppingham Rutland 137 D7
Uppington Dorset 31 F8
Uppington Shrops 132 B2
Upsall N Yorks 215 B9
Upsher Green Suff 107 C8
Upshire Essex 86 E6
Upstreet Kent 71 G8
Upthorpe Glos 80 E3
Upthorpe Suff 125 C9
Upton Bucks 84 C3
Upton Cambs 122 B3
Upton Corn 11 G11
Upton Corn 24 G2
Upton Cumb 230 D2
Upton Devon 8 G4
Upton Devon 27 G9
Upton Dorset 17 E10
Upton Dorset 18 C5
Upton E Yorks 209 C8
Upton Hants 32 D5
Upton Hants 47 B11
Upton I o W 21 C7
Upton Kent 71 F11
Upton Leics 135 D7
Upton Lincs 188 D5
Upton London 68 C2
Upton Mers 182 D3
Upton Mers 183 D7
Upton Norf 161 G7
Upton Northants 120 E4
Upton Notts 172 E2
Upton Notts 188 F2
Upton Oxon 64 B4
Upton Oxon 82 C2
Upton P'boro 138 C2
Upton Slough 66 D3
Upton Som 27 B7
Upton Som 29 B7
Upton W Ches 166 B6
Upton W Yorks 198 E3
Upton Warks 118 F2
Upton Wilts 45 G11
Upton Bishop Hereford 98 F2
Upton Cheyney S Glos 61 F7
Upton Cressett Shrops 132 E3
Upton Crews Hereford 98 F2
Upton Cross Corn 11 G11
Upton End C Beds 104 E2
Upton Field Notts 172 E2
Upton Green Norf 161 G7
Upton Grey Hants 49 D7
Upton Heath W Ches 166 B6
Upton Hellions Devon 26 G4
Upton Lea Bucks 66 C3
Upton Lovell Wilts 46 E2
Upton Magna Shrops 149 G11
Upton Noble Som 45 F8
Upton Park London 68 C2
Upton Pyne Devon 14 B4
Upton Rocks Halton 183 D8
Upton St Leonards Glos 80 C5
Upton Scudamore Wilts 45 D11
Upton Snodsbury Worcs 117 G8
Upton upon Severn Worcs 99 C7
Upton Warren Worcs 117 D8
Upwaltham W Sus 34 E6
Upware Cambs 123 C10
Upwell Norf 139 C9
Upwey Dorset 17 E9
Upwick Green Herts 105 G9
Upwood Cambs 138 G5
Uradale Shetland 313 K6
Urafirth Shetland 312 F5
Uragaig Argyll 274 D4
Urchfont Wilts 46 B4
Urdimarsh Hereford 97 B10
Ure Shetland 312 F4
Ure Bank N Yorks 214 E6
Urgashay Som 29 C9
Urgha W Isles 305 J3
Urgha Beag W Isles 305 H3
Urishay Common Hereford 96 D6
Urlar Perth 286 C2
Urlay Nook Stockton 225 C7
Urmston Gtr Man 184 C3
Urpeth Durham 242 G6
Urquhart Highld 300 D5
Urquhart Moray 302 C2
Urra N Yorks 225 E11
Urray Highld 300 D5
Ushaw Moor Durham 233 C10
Usk Mon 78 E5
Usselby Lincs 189 C9
Usworth T & W 243 F8
Utkinton W Ches 167 B8
Utley W Yorks 204 E6
Uton Devon 14 B2
Utterby Lincs 190 C4
Uttoxeter Staffs 151 C11
Uwchmynydd Gwyn 144 D3
Uxbridge London 66 C5
Uxbridge Moor London 66 C5
Uyea Shetland 312 D5
Uyeasound Shetland 312 C7
Uzmaston Pembs 73 C7

V

Vachelich Pembs 90 F5
Vadlure Shetland 313 J4
Vagg Som 29 D8
Vaila Hall Shetland 313 J4
Vaivoe Shetland 312 G7
Vale W Yorks 196 B2
Vale Down Devon 12 D6
Vale of Health London 67 B9
Valeswood Shrops 149 E7
Valley = Y Fali Anglesey 178 F3
Valley Park Hants 32 C6
Valley Truckle Corn 11 E7
Valleyfield Dumfries 237 D8
Valsgarth Shetland 312 B8
Valtos Highld 298 C5
Van Caerph 59 B7
Van Powys 129 F9
Vange Essex 69 B8
Vanlop Shetland 313 M5
Varchoel Powys 148 G4
Varfell Corn 2 C2
Varteg Torf 78 D3
Vassa Shetland 313 H6
Vastern Wilts 62 C5
Vatsetter Shetland 312 E7
Vatsetter Shetland 313 L5
Vatten Highld 298 E2
Vaul Argyll 288 E2
Vauxhall London 67 D10
Vauxhall Mers 182 C4
Vauxhall W Mid 133 F11
Vaynol Hall Gwyn 163 B8
Vaynor M Tydf 77 C8
Veensgarth Shetland 313 J6
Velator Devon 40 F3
Veldo Hereford 97 C11
Velindre Powys 96 D3
Vellanoweth Corn 2 C2
Vellow Som 42 F5
Velly Devon 24 C3
Veness Orkney 314 D5
Venn Devon 8 F4
Venn Green Devon 24 E5
Venn Ottery Devon 15 C7
Venngreen Devon 24 E5
Vennington Shrops 130 B6
Venn's Green Hereford 97 B10
Venny Tedburn Devon 14 B2
Venterdon Corn 12 G3
Vention Devon 40 E3
Ventnor I o W 21 F7
Venton Devon 7 D11
Ventongimps Corn 4 E5
Ventonleague Corn 2 B3
Venus Hill Herts 85 E8
Veraby Devon 26 B3
Vermentry Shetland 313 H5
Vernham Bank Hants 47 B10
Vernham Dean Hants 47 B10
Vernham Row Hants 47 B10
Vernham Street Hants 47 B11
Vernolds Common Shrops 131 G9
Verwood Dorset 31 F9
Veryan Corn 3 B10
Veryan Green Corn 5 G8
Vicarage Devon 15 D10
Vicarscross W Ches 166 B6
Vickerstown Cumb 210 F3
Victoria Corn 5 C9
Victoria S Yorks 197 F7
Victoria Dock Village Hull 200 B6
Victoria Park Bucks 84 C4
Victory Gardens Renfs 267 B10
Vidlin Shetland 312 G6
Viewpark N Lnrk 268 C4
Vigo W Mid 133 C10
Vigo Village Kent 68 G6
Vinegar Hill Mon 60 B2
Vinehall Street E Sus 38 C3
Vines Cross E Sus 23 B9
Viney Hill Glos 79 D11
Vinney Green S Glos 61 D7
Virginia Water Sur 66 F3
Virginstow Devon 12 C3
Viscar Corn 2 C6
Vobster Som 45 D8
Voe Shetland 312 E5
Voe Shetland 313 G6
Vogue Corn 4 G4
Vole Som 43 D11
Vowchurch Hereford 97 D7
Vowchurch Common Hereford 97 D7
Voxmoor Som 27 D10
Voxter Shetland 312 F5
Voy Orkney 314 E2
Vron Gate Shrops 130 B6
Vulcan Village Mers 183 C9

W

Waberthwaite Cumb 220 G2
Wackerfield Durham 233 G9
Wacton Hereford 116 F2
Wacton Norf 142 E3
Wacton Common Norf 142 F3
Wadbister Shetland 313 J6
Wadborough Worcs 99 B8
Wadbrook Devon 28 G4
Waddesdon Bucks 84 B2
Waddeton Devon 9 D7
Waddicar Mers 182 B5
Waddicombe Devon 26 B5
Waddingham Lincs 189 B7
Waddington Lancs 203 E10
Waddington Lincs 173 C7
Waddingworth Lincs 189 G11
Waddon Devon 14 F3
Waddon London 67 G10
Wade Hall Lancs 194 C4
Wadebridge Corn 10 G5
Wadeford Som 28 E4
Wadenhoe Northants 137 G10
Wades Green E Ches 167 C11
Wadesmill Herts 86 B5
Wadhurst E Sus 52 G6
Wadshelf Derbys 186 G4
Wadsley S Yorks 186 C4
Wadsley Bridge S Yorks 186 C4
Wadswick Wilts 61 F10
Wadwick Hants 48 C2
Wadworth S Yorks 187 B9
Waen Denb 165 B10
Waen Denb 165 C7
Waen Flint 181 G11
Waen Powys 129 E9
Waen Aberwheeler Denb 165 B9
Waen-fâch Powys 148 F4
Waen Goleugoed Denb 181 G9
Waen-pentir Gwyn 163 B9
Waen-wen Gwyn 163 B9
Wag Highld 311 G4
Wagbeach Shrops 131 C7
Wagg Som 28 B6
Waggersley Staffs 151 B7
Waggs Plot Devon 28 G4
Wain Lee Staffs 168 D5
Wainfelin Torf 78 E3
Wainfleet All Saints Lincs 175 D7
Wainfleet Bank Lincs 175 D7
Wainfleet St Mary Lincs 175 D8
Wainfleet Tofts Lincs 175 D7
Wainford Norf 142 E6
Waingroves Derbys 170 F6
Wainhouse Corner Corn 11 B9
Wainscott Medway 69 E8
Wainstalls W Yorks 196 B4
Waitby Cumb 222 D5
Waithe Lincs 201 G9
Wake Green W Mid 133 G11
Wake Hill N Yorks 214 E3
Wake Lady Green N Yorks 226 F3
Wakefield W Yorks 197 C10
Wakeley Herts 104 F6
Wakerley Northants 137 D9
Wakes Colne Essex 107 F7
Wakes Colne Green Essex 107 E7
Walberswick Suff 127 C9
Walberton W Sus 35 F7
Walbottle T & W 242 D5
Walby Cumb 239 E10
Walcombe Som 44 D5
Walcot Bath 61 F9
Walcot Lincs 155 B11
Walcot N Lincs 199 C11
Walcot Oxon 82 B4
Walcot Shrops 130 F6
Walcot Swindon 63 C7
Walcot Telford 149 G11
Walcot Worcs 99 B8
Walcot Green Norf 142 G2
Walcote Leics 135 G11
Walcote Warks 118 F2
Walcott Lincs 173 D10
Walcott Norf 161 C7
Walden N Yorks 213 C10
Walden Head N Yorks 213 C9
Walden Stubbs N Yorks 198 D5
Waldersey Cambs 139 C8
Waldershaigh S Yorks 186 B3
Walderslade Medway 69 G9
Walderton W Sus 34 E3
Walditch Dorset 16 C5
Waldley Derbys 152 B2
Waldridge Durham 243 G7
Waldringfield Suff 108 C5
Waldringfield Heath Suff 108 B5
Waldron E Sus 23 B8
Waldron Down E Sus 37 C8
Wales S Yorks 187 E7
Wales Som 29 C9
Wales Bar S Yorks 187 E7
Wales End Suff 106 B5
Walesby Lincs 189 C10
Walesby Notts 187 G11
Walesby Grange Lincs 189 C10
Waleswood S Yorks 187 E7
Walford Hereford 97 G11
Walford Hereford 115 C7
Walford Shrops 149 E8
Walford Som 28 B3
Walford Staffs 150 C6
Walford Heath Shrops 149 F8
Walgherton E Ches 167 F11
Walgrave Northants 120 C6
Walham Glos 98 G6
Walham Green London 67 D9
Walhampton Hants 20 B2
Walk Mill Lancs 204 G3
Walkden Gtr Man 195 G8
Walker T & W 243 E7
Walker Barn E Ches 185 G7
Walker Fold Lancs 203 E9
Walkerburn Borders 261 B9
Walkeringham Notts 188 C3
Walkerith Lincs 188 C3
Walkern Herts 104 F5
Walker's Green Hereford 97 B10
Walker's Heath W Mid 117 B11
Walkerville N Yorks 224 F4
Walkford Dorset 19 C10
Walkhampton Devon 7 B10
Walkington E Yorks 208 F5
Walkley S Yorks 186 D4
Walkmill Shrops 131 E7
Walkmills Shrops 131 D9
Wall Corn 2 B4
Wall Northumb 241 D10
Wall Staffs 134 B2
Wall Bank Shrops 131 E10
Wall End Cumb 210 C4
Wall End Kent 71 G8
Wall Heath W Mid 133 F7
Wall Hill Gtr Man 196 F3
Wall Mead Bath 45 B7
Wall Nook Durham 233 B10
Wall under Heywood Shrops 131 E10
Wallacestone Falk 279 F8
Wallaceton Dumfries 247 F8
Wallacetown S Ayrs 245 C7
Wallacetown S Ayrs 257 E8
Wallacetown Shetland 313 H5
Wallands Park E Sus 36 E6
Wallasey Mers 182 C4
Wallbank Lancs 195 D11
Wallbrook W Mid 133 E8
Wallcrouch E Sus 53 G7
Wallend London 68 C2
Waller's Green Hereford 98 D3
Walley's Green E Ches 167 C11
Wallingford Oxon 64 B6
Wallington Hants 33 F9
Wallington Herts 104 E5
Wallington London 67 G9
Wallington Heath W Mid 133 C9
Wallingwells Notts 187 E9
Wallis Pembs 91 F10
Wallisdown Poole 19 C7
Walliswood Sur 50 F6
Wallow Green Glos 80 F4
Wallridge Northumb 242 B3
Walls Shetland 313 J4
Wallsend T & W 243 D7
Wallston V Glam 58 E6
Wallsuches Gtr Man 195 E7
Wallsworth Glos 98 G6
Wallyford E Loth 281 G7
Walmer Kent 55 C11
Walmer Bridge Lancs 194 C3
Walmersley Gtr Man 195 E10
Walmgate Stray York 207 C8
Walmley W Mid 134 E2
Walmsgate Lincs 190 F5
Walnut Grove Perth 286 E5
Walnut Tree M Keynes 103 D7
Walnuttree Green Herts 105 G9
Walpole Som 43 E10
Walpole Suff 127 C7
Walpole Cross Keys Norf 157 F10
Walpole Highway Norf 157 G10
Walpole Marsh Norf 157 F9
Walpole St Andrew Norf 157 F10
Walpole St Peter Norf 157 F9
Walrow Som 43 D10
Walsal End W Mid 118 B4
Walsall W Mid 133 D10
Walsall Wood W Mid 133 C10
Walsden W Yorks 196 C2
Walsgrave on Sowe W Mid 135 G7
Walsham le Willows Suff 125 C9
Walshaw Gtr Man 195 E9
Walshford N Yorks 206 C4
Walsoken Cambs 157 G9
Walson Mon 97 G8
Walston S Lnrk 269 F11
Walsworth Herts 104 E4
Walters Ash Bucks 84 F4
Walter's Green Kent 52 E4
Walterston V Glam 58 E5
Walterstone Hereford 96 F6
Waltham Kent 54 D6
Waltham NE Lincs 201 G9
Waltham Abbey Essex 86 E5
Waltham Chase Hants 33 D9
Waltham Cross Herts 86 E5
Waltham on the Wolds Leics 154 D6
Waltham St Lawrence Windsor 65 D10
Waltham's Cross Essex 106 E3
Walthamstow London 67 B11
Walton Bucks 84 C4
Walton Cumb 240 E2
Walton Derbys 170 B5
Walton Leics 135 F11
Walton M Keynes 103 D7
Walton Mers 182 C5
Walton P'boro 138 C3
Walton Powys 114 F5
Walton Shrops 115 B9
Walton Som 44 F3
Walton Staffs 151 C7
Walton Staffs 151 D7
Walton Suff 108 D5
Walton Telford 149 F11
Walton W Yorks 197 D11
Walton W Yorks 206 D4
Walton Warks 118 G5
Walton Cardiff Glos 99 E8
Walton Court Bucks 84 C4
Walton East Pembs 91 G10
Walton Elm Dorset 30 D3
Walton Grounds Northants 101 E10
Walton Heath Hants 33 F10
Walton Highway Norf 157 G9
Walton in Gordano N Som 60 E2
Walton-le-Dale Lancs 194 B5
Walton Manor Oxon 83 D8
Walton-on-Thames Sur 66 F6
Walton on the Hill Staffs 151 E9
Walton on the Hill Sur 51 B8
Walton-on-the-Naze Essex 108 G5
Walton on the Wolds Leics 153 F11
Walton-on-Trent Derbys 152 F4
Walton Pool Worcs 117 B8
Walton St Mary N Som 60 E2
Walton Summit Lancs 194 B5
Walton Warren Norf 158 F4
Walton West Pembs 72 C5
Walwen Flint 181 F10
Walwen Flint 181 G11
Walwen Flint 182 F2
Walwick Northumb 241 C10
Walworth Darl 224 B4
Walworth London 67 D10
Walworth Gate Darl 233 G10
Walwyn's Castle Pembs 72 C5
Wambrook Som 28 F3
Wampool Cumb 238 G6
Wanborough Sur 50 D2
Wanborough Swindon 63 C8
Wandel Dyke S Lnrk 259 D11
Wandle Park London 67 F10
Wandon End Herts 104 G2
Wandsworth London 67 E9
Wangford Suff 127 B9
Wanlip Leics 154 G2
Wanlockhead Dumfries 259 G9
Wannock E Sus 23 E9
Wansford E Yorks 209 B7
Wansford P'boro 137 D11
Wanshurst Green Kent 53 D9
Wanson Corn 24 G1
Wanstead London 68 B2
Wanstrow Som 45 E8
Wanswell Glos 79 E11
Wantage Oxon 63 B11
Wants Green Worcs 116 F5
Wapley S Glos 61 D8
Wappenbury Warks 119 D7
Wappenham Northants 102 B2
Wapping London 67 C10
Warbleton E Sus 23 B10
Warblington Hants 22 B2
Warborough Oxon 83 G9
Warboys Cambs 138 G6
Warbreck Blkpool 202 F2
Warbstow Corn 11 C10
Warbstow Cross Corn 11 C10
Warburton Gtr Man 184 D2
Warburton Green Gtr Man 184 E3
Warcop Cumb 222 B4
Ward End W Mid 134 F2
Ward Green S Yorks 197 G10
Ward Green Suff 125 E10
Ward Green Cross Lancs 203 F8
Warden Kent 70 E4
Warden Northumb 241 D10
Warden Powys 114 E6
Warden Hill Glos 99 G8
Warden Point I o W 20 D2
Warden Street C Beds 104 C2
Wardhedges C Beds 103 D11
Wardhill Orkney 314 D6
Wardington Oxon 101 B9
Wardlaw Borders 261 F7
Wardle E Ches 167 D10

Wardle Gtr Man 196 D2
Wardle Bank E Ches 167 D10
Wardley Gtr Man 195 G9
Wardley Rutland 136 C6
Wardley T & W 243 E7
Wardley W Sus 34 B4
Wardlow Derbys 185 G11
Wardour Wilts 30 B6
Wardpark N Lnrk 278 F5
Wardrobes Bucks 84 E4
Wardsend E Ches 184 E6
Wardy Hill Cambs 139 G9
Ware Herts 86 C5
Ware Kent 71 G9
Ware Street Kent 53 B9
Wareham Dorset 18 D4
Warehorne Kent 54 G3
Waren Mill Northumb 264 C4
Warenford Northumb 264 D4
Warenton Northumb 264 C4
Wareside Herts 86 B5
Waresley Cambs 122 G4
Waresley Worcs 116 C6
Warfield Brack 65 E11
Warfleet Devon 9 E7
Wargate Lincs 156 C4
Wargrave Mers 183 C9
Wargrave Wokingham 65 D9
Warham Hereford 97 D9
Warham Norf 176 E6
Warhill Gtr Man 185 B7
Waring's Green W Mid 118 C2
Wark Northumb 241 B9
Wark Northumb 263 B8
Wark Common Northumb 263 B8
Warkleigh Devon 25 C10
Warkton Northants 121 B7
Warkworth Northants 101 C9
Warkworth Northumb 252 B6
Warlaby N Yorks 224 G6
Warland W Yorks 196 C2
Warleggan Corn 6 B3
Warleigh Bath 61 G9
Warley Essex 87 G9
Warley Town W Yorks 196 B5
Warley Woods W Mid 133 F10
Warlingham Sur 51 B11
Warmbrook Derbys 170 E3
Warmfield W Yorks 197 C11
Warmingham E Ches 168 C2
Warminghurst W Sus 35 D10
Warmington Northants 137 E11
Warmington Warks 101 B8
Warminster Wilts 45 D11
Warminster Common Wilts 45 E11
Warmlake Kent 53 C10
Warmley S Glos 61 E7
Warmley Hill S Glos 61 E7
Warmley Tower S Glos 61 E7
Warmonds Hill Northants 121 D9
Warmsworth S Yorks 198 G4
Warmwell Dorset 17 D11
Warnborough Green Hants 49 C8
Warndon Worcs 117 F7
Warners End Herts 85 D8
Warnford Hants 33 C10
Warnham W Sus 51 G7
Warningcamp W Sus 35 F8
Warninglid W Sus 36 B2
Warpsgrove Oxon 83 F10
Warren Dorset 18 C3
Warren E Ches 184 G5
Warren Pembs 72 F6
Warren S Yorks 186 B5
Warren Corner Hants 34 B2
Warren Corner Hants 49 D10
Warren Heath Suff 108 C4
Warren Row Windsor 65 C10
Warren Street Kent 54 C2
Warrenby Redcar 235 F7
Warren's Green Herts 104 F5
Warrington M Keynes 121 G7
Warrington Warr 183 D10
Warriston Edin 280 F5
Warsash Hants 33 F7
Warsill N Yorks 214 F4
Warslow Staffs 169 D9
Warsop Vale Notts 171 B8
Warstock W Mid 117 B11
Warstone Staffs 133 B9
Warter E Yorks 208 C3
Warthermarske N Yorks 214 D4
Warthill N Yorks 207 B9
Wartle Aberds 293 C7
Wartling E Sus 23 D11
Wartnaby Leics 154 E4
Warton Lancs 194 B2
Warton Lancs 211 E9
Warton Northumb 252 C2
Warton Warks 134 C5
Warton Bank Lancs 194 B2
Warwick Warks 118 E5
Warwick Bridge Cumb 239 F11
Warwick on Eden Cumb 239 F11
Warwick Wold Sur 51 C10
Warwicksland Cumb 239 B10
Wasbister Orkney 314 C3
Wasdale Head Cumb 220 D3
Wash Derbys 185 E9
Wash Common W Berks 64 G3
Wash Dyke Norf 157 F10
Wash Water W Berks 64 G3
Washall Green Herts 105 E8
Washaway Corn 5 B10
Washbourne Devon 8 E5
Washbrook Som 44 C2
Washbrook Suff 108 C2
Washbrook Street Suff 108 C2
Washerwall Staffs 168 F6
Washfield Devon 26 D6
Washfold N Yorks 223 E11
Washford Som 42 E5
Washford Worcs 117 D11
Washford Pyne Devon 26 E4
Washingborough Lincs 189 G8
Washingley Cambs 138 F2
Washington T & W 243 F8
Washington W Sus 35 E10
Washington Village T & W 243 F8
Washmere Green Suff 107 B8
Washpit W Yorks 196 F6
Washwood Heath W Mid 134 F2
Wasing W Berks 64 G5
Waskerley Durham 233 B7
Wasp Green Sur 51 D10
Wasperton Warks 118 F5
Wasps Nest Lincs 173 C9
Wass N Yorks 215 D11
Waste Green Warks 118 D4
Wastor Devon 8 F2
Watch House Green Essex 106 G3
Watchet Som 42 E5
Watchfield Oxon 63 B8
Watchfield Som 43 D10
Watchgate Cumb 221 F10
Watchhill Cumb 229 C9
Watchill Dumfries 238 D6
Watchill Dumfries 248 G3
Watcombe Torbay 9 B8
Watendlath Cumb 220 B5
Water Devon 13 E11
Water Lancs 195 B10
Water Eaton M Keynes 103 E7
Water Eaton Oxon 83 C8
Water End Beds 104 B2
Water End C Beds 103 D11
Water End C Beds 104 B5
Water End E Yorks 207 F11
Water End Essex 105 C11
Water End Hants 49 C7
Water End Herts 85 C8
Water End Herts 86 E2
Water Fryston W Yorks 198 B3
Water Garth Nook Cumb 210 F3
Water Houses N Yorks 213 F7
Water Newton Cambs 138 D2
Water Orton Warks 134 E3
Water Stratford Bucks 102 E3
Water Yeat Cumb 210 B5
Waterbeach Cambs 123 D9
Waterbeach W Sus 22 B5
Waterbeck Dumfries 238 B6
Waterdale Herts 85 E10
Waterden Norf 159 B7
Waterditch Hants 19 B9
Waterend Bucks 84 F3
Waterend Cumb 229 G8
Waterend Glos 80 C3
Waterend Herts 86 C2
Waterfall Staffs 169 E9
Waterfoot Argyll 255 D9
Waterfoot Cumb 230 G5
Waterfoot E Renf 267 D11
Waterfoot Lancs 195 C10
Waterford Hants 20 B2
Waterford Herts 86 C4
Watergate Corn 6 E4
Watergate Corn 11 E8
Watergore Som 28 D6
Waterhales Essex 87 F8
Waterham Kent 70 G5
Waterhay Wilts 81 G9
Waterhead Angus 292 F6
Waterhead Cumb 221 E7
Waterhead Devon 8 F3
Waterhead Dumfries 248 E5
Waterhead on Minnoch S Ayrs 245 E9
Waterheads Borders 270 E4
Waterheath Norf 143 E8
Waterhouses Durham 233 C9
Waterhouses Staffs 169 E9
Wateringbury Kent 53 C7
Waterlane Glos 80 E6
Waterlip Som 45 E7
Waterloo Blkburn 195 B7
Waterloo Corn 11 G8
Waterloo Derbys 170 C6
Waterloo Gtr Man 196 G2
Waterloo Highld 295 C8
Waterloo Mers 182 B4
Waterloo N Lnrk 268 E6
Waterloo Norf 126 B2
Waterloo Norf 143 E8
Waterloo Norf 160 F4
Waterloo Pembs 73 E7
Waterloo Perth 286 D4
Waterloo Poole 18 C6
Waterloo Shrops 149 C9
Waterloo Park Mers 182 B4
Waterloo Port Gwyn 163 C7
Waterlooville Hants 33 F11
Waterman Quarter Kent 53 E10
Watermead Glos 80 B5
Watermeetings S Lnrk 259 G11
Watermill E Sus 38 E2
Watermillock Cumb 230 G4
Watermoor Glos 81 E8
Waterperry Oxon 83 D10
Waterrow Som 27 B9
Water's Nook Gtr Man 195 F7
Waters Upton Telford 150 F2
Watersfield W Sus 35 D8
Watersheddings Gtr Man 196 F2
Waterside Aberds 292 B5
Waterside Aberds 303 G10
Waterside Blkburn 195 C8
Waterside Bucks 85 E7
Waterside Cumb 229 B10
Waterside Derbys 185 E8
Waterside E Ayrs 245 B10
Waterside E Ayrs 267 G9
Waterside E Dunb 278 G3
Waterside E Renf 267 D10
Waterside S Yorks 199 E7
Waterside Sur 51 D11
Waterside Telford 150 F2
Waterslack Lancs 211 D9
Waterstein Highld 297 G7
Waterstock Oxon 83 D10
Waterston Pembs 72 D6
Waterthorpe S Yorks 186 E6
Waterton Aberds 303 E9
Waterton Bridgend 58 D2
Watford Herts 85 F10
Watford Northants 120 D2
Watford Gap Staffs 134 C2
Watford Heath Herts 85 G10
Watford Park Caerph 58 B6
Wath Cumb 222 D3
Wath N Yorks 214 D6
Wath N Yorks 214 F2
Wath N Yorks 216 D3
Wath Brow Cumb 219 C10
Wath upon Dearne S Yorks 198 G2
Watherston Borders 271 F8
Watledge Glos 80 E4
Watley's End S Glos 61 C7
Watlington Norf 158 G2
Watlington Oxon 83 G11
Watnall Notts 171 F8
Watsness Shetland 313 H3
Watten Highld 310 D6
Wattisfield Suff 125 C10
Wattisham Suff 125 G10
Wattisham Stone Suff 125 G10
Wattlefield Norf 142 D2
Wattlesborough Heath Shrops 149 G7
Watton E Yorks 208 C6
Watton Norf 141 C8
Watton at Stone Herts 86 B4
Watton Green Norf 141 C8
Watton's Green Essex 87 F8
Wattston N Lnrk 268 B5
Wattstown Rhondda 77 G8
Wattsville Caerph 78 G2
Wauchan Highld 295 G11
Waulkmill Lodge Orkney 314 F3
Waun Gwyn 163 C9
Waun Powys 148 F4
Waun Beddau Pembs 90 F5
Waun Fawr Ceredig 128 G2
Waun-Lwyd Bl Gwent 77 D11
Waun-y-clyn Carms 75 E7
Waun y Gilfach Bridgend 57 D10
Waunarlwydd Swansea 56 B6
Wauncluda Carms 94 E3
Waunfawr Gwyn 163 D8
Waungilwen Carms 92 D6
Waungron Swansea 75 E9
Waunlwyd Bl Gwent 77 D11
Wavendon M Keynes 103 D8
Wavendon Gate M Keynes 103 D8
Waverbridge Cumb 229 B10
Waverton Cumb 229 B10
Waverton W Ches 167 C7
Wavertree Mers 182 D5
Wawcott W Berks 63 F11
Wawne E Yorks 209 F7
Waxham Norf 161 D8
Waxholme E Yorks 201 B10
Way Kent 71 F10
Way Village Devon 26 E5
Way Wick N Som 59 G11
Waye Devon 13 G11
Wayend Street Hereford 98 D4
Wayfield Medway 69 F9
Wayford Som 28 F6
Waymills Shrops 167 G9
Wayne Green Mon 78 B6
Way's Green W Ches 167 B10
Waytown Devon 24 C5
Waytown Devon 40 G5
Wdig = Goodwick Pembs 91 D8
Weachyburn Aberds 302 D6
Weacombe Som 42 E6
Weald Oxon 82 E4
Wealdstone London 67 B7
Wearde Corn 7 D8
Weardley W Yorks 205 E11
Weare Som 44 C2
Weare Giffard Devon 25 C7
Wearhead Durham 232 D3
Wearne Som 28 B6
Weasdale Cumb 222 E3
Weasenham All Saints Norf 158 E6
Weasenham St Peter Norf 159 E7
Weaste Gtr Man 184 B4
Weatherhill Sur 51 E10
Weatheroak Hill Worcs 117 C11
Weaverham W Ches 183 G10
Weavering Street Kent 53 B9
Weaverslake Staffs 152 F2
Weaverthorpe N Yorks 217 E9
Webbington Som 43 B11
Webheath Worcs 117 D10
Webscott Shrops 149 E9
Wecock Hants 33 E11
Wedderlairs Aberds 303 F8
Wedderlie Borders 272 E2
Weddington Kent 55 B9
Weddington Warks 135 E7
Wedhampton Wilts 46 B5
Wedmore Som 44 D2
Wednesbury W Mid 133 D9
Wednesbury Oak W Mid 133 E9
Wednesfield W Mid 133 C8
Weecar Notts 172 B4
Weedon Bucks 84 B4
Weedon Bec Northants 120 F2
Weedon Lois Northants 102 B2
Weeford Staffs 134 C2
Week Devon 8 C5
Week Devon 12 E5
Week Devon 25 B9
Week Devon 26 D2
Week Green Corn 11 B10
Week St Mary Corn 11 B10
Weeke Devon 26 F3
Weeke Hants 48 G3
Weekley Northants 137 G7
Weekmoor Som 27 B10
Weeks I o W 21 C7
Weel E Yorks 209 F7
Weeley Essex 108 G2
Weeley Heath Essex 108 G3
Weelsby NE Lincs 201 F9
Weem Perth 286 C2
Weeping Cross Staffs 151 E8
Weethley Warks 117 F11
Weethley Bank Warks 117 G11
Weethley Gate Warks 117 G11
Weeting Norf 140 F5
Weeton E Yorks 201 C11
Weeton Lancs 202 G3
Weeton N Yorks 205 D11
Weetwood W Yorks 205 F11
Weetwood Common W Ches 167 B8
Weetwood Hall Northumb 264 D2
Weir Essex 69 B10
Weir Lancs 195 B11
Weir Quay Devon 7 C8
Weirbrook Shrops 148 E6
Welborne Norf 159 G11
Welborne Common Norf 141 B11
Welbourn Lincs 173 E7
Welburn N Yorks 216 C3
Welburn N Yorks 216 F4
Welbury N Yorks 225 E7
Welby Lincs 155 B9
Welches Dam Cambs 139 F9
Welcombe Devon 24 D2
Weld Bank Lancs 194 D5
Weldon Northants 137 F8
Weldon Northumb 252 D4
Welford Northants 136 G2
Welford W Berks 64 E2
Welford-on-Avon Warks 118 G3
Welham Leics 136 E5
Welham Notts 188 E2
Welham Som 45 G7
Welham Green Herts 86 D2
Welhambridge E Yorks 207 G11
Well Hants 49 D9
Well Lincs 190 G6
Well N Yorks 214 C5
Well Bottom Dorset 30 D6
Well End Bucks 65 B11
Well End Herts 86 F2
Well Green Gtr Man 184 D3
Well Heads W Yorks 205 G7
Well Hill Kent 68 G3
Well Place Oxon 65 B7
Well Street Kent 53 B7
Well Town Devon 26 F6
Welland Worcs 98 C5
Welland Stone Worcs 98 D6
Wellbank Angus 287 D8
Wellbrook E Sus 37 B9
Wellbrook Bridge Suffs 238 D5
Weller's Town Kent 52 E4
Wellesbourne Warks 118 F5
Wellheads Aberds 302 F4
Wellhouse W Berks 64 E4
Wellhouse W Yorks 196 E5
Welling London 68 D3
Wellingborough Northants 121 D7
Wellingham Norf 159 E7
Wellingore Lincs 173 D7
Wellington Cumb 219 E11
Wellington Hereford 97 B9
Wellington Som 27 C10
Wellington Telford 150 G3
Wellington Heath Hereford 98 C4
Wellington Hill W Yorks 206 F2
Wellisford Som 27 C9
Wellow Bath 45 B8
Wellow I o W 20 D3
Wellow NE Lincs 201 F9
Wellow Notts 171 B11
Wellow Wood Hants 32 C3
Wellpond Green Herts 105 G8
Wellroyd W Yorks 205 F10
Wells Som 44 D5
Wells Green E Ches 167 E11
Wells-Next-The-Sea Norf 176 E6
Wellsborough Leics 135 C7
Wellsprings Som 28 B2
Wellstye Green Essex 87 B10
Wellswood Torbay 9 C8
Welltown Corn 6 B2
Wellwood Fife 279 D11
Welney Norf 139 E10
Welsford Devon 24 C3
Welsh Bicknor Hereford 79 B9
Welsh End Shrops 149 B10
Welsh Frankton Shrops 149 C7
Welsh Harp London 67 B8
Welsh Hook Pembs 91 F8
Welsh Newton Hereford 79 B7
Welsh Newton Common Hereford 79 B8
Welsh St Donats V Glam 58 D4
Welshampton Shrops 149 B8
Welshpool Powys 130 B4
Welshwood Park Essex 107 F10
Welstor Devon 13 G10
Welton Bath 45 C7
Welton Cumb 230 C3
Welton E Ayrs 258 D2
Welton E Yorks 200 B3
Welton Lincs 189 F8
Welton Northants 119 D11
Welton Hill Lincs 189 E8
Welton le Marsh Lincs 175 B7
Welton le Wold Lincs 190 D3
Welwick E Yorks 201 C10
Welwyn Herts 86 B2
Welwyn Garden City Herts 86 C2
Wem Shrops 149 D10
Wembdon Som 43 F9
Wembley London 67 B7
Wembley Park London 67 B7
Wembury Devon 7 F10
Wembworthy Devon 25 F11
Wemyss Bay Invclyd 266 B3
Wenallt Ceredig 112 C3
Wenallt Gwyn 146 F4
Wenallt Gwyn 165 G7
Wendens Ambo Essex 105 D10
Wendlebury Oxon 83 B9
Wendling Norf 159 G8
Wendover Bucks 84 D5
Wendover Dean Bucks 84 E5
Wendron Corn 2 C5
Wendy Cambs 104 B6
Wenfordbridge Corn 11 F7
Wenhaston Suff 127 B8
Wenhaston Black Heath Suff 127 C8
Wennington Cambs 122 B4
Wennington Lancs 212 E2
Wennington London 68 C4
Wensley Derbys 170 C3
Wensley N Yorks 213 B11
Wentbridge W Yorks 198 D3
Wentnor Shrops 131 E7
Wentworth Cambs 123 B9
Wentworth S Yorks 186 B5
Wenvoe V Glam 58 E6
Weobley Hereford 115 G8
Weobley Marsh Hereford 115 G8
Weoley Castle W Mid 133 G10
Wepham W Sus 35 F8
Wepre Flint 166 B3
Wereham Norf 140 C3
Wereham Row Norf 140 C3
Wereton Staffs 168 E3
Wergs W Mid 133 C7
Wern Gwyn 145 B10
Wern Powys 77 B10
Wern Powys 147 G9
Wern Powys 148 E5
Wern Powys 148 G5
Wern Shrops 148 C5
Wern Swansea 56 C4
Wern ddu Shrops 148 D4
Wern-Gifford Mon 96 G6
Wern-olau Swansea 56 B5
Wern Tarw Bridgend 58 C3
Wern-y-cwrt Mon 78 D5
Wern-y-gaer Flint 166 B2
Werneth Gtr Man 196 G2
Werneth Low Gtr Man 185 C7
Wernffrwd Swansea 56 C4
Wernlas Shrops 148 E6
Wernrheolydd Mon 78 C5
Wernyrheolydd Mon 78 C5
Werrington Corn 12 D2
Werrington P'boro 138 C3
Werrington Staffs 168 F6
Wervin W Ches 182 G6
Wescoe Hill N Yorks 205 D11
Wesham Lancs 202 G4
Wessington Derbys 170 D5
West Aberthaw V Glam 58 F4
West Acre Norf 158 F5
West Acton London 67 C7
West Adderbury Oxon 101 D9
West Allerdean Northumb 273 F9
West Allotment T & W 243 C8
West Alvington Devon 8 G4
West Amesbury Wilts 46 E6
West Anstey Devon 26 B5
West Appleton N Yorks 224 G4
West Ardhu Argyll 288 D6
West Ardsley W Yorks 197 B9
West Ardwell Dumfries 236 E2
West Arthurlie E Renf 267 D9
West Ashby Lincs 190 G3
West Ashford Devon 40 F4
West Ashling W Sus 22 B4
West Ashton Wilts 45 B11
West Auckland Durham 233 F9
West Ayton N Yorks 217 C9
West Bagborough Som 43 G7
West Bank Bl Gwent 78 D2
West Bank Halton 183 E8
West Barkwith Lincs 189 E11
West Barnby N Yorks 226 C6
West Barnes London 67 F8
West Barns E Loth 282 F3
West Barsham Norf 159 C8
West Bay Dorset 16 C5
West Beckham Norf 160 B2
West Bedfont Sur 66 E5
West Benhar N Lnrk 269 C7
West Bergholt Essex 107 F9
West Bexington Dorset 16 D6
West Bilney Norf 158 F4
West Blackdene Durham 232 D3
West Blackdown Devon 12 E5
West Blatchington Brighton 36 F3
West Bold Borders 261 B9
West Boldon T & W 243 E9
West Bourton Dorset 30 B3
West Bowling W Yorks 205 G9
West Bradford Lancs 203 E10
West Bradley Som 44 F5
West Bretton W Yorks 197 E9
West Bridgford Notts 153 B11
West Brompton London 67 D9
West Bromwich W Mid 133 E10
West Broughton Derbys 152 C2
West Buckland Devon 41 G7
West Buckland Som 27 C11
West Burnside Aberds 293 F8
West Burrafirth Shetland 313 H4
West Burton N Yorks 213 B10
West Burton W Sus 35 E7
West Butsfield Durham 233 C8
West Butterwick N Lincs 199 F10
West Byfleet Sur 66 G4
West Caister Norf 161 G10
West Calder W Loth 269 C10
West Camel Som 29 C9
West Carlton W Yorks 205 E10
West Carr Hull 209 G7
West Carr N Lincs 199 F8
West Chadsmoor Staffs 151 G9
West Challow Oxon 63 B11
West Charleton Devon 8 G5
West Chelborough Dorset 29 F8
West Chevington Northumb 252 D6
West Chiltington W Sus 35 D9
West Chiltington Common W Sus 35 D9
West Chinnock Som 29 E7
West Chirton T & W 243 D8
West Chisenbury Wilts 46 C6
West Clandon Sur 50 C4
West Cliff Bmouth 19 C7
West Cliff N Yorks 227 C7
West Cliffe Kent 55 E10
West Clyne Highld 311 J2
West Clyth Highld 310 F6
West Coker Som 29 E8
West Common Hants 32 G6
West Compton Dorset 17 C7
West Compton Som 44 E5
West Cornforth Durham 234 E2
West Cowick E Yorks 199 C7
West Cranmore Som 45 E7
West Cross Kent 53 G10
West Cross Swansea 56 D6
West Crudwell Wilts 80 G6
West Clyne Highld 311 J2
West Clyth Highld 310 F6
West Cullery Aberds 293 C9
West Curry Corn 11 C11
West Curthwaite Cumb 230 B2
West Darlochan Argyll 255 E7
West Dean W Sus 34 E5
West Dean Wilts 32 B3
West Deeping Lincs 138 B2
West Denant Pembs 72 C6
West Denton T & W 242 D5
West Derby Mers 182 C5
West Dereham Norf 140 C3
West Didsbury Gtr Man 184 C4
West Down Devon 40 E4
West Down Hants 47 F11
West Downs Corn 5 C10
West Drayton London 66 D5
West Drayton Notts 188 G2
West Dulwich London 67 E10
West Ealing London 67 C7
West Edge Derbys 170 C4
West Ella E Yorks 200 B4
West End Beds 121 E11
West End Beds 121 G9
West End Brack 65 E11
West End Caerph 78 F2
West End Cumb 239 F8
West End Dorset 30 G6
West End E Yorks 201 B9
West End E Yorks 208 G4
West End E Yorks 209 B9
West End E Yorks 209 G9
West End E Yorks 217 G11
West End Glos 80 F5
West End Hants 33 E7
West End Hants 33 F9
West End Hants 48 F6
West End Herts 86 D3
West End Kent 54 B2
West End Kent 71 F7
West End Lancs 195 B8
West End Lancs 211 G8
West End Leics 153 F8
West End Lincs 174 F5
West End Lincs 190 B5
West End Mon 78 F6
West End N Som 60 F3
West End N Yorks 205 B8
West End N Yorks 206 E6
West End N Yorks 207 F7
West End Norf 141 B8
West End Norf 161 G10
West End Oxon 64 B5
West End Oxon 82 E6
West End S Glos 61 B8
West End S Lnrk 269 F9
West End S Yorks 199 F7
West End Som 44 C5
West End Som 45 G7
West End Suff 143 G9
West End Sur 49 E10
West End Sur 66 G2
West End Sur 66 G6
West End W Sus 36 D2
West End W Yorks 197 B7
West End W Yorks 205 F10
West End Wilts 30 C6
West End Wilts 31 C7
West End Wilts 62 D3
West End Windsor 65 D10
West End Worcs 99 D11
West End = Marian-y-mor Gwyn 145 C7
West End Green Hants 65 G7
West-end Town V Glam 58 F3
West Ewell Sur 67 G8
West Farleigh Kent 53 C8
West Farndon Northants 119 G10
West Felton Shrops 148 D6
West Fenton E Loth 281 E9
West Ferry Dundee 287 D8
West Field N Lincs 200 D6
West Field York 207 C7
West Fields W Berks 64 F3
West Firle E Sus 23 D7
West Fleetham Northumb 264 D5
West Flodden Northumb 263 C10
West Garforth W Yorks 206 G3
West Ginge Oxon 64 B2
West Gorton Gtr Man 184 B5
West Grafton Wilts 63 G8
West Green Hants 49 B8
West Green London 67 B10
West Green S Yorks 197 F11
West Green W Sus 51 F9
West Greenskares Aberds 303 C7
West Grimstead Wilts 32 B2
West Grinstead W Sus 35 C11
West Haddlesey N Yorks 198 B5
West Haddon Northants 120 C2
West Hagbourne Oxon 64 B4
West Hagley Worcs 133 G8
West Hall Cumb 240 D3
West Hallam Derbys 170 G6
West Halton N Lincs 200 C2
West Ham Hants 48 C6
West Ham London 68 C2
West Hampstead London 67 B9
West Handley Derbys 186 F5
West Hanney Oxon 82 G6
West Hanningfield Essex 88 F2
West Hardwick W Yorks 198 D2
West Harling Norf 141 G9
West Harlsey N Yorks 225 F8
West Harnham Wilts 31 B10
West Harptree Bath 44 B5
West Harrow London 66 B6
West Harting W Sus 34 C3
West Harton T & W 243 E9
West Hatch Som 28 C3
West Hatch Wilts 30 B6
West Head Norf 139 B11
West Heath E Ches 168 C4
West Heath Hants 48 B5
West Heath Hants 49 B11
West Heath London 68 D3
West Heath W Mid 117 B10
West Helmsdale Highld 311 H4
West Hendon London 67 B8
West Hendred Oxon 64 B2
West Herrington T & W 243 G8
West Heslerton N Yorks 217 D8
West Hewish N Som 59 G11
West Hill Devon 15 C7
West Hill E Sus 38 E4
West Hill E Yorks 218 F3
West Hill London 67 E8
West Hill N Som 60 D3
West Hill Som 30 B2
West Hill Staffs 151 G9
West Hill W Sus 51 G10
West Hill Wilts 61 F11
West Hoathly W Sus 51 G11
West Holme Dorset 18 D3
West Holywell T & W 243 C8
West Horndon Essex 68 B6
West Horrington Som 44 D5
West Horsley Sur 50 C5
West Horton Northumb 264 C2
West Hougham Kent 55 E9
West Houlland Shetland 313 H4
West Houses Lincs 174 E4
West Howe Bmouth 19 B7
West Howetown Som 42 G2
West Huntington York 207 B8
West Huntspill Som 43 E10
West Hurn Dorset 19 B8
West Hyde Herts 85 G8
West Hynish Argyll 288 F1
West Hythe Kent 54 G6
West Ilkerton Devon 41 D8
West Ilsley W Berks 64 C3
West Itchenor W Sus 22 C3
West Jesmond T & W 243 D7
West Keal Lincs 174 C5
West Kennett Wilts 62 F6
West Kensington London 67 D8
West Kilbride N Ayrs 266 F4
West Kilburn London 67 C8
West Kingsdown Kent 68 G5
West Kingston W Sus 35 G9
West Kington Wilts 61 D10
West Kington Wick Wilts 61 D10
West Kinharrachie Aberds 303 F9
West Kirby Mers 182 D2
West Kirkby Mers 182 D2
West Knapton N Yorks 217 D7
West Knighton Dorset 17 D10
West Knoyle Wilts 45 G11
West Kyloe Northumb 273 G11
West Kyo Durham 242 G5
West Lambrook Som 28 D6
West Langdon Kent 55 D10
West Langwell Highld 309 J6
West Lavington W Sus 34 C5
West Lavington Wilts 46 C4
West Layton N Yorks 224 D2
West Lea Durham 234 B4
West Leake Notts 153 D10
West Learmouth Northumb 263 B9
West Leigh Devon 25 F11
West Leigh Hants 22 B2
West Leigh Som 42 G6
West Lexham Norf 158 F6
West Lilling N Yorks 216 F2
West Linton Borders 270 E2
West Liss Hants 34 B3
West Littleton S Glos 61 D9
West Lockinge Oxon 64 B2
West Looe Corn 6 E5
West Luccombe Som 41 D11
West Lulworth Dorset 18 E2
West Lutton N Yorks 217 F8
West Lydford Som 44 G5
West Lydiatt Hereford 97 C11
West Lyn Devon 41 D8
West Lyng Som 28 B4
West Lynn Norf 158 E2
West Mains Borders 271 F11
West Mains S Lnrk 268 E2
West Malling Kent 53 B7
West Malvern Worcs 98 B5
West Marden W Sus 34 E3
West Marina E Sus 38 F3
West Markham Notts 188 G2
West Marsh NE Lincs 201 E9
West Marton N Yorks 204 C3
West Mathers Aberds 293 G9
West Melbury Dorset 30 C5
West Melton S Yorks 198 G2
West Meon Hants 33 C10
West Meon Woodlands Hants 33 B10
West Merkland Highld 308 F3
West Mersea Essex 89 C8
West Milton Dorset 16 B6
West Minster Kent 70 E2
West Molesey Sur 66 F6
West Monkseaton T & W 243 C8
West Monkton Som 28 B3
West Moor T & W 243 C7
West Moors Dorset 31 G9
West Morden Dorset 18 B4
West Morriston Borders 272 G2
West Morton W Yorks 205 E7
West Mudford Som 29 C9
West Muir Angus 293 G7
West Myreriggs Perth 286 C6
West Ness N Yorks 216 D3
West Newham Northumb 242 B3
West Newton E Yorks 209 F9
West Newton Norf 158 D3
West Newton Som 28 B3
West Norwood London 67 E10
West Ogwell Devon 14 G2
West Orchard Dorset 30 D4
West Overton Wilts 62 F6
West Panson Devon 12 C2
West Park Hrtlpl 234 E5
West Park Hull 200 B5
West Park Mers 183 B7
West Park T & W 243 D9
West Park W Yorks 205 F11
West Parley Dorset 19 B7
West Pasture Durham 232 G4
West Peckham Kent 52 C6
West Pelton Durham 242 G6
West Pennard Som 44 F4
West Pentire Corn 4 C5
West Perry Cambs 122 D2
West Pontnewydd Torf 78 F3
West Poringland Norf 142 C5
West Porlock Som 41 D11
West Portholland Corn 5 G9
West Porton Renfs 277 G8
West Pulham Dorset 30 F2
West Putford Devon 24 D5
West Quantoxhead Som 42 E6
West Rainton Durham 234 B2
West Rasen Lincs 189 D9
West Ravendale NE Lincs 190 B2
West Raynham Norf 159 D7
West Retford Notts 187 E11
West Rounton N Yorks 225 E8
West Row Suff 124 B3
West Royd W Yorks 205 F9
West Rudham Norf 158 D6
West Ruislip London 66 B5
West Runton Norf 177 E11
West Saltoun E Loth 271 B9
West Sandford Devon 26 G4
West Sandwick Shetland 312 E6
West Scholes W Yorks 205 G7
West Scrafton N Yorks 213 C11
West Shepton Som 44 E6
West Side Bl Gwent 77 D11
West Side Orkney 314 C5
West Skelston Dumfries 247 F8
West Sleekburn Northumb 253 G7
West Somerton Norf 161 F9
West Southbourne Bmouth 19 C8
West Stafford Dorset 17 D10
West Stockwith Notts 188 C3
West Stoke Devon 13 G9
West Stoke Som 29 D7
West Stoke W Sus 22 B4
West Stonesdale N Yorks 223 E7
West Stoughton Som 44 D2
West Stour Dorset 30 C3
West Stourmouth Kent 71 G9
West Stow Suff 124 C6
West Stowell Wilts 62 G6
West Strathan Highld 308 C5
West Stratton Hants 48 E4
West Street Kent 54 C2
West Street Kent 55 C10
West Street Medway 69 D8
West Street Suff 125 C9
West Tanfield N Yorks 214 D5
West Taphouse Corn 6 C3
West Tarbert Argyll 275 G9
West Tarring W Sus 35 G10
West Third Borders 262 B4
West Thirston Northumb 252 D5
West Thorney W Sus 22 C3
West Thurrock Thurrock 68 D5
West Tilbury Thurrock 69 D7
West Tisted Hants 33 B11
West Tofts Norf 140 E6
West Tofts Perth 286 D5
West Tolgus Corn 4 G3
West Torrington Lincs 189 E10
West Town Bath 60 G4
West Town Devon 14 B3
West Town Devon 24 C4
West Town Hants 21 B10
West Town Hereford 115 E8
West Town N Som 60 F3
West Town Som 44 F4
West Town W Sus 36 D3
West Tytherley Hants 32 B3
West Tytherton Wilts 62 E2
West Vale W Yorks 196 C5
West View Hrtlpl 234 D5
West Village V Glam 58 E3
West Walton Norf 157 G9
West Walton Highway Norf 157 G9
West Watergate Corn 6 E4
West Watford Herts 85 F10
West Wellow Hants 32 D3
West Wemyss Fife 280 C6
West Wick N Som 59 G11
West Wickham Cambs 106 B2
West Wickham London 67 F11
West Williamston Pembs 73 D8
West Willoughby Lincs 173 G7
West Winch Norf 158 F2
West Winterslow Wilts 47 G8
West Wittering W Sus 21 B11
West Witton N Yorks 213 B11
West Woodburn Northumb 251 F9
West Woodhay W Berks 63 G11
West Woodlands Som 45 E9
West Worldham Hants 49 F8
West Worlington Devon 26 E3
West Worthing W Sus 35 G10
West Wratting Cambs 124 G2
West Wycombe Bucks 84 G4
West Wylam Northumb 242 E4
West Yatton Wilts 61 E11
West Yell Shetland 312 E6
West Yeo Som 43 G10
West Yoke Kent 68 F5
West Youlstone Corn 24 D3
Westacott Devon 40 G5
Westbere Kent 71 G7
Westborough Lincs 172 G5
Westbourne Bmouth 19 C7
Westbourne Suff 108 B2
Westbourne W Sus 22 B3
Westbourne Green London 67 C9
Westbrook Hereford 96 C5
Westbrook Kent 71 E10
Westbrook Sur 50 E3
Westbrook W Berks 64 E2
Westbrook Warr 183 C9
Westbrook Wilts 62 F3
Westbrook Green Norf 142 G2
Westbrook Hay Herts 85 D8
Westburn S Lnrk 268 C3
Westbury Bucks 102 D2
Westbury Shrops 131 B7
Westbury Wilts 45 C11
Westbury Leigh Wilts 45 C11
Westbury-on-Severn Glos 80 C2
Westbury on Trym Bristol 60 D5
Westbury Park Bristol 60 D5
Westbury-sub-Mendip Som 44 D4
Westby Lancs 202 G3
Westby Lincs 155 D9
Westcliff-on-Sea Sthend 69 B11
Westcombe Som 29 B7
Westcombe Som 45 F7
Westcot Oxon 63 B10
Westcote Glos 100 G4
Westcotes Leicester 135 C11
Westcott Bucks 84 B2
Westcott Devon 27 G8
Westcott Shrops 131 C8
Westcott Sur 50 D6
Westcott Barton Oxon 101 F8
Westcourt Wilts 63 G8
Westcroft M Keynes 102 E6
Westcroft W Mid 133 C8
Westdean E Sus 23 F8
Westdene Brighton 36 F3
Westdown Camp Wilts 46 D4
Westdowns Corn 11 E7
Westend Oxon 100 G6
Westend S Glos 79 G10
Westend Town Northumb 241 D7
Westenhanger Kent 54 F6
Wester Aberchalder Highld 300 G5
Wester Arboll Highld 311 L2
Wester Auchinloch N Lnrk 278 G3
Wester Auchnagallin Highld 301 F10
Wester Balgedie Perth 286 G5
Wester Brae Highld 300 C6
Wester Broomhouse E Loth 282 F3
Wester Craiglands Highld 301 D7
Wester Culbeuchly Aberds 302 C6
Wester Dalvoult Highld 291 B11
Wester Dechmont W Loth 269 B10
Wester Deloraine Borders 261 E8
Wester Denoon Angus 287 C7
Wester Ellister Argyll 254 B2
Wester Essendy Perth 286 C5
Wester Essenside Borders 261 E10
Wester Feddal Perth 286 G2
Wester Fintray Aberds 293 B10
Wester Galgantray Highld 301 E8
Wester Gospetry Fife 286 G5
Wester Gruinards Highld 309 K5
Wester Hailes Edin 270 B4
Wester Housebyres Borders 262 B2
Wester Kershope Borders 261 D9
Wester Lealty Highld 300 B6
Wester Lix Stirl 285 E9
Wester Milton Highld 301 D9
Wester Mosshead Aberds 302 F5
Wester Newburn Fife 287 G8
Wester Ord Aberds 293 C10
Wester Parkgate Dumfries 248 F2
Wester Quarff Shetland 313 K6
Wester Skeld Shetland 313 J4
Wester Strath Highld 300 D6
Wester Watten Highld 310 D6
Westerdale Highld 310 D5
Westerdale N Yorks 226 D3
Westerfield Shetland 313 H5
Westerfield Suff 108 B3
Westerfolds Moray 301 C11
Westergate W Sus 22 B6
Westerham Kent 52 C2
Westerhope T & W 242 D5
Westerleigh S Glos 61 D8
Westerleigh Hill S Glos 61 D8
Western Bank Cumb 229 B10
Western Downs Staffs 151 E8
Western Heights Kent 55 E10
Western Hill Durham 233 C11
Western Park Leicester 135 C11
Westerton Aberds 293 B9
Westerton Aberds 302 E5
Westerton Angus 287 B10
Westerton Durham 233 E10
Westerton Moray 302 D3
Westerton W Sus 22 B5
Westertown Aberds 303 F7
Westerwick Shetland 313 J4
Westfield Bath 45 C7
Westfield Cumb 228 F5
Westfield E Sus 38 D4
Westfield Hants 21 B10
Westfield Hereford 98 B4
Westfield Highld 310 C4
Westfield N Lnrk 278 G4
Westfield Norf 141 B9

County and unitary authority boundaries

Ordnance Survey National Grid

The blue lines which divide the Navigator map pages into squares for indexing match the Ordnance Survey National Grid and correspond to the small squares on the boundary map below. Each side of a grid square measures 10km on the ground.

The National Grid 100-km square letters and kilometre values are indicated for the grid intersection at the outer corners of each page. For example, the intersection SE6090 at the upper right corner of page 215 is 60km East and 90km North of the south-west corner of National Grid square SE.

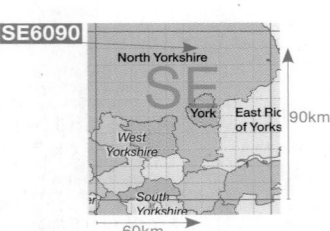
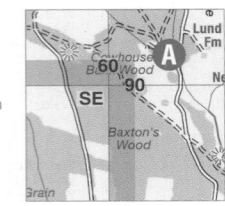

Using GPS with Navigator mapping

Since Navigator Britain is based on Ordnance Survey mapping, and rectified to the National Grid, it can be used with in-car or handheld GPS for locating identifiable waypoints such as road junctions, bridges, railways and farms, or assessing your position in relation to any of the features shown on the map.

On your receiver, choose British Grid as the location format and for map datum select Ordnance Survey (this may be described as Ord Srvy GB or similar, or more specifically as OSGB36). Your receiver will automatically convert the latitude/longitude co-ordinates transmitted by GPS into compatible National Grid data.

Positional accuracy of any particular feature is limited to 50–100m, due to the limitations of the original survey and the scale of Navigator mapping.

For further information see www.gps.gov.uk

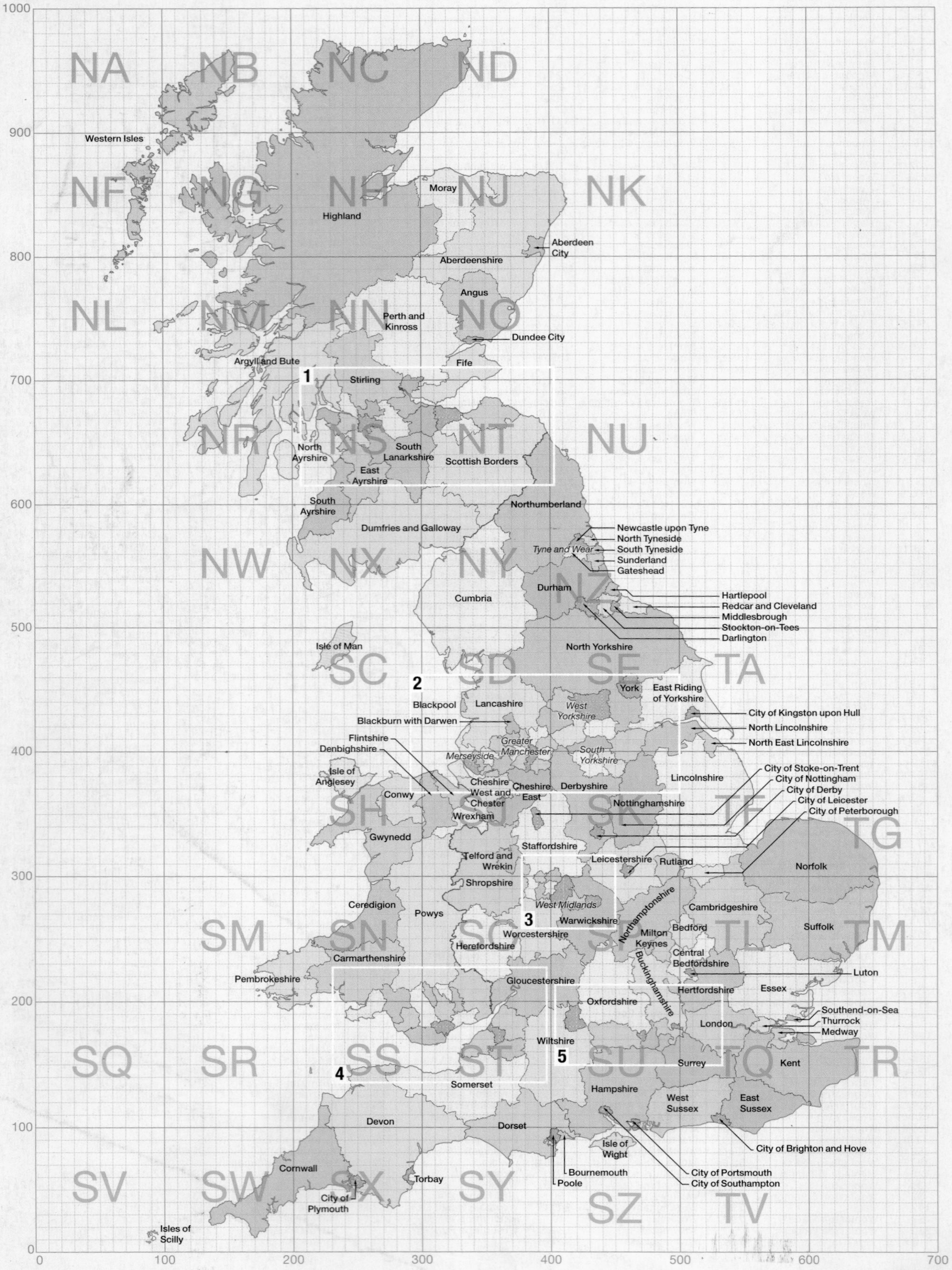

Greater London

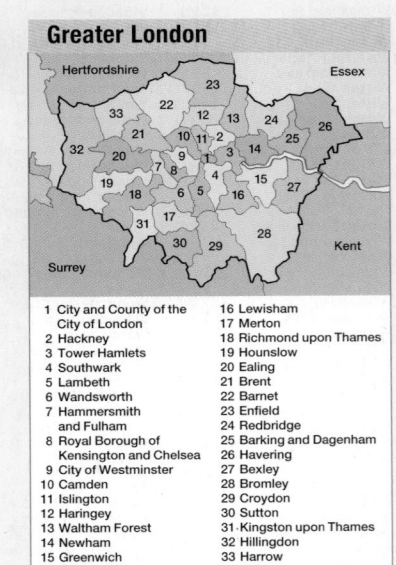

1 City and County of the City of London
2 Hackney
3 Tower Hamlets
4 Southwark
5 Lambeth
6 Wandsworth
7 Hammersmith and Fulham
8 Royal Borough of Kensington and Chelsea
9 City of Westminster
10 Camden
11 Islington
12 Haringey
13 Waltham Forest
14 Newham
15 Greenwich
16 Lewisham
17 Merton
18 Richmond upon Thames
19 Hounslow
20 Ealing
21 Brent
22 Barnet
23 Enfield
24 Redbridge
25 Barking and Dagenham
26 Havering
27 Bexley
28 Bromley
29 Croydon
30 Sutton
31 Kingston upon Thames
32 Hillingdon
33 Harrow

1 Central Scotland

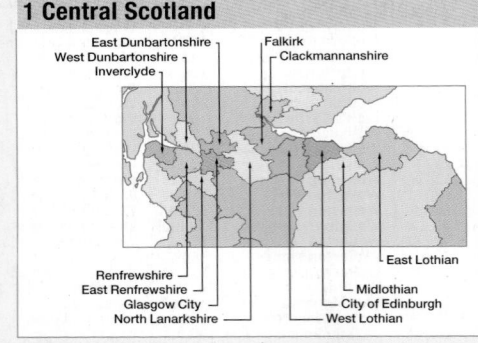

2 Northern England

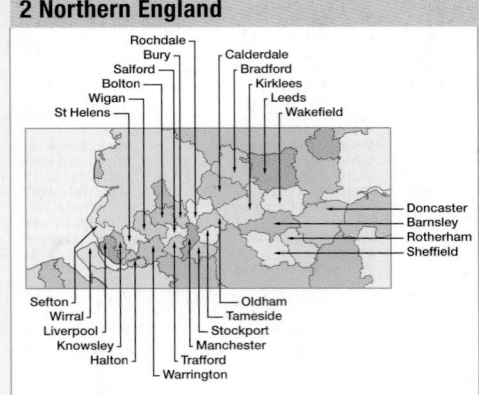

3 West Midlands

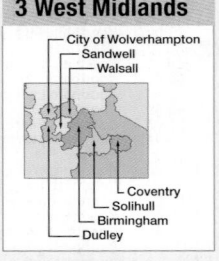

4 South Wales and Bristol area

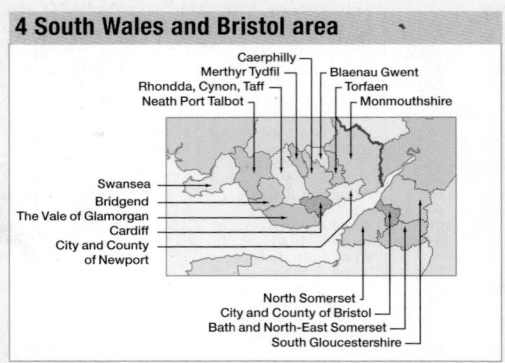

5 Thames Valley

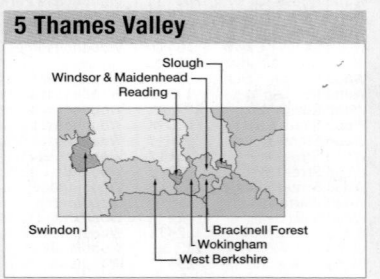